The SAGE
Handbook for
Research in
Education

Julia Conrad and Susan Anderson
Erin, Abigail, Willow, Jerad, Zane, and Sofia

The SAGE Handbook for Research in Education

Engaging Ideas and Enriching Inquiry

Clifton F. Conrad & Ronald C. Serlin
University of Wisconsin–Madison
Editors

SAGE Publications
Thousand Oaks ▪ London ▪ New Delhi

For information:

Sage Publications, Inc.
2455 Teller Road
Thousand Oaks, California 91320
E-mail: order@sagepub.com

Sage Publications Ltd.
1 Oliver's Yard
55 City Road
London EC1Y 1SP
United Kingdom

Sage Publications India Pvt. Ltd.
B-42, Panchsheel Enclave
Post Box 4109
New Delhi 110 017 India

Printed in the United States of America

Library of Congress Cataloging-in-Publication Data

The SAGE handbook for research in education: Engaging ideas and enriching inquiry / edited by Clifton F. Conrad and Ronald C. Serlin.
        p. cm.
Includes bibliographical references and index.
ISBN 1-4129-0640-7 (cloth)
    1. Education—Research—Handbooks, manuals, etc. I. Conrad, Clifton. II. Serlin, Ronald C.
LB1028.S14 2006
370′.7′2—dc22

This book is printed on acid-free paper.

05   06   07   08   09   10   9   8   7   6   5   4   3   2   1

Acquisitions Editor:	Diane McDaniel
Editorial Assistants:	Marta Peimer and Erica Carroll
Production Editor:	Melanie Birdsall
Copy Editor:	D. J. Peck
Typesetter:	C&M Digitals (P) Ltd.
Proofreader:	Cheryl Rivard
Indexer:	Kathy Paparchontis
Cover Designer:	Candice Harman

CONTENTS

Part II. Enriching Inquiry Through Identifying and Addressing Key Challenges

Section Three: Challenges in Formulating and Framing Meaningful Problems

PREFACE

Both of us, the editors of the *Handbook,* teach courses that describe and delineate research methods—one of us introducing methods to be used in what is typically defined as a qualitative research tradition, the other teaching procedures considered more appropriately applied under a quantitative research rubric. Notwithstanding differences in our syllabi, we both present research methods as tools to be used in the process of sifting and winnowing ideas in educational inquiry. In turn, we emphasize that it is the researcher's overall question that should drive the research enterprise— a compelling question that has personal as well as professional significance.

We often stress to students and colleagues that the methods we teach in our courses, as important as they are to scientific research, are techniques that are akin to instrumentation in astronomy. They allow us to see beyond the haze of the atmosphere to discern phenomena that might have otherwise gone unnoticed. But even an enlarged and clearer image often does not explain what is observed. The thrust of the research and the interpretation of findings must always go back to the animating questions of interest.

Conducting educational research that is both consequential and rigorous is intellectually demanding work. Most significant, the subject matter in education—with schooling and its effects on student learning at the epicenter of the field—is inherently difficult and challenging to study. Moreover, scholars, policymakers, practicing educators, and the public at large often have strong and competing views on the worth and rigor of the research that has been conducted. Despite these obstacles, researchers continue to make impressive contributions to our knowledge and understanding of education. Still, meaningful and first-rate research—across all subfields—is very much needed if we are to significantly advance and deepen our understanding of education.

Our students—and our faculty and practitioner colleagues—often ask us how questions of interest are obtained and how they, as scientists themselves, can come up with one or more. Clearly, this is a major mentoring challenge to us as faculty. We variously suggest that they immerse themselves in the prominent research journals in their field, see what problems are being addressed, and reflect on how the frameworks and theories guiding the research help to explain the corroborating results, are invented to explain anomalies, and help to develop and improve educational programs. We then opine that they should read the publications referenced in the most current articles, and read the previous generation of references in turn so that they can get a sense of the history of the field and see that the urgent problems and major theories can change over time, and also consider the limitations of the literature.

This endeavor to use the literature to reflect on how research questions arise is made even more difficult by the challenge that all those who mentor researchers face—knowing how best to integrate knowledge, theory, and methodology in our curriculum. If we first ask the students to read the literature to acquire the underpinnings of theory under which research results could be subsumed, then students' lack of knowledge of methods at this stage leaves them ill prepared to understand and evaluate the logic employed and the quality of the research reported. If, however, students enroll in methods courses first, then they have no body of research to provide context and motivation. Furthermore, in dealing with the current conundrum concerning how to help students formulate engaging questions without having acquired both theoretical and methodological knowledge and experiences, all of which they are now in the process of attaining, students are likely to be unable to distinguish problems that are prevalent because of extra-scientific influences from problems that go to the heart of an ongoing scientific controversy.

Unfortunately, regardless of our exhortations and our best intentions, we seem to have assigned the students a self-referentially iterative task. They ask us how questions of interest are formulated, and in response we tell them to go off, read the literature, and formulate a theory of how questions of interest are formulated. Our thinking seems to have been that once the students have developed their theory of question generation, an application of that theory in their own areas of interest will yield, with geometrical logic, the questions of interest to be fruitfully pursued.

Despite our attempts at pedagogical excellence regarding the teaching of research methods, it is by no means certain that the students will be better able to formulate their own questions of interest after this literature-searching exercise than they were before. If this is the case, then what alternative recommendations should we have given the students? One would think that by now, having been challenged by the students' plight for so long, we should be able to provide students with accumulated exemplary instances of good research, with illustrations of how fruitful and interesting questions are posed and how the pursuit of answers to these questions has led to the generation or extension of theories and to curricular improvements. This *Handbook* represents our attempt to address these challenges by providing students, faculty, and educational practitioners with a collection of essays written by scholars who have consistently demonstrated intellectual strength and curiosity in wrestling with the formidable challenges of framing and conducting meaningful inquiry.

STATE OF THE FIELD

Much has been written on the topic of educational inquiry, but the literature on educational inquiry and research methods per se continues to suffer from four major limitations. First, because research is viewed largely as a "prescribed" journey in which applying appropriate methods and techniques is the sine qua non of first-rate scholarship, developing meaningful knowledge and understanding—ironically, the goal of inquiry—is not placed at the forefront of inquiry. In turn, most texts on research methods not only fail to address adequately the context of inquiry—including animating purposes and key stakeholders—but also give woefully little consideration to identifying and exploring potentially fruitful research problems. Second, much of the literature fails to help prepare researchers to recognize and address the most fundamental challenges—before, during, and following research—in conducting inquiry. Third, qualitative and quantitative approaches are bifurcated rather than integrated into discussions of inquiry. Fourth, much of the literature advances a "one best way" approach to research that falls short of exploring a wide range of alternative and emerging perspectives on ways in which to enrich inquiry.

It is not clear whether assigning our students to discern from the research literature methods for attaining questions of interest avoids these four deficiencies. The articles and textbooks they choose to read in the pursuit of their goal will not likely reveal the motivations underlying the course of study, the failed attempts and dead ends that are more prevalent than successes in research, or especially the thought processes that lead to successes despite the failures. And even if some of these aspects are dealt with in chapters and articles, it is likely that the presentation will make it seem as if the journey from inception to conclusion was, at least in hindsight, the only logical way in which one could have proceeded.

INQUIRY THROUGH A KEYHOLE: RETRODUCTION

It might seem, from our description of our assignment to our students, that we have asked them to apply the well-known method of induction in the course of coming up with questions of interest from a reading of the literature. For instance, they could amass a set of questions that seem to have motivated various experiments, look for possible patterns in these questions that might have made them interesting to pursue, and assert by induction that the pattern that seems to have held regarding these particular questions holds in general. Or, because there is an extremely large number of ways of characterizing the question of interest in even a single experiment, the students could try to infer which of the many aspects was the key factor and generalize that this would be so in other experiments as well. Or they could find common elements among various explanations of the potential practical or theoretical value of studies and assert by induction a single theoretical explanation of the many claims to importance.

The process of formulating theories by induction from observations has been commonly held to be the generative mechanism of science since Aristotle's *Organon*. In the preface to *Novum Organum*, Bacon described a method of induction in which the scientist would question nature without biases or hypotheses and move to generalities in an algorithmic fashion, as if (in Bacon's words) by machinery. Broad (1952) described Baconian induction as "the glory of science" (p. 143). According to Thomas Reid, who popularized the works and methods of Isaac Newton during the 18th century, the success of Newton's theories led to the wide acceptance of Bacon's philosophy, for Reid (1785) claimed that Newton's methods were inductive. Indeed, Newton's famous assertion that he did not formulate hypotheses, implying that his theories were derived inductively from observation, seemed to substantiate Newton's methods as inductive.

Baconian inductive methods were actually more sophisticated than it might seem at first glance. Briefly, Bacon advocated listing all instances in which a characteristic under examination is present as well as listing the concomitant characteristics in these circumstances. He then proposed listing similar circumstances in which the characteristic under examination is not present to see, in contrast, the effects of removing the characteristic (in this manner, conducting a controlled experiment). Finally, he suggested studying the characteristic to be examined in conditions where it is present in varying degrees. This method was called "eliminative induction" by von Wright (1951).

That induction forms a crucial step in the scientific process is a view held long into the 20th century. Indeed, the scientific method as formulated by Braithwaite (1953) was depicted as cyclical, alternating between inductive and deductive phases. The view that science has an inductive phase continues to be surprisingly influential given that it has been strongly contraindicated, even from Bacon's own time. For instance, William Harvey, a contemporary of Bacon's and the person who discovered the body's circulatory system, said that Bacon wrote philosophy like a chancellor. This was interpreted by Nobel Prize winner Richard Feynman to indicate that while Bacon spoke of gathering observations, he omitted the factor of judgment regarding what to observe and what to attend to in gathering observations. And as Broad noted in virtually the same breath as he extolled induction as the glory of science, it is also "the scandal of philosophy" (Broad, 1952, p. 143).

David Hume, a contemporary of Reid, argued devastatingly that no inductive generalizations whatsoever can be logically justified, whether in pursuit of certain or probable knowledge, unless a principle of induction is presumed to hold. This principle itself, which can be variously stated as "the future will resemble the past" or as "nature is uniform," can be derived only inductively and so begs the question. Of Hume's conclusion, Russell (1945) exclaimed,

> It is therefore important to discover whether there is any answer to Hume within the framework of a philosophy that is wholly or mainly empirical. If not, there is no intellectual difference between sanity and insanity. The lunatic who believes that he is a poached egg is to be condemned solely on the ground that he is in a minority. (p. 673)

William Whewell attempted to explain the growth and stability of scientific knowledge without requiring Baconian induction. In his *Novum Organon Renovatum,* Whewell (1858) defined induction as the representation of facts with principles rather than as a generalization from facts. He argued that to explain the growth of scientific knowledge, both experience and intuition were required. Most important, he claimed that to account for how scientists discover true principles, science needs guesses. According to Wettersten (1993), Whewell's theory makes clear that "even if we start with poor guesses and treat them critically, we can come to the truth; there are many paths to the truth, but only one goal" (p. 506). Admittedly, the word "guess" is an infelicitous choice. As Medawar (1974) explained,

> It is the word that is at fault, not the conception. To say that Einstein formulated a theory of relativity by guesswork is on all fours with saying that Wordsworth wrote rhymes and Mozart tuneful music. It is cheeky where something grave is called for. (p. 281)

This view of what could be called a scientific method was also elucidated by Charles Sanders Peirce during the late 19th century. According to Peirce, all inference is either deductive or synthetic, with the latter typology subdivided into induction and what Peirce variously called hypothesis, retroduction, or abduction (Peirce, 1878). As Peirce (1958) described it, when a scientific explanation is sought,

> the explanation must be such a proposition as would lead to the prediction of the observed facts. . . . A hypothesis, then, has to be adopted, which is likely in itself, and renders the facts likely. This step of adopting a hypothesis as being suggested by the facts, is what I call abduction. . . . The first thing that will be done, as soon as a hypothesis has been adopted, will be to trace out its necessary and probable experiential consequences. This step is deduction. (p. 122)

The final step in this process is when the deduced consequences are compared with experimental results.

Feynman (1965) reiterated the notion that scientists employ guesswork, saying that a new law is first guessed, its consequences are then computed assuming that it is a correct guess, and finally the results of the computation are compared with nature. If it disagrees with experiment, then it is wrong, Feynman concluded. Feynman wrote,

In that simple statement is the key to science. It does not make any difference how beautiful your guess is. It does not make any difference how smart you are, who made the guess, or what his name is—if it disagrees with experiment, it is wrong. That is all there is to it. (p. 150)

For Whewell, Peirce, and Feynman, then, theories and hypotheses are not obtained from observations by induction. Rather, by some imaginative retroductive leap, a hypothesis is guessed that yields the observations as deductive consequences of the hypothesis.

Shank (1990) argued that, based on Peirce's insights into retroduction and his semiotic theory, the conceptual confusions created in maintaining the apparent qualitative–quantitative dichotomy can be resolved. Shank contended that the same logical processes are involved in a case study examined in a qualitative framework as in the quantitative perspective within which Peirce worked, so that the two perspectives differ in the ways in which they constitute units of analysis, but not in terms of the logic of the analysis. Common to the two perspectives are implementations of deduction and retroduction for the purposes of producing and testing explanatory hypotheses.

As Shank (1990) pointed out, it is not possible to observe and take note of all aspects of the phenomenon under study, and the number of possible explanatory hypotheses that could be imagined is virtually limitless. According to Hoffmann (2000), however, there is a relationship between the context of retroduction and the process of attaining a promising hypothesis, so that the range of explanations is limited by a complex interaction among factors at play in the given circumstance.

So it is retroduction, and not induction, that we are asking our students to perform in the course of generating questions of interest. Furthermore, they must formulate these questions within the limits imposed by aspects of the field of study, including the state of the art of theory, political realities, and funding possibilities, as well as by the circumstances in which the students find themselves, possibly involving the purposes of the studies in terms of the students' academic careers, for whom the studies may be conducted, and the ability of the students.

At a minimum, these actualities raise the question of how best to teach students how to perform retroduction, with the hope that the result of teaching them will be a good question of interest and an able scientist. From at least the time of Piaget and Ausubel during the 1960s to today's constructivism and situated learning, theory suggests that to teach abstract abilities such as retroduction, instruction must actively engage students in the process itself, but in such a manner that they are able to carry out a successful retroductive episode. So we send our students out to the literature to learn about context and limitations, extant theories, and previously tried but failed explanations. This experience can provide students with a powerful schema that will help them to incorporate the desired skills into their own inquiry that we are seeking to model in our respective classrooms.

Medawar (1974) cautioned, however, that scientific papers "actively misrepresent the reasoning that goes into the work" (p. 287) because it seems that publishable papers must be written as if inductions had occurred. It is also not sufficient to listen to what scientists say they do because their opinions will vary so widely. Medawar concluded that "only unstudied evidence will do—and that means listening at a keyhole" (p. 287).

It is our hope that this *Handbook,* by presenting detailed accounts of successful episodes of scientific activity in a variety of fields, from a variety of perspectives, in a manner that highlights the difficult exploration of ideas and actively involves the readers, will provide Medawar's necessary keyhole through which the readers can peer in the course of experiencing successful retroductive efforts regarding the engagement of ideas.

REFERENCES

Braithwaite, R. B. (1953). *Scientific explanation.* New York: Harper & Brothers.

Broad, C. D. (1952). *Ethics and the history of philosophy.* New York: Humanities Press.

Feynman, R. (1965). *The character of physical law.* New York: Random House.

Hoffmann, M. (2000). Is there a "logic" of abduction? In A. Gimate-Welsh (Ed.), *Selected papers: 6th Congress of the International Association for Semiotic Studies, Guadalajara 1997* (pp. 617–628). Mexico City: Grupo Editorial Miguel Ángel Porrúa.

Medawar, P. (1974). Hypothesis and imagination. In P. A. Schilpp (Ed.), *The philosophy of Karl Popper* (pp. 274–291). La Salle, IL: Open Court.

Peirce, C. S. (1878). Deduction, induction, and hypothesis. In C. J. W. Kloesel (Ed.), *Writings of Charles S. Peirce* (Vol. 3, pp. 323–338). Bloomington: Indiana University Press.

Peirce, C. S. (1958). *Collected papers of Charles Sanders Peirce* (A. W. Burks, Ed.), Vol. 7: *Science and philosophy.* Cambridge, MA: Harvard University Press.

Reid, T. (1785). *Essays on the intellectual powers of man.* Edinburgh, UK: J. Bell.

Russell, B (1945). *A history of Western philosophy.* New York: Simon & Schuster.

Shank, G. (1990). Qualitative vs. quantitative research: A semiotic non-problem. In T. Prewitt, J. Deely, & K. Haworth (Eds.), *Semiotics: 1989* (pp. 264–270). Washington, DC: University Press of America.

von Wright, G. H. (1951). *A treatise on induction and probability.* London: Routledge & Kegan Paul.

Wettersten, J. R. (1993). Rethinking Whewell. *Philosophy of the Social Sciences, 23,* 481–515.

Whewell, W. (1858). *Novum organon renovatum* (3rd ed.). London: John W. Parker.

ACKNOWLEDGMENTS

In a break from convention, we begin by acknowledging the support of several individuals at Sage Publications with whom we have worked closely. We have especially appreciated the fiercely intelligent and breathtakingly gentle guidance and support of Diane McDaniel, our acquisitions editor, who has deeply invested in this project from the outset and at once challenged and amused us throughout. Marta Peimer (editorial assistant) and Margo Beth Crouppen (associate editor) also were remarkably helpful from their astute judgment, to their myriad suggestions for improving the manuscript, to their own iconoclastic wit and good humor.

A highlight of this journey has been the pleasure of collaborating in this joint adventure of nearly 2 years with our section editors: from the formidably intellectual D. C. Phillips (Section One), to the multitalented Laura W. Perna and John C. Weidman (Section Two), to the sagacious Daniel Lapsley (Section Three), to the scrupulous empiricist Scott Thomas (Section Four), to the synergistic duo of King Beach and Betsy Becker (Section Five), to the imaginative Beth Graue (Section Six). This book is in substantial measure a credit to these individuals and their exemplary contributions along with those of our remarkable band of chapter authors. We also appreciate those individuals who reviewed our prospectus for this book and provided helpful feedback: Gregory R. Hancock, University of Maryland; John W. Creswell, University of Nebraska–Lincoln; and Gabriella Belli, Virginia Polytechnic Institute and State University.

We owe a special debt of gratitude to Divya Malik Gupta, our graduate assistant at the University of Wisconsin–Madison, who has invested heavily and contributed significantly to the preparation of this volume—from helping to edit chapters to reflecting on the direction and flow of the text. We are grateful for her generosity of spirit and catholicity of taste.

The following people have significantly and meaningfully influenced our thinking about inquiry: Virginia Margaret Angell Conrad, Bob Blackburn, Jennifer Grant Haworth, Stuart Rankin, Robbie Case, and Leonard Marascuilo. With a full measure of gratitude, we respectfully and gratefully acknowledge our appreciation to each of these individuals.

Finally, and most certainly, we are fortunate that we are enriched by two of the most perceptive, curious, witty, intellectually adventuresome, and lovely companions one could ever imagine—Julia Conrad and Susan Anderson—as well as a handful of highly inquisitive children and, most recently, a granddaughter (Sofia).

INTRODUCTION

Spirited engagement with ideas—the hallmark of exemplary inquiry—is muted in most contemporary texts on educational research methods. Ironically, methods texts fail to grapple with ideas both with respect to exploring meaningful problems and lines of inquiry and with respect to recognizing and addressing the fundamental but oft-ignored challenges in conducting first-rate inquiry. The purpose of this *Handbook* is to stimulate and encourage educational researchers to place the pursuit of ideas at the epicenter of their research—from framing meaningful problems to identifying and addressing the key challenges in inquiry.

The intended audience for the *Handbook* consists of three primary constituencies: (1) faculty who can use the *Handbook* in courses as their main or supplementary text as well as to inform their own inquiry; (2) students, primarily at the graduate level but including undergraduate students as well; and (3) educational practitioners, including individuals in PK–16 education, government, and the private sector who conduct applied and policy-oriented educational research. We hope that the volume addresses the needs of these three constituencies not only in the United States but also throughout the world—from the United Kingdom, to South Africa, to Latin America.

Consonant with its overarching focus on engaging ideas throughout inquiry, the *Handbook* draws on the perspectives of scholars representing not only diverse fields within the field of education—from prekindergarten, to elementary and secondary school, to higher education—but also qualitative, quantitative, and mixed-methods approaches to inquiry. The chapters in this volume are animated by scholars who have consistently demonstrated intellectual strength and curiosity, who unsettle lines of inquiry with irony and intellectual exuberance, and who have an exemplary blend of creativity and imagination in problem definition and research design as well as in the conduct of inquiry. Because they are punctuated throughout by the voices of authors who wrestle with the formidable challenges of framing and conducting meaningful inquiry, the chapters in the *Handbook* will challenge and engage the readers in their own research regardless of their particular fields of interest.

The *Handbook* is divided into two major parts. Part I consists of two sections, and Part II consists of four sections. For each of the six sections in the *Handbook,* an essay by the section editor(s) introduces the section and describes all of the chapters included in the section. In what follows, we provide a broad overview of the contents of the *Handbook,* beginning with a sketch of the two parts and then turning to a closer look at the six sections.

OVERVIEW OF THE *HANDBOOK*

Part I of the *Handbook* is focused on identifying meaningful research problems and approaches to inquiry. In the first section, several chapters explore the context of inquiry, with a dual focus on identifying and clarifying the overarching purposes of inquiry and on identifying key stakeholders. In the second section, the remaining chapters in Part I shed light on promising research questions across the field of education and on how these problems might be addressed. To invite readers to reflect deeply on their own research problems, these chapters identify and explore exemplars of fruitful research problems within and across many fields and lines of inquiry in PK–16 education. Through exploration of exemplars of promising questions and approaches to guide inquiry, these chapters advance ideas that will challenge and enlighten readers as they reflect on their own research—whatever their specific domains of inquiry.

Part II of the *Handbook* is focused on identifying and exploring the most fundamental research challenges—many often overlooked or shortchanged in the literature on research methods—in conducting rigorous inquiry as well as on advancing strategies for addressing these challenges. These challenges—key decision-making points, critical incidents, and the like—are organized into four separate sections: formulating and framing meaningful problems; preparing for inquiry; conducting inquiry; and writing, voice, and dissemination of research. Selectively drawing on their own and others' experiences for purposes of illustration, the authors of the chapters within each of these domains advance, in the spirit and language of A. N. Whitehead, "ideas of every sort"—through narratives, vignettes, and examples of key episodes in inquiry—not only to illuminate fundamental challenges and considerations in doing first-rate research but also to propose strategies for addressing these challenges.

SECTION ONE: MULTIPLE PURPOSES OF INQUIRY AND KEY STAKEHOLDERS

The opening section of the *Handbook* invites readers to enlarge their options—especially those concerning the aims of inquiry, the audiences for and with whom the inquiry is pursued, and methodological options—in conducting inquiry. In the opening chapter of Section One, D. C. Phillips argues that the "natural sciences" model of inquiry—properly understood as encompassing diverse types of inquiry for diverse purposes and with diverse methods—can serve as a liberatory model for educational inquiry. The other chapters in this section, one by Robert Floden and the other by David Plank and Debbi Harris, invite readers to reflect on the diverse audiences that educational researchers can serve—including the policy community—in concert with the challenges of serving different constituencies in their research.

SECTION TWO: MEANINGFUL PROBLEMS AND APPROACHES TO INQUIRY

As the section editors, Laura W. Perna and John C. Weidman, suggest in their introductory essay to Section Two, fruitful research begins by examining questions that have enduring significance across the entire field of education. The chapters in this section explore exemplars of research problems and approaches to inquiry, both across and within traditional lines of educational inquiry that build on, extend, and deepen our understanding of research problems—including how to develop meaningful research questions. As the chapter authors discuss various research problems and approaches to inquiry, they directly and indirectly illuminate both similarities and differences across fields of inquiry in terms of problems pursued and solutions to those problems. In so doing, they provide readers with the opportunity to learn from scholars across fields of study and thereby to inform the ends and means of their own inquiry. Indeed, the chapter authors' descriptions of and reflections on exemplars of inquiry hold the promise of encouraging even seasoned researchers to reexamine the aims and conduct of their own inquiry.

At the heart of all chapters is the shared aim of shedding light on the fundamental question facing all educational researchers: What are the most fruitful lines of inquiry? To address that question, the authors use myriad approaches—from conceptual frameworks to narratives—to illustrate and give expression to a wide range of exemplars of research. As Patricia McDonough and R. Evely Gildersleeve define the term in the opening chapter of the section, an exemplar is "a prototype of research that is a model of clarity and specificity as well as an example that demonstrates the highest level of research integrity, both theoretically and methodologically."

Across the 13 chapters in this section, the authors advance a breathtaking diversity of promising lines of and approaches to inquiry—especially through providing exemplars within the lines of inquiry they are limning. To illustrate, in reflecting on research on college access, McDonough and Gildersleeve offer a trio of exemplars to guide future inquiry. One explores connections between K–12 and higher education and between research and policy, a second stresses the ways in which public and private K–12 schools shape equal opportunity, and a third advances a "system framework" for informing such inquiry by showing the contribution of capital to understanding ongoing differences in educational equality across social class and racial/ethnic groups. The authors argue that educational inequality writ large is not only an enduring research question but also a problem that reflects the accumulation of inequities and disadvantages as a student moves through PK–12 and into higher education.

A handful of the chapters in this section identify research problems and advance exemplars within and across traditional and emerging lines of inquiry from prekindergarten through elementary and secondary education. For example, Kenneth Zeichner advances a template for enlarging inquiry on teacher education programs; Carl Grant and Vonzell Agosto revisit the enduring research problem of preparing teachers to be multicultural educators; and Joyce Epstein and Steven Sheldon describe a research agenda in which "overlapping spheres of influence"—schools, families, and communities—are examined to explore the dynamic between these spheres in "partnership" and the learning and development of students and, in turn, emphasize that interdisciplinary approaches are needed to address this agenda. And two other chapters—one by Michael Ford and Ellice Forman, the other by Juliet Baxter and Shirley Magnusson—describe major research agendas and associated methodological approaches for conducting future research on learning in science and mathematics, respectively.

The remaining chapters in the section address a wide variety of promising research problems and approaches, illuminated throughout by discussions of exemplars of inquiry. Cheryl Hanley-Maxwell and Brian Bottge advance an ambitious program for reconceptualizing research in the field of special education; Steven Schlossman, drawing on his own research, argues for the importance of tapping the "unheard voices" of children and parents in examining movements for educational reform; and Mary Lee Nelson and Cindy Juntunen identify fruitful areas for future research in counseling psychology. Identifying fruitful areas for future research in other areas are Jane Clark Lindle on educational leadership; John C. Weidman on the socialization of students in higher education; Jason Johnson, Clifton F. Conrad, and Laura W. Perna on minority-serving institutions of higher education; and David Phillips on comparative education.

SECTION THREE: FORMULATING AND FRAMING MEANINGFUL PROBLEMS

As Daniel Lapsley, the section editor, notes in his introductory essay to Section Three, "Induction into scientific practice hardly ever takes up the matter of how to formulate and frame meaningful problems," and there is "barely a word on how to ask questions, frame a problem, or generate a theory." Lapsley, in an introductory essay that could stand alone as a separate chapter, and three scholars—James Youniss, Kathryn Wentzel, and Susan Harter—identify and explore what they consider to be the most fundamental challenges in conducting high-quality research, propose strategies for addressing these challenges, and provide rationales for their proposals. Through the use of narratives, vignettes, and accounts of critical incidents and key decision-making points, the authors describe how they have wrestled with framing and formulating meaningful problems.

James Youniss addresses the challenges of "situating inquiry" and "situating self" through an autobiographical narrative. In effect, he argues, the starting point of "critical discovery" is biography. Kathryn Wentzel, in addressing the challenge of developing and nurturing researchable ideas, advances three strategies for generating interesting ideas: identifying and challenging theoretical assumptions, documenting the published literature, and generating new variables by using the person–process–context features of a developmental systems model. Finally, in an engaging first-person narrative, Susan Harter emphasizes that too often we turn our first look in problem defining in the direction of methodology rather than theory. She suggests that the challenge of framing a problem should be tightly bound to one's "burning question." All together, the chapters in this section—through nothing less than personal narratives that display highly disciplined exuberance in the quest of framing research problems—will surely invite most readers to revisit how they go about crystallizing research problems, with attention given to the ways in which both build on and disturb the conventional wisdom in the field of education.

SECTION FOUR: PREPARING FOR INQUIRY

The chapters in Section Four, under the stewardship of section editor Scott Thomas, challenge much of the orthodoxy concerning the conduct of inquiry. Perhaps most noteworthy, several authors critique and respond to the federal redefinition of what constitutes "scientific research" that has been celebrated most especially by the newly formed Institute of Education Sciences (IES). To wit, John Bean refers to the "seductive" nature of pure research, and Douglas Toma advances the innovative argument that researchers working within the tradition of applied qualitative research can frame their inquiry as "scientific" even in the restrictive language of IES—provided that they take greater initiative in explaining how their work has rigor on a par with that understood as scientific work.

All of the chapter authors in the section suggest that what John Bean calls "methodological correctness" should be superseded by the proposition that although some problems are better served or less well served by specific methodological approaches, there is no inherent association between "rigor" and "method." Bean, in concert with attacking the corrosiveness of methodological correctness, suggests that there are multiple and wide-ranging forces at play in the research process—from ego and fear to risk aversion, from groupthink to disciplinary parochialism—that pull the researcher away from the ideals of first-rate inquiry.

Building on and extending Bean's analysis, Ronald Heck provides a thoughtful consideration of challenges in the processes through which researchers identify and frame research problems. Heck cleverly explores how seemingly innocent decisions about method can have a profound impact on evidence, analysis, and conclusions. In an evocative chapter on sampling, Scott Thomas focuses on the challenges associated with the way we choose what to observe and how to observe it. And in a concluding chapter on applied qualitative inquiry, Douglas Toma conjoins many of the points made throughout this section to challenge extant norms suggesting that all rigorous inquiry is conducted in a quantitative and experimental framework.

SECTION FIVE: CONDUCTING INQUIRY

The chapters in Section Five, under the direction of section editors King Beach and Betsy Becker, address four oft-ignored challenges that are critical to conducting first-rate research: the development of the researcher as inquirer, moving from data sources to data and inference making, bringing "analytical thoughtfulness" to data analysis, and moving from findings to conclusions. The authors address these four challenges in ways that move beyond the conventional discourse about the relative merits of quantitative and qualitative research by addressing both methodological traditions without losing the meaningful distinctions between the two. It is worth noting that all four of the chapters in this section are co-authored—with each chapter including representatives of both qualitative and quantitative methods of inquiry.

Anna Neumann and Aaron Pallas explore the social and psychological challenges in becoming an educational researcher—with an emphasis on how one becomes a "practitioner" of educational inquiry. In their chapter on constructing data, Kadriye Ercikan and Wolff-Michael Roth examine and provide examples of how a researcher moves from data sources to data and data anlysis in two different types of research—high- and low-inference research—that involve both quantitative and qualitative elements. Michael Seltzer and Mike Rose, drawing on their own experiences, suggest how researchers can embrace "analytical thoughtfulness" that helps to bridge the divide between quantitative and qualitative traditions. King Beach, Betsy Becker, and Mary Kennedy, in a concluding chapter, focus on the construction of conclusions and the related challenges on which researchers should reflect—such as using their prior beliefs and knowledge to challenge their research findings.

SECTION SIX: WRITING, VOICE, AND DISSEMINATION OF RESEARCH

Under the leadership of section editor Beth Graue, the authors in the final section of the *Handbook* explore the public function of research and, in turn, challenges in making connections among research and representation, the politics of reporting one's research, the concept of "voice," and the place of practice in educational research. In the first chapter of Section Six, Beth Graue argues that writing is genre specific and that alternative genres both facilitate and constrain knowing by the ways in which they use authorial voice, the ways in which they explicate the place of the researcher in inquiry, and the degree to which their reflexivity is made public. She then advances and provides examples of four writing metaphors, exploring each with a clarity, force, and grace not often found in academic writing.

Elizabeth Creamer, drawing on her own interest and involvement in collaborative research, addresses "voice" in representation by providing diverse examples of polyvocality in single-authored texts, alternating first-person narratives, and scripts in varied formats to illustrate how different perspectives and interpretations can be shared in research writing. She vividly illustrates the ways in which traditional monovocal writing hides the voice of the author and leads readers to assign authorial meanings to research participants. Her chapter pushes readers to reflect on how their writing is nested within traditions and perspectives that may or may not fit into their own theoretical and conceptual landscapes. Finally, in a splendid final chapter—with the author demonstrating a fidelity to his voice that brings great exuberance to his topic—Gerald Bracey provides a stinging critique of the reporting of educational research through focusing on politics, ideology, and personality. He maps social networks among scholars and argues convincingly that there are many reasons beyond "good science" why research comes to light in the media and that researchers need to pay much more atttention to "getting the word out" regarding their inquiry. Fittingly, the book concludes with an animated exploration of "ideas"—ideas regarding the writing, representation, and dissemination of educational research.

PART I

ENGAGING IDEAS

*The Context of Inquiry
and Meaningful Problems*

Exploring the Multiple Purposes
of Inquiry and Key Stakeholders

INTRODUCTORY ESSAY

D. C. PHILLIPS

Webster defines "inquiry" succinctly as "attempting to learn," an account that unfortunately is silent on all of the thorny issues. Who, precisely, is making the attempt? What prompted or motivated the attempt to learn? Did the inquirer come up with the subject of the inquiry on his or her own volition, or was the inquirer commissioned to try to learn something on behalf of someone else? How will the success or failure of the inquiry be determined (and by whom)? What means—what methodology—shall the inquiry make use of? Are some methods better than others in the sense that they are likely to lead to the learning of something that is both useful and correct? Is every inquiry unique, or are there "family resemblances" that cut across different inquiries? Will the attempt be solitary, or will it involve a (large or small) team or community? What role shall the results of prior attempts play in directing the current inquiry? Such are the questions that plague a philosopher who dares to consult a dictionary.

But these issues are of more than "mere" philosophical interest; many of them have been bedeviling members of the educational research community, where for perhaps four decades (if not longer) the nature of educational inquiry has been the focus of intense debate. Educational research is of low quality because it is too focused on practice at the expense of theory, educational research is of low quality because it is too "ivory tower"—too theoretical—at the expense of focusing on practice, educational inquiry is of low quality because it lacks scientific rigor, and educational inquiry is irrelevant because it suffers from "physics envy" and mimics the (inappropriate) methods of the natural sciences. And so the debate has gone for decades, back and forth, mostly marching in place. (These various charges against research are documented in Phillips, 2005.) Now governments around the world (notably in the United States and the United Kingdom, but also elsewhere) have thrown their weight in, insisting on "evidence-based policy and practice"—not a bad idea, of course, for who wants "lack of evidence-based policy and practice"? But the small print contains a surprise: "Evidence" is characterized as being that which has been obtained (preferably) by the use of randomized controlled experiments (RCEs) or randomized field trials (RFTs). Qualitative researchers have taken up the debate with new vigor, supported by advocates of mixed methods designs. But the opposition is not silent and strikes back—with one of the responses being to hint, darkly, that use of anything except true experimental methods will identify an inquiry as being in the disreputable category of "unscientific." (The other response has been to withhold research funds from the apostates.) The stakes in this renewed, ongoing, and rapidly escalating debate are high—intellectually, socially, and educationally.

The three chapters in Section One of this volume will, it is hoped, throw light on a number of these issues (but not, of course, on all of them), and they will offer some solace to those educational researchers who wish to see an educational research enterprise that is both rigorous and relevant to the various stakeholders who wish to draw on it for guidance (or at least for succor), that is not hamstrung by a preconceived and extremely narrow view of the nature of science, and that is informed by—and draws inspiration from—having close contact with various realms of educational practice.

In Chapter 1, D. C. Phillips takes an unusual tack. Instead of arguing that the natural sciences are a stultifying model for educational research and the related social sciences to imitate, Phillips argues that the natural sciences—when properly understood—can serve as a liberating model. The case hinges, of course, on how the proviso "properly understood" is to be construed. The main theme of the chapter (backed up with numerous examples) is that the natural sciences are incredibly diverse in the types of inquiries that are conducted, the purpose of these inquiries, and the methods that are used. Natural scientists can be viewed as constructing cases that are rhetorically sound, in the sense that these are developed logically, and that marshal relevant evidence of all kinds to warrant the conclusions that are being put forward. Construing science, or even educational science, as being demarcated by the use of the RCE is to ignore the history and impressive achievements of the natural sciences, and the attempt to characterize the nature of science, and the nature of rigor, in terms of the use of a narrow range of "methods" can draw no support from the history of the sciences. (It is worth noting, in passing, that on the narrow account of science now favored in official circles, Galileo, Newton, Darwin, and many others must be considered to be "unscientific.") The chapter also stresses the vital contribution that is—and inevitably must be—made by branches of educational inquiry that are nonscientific even under the most charitable interpretation (which is not to say that they are lacking in rigor).

In Chapter 2, Robert Floden reminds the educational research community of the diverse audiences that our work serves—and how it serves them. Perhaps chief among the audiences for our work are our fellow researchers; it is from them that we usually draw our methods and theories—and often our problems. This is as it must be. But there are many other "stakeholders" in the educational enterprise whose problems sometimes concern us and who sometimes are concerned about our work. These stakeholders include parents; teachers; local education officials and program managers; state-level policymakers, politicians, and program managers; and federal policymakers, bureaucrats, and politicians. Floden reminds us of the contexts in which these individuals are operating, and he points out that the rhetorical form in which we report our work is not likely to resonate with their concerns or with their distaste for ingesting "social science findings." (Reports or stories from practitioners working in parallel contexts often have more face validity—and certainly more appeal—than do our carefully crafted, data-laden papers.) If we wish our research to have impact, we must attend more carefully to the needs, interests, and problems of those with whom we wish to communicate, and we must heed their favored styles of communication.

The final chapter in this section of the volume, authored by David Plank and Debbi Harris, in essence starts where Floden leaves off. One of the audiences for the work of the educational researcher that Floden discusses briefly is the policy community, and this becomes the specific focus of Chapter 3. In particular, the discussion grapples with the dilemmas that need to be faced when doing policy research. Researchers and policy-makers, being situated in different contexts, judge different questions to be important and have a different sense of what questions are answerable or intractable; for example, ideology is officially eschewed in research but may influence which results are accepted by policymakers. The chapter, like the previous one, remarks on the differences in rhetorical style across the research and policy contexts. Plank and Harris devote the second half of their discussion to two illustrative case studies: the debates over teacher quality and school choice. They end with a word of caution: Becoming more deeply engaged in policy research carries with it several risks for educational researchers.

Overall, then, the chapters in Section One have a liberatory intent; it is hoped that they will serve to broaden the options open to researchers—the methodological options, the types of inquiry that are mounted, the audiences for whom (and sometimes with whom) the inquiry is pursued, and the styles in which the research is reported. Broadening the options for rigorous inquiry is always a good thing.

REFERENCE

Phillips, D. C. (2005). *A quixotic quest? Philosophical issues in assessing the quality and rigor of educational research.* Unpublished manuscript, Stanford University.

1

MUDDYING THE WATERS

The Many Purposes of Educational Inquiry

D. C. PHILLIPS

Stanford University

There are more things in heaven and earth . . . than are dreamt of in your philosophy.

—Shakespeare, *Hamlet*

There is a conceit that is currently popular about an important genre of educational research—empirical research that has scientific pretensions. It is not merely a North American aberration, for it can also be found in the United Kingdom and in parts of Europe, and it is not unknown in Asia and Australasia. Put crassly, the conceit is this: In some influential quarters, empirical educational research is treated as being, in essence, a circumscribed enterprise with both narrow aims and narrow methods—despite the fact that many of the theories and much of the background knowledge on which they depend are complex and occasionally abstract and (usually) require much concentrated effort to master. Empirical educational inquiry is straightforward in principle, the story implies, because its purpose is clear-cut and narrow—namely, to establish causal relationships that can be used by planners, policymakers, and practitioners—and luckily there is a "gold standard" methodology that, if properly deployed, points the way to

rigorous work and eventually leads to reliable and hence usable findings. Doing research, on this account, is rather like gourmet cooking; if you follow the recipe, in all likelihood you will be successful, although following the recipe requires that you have had some prior experience and that you have a number of relevant skills at your disposal. Having the right recipe does not *guarantee* success, but it *facilitates* success, and in the case of some neophyte cooks, it might even be a *necessary condition* for success. The favored educational version of Julia Child's cookbook is, of course, Campbell and Stanley's (1963) *Experimental and Quasi-experimental Designs for Research,* first published as a long essay and later released in the form of a monograph.

The currently fashionable gold standard is, then, the *randomized controlled (or "true") experiment* (RCE) with related, slightly "less rigorous" designs such as the quasi-experiment and regression-discontinuity designs. The "What Works Clearinghouse" (www.wwc.org) attempts to evaluate educational research studies (from around the globe) that purport to use these designs—and currently only studies that purport to use these designs—according to their success in adhering to the "recipe" and hence according to their (supposed) trustworthiness. This whole expensive effort is funded by the U.S. Department of Education, which at the time of this writing is actively discouraging the use of other approaches to research or at least is looking with generally unfavorable funding eyes at proposals that plan to use other less rigorous methods. (For an overview of the current situation in the United States, see Eisenhart & Towne, 2003; Shavelson & Towne, 2004.)

How is this opening cannon blast, this diatribe against the setting up of a gold standard, relevant to the topic of this chapter, which after all (and unless the title is completely misleading) is purportedly concerned with delineating the range of purposes that educational research might reasonably be expected to serve? The answer, it is hoped, is obvious: If educational research is given a narrow characterization, whereby it is identified almost totally with studies that use RCEs (or related, slightly less rigorous designs), then there is something to say—but not a great deal that has not been said already. The main focal point becomes narrowed to the following: Does this treatment/ intervention cause an effect? But there is a great deal more to say if educational research, even *rigorous educational research,* is characterized more broadly and more defensibly, for the range of issues and problems that fall within its domain becomes much wider—and, dare it be said, much more interesting and possibly more socially relevant. However, it needs to be emphasized here that it is not part of the argument of this chapter that there is *anything wrong or blameworthy* about the rigorous use of true experimental and related designs; it is beyond dispute that they deserve to be part of the educational researcher's armamentarium. But it also needs to be stated clearly that they are only *part* and do not constitute anything like the *whole.* The reason why they cannot be the whole, and cannot be the entire gold standard, is that they are useful designs *only for certain purposes,* and although these purposes are important, they are quite limited in the scholarly (and even in the

scientific) scheme of things. There is more to educational research than establishing that a treatment causes an effect (and, relatedly, that the effect thus caused is of a particular size); therefore, educational research must be acknowledged as being more complicated, and as having more purposes or functions, than is dreamt of in many true experimenters' philosophy (even if their names are not Horatio). And because it has more purposes, its methodological net needs to be cast wider than the nets of true and quasi-experimental designs. To revert to the earlier analogy, cooking is hampered, not enhanced, if methodology (*one* methodology) is the prime consideration (sautéing, slow-roasting, or my favorite—deep-frying). What should determine the methodology used by the chef is the decision about *what dish it is desired to produce*—and innumerable dishes are possible.

Preparing the Ground

To lay a foundation for the main discussion, it is necessary to make a number of preliminary—but important—points.

1. The tendency to associate *rigorous scholarship or research* exclusively with *scientific research* needs to be resisted vigorously. There are a number of respectable disciplines (many antedating empirical research in education) that are sites of scholarly research in education and have their own (often long-standing and well-thought-out) canons of rigor, but that are not (and could not be) scientific under even the most charitable interpretation of the term and where the notion of a gold standard experimental methodology is ludicrous. For example, history and philosophy of education, political theory, and cultural criticism are active scholarly fields that regularly produce well-supported insights (and draw important conceptual and practical distinctions) that are mind expanding and even context setting for policymakers, practitioners, parents, and even empirical researchers. These are fields where often the conscience of society is reflected, where crucial discussions are taking place about vital matters such as the social justice ramifications of educational policies and practices, the rights of parents and

children versus those of the state, the rights of minority cultural groups versus those of the majority, the nature of fair and equitable treatment in schools and in the broader society, equality of opportunity for the sexes, the content of a liberal education, the content of the curriculum for various levels of schooling, the values we wish to pass on to the next generation of citizens, the rights of human participants in research, and whether nondemocratic beliefs and values held by some parents and students can be suppressed in the name of democracy. And the sad fact of the matter is that these fields, and work on such vital issues, are belittled—whether deliberately or unknowingly—when issues of funding and quality are discussed narrowly in terms of whether or not any particular piece of research bears the hallmark of empirical science. (All of the preceding examples have empirical dimensions, of course, but there is more to them than empirical inquiry can exhaust, and indeed research into their empirical dimensions is blind if not informed by the nonempirical discussions of matters such as social values, justice, educational ideals, and the nature of democracy.) Thus, although the main body of the chapter focuses on empirical research in education that aspires to be scientifically rigorous, it is not the intention to denigrate these other branches of inquiry or to assign them to a second-class scholarly status; it is just that there are enough fish to fry in dealing with misapprehensions about the scope of science itself.

2. The importance of the preceding point is heightened when the nature of *educational knowledge,* and of *educational problems,* is considered. Typically, problems in the natural sciences have the form of questions about matters of fact, about the truth of claims that follow from a theory, or about the nature of linkages (causal or not) between natural events and events produced in the laboratory. This is probably not a complete listing, but it is sufficient to allow me to make my point. How many chromosomes does the nucleus of a human (nonreproductive) cell contain? What is the structure of DNA? Do quarks have constituent parts? Can matter/energy escape from black holes? Are sunspot cycles related to weather patterns on Earth? What is the cause of cholera?

The field of education is interestingly different, as David Labaree puts it, because there are at least two problems that more or less condemn educational researchers to live "with a lesser form of knowledge":

> One is that, unlike workers in hard knowledge fields, they must generally deal with some aspect of human behavior. This means that cause only becomes effect through the medium of willful human action, which introduces a large and unruly error term into any predictive equation. These billiard balls are likely to change direction between the cue ball and the corner pocket. The other is that research projects in behavioral fields have embedded within them the values and the purposes not only of the researchers (like hard fields) but also of the actors under study. The result is a messy interaction of the researcher and the research subject. (Labaree, 1998, p. 5)

Thus, educational problems have the following forms (among others). Are students in U.S. high schools assigned too much homework? Does the "whole language" approach to the teaching of reading have any deleterious side effects? Can private enterprise (for-profit or not-for-profit companies) run elementary schools more effectively than do school districts? Do science textbooks trivialize ("dumb down") science, and do they sometimes omit vital topics for political reasons? Are American students overtested? What are the harmful, as well as the beneficial, effects of the "accountability movement"? What is the optimal size for a high school? Do language-minority students have a right to instruction in their own language? These and many other questions of concern are value laden (e.g., What counts as "too much" homework? What side effects are "deleterious"? What is a "political interest"? What "rights" do language-minority students have?). Furthermore, the answers to some of these questions may change over time in the sense that what was true at one time might no longer be true at another time. (An analysis of textbook content 20 years ago might well have turned up quite different results from what an analysis of contemporary books would reveal.) Lee Cronbach argued famously that in the interactive universe of the human sciences, generalizations can "decay" (Cronbach, 1975).

No doubt, with some effort, many educationally relevant questions might be subdivided into two parts: one consisting of a factual problem or series of problems (How much homework is assigned to what types of students? What extracurricular activities does this level of homework prevent students from pursuing?) and the other consisting of a question or series of questions about values or beliefs (How do those who claim this is too much justify this judgment, and do they make the case satisfactorily? Is it justified to hold that extracurricular activities— sometimes at least—are more important than homework?). But one must not lose sight of the fact that to be able to frame educationally pertinent questions, and to plan how to find the answers to them, educational researchers must not be insulated from the societal values that frame their work. After all, education is an activity that is pursued within a social setting, and problems only *become* problems within a social setting. In terms of one of the examples, it is only against a social background that harbors the value that there are some things that are more important for students to pursue than homework (e.g., sports, after-school paying jobs) that the research into quantity of homework becomes a relevant one to pursue. The moral seems clear: Researchers ought to recognize that *the domain of potential questions for educational research is virtually co-extensive with (if not wider than) the range of potential social problems.* I return to this point later.

3. Those who during recent debates have advocated the limiting of funding to educational research that is scientific because it carries out true experiments (or, more moderately, those who have advocated a massive increase in the use of true experiments) seem to come perilously close to assuming that there is a clearcut and easily policed border that demarcates science from "nonscience" or that demarcates science from other social concerns. This, however, is a pipe dream, as even a brief perusal of philosophy, history, and sociology of science since the mid-20th century makes clear. The border between science and nonscience is more like that between the United States and Mexico than it is like the former infamous wall between East Germany and West Germany (a border that,

it is salutary to remember, was never totally impermeable anyway, no matter how hard the guards tried to preserve its integrity).

Few, if any, philosophers of science have taken seriously the notion that science can be demarcated from nonscience in terms of the use or nonuse of a *specific research method* (e.g., the true experiment), and for good reason. Examination of the work of individuals who are acknowledged as being great scientists (e.g., Galileo, Harvey, Darwin, Einstein, Pasteur, Watson and Crick, Heisenberg, Hawking) fails to reveal any gold standard research method in common, in virtue of which they all could be held to be doing science. At first sight, it appears more promising to define science in terms of some underlying *logical* approach or method such as use of inductive reasoning, use of the so-called hypothetico-deductive method (HDM), or adherence to the principle of attempted refutation—but these approaches also founder. (Many apparently nonscientific endeavors make use of induction, so too much would count as science if this were set up as the criterion. Even literary hermeneutics makes use of the HDM, as Follesdal [1979], shows, and Popper's famous program to establish a "criterion of demarcation" that delineates science from nonscience, based on potential falsifiability, is a failure on several grounds; see the nontechnical account by Worrall, 2002. The main problem with all of these approaches is that many highly regarded pieces of science would be excluded if any of these criteria of demarcation of science were adopted as *the* criterion. Perhaps we must settle for John Dewey's account, where science is taken to be the clearest example of a field that engages in *competent inquiry;* on this account, there is no difference in principle between scientific inquiries and the sorts of endeavors that most of us conduct in everyday life, endeavors such as deciding which form of transport will get us to an appointment across town on time [Dewey, 1938/1966; 1933/1971].) This is not to say, of course, that everyday inquiries are always (or often) carried out proficiently in practice; humans are not by nature optimal reasoners, hence Dewey's stressing of the need for inquiries to be "competent." (For a recent discussion of common foibles in human reasoning and problem solving, see Wolpert, 1994, chap. 1.)

If the border between science and nonscience is an ill-defined porous one, then we are led to a point similar to one argued earlier, namely, that there probably is no principled way in which to completely insulate scientific activities from purposes, ideals, or values that are held in the society where particular scientific inquiries are being pursued. Although some radical sociologists and philosophers of postmodern disposition, among others, make too much of this openness and—going to extremes—hold that there is no such thing as scientific objectivity or value neutrality (for a discussion of some of the issues, and for clarification of where values ought—and ought not—to influence the workings of science, see Phillips, 1997, 2000), nevertheless a good case can be made not only that social values can influence the internal workings of science but also that in some aspects of science it is *appropriate* for them to do so. In a recent book, Philip Kitcher, a respected philosopher of science, dissects the notion that scientists—because it is not possible to pursue all of the countless issues that could be investigated—must select a subset of those issues that currently are scientifically *significant;* crucially, he also makes the case that there is no simple and atemporal way in which to determine what actually *is* scientifically significant:

> The notion of significance, I argued, is not independent of time and context, and our standards of epistemic significance, like our standards of practical significance, evolve. . . . Indeed, there's a clear sense in which the sciences are constitutive of our world, the mundane sense in which what we pick out as important and worthy of investigation at one time leads to interactions with the environment that modify it for our successors. . . . The upshot of this is that epistemic values do not stand apart from—"above"—our quotidian concerns. Rather, they are to be balanced against practical interests. (Kitcher, 2001, pp. 199–200)

This being the case, Kitcher (2001) argues that the selection of issues for investigation should take place by way of democratic deliberative processes. The resulting "well-ordered science" would not be insulated "from public discussion" (p. 201) and would likely result in research foci that are socially important but also (controversially) would lead to some potentially socially harmful lines of research being embargoed. Kitcher's position is more nuanced and better argued than this gloss suggests, and it should be stressed that he does not compromise the view that science should pursue *truth* and that objective knowledge is possible. Perhaps he could have strengthened his position even more by referring to Dewey's theory of inquiry; in a chapter titled "The Existential Matrix of Inquiry: Cultural," Dewey (1938/1966) writes,

> The environment in which human beings live, act, and inquire is not simply physical. It is cultural as well. Problems which induce inquiry grow out of the relations of fellow beings to one another, and the organs for dealing with these relations are not only the eye and ear, but the meanings which have developed in the course of living, together with the ways of forming and transmitting culture with all its constituents of tools, arts, institutions, traditions, and customary beliefs. (p. 42)

4. The penultimate point to be made in this clearing of the ground can be put succinctly: The nature of science and, crucially for the theme of this chapter, the scope of activities within science both are seriously misrepresented if science is identified solely (or even largely) with establishing that a treatment or some natural circumstance caused a particular effect. The remainder of the discussion is designed to overthrow this illiberal conception. But the point is also worth making here that the investigations of causes, when appropriate, are seriously misrepresented if it is claimed that the only rigorous way in which to carry them out is by way of true experiments or quasi-experiments. This point was made in brilliant fashion in a recent satirical (but also deadly serious) article in the *British Medical Journal.* The title nearly says it all: "Parachute Use to Prevent Death and Major Trauma Related to Gravitational Challenge: Systematic Review of Randomised Controlled Trials" (Smith & Pell, 2003). After searching a number of databases, the authors found that the belief that parachute use is effective has been supported by *no* randomized studies. Tongue-in-cheek, they suggest that such research is urgently needed because parachute use currently is supported only by

observational evidence, which of course is of dubious validity and does not establish causal efficacy.

5. Finally, before picking up the threads of the main discussion, there is a serious problem that remains to be dealt with if the subsequent discussion of the breadth of inquiries in science is to bear fruit. This problem can arise in selecting cases to serve as exemplars to delineate the range of activities to be included under the term "science" ("real scientists do X, as is revealed in the work of the experimenter Professor B, and those who do Y or Z should not be called 'scientists'") or that can arise when debate focuses on the essence of science ("although cases of X, Y, and Z can be found in the history of science, the essence of science is the doing of X," "the essence of science is establishing that C causes E"). In discussing this with colleagues and students, I have fallen into the habit of calling it the "foxtrot problem," for it is easy (and less threatening) to explain in terms of the following analogy. Suppose that one has been asked to teach a group of friends how to perform that old ballroom dance, the foxtrot. The dictionary definition will be of scant help in getting the novices started—"a ballroom dance in 2/4 or 4/4 time," *Webster's* tells us, an account that leaves lots of room for maneuver. A better stratagem might be to select an exemplar for the group to follow, but the issue of *which* exemplar will arise immediately. Perhaps a film clip of Fred Astaire? Many will reject his moves as atypical, as not being within the normal range of activities associated with the dance (it is Hollywood entertainment, not a genuine foxtrot). Others will say that only the best will do, and Astaire was the best (not forgetting Ginger Rogers, who, after all, did everything that Fred did and did it backward). Another procedure would be to go to a (now rare) tea dance, wait until the bandleader announces the foxtrot, and select a few random dancers to record for later emulation (the principle here is that the foxtrot is what dancers do when they believe they are doing the foxtrot). But again, some could offer a challenge; these might be beginners or unskilled dancers, and certainly there is no guarantee that they possess characteristics that make them worthy exemplars. Faced with this difficult situation, the hapless teacher might be excused for simply stipulating, "I've had lots of experience, and I legislate that this is what is going to constitute a foxtrot for the purposes of your instruction."

Philosophers talk about all of this in terms of stipulative and reportive definitions. (See, e.g., Scheffler, 1960. So-called programmatic definitions are excluded from the following discussion for the sake of simplicity.) A stipulative definition, as its name implies, is one where a particular meaning is stipulated, whether or not this bears any resemblance to the way in which the term being defined is commonly used. ("A person is *creative,* for the purposes of this research project, if he or she can describe 10 uses for a brick in 60 seconds" is a hoary example illustrating that an operational definition—beloved by many in the educational research community—is a type of stipulative definition.) On the other hand, a reportive definition is, unsurprisingly, one that reports how a term is used within a linguistic community. This is what dictionaries attempt to give ("Creative: Inventive; imaginative," again according to *Webster's*). It follows that reportive definitions can be true or false. (A dictionary or a definer might make a mistake when claiming "X means Y" in a certain language. This brings to mind the outrageous skit by Monty Python, where scurrilous "meanings" are inserted into phrasebooks sold to foreign tourists in England.) In contrast, stipulative definitions cannot be right or wrong, for they simply are linguistic conventions that have been legislated for a particular purpose (and although a convention can be useful or not, it cannot be "right" or "wrong"). There is freedom of stipulation, and no harm comes from exercising this freedom *so long as the stipulator does not later slip into believing that he or she has given the normal (reportive) meaning of the term in question.* (The word "creative" does not, in normal English use, mean being able to quickly think of a number of uses for a brick—when we say "Picasso was creative," we are not referring to his facility with specifying multiple uses of building materials—but nevertheless this might be a useful stipulation to make for the purposes of a piece of empirical research!)

It is not at all clear whether those who define "scientific educational research" or "rigorous educational research" in terms of RCEs or randomized field trials (RFEs), aimed at determining causation, suppose that they are giving a reportive definition or a stipulative definition (or, what comes to the same thing, think they are reporting or stipulating the central or defining feature of science). If it is the latter, then it must be stressed again that they are free to make such a stipulation, but this does not get them what they wish to attain; stipulating that this is what these expressions mean does *not* settle what "scientific research" or "rigorous research" refer to in normal discourse. Matters of research design, or of public policy with regard to what types of research ought to be funded, cannot be settled by stipulating a definition (and it is a narrow stipulation at that). The point is that issues concerning research design and public funding are ones that are discussed in professional and public forums, where terms are being used according to *normal use*. There is little doubt that in normal parlance (as would be captured in a reportive account), "science" means far more than use of the RCE. It seems incontrovertible that Newton, Einstein, Galileo, Harvey, Pasteur, Darwin, Bohr, Boyle, Rutherford, and the Curies all were doing science, yet according to the stipulative definition in terms of the RCE, none of them was. The structure of DNA, the phenomenon of continental drift, the process of biological evolution, and the expansion of the universe—not to mention the efficacy of parachutes—all were established without the benefit of true experimental or quasi-experimental designs and hence were not scientific achievements at all. And, of course, if the stipulated definition were to hold sway, the venerable periodical *Scientific American* would need to change its name to *Unscientific American*—or, perhaps more moderately, to *Nonscientific American*—for reports of randomized experiments rarely grace its pages.

DIVERSITY OF INQUIRY IN THE NATURAL SCIENCES

This lengthy but vital clearing of the ground prepares the way for the consideration of some examples of research in the natural sciences, examples that illustrate the diversity of purposes of inquiry that can be found in the natural

sciences. Then—informed by these cases, using the old culinary principle that what is sauce for the goose is sauce for the gander—the discussion turns to the many purposes of empirical research in education. The aim throughout is to "complexify"—to reassert the potential width of educational research.

The following listing of examples drawn from across the natural sciences is not intended to be exhaustive (although it is hoped that it is fairly comprehensive), nor are the categories into which the examples are sorted watertight or mutually exclusive; with more care, no doubt it would have been possible to collapse some of the categories or to tease some out into new ones not currently included. To follow this path, however, would have been to seek more precision than is necessary to illustrate the point at issue, namely, the many purposes in the service of which scientific investigation can be pursued. Finally, it becomes obvious as the discussion proceeds that several of the examples could easily have been placed into more than one category; some of them are mentioned only briefly, whereas other (perhaps less familiar) ones are described in more detail. (Some of the examples, but by no means all of them, are drawn from Lee, 2002.)

Determining Whether an Intervention or a Treatment Produces an Effect or Effects (either intended or unintended). This is the category under which the main educational use of the RCE falls, but of course there are many examples to be found in the natural (including the biological and human) sciences. As one example, after Jonas Salk had developed the first polio vaccine, he tested it on himself, but eventually a large-scale RFE was conducted to check on its safety as well as its efficacy. Did the treatment (inoculated) group enjoy more immunity from infection than the control group? Were there any deleterious side effects? As a second example, smoking is in effect an "intervention," but it is not possible in practice to randomly assign individuals to the smoking and nonsmoking conditions, so means other than the RCE (e.g., statistical analysis of medical records, matching the records of smokers with those of nonsmokers who are otherwise similar) have been adopted to make a case that firmly establishes a link between smoking and deleterious health conditions such as lung cancer and to rule out other possible causal factors. An early influential study in 1950—followed by many others that eventually cemented the case—found that of 605 men admitted to the hospital with lung cancer, fewer than 2% were nonsmokers.

Determining Whether a Purported Effect Is a Genuine One. Many apparent effects of interventions in the laboratory or in the field, or many effects that seem to arise as a consequence of some natural occurrence, are of such significance (practically or theoretically) that scientists try to replicate these findings, test to see whether they recur under more closely controlled or monitored conditions, or attempt to establish that some causal mechanism is at work. Again educational examples abound, but replication is a byword also across the natural and behavioral sciences. As one example, cold fusion, which is claimed to be a process in which atomic fusion occurs (and releases energy) in a cheap apparatus in simply equipped laboratories, was first discovered in a lab in Utah, but generally the effect has not been replicated. (There were at one time a small number of supposed positive replications, but these were later explained in terms of other mechanisms.) As a second example, "facilitated communication" was developed as a method of helping individuals unable to communicate linguistically because of autism or severe retardation. It involves a facilitator helping such individuals to type messages on a keyboard. Several qualitative studies claimed that the technique was effective—a socially important finding—but subsequent work that paid more attention to alternative explanations and to validity issues obtained evidence strongly suggesting that the messages written by the participants in the studies were (consciously or unconsciously) cued by the facilitators. (For a slightly fuller discussion and references, see Maxwell, 2004.) As a third example, some Native American tribes ingest parts of the Echinacea plant for its medicinal properties. Is there anything to this?

Determining Whether Some Predicted Process or Phenomenon Actually Occurs. The sciences contain many cases where investigations were mounted—some complex and of long duration—to verify (or refute) the claim that some as yet unobserved entity, phenomenon, or process actually exists. Often this work serves as a test of a theory. Examples include the discovery of the outer planets (e.g., the existence of Neptune was postulated to explain perturbations of the orbit of Uranus, but its existence needed to be verified observationally), the reality of continental drift, the existence of extrasensory perception (not supported), and the bending of light rays as they pass close to a large gravitational body. (This latter phenomenon, predicted by Einstein as a consequence of his theoretical work, was verified in 1919 by observations made by Eddington during an eclipse of the sun.) Some predicted phenomena, or some theories, have even been verified or supported by accident, for example, when Penzias and Wilson—working on improving microwave communication in 1964—unexpectedly detected the background radiation of the universe, a finding that strongly supported the "Big Bang" theory. (At first, they thought their historic observations were the result of malfunctioning microwave detection equipment.)

Noticing, and Then Describing and Investigating, an Unexpected Phenomenon. Sometimes scientists stumble onto things by chance (but it has been said that a prepared mind makes its own chances) and realize that they have hit on a phenomenon of great interest (as did Penzias and Wilson). The first task in such cases usually is to describe or delineate the phenomenon (What precisely is being dealt with here?). As one example, while working on bacterial infection in 1928, Alexander Fleming noted that a Petri dish containing some of his bacterial cultures had been accidentally contaminated with a mold. Luckily, he made the surprising observation that the clumps of bacteria near the site of the contamination were dying off. Puzzled by why this should be the case, he launched a research program to identify the mold, isolate the secretion it produced, and verify that it destroyed the bacteria. Eventually, of course, this led to the development of penicillin. As a second example, the physicist Roentgen discovered by chance in his laboratory that a neglected photographic plate, which apparently had not been used, had nevertheless been exposed and contained the image of the object that had been resting on it. His subsequent investigations into how this had happened revealed over many months the properties of the previously unknown "X radiation" that was being emitted during experiments he had been conducting with cathode ray tubes.

Explaining, or Determining the Cause of, Some Familiar Condition or Phenomenon. This is a very common motivation for scientific research; the world is full of phenomena that we are quite familiar with but for which (currently) no explanations are forthcoming. What is the cause of cancer? (Headway is being made here.) What is the cause of autism? Why is the sky dark at night? (If the universe is infinite in both time and space, then every point in the sky should be "occupied" by a star, making the sky white at night! This conundrum was resolved by the Big Bang theory and the accompanying posit that the universe is expanding, together with the realization that there are vast clouds of interstellar dust.) What causes the tides? (Newton cracked this mystery.) Why are pumps able to remove water from mines only to about 32 feet deep? (This puzzle led to the work of Boyle and others on air and gas pressure.) What is the cause of scurvy (the blight of mariners up until the late 18th century), and why does the consumption of citrus fruits prevent the condition from arising? (Eventually this was explained in terms of vitamin C.) How are bees able to locate sources of food? (The so-called "dance of the bees" was noted, and "decoded," by von Frisch.) How are malaria and cholera transmitted? (For a fascinating discussion of the latter in terms of maps showing the locations of the water wells in London, see Tufte, 1997, chap. 2.)

Testing a Widely Held Explanation for Some Phenomenon or Regularity. Often there is a familiar phenomenon for which an explanation has been put forward but has not been subjected to rigorous scrutiny or seems problematic given other background theories or suppositions. There are some classic illustrations of this in the history of the sciences. The explanation for childbed fever (a condition fatal to large numbers of women who had recently given birth) in terms of vapors in the air was overturned by Semmelweis (see the excellent discussion by Hempel, 1966, chap. 2). The explanation for the breakdown of foods during digestion, in terms of mechanical processes, was disproved by René de Réaumur, who inserted a piece of meat in a wire gauze container into a hawk. Protected in this manner from mechanical interference inside the digestive system, the food nevertheless was broken down. He also collected digestive juices in a sponge and squeezed them over a piece of meat that subsequently slowly dissolved (Asimov, 1964).

Determining the Function of Some Feature or Entity. Although it is not clear whether all features or entities have definite natural functions (e.g., fingerprints, the fluffy tail of a rabbit), and although it seems to be the case that some have lost their original functions (e.g., the human appendix), nevertheless it has been a motivation of many investigators to probe the possible functions of regularly occurring features. Why does the human brain have the obvious structural features that it has? (What are the functions of the cerebral hemispheres, the cerebellum, and the medulla oblongata?) Why do humans possess opposable thumbs? What functions, if any, are served by the spectacular feathers of male peacocks? (This was answered by Darwin's theory of sexual selection.) Why do many animals (e.g., amphibians, all mammals) have hearts? (The detailed functioning and structure of the circulatory system with the heart as a pump—or, in the cases of mammals, a dual pump—was elucidated by William Harvey in a brilliant series of simple "demonstrations" that were designed to eliminate reasonable alternative explanations. See Dale, 1951.)

Determining the Structure, Architecture, or Anatomy of Some Entity or Feature. Scientists have often been puzzled by questions of structure: What is the large-scale structure of the universe? What is the structure of a living cell? What is the structure of the mammalian kidney? What is the structure of the mammalian brain? What is the internal structure of the earth? What is the structure of an atom? What is the structure of DNA and other important biologically active molecules?

Making the Case for Some General or Wide-Ranging Theory or Explanatory/Predictive Model. In several long books, Darwin marshaled a variety of types of evidence to make the case that all species of plants and animals had arisen not only by evolution but also for a specific causal agency (natural selection). Theoretical physicists have developed theories about the fundamental constituents of matter (e.g., quark theory) using mathematical derivations from theoretical postulates, and predictions from these theories are tested in the now familiar large colliders (e.g., SLAC, CERN). Eddington tested the prediction about the gravitational bending of light that was made on the basis of Einstein's theory of relativity. Luis and Walter Alvarez developed a case about the extinction of the dinosaurs based on their discovery of an iridium layer in 65 million-year-old geological strata around the world. The germ theory of disease was based on the work of Pasteur and other "microbe hunters" of the late 19th century. (Eventually the research program in this area of science led to the distinguishing of bacteria from viruses and the recognition of diseases or conditions not produced by biological agents, e.g., conditions such as scurvy, a vitamin deficiency.) The search for a computer model that will allow accurate prediction of the path of a hurricane is ongoing (and each successive attempt at modeling is given a "natural test" every time a new hurricane develops).

Measuring the Age of Some Object, Measuring the Frequency of Some Event, or Measuring a Physical Constant or a Capacity. Accurate measurement has been central to many scientific endeavors. Galileo used his own pulse to time the swinging of lamps of different lengths hanging in the local cathedral (leading to the law of pendulum motion), and an accurate way in which to measure the distance of stars was crucial to the development of modern cosmological theories. Other breakthroughs have included measuring the velocity of light, determining the age of fossils and the age of the earth, dating the Ice Ages, dating the reversals of the earth's magnetic field (evidently we are overdue for another one), dating earthquakes along the San Andreas fault (of particular interest to the current author), measuring the age of the solar system, measuring the frequency of sexual activity in various human populations (of particular interest to nearly everyone), and measuring the frequency of occurrence of different blood groups in different human populations.

Developing Some Discovery Into a Usable Product or Process. Development of useful technology is often an engineering achievement, but there is a thin line between the work of engineers and the work of scientists; after all, engineers are "applied scientists." The same can be said about "materials scientists." Much work in contemporary chemistry also is of an applied nature, but it also can be considered as advancing science; synthesizing naturally occurring molecules for pharmacological use is, for example, a common enterprise. There is little doubt that the practical development of advanced scientific instrumentation, penicillin, superconductivity, radiography, inoculation, pasteurization, antiseptic surgery, the birth control pill, and radio communication and television all were important scientific achievements as well as technological achievements.

LESSONS FROM THESE EXAMPLES

A number of points emerge from these examples.

1. The first thing that is impressive about (and obvious from) these examples is the huge range of activities engaged in by scientists: establishing of causal factors; distinguishing genuine effects from spurious effects; determining function; determining structure; making careful descriptions and delineations of phenomena; making accurate measurements; developing and testing theories, hypotheses, and causal models; testing received wisdom; elucidating unexpected phenomena; and producing practically important techniques and artifacts. A moment's reflection also reveals that many of these activities have involved mathematical analysis and calculation, deductive and inductive reasoning (and almost certainly abductive reasoning as well), the development of lengthy chains of reasoning, the questioning of premises and the exposing of testable (and sometimes untestable) assumptions, a willingness to take

criticism seriously (and also, in some cases, a willingness to carry on with a line of investigation despite criticisms), and the creative design of ingenious devices and laboratory setups and demonstrations. De Réaumur constructing wire gauze containers for food, Harvey blocking a vein in his arm with pressure from a finger, Darwin observing turtles in the Galapagos and breeding pigeons on his farm, Hawking doing calculations, Kinsey and his coworkers administering questionnaires, von Frisch constructing a glass-sided beehive, Galileo rolling a ball down an inclined plane, John Snow locating on one map the locations of water wells and also the cases of cholera across London, Crick and Watson tinkering with a crude metal molecular model—all these are as much a part of science as is a modern educational psychologist consulting a table of random numbers to select members of the control and treatment groups for an RCE or an RFE.

2. Even if it were held that some of the activities just mentioned are logically or conceptually "more central" to science than the others—a view that the current author remains skeptical about—it would still need to be acknowledged that *without* careful observations, testing, measurements, construction of ingenious apparati, designing of questionnaires, making of models, calculations, implications, and so forth, scientific inquiry (however characterized) would not be able to get off the ground. A so-called "logic of inquiry" would be sterile unless there also were means for the acquisition of some substance (e.g., data, observations, hypotheses). This suggests that attempts to delineate the "central method of science"—the attempt to give a simple gold standard account of the nature of science—must always be quite arbitrary. Perhaps it was recognition of all this that led Percy Bridgman, a Nobel laureate in physics, to remark that "the scientist has no other method than doing his damnedest" (cited in Kaplan, 1964, p. 27).

3. Implicit in some of the preceding remarks is a view that hardly needs to be made explicit: Science is a creative activity at several different levels. The creativity of scientists can be tapped in realizing the need for a study (or recognizing the serendipitous opportunity for carrying one out), in deciding how to design a study, and in interpreting the results or recognizing the support that the results give to a new theory. "Doing your damnedest" presumably entails being as creative as possible, but of course neither Bridgman nor anyone else has been able to provide an algorithm for doing so. De Réaumur certainly was being creative, but he was not following some recipe when he figured out how to study digestion, and there was no handbook listing the precise steps that Harvey, Darwin, and Einstein had to follow to make their respective breakthroughs. And this is true not only for so-called "revolutionary" scientists; the nonalgorithmic nature of much of science holds true for many of those engaged in what Kuhn (somewhat controversially) called "normal science." (Sometimes this has been parodied unfairly as being "hack science.") Ingenuity was required to accurately determine the velocity of light and many other physical constants, to study the behavior of animals, and to track down the vectors of particular diseases—and it is required today in countless day-to-day activities in the laboratory and in the field.

4. Perusal of the earlier examples suggests a way of thinking about science that often has been overlooked in textbook accounts of scientific method. Many of the cases outlined earlier involved investigators *constructing a convincing case,* a case that was so competently constructed—that bound various types of evidence together with cogent argument and analysis and critique of rival hypotheses—that it would stand up to critical scrutiny and produce conviction. (Dewey's expression, used when he talked of inquiry, comes to mind here—science aims to produce conclusions that are "warrantedly assertible," with the "warrant" being a supporting argument.) In other words, pursuing a line of research and arguing in favor of the conclusions that were reached is a *rhetorical* activity. (See the symposium on rhetoric in the human sciences in Nelson, Megill, & McCloskey, 1987. See also Toulmin, 1958/2003.) Harvey constructed a detailed case about the circulation of blood in which he attempted to cover all of the known bases and convince the doubters. Darwin's great book was a lengthy case in support of his thesis that species originated by way

of natural selection, and a glance at the chapter headings reveals how thoroughly the case was developed.

Several of the examples just discussed involved scientists not developing but rather probing a case—putting it to a severe test. (Eddington's test of Einstein's case is a classic example, but so is Semmelweis's probing of the traditional case about the cause of childbed fever.) The point is that both the construction of a convincing case and the attempt to hold a case up to critical scrutiny are open-ended activities, just as a debate against an intelligent opponent is an open-ended endeavor. Once again there is no algorithm or golden rule except Bridgman's "do your damnedest" and, I would add, "be prepared to have your weak points exposed."

5. The final point about the examples to be underscored here is that although it is quite apparent that many programs of scientific research have *led to* practical applications (e.g., Roentgen's work on X-rays, Fleming's work that led to penicillin), it is important not to overlook the cases where important pieces of science *grew from* inquiries that initially were motivated by practical concerns. Finding how a disease such as cholera is transmitted, finding why water pumps have limits on their efficacy, searching for the cause of cancer, finding how to stop wine and milk from spoiling—all of these have led to major breakthroughs in our understanding of nature. Yet in many quarters, there is a prejudice against so-called "applied science," as if it were not genuine science and as if it could not lead to theoretically interesting results. The important book by Donald Stokes, *Pasteur's Quadrant,* is a strong critique of this attitude (Stokes, 1997); the title comes from Stokes's use of a two-by-two table, where the two dimensions are work that is high or low in theoretical interest and high or low in practical interest. One of the four cells or quadrants—that which is high on both dimensions—is typified by the work of Pasteur. But Pasteur was a model long before Stokes; in a work dating from the early 1960s, the following passage appears:

> Pasteur's researches into the phenomena of fermentation and decay were often directed toward solving a specific problem presented to him by brewers, dairymen, vintners, silk growers. . . . *His stimulus was almost always a practical problem, the solution of which was of economic importance.* . . . His empiricism was a means to an end: to establish once and for all that disease, both human and animal, could be traced to microorganisms. (Rook, 1964, p. 360, emphasis added)

Research in education is often regarded as an applied area, so the preceding point is of particular relevance. The attempt to unravel the intricacies of educational problems, the attempt to understand the psychology of learning and the developmental process at work in the learner, the attempt to understand the role of scientific findings and values in the making of political decisions about educational policy, the attempt to evaluate innovative educational programs and not only to document whether they produce their intended effects but also to reveal their (often vitally important) unintended consequences— all these (and countless others) may be "applied" endeavors, but they also can, and sometimes do, lead to important theoretical understandings. Many educational researchers and evaluators are working—perhaps unbeknownst to themselves—in Pasteur's quadrant. (Among the greatest examples is the work of Cronbach, whose two books on evaluation of social programs, together with his work on educational testing and measurement, have been widely influential; he was awarded the gold medal of the American Psychological Association for his disciplinary contributions. See, for example, Cronbach & Associates, 1980; Cronbach, 1982.)

THE DIVERSE FUNCTIONS OF EDUCATIONAL RESEARCH

This chapter has attempted to make a case, albeit a fairly complex one, about educational research. First, the domain of educational research is much wider than science, for historical, philosophical, and other inquiries rooted in nonscientific disciplines are an important and nondispensable part of it. Second, it is by necessity open to social concerns and is influenced by social values. (Some recent scholars have tried to make the same case about inquiry in the natural sciences, but it is not part of my current aim to join the debates over this set of issues.) The main focus, however, has been to frame how to think about empirical research in education, research that usually aspires to be in some sense "scientific." To this end, the strategy has been to suggest that too often an extremely narrow account of the nature of science has been given—one that not only is insupportable as an account of science but that also greatly restricts the scope of permissible empirical educational research. One way to put the point of the discussion is that rather than inquiry in the natural sciences being a stultifying model for educational research, quite the opposite should be the case: *A liberal view of science—one that does justice to its incredible diversity of problems, purposes, and methods—will greatly liberate empirical educational research,* and it will also illuminate what it stands to gain from nonscientific research that emanates from the disciplines more often thought of as being closely related to the humanities.

Examples can be found within the corpus of educational research that could fit into just about all of the categories used above to describe the scope of the natural sciences, but it is important to note that educational research has additional purposes not covered in the previous listing. The reason for this extra breadth was signaled earlier: Education is a social process (or family of processes) that is open to sociocultural values, purposes, and needs and interests, with the work of teachers and administrators, and the efforts of students to learn, being affected by the beliefs all of them hold, their values, their degree of motivation, and their sense of self-efficacy. Educational research that is to do justice to the nature of the phenomena being investigated must correspondingly be wide in scope. Societies generate social problems that are not found in the natural sciences:

> The morning paper reports a variety of social problems: war, pollution, traffic jams, and crimes. It also reports a decrease in automobile sales, rising prices, violence in high schools, an increase in drug use and cigarette smoking, and so on. After reading the news, readers find themselves upset about some of these reports, and wanting to do something about them. . . . In addition, those who analyze social problems often differ among themselves. Some analysts say that modern society produces more social problems than do simpler societies; others disagree. Some say that modern society produces more problems than solutions, but others argue that the real difficulty is the overproduction of so-called solutions. Trying to make sense of all this can easily result in confusion. Yet people continue to study social problems in an effort to understand how they occur and how they can be controlled. (Rubington & Weinberg, 1995, p. 3)

Wherever a social problem is found, a social scientist or an educational researcher can find there an opportunity to make a contribution.

That said, it might be well—by way of conclusion—to challenge the reader to provide an example or two of either possible or actual pieces of educational research that could fit into the earlier categories drawn from the natural sciences: determining whether an intervention or a treatment produces an effect or effects; determining whether a purported effect is a genuine one; determining whether some predicted process or phenomenon actually occurs; noticing, and then describing and investigating, an unexpected phenomenon; explaining, or determining the cause of, some familiar condition or phenomenon; testing a widely held explanation for some phenomenon or regularity; determining the function of some feature or entity; determining the structure, architecture, or anatomy of some entity or feature; making the case for some general or wide-ranging theory or predictive model; measuring the age of some object, measuring the frequency of some event, or measuring a physical constant or a capacity; and developing some discovery into a usable product or process. Then—the challenge continues—add to this list some cases of research into sociocultural matters that are not represented in the natural sciences and cases focusing on organizational or contextual factors, and then some cases of research directed at exposing social inequities and distributional problems associated with educational goods. Finally, add some examples of cases where educational researchers have come to the aid of individuals—diagnosing a learning difficulty or a misunderstanding of some key item of subject matter, helping a teacher with methods that might be more appropriate than the ones the teacher is using when he or she works with children of cultural backgrounds different from his or her own, or helping those who are running a new educational program to make it better by means of formative evaluation.

Those who take up this dual challenge will become convinced—if they are not convinced already—of the extremely broad range of issues on which educational research fruitfully can be brought to bear and the broad range of methods that are available for the researcher to use. But finally, it is important to note one important facet of educational research that will not emerge from undertaking this exercise: The pursuit of a piece of research is, at best, a fluid undertaking—as indeed is much work in the natural sciences. The researcher is always faced with difficult options, trade-offs are usually necessary as the work is both designed and executed, and there are no algorithms available to guide many of the difficult decisions that need to be made. The dynamic nature of the research process is hidden from view in the journal articles or book chapters where the results are reported; the process is sterilized for broad consumption. In building a convincing case about his or her work, the wise researcher will remain substantively and methodologically flexible and will simply do his or her "damnedest." Cronbach and Associates (1980) put it well in the context of a discussion of the applied research field of program evaluation, but their message is fully transferable to educational research more broadly construed:

> Evaluators gain much experience in the course of designing and redesigning a study. Unfortunately, little of that experience is recorded for the benefit of the evaluation community. Rarely does a research report mention the branching points where the study took one shape rather than another or explain why the final plan was preferred. Indeed, most of the choices that shape the evaluation are made rapidly and by tacit consent rather than by explicit weighing of options. Methods of evaluation would improve faster if evaluators more often wrote retrospective accounts of design choices. These accounts should reach well beyond the "tic-tac-toe" aspects of the design to consider how questions were chosen,

how resources were deployed, how quality of data was controlled, and how observations were assembled for communication. (p. 214)

References

Asimov, I. (1964). *A short history of biology.* Garden City, NY: Natural History Press.

Campbell, D., & Stanley, J. (1963). Experimental and quasi-experimental designs for research on teaching. In N. Gage (Ed.), *Handbook of research on teaching* (pp. 171–246). Chicago: Rand McNally.

Cronbach, L. (1975). Beyond the two disciplines of scientific psychology. *American Psychologist, 30*(2), 116–127.

Cronbach, L. (1982). *Designing evaluations of educational and social programs.* San Francisco: Jossey-Bass.

Cronbach, L., & Associates. (1980). *Toward reform of program evaluation.* San Francisco: Jossey-Bass.

Dale, H. (1951). Harvey and the circulation of the blood. In J. Lindsay (Ed.), *The history of science: Origins and results of the scientific revolution—A symposium* (pp. 55–64). London: Cohen & West.

Dewey, J. (1966). *Logic: The theory of inquiry.* New York: Holt, Rinehart & Winston. (Original work published in 1938)

Dewey, J. (1971). *How we think* (rev. ed.). Chicago: Henry Regnery. (Original work published in 1933)

Eisenhart, M., & Towne, L. (2003). Contestation and change in national policy on "scientifically based" education research. *Educational Researcher, 32*(7), 31–38.

Follesdal, D. (1979). Hermeneutics and the hypothetico-deductive method. *Dialectica, 33,* 319–336.

Hempel, C. (1966). *Philosophy of natural science.* Englewood Cliffs, NJ: Prentice Hall.

Kaplan, A. (1964). *The conduct of inquiry: Methodology for behavioral science.* Scranton, PA: Chandler.

Kitcher, P. (2001). *Science, truth, and democracy.* Oxford, UK: Oxford University Press.

Labaree, D. (1998). Educational researchers: Living with a lesser form of knowledge. *Educational Researcher, 27*(8), 4–12.

Lee, R. (2002). *The Eureka! Moment.* New York: Routledge.

Maxwell, J. (2004). Reemergent scientism, post-modernism, and dialogue across differences. *Qualitative Inquiry, 10*(1), 35–41.

Nelson, J., Megill, A., & McCloskey, D. (Eds.). (1987). *The rhetoric of the human sciences.* Madison: University of Wisconsin Press.

Phillips, D. (1997). Coming to grips with radical social constructivisms. *Science and Education, 6*(1–2), 85–104.

Phillips, D. (2000). *The expanded social scientist's bestiary.* Lanham, MD: Rowman & Littlefield.

Rook, A. (Ed.). (1964). *The origins and growth of biology.* Harmondsworth, UK: Penguin Books.

Rubington, E., & Weinberg, M. (Eds.). (1995). *The study of social problems: Seven perspectives* (5th ed.). New York: Oxford University Press.

Scheffler, I. (1960). *The language of education.* Springfield, IL: Charles C Thomas.

Shavelson, R., & Towne, L. (2004, April). What drives scientific research in education? *American Psychological Society Observer,* pp. 27–30.

Smith, G., & Pell, J. (2003). Parachute use to prevent death and major trauma related to gravitational challenge: Systematic review of randomised controlled trials. *British Medical Journal, 327,* 1459–1461.

Stokes, D. (1997). *Pasteur's quadrant: Basic science and technological innovation.* Washington, DC: Brookings Institution.

Toulmin, S. (2003). *The uses of argument* (rev. ed.). Cambridge, UK: Cambridge University Press. (Original work published in 1958)

Tufte, E. (1997). *Visual explanations: Images and quantities, evidence and narrative.* Cheshire, CT: Graphics Press.

Wolpert, L. (1994). *The unnatural nature of science.* Cambridge, MA: Harvard University Press.

Worrall, J. (2002). Philosophy of science: Classic debates, standard problems, future prospects. In P. Machamer & M. Silberstein (Eds.), *The Blackwell guide to the philosophy of science* (pp. 18–36). Oxford, UK: Blackwell.

2

WHAT KNOWLEDGE USERS WANT

ROBERT E. FLODEN

Michigan State University

For decades, advocates of education reforms have sprinkled the term "research-based" liberally throughout their articles and speeches. Whatever the other attractive features of a new approach, whether it be peer teaching or the use of mathematics manipulatives, saying that the approach is "based on research" seems to add appeal. Until recently, these claims about the research basis went unquestioned, both by those listening and by those making the claims. The recent No Child Left Behind legislation, however, has linked federal funding to being "research-based" and even provided criteria for applying that label. These events make it seem as though research is a key factor in the decisions of policymakers and practitioners alike.

Ironically, those who study the connection between education research and education practice come to quite a different conclusion. Despite all of the talk about working with research-based approaches and materials, much has been written bemoaning the lack of connection between research and either education practice or education policy. Researchers complain that policies often appear to be unaffected by findings from research; they likewise express the hope that practitioners may someday attend more to research than they now do. Practitioners and policymakers, for their part, note that research often yields conclusions that are too theoretical, complex, confusing, or impractical to be of much use.

To understand these contradictory claims about the links among research, policy, and practice, this chapter examines differences among the audiences for research because the differences in what audiences hope to get from research and in how they learn about research explain some of the contradictory views about research. Working from the descriptions of three different audiences, the chapter describes what representatives of each audience often say about what they hope to get from research. Much of the chapter then reviews what studies have shown about how these audiences actually use research, which often differs from what members of the audience say they hope to do. Issues in the rhetoric of research communication provide a way of understanding some of the complex issues that arise as researchers strive to demonstrate their objectivity while simultaneously trying to promote change. The conclusion speculates about the role that "engaging ideas" might have in drawing practitioners and policymakers into deliberations about the significance of research. The chapter uses the context of elementary and secondary education to explore the dynamic relationships between educational inquiry and its various audiences, but I believe that my analysis applies in large measure to higher education as well.

Although most of the chapter focuses on practitioners and policymakers as audiences for research, it also addresses researchers themselves as a third audience. Despite the stress placed in federal discussions of research on the importance of research for policy and practice, the research community remains the primary audience for research reports. Hundreds of journals publish research articles about education. Most journals are aimed at some segment of the community of scholars. Critics of education research may see writing for a research audience as too insular, that is, focused on the "ivory tower." But the growth of knowledge about education comes in large part from the interactions within the research community. That growth in knowledge may eventually be communicated to practitioners and policymakers, but the internal communications among researchers are a key part of the system.

AUDIENCES FOR RESEARCH

Practitioners, policymakers, and researchers can be thought of as three distinct audiences for research. Of course, each of these groups encompasses a variety of people with differing interests and differing ideas about what sources of information to consult. But discussions about research and its influence often point to the contrasts among these groups that are helpful in appreciating the challenges in trying to communicate across audiences.

Teachers make up the largest group of education practitioners in elementary and secondary education as well as in higher education. Variations in the grade level of subject taught may affect the availability of, interest in, and understanding of research. Although a large amount of research has been conducted on methods for teaching reading in elementary school, for example, teachers at that level often have a limited appetite for reading research studies and typically have a limited understanding of how to assess the quality of a study.

School and district administrators—as well as higher education administrators—can be thought of as some combination of practitioners and policymakers. Their daily work involves the practice of education, often working directly with pupils. It also includes making policies for schools, districts, colleges, and universities, perhaps in collaboration with teachers and faculty. Thus, administrators at different levels can be an audience for research as a way in which to inform their own practice as well as a basis for setting policies.

Policymakers include elected officials and their staffs at the district, state, and national levels. Some are school board members, others serve on state boards of education, and still others assist and advise U.S. senators and representatives. Unlike practitioners, their work does not include the direct activities of education such as teaching students, writing tests, and organizing field trips to museums. They work instead to formulate and monitor the policies that guide the education system, including policies about the selection of curriculum materials, the compensation of teachers, the length of the school day, the setting of tuition, and procedures for student financial aid. Some may have experience as practitioners, but many do not. Their engagement with education is often episodic, with a burst of activity leading to a change in education policy, the effects of which might not be known for weeks, months, or years.

Education researchers are a third audience for education research. Many of them work in higher education, where they are also education practitioners. Their areas of interest as researchers, however, may have little bearing on their practice. A researcher interested in the early development of mathematics concepts, for example, may find little in that literature that is of help in figuring out how to make the best use of small groups in teaching introductory educational psychology. Other researchers work for private firms (e.g., RAND Corporation, American Institutes for Research [AIR]), where they may devote all of their time to research or perform some mix of research, program evaluation, and technical assistance.[1] Researchers often have had experience as education practitioners, although that experience might be in the distant past.

WHAT AUDIENCES SAY THEY WANT

When asked, members of each of these audiences would typically say that they could benefit from research. At the risk of caricature, practitioners could be described as asking for answers to questions about what they should do *tomorrow* to solve a problem they are having with today in *a particular class*. Policymakers could be described as asking either for a *simple answer* to a question about the effect of a possible policy or for evidence to *support the decision* they have decided to make. What researchers say they want from research is more varied, from trying to identify a *theoretical framework* for their own research, to looking for studies that inform—and perhaps support—their *own research*, to seeking a new set of *questions* to pursue.

Practitioners' needs for knowledge arise from the immediate practical problems they face. Many problems come from a teacher's classroom. For example, a few students might be having difficulty in understanding a science concept. The teacher may be unsure which of several different approaches to try with these students, may have run out of ideas, or may be trying to decide whether it is better to spend more time on this concept or to move ahead with the class. Whatever form the problem takes, a solution must be found immediately if it is to be of much help. The teacher must go on teaching tomorrow and must either do something to address the problem or move on to other issues. Higher education practitioners dealing with students similarly are met with several issues that cannot wait long for solutions. Immediacy is a pervasive characteristic of practice. In some cases, a problem manifests itself repeatedly, for example, the problem of how to respond to a child who is "acting out" in class. Repetition of the problem gives multiple opportunities for solution, but with each repetition, what the teacher would like is an immediate solution.

Practitioners also face some problems from outside the classroom. The school system presses for higher student test scores without giving additional resources. The school adopts a curriculum that includes unfamiliar topics but does not provide time for professional development. A tragic event on campus demands a college response to help the students with emotional turmoil. Whatever the origin of the problem, practitioners' requests for knowledge emphasize the need to have something to do right away.

Practitioners also stress that it is crucial for solutions to be ones that will work in their local context. If a solution has not yet been tested with students much like those a practitioner teaches, it will be treated with caution or even with suspicion. Teachers believe that every class of students, even within a school, is unique (just as every college campus is unique), so what worked elsewhere might not work here. In short, when asked what research would be ideal to have, practitioners are likely to say that it should provide concrete solutions to the immediate problems they face—with good reason to think that it will work in their specific context.

Policymakers share with practitioners the desire for research to give quick responses to felt needs. For policymakers, the need is for decisions regarding the formulation of policies on the issues that are currently "hot" rather than regarding what to do with students on Monday. Policymakers would also like research to satisfy another constraint, namely, that its answers to questions be simple no matter how complex the questions. The messages from research should also be framed in simple language, preferably using the terms currently in use by constituents and fellow policymakers.

Current policy discussions suggest a great interest by policymakers in being able to base their decisions more on evidence, that is, more on the results of research. Organizations such as the Coalition for Evidence-Based Policy, sponsored by the Council for Excellence in Government (www.excelgov.org), promote systematic gathering of research evidence on important education issues, arguing that education should follow the lead of medicine and begin to base decisions more on evidence from rigorous research than solely on anecdotal evidence or professional judgment. In setting guidelines for continued support of federal programs, the U.S. Office of Management and Budget stipulates that "agencies should provide evidence that they have chosen and applied evaluation methods that provide the most rigorous evidence of a program's effectiveness that is appropriate and feasible" (www.excelgov.org/usermedia/images/uploads/pdfs/2006_part_guidance_-_evaluation.pdf).

Grover (Russ) Whitehurst, director of the Institute for Education Sciences, likewise emphasizes the importance of moving toward *evidence-based* education (Whitehurst, 2002). He argues that evidence from rigorous research should play an increased, but not exclusive, role in supporting decisions about instruction. He sees a role for professional wisdom but thinks that empirical evidence is needed to "resolve competing approaches, generate cumulative knowledge, [and] avoid fad, fancy, and personal bias." He goes on to suggest that the value of evidence for these purposes depends on the type of investigation that generates the evidence. For decisions about instruction, he offers a partial rank ordering, from best to worst, of sources of evidence:

1. Randomized trial (true experiment)

2. Comparison groups (quasi-experiment)

3. Pre/Post comparison

4. Correlational studies

5. Case studies

6. Anecdotes

These statements from government, agencies, and officials suggest that policymakers would like experimental research about the likely effects of different instructional practices or materials. That evidence would not be the *only* basis for decision making, but it would be a valued addition to the bases for policy decisions.

One way in which policymakers' requests for research may differ from those of practitioners is in the limits placed on acceptable answers. Whereas practitioners may *hope* that research will confirm their own beliefs, policymakers often operate in an environment in which the general direction of a policy has been set through a political process with little interest in any research that might reveal the weaknesses of that position. So, for education issues such as the academic benefits of voucher programs, the contribution that reciting the Pledge of Allegiance makes to students' democratic education, and assessment measures that influence state support for public universities, policymakers

might ask only about research that supports their previously defined positions or that could be "spun" to give apparent support. Policymakers are more likely to be influenced by research when the decisions they are making are not politically charged (Cronbach & Associates, 1980).

Researchers profess an appetite for research that reveals the complexity of an issue, makes connections to existing literature, makes an "original" contribution, and is intellectually engaging. The categories on forms used for peer review of research articles make these desired characteristics concrete and explicit. To judge whether a manuscript is worth publishing—that is, whether it is something that the journal's (researcher) audience would want to read—reviewers rate the manuscript (perhaps on a 5-point scale) on characteristics such as originality, contribution to the field, significance, and links to existing literature.

Researchers indicate a particular interest in research connected to their own work. Because they must demonstrate a mastery of the literature in their own writing, researchers are alert for reports of new studies. Those studies that are consistent with their own conclusions can be added to the lists of work cited; those that seem inconsistent could be seen as an unwelcome challenge or as a way of showing that the issue is more complex than was previously believed.

How Audiences Actually Use Research

Expressed preferences often depart from actions taken. Teachers and policymakers might say that they would like to get answers to their problems from research, but their actions often seem to belie their professions of interest. The apparent disconnect between the conclusions from research and the actions of practitioners and policymakers has itself been the object of social science research. Comparisons of researchers' expressed interest in research and their actions have received less systematic attention, so an account of education researchers' practices for research use will (ironically) be based more on casual experience.

Practitioners

Teachers—as well as administrators—are much more likely to use advice from a colleague, a friend, or a charismatic instructor at a professional development workshop than they are to use a result from research. One reason for practitioners' limited use of research is that they seldom consult the sources where research results are found. When practitioners read professional publications, they are more likely to look at *Teacher* magazine or other discipline-specific journals than to look at the *American Educational Research Journal* or the *Journal of Higher Education*. Those who come to speak at schools are more likely to be practitioners from other schools or districts than to be researchers. When speakers come, they may use the words "research-based" to characterize materials or instructional approaches they advocate, but the connection to research might be difficult to find.

Huberman (1983) gives a detailed analysis explaining why the work of teaching makes its practitioners unlikely to make decisions based on the results of research studies. Teachers are focused on the particularities of their situation. They are continually confronted with the ways in which the students in their class are distinctive and unique. As a result, they are disinclined to trust the results of studies done with other children and in other settings. Similar constraints exist when college and university faculty need solutions to problems that *their* students face.

Moreover, the features sought in a research study—careful design of instruments, attention to sample selection, close connections made between data and conclusions—are not the features that teachers look for in deciding whether to trust a conclusion. As Huberman (1983) states, "Educational practitioners tend not to judge information using such criteria as objectivity, scientific validity, or authoritativeness, but rather make a global assessment of the source's credibility, along with the plausibility of the message when filtered through their own experience and the opinion of peers" (p. 482). That is, they tend to trust information if it fits with their own experiences and with the advice of fellow practitioners, whether or not the research meets the standards of the academy.

Thus, although teachers might say that they would like solutions to their practical problems, they would rather trust their colleagues or their own experiences than trust a result from research. This does not mean that they will never try an instructional technique or a strategic method described in a research study, but they are unlikely to trust it primarily on the basis of the research. Instead, they will consider it as one of many possibilities to be tried out and perhaps adopted if they find that it works well.

Although teachers do not give priority to research in selecting particular instructional approaches, some studies of professional development have shown that teachers who read research about teaching and learning do change their practice as a result in ways that have been shown to increase student achievement. The Cognitively Guided Instruction (CGI) project, for example, gave teachers professional development sessions that taught them about how young children learn mathematics. Studies of these teachers' later classroom performance showed that they were more effective in helping pupils to learn mathematics.

This approach to professional development is consistent with teachers' reluctance to accept research as the guide to which instructional approaches should be used with their classes. The professional development taught teachers what research had found about children's learning, but it did not prescribe what teachers should do in their classrooms. Thus, teachers were able to make their own decisions about what to do with their particular students. They presumably drew on what research had found about learning, but they were able to (successfully) tailor their instruction to the particularities of their students.

Stein, Smith, and Silver (1999) describe the features that are essential for effective professional development. They note that professional developers who present material in ways that do not acknowledge local context are not likely to be successful. Although a hallmark of research is that it presents general conclusions valid across a range of contexts, that decontextualization makes it unpalatable to teachers. "New ideas about professional development suggest that 'training' will have little impact on practice unless professional developers learn to attend to the particularities of the local cultures (e.g., student background, school characteristics, district expectations) in which teachers work" (p. 266).

Policymakers

The 1960s was a decade of great optimism about the role that social science might play in guiding social policy. Books with titles such as *Systematic Thinking for Social Action* (Rivlin, 1971) proclaimed a model for social engineering in which policymakers would describe the policies they were considering, social scientists would do research on these policy options, and the policymakers would then make a research-informed choice. The major education programs of the 1960s—Head Start, Follow Through, and the like—were accompanied by large-scale research both on the overall program and on the connections between specific program features and the desired education goals. The studies of Follow Through, for example, compared different general approaches to early elementary school instruction, with some being behaviorism-based forms of direct instruction and others being versions of open education. The studies also included extensive detailed classroom observations, tracking the frequency of various teacher "moves" and measures of student engagement while looking for statistical associations with, or differences in, student achievement.

Researchers were disappointed, however, when studies of these social programs seemed to have little effect on decisions about program continuation or change. The initial study of Head Start, for example, found little effect on pupil outcomes, yet Congress voted to increase funding for the program. Did this continued support for a program that research had shown to have little value mean that policymakers, despite their avowed interest in research on the program's effects, actually ignored research?

Analyses of the connection between research and education policy (and social policy more generally) concluded that policymakers were affected by research but that the straightforward engineering conception of the link was simplistic. Contrary to the linear, rational, and predictable model often found in the literature of that period, the influence of research results was more indirect, diffuse, and dependent on the changing policy environment. David Cohen and his collaborators argued that research had a substantial impact, not through direct links from specific studies to related policy decisions but rather through an influence on the "climate of opinion" (Cohen & Garet, 1975; Lindblom & Cohen, 1979). As research results are published and discussed, they begin to shape the terms in which education problems and solutions are framed, affecting what policy choices are considered and what information is seen as relevant to assessing their viability.

Studies of research and policy also made clear that factors other than empirical results will sometimes weigh so heavily in policy decisions that research results are unlikely to affect the outcome. In some cases, policymakers may have a commitment to a principle, such as "choice" or "accountability," that they will maintain no matter what new research evidence indicates (Cronbach & Associates, 1980). Thus, academic reviews of the literature on school choice may affect the particular form that choice or accountability proposals take, but not the likelihood that policymakers will endorse a proposal with the politically appealing label. Research is also likely to have little effect on a policy choice if the political actors believe that the effects of a policy are obvious from common sense. The idea that the supply of teachers in shortage areas can be increased by loan forgiveness programs, for example, may lead policymakers to support such programs even when there are no systematic studies showing that such programs are effective. As a recent review of literature on these programs (across a range of occupations) concludes,

> However, the growth of [programs to attract students to prepare for particular occupations] cannot be attributed to research. The following statement by a state legislator typifies the political expediency and appearances that drive the growth of these programs: "What could possibly be wrong with a program that provides financial assistance for students to attend college while also addressing state workforce shortages?" (Kirshstein, Berger, Benatar, & Rhodes, 2004, pp. 4–5)

This statement illustrates the way in which policies about programs with a commonsense supporting rationale are unlikely to be much influenced by research. In a statement that reveals the way in which researchers continue to believe in a simple connection between research results and policy, this same report goes on to say, "Given the growing popularity of these programs, strong evaluations of [such programs] are needed to answer questions like this" (p. 5).

Researchers

A look at the literature on researchers' use of research reveals two apparently contradictory trends. On the one hand, the growth in researcher interest in reviews of research, especially systematic research reviews, suggests that researchers have a large appetite for work summarizing findings over a large number of studies, indicating what the major conclusions are in an area of research. On the other hand, leading members of the education research community continue to echo the complaint, also made by those outside the community, that education researchers too seldom do studies that build on previous work. Instead, each study, or at least each investigator, seems determined to do something that departs from prior work, making it difficult to see how new work has profited from what has come before.

Research synthesis has been a prominent activity in education for decades. Many publications are devoted to research reviews aimed at an audience of researchers. The journal *Review of Education Research,* which is devoted entirely to research reviews, has been published regularly for more than 70 years. During the mid-1970s, the American Educational Research Association added another journal of research reviews, the *Review of Research in Education.* "Handbooks" make up another prominent set of publications summarizing the results of research. Since the first *Handbook of Research on Teaching* (Gage, 1963) was published, the number of such handbooks has exploded, with three more editions on research on teaching, two editions on research on teacher education (with another in the works), and other handbooks on research on qualitative research (two editions), multicultural education, reading research (three volumes), early literacy research, educational communications and technology (two editions),

educational administration (two editions), Catholic education, school supervision, mathematics education, research design in mathematics and science education, and so on. A notable addition is the *Handbook of Research Synthesis* (Cooper & Hedges, 1994), also focused on education research. Needless to say, numerous handbooks (and "encyclopedias") have also been published for researchers focusing on higher education issues.

The reviews in these publications are often narrative summaries, using a variety of formal and informal methods to condense results of many studies into short accounts. Although such narrative accounts remain common, statistical methods for using multiple studies to estimate the effect of individual variables have become an increasingly important basis for reporting research summaries. Since the publication of *Meta-analysis in Social Research* (Glass, McGaw, & Smith, 1981) more than 20 years ago, the sophistication and application of meta-analysis procedures have grown dramatically. Although some of the results of meta-analysis are aimed at policymakers and practitioners (e.g., the What Works Clearinghouse [www .whatworks.ed.gov]), most are directed at researchers.

Do researchers actually read these reviews and use them in their own work? One way of gauging such use is to look at data on citations of research articles. The ISI Web of Knowledge (www.isiknowledge.com) features tools that can be used to look at the number of times during a given year that a journal is cited in another journal cataloged in the Social Science Citation Index. The Web of Knowledge also features a statistic called the "impact factor," which gives a measure of impact that adjusts for differences in the number of articles a journal publishes. That is, to take account of the fact that a journal that publishes 100 articles per year has more articles that might be cited than a journal that publishes only 10 articles per year, the impact factor is computed by dividing the number of citations to a journal during the previous 2 years by the number of articles that appeared in the journal during those 2 years.

For 2003, the Web of Knowledge indicates that a journal of research reviews, *Review of Educational Research,* had the largest impact factor (1.69) of any of the 92 education journals included in the system. (Note that this index includes only about 10% of the journals included in the ERIC list of education journals.) That journal of reviews also had the largest number of total citations—1,323 for the year. The fact that a journal of reviews is the most cited journal, and with the highest impact factor, is an indication that researchers *do* use research reviews in their own work. A typical article gets cited about 1.5 times per year during the first 2 years after publication. The distribution of citations is, of course, quite varied, with some articles being cited much more frequently. The impact for this journal also varies across years, from 1.4 to 3.0 over the past 5 years.

These data document that researchers use research articles in their own writing and that a journal of reviews is the most used. Other journals are close behind, however, so not too much should be made of the contrast between the use of review articles and the use of other research articles. These data also give a sense of the typical level of use for the mostly highly cited journal. As a point of comparison, among journals in economics, the highest impact journal (*Journal of Economic Literature*) had a 2003 impact factor of 5.2. In the biological and physical sciences (including medicine), the highest impact journal (*Annual Review of Immunology*) had an impact factor of 52.2. So, using citation rates as an indication of researchers' use of research, education has somewhat lower rates than economics but an order of magnitude less than medicine.

This relatively low rate of citation is consistent with the complaint often heard that education research does not cumulate, that is, does not add up over time. It seems as though, the complaint goes, education researchers seldom make use of the work of those who have gone before them. Rather than using the measures (e.g., surveys, observation schedules, interview protocols) developed and tested in previous studies, researchers develop new measures, making it harder to know how results from one study compare with results from another study. The National Research Council's Committee on Research in Education (CORE) addressed the issue of problems with the accumulation of education research knowledge in a series of

workshops, with summary and recommendations provided in a recent report (National Research Council, 2005).

In the CORE workshop presentations, speakers acknowledged that education research is criticized for frequent failure to accumulate knowledge within a topic area:

> Even if the quality of discrete education research studies is outstanding, if the field is not able to forge connections among them, it will amass a multitude of studies that cannot support inferences about the generalizability of findings nor sustain the long-term theory building that drives scientific progress. Forging connections among studies will enable the field to be more than the sum of its parts. Lacking the infrastructure or the professional norms to engage in efforts to connect and integrate theories and data across investigations, the scientific study of educational phenomena will be fragmented (as some currently are; see Lagemann, 2000). (National Research Council, 2005, p. 36)

The CORE workshops devoted much of their time to describing cases where knowledge did accumulate and to discussing strategies for increasing the ease with which future researchers can build more on prior work. Examples of areas where knowledge has accumulated include work on the effects of schools, where two distinct lines of research—economic studies of the production of education and classroom studies of instructional effects—have histories of drawing on prior work, revisiting existing data sets, and refining instruments rather than building them from scratch.

The discussions of what could be done to improve the cumulation of education research, however, showed that education researchers are not yet following the practices, common in some other fields, of building on the work of other researchers through data sharing, replication, and use of common instruments and key definitions. The *Proceedings of the National Academy of Sciences* requires that authors make their data available to other investigators so that the latter can attempt to replicate or extend results. In education, however, researchers often retain exclusive access to their work for years, making it difficult to conduct studies that are closely linked to what has come before. (One exception is research based on the survey data sets assembled by the National Center for Education Statistics.) Education studies commonly use measures specially developed for those particular studies. Although finely aligning a survey or observation schedule for a study may have some advantages, it makes comparing results across studies more difficult. Meta-analyses may be able to attach general labels to the varied measures, but crude classifications of instruments make it difficult to understand discrepant—or even consistent—results.

One feature of published education research that makes cumulation of knowledge more difficult is the variability across journals in the contents and formats of abstracts. For an investigator to locate work on a particular topic, an electronic search is bound to be an important component of the search. But journals that publish education research lack uniform requirements for abstracts. Indeed, abstracts often leave out much of the information needed to decide whether a study should be examined carefully:

> The task of an individual reader who seeks out the research findings of an education research article is often not an easy one. Nevertheless, the search is much more difficult when conducted on a computer. Most online and database searches for education studies or research findings yield only the barest reference information, typically providing bibliographic details and a brief, very general overview. . . . It comes as cold comfort to many a busy person in education that this detailed information is sitting on the shelves of local libraries in the form of microfiche or bound journals. (Mosteller, Nave, & Miech, 2004, p. 30)

With these various obstacles to adopting methods and measures used in prior research, it is not surprising that education research is criticized for its fragmentation and that researchers wishing to build on earlier work have a hard time doing so.

STYLE AND RHETORIC

Authors of research reports are often asked, "Who is the intended audience for this report?"

All too often, the response is similar to the following: "Several different audiences—I want to reach practitioners and policymakers as well as other researchers." That response reflects an understandable hope to gain a wide readership, but it implies that the piece will not be written with *any* of these three different audiences particularly in mind. The author may hope that clear organization and straightforward presentation will draw in all three audiences. Too often, however, the result is that the publication is used by few in any of these groups.

Perhaps the thought that one publication could suit all audiences arises from the expressions of interest that come from all three audiences: practitioners, policymakers, and researchers. As the preceding discussion pointed out, however, the audiences differ both in the specific aspects of research that are of interest and in the actual patterns of reading. Practitioners and policymakers are interested in clear-cut solutions tied to their specific problems or issues. Researchers, in looking for starting points for their own research, are interested not only in summaries of results but also in inconsistencies in results and in new questions raised by prior studies. Practitioners will find a report to be more trustworthy if it comes with the endorsement of a fellow practitioner and allows for ready adaptation to local circumstances. Policymakers value apparent consistency with political priorities. Researchers, in contrast, often put a premium on abstraction, generality, and novelty. The likelihood that a publication will be picked up by members of one of these audiences will be based in part on the ways in which the style or rhetoric of the publication appeals to what the audience is looking for and what it finds persuasive.

For a first pass, the style of research publication can be considered simply for its brevity and accessibility. Researchers who really want to be read by practitioners and policymakers are instructed to keep their writing short and free of jargon and to make connections to practical issues or current policies obvious. One need only to glance through most education journals to see that these words of advice are not given much attention in academic journals.

Journals that cater explicitly to practitioners, such as *Educational Leadership* and the *Phi Delta*

Kappan, follow these admonitions much more often. Article length is only a few pages, and the editors usually are successful in getting authors to stick to familiar language.

At another level, however, style can be considered differently, drawing on the concepts and methods of the formal study of rhetoric. During the past few decades, the rhetoric of social science has been given systematic attention by a mixture of scholars of literature, sociologists of science, and social scientists themselves. A new edition of *The Rhetoric of Economics* (McCloskey, 1998) illustrates the perspective of some who study the way in which social science is written:

> Science is an instance of writing with intent, the intent to persuade other scientists, such as economic scientists. The study of such writing with intent was called by the Greeks "rhetoric." Until the seventeenth century it was the core of education in the West and down to the present it remains, often unrecognized, the core of humanistic learning. A science like economics should be read skillfully, with a rhetoric, the more explicit the better. The choice here is between an implicit and naïve rhetoric or an explicit and learned one, the naïve rhetoric of significance tests, say, versus a learned rhetoric that knows what it is arguing and why. (pp. 4–5)

Many publications in academic education journals appear to have been written with a rhetoric, whether implicit or explicit, that is intended to argue something more or less like the following: "The study being reported represents an innovative approach to a problem of the utmost significance. The research was carried out by expert scholars, so the conclusions and implications reported should be accepted as definitive." That is to say, the message in many reports is as much about the importance of the work and the indubitability of the authors' claims as it is about the particulars of the empirical research itself. This rhetorical approach seems aimed at convincing other researchers of the quality and value of the research. It appears, in a way, as though the research authors are trying to establish their legitimacy among their colleagues as well as trying to defend their research conclusions.

The sociologist Joseph Gusfield has written eloquently about the rhetorical devices that social scientists use to convey the image of a white-coated scientist, carrying out objective research and following well-established methods, so that the conclusions drawn are based only on objective facts without any influence of the values, beliefs, or quirks of the investigator. "For the scientist . . . language is only a medium by which the external world is reported. That which is described and analyzed is not itself affected by the language through which it is reported" (Gusfield, 1976, p. 16). Gusfield argues that although scientists, including social scientists, write as though language were so transparent, their rhetorical choices matter enormously, creating impressions about the research, its content, conclusions, and "implications" that rely heavily on the way in which reports are expressed, not simply on the empirical results themselves.

Gusfield (1976) uses "drinking driver" research as an illustrative case, pointing out that although reports of the research are written as though the descriptive language is neutral, the report writer's decision to label a topic as "drunken driving," rather than "driving under the influence of alcohol," carries impressions about who is being studied, what moral significance the study has, and what sorts of solutions should be considered. Labeling the study's topic "drunken driving" carries images of social misfits who have fallen below social norms and who should probably be locked up. Labeling the topic "driving under the influence of alcohol," however, suggests that the study focuses on a situation that most people face at least occasionally, a familiar practical problem where solutions may lie with safer cars, designated drivers, or a few cups of coffee. In either case, the impression given is that the researcher is carrying out a value-neutral investigation and letting the data speak for themselves.

Reports of education research are often written in language suggesting that the definition of the problem, the investigative approach, and the interpretation of the results are based solely on science. Standard editorial guides, such as the *Publication Manual of the American Psychological Association* (APA, 2001), encourage clarity, economy of expression, smoothness of argument, and use of unbiased language. Although they do now allow for reference to the investigator in the first person (e.g., "I administered the survey to 200 teachers . . ."), the tone taken in most scholarly education journals suggests that everything done in the study follows agreed procedures and that any conclusions or recommendations are based on the data. As Gusfield (1976) puts it, the scholarly format that highlights the methods of research is a rhetorical device that puts the investigator in a technical role, carrying out the work but not directly concerned with the conclusions. "The importance of method substantiates the overall style of detachment. He [the author] means to persuade, but only by presenting an external world to the audience and allowing that external reality to do the persuading" (p. 20).

This rhetoric of science may persuade those reading the article to accept the findings reported. It would account for the relatively uncritical way in which other researchers sometimes put together literature reviews, accepting the conclusions drawn in each article they include without critically considering the way in which the conclusions may actually draw on beliefs specific to the investigator rather than being based on the research itself. It fits well with the researcher's expressed appetite for conclusions. If conclusions are simply a snapshot of the external world, then the researcher can look for articles on the topic of interest and draw information quickly from the articles by focusing on the conclusions.

But this emphasis on method and objectivity may actually work against the use of research by other consumers—practitioners and policymakers. To create the impression that the report is just a window on the world, free from interpretation and elaboration, the tone must be neutral or flat. Otherwise, the author might seem too evidently to be going beyond the evidence. As Gusfield (1976) puts it, the author's "language must not be 'interesting,' his descriptions colorful, or his words a clue to any emotion which might be aroused in the audience" (pp. 20–21). But interesting colorful language is exactly what is needed to grab the attention of practitioners and policymakers. Articles that are devoid of color are not likely to be picked up, let alone read to the end. If a report of research is to be used by these practical audiences, it must employ a rhetoric different from that used in research journals.

As noted earlier, practitioners and policymakers find accounts more trustworthy if they have been endorsed by fellow practitioners, seem easily adaptable to local circumstances, and are aligned to the policy position of the moment. Rhetorically, those attributes might be introduced by highlighting specific accounts of teaching and learning, with vivid details evocative of the specifics of practice and (for policymakers) examples that could be seen as embodying the best points of a current policy. These stimulating idiosyncratic details are just the opposite of what is needed if the intent is to create an aura of science.

Given the different rhetorical approaches needed for different audiences, it is unlikely that any piece will suit all of them, hence the likelihood that the author who tries to write for all audiences will fail—perhaps even fail with all of them. A lesson to take from this analysis is that authors of research reports should be conscious of the rhetoric they employ, making their choices explicit rather than leaving them implicit. If the intent of the argument is to persuade policymakers to adopt a particular course of action, the rhetoric must use arguments that will lead the reader in that direction. In so doing, the author must abandon the image of cool impartiality. That shift can be difficult for authors, particularly when they do not recognize that impartiality is itself a rhetorical choice, not a simple depiction of their work. Writing always entails rhetorical choices, each of which colors the report in some way. And research itself involves decisions, some of which involve personal judgment. Academic reports of research often use a reconstructed logic, giving a rationale for each facet of the work. But the study itself typically includes false starts, judgment calls, and perhaps even arbitrary choices.

DILEMMAS FOR AUTHORS

So what approach should a researcher take to engage these several groups of stakeholders? What options for communication are most likely to get the attention of researchers, practitioners, and policymakers and inform their work? One part of the answer is that stakeholders' expressed interests should be taken with a grain of salt. When someone waxes enthusiastic about the importance of research for their work, the enthusiasm may be genuine. A look at the history of the uses of education research, however, suggests that when particular research reports appear, their influence is diffuse more often than it is direct.

Researchers face rhetorical dilemmas. How the dilemmas are addressed should be tailored to the audience, but central dilemmas exist for every audience. Two important dilemmas relate to the questions of how much to simplify (including simplifying the connection between evidence and conclusions) and how much to advocate for a particular line of action.

In the first case, the question is whether to lay out the complexity, uncertainty, and ambiguity present in nearly all research or to simplify and speak with apparent certainty. The first approach may expand the audience's understanding, but it is less likely to lead the reader in any particular direction. When writing for practitioners or policymakers, laying out the whole mess might feel honest, but it can readily lead to dismissal rather than enlightenment. Even when writing for a research audience, stressing the loose ends and multiple possible interpretations may reinforce the sense that research never gets anywhere as each reader picks up on some aspect, starting down a new path without adding to a larger understanding of the terrain.

If authors choose to simplify, however, their readers may adopt new policies and practices in ways that turn possible improvements into routines and rules. The danger is that insights based on one context may be force-fit to other situations without openness to evidence about needed adjustments. Researchers working on effective teaching or successful school organization have been dismayed to find their conclusions transformed into inflexible mandates or adopted by teachers for subject matters or student populations quite different from those involved in the research. Or researchers have found themselves called on to advise on policy when research studies are incomplete or inconclusive.

The second question is whether to take a stance that highlights objectivity and neutrality or whether to be an open advocate for a line of action or research. Reports of research often conclude with ideas about what should happen given the results of the research. In some cases, the ideas are about research that should be pursued or supported; in other cases, the ideas are about directions for policy or practice. In either case, the researcher may choose to write in a way that seems to present only a factual account of research conducted or to use evocative, emotionally charged language that draws on the research but also vividly draws on ostensibly shared values to issue a call to action. This difference, perhaps put too starkly here, highlights the trade-offs. Writing as though the evidence speaks for itself may lend weight to conclusions by stressing the benefits of method. This might not open all aspects of the study to the critical scrutiny of the research audience and may fail to engage other audiences. Writing as an advocate may prompt practical action but may draw little on the insights that did come from the research study.

Dilemmas, being dilemmas, might not be resolvable. Writing about research involves making trade-offs, with no general rule for deciding where to land on these continua. Having a more sophisticated understanding of audiences for research, however, can help writers to avoid naive beliefs about how their work will be received. Both writers and readers often assume overly simple relationships among conducting studies, reporting on them, and using those reports. Writers who are aware of their rhetorical choices and appreciate the differences among their audiences should be in a better position to shape the uses of their work. They will also have reason to be modest about the influence they can expect to have.

NOTE

1. Discussions about the uses of evaluation studies parallel discussions about the uses of education research, with "evaluators" used in place of "researchers" and with "stakeholders" used in place of "practitioners and policymakers." The analysis in this chapter is generally applicable to both research and evaluation. Some examples are drawn from research, and others are drawn from evaluation.

REFERENCES

American Psychological Association. (2001). *Publication manual of the American Psychological Association* (5th ed.). Washington, DC: Author.

Cohen, D. K., & Garet, M. S. (1975). Reforming educational policy with applied social research. *Harvard Educational Review, 45*(1), 17–43.

Cooper, H., & Hedges, L. V. (Eds.). (1994). *Handbook of research synthesis.* New York: Russell Sage.

Cronbach, L. J., & Associates. (1980). *Toward reform of program evaluation: Aims, methods, and institutional arrangements.* San Francisco: Jossey-Bass.

Gage, N. L. (Ed.). (1963). *Handbook of research on teaching.* Chicago: Rand McNally.

Glass, G. V., McGaw, B., & Smith, M. L. (1981). *Meta-analysis in social research.* Beverly Hills, CA: Sage.

Gusfield, J. (1976). The literary rhetoric of science: Comedy and pathos in drinking driver research. *American Sociological Review, 41,* 16–34.

Huberman, M. (1983). Recipes for busy kitchens: A situational analysis of routine knowledge use in schools. *Knowledge: Creation, Diffusion, Utilization, 4,* 478–510.

Kirshstein, R. J., Berger, A. R., Benatar, E., & Rhodes, D. (2004). *Workforce contingent financial aid: How states link financial aid to employment.* Washington, DC: American Institutes for Research and the Lumina Foundation.

Lagemann, E. C. (2000). *An elusive science: The troubling history of educational research.* Chicago: University of Chicago Press.

Lindblom, C. E., & Cohen, D. K. (1979). *Usable knowledge: Social science and social problem solving.* New Haven, CT: Yale University Press.

McCloskey, D. N. (1998). *The rhetoric of economics* (2nd ed.). Madison: University of Wisconsin Press.

Mosteller, F., Nave, B., & Miech, E. J. (2004). Why we need a structured abstract in education research. *Educational Researcher, 33,* 29–34.

National Research Council. (2005). *Advancing scientific research in education.* Washington, DC: National Academy Press.

Rivlin, A. (1971). *Systematic thinking for social action.* Washington, DC: Brookings Institution.

Stein, M. K., Smith, M. S., & Silver, E. A. (1999). The development of professional developers: Learning to assist teachers in new settings in new ways. *Harvard Educational Review, 69*(3), 237–269.

Whitehurst, G. C. (2002, October). *Evidence-based education (EBE).* Paper presented at the Student Achievement and School Accountability Conference, Washington, DC. Available: www.ed.gov/nclb/methods/whatworks/eb/edlite-index.html

3

Minding the Gap Between Research and Policymaking

David N. Plank

Michigan State University

Debbi Harris

Michigan State University

Subway riders in London are constantly warned to "mind the gap," the dangerous and unbridgeable space between the subway platform and the train. Unwary riders who fail to heed this advice may suffer a variety of unpleasant consequences, ranging from scuffed shoes to broken ankles.

In this essay, we warn readers to mind a different gap, the one between researchers and policymakers. Researchers often bemoan the fact that policymakers fail to take research findings into account when making policy choices (Weiss, 1977). For their part, policymakers complain that research fails to provide answers to the questions they are obliged to address. There is agreement on both sides that the current state of affairs is unsatisfactory and there are frequent calls for change, but the gap between scholars and policymakers remains wide and apparently unbridgeable.

Why should this be the case? We argue that the gap between the two groups finds its origins not only in mutual obstinacy or misunderstanding (although these are common enough) but

also in a set of dilemmas that are intrinsic to the field of "policy research." These dilemmas originate in fundamental differences between the orientations and interests of researchers and policymakers. These differences inevitably produce disagreements about which questions merit study and which answers merit attention.

In the section that follows, we identify some of the crucial obstacles that must be overcome by those who venture into the realm of policy research, and we discuss the ways in which these obstacles serve to maintain the gap between scholars and policymakers. We then turn our attention to two current policy issues—teacher quality and school choice—that have attracted a great deal of recent interest from both groups. Our review of the scholarly and policy debates on these two issues illustrates some of the reasons why research findings seldom achieve immediate or lasting influence over policy choices. For each of these issues, however, we also provide examples of research that has successfully bridged the gap, influencing policymaking while maintaining academic integrity. We conclude the essay with some reflections on whether and how the divide between researchers and policymakers might be bridged, suggesting that an institutional solution may well be the best way in which to ensure that policy research is useful to policymakers in the field and simultaneously impressive to scholars in the academy.

We begin from the premise that policy research aims to answer policy-relevant questions and thereby to influence policy. We are not concerned with broader types of policy research, including research on the policy process (Baumgartner & Jones, 1993; Kingdon, 1984; Lindblom, 1959; Pressman & Wildavsky, 1984) and implementation (Lipsky, 1983; Mazmanian & Sabatier, 1989; Spillane, 2000). We recognize that scholarship on agenda setting and policy implementation has deep implications for the ways in which research influences policy, but a review of this literature is beyond the scope of our essay.

THE ORIGINS OF THE GAP

Scholars working in the field of policy research must overcome a variety of obstacles not generally faced by scholars in other fields. These obstacles find their origins in the quite different orientations and interests of scholars and policymakers with respect to the research enterprise. Under many circumstances, the demands and responsibilities of academic research conflict with the needs and expectations of policymakers. Too often, the consequence is acrimonious misunderstanding and mutual distrust, which serve to widen rather than narrow the gap between the two groups.

It is impossible to attend to all of the points of dissension between scholars and policymakers in a brief essay. In the discussion that follows, we identify some of the most salient points under three main headings: questions, answers, and arguments.

Questions

Scholars tend to be a prickly bunch, strongly resistant to the idea that anyone—federal agencies, state legislators, or deans—should tell them which research topics merit their attention.

By training and professional inclination, they are drawn to questions they find theoretically or empirically interesting, and they are rewarded for work that impresses their peers and pushes back the frontiers of knowledge. For most scholars, whether and how their work might influence policy is at best a secondary consideration.

Successful scholars focus their energies on questions that are both interesting and answerable, and they frame their questions carefully to make them tractable for research. They take great care in choosing the questions they seek to address and in designing careful research strategies to pursue the answers. Asking the right questions in the right way is the key to the success of the research enterprise.

In contrast, policymakers seek answers to questions currently featured on the policy agenda (Kingdon, 1984). Their interest in a particular question may be intense in the short run but generally persists only so long as the issue remains "above the fold" in the local newspapers. As public attention shifts, they quickly move on to other issues. Policymakers are simply not interested in the theoretical and empirical challenges that motivate scholars. They value research not because it helps to advance knowledge but only insofar as it helps them to answer the questions their constituents expect them to address.

Which Questions Are Important?

Only rarely do the questions posed by scholars coincide with those that interest policymakers. From the scholar's viewpoint, many of the questions that policymakers pose are uninteresting, whereas others have no answers. From the policymaker's viewpoint, many of the carefully framed questions posed by researchers fail to provide clear guidance on the urgent issues that they face every day.

By way of illustration, consider the divergent ways in which scholars and policymakers might frame questions related to school violence. This issue appears on the policy agenda only occasionally, often in the wake of school shootings or other high-profile incidents. When it does appear, however, it generally arrives in the company of widespread public outrage and intense pressure on policymakers to do something in response. Responding to this pressure, policymakers ask urgent but intractable questions about how to prevent further incidents and express frustration at researchers' apparent lack of concern for children's safety. From the point of view of scholarship, this sudden interest looks like ill-informed hysteria.

Scholars have in fact produced a substantial body of research on the issue of school violence, but the questions that they have addressed are quite different from those that policymakers raise. Scholars have asked whether schools are dangerous environments for children and whether schools have become more or less safe over time (DeVoe et al., 2004). They have asked about the incidence of school shootings and about the effectiveness of policy interventions aimed at preventing them (Fisher & Kettl, 2001; Moore, 2003). And they have asked questions about other forms of school violence, including bullying, that affect far more children and may be more readily susceptible to policy intervention (Moore, 2003; Smith, 2003). To policymakers seeking to prevent the next Columbine incident, however, this looks like irrelevant dithering.

Neither group is entirely correct in its characterization of the other, but the gap between the two groups is clearly wide. Scholars and policymakers ask different questions, and they frame questions in different ways. One consequence is that policy research contributes little to the policy debate, leaving policymakers to adopt policies that take little account of—or sometimes fly in the face of—scholarly research findings. In the case of school violence, for example, policymakers around the country have adopted a variety of "zero tolerance" policies, which many scholars view as ineffective or even counterproductive (Dunbar & Villareul, 2002; Newman, 2004, p. 288). Competing policies that receive greater research support are dismissed because they do not appear to answer policymakers' current questions.

Which Questions Can Be Answered?

Policymakers often ask seemingly reasonable questions that scholars cannot answer. For example, policymakers may want to know whether a given policy is better than the alternatives. Scholars, quite reasonably, want a definition of "better." Will success be judged in terms of increased student achievement or reduced dropout rates? Reduced teacher turnover or enhanced quality of new recruits? Policymakers naturally want all of these things and more; whether or not the questions they ask are amenable to research is not their concern. Without greater specificity, however, the question of which policy is better cannot be answered. Researchers may fall back on their own judgments about which inputs and outcomes are most significant, but there is no guarantee that the choices they make will satisfy the expectations of policymakers.

Even when the inputs and outcomes of interest are clearly identified, scholars may still find policymakers' questions to be intractable. Some questions cannot be answered while observing the standard canons of social science research. The variables of interest may be difficult or impossible to measure, and key contextual variables may be difficult or impossible to control. Under these circumstances, scholars may be reluctant to take on these questions, no matter how urgent they might appear to policymakers.

For policymakers, of course, the situation is rather different. Their questions demand answers. If research does not provide adequate guidance, they seek answers from other sources, as we discuss in the next section.

Faced with the gap between scholars' and policymakers' definitions of interesting answerable questions, scholars need not despair. With sufficient care, questions can be framed in ways that meet the expectations of scholars and policymakers. One example is the work by the Consortium for Policy Research in Education's (CPRE) Teacher Compensation Group focusing on the relationship between the rating scores teachers receive under various evaluation systems and their students' achievement (Borman & Kimball, 2005; Gallagher, 2004; Milanowski, 2004; Milanowski, Kimball, & White, 2004; White, 2004). This work is simultaneously interesting to academics and valuable to policymakers who are concerned with the measurement and enhancement of teacher quality.

Answers

Scholars and policymakers are likely to come to very different judgments about the usefulness of the answers these two groups propose to their respective questions, in significant part because of their dramatically different views of what constitutes "good" research. From the scholar's point of view, good research shares a number of features, including careful design, solid data, and conclusions based on cautious and responsible inference. From the policymaker's point of view, however, judgments about good research are likely to be based on criteria radically different from those valued in the academy. Compatibility with prior beliefs and political commitments, timeliness, strength and simplicity of findings, and clear implications for action all are likely to be valued above theoretical or methodological sophistication. As a result, the answers that scholars produce might be of little value from the policymaker's point of view, whereas the answers that policymakers value might not meet the standards of credible scholarship.

Ideology and Interests

Policymakers and scholars often have strongly held ideological views. Scholars are strongly enjoined to minimize the influence of their prior beliefs on their research. They are trained to observe the rules of social science and to base their conclusions on evidence and argument rather than on ideology. Policymakers have no such compunctions. For them, ideology may provide a useful filter through which to screen research findings and to decide whether they serve a larger political purpose. Findings that comport well with prior convictions or commitments may be accepted, whereas those that do not will be dismissed.

These different orientations to the role of ideology have two complementary consequences. First, policymakers may be disinclined to credit research that is not fully compatible with their ideological commitments, no matter how careful the research design or how compelling the findings. Second, policymakers' demand for research that supports or advances a particular policy agenda encourages the supply of such research from ideologically compatible, but methodologically suspect, "think tanks" and similar sources. If researchers are unable to supply the kind of information that policymakers seek, they will simply look elsewhere for it (Weiss, 1995).

Take class size reduction, for example. This idea has immediate appeal for many constituencies, including parents, teachers, and much of the general public. For most of these groups, smaller classes are obviously better. Parents prefer schools where teachers are able to lavish individual attention on every child, and teachers prefer classes that are small enough to allow them to respond to students' individual differences. Reducing class size is technically straightforward (hire more teachers), whereas alternative policies aimed at improving teacher quality may be blindingly complex. As a result, policymakers at all points on the political spectrum are under enormous pressure to adopt policies to reduce class size, and they have spent vast amounts of money toward this end. An increasingly solid body of research concludes that money spent on reducing class size might be better spent on other initiatives such as improving teacher quality (Ferguson, 1991; Ferguson & Ladd, 1996; Harris, 2002), but when research evidence conflicts with "common sense" and the opportunity to win votes, it does not carry much weight.

Timeliness

Perhaps the clearest difference between researchers and policymakers resides in their different orientations to time. As all scholars know, proper attention to the familiar steps in the research process—developing a theoretical framework, designing a study, collecting data, conducting analyses, and writing up results (not to mention seeking funding and dealing with the delays that characterize peer review and scholarly publishing)—can take a great deal of time, and shortcuts are potentially dangerous. Taking insufficient care in any of these steps can seriously, if not fatally, undermine the integrity of a research project. "Quick and dirty" alternatives to careful research are not likely to produce robust or persuasive findings, nor are they likely to win professional respect. As a result, research is generally slow to market; months, if not years, may pass between the initial formulation of a research question and the publication of results.

Policymakers operate on a very different schedule. The educational and other issues that come before them often arise in response to urgent public concerns, and they are expected to take action with appropriate dispatch. They rarely have months or years to wait for the completion of careful research because their constituents expect them to act immediately. They may well prefer good research to bad research, other things being equal, but quality according to the standards of the academy is of less concern than the immediate availability of useful findings. Getting it now may be more important than getting it right.

Simplicity and Certainty

Social science research seldom produces simple answers. In the course of their efforts to identify relationships and measure effects, researchers are trained to navigate through a minefield of potentially confounding factors, including spurious correlation, multiple causation, and "noise" in the data. The myriad choices that scholars make as they collect and analyze data depend not on rules but rather on expert judgment. As often happens, therefore, two careful researchers making slightly different but equally justifiable decisions can easily produce dramatically different findings.

Scholars similarly recognize that their findings are context dependent; relationships that are significant under some circumstances might not necessarily hold under others. Scholars are consequently reluctant to generalize beyond the scope of the specific environments they study. Policies and practices that appear to be effective in one set of schools might have quite different effects elsewhere. In addition, schools are unusually noisy environments, both literally and figuratively, and this might make it difficult to identify or measure significant relationships even when these are present.

Social scientists recognize that their findings are almost invariably provisional, subject to revision on the basis of better models and better data. They are rewarded for acknowledging and exploring the complexity of the questions they investigate. Moreover, they move forward in their work through disagreement and debate (Popper, 1959). The publication of compelling new findings spurs efforts by other scholars to refine or debunk them. Ambiguity and uncertainty define the natural state of affairs in the academy; scientific progress relies on informed dissent (Kuhn, 1970).

Scholars consequently recognize that "right" answers are hard to come by. Instead of providing unequivocal support for a specific policy position, they often answer policymakers' questions with the honest answer, "It depends."

This reluctance to generalize frustrates policymakers who must make choices for schools and students across a variety of contexts. As Green (1983) notes, "Public policy is the drop-forge or the axe of social change. It is not the knife or scalpel. . . . Policy deals always with what is good in general, on the whole, and for the most part" (p. 322). Policymakers are obliged to make use of the best blunt instrument they have in hand. Scholars are adept with the scalpel, but this is seldom a good substitute for an axe.

From the point of view of policymaking, the complexities of social science research amount to little more than hand-wringing. The qualifications and contingencies that characterize most research findings may garner the respect of other researchers, but they simultaneously disqualify most scholarly work from serious policy influence. "It depends" rarely offers helpful guidance for the binary decisions that policymakers face regularly. Policymakers must decide whether to support or oppose bills, whether or not to implement new strategies, and whether to vote yes or no. These stark choices afford little room for the complexities reflected in most social science research.

Faced with these ambiguities, policymakers may adopt either of two courses of action. On the one hand, they can simply ignore scholarly research and seek answers to their questions elsewhere. Alternatively, they can adapt scholars' answers to their own purposes by ignoring scholarly qualifications and complexity. Thus, research can be made to provide clear policy guidance, but the cost is potentially high as the integrity of the research process is compromised through oversimplification.

Arguments

In addition to posing different questions and valuing different answers, scholars and policymakers are comfortable with different kinds of arguments. The differences are both substantive and rhetorical. First, scholars and policymakers may acknowledge different arguments as trustworthy based on their respective evaluations of different warrants. Second, the rhetorical conventions that govern most research reports convey essential information to scholars but represent barriers to understanding for nearly everyone else, including policymakers.

The Problem of Warrants

In their professional capacity, scholars are uniquely responsive to arguments supported by scientific evidence obtained on the basis of solid research; arguments that rely on other kinds of warrants are discounted. In contrast, policymakers are open to arguments supported by a variety of other warrants, including compelling personal experience and common sense, which are typically dismissed by academics. Policymakers may take scientific evidence into account in their deliberations, but other kinds of evidence are often accorded equal or even greater weight.

Scholars are generally of the view that research evidence trumps other possible warrants. They are skeptical—even dismissive—of the roles that common sense, personal experience, and compelling anecdotes regularly play in policymaking. They are even cautious when considering scientific evidence. When the available research evidence is weak, scholars argue that precipitate action is not prudent until more research can be conducted; for example, they may call for the careful evaluation of pilot programs in advance of full-scale program implementation. When research evidence is strong, on the other hand, scholars may call for immediate action. They may be surprised and frustrated when policymakers fail to take the strength of their research findings into sufficient account when making policy choices, and they may be horrified when policymakers give undue weight to other sorts of warrants.

For policymakers, in contrast, research findings merit no special reverence. They may provide a useful warrant for a policy argument, but Aunt Minnie's opinion may carry equal or greater weight because of her 30 years as a teacher or parent. Under many circumstances, warrants derived from experience, authority, ideology, or common sense may provide more valuable guidance than do findings from academic research. When the "right" answer to a policy problem can be found as easily by talking to the people in line at the grocery store as by reading research reports, researchers face an uphill battle to win much attention in policy debates.

The Problem of Rhetoric

Researchers often present their findings in ways that are confusing to policymakers in reports that are less than riveting in their rhetorical style. Scholars are trained to write in formats where their arguments can be fully developed and to present their results as transparently as possible. Their lengthy reports and articles typically include a review of prior theoretical and empirical work, an explanation of methodological choices, and an exploration of competing arguments. They are expected to acknowledge weaknesses in the available data, support their conclusions by presenting detailed information on their research methods and results, and include disconfirming evidence and alternative explanations for their findings. Providing a full account of the work and how it was conducted is an essential feature of a credible and persuasive research report.

Much to the dismay of scholars, however, documents written in the familiar academic formats are unlikely to win much attention in policy debates. Like many other readers, policymakers are apt to distrust writing they do not understand and to begrudge the time it takes to sort out the rhetorical complexities and infelicities of most academic work. They are likely to find a 35-page report bristling with statistics, footnotes, and caveats to be windy, opaque, and off-putting and to conclude that it has little of value to say on the question of what to do about the problems they face. They may find a one-paragraph summary or a set of bullet points more useful and persuasive, but only if the conclusions provide a guide for action and do not include phrases such as "It's complicated" and "It depends." Such forthrightness does not come easily to most scholars.

The style of academic writing poses a further obstacle for policymakers. Researchers are trained to let their work speak for itself. Rather than seeking to persuade the reader with rhetorical flourishes and emotional arguments, scholars present their work in sufficient depth and detail to allow the reader to make an independent judgment. This is as it should be in academic writing, but for readers who lack the expertise needed to sort things out for themselves (including nearly all policymakers), the results are at best unpersuasive and at worst unintelligible. Other stakeholders—including Aunt Minnie—may be more accustomed to persuasive speaking and writing, and policymakers may be more inclined to listen to them than to scholars.

FALLING INTO THE GAP

The obstacles that scholars and policymakers must overcome to bridge the gap between them are exacerbated in specific policy debates by the ubiquity of familiar research problems. In the absence of agreement on how to address these problems, different scholars adopt different strategies, and these inevitably produce different—and sometimes diametrically opposed—findings. From the point of view of the academy, this is entirely normal and essential to the advancement of knowledge. From the point of view of policymakers, however, this is entirely chaotic and dysfunctional.

In this section, we focus on two urgent policy questions—teacher quality and school choice—and ask why research contributes so little to policymaking on these issues. The answer is partly attributable to the obstacles discussed in the preceding section but also to research problems specific to the two issues. In the case of teacher quality, the lack of valid and reliable measures for key variables precludes firm responses to the questions that policymakers seek to answer. The problem of selection bias has the same consequence in the case of school choice. In our discussion of these two issues, we also present examples of policy research that has successfully bridged the gap between academics and policymakers, engaging the curiosity of the former while providing clear guidance to the latter.

Teacher Quality

Teachers matter. Despite occasional efforts to develop "teacher-proof" curricula or classroom scripts, there is general agreement among scholars, policymakers, and parents that teacher quality has a powerful influence on student achievement. A large and growing body of research confirms this conventional wisdom (Murnane & Phillips, 1981; Nye, Konstantopoulos, & Hedges, 2004; Rivkin, Hanushek, & Kain, 2000; Rockoff, 2004; Sanders & Horn, 1998; Wenglinsky, 2000). According to Rivkin and colleagues (2000), for example, teacher quality has a larger impact on academic performance than any other school input.

Recognizing the importance of teacher quality, policymakers at the federal, state, and local levels are eager to develop policies aimed at improving the quality of teaching. In this effort, they receive unsolicited advice from unions, business organizations, colleges of education, and other interested constituencies hoping to influence the outcome. When policymakers turn to researchers for help in crafting their initiatives, however, they often come away empty-handed.

The questions that policymakers seek to answer appear to be straightforward. They want to know what attributes characterize effective teachers, and they want to know which policies help to ensure that more teachers display these attributes. Unfortunately, research offers few useful answers to these questions for two main reasons. First, there is disagreement among scholars (and others) about how to define and measure effective teaching. Are student test scores our primary concern, or are other outcomes also important? If we accept the primacy of test scores, how can we link students' scores to the contributions of individual teachers? Second, even if the obstacles to measuring effectiveness could be resolved, the available evidence about teacher attributes associated with effective teaching remains weak and equivocal. Many obvious indicators of teacher quality, including certification status and experience, appear to have limited effects on student performance. In the absence of clear strategies to overcome these obstacles, scholars cannot answer the questions that policymakers pose.

Can We Measure Student Learning?

Scholars and policymakers agree that effective teachers produce the best possible outcomes for students. But what outcomes matter most? Much of the current research on teacher quality focuses on student test scores as the principal measure of teacher quality (Hanushek, Kain, & Rivkin, 1999; Monk, 1994; Sanders & Horn, 1998). This is in large part a function of availability and ease of interpretation, as many scholars readily acknowledge. Other important outcomes, including curiosity, morally defensible behavior, critical thinking, and civic engagement (Gutmann, 1999; Kohn, 1999; Noddings, 1995), are harder to define and measure. They consequently receive less scholarly attention.

Even when researchers restrict their attention to student test scores as a measure of teacher quality, they encounter two daunting problems. First, standardized test scores are affected by many factors other than the quality of a student's teachers. Family background and prior learning have a huge influence on a student's current scores, but those factors are entirely beyond the control of the student's teacher this year. Second, even the most sophisticated assessments are subject to significant measurement error.

In an attempt to address the first of these problems, scholars and policymakers have increasingly turned to the analysis of student learning gains (Lee & Weimer, 2002; Sanders & Horn, 1998; Webster & Menro, 1997). The shift to "value-added" models is motivated by the desire to isolate the unique contributions of specific schools and teachers to student learning. In contrast to cross-sectional analyses of student achievement, these models introduce controls for family background and prior achievement by testing students at two points in time and analyzing performance changes between the two assessments. The resulting models are generally quite complex, perhaps limiting their appeal to policymakers, but they nevertheless offer a way forward on an otherwise intractable problem.

Lamentably, however, even the most sophisticated value-added models remain subject to large measurement errors stemming from three main sources. First, test scores may change from year to year for a variety of reasons, many of them unrelated to the teaching that students receive. Apart from the inevitable dispersion of scores around a student's "true" score, a flu outbreak, unusual weather, and the generosity of a "helpful" parent who brings sugar-laden doughnuts on the morning of the test all can affect test scores in a specific school or classroom (Kane & Staiger, 2002; Rogosa, 1999, 2001). These problems are exacerbated when the number of observations is small, as is regularly the case in individual classrooms.

Second, test scores at best measure only a small sample of the knowledge and skills that are taught during a given school year. Genuinely comprehensive tests would be prohibitively expensive in terms of both test development and testing time. As a result, test scores provide only a very rough measure of what children have actually learned, even in areas such as reading and mathematics. Other learning outcomes are measured with even less precision if they are measured at all.

Third, value-added models rely on the assumption that tests can be equated across grade levels (Martineau & Plank, 2004). For student learning gains to be measured accurately, two conditions must be met. First, achievement must be measured using identical equal-interval scales on which a 5-point score difference means the same thing at all points within and across tests. Second, tests must consistently assess students on the same underlying constructs; for example, reading tests must measure the same skills (e.g., vocabulary) across grades and in the same proportions across test instruments. These assumptions are routinely violated. Scholars generally agree that the standardized tests administered by most schools do not use equal-interval scales, and it is clear that the mix of skills assessed at different grade levels should and does change as children mature and advance to each new grade level. When these assumptions are violated, even sophisticated value-added assessment models might do a poor job of measuring teacher effectiveness (Martineau & Plank, 2004).

Do Teacher Attributes Matter?

Suppose for a moment that there was a simple way in which to address these problems and to measure student outcomes fully and accurately. Would we then be able to extricate ourselves from the teacher quality quagmire? Sadly, no. As we lifted one foot out of the swamp, the other foot would continue to sink. Accurate measures of student achievement would enable us to identify teachers who successfully raise student performance, but by themselves they would provide virtually no insight into the combination of knowledge, attributes, and skills that makes these teachers successful. This, of course, is precisely what policymakers need to know as they seek to design policies to recruit, reward, develop, and retain better teachers for American classrooms.

When it comes to identifying the attributes of effective teachers, researchers have barely reached the starting gate. Easily measured attributes, including experience and advanced degrees, explain only about 3% of a teacher's contribution to student achievement, leaving 97% of the variance in teacher performance unaccounted for (Goldhaber, 2001). There is some evidence that teachers with high scores on tests of verbal ability perform well in the classroom (Ballou & Podgursky, 1997; Ehrenberg & Brewer, 1995), but measures of verbal ability are rarely available to researchers, making it difficult to test this hypothesis. The selectivity of the undergraduate institution that a teacher attended (Ehrenberg & Brewer, 1994; Summers & Wolfe, 1977) and the possession of a major in the subject area taught (Monk, 1994) may also be associated with teacher effectiveness, but the explanatory power of these variables remains limited. As Woods (1994) notes, "Teachers' personal qualities are considered to be the decisive factor in effective teaching. However, it is never quite clear what these qualities are" (p. 84).

Differences in classroom practices may account for a substantial share of the unexplained variation in teacher performance (Wenglinsky, 2000), but specifying different practices and linking them to differences in student achievement is a messy, time-consuming task. Sound data on classroom practices are hard to come by, especially on a scale that would allow meaningful comparison and generalization. In short, much of what seems to matter most—teacher practices—is difficult and expensive to measure. Information regarding the other piece of the puzzle—teacher characteristics—is often unavailable and, when available, rarely proves to be particularly helpful.

Where does all of this leave policymakers? They pose a seemingly straightforward question, and scholars answer with a resounding, "Hmmm . . ." The reason why research does not have much impact in the teacher quality debate is not because policymakers are ignoring academic work or because academics are failing to address urgent policy questions; rather, it is because research cannot yet provide unequivocal answers to the questions that policymakers seek to answer. It is, therefore, little cause for wonder when policymakers throw up their hands in despair and seek information from more helpful sources such as the local union president and the mother of five who lives down the street.

All hope is not lost, however, because a reframing of the teacher quality debate can allow scholars to conduct research that is interesting to both academics and policymakers. By way of illustration, the CPRE's Teacher Compensation Group has been consistently successful in making academic contributions that are relevant to policymakers as well. They have done this by building relationships within the policymaking community over time, translating and disseminating their findings in ways that make sense to nonacademic audiences, and devoting time and energy to educating policymakers about the practical implications of their research. Their reputation has consequently grown to the point where policymakers actively seek their input on issues related to compensation policy.

For example, leaders in the Minneapolis Public Schools turned to the Teacher Compensation Group for guidance when they were attempting to develop an alternative compensation system for the district's teachers. District personnel regularly exchanged ideas with CPRE scholars and attended the annual CPRE Teacher Compensation Conference, where they networked with other districts experimenting with alternative compensation and learned about the research being done under CPRE auspices (Ritterson, 2003). The Teacher Compensation Group has consistently produced work that is of interest to policymakers and taken pains to communicate its findings in ways that make sense to that audience while observing the canons of scholarly research. The group has targeted questions of interest to policy audiences and taken advantage of its relationships with policymakers to support and advance its scholarly research. The group has managed to make a difference in the noisy volatile world of policymaking by working within an institutional framework that supports all of its endeavors, both scholarly and applied.

School Choice

Another issue that has attracted significant interest from both researchers and policymakers is school choice. The debate over vouchers, charter schools, and other school choice policies has captivated many scholars, and policymakers on both sides of the question have marshaled an impressive array of research findings to support their positions. On balance, however, it is uncertain whether research has had any influence in the policy debate beyond reinforcing the convictions of the already persuaded. Despite the proliferation of sophisticated studies conducted by admirable scholars, the findings from research on school choice have proved to be too fragile and contested to persuade key actors in the policy debate. One of the key reasons for this failure is the familiar research problem of selection bias.

Much of the policy debate on school choice has focused on the question of whether and how student achievement in "choice" schools—Catholic schools, private schools, voucher schools, and charter schools—differs from student achievement in traditional public schools. The answer to this question turns decisively on whether the students who make nontraditional choices are comparable to the children who remain in traditional public schools. If the two groups of students are indeed similar, then achievement differences across schools may rightly be attributed to differences in the schools themselves. If the two groups of students differ in significant ways, however, then achievement differences across schools may be at least partially attributable to selection bias.

Not surprisingly, therefore, the scholarly debate on school choice has featured sharp disagreements over sample selection and the constitution of appropriate control groups. The early furor over Milwaukee's voucher program originated in disagreement about which public school students were comparable to students receiving vouchers (Rouse, 1998; Witte, 1998). Recent efforts to design "voucher experiments" in New York and elsewhere have been similarly vexed by the problem of selection bias. Apparently, small shifts in the composition of control groups can produce substantially different conclusions about the efficacy of voucher schools (Krueger & Zhu, 2004; Myers, Peterson, Mayer, Chou, & Howell, 2000). In addition, students who participate in choice programs may differ from those who do not in unmeasured but important ways, including religious commitment and parental support. It has even been argued that the very fact of receiving a voucher may distinguish choice students from other students in ways that are conceptually independent of the effectiveness of the schools they attend (Floden, 2000).

On the one hand, there is a large and persuasive body of evidence suggesting that students in Catholic schools perform better than similar students in public schools (Bryk, Lee, & Holland, 1993; Coleman, Hoffer, & Kilgore, 1982), and there is a small but growing literature suggesting that at least some of the students who participate in school choice programs also experience gains (Peterson & Howell, 2003; Witte, Weimer, Schlomer, & Shober, 2004). On the other hand, there is also an extensive literature calling all of these results into question on the grounds that students who make nontraditional choices are systematically different from students who remain in traditional public schools (Fuller, Elmore, & Orfield, 1996; Krueger & Zhu, 2004). The consequence is an impasse; disputes over selection bias and the identification of appropriate control groups cloud the debate over school choice, leaving uncontested findings in extremely short supply.

That the scholarly debate on the impact of school choice policies remains stalled by the intractable problem of selection bias hardly means that research findings have been excluded from the policy debate. In fact, the policy debate over choice, charter schools, and vouchers rages on with increasing intensity, and research continues to be deployed prominently on both sides of the issue. Nevertheless, the policy debate is driven not by research findings but rather by ideology, political commitments, and other considerations. Advocates of school choice policies seize on data showing achievement gains to argue that "choice works," especially for disadvantaged students, and that publicly funded choice programs should be expanded. Opponents embrace competing research and argue that the gains associated with school choice are either illusory or too small to justify the losses by students "left behind." For now, therefore, the question of whether school choice policies lead to improved student performance remains unanswered.

This, however, is neither the only nor necessarily the most fruitful way in which to frame the debate on school choice (Plank & Sykes, 2000). Other questions might produce less contested findings and generate more useful guidance for policymakers. For example, Mintrom (2001) provides a definitive answer to the question of whether charter schools can be expected to lead to the development and diffusion of educational innovations. In Michigan and other states, one of the stated purposes for supporting the establishment of charter schools was, as stated in a Michigan state statute passed in 1993, "to stimulate innovative teaching methods." Mintrom found some evidence of innovation in Michigan's charter schools, but he also found that innovations in charter schools tend to be incremental, just as they are in traditional public schools. He also found that innovations developed in charter schools rarely spread beyond the walls of a particular school (Mintrom, 2000, 2001). His research made a significant contribution to the scholarly literature on school choice and briefly shifted the focus of the policy debate on charter schools.

Meanwhile, the debate over how school choice affects student achievement rages on fruitlessly. The gap between researchers and policymakers interested in school choice remains deep and wide, and most research findings continue to tumble into the abyss.

CAN THE GAP BE BRIDGED?

Where does this leave us? Can scholars and policymakers overcome their differences? The long-standing tradition is one of mutual incomprehension. Researchers complain that policymakers do not seek out or value their advice ("what we know"), whereas policymakers complain that research findings bear little connection to the problems they are obliged to address ("what we need"). This is mutually advantageous, at least in the short run. Neither group is obliged to change its behavior, and each is able to cast the blame on the other.

As researchers, we may find this tradition to be quite comfortable. We can win the praise of our colleagues and enjoy the rewards of academic success without worrying about the disregard of policymakers. If they choose to ignore our work, the loss is theirs, not ours.

Comfort with the prevailing situation may carry a price, however, to the extent that scholars care about what goes on in schools. When policymakers ignore research findings, they may well repeat past mistakes or adopt misguided policies. Minding the gap between scholars and policymakers is a poor substitute for action; if research is to contribute to the development of policies and the improvement of schools, we will have to find a way to build a durable bridge across the gap.

The responsibility for bridging the gap will fall mainly on scholars rather than on policymakers. Even policymakers who are eager to do the right thing have no real reason to believe that scholars have the answers they seek, and they are regularly confirmed in this judgment. Thus, the key question is how researchers can make their work more accessible and useful to policy audiences.

A relatively cheerful answer to this question comes from Weiss (1977). In her view, scholars need only to continue doing their academic work according to the canons of scholarly practice. Over time, useful findings will seep into the policy conversation, shifting the terms and boundaries of the debate. This has occurred in some important instances. For example, research findings from the Perry Preschool Project (Barnett, 1985) demonstrated that the benefits of early educational intervention far outweighed the costs, drawing the attention of policymakers to the issue of prekindergarten education. Findings from the Third International Mathematics and Science Study and other comparative assessments of student performance have strengthened efforts to raise standards and expectations in American schools (Schmidt et al., 2001). In many other cases, however, the policy debate moves forward without paying any attention to policy research while potentially useful findings languish in scholarly obscurity.

This may be the best we can do, but most policy researchers aspire to inform policy debates more directly. Individual scholars may focus their energies on questions that are of immediate policy concern, but this only begins to address the problem. They must also gain the attention of relevant policymakers, often by producing multiple representations of their work tailored for audiences such as the media and legislative aides. They must compete with lobbyists and well-funded think tanks to gain recognition. They must simultaneously tend to their academic obligations and produce work that meets scholarly expectations for rigor and theoretical reach. Some exceptionally gifted and energetic scholars can pull this off, but most cannot. Most researchers need institutional support to ensure that research findings reach policymakers in a timely and accessible way.

The rise of university-affiliated policy centers offers one promising way forward. Centers such as the CPRE, PACE (Policy Analysis for California Education), and the Education Policy Center at Michigan State University reflect efforts to institutionalize stronger connections between the worlds of research and policy. These centers strive to address issues of concern to policy audiences on reasonable timelines and to translate research findings into terms and formats that are accessible and useful to policymakers. They build institutional, as well as individual, relationships between universities and a variety of policy audiences. These institutional relationships endure beyond the terms of particular policymakers and allow both established and emerging scholars to quickly gain credibility with key constituencies.

Rather than viewing policymakers' needs as a burden, these policy centers recognize those needs as their raison d'être. They have supported excellent scholarly work while acknowledging the needs of policy audiences at every step in the research process, from formulating questions to disseminating findings. This orientation has increased their credibility to the point where policymakers may actively seek their guidance, as in the teacher compensation example described earlier. Over time, therefore, some of these centers have managed to construct bridges—still fragile and lightly traveled—across the divide that separates scholars and policymakers.

Some of the reasons why policy research has so little to say to policymakers are intrinsic to the research enterprise, but others can be changed. Scholars cannot change the political environment within which policy is made or policymakers' preferred sources of information, but scholars can change their own behavior. Policy researchers who seek to affect ongoing policy debates may, therefore, find it worthwhile to devote considerably more attention and energy to solving the problems of relevance, timing, translation, and dissemination that restrict the current impact of their work. This is a challenging task, but the reward of increased policy relevance might nevertheless make it worthwhile. University-affiliated policy centers represent one promising strategy for increasing the supply and quality of policy research.

In closing, it is important to acknowledge that deeper engagement in policy research entails significant risks, both for individual scholars and for the broader scholarly enterprise. Engagement in policy research almost inevitably requires attention to research topics and publication in formats and media that generally earn relatively little credit in the academy. Producing the kind of work that is valued by policymakers may divert time and energy away from work that would be admired by other scholars. Writing targeted to policy audiences might not always measure up to the expectations of academic audiences. In addition, the intensity of contemporary policy debates and the voracious appetite of policy audiences for politically useful research "findings" may have pernicious consequences for scholarship. Those who publish most of their work on editorial pages and in think tank broadsides may find that their work serves mainly to provide policymakers with rhetorical ammunition that reinforces prior support for or opposition to specific policy initiatives rather than with a deeper understanding of the issues.

In the realm of policy research, it is essential to strike a balance that protects the integrity of academic research even as it turns scholarly work to more practical ends. Given the urgency of the issues facing American schools and the commitment of many policy researchers to provide assistance in addressing those issues, a move toward the production of scholarship that is useful and accessible to policymakers may yield substantial rewards for schools and their students. Many researchers, therefore, may find that sacrificing some degree of scholarly autonomy and methodological elegance in exchange for greater policy influence is a worthwhile trade. It is nevertheless essential for scholars to be wary of the dilemmas and difficulties that characterize policy research and to mind their step as they stride across the gap.

REFERENCES

Ballou, D., & Podgursky, M. (1997). *Teacher pay and teacher quality.* Kalamazoo, MI: W. E. Upjohn Institute for Employment Research.

Barnett, W. S. (1985). Benefit–cost analysis of the Perry Preschool Program and its policy implications. *Educational Evaluation and Policy Analysis, 7,* 333–342.

Baumgartner, R., & Jones, B. D. (1993). Punctuated equilibria in politics. In R. Baumgartner & B. D. Jones, *Agendas and instability in American politics* (pp. 3–24). Chicago: University of Chicago Press.

Borman, G. D., & Kimball, S. M. (2005). Teacher quality and educational equality: Do teachers with higher standards-based evaluation ratings close student achievement gaps? *Elementary School Journal, 106,* 3–20.

Bryk, A. S., Lee, V., & Holland, P. (1993). *Catholic schools and the common good.* Cambridge, MA: Harvard University Press.

Coleman, J., Hoffer, T., & Kilgore, S. (1982). *High school achievement: Public, Catholic, and private schools compared.* New York: Basic Books.

DeVoe, J., Peter, K., Kaufman, P., Miller, A., Noonan, M., Snyder, T., & Baum, K. (2004). *Indicators of school crime and safety: 2004.* Washington, DC: National Center for Education Statistics.

Dunbar, C., & Villareul, F. A. (2002). Urban school leaders and the implementation of zero tolerance policy: An examination of its implications. *Peabody Journal of Education, 77,* 82–104.

Ehrenberg, R. G., & Brewer, D. J. (1994). Do school and teacher characteristics matter? Evidence from high school and beyond. *Economics of Education Review, 13*(1), 1–17.

Ehrenberg, R. G., & Brewer, D. J. (1995). Did teachers' verbal ability and race matter in the 1960's? "Coleman" revisited. *Economics of Education Review, 14*(1), 1–21.

Ferguson, R. F. (1991). Paying for public education: New evidence on how and why money matters. *Harvard Journal on Legislation, 28,* 465–498.

Ferguson, R. F., & Ladd, H. F. (1996). How and why money matters: An analysis of Alabama schools. In H. F. Ladd (Ed.), *Holding schools accountable* (pp. 265–298). Washington, DC: Brookings Institution.

Fisher, K. M., & Kettl, P. (2001). Trends in school violence: Are our schools safe? In M. Shafii & S. L. Shafii (Eds.), *School violence: Assessment, management, prevention* (pp. 73–83). Washington, DC: American Psychiatric Press.

Floden, R. (2000). *Does choice produce gains in student achievement outcomes?* East Lansing: Michigan State University, Education Policy Center.

Fuller, B., Elmore, R., & Orfield, G. (1996). *Who chooses, who loses? Culture, institutions, and the unequal effects of school choice.* New York: Columbia University, Teachers College Press.

Gallagher, H. A. (2004). Vaughn Elementary's innovative teacher evaluation system: Are teacher evaluation scores related to growth in student achievement? *Peabody Journal of Education, 79,* 79–107.

Goldhaber, D. D. (2001). How has teacher compensation changed? In W. J. Fowler, Jr. (Ed.), *Selected papers in school finance, 2000–2001* (pp. 11–30). Washington, DC: National Center for Educational Statistics.

Green, T. F. (1983). Excellence, equity, and equality. In L. S. Shulman & G. Sykes (Eds.), *Handbook of teaching and policy* (pp. 318–341). New York: Longman.

Gutmann, A. (1999). *Democratic education.* Princeton, NJ: Princeton University Press.

Hanushek, E. A., Kain, J. F., & Rivkin, S. G. (1999). *Do higher salaries buy better teachers?* (Working Paper No. 7082). Cambridge, MA: National Bureau of Economic Research.

Harris, D. N. (2002). Identifying optimal class sizes and teacher salaries. In H. M. Levin & P. McKewan (Eds.), *Cost effectiveness analysis in education* (pp. 177–191). Larchmont, NY: American Education Finance Association.

Kane, T. J., & Staiger, D. O. (2002). Volatility in school test scores: Implications for test-based accountability systems. In D. Ravitch (Ed.), *Brookings papers on education policy, 2002* (pp. 235–283). Washington, DC: Brookings Institution.

Kingdon, J. W. (1984). *Agendas, alternatives, and public policies.* New York: HarperCollins.

Kohn, A. (1999). *The schools our children deserve: Moving beyond traditional classrooms and "tougher standards."* Boston: Houghton Mifflin.

Krueger, A. B., & Zhu, P. (2004). Another look at the New York City school voucher experiment. *American Behavioral Scientist, 47,* 658–698.

Kuhn, T. S. (1970). *The structure of scientific revolutions* (2nd ed.). Chicago: University of Chicago Press.

Lee, K., & Weimer, D. (2002). *Building value-added assessment into Michigan's accountability system: Lessons from other states* (Research Report No. 1). East Lansing: Michigan State University, Education Policy Center.

Lindblom, C. E. (1959). The science of muddling through. *Public Administration Review, 19,* 79–88.

Lipsky, M. (1983). *Street-level bureaucracy: Dilemmas of the individual in public services.* New York: Russell Sage.

Martineau, J. A., & Plank, D. N. (2004). *Fairness in accountability policy: Is value-added assessment the answer?* East Lansing: Michigan State University, Education Policy Center.

Mazmanian, D. A., & Sabatier, P. A. (1989). *Implementation and public policy.* New York: University Press of America.

Milanowski, A. (2004). *Relationships among dimension scores of standards-based teacher evaluation systems, and the stability of evaluation score–student achievement relationships over time* (CPRE-UW Working Paper No. TC-04-11).

Madison, WI: Consortium for Policy Research in Education.

Milanowski, A., Kimball, S. M., & White, B. (2004). *The relationship between standards-based teacher evaluation scores and student achievement: Replication and extensions at three sites* (CPRE-UW Working Paper No. TC-04-10). Madison, WI: Consortium for Policy Research in Education.

Mintrom, M. (2000). *Leveraging local innovation: The case of Michigan's charter schools* (Working Paper No. 6). East Lansing: Michigan State University, Education Policy Center.

Mintrom, M. (2001). Policy design for local innovation: The effects of competition in public schooling. *State Politics and Policy Quarterly, 1,* 343–363.

Monk, D. (1994). Subject area preparation of secondary mathematics and science teachers and student achievement. *Economics of Education Review, 13*(2), 125–145.

Moore, M. H. (2003). *Deadly lessons: Understanding lethal school violence—Case studies of School Violence Committee.* Washington, DC: National Research Council School Violence Committee; Committee on Law and Justice; National Research Council; Board on Children, Youth, and Families; and Institute of Medicine.

Murnane, R. J., & Phillips, B. R. (1981). Learning by doing, vintage, and selection: Three pieces of the puzzle relating teaching experience and teaching performance. *Economics of Education Review, 1,* 453–465.

Myers, D., Peterson, P., Mayer, D., Chou, J., & Howell, W. G. (2000). *School choice in New York City after two years: An evaluation of the school choice scholarships program* (Interim Report No. MPR 8404-036). Princeton, NJ: Mathematica Policy Research.

Newman, K. S. (2004). *Rampage: The social roots of school shootings.* New York: Basic Books.

Noddings, N. (1995). A morally defensible mission for schools in the 21st century. *Phi Delta Kappan, 76,* 365–368.

Nye, B., Konstantopoulos, S., & Hedges, L. V. (2004). How large are teacher effects? *Educational Evaluation and Policy Analysis, 26,* 237–257.

Peterson, P., & Howell, W. G. (2003). *Efficiency, bias, and classification schemes: Estimating private-school impact* (No. PEPG 03-01). Cambridge,

MA: Harvard University, Program on Education Policy and Governance.

Plank, D. N., & Sykes, G. (2000). *The school choice debate: Framing the issues.* East Lansing: Michigan State University, Education Policy Center.

Popper, K. R. (1959). *The logic of scientific discovery.* New York: Basic Books.

Pressman, J. L., & Wildavsky, A. B. (1984). *Implementation: How great expectations in Washington are dashed in Oakland—Or, why it's amazing that federal programs work at all, this being a saga of the Economic Development Administration as told by two sympathetic observers who seek to build morals on a foundation of ruined hopes* (3rd ed.). Berkeley: University of California Press.

Ritterson, J. (2003). *Minneapolis Public Schools Teacher Academy professional pay plan report for the year ending December 2002.* Minneapolis, MN: Minneapolis Public Schools.

Rivkin, S. G., Hanushek, E. A., & Kain, J. F. (2000). *Teachers, schools, and academic achievement* (Working Paper No. 6691). Cambridge, MA: National Bureau of Economic Research.

Rockoff, J. E. (2004). The impact of individual teachers on student achievement: Evidence from panel data. *American Economic Review, 94,* 247–252.

Rogosa, D. (1999). *Accuracy of individual scores expressed in percentile ranks: Classical test theory calculations* (No. R305B60002). Washington, DC: National Center for Research on Evaluation, Standards, and Student Testing.

Rogosa, D. (2001). Shoe shopping and the reliability coefficient. *Educational Assessment, 7,* 255–258.

Rouse, C. (1998). Private school vouchers and student achievement: Evidence from the Milwaukee choice program. *Quarterly Journal of Economics, 113,* 553–602.

Sanders, W. L., & Horn, S. P. (1998). Research findings from the Tennessee value-added assessment system (TVAAS) database: Implications for educational evaluation and research. *Journal of Personnel Evaluation in Education, 12,* 247–256.

Schmidt, W. H., McKnight, C. C., Houang, R. T., Wang, H., Wiley, D. E., Cogan, L. S., & Wolfe,

R. G. (2001). *Why schools matter: A cross-national comparison of curriculum and learning.* San Francisco: Jossey-Bass.

Smith, P. K. (2003). *Violence in schools: The response in Europe.* London: Routledge Falmer.

Spillane, J. P. (2000). Cognition and policy implementation: District policymakers and the reform of mathematics education. *Cognition and Instruction, 18*(2), 141–179.

Summers, A. A., & Wolfe, B. L. (1977). Do schools make a difference? *American Economic Review, 67,* 639–652.

Webster, W. J., & Menro, R. L. (1997). The Dallas value-added accountability system. In J. Millman (Ed.), *Grading teachers, grading schools: Is student achievement a valid evaluation measure?* (pp. 81–99). Thousand Oaks, CA: Corwin.

Weiss, C. H. (1977). Research for policy's sake: The enlightenment function of social research. *Policy Analysis, 3,* 531–545.

Weiss, C. H. (1995). The four "I's" of school reform: How interests, ideology, information, and institution affect teachers and principals. *Harvard Educational Review, 65,* 571–592.

Wenglinsky, H. (2000). *How teaching matters: Bringing the classroom back into discussions of teacher quality.* Princeton, NJ: Educational Testing Service.

White, B. (2004). *The relationship between teacher evaluation scores and student achievement: Evidence from Coventry, RI* (CPRE-UW Working Paper No. TC-04-13). Madison, WI: Consortium for Policy Research in Education.

Witte, J. F. (1998). The Milwaukee voucher experiment. *Educational Evaluation and Policy Analysis, 20,* 229–251.

Witte, J. F., Weimer, D. L., Schlomer, P. A., & Shober, A. F. (2004). *The performance of charter schools in Wisconsin.* Madison: University of Wisconsin, Robert LaFollette School of Public Affairs.

Woods, P. (1994). The conditions for teacher development. In P. P. Grimmett & J. Neufeld (Eds.), *Teacher development and the struggle for authenticity: Professional growth and restructuring in the context of change* (pp. 83–100). New York: Columbia University, Teachers College Press.

*Identifying Meaningful Problems and
Approaches to Inquiry Across and Within Fields*

INTRODUCTORY ESSAY

LAURA W. PERNA

University of Pennsylvania

JOHN C. WEIDMAN

University of Pittsburgh

Fruitful research in education examines issues that have enduring (i.e., past as well as present) significance. It is also heuristic, stimulating further inquiry. According to a search at the Barnes & Noble Web site, more than 1,469 book titles contain the following three key words: *research, design,* and *education.* Many of these books undoubtedly provide important guidance about the essential components of the research process, including how to identify a research problem. Yet relatively few such resources offer suggestions for identifying potentially "fruitful" areas of educational research.

The 13 chapters in Section Two of the *Handbook* explore exemplars of "research problems"—past, present, and future—both across and within lines of inquiry. Exemplars build on, extend, and deepen our understanding of particular research problems. Together, the chapters invite readers to reflect deeply on the purposes, "ideas," "problems," and approaches guiding their own inquiry, in concert with identifying promising research problems and approaches in the field of education that might guide their future inquiry.

Drawing on their extensive knowledge and expertise, chapter authors offer their perspective on exemplars of fruitful research within major fields of educational inquiry. Many provide conceptual frameworks to guide understanding of the complex issues addressed. The authors' descriptions of and reflections about these exemplars are intended to be especially helpful not only to individuals who are learning to conceptualize research but also to experienced researchers seeking fuller understanding of fruitful approaches and topics in the various fields. It is hoped that educational researchers at all levels of expertise will benefit from the insights and perspectives shared in these chapters, as the chapters encourage readers to reflect more deeply about the problems researchers choose and the approaches researchers use to guide their inquiry.

Although the chapters address substantive problems within and across fields, the purpose of these chapters is not to discuss the entire fields of inquiry suggested by their titles (e.g., teacher education, counseling psychology, instructional leadership, comparative education). The chapters do not provide traditional reviews of the literature or comprehensive overviews of all topics within a field, nor do they include attention to all possible fields of educational inquiry.

Rather, the chapters are intended to shed light on a fundamental question for all educational researchers: What are fruitful areas of inquiry? Although the chapters vary in substance, style, and approach, several conclusions may be drawn. First, fruitful lines of inquiry examine enduring research problems. Second, fruitful lines of inquiry address research problems that are important to various stakeholders. Third, fruitful lines of inquiry may be understood, at least in part, by examining exemplars of research that have examined some aspect of the problem. In the words of McDonough and Gildersleeve in Chapter 4, an exemplar is "a prototype of research that is a model of clarity and specificity as well as an example that demonstrates the highest level of research integrity, both theoretically and methodologically." As several chapter authors note, the exemplars offered in these chapters are not representative of a particular topic but rather are appropriate and useful vehicles for understanding past, present, and promising future approaches to research in that area. The following spotlights each of the chapters in Section Two.

In Chapter 4, after providing a historical overview of the development of college access research, Patricia McDonough and R. Evely Gildersleeve offer three exemplars to guide future inquiry. The first exemplar focuses on connections between K–12 and higher education and between research and policy, the second stresses the ways in which public and private K–12 schools shape equal educational opportunity, and the third further illustrates the importance of a "system framework" by showing the contribution of capital to understanding continued differences in educational equality across social class and racial/ethnic groups. As McDonough and Gildersleeve note, educational inequality is not only an enduring research problem but also a problem that reflects the accumulation of inequities and disadvantages as a student moves from prekindergarten through Grade 12 and into higher education. The authors argue that addressing this enduring research problem more completely requires a "paradigmatic shift from a domain-specific orientation to a holistic approach that tries to capture and encompass the interconnectivity and interdependencies of inequalities." This chapter encourages researchers to adopt a more integrative approach to research on opportunity for higher education, recognizing the multiple ways in which aspects of the economic, social, cultural, and political environment constrain educational experiences over time, beginning before school entry for historically underrepresented groups.

In Chapter 5, Kenneth Zeichner shares his insights regarding research on a different enduring research problem, namely, understanding the effects of different types of preservice teacher education programs. He begins by describing the development of research on teacher education programs, noting shifts over time in the goals of, disciplinary lens applied to, and methods used in such research and discussing five categories of contemporary research on preservice teacher education. Zeichner notes that prior research examining the impact of teacher education programs is limited by the failure to consider more than the structural attributes of the program (e.g., length, institutional sponsorship). He argues that future research can advance knowledge in this area by clearly and explicitly defining and considering these and other program aspects, including curricular focus and instructional strategies, characteristics of participants and schools where they teach, and institutional and state policy context. Researchers should also recognize the need for building on the contributions and limitations of prior research, greater consistency across studies in the methods used and the measurement of relevant outcomes, and a more comprehensive set of measures of student learning.

In Chapter 6, Carl Grant and Vonzell Agosto focus on the enduring research problem of preparing teachers to be multicultural educators. The authors begin by identifying a key challenge for all educational researchers, namely, building support from key stakeholders. They argue that students, teachers, administrators, policymakers, and researchers often must be persuaded that multicultural education (and thus research on multicultural teacher education) has benefits and that these benefits are not limited to people of color. Relying on multiculturalism and social justice as conceptual lenses, Grant and Agosto identify both the contributions and limitations of prior research to understanding their research problem. The authors argue that future research will contribute to knowledge in this area by employing longitudinal research designs; examining a broader range of aspects of diversity such as ethnicity, religion, language, and sexuality; and exploring the context of multicultural education preparation.

In Chapter 7, Joyce Epstein and Steven Sheldon address the challenges of building effective school, family, and community partnerships that will contribute to improved learning and development of students. Rather than following a few lines of exemplary research, the authors focus on conceptualizing the underlying processes and applying this analytical work to developing recommendations for improving both research and program development. The chapter is framed around seven "defining principles for researchers, educators, families, and others who have a stake in improving schools and in increasing student success." Deliberately placed in the first position is the assertion that the commonly used term "parental involvement" is far more limited than the notion of "school, family, and community partnerships" that Epstein and Sheldon develop and use as the foundation of their subsequent discussion. At the core of this first principle is a framework for the interaction of "overlapping spheres of influence" in which school personnel, families, and community work together in supporting the learning and development of students. Schools are not encapsulated environments isolated from their surrounding communities; rather, they are dynamic places facing educational and developmental tasks that virtually require them to incorporate the whole range of those individuals whose lives they touch. Not surprisingly, the authors argue that to understand fully the dynamics of overlapping spheres of influence, interdisciplinary approaches are essential. They stress that because "partnership" is a multidimensional concept, approaches to research and program development require multiple perspectives to be effective. Epstein and Sheldon carefully classify and categorize their constructs (e.g., six types of "involvement," eight "essential elements" for effective partnership programs). A focus on increasing learning through subject-specific goals for students and equity is maintained throughout. The chapter concludes with a thoughtful discussion of methodological issues in the conduct of research that is both sophisticated and accessible, including indications of strengths and weaknesses of various approaches. The authors also provide concrete suggestions for how research can inform the development of partnership programs and policy, a further example of what David Plank and Debbi Harris call "minding the gap" in Section One (Chapter 3) of this volume.

In their chapter on instruction and learning in science (Chapter 8), Michael Ford and Ellice Forman discuss the contribution of, and challenges associated with, two methodological approaches to educational research: "pure science" and experimental design. The authors argue that the current debate over "acceptable" research methods may be advanced by paying attention not only to whether particular research techniques are used but also to the effectiveness of the design in accomplishing the goals of the research. As exemplars, Ford and Forman identify two research programs. One examines the effectiveness of particular instructional strategies and interventions in science education using a pure science approach; the other uses a design approach. The authors discuss the strengths and weaknesses of both of these methodological approaches in terms of their success in achieving three methodological principles: rigor, educational value, and theoretical generality.

In Chapter 9, taking a different approach to a related substantive domain, Juliet Baxter and Shirley Magnusson offer insights into the evolution of research on learning in science and mathematics. They address the conceptualization of learning or "understanding" in science and mathematics education as well as the methods used to determine students' understanding. The authors begin by recognizing the enduring contribution of Piaget's work to examining students' thinking processes and cognitive growth. Then they describe research in science and mathematics education that addresses one limitation of Piaget's work, namely, "his emphasis on content-free cognitive structures." Through this discussion, Baxter and Magnusson show that researchers have advanced both the conceptualization of learning and methodological approaches to understanding learning through paying attention to students' thinking about particular concepts specific to science and mathematics. For each of the two disciplines, the authors highlight an approach that may be especially useful for examining cognitive processes in that discipline: dynamic assessment in science education and "cognitively guided instruction" in mathematics education. The authors conclude by suggesting three recommendations to guide future research on learning in science and mathematics.

In Chapter 10, Cheryl Hanley-Maxwell and Brian Bottge use a multilevel approach to analyze research on the education of persons with disabilities: individual, small group, organization/systems-centered, and institutional/community. Using their own lines of research as exemplars, the authors "illustrate the theoretical and practical challenges and opportunities of conducting multilevel research for enhancing the lives of persons with disabilities." They address learning of complex tasks in different types of environments, including mainstream classrooms as well as more restrictive settings, focusing on the ways in which research informs the redesign of instructional practices for students with and without disabilities. In fact, the "Key Model" of learning mathematics developed by Bottge "is based primarily on theoretical constructs and practices from mainstream cognitive science." Hanley-Maxwell and Bottge make a strong case for the use of qualitative methods, including ethnographic studies, in the investigation of learning by students with disabilities as well as the effectiveness of related teaching strategies.

In Chapter 11, Steven Schlossman uses historical methods to unearth "unheard voices" of children and parents, the main target of educational reform. The author distinguishes between "top-down" approaches, which focus on organizations, laws and regulations, leaders in education, and the like, and "bottom-up" approaches, which focus on trying to find public records, biographies, diaries, newspaper accounts, and the like that cast light on historical issues through the lenses of the actors involved. Both methods enable Schlossman to "enlarge understanding of key educational actors and activities in the past." Using the modality of intellectual biography, an approach similar to the one taken by James Youniss in Section Three (Chapter 17), Schlossman describes how he came to study such topics in the educational history of children and youth as gender and social reform through the juvenile justice system, bilingual education, children's oral health, and homework. A key feature of career experience that distinguishes Schlossman from purely academic historians is his work with the RAND Corporation on applied topics of educational history that required writing for client audiences outside the academy. The author indicates that he was challenged by "the opportunity to put history to direct policy use at the federal level amid swirling political and cultural controversies."

In Chapter 12, through a historical overview of research, Mary Lee Nelson and Cindy Juntunen identify three fruitful areas for future research in counseling psychology: vocational testing and guidance, characteristics of effective counseling and therapy relationships, and training and supervision of counselors and therapists. For each of the three research areas, the authors describe the evolution of the primary theoretical, conceptual, and methodological approaches and identify, based on a discussion and critique of relevant prior research, directions for future fruitful research. Among other suggestions, Nelson and Juntunen present four constructs for developing better understandings of vocational testing and guidance: vocational interests, self-efficacy beliefs, contextual factors, and career decision making and adaptability. Through their attention to the development of each of the three areas within counseling psychology, Nelson and Juntunen illustrate the ways in which future research can build on what is known from prior research to address current knowledge gaps.

In Chapter 13, Jane Clark Lindle addresses the literature of instructional leadership at the prekindergarten through Grade 12 levels, framing her discussion in a conceptualization drawing from research on complex organizations, moral imperatives of societal institutions, and leadership in education related to curriculum and instruction as well as the monitoring of teaching and learning. She points out the strengths and many weaknesses in the extant literature on instructional leadership, highlighting exemplary research that shapes the landscape of contemporary thought and practice. Lindle also provides methodological critiques of the research, pointing out the marked differences between "espoused theory" and "theory in use," questioning the value to instructional leadership practitioners of currently favored methodological approaches.

In Chapter 14, John C. Weidman addresses issues of organizational socialization of students in higher education. He shares with Epstein and Sheldon (Chapter 7) the notion that educational institutions should not be viewed as encapsulated environments. Weidman also emphasizes conceptualization and classification of processes and influences on cognitive and affective changes in both undergraduate and graduate students, identifying common elements and pointing out ways in which conceptions and frameworks drawn from different disciplinary perspectives parallel one another. Using the types of frameworks he identifies, Weidman concludes with a discussion of exemplary research that focuses on issues related to peer socialization and effects of diversity in higher education.

In Chapter 15, Jason Johnson Clifton F. Conrad, and Laura W. Perna identify three productive areas for future research on minority-serving institutions of higher education. These three areas focus on the private and public benefits of minority-serving institutions (MSIs); the policies and practices that promote recruitment, retention, and "success" of other-race students at MSIs; and the lessons that MSIs might offer predominantly white institutions about ways in which to improve the educational experiences of all students. The authors begin by arguing that researchers should explore these questions not only because of the absence of adequate related research but also because of their importance to multiple stakeholders, particularly "individual students and their families, institutional leaders, and public policymakers." For each of the three areas, the authors provide guidance to future researchers by first describing and critiquing an exemplar of related research and then offering suggestions for additional research that will build on this exemplar to further advance knowledge.

In Chapter 16, David Phillips addresses the importance of historical inquiry for the field of comparative education, beginning with a description of five overlapping developmental stages: stories and tales brought back by travelers of what they had observed, information from travelers whose visits had a specific educational focus, accumulation of information through educational exchange, studies of "national character" in the shaping of education systems, and quantitative research leading to an increased capacity for explaining educational phenomena in comparative perspective. Phillips argues that comparative education relates most closely to the discipline of history by addressing how it contributes to explanation and prediction. Like Schlossman (Chapter 11), Phillips describes the contribution of historical perspective and methodology to understanding educational policy. Phillips, however, goes beyond the local context to the international context, discussing comparative approaches to educational history. He draws liberally from his own work on policy borrowing in education, illustrating how the influences of certain national systems of education can be seen in the educational reforms of other nations as well as how these patterns of influence must be understood in historical perspective. Phillips grounds his analysis in compelling conceptual frameworks and describes implications for policy.

In summary, the chapters in Section Two encourage readers to think about problems more generally and shed light on how to identify fruitful problems. Several chapters also link research and related outcomes of policy and educational practice. Through their discussions of particular examples and exemplars as well as their specific suggestions for future research, these chapters offer valuable guidance for educational researchers in a variety of fields.

4

ALL ELSE IS NEVER EQUAL

Opportunity Lost and Found
on the P–16 Path to College Access

PATRICIA M. MCDONOUGH

University of California, Los Angeles

R. EVELY GILDERSLEEVE

University of California, Los Angeles

The imperatives of good research design include asking precise and answerable research questions, gathering appropriate data, and making and substantiating claims. These imperatives often propel us to focus more and more narrowly on a topic, more and more narrowly on a specific research question or questions, more and more narrowly on a specific methodology.

Yet what are the implications of attending to methodological rigor in individual research studies while neglecting the perspectives and needs of the state of the art of knowledge of the field of inquiry? How often do we as a field assess the limitations of our narrow focus and privileging of precision while simultaneously holding true to the integrity of methodological rigor that demands such choices? Alternatively, how often should the researchers in a field step back, take stock of the state of the art of knowledge of their topical domain, and then try to engineer a course correction for the field or

identify the most promising lines of inquiry for the near-term future?

To address some of these questions, we have chosen to address the field of college access, including how it has been studied over the past 40 years and an assessment of the state of the art of inquiry to identify needs, promising prospects, and paradigmatic shifts. We have organized this chapter with the intent of presenting a macroperspective of the state of the art of inquiry.

The overarching goal of this chapter is to understand equal educational opportunity as a long-term systemic event and to lay bare the ways in which opportunity is constrained or enabled by our current educational structures; the free agency choices of goal-directed rational individuals; and the complex interplay of those individuals and structures throughout individuals' P–16 educational careers. We use the case of research on college access to show how one could and should reconceptualize that field of research to take a P–16 perspective and how this research perspective has and could have important implications for research, policy, and practice. Using the case of college access, we demonstrate our argument by analyzing the current state of research in this field and by offering a recent historical perspective on incipient field correctives toward a P–16 perspective. Finally, we offer three exemplars that suggest promising new directions and lead to questions and future directions for research. Thus, this chapter simultaneously embraces three foci: equal educational opportunity, college access, and exemplars of good research.

What we are emphasizing is not the need for every piece of research to incorporate this P–16 perspective but rather that periodically each domain of research needs to have some scholars take this long-term systemic field perspective to understand how aggregate individual actions influence organizations; how the actions of, say, elementary schools have implications for colleges; how institutionalized and historical legacies of racism condition the expectations and actions of both individuals and schools; and how forces such as privatization, free market competition, and legal decisions alter the terms of competition. We are proposing that taking this long-term systemic field perspective requires making some attempt at integrative inquiry (Conrad, 1989) that reviews the literature of a research domain, synthesizes what is known, offers insights, and focuses on large significant issues that need to be addressed (Conrad, 1989).

We first offer a historical perspective on the genre of college access research with an analysis of how new lines of research have developed recently. What we describe is an example of a field-level corrective, although it is one that has taken place over time and many studies, where our theoretical frameworks have multiplied, our methodological approaches have seesawed back and forth as appropriate, and our analyses at the individual level have been disaggregated across racial/ethnic, social class, and geographic/space statuses. We describe how the literature has morphed from social psychological perspectives on college choice, with studies that treated students' college choices as a process of technical fit between individuals and colleges, to

organizational analyses, which posited organizational contexts as critical to understanding the empirical patterns of individual outcomes, and cultural analyses, which focused on the role of schools' cultures in reproducing class structures. Of late, college access research has resulted in a plethora of studies that have expanded the racial/ethnic subgroups that we have deemed worthy of research and expanded our notions of geographical/spatial categorizations of students. This body of work has begun to identify the specific ways in which cultural and geographical differences affect reasons for deciding to attend college, college preparation, parental involvement, financial aid, and affirmative action, and it refutes the essentializing assumption that all low-income students are equally oppressed by structural, perceptual, and motivational barriers to college access.

Then we offer three exemplars of research that look at inquiry in a more integrative fashion. By "exemplar," we mean a prototype of research that is a model of clarity and specificity as well as an example that demonstrates a high level of research integrity, both theoretically and methodologically. We are also suggesting that some exemplars are promising new directions for research, particularly those that integrate across domains and take a long-term systemic view of the research problem.

The first exemplar of equal educational opportunities relates K–12 achievement to college access and the connection of scholarly analyses and policymaking. We see this in the efforts of Michael Kirst and Andrea Venezia's recent book, *From High School to College,* which analyzes college access as a P–16 educational pipeline problem. Kirst and Venezia (2004) look at the organization and policies of K–12 and postsecondary education and also discuss major transition points and disconnects that arise from having separate K–12 and postsecondary systems.

The second exemplar contrasts the structure, culture, and aims of K–12 schools, both public and private, using two powerful studies. The first study is a pathbreaking analysis of public schools that serve low-income urban students of color in an investigation of school conditions, state policies, and students' rights. Jeannie Oakes leads a cross-disciplinary team of prominent scholars who conducted independent studies, but collectively this research enterprise resulted in an exhaustive unpacking of school conditions to offer a rich (and depressing) accounting of how unequal educational opportunity is actively structured by state and local policies, financing schemas, and market conditions and also is enacted, reproduced, and made marginally better or worse by school leaders and teachers (Oakes, Rogers, Lipton, & Morrell, 2002). These scholars teamed with lawyers to use research evidence to successfully claim that students have a right to an equal educational opportunity framed as a simple mantra that educational opportunity minimally means access to basic educational tools—books, a teacher, and a safe place to learn. The second case represents the work of a single investigator who provides rich description and interpretive analysis of private, college preparatory independent schools. Arthur Powell identifies two hallmarks of exemplary schooling, personalization and good teaching, and shows how these elements are fundamental to educational success (Powell, 1996). Oakes and colleagues' (2002) stark representation of schools that shocks the conscience is contrasted with a representation of private college preparatory schools that alternately seems appealing, if not ideal, while at the same time seems nearly offensive in how massively unavailable it is to America's students.

Finally, the third exemplar is the work of Annette Lareau and Erin McNamara Horvat, who use the work of Pierre Bourdieu to theoretically and empirically clarify the processes of social reproduction and expose how and why individuals of different social classes and races interact with institutions in historically influenced patterns. Lareau and Horvat (1999) lay bare the history of conflict and change in the education system and the actions of teachers and administrators, all of which, wittingly or unwittingly, structure and perpetuate inequality in school settings. What makes this work an exemplar is the way in which the authors take a domain—parents' involvement in their children's elementary school education—that is often construed by teachers as "neutral, technically efficient, and designed to promote higher levels of achievement" (p. 42) and instead show parents' involvement as cultural specific and

historically conditioned. In turn, Lareau and Horvat demonstrate four critical methodological elements of inquiry. First, they clarify the needed warrants for using cultural capital and standards for demonstrating evidence of its value in school contexts. Second, they theoretically specify how race mediates class and has "an independent theoretical significance in shaping family–school relationships" (p. 38). Third, Lareau and Horvat, by carefully documenting the explicit history of legalized racial discrimination of the town where their research took place, make specific warranted claims about how that history affects the current context of family–school relationships. Finally, the authors lay bare the necessity of having a deep understanding of, and carefully implementing, the key elements that provide a theoretical framework with its integrity. What follows next is a discussion of our overarching framework, equality of educational opportunity.

Equality of educational opportunity has been a central goal of American education (Timar, Ogawa, & Orillion, 2004), yet it is also a topic that is seemingly so broad and unspecific that, from a research perspective, it can seem unwieldy and unresearchable. Instead, researchers have parsed out the components of equality of educational opportunity and taken a look at the different ways in which it has been compromised or realized. We research within the paradigms and methods of the specializations of our many subfields and often do not read across the various domains. Moreover, we do not often engage in integrative inquiry where we synthesize across the domains in an attempt to understand the whole opportunity pie as opposed to our small slice of it. College access as an equal educational opportunity research problem has important social justice, policy, economic, and human capital development implications. To take this task seriously, we must begin by looking at the whole system of education, the educational experience of individuals across this system, and the key indicators and transitions that make up the equal educational opportunity field.

Inquiry into equal educational opportunity in America needs a paradigmatic shift from a domain-specific orientation to a holistic approach that tries to capture and encompass the interconnectivity and interdependencies of inequalities. These inequalities are found throughout students' lived family and schooling experiences (early-life preschooling and K–12), their potential future experiences (postsecondary), and outside their structured schooling experiences, including but not limited to influences outside of education (e.g., privatization, profit-seeking).

We find support for our suggested paradigmatic shift from the evidence of current literature across the K–12 and higher education sectors, the limitations of that evidence, and the apparent contradictions and emerging tensions found between the evidence and its limitations. We suggest a field (or P–16 systemic) perspective as a new way in which to understand educational opportunity (Bourdieu, 1975; DiMaggio & Powell, 1983; McDonough, Ventresca, & Outcalt, 2000). In looking at the evidence in the literature across the K–12 and higher education sectors, we acknowledge the legacy of key scholarship and its findings that describes educational opportunity in America as plagued by inequitable educational advantage and disadvantage, inequitable stratification of students and resources, inequitable school contexts in which students have access (or not) to educational opportunity, and influences of familial and social forces (e.g., families, financial aid policy, the entrepreneurial admissions sector) on structuring educational opportunity. Our survey of this literature indicates that these factors and influences are cumulative and dynamic across students' educational experiences.

The limitations of this evidence, as put forth in the literature, suggest that we need new ways in which to conceive of and deploy inquiry into these issues so as to better inform the greater issue of educational opportunity. Inherently, there are tensions between the key findings and limitations of the evidence. Theoretically, a field perspective provides a useful lens to reorganize how we conceive of equal educational opportunity as a construct for investigation and as a political aim to effect change.

We begin by defining some key terms. When thinking about college access, it is apparent that there is a wide array of research methods used to study this problem and the definitions of terms used. How the problem is defined affects what one sees and, just as important, what one does not see. In our analysis of the transition from high school to college, there have been several domains of research sometimes studied as separate phenomena using different focal issues, language, assumptions, paradigms, and methods. We suggest that these domains are college access, college admissions, college choice, and (most recently) K–12 academic preparation and advising for college.

College access research, at its most macro level, starts with the assumption that the barriers to equal access are structural and that changing the structure will result in changed access outcomes. "College access" has traditionally been the phrase used by institutional, governmental, and associational policymakers. However, even these actors have different meanings in mind when using these words. College access in federal policy circles means focusing on cost and financial aid policies as a means of ensuring that all able students can go to college (Berkner & Chavez, 1997; King, 1996).

Recently, college access has increasingly taken on overtones of admissions requirements, student eligibility for entrance, and equal opportunity for all on campuses and in state systems of higher education as well as in affirmative action retrenchment public discourse. Thus, this policy research tends to include eligibility studies, aggregate analyses of federal financial aid policies and their impacts on enrollment, studies of enrollment shifts across institutions, affirmative action analyses and studies of the impact of admissions policies on high school curricula and standards, and the like (California Postsecondary Education Commission, 2004; Ikenberry & Hartle, 1998; Tienda, Cortes, & Niu, 2003).

College admissions research is macro level, assumes that institutions can bring about change in an individual's choice process, and is conducted by both scholars and institutional researchers who tend to employ large-scale quantitative econometric designs. Typically, these are studies of enrollment management, institutional recruitment or marketing, and analyses of the impact of tuition costs and financial aid policies on individual behavior (Jackson, 1982; King, 1999; Litten, 1979; Olson & Rosenfeld, 1984).

Then there are the micro-level approaches of *student college choice* (McDonough, 1997). There have been five basic approaches to the study of college choice decision making:

• *Social psychological studies* examine (a) the impact of academic program, campus social climate, cost, location, and influence of others on students' choices; (b) students' assessment of their fit with their chosen colleges; and (c) the cognitive stages of college choice.

• *Economic studies* view college choice as an investment decision and assume that students (a) maximize perceived costs–benefits in their college choices, (b) have perfect information, and (c) are engaged in a process of rational choice.

• *Sociological status attainment studies* analyze the impact of individuals' social status on the development of aspirations for educational attainment and measure inequalities in college access, emphasizing individual attributes as the key determinants of inequalities, largely neglecting the role of educational organizations. College access research in this domain analyzes the role of achievement, aptitude, and expectations, as well as race, gender, and socioeconomic status, in influencing individual educational attainment.

• *Organizational analyses* attempt to understand the empirical patterns of individual educational outcomes and analyze schools' organizational structures, resources, constraints, and contingencies (Oakes, 1989; Oakes et al., 2002) to document how different school environments produce different curricula, administrative supports, and student outcomes that lead to college access (McDonough, 1997).

• *Cultural analyses* of student college choice using different concepts, theories, and methodologies have focused on the role of schools in reproducing class structures and analyzing the internal dynamics of education systems and the specific forms of consciousness and culture that support and co-determine educational structures. Bourdieuian-based college choice analyses have looked at the interaction between individual free will and social structures (McDonough, 1997). Other researchers have used critical race theory and other frameworks (e.g., cultural wealth, cultural integrity) to analyze various racial/ethnic groups' college choice processes (Fann, 2002/2005; Gomez, 2005; McDonough, Nunez, Ceja, & Solorzano, 2003).

Finally, at a macro level yet focusing on a different set of institutions, *K–12 academic preparation and advising for college* is another related research domain. Although for some time we have focused on the need for early college plans (Alexander & Cook, 1979; Thomas, 1979), recently we have begun to focus more on college plans developing earlier (Cabrera & La Nasa, 1999). Over the past half decade, increasing attention has been focused on the domain of college preparation (Adelman, 1999; Perna, 2005). Historically, the advising area has been underresearched, although studies recently have begun to synthesize the available evidence. In this area, however, definitive quantitative evidence is still hard to come by (McDonough, 2005a, 2005b).

Although previous research has contributed in important ways to our understanding of college access, individual researchers have not looked simultaneously and thoroughly across these domains; thus, scholars have understood only a very small part of the whole field and have misrecognized important interactions and dynamics. For example, postsecondary scholars have analyzed college admissions issues; secondary scholars have studied high school preparation, achievement, and advising; and little analysis has been done on the growing entrepreneurial college admissions sector (McDonough, 1994; McDonough, Antonio, Walpole, & Perez, 1998; McDonough, Korn, & Yamasaki, 1997). McDonough and colleagues (2000) show the enhanced understanding that could come from simultaneously viewing changes in high schools, colleges, policy environments, and the entrepreneurial sector. However, field analyses are still underemployed in college access research and in understanding how educational opportunity is nourished or thwarted in the course of schooling. In this chapter, we work to fill those gaps by suggesting a research agenda and questions that suggest such a long-term view of both college access and equal educational opportunity.

THE POWER OF METAPHORS

This leads us to an important heuristic turn that we find useful in reconceptualizing college access as an issue of equal educational opportunity—the metaphor. Metaphors are, at one level, a relational way of thinking that helps us to understand and experience something in terms of its similarity to something else. It is a kind of shorthand to understanding. If we understand A already and say that B is like A, then we expect our comprehension of B to happen faster. Lakoff and Johnson (1980), in a powerful and enormously influential book, show that metaphors are the fundamental underpinning of our conceptual apparatus. The metaphors we use to understand the educational process are more than mere words; they define reality, they structure our ability to perceive new aspects of situations (e.g., they foster selective inattention), they serve as blinders to perceiving situations in alternative ways, and they limit our ability to expect things to be different in the future (Lakoff & Johnson, 1980). Metaphors often dehumanize as well as structure our subconscious categories of understanding (Sontag, 1978).

One frequently used metaphor for the vast educational enterprise is that of an educational pipeline (Astin, 1993). This pipeline begins with the earliest years of schooling and culminates either in attendance through compulsory schooling or at any other point on the postcompulsory spectrum on through the completion of an advanced degree. Other authors have used the metaphor of a river (Bowen & Bok, 1998; Olivas, 1986) to convey the idea of a large, unified, and complex education system. These metaphors move us along in understanding college access as part of a longer-term, interconnected educational process. Along the way are discrete stages with expected attitudes, resources, preparation, and behaviors that enable and constrain students for the next stage in the process. More important, educational pipelines and rivers are predicated on critical junctures, which narrow the pool of students eligible for the next stage on the path to college. The problem we find with these metaphors is that they misdirect our understanding. In pipeline terminology, students are siphoned out of the flow headed toward college, whereas in the river metaphor, tributaries at each critical stage divert some proportion of students out of the mainstream leading to college. Yet these metaphors leave us with an incomplete understanding of the process—as a whole and in stages—by which the vast majority of students become a select few. We believe that it is vital to understand this process if we are to address the many inequities in the rates of college access.

We are arguing that it is intellectually shortsighted not to think of the context of college access as part of this larger, more complex educational process. We believe that the existing metaphors of equal educational opportunity, particularly vis-à-vis college access, have a structural quality that ignores two crucial elements for understanding and rectifying the problems of college access. First, these metaphors suggest a total lack of attention to students' agency and, thus, ability to influence progress. Second, the existing metaphors neglect attention to the wider social system that envelopes the education system.

We believe that we need more powerful metaphors to understand equal educational opportunity. One suggestion we proffer is the cardiovascular system of the human body because it focuses our attention on interdependence. The cardiovascular system is composed of both a muscle (the heart) and a blood flow system (the vessels and arteries). This metaphor allows for understanding the students' flexing of their muscles and the ways in which the structure of the vessels and arteries can enable the flow of blood or constrict and thereby endanger the flow. We could use the related metaphors of clots, blockages, and hidden dangers as well as metaphors being proactive vis-à-vis diet, exercise, and the like.

A second piece of this metaphor is that it directs our attention to the rest of the human body and its systems that can dramatically affect the cardiovascular system's successful functioning. If an individual is deprived of oxygen or if his or her brain stops functioning, the cardiovascular system can be compromised. Similarly, if our schools are compromised through policies related to essential funding, discrimination, and the like, our system of equal educational opportunity is eviscerated. This metaphorical exercise is not the main point of this chapter, but we believe that it is a necessary backdrop to understand college access as part of a larger educational process that involves both structure and agency. We are not even suggesting that we have found the most useful metaphor in using the cardiovascular system; rather, we are illustrating our points about using more appropriate metaphors that capture more completely the pieces of the puzzle we are trying to understand.

Another metaphor used to describe and understand equality of opportunity in college access is often framed as the right of individuals to compete equally at any given point in their educational careers. Access to college and the equity of the collegiate opportunity structure are often described as a contest and are debated regularly in major and local newspapers and magazines, are the object of policy intervention, and are argued in district and federal courts. All of this is consistent with American democratic ideals. However, we tend to discuss college access as if it were analogous to the spin of the roulette wheel, where every moment is perfectly independent of the previous one and, thus, the conditions of competition to win are equal—the principle of ceteris paribus or "all else equal." But when looking from a P–16 perspective on the development of college aspirations and conditions for college preparation, all else is *anything but* equal. As the philosopher Edmund Burke phrased it succinctly, "The equal treatment of unequals is the greatest injustice of all." Our P–16 system has constructed an unequal contest and systematically structures the accumulation of both advantage and disadvantage. This structuring creates individuals who are unequal in how they have been prepared for the educational attainment contest. In the case of equal opportunity in college access, we are calling into question a system that differentially prepares students for college and for competition for more selective college admissions. However, we first need to return to existing problems of equal educational opportunity.

EDUCATIONAL OPPORTUNITY IN THE SOCIAL WORLD

We live not in a world of roulette but rather in a social world that comes with a history, structure,

regularities, and constraints as well as with different chances of social profits that govern its functioning. Moreover, it is a world created for particular social purposes by particular social groups that are constantly being transformed by individuals who are trying to either maintain or improve their social status. We all are self-interested individuals constantly strategizing how to manipulate objective reality and its rules so as to maximize our social status.

Our world is social because we are social. We are not atomized individuals, but we exist in schools, families, and neighborhoods and also participate in social class, racialized, and ethnic cultural practices. We learn from each other and take care of each other, but we also compete with each other for scarce resources. That means that sometimes we share our successful strategies with our friends and neighbors in our particular corner of the social world, and sometimes we ask for theirs. Moreover, in the aggregate, individual optimizers sometimes subtly, and maybe imperceptibly, effect larger-scale change that gives a select group better odds of success.

Advantaged college applicants and their parents currently "stack the deck" in their own favor by improvising admissions management behaviors such as hiring tutors, SAT coaches, and private counselors. High-socioeconomic status (SES) students attend schools that offer only courses that are college preparatory, that set expectations for high achievement, and that begin college preparation and advising when schooling begins. In short, those students live in a social and cultural environment that takes college for granted and attend schools that have strong and powerfully influencing college cultures (McDonough, 1997).

In contrast, underrepresented minorities and low-SES students are making their college access preparations constrained by their schools' and teachers' low expectations and aspirations of them; a lack of individual's, parents', and schools' knowledge of and experience with college; a lack of trained professionals to advise them; and a climate of presumed lack of merit, racial hostility, and unwelcomeness (McDonough, 1999; Oakes et al., 2002). These students struggle to get basic information and assistance, and they fight to keep their college aspirations alive against considerable structural and motivational barriers.

As social scientists, we need to rethink our understanding and research about college access by moving our analysis off the individual level and by beginning to think of the variety of organizational environments that sustain and enable, or alternatively constrain and disable, college aspirations—schools. We also need analyses that longitudinally stretch back throughout students' educational experiences and begin to tally the effects of cumulative advantage and disadvantage. We are arguing that we need analyses that are accountable to both scholarly and advocacy communities and that require constant, intimate, and reciprocal translation and utility. Finally, we are calling for new analyses that identify more clearly the moments of social inclusion and exclusion that seemingly (re)produce existing social stratifications and inequalities effortlessly. We address this issue of inclusion and exclusion later.

Educational opportunity in America is plagued by inequality. Students in every domain of education are marginalized along racial/ethnic, class, gender, geography, and a host of other categories. Marginalization from the centers of opportunity ultimately manifests itself in the unequal participation of students in higher education, where the problem of unequal educational opportunity has been documented in the underrepresentation of specific groups of students (e.g., students of color). Furthermore, although some scholars point to increased access to higher education as a sign that educational opportunity has been extended from its exclusionary past, other scholars have been quick to point out that the extension of higher education to the most marginalized groups has also been from the most marginalized sectors of higher education (Karen, 2002). Put plainly, access has been gained in less prestigious colleges and community colleges, whereas the elite sectors of higher education (major research universities and private liberal arts colleges) have remained increasingly and grossly inaccessible. Thus, inequality of educational opportunity persists, even though we take pride in our vaulted indicators of widespread college opportunity. Beyond access, we find that when members of underrepresented and traditionally marginalized groups enter higher education, their participation is again inscribed as disruptive and competing against normative notions of college participation. For many students, after having broken through the gates to the ivory tower, they find that they have simply gained access to a place that can be just as unwelcoming on the inside as it once was on the outside.

As higher education scholars, it is easy for us to locate the nucleus of educational opportunity inquiry within our own domain—colleges and universities. However, what has been made clear to us by the fruitful proliferation of scholarship on college access over the past several decades is that we cannot focus on just our own sector of the American education system if we hope to truly understand and ameliorate this problem. Although our intellectual orientation might prompt us to locate access to college as the pinnacle of educational opportunity, we must acknowledge that the inequalities in opportunity are cumulative manifestations that develop dynamically throughout and across students' educational experiences. Thus, we put forth in this chapter that the state of the art of inquiry into educational opportunity must make a paradigmatic shift. As scholars of access, equity, and equal educational opportunity, we must find ways in which to move beyond our rigidly constructed domains of K–12 and higher education. We must not be complacent with an overly simplifying all-inclusive concept of P–16 because we do not want to lose sight of categorically different contexts of schooling amid and between compulsory education and postsecondary opportunities, or the disparities between public and private schooling, or the disparities between schooling in high-SES contexts and schooling in low-SES contexts. We must move beyond the narrowly defined field of K–12 or higher education as the spaces through which we understand how our inequalities persist.

PROMISING DIRECTIONS: FIELD CORRECTIVES

We begin with a brief portrait of college access research to date. In a review of college access research in the *American Journal of Sociology,* the *American Sociological Review, Sociology of*

Education, the *Journal of Higher Education,* the *Review of Higher Education,* and *Research in Higher Education* from 1973 to 2004, McDonough and Fann (in press) found that quantitative methodologies dominate. Fully 75% of all articles published were quantitative, 20% were policy analyses or literature reviews, and a mere 5% were from qualitative or interpretive paradigms that began to appear during the 1990s.

Using six categories for analysis—student college choice, financial aid, policy, student ability and achievement, SES and families' influences, and student types (e.g., racial, nontraditional)—McDonough and Fann (in press) found that college access research began with studies of how students make their college choices and that our disciplinary lenses often served to narrow our research foci. For example, the single largest type of article in the higher education journals focused on financial aid (40% vs. no articles on this topic in sociology), whereas the sociology journals focused on parents/families and SES as related to status attainment and educational attainment (56%). Moreover, in terms of the gradual transformation of relevant topics, articles on race and ethnicity began appearing during the 1980s and analyses on school effects in the sociology journals also began appearing during the mid- to late 1980s, whereas more broadly organizational influences began during the 1990s.

Characteristically, college access has been studied as a piece of the equality of educational opportunity pipeline and has enjoyed more than 50 years of research and policy advocacy (Kinzie et al., 2004). Our free market economy and democracy has proudly featured an equal educational opportunity for a college education as a cornerstone of American public policy. Huge growth in the number of colleges and the enrollment of students, along with an extensive financial aid system and a low-priced public postsecondary sector, has made that opportunity a reality for many people (Gladieux & Swail, 1999).

Yet for all the opportunity afforded, increasingly opportunity is being lost. Although the college continuation rate of 65% of high school graduates in 2002 was quite good and historically at an all-time high, it was 25 percentage points less than the 90% of middle and high school students who expected to go to college (U.S. Department of Education, 2003).

Within our highly stratified higher education system, it is clear that by default we have retreated from our long-standing policy commitment to providing authentically equal college opportunities (McDonough, 2004). Market forces and legal mandates drive admissions offices away from expanding access and toward fiscally and competitively necessary marketing and recruitment strategies (Kinzie et al., 2004). K–12 schools attend to the federal mandate of the No Child Left Behind Act and the endless array of state accountability mandates much more than they attend to college admissions requirements (Kirst & Venezia, 2004). We have a student aid system that is geared less toward expanding opportunity for poor students and more toward making it possible to recruit middle- and upper-income students who would be attending college regardless of that aid (Heller, 2002).

The so-called level playing field of education is anything but fair or equal. The voting public has become more self-interested and short-term focused in its fiscal policies, preferring middle-class tax relief to investing in the human capital of poor underrepresented students of color. The seemingly endless media and policy reports on deteriorating school conditions and the large and persistent achievement gaps in the K–12 education system for low-income students, urban students, and students of color fall on deaf public and policymaker ears (Barton, 2004; Oakes, 2004). And crushingly, despite billions of dollars in financial aid investments, we have not been able to improve on the college participation gap between low-income and high-income students that has existed since the 1960s (Gladieux & Swail, 1999; Pathways to College Network, 2003). Thus, the pathway to college access is marked by vast disparities in college preparation, college knowledge, and college culture within schools across racial and SES lines (McDonough, 2004).

The increasing competitiveness of the global market and the shift to an information-, service-, and technology-based economy in the United States propel a growing need for college-educated professionals. Of every 10 jobs in our economy, 6 depend on highly trained workers with the requisite advanced skills that are available only to those possessing some postsecondary education or training, and these needs drive the standards movement in K–12 education (Carnevale & Desrochers, 2003; U.S. Department of Labor, 2004).

Recently, research on the problems of and prospects for improving college access has converged to a relative consensus on the major barriers. Researchers and policy advocates alike have identified six domains as comprising those major barriers of equality of opportunity to college access: financial barriers (Heller, 2002; King, 1999; St. John, 2002a), K–12 academic preparation (Gladieux & Swail, 1999; McNeil, 2003; Oakes, 2004; Pathways to College Network, 2003; Perna, 2005), K–12 focus and staff members assigned to ensure college preparation (Gandara & Bial, 2001; King, 1996; McDonough, 2004; Tierney, Corwin, & Colyar, 2004), clear and available information on college preparation and entrance as well as financial aid information (Hossler, Schmidt, & Vesper, 1999; Kirst & Venezia, 2004), family involvement (Choy, 2002; Flint, 1992; Hossler, Braxton, & Coopersmith, 1989; Hossler et al., 1999; St. John & Noell, 1989; Tierney & Auerbach, 2004), and admissions policies (Avery, Fairbanks, & Zeckhauser, 2003; Breland, Maxey, Gernand, Cumming, & Trapani, 2002; Tienda et al., 2003).

What this portrayal of the college access research needs to account for now are the promising new lines of research that have been developing over the past 5 to 10 years on racial/ethnic and geographic marginalization. As a field corrective, we put forth that college access must make two significant shifts as we become a P–16 framework. We must further disaggregate by status characteristics, such as racial/ethnic identifications and geographies/space, and we must make linkages between individual experience and policy. What follows are brief discussions of promising directions that are congruent with our field corrective.

One lens through which scholarship has been reluctant to engage in issues of educational opportunity is the geographic one. Although a growing body of literature exists that takes account of diverse physical geographies, such as rural students and education (e.g., Apostal &

Bilden, 1991; Haller & Virkler, 1993; McDonough & McClafferty, 2001; McGrath, Swisher, Elder, & Conger, 2001), scholars have yet to theorize how space matters in issues of educational opportunity. As Soja (1996) explains, when trying to understand the social world, space matters fundamentally. We act through space, co-constructing the structures in which we are subjected. Scholarship on college access already works under an assumption that space does matter. The National Center for Education Statistics (NCES) collects data that compare educational achievement across physical geographies, and from these data we see that educational opportunity is spatialized in inequitable ways. For example, NCES data in 1999 showed that rural students between 18 and 24 years of age were enrolled in school at rates more than 6% lower than the national average and nearly 8% lower than their metropolitan counterparts. Moreover, although rates were similar for black men across physical geographies, black women and Hispanic men and women from rural areas were enrolled at increasingly lower rates than their metropolitan peers. These rates were also below the differential rates for white men and women from rural areas as compared with white men and women from urban areas. Furthermore, additional data from the NCES show that despite graduating students from high school at higher rates than urban high schools, across race/ethnicity and gender, rural high schools still sent fewer students on to 4-year and 2-year colleges and universities (U.S. Department of Education, 2003).

Although the data collected documented the spatialization of opportunity, they cannot inform us about how space matters in structuring opportunity and they do not account for any human agency. These limitations stem largely from the sole reliance on physical geographic conceptions of space. Investigating space in terms of political, economic, and social geographies might prove to be useful in beginning theories of space in relation to educational opportunity. This would help to move beyond investigations that ask, "Does where one lives matter in terms of present and future opportunities?" and into a realm that seeks to understand: "How does the organization of relationships between agents (e.g., students, principals, college admissions officers, financial aid policy-makers, researchers) help to structure opportunities, and how can individuals effect change within those structures?" The latter gets closer to solutions and takes a more holistic approach to (hopefully) elicit more generative findings.

In her study of teenage girls, Thomas (2005) found that high school spaces, such as the cafeteria, are spatialized along racial lines, yet students did not perceive the segregated spaces as racialized. On further inquiry, she found that how girls located themselves within the racialized structures of various spaces (e.g., the cafeteria, shopping malls, classrooms) reflexively co-constructed girls' sense of identity. Although Thomas's work is not explicitly about educational opportunity, it points to a new direction in understanding what college access scholars have long sought to unpack—the relationships among individuals, organizations, agency, and structure. The links to college access and college choice are manifold (e.g., aspiration development, the meaning behind certain choice behaviors, perceptions of barriers).

Another way of illustrating how space matters is to examine how previous literature has not spatialized educational opportunity. For example, peer influence is a small piece of the greater college choice puzzle that scholars have felt confident in understanding for quite some time. It is commonly held that peers do influence college choice decisions but that this influence is greatest at the search phase of the decision-making process as students seek out information about postsecondary opportunities (Hossler et al., 1999). Yet Freeman's (2005) study of African American student college choice found that peers seemed to exert an important influence at all three stages of the decision process, most especially for those students who did not have the family resources to predispose them to college going at an early age. What is missing in these conflicting analyses is the spatial relations of these students to their social subjectivities. That is, we do not have a theoretical framework to understand how students' lives are organized socially and how the students exist as individuals within that organization. Investigating students' social geographies, we might ask, "How does students'

social location among peers influence the structure of their opportunity?" This might help us to understand how students' peer influences, structural influences such as school tracking, and the racialization of students in the classroom all co-conspire to affect students' access to education. In short, understanding the social world of students relies on a fundamental understanding of the matters of space.

There are a host of other problems in college access that cannot be answered from our traditional domain-specific orientations. For example, students from migrant farm families in central California have been underrepresented in California postsecondary education for as long as the land has been occupied by American settlers. Predominantly Latino, these students' experiences have been aggregated as part of the Latino college access dilemma in California. However, these students, by the nature of their families' economic and political legacies, face a different set of barriers and are armed with a different set of resources from which to exert agency (Tejeda, Espinoza, & Gutierrez, 2003). Employing individual-level analyses, although valuable, will only contribute to the canon of specific groups about which we know specific information. Without linking to wider analyses, we will not be able to systematically effect change that might alter the structures so as to provide greater amounts of agency and produce more equitable and democratic educational opportunity.

Fann (2002/2005) studied the barriers to college access of Native American high school students. American Indian students are the most underrepresented group in higher education, and virtually no research has addressed the college access experiences of American Indian students. Fann conducted a California statewide analysis of barriers to college access from the perspective of American Indian high school students to inform postsecondary outreach efforts because California has one of the largest Indian populations in the country. She found that effective ways in which to deliver college information and support to Native students who have aspirations for college require understanding what these students think regarding their opportunities for college access and how these ideas are influenced by families, tribal affiliation, peers, and schools. Fann's current research is focusing on understanding (a) how tribal sovereignty and economic development needs shape the college aspirations and behaviors of tribal citizens from both nongaming and gaming tribes, (b) how tribal needs relate to college-educated tribal citizens, and (c) how this context shapes students' aspirations. Fann's linkage of college access with Indian gaming issues points out the complex matrix of intrinsic, economic, and occupational motivations for pursuing a higher education. Her research offers a chance to understand the impact of gaming monies on the development and implementation of educational aspirations, achievements, and objectives for some Native American students that could revolutionize research given that the individual-level economic motivation is an essential underpinning of college aspirations.

Another promising line of research has looked at the impact of socially constructed statuses such as race on college choice (Allen, 1992; Ceja, 2000; Freeman, 1997; McDonough et al., 1997; Teranishi, Ceja, Antonio, Allen, & McDonough, 2004). Teranishi, Ceja, and colleagues (2004) examine the extent to which ethnicity and social class affects the college choice process of five Asian American ethnic subgroups: Chinese, Filipinos, Japanese, Koreans, and Southeast Asians. The authors confirm that Asian Americans from different ethnic subgroups do indeed approach the college choice process differentially. Chinese and Korean American students are predicted to attend more selective colleges even after controlling for other variables, whereas Southeast Asian students do not attend selective colleges.

For her book, *African Americans and College Choice: The Influence of Family and School,* Freeman (2005) took a qualitative approach that covered five major metropolitan areas and included 70 African American high school students. Her study investigates the relationship of family and school to college choice for African Americans, and she puts forth that prevailing models of college choice must "be greatly expanded to include cultural characteristics" (p. 109). Her evidence describes how school and family characteristics influence participation in higher education differentially across cultures and the ways in which students'

cultural practices are treated by schools. Freeman asserts that "to develop models based on one culture . . . does not allow for differences" (p. 109). The study from which she draws her conclusions looked beyond students' aspirations and analyzed the domain of family and school influences, allowing her to discover the nuanced ways in which school and family can both positively and negatively influence the choice process for African Americans. Freeman's work asks fundamental questions about P–16 schooling and the ways in which we understand the role that environments influence opportunity.

In a very different way, the work of St. John (2002b, 2003) merits consideration in a field-corrective way because he focuses on the access challenge by using integrative inquiry to understand how college access research has been framed from different perspectives—policy concerns about middle-income affordability, equal opportunity for low-income students, and economists' and politicians' concerns for efficient use of tax dollars. St. John then uses the synthesis of these perspectives as a jumping-off point as he offers new analyses and thoughtful proposals for solving what seem to be competing and irreconcilable dilemmas.

PROMISING DIRECTIONS: EXEMPLARS

First Exemplar: Connecting K–12 Policy and Higher Education Policy

Kirst and Venezia (2004) describe how the major barrier to students' college aspirations is a fractured K–16 education system that sends conflicting and vague signals to students and their families about how to prepare for and succeed in college. The authors document significant and persistent inequality in college counseling, course offerings, college information availability, and partnerships with local universities that could facilitate students' college visits and recruiter visits to high schools. They found that students and parents were confused or uninformed about what is expected of students when they enter college and that these misunderstandings are related to poor preparation for college. The first steps in moving to a

P–16 framework can be found in Kirst and Venezia's arguments, as they point out how the signals from higher education do not match up with the signals from high schools.

Kirst and Venezia (2004) studied students and parents from six states about their knowledge of their public colleges (flagship colleges, less selective state colleges, and community colleges) and found that less than 12% of students knew the courses required for admission, most students were confused about the expectations of college-level work, most students overestimated tuition costs (especially at less selective 4-year and community colleges), most students were unaware of college placement examination content, and college information distribution to low-income parents was inequitable. They called for aligning K–12 curricula and high school graduation requirements with college entrance requirements to ensure that students were prepared for academic success, were aware of academic expectations, and were prepared for college. They especially called for what amounts to a field corrective, namely, a shift in higher education's policy focus from preoccupation with selective postsecondary admissions to eligibility and preparatory requirements of the broad access postsecondary institutions that serve 80% of today's college students.

Kirst and Venezia (2004) contend that current K–12 and postsecondary education systems send conflicting messages about college preparation, are fractured, and create unnecessary and pernicious barriers to improving college access. This disconnect leads to inadequate high school courses, student underpreparation, and a lack of alignment between K–12 and postsecondary entrance and placement tests. As an exemplar, Kirst and Venezia's work suggests possible research questions such as the following: How are different sectors of higher education (e.g., elite institutions, comprehensive colleges, community colleges) understood by different populations of students and families (e.g., rural, non-native English speakers, students of color) in K–12? We are also prompted to investigate questions such as the following: In what specific ways are expectations from higher education institutions and organizations misaligned with preparations by K–12 systems?

Second Exemplar: Disparate K–12 Conditions, Policies, and Student Rights

At the heart of our reified system of unequal educational opportunities is a gap in schooling conditions as wide, deep, and long as the Grand Canyon. Both advantage and disadvantage accumulate beginning prior to school entry and continue throughout individuals' school and nonschool lives. Kamil and Wahlberg (2005), who write on one key educational opportunity indicator (reading), note that the road to being a high school dropout begins in early education. Evidence abounds that children who lag behind their peers to a significant degree in reading during the early grades have a low probability of catching up. The results are much more substantial for poor children.

The same can be said of the road to college access. The missions, structures, and policies of schools for low-SES non-white students differ markedly from those of schools for high-SES, primarily white students. We find that a highly productive contrast and exemplar is comparing the types of schools that do the worst and best jobs of educating students and preparing them for college.

In her introductory article to a special double issue of *Teachers College Record* (*TC Record*), Oakes (2004) describes and lays the foundation for an exemplar of the kind of research that we are suggesting might help to capture a more robust and deeper understanding of equal educational opportunity. By using the lawsuit *Williams v. State of California* as a central case to frame a holistic portrait of educational opportunity, Oakes and her collaborators marshal evidence and analyses that demonstrate how educational opportunity is a system of issues that works dynamically, interweaving through structures and agents that conflict, conflate, and reproduce inequality. *TC Record* divides the research into three sections: "Schools That Shock the Conscience" (p. 1899), "State Structures of Inadequacy and Inequality" (p. 1902), and "Broken Promises?" (p. 1904). Within this framework, Oakes and her collaborators present evidence and analyses that account for the structural barriers that prevent equal education from being attained in California as well as the agency of individual constituents in perpetuating, exacerbating, and at times challenging these structures.

We hold up Oakes's (2004) description of the *Williams* scholarship as an exemplar because of three things. First, methodologically it is responsive to Conrad's (1989) call for a stakeholder-centered model of inquiry. Oakes and colleagues collaborated with the *Williams v. State of California* legal team to plan, execute, and put into successful use its research. Second, collectively the legal and scholarly teams employed an impressive ability to pull together the work of a large number and variety of scholars to comprehensively examine an array of structural inequalities that constrict individual agency in educational settings. Finally, the researchers document a wide variety of educational conditions necessary for equality of educational opportunity to be even an approachable goal and make holistic use of seemingly autonomous issues, integrating them into a coherent field of inquiry.

Moreover, only one article in the special double issue explicitly takes on college access (Teranishi, Allen, & Solorzano, 2004). However, the unique and uniquely valuable contribution of this exemplar is that, as a whole, the work on *Williams* is intertextual. As Oakes (2004) presents the work, each piece informs the other in a coherent and well-organized medium by working within a system framework that allows—indeed, relies on—agency–structure interaction. The meaning and sensemaking that are achieved by Teranishi, Allen, and Solorzano (2004) could not be as fruitful were they not connected, and indeed embedded, in the work presented in the surrounding articles. Oakes's (2004) concise and deliberate introduction to the special issue synthesizes this intertextuality, reclaiming the fruitfulness of college access as a research question within the framework of equal educational opportunity.

Juxtaposed to the work of Oakes and her collaborators, which focuses on the limitations and barriers of public education, Powell (1996) presents an analysis of the benefits and advantages of private preparatory school education. His work illustrates the ways in which public schools do not meet standards necessary to guarantee opportunity by describing the frameworks from which private prep schools reproduce and take advantage of their privilege. A major contribution of this work is the exposition of personalization as an epistemological condition of pedagogy. Personalization in the prep school, according to Powell, is "an active participatory process, a two-way street, an obligation of everyone" (p. 205). This ethic gets embedded in systemic ways: rituals of schooling, the organization of school personnel, and student accountability practices. Moreover, in the prep world, students have a right to benefit from the powerful educational force of deep interpersonal relationships with good teachers that form the foundational underpinnings of academic learning.

Whereas Oakes (2004) contributes to the system framework by illuminating the basic necessities denied students in public education, Powell's (1996) contribution lies in laying bare how deep learning, inspiring student motivation, and out-of-classroom interpersonal connections allow mentoring, modeling, and tutoring. Powell presents personalization as an epistemic mode, an ethic of schooling, developed into pedagogy that promotes maximizing educational opportunity as the goal of education. Powell describes how teachers get constructed as caregivers and role models in prep schools. Part of the impact of personalization is a reconfiguration of how teaching happens and how the role of the teacher is organized and actualized. Prep school teachers spend less time in classrooms but more time in educationally related out-of-class contexts, and they devote more energy to fewer students, than do public school teachers (Powell, 1996). Powell's analysis looks at the holistic prep school experience, linking the personalized experiences to outcomes of opportunity. His exemplary contribution delineates the disparity between private and public education as well as the disparity across public education, be it found in high-SES versus low-SES schools or in white versus non-white schools.

One way of characterizing the Oakes versus Powell perspectives is where the bar for educational attainment is set. Oakes (2004) and her collaborators are trying to ensure that the educational floor is guaranteed, whereas Powell (1996) and independent schools are focused on raising the educational ceiling. Powell acknowledges that the sine qua non of prep school student achievement is the number of college admissions at the most selective institutions. As he puts it, "It is a concrete, public, and highly valued outcome with immediate life consequences" (p. 209).

For us, the obvious question that remains is as follows: How can we claim to have equal educational opportunity with such unequal educational positioning from these two types of schools, especially when we are as far away from ceteris paribus—all else equal—as can be imagined? In light of this exemplar, we put forth the following questions for future inquiry:

1. What role(s) can different constituents (e.g., school personnel, parents, policymakers, researchers) play in maximizing opportunity for equalizing educational experiences?

2. How can lessons from more privileged educational environments be incorporated into public reforms without sacrificing the integrity of cultural communities?

3. How might the purposes of public education, P–16, need to be realigned to provide equal treatment under the law?

Third Exemplar: Social Reproduction as a Lens on Inclusion and Exclusion

In their analysis of parental involvement and its relationship to educational opportunity across race and class, Lareau and Horvat (1999) contribute to our notion of a system framework by expanding and clarifying the uses of capital in educational (re)production. Their work accounts for the historically shaped racialized relations between schools and parents by situating the cultural practices of different families within the specific history of the school site under inquiry. Furthermore, they employ their theoretical framework, drawing on Bourdieu's notions of social reproduction, to elicit the interconnectedness among normative (or dominant) cultural practices, familial resources for activating capital, and real consequences in children's educational opportunities. In so doing, Lareau and Horvat found that how parents activated their capital directly related to how their participation in their children's schooling was received and, ultimately, to how the reality of

school experiences (and, by extension, opportunities) were changed or reinscribed. They connected the dots that seemingly effortlessly demarcated the differences between and across race and class, exposing how cultural discord was exacerbated as well as ameliorated through parental participation. The authors' findings are exemplary in that they challenge long-standing and dominant ways of thinking about parental involvement, moving beyond differences of encouragement and support.

The field-level analysis is imperative to Lareau and Horvat's (1999) contributions. By investigating the relationships between agency and structure from a field perspective, the authors are able to move from looking at micro-level occurrences to a macro perspective about how race and class played pivotal roles within a specific historical context. They hold to their theoretical framework's integrity by vigilantly delineating between the possession and activation of capital as well as by paying close attention to how each of these constructs was unpacked in practice. For example, a key illustration of their argument documents the skill with which one family's members involved themselves in their child's schooling, resulting in dramatically different consequences compared with those resulting from the practices of another family's involvement (Lareau & Horvat, 1999). These exercises of personal agency are analyzed within the context of the social setting and discussed in relation to their consequences for educational opportunity. Lareau and Horvat conclude that resources and signals become capital only when and where they are exercised in ways that brought them into symmetry with the dominant cultural practices of the school. They make a theoretical and methodological contribution by providing a stricter test of the definition of capital.

In addition, the linkages of racial status and how resources and signals become capital when and how they are deployed is a methodological and theoretical contribution that exemplifies how an integrated framework can benefit the field. Thus, although not explicitly framed as work on access to college, the findings and implications of Lareau and Horvat's (1999) study are of direct importance. Taking account of their theoretical and methodological

contributions could lead to potentially generative research questions such as the following:
How can families without traditionally dominant resources parlay their existing cultural
practices into educationally beneficial cultural
capital?

CONCLUSIONS

The promising directions we have put forth
represent possible prototypes of research that we
find meet our call for integrative inquiry. They
provide a host of new directions for research to
take up, including new populations, new methodological and/or theoretical frameworks, new
questions to ask, and (most important) new ways
of looking at the problems facing equal educational opportunity. The field correctives and
exemplars we have chosen demonstrate the
paradigmatic shift in research that we feel is
imperative to keep progressing in the field of educational opportunity and college access. These
studies integrate domains and take long-term
systemic views of the research problem. We find
optimism in the diversity of perspectives that
promise to push the field further along and could
develop meaningful discourse across research
domains by integrating our understandings along
the lines of how our exemplars have done.

Some implications that arise from our discussion and presentation of exemplary research raise
fundamental questions and provide new opportunities for how we organize inquiry. First, the idea
of scholarly collaboration gets a bit of a facelift.
Although we value collaborative research, what
we find suggested by our exemplars is an opportunity to collaborate across our specific studies
and areas of inquiry. We can collaborate in the
ways in which we share information and build on
each other's work, even going so far as to analyze
research in relation to others' work. Thus, we can
integrate domains within our field.

Second, taking a systemic perspective of
the equal educational opportunity problem
might call into question the organization of our
schools of education and research centers,
where we typically situate ourselves within
domain-specific departments or divisions. Perhaps
establishing special programs or research centers that specifically take up equal educational

opportunity, college access, and the imperatives,
directions, and exemplars of good research could
be a promising new way in which to foster and
organize integrative inquiry.

Finally, what our field correctives and exemplars make clear is that if we do not integrate
across domains in long-term systemic inquiry,
we will miss important and necessary moments
of knowledge production. We have presented an
analytic reflection to rethink the state of the field
of inquiry on equal educational opportunity. We
hope to resuscitate ourselves before we become
too distanced from the heart of the matter.

REFERENCES

Adelman, C. (1999). *Answers in the Tool Box:
Academic intensity, attendance patterns, and
bachelor's degree attainment.* Washington, DC:
U.S. Department of Education.

Alexander, K., & Cook, M. (1979). The motivational
relevance of educational plans: Questioning the
conventional wisdom. *Social Psychology
Quarterly, 43,* 202–213.

Allen, W. R. (1992). The color of success: African-
American college student outcomes at predominantly white and historically black public
colleges and universities. *Harvard Educational
Review, 62*(1), 26–44.

Apostal, R., & Bilden, J. (1991). Educational and
occupational aspirations of rural high school
students. *Journal of Career Development, 18*(2),
153–160.

Astin, A. (1993). *What matters in college? Four critical years revisited.* San Francisco: Jossey-Bass.

Avery, C., Fairbanks, A., & Zeckhauser, R. (2003).
The early admissions game: Joining the elite.
Cambridge, MA: Harvard University Press.

Barton, P. (2004). *Parsing the achievement gap:
Baselines for tracking progress.* Princeton, NJ:
Educational Testing Service, Policy Information
Center.

Berkner, L., & Chavez, L. (1997). *Access to postsecondary education for the 1992 high school
graduates.* Washington, DC: National Center for
Education Statistics.

Bourdieu, P. (1975, December 14). The specificity
of the scientific field and the social conditions
of the progress of reason. *Social Science Information,* pp. 19–47.

Bowen, W. G., & Bok, D. (1998). *The shape of the river.* Princeton, NJ: Princeton University Press.

Breland, H., Maxey, J., Gernand, R., Cumming, T., & Trapani, C. (2002). *Trends in college admissions: A report of a survey of undergraduate admissions policies, practices, and procedures.* Tallahassee, FL: Association for Institutional Research.

Cabrera, A., & La Nasa, S. (Eds.). (1999). *Understanding the college choice of disadvantaged students* (New Directions for Institutional Research, No. 107). San Francisco: Jossey-Bass.

California Postsecondary Education Commission. (2004). *University eligibility study for the class of 2003.* Sacramento, CA: Author.

Carnevale, A., & Desrochers, D. (2003). *Standards for what? The economic roots of K–16 reform.* Princeton, NJ: Educational Testing Service.

Ceja, M. (2000, November). *Making decisions about college: Understanding the information sources of Chicana students.* Paper presented at the annual meeting of the Association for the Study of Higher Education, Sacramento, CA.

Choy, S. (2002). *Access and persistence: Findings from 10 years of longitudinal research on students.* Washington, DC: American Council on Education.

Conrad, C. (1989). Meditations on the ideology of inquiry in higher education: Exposition, critique, and conjecture. *Review of Higher Education, 12*(3), 199–220.

DiMaggio, P., & Powell, W. (1983). The iron cage revisited: Institutional isomorphism and collective rationality in organizational fields. *American Sociological Review, 48,* 147–160.

Fann, A. (2005). *Forgotten students: Native American high school students' narratives on college going* (revised). (Original work [2002, November]: *Native college pathways in California: A look at college access for American Indian high school students.* Paper presented at the annual meeting of the Association for the Study of Higher Education, Sacramento, CA)

Flint, T. (1992). Parental and planning influences on the formation of student college choice sets. *Research in Higher Education, 21*(2), 21–32.

Freeman, K. (1997). Increasing African-Americans' participation in higher education: African-American high-school students' perspectives. *Journal of Higher Education, 68*(5), 523–550.

Freeman, K. (2005). *African Americans and college choice: The influence of family and school.* Albany: State University of New York Press.

Gandara, P., & Bial, D. (2001). *Paving the way to higher education: K–12 intervention programs for underrepresented youth.* Washington, DC: National Postsecondary Education Cooperative.

Gladieux, L., & Swail, W. S. (1999). Financial aid is not enough: Improving the odds for minority and low-income students. In J. E. King (Ed.), *Financing a college education: How it works and how it's changing.* Phoenix, AZ: Oryx.

Gomez, G. G. (2005, April). *Negotiating going to college: The accommodation of home and school for Mien American students.* Paper presented at the annual meeting of the American Educational Research Association, Montreal.

Haller, E. J., & Virkler, S. J. (1993). Another look at rural–nonrural differences in students' educational aspirations. *Journal of Research in Rural Education, 9*(3), 170–178.

Heller, D. (2002). *Conditions of access: Higher education for lower-income students.* Westport, CT: American Council on Education (Praeger Series on Higher Education).

Hossler, D., Braxton, J., & Coopersmith, G. (1989). Understanding student college choice. In J. C. Smart (Ed.), *Higher education: Handbook of theory and research* (Vol. 5, pp. 231–288). New York: Agathon.

Hossler, D., Schmidt, J., & Vesper, N. (1999). *Going to college: How social, economic, and educational factors influence the decisions students make.* Baltimore, MD: Johns Hopkins University Press.

Ikenberry, S., & Hartle, T. (1998). *Too little knowledge is a dangerous thing: What the public knows and thinks about paying for college.* Washington, DC: American Council on Education.

Jackson, G. (1982). Public efficiency and private choice in higher education. *Educational Evaluation and Policy Analysis, 4,* 237–247.

Kamil, M., & Wahlberg, H. (2005, January 26). The scientific teaching of reading. *Education Week,* pp. 38–40.

Karen, D. (2002, July). Changes in access to higher education in the United States: 1980–1992. *Sociology of Education, 75,* 191–210.

King, J. E. (1996). *The decision to go to college: Attitudes and experiences associated with college attendance among low-income students.* New York: College Board.

King, J. E. (Ed.). (1999). *Financing a college education: How it works and how it's changing.* Phoenix, AZ: Oryx.

Kinzie, J., Palmer, M., Hayek, J., Hossler, D., Jacob, S., & Cummings, H. (2004). *Fifty years of college choice: Social political and institutional influences on the decision-making process.* Indianapolis, IN: Lumina Foundation for Education (New Agenda Series).

Kirst, M. W., & Venezia, A. (Eds.). (2004). *From high school to college: Improving opportunities for success in postsecondary education.* San Francisco: Jossey-Bass.

Lakoff, G., & Johnson, M. (1980). *Metaphors we live by.* Chicago: University of Chicago Press.

Lareau, A., & Horvat, E. M. (1999). Moments of social inclusion and exclusion: Race, class, and cultural capital in family–school relationships. *Sociology of Education, 72*(1), 37–53.

Litten, L. (1979). Market structure and institutional position in geographic market segments. *Research in Higher Education, 11,* 59–83.

McDonough, P. M. (1994). Buying and selling higher education: The social construction of the college applicant. *Journal of Higher Education, 65,* 427–446.

McDonough, P. M. (1997). *Choosing colleges: How social class and schools structure opportunity.* Albany: State University of New York Press.

McDonough, P. M. (1999, April). *Race-based or conflict-based college admissions?* Paper presented at the annual meeting of the American Educational Research Association, Montreal.

McDonough, P. M. (2004). *The school to college transition: Challenges and prospects* (Informed Practice: Syntheses of Higher Education Research for Campus Leaders). Washington, DC: American Council on Education.

McDonough, P. M. (2005a). Counseling and college counseling in America's high schools. In D. Hawkins (Ed.), *The 2004–05 state of college admission* (pp. 107–127). Washington, DC: National Association for College Admission Counseling.

McDonough, P. M. (2005b). Counseling matters: Knowledge, assistance, and organizational commitment in college preparation. In W. G. Tierney, Z. B. Corwin, & J. E. Colyar (Eds.), *Preparing for college: Nine elements of effective*

outreach (pp. 69–87). Albany: State University of New York Press.

McDonough, P. M., Antonio, A. L., Walpole, M., & Perez, L. X. (1998). College rankings: Democratized college knowledge for whom? *Research in Higher Education, 39,* 513–537.

McDonough, P., & Fann, A. (in press). The study of inequality. In P. Gumport & A. Antonio (Eds.), *Sociology of higher education: Applying theory to practice and policy.* Baltimore, MD: Johns Hopkins University Press.

McDonough, P. M., Korn, J., & Yamasaki, E. (1997). Access, equity, and the privatization of college counseling. *Review of Higher Education, 20,* 297–317.

McDonough, P. M., & McClafferty, K. A. (2001). *Rural college opportunity: A Shasta and Siskiyou county perspective.* Technical report prepared for the University of California, Office of the President, and McConnell Foundation.

McDonough, P., Nunez, A. M., Ceja, M., & Solorzano, D. (2003, November). *A model of Latino college choice.* Paper presented at the annual meeting of the Association for the Study of Higher Education, Portland, OR.

McDonough, P. M., Ventresca, M., & Outcalt, C. (2000). Field of dreams: Organizational field approaches to understanding the transformation of college access, 1965–1995. In J. C. Smart & W. G. Tierney (Eds.), *Higher education: Handbook of theory and research* (Vol. 15, pp. 317–405). New York: Agathon.

McGrath, D. J., Swisher, R. R., Elder, G. H., Jr., & Conger, R. D. (2001). Breaking new ground: Diverse routes to college in rural America. *Rural Sociology, 66,* 244–267.

McNeil, P. M. (2003). *Rethinking high school: The next frontier for state policymakers.* Gaithersburg, MD: Aspen Institute.

Oakes, J. (1989). What educational indicators? The case for assessing the school context. *Educational Evaluation and Policy Analysis, 11,* 181–199.

Oakes, J. (2004). Investigating the claims in *Williams v. State of California:* An unconstitutional denial of education's basic tools? *Teachers College Record, 106,* 1889–1906.

Oakes, J., Rogers, J., Lipton, M., & Morrell, E. (2002). The social construction of college access: Confronting the technical, cultural, and political barriers to low-income students of color. In W. G. Tierney & L. S. Hagedorn (Eds.), *Increasing access to college: Extending possibilities for all students* (pp. 81–104). Albany: State University of New York Press.

Olivas, M. (1986). *Latino college students.* New York: Columbia University, Teachers College Press.

Olson, L., & Rosenfeld, R. A. (1984). Parents and the process of gaining access to student financial aid. *Journal of Higher Education, 55,* 455–480.

Pathways to College Network. (2003). *A shared agenda: A leadership challenge to improve college access and success.* Boston: Education Resources Institute.

Perna, L. W. (2005). The key to college access: A college preparatory curriculum. In W. G. Tierney, Z. B. Corwin, & J. E. Colyar (Eds.), *Preparing for college: Nine elements of effective outreach* (pp. 113–134). Albany: State University of New York Press.

Powell, A. G. (1996). *Lessons from privilege: The American prep school tradition.* Cambridge, MA: Harvard University Press.

Soja, F. W. (1996). *Thirdspace: Journeys to Los Angeles and other real-and-imagined places.* Oxford, UK: Basil Blackwell.

Sontag, S. (1978). *Illness as metaphor.* New York: Farrar, Straus, & Giroux.

St. John, E. (2002a). *The access challenge: Rethinking the causes of the opportunity gap* (Policy Issue Report No. 2002-1). Bloomington: Indiana Educational Policy Center.

St. John, E. (2002b). *Meeting the access challenge: Indiana's Twenty-first Century Scholars program.* Indianapolis, IN: Lumina Foundation for Education.

St. John, E. (2003). Refinancing the college dream: Access, opportunity, and justice for taxpayers. Baltimore, MD: Johns Hopkins University Press.

St. John, E., & Noell, J. (1989). The effects of student financial aid on access to higher education: An analysis of progress with special consideration of minority enrollment. *Research in Higher Education, 30,* 563–581.

Tejeda, C., Espinoza, M., & Gutierrez, K. (2003). Toward a decolonizing pedagogy: Social justice reconsidered. In P. Trifonas (Ed.), *Pedagogy of difference: Rethinking education for social change* (pp. 10–40). New York: Routledge.

Teranishi, R., Allen, W., & Solorzano, D. (2004). Opportunities at the crossroads: School segregation and disparate opportunities for higher education in California. *Teachers College Record, 106,* 2224–2245.

Teranishi, R. T., Ceja, M., Antonio, A. L., Allen, W. R., & McDonough, P. M. (2004). The college-choice process for Asian Pacific Americans: Ethnicity and socioeconomic class in context. *Review of Higher Education, 27,* 527–551.

Thomas, G. E. (1979). The influence of ascription, achievement, and educational expectations on black–white postsecondary enrollment. *Sociological Quarterly, 20,* 209–222.

Thomas, M. (2005). "I think it's just natural": The spatiality of racial segregation at a U.S. high school. *Environment and Planning A, 37,* 1233–1248.

Tienda, M., Cortes, K., & Niu, S. (2003, November). *College attendance and the Texas top 10 percent law: Permanent contagion or transitory promise?* Paper presented at the Conference on Expanding Opportunity in Higher Education: The Harvard Civil Rights Project, Sacramento, CA.

Tierney, W. G., & Auerbach, S. (2004). Toward developing an untapped resource: The role of families in college preparation. In W. G. Tierney, Z. B. Corwin, & J. E. Colyar (Eds.), *Preparing for college: Nine elements of effective outreach* (pp. 29–48). Albany: State University of New York Press.

Tierney, W. G., Corwin, Z. B., & Colyar, J. E. (Eds.). (2004). *Preparing for college: Nine elements of effective outreach.* Albany: State University of New York Press.

Timar, T. B., Ogawa, R., & Orillion, M. (2004). Expanding the University of California's outreach mission. *Review of Higher Education, 27*(2), 187–209.

U.S. Department of Education. (2003). *The condition of education, 2003* (NCES 2003-067). Washington, DC: Government Printing Office.

U.S. Department of Labor. (2004). *BLS releases 2002–12 employment projections.* Washington, DC: Government Printing Office. Retrieved April 12, 2004, from www.bls.gov/news.release/ecopro.nr0.htm

5

Studying Teacher Education Programs

Enriching and Enlarging the Inquiry

Kenneth Zeichner

University of Wisconsin–Madison

This chapter builds on and enlarges the study of an enduring problem in teacher education, namely, the nature and impact of different kinds of teacher education programs at the preservice level. It reviews the ways in which the effects of different teacher education programs have been studied in the past, and it offers suggestions for how to conceptualize and conduct studies that (a) illuminate the nature and impact of different approaches to educating teachers and (b) differentiate selection effects and influences of teaching and policy contexts from those of the teacher education programs. The integration of quantitative and qualitative research methods within coherent research programs is recommended as the optimal way in which to illuminate the complexity and impact of specific aspects of various pathways into teaching.

Teacher Education as a Field of Study

I begin by examining the nature of research in teacher education as a whole and describing the major genres of research in the field. I then focus on one particular aspect of the research, namely, studies of teacher education programs. Following a discussion of problems with existing research on teacher education programs, I draw on the work of the American Educational Research Association's (AERA) Panel on Research and Teacher Education (Cochran-Smith & Fries, 2005; Zeichner, 1999) to offer suggestions for how to strengthen this research so that it will be better able to illuminate the impact of different pathways into teaching on teachers and their pupils.

Compared with other research areas in education, such as the history of education, the psychology of learning or literacy, and mathematics education, research on teacher education is a relatively young area of study in the United States. Although there has been research about teacher education since the early part of the 20th century (Cochran-Smith & Fries, 2005; Zeichner, 1999), only since the 1970s has teacher education research emerged as a legitimate area of doctoral study in graduate schools of education. Prior to 1984 when Division K was founded within AERA, researchers who studied aspects of teacher education either iden-tified solely with the disciplines in which they received their training (e.g., sociology, history) or identified with a very small special interest group within the association (Zeichner, 1999). Now many research universities in the United States have at least one doctoral-level course in the study of teacher education, and several insti-tutions have full-fledged doctoral programs that include a series of courses examining the research literature in the field.

During its early phases, teacher education research was dominated by surveys of what prac-tices existed in the field (e.g., Conant, 1963; Evenden, 1933), studies of changes in student teacher attitudes during their participation in teacher education programs (Cyphert & Spaights, 1964), and studies that indirectly sought to iden-tify the characteristics of good teachers by sur-veying those in the field about what traits and abilities good teachers possessed (e.g., Barr, 1929; Charters & Waples, 1929). There was very little direct study of the process of teacher educa-tion at this early stage (Denemark & Macdonald, 1967).

Several scholars have attempted to identify the different programs of research in contempo-rary research concerning preservice teacher education. For example, Koehler (1985) identi-fied six different categories of research in the field: (1) studies of the skills, competencies, and attitudes of practicing classroom teachers that reflect on preservice teacher education; (2) stud-ies of the skills, competencies, and attitudes of teacher education students that reflect either on their current or past education or on the future quality of the workforce; (3) evaluations of teacher education courses, methods within courses, or complete programs; (4) studies of teacher educators; (5) studies of institutions; and (6) studies of studies and research reviews (see also Katz & Raths, 1985; Kennedy, 1996; Lanier & Little, 1986; Turner, 1975).

Cochran-Smith & Fries (2005), in an analy-sis of research syntheses, identify a shift in emphasis in research on preservice teacher edu-cation from the late 1950s onward. Their analy-sis argues that there has been a shift from an emphasis on research on teacher education as a training problem, to research on teacher edu-cation as a learning problem, to research on teacher education as a policy problem, even though all three kinds of research have existed throughout this whole period of time.

This shifting set of priorities in the research has involved an expansion in research method-ologies used to study teacher education and in the disciplinary lenses through which teacher education has been viewed. Following the nearly exclusive use of experimental and quasi-experimental comparisons of different behav-ior training methods during the 1960s and early 1970s (Peck & Tucker, 1973), research on teacher education began to incorporate natural-istic and interpretive methodologies, such as ethnography, case study, narrative inquiry, biography, and life history (e.g., Carter, 1992; Weber, 1993), as well as various critical, femi-nist, and poststructural analyses of different aspects of teacher education (e.g., Britzman, 2003; Giroux & McLaren, 1987; Maher & Rathbone, 1986; Popkewitz, 1998).

In addition to the educational psychology-trained researchers who had dominated teacher education research up to the 1980s, research-ers from other disciplines, such as sociology, anthropology, history, economics, and philoso-phy, also began to devote their attention to the study of teacher education (e.g., Clifford & Guthrie, 1988; Labaree, 2004; Steiner, 2004). In addition to a concern with the impact of teacher education on the behavior of teachers in class-rooms (Gage & Winne, 1975), researchers began to incorporate outcomes that addressed the cognitive, moral, and ethical aspects of teacher development (e.g., Feiman-Nemser, 1983; Zeichner & Gore, 1990) and focused on the connections between various policy levers, such as teacher testing and course requirements, and a variety of outcomes related to teacher quality and pupil learning (e.g., Mitchell, Robinson, Plake, & Knowles, 2001). Since the early 1990s, much of the research on teacher education has involved self-studies by teacher educators of their own practices and programs (Loughran, Harris, Laboskey, & Russell, 2004). One reason for the prevalence of self-study research is the lack of access to funding for larger-scale studies of multiple programs (Zeichner, 2005). Teacher educators who have conducted these studies argue, however, that they and their programs benefit greatly from these inquiries (Hamilton & Pinnegar, 1998) and that self-study research provides a unique perspective on teacher education not obtainable from the outside (Cochran-Smith & Lytle, 1993).

This chapter discusses a particular segment of research in teacher education that has connections to all three of Cochran-Smith and Fries's (2005) categories of research emphasis—training, learning, and policy—and that is a subset of Koehler's third research category. Specifically, I discuss the study of the nature and impact of different preservice teacher education program models or pathways into teaching since circa 1985, when this became a major policy issue in the United States. Before doing this, I place this body of research on teacher education programs within my own version of the field of teacher education research.

VARIETIES OF CURRENT RESEARCH ON PRESERVICE TEACHER EDUCATION

My own view of the current variety of research on preservice teacher education in the United States is based on a reformulation of the framework that I presented in my vice-presidential address to AERA in 1998 (Zeichner, 1999). There are several major kinds of research that have been focused on the preservice education of teachers in the United States. These include (a) surveys of current practices; (b) conceptual, historical, and comparative studies of teacher education; (c) studies of the process of learning to teach; (d) studies of teacher education participants, that is, teacher educators and teacher candidates; and (e) studies of the nature and impact of teacher education (as a whole; specific programs, courses, and program components; and instructional strategies) and of policies that affect teacher education. Following a brief description of each of these research genres, I discuss the central issue for this chapter of doing empirical research on teacher education programs.

The first type of contemporary research on teacher education consists of largely descriptive survey studies that provide information to the research, policy, and practitioner communities about the current status of teacher education in the United States and sometimes in comparison with other countries. This includes both large-scale national studies that seek to identify patterns in teacher education throughout the nation and studies that focus on documenting teacher education in specific regions or in particular specialty areas such as elementary education and bilingual education. Prominent examples of this work include the Research About Teacher Education (RATE) studies, sponsored by the American Association of Colleges for Teacher Education beginning in 1987, which described various characteristics of U.S. teacher education programs, teacher candidates, and teacher educators (Howey, 1997); regular compilations of teacher education policies in different states such as the National Center for Educational Information annual reports on alternative teacher certification policies (e.g., Feistritzer, 2004); the ERIC Clearinghouse on Teacher Education's reports about the status of professional development school partnerships (Abdal-Haqq, 1995); and the Educational Testing Service's report on teacher education policies in different countries (Wang, Coleman, Coley, & Phelps, 2003).

The second major category of research on teacher education consists of conceptual, historical, and comparative studies that go beyond presenting demographic data and examine various issues of teacher education through different theoretical lenses. One significant line of conceptual research in teacher education has sought to identify and discuss substantively different approaches to teacher education. This work has distinguished teacher education programs from one another based on the visions of teaching, learning, schooling, and society that they emphasized. Several different versions of alternative orientations to teacher education have been proposed by scholars in different countries (e.g., Avalos, 1991; Feiman-Nemser, 1990; Kirk, 1986; Liston & Zeichner, 1991; Zeichner, 2003).

In addition to the work on different orientations to teacher education, there have been philosophical analyses of the different tensions in teacher education, such as the tension between theory and practice and that between liberal and technical, as well as critical analyses of some of what McWilliam (1994) referred to as the "folkloric discourses" of teacher education, for example, that coherent programs, more school experience, and more academic content courses are necessarily desirable (Buchmann & Floden, 1993; Feiman-Nemser & Buchmann, 1985; McDiarmid, 1992). There has also been a considerable amount of effort devoted to conceptual analyses of various popular slogans in teacher education that have dominated the discourse such as reflective teaching and social justice teacher education (e.g., Valli, 1993). In addition, there have been some studies that analyzed the content of the teacher education curriculum in different programs or teacher education textbooks or course assignments in terms of the academic rigor associated with them and/or in relation to the biases they contain (e.g., Steiner, 2004; Zeichner, 1988).

Another aspect of conceptual work in teacher education has been analyses of the impact of external influences on teacher education programs such as state and federal government policies, philanthropic foundations, commercial publishers, test designers, national program accreditation standards, and economic factors. Examples of this work include Labaree's (2004) analyses of the effect of market forces on the character and quality of teacher education programs, Early's (2000) analysis of federal policymaking in the United States, and Popkewitz's (1993) international research project that examined the role of the state in teacher education in several different countries. Some of this work has employed critical, poststructural, and feminist lenses to analyze the various ways in which patterns of reasoning, norms, and patterns of communication (e.g., those stressing technical and managerial definitions of teaching) have been subtly imposed on teacher education structuring in certain possibilities while filtering out others (e.g., Gore, 1993; McWilliam, 1994).

There has also been a great deal of important conceptual and empirical work done under the label of "multicultural teacher education" that has soundly critiqued current practices in teacher education programs for their lack of attention to various aspects of cultural diversity, documented the ineffectiveness of much of what is currently being done in this area, and offered analyses as to why these problems exist and what can be done about them (e.g., Irvine, 2003; Villegas & Lucas, 2002).

Finally, within the past two decades, there has been a significant increase in historical studies of teacher education that have provided new and important insights into the role of various factors such as the feminization of teaching and the social class backgrounds of teachers and teacher educators, developments in higher education generally, and the development of teacher education in the United States. Some of this work has linked the continued marginal status of teacher education in U.S. universities to the female nature of the occupation (Clifford & Guthrie, 1988; Herbst, 1989), to differences in social class background between teacher education faculty and other faculty (Lanier & Little, 1986), and to reward systems that discourage faculty from working in a sustained way in teacher education programs (Liston, 1995).

The third major category of research in teacher education is work that has sought to illuminate the processes of learning to teach in different settings. These studies (e.g., Borko & Putnam, 1996; Darling-Hammond & Bransford, 2005; Feiman-Nemser & Remillard, 1996; Wideen, Mayer-Smith, & Moon, 1998) have used a variety of disciplinary frameworks to examine how prospective teachers' knowledge, skills, and dispositions are influenced by their participation in a teacher education program or by particular components of a teacher education program such as student teaching. This work has shown how difficult it is to change the often tacit beliefs, understandings, and worldviews that students bring to teacher education programs. In some cases, we have learned that prospective teachers transform the messages given in their programs to fit their preconceptions (e.g., Holt-Reynolds, 1992). This work has begun to tell us some things about how to increase the impact of a teacher education program on prospective teachers through means such as the organization of students into cohort groups, more connected relationships between schools and university-based courses, and the use of particular instructional strategies under certain conditions such as community field experiences, portfolio development, and action research. There have been an increasing number of longitudinal studies that follow candidates through their programs and into their early years of teaching, tracking their learning and attempting to attribute changes detected to various influences in and outside of the teacher education programs (e.g., Grossman et al., 2000; Kennedy, 1998). Some of this work has resulted in the generation of theories about the process of learning to teach (e.g., Grossman, Smagorinsky, & Valencia, 1999).

The fourth area of research on teacher education includes studies that focus on the participants in teacher education programs, namely, the candidates and their teacher educators. These studies go beyond merely describing the characteristics of these groups and attempt to identify the consequences of these characteristics. For example, Zumwalt and Craig (2005a, 2005b) analyzed the demographic and quality indicators associated with candidates in preservice teacher education programs in the United States and attempted to link particular characteristics to a variety of indicators associated with teacher quality and student learning. Lanier and Little (1986) discussed the consequences of the social class and gender patterns that exist among teacher educators for the status of teacher education in universities and for the teacher education curriculum.

The final major area of research in teacher education is concerned with illuminating the nature and impact of different approaches to educating teachers at the preservice level and of policies that are affecting these approaches. For many years, there have been debates about the efficacy of different kinds of teacher education programs (e.g., Denemark & Nutter, 1984; Hawley, 1987; Tom, 1987; Von Schlichten, 1958), and during recent years, many alternatives to university- and college-based teacher education programs have emerged and been given legitimacy by state education departments, including private for-profit programs (e.g., Dill, 1996; Morey, 2001). Although much of the discourse about the value of different pathways into teaching does not draw on evidence from empirical research, a body of research that emerged during the mid-1980s has examined the consequences for teachers and/or their pupils of entering teaching through different kinds of programs. There has also been a body of work focusing on the nature and impact of different program components, such as methods and foundations courses, and field

experiences or specific instructional strategies, such as microteaching, action research, and case studies on different aspects of teacher quality and/or pupil learning (e.g., Clift & Brady, 2005; Floden & Meniketti, 2005; Grossman, 2005). Finally, a small body of research has focused on the impact of particular teacher education policies such as those related to teacher testing and program accreditation (Wilson & Youngs, 2005). This chapter focuses on research related to teacher education programs. Because of the variety of ways that now exist for people to enter teaching, it is important to begin to develop a better understanding of the consequences of entering teaching through different kinds of teacher education programs. As is shown in what follows, currently there is very little solid research about the impact of different pathways into teaching that can inform policy and practice.

THE IDEA OF A TEACHER EDUCATION PROGRAM

One of the most important steps in doing research about teacher education programs is to define what is meant by a program type. Teacher education programs have been distinguished from one another in several different ways in the literature. The most common distinction used in research studies has been in terms of the structure of a program. Programs have been distinguished from one another by their length (e.g., 4 years, 5 years), by when they are offered (e.g., graduate level, undergraduate level), and by the institutions that sponsor them (e.g., college or university, school district, state education department, for-profit company). Programs have also sometimes been defined in terms of their admissions requirements and curricular emphases such as the amount of coursework in the arts and sciences versus education courses, whether they require a major in an academic subject, and the amount of time spent working in schools versus spent taking classes.

As mentioned earlier, teacher education programs have also been distinguished from one another in terms of their conceptual orientations (e.g., Feiman-Nemser, 1990; Liston & Zeichner, 1991) or whether they have coherent themes that tie together the various program components (Barnes, 1987). Others have defined programs in terms of whether or not they have particular features such as student cohort groups and professional development school partnerships (Arends & Winitzky, 1996). Very few dimensions beyond the general structural labels (e.g., graduate/undergraduate, alternative/traditional) have been used by researchers who have studied the nature and impact of programs.

The Inadequacy of Defining Teacher Education Programs by Structural Labels

There are several reasons why defining a teacher education program solely by a structural label, such as alternative or traditional, is a problem. First, Goodlad's (1990) national study of teacher education programs documented the ways in which the type of institution in which a teacher education program is located influences the substance of the program. Goodlad and his collaborators studied programs in 29 institutions across the United States that were representative of the different kinds of higher education institutions that offer teacher education such as liberal arts colleges, regional universities, and research universities. The high degree of institutional influence on teacher education that was found in this study strongly suggests that a 4-year program in a liberal arts college is very different from a 4-year program in a research university, for example, and that institutional type is an important factor in influencing the character and quality of teacher education programs.

Similarly, differences in state policy contexts with regard to teacher education suggest that the state in which a program exists also strongly influences the character and quality of the program. For example, a program in Texas, where the state has placed severe credit limits on professional education courses in teacher education programs, is different from a program in a state such as Wisconsin, which has encouraged the expansion of the professional education component of programs. In addition, a program in a state that has mandated the national accreditation of teacher education programs, such as New York, is not the same as a program in a state that does not require national accreditation of teacher education programs.

In addition, the character and quality of teacher education programs and the outcomes associated with them are also affected by the subject areas for which teachers are being prepared to teach. For example, Natriello and Zumwalt (1993) studied a variety of alternative and traditional teacher education programs in New Jersey and found that the greatest influence on teacher retention for the graduates of the different programs was the subject areas of the programs rather than their structural type (alternative or traditional). For example, secondary mathematics teachers who had good opportunities for higher-paying jobs outside of education left teaching at much higher rates than did elementary and English education graduates (see also Murnane, Singer, Willett, Kempe, & Olsen, 1991).

A final limitation in describing teacher education programs by their structural type alone is that teacher candidates frequently experience their programs in ways that deviate from the program labels. For example, during the 1980s, I studied a so-called 5-year preservice teacher education program at the University of Florida as part of a national longitudinal study of several programs that followed teaching candidates through their programs and into their early years of teaching (Kennedy, 1998). We were interested in learning more about how teachers learned to teach writing and mathematics to diverse pupils and the ways in which specific aspects of teacher education contributed to this learning. One of the things I discovered in this study was that very few of the students in this 5-year program actually spent 5 years in the program. Many students spent their first 2 years in various community colleges around the state, and because of the teacher shortage in Florida at the time of the study, a significant number of teacher education students left the program early and completed their final student teaching experience as full-time teachers of record. This movement of students across institutions is not an uncommon occurrence, according to a survey of teacher education students conducted by Howey and Zimpher (1989).

All of these factors mean that it does not make much sense to describe teacher education programs by only their structural characteristics, such as their length, the type of institutional sponsorship, and whether it is undergraduate or postgraduate, without considering things such as the substance of their curricula, the institutional and policy contexts in which they exist, their admissions requirements, and the characteristics of teacher candidates. Unfortunately, researchers who have studied and compared different kinds of teacher education programs and their relationships to various kinds of outcomes have rarely paid attention to these other factors.

THE EMPIRICAL RESEARCH ON TEACHER EDUCATION PROGRAMS

Between 2000 and 2004, Hilary Conklin and I conducted a review of peer-reviewed empirical studies on teacher education programs published between 1985 and 2004 as part of AERA's Panel on Research and Teacher Education that was charged with conducting an impartial and rigorous analysis of the research on various topics in teacher education (Zeichner & Conklin, 2005). In the review, we analyzed 37 studies that used a variety of research designs and methodologies and that attempted to link various kinds of teacher education programs to a variety of outcomes associated with teacher quality and pupil learning. Most of the studies were set up as comparisons of the outcomes associated with different program models. The studies were grouped into the following seven categories based on how teacher education programs were defined by researchers:

- Studies of 4-year programs versus 5-year programs
- Studies of state-sponsored alternative programs versus traditional programs
- Studies of university-sponsored alternative programs versus traditional programs
- Studies of school district-sponsored alternative programs versus traditional university-based programs
- Studies of "Teach for America"
- Comparisons of multiple alternative and traditional programs
- In-depth case studies of teacher education programs

Because of the complexity of the ways in which teacher education programs differ from one another, and because of the focus of the research on only a few structural characteristics, we were faced with the problem of defining the teacher education programs in a way that would enable us to accumulate knowledge across the individual studies. We settled on a definition of different kinds of programs that were limited by the ways in which data were presented in the studies. For example, we defined an alternative teacher certification program, which was the most ambiguously defined type of program in the studies we reviewed, as a program that allows persons to enter the teaching profession without completing a traditional 4- or 5-year university-based program. This definition included university-based postbaccalaureate programs within the category of alternative. Because of the different ways in which researchers had defined alternative and traditional programs in their studies, this definition did not enable us to use all of the data from the studies in the way we preferred, but it came the closest to doing so among all of the possible definitions. If the data had been available, we would have preferred to distinguish teacher education programs based on differences in their assumptions about what teachers need to know and be able to do to be effective instructors and how they can best acquire this knowledge and these skills (Stoddart & Floden, 1996). Clearly, there is a need for those who do research about teacher education programs to use clearer and more consistent definitions of program dimensions and types.

The studies that we reviewed examined the impact of the different types of teacher education programs on a variety of outcomes related to teacher quality and student learning. These included the numbers of teachers from different programs who entered teaching following program completion, where they taught (e.g., in schools that were difficult to staff), teachers' projected commitment to teaching as a career, and how long they actually stayed. There were also a variety of measures of teaching quality, including teachers' own sense of efficacy; their ratings of their own teaching and leadership practices; assessments of teaching based on various kinds of classroom observations done by supervisors, principals, and others; and pupil ratings of the quality of instruction. There were also a few studies that attempted to link teacher education programs to the learning of pupils taught by the graduates of different teacher education programs based on pupils' standardized achievement test scores. Finally, in some of the studies, teacher education graduates were asked to evaluate the effectiveness of their preservice programs in preparing them to do particular things in the classroom (e.g., assessment, teaching English-language learners).

Without getting into the details of the individual studies here beyond providing examples from studies of particular patterns in the research, I summarize what we learned from our analysis of the research and how I think that research on the nature and impact of teacher education programs can be improved to yield more useful knowledge. Doing research about the efficacy of different kinds of programs has become more important as the number of pathways into P–12 teaching has increased.

Problems With the Existing Research

In our review of peer-reviewed research on teacher education programs (Zeichner & Conklin, 2005), we saw several problems with how research on teacher education programs has been designed and carried out that limit its usefulness in generating knowledge that is useful to researchers, practitioners, and policymakers. First, individual research studies have been carried out as if in a vacuum. There is very little evidence in this work of researchers building on one another's work, of clear and consistent definitions of key terms, and of the use of common research instruments across studies. The result is that it is very difficult to look across the studies on teacher education programs and draw any conclusions about what we have learned about the impact of particular kinds of programs.

Second, most of the studies have examined the impact of programs that are vaguely defined according to a few structural characteristics. We know very little from these studies about the curriculum and instructional strategies used in the programs or about the social relations among candidates and between candidates and their teacher educators. We also know very little about the characteristics of the teacher candidates beyond their level or subject areas of preparation or about the contexts in which programs exist (e.g., schools used for clinical experiences, state policy contexts).

The typical study compares graduates of Program A with graduates of Program B in terms of some subset of the outcomes just listed and then draws conclusions about the efficacy of the different programs. For example, in one widely cited study, Andrew (1990) compared graduates of 4- and 5-year programs at the University of New Hampshire and concluded, "The nature of the internship and the additional course work required for the master's degree [in the five-year program] result in more effective learning about teaching" (p. 50). To some degree, the data that were presented in this research report supported this conclusion and showed more favorable results for 5-year program graduates than for 4-year program graduates in a number of areas such as entry into teaching, career satisfaction, and retention. However, there are several problems with the way in which this study was conducted that illustrate why it has been hard to conclude anything definitive from existing studies on teacher education programs.

Specifically, although on the surface the numbers indicate that the 5-year program is better than the 4-year program in terms of the outcomes of interest, there is not clear evidence in the study that the teacher education programs were responsible for these differences. Andrew (1990) recognized this problem and concluded, "We cannot eliminate the possibility that differences observed between four- and five-year program graduates in this study are not simply the result of differences in academic ability" (p. 50). Similarly, the findings of this study related to the higher retention rates of graduates of 5-year programs are of limited use because of the failure of the research report to provide information about the nature of the schools in which the graduates of the different programs taught. Teaching in schools in New Hampshire, where many of these teachers probably taught, is vastly different from teaching in, for example, Chicago or Los Angeles, and it does not make much sense to talk about the quality of teaching performance or retention without situating these data in relation to the demographic characteristics of schools.

These problems of not providing adequate information about the entering characteristics of teacher education candidates (e.g., their knowledge, skills, and dispositions related to various aspects of teaching) or about the contexts in which teachers work are characteristic of the research about teacher education programs, including in the most expensive and ambitious of these studies such as Decker, Mayer, and Glazerman's (2004) national study of Teach for America (TFA).

Another problem that is characteristic of this body of research is the consistent failure of researchers to describe the substance of the preservice programs that were attended by teachers. For example, in several of the studies of TFA, the achievement of pupils taught by TFA graduates was compared with that of pupils taught by non TFA graduates (e.g., Decker et al., 2004; Laczko-Kerr & Berliner, 2002; Raymond & Fletcher, 2002). In addition to the problem of not describing the nature of the TFA program in the specific parts of the country where it was studied, these studies provide little or no information about the preparation received by the non-TFA comparison groups. Although the studies suggest that comparisons are being made of the consequences of preparing teachers in an alternative program such as TFA and traditional university-based programs, some of the non-TFA teachers could in fact have been prepared for teaching in fast-track programs such as TFA. A number of elements of the TFA curriculum resemble those in traditional university-based programs. In many of the studies comparing outcomes associated with different kinds of programs, it is unclear how the contents of the programs being compared are similar to and different from one another.

In every type of teacher education program, there will inevitably be a range of quality and the search for the most effective structural model of teacher education is doomed to failure, just as the quest for the most effective set of teaching behaviors was bound to fail (Kliebard, 1973). Defining a program as 5-year or 4-year, or as alternative or traditional, reveals very little about the key elements of the program and does not enable researchers to link the achievement of desired outcomes to particular program characteristics.

A final limitation of the research on teacher education programs is the lack of consistency in the methods and instruments that are used to assess particular aspects of teacher education and various outcomes associated with teacher quality and pupil learning. For example, a number of the studies on teacher education programs have sought to connect the type of program experienced to the quality of teaching performance of program graduates. There are a wide variety of ways in which the quality of teaching performance has been assessed, including surveys of principals, supervisors, and mentors; use of classroom observation instruments; use of self-reports of the teachers; and ratings of teaching quality by pupils. Other than the use of rating scales that ask someone (e.g., a supervisor, a mentor) to assess the quality of a graduate's teaching in comparison with "other beginning teachers" according to unstated criteria, there is almost no overlap between the ways in which teaching performance has been assessed across the studies. The same problem exists with regard to most of the outcomes that have been included in the studies.

A second weakness in the assessment of outcomes associated with experiencing different kinds of teacher education programs is the narrowness of the way in which pupil learning has been assessed. In the few studies that have attempted to connect the type of teacher education program attended to the quality of the learning of pupils taught by program graduates, there has been nearly exclusive use of standardized achievement tests in defining student learning. The use of growth in standardized achievement test scores as a measure of pupil learning represents only a narrow range of academic performance. Although national attention is currently focused on cognitive measures of academic performance, a look at the broader history of the United States shows a strong and recurrent interest of the public in other outcomes such as students' social, emotional, aesthetic, and civic development (Goodlad, 1984).

In-Depth Case Studies of Teacher Education Programs

Most of the studies that we reviewed compared the graduates of different kinds of teacher education programs in the manner described in the preceding sections (Zeichner & Conklin, 2005). However, we also examined two in-depth case studies of sets of teacher education programs that sought to get inside the programs and illuminate their specific features that were linked to the achievement of various outcomes. In both of these studies (Darling-Hammond, 2000; National Center for Research on Teacher Education, 1991), a variety of program structures were examined and teams of researchers spent time observing classes and field experiences and interviewing the teacher candidates and their teacher educators. The research reports provide a much clearer picture than the studies discussed previously of both the programs and the contexts in which they are embedded. Both of these studies identified various program characteristics that were related to a variety of outcomes associated with teachers' knowledge, beliefs, and practices and concluded that a program's substance, rather than its structure, had the major influence on teacher learning. In the Teacher Education and Learning to Teach (TELT) study, for example, Kennedy (1998) reported that programs that had similar structures sometimes had remarkably different influences on teacher candidates, whereas programs that had different structures sometimes had similar influences on teachers, depending on their substantive characteristics.

In the TELT study and the National Commission on Teaching and America's Future (NCTAF) case studies (Darling-Hammond, 2000), researchers generated lists of program characteristics that they believed were related to the achievement of desired teacher learning outcomes. Neither study sought to connect teacher education and teacher learning to student learning. Examples of these characteristics include a shared and clear understanding among faculty, students, and school personnel about good teaching that permeates all courses and field experiences; a clear set of practice and performance standards against which candidates' coursework is guided and assessed; and courses that are taught in a manner that relates learning to real problems of practice (Darling-Hammond, 2000). Although there is some question about the adequacy of the evidence that is presented to support these conclusions (Zeichner & Conklin, 2005), these studies have begun to provide the basis for eventually being able to link specific teacher education program components to desired outcomes.

Another problem with the lists of the characteristics of good teacher education programs that have emerged from these studies is that they are stated in very general terms. For example, one of the characteristics of a good program that appears in most accounts is the presence of mentoring. Nothing is said in the presentation of these characteristics about the conditions under which these features were effective in achieving desired outcomes. For example, with regard to mentoring, we need to know things such as how the mentors were chosen, whether they work in the same schools and subject areas as their mentees, how they were prepared and are supported for their roles, and the relationship between the mentoring and teacher evaluation. Despite the limitations of the in-depth case studies of programs, they provide the basis for further research into the program characteristics that make a difference in terms of teacher and learner outcomes.

Enlarging and Enhancing Research on Teacher Education Programs

Given all of these problems with research that attempts to study teacher education programs and link particular outcomes connected to teacher quality and pupil learning, what can be done to raise the quality of research in this area so that it will produce knowledge useful to other researchers, policymakers, and teacher educators? The first thing that needs to be done is for researchers to consciously build on the work of other researchers and to view themselves as part of a research community. I have tried to convey in this chapter the complex factors that influence how a teacher education program contributes to both teacher learning and student learning. Both teacher learning and student learning are affected by a number of factors beyond the specific type of teacher education program a teacher attends. These include the individual attributes brought by prospective teachers to their programs, the specific features of these programs and their components (e.g., curriculum, instruction, social relations), the types of institutions in which the programs are located, and the like. Obviously, no single research study can adequately deal with all of this complexity. These are characteristics that can be addressed only in coherent programs of research (Shulman, 2002).

Programs of research involve researchers taking on various aspects of a general problem and adding new understandings with each new study. The general problem of the relationships between teacher education and teacher and student outcomes can be represented by the graphic in Figure 5.1. So far, I have argued that the existing research has largely sought to connect teacher education programs to aspects of teacher and student learning without taking into account the characteristics that teacher candidates bring to their programs and the many factors in and outside these programs. If researchers begin to focus on these neglected factors, better coordinate their studies, use clear and consistent definitions of key terms related to the programs and teacher and student learning, and use common research instruments

and protocols, this research will begin to produce knowledge and theoretical explanations for the ways in which teacher education influences teachers and student learning. Some of the instrumentation used in studies of teacher education programs has been made public for others to use (e.g., Kennedy, Ball, & McDiarmid, 1993), but there needs to be much more effort to develop greater consistency across studies in how various aspects of teacher education programs and their outcomes are studied.

A variety of methodological approaches are needed to implement this program of research on the relationships between teacher education and teacher and student learning. Although it is expensive and out of the reach of most individual researchers to conduct in-depth program case studies such as the TELT and NCTAF studies discussed earlier, or to conduct large-scale studies using both quantitative and qualitative methods such as the study of alternative pathways into teaching in New York City (Boyd, Grossman, Lankford, Loeb, & Wyckoff, 2003) and the Mathematica Policy Research Institute study of TFA (Decker et al., 2004), individuals and small groups of researchers can address some of the problems in the existing research even in the small-scale self-studies that dominate research in the field.

In addition to situating their own research in relation to other similar research and discussing

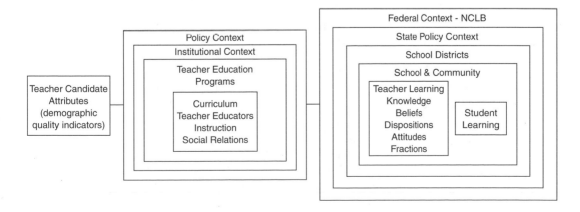

Figure 5.1   Studying the Relationships Between Teacher Education and Teacher and Student Learning

NOTE: NCLB = No Child Left Behind legislation.

what piece of the research program is being added by their research (e.g., theoretically, methodologically), researchers need to carefully describe the program or programs that are being studied in terms of the areas identified in Figure 5.1. Specifically, researchers need to describe and examine the institutional and policy contexts in which the program(s) exist; relevant characteristics of the teacher candidates and teacher educators; and enough detail about curriculum, instructional practices, and social relations in the program(s) and program organizational characteristics that the potential exists to be able to link the achievement of certain outcomes to particular program characteristics. The outcomes and the ways that are developed to assess them need to be clearly defined and linked to other work that has focused on the same issues (e.g., the development of teachers' cultural competence). Finally, if the research includes a focus on the teaching performance or the retention of program graduates, the nature of the schools in which those graduates teach needs to be described in enough detail so that the findings can be compared with those from other studies.

These recommendations apply whether the research is a small-scale study of one's own program or a large-scale national case study of many programs. They also apply whether the researchers employ sophisticated quantitative research methods (e.g., hierarchical linear modeling), ethnographic methods, or some combination of different methods. Because of the complexity of the problem of studying teacher education programs and their outcomes, I argue that the research program as a whole should include a variety of different methodological approaches. Some of the most interesting work now going on involves qualitative researchers and economists working together in research teams employing a variety of methodologies within the same study (Boyd et al., 2003). I believe that these research recommendations, if followed, can significantly enhance our understanding of the consequences of teachers entering teaching through different pathways and that they will enable us to differentiate, in ways that are not currently feasible, the ways in which individual teachers' attributes, institutional and policy contexts, and particular features of teacher education programs all contribute to desired outcomes.

REFERENCES

Abdal-Haqq, I. (1995). *Professional development schools: A directory of projects in the U.S.* Washington, DC: American Association of Colleges for Teacher Education.

Andrew, M. (1990). Differences between graduates of four-year and five-year teacher preparation programs. *Journal of Teacher Education, 41*(2), 45–51.

Arends, R., & Winitzky, N. (1996). Program structures and learning to teach. In F. Murray (Ed.), *The teacher educator handbook* (pp. 526–556). San Francisco: Jossey-Bass.

Avalos, B. (1991). *Approaches to teacher education: Initial teacher training.* London: Commonwealth Secretariat.

Barnes, H. (1987). The conceptual basis for thematic teacher education programs. *Journal of Teacher Education, 38*(4), 13–18.

Barr, A. S. (1929). *Characteristic differences in the teaching performance of good and poor teachers of the social studies.* Bloomington, IL: Public School Publishing.

Borko, H., & Putnam, R. (1996). Learning to teach. In D. Berliner & R. Calfee (Eds.), *Handbook of educational psychology* (pp. 673–708). New York: Macmillan.

Boyd, D., Grossman, P., Lankford, H., Loeb, S., & Wyckoff, J. (2003). *Examining teacher preparation: Does the pathway make a difference?* Available: www.teacherpolicyre search.org

Britzman, D. (2003). *Practice makes practice: A critical study of learning to teach.* Albany: State University of New York Press.

Buchmann, M., & Floden, R. (Eds.). (1993). *Detachment and concern: Conversations in the philosophy of teaching and teacher education.* New York: Columbia University, Teachers College Press.

Carter, K. (1992). The place of story in the study of teaching and teacher education. *Educational Researcher, 22*(1), 5–12.

Charters, W. W., & Waples, D. (1929). *The Commonwealth teacher training study.* Chicago: University of Chicago Press.

Clifford, G. J., & Guthrie, J. W. (1988). *Ed school.* Chicago: University of Chicago Press.

Clift, R., & Brady, P. (2005). Research on methods courses and field experiences. In M. Cochran-Smith & K. Zeichner (Eds.), *Studying teacher education: The report of the AERA Panel on Research and Teacher Education* (pp. 309–424). Mahwah, NJ: Lawrence Erlbaum.

Cochran-Smith, M., & Fries, K. (2005). Researching teacher education: Foreground and background. In M. Cochran-Smith & K. Zeichner (Eds.), *Researching teacher education in changing times: Politics and paradigms* (pp. 69–110). Mahwah, NJ: Lawrence Erlbaum.

Cochran-Smith, M., & Lytle, S. (1993). *Inside–outside: Teacher research and knowledge.* New York: Columbia University, Teachers College Press.

Conant, J. (1963). *The education of American teachers.* New York: McGraw-Hill.

Cyphert, F., & Spaights, E. (1964). *An analysis and projection of research in teacher education.* Washington, DC: U.S. Department of Health, Education, and Welfare.

Darling-Hammond, L. (Ed.). (2000). *Studies of excellence in teacher education.* Washington, DC: American Association of Colleges for Teacher Education.

Darling-Hammond, L., & Bransford, J. (2005). *Preparing teachers for a changing world.* San Francisco: Jossey-Bass.

Decker, P., Mayer, D., & Glazerman, S. (2004). *The effects of Teach for America on students: Findings from a national evaluation.* Princeton, NJ: Mathematica Policy Research Institute.

Denemark, G., & Macdonald, J. (1967). Preservice and inservice education of teachers. *Review of Educational Research, 37,* 233–247.

Denemark, G., & Nutter, N. (1984). The case for extended programs of initial teacher preparation. In L. Katz & J. Raths (Eds.), *Advances in teacher education* (Vol. 1, pp. 203–246). Norwood, NJ: Ablex.

Dill, V. (1996). Alternative teacher certification. In J. Sikula (Ed.), *Handbook of research on teacher education* (2nd ed., pp. 932–960). New York: Macmillan.

Early, P. (2000). Finding the culprit: Federal policy-making in teacher education. *Educational Policy, 14*(1), 25–39.

Evenden, E. (1933). *National survey of the education of teachers.* Washington, DC: U.S. Office of Education.

Feiman-Nemser, S. (1983). Learning to teach. In L. Shulman & G. Sykes (Eds.), *Handbook of teaching and policy* (pp. 150–171). New York: Longman.

Feiman-Nemser, S. (1990). Teacher education: Structural and conceptual alternatives. In W. R. Houston (Ed.), *Handbook of research on teacher education* (pp. 150–170). New York: Macmillan.

Feiman-Nemser, S., & Buchmann, M. (1985). Pitfalls of experience in teacher education. *Teachers College Record, 87,* 49–65.

Feiman-Nemser, S., & Remillard, J. (1996). Perspectives on learning to teach. In F. Murray (Ed.), *The teacher educator's handbook* (pp. 63–91). San Francisco: Jossey-Bass.

Feistritzer, E. (2004). *Alternative certification: A state by state analysis 2004.* Washington, DC: National Center for Educational Information.

Floden, R., & Meniketti, M. (2005). Research on the effects of coursework in the arts and sciences and in the foundations of education. In M. Cochran-Smith & K. Zeichner (Eds.), *Studying teacher education: The report of the AERA Panel on Research and Teacher Education* (pp. 261–308). Mahwah, NJ: Lawrence Erlbaum.

Gage, N., & Winne, P. (1975). Performance-based teacher education. In K. Ryan (Ed.), *Teacher education* (pp. 146–172). Chicago: University of Chicago Press.

Giroux, H., & McLaren, P. (1987). Teacher education and the politics of engagement. In M. Okazawa-Ray, J. Anderson, & R. Traver (Eds.), *Teachers, teaching, and teacher education* (pp. 157–182). Cambridge, MA: Harvard Educational Review Press.

Goodlad, J. (1984). *Place called school: Prospects for the future.* New York: Rand McNally.

Goodlad, J. (1990). *Teachers for our nation's schools.* San Francisco: Jossey-Bass.

Gore, J. (1993). *The struggle for pedagogies: Critical and feminist discourses as regimes of truth.* New York: Columbia University, Teachers College Press.

Grossman, P. (2005). Research on pedagogical approaches in teacher education. In M. Cochran-Smith & K. Zeichner (Eds.), *Studying teacher education: The report of the AERA Panel on Research and Teacher Education* (pp. 425–476). Mahwah, NJ: Lawrence Erlbaum.

Grossman, P., Smagorinsky, P., & Valencia, S. (1999). Appropriating tools for teaching English:

A theoretical framework for research on learning to teach. *American Journal of Education, 108,* 1–29.

Grossman, P., Valencia, S., Evans, K., Thompson, C., Martin, S., & Place, N. (2000). Transitions into teaching: Learning to teach writing in teacher education and beyond. *Journal of Literacy Research, 3,* 631–662.

Hamilton, M. L., & Pinnegar, S. (1998). The value and promise of self-study. In M. L. Hamilton (Ed.), *Reconceptualizing teaching practice* (pp. 235–246). London: Falmer.

Hawley, W. D. (1987). The high costs and doubtful efficacy of extended teacher preparation programs. *American Journal of Education, 95,* 275–313.

Herbst, J. (1989). *And sadly teach: Teacher education and professionalization in American culture.* Madison: University of Wisconsin Press.

Holt-Reynolds, D. (1992). Personal history-based beliefs as relevant prior knowledge in coursework. *American Educational Research Journal, 29,* 325–349.

Howey, K. (1997, March). *Preservice teacher education in the U.S.: The RATE project, teacher education reform, and teacher education policy.* Paper presented at the annual meeting of the American Educational Research Association, Chicago.

Howey, K., & Zimpher, N. (1989). *Profiles of preservice teacher education: Inquiry into the nature of programs.* Albany: State University of New York Press.

Irvine, J. J. (2003). *Educating teachers for diversity: Seeing with a cultural eye.* New York: Columbia University, Teachers College Press.

Katz, L., & Raths, J. (1985). A framework for research on teacher education programs. *Journal of Teacher Education, 36*(6), 9–15.

Kennedy, M. (1996). Research genres in teacher education. In F. Murray (Ed.), *The teacher educator's handbook* (pp. 120–152). New York: Longman.

Kennedy, M. (1998). *Learning to teach writing: Does teacher education make a difference?* New York: Columbia University, Teachers College Press.

Kennedy, M., Ball, D., & McDiarmid, G. W. (1993). *A study package for examining and tracking changes in teacher knowledge.* East Lansing: Michigan State University, College of Education, National Center for Research on Teacher Education.

Kirk, D. (1986). Beyond the limits of theoretical discourse in teacher education. *Teaching and Teacher Education, 2,* 155–167.

Kliebard, H. (1973). The question in teacher education. In D. McCarty (Ed.), *New perspectives on teacher education* (pp. 8–24). San Francisco: Jossey-Bass.

Koehler, V. (1985). Research on preservice teacher education. *Journal of Teacher Education, 36*(1), 23–30.

Labaree, D. (2004). *The trouble with ed schools.* New Haven, CT: Yale University Press.

Laczko-Kerr, I., & Berliner, D. (2002). The effectiveness of Teach for America and other under-certified teachers on student academic achievement. *Educational Policy Analysis Archives, 10*(37). Retrieved March 23, 2003, from http://epaa.asu .edu/epaa/v10n37

Lanier, J., & Little, J. W. (1986). Research on teacher education. In M. Wittrock (Ed.), *Handbook of research on teaching* (3rd ed., pp. 527–568). New York: Macmillan.

Liston, D. (1995). Work in teacher education. In N. Shimahara & I. Holowinsky (Eds.), *Teacher education in industrialized nations* (pp. 87–124). New York: Garland.

Liston, D., & Zeichner, K. (1991). *Teacher education and the social conditions of schooling.* New York: Routledge.

Loughran, J., Harris, M. L., Laboskey, V., & Russell, T. (Eds.). (2004). *International handbook of self-study of teaching and teacher education.* Dordrecht, Netherlands: Kluwer.

Maher, F., & Rathbone, C. (1986). Teacher education and feminist theory: Some implications for practice. *American Journal of Education, 94,* 214–235.

McDiarmid, G. W. (1992). *The arts and sciences as preparation for teaching.* East Lansing: Michigan State University, College of Education, National Center for Research on Teacher Learning.

McWilliam, E. (1994). *In broken images: Feminist tales for a different teacher education.* New York: Columbia University, Teachers College Press.

Mitchell, K., Robinson, D., Plake, B., & Knowles, K. (2001). *Testing teacher candidates: The role of licensure tests in improving teacher quality.* Washington, DC: National Research Council.

Morey, A. (2001). The growth of for-profit higher education. *Journal of Teacher Education, 52,* 300–311.

Murnane, R., Singer, J., Willett, J., Kempe, J., & Olsen, R. (1991). *Who will teach: Policies that matter.* Cambridge, MA: Harvard University Press.

National Center for Research on Teacher Education. (1991). *Findings from the Teacher Education and Learning to Teach study (TELT).* East Lansing, MI: Author.

Natriello, G., & Zumwalt, K. (1993). New teachers for urban schools? The contributions of the provisional teacher program in New Jersey. *Education and Urban Society, 26*(1), 49–62.

Peck, R., & Tucker, J. (1973). Research on teacher education. In R. Travers (Ed.), *Handbook of research on teaching* (2nd ed., pp. 940–978). Chicago: Rand McNally.

Popkewitz, T. (Ed.). (1993). *Changing patterns of power: Social regulation and teacher education.* Albany: State University of New York Press.

Popkewitz, T. (1998). *Struggling for the soul: The politics of schooling and the construction of the teacher.* New York: Columbia University, Teachers College Press.

Raymond, M., & Fletcher, S. (2002). The Teach for America evaluation. *Education Next, 2*(1), 62–69.

Shulman, L. (2002). Truth and consequences: Inquiry and policy in research on teacher education. *Journal of Teacher Education, 53,* 248–253.

Steiner, D. (2004). Preparing tomorrow's teachers: An analysis of syllabi from a sample of America's schools of education. In F. Hess, J. Rotherham, & K. Walsh (Eds.), *A quality teacher in every classroom* (pp. 119–148). Cambridge, MA: Harvard Educational Review Press.

Stoddart, T., & Floden, R. (1996). Traditional and alternative routes to teacher certification: Issues, assumptions, and misconceptions. In K. Zeichner, S. Melnick, & M. Gomez (Eds.), *Currents of reform in preservice teacher education* (pp. 80–108). New York: Columbia University, Teachers College Press.

Tom, A. (1987). A critique of the rationale for extended teacher preparation. *Educational Policy, 1*(1), 43–56.

Turner, R. (1975). An overview of research in teacher education. In K. Ryan (Ed.), *Teacher education: 74th yearbook of the National Society for the Study of Education* (pp. 87–110). Chicago: University of Chicago Press.

Valli, L. (1993). Reflective teacher education programs: Analysis of case studies. In J. Calderhead & P. Gates (Eds.), *Conceptualizing reflection in teacher development* (pp. 1–10). London: Falmer.

Villegas, A. M., & Lucas, T. (2002). *Educating culturally responsive teachers.* Albany: State University of New York Press.

Von Schlichten, E. W. (1958). Idea and practice of a fifth-year requirement for teacher certification. *Teachers College Record, 60*(1), 41–53.

Wang, A., Coleman, A., Coley, R., & Phelps, R. (2003). *Preparing teachers around the world.* Princeton, NJ: Educational Testing Service.

Weber, S. (1993). The narrative anecdote in teacher education. *Journal of Education for Teaching, 19*(1), 71–82.

Wideen, M., Mayer-Smith, J., & Moon, B. (1998). A critical analysis of the research on learning to teach. *Review of Educational Research, 68*(2), 130–178.

Wilson, S., & Youngs, P. (2005). Research on accountability processes in teacher education. In M. Cochran-Smith & K. Zeichner (Eds.), *Studying teacher education: The report of the AERA Panel on Research and Teacher Education* (pp. 591–644). Mahwah, NJ: Lawrence Erlbaum.

Zeichner, K. (1988). *Understanding the character and quality of the academic and professional components of teacher education* (Research Report No. 88-1). East Lansing: Michigan State University, College of Education, National Center for Research in Teacher Education.

Zeichner, K. (1999). The new scholarship in teacher education. *Educational Researcher, 28*(9), 4–15.

Zeichner, K. (2003). The adequacies and inadequacies of three current strategies to recruit, prepare, and retain the best teachers for all students. *Teachers College Record, 105,* 490–515.

Zeichner, K. (2005). A research agenda for teacher education. In M. Cochran-Smith & K. Zeichner (Eds.), *Studying teacher education: The report of the AERA Panel on Research and Teacher Education* (pp. 737–760). Mahwah, NJ: Lawrence Erlbaum.

Zeichner, K., & Conklin, H. G. (2005). Teacher education programs. In M. Cochran-Smith & K. Zeichner (Eds.), *Studying teacher education: The report of the AERA Panel on Research and Teacher Education* (pp. 645–736). Mahwah, NJ: Lawrence Erlbaum.

Zeichner, K., & Gore, J. (1990). Teacher socialization. In W. R. Houston (Ed.), *Handbook of research on teacher education* (pp. 329–348). New York: Macmillan.

Zumwalt, K., & Craig, E. (2005a). Teacher characteristics: Research on the demographic profile. In M. Cochran-Smith & K. Zeichner (Eds.), *Studying teacher education: The report of the AERA Panel on Research and Teacher Education* (pp. 111–156). Mahwah, NJ: Lawrence Erlbaum.

Zumwalt, K., & Craig, E. (2005b). Teacher characteristics: Research on the indicators of quality. In M. Cochran-Smith & K. Zeichner (Eds.), *Studying teacher education: The report of the AERA Panel on Research and Teacher Education* (pp. 157–260). Mahwah, NJ: Lawrence Erlbaum.

6

WHAT ARE WE TRIPPING ON?

Transgressing the Fault Lines in Research on the Preparation of Multicultural Educators

CARL A. GRANT

University of Wisconsin–Madison

VONZELL AGOSTO

University of Wisconsin–Madison

An enduring problem in multicultural education over the past 50 years has been the following: How can teacher education programs prepare, train, and/or influence preservice teachers to teach all students effectively? Or, put more simply, how do we prepare preservice teachers to become multicultural educators? The purpose of this chapter is to discuss some of the research in multicultural teacher education that speaks to and, in so doing, participates in the *life* of this enduring problem. The guiding question from which we work and invite readers to consider is as follows: In what direction might other rationales and subsequent lines of inquiry lead the research in multicultural teacher education? Although we pose many questions throughout this essay, all questions lead us back to this guiding question.

The questions we raise in this chapter have come to us through our experiences in teaching college freshmen, our informal conversations with teacher educators, and our review of academic and popular culture books and movies. These experiences, conversations, and reviews continue to present a traditional teacher who is not a multicultural educator. The implications of the absence of the multicultural educator are evident through the education-related practices and expectations that our students exhibit and do not exhibit as well as in preservice teachers' resistance to multicultural education (as reported by multicultural teacher educators).

We contend that "multicultural" does not mean "people of color," that is, all individuals except white people. It is illogical to think that improving the education system so that it well educates more students across a broader spectrum of differences can happen with an approach designed and employed solely by or for people of color when the majority of students, teachers, administrators, and education policymakers are white, not people of color. At some level, this misconception—the absences, the inequities, and our concerns about the quality of education overall—challenge and compel us to ask and respond to the following question: For whom is multicultural education not necessary?

THE WIDESPREAD NEED FOR MULTICULTURAL EDUCATION

Multicultural teacher educators tell us that many preservice teachers plan to return to their racially homogeneous middle- and upper-middle-class communities where students graduate from high school and attend college. Because of these plans, preservice teachers often argue that multicultural education is unnecessary for them or the students in their communities. In other words, preservice teachers suggest that multicultural education is not applicable to their communities now or in the future and, therefore, holds no value for them.

How do we respond to preservice teachers who think that the education system is adequate, that changing it is (and forever will be) outside their realm of influence, that the qualities and borders that frame their communities are fixed, and that what they do in their classes will not have consequences that reverberate across distance and time? Responding to these comments and questions is an expectation we have of multicultural teacher educators. We suggest that these classroom-based interactions, alongside research, are a crucial component in the development of multicultural teacher education.

Because this problem (among others) has not been resolved, many students fail to receive a quality education. A quality education would prepare students to compete for high-quality career opportunities, enjoy and provide a social and leisure lifestyle, contribute to the welfare of the global community, and recognize—as well as combat—the forces (e.g., institutions, systems, organizations, traditions) that forestall the equitable distribution and attainment of these opportunities. The education system consistently fails to provide a quality education, especially for particular groups of students (e.g., students who are economically disadvantaged, (dis)abled, members of particular racial groups, members of particular ethnic groups,

English- (as a second) language learners, and/or recent immigrants). This list is not exhaustive or static. Often excluded from this list of students who do not receive a quality education are those who do receive adequate resources and may or may not fall into one of the aforementioned historically marginalized groups—the "traditional" students. These traditional students tend to fall within the *norms* of the majority population's expectations in terms of compliance, unquestioning acceptance, promptness, attentiveness, health, attractiveness, interests, confidence, ability to prioritize school-related activities (not necessarily education), and reliance on the support of others who have *successfully* navigated the system. These students tend to be white and middle or upper class.

In addition, traditional students tend to create and meet a traditional expectation within this traditional system (e.g., remain seated, ask questions related to the subject matter, do not challenge the teacher's intellectual or ministerial authority, complete assignments promptly, seek permission). These traditional students, both current and former, reinforce the normative expectations that make the education system (for better and/or worse) resistant to rapid and sweeping change. Given the slow pace of systemwide educational change, multicultural education is in its infancy. However, the critical point here is that traditional students are, for the most part, neglected in the discourse around quality education, the rationales for multicultural (teacher) education, and the research. Many of these students become leaders (e.g., executives, deans in schools of education) who perpetuate the system because it appears to have served them well when measured by a narrow gauge of self-sufficiency. We cannot afford to neglect traditional students in our conception, practice, or research in multicultural (teacher) education. Traditional students deserve a quality education as well.

In part as a reaction to the failure of the education system in the United States of (North) America (not Mexico) to educate well its diverse student populations, teacher educators and others since the 1970s have conducted research to inform teacher education programs about how best to prepare teachers to teach students across diverse backgrounds. According to Grant and Zozakiewicz (1995), "Our responsibility is to prepare teachers who can participate in a systemic change effort to help school become the 'great equalizer' and proponent of equity for all students" (p. 272). That these inequities continue alongside newly created ones, despite the rising public attention and efforts of many to further multicultural education, begs us to ask the question: What are we tripping on?

OVERVIEW OF THE CHAPTER

In this chapter, we identify unaddressed questions and analyze research studies in multicultural teacher education to examine how current, neglected, and/or seldom interrogated rationales, lines of inquiry, and practices in research and teaching operate as fault lines or smaller ruptures. In addition, we offer suggestions for future research that builds on the lines of inquiry that studies in multicultural teacher education inspire. We use the term "fault lines" to demonstrate the complexity, tension, and urgency of the problem. Some of the fault lines that the research in multicultural teacher education reveals are embedded in the field, whereas others are superficial, at the level of practice, as isolated and individual actions. We are mainly concerned with the recurring fault lines, whether embedded or superficial. The research in the field provides a lens that captures and makes evident the fault lines that are visible and those that are not. These fault lines operate as breaks, or brakes, in the field and hinder the efforts to prepare and expand the multicultural teaching force. We hope to reveal the fault lines in the field so that workers (as researchers, teacher educators, or preservice teachers) might transgress them and continue on the path toward "producing" a greater number of multicultural educators.

We limit this discussion to researchers, teacher educators, and (preservice) teachers. We draw from conceptual, theoretical, and empirical research in the fields of teacher education and multicultural education. Transgressive, democratic, or emancipatory education, for example, have goals that overlap with multicultural education. However, we limit our survey to research in which the authors explicitly position the research within the field (in connection with multicultural education or diversity education as noted in the titles, abstracts, keywords, or introductions) and thereby directly support multicultural (teacher) education as a field of inquiry.

We recognize that our decision to use this approach limits the scope, and thus the actual representation, of those who identify as multicultural educators. Likewise, the decision of researchers to include or exclude the term "multicultural," in particular, has implications for the future of the field and its associated outcomes. However, we can only speculate about whether the absence of the term or its unprivileged position in a research article is a minor fault line that, over time, quietly serves to dismantle the field.

CONCEPTS IN CONTEXT: DIVERSITY, MULTICULTURALISM, AND SOCIAL JUSTICE

Together, multiculturalism and social justice serve as the conceptual lenses we use to discuss the research and scholarship on preparing multicultural educators to teach across a diversity of student populations. Diversity, as it is commonly expressed and defined in and outside of the academic community, provides the context for our discussion. The following statements situate history, inclusiveness, and the current significance of diversity to the question of how to prepare preservice teachers to become multicultural educators. Parrillo (1996) argues, "Diversity in America has been an ongoing social reality that has gone through many changes in the United States, not since its inception as a nation but even in its primeval colonial cradle" (p. 5). Macedo (2000) states, "Diversity embodies an insistence that no one should be excluded from the American dream of equal justice based upon arbitrary and irrelevant differences of skin color, gender ethnicity, or sexual orientation" (p. 2). In addition, Macedo claims,

> Diversity is the great issue of our time: nationalism, religious sectarianism; a heightened conscious of gender, race, and ethnicity; a greater

assertiveness with respect to sexual orientations; and a reassertion of religious voices in the public square are but a few of the forms of particularity that stubbornly refuse to yield to individualism and cosmopolitanism. (p. 1)

Sacks (2002) suggests that diversity, as an essential aspect of this world, expands our possibilities:

> The world is not a simple machine. It is a complex, interactive ecology in which diversity—biological, personal, cultural, and religious—is of the essence. Any proposed reduction of that diversity through the many forms of fundamentalism that exist today—market, scientific, or religious—would result in a diminution of the rich texture of our sacred life, a potentially disastrous narrowing of the horizons of possibility. (p. 22)

The preceding statements by Parrillo, Macedo, and Sacks help us to understand and appreciate the enduring significance of the question of how to prepare preservice teachers to become multicultural educators as well as why the question has yet to receive a satisfactory response. Currently, diversity is socially palatable as a signifier of difference for those who embrace individuality, whereas multiculturalism (when simplified to mean many cultures) alludes to a mixing of people, which some still find alarming.

Whether understood in its narrowest or broadest sense, multiculturalism stands in opposition to individualism. Individualism supports and promotes a sense of nationalism that ignores the multiplicity of its people's voices and the complexity of their dialogues, which together in tension continue to shape the United States. "The discourse of multiculturalism represents, in part, the emergence of new voices that have generally been excluded from the histories that have defined our national identity" (Giroux, 1996, p. 198). García (1982), Grant (1977), and Frazier (1977) all maintain that multicultural education is "a concept, a framework, a way of thinking, a philosophical viewpoint, a value orientation, and a criteria [sic] for making decisions that better serve the educational needs of culturally diverse student populations" (cited in Banks & Banks, 1995,

pp. 27–28). Although culturally diverse student populations may require more immediate and intensive use of multicultural practices, multicultural education is not an approach, a concept, a framework, an orientation, a criterion, a viewpoint, and/or a way of thinking that exclusively serves the needs of culturally diverse student populations.

The education literature includes different conceptual meanings of multicultural education. Definitions of multicultural education vary widely with respect to content, method, procedure, and referent group orientation. Nevertheless, some multicultural scholars are in close agreement when defining multicultural education. Banks (1993) argues, "Multicultural education is an idea, an educational reform movement, and a process whose major goal is to change the structure of educational institutions" (p. 7). We suggest that multicultural education better serves the needs of students than does education that does not consider the factors that make attributes or positions (e.g., sexuality, ethnicity, language) matter or not matter in ways that shape and define our conditions and, therefore, our lives.

Social justice, as defined by Young (1990), is "the elimination of institutionalized domination and oppression" (p. 15). Social justice goes beyond the mere distribution of benefits (i.e., income and wealth) among the members of a society to an examination of institutional and social relations. It involves the degree to which a society supports the elements necessary for a good life. These general elements are (a) "developing and exercising one's capacities and expressing one's experience" and (b) "participating in determining one's action" (p. 37). Social justice, then, involves the promotion of values of self-development and self-determination for everyone. García (1997) states, "Justice demands equality and fairness in all private transactions, wages, and property ownership, as well as equal opportunity for all to participate in the public benefits generated by society as a whole such as social security, health care, and education" (p. 247).

Cochran-Smith, Davis, and Fries (2004) connect diversity, multiculturalism, and social justice with teacher education, teacher educators, research, and policy as follows:

The strikingly different racial, cultural, and linguistic profiles of the nation's student and teaching populations, coupled with continuing disparities among racial and cultural groups in school achievement and completion rates, poverty levels, and opportunities to learn from qualified teachers, have been highlighted for some time now as a pressing—if not the most pressing—issue for teacher preparation research, practice, and policy. (p. 931)

IDENTIFYING AND EXAMINING FAULT LINES IN RESEARCH: RATIONALES, PROGRAM COMPONENTS, AND RESEARCH PRACTICES

Our purpose here is not to provide a traditional review of the multicultural research literature on teacher education and teacher educators. Instead, we use research literature to illuminate problems in research efforts aimed at addressing this question: How do we prepare multicultural educators? Our discussion does not concentrate on methodological or conceptual issues, nor does it address concerns with the reviews of the literature. Instead, we raise questions to help researchers better capture the complexity of the problems associated with preparing multicultural teacher educators—a complexity that is sometimes overlooked as a result of how researchers explore the topic and report findings.

Even the endeavor of co-authoring often results in the presentation of a unified voice. Rather than completely suppress the moments in which we merged, with difficulty, our ideas or styles into a single statement, we acknowledge that this essay is the result of a complex conversation in which we engage as co-authoring agents and engage with each other, researchers, educators, and the field of multicultural teacher education as a whole.

"How do we prepare multicultural educators?" is a question that takes into account several areas of inquiry: rationales for multicultural education, multicultural teacher education programs, the demographic profile of those who make up the cadre of multicultural teacher educators, and multicultural practices in education and research. Within each of these areas are fault lines.

Fault Lines in Rationales: Increasing Diversity, Reducing Diversity to Race/Ethnicity, and Conflating Race and Ethnicity

There are several major fault lines in the primary rationale used to argue for multicultural teacher education: increasing diversity, reducing diversity to race/ethnicity, and conflating race and ethnicity. Although several rationales supporting the need for multicultural teachers are present throughout the research (e.g., moral, civic), the one that dominates the research is the demographic rationale. Where a research article offers more than one rationale, it is the demographic rationale, rather than another rationale, that appears in the opening paragraph and thus frames the article. In dominating, the demographic rationale obscures the need to provide other rationales, especially those that would suggest that the need for multicultural educators is timeless. What rationale will we offer once the demographic shift occurs? Does the demographic rationale speak to teachers' desires for self in society improvement as well as to their desires for self in society preservation?

Increasing Diversity. The primary rationale in most of the educational literature is a demographic rationale, shift, trend, or imperative suggesting that the numbers of multicultural educators should expand because the student body is becoming more diverse. U.S. census data are used to argue that the increased immigration of students from Asian countries and the increased school enrollment of Latino students increase the need for multicultural education. This rationale positions diversity as a deficit (Ladson-Billings, 1999), whereby diversity is something with which we must contend—a challenge. Pearl (1997) reminds us, "Efforts such as multicultural education and equity pedagogy are used to interrupt notions of deficit thinking but are often 'contaminated by other forms of deficit thinking'" (cited in Brandon, 2003, p. 39).

An alternate line of reasoning might suggest that multicultural teacher education is necessary to expand the repertoire of teacher abilities and transform the teaching force from monolingual/monocultural to a force of multicultural performers who communicate multilingually depending on the students before them. Rather than speak of the demographic shift as something new and something to fear, we might welcome its potential to foster educational reform and broaden our vision of the demographic profile. What does the current and predicted demographic trend mean for educational practice, and what preparation will benefit the incoming generation of teachers? Can this demographic shift challenge researchers to expand the narrow focus on ethnic and/or racial demographic categories as the predominant markers of *diversity*?

Reducing Diversity to Race or Ethnicity. The literature claims that with the increase in student diversity and the homogeneity of the teaching force, there is a racial and/or ethnic mismatch between students and teachers (Fuller, 1992; Gay, Dingus, & Jackson, 2003; Grant & Millar, 1992; Growe, Schmersahl, Perry, & Henry, 2002; Martin, 1995; Oliva & Staudt, 2003). Much of multicultural research in teacher education argues that one of the reasons for the failure of public education to advance some groups of students (e.g., poor students and students of color from particular racial and/or ethnic groups) through secondary education and into higher education as well as it advances white middle-class students stems from the differences between students and their teachers. More generally, researchers attribute the failure to differences between students' and teachers' experiences, expectations of students, and norms associated with their racial and/or ethnic identities (e.g., American Association of Colleges for Teacher Education [AACTE], 1990; Ladson-Billings, 2001).

The multicultural literature argues that multicultural teacher education goes beyond matching teachers' and students' (pre)existing sociocultural experiences. It echoes the position of Gollnick (1992), Villegas (1991), and Zeichner and Hoeft (1996) that all teachers, regardless of their experiences or their students' experiences, must be concerned with the challenge of intercultural communication. If this is so, then must not educators and researchers begin to participate in and learn from heterogeneous communities because they (given the increased recognition of diversity) will most closely resemble the contexts in which students and teachers will become educated? Should a rationale for building a diverse teaching force broaden to consider global demographic trends, including their deeper impact on values, ideas, and daily practices and how they intersect in the lives of students?

Montecinos (2004) states, "Current efforts to diversify the teaching force have concentrated on increasing ethnic diversity as opposed to social class or gender diversity, although the teaching force is also homogeneous on those aspects" (p. 168). For example, the National Council for Accreditation of Teacher Educators (NCATE, 2002) reports that minority teachers comprise less than 15% of the teaching force. The term "minority" is generally used to refer to ethnic and/or racial composition. Thus, other social markers (e.g., social class) are omitted. Also, although race and ethnicity are often at the center of many studies, very few studies include or reveal participants' bi- or multiracial/ethnic identity alone or in combination with other characteristics such as generational and current immigrant status (e.g., Ladson-Billings & Henry, 1990; Ríos & Montecinos, 1999). If we take into account ability, class, gender, language, religion, sexuality, and/or ideology, for example, the teaching force is less diverse than most studies in the field of teacher education purport. Should the focus on race and/or ethnicity continue? The research reports conflicting findings regarding the significance of race and/or ethnicity in teachers' ability and willingness to work well across the student population.

Conflating Race and Ethnicity. It may be noted in passing that many research studies in multicultural education conjoin and conflate race and ethnicity so that they operate as one vein of the demographic shift. A broader demographic rationale recognizes that race and ethnicity are often two very different categories that become more or less (in)significant across time and space and in relation to others. As such, race and/or ethnicity are not always the most salient or prominent aspects that must be considered. Factors such as class and nationality can obfuscate experiences that, in part, become manifest in response to one's racial and/or ethnic identity or position and, thus, fracture the common experience that race and/or ethnicity alone might have engendered. In addition, race and/or ethnicity generate a multiplicity of experiences, needs, and desires to which the education system is increasingly expected to respond.

Ríos and Montecinos (1999) state, "There is evidence suggesting that teacher candidates' ethnicity does matter, with teachers from ethnic groups of color being more likely to endorse approaches to multicultural education with equity and social justice at [their] core" (cited in Montecinos, 2004, p. 173). In addition, Villegas and Clewell (1998) claim that the strengths that teachers of color may bring to the classroom are their knowledge about social/ethnic minority communities and insight into the minority experience in the United States. Gay and colleagues (2003) report that teachers of color are needed to serve as role models and for mainstream students to learn about ethnic, racial, and cultural diversity. Yet in a classic study, Risk (1970/2000) reports how schools help to reinforce the class structure of society as black middle-class teachers stereotype black working-class kindergarteners by placing them in reading groups that reflect their social classes. These studies contend that teachers' racial and/or ethnic identity does not guarantee the willingness or ability to work successfully with particular racial and/or ethnic groups of students (Ríos & Montecinos, 1999). Also, Zeichner and colleagues (1998) contend that cultural knowledge is insufficient in itself and that such knowledge "will have limited payoff unless teachers can translate these insights into pedagogical practices" (p. 167). Investigating where teachers prefer to work, a 1990 study conducted by the AACTE asked preservice teachers whether they preferred to teach in a "majority" (predominantly white) setting or a "minority" (predominantly non-white) setting. The AACTE reports that 80% of blacks, whites, and Latinos, as well as 60% of Asians, indicated a preference for a majority setting (Gomez, 1993). Along another line of inquiry related to race and/or ethnicity, Grant and Secada (1990) ask, "Is there empirical evidence that having teachers of color will positively affect the achievement scores of students of color and help white students to have a positive attitude toward students of color?"

(p. 406). Much of this literature ignores other studies reporting that the mismatch between students' and teachers' race and/or ethnicity might not be a barrier to academic achievement.

The literature also ignores students of color who are becoming teachers. On analyzing 35 published studies pertaining to multicultural teacher education courses in the United States, Montecinos (2004) warns of the scant attention afforded to teachers of color in the research literature. This omission is especially problematic for cultural groups and communities with varied ethnicities and racial identities because the omission does not make visible the nuances of common experiences, beliefs, worldviews, and rituals that inform teaching and learning behaviors.

Some of the salience of the demographic rationale is lost when researchers neglect to disclose the ethnicities of their research participants. Our suggestion is that multicultural education researchers should further disaggregate data according to class, ability, gender, sexual orientation, and other social markers to reveal aspects of diversity. Disaggregating data allows readers to consider how these aspects operate individually or through their intersections to situate and motivate, for example, students and teachers. Disaggregating data also allows for multiple readings and alternate lines of inquiry or reasoning. Narrowing diversity to race and/or ethnicity and gender, for example, allows other aspects of diversity to remain unexamined. Whether teachers' race, social class background, gender, and other social markers significantly contribute to their success in teaching students is a question very much in need of future research.

According to an analysis of research in multicultural education published between 1990 and 2001, Grant, Elsbree, and Fondrie (2004) report that "little research exists in the areas of sexuality, multiethnicity, and religion" (p. 7). Educators often teach students who might not share the same category of sexual identity. Students may identify as straight, lesbian, gay, bisexual, transgendered, queer, intersex, or pansexual (those for whom gender is not the predominant factor that determines the possibility for intimate relations or partnerships). In addition, these same students may identify as members of one or none of these current categories of sexuality, have a fluid sexuality, be questioning their sexual identity, or be in the initial stages of sexual identity formation. As more elementary and middle school students participate in gay–straight alliances and then enter secondary school better prepared to engage in discourse around issues of sexuality, it is likely that their expectations of and demands on teachers will shift. The research on sexuality in multicultural education, and in teacher education in general, is scarce. If the question of whether students' socioeconomic status, ethnicity, and/or language is a critical factor in determining their experiences and relationships with educators, as well as their performance in learning contexts, then should not research also consider whether students' sexuality may also be a critical factor in influencing students' education experience?

Fault Lines in the Program Components: Time, Out-of-School Structures, and Teaching Practices

There are several fault lines related to the research on programs that prepare multicultural teachers. These fault lines in the research range from the amount of time invested in the preparation of teachers to the attention that preparation programs give to informing students about the effect of out-of-school structures on their teaching and teaching practices. Most education programs claim that they can socialize teachers for cultural diversity (Zeichner & Hoeft, 1996). Can this socialization *really* take place? Is time a factor? The educational research literature does not provide a definitive answer. In fact, the research base on this question is thin, and concern about this as a major research question is at best modest.

Time. There is no agreement over the amount of time needed to prepare highly qualified teachers. What we know from the research literature is that the amount of time it takes, and the extent to which teacher education programs can socialize or (re)socialize teachers' practices and attitudes, varies. Research evidence notwithstanding, most traditional university teacher education programs invest 2 years toward

preparing teachers. Some programs, such as Teach for America and Troops to Teachers, contend that spending 2 to 3 years in a teacher preparation program is unnecessary and place their teachers in classrooms after approximately 5 weeks of preparation. Some states (e.g., California) contend that teachers can be prepared in a year once they earn a bachelor's degree.

Currently, there is a lack of attention given to the idea that teacher education programs are needing to re(socialize) students (i.e., prospective teachers) who have spent several prior years envisioning and fashioning their own model of a "teacher." A study of Latina/Latino (Latina/o) high school students in Texas who were participating in a preservice model for recruiting Latina/o students into teaching reports that more than 60% of the students in this program decided to become teachers before 20 years of age (Oliva & Staudt, 2003). These students, as well as other students who follow the more traditional pathways into teaching (2 years of liberal arts before entering a school of education), enter programs with preconceived ideas about the "teachers" they wish to become.

But what perceptions do students have about the teachers they wish to become? How do these perceptions influence their attitudes and behaviors toward teaching students from culturally diverse student population groups? Gomez and Tabachnick (1992) report that changing teachers' perspectives on diverse "others" is a long and labor-intensive process (cited in Gomez, 1993).

The low impact of the teacher preparation program on professional learning, including changing preservice teachers' implicit theories about teaching and being a teacher, is well documented (Flores, 2001; Pataniczek & Isaacson, 1981; Zeichner & Gore, 1990). Flores (2001) studied first-year teachers and concluded,

> Initial teacher education had a weak impact in determining beginning teachers' professional behavior. The teachers in the study referred to the gap between theory and practice and to the inadequate preparation for coping with the daily problems of the school and the classroom, especially as it [sic] regards interaction with students. (p. 138)

McDiarmid (1992) and Sleeter (1992) reached a similar conclusion, namely, that a teacher education program cannot reform in 2 years, on average, the ideas and theories that preservice teachers bring into the program with them.

What happens when preservice teachers bring into the program a level of skill, experience, and sensibility commensurate with the level that the program expects teachers to attain at the end of the program? How might a multicultural teacher education program accommodate its students? Although there are differing opinions about the lengths of time that preservice teachers need to spend in teacher education programs, there appears to be less variation in actual lengths of programs. Might a multicultural teacher education program assess students at multiple points and then determine the need to continue in the program versus completing the program or transitioning from taking a class to teaching a class?

Out-of-School Structures. Another fault line within teacher preparation programs is the lack of attention given to out-of-school structures that influence PK–12 students. Teacher education that is multicultural prepares educators to recognize that students and their learning are not isolated from societal changes. It prepares educators to consider how shifts in the economy affect family structures and community resources and how to assist students in negotiating the incongruence between home culture and school culture.

Yet the vast majority of studies that address multicultural teacher education concentrate on classroom activity. Only a few studies comment on the impact of governmental and nongovernmental regulations on teacher education and on the relationships of multicultural teacher education to the larger social, economic, and political contexts (Cochran-Smith et al., 2004). According to Torres-Guzmán (1992), "Our schools are not equipped to understand how to educate a culturally diverse youth population that finds itself in the midst of social change and must be educated for participation in social change" (p. 488). According to Duesterberg (1998), preservice students need "'more work in identifying the power relations set up by [school] configurations' in their teaching practice" (cited in Grant et al., 2004, p. 21). How might a focus on the examination of structures that sustain inequities rather than on individual attitudes or behaviors influence educators' orientations toward multicultural education?

Teaching Practices. Much research in multicultural teacher education focuses on attitudes and perspectives of preservice teachers. We must keep in mind that attitude is not behavior. Although investigations of preservice teachers' attitudes may serve as a useful preliminary tool to gauge the effectiveness of interventions, further research must investigate the extent to which various attitudes are associated with outcomes such as greater student academic success (Bakari, 2003).

The educational literature also reports that preservice teachers who engage in multicultural education tend to use a human relations approach to the exclusion of other, more progressive approaches during their first year of teaching. The focus of the human relations approach is on helping students from different backgrounds to get along better, encouraging students to help each other and feel good about themselves, and attempting to increase school and social harmony (Grant & Sleeter, 2003). Grant and colleagues (2004) report that in most of the 39 studies on preservice teachers (published between 1990 and 2001) that they reviewed, preservice teachers claimed to employ a human relations approach. Similarly, Ríos and Montecinos (1999) conducted a study of prospective teachers from diverse non-European ethnic backgrounds and found that although 20 of them initially endorsed education that is multicultural and social reconstructionist, only 4 chose this approach when considering how they might address school problems such as curricular tracking. In addition, the use of a conservative approach to multicultural education seems to carry over once preservice teachers receive their teaching licenses and their own classrooms. Fuller (1994) studied 26 recent graduates of a teacher education program with a "social reconstructionist" perspective and concluded that the "monocultural" graduates did not demonstrate "culturally informed" teaching during their first year.

The human relations approach (attitudes) is a problem when one uses it in isolation from other approaches. The reliance of teacher preparation programs on only a human relations approach limits preservice teachers' exposure to other approaches and ultimately the opportunity to see the approaches integrated. The isolated use of the human relations approach does little to challenge the status quo and correct injustices that education perpetuates (e.g., tracking or bias in testing). Beginning teachers and multicultural educators are typically at a disadvantage with the use of multiple approaches because they do not usually have school or community support in place, tenure, or credibility that comes with the reputation of being effective teachers. Ironically, the teaching shortage can offer multicultural teachers who openly challenge the status quo a bit of security when there are not other teachers who are readily available to fill their positions if they lose their jobs. Still, beginning teachers may feel pressured to refrain from using multicultural approaches due to risks (e.g., being outcast, fired). According to García (1997), "Agency for change through social justice requires courageous actions and strength of will in the pursuit of justice. It involves passion or anger, assertiveness, and endurance" (p. 247). We suggest that teachers who intend to combat injustices through education must learn to strategize, subvert, and choose their battles wisely. Thus, researchers must conduct research accordingly.

Fault Lines in Teacher Education Programs

A major fault line within teacher preparation programs involves those who educate preservice teachers, namely, teacher educators. What are the teacher educators' backgrounds, experiences, and understandings of multicultural education? Do the teacher educators have teaching experience and training in multicultural education? The majority of the teacher educators are middle-class, heterosexual, nondisabled, white male and female college graduates who have limited, if any, formal training in multicultural education and whose research and scholarship pay little attention to multicultural education. The research and demographic profile of the corps of teacher educators suggest a lack of diversity across the aforementioned aspects of difference and inexperience in navigating their lives across multiple and intersecting differences. Furthermore, they lack experience in learning and teaching the use of an approach (multicultural) that considers (rather than ignores) the potential for understanding that differences and/or identity positions might instigate. Therefore, few preservice teachers receive a multicultural education. Some of the current teacher educators are the first graduate students of the first generation of multicultural scholars. Because the first generation of multicultural scholars was small (approximately 200 teaching in the 1,200 teacher education programs), the chances of having one of these scholars as an instructor are slim at best.

To understand this rupture in teacher preparation in detail is to realize that even if a preservice teacher does have a multicultural educator, the preservice teacher is probably isolated when attempting to be a multicultural educator. He or she may work in an environment with little collegial support for multicultural education. When we discussed the initial findings that went into preparing this essay at the 2004 annual conference of the National Association of Multicultural Education, several faculty members from across the nation (many of whom are just beginning to teach) reported that they are often assigned to teach large undergraduate classes where students are overly resistant to multicultural education. Many reported that their attempts to help students learn about multicultural education often result in poor teaching evaluations. Chizhik (2003) reports similar reactions. Such an experience, they argue, leads to burnout, the decision to discontinue teaching multicultural education, and ultimately a reduced possibility that these scholars will gain the experience that could lead to improved outcomes or additional research in multicultural education.

Whereas studies conducted by teacher educators offer a firsthand account of the challenges and obstacles that teacher educators face in the classroom, they also reveal how even those teaching and researching in the field of multicultural teacher education can work against what they claim to work toward, namely, the preparation of multicultural teachers. Gay (1995) states,

> Multicultural teacher education theory–practice disparity is not so surprising given that in general the development of multicultural theory has far outstripped the development of multicultural practice, with refinements of theory depending more on proposals for what should be than on conceptualizing the lessons learned from what has been. (cited in Cochran-Smith et al., 2004, p. 934)

Fault Lines in Multicultural Teacher Education Research

There are several fault lines that arise before researchers even begin to generate data: focus on preservice or novice teachers, lack of attention given to diversity within groups, and the consideration of multiple variables and how they compose the (con)text. In multicultural teacher education and research, there is a focus on preservice teachers rather than a balanced research agenda that would include teachers who have been teaching for a number of years.

Focus on Preservice or Novice Teachers. Although several studies follow teachers into the classrooms for up to 2 years following their completion of teacher preparation programs, these studies reveal very little about how multicultural education influences teachers' practice over time or how multicultural educators develop their pedagogical practice over time. We were not able to locate any long-term studies of multicultural teacher educators that follow their practice beyond their fifth year of teaching, that is, as they advance from the novice period to the tenured period.

As Wallace (2000) describes, there are two categories into which teacher educators may be grouped: (1) those who are well versed in multicultural training and (2) those who are relatively new to multicultural training. Obtaining baseline data on preservice teachers' understanding of multicultural education would help to reveal the complexity of preservice teachers' resistance, acceptance, and growth in understanding the philosophy and practices of multicultural education. Longitudinal studies that examine how teachers continue their personal multicultural education training throughout their careers outside of or alongside inservice training may provide insights into how multicultural educators sustain their multicultural focus and use the knowledge and skills they have acquired to see subtle yet transformative acts of multicultural education, whether readily observable or embedded in practice.

"Latinos" in da House! Diversity Within "Cultural Groups." The Latina/o population in the United States grew by 57% from 1990 to 2000 (U.S. Census Bureau, 2001). This growing population promises to continue the problematization, both intentionally and unintentionally, of the rigid boundaries and prominence of race and/or ethnicity on which many studies in multicultural education rely. For example, 42% of Hispanics in the 2000 U.S. census chose "some other race" instead of one race or a combination of the five categories provided: white, black, Asian, American Indian/Alaska Native, or Hawaiian/Pacific Islander (Swarns, 2004). What is unique but not exclusive to this cultural group (writ large) is how their relationships to predominant racial categories vary across Latina/o communities (Wijeyesinghe & Jackson, 2001). The title of Swarns's *New York Times* article, "Hispanics Resist Racial Grouping by Census," reflects a growing trend of a growing population.

Montecinos (2004) argues that in positioning teachers as *ethnic-less,* multicultural teacher education undermines some of the basic principles of multicultural education. For example, neglecting ethnicity casts Latinas/os as a monolithic group instead of as a complex and multifaceted peoples who may choose to identify as Latina/o, Hispano/ic, Chicana/o, Afro-Latina/o, Afro-Caribbean, and so on (or none of these) and from which we might learn new ways of orienting ourselves in the world as and/or among others.

Although discussions of Latina/o identity will not, and should not, move researchers away from ethnicity, they may influence researchers to consider the intersectionality of cultural aspects such as language, religion, and nationality and also move researchers beyond either/or black/white and white/color binaries of race. However, multiethnic and/or multiracial cultural groups such as Latinas/os, Asian Americans, and Cape Verdeans are not isolated from the influence of the social constructions of caste, race, gender, and sexuality or from the internalization of "-ism's" and phobias. Given this, the unchanging profile of the teaching force, and the history of the public school system's failure to educate a diverse population, attention is needed to the question of how a more diverse (including and beyond race and/or ethnicity) teaching force might influence the educational system to serve students across the artificial boundaries of perceived differences.

Growth in the population of individuals who willingly and/or unwillingly identify or are identified as Latina/o may inspire researchers in multicultural (teacher) education to ask different questions. For instance, how can teacher education programs recruit and prepare more Latina/o and non-Latina/o preservice teachers? How can we modify the educational system to benefit students from the *Latina/o diaspora* with a transnational identity, splitting their time between their home country and the United States of (North) America (not Mexico)? How will the anticipated demographic shift toward a majority population of people who can trace their ancestry to Spanish-speaking forebears affect our conceptualization of the Americas? Will we come to view the United States as part of a broader America, that is, as part of rather than separate from Latin America? What educational outcomes will serve our students as territorial borders shift, dissolve, or widen?

Crossing at the Intersections: Transitory Identities. Too few studies have addressed intersecting attributes and aspects of identity or culture (Grant et al., 2004). Even when researchers describe themselves and the subjects of their studies, they tend to discuss their race and/or ethnic backgrounds to the exclusion of other attributes or aspects of their identity. When they discuss other attributes, their discussions are still limited to gender, class, and language (Brandon, 2003). Conceptions of identity as fluid, shifting, or transitory (e.g., hybridity [Bhabha, 1994]; border crossing [Anzaldúa, 1987]; cyborg [Haraway, 1991]) receive little attention in multicultural teacher education. Within these conceptions of identity is an element of strategic negotiation and transgression,

unlike the static and essentialized conceptions of identity present in much of the multicultural teacher education research. Furthermore, studies in multicultural education that refer to identities in transitory terms tend to limit their analysis to the identity or culture of the *teacher,* not the *students.* Where studies refer to transitory identities, they fail to examine how teachers' *hybrid* identities, for example, might shape their practice (e.g., Ladson-Billings & Henry, 1990; Wortham & Contreras, 2002). In neglecting to analyze transitory and multiple identities, researchers miss an opportunity to understand how teachers or students might imitate or create alternative behaviors with the intention of developing a repertoire of teaching performances. Would our teaching force reinvent itself given the expectation that teachers can and should perform multiple identities at will?

Perhaps this gap in the research of teachers' transitory identities is in part reflective of the "limited empirical evidence linking age and ethnic identity achievement," especially for individuals over 21 years of age (Ontai-Grzebik & Raffaelli, 2004, p. 562). Within this statement are several assumptions that contrast the idea of continuous (transitory/shifting/fluid) identity (re)development and that are worth pursuing before researchers embark on investigating the link between, for example, age and ethnic identity achievement. These assumptions are that development of a stable identity position is an achievement, identity (re)development comes with age rather than through various factors that have little to do with age, and identity development is a series of stages that culminate in adulthood rather than a lifelong series of processes.

Instead, we might understand identity (re)development as a broad spectrum of behaviors or conditions rather than automatically relegating it to the extreme designation of identity crises. At least, we should question how our investment in stability and order (as evident in research and educational practices in general) expands and/or limits our expectations of teachers, students, and teacher educators. Haberman (1991) argues that prospective teachers who are engaged in developing their own identities constitute a weakness in teacher reform. On the contrary, we suggest that teachers' engagement in identity development may be beneficial. We suggest that there is a great difference between engagement and consumption. In addition, Haberman suggests that mature people with diverse life and work experience may be better suited to address the serious challenges facing youth such as poverty and racism. Rather than read Haberman's two statements as built on one another, we separate his suggestion that experience is a teaching asset from his argument that recruiting and training teachers undergoing identity development is a weakness in teacher education. We suggest that multicultural teacher education would benefit from recruiting and training teachers who have a broad range of experiences as well as the ability to consider, engage, and (re)develop their own identities.

Multicultural teachers draw on components of students' (sub)cultures as well as intersecting aspects of identity. At the same time, they recognize that students function as individuals with varying degrees of membership in social groups and in response to multiple influences. Future research in multicultural teacher education should consider the intersectionalities of attributes and aspects of identity as entry points from which we position ourselves as educators, students, and researchers in the process of understanding how concurring acts of negotiation among intervening factors of power, economy, politics, time, and history influence the decisions that educators, students, and researchers make. These fuzzy areas—the borders around categories—can trouble our research and our thinking about who teachers and students are and who they become in the moments they negotiate the terrains of their classrooms.

Revealing how attributes of identity, aspects of culture, and social factors intersect and become prominent at different times in different ways with different consequences for different students makes it difficult for educators and researchers to rely too much on static descriptions of students. This complexity most accurately reflects the daily classroom. Those who aspire to become educators will take from this an understanding that teaching, learning, and producing quality research are not simple practices. When multiple and intersecting aspects of

identity are considered (e.g., race, ethnicity, sexuality, class, gender, religion/spirituality, age, (dis)ability, language) alongside notions of fluidity, hybridity, intragroup variability, and social factors, one begins to see how daunting a task it would be to prepare "types" of teachers to work with "types" of students. Rather than preparing teachers how to teach particular groups of students (them), we might begin to envision teacher education as preparing society to teach "multiculturally." To teach multiculturally involves engaging in a continual process in relation to other processes (e.g., culture).

Hidden in (the Con)Texts. According to Trueba and Wright (1992),

> Context is a dynamic, interactional notion and is understood as a determinant of human behavior. The context of classroom interactions is not a static set of situations devoid of persons interacting or the physical and human surroundings alone. Context consists primarily of individuals interacting and, by their interaction, defining the function and meaning of an interactional event. More specifically, a context is constituted by an accumulation of linguistic, paralinguistic, and kinesic features and proxemic shifts. (pp. 327–328)

Are particular settings conducive to the maintenance of unequal power relations, professionalism, and formal authority? Can we open avenues for multicultural education and research by changing the setting and the focus of our observations? In multicultural teacher education research, there is not much variation in the contexts in which preservice teachers are prepared. Moreover, the researched experiences of classroom teachers are often limited to the classroom. Physical contexts that multicultural researchers and educators seldom explore are workshops, computer labs, and academic club meetings. Perhaps these contexts are more culturally compatible or conducive to the use of (multi)culturally relevant pedagogy. Few studies in the literature on multicultural education examine how intangible factors structure learning experiences (e.g., the structure and use of time) and how their alteration might positively affect the educational experiences for a broader range of students.

Future research in multicultural education and teacher education programs might consider how switching (con)texts can alter the dimensions and dynamics of the social, epistemological, and power structures to shape the learning environment. Linking the investigation of classroom practice to, for instance, the structures of time and space that govern classroom choices, both directly and indirectly, will move multicultural teacher education research toward new questions. For instance, the theme of socio-spatiotemporality surfaces in Wortham and Contreras's (2002) observation of a bilingual classroom. The teacher in this study adjusted the socio-spatiotemporal structures of the classroom to reflect the learning styles and social patterns of her Spanish-speaking students. González (2002) outlines three cultural systems in a discussion of campus climate: (1) the social world, (2) the physical world, and (3) the epistemological world. Such an analysis reveals how one's opportunities for learning extend beyond the social and how the social is dimensional. González considers how physical structures, as part of the campus climate, shaped Chicana/o students' college experience. According to Grant and colleagues (2004), there continues to be a lack of research into the physical environments of schools.

In addition, "attempts to identify best practices for multicultural teacher education need to consider the impact of multiple social dimensions" (Montecinos, 2004, p. 168). To use a person-centered, experiential, and relational way of thinking about researching and writing about the everyday experience of multiculturalism or "narrative multiculturalism," Phillion (2002) suggests that researchers immerse themselves in the classroom so as to experience and absorb the "patterns" and "rhythms" of the classroom life and be more experiential than theoretical. As Phillion reports, "I learned to be more present with Pam [the teacher], more like a sponge, soaking up what was around me" (p. 272). Socialization occurred between the researcher and students as well. Phillion writes, "As I interacted with Pam and her students, my traditional notions of what was best for immigrant and minority children were shattered" (p. 275). Multicultural education is in part about socialization, yet researchers seldom consider how interactions among educators contribute to their practice as multicultural educators.

Multicultural educators and researchers should seek to understand how people get along in the world as they experience it and how the dimensions and facets of life become more or less pronounced within changing (con)texts and resources such as time and space. Multicultural teacher education and research can benefit from studies that acknowledge and reflect the complexities and challenges involved in the preparation of the next generation of educators. These educators will likely encounter within their classrooms and throughout their workdays diverse household arrangements, parental ages, socially acceptable lifestyles, cross-cultural alliances, and students who might describe themselves by using words with varying prefixes such as multilinguistic, intersex, and transnational. Regardless of students' attitudes, classes, identities, and cultures, there is a common goal that should guide teachers, teacher educators, and teacher training programs, namely, that all teachers should know "various procedures they can use to acquaint themselves with the specific students in their future classes" (Zeichner et al., 1998, p. 167). "Above all, they should know how to utilize the surroundings, physical and social, that exist so as to extract from them all they have to contribute to building up experiences that are worthwhile" (Parkay, 1983, p. 209). "Multicultural teacher education programs should therefore assist prospective teachers to develop a repertoire of instructional approaches that include skills in direct instruction, inquiry methods, and cooperative learning (e.g., group projects, peer centers, reciprocal teaching)" (Villegas, 1991, cited in Zeichner et al., 1998, p. 168).

Promoting Praxis: A Research-Informed Vision

A common concern evident throughout the research is how to reflect in practice what is anchored in theory. For example, how do we educate across diversity using differences as contributors to success? Whether one is teaching preservice teachers, reporting research findings, designing research, or posing questions, scholars need some vision of good practice. In the Multicultural Preservice Teacher Education Project, Zeichner and colleagues (1998) outline a vision of good practice. The design principles are organized into three main categories that emphasize issues of (1) institutional and programmatic reform, (2) personnel (staff and students), and (3) curriculum and instruction in teacher education programs. As a whole, these principles offer a lens through which researchers can analyze research and teaching in multicultural teacher education. These design principles are not prescriptive or formulaic; rather, they serve as a guide that provides educators at all levels with a means to self-check and activate warning signs while developing a common language from which educators can join forces. Mysteriously, as of October 2004, Zeichner and colleagues' article had been cited in only 11 subsequent articles.

The design principles are as follows:

1. The mission, policies, and procedures of the institution reflect the values of diversity and multicultural education.

2. The institution is committed to multicultural teacher education.

3. The teacher education program is a living example of multicultural education.

4. Admissions requirements to the teacher education program include multicultural criteria as well as academic criteria.

5. Faculty, staff, and supervisors are committed to and competent in multicultural teacher education.

6. Multicultural perspectives permeate the entire teacher education curriculum, including general education courses and those in academic subject matter areas.

7. The program fosters the understanding that teaching and learning occur in sociopolitical contexts that are not neutral but rather are based on relations of power and privilege.

8. The program is based on the assumption that all students in elementary and secondary schools bring knowledge, skills, and experiences that should be used as resources in teaching and learning and that high expectations for learning are held for all students.

9. The program teaches prospective teachers how to learn about students, families, and communities as well as how to use knowledge of culturally diverse students' backgrounds in planning, delivering, and evaluating instruction.

10. The program helps prospective teachers to reexamine their own and others' multiple and interrelated identities.

11. The program provides carefully planned and varied field experiences that explore sociocultural diversity in schools and communities.

12. The program helps prospective teachers to develop the commitment to be change agents who work to promote greater equity and social justice in schooling and society.

13. The program teaches prospective teachers how to change power and privilege in multicultural classrooms.

14. The program draws on and validates multiple types and sources of knowledge.

The process of outlining these principles involved a collaborative process of multiple steps that included a literature review, peer evaluation, public presentation, and feedback. This process aligns with the 14th principle of Zeichner and colleagues (1998), which emphasizes drawing on and validating multiple types and sources of knowledge. For the same reason why Abt-Perkins, Hauschildt, and Dale (2000) suggest that multicultural supervisors should collaborate, so should researchers. Research conducted by partners or teams fosters socialization and allows for the filter of differing, similar, and common opinions/perspectives. Abt-Perkins and colleagues emphasize the importance of collaboration in studies of supervision practices. They state, "Only such conversations will allow us to find our blind spots and silences" (p. 47).

The challenges and obstacles in conducting research are similar to those affecting the preparation of multicultural educators. The (over)-use of a (narrow) demographic rationale, the overuse and isolated use of a human relations approach, the avoidance of the structural (including power relations and their effects), and the use of a narrow lens to observe multicultural education are some of the fault lines that work against the preparation of multicultural educators and ultimately their formation into a critical mass. In what direction might other rationales and subsequent lines of inquiry lead multicultural teacher education? How long will the education community continue to face the challenges of preparing multicultural educators before co-optation, for example, makes it unfashionable and/or unprofitable? Finally, how long will society permit this question to remain an enduring unresolved problem?

CROSSING INTO THE NEXT MOMENT

To be sure, assessing multicultural education requires longer periods of observation across time in place of the periodic and episodic observations that generally feed our understanding of what teacher educators and their preservice teachers are doing in classrooms. In addition to asking whether someone is, or is not, practicing multicultural education, we might ask the question: To what extent? This question does not require an either/or response. In contrast, the question allows multicultural educators and researchers to assess their practice, for instance, in terms of the depth and breadth with which they demonstrate an integrated approach to multicultural education and the extent to which their multicultural practice is evident throughout time and their spheres of influence.

Multicultural education proposes that we examine what is invisible, covert, hidden, embedded, and often entangled in the obvious such as the identifiers we impose or reinscribe (e.g., Latina/o, people of color, white, (dis)-abled, female). It asks that we look deeply and broadly at lives and learning environments and speak of their complexities, multiple factors, and subject–object positions and, at the same time, question what, how, and why we see and speak what we do. Instances of researchers examining cross-/intercultural, -ethnic, and -racial relations may increase as the borders of single-group affiliation, social constructions,

disciplines, and geographic regions become porous and blur. Likewise, discussions of cultural groups should include the multiple ways in which members of groups align and realign over time given any number of intervening, imposing, and/or influencing conditions.

Multicultural teachers and educators should strive for robust images of "students" and "teachers" (images they intend to create or imitate for themselves or to locate in others). Furthermore, educators and researchers should integrate and incorporate multicultural education into their lives as a way of learning or understanding the world. An understanding of teaching recognizes that teaching involves continuous negotiation among intervening factors. Understanding teaching as a complex endeavor can offer a richer (con)text for preparing multicultural educators and researching multicultural teacher education. According to Grant and Zozakiewicz (1995), "It is essential that student teachers come to conceive of multicultural education as an integral and embedded part of teaching and schools; every decision, action, assignment, organizational structure, and communicative act works either toward or against the goals of multicultural education" (p. 272). Multicultural teachers, educators, and researchers must learn to recognize multicultural education in practice. This includes being able to analyze the hidden curriculum for its presence as well as the presence of the inequitable practices that it challenges. Assessing multicultural educators requires assessors for whom the lens of multicultural education is wide and telescopic.

Perhaps some educators and researchers have a limited understanding of multicultural education and its nuances. Multicultural education in practice may be grossly underrepresented in the research. Even if there are failed attempts to capture and represent in the research instances of multicultural practice, we suggest that these failed attempts are not commonplace. The teacher educators' reports of resistance among incoming preservice teachers signal that multicultural education—as a philosophy or practice (if provided)—is not internalized, embraced, or understood by preservice teachers during their PK–12 schooling. Doubts over representation call attention to the responsibility of researchers to capture and report multicultural education in practice—even when multicultural education is not the focus. Research of this kind not only will offer a truer estimate of multicultural education and educators but also will help us to understand that such practice is possible, that certain conditions make such practice possible, and that the practice and its conditions are directly and indirectly observable. These revelations move us closer to asking how.

If we submit that multicultural teacher education derives from multicultural education, then it is reasonable to suggest that the research that drives both of them should also reflect the principles of multicultural education. Researchers in the field should also analyze how they, as cultural beings operating within structures and social relations that govern their possibilities, are implicated within their studies and ultimately affect the training, preparation, and knowledge base of teacher educators, as well as preservice and inservice teachers. Researchers should also have a complex model for interrogating their practice. According to Denzin and Lincoln (2000), we are crossing into the seventh moment in social science:

> In the seventh moment, the means (methods) of social science are developed, refined, and cherished for their contributions to communities characterized by respectful and loving difference, social justice, and equal access to material, social, educational, and cultural capital (the ends of ethnography). (p. 1062)

The direction of social science research, as described by Denzin and Lincoln (2000) in the preceding excerpt, aligns ideologically with the philosophy of multicultural education. That is, researchers have available multiple strategies of inquiry and perspectives that are congruent with the aims of multicultural teacher education. Multiple strategies may be exactly what we need to help us chase the moving targets of cultural competency or cultural literacy. In part "because teachers have no alternative but to be responsive to the human world, a world continuously marked by change," the task of articulating the nature of teaching is ongoing (Hansen, 2004, p. 142). Regardless of the strategies chosen, may our actions be in combination

with "cultural humility" (S. Kapani, personal communication, October 29, 2004) while keeping in mind that multicultural education is for everyone or no one.

REFERENCES

Abt-Perkins, D., Hauschildt, P., & Dale, H. (2000). Becoming multicultural supervisors: Lessons from a collaborative field study. *Journal of Curriculum and Supervision, 16*(1), 28–47.

American Association of Colleges for Teacher Education. (1990). *AACTE/Metropolitan Life Survey of Teacher Education Students.* Washington, DC: Author.

Anzaldúa, G. (1987). *Borderlands/La frontera: The new mestiza.* San Francisco: Aunt Lute Books.

Bakari, R. (2003). Preservice teachers' attitudes toward teaching African American students: Contemporary research. *Urban Education, 38,* 640–654.

Banks, J. (1993). Approaches to multicultural curriculum reform. In J. Banks & C. A. M. Banks (Eds.), *Multicultural education: Issues and perspectives* (2nd ed., pp. 195–214). Boston: Allyn & Bacon.

Banks, J. A., & Banks, C. A. (Eds.). (1995). *Handbook of research on multicultural education.* New York: Macmillan.

Bhabha, H. K. (1994). *The location of culture.* New York: Routledge.

Brandon, W. W. (2003). Toward a white teacher's guide to playing fair: Exploring the cultural politics of multicultural teaching. *Qualitative Studies in Education, 16*(1), 31–50.

Chizhik, E. W. (2003). Reflecting on the challenges of preparing suburban teachers for urban schools. *Education in Urban Society, 35,* 443–461.

Cochran-Smith, M., Davis, D., & Fries, K. (2004). Multicultural teacher education: Research, practice, and policy. In J. Banks & C. A. McGee-Banks (Eds.), *Handbook of research on multicultural education* (2nd ed., pp. 931–975). San Francisco: Jossey-Bass.

Denzin, N. K., & Lincoln, Y. S. (2000). *Handbook of qualitative research* (2nd ed.). Thousand Oaks, CA: Sage.

Duesterberg, L. (1998). Rethinking culture in the pedagogy and practices of preservice teachers. *Teaching and Teacher Education, 14,* 497–512.

Flores, M. A. (2001). Person and context in becoming a new teacher. *Journal of Education for Teaching, 27,* 135–148.

Frazier, L. (1977). The multicultural facet of education. *Journal of Research and Development in Education, 11,* 10–16.

Fuller, M. L. (1992). Teacher education programs and increasing minority school populations: An educational mismatch? In C. A. Grant (Ed.), *Research and multicultural education: From the margins to the mainstream* (pp. 184–200). Washington, DC: Falmer.

Fuller, M. L. (1994). The monocultural graduate in the multicultural environment: A challenge for teacher educators. *Journal of Teacher Education, 45,* 269–277.

García, R. L. (1982*). Teaching in a pluralistic society: Concepts, models, strategies.* New York: Harper & Row.

García, S. S. (1997). Social justice. In C. A. Grant & G. Ladson-Billings (Eds.), *Dictionary of multicultural education.* Phoenix, AZ: Oryx.

Gay, G. (1995). Curriculum theory and multicultural education. In J. A. Banks & C. A. McGee-Banks (Eds.), *Handbook of research on multicultural education* (pp. 25–43). New York: Macmillan.

Gay, G., Dingus, J. E., & Jackson, C. (2003). *The presence and performance of teachers of color in the profession.* Available: www.community-teachers.org

Giroux, H. A. (1996). *Fugitive cultures: Race, violence, and youth.* New York: Routledge.

Gollnick, D. (1992). Multicultural education: Policies and practices in teacher education. In C. A. Grant (Ed.), *Research and multicultural education* (pp. 218–239). Washington, DC: Falmer.

Gomez, M. L. (1993). Prospective teachers' perspectives on teaching diverse children: A review with implications for teacher education and practice. *Journal of Negro Education, 62,* 459–474.

Gomez, M. L., & Tabachnick, B. R. (1992). Telling teaching stories. *Teaching Education, 4,* 129–138.

González, K. P. (2002). Campus culture and the experiences of Chicano students in a predominantly white university. *Urban Education, 37,* 193–218.

Grant, C. A. (1977). *Multicultural education: Commitments, issues, and applications.* Washington, DC: Association for Supervision and Curriculum Development.

Grant, C. A., Elsbree, R. A., & Fondrie, S. (2004). A decade of research on the changing terrain of multicultural research. In J. A. Banks & C. A. McGee-Banks (Eds.), *Handbook of multicultural education* (2nd ed., pp. 1–70). San Francisco: Jossey-Bass.

Grant, C. A., & Millar, S. (1992). Research and multicultural education: Barriers, needs, and boundaries. In C. A. Grant (Ed.), *Research and multicultural education: From the margins to the mainstream* (pp. 7–18). London: Falmer.

Grant, C. A., & Secada, W. G. (1990). Preparing teachers for diversity. In W. R. Houston (Ed.), *Handbook of research on teacher education: A project of the Association of Teacher Educators* (pp. 403–422). New York: Macmillan.

Grant, C. A., & Sleeter, C. E. (2003). *Turning on learning: Five approaches to multicultural teaching plans for race, class, gender, and disability* (3rd ed.). New York: John Wiley.

Grant, C. A., & Zozakiewicz, C. A. (1995). Student teachers, cooperating teachers, and supervisors: Interrupting the multicultural silences of student teaching. In J. M. Larkin & C. E. Sleeter (Eds.), *Developing multicultural teacher education curricula* (pp. 259–278). New York: State University of New York Press.

Growe, R., Schmersahl, K., Perry, R., & Henry, R. (2002). A knowledge base for cultural diversity in administrator training. *Journal of Instructional Psychology, 29,* 205–212.

Haberman, M. (1991). The rationale for training adults as teachers. In C. E. Sleeter (Ed.), *Empowerment through multicultural education* (pp. 275–286). Albany: State University of New York Press.

Hansen, D. T. (2004). A poetics of teaching, *Educational Theory, 54*(2), 119–142.

Haraway, D. (1991). *Simians, cyborgs, and women: The reinvention of nature.* New York: Routledge.

Ladson-Billings, G. (1999). Preparing teachers for diverse student populations: A critical race theory perspective. In A. Iran-Nejad & D. Pearson (Eds.), *Review of research in education* (Vol. 24, pp. 211–248). Washington, DC: American Educational Research Association.

Ladson-Billings, G. (2001). *Crossing over to Canaan: The journey of new teachers in diverse classrooms.* San Francisco: Jossey-Bass.

Ladson-Billings, G., & Henry, A. (1990). Blurring the borders: Voices of African liberatory pedagogy in the United States and Canada. *Journal of Education, 172*(2), 72–88.

Macedo, S. (2000). *Diversity and distrust: Civic education in a multicultural democracy.* Cambridge, MA: Harvard University Press.

Martin, R. J. (Ed.). (1995). *Practicing what we teach: Confronting diversity in teacher education.* Albany: State University of New York Press.

McDiarmid, G. W. (1992). What to do about differences? A study of multicultural education for teacher trainees in the Los Angeles Unified School District. *Journal of Teacher Education, 43*(2), 83–93.

Montecinos, C. (2004). Paradoxes in multicultural teacher education research: Students of color positioned as objects while ignored as subjects. *International Journal of Qualitative Studies in Education, 17*(2), 167–181.

National Council for Accreditation of Teacher Educators. (2002). *Professional Standards for the Accreditation of Schools, Colleges, and Departments of Education.* Available: www.ncate.org/2000/unit_stnds_2002.pdf

Oliva, M., & Staudt, K. (2003). Pathways to teaching: Latino student choice and professional identity development in a teacher training magnet program. *Equity & Excellence, 36,* 270–279.

Ontai-Grzebik, L. L., & Raffaelli, M. (2004). Individual and social influences on ethnic identity among Latino young adults. *Journal of Adolescent Research, 19,* 550–575.

Parkay, F. W. (1983). *White teacher, black school: The professional growth of ghetto teacher.* New York: Praeger.

Parrillo, V. (1996). *Diversity in America.* Thousand Oaks, CA: Pine Forge.

Pataniczek, D., & Isaacson, N. (1981). The relationship of socialization and the concerns of beginning secondary teachers. *Journal of Teacher Education, 32*(3), 14–17.

Pearl, A. (1997). Democratic education as an alternative to deficit thinking. In R. R. Valencia (Ed.), *The evolution of deficit thinking* (pp. 211–241). London: Falmer.

Phillion, J. (2002). Narrative multiculturalism, *Journal of Curriculum Studies, 34,* 265–279.

Ríos, F., & Montecinos, C. (1999). Advocating social justice and cultural affirmation: Ethnically diverse preservice teachers' perspectives on multicultural education. *Equity and Education, 32*(3), 66–76.

Risk, R. C. (2000). Student social class and teacher expectations: The self-fulfilling prophecy in ghetto education. *Harvard Educational Review, 70,* 266–301. (Original work published in 1970)

Sacks, J. (2002). *The dignity of difference: How to avoid the clash of civilizations.* London: Continuum.

Sleeter, C. E. (1992). Restructuring schools for multicultural education. *Journal of Teacher Education, 43*(2), 141–148.

Swarns, R. L. (2004, October 24). Hispanics resist racial grouping by census. *The New York Times.* Available: www.nytimes.com/2004/10/24/national/24census.html

Torres-Guzmán, M. E. (1992). Stories of hope in the midst of despair: Culturally responsive education for Latino students in an alternative high school in New York City. In M. Saravia-Shore & S. F. Arvizu (Eds.), *Cross-cultural literacy: Ethnographies of communication in multiethnic classrooms* (pp. 477–490). New York: Garland.

Trueba, H. T., & Wright, P. G. (1992). On ethnographic studies and multicultural education. In M. Saravia-Shore & S. F. Arvizu (Eds.), *Cross-cultural literacy: Ethnographies of communication in multiethnic classrooms* (pp. 299–490). New York: Garland.

U.S. Census Bureau. (2001). *Hispanic population in the United States: Current population reports, population characteristics.* Washington, DC: Government Printing Office. Available: www.census.gov/population/cen2000/phc-t1/tab04.pdf

Villegas, A. M. (1991). *Culturally responsive pedagogy for the 1990's and beyond.* Princeton, NJ: Educational Testing Service.

Villegas, A. M., & Clewell, B. C. (1998). Increasing teacher diversity by tapping the paraprofessional pool. *Theory Into Practice, 37*(2), 121–130.

Wallace, B. C. (2000). Call for change in multicultural training at graduate schools of education: Educating to end oppression and for social change. *Teachers College Record, 102,* 1086–1111.

Wijeyesinghe, C. L., & Jackson, B. W. (2001). *New perspectives on racial identity development: A theoretical and practical anthology.* New York: New York University Press.

Wortham, S., & Contreras, M. (2002). Struggling toward culturally relevant pedagogy in the Latino diaspora. *Journal of Latinos and Education, 1*(2), 133–144.

Young, I. M. (1990). *Justice and the politics of difference.* Princeton, NJ: Princeton University Press.

Zeichner, K. M., & Gore, J. M. (1990). Teacher socialization. In W. R. Houston (Ed.), *Handbook of research in teacher education* (pp. 329–348). New York: Macmillan.

Zeichner, K. M., Grant, C., Gay, G., Gillette, M., Valli, L., & Villegas, A. M. (1998). A research informed vision of good practice in multicultural teacher education: Design principles. *Theory Into Practice, 37*(2), 163–171.

Zeichner, K. M., & Hoeft, K. (1996). Teacher socialization for cultural diversity. In J. Sikula, T. J. Buttery, & E. Guyton (Eds.), *Handbook on teacher education: A project of the Association of Teacher Educators* (2nd ed., pp. 525–547). New York: Simon & Schuster.

FURTHER READING

Ball, A. (2000). Empowering pedagogies that enhance the learning of multicultural students. *Teachers College Record, 102,* 1006–1034.

Banks, J. A., & Banks, C. A. (1993). *Multicultural education: Issues and perspectives* (2nd ed.). Boston: Allyn & Bacon.

Banks, J. A., & Banks, C. A. (Eds.). (2004). *Handbook of research on multicultural education* (2nd ed.). San Francisco: Jossey-Bass.

Bennett, C. (2001). Genres of research in multicultural education. *Review of Educational Research, 71*(2), 171–217.

Britzman, D. (1991). *Practice makes practice: A critical study of learning to teach.* Albany: State University of New York Press.

Cochran-Smith, M. (1991). Learning to teach against the grain. *Harvard Educational Review, 61,* 279–310.

Cockrell, K. S., Placier, P. L., Cockrell, D. H., & Middleton, J. N. (1999). Coming to terms with "diversity" and "multiculturalism" in teacher education: Learning about our students, changing our practice. *Teaching and Teacher Education, 15,* 351–366.

Ellis, C. (2004). *The ethnographic I: A methodological novel about autoethnography.* Walnut Creek, CA: AltaMira.

Garmon, M. A. (2004). Changing preservice teachers' attitudes/beliefs about diversity: What are the critical factors? *Journal of Teacher Education, 55,* 201–213.

Gay, G. (2004). Curriculum theory and multicultural education. In J. A. Banks & C. A. Banks (Eds.), *Handbook of research on multicultural education* (2nd ed., pp. 25–43). San Francisco: Jossey-Bass.

Grant, C. A., & Ladson-Billings, G. (Eds.). (1997). *Dictionary of multicultural education.* Phoenix, AZ: Oryx.

Growe, R., Schmersahl, K., Perry, R., & Henry, R. (2002). A knowledge base for cultural diversity in administrator training. *Journal of Instructional Psychology, 29,* 205–212.

Hidalgo, N. M., Siu, S., & Epstein, J. L. (2004). Research on families, schools, and communities: A multicultural perspective. In J. A. Banks & C. A. McGee-Banks (Eds.), *Handbook of research on multicultural education* (2nd ed., pp. 631–655). San Francisco: Jossey-Bass.

Jennings, L. B., & Smith, C. P. (2002). Examining the roles of critical inquiry for transformative practices: Two joint case studies of multicultural education. *Teachers College Record, 104,* 456–481.

Kiang, P. N. (2004). Linking strategies and interventions in Asian American Studies to K–12 classrooms and teacher preparation. *International Journal of Qualitative Studies in Education, 17,* 199–225.

Ladson-Billings, G. (1995). But that's just good teaching! The case for culturally relevant pedagogy. *Theory Into Practice, 34*(3), 159–165.

LeCompte, M. (2002). The transformation of ethnographic practice: Past and current challenges. *Qualitative Research, 2,* 283–299.

Montecinos, C. (1995). Multicultural teacher education for a culturally diverse teaching force. In R. J. Martin (Ed.), *Practicing what we teach: Confronting diversity in teacher education* (pp. 97–116). Albany: State University of New York Press.

Nieto, S. (2000). *Affirming diversity: The sociopolitical context of multicultural education* (3rd ed.). New York: Longman.

Olmedo, I. M. (2004). Raising transnational issues in a multicultural curriculum project. *Urban Education, 39,* 241–265.

Saravia-Shore, M., & Arvizu, S. F. (Eds.). (1992). *Cross-cultural literacy: Ethnographies of communication in multiethnic classrooms.* New York: Garland.

Sleeter, C. E., & Grant, C. A. (1987). An analysis of multicultural education in the United States. *Harvard Educational Review, 57,* 421–444.

Sleeter, C. E., & McLaren, P. (1995). Introduction: Exploring connections to build a critical multiculturalism. In C. Sleeter & P. McLaren (Eds.), *Multicultural education, critical pedagogy, and the politics of difference* (pp. 5–32). Albany: State University of New York Press.

Speght, S. L., & Vera, E. M. (2004). A social justice agenda: Ready or not? *The Counseling Psychologist, 32*(1), 109–118.

Valencia, R. R. (1997). *The evolution of deficit thinking.* London: Falmer.

Wallace, B. C. (2000). Call for change in multicultural training at graduate schools of education: Educating to end oppression and for social justice. *Teachers College Record, 102,* 1086–1111.

Weiner, L. (1993). *Preparing teachers for urban schools: Lessons from thirty years of school reform.* New York: Columbia University, Teachers College Press.

7

MOVING FORWARD

Ideas for Research on School, Family, and Community Partnerships

JOYCE L. EPSTEIN

Johns Hopkins University

STEVEN B. SHELDON

Johns Hopkins University

I t is a social fact that children learn and grow at home, at school, and in the community. People in these three contexts affect children's learning and development, for better or for worse, from infancy through the school years and beyond. This important reality often is ignored by researchers who study only schools or only families. Educators also may focus only on the school curriculum, instruction, or testing without giving attention to students' families and communities, as if students were not also children, friends, and neighbors.

Increasingly, research and exemplary practice reveal that it is all but impossible to separate the interests and influences of educators, parents, and other educational partners on student achievement, attitudes, and behaviors. Although it is, admittedly, harder to study more than one setting at a time, it is critical for researchers to recognize the simultaneous and cumulative effects of home, school, and community on student development. It is, therefore, imperative that we "think new" about research on school, family, and community partnerships.

The field of school, family, and community partnerships is a young field of study compared with other educational research topics. Knowledge has grown over the past 25 years with sharper theory, expanded research questions, improved methods of analysis, and the interest and efforts of educators and policy leaders. Advances have been made by researchers across disciplines, and across countries, using varied methodologies to study the nature and effects of school programs and family involvement at different grade levels and in diverse communities. Many publications have summarized the results of research, documented progress in programs

AUTHORS' NOTE: This research was supported by a grant from NICHD. The opinions expressed are the authors' and might not represent the policies or positions of the funding agency.

and in policies of parental involvement, and pressed for more and better studies (Boethel, 2003; Booth & Dunn, 1995; Castelli, Mendel, & Ravn, 2003; Chavkin, 1993; Christenson & Conoley, 1992; Davies & Johnson, 1996; Edwards, 2004; Epstein, 2001; Fagnano & Werber, 1994; Fruchter, Galletta, & White, 1992; Henderson & Mapp, 2002; Hiatt-Michaels, 2001; Patrikakou, Weissberg, Redding, & Walberg, in press; Ryan, Adams, Gullotta, Weissberg, & Hampton, 1995; Sanders & Epstein, 1998a, 1998b; Schneider & Coleman, 1993; Smit, Van der Wolf, & Sleegers, 2001; Swap, 1993; see also extensive, annual bibliographies compiled by Harvard Family Research Project, 2004). Collectively, these and many other publications have shaped the field and, literally, speak volumes about topics that need more attention in future research.

In one overview of the field, Epstein and Sanders (2000) discussed several topics that needed more research, including partnerships at times of student transitions; the organization of school–community connections; students' roles in school, family, and community partnerships; results of school, family, and community connections; fathers' involvement in children's education; the impact of federal, state, and local policies; and the effects of preservice and advanced education on partnerships for future teachers and administrators. These topics, scarcely studied a few years ago, still need attention.

SEVEN PRINCIPLES TO HELP RESEARCHERS THINK IN NEW WAYS

The many thoughtful overviews and summaries of research on partnerships make it unnecessary to review the literature again. In this chapter, we look in a different direction and identify seven principles that have emerged from prior studies and from exemplary practice that should help researchers across disciplines to think in new ways about how to study the structures, processes, and results of family and community involvement in education. These principles require researchers to think in new ways to (1) broaden the familiar term of "parental involvement" to "school, family, and community partnerships" so as to recognize the shared responsibilities of educators, parents, and others for children's development and learning; (2) understand the multidimensional nature of involvement; (3) view the structure of partnerships as a component of school and classroom organization; (4) recognize multilevel leadership for involvement at the school, district, and state levels; (5) focus involvement on student success; (6) acknowledge the importance of increasing the equity of involvement of parents to promote more successful students; and (7) advance knowledge and improve practice with more and better studies. We discuss the importance of these defining principles for researchers, educators, families, and others who have a stake in improving schools and increasing student success.

1. "School, family, and community partnerships" is a better term than "parental involvement" to recognize that parents, educators, and others in the community share responsibility for students' learning and development.

The development of a theory on partnerships opened new ways in which to think about the involvement of parents in children's education. The theory of *overlapping spheres of influence* posits that students learn more when parents, educators, and others in the community work together to guide and support student learning and development (Epstein, 1987, 2001). In this model, three contexts—home, school, and community—overlap with unique and combined influences on children through the interactions of parents, educators, community partners, and students across contexts. Each context "moves" closer to or farther from the others as a result of external forces and internal actions.

The external structure of the model of overlapping spheres of influence shows that by design, the three contexts can be pulled together or pushed apart by important forces, that is, the backgrounds, philosophies, and actions of families, schools, and communities and the developmental characteristics of students. The internal structure of the model identifies the institutional and individual lines of communication and social interactions of parents, teachers, students, and community members with students and each other.

Classic sociological theories suggested that school and family organizations were most efficient and effective when they had separate goals, roles, and responsibilities (Waller, 1932; Weber, 1947). However, data on student learning indicated that students did better in school when the important people in their lives at home, at school, and in the community had common goals and played collaborative, complementary, and supportive roles (Epstein, 2001).

The theory of overlapping spheres of influence integrates and extends ecological, educational, psychological, and sociological theories and perspectives on social organization and relationships (e.g., Bronfenbrenner, 1979, 1986; Comer, 1980; Elder, 1997; Leichter, 1974; Lightfoot, 1978; Litwak & Meyer, 1974; Seeley, 1981). Based on concepts of symbolic interactionist, social exchange, reference group, and ecological theories, the theory of overlapping spheres of influence recognizes the interdisciplinary nature of school, family, and community partnerships. It emphasizes the need for reciprocal interactions of parents, educators, and community partners to understand each other's views, to identify common goals for students, and to appreciate each other's contributions to student development. For example, as the theory translates to practice, we see that teachers who hold parents as a reference group are more likely to design and conduct interactions and activities that account for the roles parents play in their children's education. Similarly, parents who understand teachers' work and school goals for their children communicate with the school and organize home activities that support their children as students (Epstein, 1987).

Concepts of social capital (Coleman, 1988; Lin, 2000) also are relevant to the theory of overlapping spheres of influence. Through their interactions, parents, educators, and community partners establish social ties and exchange information that accumulates as social capital, and this may be used to improve children's schools and learning experiences.

The theory of overlapping spheres of influence has been tested in two ways. Most often, it has been applied to study school and district programs of family and community involvement and to learn whether and how well educators, parents, and community partners interact to help students succeed in school (Sanders, 1999; Sanders & Simon, 2002; Sheldon & Van Voorhis, 2004). The theory also has served as a lens through which to examine how future teachers and administrators are prepared to understand shared leadership in schools, including educators' shared responsibilities with families and communities to maximize student learning (Chavkin, in press; Epstein, 2001, 2005a; Epstein & Sanders, 2005). For example, teachers who believe that they alone are responsible for student learning may teach differently from teachers who believe that they share responsibilities with parents and others for student success (Blackwell, Futrell, & Imig, 2003; Epstein, 2001). Administrators who believe that they and their teachers form a "professional community" may manage their schools differently from administrators who view schools as full "learning communities," including educators, students, parents, and community partners (Epstein, 2001; Epstein & Salinas, 2004; Price, 2005). By focusing family and community involvement broadly on how students learn and grow, we may improve the education of future educators as well as the policies and practices in schools.

Other useful theories and extensive research on parent involvement focus mainly on parents' motivations and actions, largely without the school context. Hoover-Dempsey and Sandler's (1997) theory of why parents get involved in their children's education, for example, emphasizes the role of parental beliefs and feelings of competence as chief determinants of parental behavior. Also, Grolnick and Slowiaczek (1994) created a multidimensional model of parental involvement that stresses the phenomenological experiences of children resulting from parent–child interactions related to schooling. In contrast, the theory of overlapping spheres of influence focuses on school–family–community interactions and the design and development of school programs as well as practices that affect parental behavior and student success in school. Taken together, the varied theories support research on different aspects of the complex work of parenting, teaching, and learning and also contribute to a fuller understanding of education and the roles of home, school, and community in child development.

The theory of overlapping spheres of influence should help researchers across disciplines to "think new" about family and community involvement in children's education. Research may focus on school-level activities that affect all families (e.g., all teachers' interactions with all families about all children at a school "open house" night) and individual-level communications that affect one family at a time (e.g., one teacher's meetings or phone calls with one parent about one child). With attention given to contexts and social relations, the theory of overlapping spheres of influence changes the narrow focus of parental involvement from what an individual parent does to a broader, more realistic representation of how students move, continuously, in and out of several contexts and how the influential people in those contexts may work together to contribute to students' education and development.

Researchers may conduct studies of the social forces that affect the external structure of the theoretical model, including how federal, state, and local policies influence the implementation of programs and actions to strengthen families, improve schools, and increase student achievement. The theory also grounds studies of the internal structure of the model by recognizing that there are many paths to partnerships in the interactions between and among teachers, administrators, counselors, parents, community partners, students, and others. For example, Sanders (1998) explored how family, school, and church affiliation supported African American teens' achievement levels and identified positive effects across contexts. Catsambis and Beveridge (2001) studied family, school, and neighborhood factors that affected high school students' math achievement and found that negative neighborhood influences may be offset by positive family involvement. Additional research is needed on whether and how all connections are affected by the design and implementation of partnership programs and practices. Questions may be asked, for example, about how much overlap of home, school, and community is necessary for students' optimal achievement at each grade level.

2. School, family, and community partnerships are a multidimensional concept.

In many early studies, definitions of parental involvement were unclear, incomplete, or confounded. It was hard to know how to categorize and measure the ways in which parents were involved in their children's education. Terms such as "parents as teachers" and "parents as learners" were not useful because they defined roles that were part and parcel of the same types of involvement. A parent could be both a teacher and a learner when working as a school volunteer and when helping students with homework, even though these are two very different activities. The early terms used to classify involvement were neither theoretically grounded nor research based but rather grew out of Head Start and Chapter 1 program descriptions that focused on parents, not on students and not on actions that could be taken at home, at school, and in the community to promote student success.

A series of studies in elementary, middle, and high schools conducted from 1981 to 1991 generated a framework of six types of involvement: *parenting, communicating, volunteering, learning at home, decision making,* and *collaborating with the community* (Epstein, 1995, 2001). The framework identifies broad separable categories of practices that involve parents with teachers, students, and community partners in different locations and for specific purposes, all contributing to student learning and success. The six types of involvement are represented by many different practices, raise specific challenges, and are responsible for producing varied results for students, families, and educators (Epstein, Sanders et al., 2002). The framework has proved to be useful in research, policy, and practice across school levels and in diverse communities (Catsambis, 2002; Epstein & Lee, 1995; Lee, 1994; Salinas & Jansorn, 2004; Sanders, 1999; Simon, 2004; see also practical examples for the National Network of Partnership Schools [NNPS], 2005).

In brief, the six types of involvement are as follows: Type 1—Parenting (helping all families to understand child and adolescent development and establishing home environments that support children as students), Type 2—Communicating (designing and conducting effective forms of two-way communications about school programs and children's progress), Type 3—Volunteering (recruiting and organizing help and support at school, at home, or in other locations to support the school and students' activities), Type 4—Learning at Home (providing information and ideas to families about how to help students with homework and curriculum-related activities and decisions), Type 5—Decision Making (having parents from all backgrounds serve as representatives and leaders on school committees and obtaining input from all parents on school decisions), and Type 6—Collaborating With the Community (identifying and integrating resources and services from the community to strengthen and support schools, students, and their families and also organizing activities to benefit the community and increase students' learning opportunities).

Schools may choose among hundreds of practices for each type of involvement to guide and encourage purposeful interactions of parents, educators, students, and others in the community. For example, there are many ways in which to use common and advanced technologies for teachers and parents to communicate with each other (Type 2); many ways in which to organize volunteers to assist educators, students, and families (Type 3); and so on. Each type of involvement requires two-way communications so that educators and families exchange information and ideas with each other and recognize and honor their shared responsibilities for children's education.

Each type of involvement poses clear challenges that must be addressed to reach all families (Epstein, Sanders et al., 2002). For example, schools may be faced with the challenge of involving parents who cannot speak or read English. Teams of educators and parents may work together to provide information in words and forms that the families understand and to implement activities ensuring that these parents, like all others, have easy access to channels of communication with teachers and administrators and opportunities for input regarding school decisions. Other challenges include getting

information to families who cannot attend school meetings, sending parents positive communications about their children's work and accomplishments so that connections are not only about students' problems, providing ways for parents and teachers to communicate so that information about students flows from school to home and from home to school, providing opportunities for many parents to volunteer at school and in other locations, preparing teachers to guide families to monitor and interact with their children about homework, ensuring that families from diverse neighborhoods are represented in the decision-making process and on school committees, and identifying and using community resources to help meet school improvement goals (Epstein, Sanders et al., 2002). By addressing these and other challenges, schools can reach out to involve parents across racial, educational, and socioeconomic groups so that they can actively support their children's education.

The framework of six types of involvement was adopted by the National PTA (2004) as its "standards" for all schools to inform and involve parents and community partners in the schools and in children's education. Furthermore, the No Child Left Behind (NCLB) Act of 2002 outlines activities for the six types of involvement in its guidelines for schools' programs for family involvement.

Researchers who are ready to think in new ways about the nature of school, family, and community partnerships may use the framework of six types of involvement in full or in part to address questions about programs, activities, and results of involvement. Research is sorely needed on the design and effects of contrasting approaches to resolve the countless challenges that arise for each type of involvement. The challenges must be solved to help all families feel welcome at school and feel ready and able to support their children (Epstein, 2001; Epstein, Sanders et al., 2002). For example, many studies in diverse communities will be needed to solve questions about the design of effective parent–teacher conferences with parents who do not speak English and to identify other effective formats for two-way communications with all families throughout the school year. Because the vast majority of parents work full- or part-time during the school day, today's schools must schedule meetings at varied times and have many different ways for parents to become and remain informed and involved with their children at home and in the community. It no longer is enough to require "bodies in the school building" as the only evidence of parents' interest and involvement in their children's education.

These kinds of "nitty-gritty" questions must be addressed to provide a stronger research base for educators' decisions about the design and content of partnership programs. The framework should help researchers to focus studies on the challenges associated with particular types of involvement, increase understanding of what schools may do to involve families in different ways, and provide parents with realistic and productive options for their involvement. Researchers also may focus on complex questions about the connections between and among the six types of involvement, that is, the sequence or mix of types of involvement that helps schools to build comprehensive and high-quality programs. The framework of six types of involvement provides an efficient way in which to categorize activities and to accumulate and synthesize results of studies so that knowledge grows and the results of research can be used by educators to improve practice.

3. A program of school, family, and community partnerships is an essential component of school and classroom organization.

The theory of overlapping spheres of influence and the framework of six types of involvement promote the view that school, family, and community partnerships should operate as an organized *program* of structures, processes, and collaborative activities to help students succeed in every school, not as a set of fragmented activities for parents. A planned program of partnership with activities linked to school improvement goals establishes family involvement as a component of school improvement, or part of the professional work of educators, just as the curriculum, instruction, and assessments are understood as essential school organizational components. The difference is that programs of partnership require educators to interact and collaborate with parents, other

family members, and community partners, not only with other educators.

A series of studies identified eight "essential elements" for effective school programs of school, family, and community partnerships: *leadership, teamwork, action plans, implementation of plans, funding, collegial support, evaluation,* and *networking.* Specifically, in longitudinal studies of more than 500 schools, Sheldon and Van Voorhis found that schools whose action teams for partnerships received technical assistance and support from district leaders and from external partners were more likely to form committees, write plans, adjust for changes in principals, reach out to more families, evaluate their efforts, and sustain their programs. These schools also addressed more challenges to involve "hard-to-reach" parents and reported that more families were involved in their children's education (Sheldon, 2003; Sheldon & Van Voorhis, 2003; Van Voorhis & Sheldon, in press). By implementing the essential program elements, elementary, middle, and high schools improved the scope and quality of activities for several types of involvement (Epstein, 2001; Sanders, 1999, 2001; Sanders & Harvey, 2002; Sanders & Simon, 2002; Sheldon & Van Voorhis, 2004).

Longitudinal studies confirmed the connections of essential program elements with increased outreach and involvement (Epstein, 2005b; Sheldon, 2003, 2005; Sheldon & Van Voorhis, 2004; Van Voorhis & Sheldon, in press). Specifically, schools that improved their programs over time increased the involvement of more and different parents as volunteers and in decision making at school. These schools also increased outreach by teachers, including greater use of homework designed to encourage parent–child interactions. The studies show, repeatedly, that more can be done to involve more families if educators, parents, and others work as a school team to plan their partnership programs, schedule activities, share leadership for activities, evaluate progress, and continually improve the quality of activities and outreach.

In schools, the word "plan" often raises concerns among educators. Currently, most schools have an annual school improvement plan that outlines major goals for students and for improving the school climate. Pressed for time, most educators are not eager to write additional, different, or extra plans for family and community involvement. Yet studies of partnership program development show that educators and parents do more together when they work as a team and write annual detailed schedules of partnership activities.

One of the most helpful new directions for applying research on partnerships in practice has been for educators to link detailed written action plans for family and community involvement to their annual school improvement plans. For example, in Buffalo, New York, plans for partnership are appended to the Comprehensive School Education Plan; in the state of Maryland, they are appended to the School Improvement Plan; and in Los Angeles, they are appended to a Single School Plan. Each school, then, has only one major plan with stated improvement goals accompanied by a detailed schedule and assigned responsibilities for family and community involvement activities. In this way, a formal program of partnerships is linked to school goals for which educators and students are held accountable, bringing parents and community partners to the central purpose of schools and schooling, and not treated as an extra burden or afterthought.

Several studies also suggest that it was necessary, but not sufficient, for schools to establish "the basics" of a partnership program such as organizing a team, writing a plan, and even implementing planned activities. To affect program quality in a measurable way, parents' responses and results for students' schools also had to address key challenges to reach all families (Sheldon, 2003, 2004, 2005).

Researchers who are ready to think in new ways about school, family, and community partnerships may conduct studies on the design and development of any or all of the eight essential elements to extend an understanding of the formation and qualities of programs of family and community involvement. The result is not a "parent program," which by its very label excuses educators from participating, but rather a "student success program"—part of school organization—that requires teachers, parents, students, and other critical partners to organize their interactions efficiently and effectively to support children's education. Two basic

questions for researchers and educators are the following. How can family and community involvement programs be organized systematically as a regular part of every school's work? Which structures, processes, and activities best help principals, teachers, parents, and others to plan, implement, and sustain partnership programs that help to boost student achievement and success?

4. Programs of school, family, and community partnerships require multilevel leadership.

Family and community involvement activities focus mainly on the school level because that is where students and their families are located every day. Nevertheless, district and state leaders have important roles to play in guiding and motivating superintendents, principals, and school teams to develop and implement policies and plans for good partnerships (Epstein, 2001; Epstein, Sanders et al., 2002).

Multilevel leadership supports the view that family and community involvement is part of school organization as district leaders help to coordinate and facilitate the smooth operation of all schools within a district. District leaders for partnerships may, for example, develop clear policies for all schools' partnership programs, organize and offer professional development workshops to school teams, help teams to write plans for goal-oriented partnership programs, share best practices, evaluate their programs, and improve from year to year.

Analysis of longitudinal data from about 80 school districts indicated that these functions and activities improved the quality of district leadership on partnerships, increased direct connections with schools, and helped schools to improve their school-based programs, as discussed earlier (Epstein & Williams, 2003; Epstein, Williams, & Jansorn, 2004; Epstein, Williams, & Lewis, 2002). The quality of district partnership programs was affected by the leaders' years of experience and time spent on partnerships, use of NNPS planning and evaluation tools, and the extent to which district leaders directly assisted their schools.

Compared with their counterparts in other districts, experienced district leaders were more likely to write annual district-level leadership plans, identify a budget for partnerships, conduct training workshops for school teams and other colleagues, offer grants or other funding to schools, recognize excellence in school programs, help schools to share best practices, and conduct other leadership actions. District leaders who evaluated their own and their schools' programs were more likely to visit their schools more often to provide support and assistance (Epstein & Williams, 2003). Regardless of their initial practices during the prior school year, district leaders who used NNPS tools and services for program development, planning, and evaluation increased the number of activities they conducted at the district level to organize their own work, facilitated their schools to address challenges to reach more families, conducted program evaluations, and increased the overall quality of their own and their schools' programs (Epstein & Williams, 2003; Epstein et al., 2004). It may be that by using planning and evaluation tools, district leaders were more serious about their work on partnerships and, therefore, guided schools to take more actions in developing their programs.

Historically, the earliest federal policies concerning Chapter 1 and Title I called for district advisory councils. These were nearly always symbolic committees that enabled a few parents to have input to district policies but that did little to increase the involvement of all families in all schools. District advisory councils still are useful, but district-level professional leaders also are needed to assist schools in understanding the importance of teamwork and how to develop their programs of family and community involvement.

State leaders for partnerships also have shown that clear policies and professional development activities can increase districts' attention to their work on partnerships with their schools (Epstein, 2001; Epstein & Williams, 2003; see also NNPS, 2005, for summaries of Wisconsin's and Connecticut's policies and programs, specifically the "In the Spotlight" section on the NNPS Web site). The importance of active multilevel leadership on partnerships is recognized and codified in the requirements for family involvement in NCLB, which redirects state and district leaders away from monitoring sites for compliance to actively helping schools to improve the quality and results of partnership programs.

Researchers who are ready to think in new ways about school, family, and community partnerships may ask questions about the effects of contrasting district and state leadership structures and processes. The 50 states and nearly 15,000 districts in the United States will respond in various ways to NCLB requirements for parental involvement. Researchers have a rare opportunity to conduct multilevel studies to identify the most effective ways in which states and districts organize their leadership on partnerships and the impact of their policies and actions on their schools.

5. Programs of school, family, and community partnerships must include a focus on increasing student learning and development.

The most common question from researchers, reporters, and educators about school, family, and community partnerships is the following: What are the effects of family and community involvement on student achievement? The question is on the right track with its focus on students. The theory of overlapping spheres of influence places students at the center of the internal structure of the model, that is, as the main reason for interactions among educators, parents, and others in the community. The theory, then, supports the intense interest in how schools' practices to involve families affect student outcomes. But the question, as typically posed, is far too narrow given that family and community involvement affects not only student achievement but also student health, attitudes, and behaviors (Epstein, 2001; Hill & Craft, 2003; Patrikakou et al., in press; Reynolds, Temple, Robertson, & Mann, 2002).

Attention to results for students is fueled by current policies and practice. For example, NCLB and most state and local policies specify that parental involvement should be designed to help increase student achievement and success in school. In practice, numerous innovative ideas are emerging on how to involve families with students on reading, math, and other subjects and on how to design involvement activities that are linked to other school goals (e.g., good attendance, good behavior) that contribute to student success (Salinas & Jansorn, 2004).

For more than a decade, research has been strengthening its base of evidence on results of family involvement for students. Many studies at the elementary, middle, and high school levels confirmed that students had higher achievements, better attendance, more course credits earned, better preparation for class, and other indicators of success in school if their families were involved in their education (Catsambis, 2002; Epstein, 2001; Lee, 1994; Muller, 1993; see also summaries of studies in Henderson & Mapp, 2002).

Types of Involvement. Researchers have extended their studies from general questions about involvement to pointed questions about how the six types of involvement affected student outcomes. For example, Simon (2001, 2004) found that when high schools conducted specific activities to increase parents' attention to teens' high school work and postsecondary planning, parents responded by conducting more interactions with their teens about those subjects. Catsambis and Beveridge (2001) pressed further, using hierarchical linear modeling (HLM) analysis to study how school, family, and neighborhood factors independently affected students' math achievement. Specifically, they showed that students in neighborhoods with high concentrations of poverty had lower math achievement test scores, but this effect was ameliorated by ongoing parental involvement in high school. These studies, conducted with large national sample surveys of parents and students at the middle and high school levels in the National Educational Longitudinal Study (NELS) data set, indicated that it is never too late to initiate programs of family and community involvement. Students benefited from their parents' interest, interactions, and guidance through high school.

Subject-Specific Goals for Students. New studies are contributing to an understanding of the importance of goal-linked family involvement to help students produce specific results. Studies of family involvement in reading have been most numerous and offer some pertinent lessons for future research.

A review of research on family involvement interventions in schools reported that these programs had mixed results for student achievement in reading and other subjects (Mattingly, Prislin, McKenzie, Rodriguez, & Kayzar, 2002). That review, however, examined diverse partnership programs with varied goals without giving separate attention to whether or how parents or other family members were encouraged or guided to support their children's learning in targeted, goal-linked ways.

Of the 41 studies reviewed by Mattingly and colleagues (2002), 16 (with a sample size of more than two students) guided parents to become involved with their children on reading and language arts activities. Of these targeted "reading" programs, 15 were reported to produce significant gains on students' reading or language arts achievement test scores and, where measured, produced differences between intervention and comparison groups on reading or language arts skills and scores. Interventions that were not closely linked to intended results, such as general communications with teachers or about school programs, improving student attendance, or improving students' skills in asking questions, did not produce gains in students' reading skills.

Another review of research conducted from 1997 to circa 2000 strengthened the importance of measuring subject-specific involvement for results in specific subjects (Henderson & Mapp, 2002). Of 51 studies, 7 examined the impact of family involvement interventions that guided parents to participate in reading-related activities. All 7 studies indicated that targeted reading-related family involvement was associated with increased student reading and language arts skills in case and control groups or as participants in the interventions over time.

These and earlier reviews (Miller, 1986; Silvern, 1985; Tizard, Scofield, & Hewison, 1982) and additional studies (Cairney, 1995; Epstein, 2001) support the position that when family involvement is focused on reading and literacy activities at home, including reading aloud and discussing stories, students' reading achievement increased. The results should help researchers to think in new ways about which interventions to increase parental involvement are most likely to affect specific results for student learning.

Many schools already are implementing subject-specific involvement activities to engage families in productive ways so as to help students reach specific goals. Schools may strengthen their partnership programs by including various activities for all six types of involvement for specific goals for students, including improving reading (Epstein, Williams et al., 2002). For example, a school may conduct workshops for parents to help them understand reading standards, host parent–teacher conferences that focus only on reading progress and next steps, use reading volunteers to help students improve reading, give reading homework to increase students' reading time and discussions of books at home, and implement other activities that emphasize the importance of the school's reading goals and parents' opportunities to talk with their children about reading. A review of literature on family involvement with students on reading indicated that, across the grades, subject-specific interventions to involve families in reading and related language arts positively affected students' reading skills and scores (Sheldon & Epstein, 2005b).

A series of school-level studies, titled Focus on Results, examined whether schools that implemented family and community involvement activities to address other learning and behavioral goals for students showed measurable changes on student outcomes over the course of a year. On achievement outcomes, schools that focused family involvement with students on math, particularly through math homework that required parent–child interactions and math materials for families to take home, increased the percentages of students who were proficient in math on state tests from one year to the next (Sheldon & Epstein, 2005a).

Family involvement also affected students' nonachievement outcomes. In schools where educators communicated well with families about attendance, the schools' rates of average daily attendance increased and chronic absence decreased from one year to the next (Epstein & Sheldon, 2002; Sheldon & Epstein, 2004). These results were reinforced by another study using longitudinal data from Ohio showing that schools in the NNPS improved attendance rates compared with a matched sample of schools that did not receive guidance on partnership program development (Sheldon, 2004). Similarly, when educators communicated effectively and involved family and community members in activities focused on student behavior and school safety, schools reported fewer disciplinary actions with students from one year to the next (Sanders, 1996; Sheldon & Epstein, 2002).

Other researchers explored the effects of family involvement with children on homework at the individual student level (Epstein & Van Voorhis, 2001). They found significant results of subject-specific family involvement for students' writing skills (Epstein, Simon, & Salinas, 1997) on science report card grades and homework completion (Van Voorhis, 2003, 2004).

The range of studies just described shows the potential for researchers to conduct many more studies on the effects of subject-specific and goal-linked activities for family and community involvement on linked student outcomes. The extant studies also revealed several difficulties that must be addressed in conducting research on the results of involvement for student outcomes. Now we discuss three challenges that make effects studies difficult.

The Challenge of Conducting Studies of Interventions. Studies of the effects of particular practices of involvement require intensive and extensive cooperation and collaboration between researchers and educators, and there are no shortcuts for the time and care needed from all participants. For example, the studies discussed previously about family involvement with students on homework required teachers to connect with students' families in targeted, well-designed, subject-specific assignments for an extended period of time of up to 1 year.

The quality of the implementation of a program or practice must be measured *before* it is possible to measure results related to the intervention. For example, a 3-year study of the Partnership Schools Comprehensive School Reform (CSR) model (Epstein, 2005b) demonstrated that a Title I elementary school could organize whole-school change that combined changes in instruction with improvements in family and community involvement focused on reading, writing, and math. Over 3 years, the CSR school improved its state achievement test scores in these subjects compared with matched schools. The CSR school also closed the gap in test scores with the district as a whole despite the fact that the district included several schools in more affluent neighborhoods with higher test scores in the base year. The school also increased the number of families involved in students' education at school and at home.

To build on current knowledge, studies of the effects of parental involvement on student outcomes must be longitudinal with data on families' prior involvement and students' prior scores on the selected outcomes, the nature and quality of schools' involvement activities, the families' responses to those activities, and the students' current outcomes. With these rich data, researchers will be able to address the basic question: How do school practices to involve families affect parents' behaviors *and* the change or continuity of student achievements and behaviors? Without the full complement of longitudinal measures, studies simply document that successful students tend to have parents who are involved.

The Challenge of Isolating Effects of Partnerships. In practice, when educators develop programs to involve families with students on specific subjects or on other goals, they may report positive results, overall, for children's achievement. For example, an action team for partnerships in an elementary school serving mainly Latino and Hmong families in St. Paul, Minnesota, wrote annual plans with many activities for the six types of involvement that focused on student learning. This school reported gains in 2004 on students' test scores of 13% in reading and 10% in math that were attributed, in part, to the hard work of the teachers and students and to family involvement and support (see NNPS, 2005, and the awards summaries in the "In the Spotlight" section on the Web site).

The example illustrates an inescapable problem for research on comprehensive partnership programs. It is difficult to isolate the effects of one program component from the effects of all other school improvement activities that are occurring simultaneously. In the school example, teachers were working with students on more demanding reading and writing standards and curricula, and more parents were involved with students on reading and writing tasks. The problem plagues all studies of school reform and can be resolved only by applying increasingly reliable measures of the nature and quality of specific practices and by using increasingly rigorous methods, including longitudinal data to account for starting points on key independent and dependent variables.

The Challenge of Explaining Negative Results. Among the most provocative and least studied patterns of results of school, family, and community partnerships are the negative associations of certain types of involvement with some measures of student achievement and behavior (Desimone, 1999; Lee, 1994; Muller, 1993; Simon, 2000). Several studies, particularly in middle and high schools, indicate that more parents communicate with teachers if their students have low achievement and poor behavior in school. In contrast, in the same schools, more parents volunteer and participate in school decision making if their students have high achievement and better behavior.

These contradictory correlations must be put in context. Without well-developed partnership programs, teachers and parents contact each other mainly when students have academic and behavior problems. If a school is not conducting some positive interactions with all families, then the number of communications between teachers and parents will be correlated with low achievement or poor behavior (Catsambis, 2002; Epstein, 2001; Epstein & Lee, 1995; Lee, 1994). This intriguing pattern of effects shows why researchers need to understand the different types of involvement and the contexts in which communications among teachers, parents, and students are conducted. Studies that delve deeper into the results of parent–teacher–student communications to solve students' academic and behavioral problems over time are sorely needed.

Despite real progress in research on results of family and community involvement for student learning and development, this remains the most important topic for new and better studies.

Researchers who are ready to think in new ways may study whether and which family and community involvement activities affect specific academic, attitudinal, behavioral, health, and other outcomes at all school and grade levels for diverse groups of students. Research is needed on whether parent–teacher communications about poor achievement and behavior have different effects at different grade levels and as a function of the roles that students play in the process.

The agenda is all but limitless because there is a long list of student outcomes that are of interest and importance in school studies (Epstein, 2001; Gerne & Epstein, 2004; Patrikakou et al., in press). These include *academic outcomes* such as readiness for school, participation in class, completion of homework, report card grades, test scores, course credits, high school completion, and enrollment in postsecondary education; *social and emotional outcomes* for students' personal development such as motivation to learn, attitudes toward schoolwork, dimensions of self-esteem, attendance, good behavior, perseverance on tasks, postsecondary planning, and positive relationships with teachers, peers, friends, and other adults in school; *health-related outcomes* for student growth and development such as nutrition, weight management, physical strength, exercise, sex education, and prevention of the use of drugs, alcohol, and tobacco as well as other health topics; and other indicators of citizenship, good character, and academic commitment. The varied outcomes may, in turn, affect student achievement and vice versa, yielding a vast agenda for studies of results of family and community involvement on student development.

Research on the effects of family involvement on student outcomes is currently a mile wide and an inch deep. Studies have identified numerous types of involvement and an array of academic, attitudinal, behavioral, and health outcomes for students. But only a few studies have been conducted on any single outcome, at certain grade levels, and in selected communities. Few studies are based on appropriate longitudinal data or other rigorous methods. We still need to know the answer to the question: Which involvement activities produce measurable results for students, and under what conditions?

Thus, the topic of whether, which, and how family and community involvement affects results for students needs many new contributions to improve the topography of the field.

6. All programs of school, family, and community partnerships are about equity.

Parental involvement programs must include all families, not just those who are currently involved or easiest to reach. This requirement, written into federal law in NCLB, also is stipulated in just about all state education policies and district mission statements. For example, NCLB's Section 1118 requires educators to communicate with all parents in languages that they will understand about their own children's achievement test scores, trends in test scores for all schools in a district and major subgroups of students, and other indicators (e.g., attendance, graduation rates, teachers' qualifications). Schools also are required to provide clear information and options to parents to transfer their children to more successful schools if the children's own schools underperform for 2 consecutive years and must provide information for selecting supplemental education services for eligible children.

The emphasis in federal policy on well-designed partnership programs that involve all families has important implications for research on school, family, and community partnerships. Many studies show that although most parents report that they want to be partners with educators, only some parents, particularly those with more formal education, higher incomes, and familiarity with schools, remain involved in their children's education across the grades (Baker & Stevenson, 1986; Dauber & Epstein, 1993; Lareau, 1989; Useem, 1991, 1992). The well-documented inequalities raise new questions about producing greater equity of family and community involvement to promote more success of students.

Typical distributions of involved and uninvolved parents can be changed with well-designed partnership programs. A growing number of studies conducted with elementary, middle, and high schools indicate that when schools conduct high-quality partnership programs, parents respond. This includes parents with less formal education or lower incomes who might not become involved on their own. Program quality and the actions taken at home are as important as, or more important than, family background variables such as race, ethnicity, social class, marital status, mother's education or work status, and language spoken at home for determining whether, how, and which parents become involved in their children's education and how students progress and succeed in school (Cairney & Munsie, 1995; Comer & Haynes, 1991; Dauber & Epstein, 1993; Epstein, 2001; Henderson & Mapp, 2002; Sanders & Epstein, 2000; Simon, 2004). These results are also represented in exemplary practice (Salinas & Jansorn, 2004).

Some research and practical reports like to discuss overinvolved and underinvolved parents (Gibbs, 2005). In fact, both groups may be assisted by well-planned partnership programs. In surveys of parents, highly involved and hard-to-reach parents report that they need more and better information from their children's schools to know how to use their limited available time to best assist their children (Dauber & Epstein, 1993). Without good guidance, the underinvolved parents wait for information and the overinvolved parents set their own agendas, whether their actions benefit their children or not.

Several decades of studies of family involvement with children about reading show how this works in practice. Many studies in this and other countries confirm that children do better in reading and other literacy skills if their families support reading at home with more books and reading experiences (Binkley, Rust, & Williams, 1996; Sheldon & Epstein, 2005b; U.S. Department of Education, 2001). Although more educated families and those with more disposable income have more books at home, schools can create more equity in involvement about reading by implementing activities that help all parents to understand their children's reading programs and to encourage reading at home. Schools also may work with local businesses to provide children with books to take home, thereby making home reading environments more equitable (NNPS, 2005; Salinas & Jansorn, 2004).

As another example, district leaders in the Seattle Public Schools are helping schools to develop partnership programs that increase the equity of involvement for highly diverse families. District leaders from several departments worked together to develop presentations, Web site communications, handbooks, and other publications for parents in 10 languages. The superintendent noted that these programs helped educators to "align parent involvement practices with academic goals, contributing to real systemic change in school buildings." During the 2003–2004 school year, the district tracked more than 260 activities for the six types of involvement attended by more than 18,360 parents, with translated materials provided at more than 60% of the activities. The work in Seattle is demonstrating that with committed district leaders, even schools in challenging communities can increase the equity of parental involvement to support students' success in school (NNPS, 2005; see these and other examples of programs and practices in the "In the Spotlight" section on the Web site).

It no longer is enough to identify inequalities in parental involvement. Researchers who are ready to think in new ways about family involvement may conduct studies designed to produce greater equity of involvement for all parents. Because families are important for students' success in school, it is important to learn how more families—ideally all families—become involved in ways that positively support their children's success in school. This requires researchers to go beyond questions of whether families are involved or not to test alternative strategies that help families and educators to build trust and respect for one another and that enable all parents to guide their children to do their best in school. Researchers may study the processes and technologies needed to involve parents who are typically hard to reach, including parents who have less formal education, speak languages other than English at home, and typically would not become involved on their own.

At its core, education is about providing equal opportunities to learn. Because it is well documented that students benefit from goal-linked family and community involvement, researchers may conduct studies that yield more and better information on which partnership approaches help to resolve the past and present inequalities in levels of involvement among diverse families.

7. Methods of research on school, family, and community partnerships must continue to improve.

The young field of school, family, and community partnerships will continue to grow if researchers ask new and pointed questions about the implementation and results of involvement activities. Knowledge will also grow with better measures, larger and more diverse samples, and the use of various methods of data collection, including surveys, case studies, experimental or quasi-experimental designs, longitudinal studies, field tests, program evaluations, and policy analyses. Researchers who are ready to think in new ways about school, family, and community partnerships will contribute new knowledge on partnerships by using the most rigorous methods of analysis that are appropriate for their questions.

After more than two decades of research on family involvement that framed the field, researchers should be ready to move from exploratory and descriptive studies to confirmatory studies and targeted evaluations about how full programs and specific practices of school, family, and community partnerships develop and affect families and students. Here we discuss a few ways in which researchers may move forward with various methods of analysis.

Experiments and Matched Samples. Experimental research and quasi-experimental research are needed to compare schools that are implementing specific partnership programs or practices with similar schools that are not (Boethel, 2003; Henderson & Mapp, 2002; Mattingly et al., 2002). Experimental and quasi-experimental methods are best suited for studying well-defined, tightly controlled interventions. For example, Van Voorhis (2001, 2003) built on early studies of the feasibility of the Teachers Involve Parents in Schoolwork (TIPS) interactive homework process (Epstein et al., 1997) by conducting a quasi-experimental study of case and control classrooms to better understand the impact of student–parent interactions about science homework. The study revealed that parents were much more involved when children led conversations and experiments with family partners at home on science and that students benefited in report card grades and homework completion, as compared with parents and students in matched classrooms who had the same homework without a family involvement component. Van Voorhis also showed that parental involvement for case and control classes did not differ in English and math—subjects that did not use the TIPS method.

Experimental designs with strict comparisons of partnership versus nonpartnership schools are difficult given widespread support for parent involvement and far-reaching federal, state, and local policies that require all schools to have programs of family and community involvement (Kessler-Sklar & Baker, 2000). When experimental or quasi-experimental conditions are not possible, researchers can improve studies of the effects of family and community involvement on student achievement and other indicators of success by using longitudinal data with well-specified effects models and closely matched samples of schools and/or students.

Well-Specified Multivariate Models. Researchers can advance knowledge by identifying the paths that connect school activities to family responses and to results for students. For example, Sheldon (2005) employed structural equation modeling (SEM) techniques to identify the connections of key program structures with the extent of schools' outreach to involve more families and with the resulting family involvement. He showed that program plans, district support, and collegial support at the school contributed to better program outreach to more families. In turn, outreach promoted greater family involvement. The processes occur simultaneously as the program grows and as plans and activities are implemented.

Notable research on other aspects of parental involvement using SEM has been conducted by Hill and her colleagues, specifically on the mechanisms by which parent–child interactions may translate into various student outcomes and how these processes vary across ethnic and socioeconomic groups (Hill et al., 2004; Hill &

Craft, 2003). SEM holds promise for testing different theoretical models of school, home, and community connections and for identifying simultaneously occurring effects such as parents' responses to school practices of involvement and results for students.

Multilevel Analysis. Researchers who are ready to think in new ways about school, family, and community partnerships can advance knowledge by studying the multilevel effects of state policies and actions on district leadership and school programs to reach all families. Multilevel analysis using HLM will be useful in separating the independent effects of policies and leadership actions that occur with a nested system (e.g., families within schools, schools within districts, districts within states). Because federal policies require states, districts, and schools to have coordinated activities for partnership program development, multilevel methods such as HLM are particularly appropriate for studying the connections and influences that occur across policy levels (Bryk & Raudenbush, 1992).

Researchers may be helped in framing new studies of family and community involvement and effects using SEM and HLM methods by tapping national data sets, such as the Early Childhood Longitudinal Study (ECLS), with ECLS-K starting with a kindergarten cohort in the fall of 1998 and ECLS-B starting with a birth cohort in 2000. The large-scale surveys included surveys of teachers, parents, and students and may encourage model testing and studies of multilevel effects of family and community involvement in schools and neighborhoods. Still, large national surveys have strengths and weaknesses. The number of items on school, family, and community partnerships may be limited, and items may be unrelated to theoretical or practical concerns. Researchers ready to think in new ways about family and community involvement still may benefit from well-designed local, regional, and state surveys, case studies, experimental studies, and action research that can delve deeply into the implementation and effects of specific practices of family involvement.

Small In-Depth Studies. Although large and methodologically sophisticated studies are needed, there still are times in a young field of study when small, in-depth quantitative and qualitative studies are appropriate. For example, over the past 20 years, most research has focused on school–family connections. Therefore, initial studies on school–community connections had to be conducted from the ground up. By using survey data from schools in many parts of the country and intensive inquiries in one elementary school, Sanders (2001) developed a useful catalogue of school–community connections and their targeted participants, that is, community connections to assist parents, students, and teachers (Sanders, 2003; Sanders & Harvey, 2002). A series of studies of three high schools in urban, suburban, and rural communities revealed how high schools can organize school–community connections to benefit all partners in education (Sanders, 2005; Sanders & Lewis, 2005). Now there is a much stronger base on which to build future studies of the effects of school–community partnerships on student learning and development.

Other topics that have not been studied much (e.g., involvement of parents in nontraditional families such as foster parents, gay and lesbian parents, and noncustodial parents; involvement at transition points; involvement to influence students' postsecondary plans; involvement to improve students' health outcomes) may benefit from small exploratory studies that help to define terms, identify activities, develop measures, and establish other parameters. In contrast, topics that have been studied extensively (e.g., teachers' and parents' attitudes about involvement and all effects studies) may be revisited but require researchers to ask more detailed questions and to use more advanced methods than in prior studies so as to make original contributions to the field.

More rigorous research on school, family, and community partnerships, using diverse methods and valid and reliable measures, should increase knowledge on the factors that produce the most effective programs and on the processes and paths that strengthen (a) leadership for partnerships, (b) the quality of program plans, (c) outreach to involve more families, (d) responses by families and community partners, and (e) the impact on student achievement and other indicators of success in school.

CONCLUSION

If family involvement is important for student success, as decades of research indicates, then we must address the fruitful question: How can more families—indeed all families—become involved in their children's education in ways that will contribute to student success?

Studies of parental involvement over the past 25 years have set a firm base on which new research can build to increase understanding of programs and practices of school, family, and community partnerships. The early work yielded a useful theory and framework of six types of involvement that have guided research, policy, and practice. Studies to date have identified and explored many aspects of the involvement of parents, teachers, administrators, and students. Researchers have begun to inspect, dissect, and identify components and effects of partnership programs in schools and school districts. By framing the field, the early work also shows that much is left to learn.

Despite the challenges of studying schools, families, and communities simultaneously, it is necessary to "think new" about how students learn and develop as they progress from preschool through high school. Well-documented problems with student achievement, motivation, attitudes about education, school behavior, and future plans are partly due to "old think" that separated school and students from home and community, leaving teachers to work on their own, isolated from other influential people in children's lives.

The seven principles featured in this chapter should help researchers to think in new ways about the structures and processes of family and community involvement that will help educators, parents, and community partners to work more systematically, organizationally, and collaboratively to support student success. The sixth principle—that involvement is all about equity—is pivotal because it requires that attention be given to all of the other principles. That is, to study how to produce more equal opportunities for family involvement and student success, it is imperative for researchers to understand that parents, educators, and others at home, in school, and in the community share an interest in and responsibilities for students' education and development. It is necessary for researchers to recognize the difference between asking or rebuking each parent, individually, to become involved and enabling every school to organize effective programs that encourage the productive involvement of all families. It is important for researchers to explore whether and how district and state leaders may work in concert with schools to establish and continually improve effective partnership programs that reach all families. Because schools are being held accountable for improving academic and other results for students, researchers must conduct studies that go beyond process outcomes for parents to study the effects of school, family, and community partnerships on academic and behavioral outcomes for students. If researchers think in these new ways, they will move the field forward with studies that go beyond documenting inequities to explore and identify programs and practices that promote greater equity in the involvement of diverse families and the effects of involvement on indicators of success for students in elementary, middle, and high schools.

All seven changes in thinking are needed to study the design and development of comprehensive partnership programs, outreach to involve all families, family and community responses, and results for students. By thinking in new ways about school, family, and community partnerships, researchers not only will extend the knowledge base but also will help educators to improve policy and practice.

REFERENCES

Baker, D. P., & Stevenson, D. L. (1986). Mothers' strategies for children's school achievement: Managing the transition to high school. *Sociology of Education, 59,* 156–166.

Binkley, M., Rust, K., & Williams, T. (1996). *Reading literacy in an international perspective* (NCES 97-875). Washington, DC: U.S. Department of Education/National Center for Education Statistics.

Blackwell, P. J., Futrell, M. H., & Imig, D. G. (2003). Burnt water paradoxes of schools of education. *Phi Delta Kappan, 84,* 356–361.

Boethel, M. (2003). *Diversity: School, family, and community connections.* Austin, TX: Southwest Educational Development Laboratory.

Booth, A., & Dunn, J. (Eds.). (1995). *Family–school links: How do they affect educational outcomes?* Hillsdale, NJ: Lawrence Erlbaum.

Bronfenbrenner, U. (1979). *The ecology of human development: Experiment by nature and design.* Cambridge, MA: Harvard University Press.

Bronfenbrenner, U. (1986). Ecology of the family as a context for human development: Research perspectives. *Developmental Psychology, 22,* 723–742.

Bryk, A. S., & Raudenbush, S. W. (1992). *Hierarchical linear modeling: Applications and data analysis methods.* Newbury Park, CA: Sage.

Cairney, T. H. (1995). Developing parent partnerships in secondary literacy learning. *Journal of Reading, 38,* 520–526.

Cairney, T. H., & Munsie, L. (1995). Parent participation in literacy learning. *Reading Teacher, 48,* 392–403.

Castelli, S., Mendel, M., & Ravn, B. (Eds.). (2003). *School, family, and community partnership in a world of differences and change* (Proceedings of the ERNAPE Conference on School, Family, and Community Partnerships). Gdansk, Poland: University of Gdansk.

Catsambis, S. (2002). Expanding knowledge of parental involvement in children's secondary education: Connections with high school seniors' academic success. *Social Psychology of Education, 5,* 149–177.

Catsambis, S., & Beveridge, A. A. (2001). Does neighborhood matter? Family, neighborhood, and school influences on eighth grade mathematics achievement. *Sociological Focus, 34,* 435–457.

Chavkin, N. (Ed.). (1993). *Families and schools in a pluralistic society.* Albany: State University of New York Press.

Chavkin, N. (in press). Preparing educators for school–family partnerships: Challenges and opportunities. In E. N. Patrikakou, R. P. Weissberg, S. Redding, & H. J. Walberg (Eds.), *School–family partnerships: Fostering children's school success.* New York: Columbia University, Teachers College Press.

Christenson, S., & Conoley, J. (Eds.). (1992). *Home and school collaborations: Enhancing children's academic and social competence.* Colesville, MD: National Association of School Psychologists.

Coleman, J. S. (1988). Social capital in the creation of human capital. *American Journal of Sociology, 94,* 95–120.

Comer, J. P. (1980). *School power: Implications of an intervention program.* New York: Free Press.

Comer, J. P., & Haynes, N. (1991). Parent involvement in schools: An ecological approach. *Elementary School Journal, 91,* 271–277.

Dauber, S. L., & Epstein, J. L. (1993). Parents' attitudes and practices of involvement in inner-city elementary and middle schools. In N. Chavkin (Ed.), *Families and schools in a pluralistic society* (pp. 53–71). Albany: State University of New York Press.

Davies, D., & Johnson, V. R. (Eds.). (1996). Crossing boundaries: Family, community, and school partnerships [special issue]. *International Journal of Educational Research, 25*(1).

Desimone, L. (1999). Linking parent involvement with student achievement: Do race and income matter? *Journal of Educational Research, 93,* 11–30.

Edwards, P. (2004). *Children's literacy development: Making it happen through school, family, and community involvement.* Boston: Allyn & Bacon.

Elder, G. H., Jr. (1997). The life course and human development. In R. M. Lerner (Ed.), *Handbook of child psychology,* Vol. 1: *Theoretical models of human development* (pp. 939–991). New York: John Wiley.

Epstein, J. L. (1987). Toward a theory of family–school connections: Teacher practices and parent involvement. In K. Hurrelman, F. Kaufmann, & F. Losel (Eds.), *Social intervention: Potential and constraints* (pp. 121–136). New York: DeGruyter.

Epstein, J. L. (1995). School/Family/Community partnerships: Caring for the children we share. *Phi Delta Kappan, 76,* 701–712.

Epstein, J. L. (2001). *School, family, and community partnerships: Preparing educators and improving schools.* Boulder, CO: Westview.

Epstein, J. L. (2005a). Links in a professional development chain: Preservice and inservice education for effective programs of school, family, and community partnerships. *The New Educator, 1*(2), 125–141.

Epstein, J. L. (2005b). Results of the Partnership Schools–CSR model for student achievement over three years. *Elementary School Journal.*

Epstein, J. L., & Lee, S. (1995). National patterns of school and family connections in the middle grades. In B. A. Ryan, G. R. Adams, T. P. Cullota, R. P. Weisberg, & R. L. Hampton

(Eds.), *The family–school connection* (pp. 108–154). Thousand Oaks, CA: Sage.

Epstein, J. L., & Salinas, K. C. (2004). Partnering with families and communities. *Educational Leadership, 61*(8), 12–18.

Epstein, J. L., & Sanders, M. G. (2000). Connecting home, school, and community: New directions for social research. In M. Hallinan (Ed.), *Handbook of sociology of education* (pp. 285–306). New York: Plenum.

Epstein, J. L., & Sanders, M. G. (2005). *Prospects for change: Preparing educators for school, family, and community partnerships.* Baltimore, MD: Johns Hopkins University, Center on School, Family, and Community Partnerships.

Epstein, J. L., Sanders, M. G., Simon, B. S., Salinas, K. C., Jansorn, N. R., & Van Voorhis, F. L. (2002). *School, family, and community partnerships: Your handbook for action* (2nd ed.). Thousand Oaks, CA: Corwin.

Epstein, J. L., & Sheldon, S. B. (2002). Present and accounted for: Improving student attendance through family and community involvement. *Journal of Educational Research, 95,* 308–318.

Epstein, J. L., Simon, B. S., & Salinas, K. C. (1997). *Effects of Teachers Involve Parents in Schoolwork (TIPS) language arts interactive homework in the middle grades* (Research Bulletin No. 18). Bloomington, IN: Phi Delta Kappa.

Epstein, J. L., & Van Voorhis, F. L. (2001). More than minutes: Teachers' roles in designing homework. *Educational Psychologist, 36,* 181–194.

Epstein, J. L., & Williams, K. J. (2003, April). *Does professional development for state and district leaders affect how they assist schools to implement programs of partnership?* Paper presented at the annual meeting of the American Educational Research Association, Chicago.

Epstein, J. L., Williams, K. J., & Jansorn, N. R. (2004, April). *Does policy prompt partnerships? Effects of NCLB on district leadership for family involvement.* Paper presented at the annual meeting of the American Educational Research Association, San Diego, CA.

Epstein, J. L., Williams, K. J., & Lewis, K. C. (2002, April). *Five-year study: Key components of effective partnership programs in states and school districts.* Paper presented at the annual meeting of the American Educational Research Association, New Orleans, LA.

Fagnano, C. L., & Werber, B. Z. (1994). *School, family, and community interaction: A view from the firing lines.* Boulder, CO: Westview.

Fruchter, N., Galletta, A., & White, J. L. (1992). *New directions in parent involvement.* Washington, DC: Academy for Educational Development.

Gerne, K. M., & Epstein, J. L. (2004). The power of partnerships: School, family, and community collaboration to improve children's health. *RMC Health Educator, 4*(2), 1–2, 4–6.

Gibbs, N. (2005, February 21). Parents behaving badly. *Time.*

Grolnick, W. S., & Slowiaczek, M. L. (1994). Parents' involvement in children's schooling: A multidimensional conceptualization and motivational model. *Child Development, 65,* 237–252.

Harvard Family Research Project. (2004). *Bibliographies of published work on school, family, and community partnerships.* Retrieved February 12, 2005, from www.gse.harvard.edu/hfrp/projects/fine/resources/bibliography/family-involvement-2004.html

Henderson, A., & Mapp, K. L. (2002). *A new wave of evidence: The impact of school, family, and community connections on student achievement.* Austin, TX: Southwest Educational Development Laboratory.

Hiatt-Michaels, D. (Ed.). (2001). *Promising practices for family involvement in schools.* Greenwich, CT: Information Age.

Hill, N. E., Castellina, D. R., Lansford, J. E., Nowlin, P., Dodge, K. A., Bates, J. E., & Pettit, G. S. (2004). Parent academic involvement as related to school behavior, achievement, and aspirations: Demographic variations across adolescence. *Child Development, 75,* 1491–1509.

Hill, N. E., & Craft, S. A. (2003). Parent–school involvement and school performance: Mediated pathways among socioeconomically comparable African-American and Euro-American families. *Journal of Educational Psychology, 95,* 934–959.

Hoover-Dempsey, K. V., & Sandler, H. M. (1997). Why do parents become involved in their children's education? *Review of Educational Research, 67,* 3–42.

Kessler-Sklar, S. L., & Baker, A. J. L. (2000). School district parent involvement policies and programs. *Elementary School Journal, 101,* 101–118.

Lareau, A. (1989). *Home advantage: Social class and parental intervention in elementary education.* Philadelphia: Falmer.

Lee, S. (1994). *Family–school connections and students' education: Continuity and change of family involvement from the middle grades to high school.* Unpublished doctoral dissertation, Johns Hopkins University.

Leichter, H. J. (1974). *The family as educator.* New York: Columbia University, Teachers College Press.

Lightfoot, S. L. (1978). *Worlds apart: Relationships between families and schools.* New York: Basic Books.

Lin, N. (2000). *Social capital: Theory of structure and action.* Cambridge, UK: Cambridge University Press.

Litwak, E., & Meyer, H. J. (1974). *School, family, and neighborhood: The theory and practice of school–community relations.* New York: Columbia University Press.

Mattingly, D. J., Prislin, R., McKenzie, T. L., Rodriguez, J. L., & Kayzar, B. (2002). Evaluating evaluations: The case of parent involvement programs. *Review of Educational Research, 72,* 549–576.

Miller, B. I. (1986). *Parental involvement effects on reading achievement of first, second, and third graders* (EDRS ED 279 997). South Bend: Indiana University.

Muller, C. (1993). Parent involvement and academic achievement: An analysis of family resources available to the child. In B. Schneider & J. Coleman (Eds.), *Parents, their children, and schools* (pp. 77–114). Boulder, CO: Westview.

National Network of Partnership Schools. (2005). *Summaries of promising partnership practices and Partnership Award winning programs.* Retrieved January 6, 2005, from www.partnershipschools.org

National PTA. (2004). *National Standards for Parent/Family Involvement Programs.* Chicago: Author.

Patrikakou, E. N., Weissberg, R. P., Redding, S., & Walberg, H. J. (Eds.). (in press). *School–family partnerships: Fostering children's school success.* New York: Columbia University, Teachers College Press.

Price, H. B. (2005, January 19). Winning hearts and minds. *Education Week,* pp. 35, 47.

Reynolds, A. J., Temple, J. A., Robertson, D. L., & Mann, E. A. (2002). Age 21 cost-benefit analysis of the Title I Chicago child–parent centers. *Educational Evaluation and Policy Analysis, 24,* 267–303.

Ryan, B. A., Adams, G. R., Gullotta, T. P., Weissberg, R. P., & Hampton, R. L. (Eds.). (1995). *The family–school connection.* Thousand Oaks, CA: Sage.

Salinas, K. C., & Jansorn, N. R. (2004). *Promising partnership practices 2004.* Baltimore, MD: Center on School, Family, and Community Partnerships.

Sanders, M. G. (1996). School–family–community partnerships focused on school safety. *Journal of Negro Education, 65,* 369–374.

Sanders, M. G. (1998). The effects of school, family, and community support on the academic achievement of African-American adolescents. *Urban Education, 33,* 385–410.

Sanders, M. G. (1999). Schools' programs and progress in the National Network of Partnership Schools. *Journal of Educational Research, 92,* 220–229.

Sanders, M. G. (2001). A study of the role of "community" in comprehensive school, family, and community partnership programs. *Elementary School Journal, 102,* 19–34.

Sanders, M. G. (2003). Community involvement in schools: From concept to practice. *Education and Urban Society, 35*(2), 161–181.

Sanders, M. G. (2005). *Building school–community partnerships: Collaboration for student success.* Thousand Oaks, CA: Corwin.

Sanders, M. G., & Epstein, J. L. (Eds.). (1998a). International perspectives on school, family, and community partnerships [special issue]. *Childhood Education, 74*(6).

Sanders, M. G., & Epstein, J. L. (1998b). School–family–community partnerships and educational change: International perspectives. In A. Hargreaves, A. Lieberman, M. Fullan, & D. Hopkins (Eds.), *International handbook of educational change* (pp. 482–502). Hingham, MA: Kluwer.

Sanders, M. G., & Epstein, J. L. (2000). Building school–family–community partnerships in middle and high schools. In M. G. Sanders (Ed.), *Schooling students placed at risk: Research, policy, and practice in the education of poor and minority adolescents* (pp. 339–361). Mahwah, NJ: Lawrence Erlbaum.

Sanders, M. G., & Harvey, A. (2002). Beyond the school walls: A case study of principal leadership for school–community collaboration. *Teachers College Record, 104,* 1345–1368.

Sanders, M. G., & Lewis, K. C. (2005). Building bridges toward excellence: Community involvement in high school. *High School Journal, 88*(3), 1–9.

Sanders, M. G., & Simon, B. S. (2002). A comparison of program development at elementary, middle, and high schools in the National Network of Partnership Schools. *School Community Journal, 12*(1), 7–27.

Schneider, B., & Coleman, J. S. (Eds.). (1993). *Parents, their children, and schools.* Boulder, CO: Westview.

Seeley, D. S. (1981). *Education through partnership: Mediating structures and education.* Cambridge, MA: Ballinger.

Sheldon, S. B. (2003). Linking school–family–community partnerships in urban elementary schools to student achievement on state tests. *Urban Review, 35*(2), 149–165.

Sheldon, S. B. (2004). *Testing the effects of school, family, and community partnership programs on student outcomes.* Baltimore, MD: Johns Hopkins University, Center on School, Family, and Community Partnerships.

Sheldon, S. B. (2005). Testing a structural equations model of partnership program implementation and family involvement. *Elementary School Journal.*

Sheldon, S. B., & Epstein, J. L. (2002). Improving student behavior and discipline with family and community involvement. *Education in Urban Society, 35,* 4–26.

Sheldon, S. B., & Epstein, J. L. (2004). Getting students to school: Using family and community involvement to reduce chronic absenteeism. *School Community Journal 4*(2), 39–56.

Sheldon, S. B., & Epstein, J. L. (2005a). Involvement counts: Family and community partnerships and math achievement. *Journal of Educational Research, 98,* 196–206.

Sheldon, S. B., & Epstein, J. L. (2005b). School programs of family and community involvement to support children's reading and literacy development across the grades. In J. Flood & P. Anders (Eds.), *Literacy development of students in urban schools: Research and policy* (pp. 107–138). Newark, DE: International Reading Association.

Sheldon, S. B., & Van Voorhis, F. (2003, April). *Professional development and the implementation of partnership programs in schools.* Paper presented at the annual meeting of the American Educational Research Association, Chicago.

Sheldon, S. B., & Van Voorhis, F. L. (2004). Partnership programs in U.S. schools: Their development and relationship to family involvement outcomes. *School Effectiveness and School Improvement, 15,* 125–148.

Silvern, S. (1985). Parent involvement and reading achievement: A review of research and implications for practice. *Childhood Education, 62,* 44–49.

Simon, B. S. (2000). *Predictors of high school and family partnerships and the influence of partnerships on student success.* Doctoral dissertation, Johns Hopkins University.

Simon, B. S. (2001). Family involvement in high school: Predictors and effects. *NASSP Bulletin, 85*(627), 8–19.

Simon, B. S. (2004). High school outreach and family involvement. *Social Psychology of Education, 7,* 185–209.

Smit, F., Van der Wolf, K., & Sleegers, P. (Eds.). (2001). *A bridge to the future* (Proceedings of the ERNAPE Conference on School, Family, and Community Partnerships). Rotterdam, Netherlands: ITS.

Swap, S. M. (1993). *Developing home–school partnerships: From concepts to practice.* New York: Columbia University, Teachers College Press.

Tizard, J., Scofield, W., & Hewison, J. (1982). Collaborating between teachers and parents in assisting children's reading. *British Journal of Educational Psychology, 52,* 1–15.

U.S. Department of Education. (2001). *The nation's report card: Fourth-grade reading 2002* (NCES 2001-499). Washington, DC: National Center for Education Statistics, Office of Educational Research and Improvement.

Useem, E. L. (1991). Student selection into course selection sequences in mathematics: The impact of parent involvement and school policies. *Journal of Research on Adolescence, 1,* 231–250.

Useem, E. L. (1992). Middle school and math groups: Parents' involvement in children's placement. *Sociology of Education, 65,* 263–279.

Van Voorhis, F. L. (2001). Interactive science homework: An experiment in home and school connections. *NASSP Bulletin, 85*(627), 20–32.

Van Voorhis, F. L. (2003). Interactive homework in middle school: Effects on family involvement and students' science achievement. *Journal of Educational Research, 96,* 323–339.

Van Voorhis, F. L. (2004). Reflecting on the homework ritual: Assignments and designs. *Theory Into Practice, 43,* 205–212.

Van Voorhis, F. L., & Sheldon, S. B. (in press). Principals' roles in the development of U.S. programs of school, family, and community partnerships. *International Journal of Educational Research.*

Waller, W. (1932). *The sociology of teaching.* New York: John Wiley.

Weber, M. (1947). *The theory of social and economic organization.* New York: Oxford University Press.

8

RESEARCH ON INSTRUCTION AND LEARNING IN SCIENCE

Elaborating the Design Approach

MICHAEL FORD

University of Pittsburgh

ELLICE ANN FORMAN

University of Pittsburgh

Many recent writings on learning and instruction in education read like manifestos for revolutionary change (e.g., Pellegrino, Baxter, & Glaser, 1999; Romberg & Collins, 2000; Shepard, 2001). These reforms go far beyond earlier attempts to modify textbooks or instructional arrangements. Instead, they require integrated shifts in the ways in which we understand learning and teaching processes as well as achievement outcomes. For example, in the fields of mathematics and science instruction, reform would require a change in focus from memorization and practice on routine algorithms to an emphasis on inquiry processes and communication. National standards documents from these disciplines are also in line with this movement (American Association for the Advancement of Science, 1993; National Council of Teachers of Mathematics, 2000; National Research Council, 1996).

These adjustments also may require a reconceptualization of educational research methods. Skepticism about the value of educational research is currently widespread and stems from an ineffective relationship between educational research and practice (Burkhardt & Schoenfeld, 2003). As a remedy, Burkhardt and Schoenfeld (2003) endorsed a shift in focus to an engineering approach for education research that values practical utility and close ties between research and practice and relies on design experiments (Barab & Squire, 2004; Brown, 1992; Collins, 1992; Kelly, 2003; Schoenfeld, in press).

AUTHORS' NOTE: We thank James Greeno and Jorge Larreamendy-Joerns; section editors Laura W. Perna and John C. Weidman; as well as Ron Serlin and Clif Conrad for their helpful and constructive comments on previous versions of this chapter.

However, design experiments in educational research have faced considerable challenges on methodological grounds (e.g., Shavelson, Phillips, Towne, & Feuer, 2003). These challenges address a general lack of logical assurance that design methodology can achieve sound products. According to Shavelson and colleagues (2003), "The issue is whether [design studies'] knowledge claims can be warranted. By their very nature, design studies are complex, multivariate, multilevel, and interventionist, making warrants particularly difficult to establish" (p. 25). This is purportedly in contrast to a higher standard of research that, Shavelson and colleagues suggested, is set by traditional "evidence-based" research methods that *can* logically ensure sound research products.

Contributing to their perceived methodological feebleness is the relatively short history of design experiments in education. Most authors point to two publications from the early 1990s, Brown (1992) and Collins (1992), as the origin of the design method despite the fact that others argue for a longer history of this approach (Cobb, Confrey, diSessa, Lehrer, & Schauble, 2003). For clarity, we find it useful to recognize that the experimental methods typically viewed as the most rigorous in educational research were borrowed from experimental psychology, which in turn adapted methods used in the physical sciences to enhance its status early in the 20th century as a "science" distinct from philosophy (Bazerman, 1988; Cole, 1996). Although recent philosophical writings highlight how design work has been, and continues to. be, integral to development of physical sciences (e.g., Baird, 2004), basic questions about the design approach in education remain in need of resolution.

Currently, educational researchers seem to face a dilemma between design experiments and more traditional "tried-and-true" methods, often captured as a zero-sum trade-off between competing value preferences. A greater value placed on relating research to practice leads some to prefer design experiments, whereas a greater value placed on rigor leads others to prefer more traditional methods. In this chapter, we depict this dilemma as an artifact of a misguided conversation about methodology.

Research methodology provides general principles that govern the extent to which research aims are met. Rather than focusing on the relationship between methods and aims, a trend in methodology has been to make judgments about research quality merely through alignment with reified templates and tools regardless of the study's aims. Consistent efforts to achieve particular aims by a community can produce refined methodological tools and frameworks as reifications of particular principles in light of those aims. For example, science has generated statistical tools that help to quantify the likelihood of inferential error given a data set, and these tools have become staples of work constructing models that explain and predict phenomena. The power of these tools and this framework has led to their reification in templates and tools, which simplify the myriad factors that affect inference during inquiry into a set of procedures capable of testing hypotheses. An unfortunate artifact of this reification is a shift in debates about methodology away from explicit consideration of research aims.

Because the aim of educational research is to improve instruction and learning, conversations about methodology need to address the relationship between research and practice. Of course, the relationship between research and practice is not, in all disciplines, considered a methodological concern. Nevertheless, education *is* a discipline driven by practical aims; therefore, it could be considered a clinical-like endeavor in a category with engineering product design, research on the diffusion of innovations, and management analysis of institutional change (Zaritsky, Kelly, Flowers, Rogers, & O'Neill, 2003).

Herein exists the source of the seeming dilemma between traditional methods and design experiments. Education has borrowed methodological templates and tools from other disciplines that may or may not be driven by similar aims. The borrowed templates and tools are necessarily accompanied by their own "logics" by which they are asserted to lead to those disciplines' aims and, indeed, come with constraints on the aims themselves. Kelly (2004) characterized such logic as a *logos,* or an "argumentative grammar" for a research discipline, "a 'separable' structure that justifies collecting certain data and not other data and under what conditions" (p. 119). Once specified, a logos serves as a general structural template by reference to which particular research activities are asserted to attain their aims. In traditional research endeavors, or "pure science" research (cf. Metz, 1995), a logos addresses how data collection and analysis techniques inform theory. Theories are the goal of pure science research; therefore, a logos that ends with theories makes sense for that class of research. However, clinical-like endeavors that have *practical* aims, such as education, require a logos that demonstrates how those practical aims are attained through their research activities.

From a pure science perspective, one way of attaining practical aims is to simply append an additional step to the pure science logos that takes theoretical products of research and studies how to apply them. Greeno (in press) referred to this particular relationship between research and practice as the "pipeline model" because it is a linear process in which each relatively autonomous stage picks up and does something with the product of the previous stage. A logos of design experiments, however, need not adhere to the pipeline model. An alternative might not involve appending an "application" step to pure science products but rather might involve an entirely different path.

How does this help us to move past the seeming methodological dilemma facing the field? Because methodological judgments necessarily refer to an underlying disciplinary logos, it would be a category error to criticize design experiments from a pure science perspective unless the underlying rationale for design experiments shared the pure science logos, as in the pipeline model. More important, identifying this category error can enable researchers to focus on the real work that needs to be done.

Just as the pure science model of research developed through history in response to particular challenges of disciplines, such as experimental psychology, so too is a design model currently being developed in education. Mayo (1996) described the development of methodological templates and tools as a process of research and critique in which errors are identified and managed. For example, the double-blind placebo control study has developed precisely because medical researchers identified systematic errors—effects by which belief alone improved health and by which experimenter bias influenced trial outcomes. Key to the process of identifying these and other kinds of errors is the notion of "severe test" (Popper, 1962). Although Mayo developed this notion for a philosophy of statistics, the idea more widely identifies a general heuristic in science: Whatever a field's level of development, research work involves continuously scrutinizing results by identifying potential errors. As the field of education pursues design experiments to improve instruction and learning, an essential part of the work is subjecting its products to severe test so as to generate an explicit methodological logos as structural template and appropriate accompanying tools.

In what follows, we discuss what a logos of design experiments in education might look like and broadly sketch key issues that need to be addressed if a design experiment logos is to be elaborated. Research efforts to improve instruction and learning generally involve designing and implementing instruction in a formal instructional setting (be it a laboratory or a classroom) and then scrutinizing learning processes and/or outcomes through assessment data. Rather than relying on production of theory exclusively as a means of improving learning and instructional practice, design work prioritizes the creation of systems that demonstrably attain valued aims in the target settings themselves, which are typically classrooms. For this work to pass muster, researchers need to demonstrate that valuable learning outcomes follow from their instructional innovations. It is also important that the results of design research can subsequently be shown to travel, that is, to improve learning and instruction in additional settings (Greeno, in press).

Against this broad backdrop, our goals in this chapter are extremely modest. Our first goal is to confront the methodological error of judging research quality by alignment with templates and tools without due consideration of aims. Our strategy is to fill out the preceding argument sketch on this issue by highlighting some challenges that a pure science approach and a design approach face in educational research, primarily through two example research programs. To organize our discussion, we offer the following three methodological principles:

- *Rigor.* Educational research should distinguish instructional effects from alternative influences on assessment performance.
- *Value.* Educational research should produce valuable learning outcomes.
- *Generality.* Educational research should provide general power to improve learning.

As Shepard (2001) lucidly demonstrated, the issues surrounding this kind of research are complex because they necessarily intertwine instruction, learning theory, and assessment strategies. To reveal the methodological issues at stake in these complex interrelationships, we draw on two bodies of recent work that focus on teaching and learning about experimentation in science education. As will become clear, these two research programs employ different instructional techniques that rest on different learning theories and employ different assessment strategies that make sense given those theoretical commitments. The choices made in each program necessarily intertwine preferences on all of these dimensions. Our focus is not to evaluate these specific aspects but rather to examine, on a more abstract level, the methodological challenges that each of these programs faces as examples of pure science and design experiment research.

As an exemplar of the pure science model, we draw from recent work by Klahr and colleagues (Chen & Klahr, 1999; Klahr, Chen, & Toth, 2001; Toth, Klahr, & Chen, 2000). As an exemplar of the design model, we draw from recent design studies by Ford (2003, in press). Our choice is driven by several considerations. First, these two bodies of work reflect some general aspects of comparison between a pure science approach and a design research approach to teaching and learning. Second, subject matter content is common across these studies in science education, conveniently allowing a better focus on methodological issues that generalize to research on teaching and learning in other subject matter domains. Finally, we find the content area of experimentation convenient because it is likely accessible to researchers generally. We offer these

examples not as representative of the gamut of studies on teaching and learning but rather to illustrate some gross features of these very different approaches.

Two examples, of course, cannot support *general* assertions about the relative value of these two methodological frameworks (i.e., that one framework is "better" or "worse" than another). Our use of the examples aims to enrich the methodological conversation in the field, first by *countering* general assertions about the methodological feebleness of design studies and superiority of traditional methods for educational research and then by indicating how the seeming dilemma facing the field can be transcended. We address the general level of methodology by drawing on the issues laid bare by these examples to sketch a logos of design experiments, highlighting the key ways in which it diverges from the traditional pure science logos. Recognizing differences in the "logics" by which (both borrowed and invented) research frameworks operate is a necessary step toward development of sound, productive, and respected educational research.

In closing, we highlight key issues that require resolution for maturation of design experiment methodology. These issues not only involve shifts in roles for educational researchers but also have implications for the roles other stakeholders play in educational research. These shifts involve assessment design, teacher professional development, and institutional supports in school districts and universities.

RIGOR

Pure Science Model

The first methodological principle for research on teaching and learning is a necessary prerequisite for subsequent inferences about educational or theoretical significance. Given an instructional event and assessed outcomes, it is crucial that we ask whether or not the documented outcomes indeed stem from instruction. If the outcomes stem from some other factor, then subsequent inferences about educational value or learning theory would be misdirected. They would not address instructional efficacy and instead would unwittingly address something else.

The pure science model of research has exhibited a sound concern for this principle. Statistical methods from behavioral and social sciences are effective when marshaled to identify contrasts between treatment groups and control groups, or between pretests and posttests, that are unlikely due to chance. Appropriate comparisons and statistical analyses provide reasonable estimates of the likelihood of error, both in terms of inferring an instructional effect when there is not one and in terms of inferring absence of an effect when there is one (type 1 and type 2 errors, respectively). By properly employing these refined tools, we can be reasonably confident in documenting effects of instruction and in not being led astray by confounds.

These tools, of course, are staples of laboratory work. In fact, as an exemplar of the sound pure science model, Klahr and his colleagues often base their classroom studies on their earlier laboratory work (e.g., Chen & Klahr, 1999). Because laboratories allow a high degree of control of contextual factors, learning gains, in a relative absence of alternative causes, could be inferred as stemming from one particular instructional treatment.

Following the laboratory work, the Klahr group then implemented its instructional innovation in classroom contexts (e.g., Klahr et al., 2001; Toth et al., 2000). In the instructional intervention, students are provided direct instruction on the control of variables strategy (CVS) and practice employing this strategy in multiple contexts, each carefully structured to highlight the efficacy of this strategy. CVS can be described as

an abstract structural rule that a relationship between a single factor and an outcome is warranted only when that factor differs across experimental conditions and all other factors are logically and experimentally controlled.[1] Conversely, a factor cannot be deemed related to a difference in outcome when other confounding factors are present in the comparison.

During CVS instruction (Klahr et al., 2001; Toth et al., 2000), students engage in hands-on practice using the CVS approach in multiple structured contexts. In one context, students are presented with two ramps, each of which operationalizes the outcome as the distance of a ball's roll after completing its run down the ramp (Klahr et al., 2001; Toth et al., 2000). Each ramp affords variance of several features between two settings; the length of the ramp can be set as short or long, the height can be set as high or low, the surface can be set as rough or smooth, and the ball can be one of two types. Each of these features may or may not affect the outcome, and students are prompted to test each factor individually. Students run the tests, observe the outcomes, and determine whether or not each feature affects the outcome. Feedback is provided so that students are told whether each of their tests is in line with or violates CVS.

Following direct instruction, practice, and feedback, students are asked to complete paper-and-pencil assessments. These assessments present students with comparisons of situations that contain multiple factors and an outcome. Figure 8.1 is an example of one such item.

Items include information about features in both pictures and words. For example, in the item in Figure 8.1 (D. Klahr, personal

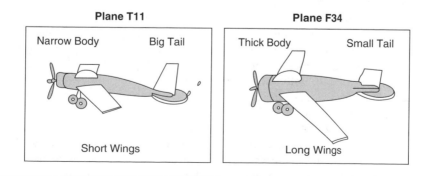

Figure 8.1   Sample Item From CVS Assessment

communication, 2001), students are prompted to answer whether this is a "good test" or a "bad test" for determining whether tail size has an effect on how the plane flies. These assessments contain approximately 16 items in various domains (e.g., planes, plant growth, foot races), and items are scored as "correct" if the student circles the appropriate response as good test or bad test for each. Each student's score is the number of items answered correctly.

The Klahr group, in various studies, employed both control group and pre/postcomparisons to demonstrate that its instructional innovation has a statistically significant effect on assessment performances. The use of these appropriate statistical tools and comparisons demonstrates compellingly that detected performance differences indeed stem from the instructional innovation for teaching students CVS.

Design Model

Research under a design model can also employ appropriate comparisons and statistical techniques to relate learning outcomes to instruction. Ultimately, under design research, the aim is a compelling demonstration that a design "works," in other words, that it reliably generates valued learning outcomes. Two key methodological challenges are to demonstrate that the instructional design, and not something else, generates measurable effects on assessment performances and that the instructional design does this reliably. Coding schemes highlight key aspects of assessment performances, and nonparametric statistical tests calculate the likelihood that any contrasts in these aspects between group performances are due to chance. Reliability is demonstrated through replication of results. Replication can be time-consuming, particularly in design work, but this is an unavoidable element of sound methodology. Similar effects documented from iterations of the same instructional design with different students provide compelling evidence that a link exists between elements of the design and assessment outcomes.

For example, Ford (2003, in press) conducted several classroom studies with instruction designed to engage students in authentic experimental practices, and this design was demonstrated to reliably produce effects on assessment tasks. Establishing "what counts" as engagement in authentic experimental practices requires a reference to disciplinary accounts of actual disciplinary experimentation. According to recent work in the philosophy of science, to count as a "practice," an account of disciplinary activity cannot be reduced to abstract logical rules (e.g., CVS) and an integrated understanding of the whole of the endeavor is fundamental to understanding the constituent parts (e.g., Rouse, 1996). This instructional approach can be distinguished from alternatives that decompose experimentation into constituent parts and focus on each part in isolation. Instruction that elicits engagement in experimental practices requires a more holistic approach because practice is something that cannot be understood in an atomistic way.

Under Ford's (2003, in press) design, students debate, enact, and revise ways in which to collect and analyze data to answer an accessible question. As an investigation unfolds, even seemingly simple experimental tasks propagate complexity. For example, in one activity (Ford, 2003), sixth graders focused on the question, "How does steepness affect speed?" The accessibility of this question in an everyday sense is clear. Yet to collect data to address this question, students had to operationally define both "steepness" and "speed." Students initially considered this task trivial, but once they suggested and enacted ways in which to collect data, trade-offs inherent in establishing effective operational definitions became apparent and students found themselves grappling with challenges of deciding on ways in which to generate a rigorous and systematic answer. An iterative cycle of enacting plans, reflecting on data, and revising procedures continued until the class was satisfied with the validity of its data and analysis.

The teacher's role in this instruction is central because without the constraints and guidance that the teacher provides, students would not encounter focused workable issues or engage experimental practices to address them. Ford's design constrained student activity by selectively highlighting issues that students confronted so that the problems "on the table" always remained focused and manageable. For example, as an investigation unfolded and decisions were faced, instruction prompted small groups to develop a solution to a focused problem (e.g., develop a measurement protocol for a variable, create a visual display that shows how results answer the question). The teacher subsequently relied on students' challenges that emerged in their group work to support debates about the benefits and drawbacks of alternative courses of action. During these debates, the teacher played the role of expert consultant, representing disciplinary constraints as the need for them arose. These constraints included ways in which student solutions should be evaluated and norms by which communication among students should be governed (e.g., students need to relate their ideas to others, students need to critique rationally by appealing to data). Ford's design is one of several examples of a pedagogical approach that has been referred to as "guided discovery" (e.g., Brown & Campione, 1996; Lehrer & Schauble, 2000). Although students work in ways that are fundamentally similar to disciplinary activity, the teacher plays a key role by engineering the environment so that complexity is managed while students grapple with some of the same problems faced by members of the discipline.

To evaluate learning outcomes, the sixth graders in Ford's (2003, in press) studies were asked, in pairs, to plan and conduct an experiment to answer the question, "If you drop a ball, how does the drop affect the bounce?" Student pairs worked for about an hour, and their performances were video-recorded. Student performances revealed appropriation of experimental practices from their instructional experiences. First, student assessment performances were analyzed with respect to similarities with the instructional unit. Several key experimental practices that were generated to address challenges during the instructional ramp activity also appeared during the assessment performances. For example, students generally took scrupulous care to standardize measurement protocols. Also, although students decided on different outcomes to answer the question (e.g., bounce height, number of bounces, time of bounce continuation), students quantified the outcome and ran multiple trials, recorded their results, and systematically summarized their results during their performances. Second, these

results contrasted with those of another group of students (randomly assigned to condition) that experienced a similar length of instruction on experimentation but with a focus on CVS (as in Chen & Klahr, 1999) rather than on engagement in authentic experimental practices. This second group of students seemed to be unable to systematize or standardize its approach to the ball drop task despite the group's earlier training on CVS. The contrasts between groups on the experimental practices identified were found to be statistically significant according to the appropriate nonparametric tests, suggesting that students in the first group had appropriated these practices from their instructional experience. Finally, these results were replicated with different students and similar outcomes.

In this way, analyses under a design model of research on teaching and learning can identify learning outcomes that stem from the instructional intervention. Like the pure science model, the design model requires scrupulous attention to aspects of assessed performance that are similar to the instructional events and can use appropriate contrasts to demonstrate statistical significance, thereby "zeroing in" on what seem to be reliable effects.

Value

Pure Science Model

The second methodological issue for research on teaching and learning involves educational value. Given a reliable effect, we are in a position to scrutinize whether that effect is educationally valuable.

Klahr and colleagues' CVS studies discussed in the preceding section present an argument about educational value that goes something like this: CVS instruction supports acquisition of abstract notions that are fundamental to experimental reasoning in science (e.g., "variable," "confound"). Because experimentation in any context can be described in terms of isolating causal factors, CVS is both common across scientific experimentation and integral to the mechanism of experimental work in science that contributes to its success. For these reasons, CVS is an educationally valuable target for instruction. If students acquire this structural mechanism, successful performance in scientific experiments generally will be supported.

Consider the assessments that detected the significant instructional effects in the CVS studies. Students were provided comparisons and asked to categorize each as a good test or a bad test. What are we to make of the effect of CVS instruction on these items? Because the performances themselves do not indicate experimental ability in an authentic context, they alone might not be educationally valuable. As a result, we must interpret these performances to explain the cause *behind* these changes in performance and then infer this underlying cause as a subsequent source of value that presumably would affect actual experimental performance. Hence, the basis for educational value rests on commitments that stem from learning theory. Although empirical data inform the inference of educational value, these data are necessarily interpreted through a particular theoretical lens. This lens carries with it assumptions, namely, that abstract structural mental representations exist, are acquired by students as a result of CVS instruction, and support subsequent generation of sound experimental comparisons. In other words, learning is seen as a process of acquisition of abstract mental entities and not as successful participation in authentic practices (Sfard, 1998). If these theoretical commitments are true, then outcomes of CVS instruction have educational value. If they are not true, then the educational value of the intervention may be questionable.

Methodologically, inferences of educational value, like inferences of instructional effects, must be subjected to severe test (Mayo, 1996). That is, stronger claims are marshaled with empirical support that rules out potential errors. In this case, an error of inferring educational value from CVS instruction is possible under each theoretical assumption; if increased performance on the CVS assessments was not caused by acquisition of an abstraction, *or* if that abstraction does not support experimental ability in more authentic contexts, then an error in the inference to educational value has been made. To remedy this methodological weakness, a severe test of educational value could scrutinize learning outcomes more closely to verify whether or not the theoretical assumptions bear out. That is, empirical evidence could be marshaled to triangulate the propositions that students acquired abstract CVS representations and that these actually function as predicted in various experimental contexts.

Design Model

The design model of research on teaching and learning offers an alternative formula for inferring educational value of instructional interventions. Recall that the primary aim of a design approach, in contrast to that of a pure science approach, is reliably generating valued outcomes. Because it is the primary aim, assessing valued outcomes is key to a design endeavor's success, both in terms of knowing when success has been achieved and in terms of refining the design to iteratively approach success. Without identifying valued outcomes, design work cannot progress. Through design iterations, it is only by reference to valued outcomes that designs can be refined to achieve their aims.

What counts as a valued outcome? In many disciplines, value judgments are made in terms of effective performance. Hence, if an instructional intervention generates performances that are valued by a discipline, then the intervention has educational value. This implies that assessments should elicit from students performances that align with key aspects of actual performance in that discipline. Assessments in mathematics should elicit aspects of performance that are key to the practice of mathematicians. Assessments in history should elicit aspects of performance that reflect the practice of historians. Assessments in science should elicit aspects of performance that reflect scientific practice. Recalling the discussion in the previous section about what counts as a practice, a methodological requirement for identifying valued outcomes in terms of practice implies that assessment data need to show not only that students can execute procedures but also that they can recognize circumstances under which those procedures are useful and can employ them appropriately.

Assessments that provide this kind of information have several features. First, they portray complex authentic situations for which disciplinary practices are relevant and useful. Second, they do not prompt students explicitly for procedures, either through problem structure or through cues, and instead allow choices about procedure application to remain the students' responsibility. Open-ended assessments allow researchers to see what students choose, thereby shedding light on how they made sense of their instructional experience. Unless assessments allow students a degree of autonomy in deciding how to reason and act in a situation that is within the spotlight of disciplinary concern, performances cannot distinguish rote learning from valued appropriation of a domain's disciplinary practices.

For example, in an assessment following Ford's (2003, in press) instructional intervention, pairs of sixth graders were asked to conduct an experiment to answer the question, "If you drop a ball, how does the drop affect the bounce?" Note that this task is both manageably constrained and considerably open. It is constrained in the sense that students are given a specific question to answer and are to show what they learned about experimentation. Given this information and some notion of experimental practice, students should be able to begin work and monitor their progress, making a decision when their answer is "good enough." It is also open in the sense that students have considerable latitude in how they choose to approach the task.

Student performances were video-recorded and analyzed, showing that students reliably employed practices they had engaged during instruction, even though the materials and research questions were quite different. Students quantified aspects of "drops" and "bounces," even though measuring tools such as rulers and yardsticks were not present at the outset of the task. (Students conducted the task in one of the school's conference rooms that contained only a table, chairs, and a blackboard. Nevertheless, they were told that they could request additional materials if they saw a need for them.) Students overwhelmingly standardized the release height of the ball for systematic testing and scrupulously collected data by running multiple trials, recording results, and systematically summarizing their data in visual displays. These features of experimental performance were reflected in

a variety of circumstances and within a variety of overall approaches that students took to the problem. For example, students operationalized "bounce" in one of several ways—as how high the ball bounces, as how long the ball continues to bounce, or as how many times the ball bounces. Hence, the appearance of standard experimental practices in student performances reflected an essential understanding of experimentation and an ability to engage in it that transcends mere procedural ability. Because these performances reflect students doing things that scientists do for some of the same disciplinary reasons, these assessed outcomes have educational value.

GENERALITY

Pure Science Model

On detecting an instructional effect, the next methodological consideration involves judging the extent to which the outcomes are theoretically informative. For the pure science model, this is of utmost importance because it is by means of sound theory that learning and instruction are improved (cf. Shepard, 2001). Theory, because it explains and predicts learning outcomes in multiple contexts, is an assertion about generality; therefore, it can be used to leverage improvements in learning and instruction beyond the context of the study.

The pure science model, for the most part, adheres to a hypothetico-deductive approach. That is, hypothetical theories of learning are constructed to account for observed phenomena, and researchers reason through the hypothetical account to generate entailments that follow from it or, in other words, are deduced from it. Researchers then collect data to check whether indeed those entailments hold in the world; that is, they test the hypothesis. Given the data that pan out, researchers are then in a position to argue about the verisimilitude of their theory of learning. The closer the theory is to the way in which learning actually occurs, the more power it will have to improve learning in other contexts.

Klahr and colleagues' studies represent a fine example of work under this model. The hypothesis is that flexible experimental performance is supported by deployment of an abstract mental representation, that is, CVS. This representation is something hypothetical in the sense that it is posited to account for observed outcomes. From CVS instruction, students purportedly generate abstract categories, such as "variable," "confound," and "good test," to which they appeal when faced with a novel experimental comparison and a prompt to judge that comparison as "good" or "bad." Increased performance on the CVS assessment is evidence for this hypothesis because it demonstrates that an entailment of the CVS hypothesis holds.

As in all scientific endeavors, this evidence is open to interpretation. Given the performance results, this account is one of several alternatives that could explain the relationship between CVS assessment performances and CVS instruction. According to the severe test heuristic, these alternatives should be scrutinized. For example, given the surface similarities between CVS assessments and CVS instruction, the possibility that enhanced performance is explained by the similarity between assessments and instruction should be entertained. It may be possible that this similarity actually embodies the very structural abstraction that the students were purported to learn.

Again, our intention is not to call into question a particular study or program of research; as all researchers know, no body of work is perfect. What we have, however, is a serious methodological difficulty that is endemic to a pure science model of research in education. Moreover, this difficulty is not unique to education but rather has concerned physical scientists and philosophers of science for hundreds of years. The crux of the problem is what Laudan (1981) termed the "problem of hypothesis." In *Science and Hypothesis,* Laudan traced this problem from Locke to Popper, highlighting contributions by many scientists and philosophers in between. The long-standing problem is that positing hypothetical entities to account for phenomena can be fruitful and is sometimes necessary for creating coherent theoretical explanations, but it also leaves scientists considerably susceptible to a bias of confirmation. Locke (1690/1864) cited this as a major source of error because, through hypothetical entities, we cling tenaciously to our preconceived ideas

and prejudge the facts on the basis of our hypotheses. Methodologically, the challenge is to use hypothetical entities to provide theoretical coherence while guarding against this danger. Laudan (1981) outlined measures that philosophers and scientists throughout history have recommended to manage the danger, and these measures generally boil down to what Popper (1962) and others (e.g., Mayo, 1996) have characterized as severe test.

The point here is that the concept of severe test, identified as fundamentally important in the history of physical science, is a general methodological guard against "the problem of hypothesis"; therefore, it is key to establishing theoretical implications. One way of submitting theories to severe test involves examining assessment data in light of *multiple* theoretical explanations—even though they may draw on ideas outside of the learning theory that informed the study's instructional design. Given that current research on learning, as a field, entertains a variety of theoretical frames, research under the pure science model should draw from alternative frames to argue for theoretical implications of assessed effects. For example, in the CVS case, theoretical implications could be strengthened with empirical data that make behaviorist, sociocultural, and other learning accounts less plausible. Theoretical claims are stronger when alternatives have been entertained and ruled out.

This methodological issue is particularly grave for the pure science model because theory is the vehicle by which both instructional practice and learning are improved in a pipeline model logos. Given this crucial role of learning theory, errors in theory could have disastrous effects, or irrelevance, for subsequent instructional practice and learning. Therefore, educational research within this model must provide compelling arguments about theoretical implications, ruling out alternative theoretical interpretations, to sufficiently address the methodological principle of generality.

Design Model

Both pure science research and design research can promote improvements in learning and instruction on a general scale, but the logos by which they do this need not be the same. In a pure science model, generalization is achieved through a universally applicable theory of learning. The research work is done within a hypothetico-deductive scheme, which tests theoretical accounts by scrutinizing whether or not they align with the way in which nature actually behaves. High-level universal abstractions are the aim of this work because through them sound instructional designs can be constructed and learning in any context can be improved.

A design logos, in contrast, need not aim only for high-level universal abstractions and instead can promote improvements in learning across contexts in different ways. In what follows, we outline two distinct ways in which design experiments generalize. First, design work informs learning theory because designs also are constrained by the way in which nature behaves. Theoretical innovations subsequently inform the construction of additional designs. Second, once designs are established, they can be moved beyond the original context. This second kind of generalization, of improvements in instruction and learning from one context to others, is what Greeno (in press) called "travel." Although universal abstractions on the level of learning theory may support travel, a design logos includes other possible mechanisms as well.

Before researchers can focus on travel, a design must be demonstrated to "work." In the previous two sections, we argued that designs that work are those in which valued performance outcomes are produced by the instructional innovation. In other words, design research first demonstrates a reliable ability to manipulate learning environments, thereby producing valued effects. Whereas the pure science model positions ideas so that they can be informed by the way in which nature behaves through hypothesis testing, a design model attains information on nature's behavior through the process of getting a design to work.

In the physical sciences, it is not uncommon for a reliable relationship between material arrangements and the behaviors of nature to be sought through design, and this kind of work can promote theoretical advances. In fact, in many historical cases, physical artifacts were designed and worked before the physical theory

had been built to explain why they did so. For example, Faraday constructed the first electric motor in the absence of accurate electromagnetic theory. Baird (2004) argued that this is far from an anomaly in the history of science; rather, it is an overlooked way in which information about nature's constraints makes its way to inform physical theory. Faraday constructed an arrangement of physical materials that worked, that is, demonstrated reliable control over nature's underlying constraints. When other scientists witnessed the surprising phenomenon of a metal wheel perpetually spinning in a pool of mercury, the phenomenon demanded—and stimulated—theoretical explanation. Through Faraday's example and other examples, Baird illustrated that mature theory often follows and, therefore, is not necessary for creating artifacts that demonstrate control over nature's constraints.

But this is only part of the story. Much is learned not only by the finished product of design but also during the design process itself. Creating a system that works, in any domain, involves an ability to craft the world's inherent constraints, whether they be material, temporal, psychological, or institutional, so as to channel events toward valued ends. During iterations in which a designer learns how the world reacts to design features, information about these constraints is gained. Although this information serves primarily to guide refinement of the design, it ultimately becomes integral for learning about the world's underlying structure and can support the development of theory. In this vein, Baird (2004) argued that even laboratory experimentation can be viewed as a special case of design because getting an experiment to work also requires considerable efforts to craft situations that channel nature's behavior, and scientists learn from these efforts. The only difference is that in laboratory experiments, the overt purpose is to inform theory.

The key is that the designer's interest encourages a flexible skeptical stance toward theory and is a disposition that encourages ideas to be subjected to severe test (Mayo, 1996). Because the aim of design work is to achieve a valued outcome, the designer has an interest in assessment data that are fundamentally different from those accorded by the pure science researcher. For the educational designer, it is of primary importance to learn from assessments how students made sense of instruction so that the design can be revised accordingly. This means that when a designer analyzes assessments, he or she looks not only for predicted effects but also for effects that were not predicted—not intended—yet seem to have been meaningful for students as well as those predicted effects that did not obtain. This information is crucial for the designer because it supports design revision, and a by-product of this is critical pressure placed on theoretical ideas.

Lobato (1996, 2003) described how a designer's critical stance toward assessment data can inform learning theory. Consider her design of instruction for teaching students about the mathematical concept of "slope." Despite high scores on initial assessments following instruction, student performances on slightly different problems, namely, to find the slope of a playground slide, evidenced a stark failure to transfer. Lobato reanalyzed student performances, found some common sources of error, and considered these in light of the instructional design. Her analysis suggested that students had drawn generalizations about the concept of slope that were unintended by instruction. Several instructional (and initial assessment) items asked students to find the slope of staircases, and the vertical and horizontal dimensions of the stairs were highlighted as "rise" and "run," respectively. In the first instructional design, stairs were used as examples because they had these features from which the concepts of rise and run were assumed to be abstracted. However, this is not the sense that students had made of the situation. When asked to identify the slope of a playground slide, students identified the rise as the length of the ladder and the run as the short horizontal platform at the top of the ladder before the slide began. This analysis suggested that students had understood rise and run to be vertical and horizontal features of objects, not the targeted abstract horizontal and vertical dimensions of an oblique line segment.

Notice that this analysis draws from student performances not only information that confirms expectations but also information that is at odds with the assumed theoretical learning mechanism. The analysis was not intended to test a hypothetical account but rather was in service of getting a design to work. Lobato (2003) wanted to know why students had not exhibited a conceptual understanding of slope, and to answer this question she scrutinized the sense that students had actually made from instruction. This work has supported a reconceptualization of transfer as what Lobato called "actor-oriented transfer."

In this way, pursuing a controllable relationship between instructional design features can lead to a theoretical advance. Consider the legendary difficulty that the pure science model has had in generating meaningful transfer, even to the extent where some researchers have speculated that transfer does not exist (e.g., Detterman, 1993). The pure science research model makes hypotheses about learning mechanisms and then designs instructional treatments and assessments for testing these hypotheses. A popular kind of hypothesis has been that abstract structural aspects of situations are those that foster transfer for the simple reason that they are general by their abstract nature. Lobato (1996, 2003) identified this structural account of learning with the expert view—that learners can apply the notion of slope to novel situations through deployment of abstract notions of rise and run. The work of the Klahr group reflects a similar commitment, namely, that CVS, as an abstract and general principle, supports experimental performance in multiple contexts.

To highlight the point that design can promote theoretical advance, consider also the results from Ford's (2003) study with sixth graders. Students who experienced instructional design based on removing sources of experimental error subsequently portrayed considerable sophistication and rigor in their approaches to the assessment question, "If you drop a ball, how does the drop affect the bounce?" In contrast to another group of students in Ford's study who had experienced CVS instruction (as in Chen & Klahr, 1999), these students more often quantified variables, standardized release height, ran multiple trials, recorded results, and summarized their results systematically, suggesting that they understood coherently how these procedures contributed to their aim. These results suggest that what Ford's (2003) students learned should not be characterized as an abstract mental representation or procedural skill; rather, it is better characterized in terms of coherent yet distinguishable dimensions of information about experimental practice. Ford (in press) employed a metaphor to characterize these dimensions as information about the "game," the "pieces," and the "players" of experimentation. Regardless of the metaphor, the point that resources for generative disciplinary work may be coherent across considerably disparate kinds of information is one that could support substantial theoretical advances on learning.

The theoretical advances pursued by Lobato (2003) and Ford (in press) stem from a critical flexible stance toward theory that design work involves. Under the pure science research model, the mechanism of transfer is predefined and uncritically assumed as it *must* be to guide instruction (to support acquisition of the abstraction) and assessment (to cue application of this abstraction) and to interpret assessed performances (to correct student responses as evidence of abstraction deployment). The pure science model does not query "what transfers" or "what similarities students draw between instruction and assessment tasks." Design studies, because they do query these issues to support design revisions, may be in a more promising position to inform the issue of transfer (Lobato, 2003) as well as other key issues in learning theory.

Although design work can inform theories of learning at the high level of abstraction, this level of theorizing is not the only way of considering generalization. As mentioned previously, *travel,* or effective movement of a design from one context to others, is another way of pursuing generalization. For a design to travel, it seems clear to us that abstractions are necessarily involved. Abstract notions are needed for communicating crucial information about a design to the stakeholders involved in making a design travel.

In contrast to the universal learning theory targeted by the pure science model, the abstractions required for design travel are likely to take quite different forms. We believe that this is an important and fruitful area for research that needs to be addressed for the educational research community to achieve its aim of improving learning and instruction.

Collins (1999) characterized a "profile" as an important product of design research. This profile is a description of a design and its function so as to communicate to other researchers the information required for the replication of a design and for a consideration of its theoretical implications. In a design logos, stakeholders involved in travel include not only other educational researchers but also teachers and administrators. A crucial issue in achieving travel for designs, then, is understanding features of profiles that support effective communication to these stakeholders as well.

Beyond Collins's (1999) profile, diSessa & Cobb (2004) offered several other forms of abstract description. Each of these forms, they noted, is on a different level of abstraction. diSessa and Cobb distinguished grand theories of learning (what we have referred to as universal) from orienting frameworks (e.g., constructivism) and frameworks for action (e.g., Brown & Campione's "fostering communities of learning," Palincsar's "reciprocal teaching," Linn's "scaffolded knowledge integration," diSessa's "learning by designing"). On a more local level, diSessa and Cobb (2004) highlighted "domain-specific instructional theories." For example, Cobb's "learning trajectory" is a design description tied to particular subject matter and a theory of how that knowledge develops with particular instructional support. Each of these different abstract forms characterizes something important about successful designs. The issue for educational researchers is to examine how these different forms promote effective communication to the necessary stakeholders and, therefore, travel.

To highlight the contrast between what is at issue here and the prevalent way in which educational researchers relate to theory, we offer the provocative possibility that due to the historic hegemony of the pure science logos on educational research, the support for travel afforded by high-level theoretical abstractions may be overestimated. Even in the physical sciences, travel of design happens without abstract theory. Consider more from the history of the electric motor. Baird (2004) noted that Thomas Davenport, a Vermont blacksmith, was interested in developing devices that would have practical utility. In 1834, he went some distance to Troy, New York, to witness an electromagnet built by a professor named Joseph Henry. A year later, Davenport succeeded in building a motor with considerable practical capabilities. The motor was an extension of the applications Henry had understood, and the design itself altered fundamentally how the magnet drove mechanical motions. The key point is that Davenport, when he witnessed Henry's electromagnet, did not understand even the contemporary electromagnetic theory, which by today's standards would be considered sketchy. Nevertheless, Davenport was able to harness a regular behavior in nature, laid bare by Henry's device, and altered the material arrangements to create different successful designs. The design traveled, seemingly without explicit support from mature, abstract electromagnetic theory.

In closing, we note that travel may best be studied not along multiple dimensions at once, as is the tendency when pursuing universal theoretical ideas, but rather along a few dimensions at a time. For example, demonstrating that a design works involves replication of a design experiment. Replication itself is a successful generalization—across time and across students. Subsequent generalization can be pursued, for example, across subject matter domains. A design, or some aspects of it identified as key, may feed an innovation in a different subject matter. Or, a dimension of generalization could focus across grade levels. Through continued design work, extending the production of valued effects beyond the original context of a study is achieving travel. This is a form of generalization not associated with a pure science logos but is key to considering the way in which design experiments, as a method, could achieve the aims of improving learning and instructional practice.

CONCLUSION

Whereas educational research has benefited by borrowing methods from other, more mature sciences, the field is at a point where methodological conversations need to reassess the extent to which these borrowed methods achieve the aims that are particular to our endeavor. In this chapter, we have highlighted some of the key challenges that the pure science model faces, drawing contrasts with ways in which the design approach can meet these challenges. As noted previously, our purpose was to counter the common assertions that, generally, design methodology cannot achieve educational aims and traditional methods can (e.g., Shavelson et al., 2003). In discussing these examples, we elucidated how the methodological error implicit in these assertions can be transcended through appeal to the overall structural relationships between methods and aims captured by research logos.

Of course, both pure science and design approaches have their respective strengths and weaknesses. Although such a "balanced" approach would not have enabled the contributions made here, it is crucial to acknowledge the importance of submitting research products from both of these approaches to severe test. We have argued that value and generality, in addition to rigor, are methodological issues that demand attention in light of education's aims. Future methodological conversations in educational research should judge the extent to which particular approaches achieve these aims, and these conversations should appeal to the concept of severe test.

To be coherent and constructive, future methodological conversations about design experiments also should appeal to a design experiment logos. That is, a design must first be demonstrated to reliably produce learning outcomes that are valuable, and for this, compelling evidence that effects are generated by instruction must be provided. Once such a design is achieved, it can generalize both by informing learning theory and by being made to travel.

This logos for design in education highlights two key areas that require concerted focus for this work to improve learning and instructional practice. One issue is assessment. For instructional designs to demonstrate outcomes that are valued, researchers need to have a thorough understanding of what activities are valued by a discipline. Fortunately, many disciplines support a scholarly community that endeavors to characterize disciplinary practice. For example, there is a large community in science studies that debates what scientific practice is and how it achieves its ends. Notably, the scholarship in science studies casts a wide net for factors that influence practice and that arguably involve not only logical and material dimensions but also social and discursive dimensions. Science educators, then, could draw on this scholarship to assess students' ability to participate in scientific practice as it is described in that literature. This may involve collaborations with scholars who study disciplinary practices or even a requirement that educational researchers themselves become familiar with characterizations of their domain's practices.

Familiarity with a discipline's practices, however, is not enough. Assessments must also be designed in such a way that performance on them will compellingly distinguish between levels of ability to engage in those practices. It has become pervasive, perhaps for reasons of economy, that high-stakes assessments often require students to demonstrate narrow procedural skills or factual knowledge without any broader ability to coordinate them or use them appropriately for disciplinary aims. Assessments need to be less constrained and more open so that students not only can demonstrate an ability to execute procedures but also can use them, as one in the discipline would, to solve rich complex problems.

The second crucial issue is understanding what it takes to make good designs travel. This, we believe, will require increased attention by educational researchers to characterizing successful designs for those audiences that influence travel. Such efforts may involve not only writing but also other communication efforts. In general, it will require a shift in the relationships among educational researchers, teachers, and administrators. Efforts in this direction may include innovative models of teacher professional development. For example, Simon (2000) drew the design experiment model into professional development for these very aims. This approach is to engage efforts to produce changes in practice, or to make travel occur, while along the way collecting information that will help to refine the professional development design. This, we believe, is a necessary and welcome step beyond the pervasive "workshop" approach to professional development.

Moreover, this approach holds promise for identifying efforts that will achieve travel of instructional designs.

The influence of the pure science vision of research on education cannot be overestimated. This is understandable because the startling success of physical science seems to affirm its methodological power. However, considerable attacks on the pure science view are becoming more frequent in the philosophical literature as alternative accounts of physical science are being explored. Rouse (1987, 1996) summarized one popular alternative that has increasingly become a focus of elaboration and extension (e.g., Baird, 2004; Kitcher, 1993; Mayo, 1996; Pickering, 1995):

> The standard model of scientific knowledge takes it to be knowledge of universal laws, valid at all times and places. . . . The problem is always how to bring universally valid knowledge to bear on local situations. . . . The new empiricism suggests an analysis moving in the opposite direction. In scientific research, we obtain a practical mastery of locally situated phenomena. The problem is how to standardize and generalize that achievement so it is replicable in different local contexts. We must try to understand how scientists get from one local knowledge to another rather than from universal knowledge to its local instantiation. (Rouse, 1987, pp. 21–22)

The fact that the physical sciences are coming to be understood in some of the same terms that characterize debates within educational methodology may make this an auspicious period for the development of our field. Whereas for physical science these issues are of import primarily for philosophical retrospection, for educational science their resolution is crucial for methodological development and success. Research on instruction and learning requires elaboration of how local knowledge can be standardized and generalized to different local contexts within a coherent methodological logos.

As methodological debates continue in education, progress will depend on maintaining an appropriate focus on educational aims. It will involve reconsideration of research quality in terms of how templates and tools achieve improvements in instruction and learning. And it will involve a reorientation to methodology as the field matures and develops templates and tools within a logos of its own.

NOTE

1. Many of the earliest CVS tasks (e.g., using a pendulum, bending rods, combining chemicals) were developed by Inhelder and Piaget (1958). They viewed CVS as one of the accomplishments of their final stage of cognitive development, namely, formal operations. CVS is often referred to as *the* scientific method.

REFERENCES

American Association for the Advancement of Science. (1993). *Benchmarks for science literacy.* New York: Oxford University Press.

Baird, D. (2004). *Thing knowledge: A philosophy of scientific instruments.* Berkeley: University of California Press.

Barab, S., & Squire, K. (2004). Design-based research: Putting a stake in the ground. *Journal of the Learning Sciences, 13*(1), 1–14.

Bazerman, C. (1988). *Shaping written knowledge: The genre and activity of the experimental article in science.* Madison: University of Wisconsin Press.

Brown, A. L. (1992). Design experiments: Theoretical and methodological challenges in creating complex interventions in classroom settings. *Journal of the Learning Sciences, 2,* 141–178.

Brown, A. L., & Campione, J. C. (1996). Psychological theory and the design of innovative learning environments: On procedures, principles, and systems. In L. Schauble & R. Glaser (Eds.), *Innovations in learning: New environments for education* (pp. 289–325). Mahwah, NJ: Lawrence Erlbaum.

Burkhardt, H., & Schoenfeld, A. H. (2003). Improving educational research: Toward a more useful, more influential, and better-funded enterprise. *Educational Researcher, 32*(9), 3–14.

Chen, Z., & Klahr, D. (1999). All other things being equal: Acquisition and transfer of the control of variables strategy. *Child Development, 70,* 1098–1120.

Cobb, P., Confrey, J., diSessa, A., Lehrer, R., & Schauble, L. (2003). Design experiments in educational research. *Educational Researcher, 32*(1), 9–13.

Cole, M. (1996). *Cultural psychology: A once and future discipline.* Cambridge, MA: Belknap Press of Harvard University Press.

Collins, A. (1992). Toward a design science of education. In E. Scanlon & T. O'Shea (Eds.), *New directions in educational technology* (pp. 15–22). New York: Springer-Verlag.

Collins, A. (1999). The changing infrastructure of education research. In E. C. Lagemann & L. S. Shulman (Eds.), *Issues in education research: Problems and possibilities* (pp. 289–298). San Francisco: Jossey-Bass.

Detterman, D. K. (1993). The case for the prosecution: Transfer as an epiphenomenon. In D. K. Detterman & R. J. Sternberg (Eds.), *Transfer on trial: Intelligence, cognition, and instruction* (pp. 1–24). Norwood, NJ: Ablex.

diSessa, A. A., & Cobb, P. (2004). Ontological innovation and the role of theory in design experiments. *Journal of the Learning Sciences, 13*(1), 77–103.

Ford, M. J. (2003). *Targeting fundamental aspects of experimentation: A comparison of alternative instructional designs.* Unpublished doctoral dissertation, University of Wisconsin–Madison.

Ford, M. J. (in press). The game, the pieces, and the players: Generative resources from alternative instructional portrayals of experimentation. *Journal of the Learning Sciences, 14.*

Greeno, J. G. (in press). Theoretical and practical advances through research on learning. In P. B. Elmore, G. Camilli, & J. Green (Eds.), *Complementary methods for research in education.* Washington, DC: American Educational Research Association.

Inhelder, B., & Piaget, J. (1958). *The growth of logical thinking from childhood to adolescence: An essay on the construction of formal operational structures.* New York: Basic Books.

Kelly, A. E. (2003). Research as design. *Educational Researcher, 32*(1), 3–4.

Kelly, A. E. (2004). Design research in education: Yes, but is it methodological? *Journal of the Learning Sciences, 13*(1), 115–128.

Kitcher, P. (1993). *The advancement of science: Science without legend, objectivity without illusions.* New York: Oxford University Press.

Klahr, D., Chen, Z., & Toth, E. E. (2001). Cognitive development and science education: Ships that pass in the night or beacons of mutual illumination? In S. Carver & D. Klahr (Eds.), *Cognition and instruction: Twenty-five years of progress* (pp. 75–119). Mahwah, NJ: Lawrence Erlbaum.

Laudan, L. (1981). *Science and hypothesis.* Dordrecht, Netherlands: D. Reidel.

Lehrer, R., & Schauble, L. (2000). Modeling in mathematics and science. In R. Glaser (Ed.), *Advances in instructional psychology: Educational design and cognitive science* (Vol. 5, pp. 101–159). Mahwah, NJ: Lawrence Erlbaum.

Lobato, J. E. (1996). *Transfer reconceived: How "sameness" is produced in mathematical activity.* Unpublished doctoral dissertation, University of California, Berkeley.

Lobato, J. E. (2003). How design experiments can inform a rethinking of transfer and vice versa. *Educational Researcher, 32*(1), 17–20.

Locke, J. (1864). *An essay concerning human understanding* (34th ed.). London: W. Tegg. (Original work published in 1690)

Mayo, D. (1996). *Error and the growth of experimental knowledge.* Chicago: University of Chicago Press.

Metz, K. E. (1995). Reassessment of developmental constraints on children's science instruction. *Review of Educational Research, 65*(2), 93–128.

National Council of Teachers of Mathematics. (2000). *Principles and Standards for School Mathematics.* Reston, VA: Author.

National Research Council. (1996). *National Science Education Standards.* Washington, DC: National Academy Press.

Pellegrino, J. W., Baxter, G. P., & Glaser, R. (1999). Addressing the "two disciplines" problem: Linking theories of cognition and learning with assessment and instructional practice. *Review of Research in Education, 24,* 307–353.

Pickering, A. (1995). *The mangle of practice: Time, agency, and science.* Chicago: University of Chicago Press.

Popper, K. R. (1962). *Conjectures and refutations: The growth of scientific knowledge.* New York: Basic Books.

Romberg, T., & Collins, A. (2000). The impact of standards-based reform on methods of research in schools. In R. Lesh & A. Kelly (Eds.), *Handbook of research design in mathematics and science education* (pp. 73–85). Mahwah, NJ: Lawrence Erlbaum.

Rouse, J. (1987). *Knowledge and power: Toward a political philosophy of science.* Ithaca, NY: Cornell University Press.

Rouse, J. (1996). *Engaging science: How to understand its practices philosophically.* Ithaca, NY: Cornell University Press.

Schoenfeld, A. H. (in press). Design experiments. In P. B. Elmore, G. Camilli, & J. Green (Eds.), *Complementary methods for research in education.* Washington, DC: American Educational Research Association.

Sfard, A. (1998). On two metaphors for learning and the dangers of choosing just one. *Educational Researcher, 27*(2), 4–13.

Shavelson, R. J., Phillips, D. C., Towne, L., & Feuer, M. J. (2003). On the science of education design studies. *Educational Researcher, 32*(1), 25–28.

Shepard, L. A. (2001). The role of classroom assessment in teaching and learning. In V. Richardson (Ed.), *Handbook of research on teaching* (4th ed., pp. 1066–1101). Washington, DC: American Educational Research Association.

Simon, M. A. (2000). Research on the development of mathematics teachers: The teacher development experiment. In A. E. Kelly & R. A. Lesh (Eds.), *Handbook of research design in mathematics and science education* (pp. 335–359). Mahwah, NJ: Lawrence Erlbaum.

Toth, E. E., Klahr, D., & Chen, Z. (2000). Bridging research and practice: A research-based classroom intervention for teaching experimentation skills to elementary school children. *Cognition and Instruction, 18,* 423–459.

Zaritsky, R., Kelly, A. E., Flowers, W., Rogers, E., & O'Neill, P. (2003). Clinical design sciences: A view from sister design efforts. *Educational Researcher, 32*(1), 32–34.

9

Learning in Science and Mathematics

The Role of Philosophy, Theory, and Methodology in Shaping Our Developing Understanding

Juliet A. Baxter

University of Oregon

Shirley J. Magnusson

California Polytechnic State University

Educational researchers have long grappled with how to improve the teaching and learning of science and mathematics. International and national studies of student achievement results suggest that many students, particularly students of color and girls, are underserved in both mathematics and science (Reese, Miller, Mazzeo, & Dossey, 1997; Schmidt, McKnight, Cogan, Jakewerth, & Houang, 1999). For some children—a small select group—mathematics comes easily. They "see" mathematical patterns and relationships wherever they are. For others—a much larger group—mathematics is an intimidating mysterious domain that requires prodigious memorization skills to produce correct answers. In science, students need to develop new ways of seeing the world, ways that might seem counter to their experiences. The challenge for teachers is to provide opportunities for all children to develop mathematical and scientific ways of knowing.

Creating opportunities that will engage all children in the study of science and mathematics is a demanding and complex task. The dynamics among curricula, instruction, assessment, and teacher education make each an important focus in the quest to enrich children's understanding. Science and mathematics curricula, as represented in textbooks, tend toward declarative knowledge and rote procedures. An oft-quoted finding from the Third International Mathematics and Science Study is that U.S. curriculum is "a mile wide and an inch deep" (Schmidt et al., 1999, p. 4). During the past decade, more challenging curricula in both mathematics and science, such as those supported by the National Science Foundation, have been published. Not surprisingly, these innovative curricula are challenging to implement, requiring teachers to qualitatively change their instruction (Senk & Thompson, 2003). When designing curricula and instruction in mathematics and science, children's understanding needs to serve as a foundation. Assessments play a powerful role in shaping both instruction and our evaluation of the effectiveness of instruction (Romberg, 1992). Efforts to assess more complex understandings and ways of reasoning require rigorous psychometrics and a nuanced understanding of what it means to understand and do mathematics and science well (Lane, 1993). Teacher education is critical in supporting teachers as they work to help more children understand mathematics and science. Research suggests that teachers need to understand the content they are to teach in a deep and profound way (Ma, 1999) as well as how children come to understand important ideas (Carpenter, Franke, Jacobs, Fennema, & Empson, 1997). Thus, all of those engaged in developing curricula, instruction, assessment, and teacher education can benefit from research that helps to explain how children understand mathematics and science.

Two related challenges face researchers as they work to inform efforts to improve curricula, instruction, assessment, and teacher education. The first challenge is to develop a clear definition of what it means to understand science and mathematics. Over the years, researchers have developed and refined how we conceptualize understanding. A closely related challenge is to develop methods for examining and analyzing students' understanding. Researchers have used an array of methods to probe children's scientific and mathematical thinking.

The purpose of this chapter is to trace the development and refinement of our conception of scientific and mathematical understanding and to examine the research methods that have supported these efforts. The discussion is highly selective, making no claims at being an exhaustive review but rather being illustrative of different approaches that have moved our thinking about children's scientific and mathematical understanding forward. We begin with a close examination of Jean Piaget's work because his research has had a lasting impact on research and theoretical development in both mathematics and science education. We argue that a major limitation of Piaget's work is his emphasis on content-free cognitive structures. Research in both science and mathematics education has focused on children's understanding of specific concepts, an orientation that has been critical to the development of theory as well as to the application of research findings to instructional settings. We discuss research in science education on content-specific learning. In mathematics education, we discuss studies of children's systematic errors and metacognition when problem solving. These two lines of work illustrate the importance of cognitive processes when learning and teaching mathematics. We then discuss two promising directions for these two fields: dynamic assessment in science and cognitively guided instruction in mathematics. We conclude the chapter with important questions still to be addressed.

The Era of the Dominance of Piagetian Theory

The work of Piaget, a biologist and developmental psychologist, has profoundly influenced how we view school science and mathematics learning. His studies of young children revealed the active and distinct ways in which children interact with the world around them. For Piaget, the child is not a tabula rasa awaiting knowledge to be inscribed by teachers and other adults; instead, the child is an active agent who builds understanding through interacting with the environment. Through his close observations of children, Piaget identified stages of cognitive growth that he saw as biologically determined yet mediated by culture and the environment. Shulman (1970) compared Piaget's description of cognitive growth to a drama: "The script or scenario describing the drama's plot and characters is given by the biological component. The role of the director—that of determining the onset and pace of the episodes—is a function of the environment" (p. 66).

According to Piaget, the interaction between the biological development of the child and the environment results in cognitive growth through a set of stages. These stages represent qualitative differences in thinking: Children do not just acquire more information as they grow older; they also think differently. In a given situation, they take more characteristics into account and see how changing one part of a system will affect other parts of the system (Resnick & Ford, 1981).

The geometric task "dot in a rectangle" illustrates the qualitatively different ways in which children of different ages think. The problem is elegant in its simplicity. The child is shown two rectangles: one with a dot and the other blank. The child is asked to draw a dot in the second rectangle that is in the same location as the dot in the first rectangle. Young children (4 or 5 years) randomly place the dot, usually noting the height of the dots but not the horizontal position. These young children are unable to consider two dimensions, horizontal and vertical, when placing the dot. Slightly older children (6 or 7 years) are able to consider the two dimensions visually when placing the dot, but when asked to use more precise measurements to position the dot, they are not able to coordinate two measurements. By 8 or 9 years of age, children are able to see that two separate measurements are needed to accurately place the dot.

Using an array of such tasks, Piaget identified the distinct ways in which children at different ages reason about the world. Children know a great deal; they navigate quite successfully through a variety of daily tasks. The implication is that learning is not simply the accumulation of more and more information but also the restructuring or reorganization of new information that is key to learning big ideas in science and mathematics. Piaget's research was an early indicator of the complexity of individual knowledge construction and the qualitative differences that occur in the development of the intellect.

The method used by Piaget and his collaborator, Bärbel Inhelder, is commonly referred to as a clinical interview. In this approach, the interviewer presents a physical phenomenon to the child and then asks the child questions about the phenomenon as it is manipulated in various ways. During clinical interviews, Piaget and his colleagues employed actual phenomena as a stimulus to elicit thinking about the physical world from which they drew conclusions about intellectual development (e.g., Inhelder & Piaget, 1954/1958). Clinical interviews are conducted one-on-one with the interviewer using a protocol that guides both questioning and the use of materials. For example, in conservation tasks, a participant is initially shown some material in a particular form (e.g., straight pipe cleaner, tall thin glass of colored water), the material is manipulated in some way (e.g., pipe cleaner is given a series of bends so that its end points designate a distance that is far less than the straightened pipe cleaner, colored water from the tall thin glass is evenly distributed into a series of short wide glasses), and the participant is asked whether the resulting change resulted in the amount of material constituting more, less, or the same as before. The physical changes affected by the interviewer do not change the quantity; however, perceptually, it can look as though the quantity has changed, and that perceptual miscue can lead participants to state that the quantity is different. These findings contribute to our knowledge of the development of understanding in science by identifying issues that children possibly have in coordinating perception and the state of physical reality, that is, recognizing the invariability in the quantity of physical materials in the different physical arrangements created.

Another type of Piagetian task seeks to ascertain whether a child can solve a problem requiring attention to all possible combinations by using a collection of four colorless liquids presented to the participant in glass containers and a fifth colorless liquid that is meant to be added to the other liquids. The interviewer starts by showing the participant that the fifth liquid, when added to another colorless liquid, can cause a color change; the interviewer has two samples of colorless liquids, and on adding some of the fifth liquid to each, the material in one glass changes color to a bright yellow. The participant is then told to find out which combination of liquids creates the yellow color. Two key elements of the materials that are unknown to the participant are that (1) the color change was due to the fifth liquid being added to a *combination* of two of the four colorless liquids and

(2) one of the remaining liquids will prevent the color from forming if it is also included in the combination. Thus, the participant must be quite systematic in examining the combinations of liquids to determine what creates the yellow color. This type of systematic activity is typical in scientific experimentation.

As a methodological approach, clinical interviews make an important contribution to the study of learning in science and mathematics. Brainerd (1978) observed that the clinical interview lies somewhere in between the typical approaches to research in psychology, namely, the experimental method and the survey method. The manipulability of the problem-solving context, and the fact that many tasks are designed such that the interviewer determines what is done next as a function of the response just given by the participant, had led to much criticism of clinical interviews providing replicable results. Brainerd described Piaget's response to this as arguing that "cognitive structures are just too complex to be revealed by less flexible, standardized research techniques" and that "one must avoid constricting children's behavior and thereby perhaps producing findings that are either trivial or, worse yet, artificial" (p. 41).

LIMITATIONS OF PIAGETIAN THEORY

An important issue in the use of Piagetian theory that was brought into relief by its differences with approaches to intellectual development in the United States is its lack of attention to learning. As Brainerd (1978) described it, "Piaget assumes that biological laws also govern intellectual development [and] treats cognitive growth as though it were a special case of growth in general" (p. 168). Piaget's writing indicates that he considered a child's developmental stage as a constraint on any learning, and he was actually quoted as saying that "teaching children concepts that they have not already acquired in their spontaneous development . . . is completely useless" (Hall, 1970, p. 30). In contrast to this view, many researchers in the United States were interested in the role of learning in intellectual development—a situation of which Piaget was initially dismissive, referring to it as an "American question" (cited in Brainerd,

1978, p. 189). Although findings from such studies did not raise questions about the issues of reasoning represented by the theory, they did contradict Piaget's thinking about the utility of teaching concepts not yet acquired spontaneously. Aspects of concrete and formal operational thinking have been successfully taught to children, often in a direct manner. For example, children as young as 3 years were successfully taught to conserve (e.g., Bucher & Schneider, 1973), children as young as 8 years who trained on the "bending rods" task successfully separated and controlled variables on related tasks (Case, 1974), and children around 11 years of age who trained on the "pendulum task" performed successfully on related tasks regarding the identification of a single variable that influenced an outcome (Siegler, Liebert, & Liebert, 1973).

In mathematics, researchers have found that young children can be taught to think in ways that Piaget termed "concrete operational" by practicing specific features of tasks. For example, Gelman (1969) focused on conservation tasks, teaching children to recognize the important features in a situation. She conducted a study in which children practiced making "same" and "different" judgments for quantities such as number of objects and lengths of sticks. In one study, children were shown three rows of objects (Figure 9.1) and asked to show two rows with the same number of dots or two rows with different numbers of dots. Children were rewarded for correct responses; thus, they were clearly told when a response was correct or incorrect. After as many as 100 practice sessions, 95% of the kindergarten-age children correctly responded to such tasks. Similarly, Bearison (1969) used a series of tasks to teach 4- and 5-year-olds how to conserve liquid quantities.

Resnick and Ford (1981) noted that children in most societies usually develop this level of thinking through normal schooling and everyday experiences. The success of a few studies (e.g., Case, 1974; Siegler et al., 1973) in supporting preadolescents to develop formal operational thinking draws into question Piaget and Inhelder's "implication that one must await children's readiness for formal operations training" (Resnick & Ford, 1981, p. 188).

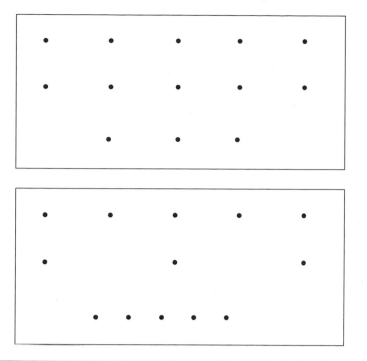

Figure 9.1   Arrangement of Chips to Practice Conservation of Number

SOURCE: Based on Gelman (1969).

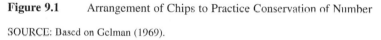

These studies from the 1970s focused on accelerating children's progression through the Piagetian stages. A related concern was matching instruction to developmental stages (Resnick & Ford, 1981). Researchers such as Hunt (1961) and Lovell (1971), foreshadowing the introduction of Vygotsky's concept of the "zone of proximal development," stressed the importance of the teacher engaging students in activities that were slightly beyond the students' capability. These researchers saw the teacher's task as creating cognitive conflict by challenging students' existing ideas and, thus, encouraging students to develop more powerful ways of thinking (Resnick & Ford, 1981).

Researchers examining cognition from a cross-cultural perspective also questioned Piaget's work. Rogoff and Chavajay (1995) traced the development of research on cognition and culture from a cross-cultural perspective and reported differences in performance within and across Piagetian stages that were a function of differences in human experience around the world tied to membership in particular cultural

groups. From the perspective of a "science" of learning and underlying assumptions of Piagetian theory, this result is problematic because in the natural sciences, relationships are expected to hold regardless of context. These and other findings suggest that culture is related to differential performance on Piagetian tasks. Rogoff and Chavajay indicated that these research results played a key role in leading Piaget to "revise his stance on the generality of the formal operational stage and led to interest in understanding the role of *familiarity* in concrete operational thinking" (p. 860, emphasis added). They cited an article of Piaget's (1972) in which he concluded that the "achievement of formal operations was tied to people's experience with the specific kind of scientific thinking that this stage focused on (such as in high school science classes) rather than being culture free and domain free" (p. 860). This quote by Piaget is significant in its admission of the problem of the "domain-free" nature of intellectual development that his theory originally assumed.

THE SHIFT AWAY FROM CONTENT-FREE VIEWS OF COGNITIVE STRUCTURES

Questions about the central role of content—that is, the subject one is thinking about—inspired a substantial body of research that took the study of learning science and mathematics in a new direction. This body of work, which began during the late 1970s and extended through the 1980s, involved investigating individuals' concepts about specific aspects of the physical world. The grounding for this work was the cognitive revolution, that is, the emergence of a focus on "what's in the head" of individuals in topic-specific ways. Instead of asking the general questions about thinking that occupied Piaget and colleagues, researchers sought to know how individuals thought about topics such as motion (e.g., Viennot, 1979), the earth in space (e.g., Nussbaum, 1979), animals as a category of living things (Bell, 1981), current in an electric circuit (Osborne, 1983), and microbes (e.g., Nagy, 1953). The focus was on ascertaining the ideas that children have about the physical world and understanding how they change and develop with teaching toward scientific concepts. In mathematics, the shift away from content-free views of cognitive structures is represented by the work on topics such as addition and subtraction (Carpenter & Moser, 1984), geometry (Clements & Battista, 1989), and probability (Shaughnessy, 1981). We discuss the research in science and mathematics in separate sections because researchers in each discipline developed content-based studies in different ways.

UNDERSTANDING LEARNING IN SCIENCE: TOWARD EFFICACY MODELS RATHER THAN DEFICIT MODELS

When the focus turned from the domain-free nature of logical thinking structures to the domain- and topic-specific nature of ideas that individuals held to explain the physical world, there was a proliferation of contexts devised to study understanding in specific areas of science (e.g., Duit, 2004). This emerging body of work represented a range of theoretical and methodological perspectives (e.g., Confrey, 1990; Driver & Easley, 1978; Driver & Erickson, 1983; Gilbert & Watts, 1983); however, the tendency was to draw broad generalizations across studies (e.g., Wandersee, Mintzes, & Novak, 1994). These generalizations—such as the assertion that when students do not have the same ideas as scientists, those ideas need to be *replaced*—have been criticized on the grounds that they are inconsistent with a constructivist epistemology (Smith, diSessa, & Roschelle, 1993). In addition, it has been pointed out that the methodologies used illuminated only the limitations of individuals' everyday sense-making, promoting deficit models, rather than illuminating what individuals are capable of learning, as in an efficacy perspective (for a discussion of this issue, see Metz, 1995).

In a similar vein regarding the study of *development* such as conceptual development, Siegler and colleagues called attention to the tendency to employ static approaches to assessing understanding, focusing on end states rather than instances of change. They argued for the need of "movies" rather than "snapshots" (Siegler & Crowley, 1991). With respect to science, snapshots may have given the impression that a conception cannot be constructed from the initial understanding exhibited, whereas movies may reveal ways in which it can, especially in contexts that promote the epistemological and ontological frames of reference that guide the development of knowledge in the scientific community. Such concerns led to the establishment of the "microgenetic" method of studying development, three attributes of which distinguish it from other approaches, namely that (1) a change is observed from its beginning to a stable point, (2) there are a large number of observations relative to the rate of change, and (3) analyses attend to qualitative as well as quantitative aspects of a change.

The microgenetic analytic approach represents a contrast to the many studies of individuals' understandings of science that have typically marked points *between* which change occurs, and from which inferences were drawn about the change, rather than observing the change in context. Strikingly, switching to microgenetic approaches represents a return to the roots of studying learning favored by Inhelder and colleagues, who wrote that the most appropriate method should "permit the subject to have the opportunity for repeated learning experiences in order to activate his existing schemes and to increase the opportunity for interaction between these schemes and the emergent schemes which result from interaction with the problem environment" (Inhelder et al., 1976, p. 58, cited in Siegler & Crowley, 1991, p. 608).

Some might consider this position to be antithetical to appropriate research practice; that is, to intervene and support students in developing knowledge would seem to invalidate one's data. To the contrary, Smagorinsky (1995) argued that "to assume that the study of learning can take place outside the bubble of the social environment of learning is to misconceptualize the role of mediation in human development and to underestimate the effects of the introduction of any research tools into the learning environment" (p. 205). Thus, one could argue that all along we have been prompting learning by asking students to complete particular tasks in our assessments of understanding. That being the case, a next step is to advance to methodologies that are purposeful in promoting learning for the purpose of studying conceptual change in particular areas. One approach that does this is dynamic assessment.

Dynamic Assessment

"Dynamic assessment" is a phrase coined by Feuerstein (1979), who is generally credited with originating the idea. These assessments are distinguishable from other approaches to assessing individual performance in that the participants (e.g., researcher and student) interact in a *guided learning* situation in which the more experienced participant "selects, focuses, and feedbacks an environmental experience in such a way as to create appropriate learning sets" (Feuerstein, 1969, p. 6, cited in Palincsar, Brown, & Campione, 1991, p. 77). Feuerstein considered this feature to be instrumental in providing information about an individual's ability to *acquire* knowledge; that is, it provides a "*prospective* measure of performance, indicating abilities that are in the process of developing . . . , [and] is *predictive* of how the child will perform independently in the future" (p. 76, emphases in original). Thus, dynamic assessments provide an indication of what children are capable of learning—their *potential* development—rather than what they have already learned.

There are two critical variables in conducting successful assessments of this nature: (1) the amount (and kind) of guidance that is provided and (2) the skills and knowledge of the guide with respect to providing assistance in appropriate ways at appropriate times. Whereas Feuerstein (1979) developed this form of assessment as a critical tool to understand the capabilities of cognitively impaired individuals, Magnusson, Templin, and Boyle (1997) employed the same idea in examining the science learning of children. In this context, they argued that the three key design elements of a dynamic assessment that is specific to a subject matter domain are (1) using a *series* of topic-specific tasks, (2) determining the desired thinking and action of the student (i.e., expected performance), and (3) determining the extent to which the guide provides guidance regarding norms of knowledge building within a domain/topic area and/or ideas to foster desired knowledge building within a topic area.

Dynamic Science Assessment

Magnusson and colleagues (1997) described a dynamic assessment in the domain of science as requiring a context in which actual physical phenomena or simulations of them are observed and manipulated and the individual is guided to make sense of what is observed according to the norms and expectations that guide knowledge production in the scientific community. Considering that a major goal of scientific activity is to develop theories to explain the physical world, and contemporary views of science indicate the prominence of theory in the interpretation as well as the explanation of physical phenomena (e.g., Suppe, 1977), they argued that a dynamic science assessment (DSA) should also engage students in the development and testing of explanations (theories) to account for the critical events/features of particular phenomena that are observed.

Magnusson and colleagues (1997) emphasized that the opportunity to manipulate a phenomenon is important because it emphasizes the active role of the individual in this type of assessment. For example, in their work with electric circuits, they provided participants with previously constructed circuits containing switches that could be manipulated as well as with extra wire that could be used to add new paths to the circuits.

The two key aspects to a DSA are the contexts chosen for the participant to interact with and the nature of the guidance by the interviewer. Regarding the contexts, Magnusson and colleagues (1997) recommended the use of a series of related phenomena, allowing assessment of whether the participant uses the same or related ideas to explain what was observed, as would be the norm in the practice of science. This feature also provides the participant with multiple opportunities to develop understanding of particular scientific concepts. For example, Figure 9.2 shows the variety of circuits used to explore students' understanding of current in a circuit (Magnusson et al., 1997), and Figure 9.3 shows contexts used to explore students' understanding of the influence of force and mass on motion (Templin, Magnusson, & Palincsar, 2005).

Regarding the guidance in a DSA, Magnusson and colleagues (1997) described three dimensions of possible guidance: (1) metacognitive mediation (common to any dynamic assessment), (2) mediation with respect to domain-specific *reasoning,* and (3) mediation with respect to domain-specific *ideas.* Guidance in the dimension of domain-specific reasoning refers to encouraging participants to follow *general* standards that guide the production of scientific knowledge such as using the same explanation in different contexts. Guidance with respect to domain-specific ideas refers to focusing students' attention on particular aspects of a phenomenon or introducing students to key concepts that would be used by scientists to explain the

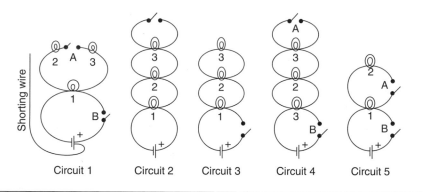

Figure 9.2   Contexts for Studying Students' Understanding of Electricity in a DSA

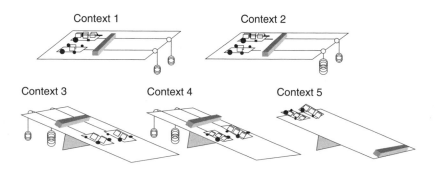

Figure 9.3   Contexts for Studying Students' Understanding of Motion in a DSA

phenomenon. For example, in the contexts for investigating motion (Figure 9.3), participants were guided to think about the influence of force and mass on the motion of the carts. In a DSA regarding sound (Magnusson, 1996), when elementary school students typically commented on amplitude differences rather than frequency differences on viewing patterns of vibrations from different pitches,[1] they were prompted to describe frequency as well. When the concept of frequency was unfamiliar to students, it was illustrated and participants were asked to try to use the concept in constructing their explanations.

A Different View of Science Learning

Contexts such as DSAs suggest conclusions about learning that are different from the ideas that prevail regarding the challenges of developing scientific knowledge. Whereas prevailing notions suggest that students' ideas are difficult to change, Magnusson and colleagues observed different results. In their study of learning about electricity, Magnusson and colleagues (1997) saw children change their concepts of models of current fairly frequently, and this was especially the case among younger children (i.e., third and fourth graders rather than fifth graders). Similarly, in a small study of children's learning that focused on understanding that light reflects off all objects and that the color of the object is due to the color of the reflected light, Magnusson, Vekiri, Lee, and Dwyer (1996) found that each of three at-risk 10-year-olds developed the targeted understanding despite reports that children have strongly held views that are inconsistent with scientific ones (Guesne, 1985).

Moreover, this type of result has been noted in earlier studies that were not conducted as DSAs. A study by Osborne (1983), in which students were shown readings on an ammeter (which measures current) that showed them how the amounts of current in a circuit compared depending on whether the ammeter was placed on one side or the other side of a lightbulb, 32 of 37 students whose initial models of current were scientifically inaccurate (because they suggested that current was consumed) changed to a scientifically accurate model of conservation of current following viewing the ammeter readings. Finally, the type of information about student learning that a DSA produces provides an opportunity to move away from deficit views into efficacy views of children's capabilities by identifying "seeds" of accurate ideas embedded within students' initial scientifically deficient models. For example, in the DSA research regarding electricity, Magnusson and colleagues (1997) identified a hierarchy of children's models of current in parallel circuits that differed in terms of how many accurate aspects of understanding about electric circuits and current were present. Models ranged from having one to several different ideas that were scientifically accurate and could be built on. The work of Clement and colleagues (e.g., Clement, 1993; Clement, Brown, & Zietsman, 1989) has taken a similar perspective on learning by seeking to identify aspects of students' conceptions that can be "anchors" from which bridges can be built to desired scientific knowledge. In only a few topic areas has this type of approach been taken, leaving much room for research to help us see how students' existing knowledge can provide a foundation from which to build rather than being seen as an impediment.

Important Next Steps for Research About Understanding Learning in Science

Whereas the vast majority of research on learning science has come from static contexts promoting deficit views that give the impression that children are bound to have difficulty in learning science because their everyday ideas are often different from those of scientists, results from DSAs present a different view. The amount of change seen in the few contexts in which DSAs have been conducted suggests promise in their ability to help uncover routes to promoting learning that are not now commonly known. Furthermore, the context of a DSA, which allows for manipulation of the nature of guidance provided to students, provides a means for the study of particular types of scaffolding in learning science that have not been studied systematically to date. Such studies have the potential to dramatically change our knowledge about teaching science as well as to illuminate the nature of learning.

In addition, there is another line of work that is important to consider relative to learning about learning science: the work of Chi and colleagues (e.g., Chi, 1992; Chi & Roscoe, 2002; Chi, Slotta, & de Leeuw, 1994; Reiner, Slotta, Chi, & Resnick, 2000; Slotta, Chi, & Joram, 1995). Chi's thesis is that learning science can be thought of as involving changes within or across ontological categories, that is, categories describing the nature of the entity. For example, physical objects such as animals represent one type of ontological category and are distinct from physical events such as running. Change within an ontological category refers to cases such as developing understanding that whales are mammals and not fish and that the phases of the moon are due to differences in how the moon looks from the earth given its position relative to the earth and the sun and are not due to changes in the moon's own shape. Change across ontological categories refers to cases such as understanding that heat is a process of energy transfer between objects or between an object and its surroundings and that a force is a process of interaction between two objects and not an entity by itself.

With these ideas about learning, it is possible to design dynamic assessment contexts that would differ according to whether the guidance attended to ontological issues. For example, general guidance supporting *metacognition* encourages students to examine how they are trying to make sense of the phenomena, whether their thinking is changing or staying the same, and whether they are considering all of the information that would be helpful to have in mind. Ontologically focused metacognitive support would prompt students to examine those same issues relative to the question of the nature of the phenomena, for example, the nature of current in an electric circuit. Students might be asked to think about what the nature of current could be like if it results in the simultaneous turning on of all the lights in a circuit once it is complete (vs. a gradual turning on of lights in turn). In guidance about *ideas* in the electricity DSA context, ontologically focused support would identify current as the result of the interaction of the materials in a circuit such as the lightbulbs (a process rather than a substance), which immediately communicates the variability

of current in a circuit (meaning that its amount can change as circuit elements such as lightbulbs are added or removed) as opposed to the constant current view that is commonly held by students.

Research with this type of manipulation of guidance would be very informative relative to helping us to understand the specific nature of support that students need to develop desired scientific knowledge. Moreover, obtaining results of such research across different topic areas would allow us to determine how far the various aspects of guidance go in supporting desired learning and the extent to which the ontological focus is particularly powerful.

UNDERSTANDING LEARNING IN MATHEMATICS: THE NEED TO MAKE SENSE

It is a great irony that so many learners experience mathematics—one of the most logical and orderly disciplines—as a set of rules and procedures that must be memorized rather than as an internally consistent network of relationships that can be tested and examined. In school settings, many learners turn to the teacher or the text for the right answers or the right procedures when solving problems rather than using the intellectual tools of mathematics to test their ideas. The ways in which learners *misunderstand* mathematics has drawn the interest of some researchers (Brown & Burton, 1978; Brown & Van Lehn, 1980; Erlwanger, 1973) because mathematics offers a rich context in which to study cognitive processes. Erlwanger's (1973) study of one student's errors focused on procedural knowledge of arithmetic operations and offered one view of the learner, a view that highlights deficits. An alternative view of the learner was captured in Schoenfeld's (1987) study of students' metacognition when problem solving.

The Study of Student Errors

Erlwanger's (1973) case study of one child named Benny is a compelling tale. Benny was a thoughtful child who diligently applied himself to his mathematics lessons, solving problems and then checking them with the answer key.

But something had gone awry for Benny. His efforts resulted in an inconsistent and contradictory understanding of mathematics. For Benny, four tenths plus three tenths equaled seven hundredths ($.4 + .3 = .07$):

> Because there's two points: at the front of the 4 and the front of the 3. So you have to have two numbers after the decimal, because . . . you know . . . two decimals. Now like if I had .44, .44 (i.e., .44 + .44), I have to have four numbers after the decimal (i.e., .0088). (p. 180)

Benny noted that sometimes the answer was in another form (e.g., 1/2 rather than 2/4) and did not match the answer key, but he knew that his answer was still right.

An especially troubling finding was that Benny's misunderstandings were not easily addressed. Over an 8-week period, Erlwanger (1973) worked with Benny twice a week for 45 minutes each session. During that time, they worked with manipulatives to develop Benny's understanding of rational numbers and operations. Benny appeared to understand the ideas. Five weeks later, Erlwanger interviewed Benny again. In this interview, Benny returned to many of his earlier rules:

Erlwanger: Suppose I had .3 + .4?

Benny: .07.

Erlwanger: How do you decide that you should have .07?

Benny: Because you use two decimals and there is one number behind each decimal. So in your answer you have to have two numbers behind the decimal, and you just add them.

Erlwanger: Your answer here [i.e., .3 + .4] is .07 and here [i.e., 3/10 + 4/10] is .7.

Benny: Right.

Erlwanger: You think that's right?

Benny: Because there ain't no decimals here [i.e., 3/10 + 4/10]. You are not using decimals. But you are using decimals up here [i.e., .3 + .4], and that makes the difference. (p. 193)

Erlwanger's (1973) case study captured Benny's struggles to learn the rules for operations with decimal numbers. Erlwanger interviewed Benny individually, observed him working in class, and talked with Benny's teacher about his progress. From these sources of data, Erlwanger was able to examine how Benny understood mathematical ideas and how the highly structured program he was studying affected his understanding. In addition, Erlwanger tutored Benny and then interviewed him to see how resistant his mathematical ideas were to instruction.

Erlwanger's (1973) study suggested that students' errors provided clues to students' understanding. Benny developed rules that he could explain and consistently apply. His errors were not simply careless mistakes or wild guesses but rather the result of rule-based reasoning. Although Benny's reversion to inaccurate rules is discouraging to see, it is important to note that he was trying to develop consistent rules for working with decimals and that the instructional context did not appear to support his efforts to evolve in his sensemaking regarding the mathematics. Studies like Erlwanger's highlight the importance of understanding how children make sense of mathematics, for they reveal the ways in which children can misinterpret and modify even a seemingly straightforward set of skills such as arithmetic operations.

Metacognition: Expert Novice Comparison

Schoenfeld's (1987) work illustrates how instruction can support students' efforts to make sense. Schoenfeld highlighted the importance of metacognition, focusing on self-regulation. Drawing parallels to reading, he noted that skilled reading relies on mastery of phonics and decoding but involves much more. Skilled readers monitor their understanding as they read, pausing to review passages that did not make sense. Self-regulation, an awareness of what is and is not making sense, is critical to reading. Schoenfeld argued that the same type of self-regulation is needed when solving problems.

Schoenfeld (1987) studied the impact of self-regulation on the work of expert and novice problem solvers. He asked college students and mathematicians to solve nonstandard problems.

He videotaped and coded each 20-minute problem-solving session, noting the time spent reading the problem, analyzing the problem, exploring solution strategies, planning, implementing the plan, and verifying the solution. The mathematician and the college students used the 20 minutes very differently. The college students quickly read the problem, selected a solution strategy, and relentlessly pursued their one strategy without pausing to consider the effectiveness of their strategy in reaching a solution. At the end of the 20 minutes, they had not solved the problem despite having recently studied the content—geometry—related to the problem. In contrast, the mathematician devoted nearly half of the 20 minutes to analyzing the problem. He attempted different solution strategies but questioned their efficacy and abandoned those that did not move him toward a solution. During his session, he explicitly noted the state of his problem solution, commenting on dead ends. The mathematician had not recently worked in the area (it had been 10 years since he studied geometry), so the specific content in the problem was more familiar to the students than to the mathematician. A telling difference between the mathematician's work and the college students' work was the absence of questions by college students about how they were progressing in their problem solution.

Schoenfeld (1987) used these findings to develop an intervention in his college-level problem-solving course. While students worked in small groups to solve problems, he would move about the room asking the following questions:

What exactly are you doing?

(Can you describe it precisely?)

Why are you doing it?

(How does it fit into the solution?)

How does it help you?

(What will you do with the outcome when you obtain it?) (p. 206)

By the end of the term, students had begun to ask the questions as they worked. Schoenfeld's analyses of videotaped problem-solving sessions at the end of the term showed that students were asking more of these self-regulating questions. They recognized and abandoned unproductive strategies, although experts tend to do so more rapidly.

With this study, Schoenfeld (1987) demonstrated that it is possible to help students develop their metacognitive skills for solving mathematics problems through specific scaffolding. Schoenfeld's questions pressed students to pause and consider how their problem-solving work was progressing. As the term progressed, students asked each other these questions, indicating that they were engaging in self-regulation. Thus, in contrast to Erlwanger's (1973) study, Schoenfeld (1987) illustrated how the instructional setting can be designed to support students' efforts to understand mathematics. The work of Carpenter and his colleagues (e.g., Carpenter & Moser, 1984) extended this line of research in their studies of children's thinking. They developed an instructional approach that rests completely on how children understand mathematics.

A Different View of Mathematics Instruction

Carpenter and his colleagues have spent many years studying how young children come to understand addition and subtraction. Based on this work, they developed an instructional approach, cognitively guided instruction (CGI), in which children's intuitive mathematical ideas form the basis for the development of more formal concepts and procedures (Carpenter et al., 1997). In a series of studies, they documented how children use base 10 materials and develop invented strategies to solve addition and subtraction problems (Carpenter, Ansell, Franke, Fennema, & Weisneck, 1993; Fennema, Carpenter, Franke, & Carey, 1993). They developed neither curricular materials nor specific guidelines for instruction; instead, they worked with teachers to help them understand how children make sense of addition and subtraction. CGI classrooms have some common features: extensive use of word problems, opportunities for children to solve problems using a variety of strategies, and whole-class or small-group discussions of alternative strategies for solving problems.

To examine how students in CGI classrooms develop their mathematical thinking, Carpenter and colleagues (1997) conducted a longitudinal study over a 3-year period. They interviewed the same children five times: at the end of first grade, in the fall and spring of second grade, and in the fall and spring of third grade. Their goal was to examine how students used invented strategies[2] and traditional algorithms when solving multidigit addition and subtraction problems. They predicted that children who used invented strategies would have a more robust understanding of addition and subtraction than would students who used traditional algorithms. They reasoned that a more robust understanding would result in better performance on extension tasks and fewer systematic errors.

To test these predictions, Carpenter and colleagues (1997) designed individual interviews to probe students' understanding of base 10 number concepts as well as their use of invented strategies and traditional algorithms to solve addition and subtraction problems. Using both physical materials and word problems, the researchers questioned each child in two 30-minute interviews. For example, in one task, based on Kamii's (1989) work, the interviewer showed each student a card with "17" written on it and asked the student to count out 17 chips. The interviewer then pointed to the "7" and asked the student to use the chips to show what that part meant. The interviewer then pointed to the "1" and asked the student to again show with the chips what that meant. This task is designed to reveal the robustness of a child's understanding of place value. A child who correctly counts out seven chips to represent the 7 in 17, but then counts out one chip to represent the 1 in 17, is still developing an understanding of the base 10 system.

The addition and subtraction problems in the interviews were designed to elicit students' invented strategies and traditional procedures. The problems were straightforward in that the task was to take an initial amount, make a change to that quantity, and then determine the result. For most of the problems, students were offered the use of physical materials (e.g., blocks) and paper and pencil. Responses were coded into categories such as incorrect, modeling or counting by ones, modeling with tens

materials, sequential invented strategies, algorithms, and buggy algorithms. Students were then categorized into groups depending on the sequence of their responses across the five interviews. Some students used traditional algorithms in the early interviews, whereas others used invented strategies most of the time with some use of traditional algorithms in the later interviews. The researchers wanted to compare children who learned algorithms first with those who used invented strategies first and then traditional algorithms.

In the last two interviews, students were given two extension problems involving three-digit numbers. They were not allowed to use physical materials or paper and pencil to solve the problems. These problems required some flexibility in thinking. For example, one problem had a missing addend: "A child has $398.00. How much more would he have to save to have $500.00?" (Carpenter et al., 1997, p. 9). The extension problems were designed to see how effectively students could transfer their addition and subtraction problem solving to other types of problems.

Carpenter and colleagues' (1997) analysis revealed that children who used invented strategies did so flexibly and were more successful at solving extension-type problems than were children in the algorithm group. In addition, children in the invented strategies group made fewer systematic errors than did children in the algorithm group. An important contribution of the CGI work is the grounding of instruction in children's thinking. The mathematical content is critical, but the ways in which children make sense of the content shape instruction.

Important Next Steps for Research About Understanding Learning in Mathematics

The work of Carpenter and his colleagues demonstrates the value of building instruction on students' understanding of specific topics. This work suggests that other mathematical topics need to be studied with the same depth. The RAND Mathematics Study Panel (2003) recommended that algebra be the focus for such study. Algebra has been studied systematically at the high school level, revealing how students understand literal terms and processes such as simplifying expressions and graphing equations (Kiernan, 1992). However, algebra is now viewed as a K–12 topic because it plays a crucial role in school mathematics, providing a gateway or insurmountable obstacle to advanced mathematics courses. Young children can develop their algebraic understanding by studying topics such as proportionality and measurement as well as linear relations and symbols (RAND Mathematics Study Panel, 2003). Careful studies of how children interpret and understand these concepts can contribute to a knowledge base for teachers. This knowledge base can inform professional development programs for teachers, "helping teachers *understand* the mathematics they teach, how their students learn that mathematics, and how to facilitate that learning" (Kilpatrick, Swafford, & Findell, 2001, p. 398).

SUMMARY AND CONCLUSIONS

In this chapter, we have tried to trace a bit of the progression of research to understand learning science and mathematics. Whereas Piagetian theory and the methodology of Inhelder provided an early foundation for understanding learning in these areas, the content-free nature of Piagetian theory gave way to research with a domain-specific focus that has attended to the nature of concepts and processes brought to bear in building ideas or solving problems in those domains. The most advanced research in both science and mathematics provides a picture of students who are very much engaged in sensemaking and building knowledge, but in ways that do not always result in desired learning outcomes. Whereas these undesired outcomes initially led to deficit views of learners, more recent work has sought to identify and understand the necessary elements required to support sensemaking that *does* result in desired knowledge building. Toward that end, the research that we described in this chapter can be grouped into three themes regarding focal points to research that we think are key to understanding and promoting learning science and mathematics.

Theme 1: Working With Specific Ideas to Learn Science and Learning From Errors in Problem Solving in Mathematics

The large body of research identifying the conceptions that students bring to science instruction has helped to illuminate a basic difference between our everyday knowledge and the knowledge of the scientific community: They differ along ontological dimensions. Changes that need to be fostered by instruction include changes within and across ontological categories, the latter of which have been demonstrated to be quite challenging to promote. However, having this understanding supports the development of new ideas about how to support learners to develop desired understandings. The methodology of DSA is an important tool to study the knowledge-building process. The guidance in DSAs can be used to specifically examine the effect of introducing *particular* ideas in fostering desired knowledge development. By manipulating the kind of information provided in the guidance (e.g., offering information about concepts such as electric current that suggest it to be a substance vs. providing information about the concepts in a way that attends to their ontological character), we can gain a better understanding of the relative benefits of different kinds of ideas to support students' work in building desired understanding. It is an important research question to ask: What is the influence on student performance in DSAs where guidance in learning about electricity focuses either on models that treat electricity as a substance or on models that treat electricity as an emergent process?

In mathematics, research revealing students' errors initially led to the encouragement of a diagnosis and remediation approach to instruction and a deficit view of the learner rather than appreciating that students actively strive to make sense of mathematics, as in Erlwanger's (1973) study of Benny. Schoenfeld's (1987) microgenetic study of metacognition showed how teachers can support qualitative and quantitative changes in students' mathematical thinking. The CGI approach sought to capitalize on students' informal understanding of mathematics by using it to help teachers develop detailed understanding of how children come to understand addition and subtraction and the types of problems that can foster their understanding. The question remains as to whether the CGI approach can support students' learning of more complex topics. An important research question in this vein is the following: How do children come to understand algebraic ideas (e.g., geometric ideas, calculus ideas), and what are the types of problems that will further that understanding?

Theme 2: The Role of Metacognition in Fostering Knowledge Building

Whereas this theme is an important principle of how people learn (National Research Council, 1999), research in science learning has illuminated particular aspects of one's thinking that are important to attend to in the knowledge-building process. The guidance in a DSA regarding the norms for producing new knowledge in the scientific community reflects one aspect of thinking to which learners should attend. Prompting learners' awareness that the knowledge they are seeking to develop requires a new perspective on the nature of reality—that is, an ontological shift across categories—may make a substantial difference in the knowledge that students can build from instruction. The methodology of a DSA can be used to systematically study the effect of this awareness by itself and in hand with guidance providing specific ideas. For example, do we see differences in performance in DSAs where guidance focuses on prompting students to attend to whether they are thinking about heat or electricity as a substance or a process? And what impact does the guidance have if it is just about prompting students to think about electricity or heat as a process versus guidance that more specifically provides information about the nature of the process?

In mathematics, we have seen that metacognition can be supported by teachers' questions that encourage students to examine their thinking while solving complex problems such as in Schoenfeld's (1987) work. The question that remains is whether there are domain-specific aspects to thinking about metacognitive processes in the doing of mathematics that are important to investigate similar to those described for science previously. One avenue for pursuing

this inquiry might build on the work of Ball and Bass (2003), who distinguished between two types of mathematical reasoning: reasoning of inquiry (i.e., problem posing) and reasoning of justification (i.e., justifying or proving mathematical claims). These types of reasoning are more common at higher levels of mathematics, but Ball and Bass urged that they be emphasized at the elementary level as well. As we identify and come to understand these types of mathematical thinking, it provides the opportunity to ask the question: How we can help children to become aware of the range of reasoning that can be productively applied to problem solving in mathematical situations?

Theme 3: Programs of Instructional Research

Both methodologies presented in this chapter—dynamic assessment and the work of Magnusson and colleagues in science, microgenetic analyses conducted by Schoenfeld in mathematics—provide examples of means of study that could be laboratory based yet highly informative regarding the nature of learning and implications for instruction. The use of dynamic assessment contexts, in which the guidance can be manipulated to ask specific questions of the nature of teacher scaffolding that would be most productive in the process of building desired scientific or mathematical knowledge, provides a logical next step in a program of research toward the design of instruction based on a science of learning. Finally, laboratory studies can be followed by classroom-based research employing the types of scaffolding found to be most effective in the dynamic assessment contexts, and the effectiveness across a range of students and within the complexity of classroom life can be examined. We argue that such programs are critical to addressing the challenges we face in reaching desired national goals for science and mathematics learning.

NOTES

1. The DSA involved the use of software that allowed a microcomputer to function as an oscilloscope.

2. Carpenter and colleagues (1997) defined invented strategies as procedures that students develop collectively or individually to solve problems. Although initially the children in CGI classrooms work extensively with physical materials to model addition and subtraction, their invented strategies do not include the use of physical materials of any kind.

REFERENCES

Ball, D. L., & Bass, H. (2003). Making mathematics reasonable in school. In J. Kilpatrick, W. G. Martin, & D. Schifter (Eds.), *A research companion to Principles and Standards for School Mathematics* (pp. 27–44). Reston, VA: National Council of Teachers of Mathematics.

Bearison, D. J. (1969). Role of measurement operations in the acquisition of conservation. *Developmental Psychology, 1,* 653–660.

Bell, B. F. (1981). When is an animal not an animal? *Journal of Biological Education, 15,* 213–218.

Brainerd, C. (1978). *Piaget's theory of intelligence.* Englewood Cliffs, NJ: Prentice Hall.

Brown, J. S., & Burton, R. B. (1978). Diagnostic models for procedural bugs in basic mathematical skills. *Cognitive Science, 2,* 155–192.

Brown, J. S., & Van Lehn, K. (1980). Repair theory: A generative theory of bugs in procedural skills. *Cognitive Science, 4,* 379–426.

Bucher, B., & Schneider, R. R. (1973). Acquisition and generalization of conservation by preschoolers using operant training. *Journal of Experimental Child Psychology, 16,* 187–204.

Carpenter, T. P., Ansell, E., Franke, M. L., Fennema, E., & Weisneck, L. (1993). A study of kindergarten children's problem-solving processes. *Journal for Research in Mathematics Education, 24,* 428–441.

Carpenter, T. P., Franke, M. L., Jacobs, V. R., Fennema, E., & Empson, S. B. (1997). A longitudinal study of invention and understanding in children's multidigit addition and subtraction. *Journal for Research in Mathematics Education, 29,* 3–20.

Carpenter, T. P., & Moser, J. M. (1984). The acquisition of additional and subtraction concepts in grades one through three. *Journal for Research in Mathematics Education, 15,* 179–202.

Case, R. (1974). Structures and strictures: Some functional limitations on the course of cognitive growth. *Cognitive Psychology, 6,* 544–573.

Chi, M. T. H. (1992). Conceptual change within and across ontological categories: Examples from learning and discovery in science. In R. Giere (Ed.), *Cognitive models of science* (Minnesota Studies in the Philosophy of Science, pp. 129–186). Minneapolis: University of Minnesota Press.

Chi, M. T. H., & Roscoe, R. D. (2002). The processes and challenges of conceptual change. In M. Limon & L. Mason (Eds.), *Reconsidering conceptual change: Issues in theory and practice* (pp. 3–27). Dordrecht, Netherlands: Kluwer Academic.

Chi, M. T. H., Slotta, J. D., & de Leeuw, N. (1994). From things to processes: A theory of conceptual change for learning science concepts. *Learning and Instruction, 4,* 27–43.

Clement, J. (1993). Using bridging analogies and anchoring intuitions to deal with students' preconceptions in physics. *Journal of Research in Science Teaching, 30,* 1241–1257.

Clement, J., Brown, D. E., & Zietsman, A. (1989). Not all preconceptions are misconceptions: Finding "anchoring conceptions" for grounding instruction on students' intuitions. *International Journal of Science Education, 11,* 554–565.

Clements, D. H., & Battista, M. T. (1989). Learning of geometric concepts in a Logo environment. *Journal for Research in Mathematics Education, 20,* 450–467.

Confrey, J. (1990). A review of the research on student conceptions in mathematics, science, and programming. In C. Cazden (Ed.), *Review of Research in Education* (pp. 3–56). Washington, DC: American Educational Research Association.

Driver, R., & Easley, J. (1978). Pupils and paradigms: A review of the literature related to concept development in adolescent science students. *Studies in Science Education, 5,* 61–84.

Driver, R., & Erickson, G. (1983). Theories-in-action: Some theoretical and empirical issues in the study of students' conceptual frameworks in science. *Studies in Science Education, 10,* 37–60.

Duit, R. (2004). *Students' and teachers' conceptions and science education* (5th ed.). Available: www.ipn.uni-kiel.de/aktuell/stcse/stcse.html

Erlwanger, S. H. (1973). Benny's conception of rules and answers in IPI mathematics. *Journal of Children's Mathematical Behavior, 1*(3), 157–283.

Fennema, E., Carpenter, T. P., Franke, M. L., & Carey, D. (1993). Learning to use children's mathematical thinking: A case study. In R. B. Davis & C. A. Maher (Eds.), *School, mathematics, and the world of reality* (pp. 93–117). Boston: Allyn & Bacon.

Feuerstein, R. (1969). *The instrumental enrichment method: An outline of theory and technique.* Unpublished manuscript, Hadassah–Wize–Canade Research Institute, Jerusalem, Israel.

Feuerstein, R. (1979). *The dynamic assessment of retarded performers: The learning potential assessment device, theory, instruments, and techniques.* Baltimore, MD: University Park Press.

Gelman, R. (1969). Conservation acquisition: A problem of learning to attend to relevant attributes. *Journal of Experimental Child Psychology, 7*, 167–187.

Gilbert, J. K., & Watts, D. M. (1983). Concepts, misconceptions, and alternative conceptions: Changing perspectives in science education. *Studies in Science Education, 10*, 61–98.

Guesne, E. (1985). Light. In E. Driver, E. Guesne, & A. Tiberghien (Eds.), *Children's ideas in science* (pp. 10–32). Milton Keynes, UK: Open University Press.

Hall, E. (1970, May). A conversation with Jean Piaget and Bärbel Inhelder. *Psychology Today,* pp. 25–32, 54–56.

Hunt, J. M. (1961). *Intelligence and experience.* New York: Ronald Press.

Inhelder, B., Ackerman-Vallado, E., Blanchet, A., Karmiloff-Smith, A., Kilcher-Hagedorn, H., Montagero, J., & Robert, M. (1976). The process of invention in cognitive development: A report of research in progress. *Archives de Psychologie, 171*, 57–72.

Inhelder, B., & Piaget, J. (1958). *The growth of logical thinking from childhood to adolescence.* New York: Basic Books. (Original work published in 1954)

Kamii, C. (1989). *Young children continue to invent arithmetic—2nd grade: Implications of Piaget's theory.* New York: Columbia University, Teachers College Press.

Kiernan, C. (1992). The learning and teaching of school algebra. In D. Grouws (Ed.), *Handbook of research on mathematics teaching and learning* (pp. 390–419). New York: Macmillan.

Kilpatrick, J., Swafford, J., & Findell, B. (Eds.). (2001). *Adding it up: Helping children learn mathematics.* Washington, DC: National Academy of Sciences.

Lane, S. (1993). The conceptual framework for the development of a mathematics performance assessment. *Educational Measurement: Issues and Practice, 12*(2), 16–23.

Lovell, K. (1971). *The growth of understanding in mathematics: Kindergarten through grade three.* New York: Holt, Rinehart & Winston.

Ma, L. (1999). *Knowing and teaching elementary mathematics.* Mahwah, NJ: Lawrence Erlbaum.

Magnusson, S. J. (1996). Complexities of learning with computer-based tools: A case of inquiry about sound and music in elementary school. *Journal of Science Education and Technology, 5*, 297–309.

Magnusson, S. J., Templin, M., & Boyle, R. A. (1997). Dynamic science assessment: A new approach for investigating conceptual change. *Journal of the Learning Sciences, 6*(1), 91–142.

Magnusson, S. J., Vekiri, I., Lee, J., & Dwyer, L. (1996). *A dynamic science assessment concerning children's developing understanding of light.* Unpublished manuscript, California Polytechnic State University. (Available from S. J. Magnusson, smagnuss@calpoly.edu)

Metz, K. E. (1995). Reassessment of developmental constraints on children's science instruction. *Review of Educational Research, 65*(2), 93–127.

Nagy, M. H. (1953). The representation of germs by children. *Journal of General Psychology, 83*, 227–240.

National Research Council. (1999). How people learn: Brain, mind, experience, and school. In J. D. Bransford, A. L. Brown, & R. R. Cocking (Eds.), *Commission on Behavioral and Social Sciences and Education.* Washington, DC: National Academy Press.

Nussbaum, J. (1979). Children's conception of the earth as a cosmic body: A cross-age study. *Science Education, 63*(1), 83–93.

Osborne, R. (1983). Towards modifying children's ideas about electric current. *Research in Science and Technological Education, 1*(1), 73–82.

Palincsar, A. S., Brown, A. L., & Campione, J. C. (1991). Dynamic assessment. In H. L. Swanson (Ed.), *Handbook on the assessment of learning disabilities: Theory, research, and practice* (pp. 75–94). Austin, TX: Pro-Ed.

Piaget, J. (1972). Intellectual evolution from adolescence to adulthood. *Human Development, 15,* 1–12.

RAND Mathematics Study Panel. (2003). *Mathematical proficiency for all students: Towards a strategic development program in mathematics education* (MR-1643.0-OERI). Santa Monica, CA: RAND.

Reese, C. M., Miller, K. E., Mazzeo, J., & Dossey, J. A. (1997). *NAEP 1996 mathematics report card for the nation and the states.* Washington, DC: National Center for Education Studies.

Reiner, M., Slotta, J. D., Chi, M. T. H., & Resnick, L. B. (2000). Naïve physics reasoning: A commitment to substance-based conceptions. *Cognition and Instruction, 18*(1), 1–34.

Resnick, L. B., & Ford, W. W. (1981). *The psychology of mathematics for instruction.* Hillsdale, NJ: Lawrence Erlbaum.

Rogoff, B., & Chavajay, P. (1995). What's become of research on the cultural basis of cognitive development? *American Psychologist, 50,* 859–877.

Romberg, T. (Ed.). (1992). *Mathematics assessment and evaluation: Imperatives for mathematics educators.* Albany: State University of New York Press.

Schmidt, W. H., McKnight, C. C., Cogan, L. S., Jakewerth, P. M., & Houang, R. T. (1999). *Facing the consequences: Using TIMSS for a closer look at mathematics and science education.* Dordrecht, Netherlands: Kluwer.

Schoenfeld, A. (1987). What's all the fuss about metacognition? In A. Schoenfeld (Ed.), *Cognitive science and mathematics education* (pp. 189–215). Hillsdale, NJ: Lawrence Erlbaum.

Senk, S. L., & Thompson, D. R. (Eds.). (2003). *Standards-based school mathematics curricula: What are they? What do students learn?* Mahwah, NJ: Lawrence Erlbaum.

Shaughnessy, J. M. (1981). Misconceptions of probability: From systematic errors to systematic experiments and decisions. In A. Schulte (Ed.), *Teaching statistics and probability* (pp. 90–100). Reston, VA: National Council of Teachers of Mathematics.

Shulman, L. S. (1970). Psychology and mathematics education. In E. G. Begle (Ed.), *Mathematics education: The sixty-ninth yearbook of the National Society for the Study of Education* (pp. 23–71). Chicago: National Society for the Study of Education.

Siegler, R. S., & Crowley, K. (1991). The microgenetic method: A direct means for studying cognitive development. *American Psychologist, 46,* 606–620.

Siegler, R. S., Liebert, D. E., & Liebert, R. M. (1973). Inhelder and Piaget's pendulum problem: Teaching preadolescents to act as scientists. *Developmental Psychology, 11,* 97–101.

Slotta, J. D., Chi, M. T. H., & Joram, E. (1995). Assessing students' misclassifications of physics concepts: An ontological basis for conceptual change. *Cognition and Instruction, 13,* 373–400.

Smagorinsky, P. (1995). The social construction of data: Methodological problems of investigating learning in the zone of proximal development. *Review of Educational Research, 65*(3), 191–212.

Smith, J. P., diSessa, A. A., & Roschelle, J. (1993). Misconceptions reconceived: A constructivist analysis of knowledge in transition. *Journal of the Learning Sciences, 3,* 115–163.

Suppe, F. (1977). *The structure of scientific theories* (2nd ed.). Champagne–Urbana: University of Illinois Press.

Templin, M., Magnusson, S. J., & Palincsar, A. S. (2005). *The development of children's understanding of motion.* Unpublished manuscript, California Polytechnic State University.

Viennot, L. (1979). Spontaneous learning in elementary dynamics. *European Journal of Science Education, 1*(2), 205–221.

Wandersee, J. H., Mintzes, J. J., & Novak, J. D. (1994). Research on alternative conceptions in science. In D. Gabel (Ed.), *Handbook of research on science teaching and learning* (pp. 177–210). New York: Macmillan.

10

RECONCEPTUALIZING AND RECENTERING RESEARCH IN SPECIAL EDUCATION

CHERYL HANLEY-MAXWELL
University of Wisconsin–Madison

BRIAN A. BOTTGE
University of Wisconsin–Madison

The field of special education became a legitimate field of educational inquiry during the 1960s. Modern special education borrowed much of its understanding about the nature of disabilities from other fields, such as medicine and psychology, where it was widely held that

> (1) disability is a condition that is inherent among certain individuals, (2) disability labels are useful in making objective distinctions between people with and without disabilities, (3) systems of services that help people with disabilities are rationally conceived and coordinated, and (4) progress toward helping people with disabilities can be made by improving diagnosis and intervention. (Bogdan & Kugelmass, 1984, cited in Skrtic, 1986)

Embedded in these assumptions was the belief that research could ultimately identify and provide evidence of successful practices for enabling persons with disabilities to lead productive and rewarding lives in educational and community environments.

Over the past several decades, researchers in special education have developed and tested a variety of approaches and techniques for helping children to achieve at higher levels in school and helping young adults to make the successful transition from school to community settings. One of the most contentious and continuing debates in special education has centered on what settings are most appropriate and effective for accomplishing these goals. That is, from what instructional placement do students with disabilities profit the most? To wit, Dunn (1968) questioned the efficacy of special education programs during the 1960s that segregated students with mild mental retardation from their peers without disabilities. Dunn believed that the goal of research and practice was to develop instructional strategies powerful enough to *fix* these students so that they could learn at rates comparable to those of their peers without disabilities. Taking a slightly different approach, Deno (1970) argued for the provision of a continuum of services that provided alternatives, ranging from segregated special education settings to integrated general education settings (cited in Edgar & Polloway, 1994). Debates such as these were important because they questioned beliefs about human development and challenged practices that denied children with disabilities access to the same education opportunities that children without disabilities enjoyed. For prior to the 1960s, persons with developmental disabilities were cared for, in large part, by institutions or government programs (e.g., developmental disability centers, sheltered workshops, hospital schools), private/parent-sponsored schools, and family members. A majority of students with mild disabilities (e.g., learning disabilities, mild mental retardation, behavior and emotional disabilities) received their education in segregated settings for most or all of the school day.

As accommodations were made for students with disabilities in more inclusive instructional settings, debate over appropriate curricular content and teaching strategies intensified. Scholars who advocated for the availability of a continuum of services (from fully included to fully segregated) believed that general education settings, along with the content and methods used, could not meet the needs of all students with disabilities. In support for their position, they cited results from studies that showed the negative attitudes of teachers toward students with disabilities, inappropriate and ineffective instruction in inclusive classrooms, lack of adequate time to develop curricular and instructional accommodations in general education (especially at the secondary level), and reliance on large-group instruction that minimized the amount of individual help that students with disabilities received (Baker & Zigmond, 1990, 1995; Lieberman, 1996; Schumm & Vaughn, 1995). Proponents of inclusive education believed that access to challenging curricula, higher expectations, and interactions with peers without disabilities were compelling reasons for students with disabilities to be educated in general education classrooms (e.g., Lipsky & Gartner, 1996).

Although discussions over placements of students with disabilities persist, current theory and practices in special education reflect an enhanced understanding of the etiology and characteristics of disabilities, how to develop and implement strategies to remediate or accommodate the disabilities, and how the educational contexts interact with student characteristics to either relieve or exacerbate student learning and performance problems. In this chapter, we begin by recognizing this enhanced understanding through summarizing the extant state of affairs for children and adults with disabilities. We go on to advance a research agenda that builds on, but goes beyond, the extant research. Specifically, we advance a single overarching question—"Regardless of instructional setting, which approaches and techniques result in the most positive outcomes for individuals with disabilities?"—to guide inquiry along with four levels of intervention for answering that question. We conclude by suggesting two lines of research to illustrate how research-based practices in special education *can* contribute to enhancing the outcomes for students with disabilities.

STATUS OF CHILDREN AND ADULTS WITH DISABILITIES: A CONTEMPORARY PORTRAIT

Results of the National Longitudinal Transition Study–2 (NLTS2) (Wagner, Newman, & Cameto, 2004) were mixed with regard to the achievement of students with disabilities. On the positive side, the study found that since 1993, grades of high school students with disabilities improved from Cs to As and Bs, with the majority of students receiving at least passing grades. It also reported that 30% of these students were taking academic courses (e.g., math, science, social studies, foreign languages) in general education settings compared with only 9% in 1993. Most of these students got along with their teachers and peers, controlled their behavior, and followed directions. Furthermore, more students had access to adaptive technology, curricular and instructional accommodations, and mental health, social work, and health services (e.g., alcohol and other drug abuse) than was the case during the previous decade. These programs appeared to be paying off because more students with disabilities were employed and attending school than was the case in the past.

The NLTS2 also provided an in-depth snapshot of students with learning disabilities and emotional disabilities. Most of these students (77%) were male, 30% lived in poverty, and 25% were reported by their parents to have low social skills. These students found schools to be extremely challenging, as 40% of them had attended five or more schools, 38% had been held back at least one grade, 75% had been suspended or expelled at least one time, and 42% had been in fights and reported having been bullied during the school year. About half of these students had received mental health services, 43% had received conflict resolution/anger management training, 34% had received substance abuse services, and 34% had case managers assigned to them (Levine, Marder, & Wagner, 2004).

The NLTS2 reported persistent academic and social problems among students with disabilities. For example, 25% of the general education teachers believed that students with disabilities were not keeping up in their work compared with students without disabilities and indicated that students with disabilities were more likely to be *less engaged* in academic class activities (e.g., class discussions, homework completion). In reading and math especially, students with disabilities achieved far below grade level, severely limiting their chances of successfully completing high school-level work. Compared with their peers, students with disabilities were also absent from school more often and experienced more school disciplinary actions, arrests, and job terminations. The importance of receiving better grades, cited as a positive outcome earlier, was lessened by the fact that there was virtually no correlation between grades and academic achievement, although lower grades were associated with consequences of problem behaviors in school (e.g., suspension) and in the community (e.g., arrest) (Wagner et al., 2004).

Low academic achievement of these students could also be attributed to high dropout rates.

For example, during the mid- to late 1980s, the dropout rate for all students was between 12% (Benz & Halpern, 1986) and 16% (Edgar, 1988). In comparison, the dropout rate was 48% for students with behavioral or emotional disabilities, 30% for students with mild cognitive disabilities, and 28% for students with learning disabilities (Wagner, Blackorby, Cameto, & Newman, 1993). A more recent report indicated that the problem is worse (National Council on Disabilities, 2000). During the 2001–2002 school year, 31% of students with mild cognitive disabilities, 35% of students with learning disabilities, and 65% of students with emotional disabilities dropped out of school.

Faced with these statistics, researchers, school officials, and adult service providers worry about the prospect of students with disabilities leading productive adult lives (Phelps & Hanley-Maxwell, 1997). Follow-up studies during the late 1980s and early 1990s showed that a large proportion of students with disabilities experienced unfavorable outcomes when they reached adulthood (Bruininks, Lewis, & Thurlow, 1989; Hasazi, Gordon, & Roe, 1985; Kortering & Edgar, 1988; Mithaug, Horiuchi, & Fanning, 1985; Neel, Meadows, Levine, & Edgar, 1988; Scuccimarra & Speece, 1990; Sitlington & Frank, 1990; Wagner et al., 1993). In large part, unemployment rates contributed to these lackluster outcomes. For example, reports cited an unemployment rate of 30% for high school graduates with learning disabilities and 50% for graduates with cognitive disabilities or emotional disabilities (Edgar, 1988; Wagner et al., 1993). More recent data indicate that of the students with disabilities who complete high school, only 27% go on to postsecondary education and only 50% continue employment 3 to 5 years after graduation (Fabian, Lent, & Willis, 1998). Furthermore, 29% of all people with disabilities live in households with income levels of $15,000 or less compared with 10% of households in which no individuals with disabilities reside. For youth with disabilities, 35% of households in which youth with disabilities reside have incomes of less than $12,500 compared with 18% of households in which no youth with disabilities reside (National Organization on Disability and Harris Interactive, 2000).

Toward a Research Agenda

Despite sobering statistics, there is little doubt that the work of special educators (e.g., practitioners, researchers) has improved the lives of people with disabilities. These significant advances have improved the quality and scope of curricula and teaching methods that teachers use in their classrooms and the programs that provide assistance to young adults as they transition from school to community settings. Yet we believe that special educators continue to debate philosophy and placement issues at the expense of testing interventions that may prove to be effective for many individuals with disabilities regardless of where they are implemented. In our opinion, the primary goal—but certainly not the only goal—of research in contemporary special education should answer this question: Regardless of instructional setting, what approaches and techniques result in the most positive outcomes for individuals with disabilities?

To answer this question, some scholars have challenged special education researchers to move away from focusing exclusively on the individual to considering how social variables and institutional factors create and maintain our conceptions of disability (Brantlinger, 1997; Oliver, 1992; Skrtic, 1986). Hanley-Maxwell, Rusch, and Rappaport (1989) proposed using a multilevel approach to describe social problems and to create and analyze the effects of interventions for persons with disabilities. In the following subsections, we describe four levels of research: individual, small-group, organization/systems-centered, and institutional/community.

Individual-Level Research. At the individual level, persons with disabilities are viewed as the source of the problem in that they deviate from the norm and are in need of transformation. Thus, change at this level relies on strategies and tactics designed to be person-centered (Hanley-Maxwell, Rusch, & Rappaport, 1989).

Many researchers in a variety of subareas within special education have focused their research at this level. As a result, the field today knows a great deal about the characteristics and needs of persons with disabilities. In addition, researchers have generated a considerable body of knowledge based on results from single-subject research in areas such as behavior intervention, social skills training, self-management development, functional skill development, reading, and math. However, this research is often conducted with the purpose of isolating the *pure* affect in controlled situations. Although these situations can be varied systematically, research focused at the individual level requires the researcher to determine how to achieve generalization and maintenance across contexts such as in the variety of postsecondary settings, tasks, people, and materials. Unanswered or partially answered questions at the individual level include, but are not limited to, those questions related to research on genetic markers for autism and other disabilities, continued development and application of assistive technology and alternative communication systems, and strategies for modifying behavioral aberrations (e.g., self-abuse, idiosyncratic speech).

Small-Group Research. When research questions are posed at the small-group level, they are directed at interpersonal issues that involve difficulties within primary groups (e.g., families, classmates, students, teachers). Thus, the problem is posed as a group problem rather than as an individual problem. Nearly all problems at the individual level can be considered as a small-group problem, considering aspects such as interactions between the primary group and one of its members, level of understanding on the part of the primary group, and levels of support provided by the primary group (Hanley-Maxwell et al., 1989).

Research conducted at the small-group level could examine the problem of unsuccessful postschool outcomes among students with disabilities as possibly related to low expectations or risk tolerance of parents for their children. Other small-group-level research might explore how attitudes of teachers, parents, or students affect the learning of students with disabilities, how environmental factors (e.g., family mobility, transportation, educational philosophies, homelessness) affect student success in learning, and how strategies to support teachers' instruction in inclusive classrooms lead to improved learning outcomes. Small-group research could also identify reasons for the high dropout rate of students with emotional disabilities. For example, research at the small-group level could examine whether the likelihood of dropping out of school is related to student–student and/or student–teacher relationships in middle school, or to victimization due to bullying in earlier grades, and could develop and test interventions to prevent the development of these interpersonal problems.

Organizational/Systems-Centered Research. At the organizational/systems-centered level, problems are considered to be the result of actions, or lack of actions, taken by organizations/systems that result from the failure of these systems to put socially desirable values and goals into practice (Hanley-Maxwell et al., 1989).

Research at this level could examine how district policies and procedures influence the instructional strategies, planning processes, and policies and how other practices (e.g., disciplinary codes, access to extracurricular activities, graduation requirements) affect the learning and behavior of students with disabilities at the school and classroom levels. Specific topics of inquiry may assess the affect of "zero tolerance" policies, school district adherence to Individuals with Disabilities Education Act eligibility and planning requirements, curricular choices on learning outcomes, staff allocation patterns on teaching strategies, and school focus (e.g., college preparatory, vocationally oriented) on graduation rates for students with disabilities.

Institutional/Community Research. Institutional/Community-level research targets institutions (e.g., state or federal government agencies, cultures) and their policies. Investigators working at this level believe that the institutions and their policies reveal society's lack of consideration for all persons. As a result, institutions and communities—rather than organizations, small groups, and individuals—cause and promote the social problems. This level of analysis entails examination of the interrelationship between individuals and social, political, legal, and economic influences. Grassroots political action and class advocacy are examples of rich contexts for research (Hanley-Maxwell et al., 1989). The civil rights movement and the lobbying for the passage of federal laws related to

improving the lives of persons with disabilities (e.g., Education of the Handicapped Act, Americans with Disabilities Act, Rehabilitation Act and its amendments) are examples of class advocacy in action. Research at this level might examine the institutional- and community-level factors that influence postschool outcomes for individuals, access to community-funded alcohol and drug treatment programs for adolescents, and work disincentives created by social security policies.

CHALLENGES AND OPPORTUNITIES IN CONDUCTING INQUIRY: IDENTIFYING APPROACHES AND TECHNIQUES

In the following sections, each of us describes our own lines of research in an attempt to illustrate the theoretical and practical challenges and opportunities of conducting multilevel research for enhancing the lives of persons with disabilities. By providing these descriptions, we are not suggesting that our work takes on more importance than that of other researchers. Rather, we offer these two cases to show how our research paths complement one another despite appearing quite different on the surface.

In the first example, Hanley-Maxwell describes the Research Institute on Secondary Education Reform for Youth With Disabilities (RISER), which examined how organizational variables affect learning in school and postschool outcomes. Specifically, the RISER agenda described how schoolwide educational philosophies influence educational opportunities for and success of students with disabilities; how planning and power structures within the schools change student and teacher sense of ownership and responsibility, confidence, and fear of risk taking (thereby limiting learning experiences); and how school districtwide and school-specific standards and assessments affect curricula and educational opportunities. From these findings, professional development opportunities were developed to enable teachers to help their students acquire the knowledge and skills for making successful transitions from school to work. The RISER research is an example of research focused on and the relationships among several levels of research: small-group, organization/systems-centered, and institutional/community.

Research Institute on Secondary Education Reform for Youth With Disabilities

In 1972, Marc Gold debunked the myth that adults with severe or profound mental disabilities could not learn complex tasks. With his Try Another Way approach, Gold demonstrated that adults with disabilities could learn to assemble bicycle brakes if they were provided with systematic instruction and task-oriented adaptations (Gold, 1980). The results of research such as Gold's, coupled with changing disability philosophies (e.g., normalization [Wolfensberger, 1972]) and federal civil rights actions (e.g., Section 504 of 1973 Vocational Rehabilitation Act amendments, Education for All Handicapped Children Act of 1975), created significant changes in quantity and quality of services provided to adults and children with disabilities. From this decade and beyond, researchers developed and tested a variety of educational service models and developed new approaches to curriculum development such as the top-down curriculum that enabled children and adults to become more active participants in their communities (Brown, Nietupski, & Hamre-Nietupski, 1976). In a significant change, these laws provided adults with severe disabilities supported employment to help them gain entry into the work world (Wehman & Kregel, 1985) and provided students with disabilities the legal right to receive a fair and appropriate public education (Education for All Handicapped Children Act, 1975).

As students with developmental disabilities began attending mainstream schools, more research focused on identifying academic, social, behavioral, and functional skills and on emphasizing interventions critical to participating in education programs with their peers without disabilities. For example, we examined the employment records of employees with disabilities who had been terminated from one or more jobs and found that supported employees were terminated for both behavioral excesses and skill deficits (Hanley-Maxwell, Rusch, Chadsey-Rusch, & Renzaglia, 1986). Implications of the study suggested that more training was needed to help potential employees learn nuances of social interaction such as social decoding, self-control, and self-management. From this research, essential skills and experiences were incorporated into secondary school curricula so that students could profit from instruction well in advance of needing to look for and assume employment. Solutions to these problems were also sought at the community/systems level, looking at the policies and delivery models of schools and adult service agencies.

Despite more emphasis on interventions and services, students with disabilities continue to make less than satisfactory transitions from school to employment. In our review of the transition literature, we found that independent living skills and academic skills were related to postschool outcomes for students with disabilities regardless of type or severity (Phelps & Hanley-Maxwell, 1997). Students who had received special education services and their employers reported that academic skills in reading, math, and writing were critical for obtaining and maintaining employment. Although there was no consensus on the level of performance required in each academic area, the key factor seemed to center on the ability of employees to apply their academic skills in solving problems and communicating solutions to them.

Higher-order thinking skills were also a critical part of postschool success along with basic academic and social skills. Research related to the role of self-determination demonstrated the importance of higher-order thinking skills. Self-determination (e.g., autonomy, self-regulation, psychological empowerment, self-realization) includes skills in self-knowledge (interests, values, assets, and needs), planning (goal setting and attainment), self-regulation, problem solving, choice making, decision making, and self-advocacy (Wehmeyer & Schwartz, 1998, cited in Hanley-Maxwell & Collet-Klingenberg, 2004). Results of this research showed that students and adults with disabilities who possess more self-determination skills achieve more satisfactory outcomes than do those who possess fewer of these skills.

Finally, the location and content of students' educational programs affect the outcomes for students with disabilities. For all graduating students with disabilities, receiving special education services in resource rooms; being included in general education classes; receiving curricula that include self-determination skills, interpersonal/social skills, and job-related skills; and having on-the-job training and career-focused and supervised work experiences and other employment during the high school years (e.g., summer jobs, part-time school year jobs) were all related to positive postschool outcomes (National Council on Disabilities, 2000; Phelps & Hanley-Maxwell, 1997).

Qualitative research became an essential tool in these investigations as we attempted to understand how students and parents viewed the process. For example, we interviewed parents whose children with and without mental retardation had recently graduated from high school or would soon graduate (Hanley-Maxwell, Whitney-Thomas, & Pogoloff, 1995; Whitney-Thomas & Hanley-Maxwell, 1996). The purpose of the research was to provide information to high school personnel about how they could develop more appropriate programs for their students. Parents articulated a three-part vision that included a safe, community-based residential environment that was independent of the students' parents; a fulfilling social network of friends and family; and productive activities to fill their time, including (but not necessarily) employment. Parents of adolescents without disabilities expressed similar wishes for the future of their children, although their anxiety was considerably less than that of the parents of students with disabilities.

Redesigning Instructional Practices

RISER explored ways in which high schools could improve outcomes for all students, including those with disabilities (Hanley-Maxwell, Phelps, Braden, & Warren, 1999). RISER focused on the concern of Kauffman (1993) that "we understand relatively little about how student placement determines what is possible and what is probable as far as instruction and its outcomes are concerned" (p. 8). To address this concern, RISER studied how high schools could be restructured so that youth with disabilities could be fully and effectively included with their

peers without disabilities in academic and social contexts. To help fulfill this promise, we decided to use a curricular model (Newmann, Secada, & Wehlage, 1995; Newmann & Wehlage, 1995) that emphasized the importance of engaging students in disciplined inquiry on authentic tasks to construct knowledge of value beyond school.

Components of the model, such as the focus on authentic tasks, are consistent with curricular goals of secondary special education (Halpern, 1992; Ysseldyke, Thurlow, & Bruininks, 1992). Newmann and colleagues (1995) described *construction of knowledge* as using *higher-order or critical thinking skills* to convert pieces of information into *new knowledge* for use *beyond school*, suggesting that mere repetition of information is unnecessary and ineffective as the only approach to learning. Special educators especially recognized the importance of teaching concepts and skills that have value beyond school. Experiential and community-based learning enhances the relevance of the content and experiences for students with disabilities, which in turn facilitates learning. Like the applied approaches of special education, authentic achievement requires that learning experiences be assessed based in part on their applications to real-world contexts and not solely by their utility in school contexts (Hanley-Maxwell et al., 1999).

Unlike the principles of authenticity and value beyond school, disciplined inquiry is not as common in special education as it is in general education. As a field, special education stresses instruction that focuses on developing students' basic foundation skills (e.g., decoding, number facts) because most students with disabilities display weaknesses in these areas. Furthermore, authentic achievement as conceived by Newmann and colleagues (1995) requires students to write elaborate explanations and justifications of their work, tasks that have not been expected of most students with disabilities. However, RISER altered the Newmann and colleagues (1995) findings to include other forms of elaborated explanations and justifications.

RISER Findings

Since the publication of *A Nation at Risk* (U.S. Department of Education, 1983), business leaders, parents, and politicians have challenged the political, economic, and social efficacy of high schools. Reform movements materialized in an effort to address the poor performance of America's youth on international comparisons of student achievement, forcing educators to consider new approaches (e.g., curriculum and instructional strategies, organizational models, support services) and to monitor the results (e.g., academic achievement gains, postschool outcomes) that these approaches achieved. Unfortunately, special education students have not been considered within these reforms, yet these students face the same world challenges that students without disabilities face (Hanley-Maxwell et al., 1999). The schools that participated in RISER research provide structures to consider as research looks for ways in which to merge general and special education reform. RISER schools demonstrate that students with disabilities can be successful in high-demand academic settings when provided with authentic learning opportunities and appropriate adaptations, revealing that changes at the small-group and organizations/system-centered levels influence the educational experiences and outcomes for students with and without disabilities.

Using a nested case study design, RISER addressed questions related to the effect of authentic and inclusive learning on the academic skills of learners with high-incidence disabilities, the effect of external and internal mandates on the curriculum and assessment practices used and the implications of those practices, the planning used to design inclusive and authentic learning opportunities and the individual programs of students, and the effect of the organizational contexts on the success of students and teachers in schools of authentic and inclusive learning. Results from the institute's research revealed that high schools using highly authentic approaches to learning improved the learning and postschool outcomes for secondary students with and without disabilities. More specifically, RISER research demonstrated that schools of authentic and inclusive learning (SAILs) support high academic standards for *all* students, including students with disabilities:

- SAILs provide instruction and assessment tasks of high intellectual quality. Under these conditions, all students, including those with mild to moderate disabilities, exhibit higher performance levels than they do under conditions of low authenticity, and in some cases students with disabilities perform at levels that are commensurate with, or superior to, those of some of their nondisabled peers.

- SAILs incorporate career development, self-determination, and postschool planning for all students.

- Although external high-stakes assessments may increase the likelihood that students with disabilities are included in assessment-relevant instruction and content, they tend to limit *all* students' exposure to authentic pedagogy.

Developing Skills and Understanding of Mathematics Among Students With Disabilities

In this example, Bottge summarizes an approach for developing the math skills of adolescents with learning disabilities and/or emotional disabilities (LD and/or ED) centered in cognitive learning theory. The rationale for his intervention is conceptualized in the "Key Model" of learning mathematics (Bottge, 2001) and is based primarily on theoretical constructs and practices from mainstream cognitive science.

Need for Mathematics Reform

Pressure to raise the academic achievement of all students, including those with disabilities, has come from government and professional groups. They have urged educators to help *all* students acquire the essential math skills for successful employment in the 21st century. These initiatives include *Goals 2000: Educate America Act* (U.S. Department of Education, 1994); *What Work Requires of Schools: A SCANS Report for America 2000* (U.S. Department of Labor, 1991); and *Preparing Students for the 21st Century* (Uchida, Cetron, & McKenzie, 1996). The most recent of these initiatives, the No Child Left Behind Act of 2001, outlines a national initiative for improving elementary and secondary education tied to high-stakes assessments (No Child Left Behind Act, 2002). To achieve the promise outlined in these initiatives, the U.S. Department of Education (2002) set six strategic goals for improving education. Goal 4 stresses the need for high-quality, evidence-based research to support Goal 2, which seeks to close the achievement gap between all groups of students in reading, science, and mathematics because success in the workplace depends on workers' ability to use their academic skills to solve important problems.

In the case of mathematics, raising achievement has been a priority for many years because U.S. students have traditionally scored lower than students in many other industrialized nations on international tests (National Center for Education Statistics, 2000). Many students with LD and/or ED have a particularly difficult time achieving at the same level as their peers without disabilities. For example, according to the National Center for Education Statistics (2005), 71% of eighth-grade students with disabilities scored below the basic level on the National Assessment of Educational Progress math test in 2003, compared with 29% of students without disabilities. It is likely that students with LD and ED make up the bulk of this low-performing group because they rank as the first (50.0%) and third (8.2%) largest among all disability categories.

Previous research demonstrated that considerable effort is needed to upgrade the skills of students with LD in whole number operations (Cawley, Parmar, Foley, Salmon, & Roy, 2001; Cawley, Parmar, Yan, & Miller, 1998), fractions computation (Behr, Wachsmuth, & Post, 1985), decimals (Woodward, Baxter, & Robinson, 1999), and problem solving (Jitendra, Hoff, & Beck, 1999; Parmar, Cawley, & Frazita, 1996; Xin & Jitendra, 1999). Although researchers identified some promising approaches for helping students with LD to develop their math skills—such as curriculum-based measurement, peer-assisted learning strategies (Calhoon & Fuchs, 2003; Fuchs et al., 1997), and schema-based instruction for solving word problems (Jitendra, DiPipi, & Perron-Jones, 2002)—most methods are designed primarily as accommodations to the general education curriculum for young children.

The goal of enhancing the math achievement of adolescents with ED appears to be even more remote because hardly any math intervention research has been conducted with this population (Mooney, Epstein, Reid, & Nelson, 2003; Pierce, Reid, & Epstein, 2004). Between 1996 and 2002, only four studies attempted to improve the math skills of students with ED, and all of them concentrated on computation skills. In fact, only one study published since 1975 attempted to increase students' higher-order reasoning skills. Just as disconcerting is the finding that of all 55 intervention studies between 1975 and 2002 that Mooney and colleagues (2003) reviewed, none emphasized interventions specific to females despite recent statistics that females comprise up to 25% of students with ED (U.S. Department of Education, 1998).

Teaching and Learning Complex Mathematics Problems

For more than a decade, we have used a method of teaching problem solving in mathematics called enhanced anchored instruction (EAI) that is specially designed to develop the math skills of low-achieving adolescents, including students with LD and/or ED. EAI is based on the concept of anchored instruction (AI), popularized by the Cognition and Technology Group at Vanderbilt (1997). AI uses video-based problems situated in authentic contexts that support students' learning in generative rather than passive learning environments (Cognition and Technology Group at Vanderbilt University, 1990; Goldman, Hasselbring, & Cognition and Technology Group at Vanderbilt, 1997). EAI extends or enhances AI by affording students with additional opportunities to practice their skills as they solve new but analogous problems in applied, motivating, and challenging contexts (e.g., building skateboard ramps, designing and manufacturing hovercrafts).

Results from previous studies show that EAI can improve the problem-solving skills of average- and low-achieving middle school students, yielding moderate effect sizes from .50 to .81 on problem-solving tests and from .37 to .62 on transfer tasks (Bottge, 1999; Bottge & Hasselbring, 1993; Bottge, Heinrichs, Chan, & Serlin, 2001; Bottge, Heinrichs, Mehta, & Hung, 2002). Elements in the Key Model emerged as important factors in improving the problem-solving performance of both average- and low-achieving students. For example, EAI problems directly immerse students in problem contexts that they find relevant and interesting, in contrast to most traditional text-based problems (Lesh & Kelly, 2000). The limited amount of reading required to solve EAI problems is a significant benefit for many students who experience difficulty with math *and* reading (Fuchs & Fuchs, 2002; Geary, 1993; Geary, Hamson, & Hoard, 2000; Muth, 1984). An unusual quality of EAI problems is that they motivate students who previously have shown a dislike for mathematics to engage in substantive effort. Teachers using EAI place high expectations on all of their students, a prerequisite for reaching high academic standards (Clifford, 1991; Darling-Hammond, 1996).

As noted previously, research in special education historically has focused on whatever deficits the student in question exhibits rather than emphasizing instructional practices that make use of learners' strengths (Ginsburg, 1997; Means & Knapp, 1991; Poplin, 1988). Recently, Fuchs and Fuchs (2001) outlined a set of principles to guide planning and delivery of mathematics instruction for students with LD. They suggested that teachers afford students with opportunities to engage in highly motivating learning activities that communicate high expectations, a theme echoed by others (Gamoran, Porter, Smithson, & White, 1997; Ring & Reetz, 2000). Thus, the role of future research should be to capture the effects of these activities in rigorous research designs (e.g., Gersten, Baker, & Lloyd, 2000) that can be applied directly to classroom practice (e.g., Lewis, Hudson, Richter, & Johnson, 2004).

Reconceptualizing Mathematics Instruction for Students With LD and/or ED

Figure 10.1 shows the Key Model, an extension of a model we had advanced previously (Bottge, 2001) and have used to guide our *theory–research–instructional development cycle.* The need for such a model was precipitated by the inability of a large number of students to achieve at satisfactory levels in mathematics and by the lack of meaningful exchanges among cognitive scientists, curriculum developers, and practitioners. Mastropieri, Scruggs, and Shiah

(1991) identified this failure to bridge learning theory and instructional processes in the disabilities literature several years ago. In reviewing 30 studies involving math instruction and students with disabilities, they found few studies that "made a systematic effort to link specific intervention procedures with specific theories, or even characterizations or learning disabilities, other than general deficits in math functioning" (p. 97). This situation contrasts with the abundance of theoretical and experimental information about normally achieving children (Ginsburg, 1997).

The base of the model is represented by a key and a lock. For the key to open the lock, the teeth of the key must lift a set of pins to the sheer line. When all of the pins are in perfect position (appropriate instruction), the plug in the lock can rotate and the lock opens (important learning). Despite teachers' best efforts, the Key Model also suggests that at times some of the pins may be out of alignment and not much learning will occur. The top half of the model shows who is generally involved in teaching EAI: math, special education, and technology education teachers. The principal is also included because of his or her importance in encouraging teachers to collaborate in both curriculum design and teaching practices.

The Key Model acknowledges and describes the potential of previous learning theories and research related to populations of students without disabilities in developing effective interventions for students with disabilities. Thus, the model is more inclusive than most found in special education. In the following subsections, the theoretical foundations that support the Key Model are described in more detail.

Meaningful Problems and Engagement. Scholars such as Dewey, Wertheimer, and Bruner advanced the notion that worthwhile problems motivate students to solve them. For example, Dewey (1938) advised teachers to arrange "experiences" that are "engaging" to students and that "live fruitfully· and creatively in subsequent experiences" (p. 28). Wertheimer (1959) advised teachers to teach as little as possible and to challenge students with tasks that they can accomplish themselves. Bruner (1960) thought that "students should know what

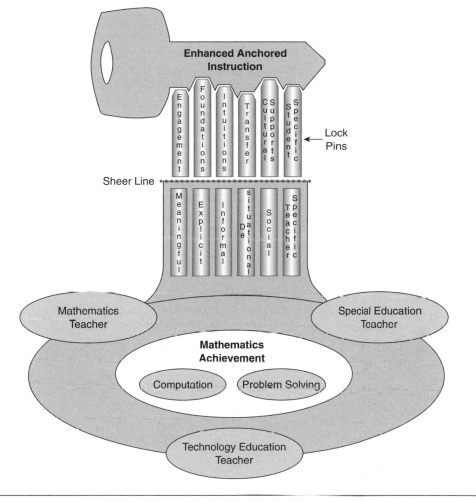

Figure 10.1   Key Teaching and Learning Factors That Affect the Mathematics Achievement of
Low-Achieving Students

it feels like to be completely absorbed in a problem" but lamented that "they seldom experience this feeling in school" (p. 50).

So, what is a problem to low-achieving students? In professional special education literature, Mercer and Miller (1992) concluded that the meaning of the word "problem" is elusive after finding 37 different descriptions of the term in 10 books and articles. But in mainstream contemporary mathematics and cognitive science literature, authors seem to agree on the nature of problem solving. For example, Polya (1962) defined problem solving as searching for an appropriate course of action to attain an aim that is not immediately attainable. In mathematics,

Schoenfeld (1989) defined a problem in relation to its effect on the learner as "a task (a) in which the student is interested and engaged and for which he wishes to obtain a resolution, and (b) for which the student does not have a readily accessible mathematical means by which to achieve that resolution" (p. 88). Both definitions suggest that a problem is not a problem unless the learner is interested in solving it. Thus, problems and problem solving are not defined solely by appearance or subject matter but rather are defined by their capacity to evoke in students a genuine interest in solving them.

However, low-achieving students do not often get the chance to work on problems that stimulate their interest. By far, the most popular method of teaching and assessing math problem solving in American classrooms relies on text-based problems. The usual method of helping low-achieving students to solve word problems is to teach them how to identify key words that trigger number operations, a procedure that imitates "drill and practice," routinizes procedures, and discourages understanding. Thus, word problems rarely appear to be authentic and important to these students (Brown, Collins, & Duguid, 1989; Lave, 1988). Lave (1993) described word problems as a school activity having "no intuitive connections with everyday experience" (p. 89).

Even when teachers offer their students interesting problems to solve, low-achieving students might not be included because they lack the "readiness" skills required for solving them. Knapp and Turnbull (1990) concluded that teaching low-order skills to low-achieving students at the expense of teaching them high-order concepts is likely to

- underestimate what disadvantaged students are capable of doing;
- postpone more challenging and interesting work for too long—in some cases, forever; and
- deprive students of a meaningful and motivating context for learning or using skills that are taught. (p. 4)

Explicit Teaching and Foundation Skills. New standards emphasize the need for teachers to offer low-achieving students more opportunities to be engaged in and solve meaningful problems. However, opportunity does not diminish the importance of providing students with the foundation skills necessary to work on these problems. One of the major research findings of the past decade is the central role that domain-specific knowledge plays in problem solving and learning in a content area (Doyle, 1983). For students with LD and/or ED, this knowledge included number facts, computational algorithms, and strategies for solving traditional text-based problems (Resnick & Ford, 1981). One of the most widely accepted methods of improving foundation skills of students with LD is called direct instruction (Carnine, 1997,

1998), which emphasizes explicit instruction of strategies combined with plenty of structured practice and systematic prompting to enable students to learn the "big ideas" embedded in mathematics concepts.

However, despite the emphasis in the cognitive literature on embedding instruction of lower-order skills in tasks that require higher-order conceptual processing, very little research of this kind has been conducted with low-achieving adolescents. Reasons for this omission can be traced to teacher practices and researcher beliefs. For example, low-achieving students are rarely called on to explain their reasoning or their strategies for solving meaningful problems (Ginsburg, 1998). Most of the emphasis on teaching foundation skills has been on elementary school students (e.g., Cawley et al., 1998, 2001; Naglieri & Johnson, 2000). And many researchers in special education think of *constructivist* methods of teaching as unstructured, lacking in specific objectives, and "logically inadequate for the task of teaching adolescents with LD" (Jones, Wilson, & Bhojwani, 1997, p. 161).

Informal Teaching and Students' Intuitions. Modern theories of teaching and learning acknowledge that students bring to the classroom a rich store of knowledge untapped by conventional teaching practices. This theme is not new, of course, especially as it relates to students with learning problems. More than 70 years ago, Whitehead (1929) called the intuitions that go unnoticed and untapped in school "inert knowledge." When people are involved in a real problem-solving situation, "its structural features and requirements set up certain strains, stresses, tensions in the thinker" (Wertheimer, 1959, p. 239). Whatever the endeavor, knowledgeable hunches and informed hypotheses help us to uncover paths to promising but unproved solutions.

In earlier research (Bottge et al., 2001), we used a video-based anchor called "Kim's Komet" from the Adventures of Jasper Woodbury series (Cognition and Technology Group at Vanderbilt, 1997) to study whether low-achieving math students could match the performance of students without disabilities on problem-solving curriculum aligned to National Council of

Teachers of Mathematics algebra standards for middle school students. Results showed that students in a remedial class matched the problem-solving performance of prealgebra students despite large differences between them prior to instruction. Classroom observations revealed that students in the remedial group called on their prior background experiences to help them solve the central problems in Kim's Komet.

The impact of *not* accessing intuition and informal knowledge became clear in a study where students with LD and/or ED attempted to solve the video-based anchor called "Fraction of the Cost" in inclusive math classrooms (Bottge et al., 2002). The problem-solving posttests revealed that few of these students understood the central concepts in the video anchor, a finding that contradicted previous research. Classroom observations showed that students with disabilities received *too much help* from their group partners without disabilities. For example, students with disabilities seldom engaged in classroom discussions about how to solve the problems in the anchor. Students who were interviewed at the conclusion of the study confessed that they were afraid of embarrassing themselves by giving "dumb" answers. In a dramatic turnaround the week after the posttests were administered, students with disabilities solved the video problems in less than 4 hours with help from a special education teacher in a resource room.

(De)Situated Learning and Transfer. Thorndike and Woodworth (1901) recognized the importance of learning transfer and concluded that subject matter learned in one discipline does not automatically improve a person's performance in another discipline. Two decades later, Thorndike (1922) noted that mathematics pedagogy made artificial distinctions between computation and reasoning, thereby hindering the transfer of skills. It viewed "reasoning as a somewhat magical power or essence" and "separated too sharply the 'understanding of principles' by reasoning from the 'mechanical' work of computation . . . remembering facts and the like, done by 'mere' habit and memory" (p. 190). Other scholars, such as Vygotsky

(1978) and Whitehead (1929), warned of "fossilized behavior" and "inert knowledge." With special populations in particular, most attempts to engender transfer across contexts have been stymied (Ginsburg, 1997).

Increasingly, educators recognize that previous theories of learning based solely on learner characteristics and learning processes are insufficient to describe the complex interactions between the learner and the setting where learning occurs. In current learning theories, contextual variables are seen as playing an important role in learning and knowledge transfer. Learning that takes contextual variables into account has been termed "situated cognition" (e.g., Brown et al., 1989; Greeno and the Middle School Mathematics Through Applications Project Group, 1998) and "cognitive apprenticeship" (e.g., Collins, Brown, & Newman, 1989). For example, Greeno and the Middle School Mathematics Through Applications Project Group (1998) described the situative perspective as focusing "attention on systems in which people interact with each other and with material, informational, and conceptual resources in their environments" (p. 23). Helping students to identify, understand, and discuss the contextual elements of problems is important for their successful work performance and everyday living.

Contextual variables may also hamper knowledge transfer when they are tied too closely to the situations in which content is learned. In fact, prior knowledge may interfere with a person's predisposition to impose structure on situations. In these cases, knowledge quite automatically infuses itself into a situation and appears to be helpful, but in fact it impairs the individual's search for the appropriate solution (Stanovich, 2003). This phenomenon appeared in several studies (e.g., Bottge et al., 2002) as students attempted to solve the EAI problems in Fraction of the Cost and Kim's Komet. In these cases, teachers had to (de)situate, or *uncouple,* the procedural misconception from the inappropriate context, *reteach* it, and then *reattach* it in its more appropriate form.

Ethnographic studies yielded insight into the role that context plays in work settings. For example, carpet layers know that carpet comes in standard widths, all of the nap must run the same way, and seams should be placed out of heavy traffic areas (Masingila, 1993). Automobile assembly workers use the English system or the metric system to measure tolerances, depending on the machine and the specific requirements of the part (Murnane & Levy, 1996; Smith, 1999). Nurses must manage the *dead space* in infusion lines to calculate the appropriate flow of fluid into patients (Noss, Hoyles, & Pozzi, 2002). In each profession, the number and nature of required math operations are determined by the problem context. Yet contextual factors are often missing from school-based problems, making the problems appear to be artificial and disconnected from life outside of school (Lave, Smith, & Butler, 1988). Thus, as Ceci and Roazzi (1994) asserted, "We cannot conclude that children lack certain cognitive abilities just because they do not exhibit them in a given context" (p. 93).

Social Learning and Cultural Supports. Vygotsky (1978) is often credited as the founder of modern sociocultural theory that calls for, among other things, the prominence of language and discourse in the learning process. He believed that higher forms of intellectual functioning arose out of cooperation and collaboration with other people. According to Vygotsky, language is one of the tools that people use to transform their behavior as they develop new understandings about the context in which they live and work. He used the term "zone of proximal development" to describe "the distance between the actual developmental level as determined by independent problem solving and the level of potential development as determined through problem solving under adult guidance or in collaboration with more capable peers" (p. 86).

Teachers use language as a tool to ask students what they understand about a topic. Vygotsky (1978) maintained that teachers could get a more accurate measure of children's understanding by guiding their inquiry with a series of questions rather than by expecting them to solve problems independently. In independent problem-solving situations, students' responses reflect learning that has already matured. If, on the other hand, we want to know students' potential for solving a problem, then we should provide just the right amount of assistance to guide their thinking toward a solution (e.g., Cobb, Yackel, & Wood, 1992).

Teacher-Specific and Student-Specific Factors. A subtle factor that influences the performance of students, especially those who are difficult to teach, is teacher expectation. Rosenthal and Jacobson (1968) endeavored to show how false-positive teacher expectations influenced changes in student achievement. Several research efforts resulted from their study to explain in more detail how teachers convey their expectations and what impact such expectations have on student motivation and performance. Brophy and Good (1974) distinguished two effects of differential treatment: direct effects (instructional materials and practice) and indirect effects (student awareness of teacher expectations that could affect motivation and self-concept). In the latter area, Weinstein and Middlestadt (1979) found that teachers had different expectations for low-achieving and high-achieving students. For example, teachers of high-achieving students expressed higher expectations and provided more opportunity for choice than did teachers of low-achieving students.

Of course, teachers' expectations are affected by their perceptions of the efficacy of their teaching. High-efficacy teachers take responsibility for teaching all students, whereas low-efficacy teachers often form biases and relinquish their responsibility to other teachers (Weinstein & McKown, 1998). This finding has important implications for special education teachers and their students. For example, students with LD often become frustrated when they cannot learn as quickly as their peers. In an effort to control their classes, low-efficacy teachers may rely on extrinsic incentive systems that emphasize repetition and short-term goals. Although these goals and systems are necessary to build a base of knowledge for students with disabilities, overreliance on such systems may actually stifle intrinsic motivation (Brophy, 1986), thereby making matters worse, especially as students reach adolescence (Wigfield, Eccles, & Rodriguez, 1998). The challenge for teachers of students with disabilities is finding ways of delivering instruction that promote high expectations for all students.

UNANSWERED QUESTIONS

Although both lines of research (RISER and EAI) have uncovered new findings that can be used to improve the lives of individuals with disabilities, additional questions have emerged. For example, a most important question from the RISER research asks how existing schools can be transformed into SAIL schools. The answer will depend on factors identified mostly at the organization/systems-centered and institutional/community levels. At the organizational level, research might explore what mix of educational arrangements at the secondary level (e.g., community based, school based) results in successful post-high school outcomes for students with disabilities. Organization-level research might also assess the benefits of implementing SAIL earlier, in elementary and middle schools, compared with waiting until high school to implement SAIL. At the institution/community level, research might explore the impact of governmental initiatives, such as the No Child Left Behind Act that mandates traditional standardized tests, on the use of authentic performance-based assessments used in SAIL.

An important question for future research with EAI asks how to merge instruction on basic math skills with the problem-solving activities. Still unclear is whether (or how much) the cognitive load placed on working memory (Sweller, 1988) due to students' lack of basic skills (e.g., nonautomatic math facts, deficient procedural knowledge of fractions computation) affects students' ability to attend to and solve subproblems embedded in EAI challenges. A second line of research might examine the controversial issue of how best to measure students' academic performance. Most high-stakes assessments are in typical text-based, multiple-choice standardized formats. However, because many students with math disabilities also have reading problems, typical text-based testing formats might not adequately measure these students' knowledge. One solution may reside in the promise of computer-based interactive assessment that enables students to *show* the way in which they would solve multistep math problems in motivating contexts. New assessment methods may motivate students to demonstrate their ability to solve problems that look more like those they will encounter in real life. The answers to these questions may come from carefully crafted research designs at the individual and group levels.

CONCLUSION

Research in special education has had a profound impact on the lives of individuals with disabilities. Most children with disabilities are now educated alongside their peers without disabilities, and young adults are making successful transitions to the community and work settings. However, as revealed in a general way by national statistics, as well as in detailed accounts by contemporary special education research, there remains much to do to enrich their lives. Remarkably, debates over the least restrictive environment (e.g., segregated vs. inclusive settings) rage on, and we expect that they will continue to do so. Yet we hope that future research would recenter itself to answer the primary question: What interventions yield positive results with what individuals under what conditions? The examples of research described in this chapter illustrate how two lines of inquiry converge to answer this most critical question. The SAIL project uses ethnographic case-based research to examine this question from several levels: small-group, organization/systems-centered, and institutional/community. Research on the effects of EAI is focused primarily at the small-group level (i.e., classroom) and employs a combination of traditional quasi-experimental group methods coupled with descriptions of classroom interactions. Although the research methodologies and focal points differ, both the SAIL and EAI research projects seek to identify school conditions (e.g., specialized instructional curricula and teaching methods) that will ultimately lead to higher achievement and more positive postschool outcomes for individuals with disabilities. The challenge is formidable, but we can meet it by focusing more attention on answering the important question, developing interventions guided by theory, and using complementary approaches of inquiry across multiple levels.

REFERENCES

Baker, J. M., & Zigmond, N. (1990). Are regular education classes equipped to accommodate students with learning disabilities? *Exceptional Children, 56,* 515–526.

Baker, J. M., & Zigmond, N. (1995). The meaning and practice of inclusion for students with learning disabilities: Themes and implications from five cases. *Journal of Special Education, 29,* 163–180.

Behr, J. J., Wachsmuth, I., & Post, T. R. (1985). Construct a sum: A measure of children's understanding of fraction size. *Journal for Research in Mathematics Education, 16,* 120–131.

Benz, M. R., & Halpern, A. S. (1986). Vocational preparation for high school students with mild disabilities: A statewide study of administrator, teacher, and parent perceptions. *Career Development for Exceptional Individuals, 9,* 3–15.

Bogdan, R., & Kugelmass, J. W. (1984). Case studies of mainstreaming: A symbolic interactionist approach to special schooling. In L. Barton & S. Tomlinson (Eds.), *Special education and social interests* (pp. 173–191). New York: Nichols.

Bottge, B. A. (1999). Effects of contextualized math instruction on problem solving of average and below-average achieving students. *Journal of Special Education, 33,* 81–92.

Bottge, B. A. (2001). Reconceptualizing math problem solving for low-achieving students. *Remedial and Special Education, 22,* 102–112.

Bottge, B. A., & Hasselbring, T. S. (1993). A comparison of two approaches for teaching complex, authentic mathematics problems to adolescents in remedial math classes. *Exceptional Children, 59,* 556–566.

Bottge, B. A., Heinrichs, M., Chan, S., & Serlin, R. (2001). Anchoring adolescents' understanding of math concepts in rich problem solving environments. *Remedial and Special Education, 22,* 299–314.

Bottge, B. A., Heinrichs, M., Mehta, Z., & Hung, Y. (2002). Weighing the benefits of anchored math instruction for students with disabilities in general education classes. *Journal of Special Education, 35,* 186–200.

Brantlinger, E. (1997). Using ideology: Cases of nonrecognition of the politics of research and practice in special education. *Review of Educational Research, 67,* 425–459.

Brophy, J. (1986). Teaching and learning mathematics: Where research should be going. *Journal for Research in Mathematics Education, 17,* 323–346.

Brophy, J. E., & Good, T. L. (1974). *Teacher–student relationships: Causes and consequences.* New York: Holt, Rinehart & Winston.

Brown, J. S., Collins, A., & Duguid, P. (1989). Situated cognition and the culture of learning. *Educational Researcher, 17*(1), 32–41.

Brown, L., Nietupski, J., & Hamre-Nietupski, S. (1976). The criterion of ultimate functioning and public school services for severely handicapped children. In M. A. Thomas (Ed.), *Hey, don't forget about me!* (pp. 2–15). Reston, VA: Council for Exceptional Children.

Bruininks, R., Lewis, D., & Thurlow, M. (1989). *Assessing outcomes, cost, and benefits of special education programs.* Minneapolis: University of Minnesota Press.

Bruner, J. S. (1960). *The process of education.* New York: Random House.

Calhoon, M. B., & Fuchs, L. S. (2003). The effects of peer-assisted learning strategies and curriculum-based measurement on the mathematics performance of secondary students with disabilities. *Remedial and Special Education, 24,* 235–245.

Carnine, D. (1997). Instructional design in mathematics for students with learning disabilities. *Journal of Learning Disabilities, 30,* 130–141.

Carnine, D. (1998). Instructional design in mathematics for students with learning disabilities. In D. P. Rivera (Ed.), *Mathematics education for students with learning disabilities: Theory to practice* (pp. 119–138). Austin, TX: Pro-Ed.

Cawley, J., Parmar, R., Foley, T. E., Salmon, S., & Roy, S. (2001). Arithmetic performance of students: Implications for standards and programming. *Exceptional Children, 67,* 311–328.

Cawley, J. F., Parmar, R. S., Yan, W., & Miller, J. H. (1998). Arithmetic computation performance of students with learning disabilities: Implications for curriculum. *Learning Disabilities Research & Practice, 13*(2), 68–74.

Ceci, S. J., & Roazzi, A. (1994). The effects of context on cognition: Postcards from Brazil. In R. J. Sternberg & R. K. Wagner (Eds.), *Mind in context: Interactionist perspectives on human intelligence* (pp. 74–101). New York: Cambridge University Press.

Clifford, M. M. (1991). Risk taking: Theoretical, empirical, and educational considerations. *Educational Psychologist, 26,* 263–297.

Cobb, P., Yackel, E., & Wood, T. (1992). A constructivist alternative to the representational view of mind in mathematics education. *Journal for Research in Mathematics Education, 23,* 2–33.

Cognition and Technology Group at Vanderbilt University. (1990). Anchored instruction and its relationship to situated cognition. *Educational Researcher, 19*(3), 2–10.

Cognition and Technology Group at Vanderbilt. (1997). *The Jasper Project: Lessons in curriculum, instruction, assessment, and professional development.* Mahwah, NJ: Lawrence Erlbaum.

Collins, A., Brown, J. S., & Newman, S. E. (1989). Cognitive apprenticeship: Teaching the crafts of reading, writing, and mathematics. In L. B. Resnick (Ed.), *Knowing, learning, and instruction: Essays in honor of Robert Glaser* (pp. 453–494). Hillsdale, NJ: Lawrence Erlbaum.

Darling-Hammond, L. (1996). The right to learn and the advancement of teaching: Research, policy, practice for democratic education. *Educational Researcher, 25*(6), 5–17.

Deno, E. (1970). Special education as developmental capital. *Exceptional Children, 37,* 229–237.

Dewey, J. (1938). *Experience and education.* New York: Macmillan.

Doyle, W. (1983). Academic work. *Review of Educational Research, 53,* 159–199.

Dunn, L. E. (1968). Special education for the mentally retarded: Is much of it justifiable? *Exceptional Children, 35,* 5–22.

Edgar, E. (1988). Employment as an outcome for mildly handicapped students: Current status and future directions. *Focus on Exceptional Children, 21,* 1–8.

Edgar, E., & Polloway, E. A. (1994). Education for adolescents with disabilities: Curriculum and placement issues. *Journal of Special Education, 27,* 438–452.

Education of All Handicapped Children Act, P.L. 94-142, 20 U.S.C. § 1400 et seq. (1975). (Note: In 1990, P.L. 101-476 changed the name of this act, including all subsequent amendments, to the Individuals with Disabilities Education Act.)

Fabian, E., Lent, R., & Willis, S. (1998). Predicting work transition outcomes for students with disabilities: Implications for counselors. *Journal of Counseling & Development, 76,* 311–316.

Fuchs, L. S., & Fuchs, D. (2001). Principles for the prevention and intervention of mathematics difficulties. *Learning Disabilities Research & Practice, 16,* 85–95.

Fuchs, L. S., & Fuchs, D. (2002). Mathematical problem-solving profiles of students with mathematics disabilities with and without comorbid reading difficulties. *Journal of Learning Disabilities, 35,* 563–573.

Fuchs, L. S., Fuchs, D., Karns, K., Hamlett, C. L., Katzaroff, M., & Dutka, S. (1997). Effects of task-focused goals on low-achieving students with and without learning disabilities. *American Educational Research Journal, 34,* 513–543.

Gamoran, A., Porter, A., Smithson, J., & White, P. (1997). Upgrading high school mathematics instruction: Improving learning opportunities for low-achieving, low-income youth. *Educational Evaluation and Policy Analysis, 19,* 325–338.

Geary, D. (1993). Mathematical disabilities: Cognitive, neuropsychological, and genetic components. *Psychological Bulletin, 114,* 345–362.

Geary, D. C., Hamson, C. O., & Hoard, M. K. (2000). Numerical and arithmetical cognition: A longitudinal study of process and concept deficits in children with learning disability. *Journal of Experimental Psychology, 77,* 236–263.

Gersten, R., Baker, S., & Lloyd, J. W. (2000). Designing high-quality research in special education: Group experimental design. *Journal of Special Education, 34,* 2–18.

Ginsburg, H. P. (1997). Mathematics learning disabilities: A view from developmental psychology. *Journal of Learning Disabilities, 30,* 20–33.

Ginsburg, H. P. (1998). Mathematics learning disabilities: A view from developmental psychology. In D. P. Rivera (Ed.), *Mathematics education for students with learning disabilities: Theory to practice* (pp. 33–58). Austin, TX: Pro-Ed.

Gold, M. (1980). *"Did I say that?": Articles and commentary on the Try Another Way system.* Champaign, IL: Research Press.

Goldman, S. R., Hasselbring, T. S., & Cognition and Technology Group at Vanderbilt. (1997). Achieving meaningful mathematics literacy for students with learning disabilities. *Journal of Learning Disabilities, 30,* 198–208.

Greeno, J. G., & Middle School Mathematics Through Applications Project Group. (1998). The situativity of knowing, learning, and research. *American Psychologist, 53*(1), 5–26.

Halpern, A. (1992). Transition: Old wine in new bottles. *Exceptional Children, 58,* 202–211.

Hanley-Maxwell, C., & Collet-Klingenberg, L. (2004). Preparing students for employment. In P. Wehman & J. Kregel (Eds.), *Functional curriculum for elementary, middle, and secondary age students with special needs* (2nd ed., pp. 205–243). Austin, TX: Pro-Ed.

Hanley-Maxwell, C., Phelps, L. A., Braden, J., & Warren, V. (1999). *Schools of authentic and inclusive learning* (Brief No. 1). Madison: University of Wisconsin, Research Institute on Secondary Education Reform for Youth With Disabilities.

Hanley-Maxwell, C., Rusch, F. R., Chadsey-Rusch, J., & Renzaglia, A. (1986). Reported factors contributing to job terminations of individuals with severe disabilities. *Journal of the Association for Persons With Severe Handicaps, 11*(1), 45–52.

Hanley-Maxwell, C., Rusch, F. R., & Rappaport, J. (1989). A multi-level perspective of community employment problems for persons with mental retardation. *Rehabilitation Counseling Bulletin, 32,* 266–280.

Hanley-Maxwell, C., Whitney-Thomas, J., & Pogoloff, S. (1995). The second shock: A qualitative study of parents' perspectives and needs during their child's transition from school to adult life. *Journal of the Association for Persons With Severe Handicaps, 2,* 3–15.

Hasazi, S. B., Gordon, L., & Roe, C. A. (1985). Factors associated with the employment status of handicapped youth exiting high school from 1979 to 1983. *Exceptional Children, 51,* 455–469.

Jitendra, A., DiPipi, C. M., & Perron-Jones, N. (2002). An exploratory study of schema-based word problem-solving instruction for middle school students with learning disabilities: An emphasis on conceptual and procedural understanding. *Journal of Special Education, 36,* 23–38.

Jitendra, A. K., Hoff, K., & Beck, M. M. (1999). Teaching middle school students with learning disabilities to solve word problems using a schema-based approach. *Remedial and Special Education, 20,* 50–64.

Jones, E. D., Wilson, R., & Bhojwani, S. (1997). Mathematics instruction for secondary students with learning disabilities. *Journal of Learning Disabilities, 30,* 151–163.

Kauffman, J. M. (1993). How we might achieve the radical reform of special education. *Exceptional Children, 60,* 6–16.

Knapp, M. S., & Turnbull, B. J. (1990). *Better schooling for the children of poverty: Alternatives to conventional wisdom.* Washington, DC: U.S. Department of Education, Office of Planning, Budget, and Evaluation.

Kortering, L., & Edgar, E. (1988). Special education and rehabilitation: A need for cooperation. *Rehabilitation Counseling Bulletin, 31,* 178–184.

Lave, J. (1988). *Cognition in practice.* Cambridge, MA: Cambridge University Press.

Lave, J. (1993). Word problems: A microcosm of theories of learning. In P. Light & G. Butterworth (Eds.), *Context and cognition: Ways of learning and knowing* (pp. 74–92). Hillsdale, NJ: Lawrence Erlbaum.

Lave, J., Smith, S., & Butler, M. (1988). Problem solving as an everyday practice. In R. I. Charles & E. A. Silver (Eds.), *The teaching and assessing of mathematical problem solving* (pp. 61–81). Reston, VA: National Council of Teachers of Mathematics.

Lesh, R., & Kelly, A. (2000). Multitiered teaching experiments. In A. E. Kelly & R. A. Lesh (Eds.), *Handbook of research design in mathematics and science education* (pp. 197–230). Mahwah, NJ: Lawrence Erlbaum.

Levine, P., Marder, C., & Wagner, M. (2004). *Service and support for secondary school students with disabilities: A special topic report from the National Longitudinal Study–2 (NLTS-2).* Menlo Park, CA: SRI International.

Lewis, T. J., Hudson, S., Richter, M., & Johnson, N. (2004). Scientifically supported practices in emotional and behavioral disorders: A proposed approach and brief review of current practices. *Behavioral Disorders, 29,* 247–259.

Lieberman L. M. (1996). Preserving special education . . . for those who need it. In W. Stainback & S. Stainback (Eds.), *Controversial issues confronting special education* (pp. 16–27). Boston: Allyn & Bacon.

Lipsky, D. K., & Gartner, A. (1996). Inclusive education and school restructuring. In W. Stainback & S. Stainback (Eds.), *Controversial issues* confronting special education (pp. 3–15). Boston: Allyn & Bacon.

Masingila, J. O. (1993). Learning from mathematics practice in out-of-school situations. *For the Learning of Mathematics, 13*(2), 18–22.

Mastropieri, M. A., Scruggs, T. E., & Shiah, S. (1991). Mathematics instruction for learning disabled students: A review of research. *Learning Disabilities Research & Practice, 6,* 89–98.

Means, B., & Knapp, M. S. (1991). Cognitive approaches to teaching advanced skills to educationally disadvantaged students. *Phi Delta Kappan, 73,* 282–289.

Mercer, C. D., & Miller, S. P. (1992). Teaching students with learning problems in math to acquire, understand, and apply basic math facts. *Remedial and Special Education, 13,* 19–35, 61.

Mithaug, D. E., Horiuchi, C., & Fanning P. (1985). A report of the Colorado statewide follow-up survey of special education students. *Exceptional Children, 51,* 397–404.

Mooney, P., Epstein, M. H., Reid, R., & Nelson, J. R. (2003). Status and trends in academic intervention research for students with emotional disabilities. *Remedial and Special Education, 24,* 273–287.

Murnane, R. J., & Levy, F. (1996). *Teaching the new basic skills.* New York: Free Press.

Muth, K. D. (1984). Solving arithmetic word problems: Role of reading and computational skills. *Journal of Educational Psychology, 76,* 205–210.

Naglieri, J. A., & Johnson, D. (2000). Effectiveness of a cognitive strategy intervention in improving arithmetic computation based on the PASS theory. *Journal of Learning Disabilities, 33,* 591–597.

National Center for Education Statistics. (2000). *Third International Mathematics and Science Study–Repeat (TIMMS-R).* Available: http://nces.ed.gov/pubsearch/pubsinfo.asp?pubid=2001028

National Center for Education Statistics. (2005). *National Assessment of Educational Progress—Mathematics 2003 results.* Retrieved January 24, 2005, from http://nces.ed.gov/nationsreportcard/mathematics/results2003

National Council on Disabilities, Social Security Administration. (2000). *Transition and post-school outcomes for youth with disabilities: Closing the gaps to post-secondary education and employment.* Washington, DC: Author.

National Organization on Disability and Harris Interactive. (2000). *NOD/Harris survey of Americans with disabilities.* New York: Author.

Neel, R., Meadows, N., Levine, P., & Edgar, E. (1988). What happens after special education: A statewide follow-up study. *Behavior Disorders, 13,* 209–216.

Newmann, F. M., Secada, G. G., &, Wehlage, G. G. (1995). *A guide to authentic instruction and assessment: Vision, standards, and scoring.* Madison: Wisconsin Center for Education Research.

Newmann, F. M., & Wehlage, G. G. (1995). *Successful school restructuring.* Madison: University of Wisconsin, Center on Organization and Restructuring of Schools.

No Child Left Behind Act of 2001, P. L. 107-110, 115 Stat. 1425 (2002).

Noss, R., Hoyles, C., & Pozzi, S. (2002). Abstraction in expertise: A study of nurses' conceptions of concentration. *Journal for Research in Mathematics Education, 33,* 204–229.

Oliver, M. (1992). Changing social relations of research production? *Disability, Handicap, & Society, 7*(2), 101–114.

Parmar, R. S., Cawley, J. F., & Frazita, R. R. (1996). Word problem-solving by students with and without mild disabilities. *Exceptional Children, 62,* 415–429.

Phelps, L. A., & Hanley-Maxwell, C. (1997). School-to-work transitions for youth with disabilities: A review of outcomes and practices. *Review of Educational Research, 67*(2), 197–226.

Pierce, C. D., Reid, R., & Epstein, M. H. (2004). Teacher-mediated interventions for children with EBD and their academic outcomes. *Remedial and Special Education, 25,* 175–188.

Polya, G. (1962). *Mathematical discovery: On understanding, learning, and teaching problem solving.* New York: John Wiley.

Poplin, M. S. (1988). The reductionistic fallacy in learning disabilities: Replicating the past by reducing the present. *Journal of Learning Disabilities, 21,* 389–400.

Resnick, C. B., & Ford, W. W. (1981). Structure and insight in problem solving. In C. B. Resnick & W. W. Ford, *The psychology of mathematics for instruction* (pp. 128–154). Hillsdale, NJ: Lawrence Erlbaum.

Ring, M. M., & Reetz, L. (2000). Modification effects on attributions of middle school students with learning disabilities. *Learning Disabilities Research & Practice, 15,* 34–42.

Rosenthal, R., & Jacobson, L. (1968). *Pygmalian in the classroom.* New York: Holt, Rinehart & Winston.

Schoenfeld, A. H. (1989). Teaching mathematical thinking and problem solving. In L. B. Resnick & L. E. Klopfer (Eds.), *Toward the thinking curriculum: Current cognitive research* (pp. 83–103). Alexandria, VA: Association for Supervision and Curriculum Development.

Schumm, J. S., & Vaughn, S. (1995). Getting ready for inclusion. *Learning Disabilities Research & Practice, 10*(3), 169–179.

Scuccimarra, D., & Speece, D. (1990). Employment outcomes and social integration of students with mild disabilities: The quality of life two years after high school. *Journal of Learning Disabilities, 23,* 213–219.

Sitlington, P. L., & Frank, A. R. (1990). Are adolescents with learning disabilities successfully crossing the bridges into adult life? *Learning Disabilities Quarterly, 13*(2), 97–111.

Skrtic, T. M. (1986). The crisis in special education knowledge: A perspective on perspective. *Focus on Exceptional Children, 18*(7), 1–16.

Smith, J. P. I. (1999). Tracking the mathematics of automobile production: Are schools failing to prepare students for work? *American Educational Research Journal, 36,* 835–878.

Stanovich, K. E. (2003). The fundamental computational biases of human cognition: Heuristics that (sometimes) impair decision making and problem solving. In J. E. Davidson & R. J. Sternberg (Eds.), *The psychology of problem solving* (pp. 291–342). Cambridge, UK: Cambridge University Press.

Sweller, J. (1988). Cognitive load during problem solving: Effects on learning. *Cognitive Science, 12,* 257–285.

Thorndike, E. L. (1922). *Psychology of arithmetic.* New York: Macmillan.

Thorndike, E. L., & Woodworth, R. S. (1901). The influence of improvement in one mental function upon the efficiency of other functions. *Psychological Review, 8,* 247–261, 384–395, 553–564.

Uchida, D., Cetron, M., & McKenzie, F. (1996). *Preparing students for the 21st century.* Arlington, VA: American Association of School Administrators.

U.S. Department of Education. (1983). *A nation at risk.* Washington, DC: Author.

U.S. Department of Education. (1994). *Goals 2000: Educate America Act,* 20 U.S.C. § 5801.

U.S. Department of Education. (1998). *Twentieth annual report to Congress on the implementation of the Individuals with Disabilities Education Act.* Washington, DC: Author.

U.S. Department of Education. (2002). *U.S. Department of Education Strategic Plan 2002–2007.* Washington, DC: Author. Retrieved December 23, 2003, from www.ed.gov/about/ reports/strat/ plan2002-07/plan.pdf

U.S. Department of Labor. (1991). *What work requires of schools: A SCANS report for America 2000.* Washington, DC: Author.

Vygotsky, L. S. (1978). *Mind in society.* Cambridge, MA: Harvard University Press.

Wagner, M., Blackorby, J., Cameto, R., & Newman, L. (1993). *What makes a difference? Influences on postschool outcomes of youth with disabilities.* Menlo Park, CA: SRI International.

Wagner, M., Newman, L., & Cameto, R. (2004). *Changes over time in the secondary school experiences of students with disabilities: A report from the National Longitudinal Transition Study–2 (NLTS2).* Menlo Park, CA: SRI International. Available: www.nlts2.org/pdfs/ changestime_exec_sum_standalone.pdf

Wehman, P., & Kregel, J. (1985). A supported work approach to competitive employment of individuals with moderate and severe handicaps. *Journal for the Association for Persons With Severe Handicaps, 10*(1), 3–11.

Wehmeyer, M. L., & Schwartz, M. (1998). The self-determination focus of transition goals for students with mental retardation. *Career Development for Exceptional Individuals, 21,* 75–86.

Weinstein, R. S., & McKown, C. (1998). Expectancy effects in "context": Listening to the voices of students and teachers. In J. Brophy (Ed.), *Advances in research on teaching* (Vol. 7, pp. 215–242). Greenwich, CT: JAI.

Weinstein, R. S., & Middlestadt, S. E. (1979). Student perceptions of teachers' interactions with high and low achievers. *Journal of Educational Psychology, 71,* 421–431.

Wertheimer, M. (1959). *Productive thinking.* New York: Harper.

Whitehead, A. M. (1929). *The aims of education.* New York: Macmillan.

Whitney-Thomas, J., & Hanley-Maxwell, C. (1996). Packing the parachute: A survey of parents' experiences as their children prepare to leave high school. *Exceptional Children, 63,* 25–42.

Wigfield, A., Eccles, J. S., & Rodriguez, D. (1998). The development of children's motivations in school contexts. In P. D. Pearson & A. Iran-Nefad (Eds.), *A review of research in education* (pp. 73–118). Washington, DC: American Educational Research Association.

Wolfensberger, W. (1972). *The principle of normalization.* Toronto: National Institute on Mental Retardation.

Woodward, J., Baxter, J., & Robinson, R. (1999). Rules and reasons: Decimal instruction for academically low achieving students. *Learning Disabilities Research & Practice, 14,* 15–24.

Xin, Y. P., & Jitendra, A. K. (1999). The effects of instruction in solving mathematical word problems for students with learning problems: A meta-analysis. *Journal of Special Education, 32,* 207–225.

Ysseldyke, J. E., Thurlow, M. L., & Bruininks, R. H. (1992). Expected outcomes for students with disabilities. *Remedial and Special Education, 13*(6), 19–30.

11

DISCOVERING UNHEARD VOICES

Explorations in the History of Education, Childhood, and Juvenile Justice

STEVEN SCHLOSSMAN

Carnegie Mellon University

What establishes and what ties together a scholar's research agenda—the lines of inquiry along which he or she seeks to make original contributions to knowledge? In my discipline of history, geography and chronology, both defined narrowly (e.g., Massachusetts during the Revolutionary era), set the main boundary lines. Within that boundary, scholars usually probe one or two specific topics or themes, such as the role of the militia and/or gender roles, and seek to explain patterns of change and continuity over time. Most often, except in textbooks, they do so from an identifiable subdisciplinary perspective such as political, cultural, or economic history. They publish their findings in historical monographs and in specialized (e.g., *Journal of Social History*) or general (e.g., *American Historical Review*) history journals.

Historians who study education—whether located professionally (as most are) in schools of education or in history departments—generally respect another boundary line that separates studies of colleges, universities, and professional schools, on the one hand, from studies of K–12 education, on the other. Both groups, however, tend to focus on schooling per se, whatever the level or type, and to do "top-down" analysis of the design, organization, funding, staffing, clientele, and especially ideas that underlay the creation of formal educational institutions. Within this conceptual framework—this "prescribed journey"—they seek to identify new questions and methods to illuminate educational experience in the past.

I consider myself to be an educational historian of the United States, primarily of the 19th and 20th centuries, although my research interests extend well beyond schooling to include the legal and cultural history of children and youth, including the operations of the juvenile justice system. Moreover, I have done substantial research that crosses the boundary line between K–12 and higher education; indeed, my empirical work touches all school levels from preschool to professional studies. But what truly motivates and ties together my research is method—and by "method," historians generally do not mean the use of approved, sophisticated analytic techniques that provide a sine qua non of first-rate scholarship, as is true in the field of education. Rather, by the term "method," historians usually mean the framing of novel questions that spur identification of untapped or little-explored databases so as to establish new lines of empirical inquiry into the past (Gaddis, 2002). And the main object of my method has been to discover unheard voices in the history of education, particularly the "bottom-up" voices of children and parents who have been the objects of reform initiatives in education and juvenile justice. To be sure, much of my scholarship inevitably also addresses "top-down" voices such as John Dewey in education and William Healy in juvenile justice. Most often, however, I have sought to identify "top-down" voices that have been largely forgotten and to incorporate them into the mainstream of American educational history.

In short, my main "research problem" has concerned how to expand contemporary understanding of key educational actors and activities in the past—not just the most famous, and not just the reformers, but also the targets of reform, mainly children and parents. This research problem has shaped my historical method, and it links the diverse set of topics that I have explored as an educational historian. In the remainder of this essay, I clarify why I chose this particular methodological approach to expand knowledge in the field of educational history and some of the professional circumstances and decision making that were critical to translating my general research problem into specific projects.

GRADUATE SCHOOL AND THE ESTABLISHMENT OF A RESEARCH AGENDA AND METHOD

I began graduate study in 1968 in a joint law and history program at the University of Wisconsin–Madison, but in 1970, as I became interested in the legal and cultural history of children and youth, I transferred to Columbia University to study with two of the reigning giants in American educational history: Lawrence Cremin and Richard Hofstadter (who died of leukemia during my first semester) (Cremin, 1961; Hofstadter, 1963). However, it was neither Cremin nor Hofstadter, but rather

Michael Katz and Anthony Platt, who provided the initial intellectual catalyst for my shift to educational history. In *The Irony of Early School Reform* (Katz, 1968/2001) and *The Child Savers* (Platt, 1969), Katz and Platt challenged several generations of conventional scholarly wisdom about the motives, methods, and results of reform movements in education and juvenile justice during the 19th and early 20th centuries (see also Cremin, 1980). They claimed that "social control," not benevolence or the expansion of equal opportunity, was the principal goal and outcome of child welfare innovations aimed at children and youth, especially the creation of public schools and juvenile courts. Both authors employed the tool of case study analysis, which was still novel in historical studies at the time. Katz, in particular, went beyond traditional kinds of "top-down" literary evidence to unearth local data, both qualitative and quantitative, to show how parents and children viewed the origins, processes, and results of educational innovation in their communities. Thus, the challenge that Katz and Platt offered to traditional scholarship was both interpretive and methodological.

At our very first meeting, Cremin raised doubts about the sufficiency or originality of the social control hypothesis to explain the dynamics of educational reform, and he urged me to read Merle Curti, Frank Tracy Carlton, and other scholars of the 1930s to gain perspective on earlier critical traditions in educational historiography (Carlton, 1965; Curti, 1935). But he strongly supported my interest in integrating new "bottom-up" voices into the study of educational reform, and he outlined a broad theoretical framework for reconceiving the entire story of American education that he believed was consistent with my approach. As I soon learned, Cremin was about to publish the first installment of his massive three-volume historical trilogy, *American Education*. In that volume on the colonial period, and in the two volumes that followed on the national period and the modern (he termed it "metropolitan") period, he radically redefined what the study of educational history was all about (Cremin, 1970, 1976, 1980, 1988, 1989). He also, from a methodological standpoint, embraced the study of individual communities and the inclusion of "bottom-up" voices as essential to recreating lived educational experience in the past. Ultimately, even though I chose a dissertation topic on the juvenile justice system that reflected my intellectual debt to Katz and Platt more than to Cremin, the new conceptual framework to which Cremin introduced me in 1970, and the concrete opportunities he provided for me to serve as both his teaching assistant and his research assistant, profoundly shaped my methods of inquiry throughout my career. And Cremin's analytic framework also reinforced my decision to center my own intellectual energies less on grand synthesis, as Cremin was doing on a scale I could hardly imagine, than on continually seeking to discover new voices in America's educational past.

In truth, for my first 18 months at Columbia, I did not have the time, resources, or good fortune to follow through on these commitments. I had no difficulty in internalizing Cremin's new, unconventional, and disarmingly broad (he liked to call it "latitudinarian") definition of education[1] or the new lingo of "educational configuration"[2] and "educational biography"[3] that he created to transform that definition into an operational research strategy. Indeed, I was intrigued and energized by how much consternation his new approach caused more traditional school-focused scholars in the field, including his distinguished Teachers College mentor (and co-author with Cremin of a classic textbook in the field), R. Freeman Butts (Butts & Cremin, 1953). But my main energies at the time had to go elsewhere, notably toward mastering the canonical literature so as to pass doctoral qualifying exams.

In addition, my intention to develop a "bottom-up" dissertation topic in juvenile justice was frustrated by my inability to gain access to original case files from early-20th-century juvenile courts. Cremin's skepticism regarding Platt's (1969) *The Child Savers* had led me to rethink his methodology; it was only on second reading that I realized that Platt's social control interpretation was seriously compromised by a lack of empirical data on how juvenile courts actually worked on a day-to-day basis. Until I could gain access to such data, I did not think I could seriously improve on Platt's research; therefore, I was reluctant to commit

to a dissertation on juvenile justice. In the meantime, I experimented with various other historical topics in Cremin's research seminar. Two of these led to journal publications while I was still a graduate student (Schlossman, 1973, 1974), but all involved "top-down" rather than "bottom-up" data, and from my standpoint, none pointed toward the kind of dissertation I wanted to do.

Fortunately, my luck in crafting a "bottom-up" dissertation changed dramatically toward the end of my second year at Columbia following an expedition to the Midwest where, after many failures, I finally managed to gain access to the case files of Milwaukee Juvenile Court for the 1901 to 1920 period.[4] With these unique documents in hand to ground the project empirically, Cremin readily agreed to supervise the dissertation. Indeed, he saw the topic as an exemplar of his new "latitudinarian" definition of education, not only because analysis of the inner workings of families—the centerpiece of Cremin's notion of "educational configuration"—was central to my project but also because I viewed the entire juvenile court experiment as a variant on "progressive" educational ideas, with probation officers cast in the role of teachers, parents cast in the role of students, and the world-famous Denver judge Ben Lindsey cast in the role of the educational philosopher John Dewey (Schlossman, 2005).

Beyond this, however, Cremin—who was already well under way in writing *American Education: The National Experience* (Cremin, 1980)—was deeply committed to the search for new "bottom-up" data sources that would allow him to bring to life the notions of "educational configuration" and "educational biography" in typical 19th-century communities. Cremin's goal was to show how similarities and differences in community-level educational configurations operated in practice to constrain or expand individual educational opportunities. Thus, my research and Cremin's research were proceeding on similar methodological tracks, and in 1973 Cremin asked me to serve as his research assistant. As I was writing the chapters of my dissertation that analyzed the previously unheard voices of children and parents in Milwaukee Juvenile Court, Cremin asked me to identify three small communities for case study analysis of educational developments in

New England, the Midwest, and the South.[5] Key in selecting each community would be whether its local (and supporting state) libraries held two different types of historical evidence: (1) data tracking key patterns of institutional growth, such as schools, churches, work environments, benevolent societies, newspapers, libraries, and railroad and telegraph linkages, as well as census and supplementary quantitative and qualitative data outlining the basic structures of family life, and (2) data capturing life histories of individuals raised in that community, whether contained in diaries (published or unpublished), letters, or other personal documents and with particular attention to that person's formal and informal education at home, at school, and in the community. Cremin asked me to locate as much untapped historical data as possible, that is, data dealing with communities and individuals about whom historians had not written much or anything previously. At the same time, at least for his case study of education in a New England community, he made clear that he was leaning toward the early industrial city of Lowell, Massachusetts, because it was the site that had inspired Lucy Larcom's famous reminiscence, *A New England Girlhood,* which was perfect, in his mind, for purposes of educational biography (Larcom, 1961).

Although my professional commitment to "bottom-up" history was already secure in my ongoing dissertation research, the months that I spent as Cremin's assistant motoring through the American countryside in search of unheard voices in American education refined that commitment and clarified its practical difficulties as a historical methodology. During the New England phase of the research, I learned not to look a gift horse in the mouth. Try though I did to persuade Cremin to focus his case study on lesser-known cities such as Fall River, Holyoke, and Pawtucket, I finally had to admit that none of the new voices I uncovered in these (and other) locales suited Cremin's method of educational biography as well as the writings of Larcom and other female and male mill operatives in Lowell. And once I located rich, previously untapped community-level data on schooling, labor, churches, newspapers, and many other dynamics of community life in Lowell, especially concerning the impact of early Irish immigration on the town's social and economic fabric (including public financing of Irish parochial schools), the choice of Lowell as a case study site had too many advantages to turn down, even though the town was already quite familiar to American historians.

After New England, I traveled south to visit state historical societies and local libraries in Virginia, North Carolina, and South Carolina. Cremin and I had already identified several autobiographies written by former slaves from those states that might serve the purposes of educational biography, but only if they could narrow the search for a case study site that contained ample data on white as well as black educational experiences. Ultimately, what determined the selection of Sumter District, South Carolina, as Cremin's case study site was not so much the family- or community-level data uncovered there for whites—although the southern educational experience generally was richer institutionally than previous literature had indicated—as two other unexpected data resources. First was the availability of manuscript census data by which to calculate how many whites owned slaves in Sumter District and the average number of slaves per farm/plantation—both key for outlining the contours of the district's educational configurations. Second, and more important to Cremin, was the discovery of a second slave autobiography within Sumter District, that of Irving E. Lowery, to compare and contrast with the more widely known slave autobiography of Jacob Stroyer (Lowery, 1911; Stroyer, 1898). This combination of African American data sources made Sumter unique among the several case study sites that I was investigating, and the final choice for Cremin was easy.

The search for new voices in the educational history of the small-town Midwest gave Cremin the most pause. No single institutional development, such as the birth of the factory or the expansion of slavery, so clearly shaped regional experience in the early-19th-century Midwest, educational or otherwise. Moreover, Cremin had not previously identified any personal narratives that pointed him toward one community or another for purposes of educational biography. In identifying criteria for prospective case study sites, we decided that it was imperative to respect settlement patterns. That is, we would not consider communities in the northern or southern tiers of states such as Ohio, Indiana, and Illinois because they tended to be dominated by settlers from the North or the South, respectively, each of whom had very different prior experiences with state funding of public schooling. Thus, my travels to the Midwest in search of new data centered on the middle geographic range of each state, where the settlement pattern more commonly mixed northerners and southerners. If anything, we believed, it was better to err on the side of southern dominance in selecting a case study site because educational historians had tended to overstate the impact of New England educational traditions in schooling the Midwest.

Cremin's final choice of Macoupin County in Illinois as his midwestern case study site rested in part on the mix of southerners, northerners, and immigrants who migrated there (although southerners predominated), in part on rich data concerning both publicly supported and denominationally supported educational activities (especially by German Lutherans), and in part by my fortuitous discovery (after lengthy residence and largely by accident) of two locally held personal narratives by individuals who had come of age in the county: John McAuley Palmer, a white who achieved considerable success as a politician, and James Henry Magee, a free black who overcame serious childhood illness and struggled during his adult career as a teacher and preacher (Magee, 1873; G. T. Palmer, 1941; J. M. Palmer, 1901). Being able to compare and contrast the voices of a little-known white and a free black man in the same county was an opportunity I had never expected to find; it clinched Cremin's choice of Macoupin County for case study analysis.

The Dissertation as a Culmination and New Beginning: Gender and Social Reform During the Progressive Era

My travels as Cremin's research assistant provided a remarkable opportunity to scour the country in search of new voices in educational history. No less important, it offered regular occasions to discuss methodological strategies and choices with him. The experience also increased my appreciation for how unique my "bottom-up" juvenile court data were for analyzing the predicaments of lower-class children and parents during the early 20th century. After completing the dissertation, I won a National Institute of Mental Health postdoctoral fellowship to revise the dissertation into a book, and I completed the book manuscript within several months (Schlossman, 1977).

Two unplanned possibilities for discovering new historical voices had emerged clearly from the dissertation project, and I was fortunate to have several more months as a postdoctoral fellow to pursue them. Both involved issues of gender, a theme of major importance during the mid-1970s as historians provided key intellectual leadership for the rise of women's studies as a legitimate scholarly field.

First, during my studies of Milwaukee Juvenile Court, I was surprised to learn that the National Parent–Teachers Association (PTA)—which was led entirely by women—was the leading advocacy group for juvenile courts during the early 20th century. Why was the PTA so involved in juvenile court if its primary focus, as suggested by its name, was to improve communications between parents and schools? Because historians of education and juvenile justice had never shown much, if any, interest in the PTA, I was optimistic that adding its "top-down" voice to historians' understanding of social reform leadership during the Progressive Era would be a notable contribution. Second, as I completed my book, I realized that boys and girls had followed fundamentally different pathways into juvenile court. Boys were charged mainly with property crimes, and girls were charged mainly with sexual offenses—actually, not so much "offenses" per se, such as prostitution, as simply sexual activity itself (for which their male partners were not held accountable). Moreover, my Milwaukee data suggested that girls were incarcerated for their "crimes" at higher rates than were boys. I noted these points briefly and tentatively in the book, but I sensed that a significant next step in my own research would be to give full voice to the distinctive experiences of girls in court and thereby to introduce gender as a key variable in historical studies of juvenile justice.

Fortunately, both lines of inquiry uncovered rich untapped veins of historical data that introduced new female voices into the discourse of Progressive Era social reform. In "Before Home Start," I probed previously ignored writings of the PTA's predecessor group, the National Congress of Mothers (founded in 1897), to analyze the remarkably broad child welfare reform agenda that this organization championed during the Progressive Era, including not only juvenile courts and various school-related measures but also scientifically grounded parent education based on G. Stanley Hall's ideas about child development (Schlossman, 1976). I also tracked radical changes that occurred in the organization and leadership of child development research and parent education during the post-World War I era. In particular, I highlighted major initiatives in parent education led by unheralded women's organizations such as the Child Study Association of America, the American Association of University Women, and the Merrill Palmer School as well as numerous contributions to child development research and practice initiated by women such as Edna White, Helen Thompson Woolley, Patty Smith Hill, Sidonie Gruenberg, and Lois Meek Stolz, all of whom educational historians had previously ignored. What began as an offshoot of my juvenile justice research ended up opening a new subfield within educational history and engaging me for nearly a decade in professional association with scholars and practitioners affiliated with the Society for Research in Child Development (Schlossman, 1978b, 1981, 1983a, 1983b, 1986a, 1986b).

In "The Crime of Precocious Sexuality," extending the little I knew about female delinquency from my study of Milwaukee Juvenile Court, I analyzed a large body of obscure early-20th-century writings on the sexual behavior of adolescent females, venereal disease, and eugenics of which historians were almost entirely unaware (Schlossman & Wallach, 1978). This "top-down," quasi-scientific literature clearly explained why girls, but not boys, were regularly charged with sex offenses in juvenile court during the early 20th century. The literature invoked the traditional Victorian double standard on sex but did so in the context of a real epidemic of venereal disease and the growing popularity of eugenic ideas that aimed to eliminate inherited mental and moral deficiency via incarceration and sterilization of promiscuous girls. In addition to these voluminous writings, I located select but revealing statistical data from juvenile courts and correctional institutions that reinforced my preliminary findings from Milwaukee. Girls throughout the nation were incarcerated in public and private reform schools at roughly twice the rate of boys, even though the girls' "offenses" were almost entirely sexual rather than criminal in nature. As with my research on parent education, this offshoot of my doctoral dissertation identified fascinating new voices that enlarged historians' understanding of the impact of gender on social reform during the early 20th century. Over the past three decades, the historical study of female delinquency has become a major subfield in women's history, the history of childhood, and the history of juvenile justice (Odem & Schlossman, 1991; Schlossman & Cairns, 1993).

A Historian at RAND: Linking "Bottom-Up" Social History to Policy Research on Children and Parents

Naturally, I was pleased with the directions in which my postdissertation research was moving, but I was also concerned that for all the new data I had located, I was not finding true "bottom-up" voices that enabled me to present children and parents as central actors—as agents in history—as the case files of Milwaukee Juvenile Court had allowed me to do. Thus, my research on parent education mainly broadened historical understanding of the middle-class and academic innovators in the field, not of the parents and children who were the targets of parent education initiatives. Similarly, my research on female delinquency and several other juvenile justice topics that I studied during the late 1970s offered new information about courts, clinics, correctional institutions, and delinquency prevention efforts in public schools but contained very few insights on the children and parents who were the clients of these institutional initiatives. Unexpectedly, it was only after I joined the RAND Corporation in 1979— ostensibly to apply historical perspective more directly toward public policy—that I found several exciting opportunities to contribute not only new historical voices but also unique "bottom-up" voices into historical scholarship on education, childhood, and juvenile justice.[6]

During my first year at RAND, I received grants from the Ford Foundation and the National Institute of Education (NIE) to conduct two historical research projects on bilingual education and delinquency prevention, respectively. Both projects were closely linked to contemporary policy issues, but each one gave me considerable methodological latitude. For parts of each project, I explored relatively familiar topics and data sources such as debates among leading bilingual education authorities in different time periods about pedagogical strategies and the views of psychologists, psychiatrists, and sociologists regarding the roles of clinics and schools in preventing juvenile delinquency. These facets of both projects were relatively straightforward to define and execute, and I completed them as expeditiously as possible to leave time for original archival research that might yield new "bottom-up" data. In the end, I was able to uncover novel data sources in both projects and to offer new perspectives on children and parents as actors in 19th- and early-20th-century education and juvenile justice reform.

In the Ford-sponsored study of bilingual education, I focused on two principal topics, neither of which educational historians knew much about and both of which held potential to enlighten the divisively ideological debates that were then taking place on the subject (these were the early years of the Reagan administration, which was strongly hostile to federal subsidy of bilingual education). First, what was the attitude of professional educators to bilingual education during the first half of the 20th century? Second, did German immigrants to the 19th-century frontier attend bilingual schools that were publicly funded? After reading widely on the first topic, I concluded that my most original contribution as a historian would be to call attention to the little-known but insightful scholarship of George Sanchez, a noted Hispanic American educator of the early 20th century, and of Herbert Manuel, Sanchez's mentor at the University of Texas (and who, despite his last name, was not of Hispanic heritage). Archival data were available for both men that shed light on the entire history of schooling in the Southwest, perhaps the least researched region in all of American educational history. I was especially intrigued that neither Sanchez nor Manuel viewed bilingual education as a "self-evident remedy" to school failures among native Spanish-speaking children. Personally, I was an advocate of bilingual education; thus, I was doubly fascinated by the doubts that both Manuel and Sanchez raised about its limitations and potential misuses in the classroom. My goal as a historian was to use new knowledge about educational controversy in the past to complicate current public debate and to demonstrate the continued relevance of Manuel's and Sanchez's views for everyone in the field (Schlossman, 1983c). (Some bilingual education advocates, it should be noted, interpreted my work as hostile to both Sanchez and bilingual education, although it was not intended to be.)

On the second topic, I was particularly intrigued by how politics had shaped both advocates' and critics' views of the history of language instruction in the United States. Critics of bilingual programs confidently asserted that publicly sponsored vernacular instruction had always been rejected as un-American, backward-looking, and pedagogically impractical because, in a pluralist society, it was impossible to accommodate the language traditions of multiple immigrant groups. Advocates of bilingual programs, on the other hand, countered that politically powerful immigrant groups, notably Germans during the 19th century, had regularly been able to force local public schools to offer subject matter instruction in German. Neither advocates nor critics, alas, seemed much interested in verifying the historical claims that grounded their contemporary politics. What, then, was the "American historical tradition" in bilingual education? I simply did not know, and my review of the relevant historical literature persuaded me that no one else really knew either (but see Fishman, 1966; Kloss, 1977).

In developing a methodology, I wanted most of all to establish a solid empirical base for challenging or confirming the contrasting political claims about the educational tactics of 19th-century Germans. If, during their heyday of political power, German parents did indeed gain public subsidy for extensive vernacular instruction, this would establish a notable historical precedent and undermine the critics' charge that bilingual programs were antithetical to American public school traditions. If, on the other hand, Germans did not try to gain, or tried but did not succeed in gaining, public funding, then advocates for bilingual programs would be forced to acknowledge that their views marked a sharp departure from educational policy and experience in the past.

Because I did not read German, I was seriously handicapped in the types of historical data that I could readily access to judge German public opinion on the subject. That is, I could not read German-language newspapers, diaries, letters, reminiscences, and the like that were potentially ideal to tap into ground-level, 19th-century German opinion. But I had neither sufficient funding nor time to invest in large-scale translation or in a German-speaking research assistant, so I decided to see whether I could develop a viable methodology based solely on English-language sources. Thankfully, from the extensive community-level research that I had done for Cremin on education in the Midwest, I already knew that 19th-century school reports tended to be remarkably rich in detail and commentary on local social and political, as well as educational, matters. Perhaps those documents might record contemporary controversies about using German or other frontier vernaculars in the classroom.

In the end, I was able to gather only scattered information about the use of German in 19th-century rural schools. Nonetheless, it seemed clear that public funding of German-language instruction was fairly widespread, at least in states where Germans were thickly settled and state authority over education was minimal. But my methodology worked out much better in four important centers of German urban settlement: Cincinnati, St. Louis, Milwaukee, and Indianapolis. In each of those cities, I was able to locate annual school reports that supplied sufficient data, both qualitative and quantitative, to develop a substantial new empirical base for understanding the role of parent advocacy in promoting bilingual education on the urban frontier. Public funding of German instructional programs was, in fact, commonplace in each community, and German parents were remarkably active in fighting politically for the programs' establishment and maintenance. But despite the political activism of German parents, the design and longevity of specific programs varied markedly from city to city; moreover, political battles were often bitter and prolonged, with outcomes varying from year to year. Staffing, supplying, and implementing bilingual programs were administrative nightmares; programs that seemed to be effective one year came apart the next year (Schlossman, 1983e).

Thus, no single or simple conclusions emerged from my analysis that indisputably reinforced or challenged the opposing historical claims of bilingual education protagonists during the early 1980s. But the historical data did introduce the voices of 19th-century parents into current debate, and the analysis also generated two conclusions that, in my judgment, spoke equally to both sides. First, even in communities where bilingual programs were sustained for many decades, no program remained politically uncontested for long. Second, in every city, daunting and recurring implementation problems were common, especially with regard to the development of curricular materials, the selection of teachers, and the refinement of age- or grade-appropriate teaching methods in the classroom. There was, in short, no golden era in 19th-century America where conflict was absent or programs were secure—no single road or final solution for diffusing the political volatility of bilingual education in a pluralist, immigrant-receiving society that saw public schooling as key to cultural assimilation. Only patience, an experimental attitude, and an open recognition of difficulties and failures enabled bilingual programs to survive in individual communities as long as they did.

My NIE-sponsored study of delinquency prevention sought to recreate the rise and demise of innovations in the field during the first half of the 20th century. The study was funded largely because policymakers had little readily available information about the past to draw on in trying to invent new programs for current application. In short, they were genuinely concerned about reinventing the wheel. The project presented many and varied opportunities for both synthetic and original research. As in my bilingual education project, my research strategy was to dedicate as many resources as possible to identify new historical voices that might contribute something unexpected to how policymakers sorted out their options in the present (Cohen & Schlossman, 1977). During the early 1980s, policy evaluations in delinquency prevention often stressed the gap between design and implementation that undermined field experiments before they could be fully tested. My research strategy was to identify new historical data that would speak directly to this current concern about program implementation as well as program design. (The pioneering studies of implementation in education by my RAND colleagues, Paul Berman and Milbrey McLaughlin, were vital in shaping my historical research strategies for analyzing both delinquency prevention and bilingual education [McLaughlin, 1989].)

Not all of my forays were successful in uncovering useful historical data. In several parts of the project, I had little choice but to focus on program design rather than implementation and to synthesize, in somewhat original ways, data that were already known to specialists in the field (Schlossman, 1978a, 1983d; Sedlak & Schlossman, 1985). In two instances, however, my methodological approach achieved more than I initially thought was possible.

First, in Berkeley, California, I learned of an innovative delinquency prevention program—the community coordinating council—that was co-invented during the 1920s by the chief of police, August Vollmer, and the superintendent of schools, Virgil Dickson (a former doctoral student of Lewis Terman's at Stanford University). In addition to several targeted programs that were run exclusively by the police, the coordinating council brought representatives from the schools and the police, mental health, and business communities together on a weekly basis to address the problems of individual troubled children before they accumulated arrest records that would require judicial intervention.

Each representative analyzed the individual child's difficulties from his or her particular professional or civic perspective, and the group as a whole developed a coordinated intervention plan that would leverage all available community resources and keep the child under close watch. Although largely forgotten in later years, the coordinating council idea was celebrated in its time and exerted considerable statewide influence in California (especially in the Los Angeles area) during the 1930s and 1940s. Luckily for me, in addition to a small archive of Dickson's administration as school superintendent, both Vollmer and the police department had established separate voluminous archives that enabled me to examine the implementation, as well as the design, of the coordinating council experiment (Liss & Schlossman, 1984; Zellman & Schlossman, 1986).

The second and more notable product of the NIE study dealt with delinquency prevention experiments in Depression-era Chicago, especially the Chicago Area Project (CAP). An offspring of research conducted by the world-famous Chicago School of Sociology (W. I. Thomas, Robert Park, Ernest Burgess, Frederick Thrasher, Clifford Shaw, Henry McKay, and many others), the CAP, unlike the Berkeley program, was already legendary in the field of delinquency prevention. In fact, I initially shied away from studying it for precisely that reason, thinking that I could draw what was useful to my project from prior historical and sociological scholarship. As I read the relevant secondary literature, however, it became clear that scholars had devoted their intellectual energies mainly (and repetitively) to articulating the CAP's theoretical premises, not to exploring how it came into being and actually worked on a daily basis—in other words, to program design, not program implementation or maintenance.

When I visited Chicago initially, I did not expect to find an archival base to support the kind of implementation research that I ideally wanted to do; after all, if such data were readily available, wouldn't the numerous previous scholars who had studied the CAP have used them? For whatever reasons, the answer was no. I found a sprawling, minimally organized but extraordinarily rich archive that contained in-depth implementation data for several of the high-delinquency neighborhoods of Chicago where the CAP had operated between the 1930s and the 1950s. Moreover, the archive contained many interviews by the CAP field-workers with youth who belonged to competing neighborhood gangs. It did not take me long to realize that this archive contained the best "bottom-up" historical data I had encountered for studying juvenile delinquency since I had completed my research on Milwaukee Juvenile Court.

Because of time and budget constraints in my overall NIE project, I was compelled to select a single neighborhood (South Chicago) to study both program design and implementation issues in-depth. While still counting my good fortune in locating such data, I was startled several weeks later to learn that another archive that contained the personal papers of the CAP's chief field-worker in South Chicago, Stephen Bubacz, had literally just opened. With these two excellent archives to draw on, I soon completed the first historical study of the CAP in action and even dared to conclude (based on statistical data that had been compiled but never brought to light) that the program may have been successful in reducing rates of juvenile delinquency in South Chicago. The analysis not only shed new empirical light on principles of implementation in the field of delinquency prevention, it also painted a vivid "bottom-up" portrait of the everyday lives of working-class children and parents struggling for individual and community survival in Depression-era Chicago (Schlossman & Sedlak, 1983; Wolcott & Schlossman, in press). Furthermore, several months after the historical research was completed, I teamed with an interdisciplinary team of RAND colleagues to investigate the logic, operations, and effectiveness of delinquency prevention programs currently in operation (early 1980s) in the same community of South Chicago. The result, *Delinquency Prevention in South Chicago,* was a uniquely integrated study of a pioneer delinquency prevention program in a single neighborhood, past and present, using both qualitative and quantitative analytic techniques. And the program, interestingly enough, appeared to be as successful in the present as in the past in reducing rates of juvenile delinquency (Schlossman, Shavelson, & Zellman, 1984).

New Subjects, New Voices in the History of American Education

During the mid-1980s, two unanticipated projects emerged, one supported by RAND and the other by a separate consulting arrangement, enabling me once again to advance my own methodological agenda and discover two sets of fascinating new voices in American educational history. The RAND project was an offshoot of the pathbreaking evaluation of the National Preventive Dentistry Demonstration Program that RAND's Stephen Klein, in coordination with several leading scholars of dentistry, was leading under a grant from the Robert Wood Johnson Foundation. Its focus was a variety of school-based dentistry initiatives, particularly the free provision of fluoride rinses and sealants to students at various grade levels. These preventive techniques were heralded by the dental profession as unprecedented in their potential to reach underserved children and attack the origins of dental disease. As the study progressed, a surprising finding emerged: The incidence of caries among children was already declining precipitously and independently of the experimental interventions. The main explanation appeared to be the dissemination of fluoride throughout American society during the 1970s via municipal water supplies and the food chain as a whole. From a cost-benefit standpoint, the RAND analysts concluded that the new school-based interventions, in addition to being more difficult and expensive to implement than their supporters had anticipated, seemed largely superfluous given the rapid general decline in children's incidence of dental caries (Bell et al., 1984).

In light of these emerging findings, Klein asked me to investigate whether schools had ever been used successfully in the past as sites to improve children's health. I already knew that during the Progressive Era, schools had employed doctors and nurses to identify and treat disease among immigrant children and that schools had cooperated with boards of health to persuade immigrant parents to approve vaccination of their children against various infectious and potentially deadly diseases. Might it not also have been possible, I wondered, that

Progressive Era schools took steps to curtail dental disease? Klein doubted this given that a central premise of the recent school-based initiatives was that they were historically unprecedented in reconceiving the role of schools as a delivery site for dental services to children. But he agreed to provide a week of funding to test out my hunch.

Suffice it to say that only a few days of intensive research in school reports and dental journals from the early 20th century were necessary to establish, first, that children's oral health was a major public health concern at the time and, second, that educators and dentists had collaborated to extend school social services to include dentistry. During the Progressive Era, both public and private funds supported school-based and free-standing dental clinics to deliver preventive and reparative services to children who could not otherwise afford them. These preliminary discoveries, Klein believed, justified further inquiry and funding. Over the next several months, I located large amounts of previously unused historical data on children's dentistry in various libraries and archives across the country. The historical research established conclusively that dentistry was part and parcel of the creation of school-based social services during the Progressive Era. Indeed, until the 1950s—with the Depression era as the high point—both preventive services delivered by hygienists and reparative treatments delivered by dentists to children in both schools and free clinics provided the majority of dental services that American children received altogether. This entire set of historical voices had been totally forgotten. The school-based dental experiments of the 1970s were obviously not as original in design or execution as their advocates believed (Schlossman, 2004; Schlossman, Brown, & Sedlak, 1986).

A second unanticipated and fruitful opportunity to identify new voices in educational history came from the Graduate Management Admission Council (GMAC, sponsor of the Graduate Management Admission Test [GMAT]), which during the mid-1980s was conducting research on long-term student demand for the MBA degree for its core constituency of leading American business schools. After several efforts

at statistical modeling, the GMAC researchers raised a sobering question: How reliably could they predict future demand for graduate business degrees if they had little understanding of how current demand had originated, and more generally, how and why had graduate business education changed over the course of the 20th century? Although I had no expertise on this topic, the GMAC asked me to assist the council in assessing how much was already known about patterns of change and continuity in MBA programs, which time periods had seen the greatest expansion of demand, and what factors had driven the change process inside and outside of the business and educational communities. The focus, I was told, should be as much as possible on major business schools, both public and private, and every effort should be made to understand both the policy decision-making process and curricular and pedagogical developments. These kinds of information would interest current business school deans and admissions officers, whose responsibility was (particularly as national ranking schemes gained popularity during the 1980s) to keep their institutions ahead of the demand curve.

As I quickly learned, very little was known about the history of American business education, especially at the graduate level. Apart from a few narrowly specialized or anecdotal studies of Harvard University and the Wharton School of Business at the University of Pennsylvania, and a consuming fascination with the origins and practice of the case method (as adapted by business schools from law schools), both historians of business and historians of higher and professional education had largely ignored the topic (but see Sedlak & Williamson, 1983). Moreover, except in a few instances, historical data on business schools, archival or otherwise, appeared to be minimal. Despite these obstacles, the GMAC agreed to fund an initial inquiry designed to illuminate the change process in graduate business education, especially during the post-World War II period. I agreed to lead the project but made my long-term involvement contingent on whether I could add genuinely new historical voices to what was already known about Harvard and Wharton.

At first, I lacked a driving question to motivate the study as a whole or to direct my methodology. But the project took off quickly once I realized that MBA programs began to expand enormously during the 1950s, that curricula and pedagogical methods were often radically transformed during the 1960s, and that not Harvard or Wharton but rather Carnegie Mellon University; the University of Chicago; Northwestern University; Stanford University; the University of California, Berkeley (UC Berkeley); and the University of California, Los Angeles (UCLA), were generally viewed as the new leaders in the field during the postwar era. Furthermore, I learned, most changes in educational philosophy and practice were somehow linked to two widely read, highly critical assessments of business education sponsored by the Ford Foundation and the Carnegie Corporation in 1959. The involvement of foundations in business education reform caught me by surprise, but it was very promising for the development of a research methodology. My earlier studies of parent education had shown how the Rockefeller Foundation, through generous and strategically aimed grants, had virtually recreated the entire field of child development during the 1920s and 1930s at institutions such as the University of Iowa, the University of Minnesota, UC Berkeley, Teachers College at Columbia University, and the University of Toronto (Schlossman, 1981). Had Ford and Carnegie perhaps played a similar change agent role in postwar business education? If so, then why?

I inquired whether the Ford and Carnegie archives (like those at Rockefeller) might be made available for my research. At Carnegie the answer was no, but Ford, which was near the end of a major effort to organize its archives for potential scholarly use, invited me to visit. Suffice it to say that the files of several grant officers and trustees of the Ford Foundation introduced me to some of the most intriguing "insider" voices that I had ever encountered in studying educational history. As early as the 1940s, and very much part of cold war economic strategies aimed against the Soviet Union, Ford (and Carnegie) had begun planning a multiple-pronged grants strategy to shake up American business schools and infuse them with mathematical methods and theoretical insights pioneered by avant-garde social scientists such as Hebert Simon and Robert Merton.

Both foundations launched their grants programs (and their critical assessments of current teaching in business schools) during the early 1950s. Within two decades, they had spearheaded a major revolution in the professorial ranks of business schools and in the subject matter, pedagogical methods, and clientele they taught, especially at the graduate level. Thus, the change process had been purposeful, centrally directed, generously funded, quick to take root, and remarkably successful in expanding the popularity of the MBA degree—findings that the sponsors of my research, quite understandably, found intriguing (Schlossman, Sedlak, & Wechsler, 1987b, 1988).

In addition to providing detailed insight into the foundation's role as a change agent, the Ford records contained pointed commentary and considerable documentation (especially correspondence but also curricular materials) gathered from several of the best-known business schools in the country. This information facilitated a next-stage research strategy, the selection of specific university sites for conducting in-depth case studies of the change process in business education during the quarter century following World War II. The methodological emphasis, to be sure, would be almost entirely on "top-down" voices at the Ford Foundation and the individual universities (e.g., presidents, provosts, deans, department chairs). Nonetheless, these were the voices of key players in American universities who historians had marginalized from the mainstream of educational history. Because the growth of MBA programs in size and prestige was one of the most dramatic developments in postwar higher education, I had no doubt that this line of inquiry would significantly expand the boundaries of traditional scholarship in higher and professional education. The contribution would be even greater if I could go beyond Harvard and Wharton and analyze the change process in other influential public and private business schools that had entirely escaped historians' attention.

But where to start? Because I was working in Santa Monica, California, and because the grant officers at Ford had viewed UCLA's business school as one of their early prime targets, I decided to begin at UCLA. Alas, there were no archives to be found in either the university or business school libraries. But in conversations with older faculty members and secretaries, I sensed that key administrative records had indeed been preserved but had been moved frequently to make way for changing uses of office space. The problem was that no one could remember where the records were currently located. After several days of fruitless search in faculty offices and file cabinets, a secretary retrieved a set of keys to open various doors and closets, the contents of which no one knew. After several failures, she opened a large closet in a student dining area; quite literally, the records I had been seeking began to fall out from the shelves of their jam-packed hiding space of many years. It took several days for me to transport and organize the records, but they were in fact exactly what I needed to begin identifying who pushed for and against change at UCLA during the 1950s and 1960s and to account for pressures inside and outside of the university in shaping the change process (grants from Ford mattered, but competition with archrival UC Berkeley was also key). This awkward uncertain hunt for fugitive administrative records in closets, file cabinets desk drawers, basements, and the like was repeated with numerous variations over the next decade as I enlarged the range of case study sites (e.g., Michigan State University, University of Washington, Ohio State University, University of Michigan, University of Pittsburgh, Northwestern University, Stanford University, Harvard University, Carnegie Mellon University, Dartmouth University, University of Western Ontario) and began the long-term process, which is still under way, of understanding how the modern American business school came into being (Gleeson & Schlossman, 1992a, 1992b, 1995; Gleeson, Schlossman, & Allen, 1993, 1994; Schlossman & Sedlak, 1985, 1988; Schlossman, Sedlak, & Wechsler, 1987a, 1989a, 1989b; Sedlak & Schlossman, 1991).

PERSONAL EXPERIENCE AND RESEARCH PROBLEMS: HOMEWORK AND THE PARENT–SCHOOL INTERFACE

Since the mid-1990s, I have extended my research agenda and method to cover one main new topic in educational history, namely, the place of homework in American schooling. In this instance, and for the only time in my career, personal experience suggested the topic. As the parent of two school-age children, I found myself deeply perplexed (in both public and private schools) by teachers' inconsistent use of homework at all grade levels—from no homework at all in the middle grades, to large assignments in the lower grades, to massive assignments equivalent to an adult work week in upper grades. When I inquired about the logic behind these assignments, I was politely told by principals and teachers that I was an overbearing parent, that my child was not "gifted," or that I was a confused "progressive" who needed a strong dose of William Bennett as an antidote to sentimentalism in education. This frustrating experience prompted two realizations I had never considered before my children attended school: first, that on academic matters (especially in the early grades), homework usually provides the main interface between teachers and parents; and second, that the experience of homework is vital in shaping the spirit of parent–school relations as a whole, for better or for worse (Gill & Schlossman, 1995).

Naturally, I set out to see what educational scholars had to say about homework and its place in American schooling today. I was pleased to learn not only that there was exemplary research on the subject but also that prominent scholars, such as Harris Cooper and Joyce Epstein, had similarly emphasized the key role of homework in parent–school relations (Cooper, 1989a, 1989b, 1994; Epstein, 1983, 1988; Epstein & Pinkow, 1988). From a historical standpoint, however, there was no scholarship whatsoever; homework might just as well have been absent from the 19th- and 20th-century American child's school experience.

Obviously, homework had a history; the problem was that scholars had ignored it. This did not surprise me because, unfortunately, educational historians have ignored many matters concerning the content and methods of day-to-day instruction in both urban and rural schools. I decided to probe whether the history of homework could be studied not solely as a tool for helping children to learn subject matter but also—and a topic that had interested me since my earliest studies of parent education—as a vehicle for examining relations between parents and schools. If the latter, the research would be especially important to pursue. Despite pioneering research by Carl Kaestle, Geraldine Joncich Clifford, and William Reese on parent–school relations during the 19th and early 20th centuries, and despite Cremin's attempt to interweave family and school experience via the concepts of "educational configuration" and "educational biography," historians still tended to write family history and school history as discrete rather than dynamically interrelated topics (Clifford, 1978; Cremin, 1976, 1977; Kaestle, 1978, 1983; Reese, 1986, 1995). A history of homework, I thought, might provide an unexpected avenue by which to explore this dynamic relationship and, at the same time, fill a major gap in historians' understanding of everyday school experiences. As it turned out, both of these possibilities were methodologically viable. Furthermore, the historical research demonstrated that homework was one of the most contested school practices in American educational history and that it had long provided parents with a regular outlet to criticize or praise teachers and to express strong views about what went on in school.

At first—and this stage, rather embarrassingly, lasted for nearly a full year of active research—I thought that the seminal period for studying homework was the 1930s. This was consistent with how previous scholars had tracked trends in attitudes toward homework during the previous half century, and I had no reason to challenge their periodization (What are the proper chronological boundaries for studying homework over time?) (Cooper, 1989a; Otto, 1941). I did, however, decide to spend several weeks using the *Reader's Guide to Periodical Literature* to confirm what I was confident I already knew. As expected, I found both plentiful discourse on homework during the 1930s and a relative absence of such discourse during the 1920s. Publications about homework abounded during the 1930s in both education journals and popular periodicals. Anti-homework sentiment was the dominant theme and a central component of "progressive" educational thought during this period. Numerous communities eliminated homework in the early grades and sharply limited its use in the junior high and high school years—a pattern that would not be substantially altered until after the launching

of Sputnik during the late 1950s. Because the documentary evidence introduced such compelling new voices into educational history, I was already preparing an article explaining why sustained dialogue about the place of homework in American schooling had first emerged during the 1930s. It simply did not occur to me to probe further back in time, even though the *Readers' Guide to Periodical Literature* and other bibliographic tools were readily available to do so. Only nagging doubts about the meaning of two obscure references I had seen to court cases involving homework in Texas and Mississippi in 1887 and 1909, respectively, delayed my completing this article (*Balding v. State,* 1887; *Hobbs v. Germany,* 1909).

Retrieving the two court cases spared me from one of the more serious mistakes a historian can make, that is, the misdating of a significant historical movement. Something was clearly happening with regard to homework during the late 19th and early 20th centuries about which I knew nothing. Therefore, I pushed my research effort backward in time and was eventually able to determine conclusively that it was during the late 19th century, not the 1930s, that Americans first began to seriously debate the pros and cons of homework. The relative lack of controversy about homework during the 1920s was the exception, not the rule. And although the views of progressive educators about homework during the 1930s remained fascinating, they could best be understood as refinements of the views of turn-of-the-century commentators such as the psychologist G. Stanley Hall, the physician–reformer Joseph Mayer Rice, and the magazine (*Ladies' Home Journal*) publisher Edward J. Bok.

Nonetheless, despite my initial misunderstanding of the chronology, my main interpretive point about the discourse on homework held up: During the first half of the 20th century, most educational scholars were sharply critical of teachers' reliance on heavy, repetitive, memory-driven homework assignments of the sort that had shaped the modal school experience since the early 19th century. As one of the educators put it, homework (especially before the fifth grade) was widely viewed as "a sin against childhood." This conclusion inevitably raised new questions about the meaning and impact of the "progressive" movement in American education during its heyday (Gill & Schlossman, 1996).

But what about parents' views of homework? Did parents mainly agree or disagree with the anti-homework sentiments of the educational experts? After all, it was the voices of parents—my own voice, in particular—that had provided the initial incentive for me to open this topic to historical analysis. My prior data collection from educational journals, popular periodicals, school board reports, and newspapers during the first half of the 20th century had left me uncertain whether parents mainly agreed or disagreed with the anti-homework position of the professional educators. Thus, after completing a follow-up article that extended analysis of educators' views on homework from the 1930s to the 1960s (Gill & Schlossman, 2000), I began to probe whether a "bottom-up" line of inquiry was possible to determine whether educators and parents mainly agreed or disagreed about homework.

Parents' views on homework did indeed prove to be a researchable topic. In the end, I concluded that during the first half of the 20th century, parents were far more supportive of homework than were educational scholars. At the early stages of the research, however, this conclusion was far from self-evident. The easiest data to obtain regarding parents' views was the parental testimony that opponents of homework had marshaled to support their negative position. But was this testimony representative of general parental sentiment? Eventually I concluded that it was not. After many months of research, I was able to locate more disinterested data—usually contained in locally administered polls or surveys of parents' views, in doctoral dissertations about educational practice and attitudes toward schooling, and in incidental comments by parents and school officials reported in annual school reports and in local newspapers—that revealed parents' voices unmediated by the views of homework opponents. Overall, these data showed that parents mainly disagreed with educators. In all regions of the country, parents supported substantial homework for their children, not only to improve academic performance but also to build character, train work habits, fill otherwise idle time, and provide a concrete starting point for facilitating parent–teacher communication. From a methodological standpoint, then, it was clearly vital to locate "bottom-up" historical data before one could reach a fair overall assessment of what parents thought about homework (Gill & Schlossman, 2003b).

But could this methodology be carried a step further to identify not only parents' but also students' views on homework during the first half of the 20th century? In other words, might it be possible—on this topic as in some of my research on juvenile delinquency—to introduce children as active historical agents with their own points of view? Alas, after several years of data collection, it became obvious that I could not produce a parallel study on children's views. The available empirical data were simply inadequate to provide a reliable answer. But what about children's homework *behaviors*? If their views were unascertainable, could their actual conduct be charted by obtaining data on how much homework they actually did? For some time, this prospect did seem alive because more than a dozen quantitative and qualitative studies were conducted during the first half of the 20th century on how much time children spent doing homework. On closer inspection, however, the studies were too local, too diverse in grade levels, too small in scale, and too inconsistent in research methods to yield reliable measures on students' homework at any one point in time, much less to chart change over time. Thus, this line of historical inquiry also had to be abandoned.

But what about the more recent past—the second half of the 20th century? At the suggestion of my Carnegie Mellon colleague, John Modell, I had already acquired some unique statistical data on homework during the 1940s, 1950s, and 1960s from the little-known Purdue Opinion Panel, a nationally representative sample of 9th- to 12th-grade students' views on a wide variety of topics related to schooling. The panel's creator, H. H. Remmers, periodically asked students about their attitudes and behaviors regarding homework and how much of it they did on a regular basis. If comparable data could be located for the period between the 1970s and 1990s, it might be possible to assess changes in students' homework behaviors over this lengthy time period and to compare behaviors with shifting currents of thought and policy regarding homework.

Fortunately, with a number of minor adjustments, it was indeed possible to link homework data from the Purdue Opinion Panel with several data sets covering more recent time periods to track homework trends among high school students for the entire half century.[7] Analysis of these data resulted in the publication in 2003 of "A Nation at Rest" (Gill & Schlossman, 2003a). Not only were high school students at the turn of the 21st century not doing more homework than they had done during the early 1980s when the modern academic "excellence" movement began, but their homework behaviors actually had not changed much (except for a brief post-Sputnik burst) since the end of World War II. In other words, the "voice" of students' behaviors—to the extent that statistical data could capture that voice—was clear: Doing a minimal amount of homework *was* the American tradition.

Not surprisingly, "A Nation at Rest" garnered considerable publicity in the educational and popular press because it confounded conventional wisdom about how much homework students were actually doing during the late 1990s (Gill & Schlossman, 2003a). From my perspective, however, the article's chief contribution lay more in the novel historical questions that preceded and motivated it, the use it made of history to illuminate and complicate current educational discourse, and the example it provided of why methodological invention is so important to discover new voices and integrate them into the tapestry of educational history (Gill & Schlossman, 2004). In these ways, despite its heavy reliance on quantification, the article was consistent with the pathway I had long followed to guide my research in the histories of education, childhood, and juvenile justice.

A CONTINUING JOURNEY

I left RAND during the late 1980s to teach in the Department of History at Carnegie Mellon, and in the main I have continued to elaborate the methodologically driven research agenda that I set in graduate school during the early 1970s. My one main deviation occurred in 1993 when

I returned to RAND as a full-time consultant to conduct a series of historical inquiries about blacks, women, and gays in the military. This research was part of a multidisciplinary study (prompted by President Clinton's directive to end discrimination in the military on the basis of sexual orientation) designed to provide the secretary of defense with information and analysis relevant to the development of policies toward openly homosexual military personnel. From the start, it was clear that there would be hardly any time to conduct original historical research. Instead, my goal would be to synthesize and interpret readily available knowledge (i.e., secondary sources and published collections of primary documents) in ways that intersected with the findings of other RAND analysts working on the same subject from different social science, legal, and medical perspectives. Assisted by an extraordinary team of Carnegie Mellon graduate students, I shuttled regularly between Pittsburgh and Santa Monica and worked long days to accommodate a tight political timetable. After several months, we produced several hundred pages of well-grounded, albeit mainly derivative, historical scholarship on each of our three topics.[8] Afterward, in collaboration with one of the graduate students, I expanded the research on African Americans into a book about the desegregation of the U.S. armed forces (Mershon & Schlossman, 1998).

Why did I agree to deviate so sharply from my own research agenda to participate in this unrelated RAND project? There were three main reasons. First, the opportunity to put history to direct policy use at the federal level amid swirling political and cultural controversies was simply too novel and challenging to turn down. Second was the undeniable attraction for a historian to work as an integral part of a research team—a collaborative role that historians are rarely asked to play in the modern world of social science research (except for the occasional historian, including myself, who is asked to participate in National Research Council studies). Third, although no time was available to identify new historical voices, I believed that the project held potential to enable history itself, as a discipline, to be heard as a distinct and equal voice in a large-scale, multidisciplinary, policy research project. As it turned out, this confidence was well placed; under the cosmopolitan intellectual leadership of Bernard Rostker, an economist, and Scott Harris, a political scientist, our voice as historians was privileged no more and no less than that of other disciplines in generating a coherent analytic perspective and specifying policy recommendations (National Defense Research Institute, 1993).

Although this venture into applied, synthetic historical research was as exciting as any I had ever tackled, the methodological challenge of discovering new voices in the history of education, childhood, and juvenile justice is still what motivates my career.

Periodically, for lack of alternative documents to evoke their voices, I have found it necessary to collect quantitative data to write about certain groups of children whose life experiences would otherwise remain lost to history. So, for example, I have analyzed statistics from 19th- and early-20th-century reform schools to demonstrate the regular incarceration of noncriminal children, from adult prisons to determine how often individuals ages 17 years or younger were incarcerated there (most were minor offenders), and from courts to analyze how race and nationality influenced judicial decision making about whether to incarcerate a delinquent child and in what type of institution to incarcerate the child. I am quick to admit that I find the collection and analysis of quantitative data intrinsically dull compared with the chockfull-of-life "top-down" and "bottom-up" documents that animate most of my historical research. Still, when such documents are unavailable, I find myself turning increasingly to quantitative analysis, especially for writing about arrested and incarcerated children whose very existence would remain forgotten if not for the collective statistical portraits that historians can draw of them from police, court, and correctional records (Schlossman, 1989, 1995; Schlossman & Cairns, 1993; Schlossman & Pisciotta, 1986; Schlossman et al., 1984; Schlossman & Spillane, 1995; Schlossman & Turner, 1990, 1993; Wolcott & Schlossman, 2004). Whatever the data sources, the prime challenge for me as a historian remains to use method imaginatively so as to generate new knowledge about otherwise anonymous children, parents, and educators in the past and to integrate that knowledge into how we design policies to educate and safeguard the well-being of children and youth today.

NOTES

1. As Cremin (1988) wrote, "I have defined education broadly, as the deliberate, systematic, and sustained effort to transmit, evoke, or acquire knowledge, values, attitudes, skills, and sensibilities, as well as any learning that results from that effort, direct or indirect, intended or unintended. The definition is intended to call attention to the wide range of situations and institutions in which education has gone forward over the years" (p. x).

2. On "educational configurations," Cremin (1977) observed "the tendency of educative institutions at particular times and places to relate to one another in configurations of education. . . . Each of the institutions within a given configuration interacts with the others and with the larger society that sustains it and that is in turn affected by it. Configurations of education also interact, as configurations, with the society of which they are part" (p. 142).

3. On "educational biography," Cremin (1976) wrote, "An educational biography is an account or portrayal of an individual life, focusing on the experience of education. . . . Individual Americans came to educational opportunities with their own purposes and their own agenda and moved through the institutions and configurations of education in their own ways" (p. 42). With regard to the 19th century in particular, Cremin (1980) noted "the striking range of human character that always issues, to greater or lesser extent, from any particular set of educational arrangements, whatever the time or the place in human history" (p. 451).

4. I have detailed this research process in the introduction to *Transforming Juvenile Justice: Reform Ideals and Institutional Realities* (Schlossman, 2005, pp. xiii–xxxi).

5. Ellen Lagemann, now dean of Harvard Graduate School of Education, served as Cremin's research assistant for his case study of New York City and for other topics as well. *American Education: The National Experience* (Cremin, 1980) was awarded the Pulitzer Prize in history.

6. Professional collaboration is one of the joys of scholarly research. Throughout my career, I have

been blessed with co-authors who have enriched my life immeasurably as a scholar. To avoid confusion and awkwardness, I have not mentioned any of the co-authors' names in the text, but each co-author is clearly identified in the references and citations. Let me extend special recognition to those colleagues with whom I have been fortunate to co-author multiple articles: Brian Gill (RAND), Robert Gleeson (Northern Illinois), Sherie Mershon (Carnegie Mellon), Michael Sedlak (Michigan State), Susan Turner (RAND), Harold Wechsler (Rochester), David Wolcott (Miami of Ohio), and Gail Zellman (RAND).

7. Data for analyzing trends during the 1970s to 1990s came from the National Assessment of Educational Progress, the National Longitudinal Survey, High School and Beyond, Monitoring the Future (University of Michigan), the Higher Education Research Institute (UCLA), and the Institute for Social Research (University of Michigan). In "A Nation at Rest" (Gill & Schlossman, 2003a), we explained in detail the adjustments we made to compare these data sets with one another and with the data from the Purdue Opinion Panel from the 1940s to 1960s.

8. It should also be noted that the RAND study argued for a very different policy solution from the one ultimately endorsed by President Clinton as, informally, "Don't ask, don't tell, don't pursue."

REFERENCES

Balding v. State, 4 579, Texas Court of Appeals (1887).

Bell, R. M., Klein, S. P., Bohannan, H. M., Disney, J. A., Graves, R. C., & Madison, R. (1984). *Treatment effects in the National Preventive Dentistry Demonstration Program* (No. R-3072-RWJ). Santa Monica, CA: RAND.

Butts, R. F., & Cremin, L. A. (1953). *A history of education in American culture*. New York: Holt.

Carlton, F. T. (1965). *Economic influences upon educational progress in the United States, 1820–1850*. New York: Columbia University, Teachers College Press.

Clifford, G. J. (1978). Home and school in 19th century America: Some personal-history reports from the United States. *History of Education Quarterly, 18,* 3–34.

Cohen, R. D., & Schlossman, S. L. (1977). The music man in Gary: Willis Brown and child-saving in the Progressive era. *Societas: A Review of Social History, 7,* 1–17.

Cooper, H. (1989a). *Homework*. New York: Longman.

Cooper, H. (1989b). Synthesis of research on homework. *Educational Leadership, 47,* 85–91.

Cooper, H. (1994). *The battle over homework: An administrator's guide to setting sound and effective policies*. Thousand Oaks, CA: Corwin.

Cremin, L. A. (1961). *The transformation of the school: Progressivism in American education*. New York: Vintage Books.

Cremin, L. A. (1970). *American education: The colonial experience, 1607–1783*. New York: Harper & Row.

Cremin, L. A. (1976). *Public education*. New York: Basic Books.

Cremin, L. A. (1977). *Traditions of American education*. New York: Basic Books.

Cremin, L. A. (1980). *American education: The national experience, 1783–1876*. New York: Harper & Row.

Cremin, L. A. (1988). *American education: The metropolitan experience, 1876–1980*. New York: Harper & Row.

Cremin, L. A. (1989). *Popular education and its discontents*. New York: Harper & Row.

Curti, M. E. (1935). *The social ideas of American educators*. New York: Scribner.

Epstein, J. L. (1983). *Effects on parents of teacher practices of parent involvement* (No. 346). Baltimore, MD: Johns Hopkins University, Center for Social Organization of Schools.

Epstein, J. L. (1988). *Homework practices, achievements, and behaviors of elementary school students* (No. 26). Baltimore, MD: Johns Hopkins University, Center for Research on Elementary and Middle Schools.

Epstein, J. L., & Pinkow, L. (1988). *A model for research on homework based on U.S. and international studies* (No. 27). Baltimore, MD: Johns Hopkins University, Center for Research on Elementary and Middle Schools.

Fishman, J. (1966). *Language loyalty in the United States*. The Hague, Netherlands: Mouton.

Gaddis, J. L. (2002). *The landscape of history: How historians map the past*. New York: Oxford University Press.

Gill, B., & Schlossman, S. (1995, June 24). Homework is a parent's eyes and ears. *Los Angeles Times,* p. B7.

Gill, B., & Schlossman, S. (1996). "A sin against childhood": Progressive education and the crusade to abolish homework, 1897–1941. *American Journal of Education, 105,* 27–66.

Gill, B., & Schlossman, S. (2000). The lost cause of homework reform. *American Journal of Education, 109,* 27–62.

Gill, B. P., & Schlossman, S. L. (2003a). A nation at rest: The American way of homework. *Educational Evaluation and Policy Analysis, 25,* 319–337.

Gill, B. P., & Schlossman, S. L. (2003b). Parents and the politics of homework: Some historical perspectives. *Teachers College Record, 105,* 846–871.

Gill, B. P., & Schlossman, S. L. (2004). Villain or savior? The American discourse on homework, 1850–2003. *Theory Into Practice, 43,* 174–181.

Gleeson, R. E., & Schlossman, S. (1992a, Winter). The many faces of the new look: The University of Virginia, Carnegie Tech, and the reform of management education in the postwar era (part 1). *Selections: The Magazine of the Graduate Management Admissions Council,* pp. 9–27.

Gleeson, R. E., & Schlossman, S. (1992b, Spring). The many faces of the new look: The University of Virginia, Carnegie Tech, and the reform of management education in the postwar era, part 2. *Selections: The Magazine of the Graduate Management Admissions Council,* pp. 1–24.

Gleeson, R. E., & Schlossman, S. (1995, Spring). George Leland Bach and the rebirth of graduate management education in the United States, 1945–1975. *Selections: The Magazine of the Graduate Management Admissions Council,* pp. 8–46.

Gleeson, R. E., Schlossman, S., & Allen, D. G. (1993, Spring). Uncertain ventures: The origins of graduate management education at Harvard and Stanford universities, 1908–1939. *Selections: The Magazine of the Graduate Management Admissions Council, 9,* 9–36.

Gleeson, R. E., Schlossman, S., & Allen, D. G. (1994). *The beginnings of graduate management education in the United States.* Los Angeles: Graduate Management Admissions Council.

Hobbs v. Germany, 49 515, Mississippi (1909).

Hofstadter, R. (1963). *Anti-intellectualism in American life.* New York: Knopf.

Kaestle, C. F. (1978). Social change, discipline, and the common school in early nineteenth-century America. *Journal of Interdisciplinary History, 9,* 1–17.

Kaestle, C. F. (1983). *Pillars of the republic: Common schools and American society, 1780–1860.* New York: Hill & Wang.

Katz, M. B. (2001). *The irony of early school reform: Educational innovation in mid-nineteenth century Massachusetts.* New York: Columbia University, Teachers College Press. (Original work published in 1968, reissued with a new introduction)

Kloss, H. (1977). *The American bilingual tradition.* Rowley, MA: Newburgh House.

Larcom, L. (1961). *A New England girlhood: Outlined from memory.* New York: Corinth Books.

Liss, J., & Schlossman, S. (1984). The contours of crime prevention in August Vollmer's Berkeley. In A. Scull & S. Spitzer (Eds.), *Research in law, deviance, and social control* (Vol. 6, pp. 79–107). Greenwich, CT: JAI.

Lowery, I. E. (1911). *Life on the old plantation in ante-bellum days.* Columbia, SC: State Company.

Magee, J. H. (1873). *The night of affliction and morning of recovery: An autobiography.* Cincinnati, OH: Author.

McLaughlin, M. W. (1989). *The RAND change agent studies ten years later: Micro perspectives and micro realities.* Stanford, CA: Stanford University, School of Education, Center for Research on the Context of Secondary Teaching.

Mershon, S., & Schlossman, S. (1998). *Foxholes and color lines: Desegregating the U.S. armed forces.* Baltimore, MD: Johns Hopkins University Press.

National Defense Research Institute. (1993). *Sexual orientation and U.S. military personnel policy: Options and assessment* (No. MR-323-OSD). Santa Monica, CA: RAND.

Odem, M. E., & Schlossman, S. (1991). Guardians of virtue: The juvenile court and female delinquency in early 20th century Los Angeles. *Crime & Delinquency, 37,* 186–203.

Otto, H. J. (1941). Elementary education. In W. S. Monroe (Ed.), *Encyclopedia of educational research* (pp. 380–381). New York: Macmillan.

Palmer, G. T. (1941). *A conscientious turncoat: The story of John M. Palmer, 1817–1900.* New Haven, CT: Yale University Press.

Palmer, J. M. (1901). *Personal recollections of John M. Palmer: The story of an earnest life.* Cincinnati, OH: Robert Clarke.

Platt, A. M. (1969). *The child savers: The invention of delinquency*. Chicago: University of Chicago Press.

Reese, W. J. (1986). *Power and the promise of school reform: Grassroots movements during the Progressive era*. Boston: Routledge.

Reese, W. J. (1995). *The origins of the American high school*. New Haven, CT: Yale University Press.

Schlossman, S. (1973). G. Stanley Hall and the boys' club: Conservative applications of recapitulation theory. *Journal of the History of the Behavioral Sciences, 9,* 140–147.

Schlossman, S. (1974). The "culture of poverty" in ante-bellum social thought. *Science and Society, 38,* 150–166.

Schlossman, S. (1976). Before home start: Notes toward a history of parent education in America, 1897–1929. *Harvard Educational Review, 46,* 436–467.

Schlossman, S. (1977). *Love and the American delinquent: The theory and practice of "progressive" juvenile justice, 1825–1920*. Chicago: University of Chicago Press.

Schlossman, S. (1978a). End of innocence: Science and the transformation of progressive juvenile justice, 1899–1917. *History of Education, 7,* 207–218.

Schlossman, S. (1978b). The parent education game: The politics of child psychology in the 1970s. *Teachers College Record, 79,* 788–808.

Schlossman, S. (1981). Philanthropy and the gospel of child development. *History of Education Quarterly, 21,* 275–299.

Schlossman, S. (1983a). The formative era in American parent education: Overview and interpretation. In R. Haskins (Ed.), *Parent education and public policy* (pp. 7–39). Norwood, NJ: Ablex.

Schlossman, S. (1983b). Juvenile justice: History and philosophy. In S. H. Kadish (Ed.), *Encyclopedia of crime and justice* (Vol. 3, pp. 961–969). New York: Free Press.

Schlossman, S. (1983c, Spring). Science and the commercialization of parenthood: Notes toward a history of *Parents' Magazine*. *Newsletter* (American Psychological Association, Division on Developmental Psychology), pp. 14–17.

Schlossman, S. (1983d). Self-evident remedy? George I. Sanchez, segregation, and enduring dilemmas in bilingual education. *Teachers College Record, 84,* 871–907.

Schlossman, S. (1983e). *Studies in the history of early 20th century delinquency prevention programs* (No. N-1945-NIE). Santa Monica, CA: RAND.

Schlossman, S. (1986a). Family as educator, parent education, and the perennial family crisis. In L. Lezotte, R. Boger, & R. Griffore (Eds.), *Child rearing in the home and school* (pp. 31–45). New York: Plenum.

Schlossman, S. (1986b). Perils of popularization: The founding of *Parents' Magazine*. In A. B. Smuts & J. W. Hagen (Eds.), *History of research in child development* (Vol. Serial 211, Vol. 50, Nos. 4–5, pp. 65–77). Chicago: Monographs of the Society for Research in Child Development.

Schlossman, S. (1989). *The California experience in American juvenile justice: Some historical perspectives*. Sacramento: California State Department of Justice, Bureau of Criminal Statistics.

Schlossman, S. (1995). Delinquent children: The juvenile reform school. In N. Morris & D. J. Rothman (Eds.), *Oxford history of the prison: The practice of punishment in Western society* (pp. 363–390). Oxford, UK: Oxford University Press.

Schlossman, S. (2004). Dentistry. In P. S. Fass (Ed.), *Encyclopedia of children and childhood in history and society* (Vol. 1, pp. 258–260). New York: Macmillan.

Schlossman, S. (2005). *Transforming juvenile justice: Reform ideals and institutional realities, 1825–1920*. DeKalb: Northern Illinois University Press.

Schlossman, S., Brown, J., & Sedlak, M. (1986). *The public school in American dentistry* (No. R-3343-RWJ/RC). Santa Monica, CA: RAND.

Schlossman, S., & Cairns, R. B. (1993). Problem girls: Observations on past and present. In G. H. Elder, J. Modell, & R. D. Parke (Eds.), *Children in time and place: Developmental and historical insights* (pp. 110–130). New York: Cambridge University Press.

Schlossman, S., & Pisciotta, A. (1986). Identifying and treating serious juvenile offenders: The view from California and New York in the 1920s. In P. Greenwood (Ed.), *Intervention strategies for chronic juvenile offenders: Some new perspectives* (pp. 7–36). New York: Greenwood.

Schlossman, S., & Sedlak, M. (1983). The Chicago Area Project revisited. *Crime & Delinquency, 29,* 398–462.

Schlossman, S., & Sedlak, M. (1985, Winter). The age of autonomy in American management education. *Selections: The Magazine of the Graduate Management Admissions Council, 1,* 16–26.

Schlossman, S., & Sedlak, M. (1988). *The age of reform in American management education.* Los Angeles: Graduate Management Admissions Council.

Schlossman, S., Sedlak, M., & Wechsler, H. (1987a, Winter). Executive education: A meeting of the minds. *Management Magazine,* pp. 10–14.

Schlossman, S., Sedlak, M., & Wechsler, H. (1987b, Winter). The "new look": The Ford Foundation and the revolution in business education. *Selections: The Magazine of the Graduate Management Admissions Council,* pp. 8–28.

Schlossman, S., Sedlak, M., & Wechsler, H. (1988). *The "new look": The Ford Foundation and the revolution in business education.* Los Angeles: Graduate Management Admissions Council.

Schlossman, S., Sedlak, M., & Wechsler, H. (1989a, Winter). Conflict, consensus, and the modernization of business education at the University of Washington, 1945–1980 (part 1). *Selections: The Magazine of the Graduate Management Admissions Council,* pp. 1–11.

Schlossman, S., Sedlak, M., & Wechsler, H. (1989b, Spring). Conflict, consensus, and the modernization of business education at the University of Washington, 1945–1980 (part 2). *Selections: The Magazine of the Graduate Management Admissions Council,* pp. 1–10.

Schlossman, S., Shavelson, R., & Zellman, G. (1984). *Delinquency prevention in South Chicago: A fifty-year assessment of the Chicago Area Project* (No. R-3142-NIE). Santa Monica, CA: RAND.

Schlossman, S., & Spillane, J. (1995). *Bright hopes, dim realities: Vocational innovation in American correctional education* (No. N-3454-NCRVE/ UCB). Santa Monica, CA: RAND.

Schlossman, S., & Turner, S. (1990). *Race and delinquency in Los Angeles Juvenile Court, 1950.* Sacramento: California State Department of Justice, Bureau of Criminal Statistics.

Schlossman, S., & Turner, S. (1993). Status offenders, criminal offenders, and children "at risk" in early twentieth-century juvenile court. In R. Wollons (Ed.), *Children at risk in America: History, concepts, and public policy* (pp. 32–58). Albany: State University of New York Press.

Schlossman, S., & Wallach, S. (1978). The crime of precocious sexuality: Female juvenile delinquency in the Progressive era. *Harvard Educational Review, 48,* 65–94.

Sedlak, M., & Schlossman, S. (1985). The public school and social services: Reassessing the progressive legacy. *Educational Theory, 35,* 371–383.

Sedlak, M., & Schlossman, S. (1991, Winter). The case method and business education at Northwestern University, 1906–1971. *Selections: The Magazine of the Graduate Management Admissions Council,* pp. 14–37.

Sedlak, M. W., & Williamson, H. F. (1983). *The evolution of management education: A history of the Northwestern University J. L. Kellogg Graduate School of Management, 1908–1983.* Urbana: University of Illinois Press.

Stroyer, J. (1898). *My life in the South* (4th ed.). Salem, MA: Newcomb & Gauss.

Wolcott, D., & Schlossman, S. (2004). Punishing serious juvenile offenders: Crime, racial disparity, and the incarceration of adolescents in adult prison in late nineteenth- and early-twentieth century Pennsylvania. In J. McCord (Ed.), *Beyond empiricism* (pp. 39–68). New Brunswick, NJ: Transaction Publishers.

Wolcott, D., & Schlossman, S. (in press). In the voices of delinquents: Social science, the Chicago Area Project, and a boys' culture of casual crime and violence. In E. Cahan, B. Beatty, & J. Grant (Eds.), *Science in service of children: Perspectives on education, parenting, and child welfare.* New York: Columbia University, Teachers College Press.

Zellman, G., & Schlossman, S. L. (1986). The Berkeley youth wars. *The Public Interest, 84,* 29–41.

12

COUNSELING PSYCHOLOGY

MARY LEE NELSON

University of Wisconsin–Madison

CINDY L. JUNTUNEN

University of North Dakota

Although the field of counseling psychology is relatively new, counseling practitioners, educators, and researchers pursue a vast array of professional topics. The goal of this chapter is not to present a review of the many areas of research in which counseling psychologists have been engaged but rather to identify major lines of inquiry—and subsidiary lines and approaches to that inquiry—that, in our view, should guide research in counseling psychology during the coming years. We have identified three major lines of inquiry—vocational testing and guidance, qualities of optimal counseling and therapy relationships, and training and supervision of counselors and therapists—as the most promising for counseling psychologists to pursue during the years ahead. In this chapter, we provide the reader with an overview of the extant literature in these three areas and identify specific lines of inquiry within each of them as well as approaches to inquiry—along with some exemplary research studies—that, we think, provide a compelling foundation for future inquiry in counseling psychology. We start with an introduction to the history of and research in counseling psychology and then go on to explore each of the three meaningful lines of inquiry.

Before turning to an overview of the literature, we wish to emphasize that we take the perspective that counseling psychology as a field has been at the forefront of psychological initiatives to address the challenge of diversity and the effects of multiple perspectives on counseling-related phenomena. To wit, early school guidance and military training efforts included attention to racial and cultural backgrounds of students, particularly with regard to the developmental needs of blacks and whites, who needed similar social and professional skill sets in segregated settings (Davenport, 1946; Phillips, 1960). As interest in multiculturalism in counseling psychology has gained tremendous momentum during the past decade, researchers of counseling phenomena are often expected to recognize the implications of cultural and other types of differences for their methods, findings, and conclusions (Ponterotto, Casas, Suzuki, & Alexander, 2001). On the grounds that this development portends well for our future inquiry, in this chapter we address the dimension of diversity not as a separate area of inquiry but rather as an important aspect of future research across these three domains of inquiry.

AN OVERVIEW OF RESEARCH IN COUNSELING PSYCHOLOGY

Research in counseling has its roots in several traditions. Early in the 20th century, most psychotherapy was delivered by psychiatrists, psychologists, and social workers trained in the psychoanalytic tradition. At that time, the U.S. military began to employ psychologists to provide vocational testing and nonpsychoanalytic personal adjustment counseling to military personnel (Whitely, 1984). To aid the placement of recruits into appropriate work roles, the military hired psychologically trained researchers to develop and test career and personality screening batteries (Dawis, 1992). In addition, the service of psychologists who could develop and administer useful personality and vocational tests was sought after both World Wars I and II when American soldiers returned from abroad in large numbers seeking employment.

By mid-century, colleges and universities were also beginning to make use of vocational and personality testing to guide students toward appropriate majors and programs, and psychologists were hired in university counseling centers to provide these services (Tyler, 1992). In short, many counseling psychologists concerned themselves with the development of norm-based tests—the goal of which was to identify *individual differences* from group norms for the purposes of classification and placement (Dawis, 1992). In this way, one of the first and most popular uses of counseling psychology—vocational testing and guidance—came into being.

During the post-World War II era, many veterans also required assistance with personal and relational difficulties attendant on adjustment to civilian life (Whitely, 1984). Clinical and counseling psychologists were employed to assist veterans and their families with mental health and adjustment issues. Because psychoanalytic practice was viewed as impractical and inaccessible to the general population, other approaches to counseling and psychotherapy were in high demand. Professional attention shifted to the work of non-analytic psychologists such as Carl Rogers and his colleagues at the University of Chicago.

Rogers (1957) proposed a theory of human development and helping that was in direct contrast to the determinism of both psychoanalytic and behavioral thought. His proposal and testing of hypotheses about the necessary and sufficient conditions for therapeutic change represented a watershed in the development of the identity of counseling psychology. Rogers's work placed the therapeutic relationship at the fulcrum of counseling and psychotherapy effectiveness, and since then, investigations about the optimal conditions and behaviors for positive therapeutic outcomes have been another major focus of counseling psychology research.

Closely linked to the interest in promoting optimal conditions for counseling relationships was a concern about providing training for counselors and therapists in the skills necessary to offer their clients therapeutic relationships. Early on, Berenson, Carkhuff, and Myrus (1966) found that deliberate training in skills related to facilitative conditions was effective. Since that time, counseling researchers have investigated the best practices in counselor training and supervision, and the field has developed technologies for both.

From our perspective, then, three critical themes have informed counseling psychology research from its inception: (1) the applicability of vocational testing and guidance to the promotion of optimal career development for youth and adults, (2) the identification of relational factors that promote success in the practice of counseling and psychotherapy, and (3) the importance of strong training and supervision of counselors and therapists.

CAREER AND VOCATIONAL RESEARCH

The earliest roots of counseling psychology research and practice can be traced to the early 1900s, when the vocational guidance movement emerged from a greater social emphasis on vocational education and school reform. In 1908, Frank Parsons established the Vocation Bureau of Boston, and his book *Choosing a Vocation* was published the following year (Parsons, 1909). This work focused on three fundamental ideas: self-exploration of personal interests, skills, and values relevant to work; knowledge of the world of work; and understanding how the two correspond. Although numerous theories have since evolved to elaborate on the process of choosing and obtaining a career, these basic ideas remain highly relevant to the work and research of counseling psychology.

A rich and active century's worth of research has evolved since Parsons first identified a goal for the new profession of vocational guidance and counseling. Overall, the findings of that research have demonstrated that career counseling is generally effective (Brown & Ryan Krane, 2000; Oliver & Spokane, 1988), but the empirical literature remains very dynamic as researchers strive to understand how and why career counseling works. In our view, four lines of inquiry are critical to understanding the status of career research: vocational interests, self-efficacy beliefs, contextual factors, and career decision making and adaptability. In what follows, we discuss these in detail after a brief overview of key career theories.

Overview of Three
Primary Career Theories

Many theories have been advanced to explain the ways in which individuals go about choosing a career. Although there is significant diversity among theories, most can be classified as either trait–factor, developmental, or social learning/social cognitive approaches (Hackett, Lent, & Greenhaus, 1991). Trait–factor theories rely on the premise that the individual has traits that are more or less well suited to the factors required for success in a given kind of work. The work of Holland (1959), perhaps the most widely studied work in vocational psychology, refers to the person environment fit to describe the matching of trait and factor. Developmental theories, on the other hand, focus on the processes and decisions made over the life span that result in a career choice and a subsequent career trajectory. Super's (1990) theory emphasizes the importance of childhood experiences in career development and the activity of choosing a career, as well as the need to attend to midlife and retirement issues, and has received the most empirical attention of the developmental theories. Finally, social learning and social cognitive theories emphasize the interaction of the environment and the individual, noting that career-related behaviors are the result of this

interaction. Self-efficacy beliefs (Bandura, 1986), which are the beliefs one has about the ability to complete a given task, are a cornerstone of this perspective on making career choices and have been the focus of a significant amount of research during the past two decades.

These theoretical frameworks are closely linked to the research in vocational assessments and career counseling. In fact, one of the major strengths of vocational research is the fact that it is firmly theory driven (Fouad, 2001) and, as such, consistently advances the knowledge base while helping to refine both theory and practice. Theory has supported the intensive study of several factors predictive of career choice, attainment, and satisfaction. The four factors that we consider to be most relevant for current and future research are vocational interests, self-efficacy beliefs, contextual factors, and career decision making and adaptability.

Vocational Interests. The most common rubric for identifying vocational interests emerged from Holland's theory of vocational choice. Holland (1959) proposed that individual personality represents one basic personality type or a combination of several of six basic personality types, which are generally treated as a typology of interests: Realistic (working with machines, animals, physical labor), Investigative (seeking answers, working with ideas, scientific), Artistic (creative, expressive, emphasizing artistic or musical skills), Social (oriented toward helping others, working with people), Enterprising (oriented toward people with an emphasis on leading and persuading), and Conventional (working with numbers, detail oriented, practical), also collectively known as RIASEC. Individuals are assumed to have a 2- or 3-point code (e.g., SAI, ECR) that represents their major interest structure. Work environments can also be coded to reflect the types of work activities that typify the position. Thus, a person with a code of SAI is assumed to be most congruent with a work environment that is also coded SAI.

Empirical examination of the RIASEC model has provided significant support for the generality of the structure of interests across cultural groups (Day & Rounds, 1998; Day, Rounds, & Swaney, 1998). Essentially, this means that although there may be differences in terms of how members from different cultural groups score on the six interest types, the underlying hexagonal (or at least circular) structure is maintained across groups. This generality, however, is not as clear for sex differences, where several studies have concluded that there are differences, yet meta-analyses have suggested that the differences are minimal (Swanson & Gore, 2000). Furthermore, there is some indication that socioeconomic status may interact with sex and ethnicity to create additional differences in the interest structure (Heppner & Scott, 2004).

Assessment plays a critical role in career counseling, and several assessment methods have been developed to measure career interests. Among the most popular interest inventories are the Self-Directed Search (Holland, 1994) and the Strong Interest Inventory (Harmon, Hansen, Borgen, & Hammer, 1994). Each is widely used in career counseling, and research and has demonstrated their excellent psychometric properties. A number of interest inventories are also available online, resulting in improved access to career counseling clients and greater ease of research administration. Notable among these is the Kuder Career Search (Zytowski, 2001), which is the latest in a long history of interest inventories initiated by Kuder in 1939.

Vocational interests have been the subject of intensive research for the past 50 years. Although much is now understood about interests and the role they play in career development, the ongoing research in this area supports the assertion that this remains a rich area of investigation that will likely continue for the foreseeable future. Importantly, research must continue to address the salience of career interests in the work lives of individuals who might not see themselves as having the opportunity to work in whatever careers they choose (Blustein, 2001; Juntunen et al., 2001). As counseling psychologists continue to improve theory and research to account for the scope of experience of a diverse population, the salience of interests in the career decision-making process will continue to be debated.

Self-Efficacy Beliefs. Career self-efficacy beliefs became a focus of empirical attention during the early 1980s when Hackett and Betz (1981) first applied Bandura's (1986) concept of self-efficacy to explain the underrepresentation of women in "nontraditional" careers, particularly those that relied heavily on math and science. A steady stream of studies followed that identified the importance of self-efficacy beliefs for academic achievement, choice of major, career interests, career decision making, and performance. This research ultimately led to the development of the social cognitive career theory (SCCT) (Lent, Brown, & Hackett, 1994).

An important strength of SCCT and the extant research on self-efficacy beliefs is the recognition of the impact of learning experiences and contextual factors on both the development and the sequelae of self-efficacy expectations. The model addresses the impact of both personal factors (e.g., gender, predispositions, race/ethnicity) and background contextual factors (e.g., family, socioeconomic) and their relationship with learning experiences, which in turn lead to self-efficacy and outcome expectations. Environmental supports and barriers are also addressed. The model assumes a dynamic process between self-efficacy beliefs and outcome expectations, which are ultimately related to the development of vocational interests, goals, and actions. The complexity of the model, and its ability to account for numerous variables likely to influence career development, provides many opportunities for intervention from a career counseling perspective and provides a rich array of research questions worthy of continued examination.

Self-efficacy remains the most widely studied component of social cognitive career theory (Lent, 2005). Empirical evidence demonstrates that self-efficacy beliefs are predictive of several key vocational constructs, including interests, choice, indecision, and exploratory behavior (Lent, 2005). Furthermore, self-efficacy theory has helped to explain differential vocational attainment for various groups, including women (Betz & Hackett, 1981); racial/ethnic minority groups (Fouad & Smith, 1996); gay, lesbian, bisexual, and transgender persons (Morrow, Gore, & Campbell, 1996); work-bound youth (Lent, Hackett, & Brown, 1999); and battered women (Chronister & McWhirter, 2003).

As demonstrated by the vast array of studies that have applied self-efficacy and social cognitive frameworks, this is an area of research that will continue to be fruitful well into the future. The applicability of SCCT to various groups and career circumstances is being examined continually. The SCCT model supports a framework for asking complex and meaningful research questions about the development of self-efficacy and subsequent career-relevant behaviors. Furthermore, the model supports sophisticated analysis procedures such as structural equation modeling and path analysis. At the current time, SCCT is perhaps the most effective career theory for identifying and examining the complex relationships among personal characteristics, learning experiences, and contextual factors.

Contextual Factors. Contextual factors have received increasing attention over the past decade, with attention being paid to personal, family, and social factors so as to understand the individual's life in context. Recently, emphasis has been shifting away from thinking of career development as relevant only to an individual pursuing a career and toward recognizing that the individual is "embedded within a family system" (Blustein, 2004, p. 603). A recent issue of *The Counseling Psychologist,* dedicated to the influence of family-of-origin factors on career development (Whiston & Keller, 2004), identified several critical areas of research worthy of further development.

Another critical contextual issue is that of the workforce and access to work opportunities. Changes in technology and globalization are having a significant effect on work and the research of work activities. A single change in the world economy can have dramatically different effects on the labor force around the globe, with some economies gaining and others being devastated (DeBell, 2004; Whiteley, 1999). Furthermore, the world labor market is increasingly being controlled by a smaller number of employers. For example, DeBell (2004) noted that transnational corporations control a vast majority of technology patents and are experiencing huge increases in assets while simultaneously laying off employees or not replacing employee positions. Such practices create instability in world employment patterns (DeBell, 2004). Increasingly, psychologists are being

urged to integrate this type of macrosystem context into their understanding of work, their career counseling work with clients, and their conceptualization of research.

Career Decision Making and Adaptability. The actual selection of a career or career training is a second enduring focus in the counseling psychology literature and includes the study of the process of making decisions as well as the potential for indecisiveness. Career indecisiveness is distinguished from indecision. Indecision is a normal developmental process that most people experience as they encounter a transition or decision point. In contrast, indecisiveness is "a personal trait which generalizes across situations demanding decisions" (Osipow, 1999, p. 148). Long a concern of vocational psychology, it becomes even more important for researchers to examine career decision making now—at a time when the majority of people will encounter multiple career decision points over their lifetimes (Gaffner & Hazler, 2002).

Early theorists suggested that a certain level of career maturity (Super, 1990) or vocational identity (Holland, 1959) was necessary to make a sound career choice effectively. These constructs brought with them an assumption that individuals approached career decision making with a level of planning that would allow them to achieve an identified goal. However, with an ever-changing labor market and the challenges of predicting which current jobs will be available and which new jobs will be developed in the near future, researchers are attending more and more to the need for career adaptability (Savickas, 2005), and the ability to plan to adapt, than to career choice. With this shift comes a focus on career transitions and changes, bolstered by the reality that many people will make changes in their careers multiple times throughout their working lives.

This emphasis on career adaptability has also brought renewed attention to critical developmental tasks, including the school-to-work transition of adolescents (Blustein, Juntunen, & Worthington, 2000; Savickas, 2005; Worthington & Juntunen, 1997). The burst of theoretical and research activity triggered by the School-to-Work Opportunities Act of 1994 (U.S. Congress, 1994) reinforced the social justice mission of counseling psychology and also reaffirmed the potential for greater collaboration between counseling psychology and schools (Romano & Kachgal, 2004). More important, this research has highlighted the need to prepare youth and adults to develop the skills necessary to both cope with and flourish in a continually changing vocational environment. Future research efforts on school-to-work transitioning will take into account developmental factors as they interact with cultural and other contextual factors.

Summary

The vocational and career counseling research literature has a 100-year history of identifying, measuring, and applying constructs critical to the development of successful work experiences. This work is applicable to adults and youth alike, and the interventions that have emerged from it are widely practiced in schools, colleges, and job and retirement programs. Importantly, the ongoing research in the field is poised to continue fostering career development in a future that is likely to be accompanied by significant labor force upheaval and change. We now go on to discuss the second critical area in counseling psychology research, namely, the therapeutic relationship.

WHETHER IT'S CAREER OR PERSONAL COUNSELING, IT'S THE RELATIONSHIP THAT MATTERS: THE LEGACY OF CARL ROGERS

Rogers hypothesized that the relationship between client and counselor is at the core of helping and that this hypothesis could be verified experimentally. In their landmark text, *Psychotherapy and Personality Change,* Rogers and Dymond (1954) presented 13 studies that addressed the efficacy of client-centered therapy and its tenets. Rogers and Dymond showcased innovations such as using electronic recordings of psychotherapy discourse to study the impact of therapeutic conditions on client outcomes. They used case studies to demonstrate process aspects of both successful and unsuccessful therapy, advancing the notion that the process of

psychotherapy itself is the critical ingredient in psychotherapy outcome. They also showcased the use of successful and unsuccessful cases to examine process differences, a strategy that has been used frequently in counseling psychology research and, we believe, will continue to show promise in efforts to reveal the characteristics of successful and unsuccessful elements of counselor and therapist in-session conduct. We now discuss the lines of inquiry within this field: research on facilitative conditions, the counseling process, resistance and reactance in the counseling relationship, and common factors that influence counseling and psychotherapy outcome.

Research on Facilitative Conditions

Central to Rogers's theory is the notion that facilitative conditions offered by therapists—unconditional positive regard, empathy, and congruence—are necessary for therapeutic change. During the 1960s, numerous researchers made efforts to operationalize these and related conditions to validate their positive impact on client self-exploration and therapeutic outcomes (Truax, 1966; Truax & Carkhuff, 1965). A resulting prescriptive technology of appropriate counseling behaviors was developed (Carkhuff & Pierce, 1975; Truax & Carkhuff, 1967). The necessary core conditions that emerged from these lines of research were empathy, respect (positive regard), genuineness (congruence), and concreteness (specificity).

Since the 1960s, counseling psychology researchers have used numerous methods and strategies to assess the quality of the counseling relationship and validate the importance of its impact on therapeutic outcomes. One such effort has involved conceptualization, operationalization, and study of the psychotherapeutic working alliance.

The Working (therapeutic) Alliance. An early detractor from Rogers's client-centered therapy approach was Edward Bordin, who believed that Rogers's rigid adherence to a nondirective counseling stance would create unnecessary resistance in clients who needed more direction in counseling. Disillusioned with strict black-and-white definitions of client-centered therapy,

Bordin sought alternative ways in which to think about the therapeutic relationship and began to investigate the psychoanalytic concept of the therapeutic working alliance.

The terms "working alliance" and "therapeutic alliance" originated in psychoanalytic discussions about the therapeutic interaction and are often used interchangeably to refer to a collaborative relationship between client and therapist that is based on an agreement to identify and treat the client's difficulties. Psychoanalytic writers distinguished the collaborative working alliance from the "transference neurosis," which referred not to the actual working relationship but rather to a fantasized relationship based on the client's unconscious projections. Beginning in the 1970s, psychoanalytically oriented researchers began trying to define the alliance operationally so that it could be measured (Luborsky, 1976; Suh, O'Malley, & Strupp, 1986).

Bordin (1979) concluded that the concept of working alliance could apply to any therapeutic or helping relationship regardless of its theoretical influence. He proposed that a positive working alliance involved three components: the *bond,* or the experienced connection between therapist and client; the *task,* or the degree to which client and therapist agree on the tasks to be undertaken in session; and the *goal,* or the degree to which client and therapist agree on the desired outcome of their work.

Using Bordin's (1979) definition, Horvath and Greenberg (1989) developed the Working Alliance Inventory (WAI), which measures the strength of the working alliance on each of Bordin's three components. The scale also yields a total alliance score. Since the development of the WAI, more than 150 studies investigating the relationship of the working alliance to counseling and therapy processes and outcomes have been conducted. Regarding the influence of working alliance on therapy outcome, a meta-analysis by Horvath and Symonds (1991) reported an effect size of .26. Individual studies have produced larger or smaller effect sizes, depending on the populations and treatments studied, sample sizes, and measures used (Horvath & Bedi, 2002).

Research on the working alliance has demonstrated the power of the therapeutic relationship to affect client change and well-being. This body of research accords well with Rogers's original assertion that the quality of the relationship is essential to the effectiveness of counseling and psychotherapy. Both of these bodies of work have demonstrated the value of the counseling *process* in determining the ultimate *outcome* of counseling. There is still much to be learned, however, about what types of processes actually strengthen the working alliance and promote stronger outcomes. Several avenues of work have attempted to highlight the nature of productive interpersonal processes in counseling and therapy.

A Window on Counseling Process: Examining the Interaction

Numerous process researchers have made attempts to explore therapy conversations to determine how counselor verbal behaviors affect client reactions as well as outcomes in terms of client change and satisfaction. Many of those studies have investigated outcomes related to therapist verbal response modes such as questions, information giving, advisement, reflection, interpretation, and self-disclosure (Elliott et al., 1987).

Hill and colleagues (1988) later demonstrated the relation of therapist response modes in relation to therapist intentions such as assessment, setting limits, supporting the client, educating the client, promoting exploration, restructuring the client's worldview, and promoting change. In that study, the authors also demonstrated the use of videotape-assisted recall with clients to examine retrospective reactions to therapist intentions and interventions. Hill (1990) observed that of all response modes, interpretation seems to be the one most frequently connected with desirable client responses.

One difficulty with the study of therapist response modes was that they used assisted recall and immediate postsession outcome measures. They did not directly examine the client's immediate in-session reactions to counselor interventions—or *reciprocity.* Studies of the interactional reciprocity between counselors and therapists have focused primarily on complementarity theory.

Studies of Complementarity in Counseling. Complementarity is a theoretical construct that refers to the degree of "fit" or how well two people's behaviors mutually satisfy their individual expectations for a relationship. A complementary interaction, therefore, implies that every behavior carries information regarding how a recipient should respond, and so each behavior elicits or constrains subsequent behaviors in a manner that affirms the role of the participants and their expectations for the relationship (Carson, 1969; Kiesler, 1979; Tracey, 1993). The complementarity model has been used to study the counseling process in several ways.

Complementarity in interpersonal relationships has been investigated using a bidimensional circumplex model that conceptualizes behaviors as occurring within the dimensions of status (dominance vs. submission) and affiliation (friendly vs. hostile) (Carson, 1969; Kiesler, 1979). Carson (1969) demonstrated the orthogonality, or independence, of these two dimensions.

According to complementarity theory, submissive behavior pulls for dominant behavior and hostile behavior pulls for a hostile complement. Thus, an interaction is complementary on the status dimension if paired with its opposite. This one-dimensional version of complementarity would be theorized to result in no apparent struggle over the control or use of power in the relationship and, as a result, has been shown to be relatively stable (Carson, 1969; Kiesler, 1979). In contrast, if the exchange were identified as anti-complementary (i.e., both individuals attempting to be dominant), this interaction would represent a struggle for control on the basis of power and would be indicative of an unstable relationship.

A one-dimensional definition of complementarity based on affiliation works just the opposite of that found to result on the status dimension. Instead of an antecedent pairing with its opposite as on the status dimension (i.e., dominant with submissive), on the affiliation dimension an antecedent exerts pull for a *matching* or similar subsequent response. The complementary pairing for a friendly behavior in a relational exchange would be another friendly response, and the complementary pairing for a hostile response would be another hostile response. Thus, a high-dominant, high-friendly message would pull for a low-dominant, low-friendly response, and a high-dominant, high-hostile message would pull for a low-dominant, low-hostile response

More recently still, the circumplex model has been used to describe the influences of both counselor and client as they are exchanged within sessions and over the course of counseling (Tracey, Sherry, & Albright, 1999). Based in part on prior research by Dietzel and Abeles (1975), Tracey (1993) proposed that successful counseling relationships would be characterized by high complementary or stable interactions during the early phase of counseling, by noncomplementary or unstable interactions during the middle phase of counseling, and by a return to complementary interactions near the end of counseling. He posited that during the middle phase of successful counseling, the counselor breaks up the client's typical manner of interacting, assuming noncomplementary positions and requiring the client to adopt a new interactional style. Tracey and colleagues (1999) validated Tracey's (1993) theory in a study of successful time-limited cognitive behavioral therapy.

On the surface, Tracey's (1993) theory makes sense. The counselor's job is, in part, to help the client behave differently. However, what if the client's typical interaction pattern is to be docile and friendly or self-effacing and slightly distrustful, that is, submissive and not very powerful? What if the client exhibits very little hostility in the relationship? Does this mean that to be successful, the counselor must introduce hostility? Tracey would say *yes* or *probably.* Friedlander (1993) would say *definitely not.* In a study of successful eclectic counseling among female counselors and female clients, Coulon (2003) found little evidence for the presence of negative messages or negative complementarity during any phase of the interactions. It is possible that for some clients who are open to and inviting of challenge, direct confrontation by the therapist is helpful. Other clients may prefer a less confrontational, more insight-focused approach. For some clients who are resistant to counselor direction, a nondirective approach may be indicated. More work is needed to uncover the types of reciprocal communication that promote positive outcomes in therapy. One line of work that shows continued promise is the study of client resistance.

Resistance and Reactance in the Counseling Relationship

The concept of "resistance," or the client's lack of willingness not only to accept the therapist's interventions but also to face the inevitable disappointments of life, has its origins in psychoanalytic thought. In counseling psychology research, the term "reactance" has been defined as both an individual trait and a psychological response to an interpersonal constraint on one's sense of autonomy. Brehm (1966) proposed a theory of psychological reactance that refers to peoples' *responses* to interpersonal impingements on their natural needs for freedom. Early studies of reactance examined its place in the success or failure of paradoxical interventions (cf. Dowd et al., 1988). On the other hand, Dowd and Seibel (1991) defined reactance as an individual *trait* that can be measured and used to estimate a client's likelihood of responding positively to directive counselor interventions. Both types of reactance have the potential to affect the nature of counseling and therapy relationships.

Beutler and colleagues (1991) found that clients with traitlike tendencies to resist authority benefited more from self-directed psychotherapy, whereas clients who were less reactive benefited more from cognitive and Gestalt-type experiential procedures. Beutler and others have concluded that therapy relationships involving less prescription or direction work better with highly reactant clients (cf. Beutler & Consoli, 1993). Perhaps, however, the picture is not quite that simple. In a multiple-site study of 681 chronically depressed clients, Arnow and colleagues (2003) studied reactance using a cognitive behavioral treatment intervention (McCullough, 2000) that begins by addressing potential client transferences (which the authors called "perturburances") involving authority figures. They found that highly reactant clients actually benefited more from therapy than did nonreactant clients. Although the authors claimed that the cognitive behavioral intervention was responsible for change in those clients, it is possible that the transference

interpretations themselves, or the therapists' ability to directly address their relationships with their clients, contributed greatly to the therapeutic change.

From these findings, one might conclude that therapists who are best at assisting clients to understand the interpersonal biases they bring to relationships and how those biases may operate in the therapy relationship are best at helping clients, regardless of how resistant clients might be and regardless of the type of therapeutic intervention. Such a relational ability might be termed a *common factor,* or a *nonspecific factor,* that accounts for positive outcomes in counseling.

Resistance or reactance may also be understood in terms of sex, ethnic, and other differences between counselor and client. In the absence of more complex information about a therapist, clients may react to the most readily observable qualities such as skin color, dress, sex, and age. In addition, research has demonstrated that many clients prefer to be matched with counselors who are similar in terms of gender (Nelson, 1993) and ethnicity (Atkinson & Lowe, 1995). Research also suggests that a client's comfort with a counselor from a different ethnic group may depend on level of ethnic identity development for both client and counselor (Burkhard, Ponterotto, Reynolds, & Alfonso, 1999). Furthermore, resistances that a client brings to counseling may also be related to cultural attitudes about authority figures and potential threats from outsiders as well as cultural beliefs about what types of interventions will be helpful (Atkinson, Bui, & Mori, 2001). Thus, any examination of client reactance, whether defined as a trait or as a reaction to counselor provocations, should include an analysis of potential cultural, gender, and other factors that might influence both client and counselor experiences of the relationship.

Common Factors in Counseling and Psychotherapy Outcomes

Although counseling psychologists have concerned themselves to some degree with identifying what types of technical interventions seem to be most efficacious, the field of clinical psychology has undertaken most of that work. The majority of outcome studies have examined the efficacy of behavioral, cognitive behavioral, and brief psychodynamic and interpersonal interventions for treating depression and anxiety disorders. Numerous meta-analyses of comparative outcome studies have demonstrated that most bona fide technical interventions do work (Wampold, 2001). Bruce Wampold and his colleagues have demonstrated that common factors actually contribute more to therapy outcome than do technical interventions (Wampold, 2001; Wampold et al., 1997).

Common factors include a broad array of influences, including the counseling relationship (e.g., therapeutic alliance, level of engagement, shared worldview, transference), client attitudes and characteristics (e.g., gender and ethnicity, positive expectancy, level of distress, motivation), and therapist characteristics and competencies (e.g., acceptance, warmth, empathy, expert role).

Multicultural counseling competencies can also be identified as common factors. Indeed, Coleman (1998) demonstrated that multicultural competencies and general counseling competencies may constitute a similar skill set. With the exception of one study that reported that counselor multicultural competency results in greater satisfaction for ethnic minority clients than for Euro-American clients (Fuertes & Brobst, 2002), there is a dearth of research on the influence of specific multicultural skills on the actual counseling process and outcome (Pope-Davis, Liu, Toporek, & Brittan-Powell, 2001).

Perhaps the most striking finding from current research on common factors is that the *person* of the counselor—however one may define "person"—appears to have a powerful influence on outcomes (Crits-Cristoph et al., 1991), ultimately accounting for a greater amount of variance in outcome than treatment modality (Wampold, 2001). Understanding this "error," or variance unaccounted for, is critical to identifying an essential ingredient of effective counseling and therapy.

Rosenzweig (1936) proposed that therapist personality factors, such as capacity to be stimulating and inspirational, must affect psychotherapy outcome. Similarly, Nacht (1962) posited that the therapist's personality and the client's reaction to it are the most significant elements in psychoanalytic psychotherapy.

Surprisingly little work has been done, however, to identify individual therapist qualities that affect the counseling relationship. Wampold's (2001) work suggests that understanding therapist factors that contribute to outcome is a critical next step in counseling and psychotherapy research.

Beyond the facilitative conditions researchers, only a few investigators have attempted to address the therapist factors question. In a review of multiple contributors to positive outcomes, Luborsky (1976) identified factors such as therapist experience, attitudes and interest patterns, and empathy and similarity between patient and therapist. Rounsaville, Chevron, Prusoff, and Elkin (1987) found that therapist behaviors such as exploration, warmth, and friendliness predicted positive outcomes. Engvik (1999) found that the most popular counselors in a training program exhibited greater agreeableness, conscientiousness, and emotional stability than did less popular counselors. However, there is much yet to be discovered about what kinds of people make the best therapists. This brings us to the third critical area in counseling psychology research—the training and supervision of counselors and therapists.

ARE GOOD COUNSELORS AND THERAPISTS BORN, OR CAN THEY BE TRAINED?

Numerous researchers have demonstrated the utility of training in basic counseling skills (Baker, Daniels, & Greeley, 1990; Berenson et al., 1966), indicating that most students can learn to actively listen, reflect the feelings of a client with some accuracy, name the meaning of a client's experience, and summarize client concerns. With the advent of interpersonal skills training programs (Carkhuff & Pierce, 1975; Ivey, 1968; Truax & Carkhuff, 1967) came a flurry of research on optimal strategies for counselor training. Taping of practice sessions and facilitated recall (Kagan, 1969) provided opportunities for researchers to observe immediate outcomes of training.

In a meta-analytic review of success of major training models, Baker and colleagues (1990) found that the Truax and Carkhuff (1967) human resources development training model was superior to the Ivey (1968) microtraining model and Kagan's (1969) interpersonal process recall model in helping novices to develop basic skills. Perhaps one reason why the Truax and Carkhuff model may be superior to other models is that it includes an experiential component.

Very early on, Truax, Carkhuff, and Douds (1964) proposed that proper training should, among other things, provide therapeutic experiences for the counselors themselves. They argued on behalf of training that promoted student self-exploration and personal growth, including group participation and intensive individual supervision. Several researchers have demonstrated that group or interpersonal therapy experiences enhance development of basic counseling skills (Carkhuff & Truax, 1965; Peebles, 1980; Selfridge, 1975). In addition, interactive multicultural awareness training is used in some counselor education and counseling psychology programs and has been recommended for enhancing counselor development of multicultural competence (Hanna, Bemak, & Chung, 1999). However, we do not know the effects of such efforts on counselor multicultural competency or actual skill with counseling clients (Pope-Davis et al., 2001). Research on the benefits of both generic and multicultural awareness training models is needed.

Over the past two decades, however, research on the efficacy of personal awareness training has lagged. This omission may be related to a decline in training program willingness to require personal awareness experiences due in part to concern about dual relationships between faculty and students. The evaluator role of faculty members contravenes their conduct of therapy with students. Ethical concerns have, however, been recently remedied by the most current ethical guidelines of both the American Psychological Association (APA, 2002) and the American Counseling Association (ACA, 1995), both of which suggest ways of managing departmental expectations about personal awareness requirements in training programs. Whereas the ACA code proscribes faculty use of student self-disclosures in any evaluations of student performance, the APA code mandates that any personal awareness requirements be implemented by individuals outside of the academic training program. These clarifications

could, and perhaps should, reinvigorate exploration of the utility of personal experiential training components in optimal counselor training and development—particularly their role in helping counselors to build awareness of how their interpersonal attitudes and styles affect others.

Supervision: A Major Focus Area for Training Research

Supervision has always been viewed as a safe place for counselors in training to learn about themselves in relation to their clients as well as to their supervisors. Most of the early literature on supervision was theoretical in nature and was influenced primarily by supervision practices in psychoanalytic training (cf. Sager, 1953).

Counseling psychologists, who choose to view supervision from a more theoretically neutral perspective than do other types of clinicians, conceptualized the role of supervisor as facilitator of supervisee development. From the counseling psychology viewpoint, training and supervision should promote personal and professional development. Historically, counselors and counseling psychologists have attempted to detail stages of counselor development (Hogan, 1964; Stoltenberg, 1981), and most models have described the process in terms of moving from dependent novice, through phases of developmental anxiety and uncertainty, to a position of integration and professional autonomy.

Borrowing notions from educational theory and research on development of conceptual level, Stoltenberg (1981) developed the *counselor complexity model,* which described novice counselors as concrete in their view of human problems and how to change them. According to Stoltenberg's theory, training and supervision facilitate the supervisee's journey toward comfort with ambiguity and the capacity to view both the client and the counseling process through a multifaceted lens. Stoltenberg and colleagues have gone to some lengths to recommend appropriate supervisor interventions for each level of counselor development (Stoltenberg, 1981; Stoltenberg, McNeill, & Delworth, 1998).

Holloway (1987) challenged Stoltenberg's theory, arguing that not all individuals enter counselor training as concrete thinkers and that new supervisees vary in terms of their ability to grasp complexity. Supervision, therefore, should be a process of assessing supervisees' cognitive developmental levels and working to facilitate subsequent growth. A part of Holloway's body of work has been to examine conceptual level as a critical factor in both therapists' and counselor trainees' abilities to build strong relationships and effect client change (Holloway & Wampold, 1986). Although others have validated these findings (cf. Borders & Fong, 1989), studies on the importance of conceptual level have been hampered by concerns about the difficulty of defining and measuring it (Holloway & Wampold, 1986). We believe, however, that the concept still holds promise, not only for identifying levels of counselor development but also for studying training factors that can enhance student capacity to manage complex interpersonal and mental tasks.

The Stoltenberg–Holloway debate (Holloway, 1987; Stoltenberg, 1981) did, in part, raise the issue of whether good counselors are born or bred. If breeding is at least part of it, then what should good supervisors do to promote optimal learning for counselors and therapists in training? Worthen and McNeill (1996) reported that good supervisors built empathic nonjudgmental relationships with their supervisees, were receptive to supervisee input, and promoted nondefensive analysis on the part of supervisees by normalizing and embracing their struggles.

Other researchers have identified how supervision can go wrong and the negative sequelae of poor supervision (Gray, Ladany, Walker, & Ancis, 2001; Nelson & Friedlander, 2001). Specifically, these researchers found that poor supervisors did not offer facilitative conditions to their supervisees, did not respect their supervisees' worldviews, ignored key points of difference between themselves and their supervisees (e.g., gender, ethnicity), and did not address obvious conflicts openly. A common pattern among poor supervisors was to exhibit feelings of being threatened by supervisee competence or expertise in areas where the supervisors themselves lacked competence or expertise. Typical responses to this type of threat involved scapegoating of supervisees, becoming dominant and controlling of supervisees, and insisting that supervisees subscribe to the supervisors'

worldviews. Poor supervisors appeared to be unwilling to acknowledge and allow their own anxieties about competence. Thus, it is not surprising that supervisees sometimes have been found to withhold critical information from their supervisors for fear of recrimination (Ladany, Hill, Corbett, & Nutt, 1996).

One of the most striking observations in the Nelson and Friedlander (2001) study was that poor supervision relationships were characterized by a high degree of role conflict or supervisee anxiety related to experienced conflict regarding supervisor expectations (Olk & Friedlander, 1992). This finding is not surprising in that supervision is by nature conflicted as a result of the clinical and evaluative nature of the relationship. Supervisors are especially challenged to help their supervisees understand the nature of supervision and their role expectations within it. Nelson and Friedlander (2001) recommended a role induction process that specifies the supervisor's expectations as well as goals and tasks for the supervisory pair. Indeed, current best practices in the supervision literature recommend written contracts that specify supervisee and supervisor roles and tasks (Bernard & Goodyear, 2004); however, research on role induction, supervision contracts, and their relation to formation of positive supervisory relationships is needed.

Another critical factor identified by Nelson and Friedlander (2001) and Gray and colleagues (2001) was that many supervisors in difficult relationships did not directly address the source of relational conflict with their supervisees. This phenomenon may be due in part to the lack of a prescriptive technology of supervisory intervention. Ladany, Friedlander, and Nelson (2005) proposed an interpersonal model of supervision that addresses how critical issues in supervision, such as racial/ethnic difference, gender difference, and sexual attraction, can be addressed respectfully within the interactional context. These types of interventions are not new; rather, they reflect a historical recognition that the "here and now" of all relationships is a powerful axis of connection and change. Research is needed to document the impact of direct, interpersonal supervision interventions on the supervisory relationship, supervisee development, and (ultimately) client progress.

CONCLUSION

In this chapter, we have identified three major research areas that, we think, should inform inquiry in the remarkably diverse field of counseling psychology during the coming years. In broad strokes, we are persuaded that the field has a remarkable opportunity to continue to pursue research that serves to advance a social justice mission in ways that recognize and build on the power of the profession to effect change for populations most in need of attention and support. Although counseling psychology researchers have frequently been at the forefront of psychological efforts to address issues of diversity, it is a propitious time, we believe, to renew our individual commitment to that challenge. Whether researchers undertake studies of career development, individual development, counseling process and outcome, training and supervision, or multicultural/contextualized influences on psychological factors, we believe that the motivation to improve our efforts to serve the most vulnerable should be a driving force in counseling psychology during the years ahead.

REFERENCES

American Counseling Association. (1995). *Code of ethics* (rev. ed.). Alexandria, VA: Author.

American Psychological Association. (2002). *Ethical principles of psychologists and code of conduct: 2002.* Washington, DC: Author.

Arnow, B. A., Manber, R., Blasey, C., Klein, D. N., Blalock, J. A., Markowitz, J. C., Rothbaum, B. O., Rush, A. J., Thase, M. E., Riso, L. P., Vivian, D., McCullough, J. P., & Keller, M. B. (2003). Therapeutic reactance as a predictor of outcome in the treatment of chronic depression. *Journal of Consulting and Clinical Psychology, 71,* 1025–1035.

Atkinson, D. R., Bui, U., & Mori, S. (2001). Multiculturally sensitive empirically supported treatments: An oxymoron? In J. G. Ponterotto, J. M. Casas, L. A. Suzuki, & C. M. Alexander (Eds.), *Handbook of multicultural counseling* (2nd ed., pp. 542–574). Thousand Oaks, CA: Sage.

Atkinson, D. R., & Lowe, S. M. (1995). The role of ethnicity, cultural knowledge, and conventional techniques in counseling psychology. In J. G. Ponterotto, J. M. Casas, L. A. Suzuki, & C. M. Alexander (Eds.), *Handbook of multicultural counseling* (pp. 387–414). Thousand Oaks, CA: Sage.

Baker, S. B., Daniels, T. G., & Greeley, A. T. (1990). Systematic training of graduate level counselors: Narrative and meta-analytic reviews of three major programs. *The Counseling Psychologist, 18,* 355–421.

Bandura, A. (1986). *Social foundations of thought and action: A social cognitive theory.* Englewood Cliffs, NJ: Prentice Hall.

Berenson, B. G., Carkhuff, R. R., & Myrus, P. (1966). The interpersonal training and functioning of college students. *Journal of Counseling Psychology, 13,* 441–446.

Bernard, J. M., & Goodyear, R. K. (2004). *Fundamentals of clinical supervision.* Boston: Allyn & Bacon.

Betz, N. E., & Hackett, G. (1981). The relationship of career-related self-efficacy expectations to perceived career options in college women and men. *Journal of Counseling Psychology, 28,* 399–410.

Beutler, L. E., & Consoli, A. J. (1993). Matching the therapist's interpersonal stance to client's characteristics: Contributions from systematic, eclectic psychotherapy. *Psychotherapy, 30,* 417–422.

Beutler, L. E., Engle, D., Mohr, D., Daldrup, R. J., Bergan, J., Meredith, K., & Merry, W. (1991). Predictors of differential response to cognitive, experiential, and self-directed psychotherapeutic procedures. *Journal of Consulting and Clinical Psychology, 59,* 333–340.

Blustein, D. L. (2001). Extending the reach of vocational psychology: Toward an inclusive and integrative psychology of working. *Journal of Vocational Behavior, 59,* 171–182.

Blustein, D. L. (2004). Moving from the inside out: Further explorations of the family of origin/career development linkage. *The Counseling Psychologist, 32,* 603–611.

Blustein, D. L., Juntunen, C. L., & Worthington, R. L. (2000). The school-to-work transition: Adjustment challenges for the forgotten half. In S. D. Brown & R. W. Lent (Eds.), *Handbook of counseling psychology* (pp. 435–470). New York: John Wiley.

Borders, L. D., & Fong, M. L. (1989). Ego development and counseling ability during training. *Counselor Education and Supervision, 29,* 71–83.

Bordin, E. S. (1979). The generalizability of the psychoanalytic concept of the working alliance. *Psychotherapy: Theory, Research, and Practice, 16,* 252–260.

Brehm, J. W. (1966). *A theory of psychological reactance.* New York: Academic Press.

Brown, S. D., & Ryan Krane, N. E. (2000). Four (or five) sessions and a cloud of dust: Old assumptions and new observations about career counseling. In S. D. Brown & R. W. Lent (Eds.), *Handbook of counseling psychology* (3rd ed., pp. 740–766). New York: John Wiley.

Burkhard, A. W., Ponterotto, J. G., Reynolds, A. L., & Alfonso, V. C. (1999). White counselor trainees' racial identity and working alliance perceptions. *Journal of Counseling and Development, 77,* 324–329.

Carkhuff, R. R., & Pierce, R. M. (1975). *The art of helping: An introduction to life skills—A trainer's guide for developing the helping skills of parents, teachers, and counselors.* Amherst, MA: Human Resource Development Press.

Carkhuff, R. R., & Truax, C. B. (1965). Training in counseling and psychotherapy: An evaluation of an integrated didactic and experiential approach. *Journal of Consulting Psychology, 29,* 333–336.

Carson, R. C. (1969). *Interaction concepts of personality.* Chicago: Aldine.

Chronister, K. M., & McWhirter, E. H. (2003). Applying social cognitive career theory to the empowerment of battered women. *Journal of Counseling and Development, 81,* 418–425.

Coleman, H. L. K. (1998). General and multicultural counseling competency: Apples and oranges? *Journal of Multicultural Counseling and Development, 26,* 147–156.

Coulon, J. C. (2003). Negative complementarity: Not an essential component of successful counseling. *Dissertation Abstracts International Section A: Humanities and Social Sciences, 63,* p. 2789.

Crits-Cristoph, P., Baranackie, K., Kurcias, J. S., Beck, A. T., Carroll, K., Perry, K., Luborsky, L., McLellan, A. T., Woody, G. E., Thompson, L. E., Gallagher, D., & Zitrin, C. (1991). Metaanalysis of therapist effects in psychotherapy outcome studies. *Psychotherapy Research, 2,* 81–91.

Davenport, R. K. (1946). Implications of military selection and classification in relation to universal military training. *Journal of Negro Education, 15,* 585–594.

Dawis, R. V. (1992). The individual differences tradition in counseling psychology. *Journal of Counseling Psychology, 39,* 7–19.

Day, S. X., & Rounds, J. (1998). Universality of vocational interest structure among racial and ethnic minorities. *American Psychologist, 53,* 728–736.

Day, S. X., Rounds, J., & Swaney, K. (1998). The structure of vocational interests for diverse racial–ethnic groups. *Psychological Science, 9,* 40–44.

DeBell, C. S. (2004, July). *What all applied psychologists need to know about the world of work.* Paper presented at the annual meeting of the American Psychological Association, Honolulu, HI.

Dietzel, C., & Abeles, N. (1975). Client–therapist complementarity and therapeutic outcome. *Journal of Counseling Psychology, 22,* 264–272.

Dowd, E. T., Hughes, S. L., Brockbank, L., Halpain, D., Seibel, C., & Seibel, P. (1988). Compliance-based and defiance-based intervention strategies and psychological reactance in the treatment of free and unfree behavior. *Journal of Counseling Psychology, 35,* 370–376.

Dowd, E. T., & Seibel, C. A. (1991). A cognitive theory of resistance and reactance: Implications for treatment. *Journal of Mental Health Counseling, 12,* 458–469.

Elliott, R., Hill, C. E., Stiles, W. B., Friedlander, M. L., Mahrer, A. R., & Margison, F. R. (1987). Primary response modes: A comparison of six rating systems. *Journal of Clinical and Consulting Psychology, 55,* 218–223.

Engvik, H. (1999). Therapeutic popularity and personality: Association between peer therapist nominations and the "Big Five" personality factors. *Scandinavian Journal of Psychology, 40,* 261–267.

Fouad, N. A. (2001). The future of vocational psychology: Aiming high. *Journal of Vocational Behavior, 59,* 183–191.

Fouad, N. A., & Smith, P. L. (1996). A test of a social cognitive model for middle school students: Math and science. *Journal of Counseling Psychology, 43,* 338–346.

Friedlander, M. L. (1993). Does complementarity promote or hinder client change in brief therapy? A review of the evidence from two theoretical perspectives. *The Counseling Psychologist, 21,* 457–486.

Fuertes, J. N., & Brobst, K. (2002). Clients' ratings of counselor multicultural competency. *Cultural*

Diversity and Ethnic Minority Psychology, 3, 214–223.

Gaffner, D. C., & Hazler, R. J. (2002). Factors related to indecisiveness and career indecision in undecided college students. *Journal of College Student Development, 43,* 317–326.

Gray, L. A., Ladany, N., Walker, J. A., & Ancis, J. R. (2001). Psychotherapy trainees' experience of counterproductive events in supervision. *Journal of Counseling Psychology, 48,* 371–383.

Hackett, G., & Betz, N. E. (1981). A self-efficacy approach to the career development of women. *Journal of Vocational Behavior, 18,* 326–336.

Hackett, G., Lent, R. W., & Greenhaus, J. H. (1991). Advances in vocational theory and research: A 20-year retrospective. *Journal of Vocational Behavior, 38,* 3–38.

Hanna, F. J., Bemak, F., & Chung, R. C. (1999). Toward a new paradigm for multicultural counseling. *Journal of Counseling and Development, 77,* 125–134.

Harmon, L. W., Hansen, J. C., Borgen, F. H., & Hammer, A. L. (1994). *Applications and technical guide for the Strong Interest Inventory.* Palo Alto, CA: Consulting Psychologists Press.

Heppner, M. J., & Scott, A. B. (2004). From whence we came: The role of social class in our families of origin. *The Counseling Psychologist, 32,* 596–602.

Hill, C. E. (1990). Exploratory in-session process research in individual psychotherapy: A review. *Journal of Clinical and Consulting Psychology, 58,* 288–294.

Hill, C. E., Helms, J. E., Tichenor, V., Spiegel, S. B., O'Grady, K. E., & Perry, E. S. (1988). Effects of therapist response modes in brief psychotherapy. *Journal of Counseling Psychology, 35,* 222–233.

Hogan, R. (1964). Issues and approaches in supervision. *Psychotherapy: Theory, Research, and Practice, 1,* 139–141.

Holland, J. L. (1959). A theory of vocational choice. *Journal of Counseling Psychology, 6,* 35–45.

Holland, J. L. (1994). *Self-directed search.* Odessa, FL: Psychological Assessment Resources.

Holloway, E. L. (1987). Developmental models of supervision: Is it development? *Professional Psychology: Research and Practice, 18,* 209–216.

Holloway, E. L., & Wampold, B. E. (1986). Relation between conceptual level and counseling-related tasks: A meta-analysis. *Journal of Counseling Psychology, 15,* 205–260.

Horvath, A. O., & Bedi, R. P. (2002). The alliance. In J. C. Norcross (Ed.), *Psychotherapy relationships that work* (pp. 37–69). New York: Oxford University Press.

Horvath, A. O., & Greenberg, L. S. (1989). Development and validation of the Working Alliance Inventory. *Journal of Counseling Psychology, 36,* 223–233.

Horvath, A. O., & Symonds, B. D. (1991). Relation between working alliance and outcome in psychotherapy: A meta-analysis. *Journal of Counseling Psychology, 38,* 139–149.

Ivey, A. E. (1968). Microcounseling and attending behavior: An approach to prepracticum counselor training. *Journal of Counseling Psychology, 15,* 1–12.

Juntunen, C. L., Barraclough, D. J., Broneck, C. M., Morin, P. M., Seibel, G. A., & Winrow, S. A. (2001). Native American perspectives on the career journey. *Journal of Counseling Psychology, 48,* 274–285.

Kagan, N. (1969). Interpersonal process recall. *Journal of Nervous and Mental Disease, 148,* 365–374.

Kiesler, D. J. (1979). An interpersonal communications analysis of relationship in psychotherapy. *Psychiatry, 42,* 299–311.

Ladany, N., Friedlander, M. L., & Nelson, M. L. (2005). *Critical events in psychotherapy supervision: An interpersonal approach.* Washington, DC: American Psychological Association.

Ladany, N., Hill, C. E., Corbett, M. M., & Nutt, E. A. (1996). The nature, extent, and importance of what psychotherapy trainees do not disclose to their supervisors. *Journal of Counseling Psychology, 43,* 10–24.

Lent, R. W. (2005). A social cognitive view of career development and counseling. In S. D. Brown & R. W. Lent (Eds.), *Career development and counseling* (pp. 101–127). Hoboken, NJ: John Wiley.

Lent, R. W., Brown, S. D., & Hackett, G. (1994). Toward a unifying social cognitive theory of career and academic interest, choice, and performance. *Journal of Vocational Behavior, 62,* 101–118.

Lent, R. W., Hackett, G., & Brown, S. D. (1999). A social-cognitive view of the school-to-work transition. *Career Development Quarterly, 44,* 297–311.

Luborsky, L. (1976). Helping alliances in psychotherapy. In J. L. Cleghhorn (Ed.), *Successful psychotherapy* (pp. 92–116). New York: Brunner/Mazel.

McCullough, J. P. (2000). *Treatment for chronic depression: Cognitive behavioral system of psychotherapy.* New York: Guilford.

Morrow, S. L., Gore, P. A., & Campbell, B. W. (1996). The application of a sociocognitive framework to the career development of lesbian women and gay men. *Journal of Vocational Behavior, 48,* 136–148.

Nacht, S. (1962). The curative factors in psychoanalysis (part 2). *International Journal of Psychoanalysis, 43,* 206–211.

Nelson, M. L. (1993). A current perspective on gender differences: Implications for research in counseling. *Journal of Counseling Psychology, 40,* 200–209.

Nelson, M. L., & Friedlander, M. L. (2001). A close look at conflictual supervisory relationships: The trainee's perspective. *Journal of Counseling Psychology, 48,* 384–395.

Oliver, L. W., & Spokane, A. K. (1988). Career-intervention outcome: What contributes to client gain? *Journal of Counseling Psychology, 35,* 447–462.

Olk, M. E., & Friedlander, M. L. (1992). Trainees' experiences of role conflict and role ambiguity in supervisory relationships. *Journal of Counseling Psychology, 39,* 389–397.

Osipow, S. H. (1999). Assessing career indecision. *Journal of Vocational Behavior, 55,* 147–154.

Parsons, F. (1909). *Choosing a vocation.* Boston: Houghton Mifflin.

Peebles, M. J. (1980). Personal therapy and ability to display empathy, warmth, and genuineness in psychotherapy. *Psychotherapy: Theory, Research, and Practice, 17,* 258–262.

Phillips, W. B. (1960). Counseling Negro pupils: An educational dilemma. *Journal of Negro Education, 24,* 504–507.

Ponterotto, J., Casas, J. M., Suzuki, L. A., & Alexander, C. M. (2001). *Handbook of multicultural counseling.* Thousand Oaks, CA: Sage.

Pope-Davis, D. B., Liu, W. M., Toporek, R. L., & Brittan-Powell, C. S. (2001). What's missing from multicultural competency research: Review, introspection, and recommendations. *Cultural Diversity and Ethnic Minority Psychology, 7,* 121–138.

Rogers, C. R. (1957). The necessary and sufficient conditions of *therapeutic* personality change. *Journal of Consulting Psychology, 21,* 95–103.

Rogers, C. R., & Dymond, R. F. (1954). *Psychotherapy and personality change.* Chicago: University of Chicago Press.

Romano, J. L., & Kachgal, M. M. (2004). Counseling psychology and school counseling: An underutilized partnership. *The Counseling Psychologist, 32,* 184–215.

Rosenzweig, S. (1936). Some implicit common factors in diverse methods of psychotherapy. *American Journal of Orthopsychiatry, 6,* 412–415.

Rounsaville, B. J., Chevron, E. S., Prusoff, B. A., & Elkin, I. (1987). The relation between specific and general dimensions of psychotherapy process in interpersonal psychotherapy of depression. *Journal of Clinical and Consulting Psychology, 55,* 379–384.

Sager, C. J. (1953). Aspects of clinical training in psychotherapy. *American Journal of Psychotherapy, 7,* 633–640.

Savickas, M. L. (2005). The theory and practice of career construction. In S. D. Brown & R. W. Lent (Eds.), *Career development and counseling* (pp. 42–70). Hoboken, NJ: John Wiley.

Selfridge, F. F. (1975). Sensitivity-oriented versus didactically-oriented in-service counselor training. *Journal of Counseling Psychology, 22,* 156–159.

Stoltenberg, C. (1981). Approaching supervision from a developmental perspective: The counselor-complexity model. *The Counseling Psychologist, 28,* 59–65.

Stoltenberg, C. D., McNeill, B., & Delworth, U. (1998). *IDM supervision: An integrated developmental model for supervising counselors and therapists.* San Francisco: Jossey-Bass.

Suh, C. S., O'Malley, S. S., & Strupp, H. H. (1986). The Vanderbilt Psychotherapy Process Scale (VPPS) and the Negative Indicators Scale (VNIS). In L. S. Greenberg & W. M. Pinsof (Eds.), *The psychotherapeutic process: A research handbook.* New York: Guilford.

Super, D. E. (1990). A life-span, life-space approach to career development. In D. Brown & L. Brooks (Eds.), *Career choice and development* (pp. 192–234). San Francisco: Jossey-Bass.

Swanson, J. L., & Gore, P. A., Jr. (2000). Advances in vocational psychology theory and research. In S. D. Brown & R. W. Lent (Eds.), *Handbook of counseling psychology* (pp. 233–269). New York: John Wiley.

Tracey, T. J. (1993). An interpersonal stage model of the therapeutic process. *Journal of Counseling Psychology, 40,* 396–409.

Tracey, T. J., Sherry, P., & Albright, J. M. (1999). The interpersonal process of cognitive-behavioral therapy: An examination of complementarity over the course of treatment. *Journal of Counseling Psychology, 46,* 80–91.

Truax, C. B. (1966). Therapist empathy, genuineness, and warmth and patient therapeutic outcome. *Journal of Consulting Psychology, 30,* 395–401.

Truax, C. B., & Carkhuff, R. R. (1965). Experimental manipulation of therapeutic conditions. *Journal of Consulting Psychology, 29,* 119–124.

Truax, C. B., & Carkhuff, R. R. (1967). *Toward effective counseling and psychotherapy: Training and practice.* Hawthorne, NY: Aldine.

Truax, C. B., Carkhuff, R. R., & Douds, J. (1964). Toward an integration of the didactic and experiential approaches to training in counseling and psychotherapy. *Journal of Counseling Psychology, 11,* 240–247.

Tyler, L. (1992). Counseling psychology: Why? *Professional Psychology: Research and Practice, 23,* 342–344.

U.S. Congress. (1994). *School to Work Opportunities Act of 1994* (P.L. 103-239). Washington, DC: Government Printing Office.

Wampold, B. E. (2001). *The great psychotherapy debate: Models, methods, and findings.* Mahwah, NJ: Lawrence Erlbaum.

Wampold, B. E., Mondin, G. W., Moody, M., Stich, F., Benson, K., & Ahn, H. (1997). A meta-analysis of outcome studies comparing bona fide psychotherapies: Empirically, "all must have prizes." *Psychological Bulletin, 122,* 203–215.

Whiston, S. C., & Keller, B. K. (2004). The influences of the family of origin on career development: A review and analysis. *The Counseling Psychologist, 32,* 493–568.

Whitely, J. M. (1984). Counseling psychology: A historical perspective. *The Counseling Psychologist, 12,* 3–109.

Whitely, J. M. (1999). The paradigms of counseling psychology. *The Counseling Psychologist, 27,* 14–31.

Worthen, V., & McNeill, B. W. (1996). A phenomenological investigation of "good" supervision events. *Journal of Counseling Psychology, 43,* 25–34.

Worthington, R. L., & Juntunen, C. L. (1997). The vocational development of non-college-bound youth: Counseling psychology and the school-to-work transition movement. *The Counseling Psychologist, 25,* 323–363.

Zytowski, D. G. (2001). *Kuder Career Search user's manual.* Adel, IA: National Career Assessment Services.

13

EDUCATIONAL LEADERSHIP

JANE CLARK LINDLE
Clemson University

The term "instructional leadership" derives from early attempts to explain the unexpectedly higher achievement of low-socioeconomic status students in high-poverty schools during the 1970s (Brookover & Lezotte, 1979; Edmonds, 1979, 1982; Edmonds & Frederiksen, 1978; Lezotte & Passalacqua, 1978). Known as *effective schools research,* these studies generated a set of characteristics common to effective schools that typically included the following list (Edmonds, 1979, 1982):

1. Instructional leadership

2. Schoolwide focus on instruction

3. Orderly and safe environment

4. High expectations for student achievement

5. Use of student achievement data for decision making and planning

Critiques and replications of this work showed a fairly stable, if contested, listing of similar constructs concerning the conditions of effective schools. Among the contests was a debate over whether a *schoolwide focus on instruction* was inclusive of, or different from, constructs of *professional development* and *professional community* (Burlingame, 1987; Hallinger & Murphy,

1986; Lee, 1991; Lieberman, 1988; Louis, 1992). A few studies added one more characteristic, noting the importance of community and family support for schools as a critical feature in high-achieving, low-income schools (Coleman, 1987; Comer, 1980; Desimone, Finn-Stevenson, & Henrich, 2000; National Center for Effective Schools Research and Development, 1989).

Increasingly, state and federal education policies used effective schools research, and school administrators demanded a sharpened and practical definition of instructional leadership. Today, the research community is engaged in a continuing effort to find a definitive explanation of complexities of leadership practices in proximity to, but still distant from, the core interactions associated with student achievement: learning and teaching.

As researchers wrestle with systematic inquiry into instructional leadership, a number of policy documents promoting lists of leader behaviors associated with higher student achievement add impetus to this work. For example, the Council of Chief State School Officers (CCSSO) conducted a series of seminars and focus groups and in 1996 promulgated six standards and nearly 200 indicators for states to use in school leader certification and assessment. The Southern Regional Education

Board used focus groups and surveys of teachers and principals engaged in one of its projects, High Schools That Work, to produce a list of 13 critical success factors associated with high-performing principals (Bottoms & O'Neill, 2001). Division A of the American Educational Research Association (AERA) distributed a task force brief listing five findings from a review of research about what effective principals do (Leithwood & Riehl, 2003). In addition, the Mid-continent Regional Education Lab (McREL), one of 10 such labs sponsored by the U.S. government, conducted a meta-analysis of research on principals producing a set of 21 responsibilities for principals that it called "balanced leadership" (Miller, 2003; Waters & Grubb, 2004; Waters, Marzano, & McNulty, 2003). This explosion of enumerated expectations surrounding educational leaders' practices focused on instruction highlights the importance of empirical work concerned with what principals do to enhance teaching and improve learning and also raises the stakes for researchers investigating the construct of instructional leadership.

This chapter spotlights the ongoing empirical endeavors delineating the construct of instructional leadership. After a brief discussion of the ways in which instructional leadership has been synthesized through academic debates and reviews, the second section covers the methodological challenges to operationalizing instructional leadership. The third section reviews several studies that have offered promising and influential developments in the knowledge base surrounding instructional leadership. The conclusion offers several suggestions for further investigation and conceptual development of instructional leadership.

CHALLENGES IN CONCEPTUALIZATION OF INSTRUCTIONAL LEADERSHIP

Although critics of the initial effective school research projects expressed concerns about the nonorthogonal and intercorrelational elements of all the effective schools' characteristics and constructs (Bossert, 1988; Purkey & Smith, 1983), the association of any leadership practices with student achievement represented a significant conceptual breakthrough for scholars and practitioners of educational leadership. Much of the knowledge base for educational leadership had been, and often continues to be, roundly critiqued for being largely derivative of corporate and public administration (Bates, 1980, 1987; Beck, 1994; Foster, 1986; T. B. Greenfield, 1982, 1985; W. B. Greenfield, 1987; Gunter & Ribbins, 2002; Hoy & Miskel, 2005; Johnson, 2004; Ribbins & Gunter, 2002).

The scope of this chapter does not permit a recitation of the multiple critiques of the knowledge base surrounding educational leadership. To capture these complex contributions to knowledge development about educational leadership and illustrate the sharpened focus on the practices of instructional leadership in schooling, Figure 13.1 offers a schematic.

The schematic illustrates the diversity of descriptions about practices of leadership applied to education from a variety of perspectives. Some of the descriptions derive from business and industrial knowledge about the work of people in organizations. Much of that knowledge was generated in studies of complex organizations from factories to the military and generally offered insights into the management of people and resources in the production of goods or accomplishment of precise goals (Burns, 1982; Callahan, 1962; Culbertson, 1988; English, 1992, 1994; Griffiths, 1988; Hoy & Miskel, 2005). In contrast, other literature on leadership appeals to the service that education provides in a social contract with individuals and society. Such neo-institutional theories suggest a deeper mission for leadership that involves attending to social ends that may be highly ambiguous, implicit, and contested in the social arenas surrounding such institutions (Cibulka, 1996; Crowson, Boyd, & Mawhinney, 1996; Dantley, 2002, 2003; Foster, 1986; Hannaway, 1993; Hanson, 2001; Hartley, 2004; Rowan & Miskel, 1999; Tyack & Hansot, 1982; Wheatley, 2002). Although some reviewers consider this perspective to be neo-institutional, historians acknowledge U.S. school managers' traditional role in upholding the common good through model moral behavior (Tyack & Hansot, 1982).

These two perspectives on leadership in organizations and institutions that barely mirror educational purposes or activities still provide

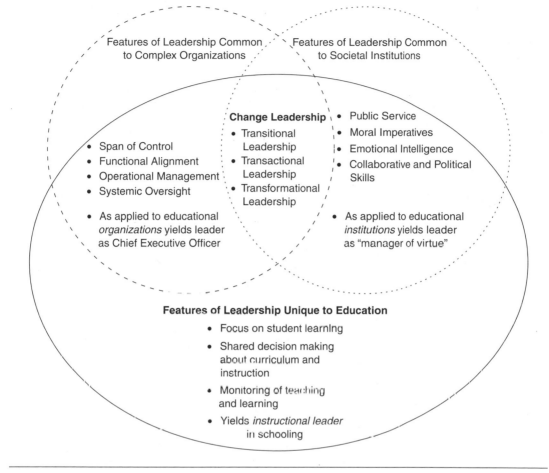

Figure 13.1   Schematic of the Conceptual Focus Offered by Instructional Leadership

some understanding of leadership practices common to most organizations and institutions. To the degree that some leadership practices are common across a variety of settings, these insights offer some use for educational researchers and practitioners. For example, all organizations and institutions face internal and external influences that either cause or respond to change. So, literature about leadership in organizations and institutions dealing with change overlaps and offers concepts addressing leadership practices that enhance or impede change such as is depicted in Figure 13.1 in the common intersection of transitional, transactional, and transformational leadership (Burns, 1982; Goldring, Crowson, Laird, & Berk, 2003; Hallinger, 2003; Leithwood, 1992). Notwithstanding the common utility of

organizational and institutional perspectives, their lack of guidance regarding educational goals sparks continuing debates that are too numerous to recite here.

Instead, the third portion of the schematic is larger than the other two so as to illustrate a direction of knowledge development in educational leadership that provides insight into educational leaders' practices. This portion of the schematic encompasses the common features of organizational and institutional leadership but also highlights a distinguishing aspect of leadership in education, that is, instructional leadership.

Despite the important opportunity to focus on a uniquely educational aspect of leadership, the conceptual topography of instructional leadership is not clear. Notably, the first

Handbook of Research on Educational Administration (Boyan, 1988) makes scant reference to school leaders' instructional responsibilities. The chapter on leadership (Immegart, 1988) calls for increased attention to leading as opposed to managing, but only the chapter on school effects (Bossert, 1988) refers to instruction, and even there the term used is "instructional management" (pp. 348–349). Bossert's (1988) delineation of instructional management divides across two school leader practices: (1) the protection of instructional time and (2) the articulation and pacing of curriculum.

In contrast, the second edition of the *Handbook of Research on Educational Administration* (Murphy & Louis, 1999) devotes three chapters to aspects of teaching and learning in one section (Louis, Toole, & Hargreaves, 1999; Prawat & Peterson, 1999; Sykes, 1999) and then revisits issues of school leadership associated with change and instruction (Smylie & Hart, 1999). In the second *Handbook*'s index, the term "instructional" occupies a section of leadership topics, but as in the first *Handbook,* neither the term "instruction" nor the term "supervision" is an index topic. Both editions of the *Handbook* include a similar number of index entries related to curriculum topics.

If either edition of the *Handbook of Research on Educational Administration* represents the extant state of research on educational administration at its point of publication, then neither one fully defines instructional leadership as a significant research topic. Some critiques of the second *Handbook* raise questions as to the extent to which the chapters present persuasive essays rather than traditional reviews of research (Björk, Lindle, & Van Meter, 1999; Donmoyer, 1999; Levin, 1999).

The issue of availability of empirical literature on instructional leadership represents a limitation of this chapter. Many of the primary sources on the topic of instructional leadership represent positions about the conceptualization of instructional leadership (Blase & Blase, 1999; Greenfield, 1987; Griffiths, Stout, & Forsyth, 1988; Hallinger, 2003; LeMahieu & Roy, 1997). These positions are important steps in establishing the foundation for empirical investigations of instructional leadership; however, such discourses also produce frustrating

paralysis in the reiterative knowledge development processes, including (a) description of phenomena, (b) variable definition, (c) instrumentation, (d) measurement, and (e) hypothesis testing (Forsyth, 2004; Pounder, 2000a, 2000b). Seemingly, the volume of opinionated descriptions surrounding phenomena associated with the construct of instructional leadership overwhelms empirical reports (Forsyth, 2004; Waters & Grubb, 2004). Furthermore, the overabundance of conceptual debates stalls progress toward empirical testing given the "loose definition of theoretical orientation" (Hallinger & Heck, 1996, p. 33) among the small number of emerging empirical studies of instructional leadership.

These studies tend to select proxies for principals' practices of instructional leadership, thereby creating subconstructs within the construct of instructional leadership. A sample of the diversity among operational definitions of the instructional leadership construct can be found in Table 13.1.

The conceptual descriptions sampled in Table 13.1 represent a chronology of ideas about instructional leadership that may have been empirically tested only once or not at all. Nevertheless, these particular examples hold influence over the field, if only in the number of repeated citations they generated. The chronology is important because it illustrates the degree to which the conceptual work fails to build and inform other work. That feature is particularly evident in the first two examples. Hallinger's co-author in their 1985 article, Murphy, played a significant role in the development of the Interstate School Leaders Licensure Consortium (ISLLC) standards roughly a decade later. Any conceptual alignment between those examples is not any more evident than it is among the other examples.

Each set of authors laments the struggle to define instructional leadership. Hallinger and Murphy (1985) observe that virtually no studies uncover what principals do to influence curriculum and instruction (p. 217). Blase and Blase (1999) offer a more comprehensive overview of instructional leadership by using literature from curriculum and supervision rather than the traditional educational administration literature. In a nearly verbatim echo of Hallinger and Murphy's

Table 13.1   Examples of Conceptual Variety in Instructional Leader Constructs

Literature	*Number and Names of Subconstructs*	*Measures*	*Data Sources*
Hallinger & Murphy (1985)	3 • Define mission • Manage instructional program • Promote school climate	Researcher-developed questionnaire plus local documentation	• Self-reports • Perceptions of subordinates and superiors
Council of Chief State School Officers (1996)	4 to 6[a] • 4 themes: (1) vision for success, (2) focus on teaching and learning, (3) involvement of all stakeholders, and (4) demonstration of ethical practice • 6 standards: (1) vision, (2) instructional culture, (3) organizational management, (4) community collaboration, (5) ethical practice, and (6) school context	Varies by state; includes knowledge assessment by Educational Testing Service— School Leaders Licensure Assessment— developed through focus group validation	• Proprietary by Educational Testing Service of School Leaders Licensure Assessment results; availability varies by state • Council of Chief State School Officers focus group results published
Blase & Blase (1999)	2 (positive themes) • Talking with teachers to promote reflection • Promoting professional growth	Researcher-developed questionnaire	• Perceptions of teachers, presumably of different principals
Bryk, Camburn, & Louis (1999)	2 • Direct supervision of teachers • Facilitative style	Researcher-developed surveys	• Perceptions of teachers across schools
Leithwood, Steinbach, & Jantzi (2002)	5 • Policy beliefs • Goals • Capacity beliefs • Context beliefs • Emotional arousal	Researcher-developed semistructured interview questionnaire	• Administrator and teacher perceptions

a. The Interstate School Leaders Licensure Consortium Standards for School Leaders lists six standards, but subsequent content analyses by the Educational Testing Service yielded four constructs (Hessel & Holloway, 2002; Holloway, 2002; Iwanicki, 1999; Latham & Pearlman, 1999).

(1985) remarks, Bryk, Camburn, and Louis (1999) decry the lack of clarity as to what principals may do to promote student learning (p. 757). Leithwood, Steinbach, and Jantzi (2002) simultaneously presume that school leaders could play influential roles in the accountability press for higher student achievement and then investigate whether either teachers or their leaders agree. The essential research question surrounding instructional leadership remains the same: What do school leaders do that enhances teaching and increases student learning?

Table 13.1 could have been extended to other studies less clearly engaged in defining instructional leadership. As another example of the diffusion of meaning surrounding the term "instructional leadership," Hallinger (2003) provides an analysis of conceptual work on the construct that notes *concurrent* rather than *synthetic* and *collaborative* development. Hallinger reports "similarities greater than their differences" (p. 331) but then proceeds to note at least six different approaches among conceptualizations of instructional leadership: (1) control and supervision of curriculum and instruction, (2) an elementary school focus, (3) strong leadership, (4) hands-on supervision of instruction, (5) narrow goals for increasing student achievement, and (6) general academic press for teachers (pp. 331–332). Hallinger also reflects on the degree to which the conceptual development of instructional leadership overlaps other descriptions of leadership as change agency. He opines that the differences offer instructional leadership as encompassing individual practices rather than distributed or shared practices and as immersed in first-order change rather than second-order change (p. 343).

In contrast to Hallinger's (2003) retrospective, which concludes that instructional leadership speaks to individual practice, work by Camburn, Rowan, and Taylor (2003) uses instructional leadership as a subconstruct in a study examining distributed leadership. Their study represents an example of a different and independent conceptualization of instructional leadership. These researchers seek to understand how shared leadership includes instructional leadership as a collective practice, not an individual practice. Camburn and colleagues investigate distributed leadership in schools using federally funded comprehensive school reform models. These researchers construct a survey that includes four instructional leadership subconstructs—setting instructional goals, developing instructional capacity, coordinating curriculum, and monitoring improvement—among multiple measures of shared leadership. They conclude that instructional leadership could be exhibited by more members of the professional community than just principals.

This small sampling of the conceptual work behind the construct of instructional leadership reveals two features about the challenges in conceptualizing the construct. First, the debates over the construct are more oblique than direct. That is, the literature with opinions about instructional leadership seems to be uninformed by empirical work testing constructs associated with instructional leaders' observed or measured practices. Among those studies validating various constructs of instructional leadership, few build on the work of others or even test competing constructions of instructional leadership for both theoretical/practical validity and reliability. Even among the exemplary studies of instructional leadership reviewed in the third section of this chapter, a couple of studies suffer from a lack of replicational work.

The ultimate problem yielded by such conceptual ambiguity is that different studies yield different results because the investigations are based on discrepant conceptualizations of instructional leadership (Hallinger & Heck, 1996, 1998). Fundamental progress in advancing knowledge about instructional leadership is blocked when studies do not replicate or generate conceptual connections across investigations (Forsyth, 2004; Towne, Wise, & Winters, 2005). The next section discusses such methodological issues further.

Although the term "instructional leadership" seems to hold promise in providing educational leaders a set of unique insights and practices for their roles in enhancing teaching and learning, the conceptual development remains ambiguous. A variety of investigators offer a diversity of constructs and subconstructs in a still early stage of theory development. The concurrent, rather than interactive and synthetic, proliferation of approaches to postulations about instructional leadership further confounds understanding about a potentially important field of study. Methodological problems stem from the current obstacles in conceptualizing instructional leadership.

CHALLENGES IN RESEARCH DESIGNS FOR INVESTIGATING INSTRUCTIONAL LEADERSHIP

Although many scholars have pointed to limitations in the research on school leaders and school leadership, these constraints seem to fit into two challenging and intertwined categories: (1) methods and (2) scale. These are intertwined issues because constraints on scale hamper methods and raise questions about most studies. The methods tend to fit the economies of scale

Methods

Method-related problems derive from reliance on data sources that represent espoused theory rather than theory in use. As noted previously, the espoused theories surrounding instructional leadership remain contested and ambiguous. Further complicating the espoused theory issue is that most large-scale studies of instructional leadership, beyond demographic descriptions, generate data primarily through perceptual surveys of the school leaders and stakeholders in schools (Blase & Blase, 1999; Bryk et al., 1999).

Instrumentation poses many limitations on research on leadership roles beyond the conceptual issues described heretofore (Hallinger & Heck, 1996). For example, the perceptions of any single group of stakeholders represent a narrow and bounded view of leaders and their work (Heck & Marcoulides, 1992). In addition, respondents to any survey may belie their espoused socially acceptable positions by their actions (Babbie, 1998). At the very least, use of perceptual data for the purposes of measuring behavior flies in the face of what the National Research Council offers as Scientific Principle 3: "Use methods that permit direct investigation of the question" (Shavelson & Towne, 2002, p. 52). If the question is "What do principals do to enhance teaching and increase student learning?" then the question dictates the necessity of collecting observation data to find out what instructional leaders do.

Certainly, the gold standard of determining the theoretical and practical value of any model of instructional leadership would include observational methods. Yet all of the large-scale studies of instructional leadership rely on researcher-developed questionnaires (e.g., Blase & Blase, 1999; Bryk et al., 1999; Camburn et al., 2003). The survey method is an efficient method for gathering large-scale opinion data, but such an approach not only creates limitations in the study of principals' behavior but also poses some issues concerning unit of analysis within certain research designs (Hallinger, 2003; Hallinger & Heck, 1996, 1998). Many of the large-scale designs use hierarchical linear modeling (HLM), but sample size requirements for HLM usually present obstacles for schools that are constrained by nonrandom participation of teachers and principals (Hallinger & Heck, 1998). For example, when teacher responses are aggregated as a measure for school as the unit of analysis, statistical requirements for independence of measures are violated (Hallinger & Heck, 1998).

One of the primary findings about methods in the study of instructional leadership reveals the critical requirement to address leadership context in the research design (Bryk et al., 1999; Hallinger & Heck, 1996, 1998). Large-scale studies of instructional leadership require models of school context due to the conceptualization of instructional leadership as embedded in the demographic factors controlling student performance and also due to the demographics that shape perceptions among stakeholders (Bryk et al., 1999; Marks & Printy, 2003). Small-scale studies offer richer insights into the influence of context but also remain limited in their generalizability, meaning that their explanatory power wanes in the face of context diversity in other locales. However, research on instructional leadership practices reveals that leadership impact on school climate and learning cultures is greater in smaller schools (Howley, 1989). The overriding design concern with context poses a double-edged sword in determining the advantages and disadvantages of scale.

Further complicating the scale issue, resource limitations mean that many of these studies come from self-reports of school practices. These studies of one's own sites also suffer from the problems with the inability to ascertain the distance between espoused practices and those in use (Anderson & Jones, 2000). However, the largest limitation of small-scale and qualitative studies is that they often are excluded from the meta-analyses of work on instructional leadership (Hallinger & Heck, 1998).

Economies of Scale

Despite burgeoning claims of the importance of leadership to student achievement, the study of school leadership rarely benefits from any major investment in its study (Hallinger & Heck, 1998; Leithwood & Riehl, 2003). What we know about school leadership depends heavily on accumulation of unpublished doctoral dissertations; small-scale funded research on specific states, school districts, or schools; funded survey research of selected practitioner perceptions; and focus groups assembled in conjunction with professional meetings and conferences (Hallinger & Heck, 1996; Waters et al., 2003). These reports result from an unsavory ad hoc approach to the study of school leadership (Young & Creighton, 2002). Thus, they are only suggestive of lines of understanding about the field. This scattered approach to research on the field merely hints at possible directions for further study (Leithwood & Riehl, 2003).

Despite multiple limitations on methods as well as challenges to the conceptualization of instructional leadership, some work provides the field with fundamental knowledge about the ways in which school leaders affect student learning. In the next section, a few studies that address the important question of instructional leadership provide insights into what principals do.

EXEMPLARY STUDIES OF INSTRUCTIONAL LEADERSHIP

Most of today's citations on instructional leadership begin with a meta-analysis conducted by Hallinger and Heck (1996, 1998), and given this influence, their work is reviewed here. As a counterpoint to Hallinger and Heck's meta-analysis, we also review recent work by McREL that included a meta-analysis of principal effects on student achievement and resulted in 21 responsibilities in a model labeled *balanced leadership* (Miller, 2003; Waters & Grubb, 2004; Waters et al., 2003). Finally, work by Marks and Printy (2003), the 2004 Davis Award[1] winners, offers a view of how the dominant use of perceptual data to measure instructional leadership can be expanded fruitfully with observational data to describe instructional leadership in a robust research design that builds on one line of conceptual work explained herein.

Hallinger and Heck's Application of Pitner's Administrator Effects Models

Hallinger and Heck's (1996, 1998) meta-analysis began with 40 studies of which the researchers were able to obtain only 38. They note that 23 were published in scholarly journals, 8 were peer-refereed papers, and 6 were found in unpublished dissertations. Unfortunately, the origin or availability of the 1 remaining source is not explained. Furthermore, neither the authors, the editors, nor the publisher of their article appeared to follow the convention of using asterisks in the reference list to signal which sources were used in the meta-analysis. As a result, only 31 of the 38 citations could be culled from their article.

Setting aside these limitations of disclosure (Shavelson & Towne, 2002; Towne et al., 2005), Hallinger and Heck's (1996, 1998) work offers a framework for understanding the indirect effect of principals' work as well as its interactive effects on teachers. Hallinger and Heck extend Pitner's (1988) model obtained from the first *Handbook of Research in Educational Administration* (Boyan, 1988). Using one level of Pitner's model, they demonstrate a consistency among studies seeking a direct linear relationship between student achievement and principals' leadership; there is none. Given that principals rarely interact directly in students' learning or assessment, such findings pose no surprises. Hallinger and Heck (1998) suggest that pursuing direct effects models, even with sophisticated techniques such as structural equation modeling, is not useful even conceptually, much less practically. As for mediated effects models, Hallinger and Heck (1998) note that multiple regression and path analysis reveal sometimes mixed, but largely positive, effects (p. 167). They conclude that the most promising approach to investigating principal effects on student achievement lies in reciprocal effects models. Whereas many studies sort through reciprocal effects to clarify mediated or direct effects, Hallinger and Heck (1996) observe that the conceptual and analytic power of effects may be embedded in the interactive and multidirectional relationships among variables of leadership. In other words, leaders do not just act on followers; rather, the relationship and effects are mutual. The reciprocal effects model removes leadership from its traditional placement as an independent variable (Hallinger & Heck, 1996).

Given the relative power among the three-model classification of research designs, Hallinger and Heck (1996) offer the following conclusions about instructional leadership. Principals make a difference indirectly in the teaching–learning dyad. Context matters in any study of instructional leadership due to the mediating effects that surround teaching and learning. Principals affect school goals by creating a purposeful focus, which in turn influences classrooms and student learning (Hallinger & Heck, 1996, 1998). Principals mediate organizational structure in ways that enhance the school community's social networks to support teaching and learning (Hallinger & Heck, 1998). These effects extend to a number of people-focused principal behaviors, including ongoing supervision in classrooms, conflict management, and guidance for improving instructional outcomes (Hallinger & Heck, 1998). In addition, principals affect the culture for learning found in schools (Hallinger & Heck, 1998). Although Hallinger and Heck list social networks, people, and culture as different findings, the conceptual distinctions are not that clear and probably reflect the ongoing conceptual messiness surrounding operationalization of instructional leadership. They conclude by addressing the further need for theoretical and practical development of specific answers to the question of how principals influence school outcomes and how their practices are mediated by school contexts (Hallinger & Heck, 1998, p. 186).

Hallinger and Heck (1996, 1998) resolve a perennial question over whether schools—or, more important, students—need principals if the sole purpose of schooling is better performance on achievement tests. In fact, Hallinger and Heck's work potentially lays to rest the overly simplistic question of whether principals directly influence students' test scores. On the other hand, their work supports a move to more complexity in the conceptualization of instructional leadership as well as more sophistication in research design, measurement, and analysis techniques to answer the question of what

instructional leaders do. Finally, Hallinger and Heck offer important evidence that the question ought to ask not only what instructional leaders do but also how they interact with school contexts and in what ways they react strategically to their environments to promote learning.

McREL's Balanced Leadership

Since the late 1990s, McREL has engaged in obtaining quantitative studies of teachers, schools, and leadership practices to apply meta-analyses that identify effects on student achievement (Miller, 2003). These studies cover more than 30 years of educational research, and McREL has distilled these results to address the question of "what works" in classrooms and schools. McREL's most recent meta-analysis used 70 studies to identify school leaders' effects on student achievement (Waters & Grubb, 2004; Waters et al., 2003).

McREL's report on this data analysis lists only 55 of those 70 studies in its reference list, and perhaps the count is really 54 given that 2 references seem to be of the same study reported in different venues (a peer-reviewed conference and a scholarly journal). Of those identifiable sources, 49 (91%) are listed as unpublished dissertations, and 11 are included in Hallinger and Heck's (1996, 1998) meta-analysis. Of those 11, Hallinger and Heck classify 6 as direct effects designs that they conclude are conceptually weak and practically useless in addressing research questions concerning instructional leadership. Given the National Research Council's calls for improvements in educational research that includes replication and generalization across studies as well as full disclosure for the purposes of professional scrutiny and critique (Shavelson & Towne, 2002; Towne et al., 2005), McREL's funded work on instructional leadership apparently suffers from several flaws in research rigor promoted by proponents of scientific research (Shavelson & Towne, 2002; Towne et al., 2005).

Apart from these limitations, McREL's work apparently aims at relieving the current licensure boundaries established by the CCSSO through its promulgation of ISLLC in 1996 (Waters & Grubb, 2004). McREL's meta-analysis offers the first step in this policy agenda. It yields 21 correlates that McREL dubs "responsibilities" that principals should practice to influence student achievement as much as 25% (Waters et al., 2003). Then, using the literature and the research team's "professional wisdom" (Waters et al., 2003, p. 3), McREL lists from 1 to 5 leadership practices associated with each of the 21 responsibilities. This arrangement produced a grand total of 66 practices[2] for a model that McREL calls *balanced leadership.*

After producing this model, McREL created a survey that it administered to practicing principals to validate the balanced leadership model and to associate the placement of practices against a model of first- and second-order change (Waters & Grubb, 2004, pp. 2–3). Apparently, the factor analysis offered validation for the model, although the report is not specific. The next step in the validation process appears to be a content analysis comparing language from ISLLC indicators (CCSSO, 1996). McREL reports that 17 (26%) of the balanced leadership practices could not be matched to any of ISLLC's 184 indicators (Waters & Grubb, 2004, pp. 5–7). Although McREL's report includes a chart, the specifics of the analysis reside in other documents available to "states" (p. 5).

The McREL work is included here because it had potential to replicate Hallinger and Heck's (1996, 1998) seminal approach to the conceptual underpinnings of research on instructional leadership. However, McREL's report displays an atheoretical approach as well as indiscriminate approach to identifying studies for its meta-analysis. It further compounds its design limitations by creating yet another survey of leadership practices that generates more perceptual data rather than obtaining any observational measures that are more likely to answer the question of what principals do as opposed to their espousal of what they ought to be doing. The problem of data sources seems to bedevil most studies of instructional leadership except our next example.

Marks and Printy's Inclusion of Observations of Instructional Leadership

Marks and Printy's (2003) research recognizes the conceptual contributions of Hallinger and Leithwood in addressing the constructs of instructional leadership, transformational leadership, and change. In particular, they designed their study of principals' influence on school performance to further describe the reciprocal effects of leadership and investigated it as a shared model (p. 371).

Marks and Printy (2003) use hierarchical linear modeling of 24 schools selected across the United States for school level (elementary, middle, and high schools) as well as their participation in a larger study of school restructuring. Data collection included surveys and interviews as well as observers trained to measure quality of pedagogy (pp. 378–379). Observers also attended meetings and analyzed documentation. Their methods control for context variables such as distribution of students across classrooms by sex, race/ethnicity, prior achievement (National Assessment of Educational Progress results), and socioeconomic status. The researchers also address school context variables, demonstrating their replication of prior research results from instructional leadership studies (e.g., Hallinger & Heck, 1996, 1998).

Marks and Printy's (2003) findings show that principals' practice includes what the researchers term "integrated leadership" (pp. 388–389). This approach represents a mid-study implementation of a combined indicator variable where principals engaged in high levels of both transformational and instructional leadership. Principals must enact change while maintaining interactions concerning curriculum, instruction, and assessment.

Despite the elegance and sophistication of this study, and despite the encouraging findings of the power of combined transformational and instructional leadership, Marks and Printy (2003) do not open the "black box" of principals' instructional leadership behaviors. Instead, they promise a further report using case study methods of observation (p. 392). Nevertheless, Marks and Printy's findings suggest utility for the focus of leadership illustrated in Figure 13.1. That is, although change is a feature of both organizations and institutions, education requires more than the generic features of leadership; education also requires an instructional focus from its leaders.

These three examples illustrate the ongoing tensions surrounding research on school leaders and student achievement. Marks and Printy's (2003) work shows the intellectual and practical progress possible when lines of conceptual analysis and persistence in the refinement of appropriate research design align. Although the studies use quantitative methods to an increasingly sophisticated degree, persisting conceptual weaknesses, an overreliance on a singular inexpensive (but arguably inappropriate) method of data generation, and perennial independent investigative efforts produce ongoing gaps in knowledge development surrounding instructional leadership.

CONCLUSION

This chapter has reviewed the conceptual and practical interest in the definition of instructional leadership for theoretical and practical purposes. As described, the promise of a unique focus on instruction in the repertoire of educational leadership has yet to be met. Although more and more sophisticated techniques have been applied to the study of the ways in which school leadership affects student achievement, no consistently sustained identifiable line—or even lines—of research emerged focused on instructional leadership. Most of the research is conceived in apparent intellectual isolation and generates constructs about instructional leadership from scratch, that is, uninformed by any other scholarship. Such a failure in scholarship is variously termed "lack of generativity" or "compartmentalization" and, regardless of the moniker, points to a lack of sophistication in the field. These independent approaches include cross-sectional, large-scale studies with an overreliance on one type of data generation—perceptual data. Smaller-scale studies also fail to reference or replicate each other and have yet to produce any meta-ethnographies.

Finally, the question remains as to what principals do to enhance teaching and improve student learning. Conceptual and empirical work to date argues that such a question is not one about the direct effects of principals' work on student achievement. Nevertheless, data collection that includes more observational studies of principals at work may provide more insights and less mystery about instructional leadership.

NOTES

1. The University Council for Educational Administration (UCEA) awards the William J. Davis Award annually to the author(s) of the most outstanding article published in *Educational Administration Quarterly* during the preceding volume year. The Davis Award was established in 1979 to honor the late former associate director of UCEA and assistant professor at the University of Wisconsin–Madison.

2. Apparently, a misprint of 3 rather than 2 practices for the responsibility of *curriculum, instruction,* and *assessment* appears in the earlier document (Waters et al., 2003, p. 9). The count of practices in that document sums to 67.

REFERENCES

Anderson, G. L., & Jones, F. (2000). Knowledge generation in educational administration from the inside out: The promise and perils of site-based, administrator research. *Educational Administration Quarterly, 36,* 428–464.

Babbie, E. (1998). *Survey research methods.* Belmont, CA: Wadsworth.

Bates, R. J. (1980). Educational administration: The sociology of science and the management of knowledge. *Educational Administration Quarterly, 16*(2), 1–20.

Bates, R. J. (1987). Corporate culture, schooling, and educational administration. *Educational Administration Quarterly, 23*(4), 79–115.

Beck, L. G. (1994). *Reclaiming educational administration as a caring profession.* New York: Columbia University, Teachers College Press.

Björk, L. G., Lindle, J. C., & Van Meter, E. J. (1999). A summing up. *Educational Administration Quarterly, 35,* 658–664.

Blase, J., & Blase, J. (1999). Principals' instructional leadership and teacher development: Teachers' perspectives. *Educational Administration Quarterly, 35,* 349–378.

Bossert, S. T. (1988). School effects. In N. J. Boyan (Ed.), *Handbook of research on educational administration: A project of the American Educational Research Association* (pp. 341–352). New York: Longman.

Bottoms, G., & O'Neill, K. (2001, April). *Preparing a new breed of school principals: It's time for action.* Atlanta, GA: Southern Regional Education Board.

Boyan, N. J. (Ed.). (1988). *Handbook of research on educational administration: A project of the American Educational Research Association.* New York: Longman.

Brookover, W. B., & Lezotte, L. W. (1979). *Changes in school characteristics coincident with changes in student achievement* (Occasional Paper No. 17). East Lansing: Michigan State University, Institute for Research on Teaching. (ERIC Reproduction Service No. ED181005)

Bryk, A., Camburn, E., & Louis, K. S. (1999). Professional community in Chicago elementary schools: Facilitating factors and organizational consequences. *Educational Administration Quarterly, 35,* 751–781.

Burlingame, M. (1987). Images of instructional leadership in effective schools literature. In W. B. Greenfield (Ed.), *Instructional leadership: Concepts, issues, and controversies* (pp. 3–16). Boston: Allyn & Bacon.

Burns, J. M. (1982). *Leadership.* New York: Perennial.

Callahan, R. (1962). *Education and the cult of efficiency.* Chicago: University of Chicago Press.

Camburn, E., Rowan, B., & Taylor, J. E. (2003). Distributed leadership in schools: The case of elementary schools adopting comprehensive school reform models. *Educational Evaluation and Policy Analysis, 25,* 347–373.

Cibulka, J. G. (1996). The reform and survival of American public schools: An institutional perspective. In R. L. Crowson, W. L. Boyd, & H. B. Mawhinney (Eds.), *The politics of education and the new institutionalism: Reinventing the American school* (pp. 7–22). Washington, DC: Falmer.

Coleman, J. S. (1987). Families and schools. *Educational Researcher, 16*(6), 32–38.

Comer, J. P. (1980). *School power: Implications of an intervention project.* New York: Free Press.

Council of Chief State School Officers. (1996). *Interstate School Leaders Licensure Consortium's Standards for School Leaders.* Washington, DC: Author.

Crowson, R. L., Boyd, W. L., & Mawhinney, H. B. (1996). Introduction and overview: The new institutionalism and the politics of reinventing the American school. In R. L. Crowson, W. L. Boyd, & H. B. Mawhinney (Eds.), *The politics of education and the new institutionalism: Reinventing the American school* (pp. 1–5). Washington, DC: Falmer.

Culbertson, J. A. (1988). A century's quest for a knowledge base. In N. Boyan (Ed.), *Handbook of research on educational administration: A project of the American Educational Research Association* (pp. 3–26). New York: Longman.

Dantley, M. E. (2002). Uprooting and replacing positivism, the melting pot, multiculturalism, and other impotent notions in educational leadership through an African American perspective. *Education and Urban Society, 34,* 334–352.

Dantley, M. E. (2003). Purpose-driven leadership: The spiritual imperative to guiding schools beyond high-stakes testing and minimum proficiency. *Education and Urban Society, 35,* 273–291.

Desimone, L., Finn-Stevenson, M., & Henrich, C. (2000). Whole school reform in a low-income African American community: The effects of the CoZi model on teachers, parents, and students. *Urban Education, 35,* 269–323.

Donmoyer, R. (1999). Paradigm talk and its absence in the second edition of the *Handbook of Research on Educational Administration. Educational Administration Quarterly, 35,* 614–641.

Edmonds, R. R. (1979). *A discussion of the literature and issues related to effective schooling.* (ERIC Document Reproduction Service No. ED170394)

Edmonds, R. R. (1982). Programs of school improvement: An overview. *Educational Leadership, 40*(3), 4–11.

Edmonds, R. R., & Frederiksen, J. R. (1978). *Search for effective schools: The identification and analysis of city schools that are instructionally effective for poor children.* (ERIC Document Reproduction Service No. ED170396)

English, F. W. (1992). *Educational administration: The human science.* New York: HarperCollins.

English, F. W. (1994). *Theory in educational administration.* New York: HarperCollins.

Forsyth, P. B. (2004, Fall). Educational administration research: Are we too broken? *AERA Division A Newsletter,* pp. 1–10.

Foster, W. P. (1986). *Paradigms and promises: New approaches to educational administration.* Amherst, NY: Prometheus Books.

Goldring, E., Crowson, R., Laird, D., & Berk, R. (2003). Transition leadership in a shifting policy environment. *Educational Evaluation and Policy Analysis, 25,* 473–488.

Greenfield, T. B. (1982). Against group mind: An anarchistic theory of organization. *McGill Journal of Education, 17*(1), 3–11.

Greenfield, T. B. (1985). Theories of educational organization: A critical perspective. In T. Husen & T. N. Postlethwaite (Eds.), *International encyclopedia of education: Research and studies.* Oxford, UK: Pergamon.

Greenfield, W. B. (Ed.). (1987). *Instructional leadership: Concepts, issues, and controversies.* Boston: Allyn & Bacon.

Griffiths, D. E. (1988). Administrative theory. In N. Boyan (Ed.), *Handbook of research on educational administration: A project of the American Educational Research Association* (pp. 27–51). New York: Longman.

Griffiths, D. E., Stout, R. T., & Forsyth, P. B. (Eds.). (1988). *Leaders for America's schools.* Berkeley, CA: McCutchan.

Gunter, H., & Ribbins, P. (2002). Leadership studies in education: Towards a map of the field. *Educational Management and Administration, 30,* 387–416.

Hallinger, P. (2003). Leading educational change: Reflections on the practice of instructional and transformational leadership. *Cambridge Journal of Education, 33,* 329–351.

Hallinger, P., & Heck, R. H. (1996). Reassessing the principal's role in school effectiveness: A review of empirical research, 1980–1995. *Educational Administration Quarterly, 32*(1), 5–44.

Hallinger, P., & Heck, R. H. (1998). Exploring the principal's contribution to school effectiveness, 1980–1995. *School Effectiveness and School Improvement, 9*(2), 157–191.

Hallinger, P., & Murphy, J. (1985). Assessing the instructional management behavior of principals. *Elementary School Journal, 86,* 217–247.

Hallinger, P., & Murphy, J. (1986). *Instructional leadership in effective schools.* (ERIC Document Reproduction Service No. ED309535)

Hannaway, J. (1993). Political pressure and decentralization in institutional organizations: The case of school districts. *Sociology of Education, 66*(3), 147–163.

Hanson, M. (2001). Institutional theory and educational change. *Educational Administration Quarterly, 37,* 637–661.

Hartley, D. (2004). Management, leadership, and the emotional order of the school. *Journal of Educational Policy, 19,* 583–594.

Heck, R. H., & Marcoulides, G. A. (1992). Principal assessment: Conceptual problem, methodological problem, or both? *Peabody Journal of Education, 68*(1), 124–144.

Hessel, K., & Holloway, J. (2002). *A framework for school leaders: Linking the ISLLC standards to practice.* Princeton, NJ: Educational Testing Service.

Holloway, J. (2002, May). A defense of the test for school leaders. *Educational Leadership, 59*(8), 71–75.

Howley, C. B. (1989). What is the effect of small-scale schooling on student achievement? In *ERIC Digest.* Charleston, WV: Appalachian Education Lab. (ERIC Document Reproduction Service No. ED308062)

Hoy, W. K., & Miskel, C. G. (2005). *Educational administration: Theory, research, and practice* (7th ed.). Boston: McGraw-Hill.

Immegart, G. L. (1988). Leadership and leader behavior. In N. J. Boyan (Ed.), *Handbook of research on educational administration: A project of the American Educational Research Association* (pp. 259–277). New York: Longman.

Iwanicki, E. F. (1999). ISLLC standards and assessment in context of school leadership reform. *Journal of Personnel Evaluation in Education, 13,* 283–294.

Johnson, B. L., Jr. (2004). Where have all the flowers gone? Reconnecting leadership preparation with the field of organizational theory. *UCEA Review, 46*(3), 16, 19–22.

Latham, A. S., & Pearlman, M. A. (1999). From standards to licensure: Developing an authentic assessment for school principals. *Journal of Personnel Evaluation in Education, 13,* 245–262.

Lee, G. (1991). Instructional leadership as collaborative sense-making. *Theory Into Practice, 30*(2), 83–90.

Leithwood, K. A. (1992). The move toward transformational leadership. *Educational Leadership, 49*(5), 8–12.

Leithwood, K. A., & Riehl, C. (2003). *What we know about successful school leadership* (brief of Report from Division A Task Force on Developing Research in Educational Leadership). Rutgers, NJ: Center for Educational Policy Analysis and American Educational Research Association.

Leithwood, K. A., Steinbach, R., & Jantzi, D. (2002). School leadership and teachers' motivation to implement accountability policies. *Educational Administration Quarterly, 38*(1), 94–119.

LeMahieu, P. G., & Roy, P. A. (1997). Through a lens clearly: A model to guide the instructional leadership of principals. *Urban Education, 31,* 582–608.

Levin, B. (1999). What is educational administration anyway? *Educational Administration Quarterly, 35,* 546–561.

Lezotte, L. W., & Passalacqua, J. (1978). Individual school buildings: Accounting for differences in measured pupil performance. *Urban Education, 13,* 283–293.

Lieberman, A. (Ed.). (1988). *Building a professional culture in schools.* New York: Columbia University, Teachers College Press.

Louis, K. S. (1992). Restructuring and the problem of teachers' work. In A. Lieberman (Ed.), *The changing contexts of teaching* (Vol. 1, pp. 138–156). Chicago: National Society for the Study of Education.

Louis, K. S., Toole, J., & Hargreaves, A. (1999). Rethinking school improvement. In J. Murphy & K. S. Louis (Eds.), *Handbook of research on educational administration: A project of the American Educational Research Association* (2nd ed., pp. 251–276). San Francisco: Jossey-Bass.

Marks, H. M., & Printy, S. M. (2003). Principal leadership and school performance: An integration of transformational and instructional leadership. *Educational Administration Quarterly, 39,* 370–397.

Miller, K. (2003, November). *School, teacher, and leadership impacts on student achievement* (policy brief). Aurora, CO: Mid-continent Regional Education Lab.

Murphy, J., & Louis, K. S. (Eds.). (1999). *Handbook of research on educational administration: A project of the American Educational Research Association* (2nd ed.). San Francisco: Jossey-Bass.

National Center for Effective Schools Research and Development. (1989). *A conversation between James Comer and Ronald Edmonds: Fundamentals of effective school improvement.* Madison, WI: Author.

Ogawa, R. T., Goldring, E. B., & Conley, S. (2000). Organizing the field to improve research on educational administration. *Educational Administration Quarterly, 36,* 340–357.

Pitner, N. (1988). The study of administrator effects and effectiveness. In N. J. Boyan (Ed.), *Handbook of research on educational administration: A project of the American Educational Research Association* (pp. 99–122). New York: Longman.

Pounder, D. G. (Ed.). (2000a). Research and inquiry in educational administration: A call for quality and utility. *Educational Administration Quarterly, 36,* 336–339.

Pounder, D. G. (2000b). A discussion of the task force's collective findings. *Educational Administration Quarterly, 36,* 465–473.

Prawat, R. S., & Peterson, P. L. (1999). Social constructivist views of learning. In J. Murphy & K. S. Louis (Eds.), *Handbook of research on educational administration: A project of the American Educational Research Association* (2nd ed., pp. 203–226). San Francisco: Jossey-Bass.

Purkey, S. C., & Smith, M. S. (1983). Effective schools: A review. *Elementary School Journal, 83,* 427–452.

Ribbins, P., & Gunter, H. (2002). Mapping leadership studies in education: Towards a typology of knowledge domains. *Educational Management and Administration, 30,* 359–385.

Rowan, B., & Miskel, C. G. (1999). Institutional theory and the study of educational organizations. In J. Murphy & K. S. Louis (Eds.), *Handbook of Research on Educational Administration* (2nd ed., pp. 359–383). San Francisco: Jossey-Bass.

Shavelson, R. J., & Towne, L. (Eds.). (2002). *Scientific research in education.* Washington, DC: National Academy Press.

Smylie, M. A., & Hart, A. W. (1999). School leadership for teacher learning and change: A human and social capital development perspective. In J. Murphy & K. S. Louis (Eds.), *Handbook of research on educational administration: A project of the American Educational Research Association* (2nd ed., pp. 421–441). San Francisco: Jossey-Bass.

Sykes, G. (1999). The "new professionalism" in education: An appraisal. In J. Murphy & K. S. Louis (Eds.), *Handbook of research on educational administration: A project of the American Educational Research Association* (2nd ed., pp. 227–249). San Francisco: Jossey-Bass.

Towne, L., Wise, L. L., & Winters, T. (2005). *Advancing scientific research in education.* Washington, DC: National Academy Press.

Tyack, D. B., & Hansot, E. (1982). *Managers of virtue: Public school leadership in America, 1820–1980.* New York: Basic Books.

Waters, T., & Grubb, S. (2004). *The leadership we need: Using research to strengthen the use of standards for administrator preparation and licensure programs.* Aurora, CO: Mid-continent Regional Education Laboratory.

Waters, T., Marzano, R. J., & McNulty, B. (2003). *Balanced leadership: What 30 years of research tells us about the effect of leadership on student achievement.* Aurora, CO: Midcontinent Regional Education Laboratory.

Wheatley, M. J. (2002, September). Spirituality in turbulent times. *School Administrator Web Edition.* Retrieved April 2, 2004, from www .aasa.org/publications/sa/2002_9/wheatley .htm

Young, M. D., & Creighton, T. (2002). Who is framing the national understanding of educational leadership preparation and practice? *Leadership and Policy in Schools, 1,* 222–241.

14

SOCIALIZATION OF STUDENTS IN HIGHER EDUCATION

Organizational Perspectives

JOHN C. WEIDMAN

University of Pittsburgh

In their recently published book reviewing research that appeared during the 1990s, Pascarella and Terenzini (2005, chap. 2) continued the pattern established in their previous volume (Pascarella & Terenzini, 1991, chap. 2) of identifying two broad clusters of conceptual frameworks that are important for understanding change in college students: developmental theories and college impact models. Developmental models of student change address "the nature, structure, and processes of individual human growth. They focus primarily on the nature and content of *intra*individual change, although interpersonal experiences are often salient components of these models" (Pascarella & Terenzini, 2005, p. 18, emphasis in original).

College impact models of student change focus more "on the environmental and *inter*individual origins of student change . . . [and] emphasize change associated with the characteristics of the institutions students attend (between-college effects) or with the experiences students have while enrolled (within-college effects)" (Pascarella & Terenzini, 2005, p. 18, emphasis in original). College impact frameworks may include characteristics of individuals (e.g., gender, ethnicity, socioeconomic status), higher education institutions as organizations (e.g., size, type of control, selectivity, mission, resources), or environment (e.g., academic, social, cultural, or political climate) created by faculty and students on a campus. Developmental and college impact frameworks are not mutually exclusive, and as the following discussion of a particular stream of research within each type suggests, there can be considerable overlap of both conceptions and contributing authors.

This chapter treats the notion of "college impact" under the broad concept of socialization, relying on the classic definition by Brim (1966): "the process by which persons acquire the knowledge, skills, and dispositions that make them more or less effective members of their society" (p. 3). Society is not necessarily a

AUTHOR'S NOTE: Helpful comments on an earlier draft of this chapter were provided by Kenneth A. Feldman and Laura W. Perna.

unitary construct given that individuals are normally thought of as participating in multiple social groups and structures (e.g., families, peer groups, occupations, organizations) simultaneously, each presenting more or less discrete and distinct expectations for their behavior (Clausen, 1968, p. 4). Hence, socialization can be thought of as having both individual (cognitive developmental) and organizational (affective interpersonal) dimensions linked through patterns of acquisition and maintenance of memberships and participation in salient groups (Weidman, 1989, p. 294). Organizational aspects of socialization are the focus of this chapter because their design and modification of an institution's social and material structure are more under the control of colleges and universities than are personality characteristics of students and, hence, are more "policy relevant" in the sense of broad usefulness for institutional reform (p. 290).

The two volumes by Pascarella and Terenzini (1991, 2005) are encyclopedic in their coverage, and interested readers are referred to their work for comprehensive inventories of research studies. Although Pascarella and Terenzini (1991, 2005) provide excellent descriptions of the developmental and college impact streams of research, their discussion of research tends not to link results to theoretical and conceptual implications. Rather, both books are organized in terms of types of outcomes. Hence, in the current chapter, two streams of research having particularly sophisticated conceptual underpinnings as well as rigorous research methods have been identified for emphasis.

The first research stream (Feldman, Ethington, & Smart, 2001; Feldman, Smart, & Ethington, 1999, 2004; Smart, 1997; Smart & Feldman, 1998; Smart, Feldman, & Ethington, 2000) is grounded in the developmental perspective of person–environment interaction (Pace, 1979; Stern, 1970), as reflected in the work on the psychology of vocational choice and the typology of academic environments developed by Holland (1966, 1997). Focusing on the socialization of students in academic majors, the research reflecting this perspective extends the framework by incorporating the broader, more sociological orientation championed by Feldman (1972; see also Feldman & Newcomb, 1969). This extension suggests

important parallels between the more psychologically and more socioculturally oriented frameworks that are addressed in a systematic comparison of college impact models.

The second research stream is grounded in a college impact perspective, as reflected in organizational sociology (Antonio, 2004, Berger & Milem, 2000b; Carter, 1999; Tierney, 1997; Weidman, 1989). It focuses on the socializing impacts of institutional diversity, especially the diversity of peer groups, in higher education.

ACADEMIC ENVIRONMENTS AND STUDENT SOCIALIZATION

Academic Disciplines (Smart et al., 2000) presents a thorough and convincing empirical study of certain effects of academic majors on students during college that is grounded in the theory of career choice developed by Holland (1966, 1997). The authors' rationale for the study is described as follows:

> Holland's theory is basically a theory of person–environment fit, based on the assumption that there are six personality types and six analogous academic environments and that educational persistence, satisfaction, and achievement of students are functions of the congruence or fit between students and their academic environments. Thus, if one wants to know more about what colleges and universities might do to facilitate the retention, satisfaction, and learning of their students, then one must understand the inherent diversity of academic disciplines and the distinctive academic environments that their respective faculties create. (p. 2)

After empirically validating the theoretical typology of academic environments for faculty (using data from the 1989 Carnegie study of the American professoriate) and students (using data from the 1986 freshman survey and a 1990 follow-up conducted by the Higher Education Research Institute at the University of California, Los Angeles [UCLA], Smart and colleagues (2000) systematically test the Holland model. They focus on three underlying assumptions of the Holland model: *self-selection,* where students choose academic environments compatible with their personality types; *socialization,* where academic environments reinforce and reward different talents; and *congruence,* where people flourish in environments congruent with their personality types (pp. 51–54). Longitudinal data from 2,309 students who were enrolled in the same 4-year college in 1986 and 1990 were used in the analysis of change due to Holland environments. Dependent variables in the change analysis were scales reflecting ability and interest in each of four personality orientations: Investigative (self-ratings on intellectual self-confidence, possessing academic and mathematical ability, having drive to achieve, making a theoretical contribution to science), Artistic (self-ratings on artistic and writing ability, becoming accomplished in one of the performing arts, writing original works, creating artistic work, developing a meaningful philosophy of life), Social (influencing the political structure, influencing social values, helping others who are having difficulties, becoming involved in programs to clean up the environment, participating in a community action program, helping to promote racial understanding), and Enterprising (having leadership ability, being popular, displaying social self-confidence, becoming an authority in one's field, obtaining recognition from colleagues for contributions to one's special field, having administrative responsibility for the work of others, being very well-off financially, being successful in a business of one's own, becoming an expert on finance and commerce) (pp. 66–67).

All analyses employ appropriate statistical adjustments to control for any underlying problems with the data as well as for relevant student characteristics such as gender. Smart and colleagues (2000) also look at differences in outcomes based on whether students were primary recruits (similar disciplines in both surveys) or secondary recruits (dissimilar disciplines) into their academic majors.

Results generally support the self-selection assumption, but with some gender differences. Both the socialization and congruence assumptions are also supported, but with some differences by gender and major field. Smart and colleagues (2000) conclude their book by discussing the importance of theoretically based schemes for classifying important dimensions of academic environments as well as for understanding more fully student learning, patterns of change and stability in college students, alternative schemas for curriculum design, and organizational diversity.

Overall, the presentations of findings and their implications in *Academic Disciplines* are far too rich for a brief review to do them justice. Of particular importance, however, is Smart and colleagues' (2000) discussion of the differences in knowledge gained about college impact by research drawing from psychological models focusing primarily on individual learning and cognitive development as opposed to those drawing from sociological and anthropological models focusing primarily on social, organizational, and cultural processes affecting both cognitive and affective outcomes of college. They are careful not to pit one conceptual approach against the other, but they do recommend future research that would extend this particular study by drawing on other, more sociologically oriented conceptual frameworks.

Certainly, the outcomes of interest (e.g., cognitive vs. affective, knowledge vs. values) play a strong part in determining the conceptual approach that is likely to be taken in research. The stakeholders being served also influence the conceptual approach being used. Student affairs professionals responsible for residential and co-curricular programming might be better served by more sociologically oriented studies of how various types of group and organizational activities might facilitate student integration into college, whereas professors concerned with having students develop knowledge of their disciplines might be better served by more psychologically oriented studies of teaching and student learning. Of course, context is always a factor no matter what the outcomes of interest are.

The work reflected in Smart and colleagues' (2000) book also serves an important heuristic function—Feldman and colleagues (1999), written while the book was in progress and containing findings addressed in Chapter 7; Feldman and colleagues (2001), written immediately after publication of the book and including a more comprehensive framework for Chapter 8 as well as a test for statistical significance; and Feldman and colleagues (2004), written after publication of the book and including data and interpretations comparing experiences and involvement of noncongruent and congruent students in their colleges. The most recently published article (Feldman et al., 2004) concludes with the assertion that the results from the book and related articles reflect a much stronger socialization effect of students' experiences in an academic major over the course of college than does previous research that placed more emphasis on psychological effects of self-selection. Feldman and colleagues (2004) argue that further research should pay closer attention to understanding the organizational and interpersonal dynamics of academic environments in higher education, particularly those reflected in the Weidman (1989) framework for understanding undergraduate socialization:

> Weidman's is one of the rare higher education models that explicitly incorporates academic environments (i.e., departments), and his discussion of the components of the normative contexts and socialization processes of academic environments and institutions could provide substantial assistance in understanding similarities and differences in exactly how the disparate academic environments in Holland's theory seek to socialize students to their respective norms and values. (Feldman et al., 2004, pp. 548–549)

Of course, there are other frameworks that have been used even more widely for the study of college impact. Given the apparent overlap of conceptions and approaches to the study of college impact, it is instructive to identify similar elements among models as applied to understanding the process of student socialization. The next section presents a conceptual framework illustrating analogous constructs that appear in different models. The chapter then concludes with a description of two lines of research that use an organizational perspective grounded in the work of Tinto (1975, 1993) and Weidman (1989) for studying peer group influence and the effects of diversity in higher education.

MODELS OF COLLEGE IMPACT: COMMON THEMES

Figure 14.1 shows a general framework for socialization in higher education that incorporates major elements of college impact models of student change developed in the work of four authors (Astin, 1970a, 1970b, 1991, 1993; Pascarella, 1985; Tinto, 1975, 1993; Weidman, 1989; Weidman, Twale, & Stein, 2001) discussed by Pascarella and Terenzini (1991, pp. 50–58; 2005, pp. 52–60). The figure includes central concepts from each framework and encompasses additional constructs suggested by research on graduate and professional students (Weidman & Stein, 2003; Weidman et al., 2001). Elements that are parallel conceptually across frameworks are also identified. Dotted lines are used to suggest that boundaries across dimensions are permeable rather than fixed.

On its horizontal axis, the model shown in Figure 14.1 reflects a basic inputs–environment–outcomes (I–E–O) structure that parallels what is described by Astin (1970a, 1970b, 1991). It is worthy of note that Astin, whose orientation is primarily psychological, also had a hand in the development of the Holland typology of majors and careers (Astin & Holland, 1961). The I–E–O structure is shared by human capital theory in economics (Becker, 1975) and status attainment theory in sociology (Sewell, Haller, & Portes, 1969). The student *inputs* to higher education are family background, beliefs and values (predispositions to influence), and prior academic preparation. *Environment* represents the organizational structures and institutional culture with which students interact. Following Weidman (1989), the model suggests that socialization occurs through processes of interpersonal interaction, learning, and social integration (Tinto, 1975, 1993) that link students with salient normative environments in higher education. Socialization *outcomes* are the resultant changes (values, beliefs, and knowledge) that occur in students. In arguing for the use of an ecological model of college impact for the study of peer culture, Renn and Arnold (2003) provide a particularly good analysis of conceptual similarities and differences between the models of Weidman and Tinto.

The bottom lines in Figure 14.1 highlight four main stages of the socialization process that can be assumed to occur during the period when students are enrolled in higher education institutions and that continue as they move into professional careers. Although socialization is construed as a temporal process, the distinct stages do not necessarily occur in a strict

Inputs
Anticipatory

Environment
Interactive Stages of Socialization:
Formal, Informal

Outcomes
Personal

Figure 14.1   Conceptualizing Organizational Socialization of Students in Higher Education

SOURCE: Adapted from Weidman, Twale, & Stein, *Socialization of Graduate and Professional Students in Higher Education: A Perilous Passage?* ASHE–ERIC Higher Education. © 2001. Reprinted with permission of John Wiley & Sons, Inc.

sequence but rather are interactive with movement in both directions (Thornton & Nardi, 1975). Prior to their entry into a higher education institution, students *anticipate* what might occur based on prior experience but incomplete knowledge. During their passage through academic programs, students encounter the normative influences of peers and faculty in both *formal* and *informal* settings (e.g., majors, peer groups, co-curricular activities), ultimately *personalizing* those experiences by either changing or maintaining perspectives held at entrance to higher education at either the undergraduate or graduate level. Students are influenced in

various ways, particularly through learning (Pascarella, 1985) or *knowledge acquisition,* again via both formal instruction and informal interaction with faculty and peers. The processes are reflected by *involvement* (Astin, 1984) in both the formal and informal structures of college *environments. Engagement* (Kuh, Schuh, Whitt, & Associates, 1991; Zhao, Kuh, & Carini, 2005) occurs as students develop attachments to persons and *environments* within higher education institutions.

Involvement and *engagement* are also fundamental dimensions of *integration* (Tinto, 1975, 1993) into the social and academic spheres as well as personal *investment* into what each sphere represents. These *investments* result in particular *outcomes,* notably *knowledge, skills,* and *dispositions,* including *commitment* to institutions (Tinto, 1975, 1993), careers, and other personal orientations that also shape individual *identity* along a variety of dimensions. The notions of *investment, involvement,* and *engagement* also appear in the "college impress model" of Pace (1979, p. 126). In the Pace framework, *involvement* is reflected in the "amount, scope, and quality" of effort that students invest (p. 127).

Finally, Figure 14.1 includes a vertical dimension that reflects the importance of communities external to higher education institutions for student socialization. Colleges and universities are not, after all, encapsulated environments. *Professional communities,* for example, have important influence on the curriculum in higher education through the promulgation of standards for professional practice and licensure. Accreditation agencies play a similar role at both the institutional and academic program levels. *Personal communities* represent significant others with whom students continue to be in contact throughout the time they are enrolled in higher education. Reference groups, both within and external to higher education institutions, can also influence change and stability in students.

Personal and professional communities often provide strong normative contexts for human social behavior. Figure 14.1 shows them as external to the higher education institutions, but they may also spill over. Normative contexts are fundamental parts of a higher education institution's organizational structure and, as such, play a key role in the socialization of students.

ORGANIZATIONAL SOCIALIZATION IN HIGHER EDUCATION

One of the most influential lines of research on organizational impacts of higher education is reflected in the work of Vreeland and Bidwell (1965, 1966; see also Bidwell & Vreeland, 1963). They use the classic essay by Parsons (1959) as the starting point for arguing that organizational units of colleges can serve as climates for the

technical (acquisition of knowledge and skills) and moral (acquisition of values, beliefs, and commitments) socialization of students. They apply this framework to the classification of both residences (Harvard houses) and academic departments, showing that these units vary both in the emphases of members (faculty and students) on technical and moral dimensions of socialization and in their corresponding impacts on students' values and attitudes. More recently, Hermanowicz (2005) shows how conceptions of institutional culture manifested by members can be useful in classifying departments according to their normative climates represented along three dimensions: elite, pluralist, and communitarian. These two approaches are alternatives to the Holland typology, but they share an emphasis on the importance of organizational structure and normative dimensions of academic majors for understanding student outcomes.

Berger and Milem (2000b) provide a particularly insightful discussion of organizational approaches to the study of college student outcomes. Drawing from the Tinto and Weidman models, as well as from other relevant literature on organizational sociology and college impact, Berger and Milem present a comprehensive review of literature leading to a conceptual model of organizational impact on student outcomes. Structural–demographic features of organizations (e.g., size, control, selectivity, Carnegie type, location) and a typology of organizational behavior (e.g., bureaucratic, collegial, political, symbolic, systemic) are also included. These authors emphasize the importance of the peer group as an important mediator of organizational influences in higher education in that peer groups serve as a locus of personal, behavioral, and structural influences. They also use their framework to assess change related to participation in various types of higher education institutions, including historically black colleges and universities (Berger, 2000; Berger & Milem, 2000a). In fact, the types of organizational perspectives reflected in this work permeate other analyses of issues related to improving campus climates for racial/ethnic diversity in higher education (e.g., Hurtado, Milem, Clayton-Pedersen, & Allen, 1999).

Two other recent studies related to issues of diversity in higher education draw on the foregoing models of college impact and suggest particularly fruitful lines of research. Carter (1999) uses the data set from the Beginning Postsecondary Students (BPS) project (1990/1992) to investigate effects of individual and institutional characteristics, student experiences, and financial aid on African American and white college students' degree aspirations. The main theoretical foundations for this study (pp. 20, 22) are sociological models of status attainment (Sewell et al., 1969) and undergraduate socialization (Weidman, 1989). Using multiple regression techniques, Carter (1999) finds many similarities between the two groups of students such as the positive effects on degree aspirations of their mother's education, their degree aspirations prior to entering college, and the size and type (e.g., 4-year) of institution. There are also notable differences such as intellectual self-confidence (positive for whites, negative for African Americans), faculty contact (positive for African Americans), percentage of African American enrollment at the institution (positive for African Americans), and peer contact (positive for whites). Effects of financial aid on students' degree expectations were not significant. Carter concludes,

> The socializing influences on students' degree aspirations differ within institutions and *between* institutions. Also, the socializing influences on students' degree expectations differ for African-American and white students. Theoretical models of African-American and white students should be tested separately for each group because African-American and white students begin college with different backgrounds, attend different types of institutions, and have different experiences in college. (p. 38, emphasis in original)

Antonio (2001a, 2001b, 2004) presents a related line of empirical research on the influence of peer and friendship groups on a student's educational aspirations and intellectual self-confidence. In the most recent of these studies (Antonio, 2004, pp. 452, 455–456), the research is grounded explicitly in the college impact models of Astin (1984, 1993) and Weidman (1989) as well as in related research on peer influences by Dey (1996, 1997) and Milem (1998). Antonio's (2004) study addresses the effects of the interpersonal environment reflected by the academic abilities and degree aspirations of students' friendship groups on members' intellectual self-confidence and aspirations. It also explores the importance of the diversity of students' best friends for change in these two areas. Longitudinal data for the study came from 2,222 third-year students at UCLA. Three indicators of interaction among students—a primary mechanism of socialization described by Weidman (1989)—are included in the analysis. Variables are entered into the regression equations in blocks reflecting the longitudinal process of college impact specified in the conceptual models underlying the research.

Similar to the findings of Carter (1999), Antonio's (2004) study suggests that "the peer factors that influence students' intellectual self-confidence and degree aspirations operate differentially by race" (p. 464). Furthermore, Antonio argues that the factors producing these "differential patterns of effects on self-concept may originate in the frequently unmeasured interpersonal environment of students" (p. 464). The findings also extend his previous research showing the relationship of the diversity of friendship groups for commitment to racial understanding and diverse interaction outside of friendship groups (Antonio, 2001a), although in the 2001 study friendship group diversity was positively related to intellectual self-confidence only for students of color. Antonio raises interesting questions about these different patterns of effects by race, concluding with a call for both methodological and conceptual elaboration of the research.

The research mentioned in this chapter to this point, although grounded in similar theoretical perspectives, has been empirical. Virtually all of the authors argue, in one way or another, that findings based on quantitative studies could or should be extended by focusing more explicitly on the specific mechanisms of socialization processes through the use of qualitative research techniques. Hence, it seems appropriate to bring in a recent qualitative study co-authored by a long-term contributor to the study of higher education (Kaufman & Feldman, 2004). True to Feldman's persistent plea for the use of sociological approaches as a way of extending the knowledge about college beyond that generated by psychologically oriented research (Feldman, 1972; Feldman & Newcomb, 1969; Feldman et al., 2004), the study by Kaufman and Feldman (2004) describes the dynamics of social interaction among college students that influence the constitution of their newly formed or modified felt identities in the domains of intelligence and knowledgeability, occupation, and cosmopolitanism. This study is based on data from 82 semistructured, open-ended interviews with a randomly selected sample of college students attending a large, diverse public university in a suburban environment approximately 60 miles from a major metropolitan area. The authors describe their objectives in the in-depth interviews as follows:

> We were particularly interested in students' interpretation of their experiences in college, how they saw themselves in comparison with other individuals, groups, and categories (social comparisons), and how they believed others viewed them. . . . In the context of a semistructured interview, respondents were able to be reflexive, to challenge their own taken-for-granted notions, and to elaborate on their newly constructed felt identities. Without allowing students to express their felt identities and place them in an appropriate context, researchers may overlook some of the nuances of the college experience and its consequences for the individual. (p. 468)

Kaufman and Feldman's (2004) carefully crafted study describes the feelings reported by students about their experiences with peers and others in the college environment that are perceived to have influenced the students' perceptions of themselves in the intellectual and occupational domains. It identifies college-sponsored, but off-campus, experiences such as studying abroad that affirm the importance of noncollege peers for socialization in higher education. The research suggests elements of anticipatory socialization in that the students describe developing symbolic commitments to professional occupations and careers. It also describes how students expand their horizons, moving toward more cosmopolitan views of the world through their negotiation of interaction with students who encompass social worlds very different from those to which they had been

accustomed prior to their university experience. Throughout their article, the authors focus their interpretation of results on exploring "the extent to which the social environment impacts the formation of individual felt identity" rather than "how students do or do not 'develop' in college" (p. 490). In so doing, Kaufman and Feldman conclude that there is considerable variability in student change during college and that change in one domain may overlap with change in another domain. They also argue that the college "charter" or mission can be a particularly important, but difficult-to-measure, source of influence, a finding supported by the work of Pike, Kuh, and Gonyea (2003) and Hermanowicz (2005).

In short, socialization processes are complex, can be complementary, and vary according to both individual characteristics and the variety of students' experiences within higher education institutions. Furthermore, as Figure 14.1 illustrates, conceptual approaches to the study of socialization in higher education institutions as organizations share commonalities across disciplines and frameworks. Hence, it is reasonable to expect that research in this area should reflect both broadly based conceptual grounding and rigorous methodological approaches to elaborate, extend, and expand our knowledge of socialization in higher education. Far too often, studies merely pay lip service to conceptual models and wind up addressing a very limited set of variables and failing to draw implications for the models when discussing results. Paying attention to stakeholders in research, whether academic or not, can also provide important clues about the types of conceptual frameworks (and their disciplinary underpinnings), as well as the types and targets of resulting recommendations, that might be used.

References

Antonio, A. L. (2001a). Diversity and the influence of friendship groups in college. *Review of Higher Education, 25*(1), 63–89.

Antonio, A. L. (2001b). The role of interracial interaction in the development of leadership skills and cultural knowledge and understanding. *Research in Higher Education, 42,* 593–617.

Antonio, A. L. (2004). The influence of friendship groups on intellectual self-confidence and educational aspirations in college. *Journal of Higher Education, 75,* 446–471.

Astin, A. W. (1970a). The methodology of research on college impact (part 1). *Sociology of Education, 43,* 223–254.

Astin, A. W. (1970b). The methodology of research on college impact (part 2). *Sociology of Education, 43,* 437–450.

Astin, A. W. (1984). Student involvement: A developmental theory for higher education. *Journal of College Student Personnel, 25,* 297–308.

Astin, A. W. (1991). *Assessment for excellence: The philosophy and practice of assessment and evaluation of higher education.* New York: Macmillan.

Astin, A. W. (1993). *What matters in college? Four critical years revisited.* San Francisco: Jossey-Bass.

Astin, A. W., & Holland, J. L. (1961). The environmental assessment technique: A way to measure college environments. *Journal of Educational Psychology, 52,* 308–316.

Becker, G. S. (1975). *Human capital: A theoretical and empirical analysis, with special reference to education.* Chicago: University of Chicago Press.

Berger, J. B. (2000). Organizational behavior at colleges and student outcomes: A new perspective on college impact. *Review of Higher Education, 23*(2), 177–198.

Berger, J. B., & Milem, J. F. (2000a). Exploring the impact of historically black colleges in promoting the development of undergraduates' self-concept. *Journal of College Student Development, 41,* 381–394.

Berger, J. B., & Milem, J. F. (2000b). Organizational behavior in higher education and student outcomes. In J. C. Smart (Ed.), *Higher education: Handbook of theory and research* (Vol. 15, pp. 268–338). New York: Agathon.

Bidwell, C. E., & Vreeland, R. E. (1963). College education and moral orientations: An organizational approach. *Administrative Science Quarterly, 8,* 166–191.

Brim, O. G., Jr. (1966). Socialization through the life cycle. In O. G. Brim, Jr., & S. Wheeler (Eds.), *Socialization after childhood: Two essays* (pp. 1–49). New York: John Wiley.

Carter, D. F. (1999). The impact of institutional choice and environments on African-American and white students' degree expectations. *Research in Higher Education, 40,* 17–41.

Clausen, J. A. (1968). Introduction. In J. A. Clausen (Ed.), *Socialization and society* (pp. 1–17). Boston: Little, Brown.

Dey, E. L. (1996). Undergraduate political attitudes: An examination of peer, faculty, and social influences. *Research in Higher Education, 37,* 535–554.

Dey, E. L. (1997). Undergraduate political attitudes: Peer influence in changing social contexts. *Journal of Higher Education, 68,* 398–413.

Feldman, K. A. (1972). Some theoretical approaches to the study of change and stability of college students. *Review of Educational Research, 42*(1), 1–26.

Feldman, K. A., Ethington, C. A., & Smart, J. C. (2001). A further investigation of major field and person–environment fit: Sociological versus psychological interpretations of Holland's theory. *Journal of Higher Education, 72,* 670–698.

Feldman, K. A., & Newcomb, T. N. (1969). *The impact of college on students.* San Francisco: Jossey-Bass.

Feldman, K. A., Smart, J. C., & Ethington, C. A. (1999). Major field and person–environment fit: Using Holland's theory to study change and stability of college students. *Journal of Higher Education, 70,* 642–669.

Feldman, K. A., Smart, J. C., & Ethington, C. A. (2004). What do college students have to lose? Exploring the outcomes of differences in person–environment fits. *Journal of Higher Education, 75,* 528–555.

Hermanowicz, J. C. (2005). Classifying universities and their departments: A social world perspective. *Journal of Higher Education, 76,* 26–55.

Holland, J. L. (1966). *The psychology of vocational choice: A theory of personality types and model environments.* Waltham, MA: Blaisdell.

Holland, J. L. (1997). *Making vocational choices: A theory of vocational personalities and work environments* (3rd ed.). Odessa, FL: Psychological Assessment Resources.

Hurtado, S., Milem, J., Clayton-Pedersen, A., & Allen, W. (1999). *Enacting diverse learning environments: Improving the climate for racial/ethnic diversity in higher education* (ASHE–ERIC Higher Education Report, Vol. 26, No. 8). Washington, DC: George Washington University,

Graduate School of Education and Human Development.

Kaufman, P., & Feldman, K. A. (2004). Forming identities in college: A sociological approach. *Research in Higher Education, 45,* 463–496.

Kuh, G. D., Schuh, J. S., Whitt, E. J., & Associates. (1991). *Involving colleges: Successful approaches to fostering student learning and personal development outside the classroom.* San Francisco: Jossey-Bass.

Milem, J. F. (1998). Attitude change in college students: Examining the effect of college peer groups and faculty normative groups. *Journal of Higher Education, 69*(2), 117–140.

Pace, C. R. (1979). *Measuring outcomes of college.* San Francisco: Jossey-Bass.

Parsons, T. (1959). The school class as a social system: Some of its functions in American society. *Harvard Educational Review, 29,* 297–318.

Pascarella, E. T. (1985). College environment influences on learning and cognitive development. In J. C. Smart (Ed.), *Higher education: Handbook of theory and research* (Vol. 1, pp. 1–61). New York: Agathon.

Pascarella, E. T., & Terenzini, P. T. (1991). *How college affects students.* San Francisco: Jossey-Bass.

Pascarella, E. T., & Terenzini, P. T. (2005). *How college affects students,* Vol. 2: *A third decade of research.* San Francisco: Jossey-Bass.

Pike, G. R., Kuh, G. D., & Gonyea, R. M. (2003). The relationship between institutional mission and students' involvement and educational outcomes. *Research in Higher Education, 44,* 241–261.

Renn, K. A., & Arnold, K. D. (2003). Reconceptualizing research on college student peer culture. *Journal of Higher Education, 74,* 261–291.

Sewell, W. H., Haller, A. O., & Portes, A. (1969). The educational and early occupational attainment process. *American Sociological Review, 34,* 82–92.

Smart, J. C. (1997). Academic subenvironments and differential patterns of self-perceived growth during college: A test of Holland's theory. *Journal of College Student Development, 38*(1), 68–78.

Smart, J. C., & Feldman, K. A. (1998). "Accentuation effects" of dissimilar academic departments: An application and exploration of Holland's theory. *Research in Higher Education, 39,* 385–418.

Smart, J. C., Feldman, K. A., & Ethington, C. A. (2000). *Academic disciplines: Holland's theory and the study of college students and faculty.* Nashville, TN: Vanderbilt University Press.

Stern, G. C. (1970). *People in context: Measuring person–environment congruence in education and industry.* New York: John Wiley.

Thornton, R., & Nardi, P. M. (1975). The dynamics of role acquisition. *American Journal of Sociology, 80,* 870–885.

Tierney, W. G. (1997). Organizational socialization in higher education. *Journal of Higher Education, 68*(1), 1–16.

Tinto, V. (1975). Dropout from higher education: A theoretical synthesis of recent research. *Review of Educational Research, 45,* 89–125.

Tinto, V. (1993). *Leaving college: Rethinking the causes and cures of student attrition* (2nd ed.). Chicago: University of Chicago Press.

Vreeland, R. S., & Bidwell, C. E. (1965). Organizational effects on student attitudes: A study of the Harvard houses. *Sociology of Education, 38,* 233–250.

Vreeland, R. S., & Bidwell, C. E. (1966). Classifying university departments: An approach to the analysis of their effects upon undergraduates' values and attitudes. *Sociology of Education, 39,* 237–254.

Weidman, J. C. (1989). Undergraduate socialization: A conceptual approach. In J. C. Smart (Ed.), *Higher education: Handbook of theory and research* (Vol. 5, pp. 289–322). New York: Agathon.

Weidman, J. C., & Stein, E. L. (2003). Socialization of graduate students to academic norms. *Research in Higher Education, 44,* 641–656.

Weidman, J. C., Twale, D. J., & Stein, E. L. (2001). *Socialization of graduate and professional students in higher education: A perilous passage?* (ASHE–ERIC Higher Education Report, Vol. 28, No. 3). San Francisco: Jossey-Bass.

Zhao, C.-M., Kuh, G. D., & Carini, R. M. (2005). A comparison of international student and American student engagement in effective educational practices. *Journal of Higher Education, 76,* 209–231.

15

MINORITY-SERVING INSTITUTIONS OF HIGHER EDUCATION

Building On and Extending Lines of Inquiry for the Advancement of the Public Good

JASON N. JOHNSON

University of Wisconsin–Madison

CLIFTON F. CONRAD

University of Wisconsin–Madison

LAURA W. PERNA

University of Pennsylvania

Minority-serving institutions (MSIs)—colleges and universities identified for their commitment to serving individuals historically underrepresented in higher education—contribute substantially to the public good. Adding to the diversity of institution types and increasing the diversity of the student population, MSIs strengthen two hallmarks of life and learning in the United States: choice and opportunity. Yet relatively little scholarship has focused on these institutions. In this chapter, we argue that contemporary scholars have an extraordinary opportunity to build on, and substantially extend, the extant literature on MSIs. In so doing, we believe that researchers can develop a deeper understanding of the

contributions made by MSIs and, in turn, influence policy and practice to continue the advancement of higher education and the public good writ large.

This chapter advances three lines of inquiry related to MSIs. We articulate how each line represents a promising approach to inquiry and suggest ways in which each may be pushed further during the coming years. The three lines of inquiry that serve as organizing questions for this chapter are as follows:

1. What are the individual and societal benefits of MSIs?

2. What policies and practices can contribute to attracting, retaining, and enhancing the

educational experiences of other-race students in MSIs?

3. What might predominantly white institutions (PWIs) learn from MSIs about "best practices" for supporting and enhancing the education of all students?

Each of these questions has connections to existing research and, in our view, has great potential for meaningful future scholarship related to MSIs. After briefly discussing why we believe that these questions can lead to research findings that are relevant to the needs of multiple stakeholders, we provide an overview of MSIs and their categorizations, with some cautionary notes about making sense of their similarities and differences. Following this synopsis, we explicate each of the three lines of inquiry.

Research along these three lines of inquiry can be meaningful, at least in part, because it would address the needs and concerns of multiple stakeholders, including individual students and their families, institutional leaders, and public policymakers. Despite the fact that the higher education student population has become increasingly diverse during recent generations, historically underrepresented students continue to be, well, underrepresented (National Center for Education Statistics [NCES], 2004). Consequently, gaps in higher education opportunity contribute to increasing economic and societal stratification in our society. To identify policies and practices that can significantly improve higher education access, retention, and success for underrepresented groups of students, leaders of both MSIs and PWIs need more knowledge and perspective that is anchored in rigorous relevant research. In spite of this great need, existing research is not sufficient for guiding such action.

A better understanding of MSIs also must be developed to inform public policy. Recognizing the important role that MSIs play in expanding higher education to populations that have not been well served by American higher education institutions and the challenges that often limit the availability of resources at MSIs, the federal government targets several sources of funds to these institutions. MSIs may be eligible for institutional grants through programs such as the Strengthening Institutions Program (Title III of the Higher Education Act of 1965), the Developing Hispanic-Serving Institutions Program (Title V of the Higher Education Act), and the Tribally Controlled College or University Assistance Act of 1978 (administered by the Bureau of Indian Affairs). During an era of restricted public financial resources and growing demands for accountability, continued and additional availability of federal and state financial support may rest, at least in part, on policymakers' understandings of the contributions that MSIs make to the public good.

BACKGROUNDS OF MSIs: RECOGNIZING THE SIMILARITIES, UNDERSTANDING THE DIFFERENCES

Understanding the different ways in which MSIs are defined, categorized, and organized is challenging, not least because the identities of colleges and universities are shaped by institutions themselves, by their students, by their communities, and by associated agencies and organizations. The U.S. Department of Education's Office for Civil Rights (OCR) publishes basic descriptive statistics related to MSIs using data from NCES's Integrated Postsecondary Education Data System (IPEDS). OCR's reports are informed by, and responsive to, a collection of federal statutes that have created and/or provided guidelines for recognition of MSIs. As such, OCR's approach is centered in a legal or bureaucratic framework for viewing MSIs. Several regional and national professional organizations that are dedicated to supporting MSIs offer their own definitions and participant lists, but these are not always aligned with those of OCR. To establish a general sense of the roles that MSIs play in American postsecondary education, we begin with an overview of the perspective provided by OCR. We then briefly describe each MSI type as defined by OCR, guided throughout by understandings communicated by the regional and national associations that represent each type of institution.

OCR may designate an institution as belonging in one or more of the following categories: minority postsecondary institutions (MPIs), historically black colleges and universities (HBCUs), Hispanic-serving institutions (HSIs), tribal colleges and universities (TCUs), and Alaska Native- or Native Hawaiian-serving institutions (AHIs). In broad strokes, MPIs are institutions in which a single minority group or combination of minority groups comprises at least 50% of the student population. The MPI and other MSI categories overlap substantially but not completely. More than 300 institutions, or about one third of all MSIs, do not meet the criteria for being an MPI; at these MSIs, fewer than 50% of the students are minorities. The remaining MSIs are designated as both MPIs and either HBCUs, HSIs, TCUs, or AHIs.

Mirroring the characteristics of colleges and universities nationwide, OCR's list of designated MSIs reflects the diversity of the nation's higher education system. MSIs include institutions that are public and private, 2-year and 4-year, single-sex and coeducational, and religious and secular. Although the vast majority of MSIs are not-for-profit institutions, a few are for-profit institutions (e.g., ITT Technical Institute of Tucson, AZ, an HSI).

In fall 2002, OCR (2004) recognized 737 MSIs located in 43 states and 81 MSIs located in 7 U.S. territories and outlying areas. These 818 MSIs accounted for approximately 17% of the more than 4,200 colleges and universities in operation throughout the United States and its territories and surrounding areas. These numbers take on new meanings and expanded complexities when illuminated within each type of identity-specific MSI.

Background: Historically Black Colleges and Universities

HBCUs not only have the longest and most well-documented history among MSIs but also are, arguably, the most contentious. The first HBCU was founded in 1837 (then the Institute for Colored Youth, now Cheyney University), and the majority of HBCUs were established during the 40 years after the Civil War. Reflecting the mores of the time, these institutions were established in large measure through the ingenuity and leadership of a relative few against the widely shared sentiment among the white majority to maintain their dominance in social and economic life. The second Morrill Land Grant Act of 1890, which mandated that states receiving federal funds for land grant institutions must either open their postsecondary institutions to black students or create separate land grant institutions for blacks, was critical to the establishment of more than a dozen HBCUs.

Black colleges and universities established firm roots in both cities and rural areas throughout the first half of the 20th century, often initially as 2-year colleges. Not infrequently, these institutions were located in geographical proximity to PWIs. Black colleges and universities were officially designated as HBCUs under the authorizing legislation of the Higher Education Act. The amended Higher Education Act of 1965 (1998) defined an HBCU as an accredited college or university that was established prior to 1964 and "whose principal mission was, and is, the education of black Americans."

In fall 2002, there were 103 HBCUs located in 20 states, the District of Columbia, and the Virgin Islands (OCR, 2004). Although 1 HBCU is located in Michigan, 3 HBCUs are located in the District of Columbia, and 1 HBCU is located in the Virgin Islands, all other HBCUs are located in 19 southern and southern border states: Alabama, Arkansas, Delaware, Florida, Georgia, Kentucky, Louisiana, Maryland, Mississippi, Missouri, North Carolina, Ohio, Oklahoma, Pennsylvania, South Carolina, Tennessee, Texas, Virginia, and West Virginia. Nearly half ($n = 48$) of the 103 HBCUs are private 4-year institutions, 40% ($n = 41$) are public 4-year institutions, 11% ($n = 11$) are public 2-year institutions, and 3% ($n = 3$) are private 2-year institutions (NCES, 2004). HBCUs include 19 land grant institutions as well as single-sex institutions, professional schools, liberal arts colleges, and research universities (Provasnik, Shafer, & Snyder, 2004).

Founded in 1969 by several presidents of HBCUs, the National Association for Equal Opportunity in Higher Education (NAFEO, 2005) is charged with advancing the interests of HBCUs, as well as predominantly black colleges and universities, to federal and state governments, businesses, and other organizations. NAFEO (2005) has 120 member institutions located in 25 states, the District of Columbia, the Virgin Islands, and Brazil.

Approximately 16% of all African Americans enrolled in higher education in fall 2001 attended HBCUs (NCES, 2004). When only 4-year institutions are considered, the share of African Americans enrolled at HBCUs increases to 21% (NCES, 2004). The critical role of HBCUs in providing access to higher education for black students is underscored by the fact that the 103 HBCUs make up less than 3% of all colleges and universities in the United States.

Background: Tribal Colleges and Universities

According to the Tribally Controlled College or University Assistance Act, a TCU is an accredited institution at which American Indians represent at least 50% of total enrollments (OCR, 2004). In fall 2002, there were 34 TCUs located in 12 states (OCR, 2004). Montana is home to the largest number of TCUs ($n = 7$), followed by North Dakota ($n = 5$) and South Dakota ($n = 4$). TCUs are also located in 5 other states in the Midwest (Minnesota, Wisconsin, Michigan, Nebraska, and Kansas), 3 states in the Southwest (New Mexico, Arizona, and California), and 1 state in the Pacific Northwest (Washington) (OCR, 2004).

Whereas most HBCUs are more than 100 years old, TCUs are relatively young. Among active TCUs, Diné College (Tsaile, AZ) has the longest history, established by the Navajo Nation in 1968 (American Indian Higher Education Consortium [AIHEC], 1999). Most TCUs were established during the 1970s and 1980s, and four were established during the 1990s. Whereas 85% of HBCUs are 4-year institutions, all TCUs were founded as 2-year institutions, with most offering certificate and associate's degree programs. Over time, four TCUs expanded their missions to offer baccalaureate degrees, and two now offer master's degrees (AIHEC, 1999). The majority (about two thirds) of all TCUs are public 2-year institutions (NCES, 2004).

Although TCUs are fewer in number and have more limited missions compared with HBCUs, TCUs and HBCUs have many similarities, particularly with respect to institutional identity. To wit, HBCUs were established to provide educational, social, and economic opportunities to a population essentially shut out from the mainstream education system. TCUs were established to provide opportunities to American Indians who were shut out of the mainstream education system as a result of not only institutionalized prejudice but also geographical separation. Like HBCUs, TCUs have embraced, since their inception, both cultural and academic educational agendas in their organizing principles. According to AIHEC (1999),

> In many ways, Tribal Colleges are similar to mainstream community colleges. However, the trait that distinguishes them from other community colleges is their dual mission: (1) to rebuild, reinforce, and explore traditional tribal cultures, using uniquely designed curricula and institutional settings; and at the same time, (2) to address Western models of learning by providing traditional disciplinary courses that are transferable to four-year institutions. (p. A-3)

Also similar to HBCUs, the institutional identities of TCUs preceded governmental legitimization. Although three TCUs were founded through federal charters, the first and majority of TCUs were established by American Indian tribes and subsequently recognized by federal agencies (AIHEC, 1999). The federally chartered TCUs are governed by national boards, and the other TCUs are managed locally (AIHEC, 1999).

The enduring role that HBCUs and TCUs have played as population-specific institutions is evident in these simple statistics. Across all HBCUs and TCUs, approximately 87% of HBCU students were black and 81% of TCU students were American Indian in fall 2002 (OCR, 2004). The high representation of blacks at HBCUs and of American Indians at TCUs stands in contrast to the relatively lower representation of Hispanics among enrollments at HSIs (53%) and of Alaska Natives and Native Hawaiians among enrollments at AHIs (approximately 45%) in fall 2002 (OCR, 2004).

Background: Hispanic-Serving Institutions

A college or university is recognized as an HSI by OCR if at least 25% of its full-time equivalent undergraduates who are U.S. citizens are Hispanic. According to this definition, there are currently 362 HSIs in the United States and outlying areas (299 in 15 states and 63 in Puerto Rico) (OCR, 2004). The highest concentrations of HSIs in the United States are found in California ($n = 115$), Texas ($n = 55$), New Mexico ($n = 27$), Florida ($n = 23$), New York ($n = 21$), and Arizona ($n = 21$). Nine other states are home to a dozen or fewer HSIs.

The U.S. Department of Education uses a more restrictive designation of HSIs for its Developing Hispanic-Serving Institutions Program. This program, which awards funds to eligible not-for-profit institutions under Title V of the Higher Education Act, defines HSIs by the aforementioned criterion (minimum of 25% Hispanic student enrollment) plus the criterion that at least 50% of their Hispanic student enrollment meets certain low-income qualifications. In 2002, 242 HSIs distributed among 14 states and Puerto Rico met this more restrictive designation (OCR, 2004). The highest concentrations of these HSIs are found in Texas and California.

Whereas the numbers of HBCUs and TCUs remain relatively unchanged from year to year, the number of institutions identified as HSIs may fluctuate from year to year because both definitions of HSIs are based on student enrollments. The Hispanic Association of Colleges and Universities (HACU), a national organization founded in 1986 to provide organization and advocacy for HSIs, offers a more identity-based definition of HSIs. To be a voting member of HACU, an institution must be an accredited nonprofit college or university with a student population that is at least 25% Hispanic. HACU also recognizes associate members—that is, accredited nonprofit colleges and universities where at least 1,000 students are Hispanic and with student populations that are at least 10% Hispanic—as well as international members (HACU, 2004). HACU (2005) counted more than 400 colleges and universities located in the United States, Puerto Rico, Latin America, and Spain among its consortium of institutions.

As noted earlier, HSIs' Hispanic student enrollment is approximately 53% (OCR, 2004). This percentage is inflated somewhat by the inclusion of HSIs located in Puerto Rico given

that Hispanics represent nearly 100% of enrollments at HSIs in Puerto Rico. At the 299 HSIs in the states, Hispanics represent an average of 43% of enrollments (OCR, 2004). Like HBCUs, HSIs include a diverse array of institutional types, including public and private institutions, for-profit and not-for-profit institutions, and a full range of colleges and universities within the Carnegie classification system. Approximately one third of all HSIs offer postbaccalaureate programs.

Background: Alaska Native and Native Hawaiian Institutions

The newest MSI designation is AHI. The categorization scheme for AHIs is similar to that for HSIs in that it is based on the demographics of student enrollments. The 1998 amendments to the Higher Education Act define AHIs as institutions with at least 20% Alaskan Native students or at least 10% Native Hawaiian students. In fall 2002, there were 12 AHIs (11 located in Alaska and 1 located in Hawaii) (OCR, 2004). The number of colleges and universities reported for Hawaii is somewhat suspect given the challenges associated with identifying the number of Native Hawaiian students. The primary source of data for the race/ethnicity of enrollments, IPEDS, includes one category for "American Indian/Alaskan Native" and no category for Native Hawaiian. Thus, designation as an AHI depends, in part, on the availability of supplemental institutional reports. At the AHIs in Alaska, Alaska Native students made up approximately 45% of the total student enrollment in fall 2002 (OCR, 2004). Native Hawaiians represented approximately 18% of all students enrolled at the one AHI in Hawaii in fall 2002 (OCR, 2004).

Recognizing the Similarities, Understanding the Differences

By necessity and design, MSIs have done, and will continue to do at least in the foreseeable future, more than their share in supporting the access and persistence of traditionally underrepresented racial and ethnic groups in higher education. They serve as gateways for specific student populations and their families as well as symbols of equity for the entire system of higher education in the United States and surrounding areas. The effectiveness of MSIs as practical gateways can be questioned, of course, and their symbolic value may be critiqued from a variety of perspectives.

Notwithstanding their similarities, we must of course not assume that all MSIs are the same either across or within groups of MSIs. Variation in definitions and categorizations of MSIs is one source of difference across groups of MSIs. MSIs also differ across and within groups owing to differences in the histories, identities, and cultures of member institutions and their surrounding communities. Moreover, MSIs vary in the extent to which they serve not only their identified student population but also other populations. Therefore, assuming homogeneity of mission, racial/ethnic representation, or some other characteristic masks true heterogeneity. It is with this sensibility that we turn to identifying and elaborating on the three lines of inquiry that we believe may serve and challenge these institutions—and PWIs—in the future.

Benefits of MSIs: For Individuals and for Society

In 1977, with support from the Carnegie Council on Policy Studies in Higher Education, Howard Bowen published *Investment in Learning: The Individual and Social Value of American Higher Education*. This volume, released in a second edition in 1997, has been highly influential, particularly with regard to the way in which Bowen framed inquiry into the benefits of higher education. His exploration of the connections and distinctions between individual and social gains afforded by higher education—without, we should add, getting mired in the "private gain versus public good" debate—created ripples that have propelled "benefits" studies on this matter in multiple disciplines for more than two decades and counting. Among the most important touchstones was Bowen's inclusion of nonclassroom experiences in his discussion of the value of higher education for individuals and his examination of the impact of the social value of higher education on equality and inequality (Bowen, 1977/1997).

The widely shared understanding of the benefits of MSIs is that they provide underrepresented individuals with otherwise unavailable access to higher education and that, in turn, both society and individuals benefit from a more diverse, well-educated public. Historically, HBCUs often provided the only access to higher education for African Americans. There was also, of course, the perverse "benefit" for the white majority that HBCUs were wholly separate from other colleges and universities. Such an egregiously discriminatory foundation was not laid so explicitly for TCUs, HSIs, or AHIs—which emerged on the scene much more recently—but the overarching principles of access to individuals and the benefits of diversity to society make them kindred spirits with HBCUs.

Further research on the individual and societal benefits of MSIs is especially important at a time when the purposes of these institutions and their progress in advancing equality of opportunity for all students are being widely debated. What are the benefits of attending MSIs for individual students? What economic benefits can be found? What do we know about the personal growth and development experienced by students that is distinctly the result of attending MSIs? What are the social benefits of MSIs? What contributions do MSIs make to the communities with which they share identities? What are the benefits of MSIs to society's educational, industrial, governmental, and corporate institutions? In short, in what ways do MSIs contribute to the public good?

An exemplar of an investigation of the individual and social benefits of MSIs is Laura W. Perna's report that was published in *Research in Education*. Perna's (2001) study focused on the comparative contributions of HBCUs and other colleges and universities to the preparation of African Americans for faculty careers. Perna's study provides a useful point of reflection for identifying ways in which future research and inquiry could advance our understandings of the individual and social benefits of HBCUs as well as other MSIs.

Building on extant research that offered evidence of the personal and academic benefits to African American students attending HBCUs, Perna (2001) looked to the 1992 National Study of Postsecondary Faculty for answers to the following questions:

> a. How do the characteristics of African American faculty who earned their bachelor's degrees from an HBCU compare with the characteristics of other African American faculty?
>
> b. How do the characteristics of African American faculty who received their doctoral degree from an HBCU compare with the characteristics of other African American faculty who have earned doctoral degrees?
>
> c. Is having earned a bachelor's degree or a doctoral degree from an HBCU related to research productivity, one indicator of faculty preparation, among African American men and women faculty?
>
> d. Is having earned a bachelor's degree or a doctoral degree from an HBCU related to satisfaction with the work setting, a second indicator of preparation, among African American men and women faculty? (p. 271)

Using both descriptive and inferential statistics, Perna (2001) identified several noteworthy relationships between HBCU enrollment and African American faculty career preparation. Although many of Perna's findings confirmed assumptions that many might have made in light of earlier research, some findings deviated from what many might have suspected. A few key findings are especially conducive to excavating the individual and social benefits of MSIs.

According to Perna (2001), African Americans accounted for 5.2% of faculty at colleges and universities throughout the United States, a figure far lower than the percentage of African Americans in the country's population as a whole (12.6%). Therein lies the basic impetus for her line of inquiry: If African American representation among higher education faculty is lagging, and we know that HBCUs have made significant contributions to the education of African Americans in general, it is important to consider the role of HBCUs in the preparation of African American faculty. The primary finding of the study offers a window into these relationships: Insofar as preparation for a faculty

career is defined by research production and satisfaction in the workplace, having earned a baccalaureate or doctoral degree from an HBCU is unrelated to the preparation of African American faculty.

The absence of a significant relationship between African American faculty career preparation and graduating from an HBCU may be interpreted in a variety of ways. On the one hand, one might hope to see that HBCUs are more influential—that they prepare African Americans for faculty careers *better than* do PWIs. On the other hand, the results show that HBCUs contribute to African Americans' faculty career preparation *just as well as* do PWIs, and this belies a common stereotype of HBCUs as being somehow inferior institutions.

Perna (2001) measured the contributions of HBCUs relative to PWIs based on the dependent variables of satisfaction with the work setting and research productivity. Other statistics identified by Perna provide insight into how receiving a baccalaureate or doctoral degree from an HBCU influences certain characteristics among African American faculty. For example, Perna noted that female African American faculty are more likely to have received their baccalaureate degrees from HBCUs than are male African American faculty. The study also found that African American faculty who earned their baccalaureate degrees at HBCUs are overrepresented among faculty at predominantly black colleges and universities (PBCUs, i.e., institutions that are composed of a majority of black students but that are not necessarily classified as HBCUs) and underrepresented among faculty at research universities. These and other findings invite research that probes the reasons for these little-understood phenomena.

Two additional results from the study offer serious points of reflection for future research and inquiry related to individual and social benefits of HBCUs. According to Perna (2001), in spite of the fact that African American faculty who obtained baccalaureate and/or doctoral degrees from HBCUs are more likely to work at PBCUs than at PWIs, African American faculty at PBCUs are less satisfied with their work settings. This may raise concerns regarding PBCUs' ability to attract and retain African

American faculty in the future. Researchers and practitioners alike should consider probing this finding to understand why satisfaction levels differ based on institutional type.

Perna (2001) also found that HBCUs have become especially proficient at generating faculty in the fields of education, engineering, and the natural sciences. Considering that the underrepresentation of African Americans is particularly severe among faculty in the sciences (NCES, 2004), this finding suggests another area where HBCUs are generating individual and societal benefits. Yet this achievement may be occurring for reasons that even HBCUs do not fully understand. Developing an understanding of this phenomenon may be valuable not only for HBCUs but also for any institutions of higher education striving to increase diversity in their graduate programs and to contribute to the diversity of American higher education faculty.

To be sure, HSIs, TCUs, and AHIs may also benefit from such inquiries because their constituencies are also underrepresented in the academic ranks. Perna's (2001) study of HBCUs summons a series of questions concerning the overall status of underrepresented minority faculty. What contributions do MSIs make to the career preparation of Hispanic and Native American faculty? How do the publication records and job satisfaction measures of underrepresented minority faculty correspond to where they earned their baccalaureate or doctoral degrees? What are the dimensions of minority participation in academic roles outside of colleges and universities such as research groups and "think tanks"? What contributions do MSIs make to the preparation of individuals for other types of careers?

More broadly, and including all MSIs, if we are to strategize ways in which underrepresented persons may move "up the educational pipeline" (Perna, 2001, p. 288) into academic roles and other major professions in the public and private sectors, then the complexities implicit in Perna's findings lead us to imagine a pipeline that is full of twists and turns, parallel and divergent paths, dead ends, and gaps in need of repair. As Perna (2001) suggested in her call for future research, we know that such a pipeline is shaped by multiple socialization factors such as attitudes and values that are influenced by many characteristics and experiences, including student–faculty relationships. Additional probing of the experiences of students using a range of methodologies is needed to provide a more detailed picture of this pipeline schematic that has been built between and within our institutions of higher learning.

More equitable participation in all facets of higher education results in a reciprocal web of individual and social benefits. First, individual students—eventual graduates—of colleges and universities benefit personally in terms of intellectual, moral, and economic development. In turn, those individuals join the proverbial "real world" and influence change in myriad ways. As Bowen (1977/1997) noted succinctly more than 25 years ago,

> Education does not automatically mitigate human inequality. It may do so, it may work in the opposite direction, or it may have little or no effect. The influence of education upon inequality depends on the social origins of the students, the numbers being educated, the capacity of the educational programs offered to meet the needs of persons of varying backgrounds and aspirations, and the degree to which egalitarian ideas are conveyed through the attitudes and values it transmits. (p. 326)

The very existence of MSIs reflects higher education's efforts to work in the "opposite direction" of human inequality. Research and inquiry that attempt to understand in great detail the ways in which MSIs are working to redress historic imbalances will help to improve policies and practices at MSIs and in the nation's system of higher education as a whole.

The whole population of students is of concern to MSIs as well. Across all HBCUs, TCUs, HSIs, and AHIs, approximately 40% of the students enrolled are white (OCR, 2004). Furthermore, MSIs routinely enroll students who are underrepresented minorities but who do not share the expressed identities of MSIs (OCR, 2004). Serving other-race students is a part of MSIs' practice by default, by mission, and (for some) in accordance with the law. The question of what MSIs can do to serve these student populations is addressed in the following section.

Enrolling Other-Race Students at MSIs: Challenges and Opportunities

Although the degree to which serving a specific minority population is a part of an MSI's explicit mission varies across and within types of MSIs, the student populations of many MSIs are made up of a significant number—if not a majority—of students from other-race groups, that is, groups other than the specified minority group. This being the case, MSIs may be challenged—like PWIs—to attract, enroll, retain, and enhance the educational experiences of multiple groups of students. There are, of course, similarities and differences in the sources and character of the challenge, and an examination of these is in part addressed here. Although an abundance of studies have focused on the experiences of black and Hispanic students at PWIs, few researchers have focused on the experiences of other-race students at MSIs. Expansions of this line of inquiry would no doubt yield many benefits, not least of which would be data and information to identify and inform policies and practices at MSIs that are likely to increase and sustain other-race student enrollments and degree completions.

If white students are overrepresented nationwide in higher education, and if MSIs are so successful in efforts to counteract prejudice institutionalized through colleges and universities, then why would (or should) MSIs be concerned with the enrollment of other-race students? This is a valid question, and the answers are at once commonsensical and open to scrutiny. Like PWIs, MSIs may be interested in the enrollment of other-race students simply for the sake of increasing their overall enrollments as well as the implicit value of diversifying the student body. Perhaps more urgently, some HBCUs—such as those in Mississippi— are faced, via court order and other mandates, with the task of eliminating the remnants of segregation and must seek to enroll non-black students to meet the demands of desegregation. An exploration of the situation faced by HBCUs illuminates ways in which this line of inquiry may be deepened and expanded with respect to HBCUs as well as other MSIs.

In collaboration with two other scholars, another author of this chapter conducted and reported on the first major study focused on identifying the factors that contribute to the matriculation of white students at public HBCUs (Conrad, Brier, & Braxton, 1997). Through individual and group interviews with 80 stakeholders (36 students, 32 administrators, and 12 faculty members) at five public HBCUs (three known for their success in enrolling white students and two under court order to desegregate), the investigators identified 14 key factors influencing white students to enroll at HBCUs. The factors were organized into three major categories: (1) academic program offerings (program offerings in high-demand fields, unique program offerings, alternative program delivery systems, graduate program offerings in high-demand fields, and positive reputation for quality), (2) student financial support (student scholarships and low cost), and (3) institutional characteristics (positive image as a multiracial institution, supportive and inclusive campus culture, white student recruitment, articulation and cooperative agreements with PWIs, positive external relations, safe environment, and attractive campus appearance).

Conrad and colleagues (1997) went on to analyze the correspondence between the 14 factors identified in their study and the primary factors that other research has found to be associated with white students' decisions to enroll at PWIs. They concluded that "the factors that attract whites to HBCUs are, for the most part, significantly different from factors that attract students to PWIs as identified in studies of mostly white student selection of PWIs" (p. 56). Of the five primary factors that Conrad and colleagues identified, only one (academic quality/ reputation) overlapped with the seven (academic quality/reputation, special academic programs, costs, availability of financial aid, location, size, and social atmosphere) that the authors had found reported in previous studies. Moreover, this particular factor ranked first for white students at PWIs but ranked only fourth for white students at HBCUs.

Conrad and colleagues (1997) concluded their report by identifying policies and practices at the state and institutional levels for encouraging white students to attend HBCUs. They urged states to create and maintain high-demand programs at HBCUs, to "sharpen the missions of all public institutions by assigning program exclusivity to various institutions" so as to avoid program duplication (a stipulation of desegregation guidelines), and to provide funding streams sufficient for other elements of institutional quality that attract white students (p. 57). At the institutional level, the authors suggested that HBCUs develop strategies for developing program distinctiveness, financial support specifically dedicated to the recruitment of white students, and other institutional enhancement initiatives.

Conrad and colleagues' (1997) study is useful for informing future inquiry on several major fronts. First and foremost, its conclusion that the criteria white students consider in their selection of HBCUs is different from the criteria they consider in their selection of PWIs provides leverage and illumination for further examination of such differences. Furthermore, this conclusion provides a starting point for considering related lines of inquiry that might be developed with respect to other types of MSIs as well as both public and private HBCUs. The remainder of this section sketches ways in which future research and inquiry might be developed with regard to attracting, enrolling, and retaining other-race students at MSIs.

Noting that Conrad and colleagues' (1997) study is nearly 10 years old, we wonder how the five campuses in their study may have changed. The interviews that informed this study took place less than 5 years after the 1992 *United States v. Fordice* decision in which the U.S. Supreme Court ruled that states must eliminate any vestiges of segregation in their public colleges and universities. Since that time, ideas and attitudes among faculty, staff, and students have likely crystallized in new ways, making them ripe for further examination. Furthermore, state and institutional policies and procedures, regardless of whether they were influenced by the publication of the 1997 article, would certainly be primed for examination at this point in time. In addition to seeing what has changed, future research should try to identify what may have been missed and probe some of the findings more deeply.

If we were to reorganize the 14 factors identified in the Conrad and colleagues' (1997) study along a continuum ranging from least subjective/most objective to most subjective/least objective, some of the most intriguing questions for a second similar study would be found at the latter end of the continuum. For example, the study identified academic program quality or reputation as one of the most frequently noted influences associated with white students' decisions to attend HBCUs. And the perceptions vis-à-vis program quality were powerful, as demonstrated by one student when she said,

> I believe that there is a different culture in the white institution than the black institution. In the black institution, a part of the culture is that the faculty is there to support a student's progress through the program. And that is not always the case in historically white universities. . . . I attended historically white universities, and they have been some of the coldest institutions I have known. (p. 47)

What is not clear from Conrad and colleagues' (1997) study are answers to the infinite *why* questions. Why are certain programs viewed as having a positive reputation? With respect to institutional characteristics, why are HBCUs seen as supportive and inclusive? Pursuing questions like these will develop a stronger understanding of how HBCUs advance these characteristics—and how students and others can develop and nurture them.

One of the limitations of Conrad and colleagues' (1997) study is that it attempted to ascertain an understanding of white students' decisions to attend HBCUs through solely reflective and perspectival questioning. That is, students were asked to reflect on their decisions to attend HBCUs after they had already made their decisions to enroll and had the experience of being at HBCUs. Faculty and administrators were asked to offer their perspectives on these same students. Additional insights may be gained through a study of white students attending high schools in proximity to HBCUs. By interviewing white students and their teachers, counselors, and parents during the period of time when students were actually in the process of making their college choices, much could be learned about the factors that shape students' decisions. Implicit in the 1997 study were thresholds encountered by white students in their decisions to attend HBCUs. A study of high school juniors and seniors may produce a more in-depth examination of the thresholds. Among the factors that contribute to these students' college choices (whether HBCUs or not), which have the weight to swing the balance? Among the potential questions to guide future research are the following. What beliefs about HBCUs are held by white high school students for whom enrollment at HBCUs is a real option given their close geographic proximity? What images of HBCUs are dominant in the culture of high schools? What do counselors and teachers and parents say about HBCUs? How does information about academic programs, such as course options and teacher quality, get communicated to high school students? What do students say to each other about HBCUs? How do the responses to questions vary among students, counselors, teachers, and parents of different racial/ethnic groups? Are there differences in how prospective black students and prospective white students view academic program offerings, high-demand fields, unique program offerings, alternative delivery systems, and multiracial images? And arguably the most revealing question: Why do students choose *not* to attend HBCUs? Answers to such questions might begin to generate a more comprehensive understanding of the college choice process with regard to HBCUs.

A line of inquiry that focuses on white students at HBCUs might not appear to be relevant to other MSIs because other MSIs do not have the mandate to desegregate as some public HBCUs do. Although the sense of urgency and stakes might not be the same at other MSIs—or at private HBCUs, for that matter—the relevance remains. Given the complexities posed by racial and ethnic identities in the United States, and the ways in which higher education feeds on and into those complexities, more information is needed about other-race students' perspectives and experiences at all types of MSIs. This is a significantly understudied area of research. Extending this line of inquiry to all MSIs generates additional questions. For example, why do white students—or black, Hispanic, American

Indian, or Asian students—who attend HSIs, TCUs, and AHIs choose to do so? Are their reasons similar to those of white students who choose to attend HBCUs?

Given the respective histories and current enrollment patterns found at other MSIs, we might begin to develop some hypotheses and more specific questions to explore such as the following. Are students who attend MSIs where white students make up the majority of student enrollment aware of those institutions' designations as MSIs, and if so, to what degree is that designation a factor in their matriculation? In what ways does the relative newness of MSIs (other than HBCUs) work for or against enrolling other-race students? Answers to questions along these lines would be helpful in developing theory that will inform practice at high schools and institutions of higher education as well as state and institutional policies. Furthermore, expanding the inquiry beyond HBCUs may, in turn, be beneficial to HBCUs' efforts to respond to ongoing desegregation challenges as greater understandings of other-race enrollments at other types of MSIs are developed.

CROSS-INSTITUTIONAL IMPROVEMENT AND INNOVATION: MSIS AND PWIS

What can PWIs learn from MSIs about best practices for supporting and enhancing the education of students at PWIs? As the previous sections have suggested, PWIs may have much to learn from MSIs with regard to advancing the progress of underrepresented students through the educational pipeline into academic positions and other areas of the world of work as well as shaping recruitment and retention efforts. The third central question advanced in this chapter is a direct exploration of such possibilities and is advanced in terms of two subquestions. First, what can PWIs learn from MSIs in terms of serving underrepresented student populations and the continued maturity of the educational pipeline? Second, what can PWIs learn from MSIs for the sake of serving *all* students at PWIs and the improvement of their core educational practices?

To be sure, serving the pipeline and institutional practices are interconnected. As Berta Vigil Laden noted in her study of "celebratory socialization" of underrepresented students at two community colleges, "Institutions can promote culturally-sensitive and culturally-specific programs in academic and student services to increase ethnic student motivation and commitment to college while also changing the institution as a result of the commitment to the students" (Laden, 1999, p. 176).

To put forth a line of inquiry that will build on and extend research related to PWI and MSI cross-institutional improvement and innovation, we use Laden's (1999) study as a theoretical and methodological exemplar. Following a description of her report on this research, we articulate sets of questions for future consideration.

Laden (1999), employing an "ecological model which considers the cultural context of students' lives" (p. 177), conducted ethnographic case studies of two community colleges in Northern California. Selected for the study because of their highly regarded efforts to support underrepresented students' transfer into 4-year institutions, the schools had minority student enrollments of 59% and 27% among total enrollments of approximately 11,000 and 14,000, respectively. According to Laden's descriptions, student services on each campus featured programs for Latino and Latina students; therefore, it is not unreasonable to assume that at least one of the institutions, if not both, is classified as an HSI. (Laden did not make explicit the identities of the colleges in this way; as a side note, this is perhaps indicative of the way in which the HSI label is operationalized in practice and research in comparison with, say, HBCUs, where the MSI identity seems to be front and center almost without exception.) Laden indicated that she spent a year performing observations, reviewing institutional documents, and conducting interviews with 38 administrators, faculty, and support staff at the two colleges.

From her analysis of these rich data, Laden (1999) identified critical characteristics of exemplary organizational models that she found at these two community colleges. At both institutions, the campus leaders—the president at

one, other executive administrators at the other, and faculty at both—actively took ownership of the transfer challenge and publicly articulated their commitment to meeting it. They executed organizational and fiscal realignments in the form of a variety of curricular, co-curricular, and outreach programs. Examples of such undertakings included in-depth outreach and orientation programs for prospective and new students of color, English composition programs that incorporated reading and writing about students' heritages, supplemental counseling and mentoring available through transfer centers, and physical spaces dedicated to providing information and assistance to facilitate the process of moving on to 4-year colleges and universities. All such initiatives were aligned with what were essentially moral imperatives adopted by the two colleges. According to Laden, "The interactions occurring among the various elements . . . have the potential for creating a web effect that leads to student empowerment and success" (pp. 190–191). Thus, the commitment to students leads to benefits not only for the individual students but also for the institutions in the forms of achieving their goals and changing structures and organizational cultures along the way.

Programs and services like those documented by Laden (1999) abound at colleges and universities of all shapes and sizes around the country, including many PWIs. In fact, we contend that one would be hard-pressed to find any PWI of average size or larger that does not have some combination of similar efforts expressly for underrepresented students. The availability of strong leadership and sufficient resource allocations for these programs and services varies, of course, and therein lies one of the tribulations routinely faced by advocates for minority students at several institutions. It is not insignificant that Laden found both creativity and commitment at those two exemplary community colleges.

In addition to aligning resources with goals, what more can PWIs learn from MSIs with regard to supporting underrepresented students through the educational pipeline? If Laden's (1999) study had any shortcoming, it might be the absence of students as direct informants in her fieldwork. She recorded some powerful statements and perspectives from the architects, builders, and managers of the efforts at the two schools, but the student voices were lacking, at least in this particular report. Future studies would benefit from asking student participants to describe and reflect on their experiences. One would not be surprised to learn that faculty and staff accounts of the value of a program or experience may be far different from the perspectives provided by students. Thus, a more inclusive approach should guide future explorations.

What can PWIs learn from MSIs for the sake of all students? Recall the statement made by a white student in the study by Conrad and colleagues (1997) concerning the supportive and welcoming nature of HBCUs in comparison with the impersonal nature of many PWIs. This student was reflecting on her experience with the whole institution, not a special program or service designed especially for white students. Having spent significant time at more than 20 HBCUs conducting research, one of the authors of this chapter (Conrad) can attest that something about many of these campuses seems to make nearly *everyone* feel welcome. We might infer from Perna's (2001) finding that African American faculty with degrees from HBCUs were more likely to work at HBCUs because they felt so welcomed and supported by these institutions that they brought them back. But what is *it?* Conrad and colleagues (1997) documented a variety of initiatives made by HBCU faculty and administrators to make the institution *seem* to embrace the multicultural heritage of all its students, but those used devices such as print and Web publications. Laden's (1999) study suggests that HBCUs may benefit from the significant contributions of strong leadership and commitment. But the applicability of findings from Laden's study of two MSIs to HBCUs is unclear given the historically conspicuous underfunding of HBCUs. We are persuaded that there are some special features of HBCUs in particular—and of MSIs in general—that research has not adequately addressed heretofore.

Some presume that such qualities of MSIs are unknowable or, even if known, are not replicable in PWIs. For example, in an essay that argued for public HBCUs to remain predominantly black, Jackson, Snowden, and Eckes (2002) stated,

> Perhaps most importantly, black culture and accomplishment are essential ingredients in the curriculum at black colleges. The attributes of the public HBCU cannot be replicated at white universities. At white universities, black students can be marginalized and the courses oftentimes ignore the contributions of blacks to the sciences, art, and literature. Continued access to HBCUs ultimately ensures full and meaningful participation of blacks in a multicultural democratic society, and the research supports these statements. (pp. 15 16)

Although PWIs cannot *become* HBCUs, and although specific structures or features of HBCUs cannot be grossly replicated at PWIs without likely resulting in an object lesson in futility, we believe that PWIs can learn and benefit from HBCUs and other MSIs. More specifically, we can study attributes of MSIs found to be linked to desirable educational outcomes and can deliberate over and experiment with how they may be adapted in the PWI context. Consider, for example, the community college in Laden's (1999) study that overhauled its curriculum by infusing it with ethnic and cultural studies themes, courses, and requirements. Like the curricular attributes referred to in Jackson and colleagues' (2002) study, such changes recognize how important it is for students to be able to see themselves, as it were, in elements of their courses. Incorporation of such principles into curriculum development at PWIs is a worthwhile endeavor. To assume otherwise, we believe, is to paint a bleak picture for the future.

On a somewhat tangential note, but important to the task nonetheless, the call for maintaining the demographic status quo at HBCUs by Jackson and colleagues (2002) rightly raises what we think is a critical question to pursue concurrent with this line of inquiry: Will increasing the number of white students who attend HBCUs result in a dismantling of those special qualities that HBCUs offer not only to black students but to all students? This seems to be a logical possibility. If so, then it poses serious questions for social policy as the future generations of our institutions of higher education are evolving.

Recall that in the study by Conrad and colleagues (1997), white students found satisfaction in the whole of HBCUs rather than in the types of specialized programs identified in Laden's (1999) study. This observation raises an interesting question: How might future research account for what are apparently two modes of cultivating student belonging and success, and how might practice be influenced? One of the ways in which the HBCUs in Conrad and colleagues' (1997) study recruited white students was to offer high-demand curricula through evening programs, in one instance resulting in a "black HBCU by day" and a "white HBCU by night." This is at least partly analogous to the special English composition programs created at the community colleges in Laden's (1999) study. Is isolation an unintended consequence of such efforts to recruit, retain, and support these specific populations of students? If we are to take the evidence from HBCUs seriously, then we believe it is fair to speculate that unless institutions change on the whole, special boutiquelike programs ancillary to the central missions of institutions might not be the most effective solutions possible. Although they may be effective for supporting targeted populations *through* the pipeline, it is not the pipeline being changed; instead, it is more like the pipeline is being retrofitted. The most compelling evidence, of course, is not found through the creation of pithy metaphors; rather, it is found in analyses of data collected in the most rigorous and conscientious ways of which we, as a community, are capable.

CONCLUSION

MSIs enroll disproportionate shares of students from African American, Hispanic, Native American, Alaska Native, and Native Hawaiian populations. Yet we know surprisingly little about the range of benefits that MSIs generate for individuals and society; the policies and practices that promote the enrollment, retention, and success of other-race students attending MSIs; or the "secrets" to MSIs' success in creating a welcoming and supportive educational experience for minority students.

Pursuing these three lines of inquiry is important not only for addressing gaps in the literature but also for identifying ways in which to address the continued underrepresentation of these groups in American higher education more generally. Although MSIs educate disproportionate shares of minority students, students from these populations continue to be underrepresented at all levels of higher education. Addressing these three lines of inquiry may help all institutions to better respond to calls for accountability and for justifications of public financial support.

We invite our colleagues to embrace these three lines of inquiry. We are strongly persuaded that by building on and extending research on MSIs, researchers can greatly enhance our understandings of their contributions to the higher learning and, in turn, the public good.

REFERENCES

American Indian Higher Education Consortium. (1999). *Tribal colleges: An introduction.* Washington, DC: Institute for Higher Education Policy.

Bowen, H. (1997). *Investment in learning: The individual and social value of American higher education.* Baltimore, MD: Johns Hopkins University Press. (Original work published in 1977)

Conrad, C. F., Brier, E. M., & Braxton, J. M. (1997). Factors contributing to the matriculation of white students in public HBCUs. *Journal for a Just and Caring Education, 3*(1), 37–62.

Higher Education Act of 1965, as amended, Title III, Part B, Section 321 (enacted 1998).

Hispanic Association of Colleges and Universities. (2004). *HACU bylaws.* San Antonio, TX: Author.

Hispanic Association of Colleges and Universities. (2005). *HACU 101.* San Antonio, TX: Author. Retrieved February 25, 2005, from www .hacu.net

Jackson, J. F. L., Snowden, M., & Eckes, S. (2002). Fordice as a window of opportunity: The case for maintaining historically black colleges and universities (HBCUs) as predominantly black institutions. *West's Education Law Reporter, 1,* 1–19.

Laden, B. V. (1999). Celebratory socialization of culturally diverse students through academic programs and student support services. In J. R. Valadez & R. A. Rhoads (Eds.), *Community colleges as cultural texts: Qualitative explorations of organizational and student culture* (pp. 173–194). Albany: State University of New York Press.

National Association for Equal Opportunity in Higher Education. (2005). *About NAFEO: Mission statement.* Washington, DC: Author. Retrieved February 25, 2005, from www.nafeo.org

National Center for Education Statistics. (2004). *Digest of education statistics: 2003* (NCES 2005–025). Washington, DC: Author.

Office of Civil Rights. (2004). *Accredited postsecondary minority institutions: 2004.* Washington, DC: U.S. Department of Education.

Perna, L. W. (2001). The contribution of historically black colleges and universities to the preparation of African Americans for faculty careers. *Research in Higher Education, 42,* 267–294.

Provasnik, S., Shafer, L. L., & Snyder, T. D. (2004). *Historically black colleges and universities, 1976 to 2001* (NCES 2004–062). Washington, DC: National Center for Education Statistics.

16

COMPARATIVE EDUCATION

An Approach to Educational Inquiry

DAVID PHILLIPS

University of Oxford

Comparing is inherent in human thinking.

—Eckstein (1985, p.167)

The making of comparisons is funda-mental to intellectual inquiry. A com-mon ground between various investigators in the field of education—whatever their partic-ular focus—has been the task of making com-parisons, of examining features of educational provision in different contexts alongside each other and reaching conclusions (judgments) about the nature of those features and the degree to which they are instructive. The work of comparativists is distinguishable from that of other educationists inasmuch as the former are concerned essentially with other countries and their cultures. This focus on education "else-where"—on "the other"—means that they must be concerned with appropriate methods to facil-itate comparison. Otherwise, comparativists use the research methods that other education specialists employ in their research: they utilize what is a large body of established approaches to investigation in education (drawing on meth-ods in a range of cognate disciplines) and add

approaches specific to the particular task of comparison.

Comparative education as a field of schol-arly inquiry covers a vast range of topics and ways of investigating them. It can consist of valuable descriptive material (cf. some of the work of the United Nations Educational, Scientific, and Cultural Organization [UNESCO] or the Organization for Economic Cooperation and Development [OECD] or the European Union's Eurydice database); of philosophical analysis of education systems; of sociological investigations; of detailed local case studies; of large-scale surveys of pupil attainment; of sophisticated statistical comparisons; of inquiry into teaching styles, teacher training, and teacher professionalism; and of a host of other areas of research.

Comparative education has had method-ologists whose views cover a broad spectrum of approaches, from the historical (Kandel), through what can be termed the "factors" (Hans), "national character" (Mallinson), "philosophical traditions" (Lauwerys), "cultural/theoretical models" (Moehlman) approaches, via attempts at defining a more "scientific" methodology (Bereday, Holmes, Noah, and Eckstein) and to various forms of interdisciplinarity (King) and to the work of the globalization and postmodern theorists who dominate today. The field is rich in tradition and variety; it draws upon considerable strengths which outweigh its weaknesses; it attracts researchers with origins in a very wide range of disciplines, each of them bringing to it perspectives which assist in its development.

In this chapter, I shall aim to consider in outline how comparative education has developed since the early years of the 19th century and illustrate its affinity with inquiry in other disciplines, especially history. I will then discuss how comparative inquiry informs the study of educational history and "policy borrowing"— followed by an exemplary model for policy borrowing—and make a case for comparative education as a quasi-discipline. Finally, I propose a simple schema for comparative inquiry which attempts to combine theoretical, methodological, and practical considerations.

HISTORICAL STAGES OF COMPARATIVE STUDIES IN EDUCATION

In considering the historical development of comparative education as an area of scholarly inquiry, various writers have postulated broad phases of development. Noah and Eckstein, to take the most prominent example, postulate five stages in the development of comparative endeavor in education. The first stage comprises for them the time when travelers brought back tales of what they had observed. Such tales formed "the most primitive . . . observations," originating in curiosity and emphasizing the exotic so as to produce stark contrast with the norm at home. "Only the rare observer could extract systematic conclusions with explanatory value from a mass of indiscriminately reported impressions" (Noah & Eckstein, 1969, pp. 4–5). Such 'travelers' tales'—often summarily dismissed by present-day commentators—nevertheless provide valuable insights into the *mentalité* of the time in which they were written and can help

us to understand the preoccupations of those formulating policy in education as education systems began to take shape.

The second stage encompasses travelers with a specific educational focus to their investigations. These visitors came with a distinct purpose—to learn from a foreign example and through such learning to help improve the circumstances in their home countries. Still, so Noah and Eckstein (1969) argue, their reports were "rarely explanatory"; they tended to concentrate on "encyclopedic descriptions of foreign school systems, perhaps enlivened here and there with anecdotes" (p. 5). But again the work of such investigators is particularly valuable to us in piecing together snapshots of the agenda in educational policy at particular times.

Noah and Eckstein's third stage is characterized by a desire to understand other nations through the detailed accumulation of information and through educational exchange. Only in their fourth stage, involving the study of "national character" in terms of its deterministic role in shaping national systems of education, can we see the beginnings of a social science approach to the understanding of what informs educational provision in any particular country. Thereafter, in the fifth stage, significant developments in quantitative research have led to an increase in the ability to *explain* educational phenomena.

These developmental stages, though in essence chronological, in fact overlap quite considerably; it has been noted, indeed, that much journalistic practice of our own times can still be located firmly even within the first stage of Noah and Eckstein's typology. And of course we can place rare early examples of attempts at the systematic collection of explanatory data—Jullien's *Esquisse et Vues Préliminaires d'un Ouvrage sur l'Education Comparée* of 1816–1817 (Fraser, 1964) is the obvious example—within the third or even the fifth stage.

There is then an essential interconnection between these five phases. Though any discipline or field of academic inquiry will move through a series of developmental stages, each will encompass the successes—and perhaps some of the shortcomings—of a previous stage or stages. And so a synthesis will emerge, carrying the burden of a complex historical parentage. The current obsession with international surveys of pupil attainment (represented in stage five in Noah and Eckstein's analysis) should not, in my view, be seen in isolation from the work of earlier comparativists who have suggested ways of interpreting and understanding data and their usefulness in terms of the development of educational policy. Comparativists should be concerned both to understand the lessons of the history of their specialism and to use history as an essential tool to understand current educational issues.

Comparing and History: Explanation, Causality, and Prediction

Although comparative education takes from various disciplines, it is with approaches to study history that it relates most. The concerns of historians involve issues which are clearly of *intrinsic* interest to comparativists, especially as they contemplate, for example, the origins of education systems and the determinants of present-day educational phenomena. We need only—in the British context—to mention (whether we agree with them or not) the work of Margaret Archer or more recently that of Andy Green on the origins of education systems and on the role of education in the creation of nation-states (Archer, 1979; Green, 1990), to demonstrate that this is the case.

In addition, the literature of historiography (with which comparativists can engage with profit), as well as devoting much space to questions of *purpose,* focuses on such interconnected and complex topics as *explanation, causality,* and *prediction*—all of which are germane to research in comparative education.

Explanation is a potentially very complex topic which needs little defense as one of the prime concerns of historical investigation. The advantage the comparativist brings is principally that of the outsider, with a new or at least different perspective on the issues under scrutiny; the disadvantage comes in the constant need to be aware of, and to disengage from, a dangerously ethnocentric standpoint, to try as far as possible to combine external objectivity with the internal perceptions that someone closely familiar with the inner or "secret" workings—to use Michael

Sadler's term—of a country's national and educational history and culture can bring. We might also recall Sadler's description of a national system of education as "the outcome of forgotten struggles and difficulties" and of "battles long ago" (Sadler, 1900, cited in Higginson, 1979, p. 49), which implies the importance of historical understanding.

The question of *causality*—also so important for historians—is of particular interest to comparativists because of the tendency to look to the historical example as a kind of proxy for experiment. The "comparative method" in sociology was devised, of course, precisely because it enabled researchers to bypass social experiment by drawing on equivalent experience in other situations. In Durkheim's (1895/1982) analysis,

> We have only one way of demonstrating that one phenomenon is the cause of another. This is to compare the cases where they are both simultaneously present or absent, so as to discover whether the variations they display in these different combinations of circumstances provide evidence that one depends on the other. When the phenomena can be artificially produced at will by the observer, the method is that of experimentation proper. When, on the other hand, the production of facts is something beyond our power to command, and we can only bring them together as they have been spontaneously produced, the method used is one of indirect experimentation, or the comparative method. (p. 147)

It is in this "indirect experimentation," much of it evident in historical analysis, that comparative education has so much to offer.

And *Prediction* is a skill which every policymaker would, quite unreasonably, like the comparativist to master. There is, however, an essential unpredictability and unreliability in human behavior which makes the anticipation of outcomes at the very least insecure. In terms of our expectations for the use of historical examples, the paradigm should be not "If you do that, this will result" but rather "If you do that, this is what has resulted in the past—and so beware."

Prediction has of course occupied the minds of philosophers since the beginnings of science. But the bottom line of discussion within the philosophy of science remains the position that there can be no absolute predictability of observed phenomena. No matter how many times the behavior of a phenomenon is observed within a particular set of circumstances, there can be no guarantee that the phenomenon in question will behave similarly when those circumstances are replicated. That said, however, it is also clear that there can be some fairly reliable "laws" on which scientific theory depends and which are generally accepted; there are even such relative certainties in the social sciences, especially (for example) in economics or in behavioral psychology. We seem happy to accommodate the fact that the "certainties" involved here are not absolute but constitute reasonable hypotheses.

It seems therefore acceptable to assume that certain types of outcome will in most cases be observed if certain types of condition are in place. If this were not the case, much work at a practical level in education would be haphazard; in fact, present and future practice is commonly informed by past practice deemed to have been successful. But, as Popper (1957/1991) observed, prediction is problematic insofar as it can both cause and prevent future events:

> A prediction is a social happening which may interact with other social happenings, and among them the one which it predicts. It may . . . help to precipitate the event. . . . It may, in an extreme case, even *cause* the happening it predicts: the happening might not have occurred at all if it had not been predicted. At the other extreme the prediction of an impending event may lead to its *prevention*. . . . The action of predicting something, and not of abstaining from prediction, might both have all sorts of consequences. (p. 15, emphases in original)

The historian will hence be wary of the many pitfalls of prediction on the basis of past events and the hindsight that accompanies our understanding of them. Santayana's (1905) well-known view (in *The Life of Reason*) that "those who cannot remember the past are condemned to repeat it" reminds us of the importance of having regard to a historical dimension in any analysis of present-day issues—even, or especially, if it is ignored by policymakers. The argument here (since the two statements are complementary) is that the fact that "peoples and governments" might not learn from the lessons of history does not imply the "unlearnability" of those lessons.

But despite this there is a skeptical view which is also of interest. The eminent British historian, Sir Michael Howard, asserts that

> it is safer to start with the assumption that history, whatever its value in educating . . . judgment, teaches no "lessons," and the professional historian will be as skeptical of those who claim that it does as professional doctors are of their colleagues who peddle patent medicines guaranteeing instant cures. The past is infinitely various, an inexhaustible storehouse of events from which we can prove anything or its contrary. (Howard, 1981, p. 8)

The view here is that lessons will not be learned, and that there are in effect no lessons to learn. But Howard goes on to postulate some principal lessons for historians to *teach*, among them:

- Not to generalize from false premises based on inadequate evidence (p. 12).
- The past is a foreign country; there is very little we can say about it until we have learned its language and understood its assumptions; and in deriving conclusions about the processes which occurred in it and applying them to our own day, we must be very careful indeed (p. 12).
- The importance of comprehending cultural diversity and equipping oneself to cope with it (p. 19).

These general lessons taught by historians are clearly of considerable relevance to comparativists concerned with the historical analysis of educational phenomena in two or more countries and its usefulness in throwing light on present-day issues. Among those who have made an impact on comparative studies in education, there are many who have had initial training as historians. It is indeed no disadvantage in this area of academic inquiry to be a trained historian, just as it is not unhelpful to be competent in several languages. But I feel confident in venturing the opinion that of all the associated disciplines, history is that which is of most immediate help to the comparativist.

COMPARATIVE APPROACHES
TO THE HISTORY OF EDUCATION

An important issue (September 2002) of the journal *History of Education* is devoted to "Comparative Approaches to the History of Education." In their introduction, the editors argue that

> because the history of education gravitates most naturally toward the study of the particular and individual context or case . . . it is essential that we should go beyond the purely local and singular, and attempt to develop connections between phenomena and problems encountered in different historical situations and in different countries and cultures. (Crook & McCulloch, 2002, p. 397)

That is to say that the same reasons we would adduce for the comparative study of present-day issues in education may be taken to apply to the study of educational history. And Crook and McCulloch (2002) list three principal benefits which can accrue from a comparative approach to the history of education:

- To establish detailed insight into comparisons and contrasts in our educational past
- To enhance our understanding of influences and interactions
- To generate or inform overarching theory and general patterns (pp. 397–398)

Despite this, however, Crook and McCulloch (2002) lament the fact that "the 'comparative' and the 'historical' have tended to develop as distinct fields of study with separate concerns and characteristics" (p. 399). This is of course very strange, since it might be imagined that the two areas of inquiry are ideally mutually dependent to varying degrees. It is a theme taken up by Robert Cowen in an article in the same issue on "time" in comparative studies, in which he argues that comparative studies "undertheorize concepts of time, while being clear about a concept of space" (Cowen, 2002, p. 413).

Nóvoa and Yaviv-Mashal (2003) have suggested an important role for the historian, which would attempt to combine time and space, and history and comparison:

> We are facing an important role for historical research within the comparative discipline, one

that would enable comparative work to trace the conceptualization of ideas and the formation of knowledge over time and space. One could picture such a theoretical framework for comparative studies as a multidimensional process in which research is grounded in "local histories" but is based and embedded in different forces, connections, times, and places. The reception of each of these histories in different "presents" will produce an individual, historically contingent social, cultural, and educational discourse. (p. 435)

This is an ambitious role indeed, but it is one that would have the distinct advantage of drawing on the strengths of historical investigation based in different localities and building upon them to establish "ways of thinking" (to use Nóvoa's [1998] term) that will form a theoretical framework of informed discourse that in turn will help to explain those "local histories."

I have attempted over recent years to address questions of *time* in comparative studies, in particular inasmuch as they relate to problems of periodization, construing discrete periods of development in education which might help in attempts to juxtapose (to use Bereday's [1964] term) educational phenomena in two or more countries and to do so on the basis of some alignment of periods between countries (Phillips, 1994, 2002). Through the very process of thinking through the problems of periodization—a topic, incidentally, that is curiously neglected by many historiographers—we are helped to challenge assumptions, for example, about the determinants of the beginnings and ends of periods or about what constitutes a "period" in terms of a discrete *mentalité* (in the usage of the *Annalistes*).

In the historiographical literature, three basic conclusions tended to be reached on the question of periodization:

- That the ordering of history is inevitably to a large extent *subjective,* though it will often be defended in quasi-objective terms
- That the essential purpose of periodization is to make sense of otherwise unmanageable time spans by identifying *unities* of some kind
- That identifying such coherence in turn depends on the identification of significant *events* that may be taken to determine change

Each of these conclusions poses obvious challenges for the comparative historian of education.

The periods that we might determine when making historical comparisons between countries—according to criteria of affinity and inner coherence of some kind—might of course not coincide. But their lack of coincidence will in any case be of interest to comparativists, since it is in contrast that much of the value of comparison consists.

We can also postulate cycles or waves of influence, with a time lag effect as new information is assimilated and the atmosphere of change drifts from place to place. And we might learn from examples of time-related phenomena described in other disciplines—Kondratieff's "long waves" or Schumpeter's cycles in economics, perhaps—which are based on the effects of an accumulation of innovations whose influence gradually wanes until a new set of discoveries emerges; or the processes which philosophers have described to account for historical progress, of the type of Hegel's (1830/1944) triadic dialectic of thesis, antithesis, and synthesis. In doing so, we should bear in mind Popper's (1957/1991) criticism of historicism in the sense of "an approach to the social sciences which assumes that *historical prediction* is their principal aim, and which assumes that this aim is attainable by discovering the 'rhythms' or the 'patterns,' the 'laws' or the 'trends' that underlie the evolution of history" (p. 3, emphasis in original).

The main message here and in my previous points is that the concerns of historiographers are also the concerns of comparative historians of education. By examining and reporting upon the particular problems we encounter in researching educational issues we can also contribute to the development of methods and approaches in historical studies generally.

POLICY BORROWING IN EDUCATION

Of the many purposes of comparative inquiry in education, that of learning from the foreign example and using evidence to help improve the situation "at home" must figure prominently. From the earliest days of comparative investigation,

the notion of educational transfer, and especially of "borrowing" ideas from elsewhere, has been in evidence in the writings of travelers and other commentators reporting on their understanding of foreign systems of education. In trying to understand the processes involved in policy borrowing, historical inquiry plays an important role. Completed instances of borrowing allow us to devise ways of analyzing these processes.

Recent work in Oxford, England, has developed models and typologies to assist in the analysis of the processes involved in "policy borrowing" in education over a long historical period. One of the principal concerns here has been the need to evaluate the degree of "embeddedness" of educational phenomena in the social, cultural, political, religious, philosophical, economic, linguistic, geographical, demographic, and, of course, historical context in which they are manifest. The historical dimension inevitably embraces all of the other dimensions in this list. I shall use this recent work to illustrate the usefulness of a historical approach and to exemplify the methodological problems encountered in historical analysis of the educational issues germane to "borrowing" (Phillips, 2004; Ochs & Phillips, 2002a, 2002b; Phillips & Ochs, 2003, 2004a, 2004b).

What we have been trying to do, using the example of British interest in educational provision in Germany from about 1800 onward, is to investigate the impetus for what we have called "cross-national attraction" in education, i.e., the development of interest on the part of one country in aspects of education in another, to assess the "externalizing potential" of policy identified as being in some degree "borrowable," and then to trace the decision making about and the implementation and ultimately the "internalization" of the policy apparently "borrowed."

It is clear, of course, that there are problems with the notion of "policy borrowing." While it has been one of the implicit aims of those concerned with the investigation of educational issues in a comparative context to identify procedures "elsewhere" which might be adopted to improve provision "at home," it is common nowadays to point out the fallacious assumptions behind the notion that policy can simply be transplanted from one national context to another. Michael Sadler's famous injunction of 1900 reminds us of the problems:

> In studying foreign systems of Education we should not forget that the things outside the schools matter even more than the things inside the schools, and govern and interpret the things inside. We cannot wander at pleasure among the educational systems of the world, like a child strolling through a garden, and pick off a flower from one bush and some leaves from another, and then expect that if we stick what we have gathered into the soil at home, we shall have a living plant. (Sadler, cited in Higginson, 1979, p. 49)

And a similar stance, with clear echoes of Sadler's text, was adopted by Isaac Kandel:

> The comparative approach demands first an appreciation of the intangible, impalpable spiritual and cultural forces which underlie an educational system; the forces and factors outside the school matter even more than what goes on inside it. Hence the comparative study of education must be founded on an analysis of the social and political ideals which the school reflects, for the school epitomizes these for transmission and for progress. In order to understand, appreciate and evaluate the real meaning of the educational system of a nation, it is essential to know something of its history and traditions, of the forces and attitudes governing its social organization, of the political and economic conditions that determine its development. (Kandel, 1933, p. xix)

Within the constraints of Sadler's important cautionary message, serious investigation of aspects of education in other countries has sought to identify what contributes to success in the hope that lessons might be learned which could have implications for policy development in the "home" context.

According to Noah and Eckstein's (1969) historical typology of inquiry in comparative education, "borrowing" constitutes the second stage (though, as we have seen, the stages overlap considerably) in the general development of the field. From the work of Jullien in 1816–1817 onward, investigators were "motivated by a desire to gain useful lessons from abroad" (p. 15):

- What might seem, however, to be an observable and straightforward intentional process (identification of successful practice → introduction into the home context → assimilation) proves extraordinarily complex and poses a number of problems for the comparativist to tackle.

- We have used the example of Germany over a long historical period to illustrate the ways in which British policymakers have attempted to employ lessons to be learnt from Germany in order to inform the debate "at home." That there was interest in education in Germany at a high level and at an early and significant date in England is shown, for example, by a report of the Select Committee of the House of Commons on the State of Education published in 1834, the year following the first vote of public funds to education in England. The material provided by the Select Committee's report illustrates the richness of the historical resource which can throw light on the use that might be made of the foreign example—what Zymek (1975) calls "das Ausland als Argument in der pädagogischen Reformdiskussion."

Our investigation generally of official documents from various points in the nineteenth century has revealed a quite remarkable level of interest in the foreign—and specifically the German—model. This interest can be traced, as the example of the Select Committee's report indicates, from the early decades of the nineteenth century and increases in scale as the need to develop a national system in England gathers momentum; it reaches its apogee at the turn of the century, when the Office of Special Inquiries and Reports, set up under Michael Sadler's directorship in London in 1895, was producing a quite extraordinary range of reports on all aspects of education in other countries, with Germany figuring prominently among them. These reports are models of precision, scholarly argument, and presentation, and are written with an elegance typical of the great documents produced by the Royal Commissions which have been such a prominent feature of educational policymaking in England. More recently, from the mid-1980s onward, the London ministry and Her Majesty's Inspectors have been producing reports on aspects of education in

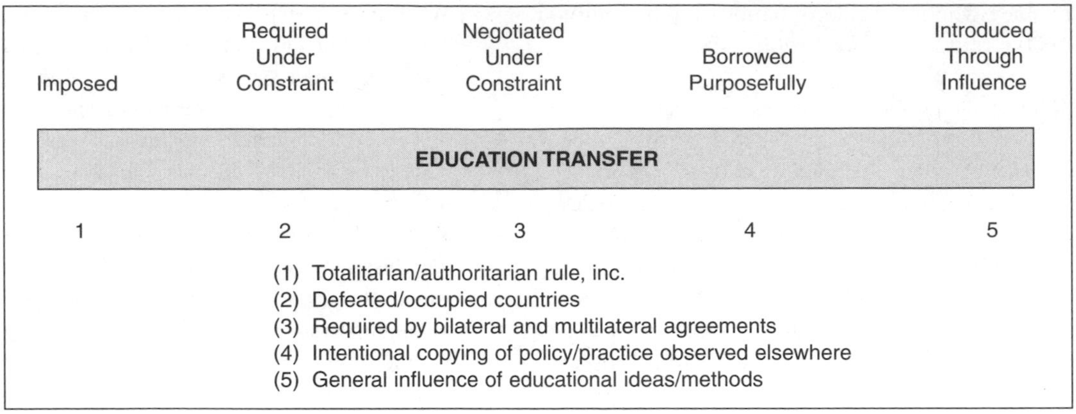

Imposed	Required Under Constraint	Negotiated Under Constraint	Borrowed Purposefully	Introduced Through Influence
		EDUCATION TRANSFER		
1	2	3	4	5

(1) Totalitarian/authoritarian rule, inc.
(2) Defeated/occupied countries
(3) Required by bilateral and multilateral agreements
(4) Intentional copying of policy/practice observed elsewhere
(5) General influence of educational ideas/methods

Figure 16.1   Continuum of Educational Transfer

other countries, with Germany still figuring prominently among them.

THE POLICY BORROWING PHENOMENON

The problems we have encountered in our investigation of "borrowing" have had to do with the identification of unambiguously clear references to the foreign example, with the association of quoted instances of "borrowable" features of education elsewhere with "home" policy, with the processes by which any "borrowed" policy is assimilated or "internalized," and with the analysis of the contextual features in which the "borrowable" policies are embedded and those in which "borrowed" polices will have to take root. On the basis of our analysis of historical examples of policy borrowing, we have been able to propose a number of models to help explain the phenomena involved.

To begin with, we can postulate a spectrum of educational transfer (Ochs & Phillips, 2002a) in which "policy borrowing" is depicted as a *purposive act* on the part of policymakers.

As illustrated in Figure 16.1, this purposive act of educational transfer might occur under different circumstances or reasons—varying from its being imposed to its being introduced through general influence of educational ideas. Also, in Figure 16.2, borrowing can be seen within a timescale that envisages the progression of a "borrowed" policy (here "policy$_1$")

through filters of interpretation, transmission, reception, and implementation (here "policy$_2$") in the "host" system. At each of these stages (filters), there is scope for analysis of the historical conditions affecting the nature of the "borrowing" process.

Kimberly Ochs and I have suggested ways of identifying and analyzing the origins of the borrowing process, the factors that trigger "cross-national attraction" in education. Examples of these factors include forms of systemic collapse, economic change/competition, political imperatives of various kinds, negative external evaluation, and general internal dissatisfaction. These factors are instrumental in policymakers' attempts to identify features of other systems that form what we term "foci of attraction," ranging from "guiding philosophy or ideology" to "techniques," as illustrated in Figure 16.3. We place these foci against a background of context, including that of historical development.

In testing this typology by means of our detailed investigation of historical instances of British policy that have been influenced by the German example in education, we have been able to trace "policy borrowing" through the four principal processes of cross-national attraction, decision, implementation, and internalization, as shown in Figure 16.4.

This composite model takes the borrowing process through a sequence of stages, each of which throws light on the historical background while in turn depending on it.

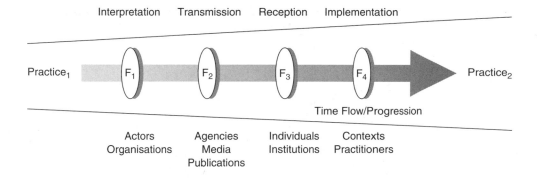

Figure 16.2   Progression of Policy Borrowing Over Time

SOURCE: Phillips and Ochs (2004a, p. 16).

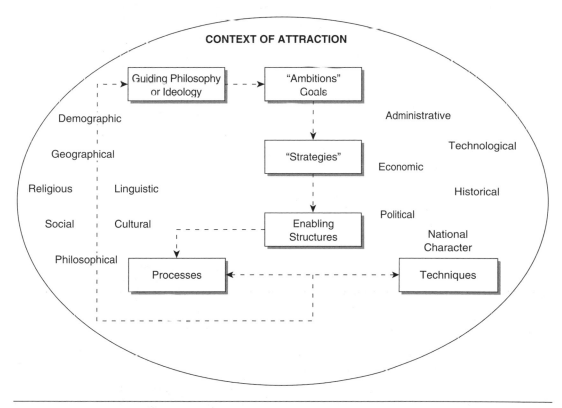

Figure 16.3   Structural Typology of Cross-National Attraction

SOURCE: Ochs and Phillips (2002a, 2002b).

I have used the example of policy borrowing in education in this chapter since it is so central to the concerns of comparativists and since it serves to demonstrate the significance of the historical understanding of educational phenomena.

COMPARATIVE EDUCATION AS A QUASI-DISCIPLINE

Comparative education as a field of scholarly inquiry has been bedeviled by methodological

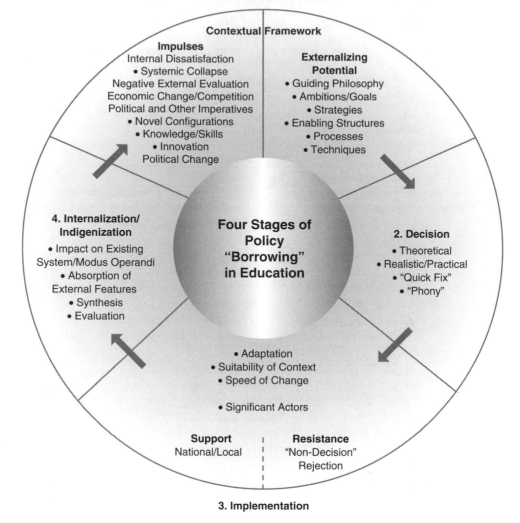

Figure 16.4   Stages of Policy Borrowing in Education

SOURCE: Phillips and Ochs (2003, 2004a, 2004b).

disputes—despite its long history and its established place in educational research. Fundamental to the controversies is the question as to whether it can properly be considered to be a discipline. Since the academic world can be very dismissive of scholarly activity that does not "belong" to a historically well-defined canon of disciplines, the problems in question have been particularly damaging.

One problem in the wide acceptance of comparative education as a scholarly discipline is what many commentators see as its essential multidisciplinarity, which prevents it from having an individual identity and gives it a multiple profile. Patricia Broadfoot has famously argued that "the comparative study of education is not a discipline: it is a context" (Broadfoot, 1977, p. 133), and her emphasis on the centrality of context provides a clear imperative to develop understanding from other contributing disciplines (sociology, history, philosophy, etc.)—in endeavors in comparative research. And so the argument goes that comparativists, belonging to a multidisciplinary subject, are essentially generalists, and among the many competences expected of them is a knowledge of and sympathy for the methods, for example, of philosophical and sociological and historical inquiry. To these contributing disciplines might be added the "culturalist" approach advocated by W. D. Halls (Halls, 1973). And we might also mention, in this connection, the work of Edmund King, who represented the epitome of the cultured humanist educationist, bringing to his research and scholarship in comparative education all the virtues of the classicist, the linguist, and the cultural historian (King, 1968). Of immediate importance here, however, is the question of context together with the fact that comparative inquiry both informs and is informed by other disciplines.

If, then, we accept that comparative education is indeed not a discipline with special rules and methods, it becomes imperative to consider ways in which it relates to and can draw upon approaches in disciplines germane to comparative inquiry in education (it is clear that it at least has certain *affinities* with several established disciplines, both in the humanities and in the social sciences). If, on the other hand, we take the view that, as a highly developed field of scholarly inquiry, it does indeed have some of the *characteristics* of a discipline, then it is important to identify what they might be.

Elsewhere (Phillips, 1999, p. 16), I have attempted a checklist of the defenses of comparative education. It

- shows what is possible by examining alternatives to provision "at home";
- offers yardsticks by which to judge the performance of education systems;
- describes what might be the consequences of certain courses of action by looking at experience in various countries (i.e., in attempting to predict outcomes, it can serve both to support and to warn against potential policy decisions);
- provides a body of descriptive and explanatory data which allows us to see various practices and procedures in a very wide context that helps to throw light upon them;
- contributes to the development of an increasingly sophisticated theoretical framework in which to describe and analyze educational phenomena;

- serves to provide authoritative objective data which can be used to put the less objective data of others (politicians and administrators, principally) who use comparisons for a variety of political and other reasons, to the test;
- has an important supportive and instructional role to play in the development of any plans for educational reform when there must be concern to examine experience elsewhere;
- helps to foster cooperation and mutual understanding among nations by discussing cultural differences and similarities and offering explanations for them;
- is of intrinsic intellectual interest as a scholarly activity in much the same way as the comparative study of religion, or literature, or government, is.

This multiplicity of purpose reinforces the view that comparative education is too broad to be considered a discipline with its own discrete methodological approaches. The term "quasi-discipline" is therefore in my view a more appropriate term to describe a field of inquiry which, while observing the rigors of a huge range of methods in the social sciences, finds its strength in their interrelationship in many and various ways.

A SCHEMA FOR COMPARISON

So far I have been concerned to demonstrate that while comparative education draws on a variety of other disciplines and their methods, it has its own traditions and a particular focus on historical analysis and on the significance of context. What is more, to recall Nóvoa's view of its positive aspects, it is essentially concerned with the relationship between theory and the world of practice, particularly in terms of "learning lessons" and "policy transfer."

In Figure 16.5, I suggest a schema for comparative inquiry, building on Bereday's (1969) model. It presupposes the centrality of context and the historical determinants of policy in education.

The schema begins with the conceptualization of issues to be addressed, seen initially in isolation from any context. It then postulates what Bereday calls a "juxtaposition" stage in which detailed analysis of the issues as manifest

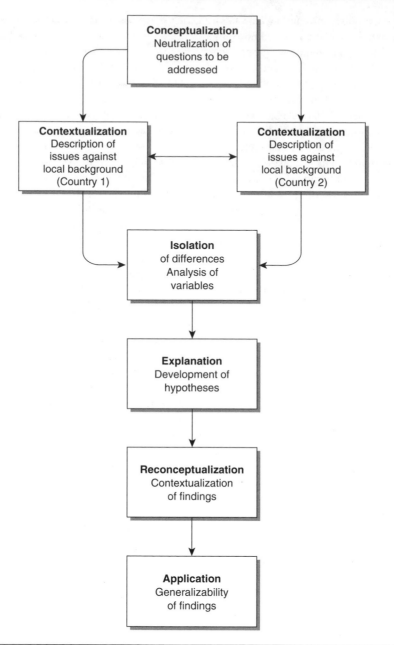

Figure 16.5 A Structure for Comparative Inquiry

in two or more contexts is undertaken. This involves, for Bereday, the analysis of historical, political, economic, and social data. Once the parallel description of data emerging from the contexts in question has been made, the differences can be isolated and an analysis can be undertaken of the variables—and their historical origins—which might account for them. This leads to an attempt at explanation (again against the background of the differing contexts and their historical determinants), to the development of hypotheses, and to a reconceptualization of the original issues under investigation. Thereafter, consideration can be given to the application of any generalizable features that emerge from the analysis.

The historical dimension to comparative studies in education is clearly essential to any understanding of present-day issues. The generalist comparativist should carry in his or her baggage the tools of the historian as well as those belonging to whatever other disciplines can contribute to the understanding of educational issues in comparative contexts.

There is a story that when clearing a house after the death of an elderly lady, her relatives found a neatly stored box with a label on it indicating its contents. It read: "Pieces of string too short to be of any use." This is a nice image for the problems of comparativists who must of necessity know about a wide range of contributing disciplines while inevitably not knowing as much about any one of them as a specialist within any of them would be required to know. The danger is that their knowledge would be, as it were, a collection of pieces of string, each of which would be far too short and which, when tied together, would not form a very strong rope. The strength of comparative inquiry lies in its ability to weave together a strong "rope" of analysis which will help to explain educational phenomena.

There is considerable potential in collective collaborative effort among educationists with a common interest in comparison. Where teams can operate, as is the case with some high-profile research projects in comparative education, the presence of a historian can be of vital importance for the quality of the collaborative research possible. The six-country European Union (EU)-funded PRESTIGE Network, for example, included alongside comparativists a historian, a political scientist, and an economist, and it also incorporated expertise in education in developing countries, in adult education, in theoretical constructs, and in EU policy. The historical dimension was very strong throughout and provided an essential underpinning of and a common thread in the Network's research output (Ertl, 2003). McCulloch & Richardson (2000) have helpfully produced an introductory text on research questions designed to inform the educationist about historical inquiry and the historian about investigation in education and, hence, to encourage such collaborative research.

I remain personally convinced of the primacy of position of historical perspectives; it is difficult to conceive of a proper analysis of current concerns in education that did not start with some kind of analysis of historical background. But in advocating a strong historical dimension to comparative studies I would also insist on the need for understanding of and sympathy with the methods of historical inquiry. Training in historical methods is as essential for the comparativist as is training in the qualitative and quantitative methods of educational research.

In summary:

- Historical analysis is central to the concerns of comparativists and provides invaluable explanatory functions;
- Historical understanding is essential in any plans for reform and development, even if it is agreed that prediction and lesson learning are not possible on the basis of historical antecedents;
- It is necessary to absorb the methods of historical inquiry alongside other methodological skills, as every comparativist is to some extent a historian.

SOME RECENT EXAMPLES OF EXEMPLARY COMPARATIVE INQUIRY

In this chapter I have only been able to exemplify work which involves the methods of historical inquiry, the intention being to demonstrate the richness and the significant potential of some current research which depends on historical understanding, while arguing that comparative education has its unique defining features, as a "quasi-discipline," in its methods and approaches.

Much interesting work is being done on the earliest origins of comparative inquiry. There is, for example, that of Almut Sprigade on the British use of foreign models in the first three decades of the nineteenth century, in the time leading up to the first voting of public funds for education—research which has uncovered much original material in journals and in the British National Archives (Sprigade, 2004). Mention might be made too of analysis of the contribution to comparative studies of Sarah Austin, the English translator of Victor Cousin (Goodman, 2002). These groundbreaking studies reveal something of the early origins of comparative education, reminding us of the longevity of comparative inquiry.

There is also the important research undertaken in Berlin, under Jürgen Schriewer's direction, which involves the most complex analysis of the internationalization of educational knowledge and painstaking investigation of the historical evolution of reference to the work of significant figures in education—John Dewey prominent among them—who have been referred to outside of their own countries and immediate spheres of influence. That important research is essentially historical in nature and throws new light on the spread of educational knowledge and thinking throughout the world.

The events of 1989 and after have spurred much analysis of the processes of transition in education, and such analysis has had a significant historical dimension. Here in particular, the work of researchers in the German-speaking world has been of considerable value in the analysis of developments which can only be understood against a thorough and scientific analysis of the historical imperatives which have produced them. And others have helped with the development of theoretical frameworks ("transitologies" in Cowen's invention) to help with the analysis of the phenomena of transition.

Meticulous work over many years on the description and analysis of education in the German Democratic Republic by a distinguished range of West German academics provided a most valuable service to policymakers, especially in the immediate post-Unification period in Germany, when a rapid and thorough understanding of the historical developments in education in that country was needed to assist in the processes of reconstruction, such as in the difficult tasks of evaluation and recommendation undertaken by the *Wissenschaftsrat*. The rootedness of educational phenomena in a political past is so obvious as to need no further explanation. But without the essential historical dimension, our understanding of what has happened since Unification in the territory of the former German Democratic Republic would be severely diminished.

Political change in South Africa has thrown up a large variety of questions relating to educational provision that again can only be properly understood through a thorough appreciation of the historical development of education in that troubled country. The sad faith in "outcomes based education" (OBE) as a curricular panacea serves to reinforce the imperative to use the comparative example to warn against policy measures. Proper analysis of the historical background to OBE would have prevented many problems in education in South Africa; the "lessons of history" might have served that country well (Jansen, 2004; Spreen, 2004).

CONCLUSION

The sources discussed in this chapter are no more than selective examples, but each of them serves to underline the importance of the historical work of comparativists; each of them depends essentially on the understanding that only the researcher with an awareness of the methods and purpose of historical inquiry can bring. We might almost say that a comparativist without historical understanding is not a proper comparativist. But we can also feel confident that the subject has its own eclectic methods, drawing on a wide range of approaches in other disciplines that together constitute its value in terms of a contribution to policy analysis and development that can lead to improvements in practice that even its critics would wish to see. If comparative education is not a discipline in the strict sense of the word, it has sufficient discipline-like qualities to be described as a "quasi-discipline" and as such plays an important role in every field of inquiry in the many subjects that make up the study of education.

Nóvoa (1998) says of comparative education that it is

> easy to praise a field which looks for explanations beyond national limits, which calls on multidisciplinary approaches, which does not hesitate to come to terms with the inevitable links between educational research and educational action; the plea in favor could go so far as to assert that comparative education is the quintessence of the educational sciences, since it is situated at . . . "a more elevated epistemological level." (p. 53) [Present author's translation from the French]

This view clearly places comparative education at the very center of inquiry in education.

REFERENCES

Archer, M. S. (1979). *Social origins of educational systems.* London: Sage.

Bereday, G. (1964). *Comparative method in education.* New York: Holt, Rinehart & Winston.

Broadfoot, T. (1977). The comparative contribution: A research perspective. *Comparative Education, 13*(2), 133–137.

Cowen, R. (2002). Moments of time: A comparative note. *History of Education, 3,* 413–424.

Crook, D., & McCulloch, G. (2002). Introduction: Comparative approaches to the history of education. *History of Education, 31,* 397–400.

Durkheim, E. (1982). *The rules of sociological method and selected texts on sociology and its method* (S. Lukes, Ed.). London: Macmillan. (Original work published in 1895)

Eckstein, M. A. (1985). The comparative mind. In P. G. Altbach & G. P. Kelly (Eds.), *New approaches to comparative education* (pp. 167–178). Chicago: University of Chicago Press.

Ertl, H. (2003). *Knowledge production in an international research and training network: Methodological and conceptual considerations.* Lisbon, Portugal: Educa.

Fraser, S. (1964). *Jullien's plan for comparative education, 1816–1817.* New York: Columbia University, Teachers College Press.

Goodman, J. (2002). A historiography of founding fathers? Sarah Austin (1793–1867) and English comparative education. *History of Education, 31,* 425–435.

Green, A. (1990). *Education and state formation: The rise of education systems in England, France, and the USA.* London: Macmillan.

Halls, W. D. (1973). Culture and education: The culturalist approach to comparative studies. In R. Evans, B. Holmes, & J. Van de Graaff (Eds.), *Relevant methods in comparative education* (pp. 119–135). Hamburg, Germany: UNESCO Institute for Education.

Hegel, G. W. F. (1944). *The philosophy of history.* New York: John Wiley. (Original work published in 1830)

Higginson, J. H. (Ed.). (1979). *Selections from Michael Sadler.* Liverpool, UK: Dejall & Meyorre.

Howard, M. (1981). *The lessons of history.* Oxford, UK: Clarendon.

Jansen, J. (2004). Importing outcomes-based education into South Africa: Policy borrowing in a post-communist world. In D. Phillips & K. Ochs (Eds.), *Educational policy borrowing: Historical perspectives* (pp. 199–220). Didcot, UK: Symposium Books.

Kandel, I. L. (1933). *Studies in comparative education.* London: Harrap.

King, E. J. (1968). *Comparative studies and educational decision.* Indianapolis, IN: Bobbs-Merrill.

McCulloch, G., & Richardson, W. (2000). *Historical research in educational settings.* Buckingham, UK: Open University Press.

Noah, H. J., & Eckstein, M. A. (1969). *Toward a science of comparative education.* London: Macmillan.

Nóvoa, A. (1998). *Histoire & comparaison (Essais sur l'Éducation).* Lisbon, Portugal: Educa.

Nóvoa, A., & Yaviv-Mashal, T. (2003). Comparative research in education: A mode of governance or a historical journey? *Comparative Education, 39,* 423–438.

Ochs, K., & Phillips, D. (2002a). Comparative studies and "cross-national attraction" in education: A typology for the analysis of English interest in educational policy and provision in Germany. *Educational Studies, 28,* 325–339.

Ochs, K., & Phillips, D. (2002b). *Towards a structural typology of cross-national attraction in education.* Lisbon, Portugal: Educa.

Phillips, D. (1994). Periodisation in historical approaches to comparative education: Some considerations from the examples of Germany and England and Wales. *British Journal of Educational Studies, 42,* 261–272.

Phillips, D. (1999). On comparing. In R. Alexander, P. Broadfoot, & D. Phillips (Eds.), *Learning from comparing: New directions in comparative educational research,* Vol. 1: *Contexts, classrooms, and outcomes* (pp. 15–20). Wallingford, UK: Symposium Books.

Phillips, D. (2002). Comparative historical studies in education: Problems of periodisation reconsidered. *British Journal of Educational Studies, 50,* 363–377.

Phillips, D. (2004). Toward a theory of policy attraction in education. In G. Steiner-Khamsi (Ed.), *Lessons from elsewhere: The politics of educational borrowing and lending* (pp. 54–67).

New York: Columbia University, Teachers College Press.

Phillips, D., & Ochs, K. (2003). Processes of policy borrowing in education: Some analytical and explanatory devices. *Comparative Education, 39,* 451–461.

Phillips, D., & Ochs, K. (Eds.). (2004a). *Educational policy borrowing: Historical perspectives.* Didcot, UK: Symposium Books.

Phillips, D., & Ochs, K. (2004b). Researching policy borrowing: Some methodological challenges in comparative education. *British Educational Research Journal, 30,* 773–784.

Popper, K. (1991). *The poverty of historicism.* London: Routledge. (Original work published in 1957)

Sadler, M. (1900). How far can we learn anything of practical value from the study of foreign systems of education? In J. H. Higginson (Ed.), *Selections from Michael Sadler* (pp. 48–51). Liverpool, UK: Dejall & Meyorre.

Santayana, G. (1905). *The life of reason.* London: Constable.

Spreen, C. A. (2004). The vanishing origins of outcomes-based education. In D. Phillips & K. Ochs (Eds.), *Educational policy borrowing: Historical perspectives* (pp. 221–236). Didcot, UK: Symposium Books.

Sprigade, A. (2004). Educational comparison in England during the first half of the nineteenth century. In D. Phillips & K. Ochs (Eds.), *Educational policy borrowing: Historical perspectives* (pp. 37–56). Didcot, UK: Symposium Books.

Zymek, B. (1975). *Das ausland als argument in der pädagogischen reformdiskussion.* Ratingen, Germany: Aloys Henn Verlag.

PART II

ENRICHING INQUIRY
THROUGH IDENTIFYING AND
ADDRESSING KEY CHALLENGES

Section Three

Challenges in Formulating and Framing Meaningful Problems

INTRODUCTORY ESSAY

DANIEL K. LAPSLEY

Ball State University

Induction into scientific practice hardly ever takes up the matter of how to formulate and frame meaningful problems. Most primers on research methods are geared to the culminating steps in research—on how to test, evaluate, and dispose of hypotheses that otherwise seem to show up, like masked wrestlers, from "parts unknown." One might gather that educational and social science is mostly a technical matter of how to grapple unruly variables into submission—of how to assert proper experimental control, fit statistical models, and draw valid inferences. Nothing is trained so assiduously as the ability to indict a study for its yield of flaws. What is absent, however, is sustained reflection on the source and object of these exertions, and this is a theoretical problem worthy of the effort. There is barely a word on how to ask questions, frame a problem, or generate a theory, and there is very little guidance on what is to count as a meaningful problem or a good idea. In the absence of these considerations, the default criterion is often sheer novelty; the good idea is that which has not yet been expressed or been found in print. Of course, the fact that an idea has never occurred to anyone is scarcely reason to invest it with meaning.

Karl Popper and the Vienna Circle of logical positivists could claim some credit for this state of affairs. "The work of the scientist," Popper (1959) asserted, "consists of putting forward and testing theories" (p. 30), although in his view only the theory-testing part of the work presented any interesting philosophical problems. How one happens to put forward a new idea was not worthy of notice. It always contains an "irrational element" (p. 32). It is strictly a psychological matter of creativity, intuition, and inspiration that can have no implication for the logical analysis of scientific knowledge. Nor is it possible to rationally reconstruct the steps by which a scientist comes to propose a theory; no logical analysis is possible for understanding how hypotheses occur to scientists or how inventions and discoveries cross their minds. For understanding "the processes involved in the stimulation and release of an inspiration" (p. 31), there is "no such thing as a logical method of having new ideas or a logical reconstruction of this process" (p. 32), but only for subsequent tests of the products of inspiration. Hence, scientific methodology, logical analysis, and rational reconstruction are reserved strictly for justification but never for discovery.

These strictures have solidified into a standard account that relegates the creation, invention, and origins of theory, and the "putting forward" of ideas, to the context of discovery—of which little can be said. Meanwhile, the appraisal of a theory's evidential warrant is remanded to the context of justification, at whose disposal is placed the whole armamentarium of a discipline's methodological, analytical, and logical tools. The context of discovery, if not entirely occult, is nonetheless beyond methodological specification and is only preparatory to the real work of science, which is to justify winners among those theories that do manage to show up for the match. One suspects that the lingering influence of the standard account in educational and psychological science has diverted attention away from the front end of discovery, invention, and theory construction and toward the back end of justification, appraisal, and evaluation.

Yet the distinction between discovery and justification, like other venerable antinomies (e.g., fact–value, is–ought), has fallen on hard times. There is a consensus that there is a kind of logic of discovery that revolves around reasonable arguments for pursuing plausible lines of inquiry and that these pursuit arguments are not irrelevant for theory appraisal. As Kelly (1987) put it, "When the one sort of procedure squeezes through the door, the other is difficult to exclude" (p. 441). Kordig (1978) argued, for example, that after the initial "hitting upon an idea," one does in fact subject hypotheses to a kind of rational appraisal. One can deem them promising, worthy of exploration, meaningful, and/or plausible to pursue—and all for good reasons. A question could be worthy of pursuit if its confirmation ("acceptability") constitutes a lethal blow against a rival, if it extends a line of research into new areas, and/or if it anticipates novel facts or upends a settled convention. Plausible hypotheses are then put to the test, with empirical confirmation supporting its acceptability but along with other considerations, including simplicity, fertility, and extensibility. But these other considerations are also good reasons to establish plausibility in the first place; they also constitute rational grounds to pursue this hypothesis but not another.

Although plausibility arguments are prior to acceptability (one does not ordinarily attempt to justify implausible hypotheses), the sort of arguments that are relevant to acceptability are also relevant to plausibility, suggesting that there is no fundamental distinction between reasons for plausibility and acceptance. The various considerations that support the acceptability of hypotheses at the back end of justification are similar to those that signal plausibility at the front end of discovery.

Gutting (1972) argued similarly that the context of discovery consists of two movements: (1) "inventive discovery," which describes initial conjecture or the thinking of hypotheses, and (2) "critical discovery," which judges whether hypotheses are plausible and worthy of pursuit. According to Gutting, critical discovery uses arguments that are guided by regulative principles. For example, critical discovery often appeals pragmatically to heuristic principles (e.g., simplicity, analogy) that "provide convenient ways of continuing research" (p. 389) when the empirical evidence does not indicate which direction it should take or what should be done next. As such, heuristics are maxims of convenience that point the way out of "desperate situations" (p. 389).

Critical discovery also appeals to metatheoretical principles that summarize the scientist's views about the nature of scientific theories or to broad metaphors and claims about the nature of the persons or the domain of inquiry (what Gutting [1972] termed "cosmological principles"). Scientists who are reflective about the metatheoretical implications of their work and of the problematic that confronts a discipline can use this reflection to guide pursuit assessment, particularly during periods of ferment and transition among paradigms. Claims about the nature of persons are often derived from the core metaphors of research programs. For Piaget, the child is a naive scientist who investigates the properties of the world; for certain cognitive scientists, the mind processes information much like a computer; and for some educational researchers, the variables that influence student achievement (e.g., class size, per pupil expenditure) are modeled much the same way functional relationships are established between inputs and outputs in the manufacture of commodities.

In addition to maxims of convenience, metatheory, and cosmological principles, one can point to the research tools of science as a bridge between critical discovery and justification. For example, Baird (1987) found the role of exploratory factor analysis useful to the logic of discovery. Gigerenzer (1991) argued for a *tools-to-theory heuristic* that envisions two steps. First, the entrenchment of research tools (e.g., statistical techniques, computers) generates new metaphors and concepts. Second, these metaphors and concepts lead to greater acceptance of theories that partake of them if the research community uses the tools extensively. The widespread use of computers, for example, generated metaphors and concepts that modeled cognition in terms of information processing (Gigerenzer & Goldstein, 1996). The widespread use of statistics encouraged models of human decision making that traded on the metaphor of the person as an "intuitive statistician" who makes interesting errors when asked to generate or consider the probability of events. In this way, discovery is "inspired" by justification rather than being independent steps in scientific problem solving (Gigerenzer, 1991).

Others have argued similarly that research programs are in fact prodded along by rational heuristics that "guide research by indicating both the method by which new theories should be constructed and the manner in which the whole program should deal with empirical refutations" (Zahar, 1983, p. 244). Indeed, Lakatos (1978) argued that all research programs have heuristics that give direction to the progressive elaboration of its core commitments, including how to fend off recalcitrant evidence and prima facie refutation, although the work of these heuristics might be apparent only with reconstruction and historical analysis of a research problem. Once again, the heuristic that gives direction to lines of research on the "front end" of discovery is relevant to the appraisal of the evidence on the "back end" of justification.

It would seem, then, that the divide between discovery and justification is not the unbridgeable chasm once feared and that the historical neglect of the context of discovery is not warranted. Of course, none of this implies that the context of discovery is amenable to anything like mechanical generation of theories or hypotheses. As Cronbach (1986) put it, "Planning inquiry cannot be the subject of prescription because planning is the art of recognizing trade-offs and placing bets" (p. 103). Perhaps it is not prescription that is wanted but rather attested strategies for placing strategic bets. Gutting (1972) suggested that a scientist who is well equipped to exploit the context of critical discovery would be conversant with metatheory, philosophy, and theology. After all, scientific practice is by and for "earthlings" (Cronbach, 1986) and, as such, trades on the full range of human experience for its inspiration, for which no discipline or reflective practice can be excluded as a possible source. We bring our complete personalities to the contest; our interpretive frameworks are forged in the heat of our biographies as much as by formal training in theory, metatheory, tools, and heuristics. Discovery is the prize of the prepared mind, to be sure, and there are no shortcuts to scientific expertise, yet our general views about the nature, purpose, and subject of inquiry—our "nonscientific conceptual schemes," as Gutting put it—are often the starting point of critical discovery and scientific refinement.

These themes are in evidence in the three chapters in Section Three of this volume. Three renowned scholars, James Youniss, Kathryn Wentzel, and Susan Harter, take up the problem of how to formulate and frame meaningful problems. The authors were invited to discuss fundamental challenges to doing first-rate research, propose strategies for overcoming these challenges, and discuss rationales for their decisions. Of course, science is not done from the safety of bleachers; it is not a formalized transcendental activity that leads easily to didactic formalisms. Rather, science takes place in the ring. Critical discovery is the result of one's wrestle with problems that seem crucial from the vantage point of one's intellectual biography. Hence, it is narrative, vignettes, accounts of critical incidents, and key decision-making points that provide the prism through which the authors describe their wrestle with meaningful problems.

In Chapter 17, James Youniss examines the problem of how to situate one's inquiry from a vantage point that is deeply reflective of his distinguished career. The biographical narrative is not mere reminiscence but instead points to an inescapable fact—that the problems of "situating inquiry" and of "situating the self" are not two different sorts of activity and that, indeed, one is parasitic on the other. To understand the narrative of one's intellectual formation is to reveal the problematic that brings it meaning. Situating inquiry requires interpretive frameworks, but these emerge from a rich and varied personal experience. The starting point of critical discovery, then, is biography. A first-person account is required to capture its regulative principles.

And what do we learn? The problem of situating must be pursued intentionally. One must seek out colleagues, engage new ideas, attend colloquia, form study groups, and work collaboratively in both formal and informal settings. A policy of intentional engagement and collaborative inquiry is of strategic importance for situating the self within the problematic of the times. Similarly, one must master the literatures of one's discipline. This means reading the classics, the standard texts, and the great works. There is no shortcut to expertise, but then there is no surer way to situate one's stance than to understand the history of intellectual problems that repose in the classic literature of one's discipline. But one should also study philosophy and be conversant with metatheory because these will provide the conceptual tools for framing one's inquiry and for addressing foundational questions. This was Gutting's suggestion, as noted earlier, yet we see how it pays off as Youniss recounts his remarkable journey from an early training in the behavioral paradigm to paradigms that were increasingly cognitive, developmental, and sociological. Finally, one should struggle to make an integrative point whenever possible and to extend integrative ideas into new domains, even if this takes one beyond the friendly confines of narrow specialization.

In Chapter 18, Kathryn Wentzel takes on the problem of how to develop and nurture interesting and researchable ideas. For Wentzel, interesting ideas that are researchable have two qualities. First, they hold personal interest, and this is critical to sustain research effort over the long haul. Second, they are interesting to the research community, to educators and practitioners, or to those who set policy. She advocates three specific strategies for generating interesting ideas: identifying and challenging theoretical assumptions, documenting the published literature, and generating new variables by using the person–process–context features of a developmental systems model. The use of these strategies is illustrated by examples from Wentzel's research on goal setting (challenge assumptions), peer relationships (document the literature), and teacher caring (generate variables).

Of course, one gains facility in executing and profiting from these strategies to the extent that one is sufficiently expert in the relevant background literatures. In each of Wentzel's examples, notice what is the opening move regardless of the strategy—an extensive and deep reading of the literature. Wentzel suggests that in addition to expertise, talent at generating ideas is also a matter of persistence and commitment to task. It requires cultivating an ability to frame an argument so that it can be sold to skeptics and doubters. She writes, "It is necessary to explain ideas in the language of other researchers, describe them in ways such that they become extensions of what has come before, and articulate ways in which other perspectives might contribute to their further development." In other words, interesting research ideas are those that contribute to an elaboration of a research program by accounting for settled facts of rival ways of framing a problem and by anticipating novel facts, some of which are corroborated. Interesting research ideas are both integrative and extensive, which are criteria by which Lakatos (1978) defines a progressive research program.

There are common themes in the chapters on situating ideas (Youniss's Chapter 17) and developing and nurturing them (Wentzel's Chapter 18), and both chapters illustrate key aspects of critical discovery noted by Gutting (1972) and Kordig (1978). Both Youniss and Wentzel emphasize the importance of personal motivations in situating inquiry and identifying interesting questions. Both insist on the importance of expertise. Both point to dispositional qualities of the researcher as critical to the success of inquiry; engagement and collaboration must be intentional (Youniss), and effort, commitment, and persistence must be sustained (Wentzel). Both illustrate key features of the philosophical analysis of critical discovery noted earlier. For example, Youniss illustrates Gutting's point that knowledge of metatheory and philosophy is foundational to situating inquiry, particularly when paradigms are rattled by winds of change. In turn, Wentzel shows how pragmatic heuristics of critical discovery can be understood in terms of intentional strategies. In addition, she shows that interesting and researchable ideas are just those that are framed as progressive elaborations of research programs, a point that underscores Kordig's (1978) claim that arguments suitable for plausibility assessment on the front end of discovery are required as well as for judgments of acceptability on the back end of justification.

Susan Harter's chapter on the challenge of framing a research problem (Chapter 13) brings closure to this section. Where do we turn to frame a problem worthy of study? Too often, Harter notes, we turn our first gaze in the direction of methodology rather than theory. We slog away using our favorite measures or paradigm. We cut our pet ideas thin but spread them wide. She deplores the tendency to reject theoretical perspective wholesale insofar as these theories, or some reconstruction of them, are often the source of new perspectives or integrative possibilities. Besides, cultivating such ruthless dismissive tendencies discourages one from stepping up to the theoretical plate in one's own right. It dampens enthusiasm for trying out new ideas, even if ill formed. Unlike the physical sciences, where new but currently untestable ideas are given a respectful hearing for quite a long time, the social sciences are more demanding of instant rationality of their theories, perhaps explaining why there are no grand theories of much of anything anymore.

Harter appeals to her own innovative and productive research to illustrate how she responds to the challenge of framing research problems. Sometimes historical frameworks (e.g., William James's notion of the self) can be exploited with profit. Sometimes theoretical perspectives that explain adult functioning must be turned on their heads to account for developmental and individual differences. Or else a construct must be assessed differently at different developmental levels. Her work on multiple pathways to low self-esteem illustrates the value of not assuming that group "main effects" always apply to subgroups. Her research on imaginary friends, multiple emotions, and multiple selves uses clinical material to inform normative developmental processes. Sometimes outcomes that are disconfirming and counterintuitive, as well as serendipitous findings, are worthy of pursuit, as are instances suggested by real-world events (e.g., school shootings) and trends in culture (e.g., physical aggression among girls, cultural importance of physical attractiveness, internalizing symptoms and eating disorders). These and other examples are marshaled to make this point: The challenge of framing a problem is bound inextricably with what is considered one's "burning question." The starting point is personal and biographical.

So with Harter's chapter, the section comes full circle. We come to see that the problem of situating inquiry, developing and nurturing ideas, and framing a problem are essential components of critical discovery that share common elements. All three chapters call for a reflective appreciation of historical frameworks, metatheory, and paradigms. All three chapters make demands on researchers for expertise, invoke intentional strategies to see clearly and differently, and insist that one seek integrative possibilities and mark progress. Indeed, what signals an important problem or a good idea is that which makes an integrative point or solves a puzzle in a way that represents progress in the elaboration of a research program, and this determination is always comparative against rivals. Finally, all three chapters show that the questions that motivate scientific inquiry are often deeply rooted in biography and personal interest. We seek answers to burning questions that are suggested by our personal experiences, and these questions also serve to situate us within an intellectual landscape. It is a great privilege to take up the life of the mind in this way, for what we often discover is that the products of our research are as crucial to self-understanding as to theoretical understanding and that the problem of situating, nurturing, and framing is both personal and scientific.

REFERENCES

Baird, D. (1987). Exploratory factor analysis, instruments, and the logic of discovery. *British Journal for the Philosophy of Science, 38,* 319–337.

Cronbach, L. (1986). Social inquiry by and for earthlings. In D. W. Fiske & R. A. Shweder (Eds.), *Metatheory in social science: Pluralisms and subjectivities* (pp. 61–82). Chicago: University of Chicago Press.

Gigerenzer, G. (1991). From tools to theories: A heuristic of discovery in cognitive psychology. *Psychological Review, 98,* 254–268.

Gigerenzer, G., & Goldstein, D. G. (1996). Mind as a computer: Birth of a metaphor. *Creativity Research Journal, 9,* 131–144.

Gutting, G. (1972). A defense of the logic of discovery. *Philosophical Forum, 4,* 384–405.

Kelly, K. T. (1987). The logic of discovery. *Philosophy of Science, 54,* 435–452.

Kordig, C. R. (1978). Discovery and justification. *Philosophy of Science, 45,* 110–117.

Lakatos, I. (1978). Falsification and the methodology of scientific research programmes. In J. Worrall & G. Currie (Eds.), *The methodology of scientific research programmes: Imre Lakatos philosophical papers* (Vol. 1, pp. 8–101). Cambridge, UK: Cambridge University Press.

Popper, K. (1959). *The logic of scientific discovery.* New York: Harper Torchbooks.

Zahar, E. (1983). Logic of discovery or psychology of invention. *British Journal for the Philosophy of Science, 34,* 243–261.

17

SITUATING OURSELVES AND OUR INQUIRY

A First-Person Account

JAMES YOUNISS

The Catholic University of America

I have had the good fortune of a long, rewarding, and enjoyable research career. Forty-plus years seem to have passed by quickly, with successes and failures, high and low moments, and more than enough surprises to have kept me going and make me believe there is more to come in the future. I took the invitation to write this chapter as an opportunity to reflect and focus on the people and conditions that helped to shape and give direction to my research. But I found this task to be challenging. I wondered whether it was possible to take something of a third-person perspective in discerning the situatedness of my research choices of topics, theory, and methods. Surely there are unconscious defenses and conscious avoidances that operate in such an endeavor, and one hopes that they would not distort the narrative to the point of rendering it a fantasy tale rather than allowing it to reveal how my career developed as it did.

The second challenge was to determine whether I could find useful lessons that might be transferable to other researchers, particularly those at earlier stages in their careers. I have tried to pass along tips to my graduate students

for years, but I never took the time to look carefully at my own life as a means to improve their lives. Having now made this effort, I realize that the conditions that prevailed during the formative years of my career differ from those confronting younger researchers today. As I note in what follows, my generation entered the discipline when academic positions were plentiful, senior researchers were eager to help us get started, funds were abundant, and confidence in the discipline's future was soaring—quite a difference from today's tight employment market, fierce competition for funds, and a discipline splintered into niches of expertise without unifying theoretical stances. Nevertheless, on the hope that some of my experiences are generalizable, I proceeded with confidence that readers are clever enough to find their own comparisons as they patiently sift through a particular narrative about a neglected topic in methodological texts—how ideas emerge and evolve in the everyday world of research.

This chapter is divided into two major sections. The first major section is a chronological narrative ordered according to coherent themes. I started my work by chancing into the study of cognitive development, and this led to the discovery of Piaget's writing, with its bold epistemology of construction that is contributed to by both subject and object. Events led next to reframing this stance in terms of the subject–subject social construction of knowledge and the study of interpersonal relationships. Subsequently, this theme was extended to the study of social history and the role that culture and institutions play in mediating development, so that political–moral identity becomes the key source of collective meaning for individual lives. This odyssey is divided into three phases: the opening, with my interest in cognitive development and search for a theoretical position; the middle, when I extended this position to explore the social nature of knowing and of research itself; and a later period, when my prior thinking coalesced into a more comprehensive perspective regarding political–moral identity, a stance that is still generating studies and theory.

The second major section is an attempt to draw from this the narrative lessons that might be of use to others who are in earlier phases of their careers. In both major sections, I have tried to identify people, places, and events that situated my thinking. I have also tried to avoid justifications of what I did and why. Still, I acknowledge that there is little objectivity in such an enterprise—which I hope is, if nothing else, enjoyable and enriching to readers.

Theoretical Perspectives and Situating Circumstances

1962–1972: Discovering Piaget's Epistemology

I entered graduate school in 1959, intellectually naive and eager to learn. My interest in experimental psychology had been stimulated by an undergraduate instructor who taught a required laboratory based on traditional philosophy of science and best methods circa the 1950s. For unremembered reasons, he asked me and another student to serve as teaching assistants the following year. So as a young and not particularly outstanding student, I was given the opportunity to envision myself as a would-be professor with inside knowledge of research.

That same teacher steered me to Hollins College, with a new graduate program in psychology headed by Frank McGuigan and with four other active faculty, including my master's thesis adviser, Allen Calvin. Although I studied there only 1 year, the faculty immersed us thoroughly in a classical introduction to the discipline. Not only were we required by a statistician professor to do several analyses of variance daily on cumbersome calculators, but we also needed to read and understand every line of Kofka's *Gestalt Psychology* and Hull's *Principles of Behavior.* In addition, we were closely walked through Geldard's *Physiological Psychology,* Boring's *History of Psychology,* and Volume 1 of Koch's *Psychology: The Study of a Science,* among others. The department speaker series that year included Kenneth Spence, B. F. Skinner, Murray Glanzer, Robert Thompson, James Gallagher, and Michael Scriven, among others, with Scriven returning in the spring semester to guide a faculty–student seminar in philosophy of science. The 1959–1960 school year afforded me a sound introduction to the discipline with a grounding that has lasted for a lifetime.

The year was exhausting but exhilarating and served as a rite of passage into a tradition that seemed well worth entering. What it did not do was alert me to the revolution that the discipline was about to undergo. To wit, during that first year, we read Skinner's *Verbal Behavior,* unaware that I would soon be reading Chomsky's incisive critique of Skinner and behaviorism. I had moved on to the Catholic University of America in Washington, D.C., to complete my Ph.D. when, in the first semester, I met Hans Furth, who became my major professor.

Furth, who had left Austria as a teenager because of the Nazi threat, was on an intellectual quest to discern whether or not thinking was dependent on language. To address this question, he devised the strategy of studying deaf children, who typically spent their early years without a system of language for communication. During those days, speech experts advised parents that if they wanted their deaf children to speak and to read lips, they should never use gestures or signs. Despite this psychologically unhealthy formula, the vast majority of deaf children matured into well-functioning adults who were gainfully employed, formed healthy families, lived in thriving communities, and demonstrated all of the normal marks of good citizenship. If language was so critical, then how was this possible?

The answer was that despite the misguided "oralism" policy, most deaf children were eventually sent to residential schools where they came into contact with peers who had been reared by deaf parents and, therefore, were versed in American Sign Language (ASL). In our studies at state residential schools up and down the East Coast, from New York to North Carolina, we saw children of, say, 9 or 10 years of age struggling with speech and lip reading in the oral environment of the classroom but communicating fluently in ASL on the playground and in the dormitory. By middle school, the students were sorted according to oral skills, but nearly all of the children were incorporated into a common peer community that shared ASL.

My dissertation was a study of the flexibility in deaf children's thinking, with results showing that they developed fluidity similar to their hearing peers. This work was published in the journal *Child Development* and fit into the series of studies that was generated from Furth's original insight. Our other studies were published in the *Journal of Experimental Psychology, Educational Psychology,* and the *Journal of Comparative and Physiological Psychology,* all scientifically respected venues during that era.

In 1965, Furth summarized this research in a book, *Thinking Without Language,* that led to a new line of inquiry. If deaf children's thinking developed in normal fashion, albeit slightly age-delayed compared with hearing–speaking children's thinking, then what was the basis for it? Most psychological theories required language or an equivalent symbol system to mediate thinking. But given our findings, something else had to be at work.

Thus, we were led to explore Piaget's theory, which based intelligence on an action system rather than a linguistic base. My introduction to Piaget took place in a reading group with Furth and two colleagues on campus, a philosopher–logician and a mathematician, who joined us out of sheer intellectual curiosity. Piaget's questions were not readily transparent to someone trained in experimental psychology, and his ideas were expressed in unfamiliar terms that seemed to

have "excess meaning." This group proved to be invaluable for me, however, because these scholars were versed in the epistemological questions that Piaget had raised and were not distracted by methodological matters. This allowed them to view the phenomena Piaget reported as clever empirical illustrations of important theoretical concepts.

This starting step framed my thinking and focused my interest on processes by which knowledge was a relationship constructed in the form of subject–object and subject–subject interactions. The premise that knowledge begins not with the word but rather with the act, and that knowledge develops through interactions, also led to the view that objects were constructed from reflection on these relationships and were not given a priori existence in the world. Thus, development did not consist in ever more valid approximations to reality but rather occurred through mental ordering of self–other (either objects or persons) relationships. These principles comprise the core of my outlook and have unified my work through the various topical turns it has taken over the years.

We perceived that our interest in Piaget's writings was part of a broader intellectual movement that was taking shape within developmental psychology, adding importance to our work. Furth and I were invited to join an informal group of scholars that met in conjunction with Society for Research in Child Development (SRCD) on- and off-year meetings. The group included Irving Sigel, Harry Beilin, Larry Kohlberg, John Flavell, Jack Wohlwill, and others. Although I was the youngster in the crowd, I was readily welcomed. Members of the group promoted my work through peer reviews that allowed me to publish in well-known journals and to gain 10 years of National Institute of Child Health and Human Development (NICHD) funding at the critical start of my career. Being seen as having competence in Piaget's theory also led to an invitation from Robert Sears to serve as associate editor of the SRCD *Monographs.* (This invitation attests to Sears's intellectual open-mindedness and to the lack of status barriers within the discipline during those days.)

President Lyndon Johnson's "War on Poverty" added practical relevance to our work, and the discipline's work, by giving immediacy to its potential application. For example, after decades of neglect, the education of Native American children was placed on the nation's political agenda. Because of our studies with deaf children, the Bureau of Indian Affairs invited us to assess educational competence in Navajo children on reservation schools that had large numbers of "slow-learning" pupils. Furth, Bruce Ross (a colleague who joined our group in 1964), and I made several trips to New Mexico and Arizona during the 1960s. Adapting our nonverbal methods, we found that nearly all of the students who had been classified as "educationally retarded" were in fact quite normal. They did not, however, do well on standardized tests of intelligence (which posed questions such as "Who was the father of our country?") conducted in English by testers who were insensitive to Navajo communication patterns (e.g., children not making direct eye contact with adults, not speaking freely to strangers).

One could hardly ask for a more conducive set of conditions for the start of an early career. I entered the discipline as it was opening up to new ideas about its purpose and methods. The populations and problems we studied were substantively important. The work was part of an intellectual movement to bring Piaget's theory to bear on the new cognitive psychology and cognitive development. Well-established scholars endorsed the work by funding, publishing, and citing it. And the political context of using research to better the lot of all children gave our studies the advantage of being socially relevant.

A demographic factor should not be left out. I was born during the Depression, nearly a decade ahead of the "baby boomers." My generation has been called the "in-betweens" who were sandwiched by the World War II veterans and the baby boomers. The former assumed positions of authority in and outside of academia until the early 1990s, when they were replaced by the baby boomers. As a result, our generation was skipped over, as illustrated by the leap in the U.S. presidency from George H. W. Bush to Bill Clinton. Without the spotlight shining directly on us, we in-betweens were a favored cohort because we completed our training when employment openings and resources such as grants were abundant in a context of little competition.

Our students, the baby boomers, were often first-generation college graduates. They were self-motivated and eager to make their mark in the intellectual world. These advantages of birth have remained with us along the age scale, giving us opportunities for research and, now, the prestige that comes with senior status.

1972–1985: Discovering the Social Basis of Knowledge and Self

My first decade as a young researcher culminated with an NICHD-sponsored sabbatical year in Central and South America, where I conducted studies of thinking with children in a school for the deaf and with hearing children living in a rural coffee-growing region of Costa Rica. During the year, I also visited Mexico, Panama, Peru, Ecuador, and Guatemala, where an NICHD study was being conducted on early childhood development in small villages around Lake Atitlan. Each country presented a new image of the contrast between wealth and extreme poverty, with my informal observations feeding directly into questions that were being asked during those days about the "culture of poverty" and whether being poor in integral communities held more favorable prospects for development than did living poor under dissembled social conditions.

The year away from Washington was enlightening and also a relief from the protest atmosphere that had permeated the city during the 1960s. Young people regularly filled the mall with antiwar demonstrations as buses were rimmed three-deep to shield the White House and teams of police patrolled the crowds. Several of us faculty members from local universities volunteered as monitors to defray confrontations between students and authorities. The Catholic University campus, which is located less than 2 miles from the Capitol, served as a hostel for student demonstrators who, for a couple of dollars, could sleep and take showers in the gym. Consequently, rallies led by nationally known activists regularly sprung up on campus, disrupting the academic routine. To add to the chaos, we frequently had to evacuate our offices because of bomb threats.

After a year away, the ideas stimulated by South and Central America made me eager to resume my research. However, I was unprepared for the culture shock when the taken-for-granted resumption proved to be a struggle. Confronting Washington again, I perceived familiar people and events differently. I recall the night when I reentered the states. The Democratic Convention had just nominated George McGovern, and Marlo Thomas was giving a speech on women's rights. Only hours earlier, my family and I had been in the freezing Peruvian Andes, where barefooted women toting children on their backs were selling thread for a penny a spool. I understood Thomas intellectually but not emotionally because my focus was fixed on South America and its centuries of struggle with human dignity, a great divide between haves and have-nots, and structural inequality between men and women.

The research I had planned suddenly did not seem so worthwhile. Reading Marquez's *100 Years of Solitude* had helped to put South America into context by showing how adaptive blurring the line between reality and fantasy can be. Something in the reverse was needed to facilitate my reentry to Washington.

Help came unexpectedly from a young colleague who asked me to co-teach a graduate seminar on moral development, with the responsibility of handling the section on Piaget's *The Moral Judgment of the Child,* which I had not previously read. The first 108 pages caught me off-guard and struck like lightning. In these pages, Piaget restated his epistemology in social interactive terms. I had already viewed the knowledge process as a mental construction about the relationship between the child's actions and objects' reactions. It now became clear that this same formula applied to interactions between the self's actions and others' actions, with both parties contributing to the relationship of knowing. This was followed by the insight that social cognition was social not because people were the object of knowing but rather because of the interpersonal process by which knowledge was collaboratively constructed.

The first 108 pages spelled out the dynamics of social interaction in terms of two prototypical human relationships: one based on reciprocity of complement and the other based on symmetrical reciprocity. The former was epitomized by children's relationships with adults, and the latter was epitomized by children's relationships with peers, especially friends. Both relationships were central to morality, but the latter was the basis for mature morality because it was guided by the norms of reciprocity and open communication that, when practiced, resulted in mutual respect. This grounded form of respect, not sure-minded individual reasoning, was for Piaget the essence of morality. Indeed, Piaget rejected the notion that mature moral knowledge could be achieved through personal reflection or the use of logic. Instead, it came from mutual understanding among persons who practiced norms of cooperation, reciprocity, and open communication.

Because of this seminar, I immediately produced a manuscript that characterized Piaget as a social theorist, coupling his ideas with those of the philosopher John MacMurray. It was accepted for publication by Klaus Riegel, the editor of the journal *Human Development.* On the basis of this paper, and another in which I contested one of Riegel's critiques of Piaget, he invited me to serve on the *Human Development* editorial board—another instance of the intellectual openness and lack of hierarchy in the discipline during this era. I remained on the journal's board through a succession of editors— Jack Meacham, Deanna Kuhn, Barbara Rogoff, and Geoff Saxe—all of whom maintained Riegel's aim of keeping psychology connected to the larger intellectual debates that start with culture and history and eventually touch on philosophy and politics.

The next step was to go to children to find out whether Piaget's ideas would be verified and whether children actually distinguished the two forms of relationship. The details of the first child's protocol are still fresh in my memory. A graduate student, who did the pretesting, asked a 5-year-old female kindergartner to tell her how a child her age would show her mother that she liked her—that she was kind to her. The child said, "She would pick up her mother's slippers and hand them to her." Not sure whether the girl understood the question, the student asked the girl again and got pretty much the same response: "She would set the table." On the third asking, the girl said, "She would obey her." And how would she show her mother that she was unkind? "She would disobey!"

The same girl was then asked about showing kindness to another child her age. The girl said, "She would play with the other girl." Again the student was not sure whether the girl understood, so she asked the question again. The girl said, "They would play *together*." When asked still again, the girl said, "They would take a walk, hold hands, and smell the flowers!" And how would she be unkind to the other child— not be her friend? "She wouldn't play with her."

This child articulated the core elements of complementary and symmetrical reciprocity that we later found repeated by hundreds of children of whom we asked similar questions during the next couple of years. This work was first reported at the 1975 Minnesota Symposium on Child Development and eventuated in two books published by the University of Chicago Press: *Parents and Peers in Social Development* (1980) and *Adolescent Relations With Mothers, Fathers, and Friends* (1985, co-authored with Jacqueline Smollar), which extended relationship development to adolescence.

It is hard to recapture the intellectual atmosphere of the 1970s. The general exploration of cognitive theories had bypassed Piaget for the more technical and scientific approach of information processing. Piaget had been reduced to a "psychologist of childhood" by the general public and as the champion of the individual's use of logic to parse the world by textbook writers. He was not viewed as a social theorist who would assert, "There is no self apart from relationship and society." Moreover, there was little work being done on children's understanding of relationships with parents and friends, and there was no theory regarding the property of reciprocity and its developing forms. So there was excitement in offering a novel interpretation of an important theory and showing that it fit children's everyday social understandings.

As with the earlier work, support came from being part of an emerging movement. As we were doing our studies on relationships, I met Robert Selman, who was studying perspective taking and thereby adding a socializing element to Kohlberg's theory. At about the same time, I met William Damon, who was about to publish similar data, having discovered the same theoretical themes in Piaget's writings regarding the social nature of knowledge and two basic forms

of relationship. His 1977 book, *Two Worlds of Childhood*, reinforced the view that Piaget offered an overlooked analysis of the social construction of knowledge, and he kindly included some of our data alongside his in making this important case.

Two other factors helped to advance the work at this time. The William T. Grant Foundation awarded us a grant for the study of children's understanding of interpersonal relationships, and a number of outstanding graduate students began coming to study in our Ph.D. program because of its orientation to Piaget's theory. Among other things, Catholic University had awarded Piaget an honorary degree in 1970, and numerous researchers from the East Coast joined us for the weekend celebration in Washington. This helped to publicize our program and attracted postdoctoral fellows who wanted to explore Piaget more deeply. One was Michael Chapman, whose 1987 book, *Constructive Evolution*, remains one of the most insightful ever written about connections between Piaget the person and his theory. (As a side note, as this chapter is being written, the "Generation 10" cicadas are reemerging in Washington from their 17-year incubation period underground. Piaget's degree was awarded 34 years ago, and as I escorted him to our home for a reception, he was delighted to learn about these cicadas. As soon as he got out of the automobile in front of our home, he bent over to scoop up a handful and put them in his suit pocket for closer inspection later that evening.)

In summary, the second phase of my work began in a rather diffuse state of culture shock, but it was put back on track through many of the same factors that had operated earlier. A generative insight was sparked by the co-teaching invitation of a colleague and recognition from scholars in the field who helped sponsor the work. The socialization of knowledge insight became part of an exciting intellectual movement and proved to be fundable. In addition, it was moved ahead with the assistance of several competent students who went on to establish productive careers. Several of these students have now had accomplished careers of their own, many have held dean and departmental chair appointments, and several have worked in decision-making policy (e.g., state commissioner of mental health, interim director of the National Institute of Mental Health, foundation officers, consultant to assistant secretaries at the Department of Health and Human Services). One can hardly overstate the value of teaching exceptionally bright students who demand clarity and are motivated to make intellectual commitments that seek measurable improvements in society.

1975–1995: From Relationship to Society and History

During the mid-1970s, Catholic University and Stanford University received long-term grants from the nonprofit organization Boystown to establish research centers on adolescent development. Our Ph.D. program was partly responsible for that grant; thus, we were relocated in a new center on campus. Suddenly we found ourselves interacting daily with sociologists, anthropologists, social workers, and educators. Coffee, lunch, and colloquia became occasions for interdisciplinary interaction that further widened my interest in the notion of social construction.

Life in an interdisciplinary setting can be unexpectedly generative. An example of one such occasion was a colloquium organized by a sociologist colleague who brought in Gilbert Steiner, the author of the 1976 book *The Children's Cause,* which offered an analysis of the roots of contemporary antipoverty programs aimed at children. Steiner argued that it was not the congressional testimony of child development experts but rather the food cafeteria workers union, dairy industry lobby, and the like that were most responsible for passage of legislation for children's programs. This kind of economic–political analysis countered the prevailing view in my discipline that research leads to facts, which in turn lead to policy, in a logical flow from abstract ideas to practical application.

This was the kind of prodding that whetted my interest in the social–political forces that operated in and around research. The opening to the broader meaning of social construction was helped along by my joining an informal reading group headed by a sociologist colleague, John McCarthy, that launched me into the then new endeavor of social history. This discipline was just taking off, with new books coming out regularly on the social–historical bases of concepts of family, childhood, womanhood, adolescence, and the like. I soon began offering a graduate seminar on "Social History and Concepts of Development," with my goal being to get students to reflect seriously on the political and economic situatedness of psychological concepts such as attachment, parent–youth relationships, adolescence, and aging.

History proved to be an effective means for getting students to think reflectively—more so than, say, cultural data from esoteric peoples. History dealt with familiar ancestors from England, France, Ireland, and Germany, for example. This course elicited some of the most creative student work I ever received, with topics including "If Attachment, Then Why Infanticide in Modern France?" "Toward Recognition of the Masses: The 1913 Armory Show," and "Why Do Contemporary, Educated Jewish Feminists Convert to Orthodoxy?"

As I was trying to understand how to incorporate history, sociology, and political forces into the study of development, a new source of intellectual stimulation arose. By the 1970s, the German government had restabilized into a functioning democracy, the economy had grown, and universities were regaining their prewar status. Within this larger normalization, the study of psychological development had a rebirth. The founder of developmental studies in the United States, G. Stanley Hall, had brought the concept from Germany to the United States during the late 19th century, and now U.S. scholars were reciprocating by sharing the advances made during the intervening years.

I was invited along with Michael Chandler, an unusually creative colleague, to lecture and participate in a series of discussions in Berlin with professors from various universities in the West. The weeklong discussions showed that our German colleagues were well versed in philosophical questions, sociological theories, and American psychological methods. Furthermore, Berlin's location, surrounded by the Soviet-led Eastern Bloc, made it the center of multicultural input, and it sensitized scholars to the social–historical groundedness of ideas.

This visit set in motion a series of exchanges that have continued to the present day with scholars from German universities—Hans Oswald, Lothar Krappmann, Manfred Hofer, Wolfgang Edelstein, Olaf Reis, and Heinz Reinders, among others. I especially treasure my visits to German universities over the past 28 years, encouraging me to explore the larger political–historical issues that underlie psychology's concerns.

Another set of relationships was established at this time with Canadian scholars at Laurentian University who introduced me to yet other cultural issues that also contextualized developmental processes, for example, views of work in youth growing up in mining areas, where cycles of employment–unemployment are structural. At the same time, a shift in the nature of work from manufacturing and mining to service in the North American economy was then just becoming evident. John Lewko, Geoffrey Tesson, and others were responsible for identifying the importance of economic forces and in spelling them out in microsociological terms that nourished my interest on the social construction of knowledge and of our discipline.

My interest in culture and history was further expanded by an evolving relationship with James Wertsch, who was then just starting the series of books that introduced American psychologists to Vygotsky and the Russian sociohistorical school of thinking. In 1986, Wertsch took six of us to Moscow, where we interacted with a number of psychologists who were carrying on the sociocultural tradition during the cold war. As with their German colleagues, many of these scholars were steeped in multidisciplinary traditions that allowed them, as Wertsch noted, to lecture on psychology with Karl Marx in one hand and the Bible in the other hand. (Our 10-day visit ended on an intriguing note as we took the inaugural Pan Am flight out of Moscow on April 30, 1986, and on landing in Frankfurt, Germany, were detained on the runway while being scanned for radioactivity. Unknown to us, the nuclear meltdown had occurred earlier in the week at Chernobyl, and we had flown through the debris.)

This phase of my work ran through the early 1990s, with other foreign visits of note. One was to Germany for a year (1993–1994) as a Humboldt scholar, and another was for 3 weeks in Tokyo on a fellowship from the Japanese Society for the Promotion of Science. The Humboldt award allowed me to experience thoroughly Berlin and parts of the former East Germany just after the Berlin Wall fell and Germany was reunited. I traveled to several universities, where my interactions with faculty proved that the government's earlier investment in developmental studies had paid off in the establishment of a younger generation of researchers who were on par with their U.S. counterparts in every dimension of importance. At the same time, it appeared that the power of culture was strong enough to merit a "German psychology" that was suited to the culture and that country's rich and peculiar Central European history.

The Japanese visit was equally informative, again showing that the younger generation was exceedingly well prepared. For example, Keiko Takahashi and Giyoo Hatano were equipping a cohort of psychologists, including a surprising number of feminists, to move the discipline ahead. As with Germany, the power of culture was patently evident, most pointedly in a psychological clash between American individualism–ego assertion and Japanese management of self through control of private and public presentations. It was obvious that psychological studies in the two places are not readily commensurable, demonstrating clearly that our discipline needed to broaden its understanding of developmental processes through serious reflection on culture. It is not that psychological processes lack generality. Rather, if they are general, then we must rediscover that through careful study of the various forms they take.

This period proved to be a time of intellectual consolidation in which my Piagetian base became integrated with a growing interest in cultural and sociological aspects of development. Culture and society are not "independent variables"; rather, they are better understood as constituting of development, so that becoming a person is co-equal with entering into human history at a particular time and place—hence the importance of studying processes by which people together co-construct reality and themselves. Of key significance is the avoidance of slipping into social determinism, on the one hand, or dead-end critique of traditional psychology, on the other.

1995–Present:
Political–Moral Development

The past decade of work is too close to the present to allow a reflective analysis; moreover, the work is still evolving. It is worth pointing out, however, the broad outlines that this work has been taking. Throughout the 1980s and 1990s, I tried to situate both the persons being studied and the theoretical approaches being taken in social, historical, and political terms. Our current work follows along this path rather closely, as I have been studying civic development and the roots of political–moral identity in young people's activism. One line of work involves studies of youth who participate in community service programs in and outside of school. Two published books on this topic have been co-authored with Miranda Yates: *Community Service and Social Responsibility in Youth* (1997, University of Chicago Press) and *Roots of Civic Identity: International Perspectives on Community Service and Youth Activism* (1999, Cambridge University Press).

The gist of our position is that identity, as it is formed during adolescence and youth, is dependent on participation in ongoing value traditions that are articulated by churches, community-based organizations, nongovernmental organizations, and other institutions that frame service activities addressing serious social problems. Service that represents a particular value tradition operates as a resource that nourishes young people's construction of identities. Rather than searching inward for identity to materialize, young people look outward by participating in traditions and trying them out as suitable or not for themselves and their generation. In so doing, they gain opportunities to partake in a known and respectable past and envision themselves as working toward the ideal future that each tradition promises.

As I envision this work evolving further, it will take seriously the role that value traditions, be they religious or political, play in promoting identity. What we learned from the 1960s is that youth who participated in these systems (e.g., by partaking in the civil rights struggle) gained lifelong advantages eventuating in continuous active citizenship through middle age. Civil rights activism demonstrates the importance of collective meaning systems in particular because it was organized by a coalition among churches, government agencies, and groups focused on social justice. It is pertinent, then, that today, when so many youth are doing community service, service opportunities are typically provided by value-bearing organizations such as churches, environmental groups, and other cause-based associations that allow youth to build identities on a respectable past and provide them with a vision of an ideal future.

ELEMENTS THAT SUSTAIN ANY CAREER

I now highlight some of the factors that led me to study the topics I did in the way that I approached them. Emphasis is given to those factors that are potentially transferable across people and time periods. There are many things we cannot control, including our birth cohort and luck. But there may be strategies we can employ to enhance our work and enrich our enjoyment of it. These are the focus of this section of the chapter.

Have a Grounding

I was fortunate to have begun graduate training when there was a consensus about the discipline's fundamental work and basic methods. I felt grounded in the sense of having shared understandings and outlooks with colleagues throughout the discipline. Although this consensus was suddenly shattered, letting in a flood of new perspectives, the basic grounding helped to serve as a compass in sorting through the new choices. One knew the strengths and weaknesses of classic positions. One also knew which new approaches were simply versions of the old models and which offered fresh solutions and why. Having been trained in traditional behavioral psychology was not a curse, but it allowed me to discern which new course I wanted to take and what its advantages might be.

Not Dismissing Philosophy
and Its Questions

We were taught that empirical psychology had replaced philosophy, raising questions that could not be answered. This belief served as a motivating device that allowed psychology departments to evolve as independent academic units and allowed psychologists to self-identify as scientists. The colleagues with whom I originally studied Piaget's writings, and subsequently those outside the United States, have helped me to understand the importance of grasping philosophical inquiry. Psychology may have moved to separate quarters on campus, but it did not escape confronting philosophical issues. Piaget's lifelong struggle to clarify the subject–object relationship in knowing, Charles Taylor's excursion into the history of the self in Western society, Anthony Giddens's efforts to spell out how people together reconstruct society's structures, and the like are not departures from our psychological mission but rather central to it.

Interdisciplinary Interaction

Psychology is the largest social science discipline by far. One can operate solely within it, assured of having an audience and not needing to look outside for reinforcement. The disadvantage is that one can easily lose sight of the larger issues being considered regarding Western culture. I was led to attend to this intellectual sphere by my sociologist, political scientist, historian, and other colleagues whose work differed from mine but had to be respected. I was forced to seek connections between their work and mine, and this effort has paid off in the belief that my research addresses issues that matter to the larger discourse going on around us. I have learned from my colleagues in these other disciplines, and as a result I am more reflective about what I choose to study and more appreciative of the various approaches they represent. In this regard, I recall being excited by an unpublished, widely circulated essay written by Lee J. Cronbach during the early 1980s. In that essay, he argued that psychology offered only one limited way of understanding humanity. Without minimizing its importance, he proposed that psychology needed the insights that other disciplines offered, in particular those coming from architecture, the arts, poetry, and the other humanities. It takes confidence to believe and act on this proposition. Psychology

is now old enough and strong enough to realize its proper place within, not apart from, the world of scholarship.

Exposure to Other Cultures

I have already mentioned the role played by interacting with scholars from other cultures. I alluded only briefly to the value that came from living for periods of time outside the United States. Adjustments to taken-for-granted expectations are important for jogging one out the belief that there is only reality to explain. Everyday rules pertaining to waiting in queues for South American buses, filling out official papers in German banks, asking questions of lecturers in Japan, and the like force one to check assumptions about norms. In turn, being taken aback by these little things of daily life translates into a more reflective approach to one's research. It also reveals that identity comes not in discovering a "true inner self" but rather in trying to enter into history by taking part in it.

Keeping Up With the Literature

There is a tendency for active researchers to focus ever more narrowly on a selected literature and to form restrictive templates of essential others whose work is to be tracked. I have fallen into this trap and devised strategies to get me out of it. One of them is to use the classroom seminar to force myself to attend to work I might otherwise not read and to explore areas of work about which I am unsure. I already mentioned the value of my seminars in social history insofar as they generated especially creative and integrative work from students. In this regard, I was able to learn from students while being reinforced to pursue this avenue of study.

A second strategy was to remain an active reviewer for journals, research panels, and publishers. Reviewers have no choice but to take others' writings seriously, and this leads to exposure well beyond material I might select for myself. Book manuscripts are particularly instructive because authors, not bound by the restrictive journal format, are freer to express a fuller and more creative view of their thinking. My own books show this same point in another way in that they, in contrast to journal articles, have reached a wider and more diverse audience and have stimulated lively correspondence with a focus more on ideas than on methodology.

Collaboration

My initial collaboration was with more senior psychologists who served as mentors. Gaining confidence from their willingness to let me learn, I was then able to work cooperatively with scholars at other universities who shared my interest for social development and construction. I also collaborated with graduate students who increasingly came to be my methodological guides to new techniques. I did not mention my administrative roles, but during my 11 years as director of the Life Cycle Institute at Catholic University, I relied on postdoctoral fellows as managers of students and connectors to the literature. I cannot imagine doing research alone, needing to function without daily discussion and forthright feedback that helps to forestall taking dead-end paths.

A special note should be made about collaborating with students. There is a line that needs to be crossed so that students feel the right to take initiatives and interact as peers. Unless this is done, students remain research assistants carrying out others' agendas. One strategy I found to be useful in this regard was to rule out as motives negative correction of others' research. Unless a positive point was to made, you probably did not understand what you were doing or trying to say. We, of course, used the work of others as "straw men" in our preliminary discussions. But once a project started, focus was on the contribution that the results would make.

Seeing one's work as part of collective movements was a key element of collaboration. This occurred in the initial effort on Piaget, recurred in the study of social relationships, and continues in our new approach to civic development. One's membership in such networks provides a wealth of intellectual resources that individuals cannot provide for themselves. This pertains not only to knowledge but also to strategic advice and emotional energy that everyone needs to persist through the lows and remain balanced through the highs.

Enjoyment

It should now be obvious that I have enjoyed my career, even as the writing of this essay has helped me to recognize the limited contributions that resulted. One source of pleasure came from the teaching of undergraduates, and I attribute this in part to my confidence as a researcher. I did not believe that I was merely conveying the accumulated knowledge of the discipline; rather, I believed that I was inviting students to see reality and themselves differently. There are any number of effective teaching styles, and it took me several years to discern what I ought to be doing in classes. I began each semester with a focus on at most 10 basic ideas regarding development. I prepared readings and materials to illustrate these points. I restricted lecturing mainly to introducing the ideas, outlining the big picture, and laying out issues. After that, it was students' responsibility to learn by writing weekly two-page essays, delivering lectures, raising questions, and taking sides in debates. Within this format, I sought out at least six students who had promise but who seemed not to know it. I communicated with them via comments on their essays and remarks on their lectures and questions. If they responded, then I encouraged them to participate in research with our group or the department's faculty.

It would be unrealistic to deny that enjoyment also came from the rewards my work generated. They include support from senior researchers whose work I respected and personal friendships with scholars who shared my theoretical interests. They also include grants that allowed my work to continue, being hosted by universities around the world, and becoming engaged in lifelong relationships with students and colleagues—people of unusual intellect and humanity.

CONCLUSION

I am sure that there are other lessons that might be gleaned from this account. I leave them to readers to decide what they might be. One never quite knows how others perceive you. In this regard, I am reminded of this point, which was made to me by a friend, an elderly novelist who for years visited our home Wednesday evenings for free-ranging conversation. One evening we talked about his writing and the basis of its success. He identified a couple of important features. First, he wrote elegantly simple dialogue "like Art Buchwald." Second, his most successful novels dealt with the Oedipal issue but in cleverly veiled ways, a trick he acquired from Victorian authors. And third, he wrote in the first-person voice. When I asked him why the first person, he answered, "How could I be expected to know what anyone else was thinking and feeling?"

18

DEVELOPING AND NURTURING INTERESTING AND RESEARCHABLE IDEAS

KATHRYN R. WENTZEL

University of Maryland, College Park

Aquick search of the Internet would suggest that ideas can easily be developed into something great; simply "tear them apart," "keep it simple," "play with them," "find courage," "stay loose," or "ask a child." Yet when confronted with actually needing to develop a new and interesting idea, the task can quickly become quite daunting and often frustrating. Ask a student to come up with a new idea, and the first response is often panic. Ask a seasoned researcher, and the response is as likely to be "Call me later" as it is to be "When can we start?" The simple truth is that coming up with good ideas is not a simple task, and the strategies for doing so are likely to be more complex than a set of motivational catchphrases might suggest. However, useful strategies for finding interesting and researchable ideas do exist. As a way of illustrating how to develop interesting research questions, this chapter describes how my own ideas concerning goal setting, peer relationships, and teacher caring have evolved over time. In this description, strategies that have proven to be useful for motivating innovative thinking, as well as for providing new perspectives on old ideas, are presented. Although it would be tempting to

claim that these strategies have always been used in deliberate fashion throughout my research career, they have not. However, they represent ways in which I have thought about and developed new ideas for research.

The chapter begins with a description of three specific strategies for finding interesting ideas: challenging theoretical assumptions, documenting the published literature, and generating new variables. Next, illustrations of how to use these strategies to develop ideas in the area of goal setting, peer relationships, and teacher caring are presented. The chapter ends with reflections on some basic principles for developing interesting ideas. Throughout this chapter, the focus of discussion is on "interesting" ideas. This focus reflects the fact that a good idea is one that is interesting enough to motivate a researcher to do something with it and also is interesting enough to motivate others to pay attention to it.

FINDING INTERESTING IDEAS: DEVELOPING METHODS TO TAME THE MADNESS

What makes an idea interesting? How does one go about developing an interesting research

315

question or hypothesis? Unfortunately, there are no quick and easy answers to these questions. However, there are several characteristics of good ideas to keep in mind when searching for that perfect idea. First, the best ideas are always those that have a high degree of personal interest; ideas to guide empirical study must be motivating enough to sustain interest throughout the often long and arduous research process. Without this level of personal investment, research can quickly become a tiresome chore. Therefore, the first prerequisite for identifying interesting ideas is to discern what is fascinating and intriguing on a personal level.

In addition, however, what makes a question interesting also depends on the research audience. Indeed, the ability to convince others that something is interesting lies at the core of any successful idea. For the most part, research ideas and questions are likely to be interesting to other scholars if they address puzzling issues or unsolved mysteries (e.g., Why do girls tend to earn higher grades than boys but do not score higher than them on standardized tests?) or if they support a set of theoretical assumptions that have been the source of intellectual debate (e.g., males are predisposed to developing more complex math skills than are females). Questions and ideas are likely to be interesting to teachers and educators if they lead to concrete solutions to difficult educational problems (e.g., how to motivate boys and girls equally to engage them in classroom activities). Finally, research ideas and questions are interesting to policymakers if they have the potential to support political agendas (e.g., Do boys and girls learn better in coed classrooms than in single-sex classrooms?) or speak to long-standing social issues (e.g., Does learning in coed classrooms level the playing field for females entering the workforce?).

Finding these interesting questions, however, is not an easy task. Knowing which puzzles are currently engaging other scholars or what types of instructional issues are posing challenges for teachers takes work and more than a cursory knowledge of the field. For instance, deciding to study sex differences in learning requires at least a core knowledge of the literature on motivation and cognitive development as well as an understanding of the literature that has documented

sex differences in the past. Identification of theoretical perspectives that might explain these differences is also a prerequisite for developing an interesting idea to guide research. Unfortunately, all of this knowledge cannot be acquired in a short amount of time. Indeed, an initial search of the relevant databases might lead to quick abandonment of an idea if the result of the search is hundreds of abstracts on a topic.

There are several strategies, however, that can help to impose an order on a corpus of empirical findings and that ultimately can lead to interesting and researchable questions. These strategies involve identifying the theoretical assumptions that guide current research on a topic, systematically documenting published findings, and generating new variables. In the following sections, each of these strategies is described in turn with examples of how it has been used in work on classroom goals and peer relationships.

Identifying Theoretical Assumptions

Thinking about and challenging theoretical assumptions is perhaps the most difficult yet fruitful strategy to employ in generating new and interesting ideas for research. At the outset, it is necessary to identify the prevailing theoretical perspectives or assumptions that guide thinking about educational issues. Deciding what these are is often easier said than done because it is common for researchers to design studies without a theoretical basis—or if conceptual models are cited in support of research, it is rare for researchers to test them formally. Therefore, it is left to the reader to discern the underlying assumptions guiding research on a topic. Although this might seem like a daunting task, quite often theoretical assumptions can be determined by simply applying common sense or the "What would your grandmother say?" rule. Indeed, simply talking to someone outside of the field about what others are studying and how they are going about it is likely to uncover important underlying assumptions and thereby help to generate new ideas and perspectives on a topic.

A good example of how to use this rule comes from my own work on the number and types of goals that students pursue when they are at school (Wentzel, 1989). During the 1980s, most researchers interested in motivation at school were investigating students' desires to achieve a standard of academic excellence, either by mastering a task or by demonstrating ability to others (e.g., Dweck & Leggett, 1988; Nicholls, 1984). The common wisdom was that an understanding of these two orientations toward achievement would explain academic performance. This assumption, however, did not seem to ring true for all students. First, it seemed to me that being a successful student sometimes required more than just attention to learning and doing well academically. Personal recollections of life in high school also suggested that even the best students often put significant amounts of effort into accomplishing things other than academics while they are at school. Conversations with family members and friends who were not studying educational psychology confirmed that being successful in school involved much more than academic pursuits. Therefore, as described in greater detail in a later section, I began to think about alternatives to the underlying assumptions that seemed to be guiding this work. If students pursue more than just academic goals at school, what are these goals and how might they also contribute to academic success?

A different tactic for challenging assumptions is to begin by identifying one's own theoretical or philosophical inclinations and considering how the application of a personal worldview might change the way in which a topic is studied. To illustrate, one can start by asking broad theoretical questions relevant to a topic. Is learning and change a fairly linear and additive process, or is change the result of complex interacting systems that create nonlinear patterns of growth? How would a constructivist (e.g., Piaget, 1965) or a social learning theorist (Bandura, 1986) describe change over time? The answers to these types of questions are likely to provide contrasting approaches to a problem. For example, a constructivist perspective on the classroom goal issue would be to focus on those things that children are intrinsically interested in doing; if the belief is that social influences are central to development, then thinking about the expectations that adults impose on children with regard to schooling would be a logical place to start. Regardless of which perspectives guide one's thinking, some new and interesting ideas are bound to develop if the status quo is challenged from a unique set of personal beliefs.

Documenting Published Findings

Perhaps the most straightforward strategy for organizing the literature on a topic is to document what has been done, with whom, and how. The identification of what has been accomplished makes it a relatively simple task to think about what still needs to be done. Ultimately, a topic needs to be narrowed to a point where the amount of information can be organized efficiently. At the outset, however, a fairly broad question should guide a search (e.g., Are peer relationships related to academic achievement?). A novice to this area would first want to read widely and become familiar with the common questions and issues pertaining to peer relationships at school as well as how studies typically are conducted. For instance, a good start would be to document information on sample characteristics, independent and dependent variables, measures, designs, and relevant findings. Once a basic overview of the field has been achieved, the search can be narrowed to answer a more specific question. For example, ideas can be generated from a subset of studies defined by age groups or specific sample characteristics (e.g., How are peer relationships related to achievement during middle childhood?), methodologies (e.g., How are peer relationships, as operationalized in terms of sociometric status group membership, related to academic achievement?), or designs (e.g., How do peer relationships predict achievement over time?).

Table 18.1 illustrates how to document the literature to answer this question: Are peer relationships related to academic achievement? The "data" shown in the table reflect a fairly broad search of the literature, with the exception that peer relationships are defined exclusively by social acceptance and sociometric status group membership (for excellent examples of this strategy, see Newcomb, Bukowski, & Pattee, 1993; Parker & Asher, 1987). As shown in the table, every study can be described as a function

Table 18.1   Documenting the Literature: How Are Peer Relationships Related to Achievement?

Study	Sample Characteristics	Relationship Assessment	Achievement Assessment	Control Variables	Design	Results[a]
1	Preschoolers and 4th to 6th graders	Observations	IQ test	Sex	Longitudinal	*
2	2nd to 7th graders	Peer ratings	Standardized	Sex	Longitudinal	*
3	2nd and 5th graders	Status groups	Academic behavior	Sex	Correlational	*
4	3rd graders	Status groups	Standardized	None	Correlational	*
5	Kindergarten	Status groups	Teacher ratings	Sex	Longitudinal	*
6	Kindergartners and 2nd and 3rd graders	Status groups	Standardized	None	Longitudinal	*
7	3rd and 7th graders and high school students	Peer nominations	Composite	None	Longitudinal	*
8	7th- and 12th-grade whites and African Americans	Peer nominations	Grades	Sex, race	Correlational	*
9	4th, 7th, and 10th graders	Peer nominations	Standardized	None	Correlational	*
10	4th graders	Teacher rating	Standardized	None	Correlational	*
11	6th and 7th graders	Peer, teacher ratings	GPA	Sex, SES	Longitudinal	*
12	4th and 9th graders	Peer rating, nominations	GPA	None	Longitudinal	*

NOTE: The information presented in this table is representative of empirical findings on this topic. More than 60 studies have been published in this area.

a. An asterisk (*) indicates that the relation between peer relationships and achievement was significant.

of sample characteristics, measures of independent and dependent variables, control variables, research design, and basic findings. By documenting these characteristics for each study, it becomes fairly easy to determine what has been done and how it has been done to answer the question. In the case of 12 studies on peer relationships and achievement, samples ranged from kindergartners to high school students. A range of measures has been used to assess peer acceptance, including peer nominations of classmates who they like and dislike, peer ratings of how much they like their classmates, sociometric status groupings (Asher & Dodge,

1986), and teacher ratings of how well students are accepted by their classmates. Similarly, a range of measures has been used to assess achievement, including standardized test scores, classroom grades, teacher ratings of academic success, and peer ratings of academic success. When included, control variables have consisted of demographic characteristics such as sex and race. Nearly half of the studies followed students over time, and in all but 2 cases peer acceptance was related significantly to academic achievement, regardless of whether assessments were made concurrently or longitudinally.

How might this exercise uncover intriguing puzzles that provide the basis for interesting ideas and research questions? A quick look at Table 18.1 leads to several conclusions about research on peer relationships and achievement. First, research in this area has been conducted on students of all ages. Second, all researchers have operationalized peer relationships in terms of peer acceptance/rejection or sociometric status groups, although multiple methods and informants have been used. Similarly, academic achievement has been operationalized in several ways using multiple informants. Despite these variations in methodologies, the group of studies presented in the table provides resounding evidence of a significant relation between peer acceptance and academic performance, such that well-accepted children at all ages perform at higher levels than do children who are rejected by their peers. Moreover, this relation is stable over time.

At first glance, one might conclude that there is not much left to be done on this topic. However, the basic strategy should be to begin simply by filling in the remaining gaps. For instance, based on the data shown in Table 18.1, it might seem expeditious to consider additional control variables that could explain the significant relations between peer relationships and achievement. However, if researchers had focused on only one age or racial group, then a potentially interesting extension of this literature would be to create questions or hypotheses concerning ways in which multiple age or racial groups might moderate the relation between peer relationships and achievement. Similarly, methodological puzzles would arise if findings had been significant for

teacher-assessed acceptance but not peer-assessed acceptance. If this had been the case, then an interesting follow-up question might focus on further explicating the contrasting perspectives on social acceptance offered by peers and teachers. If results had differed as a function of how the dependent variable was measured, then interesting hypotheses could be developed concerning the competencies required to perform well on teacher-developed tests versus standardized tests and how these might be differentially related to peer relationships.

In summary, regardless of the topic of interest, organizational charts similar to Table 18.1 can be created to provide an excellent overview of a field of study. A careful examination of the table should yield valuable information about where the field has been and where it has yet to go. Using this strategy to uncover gaps in the literature is certain to generate a few new and interesting ideas for further study. If, however, a search ends with a robust set of findings (e.g., those shown in Table 18.1) and identification of additional interesting questions proves to be elusive, then an additional strategy would be to reorganize the data using a "variable" approach. This strategy for generating interesting ideas is described next.

Generating New Variables

Generating new variables to formulate new and interesting ideas requires the same basic review of the literature that is necessary to document published findings as is shown in Table 18.1. However, this third strategy has as its starting point the three types of variables described in Bronfenbrenner's (1989) person–process–context model for designing research. In Bronfenbrenner's formulation, these are variables that have the potential to influence development and change over time. Person variables refer to characteristics of the individual such as IQ, temperament, and other attributes believed to be relatively stable over time. Context variables refer to social address or environmental factors such as socioeconomic status, family size, racial group, parents' educational attainment, and neighborhood type. Process variables refer to the mechanisms that produce change such as the quality of instruction, communication

Table 18.2   Generating New Variables: How Are Peer Relationships Related to Achievement?

Outcome	Person	Process	Context
Achievement	Sex	None	Peer acceptance versus *friendships*
	Race	*Communication of values*	*In-school relationships* versus *out-of-school relationships*
	Motives		
	Temperament	*Observational learning*	*Urban relationships* versus *rural relationships*

NOTE: The first row of the table reflects variables shown in Table 18.1. Variables in italics are examples of new variables that could be added to a study of peer relationships and achievement.

patterns, observational learning, and maturation; theoretical assumptions about development and change are the best source of process variables.

Table 18.2 shows how the data organized in Table 18.1 can be reorganized in terms of person–process–context variables. From this new perspective, it appears that relatively little is known about peer relationships and achievement. As shown, person variables have been limited primarily to sex, process variables are virtually unexplored, and context variables have been limited to peer relationships as defined by social acceptance and sociometric status. Therefore, using this organizational structure to think about the original question concerning peer relationships and achievement, an entirely new set of questions should emerge. What other contexts might be important for answering the question? How might variations across these contexts extend understanding of how and why peer relationships might influence achievement? If the definition of peer relationships were extended to include friendships and cliques, would variation in findings across these different relationship contexts change understanding of the functions of peer relationships in achievement settings? Or, how would findings change if context were extended to include out-of-school as well as in-school peer relationships or peer relationships in urban, suburban, and rural schools?

Answers to these questions would extend the field in important ways.

Similarly, questions concerning process variables also can be raised. Could communications from peers concerning academic values explain these significant findings? Could opportunities for observational learning from peers explain variations in achievement? Additional person variables also could enrich the story. Would controlling for individual differences in motives for social approval or for academic achievement influence the significance of results? Would a student's race influence the types or qualities of peer relationships that are developed at school, and could this have an impact on the association between peer relationships and achievement? How would basic temperament influence these relations? In short, a consideration of additional person, process, and context variables can add complexity to research questions and initiate the development of new ideas in ways that a simpler documentation of what has been published cannot.

Bronfenbrenner (1989) also argued, however, that each type of variable by itself can never tell the whole story. Rather, the ways in which person, process, and context variables interact with each other also need to be taken into account. Although a consideration of interactions complicates the picture even further, it reflects to a greater degree how humans learn and develop in context over time. For instance, an interesting question using an observational learning perspective (Bandura, 1986) would be the following: Do boys and girls react to modeled behavior of peers in similar or different ways? Similarly, one could ask whether behavior is more likely to be observed if it is modeled by a best friend, a group of classmates, or the highest achiever in the class or whether observational learning works better in elementary classrooms than in high school classrooms. Finally, Bronfenbrenner reminds us that development and change are not static processes. Ideally, research designs should be able to account for consistency and change in persons, processes, and contexts over time. An illustrative question would be the following: Does a peer relationship need to be stable for a certain amount of time before it has an influence on a student's level of achievement? Ideas and questions concerning time-related issues are certain to have interesting implications for theory as well as practice.

The use of a variable generation strategy enables the identification of a nearly limitless number of new and interesting ideas for research. Indeed, by now a researcher could have a list containing hundreds of interesting questions about peer relationships and achievement. The researcher's eyes may have glazed over, and he or she might have no idea of how to proceed. How can all of these possibilities help to identify an interesting question that can be addressed in a single program of research? How does one go about designing a study that takes all of these issues into account? It is clear that all possible questions cannot be answered in one study. As noted at the beginning of this chapter, a good place to start is by taking note of ideas that spark personal interest. If only one new thing could be learned about peer relationships and achievement, then what should it be? Other questions can always be tackled later.

Summary

Three strategies that can facilitate the development of new and interesting ideas for research have been described. The first strategy requires careful consideration of the underlying theoretical assumptions used to guide work on a topic.

The second strategy entails an in-depth documentation of what has been published. Finally, systematic generation of person, process, and context variables can extend research in myriad ways. Is one strategy better than another? Each strategy is useful in its own right, but these strategies can also be used in conjunction with each other to create new directions for research. At the simplest level, a researcher's strategies should result in information that will help him or her to refine current understanding of a topic by filling in the gaps and extending an avenue of research to its next logical step. Breaking new ground requires a more sophisticated and innovative look at the data by challenging assumptions or creating a more complex model of person, process, and context variables.

STRATEGIES IN ACTION: PUTTING THEM TO THE TEST

Perhaps the best way of illustrating the utility of each strategy is to describe how it has been implemented in a program of research. The following are brief accounts of how interesting questions have been developed in three interrelated areas using each of the strategies just described.

Challenging Theoretical Assumptions: What Is a Goal?

Questioning theoretical assumptions and turning them upside down to create new and interesting questions for research is challenging. However, do not shy away from attempting to do so; simple ideas, if they are new and unexplored, can go a long way. In my own experience, at least two factors have supported new thinking about theoretical issues: gaining competence in one theoretical perspective and then integrating principles from multiple perspectives. In what follows, I illustrate how I came to ask the following questions. Do students simply want to achieve a goal to do well academically, or do they pursue multiple goals while they are at school? Are academic goals the only ones important for understanding the effects of motivation on performance, or might social goals also be important? These two fairly simple questions have served as a basis for numerous studies over the years.

Like many students, I began my graduate work with multiple interests, wanting to study achievement motivation, gender differences, and social development. Having taken first a course on motivation, I quickly began reading everything I could find on the topic, especially work that focused on gender differences and socialization processes. Being interested in history, I also discovered the work of David McClelland and Eleanor Maccoby, giants in their respective fields of motivation and social development. From McClelland's (1987) work, I learned about the conceptual roots of current perspectives on achievement motivation, including the notion that motivation to achieve involves reaching standards of excellence. In addition, however, McClelland demonstrated that individuals can have multiple motives, including social needs, and that achievement motives can be "socialized" in adults by way of direct intervention. Specific socialization strategies, as described by McClelland, were creating a social environment marked by warmth, as well as by social and emotional support, and communicating expectations for reaching one's full potential (McClelland, 1965).

Maccoby's work focused on family socialization theory (e.g., Maccoby & Martin, 1983). Maccoby also wrote extensively on the development of sex differences, including differences in boys' and girls' motivation and intellectual functioning (Maccoby, 1966). Of particular interest was her suggestion that boys and girls might be motivated to achieve different things, with girls being more interested than boys in pursuing social outcomes and in achieving academically for social reasons. From her work, I also gained exposure to the literature on parents' socialization of children and ways in which to think about social factors that might contribute to differences in academic achievement. What was particularly intriguing was that both scholars—McClelland and Maccoby—discussed socialization in very similar terms, even though they were talking about very different contexts (families vs. business). In addition, both McClelland and Maccoby proposed that individuals are motivated to pursue social as well as achievement-related goals.

While reading about motivation and socialization, I also was introduced to a unique set of theoretical principles from developmental systems theory (Ford & Ford, 1987) that stood in stark contrast to many of those principles guiding work on motivation. For example, like many motivational theorists, systems theorists view behavior as goal directed, that is, having direction and purpose and being under the control and regulation of the individual. However, from a systems perspective, the context of goal-directed behavior, especially when considered in terms of hierarchically organized systems (e.g., family, peer group, school), was essential for understanding its origins. An additional systems concept was that competence was a reflection of an equilibrium established between the individual and the environment (Bronfenbrenner, 1989; Ford, 1992). Finally, the notion of equifinality—that is, that different and multiple goals can serve the same purpose—provided further impetus for the idea that a variety of goals might explain achievement-related outcomes.

Over the years, this unique set of knowledge bases has contributed to the development of interesting and researchable ideas concerning motivation and adjustment to school. McClelland's work had demonstrated that people strive to fulfill multiple motives (including social motives), Maccoby argued convincingly that there might be individual differences in the goals that children pursue at school, and systems concepts described competence in terms of the pursuit of multiple goals that resulted in person–environment fit. From the intersection of these multiple perspectives came several related ideas concerning students' classroom goals. First, it seemed to be useful to adopt a definition of school-related goals that allowed for the pursuit of more than one goal at a time and that included nonacademic outcomes. Indeed, the prevailing definition of achievement goals at the time was that students pursued one of two orthogonal goals that reflected either superior performance or mastery of a task (e.g., Dweck & Leggett, 1988). Second, if students pursued multiple goals at school, then it also seemed reasonable to expect that teachers wanted their students to achieve multiple goals that reflected social outcomes as well as academic outcomes. Finally, inserting the notion of person–environment fit into the mix, it seemed reasonable to think that students might be most successful at school when the set of goals they pursued overlapped significantly with those that teachers wanted them to pursue.

From this initial set of ideas, I designed a dissertation on multiple goals and achievement (Wentzel, 1989) and began a career of studying the role of multiple goals in students' academic success, including the role of social goals and social competence in understanding children's adjustment to school. What made these ideas interesting to me? For the most part, they posed interesting puzzles because they were based on a set of assumptions about why children succeed at school that differed from those guiding other research on motivation. What made these ideas interesting to others? At one level, they reflected common wisdom. My own experience and that of others suggested that students do pursue multiple goals at school. In addition, it was not difficult to find classroom teachers who would confirm that student demonstration of competent social behavior was a high priority in the classroom. From a scholarly perspective, the notion that people pursue multiple goals was certainly not new, nor was the notion that students might pursue social goals (Maehr, 1983). However, few scholars had studied the multiple goals of schoolchildren or empirically assessed social goals as part of a more complex profile of school-related goals. Therefore, it is possible that my introduction to these ideas came at a time when the field needed a fresh look at an enduring problem.

In summary, finding new and interesting ideas by questioning theoretical assumptions and common practice can be facilitated by developing extensive background knowledge on a topic and looking for ways in which multiple perspectives or disciplines intersect. In addition, it is always prudent to trust personal experience, talk to others, and think about what your grandmother would say.

Documenting the Literature: How Are Peer Relationships Related to Academic Achievement?

What if achieving theoretical insight and creativity proves to be too difficult? My work on peer relationships provides a good example of how to develop new and interesting questions without tackling theoretical abstractions. I embarked on a project to study peer relationships at school while working as a postdoctoral fellow. Knowing relatively little about peer relationships, I began by reading widely in the area to develop a baseline of knowledge. This initial exposure to the topic revealed several issues. First, the work on this topic was fairly atheoretical; research was primarily descriptive, documenting correlates of peer acceptance/rejection and sociometric status group membership. In addition, the findings were extremely consistent (e.g., Newcomb et al., 1993), indicating that popular and well-accepted students, when compared with average-status peers, are more cooperative, helpful, and sociable; demonstrate better leadership skills; and are more self-assertive, whereas low-accepted and rejected students tend to be less compliant, less self-assured, less sociable, and more aggressive, disruptive, and withdrawn. In addition, although researchers in this area did not seem to be particularly interested in school-related outcomes, many of them had documented that rejected or low-accepted children tended to have poor academic records (e.g., Austin & Draper, 1984).

This link to achievement led to a more focused interest in why peer relationships might be related to academic performance, and I began documenting the published research on this narrowed topic. My efforts resulted in a table that was more extensive than, but highly similar to, Table 18.1. Peer acceptance and rejection, as well as popular and rejected sociometric status, had been related consistently to academic outcomes, regardless of methods used or sources of information. Therefore, the evidence indicated a very robust phenomenon. What intrigued me, however, was that studies that included control or mediating variables that might explain this relation were rare; in the absence of theoretical perspectives, there was little empirical evidence to explain why this relation might exist. I had found a puzzle to solve.

Two additional pieces of evidence contributed to my first study of this problem. First, Parker and Asher's (1987) review of the literature on peer rejection presented the intriguing notion that peer rejection might place

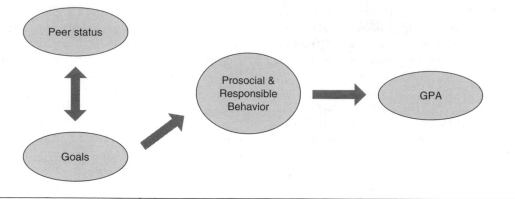

Figure 18.1   Model of Peer Status in Relation to Academic Achievement

NOTE: GPA = grade point average.

children at risk for two reasons: either (1) because not being liked might actually cause the development of undesirable outcomes over time or (2) because what a rejected child is like (a relatively stable characteristic) might lead to long-term negative consequences. In the first case, peer rejection would have a causal influence on an outcome such as achievement. In the second case, peer rejection would simply be a correlate of achievement, with a second factor having causal influence on both rejection and academic performance.

If the second model was correct, then what underlying characteristic(s) might be related to both peer rejection and academic achievement? Knowing that aggression and prosocial forms of behavior were strong correlates of peer rejection and acceptance, respectively, I then reviewed the literature on behavioral correlates of academic achievement. I found overwhelming evidence for a negative association between aggression and achievement, and from my earlier work on multiple goals, I knew there was a positive association between prosocial and socially responsible forms of behavior and achievement (Wentzel, 1991b). Therefore, I extended the findings in Table 18.1 by adding classroom behavioral styles and their corresponding goals as intervening variables that might explain the relation between peer status and academic achievement. A simplified model

that guided the resulting study is shown in Figure 18.1.

The results of this study indicated that for middle school students, demonstrations of socially responsible behavior in the classroom could explain significant relations between peer sociometric status and academic achievement, even when controlling for variables such as IQ, sex, ethnicity, school absence, and family structure (Wentzel, 1991a). In addition, the relation between peer status and classroom behavior could be explained, in part, by the social goals that students pursued at school. In short, the findings of the study extended the literature by identifying potential mediators of the relation between peer sociometric status and academic achievement. Therefore, of interest to the field was empirical evidence to support the incidental model described by Parker and Asher (1987), and part of a puzzle would be solved. Of unique interest to me was additional evidence that social factors (peer relationships, social goals, and classroom behavior) could have a significant impact on the academic lives of students.

A second example of how to develop ideas based on documentation and then extension of the literature comes from a follow-up study on peer relationships (Wentzel & Caldwell, 1997). In this case, a variable generation approach provided the primary impetus for the ideas guiding the study. Having already documented the

Table 18.3   Generating New Variables: A Follow-Up Study on Peer
Relationships and Achievement

Outcome	Person	Process	Context
Achievement	Sex	None	Peer acceptance versus friendships versus cliques
	Behavioral styles		
	Emotional distress		School

NOTE: Variables were generated for Wentzel and Caldwell (1997).

literature on peer acceptance and achievement, the initial thinking for this second study began with a consideration of person, process, and context variables (see the first row of Table 18.2). From this perspective, the field appeared to be wide-open for additional research. We first considered contextual factors that might add to the story of peer relationships and achievement. As noted earlier, a number of interesting contexts could be examined in this regard. We chose simply to expand the types of peer relationship contexts to include friendships and peer groups; to that point, no studies had reported on multiple peer contexts in relation to academic achievement. Adding additional peer contexts was potentially interesting because different processes of influence would be implied if some were significantly related to achievement and others were not. We also considered the school that students attended as a context and included samples from two different schools.

In the first study of peer relationships and achievement described earlier, behavioral styles were added as a person variable. In this new study, emotional distress was included as an additional mediator between peer relationships and achievement. Of interest here was the possibility that the quality of peer relationships might directly influence the emotional well-being of a student; in turn, emotional well-being might influence behavior as well as academic outcomes. We did not include process variables. However, we did include a time dimension by following students over a 2-year period. This allowed us to draw

some conclusions concerning the stability of predictors and outcomes over time and concerning the correlates of change. Therefore, by considering new variables, we developed a study that involved a relatively simple but new and potentially important extension of the literature. Our new set of person, process, and context variables is shown in Table 18.3.

In summary, I have illustrated how documenting published work and generating new variables led to several new ideas concerning the peer relationship–achievement connection. At the outset, a significant amount of background reading resulted in a fairly focused question about peer relationships and achievement to guide a systematic documentation of the literature (e.g., Table 18.1). In addition, I used what I knew best—the literature on motivation and achievement—to bring a fresh perspective to something about which I knew relatively little. Finally, once some familiarity with the literature had been gained, a variable approach provided the impetus to consider additional person and context variables. A third illustration of how to formulate and develop new and interesting ideas reflects the use of all three strategies. In this case, the key to developing an interesting question was the fact that some ideas simply need time to develop and mature.

Let It Stew: How Do Teachers "Care"?

This final idea has to do with the notion of a caring teacher—how teacher caring is translated into practice and how it motivates students to engage in the social and intellectual life of the classroom. The roots of this idea began immediately after graduate school while I was working on a project relating parent–child relationships and characteristics of family systems to school-related behavior and achievement. The work was highly complementary to my training in systems theory and allowed me to learn about the social and familial antecedents of adolescents' classroom behavior. At that time, it struck me that teachers were rarely included in studies of parental influence on children's adjustment to school but that they might play an important socialization role by either complementing or countering parental and family influences. Knowing little about research on teachers, I began collecting articles that explored teacher predictors of achievement as well as parent predictors of achievement. Most of this work, however, focused on parental involvement and home–school connections and did not explicate processes by which teachers might have a social impact on student outcomes independently of parents. Consequently, the idea was set aside, and work on peer socialization and school adjustment began.

While working on the peer–achievement connection, however, I began to include additional measures in my studies that reflected two social ways in which teachers might influence student motivation and achievement: by providing social support and by liking a student. Indeed, it seemed reasonable that if perceptions of social support from peers and how much peers liked a student were related to motivation and achievement, then social acceptance and approval from teachers might influence students in similar ways. The inclusion of these variables yielded two interesting findings. First, middle school teachers and peers tended to like the same students with one exception, namely, that students who were sociometrically neglected (i.e., students who were not well liked but also were not particularly disliked by their peers) were liked by teachers most; these students also were the highest achievers (Wentzel & Asher, 1995). Therefore, at least for some students, levels of support and acceptance from peers could not explain academic excellence. Second, I found that when levels of social support from families, peers, and teachers were taken into

account simultaneously, the pathway from teachers' social support to student achievement was different from the pathways from parental and peer social support to student achievement (Wentzel, 1998). Teachers' social support seemed to have a greater impact on students' interest and motivation for schoolwork, whereas parent and peer social support seemed to have the strongest relation to students' levels of emotional distress. In short, something about the social nature of teaching provided students with unique experiences relevant for understanding motivation and achievement.

This new information helped to refine my earlier interest in teachers by focusing on the notion of social support. A review and documentation of the published literature indicated that several researchers had examined social support from teachers in relation to student motivation and achievement (e.g., Goodenow, 1993). One outcome of this review, however, was an observation that nearly all of the studies had employed similar measures of social support. These measures generally asked students how much they thought their teachers cared about them. In this case, my review uncovered a conceptual puzzle: How were students defining the word "care," and what did it mean when students said that their teachers cared about them? Rather than trying to come up with a conceptual definition on my own, I asked students to provide a definition by generating characteristics of teachers who care about them and of teachers who do not care about them (Wentzel, 1997).

To make sense of the qualitative responses generated by students, I had to develop a coding scheme to analyze the data. While I read about the construct of caring, it became evident that many of the scholars writing in this area (e.g., Noddings, 1992) were describing aspects of effective parenting. Around the same time, I came across an article by Maccoby (1992) that described Kurt Lewin's work on leadership styles and group processes with school-age boys (Lewin, Lippitt, & White, 1939). In her article, Maccoby noted how Lewin's ideas about warm, democratic, and authoritative leadership styles served as the foundation for subsequent studies of families, including the research on parenting styles (Baumrind, 1971). What struck me at the time was the fact that much of what we knew about effective parenting was in fact based on a set of fairly generic social processes that could also describe effective strategies for any adult, including teachers, in working with children. This insight prompted me to use the parenting dimensions described by Baumrind (1971) to develop a coding scheme for the responses about caring from my middle school participants. Based on extensive observations of parents and children, Baumrind concluded that specific dimensions of parent–child interactions could reliably predict children's social, emotional, and cognitive competencies. These dimensions reflect consistent enforcement of rules, expectations for self-reliance and self-control, solicitation of children's opinions and feelings, and expressions of warmth and approval. It seemed reasonable to think that teachers interacted with their students along similar dimensions. The result was a set of categories that fit the data in a reliable and meaningful way (Wentzel, 1997).

The logical next step was to replicate and extend these findings to see whether this set of teacher characteristics predicted students' social and academic competencies in ways predicted by parenting dimensions. Using a variable generation strategy, I also considered additional person and context variables. I included students' beliefs about control as a person variable because my previous studies had identified these beliefs as correlates of classroom goal pursuit. In addition, others' previous work had indicated that associations between parenting styles and child outcomes might be moderated by race (Steinberg, Dornbusch, & Brown, 1992). Therefore, this additional context variable also was included in the study. Findings indicated that the teaching dimensions reminiscent of parenting styles explained significant amounts of variance in middle school students' social and academic goals, classroom behavior, and academic achievement (Wentzel, 2002). In addition, race and sex did not moderate these relations.

To some researchers in the field, this study might have seemed like a very novel and innovative approach to studying classroom processes in relation to student outcomes. From my perspective, however, the study was a natural extension of years of reading, thinking, and conducting research on goal setting, social

relationships, and academic achievement. In fact, the findings of this study have already served as the basis for further consideration of person, process, and context variables relevant to understanding teacher effectiveness. Indeed, new person variables could be added to examine the role of individual differences in moderating the effects of teacher characteristics of student motivation. Additional process variables that might interact with teaching dimensions to influence social and academic engagement (e.g., instructional techniques) also could be included. Finally, new context variables, such as subject areas (e.g., mathematics, social studies), class size, and school climate, could be explored. My choice was to add a context I now knew much about—peer relationships. This focused my thinking on issues of generalizability of the teacher effectiveness dimensions and how to refine them to include processes relevant to peer socialization practices as well as teacher socialization practices. A new model of classroom "affordances," shown in Figure 18.2, is currently serving as a foundation for a next round of studies examining the joint contribution of teacher and peer provisions to students' self-processes and motivation at different grade levels (Wentzel, 2004).

SUMMARY AND CONCLUSIONS

As a way of summarizing the suggestions presented in this chapter, I now offer a set of guiding principles that I have gleaned along the way. These reflect the basic elements from which interesting ideas are built: expertise, hard work, and perspective taking.

Become an Expert: Cultivate Unique Talents and Skills

For any given topic, there can be as many new ideas and variations on a theme as there are people to contribute. Interesting ideas, however, are unique in that they are built on a level of expertise that allows them not only to stand out but also to withstand challenges and counterarguments from others. Therefore, the development of background knowledge and some core competencies is a necessary first step to finding interesting ideas. In short, idea-generating

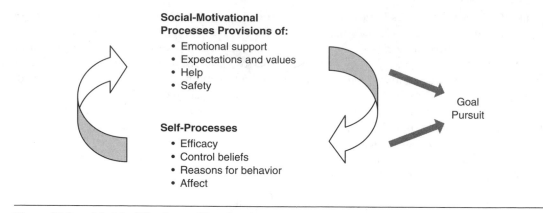

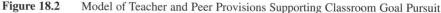

Figure 18.2   Model of Teacher and Peer Provisions Supporting Classroom Goal Pursuit

SOURCE: Reprinted from *Advances in Child Development and Behavior* (Vol. 32), K. R. Wentzel, "Understanding Classroom Competence: The Role of Social-Motivational and Self-Processes," 2004, p. 216, with permission from Elsevier.

talents will be a product of those things that are understood and known best. Whether interests concern socialization processes, educational leadership, classroom instruction, or qualitative interviewing techniques, the quality of ideas will reflect the amount of work and time taken to develop an area of expertise.

In addition to developing expertise, the idea-generating strategies that will be most useful over time will be those that reflect personal problem-solving styles and levels of comfort with taking intellectual risks. Problem-solving talents might lie in bringing people together to generate collaborative ideas rather than "going it alone," in identifying essential incremental steps to solving one seemingly intractable problem, or in challenging the status quo to uncover hidden assumptions. Similarly, ideas might come not from questioning theoretical assumptions but rather from challenging methodological traditions or applying new statistical techniques or designs to old problems. Indeed, many theoretical advances have come from the development of new methodologies and ways of assessing phenomena. In all cases, however, a solid foundation of knowledge and expertise is essential for the development of interesting and new ideas.

Commit to It: Do It

The underlying key to success at anything is hard work, persistence, and a determination to make it work. Likewise, the generation of interesting ideas reflects a commitment to working on a problem despite setbacks or periodic lack of inspiration. Ideas need to be constantly tinkered with, rebuilt, and polished over time. As noted earlier, interesting ideas also come from knowing what has been done, what has been discarded, what is taken for granted, what is in vogue, and what ideas others are working on currently. The only way of knowing all of these things is to engage in a process of constant intellectual renewal—read everything possible, talk to people, and listen closely to what others have to say. In addition, it is worth remembering that knowing comes from doing, even if some efforts are more successful than others. Indeed, not all research is published in top journals; in fact, not everything that is published will even be read by someone other than the journal editor and a few reviewers. However, the more ideas that are generated and put to the test empirically, the more likely it is that some ideas that are truly interesting will be produced. Finally, inherent in the notion of commitment is the reality that things take time. New and interesting ideas are rarely formed at the outset. In fact, some may take years to develop to a point where they are tenable. Let them stew and let them grow; their time will come.

Take the Other Perspective

In this chapter, I have focused mostly on how to develop ideas from the perspective of the researcher. However, what might be profoundly interesting to one researcher and seem like the best idea the field has seen in years might seem trivial or inconsequential to other researchers. Even when an idea seems to be absolutely brilliant, others still must be convinced; trying to "sell a better mousetrap" is a difficult chore. Making ideas interesting to others requires communicating a vision in ways that are understandable and acceptable to those who probably do not view the world through the same lens. Therefore, the selling of good ideas requires the same patience and persistence as did the development of the idea itself.

The art of framing ideas in ways that will be interesting to others also requires knowing one's audience and being sensitive to the ideas of many other scholars that might contradict one's own. It is necessary to explain ideas in the language of other researchers, describe them in ways so that they become extensions of what has come before, and articulate ways in which other perspectives might contribute to their further development. The goal should be to contribute to the collective wisdom as much as possible. It is also worth noting that scholars are likely to interpret a new idea in ways that are simply incorrect. Moreover, they will use their interpretations to support new directions in their own work. In those instances, it is best to consider that perhaps the most interesting and successful ideas are those that challenge others to think creatively and in new ways within their own frames of reference, even if their interpretations are not what were intended.

In conclusion, throughout this chapter I have offered strategies that might prove to be useful for generating new and interesting ideas. These strategies entail challenging theoretical assumptions, documenting the published literature, and generating new variables. Although the deliberate and systematic use of these strategies is likely to be most useful for new scholars and for those who wish to extend their work to new areas, these strategies also may be useful for established researchers who wish to review where they have been and think about what to do next. Indeed, challenging personal assumptions, documenting what one has accomplished so far, and considering variables that have not been studied are likely to provide a fresh look to any program

of research. In addition, it has been suggested that idea-generating talents are likely to be a product of those things that bring personal enjoyment and reflect areas of expertise. Good ideas also are more often the result of hard work and persistence than of some innate talent or one brilliant moment of insight; the development of ideas should be an ongoing process, not a product. Finally, good ideas are those that have been made acceptable to those who have not previously considered them. As Mark Twain once observed, "The man with a new idea is a crank until the idea succeeds." I hope that these suggestions will contribute to the development of many interesting and successful ideas.

REFERENCES

Asher, S. R., & Dodge, K. A. (1986). Identifying children who are rejected by their peers. *Developmental Psychology, 22,* 444–449.

Austin, A. B., & Draper, D. C. (1984). The relationship among peer acceptance, social impact, and academic achievement in middle school. *American Educational Research Journal, 21,* 597–604.

Bandura, A. (1986). *Social foundations of thought and action: A social cognitive theory.* Englewood Cliffs, NJ: Prentice Hall.

Baumrind, D. (1971). Current patterns of parental authority. *Developmental Psychology Monographs, 4*(1, part 2).

Bronfenbrenner, U. (1989). Ecological systems theory. In R. Vasta (Ed.), *Annals of child development* (Vol. 6, pp. 187–250). Greenwich, CT: JAI.

Dweck, C. S., & Leggett, E. L. (1988). A social-cognitive approach to motivation and personality. *Psychological Review, 95,* 256–272.

Ford, M. E. (1992). *Motivating humans: Goals, emotions, and personal agency beliefs.* Newbury Park, CA: Sage.

Ford, M. E., & Ford, D. H. (1987). *Humans as self-constructing living systems: Putting the framework to work.* Hillsdale, NJ: Lawrence Erlbaum.

Goodenow, C. (1993). Classroom belonging among early adolescent students: Relationships to motivation and achievement. *Journal of Early Adolescence, 13,* 21–43.

Lewin, K., Lippitt, R., & White, R. K. (1939). Patterns of aggressive behavior in experimentally created "social climates." *Journal of Social Psychology, 10,* 271–299.

Maccoby, E. E. (1966). *The development of sex differences.* Stanford, CA: Stanford University Press.

Maccoby, E. E. (1992). Trends in the study of socialization: Is there a Lewinian heritage? *Journal of Social Issues, 48,* 171–185.

Maccoby, E. E., & Martin, J. A. (1983). Socialization in the context of the family: Parent–child interaction. In E. M. Hetherington (Ed.), *Handbook of child psychology,* Vol. 4: *Socialization, personality, and social development* (pp. 1–101). New York: John Wiley.

Maehr, M. L. (1983). On doing well in science: Why Johnny no longer excels; why Sarah never did. In S. G. Paris, G. M. Olson, & H. W. Stevenson (Eds.), *Learning and motivation in the classroom* (pp. 179–210). Hillsdale, NJ: Lawrence Erlbaum.

McClelland, D. C. (1965). Toward a theory of motive acquisition. *American Psychologist, 20,* 321–333.

McClelland, D. C. (1987). *Human motivation.* New York: Cambridge University Press.

Newcomb, A. F., Bukowski, W. M., & Pattee, L. (1993). Children's peer relations: A meta-analytic review of popular, rejected, neglected, and controversial sociometric status. *Psychological Bulletin, 113,* 99–128.

Nicholls, J. G. (1984). Achievement motivation: Conceptions of ability, subjective experience, task choice, and performance. *Psychological Review, 91,* 328–346.

Noddings, N. (1992). *The challenge to care in schools: An alternative approach to education.* New York: Columbia University, Teachers College Press.

Parker, J. G., & Asher, S. R. (1987). Peer relations and later personal adjustment: Are low-accepted children at risk? *Psychological Bulletin, 102,* 357–389.

Piaget, J. (1965). *The moral judgment of the child.* New York: Free Press.

Steinberg, L., Dornbusch, S. M., & Brown, B. B. (1992). Ethnic differences in adolescent achievement: An ecological perspective. *American Psychologist, 47,* 723–729.

Wentzel, K. R. (1989). Adolescent classroom goals, standards for performance, and academic achievement: An interactionist perspective. *Journal of Educational Psychology, 81,* 131–142.

Wentzel, K. R. (1991a). Relations between social competence and academic achievement in early adolescence. *Child Development, 62,* 1066–1078.

Wentzel, K. R. (1991b). Social competence at school: Relations between social responsibility and academic achievement. *Review of Educational Research, 61,* 1–24.

Wentzel, K. R. (1997). Student motivation in middle school: The role of perceived pedagogical caring. *Journal of Educational Psychology, 89,* 411–419.

Wentzel, K. R. (1998). Social support and adjustment in middle school: The role of parents, teachers, and peers. *Journal of Educational Psychology, 90,* 202–209.

Wentzel, K. R. (2002). Are effective teachers like good parents? Interpersonal predictors of school adjustment in early adolescence. *Child Development, 73,* 287–301.

Wentzel, K. R. (2004). Social motivation and school adjustment. In R. Kail (Ed.), *Advances in child development and behavior* (Vol. 32, pp. 213–241). New York: Elsevier.

Wentzel, K. R., & Asher, S. R. (1995). Academic lives of neglected, rejected, popular, and controversial children. *Child Development, 66,* 754–763.

Wentzel, K. R., & Caldwell, K. (1997). Friendships, peer acceptance, and group membership: Relations to academic achievement in middle school. *Child Development, 68,* 1198–1209.

19

THE CHALLENGE OF FRAMING A PROBLEM

What Is Your Burning Question?

SUSAN HARTER

University of Denver

My mantra, framed on the office wall, asks, "What is your burning question?" It is what one first encounters when they enter into my scientific inner sanctum. Reactions vary from anxiety to lack of comprehension. Yet we need to deal with this issue, to guide investigators to know what constitutes a burning question of genuine interest. Having identified such a question, we can guide others, as well as ourselves, along the pathway that will challenge us to frame a problem thoughtfully. In turn, this should produce a rewarding answer. This is our mandate. In the role of research mentors, we can help students to move beyond the deer in the scientific headlights syndrome, to find their own burning question and approach it with intellectual passion, creativity, and sensibility.

I asked my first burning question at 6 years of age. I was a pupil at the University of Iowa Child Laboratory School, and our teacher had introduced a project in which a live hen, a first-time mother, would hatch eggs and raise chicks.

I was intrigued, especially when the teacher told us with great scientific authority that it would take exactly 21 days for the chicks to hatch. I religiously checked off the days on our home calendar, with my mother's help, and Day 21 fell on a Saturday. My mother had to work that day, and so on my own, unbeknownst to my mother, I trudged up to the school and peered through the slats of the outdoor wooden cage to observe what might have happened. Surprisingly, there were no other children from our class, nor was the teacher on-site for this great event. I was the lone observer. Sure enough, one by one, little chicks pecked their way out of their protective shells, to be greeted by their somewhat incredulous but welcoming mother hen.

Three years later, the saga continued with chickens yet again dominating my curiosity. Long before I knew about science officially, I had a fourth-grade pseudo-science course in which the teacher talked about something called "instinct." Animals come into the world

AUTHOR'S NOTE: The research reported in this chapter was supported by grants from the National Institutes of Health and the W. T. Grant Foundation.

knowing how to engage in certain behaviors without having to be taught. That was how I interpreted the message. I was a bit skeptical; I had to prove this for myself. So when our small multicolored banty hen, which I had named "Speckle" (male partner named "Heckle"), laid two eggs in our barn loft, I was excited. But there was yet no new experiment. (I had already documented the 21-day claim.) Unfortunately, her eggs were eaten, probably by barn rodents, and both she and I were distressed. We also had large white ducks of both genders. (On a farm, you learn Fertility 101 at a fairly early age.) So here was experiment Part A: I put a duck egg under her in the nest. Could she now hold out for 21 days? Was it the same time period for duck eggs? Part B: If the duck hatched, could it instinctively swim from birth? Part C: Would the mother adopt the duckling as her own? Would the duckling accept a chicken as a mother (what I much later learned, in my psychology courses, was termed "imprinting")? These were my burning questions, and I found answers to all of them. The duck, named "Yankee Doodle" because he was born on the Fourth of July, hatched appropriately, immediately paddled around in a vat of water I had waiting, and followed his small banty hen mother around for months. It was at first very poignant and then amusing as he grew to three times her size. Moreover, his trips to the pond caused his mother great consternation!

The Sources of Scientific Ideas

My childhood experiences have served me well in terms of thinking about the challenge of framing a research problem. Where do we turn, as adult scientists, to find a problem worthy of study? One can appreciate that in the history of ideas, there is no one source. Is this a comfort or a cause for confusion? Where should we cast our gaze? Where can our efforts at finding a burning question make a difference in terms of advancing the science of our given discipline?

There are many paths to framing a question. Yet the path we choose needs to be thoughtful, insightful, innovative, and groundbreaking to move the field forward. I have written elsewhere about not putting the methodological cart before the conceptual horse (Harter, 1999). Merely taking an existing measure or comparing two measures, without a burning question, is unlikely to generate very meaningful findings. Repeatedly administering the same measure(s) to the same or different populations, or being monogamously wedded to one's pet paradigm, is not likely to result in a scientific discovery. One needs compelling and interesting hypotheses that often require different frameworks, paradigms, and methodologies.

The sources of ideas are many as we look at the history of our discipline, and no one source is necessarily any more worthy than another (although textbooks and certain professors might tell a different story). Where do good ideas come from? Where should we focus? One can revisit historical theories that the field has deemed obsolete, thoughtfully examining whether there may be kernels of truth that can be revived. Freudian theory, Piagetian theory, Jamesian theory, and other historical perspectives have not garnered approval during recent decades. Yet there may be remnants of these grand theories that are worth exploring. There may be lingering questions and legitimate challenges that are still well worth investigating. To reject an entire theory, a popular stance among some contemporary investigators, is to diminish the importance of the very source of ideas that has spurred our fields forward. A healthy respect for our intellectual elders can only enrich our understanding of the processes that they identified years ago.

In addressing the issue of how we frame a problem, I take the reader on a journey through the history of my own work on the self-system over some 40 years, citing examples to document more general strategies for identifying important problems. In so doing, I hope to make this as concrete as the process has been for me. My goal is to identify different sources that allow one to recognize a burning question and to frame a problem. Although the examples are from our own research, I hope to transcend the particular content of this body of work and extract some guiding principles that reflect legitimate avenues of exploration rather than mere textbook formulas. I would submit that the creative geniuses in our field did not adhere to formulas.

GRAND THEORIES IN PSYCHOLOGY: WHAT DO WE RETAIN, WHAT DO WE DISTAIN?

We have a rich repository of theory in our field, much of it generated by theoretical giants who were considered deities during my graduate school days. In our courses, in our comprehensive exams, and in our research, we bowed to Freud, Erikson, Piaget, Skinner, and James at the urging of our knowledgeable professors. Their theories were the beacons that were to guide us through the process of formulating a problem that we could research with conviction. However, as the field "matured," attitudes changed and many felt that these formulations were far too vague in their conceptualization. As such, they did not lend themselves to researchable formulations. Consequently, these theories have fallen from grace, considered by some to be mere grand frames of reference of interest primarily for historical reasons. One needs to appreciate the reasons why such a shift in thinking has occurred. I was personally interested in comprehending why interest in the *self*, in particular, has waxed and waned. In examining these historical causes, I conclude that our predecessors may have had some insights that are well worth recovering and preserving.

I now give examples from my own work on the self and how, despite the negligence of interest in historical scholars of the self (notably William James and Charles Horton Cooley), there has been a resurgence in these historical frameworks that has reenergized our thinking about the self. More important, given the theme of this volume, their wisdom and insights have been transformed into researchable formulations, in the hands of thoughtful researchers, rather than relegated to the realm of mere arcane philosophical speculation. What follows is a brief discussion of these historical trends with regard to the *self*.

During the early period of introspection (at the turn of the 20th century), inquiry into topics concerning the self and psyche flourished. However, with the emergence of radical behaviorism, such constructs were excised from the scientific vocabularies of many theorists, and thus the writings of James (1892) and of symbolic interactionists such as Cooley (1902)

gathered dust on the shelf. Constructs such as self, self-esteem, ego strength, narcissistic injury, sense of omnipotence, perceived incompetence, unconscious sense of rejection, and so on did little to whet the behaviorists' appetite. It is of interest to ask why the self was no longer a welcome guest at the behaviorists' table. Several related reasons appear to be responsible.

The very origins of the behaviorist movement rested on the identification of *observables*. Thus, hypothetical constructs were both conceptually and methodologically unpalatable. Cognitions, in general, and self-representations, in particular, were deemed inappropriate because they could not be operationalized as observable behaviors. Self-report measures designed to tap self-constructs were not included on the methodological menu because people were assumed to be inaccurate judges of their own behavior. Finally, constructs assessed through introspective and self-report measures were not satisfying to the behaviorists' palate because their *functions* were not clearly specified. The very cornerstone of behaviorism rested on a functional analysis of behavior. In contrast, approaches to the self did little more than implicate self-representations as *correlates* of behavior, affording them little explanatory power as causes or mediators of actual behavior.

Several shifts in emphasis, beginning in the second half of the 20th century, have allowed self-constructs to become more palatable. Hypothetical constructs, in general, gained favor as parsimonious predictors of behavior, often far more economical in theoretical models than a multitude of discrete observables. In addition, we witnessed a cognitive revolution within the fields of both child psychology and adult psychology. For developmentalists, Piagetian and neo-Piagetian models came to the forefront. Among experimental and social psychologists, numerous cognitive models found favor. With the emergence of this revolution, scholars reclaimed the self as a *cognitive* construction, as mental representations that constitute a theory of the self (Harter, 1999). Finally, self-representations gained increased legitimacy as behaviorally oriented clinicians were forced to acknowledge that the self-evaluative statements of their clients seemed powerfully implicated in their pathology.

It was now permissible to take James's dusty volumes down from the shelf and take a closer look at the insights of this brilliant scholar of the self for clues on how to understand puzzling findings in our own research. By the 1980s, the field had moved to multidimensional models of self-evaluation that included domain-specific self-concepts (e.g., scholastic competence, athletic competence, physical appearance, conduct, social appeal), as well as global self-esteem, that reflected one's overall worth as a person independent of domain-specific evaluations of one's competence or adequacy (Harter, 1999). Designing measures to assess self-evaluations so defined was based on the premise that merely aggregating perceptions of domain-specific perceived competence and adequacy was *not* the route to understanding self-perceptions. Such an approach, used in measures designed during the 1960s, masked the differing self-evaluations that one held across different domains and ignored the many diverse *profiles* that exist across individuals. In addition, summing such scores did not yield a meaningful overall index of one's worth as a person. As more complex models of the self-system emerged, new measurement strategies were required to tap its multidimensional characteristics. Therefore, it is now common for self-esteem instruments (Bracken, 1992; Harter, 1982, 1999; Marsh, 1991) to tap domain-specific self-concepts, as well as global self-esteem, separately.

How could James's century-old theory help us to understand some puzzling findings that emerged in our own data? Using a multidimensional approach, what became clear in looking at dozens of individual protocols was that there were children who had virtually identical profiles across the five specific domains, with some scores high and some scores low across comparable domains. However, such children could have very disparate global self-esteem scores (for examples, see Harter, 1999). One child would have very high self-esteem, whereas another child would have very low self-esteem. How was this to be explained—two children who looked virtually identical in their pattern of domain-specific scores but who looked entirely different on their scores tapping their overall sense of worth as persons?

James (1890, 1892) scooped us all in arguing that our global self-esteem is *not* merely the sum of our perceptions of competence or adequacy in the self-evaluative domains of our lives. Rather, he cogently reasoned that global self-esteem is derived from our self-evaluations in domains that are deemed *important* to the self, where we have aspirations or "pretensions" to be successful, to employ James's own language of the day. From this perspective, the individual who perceives the self to be successful in domains of importance, and who can *discount* the importance of domains in which he or she is not that successful, will have high self-esteem. In contrast, individuals who continue to tout the importance of domains in which they are not successful will suffer psychologically in the form of low self-esteem. Thus, the *importance* of success was the missing link in explaining the puzzling individual profiles of children. James's insights required both a conceptual shift in our thinking, based on his innovations, and methodological innovations in the form of the actual assessment of the importance of success. More than two decades of research (Harter, 1999) have revealed that during later childhood, adolescence, and adulthood, a consideration of the importance of success in conjunction with one's self-evaluations, namely, discrepancy, is a major predictor of one's global self-esteem. From this perspective, one need not be a superstar in all of the domains that society deems important. Rather, one needs to highlight the domains in which one is successful and discount those where one has limitations.

What are the general lessons to be learned here? The first is not to relegate century-old theories to the delete file. True wisdom survives the ages if we muster the respect to seek it out. Second, we should not rush, in our data-analytic strategies, to the newest statistical package that promises elegant analyses of findings for groups of participants. This may be an ultimate goal, yet we need to examine individual protocols, puzzle over them, and thoughtfully look for patterns that may define subgroups and patterns that may defy any initial interpretation. It was in the wonderment of seemingly inexplicable profiles for individuals that we ultimately made progress. To sweep such findings under the conceptual rug and not be challenged by them will slow our scientific progress and will not allow us to grow intellectually. James, therefore, remains alive and well in our scientific consciousness and has provided numerous clues that have advanced our contemporary understanding of self-processes.

THINKING OUTSIDE OF THE THEORETICAL BOX

What burning question follows from this understanding of self-esteem? How can we build on James's insights about the self-system? What challenges are there to framing new and related problems of study? Society has been crazed about self-esteem during recent years. Schools clamor to find the magic bullet, we are besieged with self-help books, and we are assaulted by the media and parenting magazines promoting the message that we need to attend to our own self-esteem as well as the self-esteem of our children. Yet why should we be so obsessed with self-esteem if it may have no important ramifications in our lives? Merely discovering the *causes* of self-esteem does not deal with an equally important question: What are the *consequences* of high or low self-esteem? This becomes the next burning question on the journey to build a bigger and better model. After years of studying the determinants of self-esteem, I bolted out of my office chair one day and inarticulately asked myself, "What if self-esteem doesn't *do* anything?" Seligman (1993) put it a bit more eloquently, suggesting that self-esteem might merely be an *epi-phenomenon;* that is, we know its causes, but it does not seriously influence or mediate behaviors of importance or interest.

This is a critical question, to be sure. However, considerable evidence in the developmental, clinical, and social psychological literature reveals many correlates and consequences of self-esteem for children, adolescents, and adults. Here, consultation with those in somewhat different fields may be very helpful. In my own case, I was fortunate to meet a clinician, Donna Marold, who had considerable experience with adolescents with low self-esteem. She instantly identified depression and potential suicide as a powerful correlate of low

self-esteem. Eventually, the research community resonated to such insights, and the emerging literature now reveals that there is a strong statistical link (*r* values across studies range from .45 to .80) between level of self-esteem and self-reported depressed affect (for a review, see Harter, 1999). Both self-reported and diagnostic assessments of depression are also predictive of suicidal ideation and behavior.

Our own model (Harter, 1999; Harter, Marold, & Whitesell, 1992) clearly demonstrates these effects. Depression and suicidal behaviors represent serious mental health threats, indicating that we need to keep pushing our models, formulating new questions that will lead to more effective prevention and intervention efforts. We also need to consult with colleagues in different but related disciplines as consultants who can help us to sharpen our focus and formulate new problems to be addressed. Moreover, such consultants can turn into valuable collaborators, whereby two or more heads are better than one and the product reflects the greater complexity of the phenomenon. As a general reflection, early in my career it seemed that the values of academic research reflected those of our society, emphasizing autonomy, independence, and rewards for "my own idea, *my* theory." Fortunately, this solipsistic approach to research has given way to far more collaborative efforts. Universities are rewarding collaboration across fields, and (at an even broader level) large consortia across universities and research establishments are flourishing. Even Nobel prizes are awarded to research teams. Thus, one need not try to frame one's research problem, one's burning question, in a personal intellectual vacuum. One can seek out feedback, network, look to reasonable consultants, and collaborate. There will be many benefits.

ANOTHER UNHERALDED HISTORICAL SCHOLAR OF THE SELF: CHARLES HORTON COOLEY

In our search for an understanding of the causes of self-esteem, we also discovered the formulations of Cooley (1902), who put forth a very different model of the causes of self-esteem. For Cooley, the self was very much a *social* construction, built on the incorporation of the attitudes of others toward the self. Cooley made reference to the "looking glass self," by which he meant that the significant others in our lives were social mirrors into which we gaze, to divine what others think of us as people, whether we are worthy of respect or esteem. Our judgments or perceptions of their reactions will directly translate into our view of our own self-esteem, how worthy we are. We eventually will come to own these opinions of others as personal beliefs about our selves.

Is this arcane theory to be debunked? We thought not, yet Cooley was a philosophical scholar and not an empiricist. Thus, two questions arise. First, is Cooley's theory worthy of revival at the level of empirical investigation? Second, does Cooley's theory *compete* with James's theory? Should we frame this as who is right and who is wrong? In my opinion, my training and others' training historically has been misguided in that researchers, be they students or faculty, had been led to believe that formulating a good research question was to pit one theory against another. I have labeled this the "alpha male" model of research, although some women have adopted it as well. Yet we need to abandon this mentality. In the case of our own research, we have simultaneously investigated both James's and Cooley's formulations with the same participants, finding that each theory accounts for the prediction of self-esteem about equally (Harter, 1999). We have described an additive model documenting that if one feels competent in domains of importance (James) *and* has approval from others (Cooley), then such an individual will have the highest self-esteem. Conversely, one who has both low perceptions of competence in domains of importance *and* low approval from significant others will have the lowest self-esteem. The general point is not to pit one theory against another but rather to allow different perspectives to contribute to an understanding of the processes one is trying to investigate. That is, in exploring a given topic, such as the causes of self-esteem in our own research, more than one theory can contribute to an account of the phenomenon; they need not compete. They can, in

statistical terms, each contribute to the variance in our understanding the problem.

FROM THEORY, TO REALITY, AND BACK AGAIN

In the winter of 1999, I was intrigued by the continuing media account of the then nine high-profile cases of school shooters. Culling the reports across these cases, there were several commonalities. First, they all were white males, in late childhood or adolescence, from small cities or rural and suburban areas around the country. Second, many of the features in their childhoods and adolescence years were quite consistent with the predictors of low self-esteem, depression, and suicidal ideation in the model we were developing. Might this be a springboard for formulating a somewhat different challenging research problem? Too often, our research vision is occluded by the dictates of the "ivory tower" and we do not look to natural, or what are actually unnatural, occurrences in our world. We often regard the real world as a separate sphere; attention to such problems may disrupt our concentration on the somewhat limited research program that we have been singularly pursuing. Yet such real-world events provide a wake-up call. What is really going on in our society? Perhaps these questions are more important than our carefully crafted 2×2 experimental designs that can be tested only within the confines of a laboratory.

I was personally pondering whether we should extend our model even further into predictors of not only suicidal ideation but also violent ideation. The clinical literature reveals that internalizing symptoms (including suicidal thinking) and externalizing symptoms (e.g., acting out, aggression, homicide) are so highly related that it is often difficult to know whether adolescents will act out against others or themselves. On April 20, 1999, I was working at home, thinking about how we could extend our model even further, when the cable news channel CNN played out the entire tragedy occurring at Columbine High School. Columbine is 15 minutes from our house. Our daughter, at college, called me because she had learned that it was a high school in our county, although they had not yet disclosed the name. She was concerned that it might have been her nearby high school. It was not. However, she knew high school students from Columbine because she was active in competitive high school sports and had met girls there through that avenue. So this tragedy was now literally in our backyard.

Why bring this up in an essay on the challenge of framing a research problem? I bring this up because such events represent the psychological reality in which we live. We must be aware of the issues that are real, are pressing, and need to be investigated, issues that can be the sources of critical research questions. I recently heard a statistic indicating that only about 15% of our population in America either reads informative newspapers, particularly the newsworthy sections, or watches television news. Sadly, students are highly represented in this group. Are they watching television? Of course. However, are they watching television that might help them to formulate interesting research questions?

Columbine has become, unfortunately, the metaphor for the white male adolescent school shootings. There have now been 11 high-profile cases. In our own research, we chose to use this very tragic event to further our understanding of such violence in the school system. What might be our burning questions? Several. To what extent do the predictors in our model of low self-esteem, depression, and suicidal ideation map onto the lives of violent ideators in a normative group of adolescents? What might we learn from reading media accounts about factors that no one has ever seriously considered? Here, I was astounded, particularly as someone who has studied emotions, including shame and guilt, for some years. The media accounts clearly indicated that in all of these cases, the actual school shooters had been *humiliated,* repeatedly and chronically, and it was usually a humiliating event that precipitated their revenge. Yet we literally have no literature on humiliation. We have studies on how being a victim of aggression can eventually lead to acting out against perpetrators. But we have *not* attended to the emotional mediator of humiliation.

In our own research, therefore, we are studying links between suicidal ideation and homicidal ideation, including the precursors and the role of humiliation (Harter, Low, & Whitesell, 2003). The more general point is that we need to attend to current events and to be alert to clues as to dynamics that even your wisest professors or mentors (including me) have missed—in our case, the role of humiliation. I had a graduate school applicant ask me recently, "What is your program of research for the next 5 years?" This was a legitimate question, to be sure. But my response was that "I have no idea" because issues such as the school shootings, 9/11, and current concerns about terrorism loom large on our societal front, and many of these are grist for the mill in terms of what we should be studying. They become the new research problems that we need to frame thoughtfully.

When One Model Does Not Fit All

It is gratifying to develop models, piece by piece, and eventually to employ statistical techniques that validate the relationships one has articulated. In our case (Harter, 1999; Harter et al., 2003), we have now determined that competence or adequacy in domains deemed important to an individual, plus related approval from parents and peers, strongly predicts a composite of global self-esteem, affect (depressed to cheerful), and hope (hopeless to hopeful). This constellation, in turn, predicts both suicidal ideation and violent ideation. Group data from normative samples of adolescents have convincingly documented such a model. Yet is this the end of the theoretical and empirical journey? Have we answered all of our burning questions? Not necessarily.

For those of us who are interested in individual children or adolescents as clinicians, school psychologists, counselors, teachers, and parents, our ultimate goal is to understand *individuals* who may profit from interventions if they are suffering from low self-esteem, depression, and either suicidal ideation or violent ideation (or both). Our own research (Harter, 1999; Harter & Whitesell, 1996) has revealed that not all predictors in the model are relevant in the lives of troubled adolescents who suffer from these self-reported symptoms. That is, there are multiple pathways to the experience of low self-esteem, depression, and either suicidal or violent ideation (or both). Pursuing this theme, we next identified six different pathways that were common enough to identify most adolescents. For example, some experienced negative self-evaluations in the domains of physical appearance, peer likeability, and athletic competence that led to self-reported lack of peer approval and that, in turn, led to feelings of low self-esteem, depressed affect, and hopelessness about the future. For others, perceived lack of scholastic competence and perceptions of negative conduct led to lack of parental approval that, in turn, represented the pathways to low self-esteem, depressed affect, and hopelessness. These are but two examples. The general point is that those whose profession is to intervene in the lives of children and adolescents cannot be content with applying general models of symptoms despite their statistical significance with large numbers of participants. We need to take the next logical step in reframing the problem or question as follows: Which pathways are relevant for a given individual?

ISSUES OF DIRECTIONALITY: CONSTRUCTING AND DECONSTRUCTING OUR MODELS

The paper on our general model of the predictors, correlates, and consequences of low self-esteem and depression was accepted by a well-respected journal, and it makes for a good colloquium talk or class lecture and generates interest, particularly when applied to real children and adolescents, including the point that there are multiple pathways. Yet the simmering coals are not yet cold; we need to add more conceptual fuel to the fire. Statistical tests, even sophisticated path-analytical techniques, conducted with data collected at one time period do not truly address the issue of the directionality of effects. Often, we design our models to meet the prevailing theories of the day. For example, during the 1970s, the most popular models suggested that cognitions drive emotions. We fell prey to this conceptualization, reasoning that a negative cognition about the self, namely, low global self-esteem, would lead to depressed affect, an emotion. However, when

any two variables are as highly correlated as these two (correlations ranging from .65 to .80 in our own data), one must question their directionality. That is, reversing the directionality of the statistical paths or arrows, suggesting that depression might precede feelings of low self-esteem, would lead to an equally good fit for the model. Statistical techniques cannot solve this dilemma. Thus, we have a new challenge in terms of framing another problem. How does one determine the directionality of effects, and does it even matter?

I teamed up with an experienced and thoughtful clinician, Donna Marold, and we took the bold step of actually *talking* to adolescents. We put our questionnaires aside and simply asked those who were low in self-esteem, coupled with depressed affect, "Which comes first? Do you first not like yourself as a person and then feel depressed, or do you first feel depressed and then not like yourself as a person?" (Harter & Marold, 1993). The findings revealed two groups of adolescents: one subgroup whose members first experienced low self-esteem that, in turn, was followed by depression and a second subgroup whose members first felt depression that, in turn, made them not like themselves. The explanations they provided were quite convincing (Harter, 1999; Harter & Marold, 1993). Those who first felt low self-esteem gave examples of their own personal inadequacy that led them to feel depressed. Those who first experienced depressed affect reported causes in the form of actions of others against their selves (e.g., rejection, harm, loss). Thus, if we are interested in the experiences of individual children and adolescents, we need to continually reframe the problem and determine the directionality of effects *from the individual's perspective* if we are to be effective diagnosticians and healers.

Similar questions about directionality arise when one examines both James's and Cooley's positions. James argued that perceptions of adequacy in domains that were deemed important would lead to global evaluations of worth. Cooley contended that approval from significant others would be internalized in the form of global self-esteem or worth. Yet these were scholars of adult behavior. How might the directionality be affected at different developmental levels? Moreover, does it make a difference in the individual's life? We have determined (Harter, 1999) that one domain, perceived physical appearance, correlates most highly with global self-esteem if this domain is deemed important. Does this mean that one's evaluation of one's looks determines global self-esteem? Might global self-esteem influence one's perceptions of one's appearance? What might the directionality of this relationship be? Our statistical modeling once again could not answer this question.

Thus, we needed to find another avenue. Once again, we asked adolescents, "Which comes first?" We determined that approximately 70% of the adolescents indicated that they were basing their overall sense of worth on their perceptions of their appearance, whereas the remainder indicated that the directionality was the opposite. For the latter group, perceptions of their self-esteem determined how much they liked the way they looked. However, do these two orientations have any other interesting implications, and are there more questions to be asked? The answer is *yes,* there are more questions to be asked, because we found that for females, in particular, the orientation in which appearance is the basis for one's global self-esteem, whereby perceptions of one's outer physical self drives one's evaluation of one's inner self, is the more pernicious one. Females who endorse this model report that they are less attractive, have lower self-esteem, and are more depressed (Harter, 1999).

Obsessed with the concept of directionality, we asked the same question with regard to Cooley's formulation that the opinions of others are incorporated into one's global sense of self. Such a conceptualization is reasonable if one considers childhood, and Cooley (1902) acknowledged this point in talking about the growing period of youth. Might it not be the case, however, that during adolescence and beyond the directionality might be reversed, such that one would have a metatheory that if one liked oneself as a person (had high self-esteem), then others would come to approve of oneself as a person? Might there be liabilities if one chronically stares into the social looking glass for external feedback about the self? Our findings revealed just such liabilities (Harter,

Stocker, & Robinson, 1996) among that subgroup of adolescents.

We asked adolescents to endorse one of two orientations: either (1) "If others approve of me first, then I will like myself as a person," or (2) "If I first like myself as a person, then others will like and approve of me." The findings indicated that of those endorsing these two orientations, 59% selected the looking glass orientation described in the first statement, whereas the other 41% opted for the second sequence of events. That more adolescents endorsed the looking glass metatheory is not surprising given that many adolescents at this stage of development are still preoccupied with the opinions of others (Harter, 1999; Rosenberg, 1986).

Our faith in the validity of adolescents' choices was bolstered by their explanations. For example, those endorsing the looking glass self perspective offered the following types of justifications: "If other people my age don't like me as a person, then I wonder if I am a good person—I care about what people say about me"; "If no one liked you, you probably wouldn't like yourself very much"; and "If other kids approve of me and say good things about me, then I look at myself and think I'm not so bad and I start liking myself."

In contrast, those who reversed the sequence, placing opinions of the self as causally prior to the opinions of others, gave the following types of descriptions: "In seventh grade I didn't like myself as a person, so I didn't have many people that liked me, but in eighth grade I felt more confident about myself, and then I found that I had many more friends that liked me"; "The way I figure it, if you can't like the person you are first, then how do you expect other people to like you?"; and "You have to appreciate yourself first as a person. If you wait for other people to make you feel good, then you could be waiting a long time." The general point is that we cannot merely *assume* directionality, nor will our measures necessarily capture the direction of effects, unless we directly ask our participants. To the extent that their responses validate their choices, we are closer to answering questions about directionality.

However, what exactly are the *next* relevant questions at this point in our inquiry? Of what usefulness is it to learn about the folk theories of adolescents? Are we at the end of the conceptual road in documenting orientations about the directionality of the opinions of others and opinions about one's own sense of worth? Is it enough to turn Cooley's theory upside down, as it were, by suggesting that developmental issues are imperative to consider? My answer would be *no,* it is not sufficient. Are we now challenged by the need to frame a new problem for study? My answer would be *yes.* The general form of this question would be as follows: Of what relevance is it in the lives of adolescents that they possess one metatheory versus another? If their perceptions have no meaningful consequences, then our empirical journey might be taking us down a dead-end road.

Fortunately, we next discovered an intriguing fork in the road. We discovered that there are numerous potential liabilities for maintaining a major dependence on the opinions of others during adolescence. Our findings, based on a variety of newly constructed self-report measures to address these issues, revealed the following (for details, see Harter, 1999). First, looking glass self adolescents, as compared with those who consider their own opinions of self to be the most salient, are far more preoccupied with the opinions of others (not so surprising). Second, teachers blind to any hypotheses rated the looking glass self adolescents as behaviorally more *distracted* in the classroom. These adolescents were much less able to attend to or concentrate on their schoolwork, a decided liability given the importance of developing their academic skills. Third, looking glass self adolescents reported more *fluctuations in peer approval.* Fourth, and relatedly, looking glass self adolescents reported more fluctuations in *self-esteem,* an understandable link given that by definition they are basing their self-esteem on perceived peer approval. Fifth, those hermetically sealed to the social mirror also reported lower peer approval. Perhaps in their preoccupation with peer approval, they may engage in behaviors that do not garner such support such as trying too hard and employing inappropriate strategies; in so doing, they may annoy or alienate their classmates. Finally, looking glass self adolescents' level of self-esteem is decidedly lower than that of the group whose members do not consistently base their own opinions of their

worth as persons on what others think of them. This pattern among looking glass self adolescents is interpretable as follows: Because they are basing their esteem on their perceptions of the approval of others, and because they are not garnering that support, their self-esteem will suffer. Thus, the liabilities of maintaining a looking glass self are interrelated and numerous (Harter, 1999).

It seemed important to develop the logic of this extended study as a model for how one question leads to another, how one challenge provokes a new and exciting line of thought. From this perspective, there are endless fascinating questions to address; however, they must tell a story. I continue to ask my graduate students and postdoctoral trainees, when they enter my office with pounds of printouts and seem to think that these are the data, "What is the story line?" It is important to identify the narrative that our findings dictate, a narrative that will truly illuminate our understanding of the psychological processes that capture our attention. This is our ultimate goal.

THE USE OF CLINICAL MATERIAL TO HELP US FRAME RESEARCHABLE QUESTIONS

My own background is that of both a developmental psychologist and a child clinical psychologist, and this type of joint training can provide marvelous opportunities to reflect on a clinical observation and then pursue it into the realm of research. For example, over the years in my clinical work with children, I observed that young children seemed to be unable to experience multiple emotions concerning a given event. They had particular difficulty in accepting the idea that they could have both a positive emotion and a negative emotion together (Harter, 1977). Was this a pathology-driven process? Did it reflect psychological defenses? Might there be a normative developmental component? These and many other questions arose, issues not merely to confine to one's clinical notes but rather to serve as springboards to researchable formulations that could illuminate both our clinical intervention techniques (Harter, 1977) and the cognitive developmental underpinnings of children's understanding of their emotions. Elsewhere, I have reported on a five-stage normative developmental sequence that defines the development of children's understanding of multiple emotions (Harter & Buddin, 1987). We argued that those working directly with children in a mental health capacity appreciate such a sequence as a backdrop against which to evaluate their own clients' emotional understanding. The more general point is that clinical observations initially served to drive the research questions.

To give another example of this principle, a clinical graduate student, Christine Chao, approached me with some excitement about a 4-year-old client who had an imaginary friend. Was this normal? Was it pathological? Could we find some way in which to study the processes involved? Although I had never thought about the phenomenon, together we forged a conceptual plan to investigate the role of the self in the construction of imaginary friends. Might such companions be compensating for feelings of inadequacy? What other functions might they be serving? Were there gender differences in the types of imaginary friends that young children construct? We were able to answer many of these questions (Harter & Chao, 1992). The purpose here, however, is not to detail all of our findings but rather to highlight the different sources that can stimulate our curiosity about ideas to be pursued empirically.

One last example has grown out of clinical experience. Another student, Ann Monsour, also confronted me with an interesting clinical observation. She was treating a 15-year-old female client who was terribly distressed over her "different selves" who seemed to compete with one another, to be incompatible, and to cause her tremendous grief. Monsour's burning questions were whether this was normal, pathological, or something that was treatable and how this issue could be researched. Had I thought about this? No. However, this is the point about the challenge of framing a problem. How do we frame this new problem now rather than avoid it because it might not be in our area of expertise? One *develops* the expertise when one faces the challenge.

Our efforts, beginning with Monsour's initial observation, have led to numerous studies (beginning with Harter & Monsour, 1992). The scientific saga has been recorded in numerous other publications (Harter, 1999). However, we are still puzzling about the fact that in four separate studies, female adolescents reported far more conflict among their role-related selves than did male adolescents. We have yet to answer this question, and thus our challenge continues.

OPENNESS TO SERENDIPITOUS FINDINGS

Often in the context of our concentration on one phenomenon, such as the multiple selves that emerge during adolescence, unexpected observations peak our curiosity. We became struck by the fact that during mid-adolescence, teenagers (females more so than males) gave us clues that they were struggling with the fact that they had contradictory attributes in different roles (e.g., close with mother, distant with father; rowdy with friends, self-conscious on a date). Given these disparate personae, how could they possibly determine who their "true selves" were? Some agonized about this in the interviews, asking, "Which is the real me?" Others expressed it differently by writing in the initial protocol that they were their true selves with close friends but not on dates. Once again, this was not a phenomenon to which I had directed any previous attention. However, it was so salient that it called for its own line of research (for a review, see Harter, 1999). Sometimes the problem that needs to be framed comes to us if we are open to recognizing it. This realization launched a new programmatic effort, spawned by taking seriously what children and adolescents tell us. Our goal is to listen.

SHOULD WE LET FINDINGS THAT DO NOT CONFORM TO OUR HYPOTHESES YELLOW IN DRAWERS, NEVER TO SEE THE SCIENTIFIC LIGHT OF DAY?

As many of us in the research enterprise realize, it is hard to abandon our beloved hypotheses. We search for alternative answers; for example, perhaps our methodology was ill conceived. Much of such science has not seen the light of day. Editorial journal standards might not warrant the publication of data that support the null hypothesis rather than the predictions put forth by an investigator.

Creativity, honesty, and humility must come to the fore in these situations, and we must pass on these skills to our students, colleagues, and the scientific community. Many of us have had experiences in which our pet theories were not confirmed. My own dissertation was one such example. Working under the premise that institutionalized retarded children (in the IQ range of 65–75) lacked social support and approval, I reasoned that in a learning task they would do better with social reinforcement, with regard to their problem-solving performance, than without such reinforcement. The findings turned out to be opposite those from my prediction. Those in the condition with approval did worse than those without such approval. The methodology seemed sound, and thus the fault could not lie there. Having 20/20 hindsight *can* be a blessing *if* it is followed up by further studies. The hindsight was that because these children had been so deprived of social reinforcement, it was far more rewarding to them in that condition than performing some experimental learning task where there was no human contact. Further studies supported this interpretation. The general conclusion is that we cannot let unsavory data yellow in drawers. We must have the courage to interpret the fact that many hypotheses might not be confirmed, and thus we need to go back to the conceptual drawing board.

OUT OF THE MOUTHS OF BABES: CHILDREN'S SPONTANEOUS COMMENTS CAN INFORM OUR RESEARCH

We often feel the need to follow the "correct formulas" for conducting legitimate research, to not stray from the dictates of "true science." As a result, we may resist the temptation to take children's comments that seriously. However, often a child's innocent comments can represent insights that, if we were to listen, could change the course of a study or an entire research program. Such an experience happened in my own scientific efforts. It was 1977, and my interest in

self-concept and self-esteem was growing. However, I was not content with the instruments that had been developed, specifically the Piers and Harris (1964) and Coopersmith (1967) measures that merely aggregated responses to different self-evaluative comments in domains such as academics, social relations, and athletic competence. The sum of such responses was interpreted as a reflection of one's overall sense of self-esteem, an index we later learned masked the very marked differences that children report about their sense of inadequacy across different domains.

However, another problem with such instruments was that they broached the topic of adequacy in very bald "I statements" (e.g., "I am easy to like," "I do poorly at my schoolwork," "I'm not very good at sports"). On such measures, participants are given only two choices, such as true or false, about themselves. We discovered, in our own research, that self-evaluative responses on such scales were highly correlated with socially desirable responding. That is, they did not permit the children to accurately or honestly report their self-perceptions. Yet our scientific soul-searching could not provide any insights into how to solve this problem, that is, how to assess self-evaluations more accurately.

Thus, I visited a school playground looking for help from the children, the font of wisdom. I vividly recall walking up to a 9-year-old boy and, with little forethought, asking, "Do you think most kids your age think they are good at sports?" He stifled his reaction to what he thought was a most ignorant question, put his hands on his hips, and asserted, "Let's face it, some kids think they are good at sports and other kids don't think they are good at sports, right? Right!" As I drove home, I kept repeating his mantra, including the "Let's face it." This child's comment instantly became the basis for the construction of an item format that has persisted in our measures for years. For those unfamiliar with this format, we present participants with two choices in statement form. To assess perceived athletic competence, the statement reads, "Some kids think they are good at sports, but Other kids do not think they are that good at sports." The first part of the statement is on the left-hand side of the page, the second, on the right. Participants are asked to make two decisions. First they are asked, "Which statement is more like you?" They go to that side of the question and are then asked to make a second decision: "Is that statement REALLY true for you or just SORT OF true for you?" This allows for a 4-point scoring system. It also does not force the children to endorse "I statements." Rather, they identify with existing groups of children, either those who believe they are good at sports or those who do not believe so. We have used this question format in numerous scales over the years, and it continues to be successful. Moreover, others can use it as well given their own interests and content. (Coda: Somewhere in the world is a 37-year-old deserving co-author who never got his due given the rules of confidentiality!)

HYPOTHESES FROM ONE'S OWN EXPERIENCES

Is it legitimate to draw on one's own experiences as a source of researchable hypotheses? Different people may answer this question differently. I would submit, initially, that we do this unconsciously given the truism that we study what has touched us in our own lives. In certain cases, there is more consciousness such as when someone who has been abused chooses to study the etiology and consequences of abuse. My own example is less dramatic yet nevertheless a very conscious choice based on my own experience. Immersed in the topic of global self-esteem, a conceptual nucleus with many pseudopods, I reflected one day on the fact that my self-esteem was not equally high in all of the various domains of importance to me. Here, I was not thinking about specific competencies that we had already tapped in our measures; rather, I was questioning how much I liked and valued myself as a person in various *relational* contexts. A bit of introspection led me to conclude that it varied from high to low. If this was true for me, might it not be true for others? If so, at what age would such a differentiation emerge?

We began with adolescents, constructing items employing the format described previously (Harter, Waters, & Whitesell, 1998). A sample item would be the following: "Some

teenagers like themselves as a person when they are around their mother BUT Other teenagers do *not* like themselves as a person when they are around their mother." The children then indicate which is more like them and check whether that is "really true" or "sort of true" for them. The particular relationships can vary depending on the age of the participants, the contexts that the researcher deems important, and so on.

Our study provided clear evidence, by many statistical criteria, that adolescents definitely feel differently about their sense of worth in different relationships (for details, see Harter et al., 1998). Moreover, the findings indicate that feelings of worth in a given relationship directly relate to the social approval the children are receiving from significant others in that context. Thus, this represents a revisionist perspective on the looking glass self. Cooley, and later Mead (1934), suggested that we aggregate our perceptions of the opinions of significant others in forming a sense of our global sense of self-esteem or worth. We still embrace this conceptualization. Yet it is also interesting that with development and differentiation, adolescents come to refine this overall perception that will vary from one relationship to another. However, we have yet to examine the directionality of this correlation. Within a relationship, is it that the opinions of others dictate our sense of self, or does our own sense of self influence our perceptions of the approval we are receiving from others? Thus, our own experiences can represent another legitimate source of challenging questions, and the initial answers only lead to more questions to be explored thoughtfully.

CHALLENGING CLAIMS ABOUT ISSUES OF RELEVANCE TO SOCIETY

We owe a debt to those who have sought to illuminate psychological issues of very practical relevance to the public. (Too many in our related fields have worked within their ivory tower laboratories, churning out publishable studies that never go beyond the elitist journals that are shared only with like-minded scientists.) Others have had the courage to identify issues of relevance, attempting to stimulate public interest. One such goal is to redress certain societal ills.

Three such themes are identified in closing this essay on the challenge of framing a problem. Thus, it is critical that certain research-minded investigators step out of their ivory towers and challenge certain provocative claims, to do the needed empirical research that will bring a sense of balance, accuracy, clarity, and realism.

In our own research, first, we have questioned the generalization that there is rampant gender bias against girls within the school system (American Association of University Women [AAUW], 1992; Sadker & Sadker, 1994). Second, we have refined Gilligan's (1993) contention that with the advent of adolescence, most girls lose the ability to voice their opinions. Third, we have challenged the claims of Baumeister, Smart, and Boden (1996) that there is a "dark side to high self-esteem" in that it is part of a constellation that predicts violence toward others.

We believe that it is essential that dissemination of the results of potentially relevant studies *not* result in overgeneralizations that can be misinterpreted, and therefore misused, with regard to public policy. The opportunity to write this essay provides a forum to caution practitioners and to encourage researchers to empirically challenge some potential myths or generalizations that require refinement or qualification.

Gender Bias in the Classroom

During the early 1990s, many claims surfaced about discrimination against girls in the classroom (AAUW, 1992; Sadker & Sadker, 1994), and the public was duly informed through media coverage in newspapers, television specials, parent magazines, and the like. Claims included the fact that girls, as compared with boys, were getting less positive attention and encouragement around schoolwork, that their bids to answer questions were ignored, that they received much less quality time from teachers, and that basically they were relegated to the silent ghetto of the classroom. It was claimed that class materials were directed toward the interests of boys and that books and curricula focused far more on the achievements of males, all of which eroded the pride and confidence of girls. The AAUW report asserted that this gender bias had been responsible for the lowered self-esteem of girls.

However, these claims were flawed for many reasons. There were virtually no compelling empirical data, and the scant measures that were employed were inadequate. Nor was statistical evidence presented to support such claims. Moreover, there was no attempt to relate teacher behaviors directly to student outcomes. There was also no attention to whether students themselves perceived gender bias. Finally, there was no appreciation for the fact that children *bring* to the classroom an entire history of gender-related experiences beginning from early childhood, experiences that can profoundly influence constructs such as self-esteem. These experiences may have little or nothing to do with teacher treatment in the classroom.

Our own research (Harter & Rienks, 2004; Rienks & Harter, 2005) began with an attempt to determine whether students (in a racially mixed middle school) actually perceived bias in the way that teachers responded to male and female students. Our findings revealed that approximately 80% of the students did *not* see bias of the nature that Sadker and Sadker (1994) had claimed. An equally critical question was whether there were any differences between these 80% and the 20% who *did* see bias, particularly against their own gender. The results revealed that those who did perceive bias clearly, through self-report measures, identified more negative outcomes. They reported poorer scholastic competence, lower self-worth as students, less academic motivation, and greater hopelessness about future successes. Thus, they were clearly compromised in the classroom. However, to return to a theme in our research program, does this necessarily mean that for the minority who perceived bias, the directionality flowed from teacher behaviors to student outcomes? Might it be that such children came to the classroom with histories that led to negative experiences that, in turn, caused them to attribute current self-reported negative outcomes to teacher bias in their contemporary scholastic environment? This constitutes our next burning question in an attempt to explicate the complexities of potential gender bias. Interestingly, in contrast to Sadker and Sadker's claims about bias against girls, the boys in our study, not the girls, were more likely to report bias in that they felt that teachers were critical of their nonacademic conduct or behavior in the classroom.

Ability to Voice One's Opinions in the Classroom

Gilligan (1993), in her attempt to direct her attention to females who she believes have historically been neglected in the psychological literature, proposed a provocative hypothesis that clearly captured the attention of the psychological and educational communities as well as the popular press. It has been her thesis that prepubertal girls are far more clear about what they think and feel and have little hesitancy in voicing their opinions. However, with the advent of adolescence, females begin to suppress these thoughts and feelings. Gilligan and colleagues have offered several possible reasons for why many adolescent girls' voices might go underground. Realizing at mid-adolescence that they are at a crossroads, moving from the teenage years to womanhood, they look to the stereotypes of the day with regard to what it means, in our society, to be the good acceptable woman. The ideals include being empathic, caring, understanding, and *quiet*. Moreover, in becoming more sensitive to the relatively patriarchal society in which they are living, girls begin to realize that their voices are not as valued. In addition, to the extent that their own mothers are role models and buy into these premises, such female adolescents choose to emulate their mothers' own lack of voice. Finally, according to Gilligan, adolescent girls come to the realization that if they are to speak their true opinions forcefully, such expressions might well jeopardize their relationships. At best, doing so might threaten or compromise relationships; at worst, the girls might be rejected or abandoned. Unfortunately, Gilligan has not examined these issues in male adolescents.

These are clearly claims that would naturally provoke a person's interest, and they have been supported by the more popular press, for example, Pipher's (1994) book titled *Revising Ophelia: Saving the Selves of Adolescent Girls.* Although it is commendable to focus on a supposedly neglected gender, one cannot simply make claims about one gender without examining the other gender. Hamlet had his own problems with indecision and confidence; he spoke in soliloquies and monologues, not in dialogues.

Therefore, our own research has sought to examine the issue of voice in both male and female adolescents, ages 12 to 18 years (for a summary of these studies, see Harter, 1999). Basically, we have found no evidence, with cross-sectional data, that girls' level of voice declined across five different relationships. We found no significant gender differences, and those that we did find slightly favored girls' level of voice. What did we find of interest? We discovered tremendous individual differences in level of voice for both boys and girls. This was the next burning question to be addressed: What accounted for these vast differences *within* each gender? Perhaps the most critical determinant for both genders was the level of support for voice within each relational context (parents, close friends, female classmates, male classmates, and teachers). The findings were very clear. For each gender, the more support for expressing one's opinions, the higher one's level of voice within that context. Perhaps this is not a startling finding, but it had to be documented to identify a critical cause of individual differences in level of voice within each gender.

In addition, we examined gender orientation, and the results were particularly revealing for female adolescents. We identified both those with a predominantly feminine orientation and those with an androgynous orientation (i.e., those who endorsed both feminine and masculine stereotypes). We found that level of voice depended on gender orientation in interaction with the relational contexts just identified. Feminine girls expressed lower levels of voice, as compared with androgynous girls, in the more *public* contexts, namely, with classmates and teachers at school. However, feminine and androgynous adolescent girls reported equally high levels of voice within more personal relationships, namely, with close friends and parents.

What is our conclusion? Based on these findings, we would conclude that there is a subset of girls, the feminine girls (who during the late 1990s were in the minority), who do seem to stifle their voices in certain situations, namely, the more public contexts. This suggests to us that Gilligan's (1993) thesis is applicable to *that* subset of girls in *those* relational situations. Our point is that one needs to move to this level of analysis: What subsets of girls and boys, what contexts, what motives, and what predictors lead to our understanding of level of voice? This is the direction that not only will further our science but also will help us to understand the *individuals* in our lives, be they our children, our students, our clients, our friends, or other family members. Such an individual difference approach can help us to frame problems more creatively.

Is There a Dark Side to High Self-Esteem?

For many years, in examining the determinants of level of self-esteem (for a review, see Harter, 1999), we have been committed to identifying the predictors, correlates, and consequences of level of self-esteem. The work that was reported earlier in this chapter revealed that we and others have consistently found that low self-esteem is highly predictive of depressive symptoms and suicidal thinking, namely, internalizing symptoms. In reviewing and later researching the predictors of violent ideation (and media-reported behavior in the case of the school shooters), we also documented in our own work the finding that low self-esteem and its predictors can lead to violent ideation as well (Harter et al., 2003). Thus, we were intrigued when Baumeister and colleagues (1996) proposed that there is a dark side to high self-esteem. This formulation, intended for adults, suggested that high self-esteem, within a constellation of narcissism, low empathy, sensitivity to evaluations from others, and potentially fluctuating or fragile self-esteem, can lead to violent ideation or behavior in the face of psychological threats to the ego. This is certainly an interesting formulation, and in articles and the popular press (e.g., the *New York Times*), a headline reading "The Dark Side of High Self-Esteem" is certainly an attention grabber.

We sought to examine this issue among adolescents given that violent ideation and violent behavior have become of central interest during recent years. Our measures have specifically targeted thoughts of violent ideation when humiliated, namely, threats to the ego in Baumeister

and colleagues' (1996) terms. We are in agreement that such threats, resulting in feelings of humiliation, are central mediators of potentially violent thoughts that could possibly lead to violent behavior. However, is high self-esteem a villain in this psychological plot? Our own results with adolescents suggest otherwise. Our own findings indicate that humiliation in the face of threats to the ego, narcissism, and lack of empathy are key predictors of violent ideation, consistent with Baumeister and colleagues' claims. However, high self-esteem is not part of the predictive formulation. Self-esteem, as a predictor of violent ideation, is either negatively related or nonstatistically related. These results also suggest the need to thoughtfully distinguish between narcissism and high self-esteem because if they are assessed appropriately, they are not correlated (Harter & McCarley, 2004). Thus, our research does *not* reveal that there is a dark side to high self-esteem. Rather, narcissism (defined as feelings of entitlement, superiority, and self-aggrandizement) in conjunction with lack of empathy do predict violent thoughts that could lead to violent behavior. We need to move beyond the sensationalism of school shootings to develop thoughtful hypotheses about other dynamics such as how such violent thinking could compromise development in other areas such as lack of academic progress and difficulty in developing social skills. These are our challenges. We need to develop models that will assist us in identifying *individuals* who may be compromised and in need of interventions. Initially, as researchers, we look for general patterns, but we need to go beyond gender, age level, ethnicity, and other demographics to examine processes that will help us to understand individuals.

CONCLUSIONS

Our scientific enterprise has touted the hypothetico–deductive method in which "top-down" models, beginning with theory, dictate research formulations and empirical efforts. Yet increasingly, more *inductive* methods have come to the fore. Observations of real-life behaviors have come to attract the attention of many, not as conclusions but rather as grist for the empirical mill. Interesting observations and thoughtful approaches can drive our inquiry, frame specific questions, and dictate a research strategy.

As the introduction to this chapter revealed, I discovered this as a child. Could a banty hen patiently sit on a large duck egg for the requisite period of time and hatch a different species that would become her offspring? Would the duckling, Yankee Doodle, survive a child's experiment that he be required to swim immediately after his hatching? Would a petite hen and gangling duckling bond as mother and offspring? These were my own burning questions given childhood curiosity and a natural laboratory in which to investigate such issues.

We need to foster these processes in our children, in our students, and in ourselves. We need an educational system that promotes this type of curiosity and exploration. Too many children are turned off to science as it is taught in many schools today. On a beautiful sunny spring Friday, our daughter came home distraught, bemoaning the fact that she had to memorize the periodic table for her chemistry class. Sharing her distress, I suggested a better idea. It was time to plant the garden, and among other preparations, I had just purchased onion sets. "Let's try an experiment—plant half of them right side up and half of them upside down and see what happens." Gleefully, she ran out to the garden plot and we cordoned off two rows. For days, she vigilantly checked, asking eagerly but impatiently, "How long do we have to wait?" About 21 days later, we had our answer. Both rows of onions looked identical with many healthy scallions.

Our daughter was incredulous. "You mean under the ground the ones we planted upside down knew how to turn themselves right side up?" She had answered one of her first scientific burning questions with interest and enthusiasm. To this day, she recalls nothing about the periodic table. However, she has a profound memory of onions, instinct, and how to frame a meaningful question. Moreover, she will transfer these lessons to her kindergarten children and her young son.

REFERENCES

American Association of University Women. (1992). *How schools are short-changing girls.* Washington, DC: American Association of University Women Educational Foundation.

Baumeister, R. F., Smart, L., & Boden, J. M. (1996). Relation of threatened egotism to violence and aggression: The dark side of high self-esteem. *Psychological Review, 103,* 5–33.

Bracken, B. (1992). *Multidimensional Self-Concept Scale.* Austin, TX: Pro-Ed.

Cooley, C. H. (1902). *Human nature and the social order.* New York: Scribner.

Coopersmith, S. (1967). *The antecedents of self-esteem.* San Francisco: Freeman.

Gilligan, C. (1993). Joining the resistance: Psychology, politics, girls, and women. In L. Weis & M. Fine (Eds.), *Beyond silenced voices* (pp. 143–168). Albany: State University of New York Press.

Harter, S. (1977). A cognitive-developmental approach to children's expression of conflicting feelings and a technique to facilitate such expression in play therapy. *Journal of Consulting and Clinical Psychology, 45,* 417–432.

Harter, S. (1982). The Perceived Competence Scale for Children. *Child Development, 53,* 87–97.

Harter, S. (1999). *The construction of the self.* New York: Guilford.

Harter, S., & Buddin, B. J. (1987). Children's understanding of the simultaneity of two emotions: A five-stage developmental acquisition. *Developmental Psychology, 23,* 388–399.

Harter, S., & Chao, C. (1992). The role of competence in young children's creation of imaginary friends. *Merrill–Palmer Quarterly, 38,* 350–363.

Harter, S., Low, S., & Whitesell, N. R. (2003). What we have learned from Columbine: The impact of the self-system on suicidal and violent ideation among adolescents. *Journal of Youth Violence, 2,* 3–26.

Harter, S., & Marold, D. B. (1993). The directionality of the link between self-esteem and affect: Beyond causal modeling. In D. Cicchetti & S. L. Toth (Eds.), *Rochester Symposium on Developmental Psychopathology: Disorders and dysfunctions of the self* (Vol. 5, pp. 333–370). Rochester, NY: University of Rochester Press.

Harter, S., Marold, D. B., & Whitesell, N. R. (1992). A model of psychosocial risk factors leading to suicidal ideation in young adolescents. *Development and Psychopathology, 4,* 167–188.

Harter, S., & McCarley, K. (2004, April). *Is there a dark side to high self-esteem leading to adolescent violent ideation?* Paper presented at the meeting of the American Psychological Association, Honolulu, HI.

Harter, S., & Monsour, A. (1992). Developmental analysis of conflict caused by opposing attributes in the adolescent self-portrait. *Developmental Psychology, 28,* 251–260.

Harter, S., & Rienks, S. (2004, April). *Do young adolescents perceive gender bias in the classroom?* Paper presented at the meeting of the American Psychological Association, Honolulu, HI.

Harter, S., Stocker, C., & Robinson, N. (1996). The perceived direction of the link between approval and self-worth: The liabilities of a looking glass self orientation. *Journal of Research on Adolescence, 6,* 285–308.

Harter, S., Waters, P. L., & Whitesell, N. R. (1998). Relational self-worth: Differences in perceived worth as a person across interpersonal contexts. *Child Development, 69,* 756–766.

Harter, S., & Whitesell, N. R. (1996). Multiple-pathways to self-reported depression and adjustment among adolescents. *Development and Psychopathology, 9,* 835–854.

James, W. (1890). *The principles of psychology.* New York: Henry Holt.

James, W. (1892). *Psychology: The briefer course.* New York: Henry Holt.

Marsh, H. W. (1991). *Self-Description Questionnaire–III.* San Antonio, TX: Psychological Corporation.

Mead, G. H. (1934). *Mind, self, and society from the standpoint of a social behaviorist.* Chicago: University of Chicago Press.

Piers, E. V., & Harris, D. B. (1964). Age and other correlates of self-concept in children. *Journal of Educational Psychology, 55,* 91–95.

Pipher, M. (1994). *Reviving Ophelia: Saving the selves of adolescent girls.* New York: Ballantine.

Rienks, S., & Harter, S. (2005, April). *Is there gender bias in the middle school classroom according to students and, if so, are there academic correlates?* Paper presented at the meeting of the Society for Research in Child Development, Atlanta, GA.

Rosenberg, M. (1986). Self-concept from middle childhood through adolescence. In J. Suls & A. G. Greenwald (Eds.), *Psychological perspectives on the self* (Vol. 3, pp. 107–135). Hillsdale, NJ: Lawrence Erlbaum.

Sadker, M., & Sadker, D. (1994). *Failing at fairness: How America's schools cheat girls.* New York: Scribner.

Seligman, M. E. P. (1993). *What you can change and what you can't.* New York: Fawcett.

Challenges in Preparing for Inquiry

Introductory Essay

Scott L. Thomas

University of Georgia

T he opening chapter in Section Four plays on themes of "light" and "shadow" in education research. In Chapter 20, John Bean keys on a simple but relentless tension: In our quest for "truth" and knowledge, we make decisions that result in the artificial and immediate bounding of possible answers. Each of the chapters in this section systematically examines many of these key decisions and their implications for the conduct of exemplary research in education.

Our core interests as education researchers are often informed by our disciplinary orientations that, in turn, powerfully influence how we see and define problems, collect and analyze data, and turn findings into conclusions. Disciplines are defined by the theories that create an order of the environments and processes that are of interest to their inhabitants. These same theories presuppose certain conditions that may or may not be realistic from the point of view of scholars in other disciplines. As each author in this section observes, theory most often provides a starting point from which decisions about hypotheses and research design are made. But although theory provides us with a means by which to organize our thinking, observation, and analysis, it also proscribes our view of what constitutes an important problem and how one might undertake research most profitably in any given area. If one assumes that the goal of our research is to generate new and useful knowledge, therein lies a major challenge in preparing for meaningful inquiry.

In this section, three outstanding scholars—John Bean, Ronald Heck, and Douglas Toma—draw on their significant expertise and experience to speak to what they see as the major challenges facing the researcher preparing for inquiry in education, and I contribute a fourth chapter. Our charge was straightforward—to write about what we view as the most significant challenges confronting those making decisions about the goals, purposes, and execution of their research.

Of course, such a "most significant issues" list can quickly become unwieldy; therefore, we divided the task into four discrete areas to help each of us focus on a subset of critical issues. Bean, in his chapter, focuses on the tension between the pursuit of useful knowledge and the shackles of disciplines—among others—and their necessary orderliness. Picking up on Bean's analysis, Heck provides a thorough consideration of the challenges in the process through which researchers identify and frame problems for study. My own chapter focuses on challenges inherent in the ways in which we choose what to observe and how to observe it. Rounding out this section, Toma deftly draws on points raised throughout this section to challenge prevailing norms limiting the understanding of rigorous research as that conducted in a positivistic, quantitative, and increasingly experimental framework.

Methodological rigor (often termed "scientific") is a normative condition defined by current standard-bearers within a discipline or field. In education, a recognized standard-bearer is the newly formed Institute of Education Sciences (IES). At several points, authors in this section explore the implications of IES's perspective on what constitutes scientific inquiry in education (basically that which involves randomized controlled trials). One critical implication noted is that the imposition of such a standard, although intended to provide useful objective criteria for quality research, obviates entire classes of questions that can be framed and explored only through alternative approaches.

When our quest for new and useful knowledge is limited to knowledge that can be gleaned only through particular methodological approaches, the lines of inquiry that can be legitimately pursued become seriously proscribed. As Bean puts it in his chapter, "When methodology precedes identifying the problem to be studied, groupthink wins and research suffers." Each of the authors in this section is in agreement with Bean's sentiment, and each speaks to such challenges in his own way. If a common theme runs through this section, this is clearly it.

The first three chapters in the section are organized from the broader to the narrower, with the fourth chapter constituting an appeal for recasting the use of qualitative methodologies in a way that will better facilitate their recognition as legitimate avenues to new knowledge. This, of course, implies that qualitative methods are currently viewed as illegitimate avenues to knowledge, a position consistent with the IES proclamations regarding the characteristics of rigorous education research.

In Chapter 20, John Bean's wide-ranging consideration of the forces at play in the research process provides us with refreshing consideration of purposes of scholarship, the role of "truth" in the disciplines and applied fields, sources of data, ethics, and the importance of generalizability. From this rather sweeping overview of purpose, Bean then explores the powerful currents that pull the researcher away from the ideals of pure research. This exploration considers ego and fear, risk taking and risk aversion, groupthink and disciplinary parochialism, and ultimately the corrosive force of what he describes as "methodological correctness," a classic form of goal displacement.

The process through which researchers identify and frame problems for study provides the basis for Chapter 21 by Ronald Heck. Heck invites us to consider a number of salient issues in conceptualizing and conducting education research. In his chapter, Heck argues that the choices we make in approaching problems and selecting methods of investigation have major consequences for what we find. Although the point is perhaps obvious, Heck cleverly demonstrates the ways in which seemingly innocent decisions about method can have profound impacts on evidence, analysis, and conclusions. Through this demonstration, he argues that the importance of complete disclosure of conceptual and methodological decisions is key to producing defensible findings. At a minimum, such disclosure can serve to better ensure that the researcher has thought through these issues and forces the reconciliation of inconsistencies among framing, method, and conclusion.

My own chapter explores the role of sampling and the ways in which sampling is intimately connected to the researcher's epistemological base and predispositions to problems at hand. I use Chapter 22 to argue that sampling is all too often viewed as independent of the conceptual context of the study and many times results in the squandering of opportunities to achieve rigor in the overall research effort. Through this chapter, I argue that sampling strategies represent one of the most powerful contrasts between quantitative and qualitative inquiry and that this contrast hinges on the epistemological bases defining the two broad approaches to understanding social phenomena.

All three of these chapters emphasize that the broadest range of new and useful knowledge requires the recognition and appreciation of a wide range of methodological approaches. Bean refers to the seductive nature of pure research, that is, research that is designed to generate new, trustworthy, and defensible findings. There are myriad approaches to most problems we examine, and Heck shows that each approach yields different information and perhaps alternative conclusions. I believe that one of the advantages of working in a field like education is that we are able to bring so many perspectives to bear on issues that are important to us.

This is where Douglas Toma picks up with Chapter 23, the final chapter in this section. Focusing almost exclusively on applied qualitative approaches, Toma takes issue with the federal redefinition of what constitutes "scientific" educational research—a redefinition that makes no room whatsoever for qualitative research. Rather than a continuation of the hand-wringing that usually accompanies this, Toma develops a refreshing argument that those working within the applied qualitative tradition can, in fact, frame their efforts as scientific even in the restrictive language of the IES. There are several useful elements to his approach in this chapter. First, he eschews efforts to "shoehorn" qualitative work into the accepted quantitative standards. I agree that this is a losing fight and applaud Toma for adopting a different tack. Second, throughout the chapter, he encourages us to think about the choices we make about rigor in our research and reminds us that there is no one best way in which to approach most problems. Third, and most important in my view, Toma suggests that applied qualitative researchers take responsibility for explaining how their approach has rigor—a rigor that is on par with that understood as scientific work—but is necessarily and fundamentally different.

That some outside are critical of education research is due in part to our healthy tolerance—decidedly not an embrace—of multiple methodological approaches that yield, as argued throughout this section, a variety of views and at times conflicting conclusions. It is understandable that, in an applied field like education, those looking for clear and actionable answers are often frustrated by the many messages contained in our findings. Although I think it is incumbent on us as education researchers to provide clarity and guidance for improving the condition of education, I view the use of multiple approaches as a sign of our health and vitality as a field of study. Allowing ourselves to be forced into a box that enables only a narrow range of ways in which to understand very complex social and education problems would be a grave disservice to society.

I hope that the reader will use the chapters in Section Four to explore the proposition that multiple methodological approaches are an essential part of our field's intellectual vitality. Moreover, I hope that these chapters will help the reader to understand our shared belief that although some problems are better or less well served by particular methodological approaches, when the approaches are well planned and executed, there is no inherent association between rigor and method. As the authors in this section labor to make clear, regardless of our methodological orientations, we each make critical choices that—in the end—define the rigor of our effort.

20

Light and Shadow in Research Design

John P. Bean

Indiana University

Research, as a form of scholarship and creative work, is at the core of the academic enterprise. It is through research that universities contribute knowledge to society. Research provides the basis for what is taught in the disciplines and how members of a discipline understand their professional work. The design of research has a direct effect on what is discovered, the ideas that are created, and what forms of research contain legitimate professional information that is then passed on to the next generation of scholars in a field. The promise of research is that it will give us, as a society, what we need to know to improve our lives.

An axiological question arises for those planning to do research: Is research of value because it is true or because it is useful? Truth, the meaning of which is contested by philosophers, the existence of which is contested by postmodernists, and the use of which is contested by critical theorists, might be unattainable. I use the term "truth" as a shorthand to mean that which is consistent with observation—if observations can be made—and is identified through procedures accepted in the discipline.

The Bright Promise of Knowledge

Basic research emphasizes the search for disciplinary truth, whereas applied research emphasizes finding out something useful. Both goals are attractive, and one does not preclude the other. Conjoined with the axiological question is a metaphysical one: Is there an objective reality out there that we can discover, or is the world a product of the imagination, constructed in the minds of individuals and groups? Researchers design studies based on what they believe knowledge to be. The search for objective truth involves a different path from the one used in the search for individual meaning or a consensus about intersubjective meaning.

In the professions, as opposed to the basic disciplines, utility is necessary. Professionals provide service to a client based on superior knowledge developed from a long study of the disciplinary research. According to Shils (1984), what separates academic knowledge from common knowledge is that academic knowledge is developed by a rigorous methodology. Researchers in a pure discipline (Biglan, 1973) attempt to establish truth in that discipline. Researchers in a profession have as their

353

purpose not to attain pure knowledge but rather praxis, that is, to attain the best knowledge that can be applied in service of their clients' needs. To offer education as a societal good, money is spent, programs are funded, and teachers are trained and hired. If research is to inform these processes, then it is difficult to escape from pragmatism and positivism.

Research that advances methodology is of value to a field by developing better researchers, but such research is not always of direct use to their researchers' clientele. A field that emphasizes internal debates about philosophy, methodology, and/or definitions can be very lively but is in danger of becoming irrelevant. Well-designed research should deliver new understandings and new theories. The ultimate test of its value to the public will not rest with internal elaboration or with faculty members charming other faculty members; rather, it will be seen with improving understanding, teaching, learning, and organizing in a heterogeneous society. In what follows, I discuss some of the primary considerations that should inform research designs.

Theories

Educational researchers are interested in finding out how one thing is related to another, describing a set of phenomena, and establishing a basis on which to make claims, predictions, and explanations. Braithwaite (1955) writes that the purpose of science is theory and that, by extension, the purpose of research is to contribute theories or refinements of existing theories to science. Theory is a kind of abstraction, a simplification of reality that applies in similar circumstances and not just to the specific case at hand. For researchers, theories focus attention, limit choices, and provide explanations—characteristics that give good theories a central role in research design. For actors in the educational environment, they are practical for the same reasons.

Theories about the social behavior have inherent limits. These are identified by Thorngate (1976) and elaborated on by Weick (1979). Thorngate (1976) developed a postulate of commensurate complexity in which there are trade-offs among a theory being *general,* a theory being *accurate,* and a theory being

simple. A theory cannot be all three simultaneously; general accurate theories are not simple, accurate simple theories are not general, and simple general theories are not accurate. Weick (1979) provides examples of each. In developing a research design, the theory used, or the one the researcher is trying to develop, has more important effects on research design than does anything except the topic chosen for the research. Theory drives hypotheses. The choice of a theory to use or develop reflects the researcher's interest in being general, simple, or accurate and shapes the study accordingly.

Theory is emphasized in research because it provides explanation. Without meaningful descriptions of the situation—that is, without identifying new things to be understood and related to each other by theories—research would not move forward. Designing research that identifies the ways in which people in a given situation view their worlds is a sensible starting place for meaningful research. Without important things to be studied, no theories would need to be developed and a rigorous methodology to estimate relationships based on theory would not be necessary.

Topics

How does one go about selecting substantive issues connected by a theory? Texts covering research in education or the behavioral sciences tend to either be mute on the question or provide only minimal advice (Creswell, 2002; Gall, Borg, & Gall, 2002; Kerlinger, 1973; Krathwohl, 1988). The selection of topics for study is neither innocent nor rational. It is not innocent because being selected gives a topic legitimacy, creates the power of knowledge for those affected by the topic, and creates invisibility for those excluded. It is not rational because researchers choose topics to study based on professional interests, not professional mandates, and on self-interest based on what researchers value, are curious about, or perceive they will profit from. What is studied in a discipline becomes what is taught in the discipline. Just like what is included in the curriculum is a political decision as well as an educational decision, what is studied is not neutral; it implies that what is studied is valuable.

It is axiomatic that the most important part of any study is the choice of a topic; that is, research findings depend on what is being researched. A good topic, when well studied, improves descriptions in a field, better explains how theories operate in the discipline, and shows how this knowledge can be applied to benefit clients and society as a whole. The research problem to be addressed and the statement of the purpose of the study focus research activities and limit the scope of the study. If the purpose is too broad, then the research cannot be accomplished with reasonable effort. If the purpose is too narrow, then the study is trivial. The statement of purpose is the most important sentence in a research proposal. Researchers need to avoid making Type III errors—asking the wrong question or not asking the right question—or what I consider to be Type IV errors, that is, studying the wrong thing.

Identifying something as a *practical* problem usually means that the researcher has found a reason why the topic should be studied. A *research* problem is the starting place for research. Research problems involve identifying unresolved conditions or situations, and it is the research problem that is nested between the topic and the purpose. Theoretical research problems deal with "we don't know why," descriptive research problems deal with "we don't know what," and practical research problems deal with "we don't know how." Researchers are attracted to uncertainty, paradoxes, anomalies, contradictions, and ambiguities in the field. The significance of a problem is often based on the way in which it intersects with theoretical uncertainty and practical importance.

Probably the best way of finding a problem to study is to do extensive reading in an important topical area and find out what is poorly understood. Many articles contain sections that give suggestions for future research, and many articles have glaring shortcomings that suggest a problem should be reexamined from a different perspective. Some researchers choose a methodology and then try to find a problem to match it. This approach creates an unnecessary constraint on what is to be studied, and the foolishness of this sequence cannot be emphasized enough. The cart does not pull the horse.

Some researchers are told what to study by a superior such as an adviser, a provider of resources, an admired scholar in the field, or a co-investigator. So long as the relationship is not exploitative, joining an ongoing research agenda has the clear advantage of closure; the person knows what he or she will study. It has the disadvantage of not learning how to define one's own research problem. Typically, a study involves the following iterative process: Approach a topic of interest, read in the area, write a brief statement of purpose, discuss this statement with others, reflect, read, write, talk, and so on until closure on a compelling problem with a realistic scope is reached.

A hot topic is one where there is a lot of interest and a great likelihood of getting a project funded, finding others to participate in the study, and publishing the results. Good topics allow young scholars to demonstrate their research skills and increase the likelihood of getting further support for their research and publications in their fields. For better or worse, it usually means becoming more specialized. With luck, a good topic is one the researcher loves. Here, love is a passionate attachment to the research and an enjoyment of the research process. This attachment should not be confused with a lack of objectivity, but it involves caring for an increased understanding of a topic and a willingness to put forward the effort that results in influential research.

After deciding what to study and why such a study is worthwhile, the final part of designing research is to decide on the processes by which the research is to be accomplished. Many people, in thinking about research design, think that they need only be concerned with research methodology (Kerlinger, 1973, cited in Daniel, 1996). The following three questions always affect research design. What will the researcher study? Why is the research important? How will the researcher carry out the research? Only the third question is related to methodology.

Different Approaches to Research

There are many ways in which to study the same topic, and these produce different results. Mitroff and Kilmann (1978) describe four approaches to research based on a Jungian analysis of our predispositions to approach decision making and obtain information, similar to the Myers-Briggs Type Indicator tests (Myers-Briggs, 1962). They identify four approaches to research: the scientist, the conceptual theorist, the conceptual humanist, and the individual humanist. Given the topic *college student retention*, consider the way in which each methodology is chosen based on the researcher's interests, is different from the other methods, and produces different results. Descriptive phrases are taken from tables in Mitroff and Kilmann (1978) on the pages indicated.

For the *scientist*, the approach should be objective, causal, cumulative, and progressive, emphasizing reliability and external validity and separating the scientist from the observed. It aims at precise, unambiguous empirical knowledge using strict logic (Mitroff & Kilmann, 1978, p. 34). The norms of this approach are known as the CUDOS:

*C*ommunism, indicating that scientific knowledge is common property;

*U*niversalism, indicating that scientific knowledge should be independent of the personality of the individual scientist;

*D*isinterestedness, such that the scientist should observe what happens and not advocate a theory or experimental outcome; and

*O*rganized

*S*kepticism, where scientists should be critical of their own and others' ideas. (Merton, 1942/1973, p. 269)

An example of the scientific study of retention would be an organizational experiment based on the hypothesis that higher-achieving students are more likely to remain enrolled. Students would be randomly assigned to a treatment group or a control group. In the treatment group, students would participate in a retention program, such as developing study skills, but otherwise would have experiences no different from those of the control group. After a given time period, the researcher would find out whether the retention rate for students who participated in the retention program was significantly different from that for students who did not. This information would be used to support or negate the hypothesis.

The *conceptual theorist* is involved with research that is impersonal, value free, disinterested, imaginative, and problematic, involving multiple causation, purposeful ambiguity, and uncertainty. The theorist is interested in the conflict between antithetical imaginative theories, comprehensive holistic theories, and ever expanding research programs to produce conflicting schemas using dialectical and indeterminate logics (Mitroff & Kilmann, 1978, p. 56). A theorist conducting retention research would provide at least two theoretical explanations of retention behavior, use survey methods to gather information, analyze the data using statistics, find out whether the data supported one theory more than the other, and use that information to make more theories. Much of the empirical research reported in educational journals is a combination of the scientist and theorist— theory guiding social science inquiry into educational structures and processes.

The *conceptual humanist* (although I find *social humanist* to be a more accurate description) approaches research as a value-constituted interested activity, holistic, political, and imaginative, where multiple causation is present in an uncertain and problematic social environment, and with a deep concern for humanity. This approach recognizes the importance of the relationship between the inquirer and the subject and has the aim of promoting human development on the widest possible scale. The normative outcomes of such research would be economic plenty, aesthetic beauty, and human welfare. Similar to action research, the social humanist prefers small-group dynamics where both the inquirer and the participants learn to know themselves better and work together to improve the situation (Mitroff & Kilmann, 1978, p. 76). A retention researcher using this approach could develop an ongoing program of action-oriented ethnographic research studies where the researcher better understands how the issues facing students contribute to their leaving, and tries to alleviate those conditions. The purpose is to increase the overall retention rate with the belief that students who complete college lead richer lives.

An *individual humanist* addresses inquiry as a personal, value-constituted, interested, and partisan activity, engaging in poetic, political, acausal, and nonrational discourse in pursuit of knowledge. Intense personal knowledge and experience are highly valued, aiming to help *this* person to know himself or herself uniquely and to achieve his or her own self-determination. The logic of the unique and singular has mythical, mystical, and transcendental overtones that operate as counternorms to the CUDOS (Mitroff & Kilmann, 1978, p. 95). A retention study from this perspective would try to develop a detailed understanding of a single student in the full context of his or her life. It could take the form of an "*N* of 1" case study, a phenomenological inquiry into who the student is, what the student finds at school, and how staying or leaving school would be better for this particular individual.

The purpose of presenting these four perspectives—and many more can be imagined—is that there is no best way in which to study a topic. For different kinds of studies make different kinds of assumptions about what is important to know, serve different needs for different people involved in the studies, and produce different kinds of outcomes. The four perspectives were presented in what was once considered the normative order of acceptability: science-based positivistic research, theory development, action research, and phenomenology. One may be no more correct than the others. Some are more acceptable to certain audiences than to others, and each produces a particular outcome that favors some stakeholders more than it does others.

Methodology and the Scientific Approach

Methodology is often considered the core of research design. Kerlinger (1973, cited in Daniel, 1996) described as one of the research myths that research design and research methods were synonymous, even though many researchers held this view. Methodology is the tool used to accomplish part of the study, specifically, how to obtain and analyze data. It is subservient to choosing an important topic to study, matching the research problem and the methodology, and knowing what the results mean and how they can be applied. To do good research, the methodology used should be appropriate for the problem addressed. This is a necessary condition but not a sufficient one. An elegantly analyzed data set that was composed of ambiguously measured data that addressed a question of trivial importance is not likely to enter the annals of great research.

Educational research is part of social science research tradition, a tradition that was influenced by research in the natural sciences. The natural sciences use the scientific method to solve research problems or support a perspective. The method contains a series of sequential steps similar to the following: Identify a problem, gather information from the literature about this question, develop a hypothesis in the context of a theory, collect data related to the hypothesis, analyze the data, and draw a conclusion related to the truthfulness of the hypothesis and correctness of the theory.

Scientists, as logical purists, build arguments on falsifiability and the law of the excluded middle. This law states that *A* and *not-A* cannot exist simultaneously. But if *A* stands for "this program helps students to learn" and *not-A* stands for "this program does *not* help students to learn," then both can be true, as in the case of aptitude–treatment interactions; that is, a treatment could be effective for a high-aptitude student but not effective for a low-aptitude student. If both are true, then the law of the excluded middle is violated and falsifiability cannot be demonstrated. This situation is problematic for scientific research in education.

Education is not a scientifically based process, partly because the term "education" is ideological and idiosyncratic, much different from the term "temperature." At best, scientific research can shed light on narrowly defined educational behaviors, and researchers can hope for—but cannot guarantee—cumulative effect. When a government policy assumes that education is equivalent to improving the score on a test, the society will not have a moral compass and will not be educated. Feyerabend (1993) holds the view that if we do not separate scientific research and the state, as we have separated the church and the state, irreparable harm will be done.

In the same way as social science research has imitated the natural sciences, educational research has imitated social science research. Research in these areas may be separated more by the topic studied than by the rigor of the methodology. As with social science research in general, educational research might pretend a level of control so as to carry out an experiment. Researchers give themselves solace that "other things are equal," or "other effects are random," or "spuriousness is not a problem" and proceed as if the social world were simple and understandable in the same way as the traditional world of the pure sciences can be.

A Traditional Approach to Designing Educational Research

Most graduate programs in academic sub-specialties (e.g., history of education, sociology of education, anthropology of education, counseling psychology, experimental psychology, higher education, school administration, curriculum and instruction) spend at least a semester teaching research design appropriate for their field. Postmodern and critical approaches to research continue to challenge the status quo in research methods. These areas are not explored in detail here due to space limitations. My discussion revolves around quantitative and qualitative approaches to research, terms that reify categories that are themselves overlapping and arbitrary.

A simple way of looking at a proposal is to see how it answers the three questions posed earlier. What is this study about? Why is the study important? How will the researcher conduct the study? The study itself covers these three topics and answers two additional questions. What did the researcher find? What do the findings mean? Research designs revolve around a limited number of elements. Their exact use and exposition vary depending on the particular approach taken. The purpose and promise of these elements have been identified and discussed by a number of textbooks such as those of Gall and colleagues (2002) and Creswell (2002). These texts identify many of the issues facing researchers, especially those new to the process.

Although not suitable for all studies, well-designed quantitative research usually addresses the following areas: the introduction to the topic of the research, the background and context in which that topic has been studied, the importance of studying the topic (including the practical value of the study), the research problem to be addressed, the purpose of the study, the objectives or questions to be addressed, definitions and related constructs, assumptions used in the study, limitations of the study, the scope of the study, relevant theories to guide the study or how theories might be discovered, the findings of other researchers, the methodology to be used in the study (including the site, sample, or selection procedure for respondents), how the data will be gathered, how the data will be measured, how the data will be analyzed, and why these methods are appropriate. This information usually completes the design of a research proposal and appears as the first part of a finished study. Finished studies also include a description of the sample actually analyzed in the study, a description of the data (including the treatment of missing cases and possible biases), how the researcher met the assumptions required to use the statistics, presentation of the data, support or lack of support for the hypotheses or theories used, discussion of the findings, and conclusions. The final chapter typically summarizes the study, identifies the practical implications of the study, and identifies areas for future research.

Qualitative research can involve using the five research traditions identified by Creswell (1998)—biography, ethnography, grounded theory, case study, and phenomenology—which can be used singly or in combination. General headings appropriate for qualitative studies include the topic, the focus and purpose, the significance, related literature, the methodology, presentation of the data, interpretation of the data, and conclusions. Detailed headings in the introduction indicate the topic to be studied, the overall interest focusing on what will be explained or described, an organizing metaphor, the mystery and the detective, hermeneutic elements, the significance of the study, and why the reader should be interested. Next, the author describes getting information away from the source using relevant literature. The author then describes the selected qualitative method (how information is obtained and how sense is made from it) and methodological details about site selection, informant selection, data collection, data analysis, and data evaluation, all of which can be in a separate chapter, part of the first chapter, in an appendix, or woven into the chapters that present respondent information. This section is followed by one or more chapters that present the text as natural answers to natural questions in the form of stories, tables, interviews, documents, narratives, photographs, videotapes, vignettes, texts of various kinds, descriptions, and routines (see Schwartzman, 1993, from which some of these headings were taken). Raw data can be presented without comment, presented and interpreted simultaneously, or presented and then interpreted. The study ends with findings, conclusions, and recommendations for others. The structure of the study is more idiosyncratic than the more formal structure of traditional quantitative studies. In qualitative research, the sample *is* the study, and the reasons for selecting the sample need to be emphasized.

Most researchers, when approaching a topic they care about, have tentative hypotheses about what causes what or predispositions to think that the world operates according to certain principles that also apply in this area. People bias their observations based on their experience. All of us know that we have certain biases, and we can try to counter those biases in our research by looking for evidence that directly contradicts what we expect. In the unconscious, there is a second set of biases of which, by definition, we are not aware. Sometimes peer readers can help the researcher to discover what is missing or what is inappropriately under- or overemphasized in the study.

After analyzing the data in a quantitative study, the researcher presents the findings. Typically, it is rather straightforward because the data to be gathered and the analyses proposed for the data were specified in the proposal for the study. For qualitative researchers, the data, the findings, and the method might not be distinct. The narrative that presents selected questions and answers can represent findings based on data that came from the method by which questions were developed. As the previous sentence suggests, it is a convoluted process. The presentation might revolve around respondents'

experiences and understandings, a chronology of events, or themes supported by respondents' statements. In ethnographic studies, the descriptions of lives in context can stand on their own (Lawrence-Lightfoot, 1995). Thick descriptions (Geertz, 1973) might provide greater insight into the education of a student in a school than would an analysis of variables. In most studies, some analysis of the descriptions is expected. This predisposition is part of the legacy of pragmatism; researchers in education are expected to identify how knowledge gained from the study can improve professional practice.

In designing a study, the background, context, importance of the topic, and presumed practical value of the study come from the literature written about the topic or analogous literatures in similar fields. For example, the study of college student retention can be considered to be analogous to the study of turnover in work organizations, and the literature in one area can be used to reinforce the literature in the other area (Bean, 1980). The use of literature in quantitative studies, however, can differ substantially from the use of literature in qualitative studies.

In a quantitative study, the literature is used to identify the importance of the dependent variable, relevant independent variables, and theories that bind these factors together to justify the use of statistics procedures and to provide a context for the discussion. In qualitative studies, a premium is placed on the ability to see what is before the researcher. Our ability to observe is both heightened and diminished by our prior knowledge and expectations (Bean, 1997). It is heightened by making ourselves aware of important details to observe, and it is diminished because we focus only on those details. Due to the preconceived notions of the researcher, those factors actually influencing the respondents' world might not be identified. When the literature shapes the way in which we view the world, what is actually before us is replaced by what we expect to see.

A review of the literature, as a stand-alone section summarizing research in the topical area, makes little sense. The literature, as a compendium of related information, should be used to support arguments related to the importance of the subject. It should identify areas that are either well or poorly understood related to the topic, identify and describe relevant theories, identify and describe appropriate methodologies to study the topic, describe dependent and independent variables if relevant, provide definitions, and provide a context to discuss the findings from the study.

Dissertation Abstracts International, ERIC Documents, the ISI Web of Science, and the proceedings of relevant professional organizations all can be used to access current research. A condemning retort is that the literature in a study is dated. This phrase has some interesting subtexts. The first assumption is that the most recent research is the best research and that previous research is irrelevant. A second assumption is that all research is of limited generalizability over time so that if it is older than, say, 5 years, it is irrelevant. In either case, dated research is of marginal value. By extension, the research that a person is currently conducting is also of marginal value because it will be useful for only 5 years. This planned obsolescence of research becomes a justification for a frenzied increase in the rate of publication and is counterproductive in terms of identifying important and durable ideas in the field. Literature should not be weighed or dated.

In traditional quantitative research, the topic contains the dependent variable and the factors associated with it identify the independent variables that have been found to have important effects on the dependent variable. In studies that are not codifications—that is, not extensive reviews of the literature for the heuristic purpose of organizing what is known about a topic—citing the literature should be done for the purpose of building an argument, not simply to show familiarity with the canon.

Since the 1960s, the number of statistical analyses available for researchers to include in their designs have increased dramatically. Five commercial statistical packages bear the initials SAS, SPSS, BMDP, GLIM, and HLM. The development of these statistical packages has allowed ever more complex analyses to be performed. National data sets from the National Center for Educational Statistics and other sources have provided the opportunity to bring order to vast amounts of data.

For the description of large-scale phenomena, these data sets can be very valuable. For analyzing the causes of behavior, the attempt to gain a broad vision masks individual or small-group differences. Longitudinal studies almost always suffer from decay; that is, measures may differ from year to year and respondents drop out of the study, so the comparisons from year to year might not be the result of what people report; rather, it might be the result of changes in who is doing the reporting.

The availability of data and the means to analyze them raised the level of expectation in some journals that such analyses should be the norm. What is certain is that during the past 50 years, the sophistication of analyses has increased. The literature shifted from normed surveys that reported frequencies, to chi-square, to analyses of variance (ANOVAs) and simple correlations, to factor analysis and multiple regression, to causal modeling with ordinary least squares path analysis, to maximum likelihood used in linear structural relations (LISREL) modeling, and to generalized linear modeling (GLIM) and hierarchical linear modeling (HLM).

The increase in complexity is associated with an increase in agitated exchanges between statisticians about whose method is correct. An improved methodology has not been matched by these studies' becoming more influential in policymaking or practice (Kezar, 2000). The debate is sometimes invisible to the public, taking place between the author of a piece of research and the consulting editors who review the research, and sometimes it appears in journals such as the *Educational Researcher.*

Data

Quantitative studies require data that can be used in statistical analyses. The sources of data can vary widely—historical documents, governmental records, organizational records, interviews, standardized surveys, questionnaires developed as part of the research protocol for a particular study, unobtrusive measures, observations, participant observation, and so on. The quality of the research depends on the quality of the data analyzed; data analysis has only a secondary influence.

The quality of the data varies greatly. Good research design requires that the researcher understand the strengths and weaknesses of the data. Historical data can reflect the biases and ideological preferences of those who recorded it. People who provide data can intentionally distort it to put themselves in a better light, for example, reporting that they had higher grades than they actually did. Survey data might come from a biased sample reflecting only the experiences of high-socioeconomic status respondents. Questions in a survey might be ambiguously written, or a single item might contain two questions with different answers, for example, "How satisfied are you with your salary and fringe benefits?" Survey data that require a forced-choice response might not represent the real interests of the respondent. A respondent might have no opinion on most of the questions and refuse to answer them. Other respondents might not want to reveal personal information and so misrepresent their actual incomes, whether they have ever plagiarized, or how much they use drugs or alcohol. Although the questionnaire is not missing any data, the data provided might be intentionally inaccurate.

In other cases, respondents might not understand the questions, might not care about the answers given, or might become fatigued while filling out the questionnaire so that the accuracy of the responses are different for the beginning and the end of the questionnaire. A well-written question should reflect one bit of information about the respondent unambiguously and reliably, and the answer to the question should match observable facts.

It is acceptable to use problematic data if the analyst understands and acknowledges the problems that exist in the data. For example, a data set might not be random but might be completely representative of one group in the population studied. The bias in this sample can make conclusions drawn about the well-represented group accurate, but the conclusions would not apply to the whole population. Although not representative, the data might be useful to see whether a hypothesized relationship exists at all, that is, as a test of theory.

Data gathered from face-to-face interviews for qualitative research have the potential to yield a gold mine of insights into the people's lives and situations. There is no substitute for prolonged and focused conversations between trusted parties to discover what is important

to the interviewees and how respondents understand key elements in their own lives. When mishandled, interview data can reflect what the interviewees think the interviewers want to hear, normatively appropriate responses, the fears and biases of the interviewees, and the fears and biases of the interviewers. Data flaws become limitations of the study for which the only response is to caution the reader that the results are far from certain.

Ethics

Before proceeding with an examination of research methods, there are some ethical and legal considerations that have obtrusively entered the development of a research protocol. In line with designing research to be useful, it should also be designed to be ethical. The most obvious ethical problems arise when a research procedure causes harm to those who are asked or forced to participate in the process. There are several well-known cases of abuse, including psychological studies where participants were put in unusually stressful situations (Baumrind, 1964; Milgram, 1974) and medical research where participants were given diseases or intentionally denied treatment (Jones, 1993).

The bureaucratic response to these ethical violations was to create rules that would include everybody doing any kind of research that involved contact with living people. Bureaucratic actors, evaluating research they are not conducting themselves, become the gatekeepers of ethical behavior. This responsibility is misplaced; researchers themselves should be responsible for protecting the interests of participants in their studies. I am not naive enough to think that all researchers are ethical or that institutional review boards (IRBs) or protection of human subjects committees will go away. The problem is that ethical judgments about research have been made extrinsic to the research process. Researchers need to design research that does just what the committees want—to protect the participants of a study from harm. If researchers are not socialized to provide these protections, IRBs might not help. The enforcement system used, which involves taking federal support away from ethical researchers because they happen to be at an institution where one person did not comply with the guidelines, is itself unethical. IRBs have the enormous power of being able to block research, and the potential for abusing power must be kept under constant scrutiny. But who will judge the judges?

For qualitative researchers especially, complying with a written informed consent form can damage the trust required to conduct a study. The study of any group that dislikes authority is made impossible, or at least less reliable, by asking the person at the outset to sign a form that says, "You should know that this researcher does not intend to hurt you." A journalist and an ethnographer can conduct and publish identical studies. The journalist needs no informed consent from those who are interviewed for the story, whereas the ethnographer at a research institute needs IRB permission to ask the same questions. The journalist is protected by freedom of speech, whereas academic freedom, according to IRB rules, provides no such protection for the researcher.

Research should be designed to protect everyone, designed to benefit the participants in the research, and designed to protect society from ignorance. With few exceptions other than medical studies, research involving human subjects is intrusive but not invasive. Under the current guidelines for research involving human subjects, a certain percentage of the researcher's time and energy, and of the sponsor's resources, must be devoted to rituals that symbolically protect the participants in a study from being harmed. Whether these guidelines work or not is a different question. Their intentions are good, and research ethics is a serious issue. I do not know whether the current system of enforcing these ethics as an afterthought, through an outside agency just before the data are to be collected, is effective or not. The costs are real and, during an era of tight resources, should be examined carefully.

Generalizability

Generalizability is the central bulwark of the scientific research in education approach. Shavelson and Towne (2002) observe, "Regularity in the patterns across groups and across time—rather than replication per se—is a source of generalization. The goal of such scientific

methods, of course, remains the same: to identify generalized patterns" (p. 82).

Generalizability is a powerful statistical tool that allows researchers to make predictions about patterns of behavior in a population, such as the percentage of people who will vote for Ralph Nader, based on a measure of that behavior taken from a sample of the population. It is attractive to policymakers because it suggests the extent to which a particular solution will work everywhere in the population. As the behavior in question gets more complicated, such as how students learn ethical behavior, generalization is of more limited value. Lincoln and Guba (1985) describe this limitation well:

> Generalizations are nomothetic in nature, that is lawlike, but in order to use them—for purposes of prediction or control, say—the generalizations must be applied to particulars. And it is precisely at that point that their probabilistic, relative nature comes into sharpest focus. (p. 116)

Does what works 90% of the time for the participants in a study work for one particular teacher in one particular class dealing with one particular subject? Tutoring generally helps students to learn how to read, but for a student who is acting out against authority, and who views the tutor as an authority figure, tutoring might prevent the student from learning to read.

As a "reductionistic fallacy" (Lincoln & Guba, 1985, p. 117), generalization simplifies decision making and simultaneously reduces the understanding of the particular. Teachers operate in particular environments, and the findings from a "scientific" study with a high degree of generalizability do not ensure a program's utility in a given classroom. The purpose of scientific research is to eliminate uncertainty so that the operator can predict and control the future. Applied to education, this goal is not a research norm or a teaching norm but rather a political norm.

THE SHADOW OF RESEARCH DESIGN

Research is seductive because it promises to give the participants, as producers or consumers, those things that they imagine they want. We are seduced by research as a beatific process by which we can glimpse the bright light of pure knowledge. Scholars would have no agenda other than furthering knowledge, a value shared by those who fund research, publish it, and base policy on it. It would be a collegial environment where differences exist only about approach, all participants share the ultimate goals of research, and no ethical problems exist. These utopian goals include a greater understanding of individual and group processes in a given discipline with the potential to apply these findings to improve both individual lives and society collectively. Researchers design their studies for the sole purpose of sharing information to better understand the issues at hand and distribute the knowledge widely so that it can improve practice.

The shadow of research design comes as a series of dispositions and paradoxes when the person designing research must make decisions for which the search for disciplinary truth provides no direction. A researcher has some control, but not complete control, over deciding what research to conduct. A researcher has limited control, or no control, over how research is funded, how it is evaluated, and how it is used. The shadow of research appears when one confronts the lack of creativity in research and psychological barriers to the free flow of ideas. It occurs when a researcher encounters difficulties related to the disciplinary research environment and the primary and secondary social environments associated with the research.

The Loss of Creativity

If the world were static, then creativity would not be necessary; what worked in the past would continue to work in the future. In a dynamic social world existing in a turbulent ecology, the generation of new ideas is necessary for survival. In the natural world, mutation is a random process and selection occurs where the fit to the natural environment of the new form has advantages over existing forms. In the social world, creativity is the source of variation and must be present before selection can take place. Without creativity in identifying problems to be addressed or methods to be used, a field of study would atrophy.

If research has a core more important than anything else, it is creativity. Without creativity, researchers would only repeat themselves. Without creativity, the questions we pose, the starting place for research design, would be endlessly repetitive. Creativity allows the clientele of researchers—be they the public, practitioners, or other researchers—to bring new ideas into their intellectual or practical lives. They can agree or disagree with their findings. They can find fault in their methodologies. But the new ideas remain as work to be examined, understood, enacted, selected, and retained for use (Weick, 1979).

Getzels and Csikszentmihalyi (1976) describe problem finding as being at the heart of the creative process. Educational researchers who invent the best problems have the greatest chance of contributing to their fields. A good problem implies the way in which it should be studied. A superb methodology will not make up for a poor research problem. Structured processes for becoming more creative that emphasize steps to be followed have been identified (Parnes, 1992). The content of the steps is not well understood. If it were, then everyone would be creative and have plenty of excellent problems around which to design research.

To be creative, as opposed to simply novel, a researcher should be well versed in substantive knowledge of the topic and the limitations of the chosen methodology. Creativity has at its foundation a sense of play—of suspending normal constraints so as to see new patterns, possibilities, or connections. Play is usually an "idea non grata" in a workaholic environment, although the hermeneutical philosopher Godamer considered play to be an expression of great seriousness (Neill & Ridley, 1995). Play is characterized by just those things that are likely to lead a researcher into creative work, including taking risks, testing new ideas in safety, avoiding rigidity, and suspending judgment (Schwartzman, 1978).

A risk-averse, judgmental, assessment-oriented environment focused on short-term gains will have a negative effect on creativity. If proposals are assessed by published criteria, then how can new projects that do not fit established criteria be funded? We live in a judgment-rich environment where we have been socialized for years into viewing work as something that will be graded. Peer reviews, editorial reviews, administrative reviews, and granting agency reviews occur regularly. Faculty work can be assessed on an annual basis with the expectation of products in hand making the time frame for completing work within a year or less. In graduate schools, students are steered out of creative projects because such projects are too risky. It is unfortunate when research is designed not out of the possibility of success but rather out of the fear of failure. In the process, creativity—researchers' best friend and asset—is shunted to the rear. Academic reproduction (Bourdieu, 1984/1988; Bourdieu & Passeron, 1990) ensures reproduction, not evolution. Creativity suffers in the current context of conducting research, and producing valuable new understandings is ever more difficult.

Fear and the Researcher's Ego

There are a number of personal factors that affect research design. Morgan (1997) describes "psychic prisons" as a metaphor for the ways in which our imaginations become trapped. Whatever neuroses we have can emerge in the task of developing research. Researchers can fixate on certain ideas, repress others, idealize states, or project their own views on the data. A frequently occurring form of projection occurs when the conclusions of a research study are not connected to the data. Researchers project their beliefs onto the data, concluding what they wanted to conclude before they began conducting the study.

Fear has an unacknowledged influence on research design that manifests itself in a variety of ways. The first is internal censorship. Certain topics and methods are never given serious consideration because to do so would be to invite trouble, at least in the minds of the researchers. For example, during the 1970s, many people did not consider qualitative research to be an appropriate form of educational research. Fearing rejection by colleagues, granting agencies, advisers, and/or editors, researchers steered themselves away from the use of qualitative research. It was not surprising that much of the emphasis of Lincoln and Guba's (1985) *Naturalistic Inquiry* is a justification for, and not

an explanation of, this kind of study. Researchers engaged in self-censorship by avoiding black studies, women's studies, gay studies, and the study of emotional aspects of organizational behavior (Fineman, 2000).

Over the past 20 years or so, there has been a flowering of ideologies challenging the monolithic view of research that existed for the previous 20 years. Postmodern, poststructural, feminist, critical, race, and cultural studies have challenged research orthodoxy both in topic and in method. It is no longer surprising to find titles such as "Whiteness Enacted, Whiteness Interrupted" in the *American Educational Research Journal* (Chubbuck, 2004).

Fear also underlies what has been called the "imposter syndrome" (Harvey & Katz, 1985), where researchers might fear that they are fakes. This problem can show up in an obsessive need to review the literature because a researcher "doesn't know enough yet." A researcher might fear not being professional enough or not being thorough enough and might analyze data in an endless pattern of trivial changes. This fear is a pathology, not a motivator.

Research can also be conducted in service to the ego, not the discipline, where the researcher is driven by the extrinsic value of research. This drive results in designing research for maximum visibility regardless of substance. Finding the smallest publishable unit in a data set inflates one's résumé but clutters journals. The ego thrives on high levels of productivity. The discipline thrives on high levels of quality. The current research market defines what is acceptable, and clever marketing may be more important to one's ego than a quiet but long-term contribution to the field.

For quantitative researchers, the ego drives not just visibility but also theory vindication. In this instance, deductive quantitative studies start with theories, and the researcher organizes and analyzes the data in such a way as to show that the chosen theory is correct. Not only does this approach allow the researcher to tell himself or herself, "See, I'm right," but journals also are more likely to publish findings that support a given theory than to publish findings that do not support the theory.

Qualitative researchers' egos have a similar challenge—categorization vindication. In qualitative research, when the researcher is going through raw data, the data are placed into ever larger categories that, in turn, reflect broader concepts. The process consumes considerable effort, and changing the concepts requires starting over. The ego defends the first set of conceptual categories.

There is a competitive aspect to designing research. Instead of a "best knowledge for the discipline" model, it involves "I got there first," "I'm right and you're wrong," "I win the argument," "My theory is right," "I got the grant and you didn't," "My university is ranked higher than your university," and the like. These are the concerns of the ego, extrinsic to the creation of knowledge, casting a shadow on research. From the point of view of designing research to discover knowledge, it is bizarre that information is not shared. From the point of view that research is not about improving knowledge but rather is about supporting the ego, making a name for oneself, and providing research overhead to one's institution, it makes perfect sense. The impulse is to design research that wins some imaginary (or real) competition, not because it is vital to the field.

Disciplinary Norms and Groupthink

The kind of study a researcher can conduct depends on the development of the field. Mature fields, such as the arts and sciences, medicine, and engineering (Parsons & Platt, 1973), have a long tradition of theories and methods that are thought to be appropriate to use when conducting research. Cultural studies, critical theory, and other postmodern approaches have preferred methods that keep other disciplines vital by challenging their traditions. Research norms become institutionalized through accepting papers for professional meetings and publication. A disciplinary language develops, and a kind of parochialism develops in citation patterns: Cite from journals in the field only. Disciplines within education and in the professions become ever more specialized. Research followed suit and led the way to disciplinary specialization.

Research design reflects this specialization in topic and method. Specialization can have the advantage of accuracy and the disadvantage of triviality. Researchers who venture outside the norms can be transformational if they are lucky or can be ignored or ridiculed if they are not. New ideas are sometimes blocked by the disciplinary equivalent of "groupthink." Groupthink, first described by Janis (1972), includes many factors that limit creativity and risk taking, including sharing stereotypes that guide the decision, exerting direct pressure on others, maintaining the illusion of unanimity and invulnerability, and using mind guards to protect the group from negative information.

Groupthink is more than a norm; it is an exclusionary process designed to protect the group from outside influence. Groupthink in research can limit the topics studied and the methodology used. The long period during which editors silenced the voices of women, African Americans, and the gay, lesbian, bisexual, and transgendered community in education is one example. Another currently exists among those in education who support only "scientific research" (Shavelson & Towne, 2002). Berliner (2002) suggests that the problem is not one of science but rather one of politics and money. Those who label good research in education as "scientific" are stuck in groupthink, as are those who consider research method as essential and all else as trivial. When methodology precedes identifying the problem to be studied, groupthink wins and research suffers.

Methodology and Methodological Correctness

At the extreme, the result is "methodological correctness," a term I coin as a play on "political correctness." It is associated with taking oneself very seriously and is related to academic fundamentalism, where skepticism is replaced by dogma. Methodological correctness means that the purpose of research is to optimize methodology. It is an example of goal displacement, where the purpose of research is no longer to find out something important but rather to use method flawlessly. The hegemony of methodologists in determining the value of research has a chilling effect on exploring new approaches to research, on studying topics not studied previously, and on studying topics that do not lend themselves to study using preferred methods.

Institutionalized methodological correctness takes the form of guidelines, where if the guidelines are not followed, the result is funding not being given or results not being taken seriously. The U.S. Department of Education has provided *A User-Friendly Guide,* one that is not "friendly" at all, that can be paraphrased as follows: The only rigorous evidence that can be used to evaluate an educational intervention comes from research using randomized controlled trials (Institute of Education Sciences, 2003).

Simple solutions are often wrong. Randomization means that individual student differences will not be a factor in the research and that all kinds of students can expect to benefit equally from the program. The results are designed to mask individual differences to see whether the program worked for the majority. It worked if the mean of the criterion variable for the treatment group is significantly higher than the mean of the control group. Like randomization, means are designed to mask individual differences. Berliner (2002) makes the point that there are a "ubiquity of interactions" and that a program could have remarkable positive effects on a small segment of the treated population, none of which would be discovered by this research design. A program could benefit gifted students, African American students, girls, athletes, or special needs students in a manner invisible to scientific methods.

Much of the contentiousness about educational research design centers on whether the research is scientific, a desiderata identified by the National Research Council's (NRC) publication of *Scientific Research in Education* (Shavelson & Towne, 2002). The debate revolves around using scientific methodologies to examine educational issues. The NRC's position is generally supported by some (Feuer, Towne, & Shavelson, 2002; Slavin, 2002) and cautioned against or rejected by others (Berliner, 2002; Erickson & Gutierrez, 2002; Olson, 2004; St. Pierre, 2002). Research design, research funding, and politics are interconnected (Burkhardt & Schoenfeld, 2003).

If research is designed for political purposes, the methodology should be called "scientific," not "educational." True or quasi-experiments should be carried out on huge samples, and the study should employ terms such as "experimental"

and "randomized" to give the research an air of authority and scientific respectability. The results should be simple numbers based on complicated statistics with which few politicians can argue. Using these methods, different programs should receive a single outcome score that can be used to show that, for example, Program A is significantly more effective than Program B. Politicians can now say, "I have scientific proof that Program A should be funded and Program B should not." Few scholars would be so bold.

A research article, like the tip of an iceberg, contains only a small percentage of the information that the author encountered in the study. Given this situation, research becomes an enactment of the map–territory relationship, that is, the relationship between the object studied and the symbol for that object—the research report (Bateson, 2000). How complete does the symbol need to be to represent some objective reality? Borges (1998), in "On Exactitude in Science," provides a fictional example of an empire that was so enamored of mapmaking that the cartographers were encouraged to make maps that were larger and more accurate. In the end, they made a map that was so detailed, it needed to be exactly the same size as the land it described. As a map, it was perfectly useless.

In this case, greater accuracy and greater methodological correctness diminished utility. Bateson (2000) argues that maps are useful not because they are literal representations but rather because they are in some way analogous to reality. Research provides a map, an analog of reality. If Bateson is right, then it might be more appropriate to design and evaluate research not on the basis of how correct the methodology is or how literally it represents reality but rather on how useful it is for understanding and acting in our environments.

The Primary Research Audience

Research design is affected by the primary research audience for the study. For doctoral students, the primary audience is their advisers and other members of their research committees. For faculty, the primary audience is journal and publishing house editors and grantors. Refereed journal editors are the gatekeepers of much of the research that is published, which in turn influences what is taught and who is tenured and promoted at schools that value research.

Recognizing this power, a researcher responds to the real or imagined preferences for topic or method of this audience. The obvious way of finding editorial preferences is to read the journal, see what is being published, and use a similar approach to one's own study. Doctoral students would be prudent to read dissertations directed by a prospective dissertation adviser to see what these preferences actually are. This situation begs the question: Should these gate-keepers set the research agenda? Editors of research journals usually have been successful researchers in their fields and have published widely. The advisory board that hires an editor increases a journal's prestige by hiring the most prestigious editor it can find. The editor then finds other successful researchers in the field and brings them onboard. This selection procedure produces a conservative bias: Reward what has worked in the past.

One model for the editorial process is that reviewers have had long experience in the field and make prudent judgments about what studies will advance educational practice or knowledge. Another model views editorial decisions as being on show because what editors approve is published. The imposter syndrome is ever-present: "How do I, as an editor, make decisions that will make me look like I know what I'm doing?" The ordinary response is risk aversion: "If I don't take chances, I'm least likely to look like an imposter." Editors are likely to reject methodologically flawed research in favor of methodologically correct research. Imaginatively flawed research, research whose consequences are trivial for the discipline or practitioners, can be published if the methods are correct but with predictable disdain from the public (Kezar, 2000). I have heard of no cases where an editor has written an author saying, "The ideas in this article are so compelling that I'm going to publish it even though it contains obvious methodological flaws." Editorial referees work at the pleasure of the editor, and if they are to be retained, they work in line with the editorial vision. Reviewers are often shown the comments of other referees so that they can compare their responses. Feedback provides an implicit pressure to conform.

The upward drift in methodology can be considered paradoxical. To get published, authors use sophisticated methodologies. The newer and more complex the method, the fewer the people who will be able to evaluate the article and the fewer the practitioners who will be able to understand the research and judge whether using the results would be beneficial. In attempting to gain the approval of other researchers, a researcher might not care whether an article advances practice in the field. Good research can do both. Some publications do neither.

The Secondary Research Audience

It is a desirable state when secondary research audiences—other researchers, practitioners, and the public—are more important than the primary ones. From an altruistic perspective, it is for these audiences that the research is conducted. Research should be designed to be useful to the discipline and to advance theoretical or empirical understanding of what is happening in some area of education. Does this research provide new ideas, new understandings, and new practices that advance the ways in which professionals and practitioners in the field can serve the public good? An affirmative answer would justify the use of public and philanthropic resources in pursuit of educational knowledge. Good research should benefit everybody.

A measure of the value of research is not just acceptability to the editorial process, that is, the merit indicated by its publication; rather, the impact of a piece of research on theory or practice becomes the ultimate measure of its value or worth. Research that does not meet at least minimal methodological acceptability is not published and does not become available to its potential audience. Assuming that it does reach a larger audience, does it affect future research in the field?

A well-designed study should include, at the end of the article, recommendations for future research, but in practice, these recommendations tend to focus on narrow methodological concerns such as improving a questionnaire and using a different sample. The implicit recommendation for future researchers is that they continue to advance the theoretical orientation of the line of research. A second concluding section should deal with the practical applications of the study. The form of the application is along these lines: "If your educational world is similar to the one in which this study was conducted, here are the things you should do, based on my findings, that would improve educational practice and understanding in your world."

Educational research can be influential not because of its quality but rather because the findings confirm what policymakers already believe. This situation is distressing because it means that an excellent study will affect policy only if policymakers *want* it to affect policy. When two studies are excellent but lead to opposite conclusions, policymakers lose confidence in the research and return to intuition to set policy.

There have been contentious debates about educational research for at least the past century (Lagemann, 1997). Many of the issues centered on the different interests of the parties involved, with policymakers seeking politically expedient program evaluation, practitioners looking for ways in which to improve practice, and university researchers interested in improving knowledge in specialized disciplines. Each overlaps with the others, each can serve the others, and each can attack the others. The politics of educational research seems to be one of its salient features (Cooper & Randall, 1999).

CONCLUSION

The reporting of research can be viewed as storytelling, as part of a mythic process of identifying who we are. In storytelling, we seek to remember the past, invent the present, and envision the future (Keen & Valley-Fox, 1989). Research can be viewed as a similar process in remembering the past by examining the literature, inventing the present by conducting the study and describing the findings, and envisioning the future where this research influences thought, policy, and practice.

To design research is to make a map, an analogy of what happens in the world. Research design depends on what is being studied and what the researcher wants to find out. The double entendre of "wants to find out" is intentional. The researcher wants to find out

something about, say, how to improve literacy rates in rural areas. The researcher also wants to find out that his or her hypothesis is true, for example, that tutoring improves literacy.

The choice of the topic focuses the endeavor. The choice of method limits what can be discovered, emphasizing some possibilities and eliminating others. Each choice involves trade-offs. Each methodology chosen should, if done well, supply some beneficial information. There is one best way in which to find out something extremely simple such as the mean length of time it takes students to memorize a list of spelling words. As the question addressed becomes broader and more complex, it can be studied using a variety of designs. There is no best way in which to study education; each approach emphasizes some things and is silent on others. Political and research ideologies can drive research or be ignored.

Research could be designed purely on the basis of curiosity if the researcher wants to know something. The methodology is likely to be emergent as the researcher plays with the topic, thinking of it without preconception, delighting in possibility, and creating an ongoing dialogue with the topic, methods, other researchers in the field, the persons being studied, and so on.

Research can also be designed around extrinsic reasons: "How can I make myself famous, promoted, tenured, or rich on the basis of my research?" For that research, the researcher should let money and disciplinary popularity lead the endeavor. For research to affect policy, one should follow the money out of governmental or other granting agencies and heed their guidelines for topics and methods. Research should be designed to meet their expectations using methods they prefer. An effective presentation of the results might demand that they be presented in the most simple or most mystifying forms.

Designing research for altruistic purposes, to benefit humanity, is more complicated because what benefits one group might not benefit another. Any discovery can have wonderful unanticipated consequences. Basic research has grand possibilities, but the environment must thrive on patience and failure—on trying many new things that do not work to find the few that do. Such environments are rare. Research designed to solve well-defined problems, applied research, can also benefit humanity. Other applied research is intended to profit the patent holder. Research designed to provide an educational environment that will save humanity should get top billing, but who could agree on what that research would be?

Predicting the future can be fun because even if the researcher is wrong—well, nobody can predict the future. If the researcher is right, then he or she can claim great insight. Here are some things that I think might happen to research design in education during the years ahead:

• Knowledge production in all areas of education will continue to be valuable for understanding the field and for practice. Much of the research will be of interest only to other researchers. Potentially valuable findings will be ignored by practitioners who do not understand the research and will be used selectively by policymakers when they disagree with the findings.

• The debates about the design of educational research will continue indefinitely. They will not be resolved because they are, for the most part, not about method but rather about the political values implicit in choosing one method over another.

• Research designed to help improve the processes of teaching and learning will continue, but research cannot establish what should be taught and how it should be taught because those decisions are based on politics and values.

• The accretion of research findings will continue at an increasing rate. The use of these findings will lag considerably behind their development. To be published, the selection of research designs will be based on how they impress other researchers rather than on their usefulness to practitioners.

• Quantitative methodology will continue to develop more and more complicated strategies for data analysis, and these will be understood by fewer and fewer people. These studies may well provide better information related to what quantitative studies do well (e.g., generalizability, probability) but might not alter our basic understanding of the field.

• Many qualitative researchers are likely to be bullied out of thinking that description is enough. A majority of these researchers will remain defensive about their methods, which will take on more and more of the characteristics of quantitative researchers, focusing on reliability, validity, objectivity, generalizability, and so on. For example, qualitative methods will be used increasingly in hypothesis testing.

• Despite these pressures, qualitative researchers will continue to improve the understanding of local events and processes and will continue to advance theories and topics that can be further tested in large-scale quantitative research.

• Educational researchers will continue to emulate the methods of social scientists. Those with political agendas will continue to call educational research scientific research, believing that this label increases the probability that these studies will influence policymaking. Research will be designed to meet these expectations so that it can be funded. These studies will continue to ignore the varied effectiveness of educational processes depending on the individual characteristics of the teacher, the student, and the subject matter.

• Humanistic and aesthetic values will be neglected in research in the face of issues of social justice and pragmatism. Capitalistic elements related to the costs of education and the ways in which the education system provides a suitable labor force for the nation's economy will be emphasized.

REFERENCES

Bateson, G. (2000). *Steps to an ecology of mind: Collected essays in anthropology, psychiatry, evolution, and epistemology.* Chicago: University of Chicago Press.

Baumrind, D. (1964). Some thoughts on ethics of research: After reading Milgram's behavioral study of obedience. *American Psychologist, 19,* 421–423.

Bean, J. P. (1980). Dropouts and turnover: The synthesis and test of a causal model of student attrition. *Research in Higher Education, 12,* 155–187.

Bean, J. P. (1997, March). *How painting can inform qualitative inquiry.* Paper presented at the meeting of the American Educational Research Association, Chicago.

Berliner, D. (2002). Educational research: The hardest science of all. *Educational Researcher, 31*(8), 18–20.

Biglan, A. (1973). The characteristics of subject matter in different academic areas. *Journal of Applied Psychology, 57,* 195–203.

Borges, J. L. (1998). *Collected fictions* (A. Hurley, Trans.). New York: Penguin Books.

Bourdieu, P. (1988). *Homo academicus* (P. Collier, Trans.). Stanford, CA: Stanford University Press. (Original work published in 1984)

Bourdieu, P., & Passeron, J. C. (1990). *Reproduction in education, society, and culture* (R. Nice, Trans.). London: Sage.

Braithwaite, R. (1955). *Scientific explanation.* Cambridge, UK: Cambridge University Press.

Burkhardt, H., & Schoenfeld, A. H. (2003). Improving educational research: Toward a more useful, more influential, and better-funded enterprise. *Educational Researcher, 32*(9), 3–14.

Chubbuck, S. (2004). Whiteness enacted, whiteness disrupted: The complexity of personal congruence. *American Educational Research Journal, 41,* 301–333.

Cooper, B., & Randall, E. (1999). *Accuracy or advocacy: The politics of research in education.* Thousand Oaks, CA: Corwin.

Creswell, J. W. (1998). *Qualitative inquiry and research design: Choosing among five traditions.* Thousand Oaks, CA: Sage.

Creswell, J. W. (2002). *Research design: Qualitative, quantitative, and mixed methods approaches* (2nd ed.). Thousand Oaks, CA: Sage.

Daniel, L. G. (1996). Kerlinger's research myths. *Practical Assessment, Research, & Evaluation, 5*(4). Retrieved January 17, 2005, from http://pareonline.net/getvn.asp?v=5&n=4

Erickson, F., & Gutierrez, K. (2002). Culture, rigor, and science in educational research. *Educational Researcher, 31*(8), 21–24.

Feuer, M. J., Towne, L., & Shavelson, R. J. (2002). Scientific culture and educational research. *Educational Researcher, 31*(8), 4–14.

Feyerabend, P. (1993). *Against method* (3rd ed.). New York: Verso.

Fineman, S. (2000). *Emotions in organizations.* Thousand Oaks, CA: Sage.

Gall, M. D., Borg, W., & Gall, J. P. (2002). *Educational research: An introduction* (7th ed.). Boston: Allyn & Bacon.

Geertz, C. (1973). Thick description: Toward an interpretive theory of culture. In C. Geertz, *The interpretation of cultures* (pp. 3–32). New York: Basic Books.

Getzels, J. W., & Csikszentmihalyi, M. (1976). *The creative vision: A longitudinal study of problem finding in art.* New York: John Wiley.

Harvey, J., & Katz, C. (1985). *If I'm so successful, why do I feel like a fake? The imposter phenomenon.* New York: St. Martin's.

Institute of Education Sciences. (2003). *Identifying and implementing educational practices supported by rigorous evidence.* Washington, DC: U.S. Department of Education.

Janis, I. (1972). *Victims of groupthink: A psychological study of foreign-policy decisions and fiascoes.* Boston: Houghton Mifflin.

Jones, J. (1993). *Bad blood: The Tuskegee syphilis experiment* (rev. ed.). New York: Free Press.

Keen, S., & Valley-Fox, A. (1989). *Your mythic journey.* New York: Putnam.

Kerlinger, F. (1973). *Foundations of behavioral research* (2nd ed.). New York: Holt, Rinehart & Winston.

Kezar, A. (2000). Higher education research at the millennium: Still trees without fruit? *Review of Higher Education, 23,* 443–468.

Krathwohl, D. R. (1988). *How to prepare a research proposal: Guidelines for funding and dissertations in the social and behavioral sciences* (3rd ed.). Syracuse, NY: Syracuse University Press.

Lagemann, E. (1997). Contested terrain: A history of education research in the United States, 1890–1990. *Educational Researcher, 26*(9), 5–17.

Lawrence-Lightfoot, S. (1995). *I've known rivers: Lives of loss and liberation.* New York: Penguin Books.

Lincoln, Y. S., & Guba, E. G. (1985). *Naturalistic inquiry.* Beverly Hills, CA: Sage.

Merton, R. K. (1973). The normative structure of science. In N. W. Storer (Ed.), *The sociology of science* (pp. 267–278). Chicago: University of Chicago Press. (Original work published in 1942)

Milgram, S. (1974). *Obedience to authority.* New York: Harper & Row.

Mitroff, I. I., & Kilmann, R. H. (1978). *Methodological approaches to social science.* San Francisco: Jossey-Bass.

Morgan, B. (1997). *Images of organization* (2nd ed.). Thousand Oaks, CA: Sage.

Myers-Briggs, I. (1962). *Manual for the Myers-Briggs Type Indicator.* Princeton, NJ: Educational Testing Service.

Neill, A., & Ridley, A. (Eds.). (1995). *The philosophy of art.* New York: McGraw-Hill.

Olson, D. R. (2004). The triumph of hope over experience in the search for "what works": A response to Slavin. *Educational Researcher, 33*(1), 24–26.

Parnes, S. J. (1992). *Source book for creative problem solving.* Buffalo, NY: Creative Foundation Press.

Parsons, T., & Platt, G. M. (1973). *The American university.* Cambridge, MA: Harvard University Press.

Schwartzman, H. (1978). *Transformations: The anthropology of children's play.* New York: Plenum.

Schwartzman, H. (1993). *Ethnography in organizations* (Qualitative Research Methods Series, No. 27). Newbury Park, CA: Sage.

Shavelson, R. J., & Towne, L. (Eds.). (2002). *Scientific research in education* (National Research Council. Committee on Scientific Principles for Educational Research). Washington, DC: National Academy Press.

Shils, E. (1984). *The academic ethic.* Chicago: University of Chicago Press.

Slavin, R. E. (2002). Evidence-based education policies: Transforming educational practice and research. *Educational Researcher, 31*(7), 15–21.

St. Pierre, E. A. (2002). "Science" rejects postmodernism. *Educational Researcher, 31*(8), 25–27.

Thorngate, W. (1976). In general vs. it all depends: Some comments on the Gergen–Schlenker debate. *Academy of Management Journal, 25,* 185–192.

Weick, K. (1979). *The social psychology of organizing* (2nd ed.). Reading, MA: Addison-Wesley.

21

Conceptualizing and Conducting Meaningful Research Studies in Education

Ronald H. Heck

University of Hawaii at Manoa

The object of research is to understand phenomena in terms of their patterns and idiosyncratic tendencies and to formulate explanations of our experiences. Researchers construct explanations about phenomena from the interplay among their studies' conceptual underpinnings (e.g., frameworks, theories, previous research), the assumptions and methods underpinning scientific inquiry (e.g., what constitutes "evidence," the procedures and techniques used to collect and analyze data), and the blend of contextual conditions (e.g., cultural beliefs and values, historical situations, settings) in which their investigations are carried out. Obviously, these are in flux as opposed to static, and because research is a human endeavor, examining investigators' choices about the processes underlying a study's conceptualization and conduct is essential to understanding and evaluating the continuity of their explanations of experience.

Methodology concerns the process through which we construct scientific knowledge. It is the description, explanation, and justification of research methods (Kaplan, 1964). The aim of methodology is to detail the study's inquiry approach—how it is conceptualized and designed and how the data are collected, analyzed, and interpreted—as well as the theoretical and technical justifications for the scientific procedures used (Everhart, 1988). Therefore, methodology is concerned not only with the products of scientific inquiry but also with the underlying assumptions and processes associated with the construction of knowledge from a particular scientific approach.

The purpose of this chapter is to invite researchers to consider what I view as among the most salient issues in conceptualizing and conducting studies in education. My intent is to discuss the process through which researchers identify and frame problems for study. It is the appropriate application of an approach to a particular problem, rather than the approach itself, that enables judgments to be made about a study's scientific merit and its value to the field (Feuer, Towne, & Shavelson, 2002). Often we do not fully develop or share the assumptions underlying our methodological approach to studying a problem. How we account for (and disclose) our approach is essential, however, if consumers (e.g., the public, policymakers, practitioners, the research community) are to evaluate the results of our research critically (Anfara, Brown, & Mangione, 2002).

The consideration of substantive problems and how they are studied is especially important in a field like education, where there is currently a heightened demand for more research—but research that policymakers perceive is of a higher quality and greater utility than has been the case in the past (Feuer et al., 2002). Over the past two decades, there has been a heightened demand for increasing the quality of educational outcomes as well as educators' accountability for what is produced. Demands for increased productivity and accountability, coupled with a renewed recognition of the potential of research to provide information that can be used within policy circles, suggest that we have a renewed opportunity to produce studies that audiences perceive are important. This comes at a price. Recent federal legislation in education (e.g., the No Child Left Behind Act of 2001) has detailed requirements for obtaining federal research grants that prescribe acceptable research methods (i.e., experimental trails) and has promoted a rigid definition of research quality (Feuer et al., 2002). As a practical matter, the type of large-scale experimental designs now favored within federal policy circles can be very difficult and costly to implement in educational settings.

Disenchantment with educational research has come from several sources, including policymakers, practitioners, scholars, and researchers themselves. Critics of our field suggest that educational research is generally of little use to policymakers, does not attend to questions they want answered, is poorly conceived and conducted, and is seldom disseminated in ways whereby educators can put the results to use (Birnbaum, 2000). Practitioners lament the irrelevance of university research to the training and practice of educators. They often view research as too theoretical, idealistic, or general to relate directly to their specific needs. Researchers, as compared with practitioners, often view educational problems quite differently, employ varied methods of investigation, and reach very different suggested solutions (Nuthall, 2004; Robinson, 1996). Nuthall (2004) suggested the need to examine the "pragmatic validity" of accumulated research on an educational problem, that is, the extent to which it actually answers the research question posed "in a way that is comprehensible and practically useful" for practitioners (p. 273).

Some scholars (e.g., Lagemann, 1997; Nuthall, 2004) criticize the metaphor of education as science and the accompanying overreliance on experimental and quasi-experimental designs and quantitative methods of analysis in examining educational processes such as teaching and learning. Conceptual and methodological debates have created separate camps of researchers with contrasting interests and beliefs about the scholarly purposes of the field. Some advocate that educational research has not gone far enough in identifying oppressive structures and working to replace them. External pressures are heightened by the research community's own division over the nature of research and standards for its design and conduct. Such criticism of the quality and utility of educational research suggests the need to consider its theoretical underpinnings, design, and conduct.

If one of our research goals is to produce results that explain phenomena and, furthermore, can be used to alleviate or solve educational problems, then we must think about ways in which we can make accumulated, empirically based knowledge more accessible to knowledge users. Framing the research study is the key to providing results that are compelling and useful to readers; that is, studies should be assessed in terms of how they advance the field's thinking about a problem, serve as exemplars of its evolving scholarship, and contribute to the reduction or solution of important educational problems. Research methods should be suited to the problems they are intended to solve (Nuthall, 2004; Toulmin, 2001). Increasingly, both conceptual models and analytic tools that allow more rigorous and thorough investigations of educational problems are becoming available. Understanding how conceptual, methodological, and contextual issues work together to generate knowledge can help researchers to develop and conduct studies that are more informative in reducing educational problems and guiding future policy development.

DEVELOPING A RESEARCH STUDY

Several conceptual elements must be brought together to develop a research study. These include the definition, significance, and framing of the research problem; the goals of the research; the objects of study and method of investigation; and communication with potential users of the study's results (e.g., practitioners, policymakers, the public, other researchers). There are also potential constraints to consider, including time, costs, and the data needed versus what can actually be obtained. Finding a problem to research is a highly personal endeavor. Research problems can develop from personal interest and experience, situations in the workplace, empirical studies published in academic journals, grant opportunities from governmental and private funding agencies, and unfolding news events that are covered in professional newspapers (e.g., the *Chronicle of Higher Education, Education Week*). Research problems may result from ideas that we have carried with us over the years. In other cases, the "light just goes on" and the idea for a research study may evolve out of something that was covered in the media, or a problem presents itself for the first time in the course of a conversation with a mentor.

It can take some time to define the research problem and then to figure out what one wishes to find out about it. Usually the process unfolds gradually. Various iterations of attempting to frame the problem (e.g., what issues to highlight, what theoretical perspectives to bring to its study, what methodological approach to use) may bring some clarity to what is undiscovered or unique about how one wishes to examine the problem. Research will affect practice when it provides solutions to problems that are framed in ways that practitioners view them (Robinson, 1996). The art of crafting a study is to take a problem of personal interest and commitment and to frame it in such a way that its results will be important to practitioners and others—no matter what is found; that is, the importance is more in the framing than in the results themselves. If the study is well framed, it should be important—whether the results are "significant" or not.

Examining the Literature

Gaining access to the literature on a particular problem and determining what others have done (e.g., how they have viewed the problem, how they have investigated it) is a good place to begin. Published research and conference presentations provide up-to-date sources of information about educational problems. Studies that are not grounded in the appropriate research literature lack substantive and methodological guidance; that is, they do not contribute to growing evidence about an educational problem. Systematic accumulated knowledge emerges over time as a result of collective studies (Smart, 2002). One way of beginning a literature review is to examine what has been done on the topic within the past 5 years. If the topic does not exist within that time frame, then it is likely that either the topic is quite new or the topic has been previously mined and found to have a low yield. In education, the *Current Index to Journals in Education* (*CIJE*) and annual meeting programs from the American Educational Research Association (AERA) are useful resources, but they should not be considered as exhaustive.

A review of the empirical literature should be conducted with a particular purpose in mind—to assess the studies' contributions to knowledge and evolving scholarship. A literature review is not merely a chronological summary of all the previous studies in an educational domain. Rather, it is a conceptualization of the various theories, methods, patterns of findings, conclusions, and limitations of previous empirical work that set the stage for current study. It is a challenge for new or mature scholars to evaluate and integrate the work that has been undertaken on a particular topic, paying particular attention to the theories, concepts, and methodological approaches that are used to advance knowledge in the field.

Reviewers might have to deal with incomplete (or undeveloped) theories, conflicting findings, and the limitations of individual studies in conceptualizing progress in a field. For this reason, it is especially important to consider issues related to design and methods of analysis used to create knowledge in a domain given that the underlying assumptions of alternative designs and methods are critical to the credibility that can be placed in the studies' results. Sometimes apparent contradictions may be explained by differences in the theoretical and methodological assumptions of studies or by the criteria for selection in reviews (Hallinger & Heck, 1996). In the past, researchers generally gave little attention to the philosophical and theoretical underpinnings of their studies and how these affect research questions, designs, methods of data collection, and analyses. They defined some facets in detail, whereas other facets were only vaguely acknowledged or remained unstated.

The first step in a literature review is to identify a set of studies that is relevant to a particular problem. Developing a set of criteria is useful in deciding whether each study one encounters is pertinent to one's proposed investigation (e.g., related to how the problem is framed, theoretically informed, scientifically rigorous). Not all studies on a particular topic will be of equal value. For establishing scientific rigor, for example, published pieces in scientific journals with strong criteria for manuscript acceptance would be favored over chapters in books, presentations at conferences, unpublished papers, and doctoral dissertations. The second step is to analyze the results of the studies that meet the established criteria. This analysis should assess both the conceptual underpinnings (e.g., theoretical relations) in each study as well as the processes of scientific inquiry (e.g., methodological approach, participants, instruments, procedures for data collection) used to generate the results. Theories and other types of conceptual tools help to identify and structure the mechanisms that produce the phenomenon and under various conditions (Murray, 1996; Toulmin, 2001). They can be a valuable aid in helping to distinguish between what to include (e.g., setting, variables, interview prompts, analyses required) and what can be safely ignored (Sabatier & Jenkins-Smith, 1993). Work that is poorly grounded intellectually usually reveals itself through this type of scrutiny. Finally, one should reach some conclusions about the worth of the previous studies in contributing to knowledge about the problem and should determine needed next steps for generating knowledge.

Shaping the Research Questions

This preliminary process helps one begin to shape the study's research questions. The types of questions one asks will influence the data that will be collected and the way in which they will be analyzed. It is important to give attention to the phrasing of the questions to see where each would lead. Suppose that one is interested in studying student access to higher education. This topic could lend itself to myriad research questions. A question such as "What is the impact of students' course-taking profiles in high school on their probability of being accepted into particular types of universities or areas of study within universities?" might suggest a type of quantitative study examining students' background and high school course taking. In contrast, a question such as "How do students' perceptions of their likelihood of being accepted influence their choices about applying to universities?" might suggest a type of interpretive (or constructivist) lens with data collection focusing on interviews, documents, and observations. A question such as "What types of institutional processes encourage or discourage minority students from applying to prestigious universities?" might suggest using a critical lens and qualitative inquiry methods to examine how various institutional structures and processes may benefit or marginalize particular groups of students.

Conceptual models help to bound our inquiries into complex problems and processes. They direct our attention to the critical features—contextual conditions, processes, cultural norms, and belief systems—that influence how people participate in and construct educational realities. The collection of data themselves is not neutral. It is one thing to collect the facts, but the facts might not explain or lead to the understanding of the actual event (Easton, 1953). What must be done, then, is to order the facts around a conceptual framework or theory that may explain, analyze, and predict the "confusion of reality" (Marshall, Mitchell, & Wirt, 1989, p. 4).

There is no denying the bias toward narrow methods of inquiry that characterized the field of educational research during its early years. Over time, criticism regarding the continued reliance on rational models of organizational life and quantitative methods for studying schools and universities has expanded the conceptual and methodological approaches used (Bensimon & Marshall, 1997; Ladson-Billings, 2000; Parker & Lynn, 2002). Interpretive, phenomenological, and constructivist methodological approaches encourage methods (e.g., ethnography, narrative, discourse analysis) that can uncover how meaning is socially constructed among individuals participating in educational processes.

Other approaches (e.g., critical theory, feminism) entail a critique of existing social relationships (e.g., gender, race, class) that influence education and the advancement toward those that are desired (Keith, 1996). Postmodern and poststructural approaches focus on deconstructing the knowledge gained from traditional theories and raise questions about how researchers and their texts influence the construction of scientific knowledge (Lather, 1992). These latter approaches use alternative analytic frames and methods, and the results are contextualized— that is, they do not assume that educational practices affect individuals without regard to gender, social class, and ethnicity. Hence, they place these issues at the center of their theories and analyses instead of at the fringe. Unfortunately, there is often little guidance available about what lenses and methods are most appropriate for studying problems. It would be a mistake, however, to think that any single scheme would capture the breadth and depth of work on a particular educational problem.

Our orientation to a problem will, of course, have a substantial effect on the type of information we need to answer our research questions. Data collection itself involves decisions about what types of information are useful in the inquiry process and the construction of knowledge from the analysis of the data. Although the questions asked should drive the data collection and analysis, the reality is that most researchers think of themselves as doing either quantitative or qualitative investigation. It is considerably more difficult to conceptualize, conduct, and present a mixed-methods study that uses the differences in these approaches in a complementary fashion. These preliminary decisions about topic, data needed, and methods of investigation will begin to structure the data collection part of the study. The choice of conceptual framework and methodological approach underpinning a proposed study, therefore, is an essential part of the research design in helping to recognize previous work, mold the problem statement, develop the research questions, and add necessary structure to the collection and organization of the data (Miles & Huberman, 1984; Yin, 1989).

Deciding on a Research Design

Making the conceptual and methodological underpinning explicit encourages the linking of theoretical propositions to research questions, methods of conducting the study, empirical findings, and the logic of conclusions. This requires one to label the relevant propositions that are derived from the theory and/or the methodological approach being used. These activities are fundamental to the conduct of rigorous research on educational problems because, relative to one's research purposes, some conceptual groundings and methods will provide greater insights about problems and their solutions than will others. Where methodology refers to philosophical underpinnings and assumptions embedded in how researchers construct knowledge, as Everhart (1988) noted, method refers to the "moves" or logic that researchers use in conducting a study. These moves include how research questions are stated, sampling strategy, data collection procedures, and ways of structuring, analyzing, and interpreting data. Techniques are the specific means that researchers use to gather information (e.g., survey, interview, observation).

The intents of the proposed research and the relevant previous literature are useful in deciding on an appropriate research design. "Research design" is actually a broad term that can refer to a number of different aspects of the inquiry process. These include the research questions, theoretical formulations, setting, unit of analysis (e.g., individual, group, organizational), measurement of variables, sampling data collection, logic linking the data to the propositions, and criteria for interpreting the findings (Pedhazur & Schmelkin, 1991). Design concerns the assumptions underlying the manner in which the study is constructed to pursue inquiry about the phenomenon. These assumptions include one's beliefs about the nature of science, the proper conduct of the study given one's definition of science, the analysis and interpretation of facts, and the construction of the research text. The time to think about these issues is during the early stages of conceptualizing a study.

Decisions about the focus and conduct of a study are at the core of what it means to do science and produce scientific knowledge. Therefore, the study's design determines whether the research questions can be answered adequately through the manner in which the data are collected. If the design is incomplete, then it is likely that the data will not provide answers to the questions posed initially. The credibility of one's work, therefore, is largely a function of its conceptual underpinnings (e.g., theoretical approach, design) and methods used to conduct the study. This is much more a matter of how well the method addresses the particular research questions at hand than a matter of how the methods themselves are ranked according to some perceived hierarchy of scientific rigor.

A range of designs and methods can legitimately be used to address each type of research concern. The choices should be made after considering the particular purposes and circumstances of the research as well as the strengths and limitations of each approach. Research purposes are varied and, according to the National Research Council (2002), can include description (i.e., what, how many, how often), systematic effects (i.e., cause), and process (i.e., how or why something occurs). Importantly, the research questions and purposes should drive the selection of research design and methodology—not the other way around (Feuer et al., 2002). The relative control one has over actual events that may influence the phenomenon under study and the focus on contemporary versus historical phenomena can be useful criteria in selecting a research design. These decisions about design and method are also a function of one's creativity, style, and judgment (Majchrzak, 1984).

There are many different types of scholarly inquiry (e.g., think pieces, syntheses of literature, empirical studies). For this chapter, I limit the discussion to several key issues regarding empirical studies. Often-used research designs may be broadly classified as experimental (i.e., where there is a treatment and random assignment of participants to control and treatment groups), quasi-experimental (i.e., where there is the presence of a treatment but no random assignment of participants to treatment and control groups), nonexperimental (e.g., surveys or secondary data sets, where there is no treatment that has been manipulated and participants have not been assigned to control and treatment groups), case study (i.e., where the focus is on studying a contemporary phenomenon within its real-life context and the boundaries between the phenomenon and context are not clearly evident), and historical (i.e., where the phenomenon and context are also entangled but the focus is on past events).

Although there is certainly overlap among the approaches, each type of design has some distinctive characteristics. Case study designs (i.e., single and multiple cases) are useful for descriptive purposes and are applicable to studies where process (how and/or why) is a key concern because they focus on collecting data over time (i.e., as processes unfold and evolve). Case studies lend themselves to a variety of conceptual lenses and more flexible ways of collecting data. A quantitative study to describe factors influencing students' likelihood of being admitted to a university might also be conceptualized as a case study design if it is limited to studying students in one university.

Historical designs have a focus similar to that of case studies with either description or process. Historical designs differ from case designs primarily because their focus is on periods of time in the past, often where the participants are no longer available to be observed or interviewed. Where the concern is with the interplay between cultural contexts and various types of behavior, change over time, or how individuals and groups make sense of their evolving beliefs and actions, one might need to choose a design (e.g., case study) that allows more flexibility in framing the research and in collecting and analyzing the data. Further discussion can be found in a number of texts (e.g., Fraenkel & Wallen, 2000; Heck, 2004; Merriam, 1988; Yin, 1989).

DEVELOPING A CASE STUDY

In this section, my intent is to present some of the issues to consider in developing a case study. Case studies focus on understanding contemporary phenomena within their real settings where the boundaries between the context and the phenomena are not evident (Yin, 1989). Multiple sources of evidence are used to provide in-depth, contextualized understandings of the phenomena. Although case study data can be analyzed in a more quantitative manner (Bernard, 1994), case study is generally associated with an interpretivist or phenomenological methodological approach, that is, where the concern is with sensemaking or the social construction of reality. Case study, however, should not be confused with ethnography, which is a type of fieldwork that can be used in conducting case studies. Case studies typically make use of a number of different techniques of data collection (e.g., documents, interviews, observation, surveys) and analysis. As Yin (1989) noted, depending on the nature of the topic under investigation, one could also do a high-quality case study within the library without ever going into the field.

The case starts with the problem, its definition, and the rationale behind the selection of the design. One of the first considerations is to define the study's purposes and research questions. A second consideration is the scope and boundaries of the case. One should make decisions that narrow the study; otherwise, one is likely to end up with data that are too diffuse and often unrelated to what one is doing (Bogdan & Biklen, 1998). "Bounding the study" refers to consideration about the setting and data collection, so that the study will be manageable and the types of information collected will maximize the investigator's time (Merriam, 1988).

One way in which the case may be considered as bounded is when it is identified as a particular instance that is drawn from a broader class of instances (Adelman, Jenkins, & Kemmis, 1977). These decisions reflect what the proper unit of analysis is in the case. In some instances the case may be the individual (from a broader class of individuals), whereas in others

it may be a particular site. The identification of the unit of analysis depends on the particular research questions that one has developed. Another way in which the case can be considered bounded is when the issues are indicated, discovered, or studied so that a full understanding of the phenomenon is possible. This often occurs in the process of determining the relevant issues or aspects of the problem, the actors involved, the geographic location, the type of evidence that should be collected, and the priorities in doing the analysis (Yin, 1989). Time is a third consideration in bounding a case. This refers to the relevant length of time that is appropriate for studying the case (e.g., several weeks, a month or months, a year or more) or for which the data are to be collected. Time considerations are important in constructing a view of the way in which the phenomenon under study operates with sensitivity to a number of specific contexts. A final consideration in bounding the study is to determine the type of case study that will be conducted (e.g., descriptive, exploratory, explanatory) given the research purposes.

Single case studies are appropriate in situations where one's focus is on describing how a process works in a particular instance. In contrast, a multiple-site case study involves selecting several cases so as to make cross-case comparisons (e.g., Benham & Heck, 1994). These studies are appropriate when there is a need to bring together a sufficient range of cases to provide a comparison across cases where the goal is to provide validation of important parts of a theory (Yin, 1989). The goal is to build a general explanation that fits the individual cases, recognizing that there will be variation in the details of each case.

It is also important to consider whether and how previous research and existing theory should be used prior to the actual data collection. One perspective is to use existing empirical studies (i.e., their conceptual lenses, data collection procedures, and/or methods of analysis) to help frame and guide the study. A contrasting view is to avoid the use of previous studies in developing data collection and analysis procedures because they may impose particular orientations on the data as opposed to encouraging new ones to emerge. One may also decide to frame the study in a way that is different from previous studies (e.g., in terms of conceptual lenses or methods of inquiry). It is desirable to have some clear ideas about these issues because it is likely that the case will take some twists and turns during the investigation. One should keep in mind the original purposes of the study but also be able to adapt procedures as needed if unexpected events occur (Yin, 1989).

Collecting the Data

A particular strength of the case study design is the ability to bring different types of evidence to bear on a phenomenon, so it is important to include several data sources and to corroborate the information from one source with other sources. Triangulation is the process of obtaining information from several different sources, cross-checking, and verifying sources of information. Member checks refer to taking the data and interpretations back to the participants and asking them whether the results are plausible. In some cases, participants might even be involved in various parts of the research process, from conceptualizing to writing up the results. Some of the data sources often used are described briefly next (for further discussions, see Merriam, 1988; Yin, 1989).

Interviews. Interviews are a primary source of case study information. There are several types that are typically used, including structured interviews, where respondents are asked a consistent set of questions, as in a survey; semi-structured interviews, where a time schedule and set of questions may be followed, but the interviewer also may probe as needed for additional information; and open-ended interviews, where the interviewer may engage the respondent in relatively informal conversation, asking about events or perhaps even opinions and insights.

Focus Groups. Focus groups involve interviewing several participants at once. They are usually conducted in a semistructured manner, where one has a particular purpose and a set of guiding questions. The setting allows for a type of verbal exchange between participants about the issues that they or the researcher may feel are important. This setting may cause them to think about issues in ways that they might not if they were interviewed alone. Of course, this can work both ways because being in a public setting also might cause them to temper their remarks. One advantage of focus groups is that they allow one to gather multiple perspectives about issues in one sitting. Another is that they are relatively economical in that one can gather information from perhaps 30 to 40 people in three or four focus group meetings.

Documents. Documents are written material that is relevant to the development of case studies. They can provide an important indication of an organization in action. The organization's culture leaves its imprint on most of the printed material that is produced. Relevant documents may include memos, letters, meeting agendas and minutes, written reports and evaluations, and newspaper coverage. Getting access to documents, finding out where they are kept, and verifying their authenticity and accuracy are important parts of the data collection process (Merriam, 1988). Documents are typically not produced for research purposes; therefore, they might be fragmentary, might not fit the purposes of the research, and/or might be difficult to authenticate (Merriam, 1988). It is important to keep in mind that such items have a definite "organizational slant" to them, so the investigator should be aware that documents are evidence about the organization or group as seen through its own eyes. For example, minutes of meetings are often edited to present them in a concise manner. It is important, therefore, to seek clarification and corroboration of documentary evidence from other sources.

Archival Records. Related to organizational documents are various types of archival records. These may include personnel records, budget records, previous survey data, maps, and various organizational charts. These may be relevant in some case studies and much less so in others (Yin, 1989). If one is going to use these data, it is important to determine their accuracy. It is quite possible that they are incomplete or inaccurate and, therefore, might have little relevance.

Artifacts. Artifacts may include the types of computers or technology used, instruments, art, sayings or common expressions used, and other types of physical objects with some type of meaning to members of a particular group or organization. For example, if one is investigating the implementation of a technology policy, an important source of information might be the number of computers in classrooms, the amount of time they are used, the manner in which they are used, and what is produced with them.

Direct Observation. Observations, such as those made at formal meetings, during informal conversations, and those of people doing their routine work, can be another important source of information. They can provide evidence about the extent to which something is in fact being implemented. Observation can be an important part of the empirical process of triangulating what people say they do (as in interviews) and what they actually do (as in the observation of their behavior). This process of checking often turns up considerable discrepancies between what participants do and what they say they do. This represents a good example of what researchers call "espoused theory" versus "theory in use" (Everhart, 1988). Of course, putting this together also depends on one's interpretation (with potential bias) of a participant's words and actions. In the case where there are multiple observers, it becomes possible to get an assessment of the reliability of their observations.

Participant Observation. One specific type of observation is referred to as participant observation. This involves actually gaining access into a setting and getting up close to the members of a group or an organization such that one can observe and interview them to determine how they participate in and make meaning of their social and cultural situations. Participant observation allows one to note participants' behavior in actual settings as opposed to what they might say in retrospect on a survey or what they might intend to do. The sum of these various participant observation techniques is sometimes referred to as ethnographic (or fieldwork) methods.

Ethnographic methods have the longest track record of the qualitative methods in use today.

They involve the use of a set of methods to collect data, and the written record is the product of using the techniques. Ethnography represents a strategy focusing on interviews, documentary analysis, life history, investigator diaries, and participant observation (Merriam, 1988). Ethnography is a sociocultural interpretation of the data. Its goal is to reveal the context and social reality that guide people's behavior within a particular setting. The focus is on the activities and the meaning those activities have for the actors who engage in them (Everhart, 1988). Ethnography involves immersion over a substantial period in a single setting and detailed descriptive evidence from observations and interviews (Yin, 1989).

Critical ethnography carries a social concern for power inequities into the field setting. This agenda enters into the construction of the research text about the social relationships studied and highlights the further responsibility of researchers doing this type of work to promote social justice through the writing and dissemination of the research (e.g., Anderson, 1990). The critical approach to ethnography focuses on the concept that social reality is constructed from ongoing social interaction; therefore, it examines the often invisible ways in which social interaction is structured, power is exercised, and privileged interests are protected in organizational contexts (Anderson, 1990). Moreover, critical approaches raise concerns about how the research is conducted, analyzed, written, and presented to practitioners and others.

Analyzing the Evidence

During data collection, it is important to develop a database, or a filing system, where various pieces of data can be deposited. In addition, one should maintain a comprehensive and detailed audit trail. For example, a journal can be used to record daily research activities, including the location of material, the logistics of obtaining the data, decisions regarding the selection of data, what piece of data led to other explorations, emergent themes, new research ideas, problems in data collection and analysis, and decisions that were made to resolve research and writing problems (Benham, 1993). This can be instructive about how one made decisions about the data, the trustworthiness of sources, and the coding of the information. This provides an important check on one's initial perspectives versus evolving perspectives and on the subjectivity of the research process, data, and solutions.

Evidence, analysis, and interpretation tend to occur more simultaneously in interpretive types of analysis. Linking the data to propositions is the core of data analysis. The step has to do with generating concepts that can form the foundations of a theory (Glaser & Strauss, 1967). In some ways, linking data to propositions has been least well developed in case study research (Yin, 1989). The coding of the data is integrally related to their conceptualization. Conceptual categories become more abstract and, hence, further from the data.

Single Cases. There are a number of ways in which to go about analyzing the data. One way is to follow the theoretical propositions that led to the study (Yin, 1989). Linking data to propositions can occur in a variety of ways, including pattern matching (where the information in the case is compared against a theoretical proposition such as a hypothesized chronological sequence), explanation building (where one attempts to develop causal links from the study to other known aspects of the phenomenon), and emergent categories (where one attempts to create new categories from the data as opposed to imposing existing categories from previous research). Having some of these propositions at hand helps to organize the analysis and focus on key aspects of the data. This helps in building an explanation. A second strategy, especially for descriptive case studies, is to organize the case around key descriptive aspects (e.g., key events, themes, patterns) that emerge from the case (Yin, 1989). Several sources provide further discussion of some of these strategies (e.g., Heck, 2004; Merriam, 1988; Yin, 1989).

Comparisons Across Cases. Comparisons across a number of cases can produce evidence that is more compelling than a single case because they are based on more instances. In such analyses, it is important to establish the reliability and integrity of each case first. Then one can identify similarities and differences that help to build a comprehensive unified explanation. Differences across the cases, for example, suggest that the theoretical explanation must be qualified based on the presence of contextual factors that may be acting in expected or unexpected ways. In contrast, finding similarities allows one to extend the theoretical explanation across a number of differing situations. Researchers conducting cross-case comparisons often use some variation of the "comparative" method (Glaser & Strauss, 1967). This is an inductive analytic process whereby the interpretation of the data gradually evolves into some type of theoretical framework that guides further analysis. This process involves refining the emerging categories and their properties, developing a theoretical base for making comparisons among cases, and formulating hypotheses (Merriam, 1988). The theoretical base should be relatively parsimonious (i.e., have a clear formulation and a limited number of interrelated concepts), and its scope should be broad enough to allow it to be applied to a variety of situations. For example, if one has three cases, each should be constructed separately first, but in a way that also permits one to make comparisons subsequently.

Next, one must devise a conceptual scheme for comparing cases (e.g., format, criteria for comparison, essential information about each case). This is a means for displaying the relevant data from each case simultaneously. It is likely that the analysis will need to go through several iterations of this process until the criteria for comparison are satisfactory. This is an important step because the way in which the data are partitioned will dictate what one will see in the subsequent analysis. After partitioning the data successfully, one can make the comparisons, keeping in mind the study's purposes and looking for patterns that occur across the cases. One should also make note of important differences and speculate about what might explain these differences (e.g., contextual or temporal conditions). Eventually, one can make inferences based on the comparisons, for example, deriving theoretical propositions that provide a general explanation that is grounded in the individual cases (e.g., Benham & Heck, 1994).

Most important, one must construct a research text to present the analysis to readers. A good place to begin is by revisiting the goals and purposes of the study. Data can be organized and displayed to facilitate the overall presentation. Some of these techniques include putting information into different arrays, developing a matrix of categories and placing the key evidence within the categories, creating data displays (e.g., flow charts) to summarize relationships among variables, tabulating frequencies of certain events, and placing the information in chronological order using some type of temporal scheme (Miles & Huberman, 1984).

ISSUES IN DESIGNING AND CONDUCTING STUDIES USING QUANTITATIVE ANALYSES

In this section, I discuss some key issues regarding studies using quantitative analyses. Experiments and quasi-experiments, which are used for investigating causal relations, have not been frequently used in K–12 and higher education research. Currently, however, there is a greater demand for these types of studies from federal policymakers. It remains to be seen whether experiments and quasi-experiments will become more favored research designs in conducting school research. In-depth discussion on these designs is outside the scope of this chapter, but further information can be found in a number of research texts (e.g., Cook & Campbell, 1979; Fraenkel & Wallen, 2000; Pedhazur & Schmelkin, 1991). Nonexperimental designs are used most frequently in conducting educational research in higher education. They are best used for descriptive research purposes (e.g., to identify a set of relationships, to determine how many or how often something occurs) or to establish an association between certain sets of variables. Descriptive and associational studies can be important for building theory and suggesting subsequent variables to include in actual randomized field trials (Slavin, 2002).

In nonexperimental studies, one has no real control over actual events that influence what one is attempting to study. The events have already occurred. For example, one cannot manipulate students' motivation, the quality of their teachers, the grouping practices used in their classes, or their socioeconomic backgrounds in trying to determine how these variables affect learning. In nonexperimental research, one actually needs to work backward from the outcome to uncover relevant associations. Because of this, inferences about causality are weak at best. This type of design, therefore, is not as well suited as are experimental and quasi-experimental designs for determining cause-and-effect relationships because it generally relies on cross-sectional data (i.e., data collected at one point in time) and does not depend on manipulating treatment variables. Because of its reliance on cross-sectional data, it is also not well suited for studying processes that unfold over time.

Effect on Findings of Analytic Approach Chosen

It should be instructive for us to consider a couple of examples that demonstrate how the choice of research purposes and questions, designs, and techniques used to analyze the data influence the findings of quantitative studies. The appropriateness of the analytic techniques used affects the substantive conclusions that can be drawn. More rigorous analyses may lead to uncovering relationships in data that are not revealed in more simplistic analyses. At the same time, however, they are also more likely to lead to fewer findings of substance than have often been claimed in studies that employ more simplistic analytical methods (Pedhazur & Schmelkin, 1991). This can be important, especially when using nonexperimental designs. If one is doing this type of research, it will be necessary to give considerable attention to both the relationships implied in the theoretical models under consideration and the strengths and limitations of various analytic techniques that will be used to test the relationships implied by the model or models under consideration.

Consider a case where one wants to examine whether gender is related to student achievement. The research question under consideration might be the following: Does gender affect student achievement? To answer this question,

Table 21.1 Descriptive Statistics for Example

Variable	Male		Female	
	Mean	*SD*	*Mean*	*SD*
Total reading	650.88	37.01	641.50	15.80
Total math	679.75	36.54	637.00	15.80
Total language	658.13	27.78	631.67	25.57

one might collect achievement data on a number of students and have them report whether they are male or female. To illustrate this example, I compiled data for 14 students randomly selected from a larger study. Data include students' scores on a reading test, a math test, and a language skills test. Table 21.1 provides summary descriptive statistics for these students, suggesting in this small sample that females scored lower than males on each test.

The research question we posed concerns whether there is a difference in students' achievement scores associated with gender. For ease of presentation, we set aside the issue of whether there are other variables that should also be included in the model to provide a more thorough examination of whether gender differences in achievement would exist, even after other known variables related to achievement were controlled. Keep in mind, however, that in nonexperimental research, it is important to include other variables known to influence outcomes in any model tested. Otherwise, one runs the risk of presenting results that are not theoretically complete. In contrast, in experimental research, we assume that the effects of various extraneous variables on outcomes are minimized due to random assignment of participants to various treatment and control groups.

There are a number of different ways in which one could choose to analyze the data in this simple model. Linear models (e.g., analysis of variance [ANOVA], multiple regression, multivariate analysis of variance [MANOVA]) have a long tradition in the social sciences for analyzing data from experimental, quasi-experimental, and nonexperimental designs. Most prominent are univariate (which focus on a single dependent variable) and multivariate (which allow simultaneous investigation of several dependent variables) approaches.

Univariate analysis attempts to explain variability in a single outcome (or dependent) variable from information provided by one or more predictor (or independent) variables. Multiple regression is the most widely used statistical technique in social science research, but it does have some limitations; for example, it requires a single dependent variable, does not incorporate measurement errors on predictors, and is confined to a single unit of analysis. Multivariate analysis (e.g., MANOVA, discriminant analysis) is the more general case of univariate analysis. It facilitates the simultaneous examination of multiple independent and dependent variables in one model. It turns out that some of the distinctions among the various types of linear models (e.g., ANOVA, regression) are largely artificial, resulting from differences in terminology, how independent variables are measured (e.g., categorical, continuous), and historical traditions within the various social science disciplines (e.g., whether participants were studied in their natural settings such as schools, whether participants were placed in experimental settings).

Univariate Analysis

We could use ANOVA or multiple regression to conduct the analysis. Gender would be the independent variable, and each test would be the dependent variable. This approach would require three separate analyses. This strategy would get at the issue of how gender affects achievement, but in each case achievement would be described somewhat differently (i.e., in reading, in math, in language). Importantly, this analytic approach would eliminate the

Table 21.2   Multiple Regression Analyses

	Total reading		Total math		Total language	
Variable	Beta	SE	Beta	SE	Beta	SE
Female	−9.38	16.23	−42.75[*]	17.76	−26.46	14.52
Adjusted R^2	.01		.27		.15	

[*]$p < .05.$

possibility that students' reading scores are correlated with their math and language scores. This is a major limitation to consider in using a univariate approach to this problem. On the other hand, if we could establish that there are no correlations among the tests (or only small ones), then the case for using a univariate analysis would receive some support. When the correlations are calculated, however, it turns out that reading and math are highly correlated ($r = .90$), as are reading and language (.75) and language and math (.77). This suggests that we need a method that will incorporate the correlations among the dependent variables simultaneously.

If we use the separate regression models, we obtain the following results (summarized in Table 21.2). For reading, gender (coded 1 = females) is not a significant predictor of student differences, unstandardized beta = −9.38, $p = .574$. The coefficient suggests that females in the sample scored on average 9.38 points lower than males on the reading test. For language, in this small data set, gender also is not a significant predictor, unstandardized beta = −26.46, $p = .093$. For math, however, there is a substantial gap between male and female scores, unstandardized beta = −42.75, $p = .033$. If we were to summarize these data, we would likely conclude that gender affects achievement under some conditions (i.e., math) but not others.

Multivariate Analysis

More important is the issue of whether this would provide the correct interpretation of the data. Another way in which we could approach the analysis would be to use a multivariate technique. We could use MANOVA to investigate whether gender affected student achievement.

This approach has the advantage of providing an analysis of differences considering all dependent variables simultaneously. It has the effect of controlling for the correlations among the dependent variables. A set of means (called a vector) replaces the individual means for each achievement variable in the regression analysis. The hypothesis tested is that the populations from which the groups are selected have the same means for all dependent variables. The approach can be conceptualized as creating a latent (or an underlying) achievement variable (i.e., a weighted composite of the dependent variables) and then assessing whether this variable is significantly different for male and female participants.

From an analytic standpoint, the MANOVA requires that the dependent variables have multivariate normal distribution with the same variance–covariance matrix (i.e., a square arrangement of elements with the variances of the variables on the diagonal and the covariances of pairs of variables off the diagonal) in each group. The new combined dependent variable is formed to separate each group as much as possible. For multivariate analyses, therefore, it is insufficient to consider just the means and standard deviations of variables by themselves (as presented in Table 21.1). Considering each separately would increase the chances of making type 1 errors (i.e., false rejections of the null hypothesis) due to multiple tests of likely correlated dependent variables.

To test the hypothesis about the differences in scores on the dependent variables across gender, a matrix of difference scores must be created. These are formulated by subtracting each score from the appropriate group mean (Tabachnick & Fidell, 1996). The most basic partition of variance apportions variance attributed to systematic differences between males and females (the effect of gender) and unknown sources of error (variance attributed to differences in scores among individuals within groups). Determinants (which are measures of generalized variance in a matrix) of the various matrices are calculated, and ratios between them provide a test of hypothesis about the effect of the independent variable on the linear combination of dependent variables. One statistic often used for testing hypotheses is Wilks's lambda, which can be interpreted as a measure of the proportion of total variability not explained by group differences.

The results of our multivariate analysis (not shown) suggest that gender is significantly related to achievement, Wilks's lambda = .444, $p = .037$. This result implies that the previous regression results would be incomplete and would lead to an incorrect conclusion regarding the impact of gender on achievement. This is because of the regression approach's blind spot toward incorporating correlations among the dependent variables in the analysis. Unfortunately, a limitation of the MANOVA approach is that we do not get a sense of how strongly gender is related to achievement. More specifically, remember that there were wide variations in the beta coefficient for gender in the regression analyses presented in Table 21.2. Moreover, we do not get any information from the analysis directly about which tests might be more strongly associated with the underlying achievement domain developed in the analysis. Some researchers might be inclined to do follow-up analyses on each dependent variable separately; however, that defeats the goal of the multivariate analysis, which is to provide information about the effect of gender on the combined set of dependent variables.

Structural Equation Modeling Analysis

Given these specific limitations of MANOVA, we could also conduct the analysis with structural equation modeling (SEM). The term is broadly defined as accommodating the specification and testing of models that include latent variables, measurement errors, multiple indicators, simultaneity, and complex structural relationships such as reciprocal causation. SEM is a generalization of both regression and factor analysis and subsumes most linear modeling methods as special cases (Rigdon, 1998).

SEM can be used to address two basic concerns in these data. First is the development of latent constructs through measuring their observed indicators. We can define an achievement variable through scores on several tests. This part of the analysis focuses on defining the validity and reliability of constructs and their observed indicators. In the SEM approach to defining constructs, a smaller set of underlying (or latent) factors is hypothesized to be responsible for the specific pattern of variation and covariation present in a set of observed variables. Each observed variable is conceptualized as a linear function of one or more common factors and residual factors (error terms). Second, after defining the latent construct through a set of indicators, we can investigate relationships among various predictors and latent variables in a proposed model. Defining constructs in this manner helps to produce structural relationships among factors or between factors and other predictors that have been corrected for measurement error (for further discussion of SEM techniques, see Raykov & Marcoulides, 2001).

The model implied in the research questions is summarized in Figure 21.1. As summarized in the figure, the various tests are strongly associated with the achievement factor (with standardized loadings ranging from .79 to .99). This suggests that achievement is well measured by the individual tests. The unstandardized effect of female on achievement is –42.73, and the standardized effect is –.57, $p < .01$. The model fit (which can be determined from several fit indexes) can be described as adequate, $\chi^2 = 6.9$, $df = 2$, $p = .03$. This suggests only a small discrepancy between the hypothesized model and the actual data. In comparison with the MANOVA, therefore, the SEM analysis provides an estimate of observed loadings on the achievement factor and a coefficient describing the effect of gender on the achievement variable. In the model, the variance in achievement accounted for by gender is 33% (with 67% of the variance unaccounted for in parentheses in the figure).

As the example indicates, decisions we make about research questions and analytic

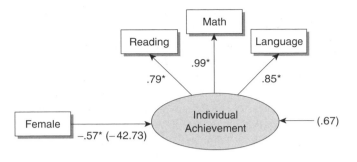

Figure 21.1   Standardized and Unstandardized (in parentheses) Effects of Gender on Achievement

$*p < .05.$

techniques influence the ways in which the data are analyzed as well as the interpretations that arise from the analysis. In this case, univariate approaches did not take full advantage of the complexity in the data structure. Approaches such as SEM and multilevel analysis (for hierarchical data structures) are fast becoming the standard analytic approaches for quantitative research in education because of their applicability to a broad range of research situations, designs, and data structures. Despite the growing recognition of their importance, however, they have not yet been fully integrated into research and statistics texts. Similarly, they are not yet an integral part of analytic techniques available in most commonly used statistical programs.

From Single-Level Analysis to Multilevel Analysis

One final example is presented to illustrate the difference between single-level and multilevel analyses of data. Many examples of educational research involve the analysis of hierarchical, or nested, data structures (i.e., where students are nested in classrooms and schools). Because of the limits of statistical techniques, until recently researchers had to decide whether to ignore the groupings and analyze the data on individuals or to ignore the individuals and analyze the data on groups only. Neither solution took full advantage of the complexity of the data structure. Concerns in various fields about how to analyze hierarchical data properly led to the development of multilevel

models as extensions of linear models over the past few decades.

A common limitation of the univariate and multivariate techniques discussed previously (e.g., ANOVA, MANOVA, multiple regression) is that they are confined to single-level analyses; that is, either individuals are the unit of analysis or groups are the unit of analysis. Multilevel modeling is fast becoming the standard analytic approach for quantitative research on schools due to its applicability to a wide range of research problems, designs, and data structures (i.e., hierarchical, cross-sectional, and longitudinal). Despite a growing recognition of its importance, however, multilevel modeling approaches have not yet been fully integrated into research and statistics texts. There are a number of approaches to the analysis of hierarchical data structures. Two of the basic approaches are multilevel regression models and multilevel structural equation models (for further discussions, see Bryk & Raudenbush, 1992; Goldstein, 1987; Heck & Thomas, 2000; Hox, 1995; Kreft & De Leeuw, 1998; Muthén, 1991, 1994; Muthén & Muthén, 1998–2004; Raykov & Marcoulides, 2001).

Importantly, the assumptions necessary for single-level techniques such as multiple regression to yield the best unbiased estimates are most realistic when the data have been collected through simple random sampling. Random sampling assumes that participants in a study are independent of each other. As groups are added to a study, however, this assumption becomes more tenuous. In large-scale educational research, simple random sampling is rarely used. Instead, various types of complex sampling strategies are employed to select students, classrooms, and schools. Clustered data, therefore, result from the sampling strategies used in large-scale databases as well as from natural groupings of students in educational institutions. The single-level regression model cannot take into consideration that the students may be clustered within a number of schools with other students having similar achievement scores and backgrounds. Because the single-level linear model assumes that prediction errors are independent for each individual student (because of simple random sampling), this assumption will likely be violated when students are actually grouped within schools.

Where data hierarchies exist, the outcomes produced will likely vary across the sample of schools in the study. Moreover, there may be variation in the relationship between some within-school variables (e.g., student socioeconomic status [SES]) and the outcomes produced. In some schools, there might be a strong relationship between student SES and outcomes, whereas in other schools, there might be no such relationship.

Given the increased availability of many secondary data sets, it is important to use analytic techniques that are most appropriate to the data collection strategy. Applying a single-level analysis produces a number of difficulties, including a forced choice over the unit of analysis (i.e., whether to analyze individuals or groups), trade-offs in measurement precision, limitations in how the model's parameters may be examined (i.e., slopes and intercepts are fixed within the sample in single-level analyses), and violations related to errors in the prediction equation (e.g., errors should be independent, be normally distributed, and have constant variance). The random error components of hierarchical data structures are more complex because the errors within each unit are dependent given that they are common to every individual in the unit. Where similarities among individuals due to groupings are present, multilevel models are acknowledged to provide more accurate assessments of the properties of groups than are single-level analyses. This is due primarily to their efficiency in calculating standard errors for each model parameter. Because tests of significance

(e.g., a t test) for variables' effects on an outcome are calculated as the ratio of each estimate to its standard error, ignoring the presence of hierarchical data structures can lead to false inferences about the relations among variables in a model (due to incorrect standard errors) as well as to missed insights about the processes being studied.

Multilevel analysis, therefore, provides several conceptual and technical benefits; because it reflects the way in which the data were collected, it allows researchers to partition the variance in an outcome into several components. The general modeling framework also allows the formulation of several useful submodels that can be used to explain the outcome's variance at different levels. In this way, it is possible to avoid problems related to choosing the unit of analysis. The presence of submodels also allows the analyst to define explanatory variables at their correct theoretical levels. For example, variables related to institutions should be estimated with respect to the number of institutions in the study, whereas variables related to individuals (e.g., age) should be estimated with respect to the number of individuals in the study.

An example may help to illustrate some of these points. Suppose that we wish to examine the impact of school quality on school outcomes, controlling for community SES (ComSES). In this example, there are a number of students within each school who are assessed through three tests (reading, math, and language). We also obtain background information on the students (e.g., their individual SES and age). Finally, we collect data on school quality and school SES.

The data could be analyzed in several ways. Similar to the last example, we could decide to conduct separate single-level regression analyses. Like before, however, those analyses would consider each achievement outcome as separate. Another limitation would be that the single-level regression would not incorporate any type of measurement error on the individual tests comprising achievement. Moreover, because the analysis is confined to a single level, it would not likely take into consideration the hierarchical data structure as well as the proper definition of variables at either the group or individual level.

As in the last example, we could decide to conduct a single-level SEM analysis. This would address the issue of considering the outcomes simultaneously and would allow the incorporation of measurement errors related to each subtest into an overall achievement variable. Here is what the results would look like if we developed and tested such a model. In this example, there are 120 students in 24 schools. The single-level model is summarized in Figure 21.2. The figure indicates that all of the subtests measure achievement well (with standardized loadings ranging from .86 to .93).

We can determine that the model fits the data well, $\chi^2 = 14.99$, $df = 8$, $p = .70$. The individual parameters indicate that the school parameters (school quality and school SES) are statistically significant, whereas the individual parameters (student SES and age) are not. The variance in achievement accounted for by this model is 26% (with 74% unaccounted for in parentheses in Figure 21.2). By not considering the hierarchical structure of the data, it is likely that the standard errors are too small. More specifically, all of the parameters in the single-level model are based on a sample size of 120, yet it is apparent that the school parameters should refer to the number of schools ($N = 24$) in the sample and not to the number of individuals ($N = 120$). This mismatch of variables in the analysis likely produces some inaccuracy for the group-level parameters (school quality and school SES).

We could also formulate this example as a multilevel structural equation model. It turns out that there is considerable variation in each outcome due to differences among schools, with the between-group variation ranging from about 16% in reading to more than 30% in math (not shown). This suggests that a multilevel model can be developed to explain the considerable variation that exists at each level (i.e., within and between schools). The resulting model is summarized in Figure 21.3.

The multilevel model also fits the data adequately, $\chi^2 = 12.69$, $df = 14$, $p = .055$. Figure 21.3 also indicates that school SES and school quality are significantly related to school achievement. Notice, however, that the sizes of the school-level coefficients in Figure 21.3 are different from those in the previous model, as are the standard errors (not shown). More specifically, the coefficients for school quality and ComSES are larger in the multilevel formulation. Notice also that the variance accounted for between groups is about 83% (with 17% unaccounted for in the figure). In contrast, the variance accounted for within groups is almost nonexistent (1%).

Overall, the multilevel model provides results that are more consistent with the complexity of the hierarchical data structures (Muthén, 1994). First, it corrects the latent constructs (e.g., achievement) for measurement errors in the observed measures. Correcting for error allows for a more accurate estimate of the

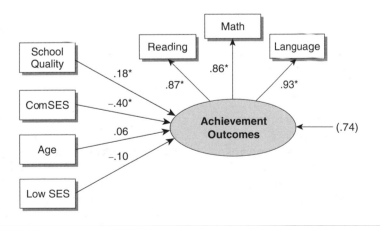

Figure 21.2   Structural Model of Individual and School Variables' Standardized Impact on Achievement

*$p < .05$.

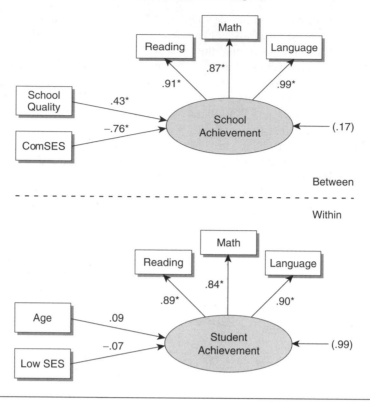

Figure 21.3   Multilevel Model of Individual and School Variables' Standardized Impact on Achievement

*p < .05.

model's structural parameters than would be possible in separate regression models. Second, the SEM approach readily allows the modeling of separate sets of variables within and between groups involving both direct and indirect effects; for example, we could also define a path from ComSES to school quality and determine the indirect effect of ComSES on outcomes. Combining corrections for measurement error (factor analysis) with path analysis provides more accurate estimates of the various ways in which the independent variables may affect outcomes. This allows the independent variables in the model to be defined at their appropriate levels in the hierarchical data structure. Because of this, hypothesis tests can be conducted more accurately given that the standard errors associated with the model's coefficients will be related to the number of units (24) or to the number of individuals (120). Third, the approach considers all of the outcomes simultaneously, thereby providing information about how the various subtests relate to each other; for example, the high loadings suggest stronger relationships among the tests.

FINAL REFLECTIONS

In this chapter, I have advanced what I view as critical considerations in developing and conducting research studies. The choices we make in approaching and framing educational problems (e.g., rationalist, constructivist, critical, postmodern), selecting methods of investigation, and collecting data have major consequences for what we find. Disclosing the conceptual and methodological moves we make is the key to producing credible and trustworthy findings. Qualitative methods of analysis represent a diverse set of inquiry techniques that can be used to examine a wide variety of problems, research purposes, and questions. They lend themselves to a number of different research designs (e.g., case study, historical research, fieldwork). They have the advantage of getting researchers up close to ways in which meaning is made in social situations.

I also demonstrated and explored how different quantitative analytic approaches used to analyze data can result in a range of different results, some of which might not take full advantage of the data structure. The benefits and consequences of each approach should be considered before choosing the approach that best addresses the study's purposes and research questions. The appropriate use of any analytic approach depends on guidance from previous research, the use of conceptual models to organize or explain relationships observed, and the collection of quality data.

Attempts to impose particular designs (e.g., experimental trials) and methods on the field undermine our free pursuit of understandings better addressed through other designs and methods. Greater sensitivity to how our research is situated conceptually, methodologically, and contextually will help audiences to understand how and why particular structures, patterns, and practices in education have existed over time. By working in concert with policymakers and practitioners to address important educational problems, we can contribute to illuminating productive practices and reducing oppressive structures in schooling.

REFERENCES

Adelman, C., Jenkins, D., & Kemmis, S. (1977). Re-thinking case study: Notes from the second Cambridge conference. *Cambridge Journal of Education, 6,* 139–150.

Anderson, G. (1990). Toward a critical constructivist approach to educational administration. *Educational Administration Quarterly, 26*(1), 38–59.

Anfara, V. A., Brown, K. M., & Mangione, T. L. (2002). Qualitative analysis on stage: Making the research process more public. *Educational Researcher, 31*(7), 28–38.

Benham, M. K. (1993). *Political and cultural determinants of educational policymaking: Their effects on Native Hawaiians.* Unpublished doctoral dissertation, University of Hawaii at Manoa.

Benham, M. K., & Heck, R. H. (1994). Political culture and policy in a state-controlled educational system: The case of educational politics in Hawaii. *Educational Administration Quarterly, 30,* 419–450.

Bensimon, E. M., & Marshall, C. (1997). Policy analysis for postsecondary education: Feminist and critical perspectives. In C. Marshall (Ed.), *Feminist critical policy analysis* (pp. 1–21). London: Falmer.

Bernard, H. R. (1994). *Research methods in anthropology: Qualitative and quantitative approaches.* Thousand Oaks, CA: Sage.

Birnbaum, R. (2000). Policy scholars are from Venus; Policy makers are from Mars. *Review of Higher Education, 23*(2), 119–132.

Bogdan, R. C., & Biklen, S. K. (1998). *Qualitative research for education* (3rd ed.). Boston: Allyn & Bacon.

Bryk, A. S., & Raudenbush, S. W. (1992). *Hierarchical linear models: Applications and data analysis methods.* Newbury Park, CA: Sage.

Cook, T. D., & Campbell, D. T. (1979). *Quasi-experimentation: Design and analysis issues for field settings.* Boston: Houghton Mifflin.

Easton, D. (1953). *The political system.* New York: Knopf.

Everhart, R. (1988). Fieldwork methodology in educational administration. In N. Boyan (Ed.), *Handbook of research on educational administration* (pp. 703–726). New York: Longman.

Feuer, M. J., Towne, L., & Shavelson, R. J. (2002). Scientific culture and educational research. *Educational Researcher, 31*(8), 4–14.

Fraenkel, J. R., & Wallen, N. (2000). *How to design and evaluate research in education* (4th ed.). Boston: McGraw-Hill.

Glaser, B. J., & Strauss, A. L. (1967). *The discovery of grounded theory.* Chicago: Aldine.

Goldstein, H. (1987). *Multilevel models in educational and social research.* London: Oxford University Press.

Hallinger, P., & Heck, R. H. (1996). The principal's role in school effectiveness: An assessment of the methodological progress, 1980–1995. In K. Leithwood, J. Chapman, D. Corson, P. Hallinger, & A. Hart (Eds.), *International handbook of educational leadership and administration* (pp. 723–783). London: Kluwer Academic.

Heck, R. H. (2004). *Studying educational and social policy: Theoretical concepts and research methods.* Mahwah, NJ: Lawrence Erlbaum.

Heck, R. H., & Thomas, S. L. (2000). *An introduction to multilevel modeling techniques.* Mahwah, NJ: Lawrence Erlbaum.

Hox, J. J. (1995). *Applied multilevel analysis.* Amsterdam, Netherlands: T. T. Publikaties.

Kaplan, A. (1964). *The conduct of inquiry: Methodology for behavioral science.* San Francisco: Chandler.

Keith, N. (1996). A critical perspective on teacher participation in urban schools. *Educational Administration Quarterly, 32*(1), 45–79.

Kreft, I., & De Leeuw, J. (1998). *Introducing multilevel modeling.* Thousand Oaks, CA: Sage.

Ladson-Billings, G. (2000). Racialized discourses and ethnic epistemologies. In N. Denzin & Y. Lincoln (Eds.), *Handbook of qualitative research* (2nd ed., pp. 257–277). Thousand Oaks, CA: Sage.

Lagemann, E. C. (1997). Contested terrain: A history of education research in the United States, 1890–1990. *Educational Researcher, 26*(9), 5–17.

Lather, P. (1992). Critical frames in educational research: Feminist and post-structural perspectives. *Theory Into Practice, 31*(2), 87–99.

Majchrzak, A. (1984). *Methods for policy research.* Beverly Hills, CA: Sage.

Marshall, C., Mitchell, D., & Wirt, F. (1989). *Culture and education policy in the American states.* New York: Falmer.

Merriam, S. B. (1988). *Case study research in education: A qualitative approach.* San Francisco: Jossey-Bass.

Miles, M. B., & Huberman, A. M. (1984). *Analyzing qualitative data: A source book for new methods.* Beverly Hills, CA: Sage.

Murray, F. B. (1996). Educational psychology and the teacher's reasoning. In F. B. Murray (Ed.), *The teacher educator's handbook: Building a knowledge base for the preparation of teachers* (pp. 419–437). San Francisco: Jossey-Bass.

Muthén, B. O. (1991). Multilevel factor analysis of class and student achievement components. *Journal of Educational Measurement, 28,* 338–354.

Muthén, B. O. (1994). Multilevel covariance structure analysis. *Sociological Methods and Research, 22,* 376–398.

Muthén, L., & Muthén, B. O. (1998–2004). *Mplus user's guide.* Los Angeles: Author.

National Research Council. (2002). Accumulation of scientific knowledge. In R. J. Shavelson & L. Towne (Eds.), *Scientific research in education* (National Research Council, Committee on Scientific Principles for Educational Research, pp. 28–49). Washington, DC: National Academy Press.

No Child Left Behind Act, P.L. 107–110. (2001).

Nuthall, G. (2004). Relating classroom teaching to student learning: A critical analysis of why research failed to bridge the theory–practice gap. *Harvard Educational Review, 74,* 273–306.

Parker, L., & Lynn, M. (2002). What's race got to do with it? Critical race theory's conflicts with and connections to qualitative research methodology and epistemology. *Qualitative Inquiry, 8*(1), 7–22.

Pedhazur, E. J., & Schmelkin, L. P. (1991). *Measurement, design, and analysis: An integrated approach.* Hillsdale, NJ: Lawrence Erlbaum.

Raykov, T., & Marcoulides, G. A. (2001). *A first course in structural equation modeling.* Mahwah, NJ: Lawrence Erlbaum.

Rigdon, E. (1998). Structural equation modeling. In G. Marcoulides (Ed.), *Modern methods of business research* (pp. 251–294). Mahwah, NJ: Lawrence Erlbaum.

Robinson, V. M. J. (1996). Critical theory and the social psychology of change. In K. Leithwood, J. Chapman, D. Corson, P. Hallinger, & A. Hart (Eds.), *International handbook of educational leadership and administration* (pp. 1069–1096). Boston: Kluwer Academic.

Sabatier, P. A., & Jenkins-Smith, H. C. (1993). *Policy change and learning: An advocacy coalition approach.* Boulder, CO: Westview.

Slavin, R. E. (2002). Evidence-based education policies: Transforming educational practice and research. *Educational Researcher, 31*(7), 15–21.

Smart, J. C. (2002, November). *Attributes of exemplary research manuscripts employing quantitative analyses.* Paper presented at the meeting of the Association for the Study of Higher Education, Sacramento, CA.

Tabachnick, B., & Fidell, X. (1996). *Using multivariate statistics* (3rd ed.). New York: HarperCollins.

Toulmin, S. (2001). *Return to reason.* Cambridge, MA: Harvard University Press.

Yin, R. K. (1989). *Case study research: Design and methods* (rev. ed.). Newbury Park, CA: Sage.

22

SAMPLING

Rationale and Rigor in Choosing What to Observe

SCOTT L. THOMAS

University of Georgia

The best research ideas and most elegant methods can be laid to waste if trained on poorly specified observations, yet the importance of the choice of sampling strategy in education research gets woefully little attention. I strongly believe that the general logic of exemplary inquiry is one that starts with theory and progresses to an assessment of the fit between what should be (theory) and what is (empirical observation). Less than thoughtful and deliberate specification of what to observe when testing propositions embedded within our theories can lead to the failure of what might be an otherwise rigorous assessment of presumed relationships. Those things we choose to observe are usually some subset of a larger population, that is, a sample. Anchored in my own research experiences—mostly with quantitative inquiry but increasingly with some qualitative approaches to supplement my research—the purpose of this chapter is to demonstrate that sampling is far more than simply a way in which to collect data for a study. Sampling is, in fact, a much more integral part of the overall research design than many scholars consciously acknowledge. In what follows, I argue that the

motivations for sampling provide one of the more powerful contrasts between qualitative and quantitative inquiry—two broad approaches to understanding social phenomena that are defined by fundamentally different epistemological bases.

Throughout this chapter, I highlight two distinct classes of sampling strategy, probability and nonprobability, that map nicely onto the qualitative–quantitative orientations of education research. Within each class, I provide examples of the variations that are often used in education research to produce exemplary studies. Through this presentation, I attempt to call attention to the reality that sampling strategy is an essential component of the overarching research design being employed. Of course, research design is fundamentally related to the types of questions being posed; furthermore, research questions are organically connected to the epistemological orientation of the researcher. This chapter speaks to my belief that the chain connecting sampling choices to the presuppositions and foundational knowledge of the researcher should be used to firmly anchor decisions about sampling.

Why sample? The most obvious answer is that in many instances an examination of an entire population (a census) is unrealistic. Trying to poll all adult males in the United States, for example, would prove to be a logistic quagmire. So for the sake of efficiency, researchers might opt to draw a sample from this larger population. Although assembling such a large population would be problematic enough, one might also wonder how the polling would take place. How many pollsters would be required to contact each adult male in the population? The costs of hiring so many pollsters would likely prove to be prohibitive. Moreover, it is likely that even with every available pollster in the country working on the project, the amount of time it would take to canvass the population in question would undermine the ability to query sample members about anything that was at all time relevant.

It turns out that, as I discuss in this chapter, samples can actually provide more accurate information than collecting data on each and every member of a large population. The variability of pollsters in questioning or observing population members can be greatly reduced by focusing energies on a much smaller group. Clearly, it would be much easier to consistently train and supervise 10 pollsters rather than 10,000. The quality of the data collected is directly related to the expertise of those asking the questions, administering the tests or questionnaires, or making the observations.

There are other compelling reasons to sample. These include the desire to commit energy to develop an in-depth understanding of particular members of a larger population. If administering predeveloped questions to large numbers of people is challenging, then using semistructured interview techniques to derive deeper understanding enabled only by allowing researchers greater flexibility with the direction of the questioning forces the use of even smaller subsets of the larger population.

Or consider research resulting in the destruction of sample elements (something we seek to avoid in social science research). What if Ford and Volvo adopted a census-based approach to the comprehensive testing of the safety of their automobiles? Every one of their vehicles would need to undergo crash testing! In the end, they may have collected all the information possible to assure their shareholders that their vehicles were safe, but at what cost? There would be no automobiles left to sell, and the data collected would likely be less accurate than would be the case if a thoughtful sampling strategy had been used.

The choice of what and when to observe offers a critical opportunity to test for the presence or absence of traits or behaviors suggested by theories. One might choose to conduct such a test on samples typical of a larger population, or one might purposively pursue the nontypical observations to test theoretical elements at the extremes. The thoughtful adoption and incorporation of sampling strategies provide such opportunities.

SAMPLING LOGIC

There exist two broad classes of sampling schemes: probabilistic and nonprobabilistic. Probabilistic strategies generally make use of larger numbers of sample elements (e.g., people, schools, counties) and are defined by each element having a known and positive probability of inclusion in the sample. Thus, probability samples require a clearly defined population from which a sampling frame can be constructed and a sample can be drawn. Quantitative analytical approaches involving inferential statistics rely on probabilistic samples that allow one to generalize and gauge sample representativeness and to control for sample bias.

Noninferential quantitative and qualitative analytical approaches rely on nonprobabilistic samples to enable a richer understanding of specific processes underlying particular phenomena—with little concern for systematic representation of a broader population. (As is mentioned later, however, probability sampling can play a part in qualitative work.) In contrast to quantitative analytical approaches seeking to control for biases that may compromise comparisons and generalizations, qualitative analytical approaches often actually seek to capitalize on such bias to derive in-depth understanding rather than empirical generalizations. This difference in sampling approaches represents what I believe to be one of the most powerful contrasts between quantitative and qualitative research approaches. From my perspective, sampling plays a defining role in this distinction.

Probability Sampling in Quantitative Research

Quantitative research is often concerned with the description of characteristics of a large group and/or the identification of differences between groups. Probability theory provides a basis by which one can estimate the degree to which any given sample may be representative of a target population. This knowledge enables the use of inferential statistical procedures that form the backbone of quantitative analytical approaches.

For reasons of economy, efficiency, and accuracy, quantitative researchers rely on samples of cases to inform their knowledge about characteristics of the larger populations from which they are drawn. Consider, for example, polls of people's opinions about public higher education (e.g., Immerwahr, 2004), examinations of characteristics related to high school mobility behavior (e.g., Rumberger & Thomas, 2000), or assessments of differences in men's and women's performances in mathematics courses (e.g., Baxter, Shavelson, Herman, Brown, & Valadez, 1993). In each of these examples, we would rely on samples of much larger populations to provide data for inferences that would be made back to the larger populations from which they were drawn. Probability theory provides the means by which we can draw conclusions from a sample and—with a stated degree of confidence—assert that those conclusions apply to the broader population as well. Note again that this is a distinctly different purpose from that driving most research in the qualitative tradition.

Although probability theory provides a means by which we can generalize our findings from samples to larger populations (with an estimated degree of confidence), the details of probability and sampling theory are beyond the scope of this chapter and the interested reader is referred to some of the many fine texts available on those subjects (e.g., Cochran, 1977; Henry, 1990; Lohr, 1998; Ross, 2002; Salant & Dillman, 1994). If there is magic in inferential statistics, it can be found in the area of probability theory. But if that power is to be realized, it is necessary to understand the principles of probability sampling, a basic and required ingredient for the magic of generalization.

I find it impossible to talk usefully about sampling without firmly connecting this activity to underlying statistical realities. First and foremost, we use sample data to generate statistics that help us to gauge confidence in generalization, compare characteristics of groups, and/or develop predictions based on multiple characteristics of sample members. Statisticians and applied researchers alike are interested in techniques that yield unbiased estimates of characteristics of the larger population. Quantitative researchers use statistics calculated from sample data to estimate key parameters of the population, with two key estimators underlying inferential statistics being those of the population mean and population variance. Choice of sampling strategy, it turns out, can introduce important biases into these estimators, biases that have powerful consequences for decision making based on sample data. In the sections that follow, I introduce several different sampling strategies, from basic to complex. My interest is in conveying the conceptual elements of the sampling process and the several major sampling strategies I have found to be most useful. The interested reader is advised to consult other sources to better understand the statistical consequences of particular choices and the ways in which these consequences can be addressed meaningfully. My focus in these sections is on distinctions among the various options available to quantitative researchers. I emphasize that judicious choice among the many alternatives available is a necessary condition for exemplary research.

The Sampling Process

There are several distinct stages in the sampling process.

- *Population.* First, one needs to identify the population from which the sample is to be drawn. For example, perhaps one is interested in describing characteristics of public elementary school principals. In that case, public elementary school principals would be the population of interest.

• *Sampling Frame.* Second, from within that population, a sampling frame needs to be defined. A sampling frame is an identifiable and discrete set of population elements that is possible to measure. This is basically a list of the members (or some significant subset of members) of the population of interest. As such, the sampling frame represents the largest sample that can be drawn from the population. Following from the previous example, a sampling frame for the population of public elementary school principals might be obtained from the National Association of Elementary School Principals (NAESP). At a minimum, the NAESP might be able to provide one with a list of its membership. An alternative could be a list generated from the National Center for Education Statistics Common Core of Data.

• *Sample Selection.* Finally, from the sampling frame, one can then employ some strategy to extract the actual sample. If inferential statistical methods are part of the analysis plan, any of these strategies will be defined by some probabilistic element in the selection process.

The most widely known and commonly used of these strategies for selecting a probability sample from a sampling frame are outlined in the sections that follow. Although there are many such procedures and countless variations and extensions within each, I limit my focus to four of the major strategies. The first of these, simple random sampling, is offered only to provide a comparative base for understanding the virtues and vices of the other three: systematic, stratified, and cluster sampling. Recall that a primary goal of sampling methods in quantitative research is the specification of a representative sample. Each of the methods outlined in the following sections promotes this goal.

Simple Random Sampling

The logic of the simple random sample is perhaps the easiest to understand, but this sampling strategy is not widely used due to limiting inefficiencies. A simple random sample is a sample whose members are chosen randomly

from a population whose members all have the same probability of being selected into the sample. For example, assume a population of 1,000 high school students from which I intend to construct a sample of 100. The probability of any student being selected into the sample is roughly 100/1,000 or .10. (The term "roughly" is used here because the probabilities will change ever so slightly if one samples without replacing the names of those selected in the previous step. This becomes less of an issue as the sample proportion, .10 in this example, grows smaller.)

To select sample members from the sampling frame, I might first assign identification numbers to each member in the sampling frame. If there are 1,000 members in the frame, three-digit numbers will suffice (provided that 000 is used as an identifier). Using a random numbers table (available in most statistics texts), I could enter the table and extract 100 unique three-digit identifiers that would define the sample members to be selected. Although the use of a random numbers table is good to make the point, virtually any statistical or database software package will allow the user to randomly extract x of y cases in a data file. Voila!—a simple random sample is born.

The random part of simple random sampling is essential to ensure that the sample drawn is not systematically biased in favor of or against particular characteristics of specific sample members. For example, if 800 of the 1,000 students in the population have brown eyes, then chances are that about 80 of 100 sample members will have brown eyes. Random selection more often than not yields a sample whose members are more representative of the members of the population from which it was drawn. Note here that random selection (used when sampling) is distinct from random assignment. Random selection deals with how one selects a subset of elements from a larger population. Random selection concerns the external validity of a study (the ability to generalize its results). In contrast, random assignment deals with the way in which one divides a sample into different groups (most often in experimental designs). Random assignment, therefore, addresses the issue of a study's internal validity (the ability to infer causality). Random sampling is presented here exclusively in the context of random selection.

In short, the distinguishing characteristics of a simple random sample are that (a) a single comprehensive sampling frame exists (suggesting that all members of the population are known) and (b) sample members are randomly selected from that list for inclusion in the sample. Simple? Conceptually *yes* but practically *no.* Rarely is simple random sampling used in real-world social science research. Lists of large populations are relatively hard to locate, and accurate lists are even more difficult to locate. Accurate and numbered lists (to facilitate random selection) of relatively large populations are rare indeed. I have found that geographical realities also intervene. Consider the logistic and economic considerations of assembling a simple random sample of adult males in the United States. Assuming that a list existed, the inefficiencies of needing to travel hither and yon to reach sample members are significant.

Other considerations, such as interests in subgroups of a population, further erode the utility of the simple random sample as an ideal strategy for assembling a sample. If one were interested in the specific characteristics of left-handers relative to right-handers, a very large sample would need to be drawn to ensure inclusion of enough lefties for a statistically sound analysis and useful comparison. Consider our previous sample of 100 high school students. If the population proportion of lefties is .10, then through random selection one would expect about 10 sample members to be left-handed. The laws of probability and knowledge of inferential statistical principles suggest that generalizing from a sample of 100 is almost always a better bet than generalizing from a sample of 10.

Challenges to simple random sampling such as these encourage the use of alternative probability sampling strategies. One remedy sought through these alternatives would address the difficulty in working with large unnumbered sampling frames such as those from membership lists. Other remedies considered address potential interests in subpopulations. This latter class of remedies involves alternatives that include, in the sampling process, information about specific characteristics of the population or its subgroups. Characteristics of interest may include physical attributes, geographic location, or self-identification categories such as Democrat or Republican. Inclusion of such characteristics in the sampling process requires important modifications and restrictions to the random sampling strategy. These are considered in what follows.

Systematic Sampling

In contrast to randomly selecting each individual sample member from a list of population elements, systematic sampling relies on an initial random start on the selection and then moving down the list selecting elements at a particular interval (e.g., every 5th element after the random start). If, for example, one had a list of 1,000 high school students from which one wanted to draw a sample of 100, then one would randomly select a starting point within the sampling frame of 1,000 and take every 10th observation thereafter. Assume that the researcher used a random numbers table to draw the starting point and that turned out to be the 550th name on the list. Using a forward counting scheme, one would select into the sample the 560th, 570th, and 580th students on this list, and so on, until one had identified a sample of 100 (one would stop with the 540th student listed after circling back to the beginning of the list after selecting the 990th student). The researcher could have just as easily assumed a reverse counting scheme and achieved the same result.

Note that because both the size of the sampling frame and the size of the desired sample are known, it is easy to identify the interval that should be used to draw sample elements from the sampling frame (simply divide the sample frame number by the desired sample size). The resulting value, 10 in the previous sample above, is known as the sampling interval. Systematic samples greatly reduce the effort required for the manual extraction of a sample using a simple random sample strategy. Moreover, if the sampling frame is itself randomized before drawing a systematic sample, the results are virtually the same.

Although the relative merits of the systematic random sample strategy are widely recognized, one major pitfall exists. If the sampling frame used is ordered in such a way that patterns are found in the ordering, the resulting sample can be radically biased (something that probability samples are designed to avoid). This threat is called "periodicity." Consider a sampling frame of student residence hall occupants in a building where there are an equal number of rooms on each of the 20 floors. Clearly, there is a possibility that the sampling interval could coincide with room arrangements on each floor. This would be particularly problematic if rooms were laid out in the same way on each floor and might result in the researchers selecting only occupants residing in "triples" (rooms with three occupants) or "doubles." Or perhaps the period would coincide with the arrangement of rooms designed for students with physical impairments. The periodicity threat requires that the researcher carefully review the ordering of the sampling frame before employing a systematic sampling strategy. Remedying periodicity is relatively easy, and systematic sampling can provide a superior alternative to simple random sampling. Note, however, that neither the simple random sample strategy nor the systematic sample strategy helps one to ensure that elements with particular characteristics are included in the sample in numbers sufficient for subgroup analysis or comparisons (remember the lefties!).

Stratified Sampling

Simple random and systematic sampling strategies provide us with the ability to estimate the amount of error that exists in any given sample. This error is a function of the size of the sample and the variance in the population. Simply put, smaller samples from more heterogeneous populations are likely to be less representative of their parent populations than are larger samples from more homogeneous populations. The bodies of work defining sampling and probability theory provide us with this knowledge.

Stratified samples capitalize on these realities by dividing the population into more homogeneous subgroups before randomly selecting sample elements. If we hope to ensure the proper proportions of lefties, then we can split the population into lefties and righties and draw random samples within each group in line with the known population proportions of

roughly .10 and .90, respectively. So if we were constructing a sample of 100 students (from the earlier hypothetical population of 1,000), we would divide the sample into lefties and righties and then randomly sample 10 from the lefty population and 90 from the righty population. This would guarantee that the sample proportions were equal to the known population proportions, thereby reducing the sampling error on this variable to zero.

Without stratification, simple random samples are by chance likely to yield proportions approximating population values but not right on those values. If dexterity were an essential variable in the study, then we would benefit from controlling for it as exactly as possible through the sample. A threat to the effective use of stratified sampling is error in the classification of elements on grouping variables. Misclassification of cases can wipe out all of the advantages realized through stratification; therefore, great care should be given to the coding of data within the sampling frame itself.

Stratified Samples and Unequal Probabilities of Selection

To this point, selection has been based on each element having an equal probability of being selected into the sample. Simple random sampling and systematic sampling ensured this, and stratified samples employed random selection with equal probabilities of selection within each stratum (i.e., lefties and righties in the previous example), thereby yielding equal probability albeit through partial probabilities resulting from dividing the population prior to sampling. It is essential to recognize that whereas simple random sampling and systematic sampling are alternative strategies, stratified sampling is a modification of these approaches. Although important, the promise of stratified samples has been only partially fulfilled by ensuring equal proportions of key population subgroups. Its more complete promise is found through the relaxation of the equal probability of selection criterion—yet an additional modification.

Although stratified sampling can be used to ensure the presence of representative proportions of subgroup membership, it does nothing to ensure that there are adequate numbers of sample elements within any group to allow meaningful statistical analysis or comparisons. To accomplish that, one needs to sample proportionally smaller strata in ways that overrepresent the true population. This is called "oversampling." Suppose that one wished to understand differences between white freshmen and African American freshmen on a predominantly white university campus (e.g., 85% of freshmen are white). If the freshman class is composed of 1,000 students, 150 or fewer will be of African American descent (this number will be smaller assuming that other racial/ethnic groups are also represented in the freshman class). If one draws a random sample of 300 students, then fewer than 45 could be expected to be African American. A stratified sample could be devised to ensure proportionate representation but would still yield a relatively small number of African Americans in the sample for analysis (i.e., 45 or fewer).

To get around this problem, one might choose to oversample within the African American stratum. Rather than choosing a number corresponding to the population proportion of African Americans, one might opt to select a number that is twice the population proportion (i.e., a maximum of 90 in the latter example). Although this yields a larger number of members of a relatively small but important subgroup, it relaxes the assumption that each member of the population has an equal probability of being included in the sample. African Americans are twice as likely as non-African Americans to be chosen for inclusion in the sample. As such, any analysis of resulting data would be biased in favor of the characteristics of African American freshmen (they are considerably overrepresented in the sample). To address this bias, one must develop a set of statistical weights that readjust the sample back to its original proportions during the analysis. Weights alter the effective contribution of specific observations during the analysis. An easy way of understanding this is to view all samples as being weighted by 1. That is, each observation makes an equal contribution during the calculation of certain statistics such as means and variances. When sample elements are selected with disproportionate probability, the weight of 1 will need to be adjusted to deflate the

resulting overrepresentation of those sample members.

Regardless of choices about proportionate or disproportionate sampling within strata, the stratified sampling strategy affords the researcher the ability to generate estimates for particular subgroups defined by the strata. By reducing sampling error through the explicit stratification on known population values, this strategy can also yield more statistically efficient parameter estimates than could a simple random sampling strategy. Finally, the stratified sampling strategy allows for flexibility in data collection methods across strata. So long as the elements within each stratum are selected randomly (through simple random or systematic sample methods), data collection approaches can vary across strata defining the sample. This affords the researcher the ability, for example, to interview sample members in one stratum and to administer questionnaires to members in another stratum.

Challenges associated with stratified sampling often include problematic definitions of boundaries for strata and more complex statistical estimation procedures that are necessary to account for multiple partial probabilities of inclusion and, in the case where disproportionate sampling is used, the development of sample weights. So although these modifications of simple random sampling strategies allow for possible reduction in sampling error, they also have costs that should be carefully considered.

Cluster Sampling

There are, of course, many instances in which an adequate sampling frame simply does not exist. For example, how would one obtain a nationally representative sample of elementary school students? No nationally comprehensive register of elementary school students exists across states. Even within states, such lists would be difficult to obtain. Cluster sampling allows one to proceed even without a clear sampling frame at the desired unit of analysis (students in this case). Even if such a sampling frame were to exist, a simple random sample could potentially yield a sample in which no sampled student shared the same school with others in the sample. This, of course, would prove to be a logistic nightmare in terms of accessing students who would be widely distributed across schools in geographically distant locations and with widely varying policies relating to researcher–student contact.

The basic idea behind cluster sampling is that sample elements can be nested within higher-order units. In the sampling strategies I have introduced to this point, the population elements were viewed in what might be understood as a single sampling unit—the population. Often, population elements are naturally or artificially nested within other higher-order units such as households, families, neighborhoods, or schools. Although no comprehensive list of elementary school students exists, it is relatively easy to locate comprehensive lists of elementary schools. With such a list in hand, we can first randomly sample a group of elementary schools and then randomly sample from the cluster of students contained within each of the schools selected into the sample. In this example, clusters were sampled only once (i.e., schools). This type of sampling strategy is referred to as a single-stage cluster sample.

Now imagine a situation in which a research design called for interviews with ninth-grade students enrolled in public or private schools within a particular geographic region. Simple random sampling would require a comprehensive sampling frame (which does not exist) and would yield a sample necessitating our visiting a large number of schools to conduct the interviews (driving up the costs of the project and unnecessarily fatiguing our research team in a way that could result in less accuracy in data collection). Such challenges can be obviated through the use of a multistage cluster sampling strategy. Imagine multiple sampling units— schools nested within school districts nested within counties nested within states nested in the target region. One possibility with this structure would be to employ a two-stage cluster sample strategy in which districts are randomly sampled in a first stage and schools in a second stage.

With a little thought, one can also see how stratification could be employed within a cluster sampling framework. For example, we sometimes wish to ensure adequate representation of public and private schools. This would require the partitioning of schools within districts at the second stage of the cluster sampling process. The sample could also be stratified at the level of the student, for example, to capture specific proportions of students from particular racial backgrounds. Additional modifications could also be made to ensure that school size was factored into the selection process through an adjustment of school selection probabilities (i.e., disproportionate sampling) that corresponds to school size. Note that this latter modification would again require the specification of statistical weights to ensure the representativeness of the final sample.

Two primary advantages of cluster sampling strategies are (1) flexibility in sampling frames and (2) a reduction in the geographic dispersion of sample elements. With additional modifications, cluster sampling becomes a very powerful strategy for constructing probability samples. Consider that most large-scale secondary data sets used in education research employ some type of cluster sampling in data collection. The interested reader is encouraged to review the sampling strategies for data sets such as the National Educational Longitudinal Study of 1988, Baccalaureate and Beyond, and the National Study of Postsecondary Faculty (National Center for Education Statistics, n.d.).

Despite these attractions, cluster sampling presents important statistical vulnerabilities. Ron Heck (my colleague and a contributor to this section) and I have written an article outlining the importance of these threats and potential safeguards that should be employed in analyses using these sampling designs (Thomas & Heck, 2001). First, the precision of estimates using data collected through cluster sampling is in part dependent on the clusters selected at each stage. Although random selection at each stage encourages the heterogeneity of sample elements, this is not ensured. This reality becomes more important as the number of elements within each sampling unit decreases. In plain language, cluster samples—relative to simple random samples—are likely to yield greater variance in statistical estimators. This has important implications for hypothesis testing.

A second vulnerability of cluster sampling strategies results from the clustered nature of the lower stages (students in the example used here). If the clusters of students are internally homogeneous—that is, if students within schools are more similar than students across schools—then the estimates of overall variance on measures will be lower than would be the case if a simple random sampling strategy were used (Muthén & Satorra, 1995). Simple random sampling requires the researcher to assume that all observations are independent (i.e., individuals within similar subunits and schools share no common characteristics or perceptions). Consequently, as similarities among individuals within groups become more pronounced in the sample, estimates of variances and standard errors derived from such data become more biased (Muthén & Satorra, 1995).

Although we can readily attend to these vulnerabilities, it is incumbent on us as researchers to be aware of the advantages and threats inherent in particular sampling choices. In short, although probability sampling is the coin of the realm for selecting large representative samples in education research, not all probability samples are alike and each requires careful thought in terms of its implications for the overall study purposes and for estimators used to test hypotheses.

Nonprobability Sampling in Quantitative Research

There are, of course, many reasons why probability samples may prove to be an unrealistic or inappropriate option in certain situations. Research focused on obscure or deviant populations are one example. How would one develop a sampling frame for minors with substance abuse problems? Or what if the population of interest was college students with reading deficiencies? Hard-to-define, relatively unbounded, or socially marginalized populations often require the use of alternate, nonprobabilistic sampling strategies. Although the rationale for such choices may be sound (and more appropriate given the goals of the research), the use of nonprobabilistic sampling strategies prohibits the meaningful use of inferential statistical methods. Again, this is not always a bad compromise. It does nonetheless represent a set of trade-offs that need to be consciously evaluated and acknowledged by the researcher.

Several options are available to the researcher using nonprobability sampling methods, and I believe that some are more systematic and defensible than others. Perhaps the least systematic and defensible approach is the *convenience sample,* in which the researcher collects data from elements that are convenient to him or her at the time. The classic example here is the ubiquitous "students in my Psychology 101" sample. Neither random nor representative, little can be inferred from such a collective, and samples such as these would best be avoided at all costs.

Regardless of the rigor of the nonprobability sampling scheme, once one enters the realm of nonprobability sampling, the only valid use of quantitative methods is that describing the characteristics of those sampled. Any attempt to generalize is rendered invalid when probability samples are not employed. For this reason, the most effective use of nonprobability samples is seen in qualitative research settings. Revisiting the opening paragraphs of this chapter, such sampling choices provide perhaps the starkest contrast between principles of qualitative research and those of quantitative research. In the sections that follow, I expand on this theme and provide examples of some of the sampling strategies used more frequently in noninferential research.

Sampling in Qualitative Research

A primary goal of the quantitative analyst is to employ random sampling strategies that help to ensure the development of an unbiased sample, that is, one as maximally representative of the broader population as possible. This goal often discourages artificial heterogeneity in the sample. Qualitative researchers, on the other hand, have different goals and limitations driving the choice of sampling methods. Choice of sampling strategy is perhaps more critical to the qualitative researcher than to the quantitative analyst.

A hallmark of useful sampling strategies is that they are purposively chosen to accomplish specific goals related to the inquiry. In qualitative inquiry, the purposive nature of the choice is much more tightly bound to the framework or theory guiding the research effort. In neither qualitative nor quantitative work is mere convenience a sufficient purpose for assembling a sample. Many are quick to lump sampling methods into categories of probability and convenience. This represents a fundamentally incorrect understanding of the role of sampling in the larger research process. Whereas competent quantitative research relies on probability sampling, competent qualitative research is defined by purposive choices about what, when, and how to observe behaviors or characteristics of sample elements.

Whereas probability sampling strategies come in many different stripes, nonprobability strategies also take on a variety of forms—each with its own purpose and place in the qualitative research process. Maxwell (1996) identifies four possible sampling goals for qualitative researchers. Each of these goals suggests a particular sampling strategy and serves to discourage others. The first goal, similar to that motivating the quantitative analyst, is achieving representativeness of the population of interest (p. 72). Unlike the relatively large sample sizes used in probability sampling strategies, purposive sampling often incorporates choices that result in inclusion of the typical range of cases defining the population of interest. That the sample members are relatively typical of the population helps to obviate the concern that data collected are representative of deviant or outlying cases in the population. Whereas probability samples accomplish this through random selection, the qualitative researcher purposively chooses the elements to reflect the general characteristics of the population.

A second goal identified by Maxwell (1996) runs directly counter to this first one. Often, the qualitative researcher is inherently interested in the nontypical cases as much as in those cases viewed as typical of the population. This goal can be addressed by purposively devising a sample that captures the dimensions of variation that are presumed to be most important to the research problem at hand. Construction of such a sample ensures maximal heterogeneity rather than the typicality targeted with the first goal. If the first goal focuses on the typical, then the third goal identified by Maxwell embraces the extremes. Often, nonprobability samples are

constructed to ensure a focus on atypical extreme cases that might be presumed to best support (or challenge) theories guiding (or being developed through) the study. Focusing exclusively on the extremes can help the researcher to accomplish this goal. Multiple-case qualitative studies provide an opportunity to establish specific comparisons that might allow the researcher to test reasons for differences that exist within the broader population. Such comparisons constitute a fourth possible sampling goal for qualitative researchers (p. 74).

Whereas the first goal, typicality or representativeness, has an analog in probability sampling, the latter three serve to distinguish fundamental differences in purpose between qualitative and quantitative work. As was shown earlier in this chapter, there exists a multitude of probabilistic sampling strategies to accomplish specific aims relating to generalizability and inference. It should not be surprising, therefore, that a comparable range of strategies is available to the qualitative analyst relying on purposive techniques to assemble samples of cases.

Of 16 sampling strategies identified by Patton (2002, pp. 243–244), 14 fall under the general category of purposeful sampling. Although it could (and perhaps should) be argued that Patton greatly simplifies the range of choices available in the general category of random probability sampling, his identification of the wide range of purposive nonprobabilistic strategies is nonetheless impressive. I believe that Patton's listing enables an easy mapping of potential strategies to Maxwell's four goals. I see strategies such as typical case sampling, maximum variation sampling, and extreme case sampling as being directly related to Maxwell's identification of sampling goals motivating the qualitative researcher.

Note here also that although sampling strategies can be divided into probabilistic and nonprobabilistic approaches, there are instances in which probability samples are used within larger nonprobabilistic designs. For example, the qualitative researcher faced with the selection of sample elements from within a particular purposively chosen subgroup may opt for random selection rather than purposeful selection. Such a choice usually does not, however, enable one to correctly employ inferential statistical techniques. In most cases, the orientation of the larger research design would itself discourage such a temptation. Implicit in this observation is evidence of the epistemological friction often challenging mixed-methods approaches to inquiry in education.

Essential to the intelligent choice of a non-probabilistic sampling strategy in qualitative research is a clear mapping of sampling strategy to qualitative research goal. Because statistical inference is not a viable option (or a goal), the careful matching of strategy to purpose is critical in defining the value of the research design and eventual analysis. For example, although snowball sampling techniques—in which the researcher uses previously identified group members to identify additional members of the population—can serve to generate a sufficient number of cases for some types of analysis, the research design and goals may be served by using a method that is designed specifically to maximize heterogeneity within the sample.

There are myriad ways in which to develop a sample, with some being easier than others. What do the goals of the research suggest in terms of choosing cases for study? The best choice will not always be the easiest or most convenient for the researcher. Given the multiplicity of possible goals in the realm of qualitative inquiry, the choice of sampling strategy can be much more critical to the success of the research than are those options facing quantitative researchers.

CONCLUSION

From my perspective, altogether too frequently in education research, sampling strategy is viewed as simply a way in which to collect data. It is, as I hope this chapter has shown, much more than that. Sampling strategy should be an integral part of research design. As I asserted at the beginning, research design is fundamentally related to the types of questions being posed; furthermore, research questions are organically connected to the epistemological orientation of the researcher. This reality firmly tethers sampling choices to the presuppositions and foundational knowledge of the researcher. Another way of thinking about this is that although there are myriad choices of sampling strategy, the range of those choices is in fact quite limited when one considers restrictions inherent in the epistemological and theoretical orientations to the problem. Above all, in my ongoing relationship with sampling issues, I have learned that there is always a best choice of sampling strategy—a best choice that can set a research effort apart from others. Conducting research that may eventually be recognized as exemplary requires that this choice be deliberate and defensible based on the intellectual principles shaping the inquiry.

REFERENCES

Baxter, G., Shavelson, R. J., Herman, S. J., Brown, K. A., & Valadez, J. R. (1993). Mathematics performance assessment: Technical quality and diverse student impact. *Journal of Research in Mathematics Education, 24*, 190–216.

Cochran, W. (1977). *Sampling techniques* (3rd ed.). New York: John Wiley.

Henry, G. (1990). *Practical sampling.* Newbury Park, CA: Sage.

Immerwahr, J. (2004). *Public attitudes on higher education: A trend analysis, 1993 to 2003.* Washington, DC: National Center for Public Policy and Higher Education. Available: www .highereducation.org/ reports/pubatt

Lohr, S. (1998). *Sampling: Design and analysis.* Pacific Grove, CA: Duxbury.

Maxwell, J. (1996). *Qualitative research design: An interactive approach.* Thousand Oaks, CA: Sage.

Muthén, B. O., & Satorra, A. (1995). Complex sample data in structural equation modeling. In P. Marsden (Ed.), *Sociological methodology* (pp. 267–316). Washington, DC: American Sociological Association.

National Center for Education Statistics. (n.d.). [Surveys and program areas]. Available: http:// nces.ed.gov/surveys

Patton, M. (2002). *Qualitative research and evaluation methods* (3rd ed.). Thousand Oaks, CA: Sage.

Ross, S. (2002). *A first course in probability and statistics.* Englewood Cliffs, NJ: Prentice Hall.

Rumberger, R., & Thomas, S. (2000). The distribution of dropout and turnover rates among urban and suburban high schools. *Sociology of Education, 73,* 39–67.

Salant, P., & Dillman, A. (1994). *How to conduct your own survey.* New York: John Wiley.

Thomas, S. L., & Heck, R. H. (2001). Analysis of large-scale secondary data in higher education: Potential perils associated with complex sample designs. *Research in Higher Education, 42,* 517–540.

23

APPROACHING RIGOR IN APPLIED QUALITATIVE RESEARCH

J. DOUGLAS TOMA

University of Georgia

In quantitative research, standards related to validity, reliability, generalizability, and objectivity are well established. Recent federal policy has embraced these standards, establishing guidelines for funding research about education based on the application by researchers of "scientific" principles that guide inquiry in the basic sciences. The U.S. Department of Education now essentially mandates experimental approaches and quantitative methods. These are based on the assumptions that researchers can develop and apply perfect instruments in wholly objective ways, can generalize from samples to broader populations, and should focus on replication of earlier work. Many researchers working in qualitative traditions have responded in two ways. As an initial matter, they have reminded themselves (and, I hope, others) that their work rejects ideals such as perfection and objectivity—as well as fully discovering some truth and reality. To do so begs a second question: Is there a place for qualitative approaches within the "scientific" frame that is the basis of federal policy and continues to be so valued across academe?

I suggest here that researchers doing work within the qualitative tradition can, indeed, frame their efforts as sufficiently "scientific," even under the restrictive terms that the federal government has mandated (and that some others

have accepted without really thinking about them). The same logic applies to doctoral students convincing dissertation committee members unfamiliar with qualitative approaches that these are worthy as dissertation work, that is, rigorous. It also relates to the application of inappropriate standards to qualitative work by those editing and reviewing for scholarly journals. I do not suggest that qualitative researchers labor to shoehorn their work into the accepted quantitative standards—an all too common approach, regrettably. Perhaps in so doing, they can more readily win acceptance from those who cannot see beyond the scientific approach. But framing qualitative work this way essentially destroys its strength, as I argue in what follows. It makes no sense to use qualitative methods to attempt to craft and deliver perfect instruments, copy earlier approaches exactly, apply all of the findings and conclusions from one case to another, and approach research with a completely objective relationship between researcher and participant.

Instead, I suggest that qualitative researchers take responsibility for explaining how their approach has a rigor—one that equals the rigor of scientific work but that is necessarily dissimilar given the fundamental differences between the qualitative and quantitative traditions. Those working in the former need not explain

405

themselves; again, questions of rigor are settled here. Qualitative researchers need to do more— and always have done more. They have available a parallel set of standards that fits different assumptions and approaches related to qualitative traditions, particularly more applied work such as case studies. These are credibility, transferability, dependability, and confirmability, which map onto validity, reliability, generalizability, and objectivity in quantitative and experimental research. These provide a starting point, at least. I argue here that these standards will likely be only marginally satisfying for qualitative researchers, including those who work, as do I, with case studies, which is the qualitative approach most likely to be in accord with the quantitative tradition given its focus on application and audience interested in setting polices and improving decision making.

My own preference is to go further. I encourage qualitative researchers to use the unsettled nature of standards for assessing rigor in qualitative research to challenge their own thinking about rigor and how they express this in the context of their writing. Those researchers working in phenomenology and ethnography, in particular, can find these parallel standards to be a poor fit. Accordingly, new conceptions of and approaches to rigor have emerged. In what follows, I address these in the context of discussing the characteristics of more policy- and practice-focused qualitative research, such as the case study work to which I pay particular attention, relevant to exploring rigor in qualitative research. But I encourage readers to read further because I only introduce these areas— and they are much more complicated and interesting than I can portray here. I also encourage case study researchers to look not only to the "right" for standards of rigor (the parallel standards) but also to the "left" (the alternative approaches). I return to these alternative frameworks in the conclusion, where I suggest how qualitative researchers can embed these standards into research designs along with more traditional standards of trustworthiness.

In short, I recommend that qualitative researchers, particularly those with more applied ends in concentrating on policy and practice (the audience I address most directly here), develop

expansive definitions of and standards related to rigor. I encourage them to read broadly and go further, perhaps using parallel standards as a foundation. I ask them to embrace using alternative ideas to complicate parallel standards and to make them more applicable to what really matters in qualitative work. These alternative standards, such as authenticity (Lincoln & Guba, 2000) in particular but also interpretive validity (Altheide & Johnson, 1994) and transgressive validity (Lather, 1993; Richardson, 1997), focus on representing participants and facilitating change. They apply somewhat, but not always fully, to case study research and the other more applied qualitative work that is my main interest here. They are likely more applicable to less applied traditions such as ethnography and phenomenology. The same is true of more descriptive, impressionistic, confessional, or theoretical studies or action research.

It is up to the qualitative researcher who wants to make the most complete case possible for rigor to draw on the parallel and alternative approaches selectively, developing a set of standards related to rigor that make sense to him or her. Thus, I am suggesting a more individualistic approach to rigor in qualitative research. I am not offering a checklist or recipe—or, at least, not a very detailed one. And my approach is certainly not likely to be a very satisfying one to someone looking for a single source to answer the question: What is rigor? Instead, I am issuing an invitation to each qualitative researcher to develop his or her own approach.

Demonstrating rigor is essential in all traditions—qualitative and otherwise. But in qualitative work, it is far from clear what the standards are or should be. It is up to the individual researcher, I contend, to become familiar with various conceptions and approaches—and to apply those that resonate to his or her own beliefs and values, working out the conflicts and inconsistencies that are almost certain to arise with any set of decisions. I also remind researchers that, as in life, there are few if any absolutes in research; the best that one can do in qualitative research is to approach rigor. Qualitative researchers understand this given that the nature of qualitative work does not even encourage, much less allow, researchers to approach, much less achieve, absolutes.[1] As usual, the task for qualitative researchers is less clear-cut and thus more difficult, requiring them to be more reflective and tolerant of ambiguity. But in so doing, qualitative researchers can find particular satisfaction.

EXPLORING QUALITATIVE RESEARCH

To begin, it makes good sense to address first what qualitative research is and how it is different from quantitative and experimental work. In so doing, how these differences demand separate standards for rigor for qualitative approaches becomes clear.

Qualitative research is holistic, empirical, interpretive, and empathetic (Stake, 1995). It is *holistic* in its concern with process and context rather than simply outcomes or focusing on differences and comparisons, as in quantitative and experimental research. The qualitative researcher seeks an overview of a given context— its logic, arrangements, and rules (both explicit and implicit) (Miles & Huberman, 1994). Thus, qualitative research concentrates on "broad, panoramic views rather than micro-analyses. The more complex, interactive, and encompassing the narrative, the better the qualitative study" (Creswell, 2003, p. 182). The opposite is the object in quantitative and experimental work; the idea is to simplify so as to say with confidence why something is occurring. Qualitative research is more interested in questions of "how." This alone suggests that different standards related to rigor are appropriate for the two approaches.

Qualitative research is *empirical* because it occurs in natural settings, centering on work in the field. In case studies, the most applied tradition generally within qualitative research, the setting is the case, a social unit—a bounded complex system of information (Creswell, 1998). In qualitative work, the researcher serves as the primary instrument for data collection and data analysis (Miles & Huberman, 1994), which occur simultaneously and focus on observations by both researchers and informants. In quantitative and experimental work, there are set, orderly, and discrete steps with a clear divide between researchers and participants, both of whom are essentially interchangeable; the same results would occur no matter who conducted the study or who specifically was in the sample. Qualitative research is, by nature, descriptive and detailed, favoring natural language (Merriam, 1998; Stake, 1995). It is also inductive, building concepts and theories from details and encouraging researchers to explore rival structures and alternative explanations (Stake, 1995). In other words, data analysis in qualitative research constantly pushes and pulls at the conceptual framework used and the research questions posed, possibly suggesting the need for either to evolve in whole or in part (Creswell, 2003). Qualitative research is not about proving or falsifying hypotheses, so quantitative and experimental conceptions of reliability based on replication, which are inherently deductive, are likely to be inapplicable to qualitative work, which is inductive in nature.

Indeed, qualitative research is *interpretive,* focusing on gaining meaning and understanding and building concepts and theories. It does so through the intuition of the researcher, who works to become an insider (Miles & Huberman, 1994). Qualitative researchers gather detail through multiple, usually interactive methods, identifying and systematically reflecting on their role in the inquiry and acknowledging and accommodating personal biases, values, and interests (Creswell, 2003). Methods include interviews, observations, document reviews, and physical artifacts (Creswell, 2003; Yin, 1994). As such, qualitative research assumes that many interpretations are possible (Miles & Huberman, 1994) and invites the reader to make his or her own interpretations, assisting the reader through providing considerable detail (Stake, 1995). It is not about offering a particular explanation, as in quantitative work. Qualitative researchers can, but need not, hold objectivity to be a standard or an ideal; indeed, there is an inherent subjectivity in the researcher-as-instrument for collecting and analyzing data.

Qualitative work is, finally, *empathetic,* concentrating on the frames of reference and values of those involved through a planned design that evolves during the course of research (Stake, 1995). It should already be clear that standards based on absolutes—such as validity (perfect instruments) and objectivity (interchangeable researchers) in quantitative and experimental work—are inapplicable to qualitative research unless adjusted considerably to reflect its nature.

It is also important to note, briefly, that there are quite different traditions in qualitative research—each tradition quite different and each in need of its own standards related to rigor, I suggest. Creswell (1998) categorizes qualitative research into five traditions.[2] These traditions share some basic standards of quality and verification such as competence in data collection and analysis and making explicit the assumptions of the researcher. Each tradition also has its own standards or common standards that are particularly important within that tradition, as with the importance of triangulation of information and member checking in qualitative research generally.

Biography, the first of Creswell's (1998) five traditions, explores the life of an individual primarily through interviews and documents, focusing on stories, epiphanies, and historical content and drawing a detailed overall picture. *Phenomenology* centers on understanding the essence of experiences about a phenomenon through long interviews, concentrating on describing the essence and meanings of the experiences. *Grounded theory* attempts to generate categories through multiple interviews, building a theory or model. *Ethnography* works to describe and interpret the behavior of a cultural group through observations, interviews, and artifacts collected over an extended period.

Case studies, the fifth tradition, develop an in-depth analysis of a single case or of multiple cases, carefully bounded by time and place (Creswell, 1998). Researchers draw on multiple sources—documents, interviews, observations, artifacts, and the like—focusing sharply on context to describe the case, generate themes, and make assertions. Case studies may be either unique (intrinsic) or representative of a broad issue (instrumental) and can be selected based on purposeful sampling—choosing cases because they are interesting or convenient as opposed to drawing a random sample (Creswell, 1998; Gall, Borg, & Gall, 1996). Case study research does not usually involve a large number of cases, although multiple cases allow for cross-case analyses organized by themes and are thought to facilitate applying generalizing to other settings (Creswell, 1998).

Case studies are the preferred method for studying interventions or innovations. They typically do not address the needs of participants, as would participant research, but instead focus on those who set policy, according to Lancy (1993). Indeed, case studies are not infrequently done under contract, and the researcher generally addresses questions shaped in advance, is not always concerned with applying theory or generating knowledge, and often focuses on evaluation and generating recommendations for improved practice (Lancy, 1993). As such, case studies are, once again, perhaps the most applied of the approaches to qualitative research, particularly if application is focused on informing and improving policy.

So alternative standards of rigor related to empowering the participants of research may be less important in case study research than in other applications of qualitative work focused on here. This depends, of course, to what ends the researcher intends to use a given approach—and, I argue, standards of rigor need to change accordingly. Here is where I turn next, concentrating first on parallel standards of rigor and then on the alternative approaches that recognize these different ends researchers have for qualitative research. Again, I invite qualitative researchers generally—and those, like me, who work with case studies, more particularly—to consider both sets of standards, selecting from both what fits the approach they use and the ends they intend for their work.

APPROACHES TO ASSESSING QUALITATIVE RESEARCH

Lincoln and Guba (2000) note that what they call the goodness or quality criteria vary by inquiry paradigm.[3] Qualitative research and particular approaches, such as case studies, phenomenology, and grounded theory, are not paradigms but rather occur within particular paradigms. Both positivist inquiry and postpositivist inquiry are based on discovering a reality, differing in that postpositivists see the tools to do so as being imperfect, thereby introducing some degree of probability into findings. Both view findings in terms of truth, with postpositivists using truth as a standard and not an achievable end, again recognizing the inherent inability to measure with absolute confidence in the social sciences. Postpositivists also hold objectivity to be a standard and not an absolute, accepting a modification of the traditional positivist approach that creates an unqualified barrier between researchers and participants, thereby accommodating qualitative methods. Whereas positivists focus on verifying hypotheses through pure experimental methods—it would not matter if one researcher were substituted for another—postpositivists accept that pure dualism between researchers and participants is unlikely and adjust their methods accordingly (including experimental methods). In short, postpositivists focus on finding what is real and true to the extent that they can, attempting to do so as objectively as possible.

Those who work in the critical theory, constructivist, and participatory paradigms abandon objectivity, even as a regulatory standard, according to Lincoln and Guba (2000). They operate in a more transactional way, connecting directly with their participants—not discovering findings *from* them but rather negotiating *with* them to create findings. Critical theorists and constructivists differ most in their views of ontology. Critical theorists believe in a historical realism that both prompts and permeates their findings. For them, reality is shaped by social, political, cultural, economic, ethnic, and gender values. So, the historical situatedness of research is the appropriate criteria in that it takes account of these reality-shaping values (Guba & Lincoln, 1994). Constructivists focus more on how individuals construct their lives, arguing that reality is more relative and locally situated and constructed than a positivist would contend. Participatory paradigm research also has a more relativist reality—one that is experiential and grounded in practical knowledge—and creates findings subjectively, focusing on conducting research in democratic ways with findings that prompt collaborative practical action. Although case study research fits within these three paradigms, its grounding in application and basic concern with generating recommendations for improved practice may be more consistent with a postpositivist approach. I explore this notion more fully later.

Given the differences between and among these paradigms on questions of ontology, epistemology, and methodology, what Lincoln and Guba (2000) call goodness or quality criteria appropriate for each differ. Positivists and postpositivists use conventional benchmarks of rigor—validity, reliability, generalizability, and objectivity—adapting these when using qualitative approaches as needed (and as I discuss in detail in the next section). For those in the critical paradigm, what matters is how completely work is situated in history, how fully it erodes ignorance and misapprehensions related to that history, and how well it stimulates action toward social transformation, equality, and social justice. So quality here is not framed in terms of positivist-style rigor; rather, it is framed as action toward empowerment and emancipation—toward more equity and justice. Constructivists and participatory researchers also focus on action, but more in terms of inquiry being incomplete without the research prompting improvement. Validity for them might mean, according to Lincoln (1994), that a study is "sufficiently grounded, triangulated, based on naturalistic indicators, carefully fitted to theory (and its consequences), comprehensive in scope, credible in terms of member checks, logical, and truthful in terms of its reflection of the phenomenon in question" (p. 579).

Mason (2002) notes the challenges to established measures of quality as applied to qualitative research but does not believe that these are problematic in themselves provided that they are framed in qualitative terms. Validity, she suggests, is useful in qualitative research in that it suggests that the researcher is observing, identifying, or measuring what he or she purports. The focus here is on the quality of the methods used, not on how a research strategy is a valid way in which to pursue a set of research questions. The same is true of generalizability—the ability to make some form of wider claim based on a study—and reliability when framed as the accuracy of qualitative methods and techniques. Mason contends that qualitative researchers must, at least, satisfy themselves that they have not misrepresented data and have not been careless in recording and analyzing data. This standard would seem to apply across qualitative approaches.

Those working in constructivist paradigms, in particular, tend to split on the question of whether to apply traditional conceptions of rigor, with "radical reconfigurations of validity [proposed that] leave researchers with multiple, sometimes conflicting, mandates for what constitutes rigorous research" (Lincoln & Guba, 2000, p. 178). The former group of constructivists frames goodness or quality criteria as trustworthiness and authenticity. The latter group concentrates on interpretation. I suggest that the former applies to case study research on improving policy and practice quite well—and that at least the logic of the latter also does.

Approaches based on trustworthiness and authenticity do not dismiss validity, instead recasting it in more relativist terms and highlighting rigor in the application of method—not simply its conception—as in quantitative approaches. Findings must relate to some reality (authenticity) and to how others construct their world (trustworthiness) such that a reader would be confident in acting on the conclusions, implications, and recommendations they yield. These constructivists have generated distinct authenticity criteria. First, *fairness* is including and balancing the perspectives and voices of those studied. Second, *ontological and educational authenticity* is a raised awareness by participants in the research and those who surround them within an organization. Third, *catalytic authenticity and tactical authenticity* encourage action among participants in the research and involvement of the researcher in training others to act (Lincoln & Guba, 2000). In other words, Lincoln and Guba (2000) recommend that emerging approaches to qualitative research focus on building relations with participants, taking stances, and enabling and promoting justice—and that work should be judged accordingly.

Another group of constructivists has developed alternative constructions of rigor, framing research in terms of interpretation: Can the constructions that researchers and informants create together be trusted? These theorists put less emphasis on traditional scientific criteria—those on which the concept of trustworthiness is built—and more emphasis on practical wisdom and moral discourse. Indeed, qualitative methods and alternative paradigms emerged in the social sciences because of skepticism related to the objectivity at the foundation of scientific practices, particularly in its exclusion of individual experiences (Gergen & Gergen, 2000). Janesick (2000) concludes, "I think it is time to question that trinity [of validity, generalizability, and reliability] and the use of psychometric language, and in fact to replace that language with language that more accurately captures the complexity and texture of qualitative research" (p. 393). Unlike Lincoln and Guba (2000), with their trustworthiness and authenticity approach, these approaches abandon trustworthiness and extend or rework the notion of authenticity.

Still, there is no one alternative construction of rigor. Some of these constructivists argue for a transgressive validity that encourages research that is disruptive of the status quo, encouraging transformation by participants (Lather, 1993; Richardson, 1997). Such approaches introduce axiology—the branch of philosophy addressing ethics, aesthetics, and religion—into the rigor discussion (Lincoln & Guba, 2000). Denzin (1994) suggests that these new approaches, in rejecting conventional measures of rigor, take a more local, personal, and political turn. Thus, interpretation is more important than causation. Accordingly, in making a case for what they term "interpretive validity," Altheide and Johnson (1994) suggest: (a) substituting the concepts of usefulness—enlightening those who read the report—for objectivity; (b) underscoring conceptual completeness, including drawing on multiple voices and tacit knowledge; (c) considering researcher positioning, that is, how the researcher is aware of his or her relationship to the situation being studied; and (d) developing a writing style that achieves verisimilitude, telling a story so richly that the reader can feel it. Once again, I suggest that some of these alternative approaches extend, to some degree, to case study research.

Denzin and Lincoln (1994) group these positions on what constitutes rigor in qualitative research into four categories. The first is *positivism,* the same categories used in quantitative research—validity, reliability, generalizability, and objectivity. *Postpositivism,* the second category, argues for a set of criteria unique to qualitative research. Here, there is agreement about the need for different standards that are appropriate for quantitative research, but there is less accord about what these standards should be. Thus, traditional concepts such as validity are acceptable, but only if they are reframed to fit qualitative research (Gall et al., 1996). Constructivists frame these distinct standards as trustworthiness and authenticity, whereas critical theorists focus on action, praxis, and historical situatedness. The third category is *postmodernism,* which contends that no criteria are appropriate for assessing qualitative research. The fourth category, *poststructuralism,* argues for an entirely new set of criteria divorced from positivism and postpositivism, one stressing subjectivity, emotionality, feeling, and the like.

I agree with Creswell's (1998) recommendation that qualitative researchers draw from across these categories, as appropriate, when working in a particular tradition in qualitative research. Creswell uses the term "verification" instead of "validity" to describe the extensive time in the field, thick description, and closeness to participants that are hallmarks of qualitative research—and its great strength. He adopts the concepts of trustworthiness and authenticity. I suggest that the former clearly applies to applied qualitative research, such as case studies, and that the latter does as well depending on how applied the work is. For instance, when work is intended for external audiences of policymakers, as much case study research is, it may be less important to raise awareness (ontological and educational authenticity) and encourage action (catalytic authenticity and tactical authenticity). The standard of fairness in authenticity (including and balancing voices) should apply to case study work generally, and the same is true of using sound procedure when working in any tradition, as Creswell recommends. Creswell also advocates drawing on postmodern approaches, such as those proposed by Lather, when doing qualitative work in a postmodern tradition.

In addition to advancing trustworthiness and authenticity as goodness or quality criteria, Lincoln (1994) recommends that standards of the inquiry community, as in evaluating articles for publication, are important. Zaruba, Toma, and Stark (1996) suggest that peer reviewers deem good qualitative research as being (a) thorough in both execution and presentation, (b) informed about both methods and topic,

(c) well written and well organized, (d) balanced and inclusive, (e) useful, and (f) educative on both substance and method.

Creswell (1998) and Lincoln (1994) have the right idea, I suggest, drawing what is useful from various approaches to ensuring rigor in qualitative research. In applied qualitative research, trustworthiness fits, as do some of the more interpretive standards. I explore these standards later, focusing on the four elements of trustworthiness. Once again, case study research is typically, but not always, more applied in nature than are the other four traditions— biography, phenomenology, grounded theory, and ethnography—and case study research is less focused on interpretation as an end in itself (like biography, phenomenology, and ethnography) or on generating theory (like grounded theory). Although each tradition focuses on providing detail and context, case study research uses these to make assertions related to specific research questions. These assertions may relate to improving a given setting—say, an organization—but are also commonly directed toward outsiders, including those who make policy. (It is unlikely that case study work will focus on being disruptive of the status quo, as those who propose a transgressive validity recommend.) Thus, given its nature and ends, fitting case study research and other, more applied applications of qualitative approaches into the postpositivist trustworthiness framework may be less problematic, particularly when one can select aspects of the authenticity and interpretive approaches such as fairness.

Once again, I encourage qualitative researchers to go further when it makes sense for them to do so, integrating alternative constructions of rigor into their individual decisions about the standards to which they will hold themselves. Different approaches and different ends require different standards from those working with qualitative methods. Those qualitative researchers interested in not only offering recommendations but also raising awareness and encouraging action among those they study are likely going to look to alternative approaches to rigor. And it is incumbent on all qualitative researchers, even those working in ways and toward ends most in line with the quantitative and experimental traditions, to understand various approaches to rigor, choosing among them as makes sense. Because trustworthiness and authenticity (the parallel standards plus attention to balancing perspectives of, raising awareness in, and encouraging action among participants) will satisfy much of what most applied qualitative researchers require, I focus here on encouraging them to read further about other approaches to rigor that intrigue them based on what they want out of their work.

APPROACHING TRUSTWORTHINESS IN APPLIED QUALITATIVE RESEARCH

Establishing validity, reliability, generalizability, and objectivity in quantitative research is relatively straightforward. In the simplest terms, findings are *internally valid* when the researcher can draw meaningful inferences from instruments that measure what they intend to measure. Threats to internal validity are aspects of procedures, treatments, or experiments that would cause the researcher to draw incorrect inferences from the data. For instance, an instrument might change during an experiment, members of the control group and the experiment group might talk with one another, or participants might mature during an experiment and change their views (Creswell, 2003). Poor construct validity—using inadequate definitions or measures of variables—might cause problems here (Creswell, 2003). Yin (1993) suggests that because most instruments are less accurate than desired, using multiple measures of the same construct is desirable. In qualitative research, using multiple data sources—the concept of triangulation—is routine practice given the inherent imprecision of data-gathering tools such as interviews.[4]

Findings are *reliable* when various researchers using the same approach would find the same result. In both qualitative and quantitative research, establishing protocols and recording the steps followed enhance reliability (Yin, 1993). Findings are *externally valid*—or generalizable—when they extend to certain individuals and settings beyond those immediately studied. Threats here arise when researchers draw incorrect inferences from the sample to people, settings, or situations not sufficiently related to

the sample such as a different racial, ethnic, or socioeconomic group (Creswell, 2003).[5] Findings are *objective* when the influence of the researcher in collecting, analyzing, and reporting data is negated—or, in qualitative terms, is understood, reported, and (when appropriate in much applied qualitative work) managed.

In qualitative work, these standards are broadly termed "trustworthiness," as noted previously. Lincoln and Guba (1985) suggest that qualitative researchers establish the trustworthiness of their findings by demonstrating that they are (a) credible, (b) transferable, (c) dependable, and (d) confirmable. These notions are parallel to internal validity, external validity, reliability, and objectivity, respectively, in quantitative work but are applicable only when reworked to fit qualitative inquiry (Marshall & Rossman, 1999).[6] As Miles and Huberman (1994) write, "We need methods that are credible, dependable, and replicable in *qualitative* terms" (p. 2, emphasis in original).

Once again, even though there are parallels between the two, the criteria for rigor in qualitative research differ from those for rigor in experimental and positivist research (Creswell, 2003; Marshall & Rossman, 1999). Simply following a set of methods does not guarantee validity in qualitative terms as it might in early conceptions of positivism, although later postpositivist views appreciate validity as more of a goal than a product (Maxwell, 1996). Maxwell (1996) observes, "Instead, it depends on the relationship of your conclusions to the real world, and there are no methods that can assure you that you have adequately grasped those aspects of the world that you are studying" (p. 86). Stake (1995) accepts "consequential validity" as the standard in qualitative case study research (and other applied qualitative work)—the consequences of applying the conclusions, interpretations, and recommendations of the work. Thus, the case study researcher has a responsibility to minimize misrepresentation and misunderstanding, including through triangulating data sources and then presenting a "substantial body of uncontestable description" (p. 110). Such description represents what others would have noticed and recorded if they had been on-site. It affords the reader the depth needed to come to an alternative interpretation (Stake, 1995).

Even with these adjustments to make standards applicable to qualitative research and appropriate for it, they still parallel validity (both internal and external) and reliability in quantitative research. Indeed, assuring the reader of adherence to such standards is critical for qualitative research to be deemed convincing—answering the question of "Why should we believe it?" in persuasive ways (Maxwell, 1996). This answer is essential in applied qualitative research given that it so often is directed toward making recommendations. One explanation of the logic of using alternative terms to describe what is essentially a positivist framework is that doing so encourages the acceptance of qualitative research in a quantitative world (Creswell, 1998). I see the utility in this argument and am not against using alternative terms, although I do not find the use of alternative terms by themselves to be satisfying. There are still arguments that quantitative language is not congruent with qualitative work. However, reframing concepts such as internal validity as credibility, external validity as transferability, reliability as dependability, and objectivity as confirmability can serve the applied qualitative researcher well. And linking trustworthiness, as appropriate, with emerging thinking that extends concepts such as validity only makes qualitative standards of rigor more robust.

It is up to qualitative researchers to determine whether these resonate with what they are attempting to do and how they are trying to do it—and whether the parallel standards (trustworthiness and authenticity) that I now explore one by one are alone sufficient or whether other standards provide a useful supplement. It is also possible and acceptable, of course, that qualitative researchers, even those interested in application, cast aside these parallel standards in favor of another approach to rigor. They need only explain their logic and approach clearly, which is always the responsibility of qualitative researchers given that standards of rigor are unsettled. Returning to the beginning of the chapter, doing so well may be sufficient to satisfy the restrictive reading of rigor that has emerged in federal policy. If nothing else, it is the only chance that qualitative researchers have. I am disappointed when qualitative researchers attempt to wedge their work into the quantitative and experimental frame. It makes more sense, perhaps building from it, to find a set of standards appropriate not only to qualitative research but also to what the researchers are interested in doing with it.

CREDIBILITY

As with all qualitative research, the credibility of a qualitative case study "depends on the degree to which it rings true to natives and colleagues in the field" (Fetterman, 1989, p. 21). Credibility is established if participants agree with the constructions and interpretations of the researcher, that is, that the description of the case is accurate based on the understanding of those studied. In other words, the case is credible when what the researcher presents describes the reality of the participants who informed the research in ways that resonate with them. Reporting processes and interactions within the boundaries of the cases with sufficient depth to really highlight their complexity satisfies the credibility standard (Marshall & Rossman, 1999). The key notions here, of course, are carefully bounding the case and explaining it as richly as possible.

Reliability (dependability) and generalizability (external validity) have limited applicability in qualitative inquiry according to Creswell (2003), but credibility (internal validity) is the strength of qualitative work. Whether responses are consistent or stable (reliability) or whether they apply to new settings (generalizability) is a secondary issue in most quantitative work. This is not to say that reliability and generalizability are inapplicable. At the analysis stage, for instance, multiple members of a research team may work independently generating categories and then comparing the outcomes against each other. Or case studies may have aspects of generalizability, relating in rather direct ways to similar settings or situations.

Credibility is far more central in qualitative inquiry. Qualitative researchers validate their findings throughout the various steps of the research process, and conveying these steps is central in ensuring the accuracy of findings (to the extent possible) and thus their credibility (Creswell, 2003).[7] The goal here is, once again, to suggest "whether the findings are accurate from the standpoint of the researcher, the participant, or the accounts of the reader" (pp. 195–196). Miles and Huberman (1994) frame credibility in qualitative research in terms of the researcher-as-instrument: As "essentially a person—more or less fallibly—is observing, interviewing, and recording, while modifying the observation, interviewing, and recording devices from one field trip to the next," the researcher himself or herself is what determines credibility (p. 38). Miles and Huberman suggest that markers of a good qualitative researcher-as-instrument include familiarity with the phenomenon and setting under study, strong conceptual interests, a multidisciplinary approach, and good "investigative" skills (e.g., doggedness, the ability to draw people out).

Miles and Huberman (1994) define credibility as "truth value"—whether the findings make sense to those studying and to those who read the study. In other words, is what is depicted authentic—what happened, what it means to people, how various concepts might explain it, and an evaluation of it (Maxwell, 1996; Miles & Huberman, 1994)? Credibility is qualitative research, according to Miles and Huberman (1994), and is the product of (a) a comprehensive and context-rich account that is sensible, convincing, and plausible for the reader, creating a "vicarious presence" for him or her; (b) converging conclusions from the triangulation of complementary methods and data sources; (c) a coherent set of findings linked with theory, either prior or emerging; (d) identification of areas of uncertainty, negative evidence, and rival explanations; (e) conclusions that are considered as accurate by participants in the research; and (f) the accuracy of predictions, if any, made in the study.[8]

Creswell (2003) suggests eight strategies that qualitative researchers can use to ensure and demonstrate the accuracy and authenticity of their work, that is, its credibility. (He also outlines these in his 1998 book.) The most straightforward of these is to triangulate data sources, for example, drawing on documentary evidence and observations in addition to interviews. Member checking—asking participants to check how their own comments have been interpreted—is also commonly used to advance credibility (Gall et al., 1996; Morse, 1994; Stake, 1995). Member checking may take the form of debriefing sessions with interviewees immediately following interviews to test the initial understanding by the researchers of the data gathered. Another aspect of member checking is through later contact with key research participants to test the evolving analytical categories generated by the researchers—and even to check emerging interpretations and conclusions. Creswell (2003) also suggests that researchers enhance credibility through conveying findings through rich thick description, clarifying the bias that researchers bring to the work, and presenting negative or discrepant information that runs counter to themes generated. More complicated approaches include spending prolonged time in the field, using a peer debriefer to ask questions about the accuracy of the account and how those other than the researchers will understand it, and using an outside auditor to examine the process and results of the project.

TRANSFERABILITY

A case study, like other applied qualitative work, must be useful in illuminating another context if it is to be deemed transferable; it should be applicable to another setting or group. In case study research especially, the case (or cases) explored needs to be useful to others in similar situations—those with similar research questions or problems of practice (Marshall & Rossman, 1999). Lancy (1993) compares generalizability to the concept of legal precedent, where the applicability of a particular precedent case is argued between the sides in a lawsuit, with the court making the final decision. Similarly, the reader determines the transferability of a case study, as with any applied qualitative approach.[9]

Although there are limitations to transferability, Marshall and Rossman (1999) argue, findings can still relate to other cases and contexts. This is especially important in case study research, where researchers use the lessons of one case to make recommendations that can apply to others. Good qualitative work tends to be "tied into 'the big picture,'" with the researcher looking "holistically at the setting to understand linkages among systems and . . . [tracing] the historical context to understand how institutions and roles have evolved" (p. 197). Accordingly, Lincoln and Guba (1985) suggest that the only way in which to establish transferability is to create a "thick description of the sending context so that someone in a potential receiving context may assess the similarity between them and . . . the study" (p. 126). Only through thick description can a case study or applied qualitative work generally inform theory and practice.[10]

As noted previously, although generalizability (transferability) has a place in qualitative research, it is less important than internal validity (credibility). It is also, as Marshall and Rossman (1999) contend, the grounds on which qualitative research is most often criticized. Thus, they rightly underscore the importance of using a theoretical framework to organize data collection and demonstrating "how data collection and analysis will be guided by concepts and models" (p. 193). Stating the theoretical parameters of the research and thus connecting it with a body of theory allows those who make policy or design research to determine whether the findings of a case study are applicable whether they are transferable. Similarly, Marshall and Rossman argue that qualitative researchers should articulate in specific terms when they relate their work to previous studies (whether or not they share a similar theory).

Marshall and Rossman (1999) also identify triangulation of data sources as contributing to transferability: "Designing a study in which multiple cases, multiple informants, or more than one data-gathering method are used can greatly strengthen the study's usefulness for other settings" (p. 194; see also Gall et al., 1996). Stake (1995) agrees, suggesting that in addition to triangulating data sources and methods, it is helpful to use multiple researchers (investigator triangulation), particularly if they represent different theoretical perspectives. However, Mason (2002) critiques triangulation, suggesting that it assumes a single knowable reality and that all researchers need to do is come up with enough triangulation points to measure it.

Miles and Huberman (1994) discuss transferability in terms of whether a set of conclusions

has any larger import. They note that qualitative studies can be connected based on similar settings or shared theories. Accordingly, it is necessary to include (a) a complete description of the setting, including its boundaries, to facilitate comparisons; (b) an explanation of how the cases selected might be transferable to similar settings and across common theoretical frameworks (and a discussion of what might limit relating the case to other situations); (c) sufficiently "thick" description of the findings such that the reader can assess the transferability of the case and the case resonates with him or her; (d) findings that are congruent with, connected to, or confirmatory of prior theory; (e) a description of processes and outcomes if the conclusions are generic enough to apply to other settings; and (f) a statement of how the findings could be explored further and whether similar cases have yielded similar results. Miles and Huberman add that the degree to which others can apply the conclusions, implications, and recommendations of a study is also a measure of its validity (broadly defined) as well as its transferability. In other words, does the research cause its "users," including those studied, to make better decisions by being better informed? Is the study accessible, does it offer usable knowledge, does it prompt change, and so on?

Gall and colleagues (1996) suggest that the responsibility for generalizing findings lies not with the researcher but rather with the reader, who must apply the report to his or her own circumstances. The researcher, of course, aids the reader by providing thick description, signaling in the discussion to where the case might be applicable, and conducting a cross-case analysis in multiple-case studies. Transferability is enhanced when the researcher reports the study "in a manner accessible to other researchers, practitioners, and policymakers," making an "adequate translation of findings so that others will be able to use them" (Marshall & Rossman, 1999, p. 197). This logic even extends to something akin to replication. Marshall and Rossman (1999) suggest that "the burden of demonstrating the applicability of one set of findings to another context rests more with the researcher who would make the transfer than with the original researcher" (p. 193). In other words, the researcher needs to describe the case in sufficient terms—that is, detailed enough—for a later researcher to ascertain whether the case is similar enough to be relevant.

DEPENDABILITY

In qualitative research, dependability involves accommodating changes in the environment studied and in the research design itself. This occurs as the understanding of the researcher becomes more refined over the course of data collection (and even during analysis, which occurs, in part, concurrently with collection). An evolving research design, in particular, is a departure from the idea of reliability in the quantitative tradition. For qualitative researchers, there is not an unchanging universe where pure replication is possible and desirable. Instead, as Marshall and Rossman (1999) note, in qualitative research "the social world is always being constructed and . . . the concept of replication is itself problematic" (p. 194). Indeed, research questions in qualitative research, although posed at the outset (particularly in case study work), tend to evolve in response to emerging data, with the researcher perhaps reshaping or eliminating preliminary questions and adding others.

Nevertheless, researchers must report results, preferably doing so with reference to possible changes over time. Findings must go beyond a snapshot; if the study were conducted again with the same participants in the same context, there should be similar results (Marshall & Rossman, 1999). In qualitative inquiry, this often means collecting data over time. Still, qualitative research purposely does not control the conditions of research so as to advance its replicability, as Marshall and Rossman (1999) suggest:

> Qualitative research does not claim to be replicable. The researcher purposefully avoids controlling the research conditions and concentrates on recording the complexity of situational contexts and interrelations as they occur naturally. The researcher's goal of discovering this complexity by altering research strategies within a flexible research design, moreover, cannot be replicated by future researchers, nor should it be attempted. (p. 195)

One might contend that no social science research can be replicated because situations inevitably change. But probably the more persuasive argument for qualitative researchers is that careful recording of what they changed in the research design and why they changed it not only allows future researchers to inspect their procedures, protocols, and decisions but also enables them to reanalyze the data (Marshall & Rossman, 1999).

Even though qualitative designs evolve, Miles and Huberman (1994) define dependability as "whether the process of the study is consistent, reasonably stable over time and across researchers and methods" (p. 278). They argue that several elements contribute to dependability: (a) a study design congruent with clear research questions; (b) an explicit explanation of the status and roles of the researcher within the site; (c) findings showing meaningful parallelism across data sources; (d) specifying basic theoretical constructs and analytical frameworks; (e) collecting data across a full range of settings, respondents, periods, and the like; (f) parallel approaches among researchers on a given team in collecting and analyzing data;[11] and (g) the presence of peer or colleague review. Related to points (d) and (e), Morse (1994) adds the selection of information according to the theoretical needs of the study (appropriateness) and amount of data collected (adequacy), respectively, as measures of rigor related to dependability.[12]

Accordingly, Marshall and Rossman (1999) suggest that the explanation of the design and methods should include a rationale for qualitative research generally and a discussion of the particular genre of the qualitative tradition in which the researcher is working. They also contend that the trustworthiness of qualitative research is advanced by a full description of the research design, the details of which I explore in the next section. The description should include discussion of, among other things, (a) researcher self-reflection toward articulating biases; (b) concrete strategies for confronting bias in collecting and analyzing data; (c) steps for addressing ethical concerns in qualitative research; and (d) commitment to challenging one's own interpretations, including a search for alternative explanations and negative instances.

Maxwell (1996) describes the failure to attend to the latter as one of three major threats (along with failures in description and interpretation) to what he calls validity. The challenge here is not to eliminate the values and expectations that a researcher brings to a study, as with the objective approach in the positivist tradition, but rather to appreciate and discuss how these influence the conduct and conclusions of the study (Mason, 2002). Maxwell (1996) also deems reactivity—that is, the influence of the researcher on the setting or individuals studied—as a threat to validity. He suggests that the researcher continually searching for evidence that challenges his or her conclusions is the best hedge against these threats. Instead of holding these threats constant in some manner, as with a quantitative approach, the research can (a) build lists of alternative plausible explanations or interpretations that can be ruled out; (b) identify and analyze discrepant data and negative cases; (c) triangulate data collection, drawing on a diverse range of individuals and settings using a variety of methods; (d) solicit feedback from those familiar and unfamiliar with the case, including the participants in the research through member checking; (e) provide rich data and some simple statistical evidence; and (f) compare cases (which is not to say that control groups or comparative studies are necessary in qualitative research as they are in quantitative approaches).

CONFIRMABILITY

Confirmability is the concept that the data can be confirmed by someone other than the researcher. It is akin to objectivity within the quantitative tradition, but it is different. Objectivity here does require that another researcher can confirm findings, but it is not the researcher who is objective; rather, it is the findings themselves. Drawing on Lincoln and Guba (1985), Marshall and Rossman (1999) note that findings should reflect the participants and inquiry itself and not a "fabrication" from the "biases and prejudices" of the researcher (p. 192). They identify the line between bias and the subjectivity inherent in qualitative research that is embedded in the relationship between the

researcher and participants needed to delve deeply into a participant or case. Some subjectivity is inherent in qualitative research; the researcher will shape the research. Nevertheless, if done well, qualitative inquiry enables the researcher to enter the world of the participants in the research, providing deep understanding of complex social systems (Marshall & Rossman, 1999).

Miles and Huberman (1994) frame confirmability as "relative neutrality and reasonable freedom from unacknowledged researcher biases—at the minimum, explicitness about the inevitable biases that exist" (p. 278). In other words, findings and conclusions depend on the participants more than on the inquirer. Miles and Huberman suggest, in essence, that confirmability depends on the researcher's (a) being clear in demonstrating through an audit trail how he or she framed the study and collected and analyzed data; (b) being aware of his or her own assumptions, values, and biases as they influenced the study; and (c) considering rival conclusions fully. Techniques in doing the latter include considering outliers by comparing them with more mainstream examples, matching patterns by considering conclusions in terms of predictions from theory, making long-term observations, and making a representativeness check by considering whether interpretations relied too heavily on elite or convenient informants (Gall et al., 1996).

Once again, results are greatly diminished if there is bias in interpretation. Marshall and Rossman (1999) offer several strategies for reducing such bias, again drawing on Lincoln and Guba (1985): (a) having a "devil's advocate" to critically question one's interpretations, (b) developing systems to search for negative instances and alternative instances, (c) developing a second set of "judgment-free" notes before developing categories, (d) citing writing on bias in qualitative research, and (e) conducting an audit of data collection and analysis strategies. Indeed, the principal means of establishing confirmability in a study, as with dependability, is through an audit. To ensure confirmability (and dependability), Lincoln and Guba (1985) recommend creating an audit trail—one that would allow an external auditor to examine both the processes and products of the study. An audit trail might include (a) raw data, including tapes, interview notes, and documents; (b) products of data reduction and analysis, including field notes, interview and document summary forms, and case analysis forms; (c) products of data reconstruction and synthesis, including category descriptions and case reports; and (d) process notes, including notes on methodological decisions and trustworthiness criteria (Gall et al., 1996; Lincoln & Guba, 1985; Morse, 1994).

Morse (1994) suggests that a form of member checking, using multiple investigators on a research team, is another measure of rigor in qualitative research. All investigators can, for instance, code the various transcripts to see whether they come up with the same categories and can negotiate to reconcile any differences. Maxwell (1996) identifies member checking as a restraint on the possibility of the researcher's imposing his or her own meaning on data rather than understanding the perspectives of those studied and the meanings they attach to their words and actions—a threat to validity.

DESIGNING RIGOROUS APPLIED QUALITATIVE RESEARCH

In my own research, I have not used each approach discussed heretofore for every project, tailoring these checks on credibility to the given project. I have used just about all of these approaches at one time or another and have found satisfaction in doing so. Having some assurance that one's findings and conclusions are perceived by those most closely involved in a case as a fair representation of what is going on there addresses a regular concern among qualitative researchers.

Applied qualitative research is effective only, at a minimum, if the researcher understands rigor, if the work is anchored in trustworthiness, and if the researcher integrates mechanisms to ensure that credibility, transferability, dependability, and confirmability are incorporated. Incorporating elements of various extensions and alternatives to trustworthiness into a research design, as they fit, only enhances rigor. Or one can adopt—and make sure to explain— the whole one of these alternative approaches to underscore the rigor in his or her work. What

really matters is that qualitative researchers must adhere to some appropriate set of standards in conducting their work. Qualitative work is increasingly prominent in social science research, but it continues to be an alternative paradigm. Thus, qualitative researchers need to describe the standards of rigor applicable to their work, lest they risk having standards appropriate for the quantitative tradition but unsuitable for qualitative inquiry. Only through a clear set of statements outlining what good qualitative work is—and what it is not—can researchers protect against inapplicable questions and criticism.

One needs to raise the following general issues in a qualitative study design. I frame these in terms of proposing a study, as in a dissertation proposal, but they are equally applicable in the past tense, as in describing a completed study.[13] Within the discussion of the issues, I embed the four trustworthiness standards and aspects of authenticity and interpretive validity that are generally applicable to applied qualitative research. Doing so is more logical than trying to work the categories, which parallel the steps in conducting any qualitative study, into the four trustworthiness categories. Accordingly, the subsequent discussion follows the process of qualitative research, not the standards that should measure its rigor. It also reinforces the need to underscore rigor issues when proposing or describing applied qualitative research. These should be ingrained into every step in the process.

SIGNIFICANCE, RESEARCH QUESTIONS, AND CONCEPTUAL FRAMEWORK

In introducing his or her topic and research questions, the researcher has likely spoken to their significance in improving policy or practice, both in terms of the specific case (or cases) studied and in terms of other settings and situations more generally. This gets to the trustworthiness standard of transferability—whether a case is illuminating in another context. It also underscores usefulness, which Altheide and Johnson (1994) include in their interpretive validity framework. The same is true of defining research questions clearly. These matter in the determination the reader will make about whether the case (or cases) discussed applies to other situations. Once again, these research questions may evolve during the course of a qualitative study, and discussing this is part of ensuring the dependability of the study, which is one of the measures of trustworthiness. Finally, qualitative research is typically grounded in larger phenomena and theoretical constructs; theory and previous research inform a qualitative study. The researcher needs to include what conceptual frameworks he or she is using in generating research questions and organizing data collection (Marshall & Rossman, 1999).

ASSUMPTIONS, APPROACH, AND STANDARDS

In qualitative research, the basic assumptions of the researcher on questions about the nature of research itself are not a given. So it is important for the researcher to address his or her foundational assumptions about what can come to be known (ontology) and how we can come to know it (epistemology). In quantitative research in the social sciences, these is largely settled; postpositivists believe that there are some reality and some truth that we can discover (albeit incompletely) and that we should approach research with objectivity as a standard (albeit imperfectly). Qualitative researchers can hold these same basic assumptions. If they do not, however, then failing to report them to the reader risks having an inapplicable set of standards applied to their work; a critique of the research proposal might inappropriately challenge a lack of objectivity. Even for those working in the postpositivist tradition (again, researchers working in different inquiry paradigms can use qualitative research), outlining basic assumptions will avoid the possibility of a constructivist's applying the wrong set of standards.

It is also important to discuss what qualitative research is and how (and perhaps why) it is different from quantitative and experimental approaches. The researcher also needs to include a discussion about why using a qualitative approach is a good way in which to study the questions at hand as well as what might be the disadvantages of this approach. Marshall and Rossman (1999) suggest that working

outside of the "received view"—the traditions in quantitative social science research—means that including a statement relating to the potential value of qualitative research is imperative. Here, one might suggest how qualitative research is a reaction to assumptions about, say, epistemology associated with the quantitative research—that researchers should be objective.[14] One might also suggest the link between qualitative research and specific types of research topics or research settings such as how it is particularly well suited for studying organizational behavior. Once more, qualitative approaches are grounded in different assumptions and should be judged by different standards. It is incumbent on the researcher to clarify these for the reader, addressing the utility and challenges associated with applied qualitative work as well as the unique measures of soundness appropriate for it. In essence, the qualitative researcher needs to make a case for the qualitative approach. Doing so will eliminate or reduce potential criticism of the approach from those grounded in other traditions—questions such as "How can one generalize from $n = 1$?"

Furthermore, the research design should outline and briefly illustrate the standards of rigor being applied, perhaps using the trustworthiness approach (credibility, transferability, dependability, and confirmability) or perhaps adding authenticity standards, taking an alternative approach, or adopting some aspects of various approaches.

SETTING AND SOURCES

A full description of the setting or settings being studied, including why the researcher selected the case (or cases) he or she did, is critical in making a case for transferability in qualitative research. Purposeful sampling is appropriate in qualitative research—choosing cases because they are interesting, convenient, representative, and so on instead of drawing a sample from a population. Because there is no sample, the researcher needs to ask whether the reader has enough information to understand the context of the study in terms of how it might apply elsewhere. (It is also good to ask whether the description includes only what is relevant.)

Given that the reader needs context to determine transferability (or usefulness in interpretive validity) to other cases, a detailed description is necessary; the reader cannot simply assume that a sample is applicable to the rest of the population as in quantitative research. The researcher should also briefly explain what purposeful sampling is and why it is appropriate in qualitative research, thereby avoiding an inapplicable critique related to sampling.

For the applied qualitative researcher doing interviews, an account of what types of people the researcher is intending to interview and why these are worthwhile people to interview is important in assessing the confirmability of a study. It is necessary in case someone were to check the data later. The decision of what people to interview is somewhat like purposeful sampling; there is no formula for doing it. Instead, the researcher finds those people who are interesting, accessible, representative, and the like.[15] Research designs should also include a short account of how the researcher is going to find these people. Will the researcher use key informants (insiders who can provide knowledge of the setting and perhaps even access to it), a snowball approach (asking each person contacted to name others who might be informative), himself or herself as a key informant, or some combination of these? It is also important to include whether the researcher might have any trouble in getting access to these people—and, if so, how he or she intends to overcome this. The same is true of discussing any concerns related to establishing rapport, gaining trust, understanding the language and culture of the interviewees, and so on. Finally, because the qualitative researcher determines when to stop interviewing when he or she has exhausted available sources or is not hearing anything new (or what he or she is learning is of only marginal importance), it is important to include a discussion of this in the research proposal. These latter points, in particular, relate to the dependability of a qualitative study—how well it accommodates changes in the environment study and thus in the research design.

The applied qualitative researcher typically triangulates his or her data collection through supplementing interviews with focus groups, document review, observation, and the like.

Thus, the researcher should include discussion of the availability of not only people to interview but also his or her access to relevant documents. As with interviewing, this is important for establishing the confirmability of the case. The researcher should also reference why triangulation is so important in qualitative research—that other data sources can uncover material that clarifies interviews or even contradicts them. Telling a complete story enhances the credibility of a case, increasing the likelihood that it will "ring true" to those in the field. Also, because data uncovered through interviews and other sources is often unexpected—perhaps to the point of causing the researcher to adapt his or her research questions and research design—triangulation relates to dependability (the ability to accommodate changes).

Data collection raises not only the issue of what the researcher is looking at but also the issue of who the researcher is. The researcher needs to address the possible relationships between himself or herself and participants in the research such as the people being interviewed. This provides a good opportunity to note how the researcher is addressing objectivity and bias—and how this can differ from the norm in quantitative approaches. It also prompts a discussion of any ethical issues that might arise in the course of conducting the study.

COLLECTION, RECORDING, AND ANALYSIS

An applied qualitative research design, whether a case study or otherwise, should also include an account of what general types of questions the researcher is going to ask the people he or she is interviewing. The researcher need not be as specific as he or she might be in an interview protocol but should at least list the general themes of the questions. In fact, not including a protocol underscores how flexibility in design is an important part of a qualitative study—that qualitative designs, while posing research questions and grounded in theory, typically evolve as the data collection unfolds. Once again, this provides context to the reader, deepening his or her understanding of the larger research questions, thereby enhancing the credibility and transferability of the study. It is also important in confirmability, of course. In addition, as noted previously, the researcher should address how he or she is using a conceptual framework to organize the categories of questions he or she is asking.

Furthermore, the researcher should reference whether he or she is using focus groups or other variants on interviewing and what type of approach he or she is taking. Approaches range from more open-ended approaches, where the researcher tends to "change on the fly," to more closed-form, carefully scripted ones.[16] The former approaches underscore the dependability of a case study or some other applied qualitative report—how well it accommodates changes. Finally, pilot-testing is important in generating questions and approaches to questioning and can contribute to the credibility of the study given that good inputs (questions) tend to produce good outputs (answers).

Confirmability in a case study depends on the exercise of care in recording data, whether through notes, audio recording and transcription, or memoranda to the file (both analytical and methodological); these allow someone to reconstruct the data from which a researcher generates findings and draws conclusions, discusses implications, and makes recommendations. In applied qualitative research, the collection, recording, and analysis of data can—and should—be simultaneous. While collecting and recording data, the researcher tests ideas and even potential conclusions. The researcher also considers and records his or her own position—his or her relationship to the situation being studied, which is an aspect of dependability in trustworthiness (and also is central to the alternative interpretive validity framework discussed here). The researcher should also suggest how he or she will store the data, including how he or she will secure the data, as is necessary if maintaining confidentiality is part of the research design.

It is also important, in demonstrating confirmability, that the researcher discuss how he or she will analyze his or her data. The essence of analysis in applied qualitative research done inductively is to compare data with other data to see whether they are in different categories and then to compare categories with each other and with other instances. The goal here is to ensure

that the derived categories are internally consistent (internal convergence) but distinct from one another (external divergence) (Marshall & Rossman, 1999). A typical inductive analytic procedure (or analytic framework) is to (a) organize the data; (b) generate categories, themes, and patterns; (c) code the data;[17] (d) test the emergent understandings; (e) search for alternative explanations; and (f) write the report (Marshall & Rossman, 1999). According to Merriam (1998), doing this while collecting data causes the researcher to make sense of categories early, improve the questions asked, narrow the study (reminding himself or herself to focus on what is most interesting), cut down on volume, and fill in the gaps. (It is also possible to prefigure categories working deductively.) And there is a parallel between data collection through changing on the fly and data analysis; categories will change, just as questions change as the research unfolds.

An account of one's position as researcher is essential, addressing questions such as whether he or she is an insider or outsider, experienced or inexperienced in the area he or she is exploring, more objective or more biased, and so on. This matters particularly in a qualitative study given that objectivity is not presumed as it is in, say, a clinical setting or in a traditional quantitative study in the social sciences. Once again, qualitative research, including that in applied applications, is simply different from work in the quantitative tradition. Qualitative approaches require a particular set of standards related to rigor and need the researcher to make a case to the reader to ensure their application. My purpose has been to outline these standards as relevant to applied qualitative research, some of the issues they raise, and how they might be integrated into research designs.

NOTES

1. I would say the same about quantitative and experimental traditions, but a critique of whether work there can really be completely valid, reliable, generalizable, and objective is beyond where I wish to go here.

2. Marshall and Rossman (1999) add ethnomethodology, historical social science, participant inquiry, and clinical research to the list.

3. The reader may also refer to Guba and Lincoln (1994) for an earlier and more streamlined discussion of these issues that includes a more detailed discussion of the ontological, epistemological, and methodological bases of the paradigms.

4. Yin (1993) divides standards into four categories: construct validity, internal validity, external validity, and reliability. I embed his construct validity into the internal validity category. Yin defines internal validity as relevant only to explanatory or causal studies, not to descriptive or exploratory ones, in terms of causation—certain conditions leading to other conditions.

5. Creswell (2003) notes that validity concerns include drawing inaccurate inferences from data due to inadequate statistical power or the violation of statistical assumptions.

6. Marshall and Rossman (1999) remind us that alternative strategies for judging the soundness of qualitative research continue to emerge.

7. Yin (1993) connects tests of construct validity, internal validity, external validity, and reliability with particular techniques used at various stages in the research process. For construct validity, for instance, these techniques might include triangulation, chains of evidence, and member checking.

8. Maxwell (1996) offers an approach more grounded in the quantitative and experimental traditions. Credibility, which he terms "validity," involves ruling out rival hypotheses that are threats to validity. Quantitative researchers design, in advance, controls that will deal with validity threats, both anticipated and unanticipated, through means such as control groups, random sampling, hypotheses, and tests of statistical significance. Qualitative researchers rule out these threats during the research using evidence collected to make these alternative hypotheses implausible. Indeed, qualitative researchers verify credibility throughout the steps in the research process, not just at the beginning and the end (Creswell, 2003).

9. Maxwell (1996) divides transferability, which he terms "generalizability," into internal and external, with the former relating to conclusions relative to the case itself and the latter relating to settings beyond the case. Internal generalizability, he argues, is more important in qualitative research. But that is not to say that external generalizability is impossible. Even if multiple cases are not formally sampled from a given population, they may still relate to one another if, as Maxwell suggests, (a) no obvious reason not to believe the results applies more generally (face validity), (b) the theory used may extend to other cases,

and (c) the cases simply are similar in terms of dynamics and constraints involved.

10. Thick description is, one could reasonably argue, necessary to reach the ontological and educational authenticity (raising awareness of participants in the research and of those who surround them within an organization) and the catalytic authenticity and tactical authenticity (encouraging action among participants in the research and involvement of the researcher in training others to act) that Lincoln and Guba (2000) propose as extended standards of rigor.

11. Creswell (2003) notes that researchers can frame reliability in essentially quantitative terms of stability or consistency of responses in checking for consistent patterns of theme development among several investigators on a research team.

12. Maxwell (1996) identifies inaccuracy or incompleteness in the data collected as a threat to validity of the description of a case.

13. For a more complete discussion of research design in applied qualitative inquiry, the reader can refer to any of the standards texts in the area, including Creswell (2003), Marshall and Rossman (1999), and Merriam (1998).

14. Of course, case study research has been critiqued, including by critical and postmodern scholars, as not sufficiently recognizing conflict and oppression. It does not acknowledge that research is fundamentally about issues of power, reports are never neutral, certain "truths" are excluded from traditional knowledge production, and knowledge should lead to radical change or emancipation, including through action by the researcher, and so on.

15. It is acceptable in applied qualitative research to acknowledge "do-ability" concerns, such as access and expense, given that few researchers have unlimited budgets and time.

16. More particularly, this range of approaches includes, from open to closed, (a) having questions emerge from immediate context and be asked in the natural course of events (informal conversational); (b) selecting topics in advance but deciding sequence and phrasing during the interview, thereby encouraging comprehensiveness through probing (interview guide); (c) asking the same open-ended questions in the same order but with different follow-up questions to probe more deeply (standard open-ended); and (d) asking closed-form (yes or no) questions with no follow-up questions.

17. Coding provides a shorthand to categorize data while reviewing transcripts and retrieving data. It

involves sorting bits of information into groups that have something in common by looking for regularities (Merriam, 1998).

REFERENCES

Altheide, D. L., & Johnson, J. M. (1994). Criteria for assessing interpretive validity in qualitative research. In N. K. Denzin & Y. S. Lincoln (Eds.), *Handbook of qualitative research* (pp. 485–499). Thousand Oaks, CA: Sage.

Creswell, J. W. (1998). *Qualitative inquiry and research design: Choosing among five traditions.* Thousand Oaks, CA: Sage.

Creswell, J. W. (2003). *Research design: Qualitative, quantitative, and mixed methods approaches* (2nd ed.). Thousand Oaks, CA: Sage.

Denzin, N. K. (1994). The art and politics of interpretation. In N. K. Denzin & Y. S. Lincoln (Eds.), *Handbook of qualitative research* (pp. 500–515). Thousand Oaks, CA: Sage.

Denzin, N. K., & Lincoln, Y. S. (Eds.). (1994). *Handbook of qualitative research.* Thousand Oaks, CA: Sage.

Fetterman, D. M. (1989). *Ethnography: Step by step.* Newbury Park, CA: Sage.

Gall, M. D., Borg, W. R., & Gall, J. P. (1996). *Educational research* (6th ed.). White Plains, NY: Longman.

Gergen, M. M., & Gergen, K. J. (2000). Qualitative inquiry: Tensions and transformations. In N. K. Denzin & Y. S. Lincoln (Eds.), *Handbook of qualitative research* (2nd ed., pp. 1025–1046). Thousand Oaks, CA: Sage.

Guba, E. G., & Lincoln, Y. S. (1994). Competing paradigms in qualitative research. In N. K. Denzin & Y. S. Lincoln (Eds.), *Handbook of qualitative research* (pp. 105–117). Thousand Oaks, CA: Sage.

Janesick, V. J. (2000). The choreography of qualitative research design: Minuets, improvisations, and crystallization. In N. K. Denzin & Y. S. Lincoln (Eds.), *Handbook of qualitative research* (2nd ed., pp. 379–399). Thousand Oaks, CA: Sage.

Lancy, D. F. (1993). *Qualitative research in education: An introduction to the major traditions.* White Plains, NY: Longman.

Lather, P. (1993). Fertile obsession: Validity after poststructuralism. *Sociological Quarterly, 34,* 673–693.

Lincoln, Y. S. (1994). The fifth moment. In N. K. Denzin & Y. S. Lincoln (Eds.), *Handbook of qualitative research* (pp. 575–586). Thousand Oaks, CA: Sage.

Lincoln, Y. S., & Guba, E. G. (1985). *Naturalistic inquiry.* Beverly Hills, Park, CA: Sage.

Lincoln, Y. S., & Guba, E. G. (2000). Paradigmatic controversies, contradictions, and emerging confluences. In N. K. Denzin & Y. S. Lincoln (Eds.), *Handbook of qualitative research* (2nd ed., pp. 163–188). Thousand Oaks, CA: Sage.

Marshall, C., & Rossman, G. B. (1999). *Designing qualitative research* (3rd ed.). Thousand Oaks, CA: Sage.

Mason, J. (2002). *Qualitative researching* (2nd ed.). Thousand Oaks, CA: Sage.

Maxwell, J. A. (1996). *Qualitative research design: An interpretive approach.* Thousand Oaks, CA: Sage.

Merriam, S. B. (1998). *Qualitative research and case study applications in education.* Thousand Oaks, CA: Sage.

Miles, M. B., & Huberman, A. M. (1994). *Qualitative data analysis: An expanded sourcebook* (2nd ed.). Thousand Oaks, CA: Sage.

Morse, J. M. (1994). Designing funded qualitative research. In N. K. Denzin & Y. S. Lincoln (Eds.), *Handbook of qualitative research* (pp. 220–235). Thousand Oaks, CA: Sage.

Richardson, L. (1997). *Fields of play: Constructing an academic life.* New Brunswick, NJ: Rutgers University Press.

Stake, R. E. (1995). *The art of case study research.* Thousand Oaks, CA: Sage.

Yin, R. K. (1993). *Applications of case study research.* Newbury Park, CA: Sage.

Yin, R. K. (1994). *Case study research: Design and methods* (2nd ed.). Thousand Oaks, CA: Sage.

Zaruba, K. E., Toma, J. D., & Stark, J. S. (1996). Criteria used for qualitative research in the refereeing process. *Review of Higher Education, 19,* 435–460.

Section Five

Challenges in Conducting Inquiry

INTRODUCTORY ESSAY

KING D BEACH, III

Florida State University

BETSY JANE BECKER

Florida State University

The chapters in Section Five deal with four challenges in conducting inquiry that are central to the processes of conducting first-rate research but are generally overlooked in scholarly discourse about methodology: the development of the researcher as inquirer, moving from data sources to data and the forms of inference involved, bringing "analytic thoughtfulness" to analyses, and moving from findings to conclusions.

Anchored in one of the animating purposes of this volume—namely, to move beyond the seemingly endless debates about the relative merits of quantitative and qualitative research—we early decided to invite chapters that deal with both methodological traditions in ways that integrate the two but that do not reduce the analytic richness of their distinctions. Our desire to take this on is perhaps also a delayed reaction to the academic eyebrows that were raised in response to our relationship when the second author (Betsy Becker), a statistical methodologist and an expert in meta-analysis, and the first author (King Beach), a cultural psychologist trained in both traditions but better known for his qualitative work, first began dating.

We strongly believe that there should not be such a divide as appears to exist from the wrangling in the literature (e.g., Cizek, 1995; Howe, 1988) and in the politics of the day (Whitehurst, 2002). We argue (as do others, e.g., Pallas, 2001; Salomon, 1991) that this divide is counterproductive. The two methodological traditions—qualitative and quantitative—have different histories, different conceptual baggage, and different institutional reifications, and they are positioned differently in the current political climate. Little of this should have anything to do with how and why we make methodological decisions in educational research. We set out to find authors who held some version of this view and would address this issue explicitly in their writings, that is, would be sure that qualitative and quantitative methodological issues were interwoven in their respective chapters.

A part of the way in which we tried to accomplish our goal was to be sure that each chapter had authors who were scholars with expertise in both quantitative and qualitative research. To this end (and also because we believe that good collaborations produce a synergy that individuals cannot achieve), we wanted each chapter to be co-authored, and we invited people to collaborate on each one. Some of our collaborators had worked together and been co-authors before (Anna Neumann and Aaron Pallas, Betsy Becker and Mary Kennedy). Others did not know each other before this project began (Kadriye Ercikan and Wolff-Michael Roth) or had not collaborated in print (Michael Seltzer and Mike Rose). As we said when we invited our authors to join the project, this was "an unusual invitation" because we proposed collaborations between researchers whose interests and talents we found to be complementary, but many of whom had not written together prior to our invitation. To our delight, all of the collaborations worked well, and additional team efforts beyond the work presented here are already under way. We describe each chapter next, with a brief introduction to its authors and an overview of the topics they address in their work.

In Chapter 24, Anna Neumann and Aaron Pallas discuss the development of researchers. Neumann and Pallas are former colleagues of ours at Michigan State University, and we knew that they shared our interest in the graduate training of future researchers. We also knew that they had an ongoing and broader scholarly interest in how researchers are trained and in how individuals develop as researchers and scholars during graduate study and over the course of their work lives (e.g., Neumann, Pallas, & Peterson, 1999; Pallas, 2001).

In their chapter, Neumann and Pallas take a scholarly look at the social and psychological "tasks" involved in becoming a researcher. They focus first on the learning that is required of new researchers—learning about the substantive material or content of the educational matters they wish to study as well as learning *how* to study those matters through the study of research methods. Neumann and Pallas then move to a level once removed from the study of research—to the consideration of how novice researchers become practitioners of educational research, particularly through communities of practice in the sense developed by Wenger (1998). They write about how researchers are inducted into research communities as well as how researchers may need to access resources external to their multiple communities of practice.

Through the lens of theories of professional socialization, Neumann and Pallas consider the roles of those who influence the developing researcher. Lastly, they look at the role of cultural capital in the development of the researcher. Neumann and Pallas do not present a "how to" guide on becoming a researcher, but many of their observations suggest ways in which novice researchers can further their understanding of their own research identities both in and apart from research communities. Moreover, the treatment of cultural capital in their chapter may suggest ways in which researchers can navigate more successfully the academic contexts in which they work.

In Chapter 25, Kadriye Ercikan and Wolff-Michael Roth have collaborated to write about constructing data. We proposed this collaboration because of the proximity of the universities where these two scholars reside (both are located in British Columbia, with Ercikan residing in Vancouver and Roth residing in Victoria) and because we knew that both authors were widely read, thoughtful, and open-minded about research methods.

In their chapter, Ercikan, a measurement expert, and Roth, a science education researcher, examine how one moves from data sources to data, and then plans for analyses of those data, in two different sorts of research: high-inference research and low-inference research. After first arguing that all phenomena involve both quantitative and qualitative elements, Ercikan and Roth define high-inference research to be research with the goal of generalization beyond the immediate research context. In low-inference research, they argue, claims are not meant to be extended beyond the sample or situation being studied. The authors use two examples to illustrate the concerns in constructing data in these two types of research.

The problem of whether the results of tests given as part of Canada's national assessment system (the School Achievement Indicators Program) are equivalent when given in English and French is used as a high-inference example. Ercikan and Roth argue that inferences are to be made for students across Canada but are based on studies of the measurement instruments done with much smaller samples. The example of low-inference research in their chapter was set in a science classroom where Roth and his colleagues were studying science learning. A wide variety of data collection activities were used, including videotaping, ethnographic observations, and interviews.

For each example, Ercikan and Roth show how both quantitative and qualitative data were developed from their data sources, in accordance with the key questions to be asked but in a dynamic way. As some questions were answered and new questions emerged, new data were drawn from the data sources in ways that pursued the issues of interest. The authors close their chapter by reviewing similarities and differences between high- and low-inference research.

The subsequent chapter was written by two colleagues from the program in methodology for social research at the University of California, Los Angeles. In Chapter 26, Michael Seltzer and Mike Rose examine ways in which researchers can bring to bear "analytic thoughtfulness" in their work and, in so doing, help to bridge perceived divides between quantitative and qualitative traditions. Seltzer and Rose recount how over several years they have read and discussed each other's work, probing into the issues behind very different types of analysis. On the "quantitative side," Seltzer has used hierarchical linear modeling to study the effects of schools and schooling as well as individual growth and development. Rose, on the other hand, has focused on educational issues via the use of observational studies, historical inquiry, and other, more qualitative research methods.

The interplay of ideas in the discussions Seltzer and Rose have shared, along with the experience of teaching together, has led them to propose a series of strategies for thinking analytically that may be brought to bear in many research domains. The authors begin by emphasizing the role of context in quantitative analysis, including "the need to consider the setting, the time, the events, and the social forces that affect, or even constitute, a given body of data." They provide examples of research where context is critical—turn taking in classroom conversations—for a qualitative illustration, and they provide a quantitative example in the evaluation of the effects of the University of Chicago School Mathematics Project Transition Mathematics curriculum on geometry readiness.

Next, Seltzer and Rose encourage the researcher to be skeptical of results, to pose rival hypotheses, and to seek disconfirming cases. In so doing, they examine Campbell and Stanley's (1963) threats to validity and take a close look at a study of a crackdown on speeding that took place in Connecticut during the 1950s. Although this example does not seem at all related to educational research, it provides an array of alternative explanations of a drop in fatal accidents that challenge the simple explanation that the traffic crackdown was effective. A second analysis, of a program for bilingual education, provides a more familiar educational example with other interesting alternative possibilities to consider. The authors close their chapter with a rationale for, and a sampling of, ways of "getting close to" the data. They bring in the idea of the data having a "story" that is to be told and unfolded through careful and thoughtful data analysis, whether quantitative or qualitative. It is unusual to hear the word "story" used in connection with *quantitative* analysis; so often we hear students talk about how they want to use *qualitative* methods to tell a story. But Seltzer and Rose convince us that this is a useful device for delving more deeply into analyses—at least more deeply than is typical in many quantitative analyses. Finally, Seltzer and Rose encourage researchers to find strong collaborators whose strengths are different from their own. If this chapter is any indication of the possible fruits of such collaborations, we are convinced that such collaborations are a good idea.

The final chapter in the section concerns conclusions. In Chapter 27, King Beach, Betsy Becker, and Mary Kennedy examine the analytic moves that are made in going from findings to conclusions. Their chapter begins with an examination of what books on educational research methods and guidelines from the literature say about the content of conclusions and how to draw them. Surprisingly, little has been written on this important topic, although some consensus exists that conclusions should summarize the findings of the research, the strengths and weaknesses of the design, and the generalizations that can be drawn. Beach and colleagues then move to the influences that researchers bring to bear when drawing conclusions; the roles of prior knowledge and beliefs in interpreting findings are considered, as is the role of scientific reasoning. Other research literatures show that even when very simple reasoning tasks are involved, prior knowledge and beliefs can lead to questionable judgments. Beach and colleagues argue, however, that if researchers can reflectively use their prior beliefs and knowledge to challenge their findings, then they will be more likely to move toward the generation of new ideas and a better understanding of their own results. Finally, in considering threats to strong conclusions, the authors examine and critique conclusion sections from several published research articles in the area of teacher qualifications to delve deeply into potential flaws (and strengths) of their conclusions.

REFERENCES

Campbell, D. T., & Stanley, J. (1963). Experimental and quasi-experimental designs for research on teaching. In N. L. Gage (Ed.), *The handbook of research on teaching* (pp. 171–246). Chicago: Rand McNally.

Cizek, G. (1995). Crunchy granola and the hegemony of the narrative. *Educational Researcher, 24*(2), 26–28.

Howe, K. (1988). Against the quantitative–qualitative incompatibility thesis. *Educational Researcher, 17*(8), 10–16.

Neumann, A., Pallas, A. M., & Peterson, P. L. (1999). Preparing education practitioners to practice education research. In E. C. Lagemann & L. S. Shulman (Eds.), *Issues in education research: Problems and possibilities* (Commission for Improving Educational Research, National Academy of Education, pp. 247–288). San Francisco: Jossey-Bass.

Pallas, A. M. (2001). Preparing education doctoral students for epistemological diversity. *Educational Researcher, 30*(5), 6–11.

Salomon, G. (1991). Transcending the quantitative–qualitative debate: The analytic and systemic approaches to educational research. *Educational Researcher, 20*(6), 10–18.

Wenger, E. (1998). *Communities of practice: Learning, meaning, and identity.* New York: Cambridge University Press.

Whitehurst, G. J. (2002). *Statement of Grover J. Whitehurst, Assistant Secretary for Research and Improvement, before the Senate Committee on Health, Education, Labor, and Pensions.* Washington, DC: U.S. Department of Education. Retrieved April 3, 2005, from www.ed.gov/news/speeches/2002/06/06252002.html

24

WINDOWS OF POSSIBILITY

Perspectives on the Construction of Educational Researchers

ANNA NEUMANN

Teachers College, Columbia University

AARON M. PALLAS

Teachers College, Columbia University

Within the field of education, a major aim of doctoral preparation, postdoctoral training, and the early years of the professorial career is to learn to conduct research and to position oneself as a competent and contributing educational researcher. These tasks are inherently social in that they take place in the context of communities of research. They are also psychological in that they involve changes in the hearts and minds of those seeking to make research a recurring activity in their lives. Learning research and constructing the self as an educational researcher are careerlong tasks that typically are launched during doctoral study. Even more important than these activities, however, is *learning how to learn* as the vividness of graduate school fades with time and new challenges. Learning both about how to enact educational research and how to keep learning research throughout one's career will shape the quality of that career and, thus, the quality of one's contribution to educational research. Given escalating calls for the improvement of educational research (Shavelson & Towne, 2002), we can think of no more important undertaking for education and educational research than helping beginning educational researchers to make good choices about how to learn about educational research throughout their future years (Argyris & Schon, 1978).

The enormity of this project—learning to engage within multiple professional communities, rethinking what and how one knows, connecting one's personal values and intellectual

AUTHORS' NOTE: The research reported in this chapter was made possible by a grant from the Spencer Foundation. The data presented, the statements made, and the views expressed are solely the responsibility of the authors. Our thanks go to Matthew Prentice for contributions to the framing of these ideas, to section editors King Beach and Betsy Becker for thoughtful comments, and to the Spencer Foundation for project support.

aims, and learning to do this not just once and for all but also throughout the length of a career—broaches the question of how entrants to the field learn research and become researchers. What can doctoral study provide these individuals to help them scale the task that lies before them, not just through coursework, qualifying exams, and their dissertations but also well beyond? What can beginning educational researchers learn—about their work, themselves, and their communities—that they will keep, for further development and change, throughout their future careers? This chapter grows from the assumption that in its historic and current form, doctoral study in the field of education addresses the task at hand partially and sometimes superficially. Yet this criticism is not new. Even scholars who have led the construction of educational research as a field of professional and intellectual endeavor have questioned the quality of research and the value of the knowledge it yields. Speaking for the National Academy of Education more than three decades ago, Cronbach and Suppes (1969) wrote,

> We believe that not more than one-tenth of the doctoral dissertations in Education and not more than one-tenth of the work published in the less-well-edited journals, even today, are respectable works of serious inquiry. The rest have had their function as training exercises and as tokens required for professional stature, but they have degraded the term "contribution to knowledge." (p. 226)

Although there have been many important advances in our understanding over the past two decades, there are persistent concerns regarding the quality of the research produced by educational researchers (Miller, 1999; Viadero, 1999). How might we conceptualize the problem at the heart of educational research? We argue in this chapter that a major problem underlying researcher learning and development in the field of education is the failure of the field to appreciate the multiple and diverse knowledge contexts within which the learning of educational research must occur.

In this chapter, we discuss four images of knowledge context that we believe are central to the construction of doctoral programs in the field of education. Our aim is to present these images of context as locations of researcher learning, as perspectives for framing *what* is to be learned by researchers, and (not least) as substantive aims for researcher learning and development that may be embedded in doctoral curricula in education.

We view beginning scholars' learning of research as being shaped by (a) the nature of educational knowledge they pursue, (b) prevailing notions of research expertise and research activity in education, (c) the personal histories and beliefs about knowledge that learners bring with them to graduate school and to their first postgraduate positions, and (d) the distinctive cultures of the disciplines and institutional environments in which they work. Each of these respective broad contexts of learning is related to a form of knowledge to be developed throughout one's early career: (a) to subject matter, (b) to the professional practices of research, (c) to researcher identity, and (d) to knowledge of cultural resources.

Because the learning of research and the development of researchers is a complicated matter, and a topic that has not been well conceptualized within the field of education, we rely on several prominent learning and developmental perspectives to help in the conceptualization. Although the perspectives overlap, they do offer distinctive avenues of thought for exploring what it means to learn research and develop as an educational researcher—in brief, *to construct one's self as an educational researcher.* We suggest that such construction involves development—activities of growth and becoming—with four distinctive aims in mind: becoming a learner of an educational subject (the subject matter perspective), becoming a practitioner of educational research (the practice perspective), becoming an object and subject of professional identity (the professional socialization and identity-crafting perspectives), and becoming a cultural actor (the cultural capital perspective). We hope that our representation of these diverse views on researcher development will lead research mentors to consider the breadth of the curricula they offer their students—both for their learning about educational research now and for their learning to learn, as researchers, throughout the rest of their lives. In addition, reflecting on these perspectives may help researchers to understand barriers to their learning and to develop strategies for lifelong learning about research.

The Subject Matter Perspective: Becoming a Learner of an Educational Subject

Teachers are qualified to teach because they have *something* to teach (Shulman, 2000), and professors profess because they have something to profess. Concomitantly, researchers engage in research because they (and their disciplinary colleagues) know something about a particular subject and seek to know more about that subject—to know it better or more deeply. Each of these roles (teacher, professor, or researcher) assumes the existence of a "subject" (or subject matter knowledge) at its core—something taught, something professed, something inquired into, or something created. The roles without the subject matter knowledge—whether labeled as content, topics, subject, discipline, or scholarship—are meaningless. This implies that we cannot speak of educational researchers in the abstract; educational researchers study something in particular.

Within the subject matter view on researcher learning and development, a researcher positions herself or himself to become a deep learner of an educational subject for a lifetime, even as that subject shifts and changes, in part through her or his own (and others') learning, defined as processes of knowledge construction. In this view, an educational researcher is a learner whose learning, amid others' learning, substantiates academic and public knowledge of a subject domain. The view derives from two assumptions: (1) that a subject for learning exists and (2) that the subject is unique enough, or particular enough, in its construction to warrant an equally unique education into how to study it. Research in a certain subject matter, although resonant of research in other subject matters, assumes deep particularistic knowledge of, and facility in, that subject's epistemic "syntax" (Schwab, 1978). In this perspective, researchers of teaching and learning in

mathematics need to understand modes of thought that, in and of themselves, express mathematical knowing—identifying it as distinctive, that is, as knowledge apart from geography, literature, and science, among others. Much the same is true for studies of teaching and learning in other fields regardless of epistemic differences that may divide the field within itself, at times aligning its parts with other fields (Becher, 1989; Graff, 1992; Rosenau, 1992).

The scholarly work that researchers carry out includes the creation of knowledge, but it also may involve the application of knowledge, teaching, outreach, and dissemination. A scholar's engagement with her or his subject, by way of any one of these professional (e.g., professorial) tasks, influences the scholar's understanding of that subject when engaged in the other tasks. For example, an academic scientist who realizes a fundamental association of ideas in the process of talking with students in class is likely to take her or his new (or renewed) understandings to the research lab, much as the academic scientist's lab-based experiences of a particular scientific phenomenon are likely to enrich her or his teaching of that topic. In other words, a professor's experience of an insight into her or his subject does not stop at the professor's classroom door, nor does it stop at the door of her or his research space.

In this sense, all professional tasks and activities (e.g., research, teaching, service) that require the beginning or aspiring scholar to work with subject matter are contexts within which she or he may elaborate (e.g., extend, revise, reshape, reorganize) her or his subject matter knowledge—assuming, of course, that those contexts bear such content and that they reflect more than a generalized (nonspecific) organizational labor or content distant from the scholar's own content. Such elaboration may be quite basic, for example, when the scholar learns material that others already know but with which she or he has little acquaintance. But professors' subject matter knowledge elaboration may be more complex, for example, when the scholar engaged in teaching gains insights previously unarticulated in research literatures (Neumann, 2000). We must then view developing researchers as finding a subject and committing themselves to its exploration or construction over time and in diverse settings, for example, in teaching as much as in research.

Reaching Beyond "That" and "How" in Subject-Based Inquiry

Conventional knowledge suggests that beginning scholars learn the primary content knowledge of their fields—ideas, theories, principles, constructs, and themes—in substantive courses and seminars, in tailored programs of reading and discussion, and in other experiences in graduate school or in structured postgraduate experiences. Presumably, they gain knowledge of how to engage in research from methods courses, apprenticeships, assistantships, and (not least) the firsthand engagement in research that writing a dissertation requires. This structure assumes an image of content knowledge being passed concretely, in well-organized form, from teacher to student, to be consumed and later used in professional endeavors such as research and teaching. To paraphrase Broudy (1977), such learning poses a picture of novice scholars engaged in "learning that" for the substantive material (content) and "learning how" for the methodological.[1] For example, many doctoral programs present themselves as offering substantive courses and related activities (e.g., guest speakers) that represent the working ideas and understandings of a field. These are sites for doctoral students to engage in "learning that." Such doctoral programs also present themselves as offering research (usually methods) courses and training experiences that lay out how such ideas are developed, elaborated, refined, and/or revised—in brief, presenting strategies, methods, and techniques of research accepted by (and acceptable to) a scholarly community. Through these curricular and co-curricular experiences, doctoral students engage in "learning how." Because images of "learning that" and "learning how" historically have dominated discussions of what goes on in school, it should be no surprise that the structure of doctoral programs reflects this image as well.

We argue that the learning of subject matter involves deep learning, well beyond the attention to "that" and "how." It requires engagement with the epistemic structuring of knowledge in disciplines or subject domains, both substantively

and syntactically (Schwab, 1978). This is likely to involve not only the learning of "truths out of nowhere," as Schwab (1978) notes, but also the drawing of "conclusions from evidence" or the making of "decisions from thought about alternatives and their consequences" (p. 270). It is also likely to involve appreciation for uncertainties in fields of study and close attention to the nature of the data or "first-order materials" (p. 270) of a field, including their description and assessment, and inference from and analysis of them. In Schwab's words, this involves learning to "construct [one's] own narrative of enquiry" within a field or subject domain (p. 271). For Schwab, as for Dewey (1902/ 1964), experience is the source of knowing. Schwab (1978) explains that "what we are, what we know, *how we have been bent,* and what we remember determine what we experience [learn, come to know] in the present" (p. 272, emphasis added). Conceptions of "learning that" and "learning how" fail to capture the depth of subject-situated learning implied by this imagery of a person, in the present day of her or his research, drawing consciously and unconsciously from a storehouse of deep conceptual understanding of a subject known through experience ("how we have been bent" in our knowing). Such knowing—what Broudy (1977) terms "knowing with"—can scarcely be articulated, although it manifests itself in the form and quality of the subject matter knowledge a scholar creates. Therefore, experiences that encourage in scholars a deep "knowing with," in the context of subject-situated research endeavors, are primary in the learning of research. They represent opportunities to develop and elaborate an *investigational content knowledge* of sorts.[2] However, the question of what constitutes such learning for beginning researchers is a significant and unaddressed question and clearly an issue for further discussion.

Framing Educational Research as Subject Matter Learning

In this section, we rely on the writings of John Dewey, Joseph Schwab, and Lee Shulman on learning to conceptualize the development of educational researchers as learners of particular subjects. We do so on the assumption that the construction of subject matter is central to both learning and research and, thus, that we can draw on existent frameworks for understanding one (learning) to understand the other (researching).

The Centrality of Experience in Learning and Research. Subject matter is material that learners—teachers and students alike—must "psychologize" in the sense of turning subject matter, abstracted from others' lives, into the experiences of learners' lives (Dewey, 1902/ 1964). Experience, including personal experience of the subjects learned in school and the subjects created in research settings, is critical to understanding the content and quality of knowledge constructed. To understand researchers' inquiries into their subjects of study, it is helpful to explore their experiences as learners of these subject matters.

Disciplinary Knowledge and Reflection in Researching as Learning. Subject matter learning encompasses attention not only to thoughts as "products" of learning, or scholarly activity, but also to the processes of the mind (Schwab, 1978) and the nature of the experiences (Dewey, 1902/1964) that bring the thought (subject) into being. This entails attention to the knowledge construction experiences of learners during the moments of their learning. It also requires attention to the knowledge construction experiences of the multitudes of learners who worked, psychologically, with a particular substantive idea (the subject) through the ages, granting that idea the status of "knowledge" (Schwab, 1978). The experiences of the learner now, relative to the recorded experiences of the learning of scholars of past ages, come together in present-day experience, and both require attention in the construction of a learning agenda.

Two research experiences, then, are central: (1) the researcher's sense of connection to the thinking of her or his disciplinary forebears, the tradition of thought being joined (Hansen, 2001), and (2) the researcher's awareness of her or his own thinking and learning in the moment, a reflecting in action (Schon, 1983, 1987). The former emphasizes the significance to research of the researcher's acquired disciplinary knowledge, whereas the latter emphasizes the researcher's personal awareness of and responsiveness to

her or his own engagement of that knowledge. Both are part and parcel of subject matter learning.

The Representational Qualities of Knowledge in Learning and Research. Learning in the current moment must consider both the formed, or crafted, material that is being passed on (the "substance" of learning) and the process of its formation as well as paths of further inquiry, and further shaping, open within it (for further discussion of the "syntax" of school knowledge, see Schwab, 1978). One outcome of this view of knowledge is an appreciation for its representational qualities—for its responsiveness to reshaping and rearticulation and, thereby, perhaps its extension or remaking.

Knowing how to represent knowledge in multiple ways often is associated with good teaching (Shulman, 1986, 1987)—for its ability to enable a teacher both to discern the many ways in which students represent what they know and to match a particular representation with the needs of a particular group of students. However, appreciation of the representational qualities of knowledge also may be associated with good research or thoughtful inquiry—as in the case of a researcher who struggles to represent what she or he is learning in multiple ways to multiple audiences, based on what an audience knows already, or in the case of a researcher who regularly invites others into conversations that may question or re-present established disciplinary (or field-based) understandings of a subject of interest (Neumann, 2000).

A view of research as learning subject matter requires attention to researchers' mindful (and sometimes critical) formulation and reformulation of their subjects of study in the context of evolving research traditions. The notion of a research tradition implies that the subject matter, or disciplinary content, that defines an area of study shifts and forms anew over time. Mindfulness requires attention to experience, particularly the personal experience of an individual's relation to her or his subject matter, which also evolves over time. A researcher learns uniquely within the tradition of thought in which she or he has been immersed, yet in so doing the researcher contributes personal meanings—sometimes reworked understandings—to that tradition, meanings that others take up for their own unique views.

THE PRACTICE PERSPECTIVE: BECOMING A PRACTITIONER OF EDUCATIONAL RESEARCH

Another way of thinking about *what* beginning educational researchers learn, as they construct themselves as researchers, recognizes that educational researchers are at once individuals and members of a community of educational researchers. In becoming educational researchers, individuals join that community, becoming increasingly central to its efforts. What joins these individuals is their shared pursuit of a common agenda—increasing the stock of knowledge about how education, in its many contexts and configurations, takes place. To further this goal, educational researchers think in particular ways and do certain things. We can describe the things that educational researchers do as the *practices* in which educational researchers engage to advance the goal of increasing understanding of educational phenomena. These practices are a way of negotiating meaning through social action. Drawing on the work of Wenger (1998), we specify a view of educational research as a practice to be learned. In this view, *what* novice scholars learn is the practice of educational research. Through protracted engagement with other community-based researchers about the community's practice-based concerns, an individual becomes a practitioner of educational research.

Defining Educational Research as Practice

Conceptualizing practice as the "what" of researcher learning requires an attention to educational researchers' *doing and knowing* as constitutive of practice. Doing without knowing is not a practice (although the knowing can be tacit). This distinction, between doing minus thought and doing and thought as intertwined, parallels Geertz's (1973) distinction between a

person whose eye twitches involuntarily (with no meaning intended) and a person whose identical eye movement constitutes a purposeful wink. Similarly, knowing without doing is not a practice either, given that a practice involves purposive action. In the context of educational research, the purpose of action is to deepen or extend understanding of educational phenomena.

Locating the Practice of Educational Research

The learning of educational research, construed as the learning of the practices of educational researchers, implies that the relevant learning cannot be constructed on one's own. Such learning occurs in a *community of practice*—a community of practitioners with a broad set of interests and commitments. An individual in isolation from a community cannot create the practices of, or introduce new practices into, that community without engaging with it. An individual's own actions cannot be defined as "practices" until they are acknowledged by the relevant community of practice. An individual cannot construct herself or himself as a practitioner without engaging with others in shared practice, learning from them as well as with them. In this way, the practice of educational research and its learning are explicitly social. And because communities evolve over time, the practice is also historically situated.

Defining Communities of Practice

We have described the practices of the educational research community as one target of beginning scholars' learning. But individuals often are members of multiple communities, and this "multimembership" (Wenger, 1998) adds complexity both to the ecology of communities of practice and to practitioner careers. Beginning scholars often seek membership not only in a community of educational research practitioners but also in communities of students, professors, college teachers, and disciplinary scholars. Each of these can be construed as a distinct community of practice.

The complexity of this view of researchers belonging to multiple communities of practice simultaneously may appear to blur the core idea of a community of practice. What, then, counts as community? Wenger (1998) addresses this concern by stating that not all social collectivities can or should be considered communities of practice. There are three defining features of a community of practice, in Wenger's view. First, a community of practice involves a negotiated enterprise. That is, individuals in a community of practice collectively negotiate their goals as a community. These goals may change over time and space. The presence of a negotiated enterprise means that community members are more willing to hold their actions accountable (and more willing for others in the community to hold them accountable) to the community's joint enterprise than to some other enterprise. Second, a community of practice involves mutual engagement among its members. This need not imply that every member of a community of practice must routinely engage in face-to-face conversation (in fact, geographic proximity is not necessary at all); rather, it means that there is sustained social interaction among the members. In a community of practice, members know one another, and they know and can evaluate each other's competencies and actions. Third, a community of practice has a shared repertoire of resources and practices. Members of a community of practice draw on a shared history of experience that gives a common meaning to resources and artifacts, including ways of communicating and rules and procedures for how the community operates.

Communities of Practice: The Case of Educational Research

Because a defining feature of a community of practice is dense social interaction within the community, a community of practice is inherently local, and a macro-level social organization, such as the American Educational Research Association (AERA), is unlikely to constitute a community of practice. There are too many discontinuities in mutual engagement, joint purpose, and shared repertoire of resources and practices within AERA to characterize it as a community of practice. And yet the members of an organization such as AERA clearly share some attributes—a common general purpose, norms for journal publication, participation in the annual meeting, and patterns of governance, among others. Members may engage in common experiences (e.g., reading AERA journals, attending the presidential address at the annual meeting), thereby developing shared understandings of what educational research means and what AERA's history represents. But these *general* identifications with AERA fail to touch the particularity of substantive research activity and researcher identity.

Conversely, a special interest group (SIG) within AERA may be defined more comfortably as a community of practice because it is not so large that mutual engagement is precluded. For example, the structural equations modeling SIG sponsors a number of sessions at the annual meeting, where papers on structural equations modeling are presented. The audience for such papers typically includes other members of the SIG who share a common language peppered with terms such as "modification indexes" and "underidentification." Members of the structural equations modeling community rely on a shared set of computer programs for estimating these models (e.g., LISREL, EQS, Amos), subscribe to shared listservs (e.g., SEMNET), and read the same journals (e.g., *Structural Equation Modeling, Multivariate Behavioral Research*). Members of this community know who the acknowledged experts in structural equations modeling are, and they follow one another's work.

We should note that the community of practice is not the SIG itself. One can be a structural equations modeling practitioner without being a member of the SIG, and membership in the SIG does not confer membership in the practitioner community sui generis. Communities of practice need not be isomorphic with organizational categories and boundaries. But there may be a great deal of overlap between membership in the community of practice and membership in the SIG.

Because bureaucratically reified bodies rarely are communities of practice, a better example might be an "invisible college" of literacy scholars, representing diverse disciplines and educational specialties and sharing in some (formal) AERA subcommunities (e.g., SIGs, divisions) but perhaps not others. Individuals belonging to this invisible college of literacy scholars may talk regularly or irregularly, yet they are likely to be linked—for example, through e-mail conversations or yearly dinner meetings informally scheduled for the annual AERA conference—and they may collaborate on research or otherwise share ideas over time. Yet this group of literacy scholars has no formal reified status, either within or outside of AERA. Perhaps these scholars' fluidity defines their sense of community; they cohere not from obligation or bureaucratic necessity but rather from voluntary personal desire.

In contrast, individuals within AERA who are not part of these two communities of practice (the structural equations modeling SIG and the invisible college of literacy scholars) would not share the understandings central to each, or at least they would not embrace such understandings as deeply as community or group members do. The language used in paper presentations and journals might well be unintelligible to them, to the point where individuals outside these communities might not understand issues central to each—problems central to structural equation modeling (in the case of the SIG) and problems central to the study of literacy (in the case of the invisible college), which issues are deemed important and why, and who is known to be making progress in addressing them. These discontinuities—in mutual engagement, joint purpose, and shared repertoire of resources and practices—imply that neither AERA as a membership organization nor the community of educational researchers writ large can be construed as a community of practice.

And yet there surely are some continuities across the communities of practice that constitute the community of educational researchers or the membership of AERA. Wenger (1998) develops the concept of a *constellation* of communities of practice, in which the metaphor of a constellation of independent but related stars is used to denote a grouping of communities of practice that are related by some form of continuity in meaning—whether purpose, membership, identity, artifacts, history, or environment. Thus, AERA might be considered a constellation of local communities of practice that share some, but by no means all, practices.

The same applies to graduate schools of education that prepare educational researchers.

It might be surprising that it is difficult to characterize the faculty of a particular school of education as a *community of the practice of educational research.* The faculty of a particular "ed school" do share a common institutional environment, have a shared history (e.g., a budget crisis, an innovative teacher education program, an oppressive provost), interact with one another concerning teaching and program issues, and often share a commitment to sustain and nourish the school. But this points to all of the faculty of that school sharing membership in a *community of the practice of being a professor at a particular school* rather than sharing membership in a *community of the practice of educational research* (Pallas, 2001).

Locating the Construction of Educational Researchers Within Communities of Practice

The local nature of communities of practice, and their distinction from encompassing "constellations," invites the question of the appropriate level of analysis for studying the learning and development of educational researchers. When neither the community of educational researchers writ large nor even the faculty of a particular school of education can be characterized as a community of the practice of educational research, can we identify one or more communities of practice within which novices construct themselves as educational researchers? This question directs attention to novice researchers' positioning within their own communities of practice and within larger constellations of communities of practice.

Induction Into a Community of Practice. A major concern of any community of practice is reproduction—the maintenance of the community as it evolves over time. Through time, community members age and must be replaced by new members if the community is to survive. But a binary categorization of "newcomers" and "old-timers" ignores what Wenger (1998) refers to as a "trajectory" of participation in a community of practice. Over time, an individual's identity and role as a member of a community of practice shifts. Newcomers to a community are on a trajectory leading to full participation and community membership, which is accompanied by the development of an identity commensurate with full membership. Conversely, the most senior members of a community are on a slow trajectory leading toward peripheral participation and the gradual loss of identity as community members.

Generational encounters between newcomers and old-timers are opportunities for learning and the development of changed practices. Newcomers strive to learn the meanings associated with the shared experiences and histories of the established members of the community; these meanings are a source of community stability. Old-timers engage with the ways in which newcomers negotiate meaning and with new meanings that such newcomers are likely to construct. Without an influx of new members, the community lacks the capacity to learn and develop new practices. Without the anchoring of established members, a community may fragment or dissolve.

Lave and Wenger (1991) coined the phrase "legitimate peripheral participation" to represent newcomers' learning in a community of practice. In their view, newcomers become members of communities of practice through a gradual process of legitimate peripheral participation during which individuals simultaneously learn the practices of the community and develop an identity as community members. A powerful metaphor for this process is the apprenticeship. Apprenticeships need not depend on a dyadic master–apprentice relationship; indeed, one of the important contributions of Lave and Wenger's conceptualization is the recognition that an apprentice is engaging with a community, not just a single master practitioner. In an apprenticeship model, an individual learns more through legitimate peripheral participation than through formal teaching as is found in classrooms. Learning practices in the context of community peripherality provide a perspective that allows novices to develop an analytic understanding of practice. In Lave and Wenger's words,

> An extended period of legitimate peripherality provides learners with opportunities to make the culture of practice theirs. From a broadly peripheral perspective, apprentices gradually assemble a

general idea of what constitutes the practice of the community. This uneven sketch of the enterprise (available if there is legitimate access) might include who is involved; what they do; what everyday life is like; how masters talk, walk, work, and generally conduct their lives; how people who are not part of the community of practice interact with it; what other learners are doing; and what learners need to learn to become full practitioners. It includes an increasing understanding of how, when, and about what old-timers collaborate, collude, and collide, and what they enjoy, dislike, respect, and admire. In particular, it offers exemplars (which are grounds and motivation for learning activity), including masters, finished products, and more advanced apprentices in the process of becoming full practitioners. (p. 95)

Peripherality within community offers newcomers to practices—in this case, the practices of educational research—opportunities to develop their knowing in the context of their own and others' joint activity. Pallas (2001) describes some of the challenges that stem from deep immersion in a community of practice, insulated from other ways of understanding the educational phenomena studied by the community.

Tapping Resources External to Community. A critical feature of communities of practice is that they are bounded, such that it is possible to distinguish members of the community from nonmembers and to distinguish a particular community's practices from the practices of another community. But these boundaries are permeable, such that individuals can participate in multiple communities of practice simultaneously and, through this participation, introduce elements of the practices of one community into the practices of another community. Wenger (1998) refers to this process as "brokering." A broker must have both the social and technical skills to discern how to link the practices of one community to those of another community and to be able to translate the community-specific meanings of reifications (e.g., artifacts) into the language and reifications of another community. Brokers also must have the legitimacy to command the attention of the members of a community and to introduce changes in the community's practices. Two key concerns during scholars' early careers are the extent to which beginning scholars can access resources brokered by senior members of their own or other fields and the extent to which they themselves may begin to engage in brokering among the communities of practice in which they reside.

BECOMING AN OBJECT AND A SUBJECT OF PROFESSIONAL IDENTITY: PROFESSIONAL SOCIALIZATION AND IDENTITY-CRAFTING PERSPECTIVES

In addition to constructing knowledge of subject matter and practice, new scholars are constructing knowledge of themselves as professionals and as members of professional communities. We might add that they are also being professionally constructed by others, sometimes consciously and willingly and other times not. Novice educational researchers are learning about themselves as extenders or creators of particular subject matters, as research practitioners, as members of multiple communities (research communities in particular, but also communities of origin, professional communities, etc.), and as participants in smaller and larger research relationships (e.g., work with collaborators, participation in an international web of scholars). The knowledge of self they create in these contexts influences their choices and conceptualization of their first research topics and, subsequently, the formulations of their research agendas. Self-knowledge, as well as other moral or ethical considerations, may also influence how researchers position themselves in relation to those they study. All theories of how individuals develop as professionals attend to the developing person *and* the context(s) of professional development, with the key differences among these theories located in how much attention they give to persons, contexts, or the interactions between them. In this section, we summarize two approaches to understanding the developing person as professional: a stage theory of professional socialization that foregrounds the developing researcher and an ecological theory of scholarly identity development that strives to capture the person–context dialectic of development.

The Developing Researcher: Stage Theories of Professional Socialization

Professional socialization is typically viewed as a developmental process in which individuals are recruited to professional training, exposed to a set of common and unique socializing influences, and inducted into the profession (see, e.g., Merton, Reader, & Kendall, 1957). The model underlying most writings on professional socialization, referred to as the induction approach (Simpson, 1979), sees socialization as something that is "done to" neophytes seeking entry into the profession. This model emphasizes those features of the professional school and the professional culture that facilitate the learning of appropriate skills and values; students themselves are viewed as relatively passive participants in the process, and what students learn is largely left unspecified. Thus, in this view, novice educational researchers are objects of socializing forces. Socialization, and sometimes resistance to it (Reinharz, 1991), creates the educational researcher.

Most developmental theories of professional socialization consist of three developmental stages: entry, "studentship," and apprenticeship. We believe that these stages may overlap, although they often are portrayed as discrete.

Entry. Entry into professional socialization pertains to the beginning phases of the socialization process, particularly the anticipatory experiences prior to professional school matriculation and the encounter experiences during the first year of study. At the time of entry into a professional program, students may already have some knowledge and beliefs about the nature of the profession stemming from their prior education and experience. For example, education doctoral students may have had formal coursework in educational research or other forms of research, may have been exposed to educational research in their prior coursework or in their work as practicing educators, or may have engaged in research activities themselves. Moreover, their beliefs about education and about society, as well as their personal backgrounds and experiences, may predispose them to particular beliefs about research.

Studentship. "Studentship" pertains to that phase of the professional socialization process during which a trainee's primary role identification is as a student. Rosen and Bates (1967) argue that before an individual can be inducted into the profession, she or he must be inducted into the role of graduate student:

> Before becoming a professional the neophyte must learn to be a student, and this includes much more than the acquisition of the professional knowledge or skills essential for his career plans. He enters a society of graduate students complete with its distinctive subculture. He must learn its norms, find a place in its competitive structure, give [support] to and receive support from peers, and learn the prevailing folklore of how to cope with the agents in whose hands his fate lies for several years. (pp. 75–76)

Sherlock and Morris (1967) suggest that during the studentship phase of professional education, students develop a sense of solidarity, common purpose, and shared norms. They believe that cohorts can be strong socializing agents, claiming that "a cohort of students spending almost all of their time together tends to form intense loyalties, allegiances and, in a few cases, antipathies. The transformation of the student class into a reference group, with associated development of shared perspectives, occurs quite rapidly" (p. 40). During the early years of professional study, students face common problems, are thrust into close proximity with one another by the organization of the curriculum into shared core courses, and thereby develop a sense of solidarity. During this early phase, the students may identify more with one another than with the faculty, may rely heavily on one another, and may in fact resist (either covertly or overtly) faculty efforts to induct them into professional roles.

Apprenticeship. The relations between students and faculty take on even greater importance during the apprenticeship stage of professional preparation. During apprenticeship, students learn the professional role through intensive interaction with a small number of faculty. This increased interaction with faculty around specific problems of practice (e.g., a particular research question) ultimately results in students' having more in common with the faculty to whom they are apprenticed than with each other and a gradual increase in the adoption of professional values and commitment coupled with a weakening of the social bonds that tie students together.

The apprenticeship phase of professional preparation may result in greater technical knowledge about the practice of the profession as well as greater identification with and commitment to the professional role. Evidence of the latter point is presented by Weiss (1981), who notes that doctoral students who describe themselves as apprentices are more highly committed to their fields of study than are those who describe themselves as merely students. Moreover, she found that students who believe that their primary professors see them as colleagues both engage in more professional behaviors and have a higher professional self-concept than do those students who believe that their primary professors view them as apprentices or students.

These benefits may be tempered by some potential drawbacks to socialization that are rooted in close ties to a single professor. A doctoral student or beginning assistant professor may be identified as having the same substantive and methodological interests as her or his adviser, whether or not that is actually the case. Moreover, Merton (1968) warns that the scholarly contributions of collaborative work between student and adviser are likely to be attributed to the adviser, even if the student is the primary architect of the work.

Although stage theories illuminate some contexts of development (e.g., peers, faculty), larger and more complex contexts—such as the unique configuration of graduate programs, the culture of the discipline or field, and larger cultural and historical patterns—are not addressed. An ecological view expands on this vision of learning research and becoming an educational researcher.

The Person–Context Dialectic: Ecological Theories of Scholarly Identity Development

Development as a person and as a professional involves construction of knowledge about oneself—in this case, who one is as a scholar and as a professional learner in education; what issues, subjects, problems, and questions one cares about and why; and, possibly, how one enacts the educator role through the medium of educational research. We describe this process as the construction of a *scholarly identity*—self-knowledge expressed in the terms of scholarship.

We define "identity" as who a person understands herself or himself to be in intersection with who others understand her or him to be. This definition is *temporal* in that identities develop and, in some cases, erode over time in response to changes in an individual's life circumstances. It is *relational* in that identity is determined by the understandings of the individual and of multiple others, both known and unknown, in her or his life. The definition is also *experiential* in that identity grows from consciousness of one's self and surroundings realized in the present or remembered. By extension, "scholarly identity" speaks to how an individual sees herself or himself, or is seen by others, as a researcher and teacher of a particular subject matter. We discuss here three dynamics in the development of scholarly identity that may be useful for understanding the development of beginning educational researchers.

Scholarly identity is situated in community. Identity is often construed as socially constructed (Berger & Luckmann, 1967; Goffman, 1959) and as being responsive to the diverse and shifting contexts of daily life (Gergen, 1991). We sharpen this conception by viewing identity as forged both through participation in purposive communities and through personal contemplation, which may involve the interrogation and critique of community practices (Myerhoff, 1978). Situating identity in purposive communities highlights the power of community processes and resources to define who a person is and what it means to be that person (Brown & Gilligan, 1992).

But the creation of identity need not be a fully passive endeavor. An individual may question who others believe her or him to be (Behar, 1993; Kondo, 1990), thereby "pushing back" against the identity that the community is constructing for her or him. In so doing, the individual may assert an alternative sense of self (Krieger, 1991), perhaps derived in other locations (and communities) in her or his life, and find ways in which to bring that alternative to bear on current constructions of what it means to be a researcher and to engage in research (see, e.g., Delgado-Gaitan, 1997; Ladson-Billings, 1997).

An individual may strive to influence an educational research community by redefining what education itself entails, by introducing new members into the community, or by promoting social change that results in changed community norms, to name but a few examples. For example, Ladson-Billings (1995) sought to redefine what it means to be a competent literate adult and citizen and to educate with this aim in mind, as well as what—in light of this revised definition—the doing of educational research entails (Ladson-Billings, 1997; Neumann, Pallas, & Peterson, 1999). In these respects, individuals can be active producers of their own development (Lerner & Busch-Rossnagel, 1981). They may play a role in constructing themselves as educational researchers or, at least, in crafting or recrafting the contexts and conditions that, through time, can frame their researcher identities, their research as a form of work, and the research efforts of their scholarly communities. In contrast to the socialization view of researcher development, the ecological view positions novices as potential authors (or active co-authors) of segments of their researcher identities.

Communities are sources of identity. Although the image of researchers creating identity in response to their critiques of the everyday life of the community that surrounds them is appealing, the power of that daily life, and of culture itself, to shape identity cannot be underestimated. Culture may be viewed as inscribed in community life (Bronfenbrenner, 1979), and diverse communities are likely to exert normative holds on their inhabitants, either as expressions of the larger culture of which they are a part or as expressions of their own unique constitutions (see, e.g., Kunda, 1992).

Much writing on colleges and universities as identity-inscribing institutions, or as faculty-socializing communities, considers institutions' powers to shape the thoughts and behaviors of their members and to create professors in the image of the prevailing local professional culture. A related literature on the institutional contexts of socialization emphasizes the power of these contexts to harm or even destroy the personal sources of professional identity (see especially Kunda, 1992). Thus, researchers' scholarly identities may be constructed in contexts that are nurturing or in conflictual contexts that inspire resistance or defense. If researchers do not create their identities in line with community norms, then they are likely to create them in opposition to them (see, e.g., Reinharz, 1991).

The question remains as to what aspects of community are likely to shape identity. Beyond sociological images of community norms as shapers of identity lie images drawn from psychology of community-situated epistemologies as shapers of identity. We define "epistemology" as conceptions of knowledge and knowledge creation that grow from assumptions about the "nature, validity, and limits of inquiry" and "ontological dimensions such as the nature of reality" (Rosenau, 1992, p. 109). These conceptions, created through repeated interaction over time, contribute to the framing and evaluation of research, inquiry, and learning generally in academic communities such as graduate schools of education and sociology and psychology departments (Pallas, 2001). Such epistemologies are historically and culturally rooted (Neumann et al., 1999).

We may assume from this view of epistemology as a rubric for the conceptualization of research, and the careerlong social and cultural formation of researchers, that culture (whether widespread or local) acts, in part, through epistemology to shape how individuals construct the researcher role and to also shape conceptions of acceptable, meaningful, and ethical research. Although researchers may, over time, gain reflective distance on the epistemological structuring of a research enterprise, the power of that enterprise remains a significant force in the academic career. A field's epistemology might not clearly determine careers, including researcher identities, but its presence and pervasiveness—and researchers' needs to respond to it, occasionally through resistance—shape the thought, including self-conceptions, of researchers who grow within it. Recent writings in feminist research suggest, in fact, an epistemology of resistance that is grounded in the "standpoints" of individuals who are situated collectively on the undersides of a social–cultural structure (an unarticulated context of sorts), much as women have been historically—or, perhaps more discursively, an epistemology of emotion that strives to voice the feeling and experience of being in a particular standpoint as central to "self." In this view, researcher identity, although inescapably shaped by dominant social epistemologies, allows space for self-creation through "a different voice," and thereby a different frame of mind, derived through existence in less visible social spaces.

Community dynamics create and recreate identity. One of the complications of an ecological view of identity development is represented in our use of terms such as "others," "relationships," and "communities"—the idea that identity is somehow negotiated between self and persons existing beyond self. And along with these multiple *others* (both individual and collective) impressing themselves on a person's identity, we also must attend to the potential impresses of *situations, life events and activities, historical time, economy, culture in its many dimensions,* and *society and social groupings writ large* (for a thorough discussion of the ecology of human development, see Bronfenbrenner, 1979).

What emerges in this yet more complex consideration is an identity composed of multiple, shifting, and "relationally defined selves . . . selves inextricable from context" (Kondo, 1990, p. 33), not as a singular, fixed, or continuous self. In this view, work—even scholarly work—is simultaneously a context and a medium for expression and formation of self. And biography (life as lived in social and cultural context), as well as autobiography (one's personal sense-making of one's own life), also are contexts for the realization of scholarly identity. Thus, a beginning scholar just entering graduate school, or stepping into her or his first professional position, draws on knowledge not only from the curricula, readings, and interactions at the scholar's professional disposal but also from the personal, perhaps nonprofessional, "curricula" of interactions, relationships, and communities situated elsewhere in her or his life (both present and past) (Behar, 1993, 1996). All of these contexts lend the role of educational researcher unique substance, perspective, and form.

Although context is a powerful contributor to identity, community contexts are especially noteworthy. The communities to which researchers belong—whether campus based, disciplinary, or professional—are likely to "bend" (Schwab, 1978, p. 272) the ways of thinking of their members, either subtly or dramatically, by invoking social norms or offering epistemologies for thought about all aspects of the research process, from which problems are important to how conclusions should be communicated to various audiences. Such "bending" may also represent responses by developing researchers to intellectual and professional resources accruing uniquely in diverse academic settings or to the absence of these resources. For example, a beginning scholar moving into a land grant university can capitalize on the intellectual resources that state or community service might provide for her or his research agenda, assuming a good match between such service obligations and the content of the scholar's studies; in this sense, community service is a resource for research and for researcher identity building. The same scholar can feel a sense of intellectual loss or resource loss if local colleagues have little understanding of her or his unique perspective on a topic meaningful to all of them.

Although we focus here on intellectual resources afforded to or withheld from scholars in academic communities—such as their particular graduate schools or the departments they join as beginning faculty—much the same can be said about practitioner communities, communities of origin, and others within which these scholars spend portions of their lives, whether earlier or later. These milieus also have the power to bend beginning scholars' minds in particular ways that, through memory, may shape the course of their research even years later (Neumann, 1999).

CULTURAL CAPITAL PERSPECTIVE: BECOMING A CULTURAL ACTOR

As we have already indicated, doctoral students and postdoctoral scholars do not learn about subject matter, practice, and themselves in a vacuum; they do not construct themselves, as educational researchers, in a vacuum. Rather, the knowledge that novices construct—about research, about practice, and about themselves and others—is situated in social and political contexts, the normative contours of which researchers must learn. Academic programs and departments, disciplines and subdisciplinary specializations, and professional communities typically display pockets of shared norms, values, and interests (in addition to shared substantive knowledge) for thought and action, and these serve to guide and, to some extent, regulate members' activities. These norms, values, and interests position these academic collectivities as "tribes and territories" within larger academic cultures (Becher, 1989) or as cultures in and of themselves (Birnbaum, 1988). Whether local or global, these social contexts host curricula of social knowledge that entrants must learn.

One of the most important kinds of social knowledge that beginning researchers construct is how to enter and navigate the social contexts in which they live and work. We focus here on the two communities most often discussed in writing about higher education: the disciplinary or subject matter field with which beginning scholars affiliate and the local collegial, departmental, and institutional settings of their work. Because knowledge of these social contexts is durable and valuable, and because this knowledge stems from cultural understanding, the term "cultural capital," borrowed from the writings of Bourdieu (1985), is apt. Cultural capital designates knowledge of and facility with cultural practices and cultural artifacts and their use, in this case, for individual scholars' career advancement. In this section, we draw heavily on Bourdieuan conceptions of cultural capital to represent the kinds of social knowledge that researchers may require to negotiate successfully the range of social opportunities and constraints that comprise their communities and careers.

The Nature of the Knowledge That Constitutes Cultural Capital

Cultural resources, including the practices and artifacts associated with them, are often opaque; they usually are not explicit or systematically formulated. Their obscure, and sometimes arbitrary, qualities help to distinguish the actions of insiders from those of outsiders, and of experts from novices, because one must master a set of imprecise and indistinct norms for full membership and expert status. Once learned, however, such knowledge of cultural resources reflects a certain sense of ease and obviousness to its users. Thus, what experts consider to be common knowledge, novices may find to be unfathomable. Moreover, the fluent enactment of cultural norms is a sign of belonging, achievement, and status, whereas tentative or awkward enactment is a sign of learning, becoming, and striving to join. The difference, not always apparent to newcomers, is obvious to longtime members of a community. A beginning scholar, for example, may know how to access disciplinary ideas and might even comprehend them well, but it may take time for her or him to learn how to represent such ideas to colleagues in ways that they can hear and connect to issues of the day. Thus, to converse in scholarly ways, a beginning scholar needs to grasp not only the subject matters of her or his field but also how members of the field talk about and make sense of those subjects.

Cultural Knowledge That Novice Scholars May Gain in Pursuit of Cultural Capital

For novice researchers, learning to navigate the cultural practices of the academy is not merely a status game. Failure to gain cultural fluency limits access to graduate programs, postdoctoral opportunities, publication, professional interaction, and employment. So to move from novice to expert, beginning researchers strive to master the cultural dimensions of academic work. Although there is plentiful cultural knowledge to be gained during the early career, we emphasize here three exemplars: knowledge of publication processes, knowledge about job hunting and academic workplaces, and knowledge about access to "cultural experts."

Knowledge of Publication Processes. In the academic community, the primary route to status and power is publication. This much novices usually know, but the process of publishing, and

the relative status of various publication outlets, is not as obvious. In moving from novice to expert, beginning researchers seek to understand how to publish as well as where to publish. Journals have different standards, formats, preferences, and statuses. Beginning scholars also attempt to understand what a publishable manuscript is in terms of what it says, how it says it, what it looks like, and who it goes to. Some journal editors are sensitive to the relative ignorance of novice scholars and make special efforts to help them understand the publication system, but many are oblivious to the issue.

What a manuscript says is grounded not only in the subject matter it explores but also in the form that exploration takes. The questions that one investigates (including their articulated form), the method of data gathering, and the structural and discursive character of the manuscript all are cultural in that they reflect norms of intracommunity communication. Novices learn what theories, perspectives, and questions are valued and by whom. How to organize a research report and how to represent content are also conventions to be mastered in line with community expectations and established understandings.

As this suggests, academic fields and disciplines are marked by distinctive dialects. The choice of language, acknowledgment of and engagement with selected ideas, and positioning of one's work relative to such ideas and their proponents all represent cultural knowledge of value, and all contribute to the ability of beginning scholars to publish successfully. Beyond knowledge of the manuscript submission process, novices typically need to learn how to interpret manuscript rejections and calls for revision, for these too contain culturally coded information about a manuscript's future prospects.

Because much scholarly work in education involves some kind of data collection, the movement from novice to expert also requires knowledge of funding and grant opportunities. What a proposal should look like, who is inclined to support what type of research, and how to use money efficiently and toward desirable ends are types of cultural knowledge that novices may need to function as full members of their scholarly communities. Convincing a foundation or government agency that what *the scholar* wants to study is what the foundation or agency is *really* interested in, regardless of the content of its call for proposals, is a highly valuable form of cultural knowledge that can be converted into research dollars that are valued almost universally.

Knowledge About Job Hunting and Academic Workplaces. Even if a novice learns the cultural knowledge surrounding the publishing process, the transition to expert researcher requires knowledge about how to parlay previous successes (usually during the graduate student years) into a job that allows for further research. Thus, beginning scholars typically need to learn the cultural practices of job hunting, and they must gain facility with the artifacts created through these practices. How one prepares a curriculum vitae and application letter, secures interviews, behaves in interviews, talks about one's own research in the required "job talk," and so on are significant social rituals of the academy that novices seek to learn. Learning these rituals involves more than learning norms or rules of behavior. It involves learning to represent oneself to others in meaningful ways. Some academic programs offer proseminars, or other formal or informal activities, to provide novices with "low-stakes" experiences prior to serious efforts at job hunting.

Beyond securing jobs, beginning scholars can benefit from learning about their new workplaces. Departmental conventions and colleagueship are infused with cultural meaning, and beginning academics are likely to learn these meanings if they have prior exposure (in graduate school or elsewhere) to some of the more generalizable features of professorial and collegial life (e.g., which committees to avoid, the role of consensus and critique among colleagues, relations between research and teaching). Thus, new scholars engage in the construction of cultural capital not only in disciplinary communities but also in more local institutional communities.

Knowledge About Access to "Cultural Experts." Explicit in the cultural capital literature, and implicit in much of the literature on mentoring, is the assumption that *who* a student has contact with is as important as the content learned (although often the *who* and *what* are linked). The ability of a novice to learn cultural practices is mediated by the degree to which an expert is willing to teach her or him, the expert's own mastery of the culture, and the degree to which the expert's knowledge is supraliminal and accessible. Thus, where one studies and with whom are important sources of cultural capital. A doctoral student's ability to develop relationships with key people in a field confers a sizable advantage for learning the murky but essential cultural expectations of the field.

Such relationships hold value after graduate school as well. Who the beginning scholar chooses to collaborate with may hasten her or his academic progress, grant access to advice and professional resources, and lead others to associate her or him with a particular project or line of work. In postdoctoral careers, as in predoctoral careers, social–intellectual connections and interactions are key for both substantive and cultural reasons. Terrific scholars are not always terrific mentors, and one cannot always collaborate with an admired senior colleague, but novices can cultivate these relationships, particularly during an era when communication need not be face-to-face.

Framing Cultural Capital: The Contributions of Pierre Bourdieu

To this point, it might be difficult to distinguish this discussion of cultural knowledge and cultural capital from the previous discussion of communities of practice. We draw on the work of Pierre Bourdieu to elaborate the distinction, which turns on questions of power and inequality. Bourdieu's (1985, 1988) work emphasizes the role of durable media of exchange (which he calls capital) in the maintenance of social structures. The theory he has developed describes how capital influences actors' worldviews in such a way as to perpetuate a stable social system that reproduces social inequality. In the following sections, we discuss selected elements of Bourdieu's conception of cultural capital, a Bourdieuan view of academic contexts, and a Bourdieuan interpretation of the dynamics of success and failure in academe.

Selected Elements of Bourdieu's Conceptions of Cultural Capital. Bourdieu conceives of society as a collection of relatively autonomous *fields,* the social spaces in which competition for capital and power takes place. Fields such as the academy develop their own internal mechanisms—"rules" that define the basis and direction of competition. A field is like a game; within a field, there is an agreement among the actors that it is worth competing (playing) for the capital (stakes). Also, the rules (whether codified or not) help to proscribe and prescribe various strategies.

According to Bourdieu, actors competing within a field are inherently interested in that they direct their actions toward the accumulation of capital. Money is an obvious type of capital, but the types of capital that are valued vary among fields. Beyond physical and economic capital, cultural capital (knowledge of, and facility with the use of, cultural resources such as practices and artifacts), social capital (acquaintances and networks), and symbolic capital (a worldview or *habitus*) may be valued forms of capital.

As actors compete within a field, they seek to influence the "rules" of the game so that they have an advantage. Those who have large amounts of various kinds of capital are in the best position to effect changes; thus, they attempt to implement a system that will perpetuate their relative advantage. Actors from privileged groups form social networks that ensure they will have ready access to high-paying and/or high-status positions. Entrance into this privileged social network is controlled by distinct cultural practices. Lastly, actors, regardless of their social position, are brought up in such a way that their attitudes, preferences, beliefs, and expectations reinforce their social origins. This worldview, or habitus, is a resource for forming strategies for action, which in turn affect the amount and type of capital that actors are likely to accumulate.

A Bourdieuan Perspective on Academic Contexts. Bourdieu suggests that the academy's role as a legitimating force in society helps to shape its internal dynamics. Within the academic field, members compete for legitimating symbolic capital, which can be converted into cultural and economic capital. When a scholar's ideas are perceived as legitimate, those ideas can lead to grants and publication in prestigious outlets, both of which can have direct and indirect effects on the accumulation of cultural and economic capital.

Scholars compete for symbolic capital, and this competition often plays out in struggles for theoretical hegemony. The existence of disparate theoretical orientations can undermine the value of symbolic knowledge because the existence of multiple perspectives mitigates against an "objective" context-independent stance. Examples abound in virtually all fields. For example, the rise of neoinstitutional theory in the study of educational organizations challenged the dominance, and hence the value, of the prevailing technical–rational understanding of organizations in that technical–rational theory no longer had an exclusive claim on how to make sense of organizations (Scott, 2001). Similarly, in educational measurement, nonparametric approaches to estimating item characteristic curves in item response theory (Sijtsma & Molenaar, 2002) pose a threat to the more conventional parametric approach because they do not require untestable or unrealistic assumptions about the data. Thus, the rise of one or more alternative perspectives endangers the value of current stores of symbolic capital and threatens to reduce the resources and prestige of disciplinary scholars who promote a hegemonic view. To prevent this, scholars band together to maintain the dominance of their favored perspective. One can, for example, view the emergence of the National Association of Scholars, primarily an organization of conservative literary scholars, as a response to the threat that postmodern literary theory poses to the standing of their ideas and, thus, to their own standing in the academy.

A key strategy for maintaining theoretical dominance in academe is controlling the dissemination of knowledge. Control over knowledge dissemination can favor a particular perspective, enlarging its symbolic capital while diminishing the presence (and thereby the symbolic capital) of competing perspectives. Scholarly journals, professional associations, and university presses are, therefore, sites of intense struggle because they are the forums for knowledge dissemination. The structure of these forums is such that a (relatively) small cadre of persons has control over whose knowledge is dispersed or suppressed, making it very difficult for individuals with alternative views to wrest control from a dominant group.

A Bourdieuan Interpretation of Who Succeeds in Academe. From a Bourdieuan perspective, symbolic capital plays a central role in the structuring and maintenance of the academic field. An individual's success within the academic field will depend in large part on how her or his habitus understands and activates symbolic capital. Thus, a beginning scholar whose social and intellectual origins readied her or him to interact professionally in the symbolic landscape of the university is in a far better position to further her or his accrual of symbolic capital than is a beginning scholar without such privilege. This presents many challenges in striving for an inclusive academy because the operation of symbolic capital typically is concealed. Those who have been isolated from the academy, such as members of racial and ethnic minority groups, are often ill informed about the currency that propels it. Thus, a Bourdieuan perspective sees an individual's success or failure in academia as the convergence of social group dynamics, field interplay, and personal–social worldview, all of which are necessary, but none of which is sufficient, to understand how the academy operates and what academic success entails.

In summary, when we construe cultural capital as the object of doctoral students' and postdoctoral scholars' academic pursuits, we largely set aside issues of the subject matter learned except insofar as subject matter content (including its representation) displays cultural qualities. Theories of cultural capital suggest that socially created and maintained patterns of knowledge creation and representation, and ideas about acceptable behavior and self-presentation, are themselves subjects of learning. Without this learning, professional success—viewed as successfully negotiating academic cultures—is unlikely. Beginning researchers' access to and activation of cultural capital are significant aspects of the learning and developmental challenges that beginning researchers face.

CONCLUSIONS AND CHALLENGES

How do beginning scholars in education construct themselves as educational researchers? We have offered four windows onto this question, each revealing a distinctive vision of what, ideally, an educational researcher can be. The subject matter window suggests that an aspiring educational researcher constructs herself or himself as a learner of an educational subject. This window portrays the ideal researcher as skeptical and imaginative, as committed to thoughtful and careful knowing and learning about important issues and subjects in education. The practice window defines the educational researcher as a community-based practitioner of research. This window reveals the ideal researcher as being attentive to research, as engaging collectively, and as working with and among persons who hold themselves and each other accountable to a shared communal endeavor. In this view, the researcher joins with others, learns from them, and contributes back. The dual-paned professional socialization and identity-crafting window represents the researcher as a professional, constructed either by external socializing forces or by internal drives—or possibly both. The ecological view in particular shows that being a researcher is both personal and professional. The ideal researcher, in this view, understands that although research is social and public, it is also a medium for a researcher to say or create something important from the knowledge of her or his life. And the cultural capital window represents the researcher as a culturally competent actor, drawing resources skillfully from surrounding contexts to advance her or his research aims. The researcher knows that educational research has exchange value, that it must be worked at, and that it is an accomplishment even as it is a way of life.

We suggest, in closing, that none of these windows alone can fully portray—or guide the creation of—thoughtful, imaginative, pragmatic, committed, clearheaded, and "savvy" educational researchers. It would be a mistake for a researcher preparation program to commit itself to just one of these windows. Although we dare not fool ourselves into believing, simply, that a panoramic view will resolve all researcher preparation problems, we do suggest that casting an eye at the scenery may strengthen researcher development programs in two ways. First, it may enlarge the scope of novice educational researchers' learning about what inquiry means and entails and may help researchers to think about how to improve the educational research that they and others carry out. Second, it may enlarge the scope of novices' future learning—informing them as to what they can learn about educational research and about themselves as educational researchers.

NOTES

1. Although concerned with learning, Broudy (1977) uses these terms in reference to "knowing."

2. We proffer the term "investigational content knowledge" as a parallel to Shulman's (1986, 1987) presentations of "pedagogical content knowledge" as conceptions of subject within a teacher's evolving understandings of what she or he teaches, within learners' changing conceptions of what they are learning in that teaching, and within the shaping of subject matter understandings that occur among them over time (see also Wilson, Shulman, & Richert, 1987). Investigational content knowledge refers, similarly, to the "psychologizing" (Dewey, 1902/1964) of a subject among researchers as they negotiate meaning, based on progressive inquiry into a subject. It consists of researchers' understandings of a subject's qualitative forms and their conceptions of paths of inquiry through it as well as tools to assist in inquiry. Investigational content knowledge can be distinguished from general investigational knowledge (i.e., knowledge about how to do research *in general*) in much the same way as Shulman distinguishes pedagogical content knowledge from general pedagogical knowledge (i.e., knowledge about teaching in general, e.g., maintaining classroom order).

REFERENCES

Argyris, C., & Schon, D. A. (1978). *Organizational learning.* Reading, MA: Addison-Wesley.

Becher, T. (1989). *Academic tribes and territories: Intellectual enquiry and the cultures of disciplines.* Buckingham, UK: Society for Research Into Higher Education and Open University Press.

Behar, R. (1993). *Translated woman: Crossing the border with Esperanza's story.* Boston: Beacon.

Behar, R, (1996). *The vulnerable observer: Anthropology that breaks your heart.* Boston: Beacon.

Berger, P. L., & Luckmann, T. (1967). *The social construction of reality: A treatise on the sociology of knowledge.* New York: Doubleday.

Birnbaum, R. (1988). *How colleges work: The cybernetics of academic organization and leadership.* San Francisco: Jossey-Bass.

Bourdieu, P. (1985). The forms of capital. In J. G. Richardson (Ed.), *Handbook of theory and research for the sociology of education* (pp. 241–258). New York: Greenwood.

Bourdieu, P. (1988). *Homo academicus.* Stanford, CA: Stanford University Press.

Bronfenbrenner, U. (1979). *The ecology of human development: Experiments by nature and design.* Cambridge, MA: Harvard University Press.

Broudy, H. S. (1977). Types of knowledge and purposes of education. In R. C. Anderson, R. J. Spiro, & W. E. Montague (Eds.), *Schooling and the acquisition of knowledge* (pp. 1–17). Hillsdale, NJ: Lawrence Erlbaum.

Brown, L. M., & Gilligan, C. (1992). *Meeting at the crossroads: Women's psychology and girls' development.* Cambridge, MA: Harvard University Press.

Cronbach, L. J., & Suppes, P. (Eds.). (1969). *Research for tomorrow's schools: Disciplined inquiry for education.* New York: Macmillan.

Delgado-Gaitan, C. (1997). Dismantling borders. In A. Neumann & P. L. Peterson (Eds.), *Learning from our lives: Women, research, and autobiography in education* (pp. 37–50). New York: Columbia University, Teachers College Press.

Dewey, J. (1964). The child and the curriculum. In R. D. Archambault (Ed.), *John Dewey on education: Selected writings* (pp. 339–358). Chicago: University of Chicago Press. (Original work published in 1902)

Geertz, C. (1973). Thick description: Toward an interpretation of culture. In C. Geertz, *The interpretation of cultures: Selected essays* (pp. 3–30). New York: Basic Books.

Gergen, K. (1991). *The saturated self: Dilemmas of identity in contemporary life.* New York: Basic Books.

Goffman, E. (1959). *The presentation of self in everyday life.* Garden City, NY: Doubleday.

Graff, G. (1992). *Beyond the culture wars: How teaching the conflicts can revitalize American education.* New York: Norton.

Hansen, D. T. (2001). *Exploring the moral heart of teaching.* New York: Columbia University, Teachers College Press.

Kondo, D. K. (1990). *Crafting selves: Power, gender, and discourses of identity in a Japanese workplace.* Chicago: University of Chicago Press.

Krieger, S. (1991). *Social science and the self: Personal essays on an art form.* New Brunswick, NJ: Rutgers University Press.

Kunda, G. (1992). *Engineering culture: Control and commitment in a high-tech corporation.* Philadelphia: Temple University Press.

Ladson-Billings, G. (1995). Toward a theory of culturally relevant pedagogy. *American Educational Research Journal, 32,* 465–491.

Ladson-Billings, G. (1997). For colored girls who have considered suicide when the academy's not enough: Reflections of an African American woman scholar. In A. Neumann & P. L. Peterson (Eds.), *Learning from our lives: Women, research, and autobiography in education* (pp. 52–70). New York: Columbia University, Teachers College Press.

Lave, J., & Wenger, E. (1991). *Situated learning: Legitimate peripheral participation.* New York: Cambridge University Press.

Lerner, R. M., & Busch-Rossnagel, N. A. (Eds.). 1981. *Individuals as producers of their development: A life-span perspective.* New York: Academic Press.

Merton, R. K. (1968). The Matthew effect in science. *Science, 159*(3810), 56–63.

Merton, R. K., Reader, G., & Kendall, P. L. (1957). *The student-physician: Introductory studies in the sociology of medical education.* Cambridge, MA: Harvard University Press.

Miller, D. W. (1999, August 6). The black hole of education research. *Chronicle of Higher Education,* p. A17.

Myerhoff, B. (1978). *Number our days.* New York: Simon & Schuster/Touchstone.

Neumann, A. (1999, April). *Professing passion: Views of passionate thought in scholarship.* Paper presented at the annual meeting of the American Educational Research Association, Montreal.

Neumann, A. (2000, April). *Toward a profession of learning: Exploring how university professors learn their subjects through teaching.* Paper presented at the annual meeting of the American Educational Research Association, New Orleans, LA.

Neumann, A., Pallas, A. M., & Peterson, P. L. (1999). Preparing education practitioners to practice education research. In E. C. Lagemann & L. S. Shulman (Eds.), *Issues in education research: Problems and possibilities* (pp. 247–288). San Francisco: Jossey-Bass.

Pallas, A. M. (2001). Preparing education doctoral students for epistemological diversity. *Educational Researcher, 30*(5), 6–11.

Reinharz, S. (1991). *On becoming a social scientist: From survey research and participant observation to experiential analysis* (2nd ed.). New Brunswick, NJ: Transaction.

Rosen, B. C., & Bates, A. P. (1967). The structure of socialization in graduate school. *Sociological Inquiry, 37,* 71–84.

Rosenau, P. M. (1992). *Post-modernism and the social sciences: Insights, inroads, and intrusions.* Princeton, NJ: Princeton University Press.

Schon, D. A. (1983). *The reflective practitioner: How professionals think in action.* New York: Basic Books.

Schon, D. A. (1987). *Educating the reflective practitioner: Educating the reflective practitioner for teaching and learning in the professions.* San Francisco: Jossey-Bass.

Schwab, J. J. (1978). Education and the structure of the disciplines. In I. Westbury & N. Wilkof (Eds.), *Science, curriculum, and liberal education: Selected essays* (pp. 229–272). Chicago: University of Chicago Press.

Scott, W. R. (2001). *Institutions and organizations* (2nd ed.). Thousand Oaks, CA: Sage.

Shavelson, R. J., & Towne, L. (Eds.). (2002). *Scientific research in education* (Committee on Scientific Principles for Education Research, Division on Behavioral and Social Sciences and Education). Washington, DC: National Academy Press.

Sherlock, B. J., & Morris, R. T. (1967). The evolution of the professional: A paradigm. *Sociological Inquiry, 37,* 27–46.

Shulman, L. S. (1986). Those who understand: Knowledge growth in teaching. *Educational Researcher, 15*(2), 4–14.

Shulman, L. S. (1987). Knowledge and teaching: Foundations of the new reform. *Harvard Educational Review, 57*(1), 1–22.

Shulman, L. S. (2000, May). *Students and teachers: What should they know?* Address presented at a conference on "The Future of Education," Northwestern University, Evanston, IL.

Sijtsma, K., & Molenaar, I. W. (2002). *Introduction to nonparametric item response theory.* Thousand Oaks, CA: Sage.

Simpson, I. H. (1979). *From student to nurse: A longitudinal study of socialization.* Cambridge, UK: Cambridge University Press.

Viadero, D. (1999, June 23). What is (and isn't) research? *Education Week,* pp. 33–38.

Weiss, C. S. (1981). The development of professional role commitment among graduate students. *Human Relations, 34*(1), 13–31.

Wenger, E. (1998). *Communities of practice: Learning, meaning, and identity.* New York: Cambridge University Press.

Wilson, S. M., Shulman, L. S., & Richert, A. E. (1987). "150 different ways" of knowing: Representations of knowledge in teaching. In J. Calderhead (Ed.), *Exploring teachers' thinking* (pp. 104–123). New York: Holt, Rinehart & Winston.

25

CONSTRUCTING DATA

KADRIYE ERCIKAN
University of British Columbia

WOLFF-MICHAEL ROTH
University of Victoria

W e focus this chapter on the construction of data in educational research, where we understand the term "data" to mean those mathematical or textual elements that researchers use in support of their claims. Articulating issues in the construction of data that are valid for educational research in general is not an easy task because there are very different traditions or research paradigms. Ordinarily, these traditions are differentiated by the adjectives "quantitative" and "qualitative." We do not find these terms to be useful, however, because all phenomena are characterized by the mutual constitution of quantitative and qualitative elements (Hegel, 1969). Accordingly, all so-called quantitative research requires qualitative processes (e.g., making judgments, distinguishing categories), and all so-called qualitative studies involve quantitative processes (e.g., counting and descriptive statistics [sums, averages, percentages]; terms such as "more," "less," and "increasing"). Other difficulties that exist in discussing data construction in general pertain to the different and sometimes

incompatible discourses that exist in the alternative traditions. Our first task, therefore, is to articulate a language that is subsequently used to discuss issues in two types of research, distinguished by the adjectives "high-inference" and "low-inference."

BASIC FRAMEWORK

In this chapter, we describe fundamental issues concerning the construction of data in high-inference and low-inference research methods. We denote as high inference those studies in which researchers are interested in generalizing findings beyond the context of the research. For example, researchers may be interested in examining gender differences in mathematics learning and performance. In this research, researchers often already have their research questions formulated at the onset of the research, such as whether there are gender differences in mathematics learning, and are interested in testing hypotheses and generalizing

AUTHORS' NOTE: The co-authors contributed equally to the chapter, and the authors' names are in alphabetical order.

findings beyond samples and contexts used in their research. In high-inference research, researchers are interested in examining gender differences in mathematics *in general* rather than gender differences in a particular classroom or context.

We denote as low inference those studies in which results (claims) are not extended beyond the sample or situation. Research questions are often developed during the process of research. The degree to which the results generalize to situations other than those represented in the data sources must be tested empirically in other research that involves these other situations. In low-inference research, researchers may examine mathematics learning in one or two classrooms in an effort to understand potential factors that lead to differential mathematics learning or motivation for mathematics learning. As we discuss and demonstrate in this chapter, quantitative and qualitative are properties of data rather than types of research or types of inferences that researchers are interested in making. Research activities may differ in terms of their purposes, such as high or low inference; however, both types of research may very well involve qualitative data as well as quantitative data.

In this chapter, constructing data is viewed as an integral component of the evidence-gathering process in research. The evidence-gathering process may be aimed at answering a set of research questions and testing hypotheses, as in the case of high-inference research. It may also be part of an exploration to refine and identify research questions, as in the case of low-inference research. Our emphasis is not on the critical differences between the two approaches themselves; instead, we highlight the differences in purposes of the two types of research and how these differences may influence the data construction process. There are, however, distinctions in the two approaches regarding the terminologies used, what constitutes data sources, how data are derived from these data sources, and who constitutes participants in research.

Here we understand *data sources* as contexts, people, methods, tools, and educational outcomes that we may want to explore so as to understand or make decisions in educational research. In mathematics gender differences

research, data sources may include different groupings of students in mathematics instruction/learning, computer programs, demonstrations of mathematical performance on different mathematical tasks, and teacher–student and student–student interactions. Research is based on representations of these contexts, people, and educational outcomes, including responses to surveys or tests as well as observations, videotapes, and audiotapes. From these representations, researchers construct the data proper through an *interpretation model.* The interpretation model could include scoring rubrics in a mathematics test or coding protocols for videotapes of student–student interaction in a classroom. Different interpretation models would be used in constructing data from students' responses to test questions, depending on the research questions. For example, if the students were asked to write a report on a science experiment, then different interpretation models would be used in constructing data for assessing their scientific literacy, mathematical competency, or English-language competency.

The distinction between data source and data also allows us to understand that the same data sources may be used in both low-inference and high-inference research and may lead to different data. For example, the same videotapes may be used to construct data for assessing mathematical knowing and understanding and for revealing patterns in student–student interaction during peer tutoring. Interpretations may result in data that assign scores to students' responses or may result in counts of some behavior of interest within and across videotapes. These could be ordinal data (e.g., 1, 2, 3, . . . , where higher numbers indicate higher degrees of competency) or categorical data (e.g., types of problem-solving strategies, types of interactions).

In low-inference research, data are used to substantiate claims (e.g., how female and male students interact with each other in a mathematics learning context) and to make inferences about the contexts and people (e.g., beliefs about mathematical competence, cognitive structures, intentions for further mathematical study or careers that involve mathematics); the inferences do not go beyond the contexts, people, and educational outcomes present in the data sources. In high-inference research, the data are used to make inferences that go beyond the actual contexts or people on which the data are based. For example, group differences such as those between fourth-grade Canadian boys and girls who participate in a study are to be generalized to all Canadian fourth-grade boys and girls. Therefore, questions about the degree to which data sources are representative of the population about which researchers want to make some general claims is a central issue in high-inference research. To be representative, the sample (group of participants in the study) should include the same variations that would be expected in the population (i.e., the group to which results are generalized), including age, region, culture, language background, and curricular exposure. In addition, the mathematics tests used for assessing mathematics competency should be consistent with the mathematical competency that the researchers are interested in examining and should include all aspects of this mathematical competency. For example, if the researchers are interested in examining how well students can apply mathematical concepts to scientific problem solving, then the test should include a sufficient number of questions to assess this component of mathematical competency as well as all other components of mathematical competency that the researchers are interested in examining.

Low-inference research and high-inference research do not distinguish themselves in the use or nonuse of quantitative data (e.g., numbers, counts). For example, some high-inference research, such as phenomenological studies that target understanding the structure of experience, might not use numbers at all; however, they might use terms that distinguish degrees of something such as degrees of understanding (Heidegger, 1977), degrees of sharpness in visual perception (Merleau-Ponty, 1945), or degrees of temporal distance (Husserl, 1991). What is the common essence of some human experience that might express itself in similarities or differences? This common essence may be derived based on studies of sound involving only one person (i.e., $N = 1$) and consistently confirmed in other studies if properly performed (Varela, 2001). Similarly, some low-inference research counts the number of incidences of some phenomenon or provides

frequencies for particular behaviors. For example, a researcher might report the frequencies of different categories of responses in a class of 20 or 30 students.

In the sections that follow, we present some research scenarios from our own individual research programs that involve both high- and low-inference research, and we highlight the similarities and differences in alternative approaches to research. These examples of research are presented and discussed in an effort to exemplify identification and definition of data sources, construction of data, challenges in research that are related to data, and the necessity of different modes of constructing data to address research questions

CONSTRUCTING DATA IN HIGH-INFERENCE RESEARCH

Most educational research requires data about student competencies, motivation, thinking skills, and the like. These are constructs, that is, entities that cannot be observed directly by the researchers. The researchers need to create data about the students' status regarding these constructs using indirect methods. Therefore, most educational data construction involves assessment of nonobservable psychological constructs that are thought to underlie the actually observable behaviors. Our understandings of some psychological construct—how it develops, how it is related to other constructs, and how it might be related to certain behavior, actions, and performance—are at the core of selecting or developing the right measurement instrument. Measurement instruments constitute primary tools for the collection of data sources. How well the measurement instruments match research purposes and the properties of such instruments are critical aspects of the validity of inferences from high-inference research. At least two typical research scenarios can be identified pertaining to measurement instruments that highlight different types of measurement issues involved in research. We refer to these as research scenarios on (1) the development of measurement instruments and (2) the identification of measurement instruments. These scenarios give us the opportunity to elaborate on measure development issues in general, the match between measures and research purposes, and limitations in research due to measurement issues that are at the core of all research scenarios. The next two subsections describe and discuss these research scenarios.

Development of Measurement Instruments

In this first scenario, the researchers have done a thorough review of the literature and identified an important research question and key constructs relevant to their research question. The main data construction issue is the development of measures that will provide adequate measurement of the construct in which the researchers are interested. For example, in developing tests to assess mathematical competency of seventh graders in the nation, such as those used in the School Achievement Indicators Program (SAIP, Canada's national survey of achievement), the tasks and associated assessed skills that the researchers choose to use in the assessment of mathematical competency skills need to be consistent with the definition of mathematical competency that the researchers have in mind or the way in which they are defined by an identified national curriculum. In addition, to be generalizable, these tasks need to span the range of all possible components of the mathematical competency that the researchers are interested in assessing. The tasks need to be presented in such a way that the language of the test items does not interfere with students' ability to demonstrate their mathematical competency. Many of these tasks should be available to give students numerous chances to demonstrate their competency, to provide multiple observations of this competency, and to rule out the possibility that students accidentally succeeded or failed on a task.

In developing measurement instruments, the researchers are required to make many choices. The first set of choices is related to the development and selection of tasks. The researchers can develop tasks that may be in a multiple-choice format, in a short-answer response format, or performance tasks that involve hands-on problem solving. The researchers may want to use as many extensive performance tasks as possible;

however, responding to these types of performance tasks can take students a long time and, therefore, may result in an unreasonably long testing time. In addition, scoring of student responses from such tasks is highly labor intensive; therefore, the use of performance tasks may result in very high costs. On the other hand, using multiple-choice questions may limit the types of competencies the researchers can assess, such as mathematical communication, and may have negative effects on communicating to the educational community what the important mathematical competency components are.

In addition to the format of the tasks, the researchers need to decide on the types of contexts in which the tasks can be and need to be presented. Whether these contexts, such as the division of pizza slices in a fractions problem, enhance the mathematics assessment, whether they introduce an artificial context that is not necessary, and whether they can introduce bias against some ethnic or gender groups must be determined. How many tasks can be included given the testing time constraints? What are the funding constraints that may limit the number of performance tasks that can be used in the assessment? How many and which tasks should be selected so that all components of mathematical competency are included in the assessment? Mathematical communication is an important component of mathematical competency, so it must be ascertained to what extent the tasks that assess mathematical communication are also assessing English-language competency and to what extent the test will be biased against those students whose primary language is not the language of instruction. These are only some of the questions that the researchers need to consider when developing and selecting tasks for the test.

Students' responses to the tasks then become the "raw data" or data sources from which evidence (data) is developed in support of the claims regarding students' competencies. The researchers need to use an interpretation model to convert the data sources into evidence in support of the existence or lack of a certain degree of competency. The interpretation model is a set of rules that determine what aspects of student responses are relevant to the target inferences and how different characteristics of responses may indicate differing degrees of competency. For example, in a mathematics test, the interpretation model includes scoring rubrics that describe what aspects of students' responses are relevant to successful completion of a mathematics problem-solving test item and how various responses, with different degrees of completion and mathematical accuracy, may indicate different levels of competency. A student's successful completion of tasks or provision of correct responses is treated as evidence supporting a certain degree of competency that is required to complete the task, whereas a student's unsuccessful completion of tasks or provision of incorrect responses is interpreted as a lack of the required level of competency.

The interpretation model can be applied to produce a set of scores, higher levels of which indicate higher degrees of competencies. Psychometric models with different degrees of complexity, such as classical test theory models, item response theory models, and latent class models, are then used to summarize this evidence. The result is a set of scores that may be one-dimensional, may be multidimensional, or may indicate class memberships. Assessment design and development issues that are at the core of such data construction efforts can be found elsewhere (Ercikan, 2005; National Research Council, 2001).

Identification of Measurement Instruments

The second scenario is similar to the first one except that the researchers choose to use a measure that has already been developed. Using an existing measure, instead of developing a new measure tailored to the purposes of the research, can have implications for the validity of research findings, and making such a choice requires investigation of the appropriateness of the selected measure for the research purposes. In the *measure identification* scenario, the researchers are typically constrained by availability and familiarity of measures, their conceptualization of how the construct should be measured, costs associated with measurement and data collection, and availability of the desired research participants (subjects) and contexts relevant to the study. If the researchers are

selecting a measure from an existing set of possible measures, the establishment of validity of interpretations for one population, such as adults, is not sufficient to expect or assume similar levels of appropriateness of interpretations for other populations, such as children. The researchers are often aware of the degree of inappropriateness of using with one age group a set of measures developed and validated for another age group. Unfortunately, the same degree of awareness does not exist for appropriateness of measures for different cultural and language groups or for people from different countries (Hambleton, 2004).

The widespread use of translated or adapted versions of tests in multicultural research or international assessments demonstrates the need for, and interest in, using the same measure in multiple languages and cultures. However, differences due to culture and language are often not taken into account when scores from these measures are used. Extensive research now demonstrates that measures in fact cannot be assumed to measure similar constructs when administered in different languages (Allalouf, Hambleton, & Sireci, 1999; Ercikan, 1998, 2002, 2003; Ercikan & Koh, 2005; Gierl & Khaliq, 2001; Sireci, Fitzgerald, & Xing, 1998). In this scenario, the validity of the research and the validity of interpretations are critically tied to the appropriateness of the measures selected for the purposes of research. Therefore, the researchers are required to provide evidence of such appropriateness.

PSYCHOMETRIC PROPERTIES OF MEASUREMENT INSTRUMENTS

The impact of different measure properties and the appropriateness of measures are at the core of validity of interpretations of all educational research. In both of the research scenarios just presented, a set of measures is at the core of the data construction process, and the primary research regarding data construction is the degree to which these measures are appropriate. This type of research requires data to examine properties of measures and their appropriateness for different uses. The following subsections discuss and exemplify the various types of research questions that psychometric research may involve and the range of data construction efforts that may be needed to explore these questions.

Examples of High-Inference Research

In this subsection, we articulate typical features of high-inference research and exemplify them in a case study assessing the equivalence of English and French versions of a school achievement test. The research described and discussed in this subsection explored the properties of tests that may have significant implications for data obtained from these tests.[1] The general research question was as follows: Can the English and French versions of tests be considered equivalent, or do the tests provide biased information about student competencies? The impetus for this research question was the fact that in Canada most tests are administered in both English and French, the two official languages of the country, with little or no evidence of the equivalence of the two versions of the tests. The comparability of constructs assessed by the two language versions of the tests is critical to all decisions and research projects that use results from these assessments. The purpose of this research was to examine the degree of differences that can be expected between the two language versions of these tests and to identify sources of differences. Data from the SAIP were used to evaluate the comparability of test items and of assessment results from the English and French versions of tests in three content areas: language arts, mathematics, and science. The data sources consisted of students' responses to test questions and identification of the language in which their test was administered.

There are many challenges in deciding which measures to use and the degree to which data from these measures will provide relevant information to address research questions adequately. In this research, the first challenge was the degree to which the types of differences that can be identified in the SAIP can be generalized to other tests. First, these tests are developed by professional content area experts in language arts, mathematics, and science and are adapted by professional bilingual translators. Given this, can the differences observed in this research be considered the minimum level of differences that might be observed in other tests for which professionals do not develop and translate the tests? The second challenge is whether the qualities of the data from the SAIP are adequate for making meaningful and valid inferences. For example, do the tests provide accurate measures of competencies in each of the three content areas? If separate measures of competencies in the two languages are not accurate—in other words, if they have high standard errors of measurement—then statistical comparisons of equivalence will not be accurate.

Comparisons of equivalence often use statistical estimates of overall competency in the substantive area. If this estimate of competency is not accurate, then investigations of equivalence are jeopardized. Another quality of assessment data is the degree to which each sample is representative of the language group as a whole. In the SAIP research, the tests tended to be long; therefore, the scores had good measurement accuracies. The two language samples were representative samples of 13- and 16-year-olds from each language group. Therefore, the two major challenges in data construction were met in this research.

Many other challenges were not met during the first phase of the study. One of the first challenges in high-inference research is the degree to which the findings can be attributed to the hypothesized sources of differences. From basic knowledge of research design, we know that we cannot infer causal relationships among variables unless we account for all possible alternative explanations, often through experimental designs. In construct comparability research, to what extent can we infer that the differences we identify are due to translation errors, differences in the two language versions of tests, or different language conceptualizations of constructs? Is it possible for the language differences to be confounded by other factors such as cultural differences, curricular differences, and education resource differences between the two groups? The statistical identification of differences does not provide answers to these questions. The next subsection describes additional data construction efforts to examine the sources of differences between the two language versions of tests and elaborates on the need for multiple sources and types of data to address these research questions.

Multiple Modes of Constructing Data to Address Research Questions

Four different approaches (Figure 25.1) were taken to examine the sources of differences identified in this psychometric research: judgmental review, replication, think-aloud protocols, and experimental design. Each of these approaches provided different types of evidence in support of or against the idea that performance differences were due to language differences between the two language versions of tests. All of the statistical comparisons were conducted for both the 13- and 16-year-olds.

This *replication* approach was expected to provide further evidence of a language differences interpretation if the differences were replicated for both age groups. Replication studies are a common way of verifying and validating findings in research. In our research, the assessments were administered to the two age groups not with replication purposes in mind but rather for the convenience of using the same assessment for two groups as well as for the examination of growth in learning from one age group to another. Because our study was based on assessment data that had already been collected as a national survey of achievement, we decided to take advantage of this feature of the data.

The evidence regarding language differences between the two language versions of tests cannot be determined without a review of the test items by bilingual experts. The *judgmental review* approach provided such evidence. We did not consider any alternative approaches to the judgmental reviews because this is the only way of examining linguistic comparability of test items, with possible variations in how the judgmental reviews are actually conducted. Even when language differences are identified by judgmental reviews, it is not certain whether these differences lead to performance differences between the two groups or whether these are the sources of differences identified by statistical methods.

The *think-aloud protocols* approach allowed us to examine students' thinking processes as the students responded to the test questions and to examine whether the language used in the test items may have affected these thought processes. There are several methods for examining students' thinking processes, including examining student concept maps and interviewing students after they complete test questions. These methods, among other possible methods, may reveal information about how students interpret test questions and use information from test questions. Given the purposes of our research, the think-aloud protocols approach had some advantages over these methods. It allowed us to document the thinking processes

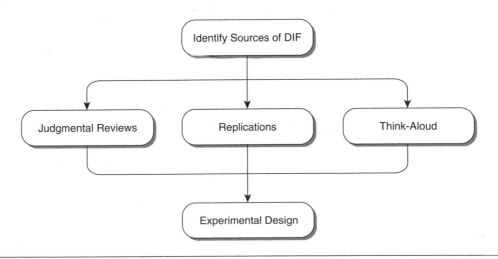

Figure 25.1   Four approaches to identifying sources of DIF are shown in the illustration.

as the students took the tests, ask students questions that targeted their understanding of the test questions, and examine whether any aspects of the test questions helped or hindered students' ability to answer the questions. All of these approaches led to further insights about sources of differences yet lacked support for causal interpretations.

The *experimental design* approach was used to test a set of hypotheses, developed using findings from the other approaches, regarding what language aspects of test items may be the sources of differential item functioning (DIF). The experimental design approach is the only way of establishing causal relationships between linguistic differences and performance. Therefore, an alternative approach was not considered for exploring such a relationship. In these four approaches, four different types of data sources were assembled to identify DIF of the English and French versions of the "same" test. The four approaches are described in the following subsections.

Judgmental Review. In the absence of experimental design, research is an evidence-gathering effort to support or contradict interpretations. Therefore, once a tentative interpretation is derived from data at hand, additional sources of evidence to support that interpretation, or other possible explanations of that interpretation, are the focus of further explorations. Following the statistical analyses, we asked bilingual experts to conduct a judgmental review of test items in an effort to identify possible sources of statistically identified DIF and possible adaptation problems. There are many variations of judgmental reviews that could have been used. We could have varied the number of reviewers, the expertise of the reviewers (e.g., their proficiency levels in the two languages), whether they review all of the test items or only a subset, whether they review the test items independently or jointly, and/or how their judgments are summarized and used. We chose to use four bilingual French–English translators, who completed a blind review of all the items to identify potential sources of statistically identified DIF. The translators were fluent in both languages and had extensive teaching experience. The adaptation review process required not only the identification of differences in the two language

versions but also judgments about the extent to which the differences were expected to lead to performance differences between the two language groups. Therefore, experience in teaching and familiarity with student thinking processes were also considered to be important characteristics of translators.

During this research phase, the data sources were the English- and French-language versions of test items. The interpretation model involved a comparison of meaning, structure, expression, format, and level of information provided to examinees in the two language versions of test items. Based on these comparisons, the reviewers created data that identified the level of comparability between the two language versions. The level of comparability ranged between 0 and 3. We used a rating of 0 or 1 to indicate minimal or no difference in meaning between the two versions, a rating of 2 to indicate differences in meaning between the two versions but not necessarily leading to differences in performance between the two groups, and a rating of 3 to indicate differences in meaning between the two versions that are expected to lead to differences in performance between the two groups.

This judgmental review phase of the study helped to identify those items that clearly had adaptation problems and those that had differential meaning, content, or format in the two languages. In the SAIP study, 38% to 100% of the DIF items in the three content areas were identified as having adaptation-related differences. The associations between these differences and the statistical differences identified cannot be causal; therefore, this additional step in examining comparability of constructs between the two language versions of tests gets the researchers one step closer to identifying sources of differences but not with certainty. Even with this uncertainty, the judgmental review phase is necessary to identify sources of DIF. Without this step, it would not be possible to tell whether there were language-related differences in the two language versions of the test items, even if we did not know with certainty whether these differences were the sources of the psychometric differences identified.

Replication. In construct comparability research, one way of finding evidence to support the interpretation that DIF arises from adaptation differences is by examining whether similar levels of psychometric differences were identified between the two language versions of tests for other groups of students who took the tests; in other words, replication of DIF findings is sought in several samples. We implemented the replication by comparing the findings for two age groups (13- and 16-year-olds) receiving the same sets of test items. In our construct comparability research, all of the reading items showing DIF were identified as having adaptation-related differences. These could be differences in the difficulty levels of vocabulary used in the two languages, differences in the clarity of the test questions, or change in the meaning of the test questions, among many other types of differences. The results of the replication study are summarized in Table 25.1. In the reading comparisons, of the 4 DIF items identified as having adaptation-related differences for the 13-year-olds, 3 were also identified as showing DIF for the 16-year-olds. In mathematics, of the 17 DIF items identified as having adaptation-related differences for the 13-year-olds, 9 were replicated for both age groups. In science, 28 of the DIF items were interpreted as having adaptation-related differences for the 13-year-olds. For the 16-year-olds, 22 of the DIF were interpreted as having adaptation-related differences, and 17 of these were the same as the items identified as DIF for the 13-year-olds. The age replication component of this research provided

further support for most of the DIF items interpreted as being due to adaptation differences.

Think-Aloud Protocols. A more direct way of determining whether adaptation differences caused DIF is to actually look at how examinees interpret test questions, how they use information from test items, and whether there are differences in these methods between the two language groups. The next phase in this research used the think-aloud protocols to examine student thinking processes during test taking and examined whether these processes were similar for the two language groups (Ercikan et al., 2004). The think-aloud protocols were defined as structured interview protocols that encourage examinees to think aloud, talk about their interpretations of test questions, and articulate solution strategies they use as well as difficulties they are having as they respond to test questions. In this research, participants consisted of two groups of 13-year-olds: a sample of 36 English-speaking students and a sample of 12 French-speaking students from schools in a large urban center in British Columbia.

The think-aloud protocols consisted of a set of questions that test administrators posed to participants on completion of each mathematics or science item. The questions were intended to tap four themes: (1) participants' understanding of the intent of each mathematics/science item, (2) the steps that participants took to answer the item, (3) the reasons for selecting the answer

Table 25.1 Replication of DIF Items Across Age Groups and Judgmental Review Ratings

Content Area	Judgmental Review Rating	13-Year-Olds	16-Year-Olds	Common Across 13- and 16-Year-Olds
Reading	0–1	0	0	0
(22 items)	2	3	3	2
	3	1	4	1
Mathematics	0–1	30	25	17
(125 items)	2	11	9	5
	3	6	6	4
Science	0–1	24	27	18
(144 items)	2	17	12	10
	3	11	10	7

NOTE: Judgmental review rating 0–1: no or minimal difference in meaning between the two versions; 2: clear differences in meaning between the two versions that might not necessarily lead to differences in performance between two groups; 3: clear differences in meaning between the two versions that are expected to lead to differences in performance between two groups.

that they chose, and (4) the aspects of the item that facilitated and hindered the problem-solving process. For each item, an interviewer instructed participants in a videotaped session to read the question and then verbalize their thought processes as they attempted to answer the item. If any information was not evident from the spontaneous thinking out loud, then the interviewer explicitly asked participants to provide further information after they had completed the question. Once a full understanding of participants' thought process was obtained, participants were instructed to proceed to the next item and so on until the protocols were completed. Even though the primary goal of the study was to determine whether data from the think-aloud protocols supported the hypothesized source of DIF, students were not prompted to confirm or deny certain possible characteristics of items. For example, if difficulty of vocabulary was the hypothesized source of DIF, students were not asked whether they found a specific word hard to understand or whether they were familiar with it. Instead, students were prompted to respond to the same set of questions on the think-aloud protocols independent of the hypothesized source of DIF. This was done to minimize any kind of bias that might be created by the researchers administering the think-aloud protocols. In fact, the researchers were not aware of the hypothesized sources of DIF during the data collection (Ercikan et al., 2004).

The think-aloud protocols data provided support for language differences as sources of DIF for 7 of the 20 items, 6 of which were hypothesized to have language differences as a source of DIF. For the remaining items, the think-aloud protocols did not provide supporting evidence for the hypotheses. This was not necessarily because these hypotheses were not reasonable; instead, it might have been because our think-aloud protocols did not induce the kind of responses from students that would support these hypotheses or because of the limitations in our sample of students.

The construction of the data source during the think-aloud phase of the study was a very time-consuming effort. It required approximately 1 hour of interviewing and videotaping for each participant (a total of nearly 50 hours). Recordings of the interviews were transcribed by hired individuals and were reviewed for accuracy by members of the research team. The transcriptions took approximately 5 hours for each interview for a total of more than 200 hours of transcription time.

The transcriptions of interviews constituted the data source in this research. The resulting text file was then used to extract data relevant to our research questions using an interpretation model, that is, by coding different qualities of student think-aloud transcriptions. The focus of the coding was to determine the following information for each item in the protocols: (a) whether or not students answered the question correctly, (b) students' understanding of the meaning of the question, (c) whether or not students found the question to be difficult to answer, (d) what aspects of the question were useful for solving the problem for students, and (e) what aspects of the question students found to be confusing or difficult to understand. Sample responses from the interviews are presented in Figure 25.2. Persons who spoke both French and English coded the data. Organization of the data for analysis was facilitated by the use of the NVIVO 2.0 qualitative data analysis computer program (QSR International, 2003).

The think-aloud protocols approach has proven to be useful in identifying sources of DIF, not as a preferred method, but rather more as a complementary method to other methods such as judgmental reviews and statistical methods. Some of the evidence obtained from using this approach, in support of the hypothesized source of DIF, could not have been obtained using either judgmental reviews or statistical analyses.

Experimental Method. The three approaches just described—replication, judgmental review, and think-aloud protocols—together provided insights about what the sources of differences may be. Yet these insights are tentative until they are tested formally. The fourth approach in identifying sources of DIF was an experimental study to test a formal set of hypotheses. These hypotheses were developed based on the replications, judgmental reviews, and think-aloud results and are related to whether different vocabularies, item formats, and language

Student's Understanding of the Meaning of the Question
I47: So what was this question actually asking you to do?   P47: Um, just find out how much it would cost for a 10-hour repair.   I32: What was this question asking you to do?   P32: Find a pattern in the cost.   I3: What do you think this question was asking you in your own words?   P3: How much the clock hand moved, or how much time is in between 3:25 and 3:45.   I10: So what were you supposed to do with this question in your own words?   P10: Figure out how many cities were under 25 degrees Celsius.   I50: So what was this question actually asking you to do?   P50: How much it would cost to purchase T-shirts for a variety show.
What Aspects of the Question Were Useful for Solving the Problem?
I66: And were there any hints in the question that helped you to solve it?   P66: The word "marine."   I53: Was there anything in there that helped you?   P53: Well, just, um, "to get the same results" is in the question, that made it easier.   I36: And what helped you to figure out that that was the final answer?   P36: Uh, the chart helped.   I37: How did it help?   P37: It shows what days he worked, when he worked, and how long.   I112: What helped you to figure out the answer?   P112: The picture.
What Aspects of the Question Did the Student Find Confusing or Difficult to Understand?
I28: So are there any words in there that you don't know?   P28: Well, the "line-ear" equation.   I. What made it difficult?   P83: Describe the oxygen cycle in nature. Use a labeled diagram if you wish. I haven't done this yet in classes or anything, so I'm not really sure what the cycle is.   I48: What made it difficult?   P48: Um, well, 'cause we had to calculate the add every additional 400 kilometers. And we had to figure out that you have to divide it by the 2,300 kilometers that he had left, and it took a while to figure that out.   I74: What made it hard?   P74: Well, I don't really know what cattails are, so I just looked at the diagram and I eliminated the least related ones, then I guessed between A and B.   I113: What is it about this question that is difficult to understand?   P113: Well, it says there are many variations among individuals of "variate."

Figure 25.2   Sample responses from the interviews are shown in the table.

styles used in the test items affected student performance. In constructing data for this phase, different qualities of test items that were suspected of being the sources of differences between the two comparison groups were manipulated, and two versions of test items were administered to randomly equivalent groups of students.

DATA SOURCES AND DATA IN LOW-INFERENCE RESEARCH

In this section, the relationship between data source and data is exemplified for low-inference research, and possibilities arising from an existing data source are articulated by drawing on materials collected during a study in a split sixth- and seventh-grade classroom taught by Wolff-Michael Roth. Data are what researchers use in support of the claims made about a situation under investigation. Thus, the set of videotapes shot in this classroom constitutes a source from which many different kinds of data can be constructed.

Construction of Data Sources

The study was designed to investigate knowing and learning when a science classroom is conceived of as a design studio and where, because of student–student interaction, one could investigate the relationship between individual learning and collective learning. For most of the time, students designed machines, encompassing the entire process from envisioning machines to completing a prototype model. The research team included the teacher (Roth), two graduate research assistants (gRA1 and gRA2), and a nonstudent research assistant (RA).

All lessons of the 4-month curriculum were recorded continuously using two cameras (operated by gRA1 and RA). During whole-class activities, the second camera served as a backup and was used to ascertain whether student utterances were recorded as completely as possible even when a student spoke quietly. In addition, two audiotape recorders were used to capture (a) students when they presented their designs in whole-class sessions, (b) the teacher's interactions with students during small-group work, and (c) interviews conducted in the setting by gRA2 while students worked independently on their design projects. Although it is never possible to "capture everything," capturing as much detail as possible in the course of a design experiment (Brown, 1992) allows researchers to identify salient factors that mediate learning at the level of the individual, small groups, and the whole class. In subsequent investigations of this type, therefore, we operated three cameras and made use of additional observers, allowing us to record half of the students during the learning process (e.g., Roth & Duit, 2003). In addition, we recorded the teacher continuously, implemented a massive interview schedule paralleling the classroom research by interviewing nearly half of the 26 students five times for 1 hour, and administered five instruments assessing knowledge, views, and attitudes. Roth could have used some standardized assessment of scientific understanding. Because Roth was more concerned with ecological validity, however, he had rejected them already in his grant application, opting instead for the construction of test items and test formats that would allow him to assess in ways where the students themselves had the sense that they had exhibited all of their understandings.

In videotaping, we decided to interfere as little as possible with ongoing activities. Students were not asked to remain at one place or to reduce the noise they made, although this would have improved video and sound quality. We felt, however, that making such changes would have been counterproductive to observing the knowing and learning as they occur in a setting conceived of as a design studio (Roth, 1998a). Ethnographic observations by the two gRAs were documented in field notes and as photographs. Although our ethnographic observations are generally unstructured, in the current case we had decided to confirm and disconfirm qualitative hypotheses from an earlier investigation about how knowledge comes to be shared in a classroom community (Roth, 1998a). We used the term "confirmatory ethnography" for this part of the work. After each lesson, team members debriefed the teacher (Roth), and these debriefings were also documented as observational field notes. Based on these observational field notes and on our experience during transcription, we prepared theoretical field notes that also became part of the data corpus. These theoretical field notes drove further collection of data sources.

The entire curriculum development effort, all curricular materials, and the artifacts used during teaching became part of the data sources. All curriculum planning meetings and interviews were recorded. Further ethnographic fieldwork was conducted in class during students' other courses, and informal interviews were completed with the students' teachers.

Prior to and at the end of the unit, we tested students in a number of ways. First, students prepared a semantic map of all the ideas they associated with simple machines. Second, students responded to questions about three instances that illustrated the application of levers, pulleys, and inclined planes. Third, the pretest phase included interviewing 13 (of 26) students about their ideas on simple machines, requesting elaborations of their written answers, and observing their qualitative and quantitative responses to problems. The students were selected to represent the class in terms of gender and grade level and had to be willing and able to articulate themselves in conversations with unfamiliar people. Fourth, the posttest was designed in the same way except that we invited pairs of students to talk about their answers on the test and about three practical problems. Fifth, all students participated in these debriefing conversations. For the three practical situations, students had available the necessary artifacts to model solutions to the following questions: "How would you use a pulley to decrease the effort?" "How would you use two logs to get a car out of a ditch?" and "How would you set up a ramp to bring a heavy load to a higher ground?" With many student groups, this led to situations that resembled conversations among students rather than interviews. By debriefing students in pairs, we hoped to address in part the problematic issue of ecological validity. During the lessons, emphasis was placed on material and discursive practices embedded in a social matrix, so we attempted to increase ecological validity by reproducing this social situation to some extent through paired interviews for the posttest. Some students agreed that debriefing in groups better reflected their learning in this class; for example, one student remarked, "It's much better with a partner. We worked on most stuff together, and although you sometimes argue, it's easier with two." All written work became part of the corpus, as did the videotaped debriefings and their transcripts. We explicitly avoided using standardized examinations because these generally do not test cognition of specific domains extensively and in-depth. Furthermore, the outcomes of such tests are frequently used for political purposes in the spirit of "accountability" (e.g., Hodgkinson, 1995) and may have detrimental effects on classroom processes and learning (e.g., Darling-Hammond, 1994; Rodriguez, 1997).

This particular research project followed on the heels of two similar design experiments in the same school. We had developed a good sense of the kind of data sources that were appropriate for each grade level. This was not the case when we started. For example, in a fourth-grade classroom, it turned out that the students in general, and the girls in particular, were rather timid and hesitated when expressing themselves. We had to make a choice about how to get students to express their knowledge and understanding prior to the beginning of our intervention. Therefore, we had to discard our plans to interview students individually. Although group interviewing has its disadvantages given that one cannot probe every student in-depth, we opted to try this technique with groups of five to seven students.

In our seventh-grade study, we ended up with an extensive database involving considerable costs, both financial (three RAs) and temporal (four times a week, approximately 2–3 hours in the school and 2 hours to commute to the research site, for 4 months). The costs were incurred in part because of concerns with making the database sufficiently extensive that any emerging hypotheses could be tested even after completion, in part for triangulation purposes (Lincoln & Guba, 1985), in part because access to suitable sites to conduct such larger studies is often limited, and in part because the curriculum development and teaching placed additional burdens on a researcher accomplishing his regular professorial duties.

Preparing for Data Construction

Low-inference research is conducted to find out how people (here students and teachers) make sense in and of their lifeworlds, how their everyday ways of acting are patterned (the structures of their practices), and why they do what they do (the grounds for their actions). In new kinds of situations not (or seldom) studied before, this requires researchers to collect materials from which the sensemaking of research participants can be inferred. What is relevant or interesting emerges from a dialectic tension between the materials at hand and the researchers' interest.

The entire team transcribed videotapes and audiotapes to make conversations available, as text for analysis and as feedback to direct further curriculum design and planning, as quickly as possible. Therefore, we chose to prepare them in a "quick and dirty way" rather than spending too much time in trying to make them suitable for publication purposes. These first transcriptions contained speaker names, spoken text, and some transcriber commentary (Figure 25.3). As is typical for design experiments (Brown, 1992), observations and interpretations during the process of building the data corpus directed subsequent design of teaching materials, social configurations, physical arrangements, temporal organization of activities, and time allotments.

WMR:	there was a question? (2)
Shamir:	but, when we were pulling on that other one, we were pulling, we were just pulling the banister string
WMR:	no, you were pulling here, this pulley (open end)
Shamir:	yea, but it was attached to the banister, if we pulled really hard then the (.)
Don:	i know, i //know]
Shamir:	if we] pulled the hardest, then the banister would fly
Daniel:	we were pulling where the pulley is ((WMR walks to the block and tackle))

Figure 25.3   This example of a first transcription contains rough estimates of pauses (indicated by single parentheses, e.g., "(2)" or "(.)" [= less than 0.2 second]), overlaps (indicated by slashes and brackets, e.g., "//know]" was overlapped by "/if we]"), and comments (enclosed by double parentheses "((" and "))"). WMR is the teacher.

To identify relevant and interesting issues, formal analyses were conducted throughout the research process. Formal data analyses were conducted in sessions with two to four members of the research team, according to precepts of interaction analysis, on the basis of videotaped data sources (Jordan & Henderson, 1995). The videotapes were played, stopping and replaying them as often as needed and whenever a team member felt that something remarkable had happened. This event was then discussed until the participants felt that nothing more could be said. In this way, a brief event (1–5 minutes) may lead to a 2-hour research session. (At the same time, we also ascertained the accuracy of the transcript as to the utterances, overlaps, emphases, etc.) When the researchers deemed this event to be interesting, all data sources were then searched to see whether it was similar to other situations and, therefore, represented a class of events. These analysis sessions were taped and recorded in field notes, and a flip chart was used to allow a permanent record of notes and drawings to be made during the meetings. Tapes, field notes, and flip charts were added to the existing data sources. In our experience, what different members of a team see in the data sources and how what they see is patterned may be quite different initially, but as the team works together, both what they see and how they see it become increasingly similar (on this point, see also Schoenfeld, 1992). This can be used to an advantage. Initial differences lead to the identification of different patterns, whereas the increasing similarity in perceiving particular events can then be used to individually analyze data sources and thereby increase a team's efficiency.

MR: and like this? (3.4) is that what you mean?

Jenni: yeah

Sham: yeah

MR: how is that different from this //one?]

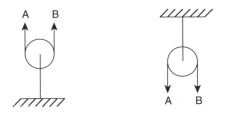

Figure 25.4   This example of a second-level transcription contains the length of pauses measured to 0.1 second accuracy ("(3.4)"), overlaps ("//one?]"), a gloss of the action ("[ends drawing]"), and the diagrams currently on the chalkboard.

In such meetings, we frequently identified some events as "interesting." We then transformed transcripts to include information that was relevant to the construction of data. For example, the transcript from the lesson excerpted earlier included drawings of the diagrams that the teacher and students had made on the chalkboard while discussing the outcomes of an earlier tug-of-war in which a pulley system had been used, leading to the fact that the teacher had won the competition against 20 students (Figure 25.4).

Evolving Interests and Construction of Data

What researchers need as data to support a claim depends on the research question, which itself is a function of the current status of the field or discipline. In the following subsections, several examples are used to show how different interests and questions led to the construction of different types of data from the raw and transformed materials. The videotapes and first transcripts constituted the sources for the construction of data.

Example 1

The researchers knew from the literature on workplace studies that artifacts and representational tools (e.g., whiteboard, chalkboard, computer screen) used in meetings mediated the interactions and content of conversations. In education and learning sciences, there had been no studies of how the content and form of classroom discourse were influenced by different combinations of artifacts (e.g., overhead transparencies, physical models), group size, and physical arrangements in and of the classroom. This tentative focus led to the identification of different interactional spaces, participant roles, and levels of participation in classroom conversations and, concomitantly, to different discursive forms and content. Three hunches (hypotheses) emerged to become more salient than others during the initial (collective) study of the videotapes. First, the artifacts appeared to have important functions in maintaining and sequencing conversations. Second, depending on the situation and the role of participants, the artifacts seemed to serve as resources for students' sensemaking. Third, each of the different activity structures of the curriculum supported different dimensions of participation in conversations. Why these three were more salient and more interesting than the others is a question that we cannot answer with certainty, but greater salience of data and research foci involves a dialectical process (Roth, 2005). In the current situation, this dialectical process likely involved the relationships among the existing literature in workplace studies, the absence of similar studies in education, and the researchers' existing predilection for group processes so that the new interest in the study of the interaction of physical arrangements, group size, and nature of representational artifacts emerged.

In support of any of these hunches, developed during the analyses of individual episodes, two kinds of data were needed. First, maps that showed how individuals were positioned with respect to one another and the focal artifact were required. Using a drawing program, we generated a map of the classroom, onto which we laid a new transparency sheet for each lesson, and felt markers were used to track student positions throughout each lesson. Second, transcripts that showed how the interactions unfolded in the situations described by the different maps were needed. Given the extensive nature of the database described, the researchers had considerable sources for testing the hunches. For example, Figure 25.5 shows the teacher's movement in the course of one whole-class discussion concerning an artifact that three students had constructed. The gray-shaded area shows the extent of the "stage," and the dark rectangle shows the artifact. Closer analysis led to the hypothesis

that individuals positioned in the gray-shaded area dominate the conversation. To substantiate or refute this hypothesis, three types of transcripts were selected, distinguished by different positions the teacher had with respect to the presenting students (Roth, McGinn, Woszczyna, & Boutonné, 1999). Thus, when the teacher was in the back of the classroom (Positions 1, 4, and 8), his influence on the conversation was as negligible or as important as that of any other student called on by the presenting students, who also chaired the session (Figure 25.5). The teacher's influence on the conversation was greater when the teacher was "in the wings" (Positions 3, 6, and 10). His impact on the conversation was as dominant as that of the presenting students when he "entered the stage" defined by the gray-shaded area (Positions 2, 5, 7, 9, and 11).

From these analyses emerged new interesting hypotheses. If participation in the conversation changes as a function of the teacher's distance from the gray-shaded area, would the same be the case for students other than the presenters? This new question required the researchers to search their entire database for all of those

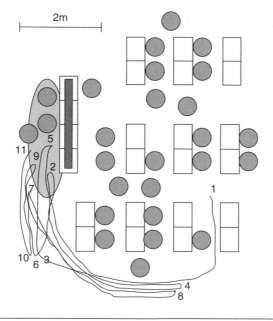

Figure 25.5   During a typical whole-class conversation about a student-designed artifact, the teacher had positioned himself in three distinct locations: directly next to the presenting students, to the side ("in the wings"), and in the back of the classroom. Depending on his location with respect to the focal area, the teacher influenced conversations to different degrees.

situations where students other than the presenters—or, in small-group work, students other than those in the group—entered the stage. These episodes could then be analyzed in terms of the contributions or impacts of the respective student(s) on the ongoing conversation. Here again, what was to become data was defined by the ongoing analyses, leading to a search through the database (i.e., the source) to identify what had been framed as the data relevant to the current question.

Example 2

A second set of issues concerning the nature of the data evolved from questions about achievement. The educational community in general and researchers of cognition in particular are concerned with questions such as the following: "What did students achieve as part of an innovative curriculum?" and "How did identifiable groups of students (in this class) achieve with respect to each other?" These are low-inference questions so long as the analyses are conducted for *this* classroom and are not generalized toward sixth- and seventh-grade students in general, but they are high-inference questions if the results from this class are generalized to a larger population of students doing the same curriculum. Although achievement might not have been the primary interest of the researchers, who were more concerned with levels of student participation and the interaction of processes at the individual and collective levels, the collective interests of their discipline were also addressed in their project. Past research on national and international (e.g., Third International Mathematics and Science Study [TIMSS]) achievement levels frequently identified grade and gender differences in science achievement; older students generally are higher achievers than younger students, and male students generally outscore females, in science. To assess whether there were differences in achievement across gender and age levels in their study, the researchers needed to search their database again, but this time for a different type of data. They were aware that any statistical calculations intended to test these general trends would have to be interpreted cautiously because of the small sample size.

The researcher had administered written tests and set up various tasks in which students orally responded to a variety of practical tasks. The raw data would consist of how each student did on the different tasks, coded as either 1 (correct) or 0 (incorrect). The relevant data sources were the written responses on the posttest and the transcripts of the videotaped interview sessions. Cautioning readers to keep the low power of the statistical tests in mind, we reported the results of a 2 (boys or girls) $\times$ 2 (sixth grade or seventh grade) multivariate analysis of variance (MANOVA), with students' written and oral posttests as dependent variables. No statistically significant effect for the gender (Wilks's lambda = .998, p = .98) or grade (Wilks's lambda = .954, p = .62) main effects or for the interaction (Wilks's lambda = .826, p = .15) was found (Roth et al., 1999). If the classroom was taken to constitute a sample from a population of sixth- and seventh-grade students doing this special design-centered curriculum, then these results would imply that the frequently occurring gender and age differences do not exist in the current classroom after instruction. Alternatively, if there are true differences in the population, then the statistical power in this study may have been too low to detect them.

The data in support of this tentative claim are the results of having used a particular statistical model; the inference is high because it makes claims about the curriculum in general. On the other hand, one could have simply reported the posttest means by gender and grade level, in which case the level of inference would have been low, but then so would have been the generalizability. That is, these statistics were used to make inferences about populations, about boys and girls in general, rather than being descriptive, in which case one would have simply reported the means for boys and girls and the different grade levels (i.e., descriptive statistics).

While assembling the raw data into a data table, the researchers noted something else that they had not considered before. Five of nine students identified by the school as cognitively or socially handicapped achieved in the top 30%. Although the research team did not pursue a possible hunch of the differential effect of the curriculum on students with different prior knowledge or achievement, this result, based on a simple tabulation of test scores by type of student, could have provided an interesting lead for future research. But another issue emerged for the researchers that was even more interesting given their predilection for, and knowledge of, situated cognition.

As the primary researcher repeatedly worked through the entire data set, he was struck by the variations in the responses that individual students appeared to give to structurally identical test items. This was interesting, especially in the context of the efforts of international testing consortia (e.g., TIMSS, Programme for International Student Assessment [PISA]). His hunch was that the results achieved in the research project could enlighten the educational community about the problematic nature of assessment formats in assessing knowing and learning not only in different language communities (as in the first section of this chapter) but also within more homogeneous groups. Having students respond to questions in a variety of circumstances, both before and after the unit, allowed an investigation about how the testing format influenced the students' answers, and therefore inferences, about their understanding and knowledge. If one assumed that knowledge is a property of the individual, such as in the high-inference examples used in the earlier part of the chapter, then this research points to the multidimensionality of knowledge even within the same domain. Alternatively, one may choose a different unit of analysis such as *person-in-setting,* as proposed by the educational psychologist Richard E. Snow, known for his work on aptitude–treatment interactions. In this case, multiple items or tests given to a student provide a sample of the student, whereas the same test given to many students provides a sample of the test (e.g., Corno et al., 2002). Supporting a claim about how different testing formats mediated student responses required a different kind of data from the kind used for achievement comparisons.

One piece of data was a table in which the response patterns of 13 students, interviewed during the pretest, were mapped in two conditions: an equal-arm balance that had continuously numbered distance markers on one side and was unmarked on the other side (Figure 25.6).

The data show unequivocally that (a) no individual student reused a strategy when the equal-arm balance was turned around to display numbered equidistant markers representing distances and (b) the sample changed in its entirety from using one set of strategies to another set (Roth, 1998b). There was no overlap in the two sets of strategies; if there was, it would have shown up as entries in the main diagonal. In the context of other studies, the researcher and his various collaborators came to the conclusion that interviews (Welzel & Roth, 1998) and better test instruments (McGinn & Roth, 1998) are not enough to arrive at suitable assessments of knowledge and understanding. These interviews alone did not allow us to take the analysis further, but subsequently additional data sources allowed us to show that students perceive the balances in different ways (i.e., they had what cognitive scientists call different "domain ontologies"), leading to different actions as well.

In this example, the analysis was qualitative in that it constructed categories of strategies on the basis of all responses to questions presented in two formats. The analysis was also quantitative in that it counted how many instances existed in each category (e.g., three students referenced locations on the marked lever but used trial-and-error procedures on the unmarked lever). The low-inferential nature of the study was not changed by the fact that the number of students using the same pair of responses was entered into a matrix; my counting itself did not make this a quantitative study because no inferences were made as to the frequencies with which students of this kind would respond on these tasks. That is, this is an example of low-inference research enacting qualitative and quantitative analyses.

Example 3

Several years later, the researcher became interested in the question of how scientific representations were used in scientific communities to mediate face-to-face interactions. He returned to the original videotapes to look at episodes where students and the teacher were engaged in conversations over and about a variety of representations. Contrasting the standard assumptions in science education at the time,

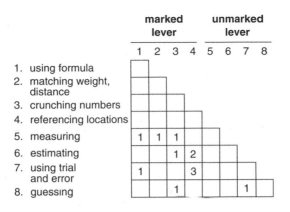

Figure 25.6 The figure shows the frequencies for strategy pairs used on marked and unmarked levers. The data support the claim that (a) structure of artifact changes the strategies that individual students use to solve problems and (b) an entirely different set of strategies was used.

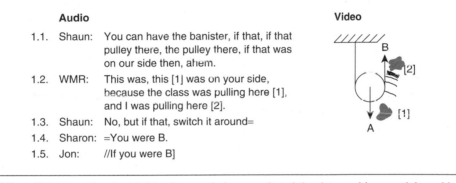

Figure 25.7 This example of a third-level transcription constituted the data used in an article making an argument that in understanding "conceptual" talk and thinking in science classrooms organized as linguistic communities, one must account for the fundamental interdependence of "hands, eyes, and signs."

according to which conceptual knowledge is expressed in language, the researcher developed the following hunch: To account for the content and process of interactions in science classrooms—that is, the scientific conceptions that are brought to bear on a debate—the fundamental interdependence of gestures, perceptions, and speech had to be accounted for. This required data that provided readers with gestures and perceptually salient chalkboard diagrams in addition to the words normally reported by educators (Figure 25.7). This claim, suitably supported by the data, undermined a common practice in science education, that is, to concentrate on words alone when identifying and testing student conceptions (Roth, 1996).

This initial research on the reported variations of performance across test format and the role of gestures and perceptions gave rise to a deepening interest in how the human body mediates knowing and learning. Do gestures and other bodily movements accompany and mediate scientific and mathematical cognition? Questions of this kind lead to claims that require data very different from the data presented so far. For example, in an article published in the *Journal of Pragmatics* (Roth, 2000), evidence (data) was presented for three major claims. First, in the absence of scientifically appropriate discourse, students' gestures already pick out, describe, and explain scientific phenomena. Second, during the initial appearance of scientific discourse, deictic and iconic gestures precede the associated utterances. Third, as students' familiarity with a domain increases, scientific talk takes on greater importance and gestures begin to coincide with the talk. This required data that showed how gestures and discourse were coordinated in time and also how words and actions, which must be brought about by the body, constitute and make scientific concepts available to others in real time. For example, Figure 25.8 constitutes a piece of data of the type presented in this article and others on the topic. It shows how the student, while uttering "You can pull on here," moved his arm upward. Here he not only said something but also activated his muscles to move the arm upward, and the video also showed a slight backward movement of the upper body. That is, in this brief episode, the relevant cognition also involved a physical action and a bodily response to the change in equilibrium as the stretched left arm was raised upward along the diagram. Readers can also see how the hand moved up to the line that supports the pulley, the place where the "you" can pull, and which words are associated with a particular position of the hand. Without active perception, it would have been unlikely that the hand had been exactly on the diagram where it was supposed to be.

This research began an extensive investigation of gestures, on the one hand, and of the literature in psycholinguistics, psychology, anthropology, and applied linguistics (in education, there was virtually no research concerning the role of gestures in content learning), on the other. This research provided further evidence of the fact that students were using gestures before they could describe and explain phenomena in words and that when the words first emerged, they tended to lag behind the corresponding gestures (Roth, 2003).

SIMILARITIES AND DIFFERENCES IN HIGH- AND LOW-INFERENCE RESEARCH

Research Question and Constructing Data

In high-inference research, a set of explicit research questions is the starting place for identifying data sources and constructing data. Examples might include "How do two mathematics instruction practices differ in their

Figure 25.8 This example of a fourth-level transcription constituted the data for an article on linguistics, arguing that (a) as students' familiarity with a domain increases, scientific talk takes on greater importance and gestures begin to coincide with the talk, and that (b) gestures involve bodily actions that constitute the nonverbal aspects of scientific concepts. The arrows mark the phonemes where the images coincide with speech.

effectiveness?" and "Are there gender differences in the way females and males use computers in their mathematical learning activities?" In the high-inference research described earlier, the research started with a well-defined research question concerning the degree of comparability between English and French versions of the SAIP and the sources of differences. In low-inference research, on the other hand, data sources relevant to the general research question may be the starting place; therefore, the first step in low-inference research is the identification of data sources. Thus, the videotapes collected in the sixth- and seventh-grade classroom permitted the generation of hypotheses about the role of gestures in the construction of scientific knowledge about simple machines and the forces operating in them. Because people make their sense of what is going on available to one another during interactions (Schegloff, 1996), videotapes are an ideal data source and starting point for low-inference research.

Common in both types of research is the need for different modes of constructing data. In the high-inference research examples discussed in this chapter, the research had four different approaches, each of which required different kinds of data and different modes of data construction. The first was the data constructed through large-scale survey testing of a nationally representative sample of eighth-grade students using the SAIP. The second required a set of judgments from reviews of English and French versions of test items by bilingual experts. The third required data about student cognitive processes during test taking. The data sources were students' responses during the think-aloud process, and the data were the extraction of the relevant components of what students said in relation to the research questions. The fourth approach, similar to the first one, involved data about student performance on different versions of test questions. These different phases and data construction efforts were *planned at the beginning* of the research project.

In low-inference research, research questions do exist before researchers begin assembling the data sources, but they are framed more broadly and frequently in process terms. Examples might include "How do students make sense of

tests?" "How do students make collaborative design activity work?" and "How does the language in whole-class interactions change when teachers change locations within the classroom?" Researchers then seek to identify patterns within the set of data sources they assemble and normally make claims that do not go beyond the particular set, although in some instances the set may be very large. (For example, a conversation analyst might look at more than 500 telephone interactions during 9-1-1 emergency calls.) The fundamental assumption underlying low-inference research is that each case expresses the concrete possibilities of acting and understanding in a particular culture; that is, any patterns identified are concrete realizations of general possibilities. Because low-inference researchers are frequently interested in how participants understand their situation, they may change their research questions while doing fieldwork so that the questions reflect participants' understandings.

Similar temporal shifts exist in the determination of the nature of the data and the interpretive model. In high-inference research, the nature of the data and the nature of the interpretive model are determined at the very beginning of the research. In low-inference research, the nature of the data and the nature of the interpretive model arise during the research process. In ethnomethodology, for example, researchers not only describe the ways in which people make sense of and act in their everyday situations but also must use the same (ethno)methods as their research participants for interpreting the data.

Research Process

In descriptions of research, details are important in low-inference research because researchers believe that all of these details may contribute to or interact with the research process. In high-inference research, on the other hand, the research is expected to be conducted in a predetermined uniform manner that guarantees the comparability of results across situations or, in other words, guarantees the generalizability of results. For example, if a set of tests is being administered, test administration procedures are expected to be uniform across classrooms or schools. Variations across different settings are almost guaranteed due to factors such as interactions between test administrators and students, students' needs, and weather. The research design in high-inference research treats such variations as random. Even though some statistical models exist for accounting for such variation, the error due to this random variation in most cases is not accounted for in the formal statistical models used for summarizing data or for testing hypotheses.

In low-inference research, efforts are made to maintain a "natural" mode of operation. In high-inference research, to determine the effects, there is an explicit intervention that is intended to change the natural course of things. Yet details of the research process are just as important in high-inference research in making meaningful interpretations. For example, during the last phase of the high-inference research described earlier, students will be split into randomly equivalent groups and will be administered different versions of a test. The equivalence of the two random groups is critical to the validity of interpretations from this phase of the study. Therefore, the description of the randomization process, details of the test administrations, and characteristics of the two groups of students are just as important in high-inference research as they would be in low-inference research.

Constructing Data

The example from low-inference research showed that there are interactions between participant/test takers and the instrument used to measure knowledge, and space limitations prohibit showing that there are similar interviewer–interviewee interactions that have been shown to exist even under the most rigorous schedules for high-inference research (Suchman & Jordan, 1990). Acknowledgment of the interaction between participants and test instruments is a general feature of most low-inference research. In typical high-inference research, the measure/ test is distinct from the participant/test taker, even though interactions between the two can be considered and modeled. Thus, even in the analyses of interviews that do not draw on statistical inferences, the participants' responses sometimes are taken to be independent of the interviewer questions and interview context. In both types of research, when such interactions are not taken into account, the inferences made by researchers may be inappropriate.

Nearly all psychometric models used in high-inference research require independent responses from participants. This assumption of independence creates constraints on what types of data are constructed and how they are constructed. For example, having participants work in pairs or groups generates data that violate the independence assumption. Low-inference research, on the other hand, generally is interested in how people make sense. Therefore, observing participants in their natural settings generates data that reveal the kind of information they make available to one another in problematic situations. In the first situation, the think-aloud protocols are used to elicit data to make inferences about individual problem-solving capabilities. In the second situation, researchers will typically ask participants to work in pairs because participants inherently make available to one another any problems experienced at the moment. In both situations, researchers collect protocols and transcripts, but these are used with different underlying assumptions (independence vs. ecological validity). The choice is (consciously or not) mediated by researchers' presuppositions about the appropriate unit of analysis. *If* knowledge is presupposed to be an attribute of the person, *then* the first situation will be chosen irrespective of the level of inference. *If,* on the other hand, knowledge is presupposed to be an attribute of person-in-setting transactions *and* always to be made available as needed by co-participants to one another, *then* the second situation will be chosen.

The examples from our research show that hypotheses can be found in both types of research; however, the hypotheses are found in different stages of the research and have different functions. In typical high-inference research, hypotheses are logical derivations from the research questions, and they determine what the relevant data sources are, what interpretation models should be used in constructing data, and thus the nature of the data at the beginning of research. In the examples discussed under high-inference research, we see that even though some of the hypotheses are indeed determined at the beginning of research, hypotheses for different phases of the research are based on findings from the previous phase. In low-inference research, hypotheses are usually found at the end of the research process, where researchers may articulate in which way their findings bear on situations other than the one they researched. This form of research is conducted because theories about phenomena that allow hypotheses to be generated do not yet exist.

CONCLUSIONS

As can be seen clearly from our examples and discussions, there are more similarities than differences between low-inference and high-inference research. Researchers needing to decide on an approach to research should make choices that best fit their research questions and the objectives of their research. For example, in policy-oriented research targeted to making decisions for groups, high-inference research will tend to provide the needed generalizability, whereas in research targeted to informing decisions about individuals, low-inference research would be preferable because of its attention to the particulars of participants and their situations. We also highlighted in this chapter that both high-inference and low-inference research may use qualitative (i.e., categorical) data as well as quantitative (i.e., numbers) data. Therefore, qualitative and quantitative terminologies do not provide useful distinctions in understanding research processes and requirements in general and the construction of data in particular.

High-inference research is interested in identifying patterns that describe groups or classes of participants. For example, a researcher might be interested in the covariation of IQ scores with achievement test scores. In low-inference research, the deviations from the group norm might be the most important component of the data (Holzkamp, 1991). For example, there is a correlation between IQ scores and achievement scores (Reschly & Grimes, 1992). High-inference research identifies such correlations, whereas low-inference research may focus on the reasons why an individual high-IQ student does very poorly on an achievement test specifically and in school more generally.

Both types of research involve interpretation models in constructing data. These models provide different ways of extracting data from data sources; therefore, subjectivity is involved in both approaches. For low-inference research, where many different interpretations of data can be found, it might be necessary to better specify the interpretation models used. Similarly, in high-inference research, the researcher needs to be aware of the possibility of multiple interpretation models and outline the reasons for choosing one model over another.

High-inference research is very prescriptive about how results are interpreted. For example, what constitutes a significant difference above and beyond reasonable doubt, or associations between different research variables, might not be interpreted as causal unless an experimental design had been used. Such requirements for low-inference research are not articulated very clearly in most studies of this kind, yet to make appropriate interpretations, similar rigor needs to be enacted. One might, for example, expect low-inference research to be very explicit about the interpretive processes and assumptions that are used to make claims about patterns and to instantiate an audit trail that allows others to retrace the emergence and changing nature of the patterns.

It is important to highlight here that researchers may choose methods and approaches that are most familiar to them, methods in which they have had training, or types of research for which they have sufficient resources. This leads many researchers to employ only one technique of data construction, that is, "monomaniacs of log–linear modeling, of discourse analysis, of participant observation, of open-ended or in-depth interviewing, or of ethnographic description" (Bourdieu, 1992, p. 226). This is unfortunate because choosing data construction or analysis methods on the basis of a method, rather than according to the question at hand, has the potential of jeopardizing what research can uncover. Therefore, we have argued in this chapter that researchers should choose the research method that best addresses the research questions. The types of research questions asked will determine the types of inferences needed. All types of research questions—such as "What is happening?" "Is there a systematic effect?"

and "Why or how is it happening?"—require different forms of inquiry with differing levels of inference. As the National Research Council's committee on research methods identified, the types of research questions asked in an area depend on the developments in that area (Shavelson & Towne, 2002). The three types of research questions just listed correspond to different stages of development in a particular area and correspond to different levels of inference, from low- to high-inference research. Therefore, the most appropriate approach is not always the one that leads to the highest level of inference; rather, it is the approach that addresses the research question the best.

NOTE

1. A more detailed and extensive description of this research can be found elsewhere (Ercikan, Gierl, McCreith, Puhan, & Koh, 2004).

REFERENCES

Allalouf, A., Hambleton, R., & Sireci, S. (1999). Identifying the causes of translation DIF on verbal items. *Journal of Educational Measurement, 36,* 185–198.

Bourdieu, P. (1992). The practice of reflexive sociology (the Paris workshop). In P. Bourdieu & L. J. D. Wacquant (Eds.), *An invitation to reflexive sociology* (pp. 216–260). Chicago: University of Chicago Press.

Brown, A. L. (1992). Design experiments: Theoretical and methodological challenges in creating complex interventions in classroom settings. *Journal of the Learning Sciences, 2,* 141–178.

Corno, L., Cronbach, L. J., Kupermintz, H., Lohman, D. F., Mandinach, E. B., Porteus, A. W., & Talbert, J. E., for the Stanford Aptitude Seminar. (2002). *Remaking the concept of aptitude: Extending the legacy of Richard E. Snow.* Mahwah, NJ: Lawrence Erlbaum.

Darling-Hammond, L. (1994). Performance-based assessment and educational equity. *Harvard Educational Review, 64,* 5–30.

Ercikan, K. (1998). Translation effects in international assessments. *International Journal of Educational Research, 29,* 543–553.

Ercikan, K. (2002). Disentangling sources of differential item functioning in multi-language assessments. *International Journal of Testing, 2,* 199–215.

Ercikan, K. (2003). Are the English and French versions of the Third International Mathematics and Science Study administered in Canada comparable? Effects of adaptations. *International Journal of Educational Policy, Research, and Practice, 4,* 55–76.

Ercikan, K. (2005). Developments in assessment of student learning. In P. Winne & P. Alexander (Eds.), *Handbook of educational psychology* (2nd ed.). Mahwah, NJ: Lawrence Erlbaum.

Ercikan, K., Gierl, M. J., McCreith, T., Puhan, G., & Koh, K. (2004). Comparability of bilingual versions of assessments: Sources of incomparability of English and French versions of Canada's national achievement tests. *Applied Measurement in Education, 17,* 301–321.

Ercikan, K., & Koh, K. (2005). Construct comparability of the English and French versions of TIMSS. *International Journal of Testing, 5,* 23–35.

Ercikan, K., Law, D., Arim, R., Domene, J. F., Lacroix, S., & Gagnon, F. (2004, April). *Identifying sources of DIF using think-aloud protocols: Comparing thought processes of examinees taking tests in English versus in French.* Paper presented at the annual meeting of the National Council on Measurement in Education, San Diego, CA.

Gierl, M., & Khaliq, S. (2001). Identifying sources of differential item and bundle functioning on translated achievement tests: A confirmatory analysis. *Journal of Educational Measurement, 38,* 164–187.

Hambleton, R. K. (2004). Issues, designs, and technical guidelines for adapting tests into multiple languages and cultures. In R. K. Hambleton, P. F. Merenda, & C. Spielberger (Eds.), *Adapting educational and psychological tests for cultural assessment* (pp. 3–39). Mahwah, NJ: Lawrence Erlbaum.

Hegel, G. W. F. (1969). *Science of logic* (A. V. Miller, Trans.). New York: George Allen & Unwin.

Heidegger, M. (1977). *Sein und Zeit.* Tübingen, Germany: Max Niemeyer.

Hodgkinson, D. (1995). Accountability in education in British Columbia. *Canadian Journal of Education, 20,* 18–26.

Holzkamp, K. (1991). Experience of self and scientific objectivity. In C. W. Tolman & W. Maiers (Eds.), *Critical psychology: Contributions to an historical science of the subject* (pp. 65–80). Cambridge, UK: Cambridge University Press.

Husserl, E. (1991). On the phenomenology of the consciousness of internal time 1893–1917 (J. B. Brough, Trans.). Dordrecht, Netherlands: Kluwer.

Jordan, B., & Henderson, A. (1995). Interaction analysis: Foundations and practice. *Journal of the Learning Sciences, 4,* 39–103.

Lincoln, Y. S., & Guba, E. (1985). *Naturalistic inquiry.* Beverly Hills, CA: Sage.

McGinn, M. K., & Roth, W.-M. (1998). Assessing students' understandings about levers: Better test instruments are not enough. *International Journal of Science Education, 20,* 813–832.

Merleau-Ponty, M. (1945). *Phénoménologie de la perception.* Paris: Gallimard.

National Research Council. (2001). *Knowing what students know: The science and design of educational assessment.* Washington, DC: National Academy Press.

QSR International. (2003). NVIVO (Version 2.0) [computer software]. Thousand Oaks, CA: Scolari–Sage Publications Software.

Reschly, D. J., & Grimes, J. P. (1992). State department and university cooperation: Evaluation of continuing education in consultation and curriculum-based assessment. *School Psychology Review, 20,* 522–529.

Rodriguez, A. J. (1997). The dangerous discourse of invisibility: A critique of the National Research Council's National Science Education Standards. *Journal of Research in Science Teaching, 3,* 19–37.

Roth, W.-M. (1996). Thinking with hands, eyes, and signs: Multimodal science talk in a Grade 6/7 unit on simple machines. *Interactive Learning Environments, 4,* 170–187.

Roth, W.-M. (1998a). *Designing communities.* Dordrecht, Netherlands: Kluwer Academic.

Roth, W.-M. (1998b). Situated cognition and assessment of competence in science. *Evaluation and Program Planning, 21,* 155–169.

Roth, W.-M. (2000). From gesture to scientific language. *Journal of Pragmatics, 32,* 1683–1714.

Roth, W.-M. (2003). Gesture–speech phenomena, learning, and development. *Educational Psychologist, 38,* 249–263.

Roth, W.-M. (2005). *Doing qualitative research: Praxis of method.* Rotterdam, Netherlands: SENSE Publications.

Roth, W.-M., & Duit, R. (2003). Emergence, flexibility, and stabilization of language in a physics classroom. *Journal for Research in Science Teaching, 40,* 869–897.

Roth, W.-M., McGinn, M. K., Woszczyna, C., & Boutonné, S. (1999). Differential participation during science conversations: The interaction of focal artifacts, social configuration, and physical arrangements. *Journal of the Learning Sciences, 8,* 293–347.

Schegloff, E. A. (1996). Confirming allusions: Toward an empirical account of action. *American Journal of Sociology, 102,* 161–216.

Schoenfeld, A. (1992). On paradigms and methods: What do you do when the ones you know don't do what you want them to? Issues in the analysis of data in the form of videotapes. *Journal of the Learning Sciences, 2,* 179–214.

Shavelson, R. J., & Towne, L. (Eds.). (2002). *Scientific research in education.* Washington, DC: National Academy Press.

Sireci, G. S., Fitzgerald, C., & Xing, D. (1998). *Adapting credentialing examinations for international uses* (Laboratory of Psychometric and Evaluative Research, Report No. 329). Amherst: University of Massachusetts, School of Education.

Suchman, L. A., & Jordan, B. (1990). Interactional troubles in face-to-face survey interviews. *Journal of the American Statistical Association, 85,* 232–244.

Varela, F. J. (2001). Consciousness: The inside view. *Trends in Cognitive Sciences, 5,* 318–319.

Welzel, M., & Roth, W.-M. (1998). Do interviews really assess students' knowledge? *International Journal of Science Education, 20,* 25–44.

26

CONSTRUCTING ANALYSES

The Development of Thoughtfulness in Working With Quantitative Methods

MICHAEL SELTZER

University of California, Los Angeles

MIKE ROSE

University of California, Los Angeles

During the past several years, we have had the opportunity to engage in numerous discussions about research methodology and about methods training for graduate students in education. One of us is a quantitative methodologist who is particularly interested in the use of hierarchical linear modeling in multisite evaluation studies, and the other works predominantly with qualitative methods and has a special interest in writing as a tool for analysis and reflection in the research process. Both of us are on the faculty of a social research methodology division. This chapter grows out of various kinds of work we have done together, research and teaching that, over time, has led to a mutual sense that traditional methods training might not address an important dimension of methodological proficiency— what we will call "analytic thoughtfulness." In this chapter, we focus on quantitative methods, although what we discuss has application to— and can involve—qualitative methodology as well.

In our experience, typical methods training tends toward developing in young researchers a technical proficiency. This makes sense; one needs to know the specifics of statistical formulas and design to do the work at all. In addition, such training, when done well, does urge students to ask hard questions of their analysis (e.g., Are there disconfirming data?). This certainly contributes to thoughtful inquiry. But do we address this quality explicitly and adequately? Do we sufficiently call attention to, and help foster, what Schön (1984) long ago called "reflective practice"? This entails thinking about what we are doing, why we are doing it, what might be flawed about it, and how best to convey the important aspects of the process to others.

One development in research methodology that, we think, can contribute to thoughtfulness in young researchers has been the call over the past decade or so for a bridging of the quantitative–qualitative divide. The increasing interest in mixed methods certainly echoes that call.

These developments have special resonance for us given the way in which our different backgrounds are often brought together in the mentoring and teaching we do. It seems to us that complementing or combining disparate research traditions, if done in a principled way, demands some reflection on purpose, some meta-level consideration of what one is doing and why (Tashakorri & Teddlie, 2003), and some degree of analytic thoughtfulness. There certainly are cases where the mixing of methods is mechanical and unreflective, but if it is done well, one is almost forced to go beyond the requirements of technique and procedure and to consider questions of epistemology and purpose.

One way of getting to such questions—which we think are related to a thoughtful stance toward one's research—is to directly address assumptions, philosophical underpinnings, and the like. Some courses and textbooks do just that. But the treatment can be a bit abstract—not clearly tied to one's analysis of data—so we have been wondering how faculty might, in practice, help students in more specific ways to develop this thoughtful stance in the actual *doing* of analysis.

Because these speculations of ours arise from our work together, it might help us to lay out our case if we briefly recount some of this mutual experience. Over the past 4 years or so, we have had the occasion to critically read each other's work, to dig deep into papers we were writing separately that involved quite different modes of analysis—hierarchical linear modeling, in one case, and life history, historical inquiry, and observational inquiry, in the other. What we observed during such sessions was the way in which the best feedback—the feedback that helped to crack the toughest technical *or* conceptual problems—was often hard to classify as, for example, being clearly from the quantitative or qualitative toolbox. A technical point quickly morphed into further questions about judgment and audience, or an appreciation of a narrative led to a discussion of validity. Of course, the specifics of our disciplinary training made our work possible in the first place, and it came into play in our discussion, but a fair amount of our critical reflection also took place in some further domain that involved language, purpose, the history of a technical procedure, implications, and the like.

Another kind of experience came as we co-taught a research practicum and reread together some of our field's classic pieces on method, for example, Campbell and Stanley's (1963) "Experimental and Quasi-Experimental Designs for Research on Teaching," Cronbach's (1975) "Beyond the Two Disciplines of Scientific Psychology," and Geertz's (1973) essay on "thick description" in *The Interpretation of Cultures.* As expected, technical issues that are identified with particular research traditions arose, for example, issues of design or of generalizability. But what struck us was the way in which our reading together led us to think across traditional methodological borders, for example, to consider the conceptual heuristic value of thinking about qualitative inquiry through the lenses provided by Campbell and Stanley (1963)—not to dismiss the legitimacy of qualitative research but rather to think about its own systematic character and, beyond, to ponder the ways in which educational researchers try to bring order and procedure to bear generally as we inquire about social phenomena. We think here of Yin's (1994) attempt to tease out the fundamental logic that underlies all good research, for example, the importance of considering rival hypotheses. But to go a little further, we were impressed with the way in which these classic texts spoke to each other and, collectively, could lead to rich conversations about the way in which inquiry works and the motive and purpose for doing it.

The final source of our reflections in this chapter is the mentoring and advising we have done together with students in our methodology division. We were struck, for example, by the difficulty of getting students to see beyond the technical aspects of quantitative analysis, to appreciate and learn to engage the interpretive dimension of statistical procedures—the qualitative element, so to speak (Shadish, Cook, & Campbell, 2002). As one small example, we began asking students to try to imagine the human reality behind a particular set of numerical data—kids in different schools taking a standardized test, families represented in shifting residential patterns, or outliers in a domestic violence population. We wanted to get them to think about the possible lived experience behind data as one way in which to see whether the data made sense.

The sum of these experiences has led us to wonder how we might talk about the analysis of quantitative data so that, on the one hand, we honor the unique aspects of a particular methodological approach but that, on the other, we seek qualities that go beyond both technical proficiency and the familiar categories we use to define methods. With this goal in mind, we offer a series of propositions that, we believe, can lead to more thoughtful analysis—to a reflective supple practice.

We should be clear that this chapter does not provide the "how to" details, that is, the techniques of specific modes of analysis. These techniques can be learned through coursework and specialized textbooks. This chapter could best be read during or after such training. Imagine reading it alongside a text on regression analysis or on hierarchical linear modeling. Our hope is that the following propositions will help in the process of converting analytic techniques into ways of thinking analytically. Consider them as strategies of inquiry that make explicit some of the intellectual moves that experienced researchers acquire through long practice.

We begin by discussing the importance of context in quantitative analysis—the need to consider the setting, the time, the events, and the social forces that affect, or even constitute, a given body of data. We then give a reminder to be skeptical of the results of one's analysis, to pose rival hypotheses and seek disconfirming cases. Both of these propositions are central to thoughtful analysis, so we devote a fair amount of space to them and provide several extended examples. We then discuss the importance of conducting extensive and careful exploratory analysis—in a sense, "getting close" to the data—before turning to the use of statistical models. We conclude the chapter by offering a few further propositions that follow from the discussion of context and rival hypotheses, propositions that further contribute to the development of thoughtful analysis.

The Importance of Context

Educational researchers are certainly aware of the notion of context, both from the traditional academic psychology perspective (one needs to

be knowledgeable about the context of one's study to control for threats to validity) and from more qualitative orientations, where context is a fundamental part of one's inquiry. "Meaning in context," asked Mishler (1979), "is there any other kind?" We are struck, however, by how often context seems to be underappreciated or is defined in narrow ways as the most immediate environment of a study.

Of course, any study must set limits, that is, restrict the scope of its investigation. And it would be an epic study indeed that gave full treatment to all of the contextual factors of an investigation. But these restrictions should not forestall a richer appreciation of context than is typical. Such appreciation can enhance the legitimacy of the study and possibly raise further interesting questions.

Let us begin consideration of this issue with a brief qualitative example—a study of the conversational turn-taking patterns in a classroom. If well done, such a study would most likely consider the context of the classroom itself—the way in which seating is arranged, the physical layout of the room, and the kinds of students in the room. Opening the contextual lens wider, however, one might ask whether there are things going on in the school that might affect the talk in this classroom. Is there a new administration, with new ideas about instruction, or a professional development program that involved some significant percentage of the teachers? Open the lens wider, and one could note whether the community is undergoing significant demographic and/or economic changes that would affect the population in a particular classroom. Open it wider still, and one would be mindful of large-scale district, state, or federal policy initiatives that could influence the way in which teachers and students talk to each other. The No Child Left Behind legislation is profoundly affecting instruction in some districts—and thus in some classrooms.

At first blush, attending to context might seem incompatible with the use of quantitative methods. The application of quantitative techniques (e.g., regression, analysis of variance) centers on investigating patterns of covariation between key predictor and outcome variables, for example, how student participation in different reading interventions relates to differences in improvement in reading skills. Such analyses lack the holistic quality—the attention to the multiplicity of factors at work in particular settings—that tends to characterize qualitative research.

However, we would argue that an awareness of the importance of context is central to good quantitative inquiry. As an example, let us consider efforts to discern key patterns of results in a large-scale evaluation of an innovative prealgebra curriculum called Transition Mathematics (TM) that were put forth by researchers at the University of Chicago during the 1980s (University of Chicago School Mathematics Project, 1986). The account we give here is somewhat detailed, but please bear with us. We refer back to this example as the chapter unfolds.

The sample for this study consisted of 20 carefully matched pairs of classrooms located in various school districts throughout the United States. Within each pair, one class was taught by a teacher who implemented the TM curriculum, and the other class was taught by a teacher who used the prealgebra curriculum already in place at that particular site. The teachers who participated in this study tended to have appreciable teaching experience.

We focus on student performance on a 19-item posttest that assessed student readiness for geometry. In large-scale evaluations such as this, questions regarding the overall effectiveness of a program with respect to key outcomes have traditionally been of interest to evaluators and policymakers. Thus, we begin by attempting to address the following question: What is the expected difference in performance between students who work with TM materials and those who do not?

When we compare the average geometry readiness score for the entire sample of TM students with the average score for students who worked with more traditional materials, we find that there is a statistically significant difference of about 1 point (i.e., 1 item) favoring TM. Although this result is statistically significant, it is clearly modest from a practical standpoint.[1]

But is this single-number summary an adequate account of the effects of TM on geometry readiness? How useful is this analysis to school superintendents who might be faced with deciding whether or not to adopt TM, to teachers who might be interested in using TM with their students, or to researchers whose interests center on teaching and learning mathematics?

Let us take a closer look at the design and sample of the TM study. First, it is important to be mindful of the fact that the sample for this study consists of 20 matched pairs of classes located in an array of sites throughout the United States. These locales range from upper-middle-class neighborhoods in the Chicago area, to inner-city neighborhoods in Cincinnati, to agricultural communities in the state of Mississippi. Second, there are appreciable differences across sites in terms of students' prior preparation in mathematics as well as in other subject areas. Third, a key element of the study is that 20 teachers implemented the TM curriculum and 20 teachers used more traditional textbooks with their students. This is a critically important point because we know that even the most experienced math teachers can vary substantially in their notions of which topics merit extra emphasis, how certain topics are best taught, and how best to organize and manage classes for instruction. For example, the particular implementation of TM experienced by the TM students at one site may have differed markedly from the implementation of TM at other sites.

When we start to think about these aspects of the TM study, we begin to sense that our single-number summary, in Cronbach's (1976) words, may conceal more than it reveals (p. 1). In fact, perhaps it is best to view the 20 sites in this study as constituting a set of 20 "mini-studies" of TM. Thus, a productive way of beginning to dig beneath our single-number summary would be to compare the performance of students in TM and comparison classes site by site. For each site, we subtract the mean geometry readiness score of the comparison class students at that site from the mean geometry readiness score of the TM students. The resulting differences, which we might term TM/comparison class contrasts or site TM effects, are displayed in Table 26.1.

As can be seen in Table 26.1, the variability in TM/comparison class contrasts is striking. Specifically, the TM students outperformed comparison class students by as much as 4.5 points at some sites, whereas there was virtually

Table 26.1 Site-by-Site Analysis: Estimates of Site TM effects

Site	TM Effect Estimate	SE	Implementation of Reading[a]
1	−0.23	0.96	0
2	2.16[b]	0.89	1
3	0.38	0.75	0
4	−0.24	0.99	0
5	0.29	1.22	0
6	1.68	1.12	1
7	1.27	0.79	1
8	−2.52[b]	1.25	1
9	4.42[b]	0.85	1
10	3.63[b]	1.52	1
11	−2.21	1.13	0
12	0.79	1.06	1
13	1.15	1.52	0
14	4.09[b]	1.27	1
15	0.94	1.37	0
16	−1.39	1.27	1
17	1.65	1.09	0
18	0.78	1.12	1
19	2.47[b]	1.06	0
20	4.56[b]	1.72	1

SOURCE: Adapted from Seltzer, M. (1994), Studying variation in program success: A multilevel modeling approach, *Evaluation Review, 18,* 342–361. Reprinted by permission of Sage Publications.

NOTE: Details regarding the calculation of the estimates presented in this table can be found in Seltzer (1994).

a. 0 = low; 1 = high.

b. TM effect estimate that is more than twice its standard error.

no difference at all at other sites. Furthermore, one can see that comparison class students outperformed TM students by appreciable amounts at two sites.

The marked heterogeneity that we see in results is not too surprising when we begin to think more qualitatively about the introduction of new programs into different school and classroom settings. When teachers implement a new program in their classrooms, an array of challenges and difficulties will likely arise. For example, a TM teacher, sensing that her students are struggling with certain concepts, might supplement various lessons with materials from another text. Another teacher whose students are

also encountering some difficulties might make very subtle yet powerful adjustments. A third teacher, sensing that his students are well prepared for TM and very engaged with the curriculum, might feel confident that his students will eventually firmly grasp certain difficult concepts when these concepts are presented and used in slightly different ways in later chapters of the text. Yet another teacher might feel compelled to skip certain topics and spend extra time on material that is certain to appear on a districtwide achievement test.

Thus, when we begin to think about the lived experience of teachers and students in different classrooms and at different evaluation sites— about various constraints that may be at work, about the dynamic nature of instruction, and about various contingencies that might arise—it is clear that the extensive variability in results that we see in Table 26.1 is more likely the rule, rather than the exception, in educational evaluations. But note, importantly, that our single-number summary masked this variability. On the basis of that summary, decision makers might mistakenly conclude that the effects of TM are uniform across sites.

Although the results in Table 26.1 begin to provide us with a more realistic picture of the effects of TM, they might in fact be a source of bewilderment and dismay for decision makers. For example, a school superintendent who is considering adopting TM might wonder whether TM will work extremely well in her district (as in the case of, e.g., Site 20) or whether TM will yield virtually no advantage (as in the case of, e.g., Site 5).

But at the same time, the heterogeneity that we see also encourages us to ask why TM appeared to be so much more successful at some sites than at others. That is, are certain key factors (e.g., particular facets of implementation) critical to the success of TM? Is TM more effective in settings where students enter prealgebra with a fundamental understanding of particular mathematical concepts?

In this connection, the naturally occurring variations in results across sites, on the one hand, and in site characteristics and implementation, on the other, provide opportunities to try to identify possible systematic connections between the two. Certainly, an appreciable

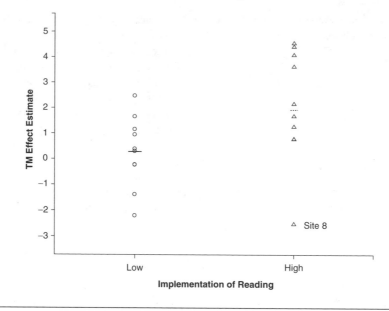

Figure 26.1   Site TM Effect Estimates Versus Level of Implementation of Reading

NOTE: Circles and triangles are used to represent low- and high-implementation sites, respectively. The mean of the TM effect estimates for the 10 low-implementation sites is represented by a solid horizontal line, and the mean of the TM effect estimates for the 10 high-implementation sites is represented by a dashed line.

amount of the variability in results that we see is very likely due to unique, site-specific factors (e.g., certain teachers in the study may have been highly skilled, certain unexpected events may have occurred). But it may also be the case, for example, that differences in certain aspects of implementation are systematically related to differences in the effects of TM.

One of us explored these possibilities through a series of analyses (Seltzer, 1994, 2004). In particular, one of the distinctive features of TM is that reading is included in every unit of the text. The developers of TM view daily discussion of the reading passages, which explicate key concepts and ideas, as a critically important element of the program. Information regarding this aspect of implementation was obtained via a teacher questionnaire administered at the end of the study.

As can be seen in Table 26.1, 10 TM teachers indicated that they discussed the reading in the text on a daily basis ("high implementation") and 10 indicated that reading was discussed frequently but not on a daily basis ("low implementation"). When we focus our attention on the high-implementation sites, we find that the

TM/comparison contrasts tend to take on relatively large positive values. In contrast, we find that the TM/comparison contrasts for many of the low-implementation sites are negligible.

Figure 26.1, which graphically displays the set of TM/comparison contrasts for the 10 low-implementation sites next to the set of contrasts for the 10 high-implementation sites, brings this pattern to light more clearly. The plot also helps us to see that the mean (expected) effect of TM in low-implementation sites is approximately 0.25 point, a result that is negligible from a practical standpoint and, as we might suspect, is not statistically significant. In essence, we find no difference, on average, in geometry readiness scores between TM and comparison classes when implementation of TM is low. However, the expected effect of TM in high-implementation sites is approximately 2 points, a result that is twice as large as the overall estimate of the effect of TM computed at the outset and that, not surprisingly, is statistically significant. Thus, the use of the reading in the TM text appears to play a critical role with respect to the success of TM.

The plot also helps us to see that the story is not so simple. For example, we see appreciable variability in results among the 10 low-implementation sites as well as among the 10 high-implementation sites. So clearly, other factors are at work—some site specific (e.g., the occurrence of certain disruptive events) and others perhaps systematic (e.g., differences across sites in other important facets of implementation). In addition, the plot draws our attention to a discrepant case, that is, Site 8. Site 8 is a high-implementation site, yet the TM/comparison contrast for this site takes on a large negative value. One possible explanation for this large negative effect centers on difficulties experienced by many of the TM students at this site in reading the text; for many of these students, English was their second language. Although we cannot say with certainty that this accounts for the pattern of results at Site 8, it is consistent with the notion that reading plays a key role in the TM curriculum. We take a further look at the use of reading in the TM text in a later section of the chapter.

All researchers—irrespective of whether they work primarily with quantitative or qualitative methods—know firsthand that the educational experiences of children can vary markedly from school to school and, indeed, from classroom to classroom within the same school. However, there may be a tendency for us to lose sight of this to some extent when we are engaged in quantitative inquiry. In analyzing data from a multisite evaluation study, for example, there may be a tendency to think in terms of *the* effect of a program. And in connection with this, there may be an emphasis on obtaining an estimate of a program's overall effect.

In contrast, we have tried to communicate the value of breaking down results site by site and attending to the natural variation in results and students' educational experiences across sites. In conducting such analyses, we essentially used the same kinds of statistical tools that were used in computing a single-number summary of the effectiveness of TM. That is, we computed and compared means for various subgroups in our data. But note that in moving beyond a single-number summary and a conception of the effect of a program, our use of these statistical tools was guided by an awareness of the importance of context—an awareness that the effects of a program can vary markedly across different sites.

The preceding ideas apply more generally to other types of research (e.g., large-scale surveys, nonexperimental studies of teacher practice) and to other relationships of potential interest (e.g., minority gaps in achievement, relationships between socioeconomic status [SES] and achievement). For example, much attention has centered on the minority gap in achievement in the United States, on gender gaps in mathematics and science achievement, and the like. Although an estimate of an overall minority gap, for example, is not without importance to policymakers, we know from large-scale data sets (e.g., High School and Beyond) that the difference in achievement between minority and nonminority students varies substantially across schools (Lee & Bryk, 1989). In some schools the difference is substantial, whereas in others there is no evidence of a gap. The question then becomes the following: What are the key factors underlying this variability? In particular, how do differences in various school policies and practices relate to differences in the magnitude of minority gaps? Similarly, we find substantial variability across schools in the relationship between the SES of students and achievement. This, in turn, has prompted investigations of why differences in SES appear to be very consequential in some schools but inconsequential in others (see, e.g., Raudenbush & Bryk, 1986).

Such analyses can be carried out by breaking down results site by site (e.g., school by school) and then looking for systematic patterns in results across sites. A more formal approach would involve the use of multilevel models, also known as hierarchical models (see, e.g., Raudenbush & Bryk, 2002). But the essential idea here is that it is critically important to have an awareness that relationships of interest can vary substantially across contexts. This broader conception can guide our analyses in extremely productive ways.

Although attending to context is perhaps more difficult for developing researchers than for experienced researchers, it is useful to consider why we do not do it more frequently—why we do not think more qualitatively—when using quantitative techniques. One might speculate that part of the problem is due to the fact that prior to the development of current multilevel modeling frameworks (e.g., hierarchical modeling), the statistical techniques available to researchers were inadequate for bringing context into the picture in quantitative analysis (e.g., studying differences in results across schools). But there is nothing inherent in statistical techniques (e.g., multiple regression, simple descriptive techniques) that precludes us from applying them to our data school by school, for example, and from investigating the extent to which relationships of interest vary and why they vary. Making the jump to proceeding in this manner is not simply a technical matter; rather, it is an intellectual move rooted in an awareness of the importance of context. It is this caste of mind, coupled with a thoughtful and creative use of time-honored statistical techniques (e.g., regression), that characterized the work of Burstein (1980), Cronbach (1976), and other scholars who helped to lay the conceptual and technical groundwork for hierarchical modeling.

We now turn to the importance of attending to alternative explanations. As will be seen, the need to carefully consider context also figures prominently in this next section.

ATTENDING TO ALTERNATIVE EXPLANATIONS

"Are there important factors or considerations I am overlooking or have failed to take into account? Do I have it right?" Whether a researcher is conducting a historical analysis, engaged in ethnographic work, or conducting a field experiment, the ability to step back and carefully consider such questions is, we believe, a key element of thoughtful inquiry. Asking such questions needs to occur during all phases of a project (e.g., during the conception and design of a study, during the data collection and analysis phases of a project, when one is writing informal accounts of preliminary findings, when one is writing a research article). Furthermore, this prized habit of mind manifests itself in a broad range of research activities—making deliberate searches for disconfirming evidence, measuring potential confounding factors, assessing the plausibility of alternative explanations (rival hypotheses), and looking at one's initial account or interpretation of events through the lens of another theoretical perspective. In addition, addressing such questions can involve drawing on a variety of evidence and employing a number of different research techniques, even within the context of a single study.

The importance of attending to alternative explanations and disconfirming evidence figures prominently in numerous pieces in the quantitative methods literature, particularly Campbell and Stanley's (1963) classic chapter on experimental and quasi-experimental designs in field settings in the first edition of the *Handbook of Research on Teaching*. Campbell and Stanley's chapter was motivated by a number of fundamental difficulties and challenges that arise when we attempt to study the effectiveness of complex programs in field settings. A starting point for Campbell and Stanley was the notion of "theory-ladenness," that is, the notion that what we attend to and the interpretations that we attach to what we observe are shaped by our theoretical orientations, the background knowledge and conjectures that we bring to our studies, and the like. A second source of complexity is the fact that in studying the effects of programs, we are typically interested in studying phenomena that are not directly observable such as changes in students' understandings of various mathematical concepts and changes in students' metalinguistic awareness.

Third, when we move from controlled laboratory settings to field settings, the interpretation of differences in outcomes between individuals in treatment and those in comparison conditions can become exceedingly problematic. That is, the possibilities that such differences may have been caused by factors other than the treatment can increase greatly. Such factors were termed threats to internal validity by Campbell and Stanley (1963). For example, consider a study of an innovative reading curriculum in which treatment group participants also had the opportunity to participate in a special reading program recently implemented in nearby public libraries. This would be an example of a potential threat to valid causal inference (i.e., a possible rival hypothesis or alternative explanation) that comes under the rubric "history" in Campbell and Stanley's chapter. For Campbell and Stanley, the soundness of our inferences concerning the causal effects of programs depends crucially on the extent to which we are able to rule out possible threats to internal validity.

Through careful reviews of the research literature in a number of disciplines, Campbell and Stanley (1963) identified various common threats to internal validity (e.g., history, maturation, selection) and evaluated the strengths and weaknesses of various experimental and quasi-experimental designs in light of these threats. They also focused on problems concerning generalization, that is, external validity.

Campbell and Stanley (1963) presented several tables that summarize whether or not particular designs logically control for various threats to validity. These tables are probably familiar to many readers who have taken a course in quantitative methods. Unfortunately, there is a risk of using them in a mechanical way—as a kind of checklist—in assessing the adequacy of causal conclusions in any given study. For example, if one sees that a researcher has employed a design that does not, according to these tables, logically control for certain threats to internal validity, then one might without any reflection conclude that the chances of drawing valid causal inferences based on this study are hopeless. Similarly, if a design that logically controls for all threats has been used, then one might automatically conclude that the study's conclusions are sound.

However, using these tables in such a manner is at odds with how Campbell and Stanley (1963) viewed the role and use of their threats-to-validity framework in the inquiry process. It is antithetical to the careful thought, investigative behavior, and judgment that characterize identifying and investigating the plausibility of possible threats to validity in a given study.

Consider Campbell and Ross's (1968) study of the impact of a crackdown on speeding initiated in the state of Connecticut at the start of 1956. Traffic fatalities had reached an alarmingly high level in Connecticut in 1955, and it was hoped that stiffening the penalty for speeding (i.e., suspending the license of any person convicted of speeding) would result in a reduction in highway fatalities. As it happened, the traffic fatality rate decreased markedly in 1956. Connecticut's governor interpreted the observed difference in traffic fatalities between 1955 and 1956 as an indication of the efficacy of the crackdown.

But Campbell and Ross (1968) warned of the danger of jumping too quickly to such a conclusion, and they went on to consider and investigate an array of factors that could potentially account for such a reduction in highway fatalities. For example, if there had been substantially less rainfall and snow in Connecticut in 1956 than in 1955, or if there had been an improvement in certain safety features of 1956 model cars, then such factors could very well account for the observed reduction in fatalities. On investigating weather records, information regarding safety features of cars, and the like, Campbell and Ross concluded that these alternative explanations could be ruled out. They also considered whether there were changes in procedures for collecting information regarding traffic fatalities and for computing fatality rates during this period. In addition, they considered whether traffic fatalities in 1955 were aberrantly high and, if so, whether the drop in fatalities in the following year represented a return to more typical rates that could have occurred even in the absence of the crackdown.

Each of these alternative explanations can be categorized in Campbell and Stanley's (1963) framework (e.g., history, instrumentation, regression artifacts). However, detailed familiarity with the nature of the program that one is studying, and with the local settings in which the program has been implemented, is essential in efforts to identify specific rival explanations that may be at work (e.g., possible changes in weather conditions, an aberrant fatality rate one year followed by a return to a more typical rate the next year). All of this points again to the importance of knowing the context of a study. Given the particulars of a study (e.g., its design, its implementation, various events that occurred during the course of the study), one must think hard about the array of possible factors that might very well account for the patterns observed in one's data.

Furthermore, assessing the plausibility of such factors is far from a mechanistic process. It can involve drawing on logs and archival records, it can involve collecting additional data through interviews and observation, and it can involve drawing on relevant information from other studies. In addition, it often can involve conducting statistical analyses that attempt to control for possible confounding variables. But what the preceding example makes clear is the qualitative nature of the process—the kind of thinking and investigative behavior—involved in identifying and assessing the plausibility of threats to validity.

The nature of this process stands in stark contrast to a mechanical use of the tables of threats to validity in Campbell and Stanley's (1963) chapter. In fact, one thing that is often overlooked in inspecting these tables, or omitted from reproductions of them in various texts, is the following footnote:

> It is with extreme reluctance that these summary tables are presented because they are apt to be "too helpful," and to be depended upon in place of the more complex and qualified presentation in the text. . . . In particular, it is against the spirit of this presentation to create uncomprehended fears of, or confidence in, specific designs. (p. 178)

The type of design employed in the Connecticut crackdown study—an interrupted time-series design—is logically vulnerable to numerous threats to internal validity. But it might be the case that in certain studies that employ this design, careful detailed investigations of the kind discussed earlier may lead us to conclude that such threats very likely do not account for the patterns observed in the data. Hence, our chances of drawing sound causal inferences in such situations may be fairly good, even though the design used *in theory* is susceptible to particular threats. At the same time, randomized experiments, which appear to logically control for an array of threats to internal validity, may "break down" down in particular instances and in various ways. As Holland (2001) noted, randomized field experiments are quasi-experiments waiting to happen. For example, problems in implementation, including non-compliance, can make drawing valid causal inferences quite challenging. Also, Campbell and Stanley (1963) discussed subtle ways in which attrition can bias the results of an experiment. Thus, in the case of randomized experiments, detailed information must be collected

regarding who drops out of a study and why they drop out, regarding difficulties in program implementation, regarding the occurrence of unusual events, and the like. Without detailed information of this kind, we are vulnerable to drawing highly misleading inferences from even the "strongest" experimental designs.

In the preceding discussion, we briefly mentioned the use of statistical techniques in controlling for possible confounding variables. This is something that we now discuss a bit further. Covariate adjustment—that is, controlling for possible confounding factors through the use of statistical techniques (e.g., multiple regression and its extensions)—might be considered the "bread and butter" of quantitative social science inquiry. This is due to the fact that there are many instances in education and related fields where the aim—either explicitly or implicitly—is to draw causal inferences about particular processes, policies, or practices but where random assignment is not possible. Examples would include studies of the relative effectiveness of Catholic high schools and public high schools and studies of various interventions in which random assignment is not feasible. Although 12th-grade mathematics achievement may be higher among Catholic high school seniors than among public school seniors, Catholic school students are, on average, more advantaged in terms of SES and other factors related to 12th-grade achievement. Thus, the difference in achievement that we observe may be due in large part to differences in SES and other confounding variables. The same would apply to quasi-experiments in which children who participate in a program of interest (e.g., an innovative after-school program) and those who participate in a more conventional program differ in terms of prior achievement and various background characteristics. This would also apply to settings in which randomized experiments have broken down, for example, experiments in which attrition renders treatment and comparison groups nonequivalent in important ways.

Through covariate adjustment, we attempt to obtain estimates of differences in outcomes for the groups we wish to compare (e.g., Catholic and public high school seniors, treatment and comparison group students in quasi-experiments) that adjust for (hold constant) confounding variables. The rub, however, is that our ability to draw sound causal inferences via covariate adjustment depends crucially on whether we are able to identify and measure *all* key confounding variables.

This obviously is a formidable task. In any given study, this requires extensive familiarity with the relevant research literature, with the study's sample and design, with various difficulties that may have occurred during the course of the study, and the like. However, for students in particular subfields, the use of covariate adjustment may come to be viewed as a mechanistic process. In a given area of research, certain covariates may appear again and again in the research literature. And in quantitative methods courses, students may see certain covariates used repeatedly in illustrative examples, for example, measures of SES and prior achievement.

Of course, the sets of covariates that are commonly used in particular kinds of investigations are used for good reasons. Undoubtedly, they measure important ways in which groups of interest are likely to differ. But something of crucial importance that we think is often missed—something that helps us get to the heart of the matter in identifying key confounding variables that we might otherwise overlook—is the need to try to understand the selection process by which individuals wind up in the different groups that we wish to compare.

Consider, for example, a discussion that took place in a section of an introductory statistics course taught recently by one of us. The discussion focused on a study of the relative effectiveness of two bilingual education strategies: Structured Immersion English (SIE), in which all instruction is conducted in English, and Early Exit (EE), a more standard form of bilingual education in which a portion of instruction is carried out in the child's primary language, which was Spanish in this particular study (Ramirez, Pasta, Yuen, Billings, & Ramey, 1991; Ramirez, Yuen, Ramey, & Pasta, 1991). In EE, teachers first tend to help children learn to read in their primary language and then help them to make the transition to reading in English.

The children in the sample we focused on in class were located in three different schools, each of which had an SIE program and an EE program. In each of these two-program schools,

some children were assigned to SIE and some to EE just prior to the start of kindergarten. However, their assignment to SIE or EE was not random.

The discussion in the statistics class centered on the relative effectiveness of SIE and EE with respect to reading (English) posttest scores in the spring of the first grade. Overall, we find that reading posttest scores are appreciably higher for EE students, a finding that is consistent across the three schools. But can we claim that EE is more effective than SIE?

Ramirez and colleagues (Ramirez, Pasta, et al., 1991; Ramirez, Yuen, et al., 1991) pointed out that the EE and SIE students were similar in terms of key pretest measures obtained in the fall of kindergarten and in terms of several other available covariates obtained via interviews with the children's parents in the spring of kindergarten (e.g., percentage of time that parents spoke English at home, level of mother's education). Nearly all parents stated that they spoke only Spanish at home.

But were there other ways in which the EE and SIE students may have differed? Were there unmeasured confounding variables at work, and if so, what might they be?

Although the EE and SIE students do appear to be similar with respect to a variety of available covariates, the students in the introductory statistics class still seemed to be concerned that assignment to SIE and EE was not random. At that point, the instructor mentioned the value of trying to understand why it is that students may wind up in one program rather than another. After a long silence, one of the students in the class, who is a parent, raised her hand and spoke. This was a student who was pretty anxious when it came to statistical formulas and equations. But as she spoke, she seemed to be on familiar turf. She pointed out that parents who knew little English, but who wanted to help their children as much as possible with homework assignments and with various skills and topics that were being taught in class, might choose to enroll their children in EE because a portion of the instruction in EE—in particular, reading—is in Spanish.

There was a sense in the room that this student had put her finger on an important way in which the SIE and EE students may have differed. If she were right, then the higher reading posttest scores that we see for EE children could be due in part to the parents of the EE children taking a stronger interest in their children's schooling, reading to them more often, and providing more help with schoolwork.

Unfortunately, information concerning the process by which children wound up in SIE or EE programs appears not to have been collected. In interviews with parents, Ramirez and colleagues (Ramirez, Pasta, et al., 1991; Ramirez, Yuen, et al., 1991) did collect some information on the extent to which parents were involved in their children's schooling. However, comparisons of the SIE and EE children with respect to these variables were not presented in the two-volume report detailing the design and results of the study. And so we do not know whether the EE and SIE students differed with respect to these factors, nor do we know how the reading posttest scores for these groups of children would compare if we were to adjust for them.

But even if this student's hunch regarding the desirability of enrolling children in EE were incorrect, this example begins to help us see the value of trying to understand the process by which individuals wind up in the groups we wish to compare. We begin to see how it can help us to identify subtle yet extremely important ways in which groups of interest may differ—ways that extend beyond pretest differences and differences in SES.

How do we learn about such processes? In a given study, it can involve drawing on relevant theory and previous research. As the preceding example makes abundantly clear, it can also involve drawing on our experiential knowledge of schooling and imagining the kinds of factors that very well may be at work. Furthermore, it can involve studying such processes "up close" by interviewing the parents of the children in a study, or teachers and other school personnel, who may be able to provide some insight.

Thus, in the case of the Catholic school example, when we consider families that are similar in terms of their religious backgrounds and their economic resources, a key question is as follows: Why do some parents choose to enroll their children in Catholic high schools, whereas others choose to enroll their children in public high schools? Are there factors at work in this process that point to important ways in which children enrolled in Catholic schools may differ from their public school counterparts— ways that may have implications for their intellectual growth and success in school? If so, such factors need to be measured and employed as covariates in our analyses if we hope to draw valid causal inferences regarding the effects of Catholic school on student achievement.

Finally, returning to the TM study, note that TM teachers were not randomly assigned to different levels of implementation. Rather, for reasons that are unclear, 10 TM teachers discussed the reading in the text with their students on a daily basis and 10 did not. Put differently, the TM teachers self-selected into different levels of implementation. As such, we must be mindful of the fact that differences in implementation may be confounded with other factors (e.g., differences in teacher experience, differences across sites in the prior preparation of students) that are associated with student outcomes. Seltzer (2004) studied the relationship between implementation of reading and program effectiveness, adjusting for various available covariates (e.g., how far in the text each TM teacher had gotten by the end of the school year), and found that even after making such adjustments, implementation still appeared to play a key role. But what was missing was information on why teachers used the reading in the text in different ways—factors that may be connected with subtle yet important ways in which these teachers differed in their instructional practices. Such information would need to be obtained through interviews of teachers and careful classroom observation.

Certainly, the use of covariate adjustment requires a fairly high degree of technical proficiency. But what is clear from the preceding discussion is that thoughtful use of this tool has a distinct qualitative nature. It involves drawing on one's experiential knowledge of schooling and on information obtained from "up close" careful study of the process by which students (and teachers) wind up in different groups of interest. It is important that we try to cultivate an awareness of this in our quantitative methods courses.

The Importance of Getting Close to the Data

In their quantitative methods courses, developing researchers learn about the logic of various complex modeling techniques (e.g., multiple regression, structural equation modeling, hierarchical modeling), how to implement such techniques using available software programs, and how to interpret computer output. In essence, students acquire a certain degree of technical proficiency.

Such techniques are extremely valuable in studying the effects of school policies and practices on student learning, in studying various developmental processes, and the like. However, there is a tendency for many researchers—both experienced and inexperienced—to apply these techniques in fairly mechanical ways and to reach for them too quickly in the course of a research project.

The thoughtful application of formal modeling techniques requires extensive, careful, exploratory data analysis involving the use of less formal techniques. It is essential to "get close" to the data by breaking them down and summarizing them in various sensible ways, by constructing useful plots that can help to illuminate important patterns, by searching for outlying cases, and so on.

Such analyses can help bring to light key patterns that could easily go unnoticed if we were to jump immediately to the use of complex models. The application of formal models for studying change (e.g., growth models) provides compelling examples of this point. For example, in studies of how differences in students' home environments and educational experiences relate to differences in the development of their literacy skills, or in studies of the long-term effects of interventions, students are assessed at multiple points in time. In what might be termed "mechanical" applications of growth modeling, student change in outcomes of interest is often modeled as a simple linear function of time; that is, an individual's growth trajectory is assumed to follow a straight line. However, patterns of change are frequently more complex. Careful inspection of plots of students' time-series data may reveal that spurts in growth occur at particular points in time, that rates of student progress decrease abruptly after an intervention comes to an end, and the like (see, e.g., Singer & Willett, 2003; Svartberg, Seltzer, Stiles, & Khoo, 1995). When exploratory analysis of this kind does not precede and accompany the model-building process, we run the risk of fitting models that conceal important patterns and that give rise to results that have little fidelity to the data. Although this particular example focuses on studies of change, the importance of "getting close" to the data extends to all formal modeling settings.

Conducting Thoughtful Research

We have spent some time discussing the value of knowing the context of a study—the nature of the site of the study, its characteristics, and the people who populate it. In addition, we tried to illustrate the importance of considering alternative explanations for the results of a study, weighing interpretive options, and taking another line of sight on the numbers. We also briefly discussed the need to conduct extensive exploratory analysis before turning to the use of formal modeling procedures.

Because qualitative methods have such an explicit interpretive dimension to them, it seems—at least on the face of things—that to use qualitative methods is, de facto, to be deliberating and judging throughout the process. Such continued reflection may, at first glance, be less evident with quantitative methods.

But we try to help our students understand that the effective use of statistical methods involves more than a mastery of technical procedures—that one could do everything by the book, so to speak, but not be a very good quantitative methodologist. Statistical thoughtfulness begins, of course, with the framing of research questions and an appropriate design. A good deal of thought is required here. But in addition, we encourage students to ask questions along the way, to see a statistical procedure as a way not only to test a hypothesis but also to probe it. Put another way, one sets out not only to solve a problem but also to think about it, possibly reframe it, and perhaps see new problems. This is not thinking *by* the numbers; rather, it is thinking *with* and *through* numbers.

A further point to consider is that the numbers that one presents tell a story about the object of the study. How a researcher frames a chart or table, how data are presented, how text is used to guide the reader—all of these contribute to the persuasiveness of the numbers and to the tale they tell. What are the major findings? Are there important patterns in the data? What do you not want the reader to miss?

We like to ask students about the "plot" of a study. What is the story of these data? Are you adequately conveying that plot through written text and the effective use of tables and figures? And, as with any story, there may be discordant notes, odd twists and turns, as in the case of the outlying site in the TM example. Are these odd findings the result of procedural missteps, or are they part of the story the data tell? If the latter, have you created an adequate plot line to tell that story? Is the tale you tell reductive or complex enough to represent your findings?

Trying to think well with numbers and crafting the best story with them require the kind of burrowing into context or shifting of perspective that we have been discussing. The researcher might have to get in close to the data—as in the TM example—or, conversely, might have to consider the data in broader terms, as was evident in the Connecticut crackdown study. Or the researcher might benefit from looking at the study's results from several theoretical or disciplinary perspectives. It is worth repeating here Campbell and Stanley's (1963) observation about the "theory ladenness" of inquiry. We see data through the theoretical lenses we wear. What might happen, then, if we—perhaps with the help of others with different training—try to look at results with the perspective afforded by another theory or even another discipline? A sociologist or anthropologist, for example, might ask thought-provoking and generative questions of the TM or Connecticut crackdown study. And such questions might spark an alternative explanation of one's findings.

Although we have focused on the development of thoughtfulness in working with quantitative methods, many of the issues that we discussed in this chapter have relevance for the thoughtful use of qualitative methods. For example, Erickson's (1986, 1998) discussion of the importance of computing frequencies and percentages of the occurrence of various actions and activities in given settings, of the kinds of things said by study participants, and the like helps us to see that numbers are good to think with in qualitative analysis; in particular, they give us a sense of what is typical and atypical and help us to discern key similarities and differences between various classes or groups that we wish to compare. Also, our discussion of alternative explanations brings to mind Erickson's warnings of the dangers of attending solely to events and actions that confirm one's initial assertions or hunches. Making deliberate searches for disconfirming cases, both during the data collection process and when one is analyzing the data corpus, is a hallmark of careful qualitative inquiry for Erickson. In addition, our concerns regarding statistical analyses that conceal important patterns, and yield results that have little fidelity to the data, bring to mind a set of questions that are applicable to researchers engaged in qualitative inquiry: Is the story you tell adequately reflective of the data? Is it nuanced enough, layered, and not a simplified tale laid onto a messy human reality?

This is just a very brief sketch of some of the connections and common ground that we see, and we look forward to undertaking a more thorough in-depth exploration at a later point in time.

When we think about the aspects of thoughtful quantitative analysis that we have emphasized in this chapter, it is clear to us that there are other points we would like to have discussed, including the importance of attending to confidence intervals (or posterior intervals) in drawing inferences concerning parameters of interest and the need to "look longitudinally" in many research settings in education and related fields (see, e.g., Singer & Willett, 2003). However, due to space constraints and the kinds of ideas we wanted to explore (e.g., the qualitative dimension of quantitative inquiry), we centered our attention on the various issues and propositions discussed in the chapter.

These propositions take us back to the beginning of the chapter—to the work we have done together. We certainly realize how difficult it is for a single researcher—especially someone fairly new to the field—to be proficient in more than one method or theoretical orientation. We do believe, however, that it is possible to form professional relationships—as we have—that can assist quantitative researchers in thinking more carefully and widely. But what we are calling for also goes beyond the particulars of professional relationships. What concerns us is that the very nature of too much academic training—with its methodological and disciplinary territoriality—can have the unfortunate effect of narrowing one's intellectual scope and sweep, thereby limiting the development of analytic thoughtfulness. All of us—quantitative, qualitative, and mixed-methods researchers alike—need to work against such limitations. We hope this chapter provided a few useful suggestions on how to do that.

NOTE

1. Given the matching procedure used in this study, it is not surprising that one obtains a similar result if one also holds pretest performance constant.

REFERENCES

Burstein, L. (1980). The analysis of multi-level data in education research and evaluation. *Review of Research in Education, 8,* 158–233.

Campbell, D. T., & Ross, H. (1968). The Connecticut crackdown on speeding: Time-series data in quasi-experimental analysis. *Law and Society Review, 3,* 33–53.

Campbell, D. T., & Stanley, J. (1963). Experimental and quasi-experimental designs for research on teaching. In N. L. Gage (Ed.), *The handbook of research on teaching* (pp. 171–246). Chicago: Rand McNally.

Cronbach, L. (1975). Beyond the two disciplines of scientific psychology. *American Psychologist, 30,* 116–127.

Cronbach, L. (1976). *Research on classrooms and schools: Formulations of questions, design, and analysis* [occasional paper]. Stanford, CA: Stanford Evaluation Consortium.

Erickson, F. (1986). Qualitative methods in research on teaching. In M. C. Wittrock (Ed.), *The handbook*

of research on teaching (3rd ed., pp. 119–161). New York: Macmillan.

Erickson, F. (1998). Qualitative research methods for science education. In B. J. Fraser & K. G. Tobin (Eds.), *The international handbook of science of education* (pp. 1155–1173). Dordrecht, Netherlands: Kluwer Academic.

Geertz, C. (1973). *The interpretation of cultures.* New York: Basic Books.

Holland, P. (2001). *What every statistician ought to know (remember?) about causation.* Paper presented at the first annual meeting of the Campbell Collaboration, Philadelphia.

Lee, V., & Bryk, A. (1989). A multilevel model of the social distribution of educational achievement. *Sociology of Education, 62,* 172–192.

Mishler, E. G. (1979). Meaning in context: Is there any other kind? *Harvard Educational Review, 49,* 1–19.

Ramirez, D., Pasta, D., Yuen, S., Billings, D., & Ramey, D. (1991). *Final report: Longitudinal study of an English immersion strategy and an early-exit transitional bilingual education program for language-minority children* (Vol. 2). San Mateo, CA: Aguirre International.

Ramirez, D., Yuen, S., Ramey, D., & Pasta, D. (1991). *Final report: Longitudinal study of an English immersion strategy and an early-exit transitional bilingual education program for language-minority children* (Vol. 1). San Mateo, CA: Aguirre International.

Raudenbush, S., & Bryk, A. (1986). A hierarchical model for studying school effects. *Sociology of Education, 59,* 1–17.

Raudenbush, S., & Bryk, A. (2002). *Hierarchical linear models: Applications and data analysis methods.* Thousand Oaks, CA: Sage.

Schön, D. A. (1984). *The reflective practitioner: How professionals think in action.* New York: Basic Books.

Seltzer, M. (1994). Studying variation in program success: A multilevel modeling approach. *Evaluation Review, 18,* 342–361.

Seltzer, M. (2004). The use of hierarchical models in analyzing data from experiments and quasi-experiments conducted in field settings. In D. Kaplan (Ed.), *The handbook of quantitative methods for the social sciences* (pp. 259–280). Thousand Oaks, CA: Sage.

Shadish, W., Cook, T., & Campbell, D. T. (2002). *Experimental and quasi-experimental designs for generalized causal inference.* Boston: Houghton Mifflin.

Singer, J., & Willett, J. (2003). *Applied longitudinal analysis: Modeling change and event occurrence.* New York: Oxford University Press.

Svartberg, M., Seltzer, M., Stiles, T., & Khoo, S. (1995). Symptom improvement and its temporal course in short-term dynamic psychotherapy: A growth curve analysis. *Journal of Nervous and Mental Disease, 183,* 242–248.

Tashakorri, A., & Teddlie, C. (Eds.). (2003). *Handbook of mixed methods in social and behavioral research.* Thousand Oaks, CA: Sage.

University of Chicago School Mathematics Project. (1986). *Transition mathematics field study* (Evaluation Report No. 85/86 TM-2). Chicago: University of Chicago, Department of Education.

Yin, R. K. (1994). Evaluation: A singular craft. *New Directions for Program Evaluation, 61,* 71–84.

27

CONSTRUCTING CONCLUSIONS

KING D BEACH, III

Florida State University

BETSY JANE BECKER

Florida State University

MARY M. KENNEDY

Michigan State University

I n this chapter, we examine the kinds of issues and challenges that researchers face in the process of developing their conclusions. We begin by examining what has been written about conclusions. Primarily, we find discussions of the potential components of conclusion sections of research reports, which differentiate conclusions from other aspects of the research "product." However, the specific components of conclusion sections are likely to be tailored to the intended audience and purpose of each research report—research limitations, future studies, researchers' subjective experiences, expansion of findings to conclusions. In this chapter, we do not focus on the range of potential components; rather, we examine specifically how researchers move from their findings to conclusions. This act of construction is most important, we believe, but surprisingly, little has been written about it in the research handbooks we examined. We also argue that

despite this underrepresentation in the literature, moving from results to conclusions is not a simple task. We illustrate this with some of the literature concerning scientific reasoning, researcher biases, and expectancy effects.

Next we address three areas that pose significant challenges to researchers as they move from findings to constructing conclusions. First, we discuss some of the challenges involved in connecting premises, findings, and conclusions. We then discuss the tension inherent in using both prior knowledge and knowledge in the form of findings to formulate conclusions. Finally, we address the role of generalization (and generalizability) in drawing conclusions, including how generalization can manifest differently in different research traditions. We conclude with our own conclusions about constructing conclusions.

Before we begin, we identify ourselves and our interest in conclusions. One of us (King

---

AUTHORS' NOTE: Authorship order was determined alphabetically.

Beach) is a cultural psychologist who has training in both quantitative and qualitative methodologies but who draws more heavily from the qualitative tradition in his current work. Another (Betsy Becker) is an educational statistician specializing in meta-analysis. The third (Mary Kennedy) was originally trained as an experimental educational psychologist but has spent the past 15 years engaging mainly in qualitative research on teaching. For the past 4 years, Becker and Kennedy have been collaborating on an extensive synthesis of the literature on teacher qualifications and, through that work, have examined many study reports and their conclusions. We have observed a great diversity of conclusions in that process. Also, all three of us have served on editorial boards or as journal editors or referees, and we have read a diversity of articles and their conclusions in those capacities. One observation from these experiences is that journal referees tend to focus on the methods and findings reported in manuscripts rather than on the stated conclusions. As a result, we suspect that authors do not get much feedback on the nature of their conclusions. This may also lead to the diversity in conclusions that we already mentioned. Finally, all three of us have taught (individually and together) courses on educational research methods, including courses on quantitative methods, qualitative methods, or both. We have noted that although it is fairly common to ask students (and others) to evaluate conclusions drawn by other researchers, it is not as common for students to be asked to prepare full conclusions based on the analyses about which we are teaching them. We suspect that this may be a shortcoming of instruction in educational research methods.

WHAT IS A CONCLUSION?

The American Heritage Dictionary of the English Language defines the word "conclusion" as "the closing or last part, as of a discourse, often containing a summing up of the preceding" and also a "judgment or decision reached after deliberation" (Morris, 1976, p. 276). In research reports, the conclusion is not merely an ending; it is often both a summary and a place to set out next steps, a brief review

of results plus conjectures about both causes and consequences. Some conclusions might go too far, and others might not go far enough. In this first section of our chapter, we examine what has been written about conclusions and find that although it is fairly easy to find recommendations about the components of conclusion sections of research reports, little has been written about how to arrive at the conclusions themselves.

What Research Methods Books Say About Conclusions

Considering the importance of conclusions, it is surprising how very little is written about what conclusions entail and how to draw them. We examined a small set of widely used research methods texts to see what they say about conclusions. It is possible that other texts we did not review are very different from these, but we found considerable consistency among these well-known texts.

In their widely used text on research methods, Gall, Gall, and Borg (2005) include 15 chapters, and none fully concerns conclusions. In 5 chapters on quantitative research designs, we found only two paragraphs about conclusions (including text on interpretation and discussion of results). Gall and colleagues write that the purpose of the conclusion section "is to explain the meaning and implications of the results" and that it is a place for the researchers "to express their interpretations of the results, evaluate shortcomings, . . . draw conclusions, . . . and make recommendations for further research" (p. 144). They add that "a more personal perspective is necessary" (as compared with the results section), but they also argue that an evaluation of researchers' conclusions requires an assessment of whether the researchers' results support their judgments. Other textbooks provide similarly terse treatments of conclusions. For instance, Fraenkel and Wallen (2003) give a diagram of the research process that ends with data analysis (p. 20). They devote only 2 pages (of a 623-page book) to conclusions ("discussions," in their terminology). They suggest that this section of a research report should include a summary of the study itself (questions asked, study design, and results) and the three components listed by Gall and colleagues (2005): implications, limitations, and suggestions for future research.

One of the best treatments we found was in Wiersma (2000), who devotes more than a page early in his book to the summary and conclusions of research and who returns to the topic in most procedural chapters as well as in chapters devoted to communicating about research and evaluating research. Wiersma lists several components of conclusions, including a summary of results, an interpretation of analyses, and conclusions as related to the research problem together with conclusions about hypotheses (if any were tested). He notes that "drawing conclusions requires interpretation, synthesis, and insights, activities that are difficult to specify as tasks" (p. 22), as opposed to the primarily procedural steps underlying most of the research process. Wiersma makes nine suggestions to help in this task, including addressing internal and external validity issues, connecting the results to theory, focusing on the meaning of the results ("rather than the results per se" [p. 22]), searching for inconsistencies with other results (and explaining or identifying possible causes of the inconsistencies), and suggesting future research.

Later in his book, Wiersma (2000) adds that limitations of the research should be described and suggests that it should be clear which conclusions follow from which results. Also, he urges the researcher to address the importance of the results to education, an admonition that can extend to whatever realm is relevant to the study. Wiersma argues for overexplanation to make one's reasoning evident, but he also argues that interpreting results (at least of experiments) is "a common-sense process" (p. 123). So it seems that even though Wiersma devotes some attention to conclusions, he gives an impression that much of the business of reaching conclusions is straightforward and requires little instruction or explanation.

In his book *Writing Up Qualitative Research,* Wolcott (2001) suggests that we "give serious thought to dropping the idea that your final chapter must lead to a conclusion or that the account must build toward a dramatic climax" (p. 120). He goes on to state his preference for *not* moving far beyond the boundaries of the

material being analyzed and for *not* couching personal opinions and beliefs as anything other than that. Thus, Wolcott is concerned with some of the same issues as are the authors cited previously, but he takes a rather different tack in suggesting three alternatives to concluding a study: summary, recommendations/implications, and personal reflections. These are not inconsistent with some of what the other texts suggest might be contained under conclusions. Wolcott does devote more space to this issue (eight pages) than do the other authors, and much of this is spent arguing against overstepping the limits of one's data and defensible interpretation.

We are in agreement with both Wiersma's and Wolcott's concerns that researchers not overstep the warrants of the research evidence in formulating conclusions. Wolcott's (2001) approach to this issue is to write one or more sections that have a more specific purpose and focus. The approach taken by Wiersma (2000) involves a more careful and explicit laying out of the reasoning behind the shift from findings to conclusions. Both are viable ways in which to avoid overreaching one's research evidence while moving beyond the specificity of one's findings.

What Study Quality Guidelines Say About Conclusions

Another place where we find information about what a conclusion is (or ought to entail) is in the literature on the quality of research studies. Research and arguments on this topic have appeared with increasing frequency in the medical realm due in part to recent attention to evidence-based decision making (or "evidence-based medicine," e.g., Sackett, Rosenberg, Muir Gray, Haynes, & Richardson, 1996). Several sets of guidelines have been proposed to describe components of high-quality studies and meta-analyses. We examine the two sets that pertain to reporting individual studies. One of the earliest sets of study guidelines is the CONSORT statement originally published in 1996 (Begg et al., 1996; Moher, Schulz, & Altman, 2001). This set of 22 characteristics of a quality study was developed by a group of medical researchers, statisticians, and journal editors and was meant to apply to randomized controlled trials. In the realm of conclusions, the CONSORT statement asked for interpretations of results, discussion of sources of bias and imprecision, information on generalizability, and a more general interpretation of the study's findings. (The checklist is available online at www.consort-statement.org/statement/revised statement.htm#checklist.)

A more recent set of guidelines developed for application to studies using nonrandomized designs is known as the TREND (Transparent Reporting of Evaluations with Nonrandomized Designs) guidelines (Des Jarlais, Lyles, & Crepaz, 2004). TREND asks for the same components mentioned by CONSORT but also requests an explanation of the mechanism(s) by which the intervention is supposed to work, a discussion of barriers to and success of the implementation, information on implementation fidelity, and commentary on the programmatic and policy implications of the study.

These recommendations for drawing conclusions make sense for some rather specific quantitative study designs, but they do not cover the variety of research genres found in education and the social sciences. They also do not represent a standard of rigor to which other research genres should aspire when constructing conclusions. Rather, they achieve rigor because they are tailored for particular forms of research.

Common Threads

Most of these treatises on conclusions appear to agree that conclusions should cover the implications of one's findings (e.g., remarks on generalizability), the limitations or weaknesses of the research, and suggestions for future research. Most differentiate between findings (the results of a study) and interpretations, explanations, and extensions of those findings. Some authors argue that one should include a brief restatement of results in the conclusion or discussion section, whereas others do not. Most suggest that multiple aspects should be included in a study conclusion, with the exception of Wolcott (2001), who argues for addressing the aspects separately rather than wrapping them together in a grand finale. Wiersma (2000) argues that "conclusions are the inferences and the like that the researcher draws from the results" (p. 395).

Notice that even though these authors tend to agree in general about the components that should be included in conclusion sections (methods books cover these components in a fair amount of detail), the particulars of these components will typically be very specific to the product being written. For instance, an executive summary of a research study being prepared for policymakers might present little detail on the methodological flaws of a study, instead emphasizing the implications for future education policy. Researchers who know their audiences will be able to choose the appropriate "ingredients" for the conclusion sections of their reports.

What has been given short shrift is the process of actually formulating the conclusions—the act of going beyond a simple restatement of findings. This process leads to many of the challenges that researchers face in constructing conclusions. In extending from findings to conclusions, researchers rely on their prior knowledge, hopes, and biases, and herein many pitfalls await researchers. As we will see in the next section, the empirical literatures on the conduct of research and the nature of scientific reasoning suggest that the process of drawing conclusions is not mechanical, simple, or easily done.

DRAWING CONCLUSIONS IS NOT A SIMPLE PROCESS

Much empirical research has investigated the nature of scientific and inferential reasoning involving analytical skills similar to those used by researchers in drawing conclusions. Other research studies have examined the possibility of bias in the conduct of research and in the decision making of researchers. The findings in these two broad areas show that errors can occur in doing even simple (albeit laboratory-based) reasoning tasks and that biases can result when one's beliefs and values are at odds with research findings. Activities such as assessing what findings represent and evaluating the quality of hypothetical studies were examined. We do not review these extensive literatures here; instead, we draw on several existing reviews of relevant research and theory to emphasize that the act of drawing conclusions in research is never a simple, totally rational, purely logical process.

Reasoning

Research on inferential reasoning shows that drawing a conclusion from uncomplicated evidence or even logical principles is not a simple process. Psychological researchers (e.g., Johnson-Laird & Byrne, 1991; Rips, 1994), philosophers, and others have examined the role of formal logical reasoning in human thinking. Although often the empirical studies in this domain concern very simple logical structures, their results provide some evidence that inferential reasoning is difficult. Recent literature reviews concerning reasoning and the issue of whether humans are rational thinkers have been published by Evans (2002), Shafir and LeBoeuf (2002), and Zimmerman (2000).

Evans (2002) reviews several decades of research on deductive reasoning. He first lays out the "deductive paradigm" whereby researchers have studied the logical evaluation of premises and conclusions, often using syllogisms such as the following:

Some A are B.

No B are C.

Therefore, some A are not C. (p. 979)

Much of this work, Evans argues, was based on the view that most or all human reasoning must be logical, and it examined axiomatic logical structures developed initially by mathematicians to evaluate the validity of mathematical proofs. The results of this work and concurrent research on decision making showed that people did not always succeed at simple rational logical reasoning, and the work of Tversky and Kahneman and their colleagues (e.g., Kahneman, Slovic, & Tversky, 1982) suggested that when individuals attempted to reason under uncertainty conditions, they were subject to cognitive constraints and biases that limited their ability to make "correct" logical decisions.

Although the bulk of this research led to the conclusion that participants untrained in logical thinking "make many errors when their performance is compared with the dictates of standard textbook logic" (Evans, 2002, p. 982), further research indicated that both the context and content of the syllogistic tasks influenced performance. One finding relevant to our topic is the belief bias effect, whereby participants describe as "valid" conclusions that are in line with their prior beliefs. That is, we all tend to seek information that confirms, rather than challenges, the ideas we already have. We "see" things that confirm our ideas (see, e.g., Edwards & Smith, 1996; Nickerson, 1998).

Much psychological research on reasoning has been designed to support or refute the idea that people reason rationally, that is, that their thinking should conform to logical rules and "should not be formed or changed based on immaterial factors related to, for example, mood, context, or mode of presentation" (Shafir & LeBoeuf, 2002, p. 493). Shafir and LeBoeuf (2002) also report,

> Many studies from the past three decades, however, have documented numerous ways in which judgments and decisions do not cohere, do not follow basic principles of logic and probability, and depend systematically on just such irrelevant factors. People use intuitive strategies and simple heuristics that are reasonably effective some of the time but that also produce biases and lead to systematic error. (p. 493)

Shafir and LeBoeuf (2002) review results in support of this statement concerning how irrelevant factors (e.g., mood, anticipated regret) affect reasoning (in studies of logical thinking such as those mentioned previously), judgment (e.g., in situations where one may have to consider several attributes of a situation and predict the likelihood of some outcome), and choice, among other outcomes. These authors also point out that critics of the research traditions described previously have faulted the work as being inapplicable to real decisions because it is overly simplistic and irrelevant or uninteresting to participants and, thus, is invalid as a representation of real-world thinking.

However, at least one response to these criticisms is relevant to our topic, and that concerns expertise. Shafir and LeBoeuf (2002) cite studies showing that reasoners with high levels of expertise in an area (e.g., physicians) are also prone to errors in decision making, even when tasks are meaningful and relevant. Similarly, other research reviewed by Shafir and LeBoeuf suggests that training ameliorates, but does not remove, erroneous strategy use (e.g., Fong & Nisbett, 1991).

A final review that is targeted more at the construct of scientific reasoning is Zimmerman's (2000) examination of studies from both psychology and science education. Zimmerman considers studies that were designed to assess "strategies involved in hypothesis generation, experimental design, and evidence evaluation" (p. 101), including reasoning about causal inferences and covariation. Unfortunately for our purposes, much of the research in this realm is limited to samples of schoolchildren or college students, sometimes in the context of science classes. However, scholars in this area have argued that reasoning is not totally dissimilar for adults and professional scientists (e.g., Kuhn, 1989). Zimmerman's (2000) survey of this work led her to report that the skills involved in evaluating evidence develop as one ages, although she argues that they "do not develop to an optimum level even among adults" (p. 118). Also, she notes a tendency for research participants to want to align theory and evidence, even when they were in disagreement. Here Zimmerman notes that individuals may choose to "ignore, distort, or selectively attend to evidence that is inconsistent with a favored theory" (p. 188) or to modify their statements of the theory to make the theory fit better with the evidence (and perhaps be unaware that they are making this adjustment). A quote from Kuhn (1989) characterizes well the findings of this line of work:

> In scientific exploration activities, lack of differentiation and coordination of theory and evidence is likely to lead to uncontrolled domination of one over the other. Exploration may be so theory-bound that the subject has difficulty "seeing" the evidence, or so data-bound that the subject is confined to local interpretation of isolated results, without benefit of a theoretical representation that would allow the subject to make sense of the data. (p. 687)

Finally, Zimmerman (2000) remarks on a set of studies that she labels self-directed experimentation studies, where participants' causal inferences are examined in light of participants' own theories about the factors involved in a causal relation as well as evidence generated over time about requirements of causal inference such as temporal priority and contiguity in time and space. The studies of Schauble (e.g., Schauble, Glaser, Raghavan, & Reiner, 1991) and Dunbar and Klahr (1989; see also Klahr, 2000) are prominent in this domain. Of import for our argument is that both adults and children in these studies drew on their prior beliefs and that task complexity also influenced adults' propensity to demonstrate more sophisticated reasoning skills. Adults tended to consider more alternative hypotheses about the causal process under investigation than did children, and adults developed more knowledge about the causal process as well as new strategies for reasoning about it.

Researcher Expectations and Biases

The reviews just described suggest that individuals who are asked to reason about particular scientific interpretations are influenced by prior beliefs and knowledge as well as task characteristics. Another literature concerns the expectancy bias that researchers bring to the process of reporting research results. Work in this area suggests that some of the same biases observed for laypersons and children learning about science are seen among trained researchers. A number of literature reviews discuss expectancy effects and biases, specifically the work of Cooper and Hazelrigg (1988), MacCoun (1998), and Rosenthal (e.g., Rosenthal, 1976; Rosenthal & Rubin, 1978). Here we focus on the review by MacCoun (1998), which discusses biases in the interpretation of results.

MacCoun (1998) reviews a variety of studies on biases that participants may bring to bear in accomplishing realistic tasks similar to the work of scientists and researchers. Some studies asked participants to review "manuscripts" or hypothetical studies containing results that were either consistent with or at odds with the theoretical orientations of the participants. The quality of the evidence in these hypothetical studies was also varied to be either weak or strong. Ratings of the perceived quality and persuasiveness of

Constructing Conclusions • 499

the pseudo-studies were obtained, and in some studies, reports of attitudes about the topics of the pseudo-studies were also taken. Results supported what MacCoun terms "biased assimilation" in that participants gave more positive evaluations to studies that supported their prior beliefs, regardless of the research methodology (weak or strong) that was described.

MacCoun (1998) also reviews the theories that have been put forth to explain the findings of biased thinking among researchers. Such hypotheses include the use of problematic strategies, such as the positive test strategy (where a reasoner tests a hypothesis by looking only for instances where they are expected to occur and not disconfirming evidence), and the presence of motivated cognition. According to MacCoun, this latter theoretical perspective (motivated cognition) includes the cognitive dissonance model, wherein individuals are expected to seek out information supportive of their views, and the model of motive-driven cognition, where things such as a need for closure or a desire to defend a particular position may lead researchers to form (weak) hypotheses and make (erroneous) causal attributions simply to reach a conclusion more quickly or to support a point of view. Both of these potential causes of bias could be in play as researchers attempt to draw conclusions from their own research results.

MacCoun (1998) reviews evidence in support of a variety of other potential biases, including "leniency bias," where scientists were "more willing to publish studies with important findings" (p. 275), and "oversight bias," where researchers rated identical research methods more positively when the topic of a hypothetical study was viewed as being more important. Clearly, to the extent that researchers believe that their own research is important, they may be susceptible to this latter bias. MacCoun concludes with the following statement:

> [There is] a wealth of evidence that biased research interpretation is a common phenomenon, and an overdetermined one, with a variety of intentional, motivational, and purely cognitive determinants. But there is danger of excessive cynicism here. The evidence suggests that the biases are often subtle and small in magnitude;

few research consumers see whatever they want in the data. The available evidence constrains our interpretations—even when intentions are fraudulent—and the stronger and more comprehensive the evidence, the less wiggle room available for bias. (p. 281)

Constructing research conclusions is never simple or straightforward, although the relative lack of attention paid to the process in research handbooks and guidelines seems to suggest otherwise. Our message to readers is that as they prepare their own research conclusions, or read the conclusions of others, they should be aware of potential biases and pursue in their own work what MacCoun (1998) describes as "heterogeneous inquisitorialism—a partnership of rigorous methodological standards, a willingness to tolerate uncertainty, a relentless honesty, and the encouragement of a diversity of hypotheses and perspectives" (pp. 281–282). In the remainder of the chapter, we attempt to suggest some ways in which this may be achieved in the process of drawing conclusions, highlighting as well some potential pitfalls in three areas of concern: connecting premises and findings with conclusions, the role of prior knowledge, and generalizability.

CONNECTING PREMISES, FINDINGS, AND CONCLUSIONS

One of the hardest tasks in developing strong conclusions from one's research is to make reasonable connections among the components of the research study and to connect information drawn from the study to the surrounding context. This context includes prior knowledge, the premises of the study, and beliefs and values that go beyond the study itself but may have motivated the research in the first place. The challenge for researchers, given that prior beliefs, knowledge, and values can influence conclusions for better or for worse, is to find a way in which to capitalize on these influences.

In this section, we examine a few common problems that researchers face in making these connections. We suspect that authors sometimes reframe their premises when their findings do not fit with their expectations (or capitalize on an unexpected result), although there is no obvious way of assessing this by simply reading research reports. Sometimes researchers report conclusions that appear to be more like wishful thinking than reports of real findings because they do not match up with analyses that were done. In this section, we examine a case of this phenomenon. We also discuss the pitfalls associated with moves from a *de*scription of findings to a *pre*scription—what we call the shift from "is" to "ought." We look at examples of these moves and argue that they do not lead to strong reporting of conclusions.

Alignment of Premises and Findings

Researchers often find unexpected results. Moreover, occasionally unexpected results may be more interesting than what the researchers set out to examine, and in such cases researchers might reframe a paper to focus on these more interesting (novel) outcomes. They might even write reports to make it seem as though these results were predicted all along. For this reason, we doubt that it is sensible to view research reports as representations of what the researchers were actually thinking as they planned and engaged in the study unless that process is made an explicit part of the interpretation—surprises, reversals, warts, and all.

One suggestive finding in regard to the framing of conclusions is seen in Becker's (1988) synthesis of studies of gender differences in science achievement. Gender differences may be included in research sometimes because they are easy to measure, sometimes because they might be useful control variables, and sometimes because the researchers have a practical or theoretical interest in gender differences. How researchers draw conclusions about their findings can be very different, depending on these different initial purposes. Becker coded articles according to whether they appeared to focus on gender as a primary issue and asked whether the size of gender differences related to having a reported practical or theoretical focus on gender. She found 8 studies (of 28) that appeared to focus on gender (according to their introductions, literature reviews, and conclusions of the reports). These studies showed significantly larger gender differences than did other studies

(with a standardized mean difference of 0.29 standard deviation units vs. 0.11 units for the other studies). One hypothesis that could account for this finding is that researchers who began with an initial interest in gender differences designed their studies in ways that would reveal these differences (possibly an instantiation of researcher expectancy effects mentioned previously). Another is that researchers who found large differences redefined their studies in retrospect to give the appearance that this was what they sought all along.

A different, but equally problematical, version of how premises align with findings occurs when findings consist of discovering an instance of one's initial theoretical construct. One of us (Beach) has reviewed numerous journal manuscripts that use a sociocultural theoretical framework. In this view, knowledge is by definition taken to be socially constructed rather than emerging from a purely private mental act. This is the theoretical and analytic framing for the study. Unfortunately, it is also sometimes taken to be a primary finding of that same study; authors might state that they found knowledge to be socially constructed during the event that was studied. Finding an instance of one's theoretical construct provides no new understanding; therefore, it is difficult, if not impossible, to legitimately expand on such as a conclusion. Both portraying unexpected findings as if they were anticipated and discovering findings that are merely instances of one's premise are problematic.

Wishful Thinking? Conclusions That Do Not Match Findings

Wishful thinking is much more pernicious than the phenomena we just discussed. Several varieties of wishful thinking can be found, for instance, when a trend (or difference) is not quite significant but the researchers discuss it in detail anyway, perhaps because they wanted that effect to be important or because the researchers felt that, to be thorough, each effect had to be discussed. Often researchers describe these findings as "nearly significant" or "having a pattern that is consistent with the hypothesis, even though not significant." Although such examinations of evidence may be an important part of a thorough discussion of findings, authors need to be careful not to build extensive conclusions from "nearly significant" findings unless it is the lack of significance that is built on by the authors.

Another variety of wishful thinking is to report on relations or other effects that were not actually studied. This can occur when variables actually studied are redefined in the conclusion section or are combined to create a new, more global construct that was not studied but that is discussed in the conclusion. Sometimes authors make claims about effects that were not examined, drawing out results from related, but different, analyses. This kind of wishful thinking appears in Hawk, Coble, and Swanson (1985), a widely cited article on teacher certification. The study involved 18 pairs of math teachers (one certified in math and the other in a different field in each pair) who were tested for their algebra and arithmetic knowledge and observed on five dimensions of the Carolina Teacher Performance Assessment System (CTPAS). Teachers' degrees held, their years of experience teaching, and their years teaching math were noted. Finally, two math tests were given (twice) to students of these teachers—as pretests and posttests. A general math test and an algebra scale were administered (although only 5% of the students took the algebra test on both occasions).

Seven *t* tests and three chi-square tests were used to examine differences between in-field and out-of-field teachers. Only two variables showed significant differences: teacher knowledge of algebra and the instructional presentation dimension from the CTPAS. No other teacher variables showed significant differences, and for most variables, means and/or test values were not shown. The nonsignificant variables included four other measures of "effective teaching practices" (Hawk et al., 1985, p. 14) such as instructional monitoring and instructional feedback. In addition, two other measures of teacher knowledge (general math knowledge and holding an advanced degree) were not significant. Surprisingly, this relatively weak result (only 2 variables of 10 showing significance) was summarized by the authors as showing that "in-field certified teachers know more mathematics and show evidence of using more effective teaching practices than their out-of-field counterparts" (p. 15).

What is notable about Hawk and colleagues' (1985) article is that the results section concerned relations that could have been studied but were not. In the results section, the findings were summarized and three conjectures were made (although they were stated as results). The first conjecture was that "teachers who are more knowledgeable in mathematics are more successful in presenting material to students" (p. 15). We argue that this is just a conjecture because the correlation between knowledge of math and success in presenting material was not measured. In addition, although teacher algebra knowledge and instructional presentation both showed differences between in-field and out-of-field teachers, two other measures of teacher knowledge showed no difference. Thus, the broad statement made by the researchers seems a bit exaggerated.

A second conjecture followed the first. Hawk and colleagues (1985) next argued that "the combination of knowledge and instructional presentation skills may be the resulting cause of the in-field teachers' students achieving at a greater level" (p. 15). This claim again concerned relations among variables that showed significant in-field versus out-of-field differences (the student outcomes and teacher algebra knowledge and instructional presentation). However, again no correlations were analyzed, even though measures of all the variables were available. This connection is even more tenuous because, as we noted previously, the findings only weakly support in-field versus out-of-field differences in knowledge and instructional skill.

The final conjecture related teacher background to student outcomes and CTPAS scores. Hawk and colleagues (1985) wrote that "it would appear fair to conclude that neither years of teaching [n]or degree level held any significant bearing on student achievement in math or the classroom performance of teachers included in the study" (p. 15). However, although two analyses of covariance did show that the students of in-field teachers scored significantly higher on both student math outcomes, relations of these outcomes to years of teaching and degree level were not tested, even though data existed to allow examination of each one. We would argue that it is *not* fair to make this conclusion—and certainly not when analyses that could support or refute the finding had not been done.

The lesson to be drawn from this example is that conclusions are stronger when they are based on the analyses actually conducted. Differences that are found should not be exaggerated. Hawk and colleagues (1985) could have computed descriptive statistics or tests to address their claims. The influence of research is likely to be reduced when untested "findings" are presented as facts.

Shifting From "Is" to "Ought"

Research projects such as "design experiments" (Brown, 1992) are specifically intended to study and make decisions about how something ought to be accomplished in education. These studies generally incorporate the values and purposes of a community, an institution, society, or some other social organization into the structure of the study. For most other studies, if there is to be an "ought," the shift from describing or explaining what "is" in a particular set of circumstances to prescribing what ought to be done usually takes place during a movement from findings to conclusions. Several difficulties can and often do occur here. (For a related discussion of this issue in developmental psychology, see Bronfenbrenner, Kessel, Kessen, & White, 1986.)

One difficulty arises when the study findings are given as the sole warrant for shifting to a concluding discussion of what *ought to be done* in education. Deciding what should be done engages not only research findings but also *values* about what should be learned, how it should be learned, by whom, and for what purposes. Thus, giving research findings sole credit for a concluding discussion of what should be done differently in education positions the findings as "values disguised as findings" or as "values in drag." Making values explicit alongside findings affords an opportunity for the reader to bring different values to the findings, critique the author's conclusions, and possibly provide an alternative argument for what "ought to be done."

A related version of this problem occurs when the researcher draws prescriptive conclusions about what ought to be enacted, but the conclusion could just as easily have been drawn without having done the study. Usually prescriptive conclusions that are disconnected from findings in this way are disguised values, but they typically are also extremely general and appeal to common sense based on the extant view of what constitutes good pedagogy at the time the article is published.

It is important to specify what one's warrants are for moving from findings that describe the way things are to conclusions that make claims of a more prescriptive nature. Making explicit the values driving this move is one of those warrants. It might also be useful to consider a more nuanced range of conclusion prescriptiveness that includes "what may be" and "what could be" as well as "what is" and "what ought to be" (Schofield, 1990).

Juxtaposing Prior Knowledge and Findings

The preceding sections have shown many ways in which conclusions can reflect prior beliefs and values, prior assumptions and expectations, and even prior wishes and hopes. Every researcher is susceptible to these prior ideas, and every researcher must work actively to find plausible connections between new findings and prior ideas. This is the central challenge facing every researcher who tries to draw conclusions from findings.

Here is our dilemma. It is impossible to construct conclusions without relying on prior knowledge. At the same time, if the meaning of research findings is dictated solely by prior knowledge, then we cannot learn from new studies. The problem that researchers face, therefore, is not one of how to put aside prior knowledge but rather one of how to capitalize on prior knowledge and use it to extract as much *new knowledge* as possible from the findings. Researchers must think of prior knowledge and research findings as two sets of knowledge that must be reconciled or juxtaposed in some way—as pieces of a puzzle must fit together. One's ability to learn from research depends on one's ability to accomplish this juxtaposition.

The task is much harder when the findings do not seem to follow from your prior knowledge.

In this case, the temptation is to excuse one set of knowledge as false and to embrace the other as true. For instance, if a researcher decides that her prior knowledge is really true, then she can use it to construct a story for why the findings are really false. Perhaps she identifies problems with the research design that would not have been emphasized if the findings had matched her expectations (e.g., Mahoney, 1977). Another researcher may cover his findings with a thick layer of interpretation that explains the discrepancy and leaves his knowledge unchallenged. Alternatively, if the researcher decides that the findings are true, then he could embrace them as revelatory and claim that they reverse everything we have known before. None of these approaches is really credible. Our prior ideas are voluminous; they form complex intertwined webs that link knowledge, beliefs, attitudes, and values; and they derive from many sources. It is hard to imagine a single study that would discredit all of this. At the same time, if a study is designed specifically to expose a particular phenomenon and the researcher does not see what she or he expected to see, it is hard to believe that the fault lies entirely in the research methods given that they were, after all, devised expressly to reveal this phenomenon.

There are, of course, many options between these two extremes. If we envision a continuum of strategies for juxtaposing these two sets of knowledge, it might look something like the list of options that follow. Those at the beginning of the list favor prior ideas to the detriment of research findings, whereas those at the end favor research findings to the detriment of prior ideas.

A. *Prior ideas are used to deny findings.* In this case, the researcher claims that his or her own findings are not really valid due to methodological anomalies. Hence, prior ideas remain true despite the research findings.

B. *Prior ideas are used to define findings.* In this case, the research findings are defined according to prior ideas. Findings are packaged with a set of labels, concepts, and constructs that come from prior ideas, so that anything unusual about them is hidden under an interpretive blanket.

C. *Prior ideas inadvertently curtail interpretation of findings.* In this case, prior ideas offer one interpretation of the findings and mask other plausible possibilities in such a way that the researcher is unable to learn anything new from the study.

D. *Prior ideas facilitate interpretation of findings.* This is the first variation in which we see prior ideas increasing our potential to learn something new. In this case, the researcher is able to draw on and juxtapose prior ideas with findings in a way that the contrast allows a new interpretation, or a new idea, to be born.

E. *Prior ideas challenge findings.* In this case, the discrepancy between prior ideas and the study findings forces the researcher to reconsider both and to generate a new idea that improves on prior ideas and renders the findings more meaningful as well. This occurred in a study by Kennedy (1999) discussed later.

F. *Prior ideas are amended by findings.* This approach to constructing conclusions occurs when the researcher revises his or her prior ideas in response to study findings in a way that acknowledges much of the prior ideas but also acknowledges the new findings.

G. *Prior ideas are replaced by findings.* This final option is in fact so rare that we list it here only as a hypothetical possibility.

Setting Option G aside, we notice that prior ideas have the upper hand in most of the other options. That is, there are more ways for prior ideas to dominate findings than there are for findings to dominate prior ideas. Hence, researchers need to learn how to harness their prior ideas so that they do not serve merely to negate, define, or interpret their findings but rather challenge the findings in ways that stimulate the researchers' thinking and increase learning. In fact, the most illuminating approaches are those that force these two sets of ideas to challenge each other. Challenges maximize one's ability to learn from the study and to construct a conclusion that pushes both prior ideas and new findings against each other to form a new idea.

Powell's (1997) comparison of two novice high school chemistry teachers, one who had been trained in a traditional teacher education program and one who had been a professional chemist before entering teaching, provides a useful example of how prior ideas and research findings can challenge each other. Powell's *expectation* was that the experienced chemist would be a superior teacher because of his practical experience and his situated understanding of the subject. Powell reasoned that the experienced chemist's understanding of the subject would enable him to offer students a more lively and interactive experience with chemistry. But as he observed the two teachers over the course of a year, Powell found that the two teachers' approaches to chemistry teaching were very similar. The chemist adopted a very restrained and controlled approach to teaching because he could not manage his students, whereas the traditionally prepared teacher adopted a restrained and controlled approach because she was too unsure of her content ideas to allow for free-ranging discussions. Powell yielded to his findings and concluded that real-world experiences and situated understanding of content alone could not ensure better teaching. Notice that, in drawing this conclusion, Powell did not need to concede every advantage to the chemist's knowledge. That is, he could still cling to his prior idea that situated understanding of chemistry would be superior to textbook knowledge while conceding that it was apparently not sufficient to provoke major changes in teaching practice.

One especially useful strategy for producing new ideas is to generate multiple plausible hypotheses that could account for one's findings. A recent study by Kennedy (1999) illustrates this strategy. The study was designed to test several different hypotheses about the types of research that would be most helpful to teachers. At the time the study was done, a debate was under way about how to make research more useful to teachers. Some researchers argued that experiments would be more useful because experiments provide more authoritative results (e.g., Campbell & Stanley, 1963; Clifford, 1973; Greene, 1998; Grossen, 1996; Hargreaves, 1997; Pressley & Harris, 1994). Others suggested that teachers need case studies because these present their findings in a narrative form that better matches the way in which teachers think about their practice (e.g., Bolster, 1983; Stake, 1978). Still others argued that teachers would respond more to research conducted by teachers themselves on the grounds that these researchers would address problems that are important to teachers (e.g., Cochran-Smith & Lytle, 1990; Lytle & Cochran-Smith, 1994).

To test these various hypotheses, Kennedy (1999) asked a sample of teachers to read bundles of studies, with each bundle of studies constructed to contain different genres of research that addressed similar content. She then interviewed the teachers, asking them their perceptions of the validity of each study as well as how relevant it was to their own practice and how much it might influence their own thinking. Finally, she ranked the five studies in each bundle according to the number of teachers who found the study to be most persuasive or most relevant to their own practice or to have influenced their thought the most. The rank ordering did not give immediate support to any of the hypotheses. For example, a nonexperimental comparison study was nominated as most persuasive more often than was a randomized experiment, and a conceptual analysis was nominated more often than was either a case study or a survey. The patterns did not allow for any parsimonious conclusion favoring a particular research genre or favoring any of the hypotheses that were in the extant literature.

If Kennedy (1999) had used her prior ideas to dictate her conclusions, then she might have found a way in which to disregard some of these findings, arguing that teachers might not have really understood one of the studies or that one of the studies had a flaw that limited its value to teachers, even though the genre itself was generally useful. Instead, Kennedy used the patterns of findings to challenge the hypotheses, and she returned to her data to learn more about what teachers saw in these various studies. The conclusion that she constructed offered a new interpretation of the kind of research that was most useful to teachers. She argued that the qualities of research that appealed to teachers had to do with the questions that were asked and not with the methodology that was used. The studies that were ranked highest had to do with the relationship between what teachers did and what students learned. They did not address only student learning or only teaching practices but instead focused on the relationship between them.

Another strategy is to draw on prior ideas from a slightly different domain to challenge one's findings. This strategy was used by Ingersoll (2003a), who was interested in the prevalence of out-of-field teaching—that is, the extent to which teachers are teaching school subjects that they are not certified to teach—and in the causes of out-of-field teaching. It might be easy to assume that out-of-field teaching would occur when there are shortages of qualified teachers, but Ingersoll knew from his own prior research (Ingersoll, 2003b) that school principals can assign courses to teachers for a wide range of quirky reasons, for instance, as punishments or rewards. This knowledge pushed him to dig deeper into the out-of-field teaching phenomenon, and through his research he learned that the prevalence of such teaching is indeed a function of local idiosyncrasies rather than of broader social or supply-and-demand trends. Without calling on his prior knowledge of school cultures, Ingersoll might have simply attributed out-of-field assignments to teacher shortages, a popular off-the-rack interpretation of assignment patterns.

In both of these cases, the authors were not relying on prior ideas to lay a ready-made interpretation over their findings but instead were using their prior ideas to render the findings problematic, to raise questions about the findings, and then to push themselves toward more sophisticated conclusions than would have otherwise been possible.

Prior ideas, when used to advantage, can figure in our thinking about all of the parts of conclusions that were listed at the start of this chapter. And to the extent that we let prior ideas challenge our findings, they can help us to clarify compromises made in the research process and to ferret out limitations that might not have appeared obvious at the outset.

CONSTRUCTING GENERALIZATIONS IN FORMING CONCLUSIONS

The generalizability of findings and interpretations often appears as an issue in drawing conclusions because of the expansive nature of conclusions. Although overgeneralization is perhaps a more common problem because of

conclusions' expansiveness, undergeneralization also occurs, often because a researcher does not carefully consider and articulate the bases for generalization. Misunderstandings of the implications of sample size and sample representativeness frequently drive inappropriate claims of generalization in research conclusions from both methodological traditions. The larger the sample size, the greater the possibility that the sample and the research findings are representative of the population that was sampled, all other things being equal. However, it is rarely the case that all other things are equal. A large sample that is biased, for instance, is not useful for generalizing to a larger population. On the other side, a small but purposefully clustered sample of sixth-grade students that includes students from lower- and upper-socioeconomic status (SES) families in proportion to their representation in the district population is more class representative of and generalizable to the district population of sixth graders than is a larger sample that includes half of the district's sixth-grade students but in proportions counter to the actual proportions of lower- and upper-SES sixth-grade students in the district.

Findings from a comparative case study of two teachers' sixth-grade science teaching, for example, are legitimately generalizable if the cases are convincingly specified as examples of categories of general interest and if a convincing argument is made for the plausibility of the generalization. The potential warrants for case-based generalizations of findings rely not on sample size and probability but rather on specification and plausibility. Qualitative case study authors sometimes limit the generalizability of their findings by underdeveloping arguments for the plausibility of generalizing to other situations and by failing to make claims of interpretive usefulness in understanding those other situations. Sometimes, of course, attempts are made to generalize findings from cases without the construction of plausibility arguments. It is also legitimate for researchers to provide thick description and no warrants for generalizability, leaving any inferences to other events and situations to be made by the reader.

What is clear from this discussion is that there are several different ways in which to conceptualize generalizability, and it is important to be explicit about what sort of generalizability is being argued for in a conclusion and what the warrants are for making such a generalization. Kvale (1996) makes a nicely articulated set of distinctions among three forms of generalization based on the work of Stake (1994): naturalistic, statistical, and analytic. *Naturalistic generalization* grows from people's personal experiences and the expectations and anticipations that are based on those experiences. The knowledge involved is often tacit and does not take the form of formal prediction. If verbalized, however, it can be a form of propositional reasoning. We all make these sorts of generalizations on a daily basis. *Statistical generalization* is formal and explicit and is based on probabilities stemming from the relation of a sample to a population. *Analytical generalization* involves a well-articulated and reasoned argument for how the findings from one study can be used as a guide to understanding a new situation or event. This reasoned argument could take the form of precedent or rules for making inferences to a hypothesized general case. Kvale's (1996) categories of generalization are a useful heuristic, reminding us that whatever approach we take to making generalizability claims from our findings, it is a choice among a wider range of possibilities that are afforded or constrained by the purpose and nature of our study. Decisions about generalizations made in moving from findings to conclusions cannot be made effectively as an afterthought.

Another choice made by researchers, although often implicitly or by default, concerns the degree to which the researcher *develops warrants and claims* for the generalizability of findings and the degree to which these warrants and claims are left to the reader to construct. This issue partially intersects with the type of generalizability argued for by the researcher. Statistical or probabilistic generalization necessarily involves considerable researcher effort to specify the range and limits of generalizability along with its warrants. This is not to say that the reader of such research has no responsibility for constructing generalizations. Rather, the nature of reader-based generalization is heavily a function of the researcher's efforts to warrant certain generalizations from findings and to rule out others.

Analytic generalizations are more open to variation in the degree to which the researcher or the reader is expected to construct generalization claims. The researcher is responsible for providing sufficient context and detailed description if responsibility for generalization is to reside largely with the reader. In clinical medicine and law, this expectation of reader interpretive agency is built into the assumptions of these disciplines (cf. Kennedy, 1979). The social sciences and education are far more variable in how and why findings are generalized; thus, the researcher should be explicit in communicating this expectation to the reader when framing the study findings. When a researcher takes on more responsibility for drawing analytic generalizations in making conclusions, the warrants take the form of plausibility arguments, based both on evidence from the study and on knowledge of the situations to which the researcher generalizes. Researchers seeking to warrant claims of analytic generalizability need more specific and detailed knowledge of the targets of their generalization than do researchers who warrant generalizations using probabilities.

It should be clear from this section that constructing generalizations, and warrants for those generalizations, when moving from findings to conclusions is neither simple, automatic, nor devoid of researcher options. Determining what type of generalization, what its warrants are, and who has primary agency for making generalizations are all points of decision for the researcher.

CONCLUSIONS ABOUT CONCLUSIONS

We began this chapter by examining what has been written about conclusions, only to find that most of what is written concerns, at its core, what to do with a piece of text labeled "conclusions." The real challenge, we believe, is not in writing some part of a document but rather in arriving at the content to be discussed; that is, the hard part is the act of moving from one's findings to the conclusions that one wants to broadcast to the world. We then laid a background for being skeptical of our abilities to easily and mechanically move from findings to conclusions, and we argued for some specific ways in which to capitalize on the tension between our prior knowledge and our findings to arrive at defensible conclusions. We suggested that by consciously juxtaposing our prior knowledge, beliefs, and values against our findings, it is possible to challenge those prior views and to learn something new. We argued that posing (and critiquing) multiple research questions or hypotheses is one way of challenging our prior views and that drawing on work in a different domain may also provide insights. Next we argued that premises, findings, and conclusions should be clearly and justifiably connected with one another. Although much of arriving at conclusions involves inferences based on our own results (and we urge researchers not to go far beyond what their analyses support), often we want to argue for what should be done or what ought to occur in some educational context based on what we have found. We believe that bringing values explicitly "to the table" along with findings is the only way in which to warrant statements of what ought to be done. In most cases, the move from "is" to "ought" cannot be justified in light of findings alone. Finally, we argued for explicit consideration of the particular form of generalizations desired as a part of a conclusion as well as the warrants for those generalizations.

To close, we reflect on how our values and beliefs informed the writing of this chapter. The three of us differ in our methodological training, in our current methodological proclivities, and in the underlying epistemological assumptions of our work. However, our collaboration on writing the chapter made it clear that the three of us value transparency and explicitness in the reporting of research, regard the careful warranting of claims as central to good research, and find seamless linear descriptions of the research process to be slightly disingenuous and at times downright misleading. As we passed versions of this manuscript back and forth, sometimes one of us might have said, "I don't understand what you mean here" (about our own writing) or asked, "Do we agree with this?" (in regard to a quote or conclusion about another author's work). This would prompt the original author of the text to clarify, to make an explicit recommendation (e.g., "Researchers should do X"), or on occasion to state, "We believe X"—essentially to elaborate on our beliefs about what we had written. Although each of us brought his or her values to the table, so to speak, it was through the collaborative effort that much of this became explicit to us and, hopefully (because we produced a written record), has become more explicit to the reader as well.

The work of constructing research conclusions is not, and should not be, automatic or simple. We hope that by making explicit some of the options, challenges, and pitfalls in drawing conclusions, this chapter makes the process a bit more reflective and transparent without diminishing the overall challenge of doing it well.

REFERENCES

Becker, B. J. (1988). Gender and science achievement: A reanalysis of studies from two meta-analyses. *Journal of Research in Science Teaching, 26,* 141–169.

Begg, C., Cho, M., Eastwood, S., Horton, R., Moher, D., Olkin, I., Pitkin, R., Rennie, D., Schulz, K. F., Simel, D., & Stroup, D. F. (1996). Improving the quality of reporting of randomized controlled trials: The CONSORT statement. *Journal of the American Medical Association, 276,* 637–639.

Bolster, A. S. J. (1983). Toward a more effective model of research on teaching. *Harvard Educational Review, 53,* 294–308.

Bronfenbrenner, U., Kessel, F., Kessen, W., & White, S. (1986). Toward a critical social history of developmental psychology. *American Psychologist, 41,* 1218–1230.

Brown, A. L. (1992). Design experiments: Theoretical and methodological challenges in creating complex interventions in classroom settings. *Journal of the Learning Sciences, 2*(2), 141–178.

Campbell, D. C., & Stanley, J. (1963). *Experimental and quasi-experimental designs for research.* Chicago: Rand McNally.

Clifford, G. (1973). A history of impact of research on teaching. In R. M. Travers (Ed.), *Second handbook of research on teaching* (pp. 1–46). New York: Macmillan.

Cochran-Smith, M., & Lytle, S. (1990). Research on teaching and teacher research: The issues that divide. *Educational Researcher, 19*(2), 2–11.

Cooper, H., & Hazelrigg, P. (1988). Personality moderators of interpersonal expectancy effects: An integrative research review. *Journal of Personality and Social Psychology, 55,* 937–949.

Des Jarlais, D. C., Lyles, C., & Crepaz, N. (2004). Improving the reporting quality of nonrandomized evaluations of behavioral and public health interventions: The TREND statement. *American Journal of Public Health, 94,* 361–366.

Dunbar, K., & Klahr, D. (1989). Developmental differences in scientific discovery strategies. In D. Klahr & K. Kotovsky (Eds.), *Complex information processing: The impact of Herbert A. Simon* (pp. 109–143). Hillsdale, NJ: Lawrence Erlbaum.

Edwards, K., & Smith, E. E. (1996). A disconfirmation bias in the evaluation of arguments. *Journal of Personality and Social Psychology, 71,* 5–24.

Evans, J. S. (2002). Logic and human reasoning: An assessment of the deduction paradigm. *Psychological Bulletin, 128,* 978–996.

Fong, G. T., & Nisbett, R. E. (1991). Immediate and delayed transfer of training effects in statistical reasoning. *Journal of Experimental Psychology: General, 120,* 34–45.

Fraenkel, J. R., & Wallen, N. E. (2003). *How to design and evaluate research in education* (5th ed.). Boston: McGraw-Hill.

Gall, J. P., Gall, M. D., & Borg, W. (2005). *Applying educational research: A practical guide* (5th ed.). Boston: Pearson/Allyn & Bacon.

Greene, J. P. (1998, April 29). Rescuing educational research: A rule of thumb for fending off the "nihilism" of competing claims. *Education Week,* p. 52.

Grossen, B. (1996, Fall). Making research serve the profession. *American Educator,* pp. 7–8, 22–27.

Hargreaves, D. H. (1997). In defense of research for evidence based teaching: A rejoinder to Martyn Hammersley. *British Educational Research Journal, 23,* 405–419.

Hawk, P. P., Coble, C. R., & Swanson, M. (1985). Certification: It does matter. *Journal of Teacher Education, 36*(3), 13–15.

Ingersoll, R. M. (2003a). *Out of field teaching and the limits of public policy.* Philadelphia: University of Pennsylvania, Consortium for Policy Research in Education.

Ingersoll, R. M. (2003b). *Who controls teachers' work? Power and accountability in America's schools.* Cambridge, MA: Harvard University Press.

Johnson-Laird, P. N., & Byrne, R. M. J. (1991). *Deduction.* Hillsdale, NJ: Lawrence Erlbaum.

Kahneman, D., Slovic, P., & Tversky, A. (1982). *Judgment under uncertainty: Heuristics and biases.* Cambridge, UK: Cambridge University Press.

Kennedy, M. M. (1979). Generalizing from single case studies. *Evaluation Quarterly, 3,* 661–678.

Kennedy, M. M. (1999). A test of some common contentions about educational research. *American Educational Research Journal, 36,* 511–541.

Klahr, D. (2000). *Exploring science: The cognition and development of discovery processes.* Cambridge, MA: MIT Press.

Kuhn, D. (1989). Children and adults as intuitive scientists. *Psychological Review, 96,* 674–689.

Kvale, S. (1996). *InterViews: An introduction to qualitative research interviewing.* Thousand Oaks, CA: Sage.

Lytle, S., & Cochran-Smith, M. (1994). Inquiry, knowledge, and practice. In S. Hollingsworth & H. Sockett (Eds.), *Teacher research and educational reform: Ninety-third yearbook of the National Society for the Study of Education, Part I* (pp. 22–51). Chicago: University of Chicago Press.

MacCoun, R. J. (1998). Biases in the interpretation and use of research results. *Annual Review of Psychology, 49,* 259–287.

Mahoney, M. J. (1977). Publication prejudices: An experimental study of confirmatory bias in the peer review system. *Cognitive Therapy and Research, 1,* 161–175.

Moher, D., Schulz, K. F., & Altman, D. G., for the CONSORT Group. (2001). The CONSORT statement: Revised recommendations for improving the quality of reports of parallel-group randomised trials. *Lancet, 357,* 1191–1194.

Morris, W. (Ed.). (1976). *The American heritage dictionary of the English language.* Boston: Houghton Mifflin.

Nickerson, R. S. (1998). Confirmation bias: A ubiquitous phenomenon in many guises. *Review of General Psychology, 2,* 175–220.

Powell, R. R. (1997). Teaching alike: A cross-case analysis of first-career and second-career beginning teachers' instructional convergence. *Teaching and Teacher Education, 13,* 341–356.

Pressley, M., & Harris, K. R. (1994). Increasing the quality of educational intervention research. *Educational Psychology Review, 6,* 191–208.

Rips, L. J. (1994). *The psychology of proof: Deductive reasoning in human thinking.* Cambridge, MA: MIT Press.

Rosenthal, R. (1976). *Experimenter effects in behavioral research* (rev. ed.). New York: Irvington.

Rosenthal, R., & Rubin, D. B. (1978). Interpersonal expectancy effects: The first 345 studies. *Behavioral and Brain Sciences, 3,* 377–415.

Sackett, D. L., Rosenberg, W. M. C., Muir Gray, J. A., Haynes, R. B., & Richardson, W. S. (1996). Evidence based medicine: What it is and what it isn't. *British Medical Journal, 312,* 7023.

Schauble, L., Glaser, R., Raghavan, K., & Reiner, M. (1991). Causal models and experimentation strategies in scientific reasoning. *Journal of the Learning Sciences, 1,* 201–238.

Schofield, J. W. (1990). Generalizability in qualitative research. In E. Eisner & A. Peshkin (Eds.), *Qualitative inquiry in education* (pp. 201–232). New York: Columbia University, Teachers College Press.

Shafir, E., & LeBoeuf, R. A. (2002). Rationality. *Annual Review of Psychology, 53,* 491–517.

Stake, R. E. (1978). The case study in social inquiry. *Educational Researcher, 7*(2), 5–8.

Stake, R. E. (1994). Case studies. In N. K. Denzin & Y. S. Lincoln (Eds.), *Handbook of qualitative research* (pp. 236–247). Thousand Oaks, CA: Sage.

Wiersma, W. (2000). *Research methods in education: An introduction* (7th ed.). Boston: Allyn & Bacon.

Wolcott, H. F. (2001). *Writing up qualitative research* (2nd ed.). Thousand Oaks, CA: Sage.

Zimmerman, C. (2000). The development of scientific reasoning skills. *Developmental Review, 20,* 99–149.

Section Six

*Challenges in Writing, Voice,
and Dissemination of Research*

INTRODUCTORY ESSAY

BETH GRAUE

University of Wisconsin–Madison

Remember this old problem: "If a tree falls in the forest and there is no one around to hear it, does it make a sound?" It serves as a model for the chapters in this Section Six, which address the question: "If a researcher does work that no one reads, is it research?" The three chapters in this section explore the public function of research, examining the ways in which various models of inquiry frame this stage of the developmental cycle and the major challenges—some often invisible—on which scholars are advised to reflect. They examine connections among research and representation, the politics of reporting, the notion of voice, and the place of practice in education research. At the risk of belaboring the tree–forest metaphor, here are a few twists that are presented in this section:

- If a tree falls in the forest and only botanists hear it, does it make a sound?
- If a tree falls in the forest and no one recognizes it as a tree, does it make a sound?
- If a tree falls in the forest and the story ends up being about the botanist, does it make a sound?
- If a tree falls in the forest and it has no impact on the ecology of the forest (either locally or globally), does it make a sound?
- If a tree falls in the laboratory, does it make a sound?

One of the challenges that researchers face when trying to share their work is writing it up. Researchers are typically so busy writing up their research that little attention is paid to writing. Examining the textual practices of writing, Beth Graue argues in Chapter 28 that writing is quite genre specific, with researchers choosing a way of telling their story that enacts theoretical perspectives on how the world works. These genres facilitate and constrain knowing by the ways in which they use the authority, by the researcher's place in inquiry, and by the degree to which reflexivity is made public. Graue suggests four metaphors for writing—writing as reporting, writing as interpreting, writing as constituting, and writing as praxis—and illustrates them through examples. Each metaphor gives the author a different role, connections to audience, and moral responsibilities to the practice of education. As a result, each genre has different standards by which we judge the quality of the writing.

Although constructivism has brought the notion of multiple realities into mainstream education research, many researchers continue to homogenize those realities when they write. Except for writers who explicitly use "alternative" formats, it is most often the case that researchers present a unified way of looking at those multiple realities, even when they work in teams. In Chapter 29, Elizabeth Creamer problematizes that practice by examining the notion of voice in research. Coming out of her interest in research collaboration, Creamer provides examples of polyvocality in single-authored texts, alternating first-person narratives, and scripts in varied formats to show how different perspectives can be shared in research writing. Through her examples, she illustrates the ways in which traditional monovocal writing hides the author and can lead the reader to assign authorial meanings to research participants. Furthermore, Creamer illustrates how these polyvocal texts cause us to question the modes of authority embedded with research texts, opening up new ways of thinking about lived experience.

The animating point of Creamer's chapter—that polyvocal collaborative research works against the notion of a single truth—pushes us to think about how our writing is located within traditions and perspectives that may or may not fit into our theoretical/conceptual landscape. We could certainly stretch the conceptions of standards for communication if we allowed our writing strategies to diverge from a single linear story to multiple accounts within a single telling. The problem is that the omniscient narrator is much easier to pull off with bad writing than is a complex telling, and unfortunately, my hunch is that many of us are better researchers than we are writers.

Working across the genres and across the chapters in this section is the challenge of writing contributing to the social practice of education. Given the public nature of education—its importance to the present and future—it makes sense to ask how research writing connects to policy, practice, and public discourse.

In this context, a recent National Public Radio segment suggested that astronomer Carl Sagan had diminished stature in the scholarly community because of his efforts to make astronomy accessible to the public. That communication with the masses would be detrimental to a researcher's reputation might initially seem curious. Is the academy so insular and junior high school-like that researchers cannot even talk to those outside the circle of friends? What this story highlights is that reporting research is anything but a neutral activity; it is rhetorical, political, and wholly focused on the notion of audience. Investing in public communication can be seen as subtractive, complementary, or vital to the work of researchers. Unfortunately, we have had very little discussion of communication, particularly beyond the borders of the scholarly community. Gerald Bracey's contribution (Chapter 30), titled "Getting the Word Out," is a wonderful tool to help us understand the complexity of research communication, particularly as it relates to working with the media.

Most handbook chapters are crafted to be untethered to specific times and places. As reference resources, their applicability rests on not having a "use by" date. Bracey writes against that model by showing us that context, in all its complexity, is everything. Focusing on the links between researchers and the media, Bracey provides a "no holds barred" critique of reporting of education research, focusing on politics, ideology, and personality. Here we finally get the back story—the ins and outs, the accusations and retorts, the readings of motivations and recriminations. From a detailed analysis of diverse media, Bracey illuminates the researchers behind research, mapping social networks among scholars and showing that there are many reasons beyond "good science" why research comes to light in the media. All research is situated in particular value systems, and Bracey shows how readings from the left are in conflict with readings from the right. His contrast between scientists as truth tellers and scientists as position promoters will probably have different actors depending on which side of the political spectrum one resides. The contrast—and the accompanying challenge it invites us to reflect on—is a useful antidote to the assumption of neutrality that afflicts many of us who consume education research without thinking about how and why it came to light. In Section Six, the chapters by Bracey, Graue, and Creamer remind us of the critical importance of never forgetting that whether a tree makes a sound or not depends on the manner in which it falls.

28

WRITING IN EDUCATION RESEARCH

BETH GRAUE

University of Wisconsin–Madison

Research is complete only when the results are shared with the scientific community.

—American Psychological Association (2001, p. 3)

Writing is a practice that connects members of the academic community. It provides cultural capital, builds a knowledge base, and translates into economic capital. It is the prime artifact of the scholarly process, the trail of breadcrumbs we leave to show our path of inquiry. Given the importance of writing in the practice of research, it is too easily thought of as a "one size fits all" model. But there are many ways to write, many sets of standards for judging writing, and many theorizations of communicating research results. Not surprisingly, given the diversity of perspectives in education research, the case of writing is a wonderful enactment of epistemology in practice. How scholars think about writing shapes how they approach the writing task, what writing means, and the standards used to judge the adequacy of examples of written communication.

In this chapter, I explore conceptualizations of writing in education research, arguing that writing is a social practice that shapes texts, writers, readers, and the knowledge produced in inquiry. In addition, I argue for genre-specific metaphors in the academy that shape the use of writing and the parameters for practice, agreeing with Laurel Richardson that

> all the social sciences have prescribed writing formats—none of them neutral, all of them value constituting. *How* we are expected to write affects *what* we can write about. . . . The conventions hold tremendous material and symbolic power over social scientists. Using them increases the probability of one's work being accepted into core social science journals, but they are not prima facie evidence of greater—or lesser—truth values or significance than social science writing using other conventions. (p. 16, emphases in original)

AUTHOR'S NOTE: I am grateful to Simone Schweber and Mary Gomez for their helpful suggestions as I conceptualized this chapter.

I hope that this chapter is viewed as more than a cumbersome typology of writing styles used in education research. Although for some the description of different categories is enough, for me the recognition and discerning of these categories can promote a more reflexive approach to writing than I have seen in education research. And even more than reflexivity, I would hope for better writing, for much as Richardson (1990) notes, I continue to be astounded by the amount of bad writing that finds its way to the published page in education research. I begin with a general discussion of writing.

WHY WE WRITE, HOW WE READ

Few tasks in academia are as mysterious, emotional, or culturally important as is writing. And few are as private and quirky. Howard Becker and Harry Wolcott describe the rituals performed by researchers as they ready themselves for the wild ride of writing (Becker, 1986; Wolcott, 1990). Munching crackers, cleaning, pencil sharpening, and reading are time-honored tools of the researcher perched at the dangerous edge of putting words down on paper. What promotes such strange behavior? Why would one choose to clean the toilet rather than write? Rose and McClafferty (2001) suggest one possible reason:

> Writing is one of the primary sites where scholarly identity is formed and displayed. Whether through papers written for coursework, for conferences or journals, or simply correspondence, scholars often form their impressions of their colleagues based on the written word. (p. 30)

From this perspective, writing is more than description or even analysis; it is an elaborate performance of identity that connects an author and his or her work to a community. In fact, thinking this way requires a subtle shift in role. If we think of how writing is part of the process of affiliation within scholarly communities, then rather than being merely researchers or social scientists, researchers who write are also authors who work through language.

A first step in conceptualizing writing as a social practice is understanding that the text we create is uniquely situated in communities with specific expectations and needs. Madigan, Johnson, and Linton (1995) apply the notion of discourse to the research writing, suggesting that the varied communities of researchers develop strategies and standards that shape the products of research in significant ways:

> Bizzell (1986) has used the term *discourse community* to refer to a group of individuals who share common goals and beliefs and who have established mechanisms for communication. Texts within the discourse community are produced and judged in relation to the community's implicit norms. The community's writing genre serves as both a model for writers and as a template for readers (Todorov, 1990). Both writers and readers come to find prose that contains the typical textual features of the discourse community to be appropriate, persuasive, and interesting. (p. 429, emphasis in original)

Through an analysis of the articles written in different disciplines, Madigan and his colleagues illustrate how stylistic guidelines shape not only the form of a text but also the types of knowledge presented, going so far as to describe how they shape the thinking of the author and reader in a way that socializes individuals into specific paradigms. This way of conceptualizing writing has been used to describe scholarship in disciplines as diverse as psychology (Bazerman, 1987; Madigan et al., 1995), physics, biology (Berkencotter & Huckin, 1993; Myers, 1990), and political science. More than merely a matter of style, which implies that one chooses a way of writing as one might choose which shirt to wear, Madigan and others argue that the content of writing follows its form, making it constitutive of the types of knowing it portrays.

In the remainder of the chapter, I describe four metaphors for writing that shape both knowing and telling in education research. Loosely related to general notions of paradigm, these metaphors have within them conceptions of ontology, epistemology, and authority. As such, they employ genre-specific standards for adequacy. Although this kind of diversity generates a richer array of writing forms, it also poses thorny problems when evaluating writing across the metaphors. These metaphors portray writing as (a) reporting, (b) interpreting, (c) constituting, and (d) praxis. Although these are distinctly different uses of writing with distinctly different forms and functions, all fall within the parameters of research and all deserve consideration.

WRITING AS REPORTING

> The scholarly literature in education and other academic fields is like a wall that is built one stone at a time, each stone filling a hole previously unfilled, each one mortared and connected to those that came before and after it, supported by those that came before. (Murray & Raths, 1994, p. 197)

Used mostly by realists, positivists, constructivists, and modernists, this genre of research writing is in some ways the most difficult to write about because it continues to be the norm in education research. Especially reflecting the historical foundations of the field in psychology, this kind of writing attempts to reflect the writing practices typical of the "hard sciences." Writing as reporting comes out of the assumption that the world is observable and understandable and that the role of the researcher is to describe phenomena that have been carefully measured or arrived at through specific procedures. It is a "just the facts" approach to the writing task, something that reports the results of research with the findings having been revealed. As an afterward to research, the approach to writing is primarily technical or procedural—and is, in turn, governed by stylistic rules for manuscripts. It is exemplified by the *Publication Manual of the American Psychological Association* (APA, 2001), the codification of guidelines developed by the APA and used by researchers in education:

> You can achieve clear communication, which is the prime objective of scientific reporting, by presenting ideas in an orderly manner and by expressing yourself smoothly and precisely. By developing ideas clearly and logically and leading readers smoothly from thought to thought, you make the task of reading an agreeable one. (p. 31)

One way to contrast the varied approaches to writing is through illustrations of the relations among the entity studied, the researcher, and the written product of the research. In the case of writing as reporting, this relation is primarily linear, where data represent measures taken of the field and then presented through written documents, as shown in Figure 28.1:

Figure 28.1   Relationship Among the Field, the Researcher, and the Written Product of the Research in *Writing as Reporting*

a. The "field" referred to here is the field that provides the source of data.

The reality of the field is disclosed through data and documented by the researcher through writing. The researcher is, therefore, only vaguely apparent in this model, a shadowy presence in the overall production of knowledge.

A recent issue of the *Early Childhood Research Quarterly* (Volume 19, Number 2) provides an illustration of this approach. Each of the eight articles in it adheres to the form and structure of the APA guidelines, beginning with a general introduction that presents the problem of interest, followed by a literature review, a description of data and methods, a report of results, and a discussion—often including an implications section. The reports are strikingly similar in form, standardized in look and texture. The sections are conceptually separate so that, for example, no discussion of findings occurs in the results section and no discussion of implications appears in the literature review.

Parsimony is promoted throughout. Clear communication, smooth expression, and a single storyline set up one reading for the data. Although most reports include a discussion of the limitations of the study, these limitations are never terminal. The similarity of form of these articles promotes the appearance of convergence in thinking, which in turn provides authority. The staging of a single "correct reading" of the problem and data suggests the image of a unified field of agreement on practices and conclusions.

Writing as reporting is writing science, which has different practices from other, more recreational forms of writing:

> Scientific prose and creative writing serve different purposes. Devices that are often found in creative writing—for example, setting up ambiguity, inserting the unexpected, omitting the expected, and suddenly shifting the topic, tense, or person—can confuse or disturb readers of scientific prose. Therefore, try to avoid these devices and aim for clear and logical communication. (APA, 2001, pp. 32–33)

Writing as reporting is designed to signal a stance of certainty; it is dispassionate and clear, providing the reader with a message that is unencumbered by alternative readings or literary tropes. It is also represented in realist approaches to qualitative research such as grounded theory, an approach that is based on the idea that theory can be generated from systematically collected data (Strauss & Corbin, 1990). In what Charmaz (2000) calls "objectivist grounded theory," criteria for judging empirical reports are related to procedures— validity, reliability, and credibility of data; methods for collecting and analyzing data; and the degree to which assertions are grounded in data (Strauss & Corbin, 1990). Although there is recognition of writing *for* an audience, the link between procedures and form of writing is so tight that they become one—the researcher writes what he or she did:

> A grounded theorist's proclivities toward objectivism or constructivism also come through in his or her writing about research. The image of a scientific laboratory comes to mind with objectivist

grounded theory, reflected in carefully organized and stated written reports of concepts, evidence, and procedures. (Charmaz, 2000, p. 526)

Another example in the qualitative genre is Miles and Huberman's (1984) approach exemplified by their assertion that

> social phenomena exist not only in the mind but also in the objective world—and that there are some lawful and reasonably stable relationships to be found among them. . . . Our task is to express them as precisely as possible, attending to their range and generality and to the local and historical contingencies under which they occur. . . . Our stance necessarily involves *orderliness,* a certain degree of formalization of the analysis process. . . . We are committed to clarity in qualitative analysis procedures, a commitment that requires a good deal of explicit structure in our approach to inquiry. (pp. 19–20, emphasis in original)

The Miles and Huberman (1984) approach to inquiry is highly focused on good methods, with all attention assigned to the analytical process and documenting that process for both the analyst and the interested reader. Their concern about documentation comes out of their commitment to verification and replication in research—that our colleagues must be able to do our work in another context or at least in their heads. The ability to imagine the methods and techniques is fostered through the many displays that array data in varied relations to promote understandings of underlying structural characteristics.

As I have examined this approach to writing, I consistently found myself at once baffled and paralyzed by the lack of explicit discussion about writing by those who practice *writing as reporting.* Unlike scholars employing other perspectives, reporters do not talk about reporting. Their job is to report. Thinking about reporting does not make sense in the ontological field, where writing is essentially a by-product of scholarly activity. Researcher authority comes out of appropriate use of research tools and procedures; writing is a matter, therefore, of representing that process faithfully. The reality rendered by the writer is wholly transparent, something that comes about through good technique. The writer/researcher is like a slide projector, illuminating the image generated through scholarly activity.

WRITING AS INTERPRETING

> The world does not arrange itself into chapters and subheadings for our convenience. There are many contrasting arrangements and "literary" styles that we can impose, more or less legitimately, on the world. The author who fails to reflect on the processes of composition and compilation may find that a version has been constructed without adequate explicit understanding. (Hammersley & Atkinson, 1995, p. 240)

In contrast to conceptualizing writing as reporting, some researchers take up writing as an interpretive process. In the same way as writing as reporting represents the epistemological stance that knowing and telling are separate, writing as interpreting conflates the two. It is a semiotic representation of the process of understanding; meaning making by participants in research is made through meaning making by researchers. It is paradigmatically expressed in Clifford Geertz's description of the work of an ethnographer:

> The ethnographer "inscribes" social discourse; *he writes it down.* In so doing, he turns it from a passing event, which exists only in its own moment of occurrence, into an account, which exists in its inscriptions and can be reconsulted. . . . So there are three characteristics of ethnographic description: it is interpretive; what it is interpretive of is the flow of social discourse; and the interpreting involved consists of trying to rescue the "said" of such discourse from its perishing occasions and fix it in perusable terms. (Geertz, 1973, pp. 19–20, emphases in original)

In conceptualizing the researcher as a writer, writing is pulled into the research activity. Rather than an afterward to scientific activity standing outside it, writing is viewed as an integral part of an interpretive process that can only partially represent complex social worlds. Writing is the scholarly instantiation of the

cultural meaning making. Researchers understand and represent through their written products. This stance has been particularly important for ethnographers, for whom recognition of the interpretive aspect of their craft was foundational. Paul Atkinson describes this theoretical position:

> Writing up, then, is not the mechanical collation and reportage of raw data. It is part of a complex layering of textual production. The ethnography is a version of social reality that is inseparably a matter of textual representations. . . . Our sense of the social world is shaped by the sense of what can be written about. . . . The decisions taken by the ethnographer have profound implications not just for how readable the text may be, but also for how the actors it portrays are "read" and understood. Here, as elsewhere, textual conventions do not merely raise technical or methodological issues: they have *moral* consequences. (Atkinson, 1992, p. 6, emphasis in original)

Atkinson further elucidates the produced nature of knowledge through writing through the following semiotic triangle, as shown in Figure 28.2:

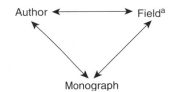

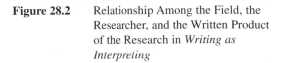

Figure 28.2 Relationship Among the Field, the Researcher, and the Written Product of the Research in *Writing as Interpreting*

a. Again, the term "field" represents fieldwork rather than the scholarly field.

For Atkinson, the field is known through the author, the author is known through the field, and both are represented by the monograph. Several important implications can be drawn from this image. The first is the inherent connectedness of the researcher, the field, and the text. The researcher brings a perspective that shapes what can be known in the field that is inscribed in writings. It is also the case that the field and the written literature shape the author. It is the recursive nature of interpretive practice that makes it a more contingent perspective on knowing (Emerson, Fretz, & Shaw, 1995) based on a relativist ontology. A single true story is not assumed but rather considered an impossibility. Instead, there are always, and necessarily, multiple potential interpretations.

The authority of an account comes out of its plausibility, conferred by the reader in response to descriptions of fieldwork and interpretations of interpretations. In contrast to writing as reporting, nested within this notion of plausibility is a recognition that methods and findings are mutually constitutive; knowing what a researcher knows is inseparable from how he or she knows it (Emerson et al., 1995). But although the data field, text, and researcher are related, they are not one and the same. Although the researcher is an author who interprets, he or she is not the story. This distinction is a complex one. When writing is interpretation, an interpreter is implied. There is recognition of the interpreter's role in the field, in the construction of the narrative, but he or she is not the central character of the story. In fact, stories of the researcher are used in service of two goals: to illustrate a conceptual point and/or to provide a textual dimension to understanding the methods used (which essentially is an element of validity). When writing is interpretation, the writer is himself or herself a tool in the study and is used as a means to the end of articulating one reading of lived experience.

An example of this approach is Annette Lareau's *Unequal Childhoods: Class, Race, and Family Life* (Lareau, 2003; see also her earlier work, *Home Advantage* [Lareau, 1989]). In this text, the author provides a rich accounting of her fieldwork—the decisions she made, the researchers involved in the project, the dilemmas of interaction. It is supplemented by a detailed chronological accounting of fieldwork. But these accounts are separate from the core of the book, situated in appendixes. Lareau's painstakingly crafted descriptions of the lives of eight children and their families take center stage with Lareau as director. The authority of this work comes out of the coherence of the descriptions and their support of theory. Inclusion of the material provides insight into the development of the interpretation provided here. It gives a sense of the labor that produced the interpretations. It locates the interpretations through a small glimpse into researcher biography and identity, as when Lareau writes, "Frankly, part of my motivation for undertaking the project was a long-standing desire to better understand the inner workings of families. As a child I longed to have a 'normal' family. My parents' unusual, even eccentric, characters made me attuned to variations in family life" (Lareau, 2003, p. 267). Equally important, however, is the status of these revelations. They are a sidebar, something that complements but does not supplant the main story Lareau is there to tell. We are witness to the lives of eight families, told through Lareau's account. If this were a play in a theater, then Lareau's personal story would be part of the director's biography rather than written into the play itself.

Sara Lawrence-Lightfoot's portraiture marks a second type of writing as interpretation. As she recalls being the object of an artist's gaze, Lawrence-Lightfoot (2005) depicts the artist's interpretive rendering of her essence, recognizing that it is not her reflection but rather someone's representation:

> From these two experiences of sitting for portraits, I learned my first methodological lessons. I learned, for example, that these portraits did not capture me as I saw myself, that they were not like looking in the mirror at my reflection. Instead, they seemed to capture my "essence"; qualities of character and history, some of which I was unaware, some of which I resisted mightily, some of which felt deeply familiar. But the translation of image was anything but literal. It was probing, layered, and interpretive. In addition to portraying my image, the piece expressed the perspective of the artist and was shaped by the evolving relationship between the artist and me. (p. xix)

The practice of portraiture, and the artist's engagement in the process, is enacted in Lawrence-Lightfoot's (2003) *The Essential Conversation*. She begins the book with a self-portrait recalling her parents' interactions with a teacher with low expectations. She describes how after a period of illness she returned to school and was shocked by her parents' initial passivity when her teacher told them that she would need to repeat second grade because she was not college material. She tells the story of her parents' rewriting the teacher's description of their daughter, telling her that the teacher was wrong and that she was indeed very capable of success. She fast-forwards to examples of their resistance against school practices, providing insight into the tense relations between home and school that particularly characterize families of color and white middle-class teachers. This story of childhood situates Lawrence-Lightfoot as one uniquely capable of interpreting the relations between home and school, having experienced the tensions between parents and teacher as a child, a researcher, and as a parent. As the book unfolds, the focus shifts from Lawrence-Lightfoot as the object of the narrative to the portrayal of 10 teacher-mothers and their practice as educators straddling the home–school divide. A key aspect of her argument is her assertion that teachers and parents use their experiences as children as the foundation of home–school relations. Her initial portrait is used as a metaphor, her experience as a foundation for her understanding of their experience based on their foundation. The symmetry of this portrayal is narratively compelling, a beautiful illustration of these relationships at both the theoretical and textual levels. And just as Lareau's inclusion of her experience is instrumental, so too is Lawrence-Lightfoot's providing a touchstone for the plausibility of her interpretations. Atkinson's semiotic triangle is recreated in both of these examples with understanding fashioned from the connections among the author, the field, and the text. The author interprets the field and creates the text, which is then interpreted by the reader who reads the field and the author:

> In short, anthropological writings are themselves interpretations, and second and third order ones to boot. (By definition, only a "native" makes first order ones: It's *his* culture.) They are thus fiction, fictions in the sense that they are "something made," "something fashioned"—the original meaning of *fictio*—not that they are false, unfactual, or merely "as if" thought experiments. . . . It is not against a body of uninterpreted data, radically thinned descriptions, that we must measure

the cogency of our explications, but against the power of the scientific imagination to bring us into touch with the lives of strangers. (Geertz, 1973, pp. 15–16)

If the researcher is a projector in writing as reporting, we might imagine the researcher in writing as interpreting much the same way as Lawrence-Lightfoot does, as a portrait artist. Working to depict an essence, the artist-researcher has a distinct style that is reflected in the artistic product but that is secondary to the subject of interest.

Writing as Constituting

> Writing is not simply a true representation of an objective reality, out there, waiting to be seen. Instead, through literary and rhetorical structures, writing creates a particular view of reality. . . . In our work as researchers we weigh and sift experiences, make choices regarding what is significant, what is trivial, what to include, what to exclude. We do not simply chronicle "what happened next," put place the "next" in a meaningful context. By doing so, we craft narratives; we write lives. (Richardson, 1990, pp. 9–10)

Richardson (1990) argues that writing makes a world for both readers and writers, enacting narrative conventions such as chronology, metaphor, and synecdoche to produce meaning. Instead of conceptualizing writing as reflective, she suggests that it *creates* realities. In so doing, Richardson vaults over the science–literature divide that asserts that science describes while literature creates. In its place, Richardson (1997) suggests a postmodern understanding of writing, one that recognizes the following:

> Working within the "ideology of doubt," experimental writers raise and display postmodernist issues. Chief among these are [the following:] How does the author position the self as a knower and teller? Who is the writer? Who is the reader? For the experimental writer, these lead to the intertwined problems of subjectivity/authority/ authorship/reflexivity, on the one hand, and representational form, on the other. Postmodernism claims that representation is always partial, local,

and situational and that our self is always present, no matter how much we try to suppress it—but only partially present, for in our writing we repress the parts of ourselves too. Working from that premise, we are freed to write material in a variety of ways: to tell and retell. (p. 91)

Within this conceptualization of writing, there is a recognition that the content of research is not given or merely relayed by the researcher. Instead, writing is simultaneously empirical, literary, political, ethical, and wholly constituting—of the content and the author. It is based on this contention:

> The possibility that we might constructively and legitimately think and speak from multiple positions within multiple discourses, not being *identified* with or bound by one is extraordinarily liberating and empowering. . . . For, once coming to a kind of agency where one is able to see the discursive practices that hold us in one place, we are better able to shift to another place—still within discourses but better able to see the ways we are bound and to loosen those ties even for small moments of time. (Laws, 2004, pp. 126–127)

Those who see writing as constituting reject the idea of a single reality that is told or interpreted. In its place, they see multiple stories chosen by multiple tellers for multiple audiences. Key to this position is the commitment that there is not a single reading or writing of lived experience. The act of writing becomes a central part of inquiry, with the researcher taking up the complex roles of author and inquirer. The goal of such writing is to evoke, provoke, interrupt, illuminate, and engage using whatever tools the author finds necessary.

Uncoupled from the notion of the single reality or format, postmodern authors have used a variety of genres and representational strategies to share their work. Academic journals that formerly hosted only texts in the "scientific" format now include works of ethnographic fiction, poetry, narratives of self, and drama. These works force us to confront our conceptions of what is real, what is social science, and what standards we use to judge the merits of inquiry.

An example of this kind of approach from my own work is the *fictionalized vignette,* a short snapshot that works to crystallize a particular idea for the reader (Graue & Walsh, 1998). Although empirical in their foundation, vignettes represent impressions of plausibility—things that might not have been directly seen but that are reasonable in the social and cultural understandings generated in fieldwork. Their purpose is primarily rhetorical:

> They are framed in terms of arguing certain ideas. The fact that scenes might be fashioned from bits and pieces of field experience rather than intact chunks is premised on the power of story to leverage understanding rather than the necessity for fidelity to certain kinds of knowing (direct observation, for example). They rely on a different kind of authority. . . . Fictionalized vignettes gain their warrant from the ability to *tell* something to someone. The meaning of the vignette is jointly constructed by the author who is speaking to the reader for a purpose. (pp. 223–224, emphasis in original)

Fictionalized vignettes are powerful formats for describing lived experience. They situate an empirical idea in a human context. They provide plot and structure to the telling. They are judged by their ability to clearly portray some theme, to link the researcher's insight to the reader's interest. They do not stand alone but rather are read in conjunction with other data presentations, providing a crystallization (Richardson, 1997) of understanding for both the reader and the author. They capitalize on our narrative inclinations—our need to understand and live through story.

I developed the following fictionalized vignette to give a multilayered account of beliefs and practices related to kindergarten readiness. Its main character, Jared, is seen by his teacher as a prototypical "unready" boy, immature and volatile in the classroom. I framed this story around a typical occurrence, a collision in the block corner, from two perspectives: Jared's and his teacher's (Mrs. Warren). Notwithstanding my skill and experience as a field-worker, I cannot read the minds of those with whom I work. Instead, ideas are woven together from interviews and extended observations of parents, teachers, and children:

Building Images of Kindergartners

Jared stands in the corner of the block area, admiring his tall, tall building. It has three towers, two bridges, and [a] place for animals—the best he has ever built. Until now he hadn't noticed anything else in the room. When Mrs. Warren told them that it was time for centers, he bounded off to the block corner, ready to begin building this thing he had been planning since he got up this morning. How tall could he make it? How many blocks would the other kids let him have? He smiles, realizing that he is the only one there; everyone else is working on jobs or doing something else. He knew he could do it—his mom called him something, something that he was going to be when he grew up. An archi- . . . hmmmm . . . what was it[?]

Out of the corner of his eye, he sees a flash of brown. Trevor flies through the air and hits the building right in the middle, knocking over the first, which hits the second, and then the third tower. The animals lie under a mountain of wood and the bridges are flattened. Glancing back only briefly, Trevor walks off to the computer area. "TREVOR!" Jared wails. "He knocked over my beautiful building!" Tears immediately roll down his round red cheeks and he is immobilized. "Mrs. Warren . . ."

Just seconds before the crash, Mrs. Warren looks up from the group she is working with on the other side of the room. Every day this week, she thinks, Jared has played in the block area. Every day this week, he has passed up a chance to do his job. He'll spend recess today and all play time tomorrow finishing things that most children had done days ago. How will he make it in first grade? All he wants to do is play! She looks back to her group, then hears Jared's wailing. Oh, boy. And this crying—that's not going to play very well with any of the first-grade teachers either. Slowly she gets up, trying to think of how to smooth this over without playing into his continual need for individual attention. How do you get kids to deal with frustration? And how do you do it with children as immature as Jared? "Mrs. Warren," Jared cries, "Mrs. Warren, he knocked down my city! He broke the buildings!" He is gasping for air and gesturing wildly. The pile of blocks shows no resemblance to the wonderful thing he had done. "I'm a good builder—that's what big kids do!" Jared thinks to himself. "He's crying like a 4-year-old," Mrs. Warren thinks as she shakes her head. Trevor watches all this from the corner with a slight smile. (Graue & Walsh, 1998, pp. 225–226)

I wrote this vignette a few years ago to put human faces on the abstract theoretical constructs of readiness. I wanted to show the relational nature of readiness decisions, their temporal development, and the ways in which children had varied awareness of their meaning. What is a moment of triumph for Jared is seen by Mrs. Warren as an indicator of immaturity, reinforced by Jared's reaction to Trevor's treachery. The fact that it was never directly observed does not reduce its utility; we judge its value by what it teaches us, not whether it occurred per se. For those who use writing as constituting, validity (in terms of the degree to which the writing represents some view of reality) is less important than crystallization (its promotion of understanding through different forms of telling). The authority of the text comes out of its ability to engage the reader.

In the other conceptions of writing, I presented models of the relations among data, researcher, and text that had variously discrete boundaries. In an attempt at symmetry, I worked to develop an image of these relations in writing as constituting and found that I had to use a very different type of representation. Figure 28.3 is my rendering of writing as constituting, which portrays the complex relations that produce research texts. The author produces the text, and the text produces the author. In turn, the author might have multiple roles, including being a character:

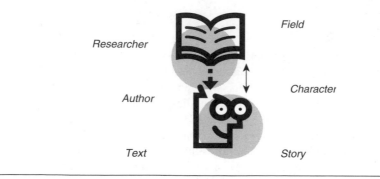

Researcher

Field

Author

Character

Text

Story

Figure 28.3   Relationship Among the Field, the Researcher, and the Written Product of the Research in *Writing as Constituting*

Dorinne Kondo's *Crafting Selves* illustrates the notion of writing as constituting. She begins her book on identity and gender in Japan with a vivid description of her Tokyo neighborhood—a "bustling, noisy, yet somehow comfortable chaos" (Kondo, 1990, p. 3). Using a self-as-camera approach, she describes the restaurants, the subway, the unique sounds and smells. What is unique about this text is how the author uses this "tried-and-true ethnographic tool." Kondo then moves to a discussion of how she has used the "setting" trope to decenter her authority. Instead of trading on her evocation of place as a tool for persuasion, her discussion jars the reader into recognition of its rhetorical purpose. While recognizing its power to recreate the field, even for herself as author, Kondo shows how authorial tactics stage a setting in a particular way.

Kondo (1990) enacts this illustration by developing a first-person narrative of her experiences as a Japanese American coming to understand the negotiation of identity in the Japanese workplace. She becomes a full actor, a character in the story of identity, woven in and out of the text of her experience. She works to illustrate the following:

First, that any account, mine included, is partial and located, screened through the narrator's eye/I; second, to emphasize the processual and emergent nature of ethnographic inquiry and the embeddedness of what we call theory in that process; and third, to argue that the liveliness and complexity of everyday life cannot be encompassed by

theoretical models which rely on organizational structures, "typical" individuals, referential meanings, or invocations of collective nouns like "the Japanese." (p. 8)

Kondo is a constant presence in this text, one of the cast of characters that help bring the plot to life. The following excerpt is illustrative of her place as a scholar, an actor, and a tool in telling:

Promptly at four P.M., the hour when most Japanese housewives do their shopping for the evening meal, I lifted the baby into her stroller and pushed her along ahead of me as I inspected the fish, selected the freshest looking vegetables, and mentally planned the meal for the evening. As I glanced into the shiny metal surface of the butcher's display case, I noticed someone who looked terribly familiar: a typical young housewife, clad in slip-on sandals and the loose, cotton shift called "home wear" (*homu wea*), a woman walking with a characteristically Japanese bend to the knees and a sliding of the feet. Suddenly I clutched the handle of the stroller to steady myself as a wave of dizziness washed over me, for I realized I had caught a glimpse of nothing less than my own reflection. . . . In order to reconstitute myself as an American researcher, I felt I had to extricate myself from the conspiracy to rewrite my identity as Japanese. (p. 17)

This is a telling moment in Kondo's narrative. She simultaneously identifies a cultural constant—a typical Japanese housewife—and recognizes that it is not an other but rather herself. This moment serves as a metaphor for her conceptualization of identity and gender— constructed discursively, often hybrid and intensely local. Her story of becoming Japanese and disengaging to theorize the process could not have been as powerful without her voice and her first-person account.

Kondo's narrative exemplifies an issue that most clearly distinguishes writing as constituting from the other types of writing—attention to the writer's voice. The location of the author in writing is a key aspect of this approach, stemming from the concern about colonizing power of the omniscient narrator. Rather than having someone behind the scenes narrating the stories of others, authors moved to an active voice, used the pronoun "I" to stand for themselves in research texts, and reflected on their role in the production of knowledge. A logical outgrowth of the recognition of the literary turn in qualitative research, this development is nonetheless one of the most contentious practices in research writing. Ruth Behar aptly captures the concerns around moving away from a more disciplined, distanced form of writing:

> No one objects to autobiography, as such, as a genre in its own right. What bothers critics is the insertion of personal stories into what we have been taught to think of as the analysis of impersonal social facts. Throughout most of the twentieth century, in scholarly fields ranging from literary criticism to anthropology to law, the reigning paradigms have traditionally called for distance, objectivity, and abstraction. The worst sin was to be "too personal." (Behar, 1996, pp. 12–13)

In the movement away from technical, methodological dictates for judging research using writing as reporting, and in basing standards for writing on postmodern ideas of multiple realities, stories, and authors, qualitative researchers have arrived at a conundrum: What constitutes a good story? In recognizing that the researcher is an author, is the only solution to write oneself into the text?

Bill Tierney outlines these concerns about the world we constitute when we write ourselves into our research texts. He is particularly focused on the genre of autoethnography, which takes as its subject the author's experience. Although he shares interests in voice and alternative writing formats, he fears that we have instituted a new orthodoxy in writing:

> Just as I once was concerned with the unreflexive absence of the author from the narrative, I am equally concerned with the unreflexive insertion of the author into the narrative. . . . An additional concern I have with the move toward reflexivity is that it appears to be a movement away from trying to understand the world of the "other" and toward a more cathartic psychological agency of the self. This form of reflexivity represents a turn away from praxis and toward humanist, modernist ideals that focus on the concerns and inner worlds of the author. (Tierney, 2002, p. 392)

A main concern for Tierney is the inward focus of these new texts, which he sees as potentially narcissistic and lacking attention to real-life problems. Worried that research will lose its connection to praxis, Tierney suggests that we continue to reflect on the forms our research writing might take, not settling for entertainment value or emotional provocation.

Few authors who view writing as constituting would argue with Tierney's (2002) main contention that we must be more thoughtful in our use of writing formats. The standard for judging the efficacy of any writing pairs the rhetorical rationale that propelled the use of varied writing formats in the first place and the skill of the author in deploying that format:

> The line between narcissism and effective ethnographic writing lies often, however, in the writing abilities of the author and in his/her ability to make use of his/her own experiences as a way to teach us about our craft itself and/or the social worlds of those "others" who are the participants in our research. (Reed-Danahay, 2002, p. 424)

From this perspective, any choice we make in writing must be a reasoned choice that rests on its pedagogical potential. Our writing tools should enhance our ability to share a particular lived experience with our readers. Sometimes the lived experience of the author is relevant, sometimes it is not.

As we explore the parameters of new writing formats, as we learn to make judgments about research that reach beyond notions of validity, we work through the tensions embedded in exploration and evaluation, both of which are necessary but sometimes in conflict. It might help if we recognize that we are working to "map an intermediate space we can't quite define yet, a borderland between passion and intellect, analysis and subjectivity, ethnography and autobiography, art and life" (Behar, 1996, p. 174). The image that comes to my mind when I think of writing as constituting is of performance art—highly varied in form, sometimes incredibly engaging, and other times just plain weird. Sometimes the artist is explicitly seen as part of the presentation and it is critical to my understanding, other times it is a matter of "too much information." Often judgments are a matter of highly personal taste, linked to assumptions about appropriate boundaries between researcher and subject.

Writing as Praxis

> Reflections on our responsibilities as social researchers must punctuate all texts we produce. Without such reflection, in the name of neutrality or researcher dispassion, we collude in a retreat from social responsibility and the academy remains yet another institution without a soul in a world increasingly bankrupt of moral authority. (Weis & Fine, 2000, p. 66)

The final category of writing does not stand alone in the typology as the others do but rather might be thought of as a possibility that weaves through the previous three. As a cross-cutting construct, it reflects the assumptions and practices of each of the other categories. In this final section, I briefly describe a perspective on writing that locates it within the realm of action. As a starting point, I build on the definition of praxis as doing and suggest that writing as praxis focuses on the degree to which education research connects with communities of practice.

Praxis is anchored on one end by a distanced view of the writing enterprise, which assumes that actions that come out of research are self-evident, a logical outgrowth of the knowledge produced. It is most frequently used within the writing as reporting genre. Within writing as reporting, praxis is a matter of implications—if we find x, then we should do y. Because good research is neutral and has a single appropriate reading, the actions we should take are logical and universally applied. Never seen as a form of advocacy, this kind of writing provides tools for decision making by others than the researcher. Good tools lead to good decisions, and the goodness of tools is related to the validity of the research rather than to the text that reports it. The absence of the author in this genre reinforces the notion of objectivity and the image that this is "just the facts."

At the other end are scholars such as Weis and Fine (2000), who advocate passionately for research and writing for social justice. From this perspective, research and its reporting must work to change social relations, particularly for those who are traditionally marginalized. Among the tasks for writers is the identification of problems and themes of social importance, connection of themes to political and historical conditions, communication of results to relevant audiences whose members can take action, respectful and trustworthy presentation of those who typically are not given voice, and provocation to change. What is meant by social change is highly contentious and dependent on the norms of inquiry enacted by the researcher. At issue are the outcomes of the act of writing and research. The nested nature of standards, assumptions, theories, and practices come to life in a particularly vibrant way when we explore writing as praxis, reminding us that there is no untheorized stance to inquiry, that all choices represent philosophical assumptions.

Whereas writing as reporting tends to coincide with an information provision form of praxis, the other two models slide across the continuum depending on the author. The potential action that might be taken up from research is situated within the intentions of the researcher and those of the reader—a dialogical relation that makes praxis situational.

Praxis within the writing as interpreting mode is a matter of understanding. Through the telling of situated social stories, researchers hope to engage their readers in cultural meaning making that links the reader's experience with the writer's data. Action coming out of research is implied but is as contextual as the data that suggested it. In the still psychologically oriented world of education research, this kind of contingent reading is maddening. I still sting from the grant reviewer who said to me, "We don't need another study that says, 'It depends.' We need to KNOW!" A hermeneutical form of praxis takes meaning making as a main form of action, which is a traditional foundation for writing as interpretation.

The nature of praxis within writing as constituting is in the eye of the beholder. Some hope that their stories, by their very nature, will provoke action. But in a story, that action must be taken up by someone who recognizes the import of the story. The reader must be grabbed by the narrative and moved to do something. And in much the same way as performance art is effective for some and not for others, not all of this work promotes praxis. In fact, the praxis might be located within the telling of the story in the first place—an act of giving voice.

The relations among the writing as praxis continuum are represented in the following table:

Writing provokes, stimulates, is context dependent	Writing provides new understanding	Writing provides information
Ideologically saturated		Nonideological

I could spend the rest of the chapter building a typology of praxis writers but recognize that it would probably be as reflective of my own perspective on praxis as it is on the position/ potential of various types of work. Instead, I end the chapter by asking questions that you, the reader, might pose as you consider your own writing. It is my attempt to sustain and disrupt the one-sided conversation I have had with you in this work, to connect to your own work to see where it might lead you:

- For whom do you write?
- Who is heard in your writing?
- What action can be taken as a result of your work?
- Who benefits? Who is potentially harmed?
- What forms of authority do you use to make your case?
- Are there other audiences whose members could benefit from your knowledge?
- How might your writing change to fit these other audiences' needs?
- Would a new writing format change what you could know?

REFERENCES

American Psychological Association. (2001). *Publication manual of the American Psychological Association* (5th ed.). Washington, DC: Author.

Atkinson, P. (1992). *Understanding ethnographic texts* (Sage Qualitative Methods Series, No. 25). Newbury Park, CA: Sage.

Bazerman, C. (1987). Codifying the social scientific style: The APA publication manual as a behaviorist rhetoric. In J. S. Nelson, A. Megill, & D. N. McCloskey (Eds.), *The rhetoric of the human sciences* (pp. 125–144). Madison: University of Wisconsin Press.

Becker, H. S. (1986). *Writing for social scientists: How to start and finish your thesis, book, or article.* Chicago: University of Chicago Press.

Behar, R. (1996). *The vulnerable observer: Anthropology that breaks your heart.* Boston: Beacon.

Berkencotter, C., & Huckin, T. N. (1993). You are what you cite: Novelty and intertextuality in a biologist's experimental article. In M. R. Blyler & C. Thralls (Eds.), *Professional communication: The social perspective* (pp. 107–127). Newbury Park, CA: Sage.

Bizzell, P. (1986). What happens when basic writers come to college. *College Composition and Communication, 37,* 294–301.

Charmaz, K. (2000). Grounded theory: Objectivist and constructivist methods. In N. Denzin & Y. Lincoln (Eds.), *The handbook of qualitative research* (2nd ed., pp. 509–535). Thousand Oaks, CA: Sage.

Emerson, R. M., Fretz, R. I., & Shaw, L. L. (1995). *Writing ethnographic fieldnotes.* Chicago: University of Chicago Press.

Geertz, C. (1973). *The interpretation of cultures.* New York: Basic Books.

Graue, M. E., & Walsh, D. J. (1998). *Studying children in context: Theories, methods, and ethics.* Thousand Oaks, CA: Sage.

Hammersley, M., & Atkinson, P. (1995). *Ethnography: Principles in practice* (2nd ed.). London: Routledge.

Kondo, D. K. (1990). *Crafting selves: Power, gender, and discourses of identity in a Japanese workplace.* Chicago: University of Chicago Press.

Lareau, A. (1989). *Home advantage.* London: Falmer.

Lareau, A. (2003). *Unequal childhoods: Class, race, and family life.* Berkeley: University of California Press.

Lawrence-Lightfoot, S. (2003). *The essential conversation: What parents and teachers can learn from each other.* New York: Random House.

Lawrence-Lightfoot, S. (2005). Reflections on portraiture: A dialogue between art and science. *Qualitative Inquiry, 11*(1), 3–15.

Laws, C. (2004). Poststructuralist writing at work. *International Journal of Qualitative Studies in Education, 17*(1), 113–127.

Madigan, R., Johnson, S., & Linton, P. (1995). The language of psychology: APA style as epistemology. *American Psychologist, 50,* 428–436.

Miles, M. B., & Huberman, A. M. (1984). *Qualitative data analysis: A sourcebook of new methods.* Beverly Hills, CA: Sage.

Murray, F. B., & Raths, J. (1994). Call for manuscripts: *Review of Educational Research,* 1994–96. *Review of Educational Research, 64,* 197–200.

Myers, G. (1990). *Writing biology: Texts in the social construction of scientific knowledge.* Madison: University of Wisconsin Press.

Reed-Danahay, D. (2002). Turning points and textual strategies in ethnographic writing. *International Journal of Qualitative Studies in Education, 15,* 421–425.

Richardson, L. (1990). *Writing strategies: Reaching diverse audiences* (Sage Qualitative Methods Series, Vol. 21). Newbury Park, CA: Sage.

Richardson, L. (1997). *Fields of play: Constructing an academic life.* New Brunswick, NJ: Rutgers University Press.

Rose, M., & McClafferty, K. A. (2001). A call for the teaching of writing in graduate education. *Educational Researcher, 30*(2), 27–33.

Strauss, A., & Corbin, J. (1990). *Basics of qualitative research: Grounded theory procedures and techniques.* Walnut Creek, CA: AltaMira.

Tierney, W. G. (2002). Get real: Representing reality. *International Journal of Qualitative Studies in Education, 15,* 385–398.

Todorov, T. (1990). *Genres in discourse* (C. Porter, Trans.). New York: Cambridge University Press.

Weis, L., & Fine, M. (2000). *Speed bumps: A student-friendly guide to qualitative research.* New York: Columbia University, Teachers College Press.

Wolcott, H. (1990). *Writing up qualitative research* (Sage Qualitative Methods Series, Vol. 20). Newbury Park, CA: Sage.

29

Experimenting With Voice and Reflexivity in Social Science Texts

Elizabeth G. Creamer

Virginia Tech University

Imagine this. A huge canvas hangs before you, a multilevel panorama depicting all manner of human, superhuman, and animal life. It carries the signature of one painter, but it was produced by dozens of hands that history has overlooked. Some of those faces, now nameless, are captured in the frieze, as is who claims to be its primary architect. How did all of these people interface to produce this masterpiece? What cultural conventions make it acceptable to assume that their contributions are merely technical when, in fact, the allegory depicted unfolded in increments over the course of years of unrecorded false starts and conversations? These are the questions that propel this chapter. The questions arise from the critique presented by this chapter of the textual convention of using a single monolithic voice in texts that claim to be the result of collective authorship.

The nature of dual authorship is both unproblematized and unexplored (Gottlieb, 1995). It is rare to encounter co-authored or multiple-authored texts where collaborators are explicit about the roles they played in constructing the text or to find the kind of personal and reflexive narrative that offers the reader a glimpse of how

collaborators grappled with substantive differences in interpretation or theoretical perspective to reach consensus. Although these issues might not resonate with academics who pursue collaboration exclusively as a speedy route to flesh out a publication record, they are particularly salient for those who pursue collaboration as a way to promote learning and achieve significant new theoretical insight (Creamer & Lattuca, 2005). It also has implications for feminists, critical theorists, and practitioners of participatory research who seek a stage that offers team members equal voice in a publication (see, e.g., Kochan = Mullen = Mullen = Kochan, 2001[1]) and for those who struggle to avoid disenfranchising co-researchers in the field (see, e.g., discussion of Clark et al., 1996, later in this chapter).

The term "voice" refers to how authors represent themselves and their participants in the texts they produce (Hertz, 1997). The sociologist Rosanna Hertz argues that reflexivity encompasses voice and is concerned not only with what is known but also with how it is known. "Social scientists tend to devote far more time and energy to depicting what they know than they do to explaining how they know," observes Hertz (1995, p. 429). Reflexivity about the creative process is a more frequent preoccupation among humanists than it is among social scientists.

Authors of much academic prose use an impersonal voice that communicates authority but absents them from the text. Changes reflected in recent editions of style manuals in the social sciences direct authors to avoid passive voice and to communicate agency for thought and action through the use of first person. Authors of collaboratively produced documents often resort to the use of first-person plural, or the collective "we," a convention that homogenizes all authors into a single authorial voice. To add to the confusion, it is not uncommon for a single author to refer to himself or herself by the first-person plural, "we." The inability to deviate from the convention of a single authorial voice even in collaboratively produced documents is a testament to the tenacity of the Western assumption of creativity and original insight as being the product of the solitary mind.

The voice adopted by authors varies by the methodological and theoretical tradition they use (Hertz, 1997). These are what I would characterize as differences in timber or tone. Egon Guba and Yvonna Lincoln implicitly assume a single authorial voice throughout their seminal piece about the key distinctions among inquiry paradigms (Guba & Lincoln, 1994). They describe the voice adopted by positivists and postpositivists as that of a "disinterested scientist" that is consistent with the stance of a dispassionate or distanced knower (p. 112). Critical theorists use "I," are reflexive about their stance, and use the voice of a "transformative intellectual," advocate, or activist (p. 112). Constructivists use the voice of a "passionate participant" to facilitate "multi-voiced reconstructions" (p. 112). Guba and Lincoln characterize voice in constructivist accounts as "'multivoice' reconstructions of his or her own reconstructions as well as those of all other participants" (p. 115). Tellingly, and with a full measure of irony, Guba and Lincoln's use of the words "his" and "her" in this last passage reveals that although they can imagine a single author engaging multiple viewpoints and participants who make meaning of their experiences in very different ways, they cannot escape the assumption that the textual product of a scholarly investigation inevitably assumes a singular voice.

"Polyvocalism" refers to representing multiple viewpoints and voices in textual form. It has also been referred to as "polyphonic" and "multivocal." It is a form of reflexivity where authors strive to achieve transparency with the reader by weaving evidence of their multiplicity in the text. Laurel Richardson and Rosanna Hertz identify it as one of several forms of experimental social science writing (Hertz, 1997; Richardson, 1994). Polyvocalism can take several forms, including (a) presenting different viewpoints as understood by one person and (b) engaging different viewpoints of the authors of a collaboratively produced text. Exploring differences in viewpoint between researcher and participant(s) is another type of polyvocalism. Representing differences in viewpoints among participants in what John Van Maanen calls "jointly told tales" (Van Maanen, 1988) is a form of polyvocalism that has received considerable attention in the research literature (e.g., Fine, 1994) and one that I leave to others to pursue.

The call for pluralistic discourse is firmly rooted in the postmodern perspective. In a cogent summary of the central tenets of postmodernism, William Tierney and Robert Rhoads point to how postmodern researchers approach their work not with the goal of creating a "meta-narrative" but rather with the goal of representing multiple realities. The call to present reality as pluralistic is explicit in Tierney and Rhoads's (1993) description of the postmodern stance:

> Research efforts work from the concept of difference and conflict rather than similarity and consensus. The Durkheimian notion of reality that seeks to synthesize knowledge—and, of consequence, people—to abstract norms again is rejected. In its place is the assumption that research studies need to be built where multiple, competing interpretations exist around what counts for reality. Such interpretations will always exist, and the researcher's task is not to find "true" interpretations, for no such analysis exists. Different individuals and different groups hold unique perspectives on a particular topic, and the challenge is not to anoint primacy to one interpretation but rather to

present those voices that have been silenced and to question the pervasiveness of dominant interpretations. (p. 326)

Although many authors have explored the implications of the postmodern framework to academic writing (see, e.g., Richardson, 1988, 1994; Schneider, 1991; Wolf, 1992), the concept of pluralistic discourse has been applied almost exclusively to creating strategies to represent participants' voices. Few authors have considered the implications of challenging an approach to academic writing that violates what Richardson (1988) calls "a major pretension of science," that is, the use of a "single, unambiguous voice" (p. 201).

Experimental texts have been used to respond to the critique presented by postmodernism to decenter authority by acknowledging the co-constructed nature of most scientific creativity, thought, or insight, regardless of the attribution reflected in a list of authors. Unlike postmodernists who have experimented with narratives that soften the line between fact and fiction (see, e.g., Wolf, 1992, discussed in the next section), my critique is about the lack of reflexivity about authorial voice, particularly when the text is co-authored. I am not in the camp that argues that social scientists should abandon the discourse of scientific realism or in the production of texts that are so multivoiced as to make the principal argument(s) or story opaque to the reader. Nor am I a proponent of shifting the focus of research inquiry from understanding social phenomena or the lived experience of participants to autoethnography or self-examination of the interior landscape of the researcher that authors such as Susan Krieger pursue (Krieger, 1991).

OVERVIEW OF THE CHAPTER

The purpose of this chapter is to demonstrate ways in which social scientists have presented more than one authorial voice in academic texts. My goal is not to provide a comprehensive review of experimental texts that are polyvocal but rather to provide one that presents selected examples illustrating how social scientists have used polyvoiced or multivoiced

texts to advance an argument. The effort I undertake is an interdisciplinary one because it applies literary analysis, a tool of humanists, to texts produced by social scientists, including educational and human science researchers. The investigation raises questions about how collaborators can achieve a synthetic or integrative quality without forcing the adoption of a singular voice.

The focus of this chapter is on unconventional strategies that social scientists have used to represent the thoughts and actions of others. In exploring alternative forms of representation, the chapter reflects my long-standing interest in academics as writers and collaborators (Creamer, 1999, 2001, 2003a, 2003b, 2004). It includes examples of issues related to voice and representation that I have pursued in publications about the collaborative process but also from another genre entirely—reflexive narratives about how writers construct texts that Richardson (1994) calls "writing stories."

My interest in the role of imbricating disparate views to create theory emerged from interviewing long-term collaborators, including academic couples. Variations by inquiry paradigm in approaches and assumptions about the role of differences in interpretation led to my interest in the dialogical and dialectical nature of knowledge construction. A concern for how conventional approaches to representation and hierarchical arrangements can silence or disenfranchise a collaborator with a minority opinion—something that I pursued in a case study (Creamer, 2005)—is the link between my prior work and this exploration of polyvocality.

In the main section that follows, I present a number of examples from the literature in social sciences illustrating different strategies that have been used to incorporate multiple interpretive stances in a text. I begin with examples of strategies that authors of single-authored publications have used to represent multiple realities and to reflect the dialogical nature of knowledge production, even when it occurs in a dialogue with self. The next subsection describes several approaches to using alternating first-person narratives. The subsequent subsection deals with the use of interviews, reader's theatre, and other variations of the script format to capture multiple voices and interaction.

EXAMPLES OF POLYVOCALISM IN THE SOCIAL SCIENCES

One of the challenges of the critique of modernism presented by postmodern writers is to question the line between fact and fiction. Fiction writers and other imaginative writers, such as playwrights, have many tools at their disposal to present multiple realities. They advance multiple viewpoints by using literary devices such as dialogue and internal monologues, passages from long-lost letters and journals, metaphors, and evocative settings or by presenting chapters that alternate speakers and points of view. Fiction writers often use these tools to pursue an interior landscape, whereas social scientists are more likely to deploy them in a bid to reach a wider audience and, generally, to communicate knowledge about some external phenomenon. Most social scientists are satisfied with borrowing literary devices to advance their narratives without turning their accounts into works constructed primarily from the imagination.

Single authors have used a number of strategies to represent the dialectical process used to achieve new insight in academic texts. In the subsection that follows, I discuss how Neumann (1997), Wolf (1992), and Schneider (1991) have used experimental formats to represent different interpretations of a single author.[2]

Single Author, Multiple Realities

In a chapter in *Learning From Our Lives: Women, Research, and Autobiography in Education,* Anna Neumann recounts the experiences of her mother as a Holocaust survivor in part to explore postmodern questions about the nature of "truth" and reality as presented in narratives. Neumann (1997) presents three versions of her mother's story, each one created for a different audience. The first version of the story is how Anna herself recollected the story from what she was able to glean through fragments of conversations that occurred over the course of her childhood. It is a sanitized version of the story, marked by silences and shaped to protect Anna from the harsh realities of the Holocaust. The second version of the story is a transcript of a conversation that Anna and her husband, Aaron, had with Anna's mother about her experiences. The third version is an official account that Anna's mother composed for the German government in an application for reparations.

Neumann (1997) presents the story in three iterations to dramatize the fluid nature of the story, how it evolved over time, and how her mother shaped the telling to the audience. Neumann introduces a textual symbol, a bracketed asterisk [*], to indicate when a piece of information was corrected or revised in a later (re)telling of the story. Neumann never shifts the focus away from her mother's story. The polyvocalism she achieves is to recognize how the narrator and the narration changed with the audience.

Richardson (1994) identifies Marjory Wolf's work as an example of polyvocalism in scientific writing that reflects a postmodern mind-set. Wolf, an anthropologist, uses different genres, directed at different audiences, to tell the same story. In *A Thrice-Told Tale: Feminism, Postmodernism, and Ethnographic Responsibility,* Wolf (1992) "turns the story" (Creswell, 1998) of an event that occurred while she was conducting fieldwork in Taiwan in three different ways: as a short story, in unanalyzed field notes written by a principal member of the field staff, and as a journal article. Each text took a different perspective and was written in a different style, but involved the same set of events.[3]

Wolf (1992) is a bit disingenuous, however, in that her primary motive in using an experimental approach to ethnography is not to embody multiple perspectives but rather as a vehicle to ruminate about issues raised by feminist scholars about polyvocality, reflexivity, voice, audience, and colonial discourse in traditional ethnographic texts. Her creations ultimately turn out to be subversive because she uses them to illustrate that they are every bit as partial in the truths they represent as are ethnographies presented as traditional "realist tales." Wolf writes, "As ethnographers, our job is not simply to pass on the disorderly complexity of culture, but also to try to hypothesize about apparent inconsistencies, to lay out our best guesses, without hiding the contradictions and instability" (p. 129).

Experimental forms and reflexivity can readily become self-indulgent and easily shift the focus, Wolf (1992) argues, from the culture and people that are the subject of ethnography to the ethnographer himself or herself. In her engaging style and elegant prose, she questions experimental writing when it becomes accessible only to a narrow circle of the intellectual elite. Wolf writes, "The message of exclusion that attaches to some of these texts contradicts the ostensible purpose of experimental ethnography, to find better ways of conveying some aspect of the experiences of another community" (p. 138). She questions whether experimental texts open or delimit the audience for scholarly work.

Wolf's (1992) caution about the inaccessibility of some experimental texts is a good preface to a hermeneutical analysis by Joseph Schneider, a sociologist. Like Wolf, Schneider (1991) designed a text that serves as a vehicle to express his viewpoints about conventions of textual authority and to engage in a dialogue with the same cast of postmodernists that inflame Wolf. Schneider uses an experimental form—which he identifies as performance text and script—to represent imagined conversations with a quirky range of invented characters. Schneider introduces an additional layer of intrigue by embellishing the text in a number of ways, including by bolding some of the text to show inherent contradictions in the speaker's comments and setting off other passages in brackets to indicate overlapping talk [when more than one person is talking at the same time].

Schneider (1991) begins his text placidly, presenting himself as the author, referring to himself as "Joseph," and engaging an invented second voice he addresses as "you." Wedged in an aside, he offers this rationale for the double voice: "Turning the sociologist into characters in the script makes them less authoritative and easier to argue with, especially **if you give** them several voices and **let** them disagree with each other" (p. 304). The use of bold in this passage is Schneider's way of demonstrating that even in an experimental text, the author is in control of the text.

Schneider (1991) ratchets up the chatter when he moves from two voices to multiple voices in the fourth part of his text. He engages three authors simultaneously in an imaginary dialogue and eventually keeps introducing new characters until that text becomes a virtual cacophony of voices wandering in and out of the text and interrupting each other mid-sentence.

Schneider (1991) is persuasive in convincing the reader of his principal point by performing through text the bedlam that can ensue when multivocality is taken to the extreme. What I take to be the heart of his argument appears rather randomly, well into the article, when he starts a section by asking, "But how do we get anywhere if all these voices have equal integrity as realities? How do I know which is right, or more right than others? How do I decide? What's the point?" (p. 307).

Like Wolf (1992), Schneider (1991) is arguing that social scientists have an obligation to "tell the story" and to accept responsibility for their role in shaping the analysis and interpretation. If Schneider's text can be said to succeed despite taxing the reader's perseverance and goodwill, it is because the text performs its point. Through the cacophony that arises from juxtaposing discordant voices, Schneider performs the point that there is a limit to how many voices can be embodied as distinct entities in a polyvocal or multivocal text.

Writers of single-authored texts have found a number of ways in which to engage competing interpretations, even if they often do it for the purpose of shoring up a single thesis. The accounts of Neumann (1997), Wolf (1992), and Schneider (1991) each present the author's voice in a different way. Neumann is very much embodied in her narrative, not just as an intellect with a theoretical orientation but also as a palpable presence with deep ties to the mother at the center of her narrative. Wolf and Schneider take more circumlocution to make their points than does Neumann, and they leave more responsibility to the reader to reach conclusions about their multilayered texts. Both trust that the reader will faithfully pursue their texts in a linear fashion, methodically moving line by line, page by page, from front to back—something that is at odds with my image of the reader as someone perpetually on the verge of wandering off. Wolf and Schneider are clearly present as a voice in their texts, but the voice is a disembodied, entirely visceral one. Both succeed at achieving polyvocality without necessarily demonstrating the ways in which those different viewpoints can be integrated to create new insight.

Alternating First-Person Narratives

Richardson (1990) is a proponent of borrowing literary devices from fiction writers as a way of capturing the lived experience of participants. At its best, the gradual unfolding of a story invites the reader to more fully imagine the setting and to follow the line of thinking as understanding and interpretation emerge. Alternating first-person narratives share the advantage of immediacy. They also provide a textual geography that allows a sustained argument about different interpretations to develop. First-person narratives offer an engaging way for social scientists to produce multivocal texts while remaining firmly ensconced in the empirical side of postmodern questions in terms of the line between fact and fiction and the line between science and literature.

The two accounts I discuss in this subsection use alternating first-person accounts to share insight about the experience of conducting research. These fit Hertz's (1997) definition of self-reflexive accounts because they capture not only what is known but also how it is known. In both cases, the authors are also research participants. Detailed self-reflexive field notes kept throughout the investigation provided the vehicle for the authors to capture the evolution of their thoughts and feelings retrospectively. The two publications differ in the extent to which they reconcile the implications of the differences in perspective, but both are effective in achieving polyvocalism.[4]

Gottlieb and Graham (1994) and Ellis, Kiesinger, and Tillmann-Healy (1997) achieve polyvocal texts by presenting alternating first-person accounts in sections of the text that are clearly labeled with the author's name. These are not scripts because they are not an attempt to capture a conversation. The use of alternating first-person accounts allows the authors not only to be embodied in their texts but also to be very much present as distinct voices, both intellectually and at a personal level through the description of emotion and description of action. The texts differ in that they use alternating first-person accounts for slightly different purposes.

In the preface to the 1994 edition of their jointly authored memoir, Alma Gottlieb and Philip Graham, a wife-and-husband team writing from a foundation in constructivism, describe their work as a literary construction or memoir that chronicles their experience doing fieldwork for Alma's dissertation in Africa between 1979 and 1980. More than 10 years later, they used copies of letters that Philip wrote, Philip's daybooks and journals, thousands of pages of field notes that Alma prepared, and photographs to reconstruct their experiences day by day. In the preface, Alma describes one of their goals as to "imagine the hidden reasons behind what people do—the *whys* that give life meaning" (Gottlieb & Graham, 1994, p. xvii, emphasis in original) and to "recapture the immediacy of the moment by recreating for the reader the emotional landscapes that marked our immersion in a radically different culture" (p. xvii). Philip captures the intent to maintain distinct perspectives (what I call polyvocalism) when, in his portion of the preface, he points to the parallel worlds marked by the title of the book by saying that he and Alma sought "to explore several sets of parallel worlds, one being the different perspectives of an anthropologist and a fiction writer" (p. xix).

That Gottlieb and Graham's (1994) intent is to maintain two equally strong voices is evident in their decision to advance their chronological narrative by alternating short sections, each dated and clearly marked with one of their names. They allow different interpretations of the same event to stand without contradiction as part of a rueful acknowledgment of partiality of "truth."

Carolyn Ellis, Christine Kiesinger, and Lisa Tillmann-Healy, three feminist writers, achieve a polyvocal narrative through alternating first-person accounts. From my perspective, Ellis and her co-authors' (1997) chapter is the best single example of how synthesis can be achieved without forcing a singular voice. Alternating first-person narratives create multiple layers of understanding of the two highly personal subjects of the text: women's relationship to food and interactive interviewing. The use of the first-person "I" and variations in textual formats, such as italics and bracketing, point to analytical insight about differences in the authors' personal experiences and viewpoints.

Authorial voice is approached differently in the two texts. Gottlieb and Graham's (1994) account is unusual in that it is narrated by two equally strong voices that are integrated by the act of moving the chronological narrative forward. Ellis and colleagues' (1997) text has a lead author who is described as the "senior researcher" but still manages to achieve multi-tonality. Ellis's voice weaves the first-person accounts together with analytical comments in bracketed asides. It is clear that Ellis took the lead in writing the final section that strives to integrate the perspectives provided by the two first-person narratives. In this case, the lead author's voice serves as a vehicle to accomplish a unified perspective without smoothing over differences in experience and interpretation that distinguish the two co-authors.

In addition to the potential to sustain prolonged reflection about differences in experiences and interpretations, alternating first-person narratives offer several advantages to social scientists. Authors can be embodied as distinct entities or voices in the text, providing a form of accountability that clarifies ownership for feelings and ideas that might ultimately translate to an appropriate allocation of credit. The reader is not abandoned to the task of deciphering which of the co-authors exercised ownership for the different parts of a publication. In both cases, the narrative creates the integrative structure that moves the story forward through a series of settings and scenes.

The multiple layers of voices and interpretations offered by alternating first-person accounts challenges writers to take advantage of a wider variety of textual cues than are typically used by authors of conventional academic texts. My only reservation is that although Ellis and her co-authors (1997) clearly identify the author of each voice appearing in their text, they take it for granted that an engaged reader will detect that they vary textual style to demarcate passages that are analytical and interpretive. Authors of polyvocal and other types of experimental text are pressed to find ways in which to clearly communicate the meaning of unconventional uses of textual symbols.

Script Formats

The script format provides a way to capture conversations, whether real or imagined. In this context, I am especially fascinated with how a dialogical exchange can be captured in a script format. This occurs when the authors of a text advance a coherent argument by knitting together different points of view. This has been achieved by using the transcript of an interview (Beld, 1994), reader's theatre (Clark et al., 1996), and what Richardson (1995) labels as an "ethnodrama."[5] A script format can create a conversational tone that stands in stark contrast to the formal language in most academic texts without necessarily genuinely engaging diverse points of view. Scripts are at their best when one or more of the authors takes on the synthetic role of integrating the parts into a whole, a task that requires considerable familiarity with the viewpoints of others making a significant intellectual contribution to the text and more prolonged engagement than many academics can find time to manage.

Interviews

Jo Beld's transcript of a conversation with Yvonna Lincoln and Egon Guba, authors of the paradigm-shifting book *Naturalistic Inquiry* (Lincoln & Guba, 1985), achieves polyvocalism by virtue of presenting more than one distinct voice, capturing the dialogical nature of collaboration and learning, and being reflexive about the construction of the text. Acknowledged as constructivists, three distinct voices are maintained in the transcript of the interview authored by Beld (1994): those of Guba, Lincoln, and Beld. Beld is curiously depersonalized in the text by the reference to her not by her name or initials but rather by the initials of the journal (*QSE* for *Qualitative Studies in Education*). Beld embodies herself in the text by embedding a few details about her own life experiences in questions she asks. Differences in viewpoint between Guba and Lincoln are juxtaposed throughout the text, giving it a dialogical quality. Some differences are acknowledged, as is the case when Guba says of Lincoln, "I don't quite agree with what she says here" (p. 108). The implications of the differences are explored, not leaving the reader to detective work of uncovering them. Finally, Beld is reflexive about the process of producing the text, if only in the single sentence, "True to constructivist principles, the three of us cooperated in an iterative fashion, deciding what to cut, what to keep, and what to clarify" (p. 100).

One disadvantage of the presentation of the results of an interview in a script format is that one person generally assumes the role of naive interlocutor. This is the person who controls the text by the questions he or she has chosen to ask but who is often only minimally visible in the text. As is the case with alternating first-person accounts, differences in the number of lines of text are readily apparent and can communicate what James Clifford and George Marcus label as "hierarchical arrangement of discourse" that may communicate unintended messages about differences in status and power (Clifford & Marcus, 1986). Alternatives such as the free-flowing conversation between Myles Horton and Paulo Freire reproduced in *We Make the Road by Walking* (Horton & Freire, 1990) are more helpful examples for writers who are committed to producing texts that project equally strong voices.

Reader's Theatre

Carolyn Clark and her collaborators present a text that contains an analytical forward prepared largely by the lead author, followed by a section of text that several members of the team performed orally. Reader's theatre is an experimental format that is written to be performed. Clark and others on a 10-member team of K–12 researchers and educators created the script from transcripts of group meetings and individual entries in reflective notebooks. Clark and her collaborators (1996) saw the reader's theatre format as a way to demonstrate "dialogue as a central and shared feature of collaborative research" (p. 197) and as a way to "honor" the voices of everyone on the team. Foregrounding different voices and perspectives was an intentional part of their agenda: "The reader's theatre form allows us to highlight—rather than gloss over—the differences in our collaborative experiences, permitting us to 'speak' in a way in which more traditional social–scientific forms of reporting might not" (p. 201).

Several characteristics of Clark and her collaborators' (1996) publication make it less successful than other stratagems to achieve polyvocalism. One simple reason is that it is probably beyond a realistic scope of most textual presentations to effectively distinguish the opinions of 10 people, especially given that in the spirit of enfranchising their co-researchers in the field and avoiding metanarratives, the researchers avoided a theoretical overlay or integrative comments.

Clark and her collaborators (1996) are reflexive about the stumbling blocks they encountered in trying to represent their experience as collaborators as they moved from reader's theatre to the conventional format of a journal article. In addition to the constraint that "some 'one' holds the pen," they found that the act of writing forced them into a monological approach to thinking that contravened the dialogical strategy they intended to adopt. Of this experience, they note, "'Writing down,' then, compels us toward a monologic text which may not represent the very dialogic nature of our work and interactions or the diversity of frames which each of us (and our listeners/readers) might bring to its interpretation" (p. 199). Their comments point directly to the constraints that the written form, at least as academics have conventionally envisioned it, presents to collaborators trying to capture the products of a dialogical process.

Ethnodrama

In "Writing-Stories: Co-authoring 'The Sea Monster,' a Writing-Story," the sociologist Laurel Richardson presents a playful rumination about many issues related to scientific writing and postmodernism, including about voice and embodiment, the distinction between fiction and ethnography, and the meaning of authorship. Offering ethnodrama as a text that performs its point, Richardson (1995) presents a multilayered text that includes a section with a co-authored play, bracketed at the beginning by a reflective foreword and at the end by an afterword that contains the author's reflections on how the text was produced (the "writing-story"). Adding to its unconventionality, the article that appeared in the journal *Qualitative Inquiry* is single-authored but contains a section where Richardson adds attribution to her spouse, Ernest Lockridge.

Richardson (1995) offers ethnographic dramas, with distinct acts, characters, and asides devoted to an interior monologue, as an effective way to embody the author(s) and to orchestrate different viewpoints, styles, and perspectives. The ethnodrama "performs what it preaches" (p. 199) and demonstrates by showing, as does the piece by Schneider (1991) discussed earlier in the chapter. "Showing," Richardson (1995) writes,

> can happen when different voices deeply penetrate our texts. Voices do not deeply penetrate our texts when they are interview snippets or homogenized story (re)telling. They do penetrate more when the voices become characters in dramas, but most deeply when the voices become embodied, take form as legitimated co-authors, writing different meanings in different styles, rupturing *our* texts. (p. 200, emphasis in original)

Richardson (1995) deploys abrupt shifts in tone and style intentionally to mark differences between the characters and to disrupt the idea of a "unified self, author" (p. 199). This leads to the suggestion that rather than smoothing over differences in style and tone, co-authors should seek to amplify them as a way to embody themselves and communicate the contribution of differences to their interpretation.

Multivoiced texts, particularly those where the speaker's are embodied as distinct voices, inevitably introduce a whole new set of questions about appropriate attribution practices. Beld's (1994) transcript of an interview with Lincoln and Guba, for example, is single-authored, even though it is acknowledged that the interviewees played a part in co-constructing the final product appearing in the publication. Richardson's (1995) journal article carries her name alone, but a section of the article, the ethnodrama, is labeled as co-authored. Richardson is reflexive about the meaning of authorship and, in the afterword, defines it as who "owns" or "controls" the text. Reasoning that marked differences in tone and voice warranted recognition of her spouse, Ernest, as co-author of a portion of the text, Richardson explains that co-authorship is not tantamount to co-authority: "I had given Ernest co-authorship but not co-authority" (p. 200). Richardson's reflexivity about attribution is rare for a co-authored text. It offers the reader insight into how the text was co-constructed, a strategy that is submerged in most monological texts.

REFLECTIONS

The authors of the experimental texts identified in this chapter explore, and sometimes perform, questions about textual conventions and representation raised by both constructivists and postmodernists, including the call for more multivocal texts. Whereas others have explored the implications of this call for foregrounding multiplicity among participants in research projects, I have undertaken in this chapter the task of exploring the implications of the postmodern agenda for representing multiple voices in texts, including co-authored texts. The postmodern call is reflected in both Neumann's (1997) and Gottlieb and Graham's (1994) use of multiple narratives to point to the partial and often contradictory nature of "truth" and reality. Schneider (1991) and Richardson (1995) create texts that perform the point that even in an experimental text, a single author still controls the text. Wolf (1992) and Richardson (1995) explore the boundaries between fiction and ethnography and the "blurring of genres" by sociologists' and anthropologists' use of literary tools. Neumann (1997) and Ellis and her co-authors (1997) consider the implications of situations where the researcher and the researched are one and the same. Alternating first-person accounts, variations of a script format, and reflexive writing-stories, including the ethnodrama suggested by Richardson (1995), offer ways for writers to demystify the process of knowledge construction by being reflexive about how texts were co-constructed and how different viewpoints were taken into account.

Just as authors publishing without an acknowledged collaborator have sought to shed light on how the creative process involves internal dialogue, examples are provided in this chapter about how collaborators have produced multiphonic texts that are reflexive about the contribution of dialogical exchanges to a final product without losing the thread of coherent argument. Whereas Schneider (1991) and Clark and her collaborators (1996) demonstrate that the thread of an argument can be dismantled when too many voices are introduced, Patti Lather and Chris Smithies invent a powerfully evocative way to communicate disparate views and embodied voices by the use of a multilayered, unconventional textual format (Lather & Smithies, 1997).

Polyvocalism that is undertaken as more than a token way to advance an argument challenges the assumption that no matter how many authors contribute, a single person must be "in charge" of the text.[6] Texts written with sections that have both alternative first-person narrators and a script format, such as appears in an interview where the speaker is identified, readily provide a format for co-authors to express different viewpoints, experiences, and interpretations. By using alternating first-person accounts that present equally strong voices, Gottlieb and Graham (1994) demonstrate that it is possible for two writers to share equal responsibility for a publication. One of the challenges is to pursue the collaborative process far enough that differences in viewpoints are not just juxtaposed or accommodated, as Clark and her collaborators (1996) represent in their use of reader's theatre, but to move to the next level of synthesis and integration regardless of how time-consuming and exhausting this process might be (Creamer, 2003b).

Authors of experimental texts have invented a variety of unconventional textual devices to communicate their postmodern messages. Neumann (1997), for example, inserts the symbol [*] to signal inconsistencies in her mother's narratives, and Ellis and her co-authors (1997) bracket and italicize text to demarcate the interpretive and analytical insight that link the first-person accounts of the co-authors. Lather and Smithies (1997) divide their text at a horizontal midpoint in a powerfully effective way of standing side by side with the women with HIV/AIDS who were the informants for their poignant study. These and other disruptions of the visual blandness of texts, such as the use of a two- or three-column format to represent different voices, are helpful ways in which authors can demarcate different voices and their contributions to new insight.[7] The options for new spatial arrangements of the written page will only expand as more and more texts are designed to be read on desktop and portable computers. An examination of the ways in which social scientists have used diverse textual typography in experimental texts would provide a provocative extension of this investigation of stratagems to accomplish multivocality.

That examples of publications embodying the process of knowledge production emerging from internal and externalized dialogues are more readily found as single-authored works than as multiple-authored works reveals a great deal about the politics of the academy. Naming conventions (e.g., "lead" author) and citing conventions mirror that the fundamentally individualistic nature of the academic reward structure persists despite calls for interdisciplinary collaboration and the growth of large-scale, team-based research led by more than one principal investigator. Naming practices may simply be a reflection of who the academy empowers to affix a signature.

Feminists, critical theorists, and those involved in participatory research with practitioners in the field are among those most likely to be pressing for changes in attribution practices for collaborative scholarship. Current conventions for attribution fall short of imagining situations where more than one person "holds the pen" or where several people have a significant intellectual investment in new insight without necessarily wielding the pen that translates those conversations to the written word. Richardson's (1995) strategy to acknowledge a co-author in one section, but not in the whole article, offers collaborators a new strategy for attribution. Professional associations are pressed to create ethical guidelines that acknowledge insight that arises from a genuine and deep engagement in a dialogical process to create knowledge.

Like our assumptions about the word "author," the vignette that introduces this chapter raises questions about the meaning of the signature of a single painter on a panoramic canvas. Because it is often assumed that one person is fundamentally responsible for the creative and scientific insight presented in a scholarly publication, there is the assumption that a single creative architect designed a visual masterpiece in minute detail and that a bevy of lower-order minions merely executed the blueprints prepared by a "master" mind.

Another, more plausible scenario about the canvas described in the opening paragraph is that the final product underwent many revisions and unfolded over the course of countless unrecorded exchanges with unnamed others, with the end product being substantially more sophisticated than what was originally envisioned. This alternative interpretation is reflected in a brief exchange between the characters who introduced this chapter. The mural's architect, a Renaissance man who fancies himself as both a teacher and a painter, has just returned from an extended trip to the north where he met with his patrons. The exchange occurs between the master and a nameless apprentice in the cavernous space that houses the colossal mural emerging from the dank walls. Forgiving the all-male cast that is a nod to historical accuracy, the conversation might have gone something like this:

Master: (with mild curiosity) I see that you have been busy while I was away.

Apprentice: (with hesitant pride) Yes, sir.

Master: I told you to paint the first level of hell in the section you were assigned. What is this with all these roses? And I see that you have painted a fuzzy sketch of yourself peeking from behind Bacchus, who holds two truncheons of frothing ale.

Apprentice: Yes, sir. I was just thinking, sir, that hell could be a surfeit of beauty. A vase full of roses may be a thing of beauty, but dozens of them crammed into a tiny vestibule could be stifling.

Master: Hmmm, I never thought of that. That is an interesting idea. What about the self-portrait? We never talked about doing something like that. What is that all about?

Apprentice: Oh, sir, I had some time on my hands. I was just playing around. I meant to paint over it before you got back. Should I do that, sir?

Master: No, no. Leave it alone for the time being. I've got to think about this idea about the roses. It's a good one, but it has caused me to reconsider what the lout is doing in the second level of hell. Carry on. I will get back with you.

This brief script not only captures the dialogical nature of scientific creativity but also illustrates one of several ways in which the voice of collaborators and their different viewpoints can step forward and stand side by side on the written (and digital) page.

Notes

1. Kochan and Mullen sought to be inventive in communicating their equal contribution; hence, they switched their last names and used equal signs instead of commas. Although this publication is sometimes cited in a traditional format, I wanted to honor the way it appears on the article.

2. Alan Peshkin offers a thought-provoking example in a text that reproduces an internal dialectical exchange by setting off alternative interpretations or what he calls "counterpoint of problematics" in text that is italicized (Peshkin, 2000).

3. *Drinkers, Drummers, and Decent Folk* (Stewart, 1989) is another experimental text that uses different genres to represent an ethnographic account.

4. Like the Gottlieb and Graham (1994) joint memoir told in alternating first-person accounts, the powerfully evocative story presented in *Cancer in Two Voices* by two feminists, Sandra Butler and Barbara Rosenblum, is advanced through alternating first-person accounts (Butler & Rosenblum, 1991). Butler produced the narrative after Rosenblum's death from a pastiche of sources, including reflective pieces of writing and journal entries that she and her partner maintained during Rosenblum's illness with the goal of bringing attention to the "unrecorded story" of a woman's battle with breast cancer.

5. A husband–wife team, Arthur Bochner and Carolyn Ellis, used a script format to introduce a text they co-authored (Bochner & Ellis, 1996). The script format provides an effective avenue by which to embody the distinct voices of the co-authors and the warmth of their personal relationship, but it falls short of the full potential of polyvocality because the two authors are essentially in agreement.

6. Stephen Ritchie and Donna Rigano describe how their thinking became considerably more nuanced after they sat side by side and co-constructed a manuscript at the computer (Ritchie & Rigano, 2003). Subtle differences in meaning and thinking emerged during the process. The computer provided the vehicle to share "the pen" or authority for the text.

7. In the same volume about voice and representation (Tierney & Lincoln, 1997), Patti Lather and Greg Tanaka experiment with using divided texts as a way to juxtapose narrative and analysis (Lather, 1997; Tanaka, 1997).

REFERENCES

Beld, J. M. (1994). Constructing a collaboration: A conversation with Egon G. Guba and Yvonna S. Lincoln. *Qualitative Studies in Education, 7*(2), 99–115.

Bochner, A. P., & Ellis, C. (1996). Talking over ethnography. In C. Ellis & A. P. Bochner (Eds.), *Composing ethnography: Alternative forms of qualitative writing* (pp. 13–45). Walnut Creek, CA: AltaMira.

Butler, S., & Rosenblum, B. (1991). *Cancer in two voices.* San Francisco: Spinster Book.

Clark, C., Moss, P. A., Goering, S., Herter, R. J., Lamar, B., Leonard, D., Robbins, S., Russell, M., Templin, M., & Wascha, K. (1996). Collaboration as dialogue: Teachers and researchers engaged in conversation and professional development. *American Educational Research Journal, 33*(1), 193–231.

Clifford, J., & Marcus, G. E. (1986). *Writing culture: The poetics and politics of ethnography.* Berkeley: University of California Press.

Creamer, E. G. (1999). Knowledge production, publication productivity, and intimate academic partnerships. *Journal of Higher Education, 70,* 261–277.

Creamer, E. G. (2001). *Working equal: Collaboration among academic couples.* New York: Routledge Falmer.

Creamer, E. G. (2003a). Exploring the link between inquiry paradigm and the process of collaboration. *Review of Higher Education, 26,* 447–465.

Creamer, E. G. (2003b). Interpretive processes in collaborative research in educational settings. *Academic Exchange Quarterly, 7,* 179–183.

Creamer, E. G. (2004). Collaborators' attitudes about differences of opinion. *Journal of Higher Education, 75,* 556–571.

Creamer, E. G. (2005). Insight from the perspective of multiple disciplinary angles: A case study of an interdisciplinary research team. In E. G. Creamer & L. R. Lattuca (Eds.), *Advancing faculty learning through interdisciplinary collaboration* (New Directions for Teaching and Learning, No. 102, chap. 4). San Francisco: Jossey-Bass.

Creamer, E. G., & Lattuca, L. R. (Eds.). (2005). *Advancing faculty learning through interdisciplinary collaboration* (New Directions for Teaching and Learning, No. 102). San Francisco: Jossey-Bass.

Creswell, J. (1998). *Qualitative inquiry and research design: Choosing among five traditions.* Thousand Oaks, CA: Sage.

Ellis, C., Kiesinger, C. E., & Tillmann-Healy, L. M. (1997). Interactive interviewing: Talking about emotional experience. In R. Hertz (Ed.), *Reflexivity and voice* (pp. 119–149). Thousand Oaks, CA: Sage.

Fine, M. (1994). Working the hyphens: Reinventing self and other in qualitative research. In N. K. Denzin & Y. S. Lincoln (Eds.), *Handbook of qualitative research* (pp. 70–82). Thousand Oaks, CA: Sage.

Gottlieb, A. (1995). Beyond the lonely anthropologist: Collaboration in research and writing. *American Anthropologist, 97*(1), 21–25.

Gottlieb, A., & Graham, P. (1994). *Parallel worlds: An anthropologist and a writer encounter Africa.* Chicago: University of Chicago Press.

Guba, E. G., & Lincoln, Y. S. (1994). Competing paradigms in qualitative research. In N. K. Denzin & Y. S. Lincoln (Eds.), *Handbook of qualitative research* (pp. 105–117). Thousand Oaks, CA: Sage.

Hertz, R. (1995). Separate but simultaneous interviewing of husbands and wives: Making sense of their stories. *Qualitative Inquiry, 1,* 429–451.

Hertz, R. (Ed.). (1997). *Reflexivity and voice.* Thousand Oaks, CA: Sage.

Horton, M., & Freire, P. (1990). *We make the road by walking: Conversations on education and social change* (B. Bell, J. Gaventa, & J. Peters, Eds.). Philadelphia: Temple University Press.

Kochan, F. K. = Mullen, C. A. = Mullen, C. A. = Kochan, F. K. (2001). Collaborative authorship: Reflections on a briar patch of twisted brambles. *Teachers College Record.* Available: www.tcrecord.org/content.asp?/contentid-10661

Krieger, S. (1991). *Social science and the self: Personal essays on an art form.* New Brunswick, NJ: Rutgers University Press.

Lather, P. (1997). Creating a multilayered text: Women, AIDS, and angels. In W. G. Tierney &

Y. S. Lincoln (Eds.), *Representation and the text: Re-framing the narrative voice* (pp. 233– 258). Albany: State University of New York Press.

Lather, P., & Smithies, C. (1997). *Troubling the angels: Women living with HIV/AIDS.* Boulder, CO: Westview.

Lincoln, Y. S., & Guba, E. G. (1985). *Naturalistic inquiry.* Beverly Hills, CA: Sage.

Neumann, A. (1997). Ways without words: Learning from silence and story in post-Holocaust lives. In A. Neumann & P. L. Peterson (Eds.), *Learning from our lives: Women, research, and autobiography in education* (pp. 91–120). New York: Columbia University, Teachers College Press.

Peshkin, A. (2000). The nature of interpretation in qualitative research. *Educational Researcher, 29*(9), 5–9.

Richardson, L. (1988). The collective story: Postmodernism and the writing of sociology. *Sociological Focus, 21,* 199–208.

Richardson, L. (1990). *Writing strategies: Reaching diverse audiences* (Sage Qualitative Research Methods Series, No. 21). Newbury Park, CA: Sage.

Richardson, L. (1994). Writing: A method of inquiry. In N. K. Denzin and Y. S. Lincoln (Eds.), *Handbook of qualitative research* (pp. 516– 529). Thousand Oaks, CA: Sage.

Richardson, L. (1995). Writing-stories: Co-authoring "The Sea Monster," a writing-story. *Qualitative Inquiry, 1,* 189–203.

Ritchie, S. M., & Rigano, D. L. (2003, July). *Metaphors that guide our research writing.* Paper presented at the annual conference of the Australasian Science Education Research Association, Melbourne.

Schneider, J. W. (1991). Troubles with textual authority in sociology. *Symbolic Interaction, 14,* 295–319.

Stewart, J. O. (1989). *Drinkers, drummers, and decent folk: Ethnographic narratives of Village Trinidad.* Albany: State University of New York Press.

Tanaka, G. (1997). Pico College. In W. G. Tierney & Y. S. Lincoln (Eds.), *Representation and the text: Re-framing the narrative voice* (pp. 259– 304). Albany: State University of New York Press.

Tierney, W. G., & Lincoln, Y. S. (Eds.). (1997). *Representation and the text: Re-framing the narrative voice.* Albany: State University of New York Press.

Tierney, W. G., & Rhoads, R. A. (1993). Postmodernism and critical theory in higher education: Implications for research and practice. In J. C. Smart (Ed.), *Higher education: Handbook of theory and research* (Vol. 9, pp. 308–343). Edison, NJ: Agathon.

Van Maanen, J. (1988). *Tales of the field.* Chicago: University of Chicago Press.

Wolf, M. (1992). *A thrice-told tale: Feminism, postmodernism, and ethnographic responsibility.* Stanford, CA: Stanford University Press.

30

GETTING THE WORD OUT

Challenges and Opportunities in Explaining Educational Research to the World

GERALD W. BRACEY

The educator/journalist George Kaplan once wrote that part of education's problem with getting its story out is that education's story doesn't break—it oozes (Kaplan, 1982). And it was true at the time that education changed incrementally, that research studies offered at most small steps, not great leaps or breakthroughs. The pace has changed since Kaplan penned his words in 1982. We can date the change to 1983 and the appearance of *A Nation at Risk*—the document that is often referred to as the "paper Sputnik" and that riveted attention on education more than did the original Sputnik (National Commission on Excellence in Education, 1983).

As the cold war began during the late 1940s, focus on schools came indirectly through defense; the United States needed more and better mathematicians, scientists, and engineers to keep the Russians from beating the Americans in the space and weapons races. Those engineers would come from the colleges and universities, but some attention trickled down to secondary schools that, of course, supplied the students to institutions of higher education. Defense analysts of the time—such as Allen Dulles, the Central Intelligence Agency chief, and Admiral Hyman Rickover, the "father" of

the nation's nuclear navy—thought that the schools did not make the grade. So far as I can determine, this was the first time in the nation's history that people perceived high schools as integral to national defense. Not all criticism concerned defense. Arthur Bestor's influential *Educational Wastelands: The Retreat From Learning in Our Public Schools* was a critique of the schools in general, the life adjustment curriculum in particular, and the colleges of education especially (Bestor, 1953). In this climate of disdain, when the Russians launched Sputnik in October 1957, the basketball-sized satellite's success proved to the critics that they had been right all along.

A Nation at Risk, in contrast, spoke directly to the K–12 enterprise. Now the threat was not so much that enemies would annihilate the United States as that "friends," especially Germany, Japan, and South Korea, would outsmart the Americans and take away their markets. Backed up with selected and spun statistics, *A Nation at Risk* delineated its central thesis—"to keep and improve on the slim competitive edge we still retain in world markets, we must dedicate ourselves to the reform of our education system." *A Nation at Risk*'s central thesis held that high performance in K–12 education, as measured by tests, was responsible for a nation's economic well-being. The thesis was widely and wildly believed—but false. Today, for example, Japanese students still outperform American students by wide margins, but while the United States was enjoying the longest economic expansion in history, Japan was mired in recession and its economy was still sputtering in 2005. Singapore, usually outdistancing even other Asian nations by wide margins on tests of mathematics and science, declared itself in recession in 2001. Even while the United States suffered its recession from 2001 to 2003, it continued to hold the number two rank in the World Economic Forum's ratings of countries for global competitiveness. In the United States, economic cycles come and go independent of any changes in test scores (Bracey, 2005).

Ironically, President Ronald Reagan almost refused to sign the *Nation at Risk* report because it addressed nothing in his education agenda— vouchers, tuition tax credits, the restoration of prayer in school, and the abolition of the U.S. Department of Education. But he did sign it, and probably to his surprise, *A Nation at Risk* became a popular hit as well as an influential policy document, with the *Washington Post* carrying no fewer than 28 articles on it during the first month after publication. Although *A Nation at Risk* announced that a "rising tide of mediocrity" threatened the country, its immediate impact was to produce a rising tide of education reform reports and media coverage.

If the media were slow to notice education in general, they moved at a glacial pace to acknowledge educational research. In 1983, the editors of *Phi Delta Kappan* asked me to write a monthly column, in accessible English, summarizing educational research that might be of interest and value to practitioners and policymakers not trained in research design and statistics. Original research abounded, the editors believed, but few translations of that research into terms understandable in school buildings existed. Early on, I complained in a column that I had difficulty in filling it. Too much research was written by and for academia. I even went so far as to suggest abolishing journals for some period (Bracey, 1987). That, too, has changed.

This chapter explores the relationships among educational research, politics, and the media. It first looks at some "natural" proclivities of media to publish certain types of studies and then moves on to describe some troubling trends in how educational research, and indeed science itself, is used and misused in nonscientific circles. The general trend is illustrated in the concrete by tracing the events that followed a newspaper report of an analysis of National Assessment of Educational Progress (NAEP) charter school data. From there, the chapter describes the U.S. Department of Education's efforts to define what constitutes adequate research in the context of definitions and concerns from others. The chapter then returns to the interests of media and the conflict between those who would use the media to advance political and ideological agendas and those who wish to have research covered by the media as part of a more objective process.

WHAT DO THE MEDIA CHOOSE TO REPORT?

The value, ethics, and tactics of getting anyone, much less the media, to take notice of research have changed much over the past 40 years. I recall quite well that in my first year of graduate work in psychology in 1963, I wrote up a study and stated in the discussion section that a particular finding was "interesting." The professor for whom the research had been done found the report to be generally acceptable but returned it with "interesting" struck through in red pencil and the comment, "The *reader* will decide if the result is interesting."

Today, it is common to call attention to findings that strike the researcher as interesting or important. Whether or not they strike the media that way is, unfortunately, rather predictable, reflecting an old journalism saw that "if it bleeds it leads." Some years ago, I sent a manuscript to the *Columbia Journalism Review* lamenting the tendency to report only the negative. The editors rejected the manuscript because the sentiment was too familiar. (*Educational Leadership* later published it, but it was likely unseen by the audience for which it was originally intended [Bracey, 1994].)

Two U.S. Department of Education staffers, Laurence Ogle and Patricia Dabbs, observed the differential media treatment of positive and negative news directly and with some puzzlement. The two assisted with the releases in 1996 of NAEP geography and history assessments. The geography results were generally positive. Recounting the event in *Education Week,* Ogle and Dabbs (1996) wrote,

> The geography press conference was attended by the president of the National Geographic Society and the mood of almost all of the speakers was clearly upbeat. They noted, for example, that more than 70 percent of students at the 4th, 8th, and 12th grades had attained at least the "basic" level. ... The reporting in the press of the [geography] results, however, was lackluster and negative at best. Few agencies picked up the story.

The contrast between the geography and history releases was stark. Rene Sanchez, then education writer for the *Washington Post,* called the results "dismal." Lewis Lapham at *Harper's* designated them a "coroner's report." Reporters clamored to get at Ogle and Dabbs:

> Returning to our offices, we found our voice mail jam-packed with media requests for additional information. News accounts were on the radio and reports were even spotted on the Internet [these events transpired before e-mails flooded in-boxes and before the Internet had become *the* mode of information exchange]. Requests for additional information flooded in from radio and television stations, newspapers, and a few talk-show hosts, ... Even television's late-night comedy king, Jay Leno, spoke about (and ridiculed) the results. Clearly, the coverage of the negative news [about history] eclipsed the relatively good news about geography. (Ogle & Dabbs, 1996)

Sometimes journalists *provide* the negativity. A Stateline.org article by Kavan Peterson quoted Achieve Inc.'s Mike Cohen on survey results from his organization, "While American public high schools are doing a reasonably good job with a majority of their students, they are seriously failing a substantial minority of young people across the nation." Cohen's quote indicates a problem, no doubt, but the headline over the story read "High Schools Failing Generation Next," and the sentence following the quote read

"The survey underscores the dismal high school achievement rates . . ." (Peterson, 2005). Peterson's story played true to the headline (this is not always the case) and went on to produce a manufactured crisis.

Sources of Media Stories

Ogle and Dabbs's experience brought to mind an earlier experience with what I have come to call the "neurotic need to believe the worst." It afflicts the media especially, but also the general public, as illustrated by the general acceptance of "the lists."

I encountered the lists in 1986 on my first day on the job at the Cherry Creek Colorado School District. They were affixed to a bulletin board outside my office. The first list described the worst, most common problems in the schools during the 1940s. The second list provided these problems for the 1980s. The first list included offenses such as chewing gum, talking out of turn, and cutting in line. The second list was full of violence, gangs, drugs, alcohol, and teen pregnancy.

I recall thinking at the time that I was fortunate to be working in a district where these problems presented themselves so minimally. If I had given more thought to the matter, I might have noticed that no Colorado district—not even Denver, afflicted with the difficulties common to urban districts—suffered these problems as much as the lists implied. But I gave it no further thought. Fortunately, Barry O'Neill at Yale University viewed the lists with more curiosity and a more jaundiced eye and set out to track down their origins.

In the process, O'Neill found that the lists were widely accepted across the political spectrum. Conservatives William J. Bennett, Rush Limbaugh, Phyllis Schlafly, and George Will had affirmed their truth. But so had liberals Herb Caen, Carl Rowan, and Anna Quindlen. Their origins were variously attributed to CBS News, CQ Researcher, and the Heritage Foundation (the lists on my bulletin board gave the Fullerton [California] Police Department as the source).

O'Neill, however, tracked the lists to a single person, T. Cullen Davis of Fort Worth, Texas. Davis, it seems, had experienced an epiphany on being found not guilty of murdering his wife's lover. He had taken a hammer to his collection of jade and ivory sculpture, declared himself a born-again Christian, and used his new religious fervor to launch a crusade against the public schools. O'Neill inquired about Davis's methodology in constructing the lists. "How did I know what offenses in the schools were in 1940?" Davis asked. "I was there. How do I know what they are now? I read the paper" (O'Neill, 1994).

How Valid Are the Educational Stories in the Media?

Unfortunately, reading the newspaper can lead to a distorted view of how schools perform. Richard Harwood, former *Washington Post* ombudsman, once observed that "for twenty years, content analysis studies have shown that 70 to 90 percent of our content is at heart the voice of officials and their experts, translated by reporters into supposedly 'objective' news" (Harwood, 1994). Such "news" usually advances some agenda desired by the news provider.

No doubt this is why the first law of journalism of the great muckraking journalist I. F. "Izzy" Stone was that "governments lie." When not engaging in outright lies, governments seek "political statistics." Winston Churchill provided a succinct operational definition of a political statistic:

> I take it, young man, that you wish to become a member of parliament. The first lesson you must learn is that when I ask you for statistics on infant mortality, I want statistics that prove that fewer infants died when I was Prime Minister than when anyone else was Prime Minister. That is a political statistic. (Wainer & Koretz, 2003)

Examples of political statistics in education are much in evidence and appear to be on the increase. For instance, a former *USA Today* reporter once wrote about a Western Michigan University evaluation of charter schools in Pennsylvania. The article claimed that the charter schools that had been open for 2 years showed greater test score gains than did regular public schools. Alas, perhaps confronted with a deadline, the reporter did not actually read the

evaluators' full report of nearly 200 pages. If she had done so, she would have noticed that the conclusion applied to only two charter schools and was presented in a most tentative fashion. Instead, the reporter relied on, and wrote nearly verbatim from, a set of political statistics, a press release prepared by the offices of two charter enthusiasts: Tom Ridge, then governor of Pennsylvania, and Eugene Hickok, his secretary of education (Henry, 2001).

Reporters often seek reactions and opinions from people who might challenge a particular political statistic. Such opinions must be quickly forthcoming, however, and reporters are often forced to write their stories without hearing back from all of the sources they sought. This can leave the verification or disconfirmation process wanting. When I once asked a reporter why he so often cited a person whose intellectual capacity and integrity I questioned, he replied, "Because she's always quick to return calls." Academics enjoy leisurely time frames. Journalists do not.

A Troubling Trend: Scientifically Based Research Versus Ideologically Driven Research and the Rush to Print

There will be political statistics so long as there are politicians. Recently, however, we have witnessed a trend to cloak ideological goals in scientific garb and to suppress science that does not advance an ideology. This is, to say the least, disturbing. For instance, the No Child Left Behind law uses the phrase "scientifically based research" 111 times. Yet no research base supports its principal program in Title I of the act, which requires schools to test every child in Grades 3 to 8 in reading and math (and, beginning in 2007, in science). Nothing in the research literature supports the notion that testing children every year, disaggregating the data, and pronouncing an entire school a failure if even one small group of the children fails to make "adequate yearly progress" is an appropriate or effective way in which to improve education. In his American Educational Research Association (AERA) presidential address,

Robert Linn, co-director of the Center for the Student of Evaluation, Student Standards, and Testing (CRESST) at the University of California, Los Angeles, and the University of Colorado and widely regarded as one of the most thorough and reasonable people in the field, pronounced the No Child Left Behind requirements "quite unreasonable" (Linn, 2003).

In fact, in view of the Bush administration's ardor for "faith-based" programs and policies, many have questioned the administration's true commitment to science. A statement from the Union of Concerned Scientists accused the administration of deliberately manipulating, suppressing, and ignoring scientific advice it did not agree with while stacking advisory panels only with people who had met an ideological litmus test (Viadero, 2004). Harvard's Howard Gardner framed the essential issue well:

> Is science a disinterested effort to find out what the world is really like . . . or is science simply a tool that we use to promote a certain point of view that we have and if the evidence supports us, great, and if not we squelch it or we don't put it on the web, or don't even find that kind of thing. The question we have to ask ourselves is, Do we want to live in a world where you can't count on scientists calling it the way it is, or simply accept that there are scientists on the left and scientists on the right? (Rehm, 2004)

Representative Henry Waxman, a California Democrat who is called "science's bulldog" by *Scientific American,* maintains a Web site, titled *Politics and Science* (http://democrats.reform .house.gov/features/politics_and_science/index .htm), and regularly reports on what he perceives as failings in the administration. Waxman's staff has issued a report, *Politics and Science in the Bush Administration,* which affirms many of the contentions voiced by the Union of Concerned Scientists.

Waxman's reports cover a wide range of situations where science was subordinated to politics and ideology. For instance, it noted another report, *Missing: Information About Women's Lives* (National Council for Research on Women, 2004), which claims information has been routinely withdrawn or altered on Web sites operated by the Centers for Disease Control and Prevention, the National Cancer Institute, and the U.S. Department of Health and Human Services (HHS) to render those sites' presentation of findings more in line with Bush administration ideology. On his Web site in September 2004, Waxman also reported on a new policy at HHS that requires the World Health Organization to submit requests for expert scientific advice to political appointees at HHS, who then decide which HHS scientists will be permitted to respond (http://democrats. reform .house.gov/features/politics_and_science/ index.htm).

This tendency to subordinate the facts of science to the desires of ideology and even religion did not begin with the Bush administration and will not terminate when Bush's term ends. Nevertheless, the trend accelerated under Bush, such that *New York Times* reporter Ron Suskind's long article in the newspaper's *Sunday Magazine* was titled "Without a Doubt." In a telling paragraph, Suskind wrote, "This is one key feature of the faith-based presidency: Open dialogue, based on facts, is not seen as something of inherent value" (Suskind, 2004). In fact, Suskind went on to observe that facts could create doubt, which could affect both decisions and the decision maker. In the Bush administration, "My mind's made up, don't confuse me with facts" ceases to be a lame old saw.

A faith-based, or at least something less than science-based, approach to dealing with issues heretofore considered scientific (e.g., how to teach beginning reading, the relationship between abortion and later breast cancer) puts a new burden on the media. What are the criteria now for deciding where truth lies? The next section illustrates the difficulties.

THE NAEP CHARTER SCHOOL STUDY AND ITS AFTERMATH: DIFFICULTIES FOR MEDIA AND CONSUMERS OF MEDIA ALIKE

When educational researchers have published reports on politically or ideologically charged topics, the debate has occasionally spilled into the media, but usually some time after the debate has been in progress. One might see opposing articles in the same publication as the original article or, occasionally, a special issue of the periodical devoted to the topic. From time to time during recent years, education writers who specialize in writing columns and writing about issues rather than stories about events will give a topic a wider audience. For example, Michael Winerip of the *New York Times* has written on controversial voucher data, and Samuel G. Freedman, also of the *Times,* and Jay Mathews of the *Washington Post* have treated conflicting views on No Child Left Behind.

Various reporters have written about "fuzzy math," bilingual education, class size, phonics versus whole language, and the heritability of IQ. Although researchers hold strong views on these issues, seldom has the dialogue ventured beyond the polite prose of academic discourse. Thus, the impolite eruption from charter supporters reacting to a straightforward article in the *New York Times* came as a surprise. The following is a chronicle of the madness.

On Tuesday, August 17, 2004, the *Times's* front page carried a story indicating that charter schools did not perform as well as public schools (Schemo, 2004a). The story derived from NAEP results collected by the U.S. Department of Education and analyzed by the American Federation of Teachers (AFT). The department assembled these data as part of the regular NAEP reading and mathematics assessments early in 2003. By the fall of 2003, the regular data had been analyzed and placed on the department's Web site. The charter school data, however, remained unanalyzed until the AFT, after unsuccessful attempts to prod the department into action, undertook an analysis itself.

The AFT reported overall results, results with schools matched for location, and results with schools matched for percentage of children eligible for free and reduced-price meals. In all three conditions, regular schools outperformed charter schools. When matched for ethnicity, blacks in charter schools and public schools did not differ, but the black–white achievement gap in charter schools was as large as in regular schools.

Depending on the edition one received, the *Times* headline read either "Charter Schools Trail in Results, U.S. Data Reveals" or "Nation's Charter Schools Lagging Behind, U.S. Test Scores Reveal." A *Times* editorial the next day called the results a "devastating setback for No Child Left Behind which authorizes failing schools to convert to charter status" ("Bad News," 2004). The law authorizes the conversion if a school fails to make "adequate yearly progress" for 5 consecutive years. Many people anticipated that this would be an oft-chosen option given the popularity of charter schools generally and the logistical difficulties of the other options. But if charter schools underperform regular schools, then what would be the point of a conversion?

It was not surprising to find organizations formally committed to charter schools defending their institution. The same day as the article appeared, Marquette University's Howard Fuller, chairman of the Charter School Leadership Council, issued a press release denouncing the analysis and the *Times,* accusing the New York newspaper of giving "short shrift" to the "remarkable gains" children show once they enter charter schools (Fuller, 2004). Equally quickly, the National Charter School Clearinghouse said that the *Times* article was terribly misleading and that the article used data that were badly flawed and provided by a teachers union that was hostile to greater parental choice.

In fact, the AFT analysis examined 1 year's data and thus had nothing to say about gains. The "flawed data" contention, made later in other publications, apparently derived mostly from a misinterpretation of the NAEP sampling design. The data had *limitations* because they measured a single point in time, but they were not flawed. At the time, only one study on charter achievement had tracked students longitudinally to examine gains. The gains it reported could hardly be called "remarkable," and even those modest gains had been challenged with a contention that they stemmed from the attrition of low-scoring students from charter schools, not from improvements by those who remained in the charter schools (Martin, 2001; Solmon, Paark, & Garcia, 2001).

What was surprising was the massive attack against the analysis and the coverage by researchers and reformers without any connection to any charter organization. On Wednesday, August 18, the *Wall Street Journal* carried an op-ed from William Howell, Paul Peterson, and Martin West of Harvard University titled "Dog

Eats AFT Homework" (Howell, Peterson, & West, 2004). This attitude of ridicule would be seen in several other retorts. For instance, editors at the *Chicago Tribune* called the analysis "as novel as a lava lamp, as revelatory as an old sock, and as significant as a belch" ("The Facts About Charter Schools," 2004).

The original Tuesday article quoted Chester Finn, charter advocate and president of the Thomas B. Fordham Foundation, as saying that "the scores are low, dismayingly low" and that "a little more tough love is needed for these schools" (Schemo, 2004a). Wednesday, however, found Finn declaring in an op-ed for the *New York Post,* "This week's firestorm over the performance of charter schools can be traced to a mischief bearing grenade hand-delivered by the charter hating American Federation of Teachers to the *New York Times*" (Finn, 2004).

On Wednesday, the *New York Times* devoted most of a Section A article to quotes from Secretary of Education Rod Paige defending charter schools (Schemo, 2004b). Wednesday also found Andrew Rotherham writing "Live by the Sword, Die by the *Times*" for www.eduwonk .com, the blog of the Progressive Policy Institute (no one had accused charter schools of "living by the sword"). As the saga continued, Rotherham updated the blog with headlines such as "Charter Cheap Shot, Day III" and referred to the AFT analysis as "nefarious." On the Center for Education Reform (2004) Web site, President Jeanne Allen wrote, "The AFT has been working on their plan for months to twist NAEP data and attack the nation's unsuspecting 3,000 charter schools with a full-force media blitz." Allen did not explain how a single article, even on the front page of the *New York Times,* could constitute "a full-force media blitz."

Also on Wednesday, Allen debated the AFT's Bella Rosenberg, a principal author of the AFT report, on NPR's *Tavis Smiley Show.* On Thursday, the U.S. Department of Education sent Nina Rees (formerly of the Heritage Foundation) to do battle with Rosenberg on PBS's *News Hour with Jim Lehrer.*

On Thursday, August 19, the *New York Post* editorialized, "The AFT hates them (charter schools) because they threaten the union's public school monopoly" ("Kids Come Last," 2004), while in the *New York Sun* the Manhattan

Institute's Jay P. Greene published an op-ed attacking the study (Greene & Forster, 2004). The *New York Times* continued its attention to the matter on Thursday with an op-ed by the Reverend Floyd Flake, a former New York congressman—and president of the Charter Schools Division of Edison Schools Inc., something the *Times's* credit line did not mention (Flake, 2004).

Perhaps to add some technical weight to the argument, Robert Lerner, acting commissioner of the National Center for Education Statistics, claimed in a letter to the editor of the *New York Times* that the "report is not a true picture of what is happening nationally" (Lerner, 2004). Lerner did not explain why NAEP would *not* provide a national picture—the N stands for "national," after all.

The saga reached a bizarre climax on August 25 when Section A of the *New York Times* carried a full-page advertisement attacking the study and the *Times* story. A total of 31 professors, assembled by Harvard's Peterson, signed the ad. Allen's Center for Education Reform bore the ad's $125,000 cost. The ad carried the headline "Charter School Evaluation Reported by *The New York Times* Fails to Meet Professional Standards." The ad also appeared in the September 15 edition of *Education Week* with only 29 signers and can be found on the Center for Education Reform's Web site (http://edreform.com/_upload/newyorktime-sad.pdf). (The two individuals who had removed their names stated that they had no idea what they were getting into.)

Among the flaws that the signatories found in the *Times* coverage was one on "journalistic responsibility": "The news media has an obligation to assess carefully any research sponsored by interest groups engaged in policy analysis. Such studies need to be vetted by independent scholars, as is commonly done in coverage of research on the biological and physical sciences."

This was a curious stance given that some signatories had routinely failed to adhere to this principle. Lawrence Mishel, a researcher at the Economic Policy Institute, observed, "Many of these guardians of professional research standards have repeatedly violated the principles they now proclaim" (Mishel, 2004).

With the data abroad in the land, it made no sense for the U.S. Department of Education to pretend that they did not exist, and the department delivered an "official" report that confirmed the AFT's earlier analysis (U.S. Department of Education, 2004a). Of the 22 comparisons in reading and math, 20 favored public schools. The NAEP data were not the only charter-unfavorable results that the department did not present in a forthcoming manner. The department withheld another charter-unfavorable study until it was obtained by the *New York Times* through a Freedom of Information Act request 5 months after the contractor had delivered the final report (Dillon & Schemo, 2004).

Still, at the press conference releasing the report, Darvin Winick, chairman of the National Assessment Governing Board, and Eugene Hickok, then deputy secretary of education, engaged in rhetoric designed to shore up charter schools. Winick emphasized the tentativeness of the data, and Hickok said that "we're big fans of charter schools." Both noted that differences between charter schools and public schools were small. Nick Anderson of the *Los Angeles Times* wondered why, given charter schools' promise to improve achievement, Winick and Hickok were so satisfied with the near parity of the test scores. "The charter schools are doing the same with less money," said Hickok. "Does that mean that money really does matter?" asked Anderson in a follow-up question. There was no response.

Indeed, at some moments during the press conference, one could not help but remember Garrison Keillor's description of Minnesotans as people "who can look reality square in the eye and deny it." Hickok stated, "Charter schools that don't work don't stay open." Yet the study that the U.S. Department of Education (2004b) withheld until the *New York Times* request through the Freedom of Information Act concluded, "Charter schools rarely face sanctions (revocation or nonrenewal). Furthermore, authorizing bodies impose sanctions on charter schools because of problems related to *compliance with regulations* and *school finances,* rather than *student performance*" (emphases in original).

The "promote a particular viewpoint" approach to science and the willingness to contradict findings both make it more difficult for journalists and the public alike to ascertain where the truth lies. On a listserv in connection with another disputed topic, beginning reading instruction, a correspondent recently wrote that "facts don't count." Indeed, it would appear that when it comes to charters and some other free market issues, the "Without a Doubt" mentality that Suskind (2004) reported has seeped into the U.S. Department of Education and has taken hold in some quarters of academia as well.

RESEARCHERS AS THEIR OWN WORST ENEMIES

The American Psychological Association (APA) style manual that I used in graduate school systematically reinforced bad writing. Although the current edition represents an enormous improvement, nothing in a researcher's training systematically reinforces good writing. One could argue, I think, that a doctorate should be conditional on writing at least one prior paper that conforms to the Strunk, White, and Angell (2000) style manual. The traditions surrounding the demonstration of scholarship in the thesis probably preclude those qualities in the thesis itself.

As I prepare my monthly research column for *Phi Delta Kappan,* I see many journal articles that could be shortened and note that virtually all could be brightened. When I review a manuscript and later receive the comments of the other reviewers, these others never mention style—only content. Editorial policies of research journals naturally allow writers to use as many words as they think are necessary to say what they need to say. That is good policy, but without any attention to writing, it is bad discipline for the writer (and bad news for the reader).

Because I write for nonresearch journals and the popular press, I sometimes receive drafts of would-be op-eds and letters to editors from colleagues in academia. My first response is that the pieces are invariably too long. No newspaper editor—outside of *Education Week* or the *Chronicle of Higher Education*—will look at a 1,000-word letter or an 1,800-word op-ed. The usual limits for these two forms are 200 and 650 to 750 words, respectively. The *New York Times* guidelines specify a maximum of 150 words, and the newspaper almost never publishes letters longer than that.

Occasionally, *USA Today* will contact me to write an "opposing view" editorial in reaction to the editors' own perspective. I get 350 words. It is a great exercise in discipline to try to write something both meaty and persuasive in 350 words—or to write an op-ed that is 650 to 750 words. The reader might wish to try doing so as an exercise.

Others have observed that researchers do not always act in their own best interest in communicating with the media. As David Savage, who worked in the National Institute of Education and later spent a decade covering education for the *Los Angeles Times,* put it,

> To read or listen to a typical education research report is to feel like a junior high school student in French class. You are inclined to look around to see if the others understand what is being said. Dense, abstract prose simply obscures the meaning—if there is any—of what is written or said. Several years ago, when I taught a news writing class for university studies in Los Angeles, I used journal articles in education as fine examples of lousy writing. I urged the students to use concrete nouns and active verbs. The verbs moved the sentence. In the education articles, I could read a page of prose without striking an active verb. There were only abstract nouns and passive verbs. . . .
>
> Abstract prose that is so light as to float off the page gives a hint that there may be little or no substance there. Often, such writing reads like an attempt to mask muddled thinking. (Savage, 1992, p. 212)

Well, we could chide Savage for saying that abstract research prose is "dense" in the first paragraph and "light" in the second paragraph, but his message still comes through. In a brief, nonrandom attempt to see whether Savage's critique still applied, I opened a recent issue of *Educational Evaluation and Policy Analysis* to the "Discussion" sections of two articles. I first read the following:

> Researchers have long documented and theorized how local school leaders manage and weaken external policy influence. Administrative strategies,

including the creation of loosely coupled systems, decoupling organization from practice, establishing logics of confidence, and adhering to the strong and socially embedded norms of practice, enable schools to maintain organizational and instructional stability in the face of repeated external attempts to alter school, teacher, and student performance. Institutional theorists argue that these strategies serve to stabilize organizations by establishing common criteria by which organizations are publicly assessed. These criteria, however, have traditionally been easily inspected and often removed from the technical core of the organization. More recently [researchers] suggest that the increasingly rationalized environment of public education is focusing more attention on performance outcomes—outcomes less reliant on superficial organization and more closely linked to classroom learning.

The authors do provide citations for the various strategies listed, but the paragraph approaches—to my mind—gibberish. And what about "the increasingly rationalized environment of public education"? Unless "rationalized" is a technical term familiar to those in the field of organizational theory, it is in a strange place; most people would contend that public education is increasingly politicized and irrational.

The second passage read as follows:

> We conducted similar analyses in which the dependent variable was a dichotomous variable that took on the value of one if voters in a district rejected an initial budget proposal put forth by a school board and then the school board either went directly to a contingency budget or went to a contingency budget after a second budget proposal was defeated and took on the value of zero if a budget proposal by the school board was accepted by the voters on an initial or second vote.

This sentence confronts the reader with 87 words and no punctuation marks to guide the reader's understanding. Unlike the previous paragraph, this sentence contains few technical terms and thus is easy for a second party to make more coherent:

> We conducted similar analyses with a dichotomous dependent variable. It took on the value of

"1" under two conditions: first, if voters rejected an initial school board budget proposal, and the board then proposed a contingency budget, or second, if voters rejected a second budget and the board went to a contingency budget. It took on the value of "0" if voters accepted a budget on a first or second vote.

The second version contains 71 words. In writing, the Bauhaus credo—"less is more"—often applies. Both versions contain no passive sentences, and both have a Flesch reading level of 12.0. The first version, however, has a Flesch reading ease of 0.0, whereas the second version has a reading ease of 38.6. In the Flesch system, 0 to 29 is very difficult postgraduate prose. The rewrite puts the reading ease at the college level.

Of course, as Savage (1992) noted, if the muddied prose conceals muddled thinking, then clear writing will simply reveal that more readily to the reader. In 1989, at a symposium that resulted in a 1992 book, AERA's Gerald Sroufe had this analysis on the thinking underlying educational research:

> Much education research is not suitable for informing education policy. It is shallow, poorly conceived, poorly executed nonsense. The field recognizes that exponential growth in research journals in education is a phenomenon of the promotion system rather than the knowledge system. Only established scholars can afford not to publish work that they regard as inferior; most will send their manuscripts around until they find an outlet somewhere. Such research is self-serving, career-building work, of little consequence to anyone but the author. (Sroufe, 1992, p. 230)

Thinking about the thousands of presentations made at AERA each year, I wondered whether Sroufe had changed his mind during the ensuing 15 years. *Yes* and *no,* he said. On the downside, irrelevant research abounds because

> anyone can hang out the "researcher" shingle, and any document can be referred to as research, especially by the media. Education research is an open system and the traditional bodies that conferred legitimacy (e.g., university press, universities themselves)—however lamely—are sorely challenged by a host of newcomers and new technology.

A huge amount of the total sum of education research continues to be generated by poorly funded graduate students. Finally on the negative side, many researchers do have a "tin ear" when it comes to policy relevance and the most embarrassing aspects of grant proposals or research reports are often the sections that seek to deal with policy implications. Often they are ill informed about policy processes, grandiose in their expectations, and intolerant of restraints on policy makers. These same problems carry over to media. (personal communication, October 29, 2004)

On the upside, Sroufe stated that a number of educational research centers, the regional laboratories, and some individual researchers "have learned how to translate their work to policy makers and the media. . . . There are increasing expectations that quality, policy-relevant research is what is valued; I find this in contemporary grant programs, [in] foundation expectations, and in some doctoral training programs."

Perhaps we will see the emergence of a new "index" in the promotion and tenure evaluations of researchers. In the beginning was the publications record, weighted for where the work appeared and worth much more if the researcher were the sole or senior author. Then came the citation index. How often do other scholars cite a researcher's work? With current information technology, we could add how often a person's work is cited by the media and in actual policymaking documents. Some policy-oriented researchers seem to be validating the worth of their work in this way.

What Are Journalists Interested In?

At a 1989 symposium on educational research and the media, Juan Williams, then of the *Washington Post,* cast the media's interest in education in stark and narrow terms:

> The truth is, reporters and editors and, most important, readers are interested in education only as a function of political power. A major proportion of any jurisdiction's tax dollars goes into schools. Politicians have to make up those school budgets and defend them. The school or university budget has to be both sufficient to the task of

educating young people and simultaneously able to withstand charges that it is really a pork-barrel project, wasting the tax-payers' money. . . . Newspaper editors, as the public's watchdogs, want to know if the taxpayers are being cheated out of their money. . . .

If the teachers are on strike, that means the schools are not open, and that means the taxpayers are being cheated out of their money. If a youngster graduates without being able to read, the taxpayers are cheated. If schools are havens for drug dealers and violence, the taxpayers are being cheated. That is news. . . .

Now, for people doing research on schools to think that newspapers are going to give attention to how best to train teachers, or to the pros and cons of instructional techniques, or even to the issue of what is being taught to young people, is just plain wrong. Unless it is sex education or religious teachings, the general public is not interested in what is taught or how it is taught. This may be sad, but it is true. And no matter how hard the educational research community complains, this will not change. (Williams, 1992, p. 219)

There are, at least two problems with Williams's (1992) formulation. First, almost any issue in education *can* be reduced to "taxpayers are being cheated." It is a theory that explains too much. For instance, the noisy debate over phonics versus whole language *can* be seen that way. If whole language works better but schools are using phonics, then the taxpayers are being cheated. Few participants in the debate and few who watched the debate probably thought of it that way. Similarly, the "math wars" seem to reflect a general interest in what is taught, and how it is taught, independent of financial concerns.

Second, at the time, Williams was the national education reporter for the *Post* and speaking from a national perspective. If he had in mind the metro section of his newspaper, he would have remembered a number of stories on local problems and local successes that perhaps *could* be cast in his taxpayer argument but that most would refer to as "local color." And as perhaps a sign that some things do change, the *Post* has moved some of the stories to Section A; they appear every Tuesday. (Similarly, the *New York Times* and the *Christian Science Monitor* have regular weekly features.)

Still, because of its hard line and because it had been 15 years since Williams had formulated his arguments, I sent the preceding quote and more of Williams's (1992) text to members of the Education Writers Association. I asked them whether Williams was right then and, if so, whether he is right now. That only 13 of 775 members replied might or might not say something about the media's interest in educational research.

Just as Williams's position as a national reporter colored his perspective, my respondents' answers also depended in part on their positions. Answering in terms of small and midsized cities, respondents said *yes* (i.e., that Williams was right then and is still right now), although one, who asked for anonymity in a personal communication (October 1, 2004), said the reasons for *yes* had changed. Reporters for smaller newspapers today, he contended, had less experience and exited the education beat faster. "Not only are reporters inexperienced," he went on, "because of budget cuts they are spread pretty thin. If a reporter has three or four stories to write in a day, you can bet they are just going to bang them out quickly without too much regard for nuance."

The respondent added, "The tightening of newsroom budgets means small papers rely on the AP [Associated Press]. . . . The AP is basically a superficial regurgitation; there's not a whole lot of depth in reporting." I would tend to agree, but there are some AP reporters, such as Ben Feller and Greg Toppo before he migrated to *USA Today,* who wrote analytic stories. However, newspapers often trim the AP wire stories, sometimes to the point of making them virtually meaningless.

Mathews of the *Washington Post* said that Williams's comments were much less true today than they were 15 years ago:

When I was a 26-year-old education reporter for the *Post,* I spent most of my time at school board meetings watching the power relationships he described. . . . We still do that kind of reporting, but in the last 15 years I think we have learned that the minutiae of classroom life, exactly how good teachers motivate and instruct kids, is more important than the money. (Mathews, personal communication, October 29, 2004)

Mathews (2000) had earlier described newspaper interest this way:

> A typical front page story in the *Washington Post* or the *New York Times* will begin with an anecdote about a person and a problem, tell the reader by the fourth paragraph about why this problem is important, show how the person is addressing the problem, and cite examples of similar people and problems elsewhere, the wider its importance the better. (p. 450)

Research studies often fail to capture editors' interest because they lack a sense of the personal. Researchers forget that "news making is a business, not a science" (Mathews, 2000).

Mathews (2000) omitted from this formulation qualities he mentioned later in the article, qualities that present a broader perspective than did Williams: "If the [research] study is to be noticed, it must shed new light on some significant political, economic, social, or ideological conflict. Newspapers and television stations love a good fight" (p. 451). I would also note that a startling opening line can by-pass the personal. A November 5, 2004, story in the *Philadelphia Inquirer* opened with "All children are born dyslexic—it's just that 'some are easy to cure'" (Langland, 2004)—a rather different slant from the usual on reading difficulties.

William O. Celis, who taught journalism at the University of Colorado, currently teaches at the University of Southern California, and covered education for the *New York Times* from 1990 to 1995, agreed with Mathews that "education coverage has come a long way in the last two decades." Celis dated the change from the mid-1980s with states requiring higher performance from students. Celis also indicated that he and others spent many hours at school board meetings in the past, but today more and more stories came from inside the classrooms. "The preponderance of school board stories about politics and squabbles gave way, for the first time, to meaningful stories about what happened inside classrooms because, I believe, editors recognized that this was an important story and because readers demanded more [of these stories]" (personal communication, October 31, 2004).

For his part, Williams retained his earlier position:

> The real reason there is more coverage of education issues today in the front sections is that . . . there is a raging national argument over the general quality of public schools. . . .
>
> The big change is that . . . the stakes have gone up. Previously schools coverage was primarily a local beat. When a national report on education was issued by the relatively new Department of Education it was an exceptional event. Today, the Secretary of Education condemns [teacher] unions as "terrorists" and there is a backlash against the focus on testing. This is all widely covered in newspapers. It is evidence of continuing interest in schools as a political, budgetary story. It is not evidence of a different approach to education coverage emerging. (personal communication, November 28, 2004)

I would both agree and disagree. The charter school imbroglio described earlier is the kind of story Williams has in mind. On the other hand, the pieces by Jay Mathews and Valerie Strauss in each Tuesday's *Washington Post,* and the articles by Samuel G. Freedman and Michael Winerip in each Wednesday's *New York Times,* represent to me a different, broader perspective on education coverage. And these articles are not about local concerns but rather about national issues, such as No Child Left Behind, or about general issues, such as what teachers perceive as their purpose.

What does this increased attention to education—a November 2004 Google search on "No Child Left Behind" found 1,520,000 items—mean for coverage of educational research? The answer is a resounding *it depends.* At one end of what might be seen as a continuum is H. Thomas James of the Spencer Foundation:

> We tend to be skeptical about the claims of scientists who set about to do research intended to be directly relevant to policy making. We believe rather that the processes of basic inquiry and the processes by which policy is made are quite different, and should not be confused. . . . The questions the scholar asks are not necessarily the questions the policy maker wants answered, and they should not be. The research is distracted by immediacy, and functions best when allowed to examine and test new knowledge about a subject in relation to

all that has been discovered earlier, adjusting theories and concepts in ways that fit the data, and by so doing, increasing our understanding of ourselves and the world we live in. (James, 1981)

Many educational researchers feel this way. For his part, James said that nothing had changed his mind during the 23 years since he wrote the statement (personal communication, November 15, 2004). On the other hand, the media are paying more attention, for better or for worse, to research with immediate policy implications. And some, such as Greene of the Manhattan Institute, cater to the desire for policy-relevant research. An article about Greene said that he "especially wants to influence the 'policy elite' he considers his primary audience and quoted Greene as saying, "I like the idea that our work is timely and useful" (Hegarty, 2003). But such catering is sometimes accompanied by denigration of traditional research. Frederick Hess of the American Enterprise Institute said, "For 50 years, people have looked to academics as the guys in robes, the monks that you go to for neutral opinions and wisdom. Now we know they've got their biases and their opinions like everyone else" (Hegarty, 2003).

Hess's statement strikes me as irresponsible and dangerous. Traditional researchers might have biases, but they also have generally accepted standards for warranting knowledge. They also have methods for keeping biases out of the analyses. For all its rigidity, the U.S. Department of Education's emphasis on random assignment is an attempt to reduce threats to validity. Without standards for warranting evidence, the field would decline into one where ideology trumps data and where "truth" is what those in power say it is—very Orwellian.

If all one can say about academic researchers is that they have "opinions like everyone else," then disciplines are reduced to "he said she said" arguments and to the use of science to promote a point of view. It appears that in a clash between scientists as truth tellers and scientists as position promoters, the latter have the upper hand at the moment. How long this state of affairs continues to exist remains in no small measure in our hands both individually and collectively.

REFERENCES

Bad news on the charter front [editorial]. (2004, August 18). *New York Times*, p. A22.

Bestor, A. (1953). *Educational wastelands: The retreat from learning in our public schools.* Urbana: University of Illinois Press.

Bracey, G. W. (1987, March 25). The time has come to abolish research journals: Too many are writing too much about too little. *Chronicle of Higher Education*, pp. 44–45.

Bracey, G. W. (1994). The media's myth of school failure. *Educational Leadership, 84*(1), 80–83.

Bracey, G. W. (2005, February 2). Education's Ground Hog Day, *Education Week*, pp. 38–39.

Center for Education Reform. (2004, August) *AFT at it again.* Available: www.edreform.com/index.cfm?fuseaction=section&psectionid=59&csectionid=126

Dillon, S., & Schemo, D. (2004, November 24). Charter schools fall short in public schools matchup. *New York Times*, p. A21.

The facts about charter schools [editorial]. (2004, August 18). *Chicago Tribune*, p. A27.

Finn, C. E., Jr. (2004, August 19). Defaming charters. *New York Post.*

Flake, F. H. (2004, August 19). Classes of last resort. *New York Times*, p. A31.

Fuller, H. (2004, August 18). *Charter School Leadership Council responds to misleading* New York Times *article* [press release]. Milwaukee, WI: Charter School Leadership Council.

Greene, J. P., & Forster, G. (2004). *Can disadvantaged children learn? The Teachability Index* (Working Paper No. 6). New York: Manhattan Institute.

Harwood, R. (1994, May 28). Reporting on, by, and for an elite. *Washington Post*, p. A29.

Hegarty, S. (2003, September 2). He proffers proof in voucher fights. *St. Petersburg Times.*

Henry, T. (2001, March 28). Score goes up for charters. *USA Today*, p. D9.

Howell, W. G., Peterson, P. E., & West, M. R. (2004, August 19). Dog eats AFT homework. *Wall Street Journal*, p. A10.

James, H. T. (1981). The president's comments. *Annual report: The Spencer Foundation, 1981.* Chicago: Spencer Foundation.

Kaplan, G. R. (1982). *Images of education: The mass media's version of America's schools.* Washington, DC: Institute for Educational Leadership.

Kids come last [editorial]. (2004, August 19). *New York Post.*

Langland, C. (2004, November 5). Provocative report issued at dyslexia conference. *Philadelphia Inquirer.*

Lerner, R. (2004, August 23). [Letter to the editor]. *New York Times.*

Linn, R. L. (2003). Accountability, responsibility, and reasonable expectations. *Educational Researcher, 33*(8), 3–13.

Martin, M. (2001). *The Goldwater Institute's charter school hoax.* Available: www.azsba.org/hoax auh2o.htm

Mathews, J. (2000). Writing for Rosie: How a journalist uses (and doesn't use) research. *Journal of Literacy Research, 64,* 449–456.

Mishel, L. (2004, September 23). Schoolhouse schlock. *The American Prospect.*

National Commission on Excellence in Education. (1983). *A nation at risk.* Washington, DC: U.S. Department of Education.

National Council for Research on Women. (2004). *Missing: Information about women's lives.* Retrieved November 6, 2004, from www.wcrw .org/misinfo/report.pdf

Ogle, L., & Dabbs, P. (1996, March 6). Good news bad news: Does media coverage of schools promote scattershot remedies? *Education Week,* p. 46.

O'Neill, B. (1994, March 6). Anatomy of a hoax. *New York Times Sunday Magazine,* pp. 46–49.

Peterson, K. (2005, February 7). *High schools failing generation next.* Available: www.stateline.org

Rehm, D. (2004, March 4). *The Diane Rehm Show.* Available: http://wamu.org/programs.dr/04/03/ 04.php

Savage, D. (1992). The press and education research: Why one ignores the other. In R. F. McNergney (Ed.), *Education research, policy, and the press* (pp. 1–30). Boston: Allyn & Bacon.

Schemo, D. J. (2004a, August 17). Charter schools trail in results, U.S. data reveals. *New York Times,* p. A1.

Schemo, D. J. (2004b, August 18). Education secretary defends charter schools. *New York Times,* p. A18.

Solmon, L. C., Paark, K., & Garcia, D. (2001). *Does charter school attendance improve test scores? The Arizona results.* Phoenix, AZ: Goldwater Institute.

Sroufe, G. (1992). Educational research, the press, and national educational policy: A skeptic's view. In R. F. McNergney (Ed.), *Educational research, policy, and the press* (pp. 213–233). Boston: Allyn & Bacon.

Strunk, W., White, E. B., & Angell, R. (2000). *Elements of style* (4th ed.). New York: Longman.

Suskind R. (2004, October 7). Without a doubt. *New York Times Sunday Magazine,* p. 44.

U.S. Department of Education. (2004a). *America's charter schools: Results from the NAEP 2003 pilot study* (NCES Report No. 2005–456). Washington, DC: Author.

U.S. Department of Education. (2004b). *Evaluation of the public charter schools program: Final report* (Report No. 2004–08). Washington, DC: Author.

Viadero, D. (2004, March 30). In Bush administration, policies drive science, scholars group claims. *Education Week,* p. 20.

Wainer, H., & Koretz, D. (2003). A political statistic. *Chance, 16*(4), 45–47.

Williams, J. (1992). The politics of education news. In R. F. McNergney (Ed.), *Education research, policy, and the press* (pp. 177–200). Boston: Allyn & Bacon.

AUTHOR INDEX

Subject Index

ABOUT THE EDITORS

Clifton F. Conrad has been Professor of Higher Education at the University of Wisconsin–Madison since 1987. He previously taught at the University of Denver (1975–1977), the College of William and Mary (1977–1981), and the University of Arizona (1981–1987), where he also served as a department chair and as associate dean for academic affairs. His research program is centered on college and university curriculum at the undergraduate and graduate levels, in the liberal arts and sciences, and in professional fields. Books that he has authored or co-authored include *The Undergraduate Curriculum, A Silent Success: Master's Education in the United States,* and *Emblems of Quality in Higher Education: Developing and Sustaining High-Quality Programs.* Although he has published quantitative studies in journals such as the *American Educational Research Journal* and the *Journal of Education Finance,* the majority of his research has been fueled by qualitative approaches to inquiry—work that appears in journals ranging from *Sociology of Education* to the *Journal of Higher Education.* A former president of the Association for the Study of Higher Education, since 1980 he has been a key expert witness and consultant to the U.S. Department of Justice and the Office of Civil Rights (U.S. Department of Education) in major civil rights cases and inquiries involving race and gender in higher education in nine states. Two of these cases led to landmark decisions by the U.S. Supreme Court, including one in which his scholarship was cited approvingly and verbatim.

Ronald C. Serlin is Professor in the Department of Educational Psychology at the University of Wisconsin–Madison. He teaches an introductory sequence in statistics as well as courses in nonparametric statistics, multivariate statistics, and the philosophy of science and statistics. His mastery in teaching earned him a Chancellor's Distinguished Teaching Award early in his career. His expertise as a statistical consultant has led to long and fruitful collaborative efforts with colleagues in the School of Nursing and the departments of Neurology, Art Education, and Journalism and Mass Communication, among others. Currently, he is engaged in two major lines of research. One investigates the philosophical underpinnings of statistical hypothesis testing, an effort linking modern philosophy of science and statistical practice to delineate the role of statistics in the scientific endeavor. The other examines the effects of violations of assumptions on known and proposed parametric and nonparametric tests, a knowledge of which helps to increase the validity of statistical conclusions. He has published regularly in *Psychological Bulletin* and *Psychological Methods* and in wide-ranging journals such as the *Journal of the American Medical Association,* the *Journal of Research in Music Education,* and *Pain.* An article that he co-authored won the annual research report awards competition for Division D of the American Educational Research Association. He won an award for Outstanding Contributions to Nursing Education, and he recently won a School of Education Distinguished Achievement Award. He is now serving his third nonconcurrent term as department chair.

ABOUT THE SECTION EDITORS

King D Beach, III, is Associate Professor of International and Sociocultural Studies at Florida State University. A cultural psychologist and educator, he studies the generalization of knowledge and identity between schools and other social organizations such as families, communities, and workplaces. His research includes the United States, South Asia, and Southeast Asia. He has served on a number of advisory and editorial boards, including *Mind, Culture, and Activity* and the *American Educational Research Journal,* and as educational consultant to the United Nations Development Program and the U.S. Agency for International Development. His current projects include American children's emergent understandings of money between home and school and action research on transitions between Indian alternative and governmental schools serving children who are at risk. He also participates in a Spencer Foundation effort that brings sociocultural theories to issues of opportunity to learn and assessment in schools.

Betsy Jane Becker recently joined the faculty of the College of Education at Florida State University, where she is Professor in the Program in Measurement and Statistics. For the previous 21 years, she was in the Measurement and Quantitative Methods program at Michigan State University. She has published widely on statistical methods for meta-analysis and has substantive interests in the relation of teacher qualifications to measures of the quality of teaching as well as interests in gender differences in math and science achievement. She serves as co-convener of the Methods Training Group for the Campbell Collaboration and is a member of the Technical Advisory Group for the "What Works Clearinghouse." She also is a member of the Design and Analysis Committee for the National Assessment of Educational Progress and serves as associate editor of the journal *Psychological Methods.*

Beth Graue is Professor in the Department of Curriculum and Instruction at the University of Wisconsin–Madison, where she teaches courses in early childhood education and research methodology. She is a former kindergarten teacher, and her research focuses on practices in primary education, including readiness for school, home–school relations, and class size reduction. She has served as associate editor of the *Review of Educational Research* and as chair of the Qualitative Research Special Interest Group, and she is currently chair of the Early Childhood/Child Development Special Interest Group of the American Educational Research Association. She is the author of *Ready for What? Constructing Meanings of Readiness for Kindergarten* and *Studying Children in Context: Theories, Methods, and Ethics* (with Daniel Walsh). She is currently engaged in a large-scale field study of a state class size reduction program.

Daniel K. Lapsley is Professor and Chair of the Department of Educational Psychology at Ball State University. He is the author or editor of six books and numerous articles and chapters on various topics in child and adolescent development and educational psychology, particularly in the areas of social cognition, personality development, moral psychology, and moral education. He currently serves on the editorial boards of the *Journal of Educational Psychology, Child Development,* the *Journal of Adolescent Research,* and the *Journal of Early Adolescence.*

Laura W. Perna is Associate Professor at the University of Pennsylvania. Her scholarship examines the ways in which individual characteristics, social structures, and public policies enable and restrict the ability of women, racial/ethnic minorities, and individuals of lower socioeconomic status to obtain the economic, social, and political opportunities that are associated with two aspects of higher education: access as a student and employment as a faculty member. Her research has been published in the *Journal of Higher Education,* the *Review of Higher Education, Research in Higher Education,* the *Journal of College Student Development,* and the *Journal of Student Financial Aid* as well as in technical reports, monographs, and edited books. She received the 2003 Promising Scholar/Early Career Achievement Award from the Association for the Study of Higher Education.

D. C. Phillips is Professor of Education, and by courtesy Professor of Philosophy, at Stanford University, where he has also served as Associate Dean for Academic Affairs and Interim Dean of the School of Education. A philosopher of education and philosopher of social science, he is the author of more than 100 essays in books and refereed journals and is the author, co-author, or editor of 11 books, most recently *Postpositivism and Educational Research* (with Nicholas C. Burbules) and *The Expanded Social Scientist's Bestiary.* He was a member of the National Research Council panel that wrote the *Scientific Research in Education* report. He is a member of the U.S. National Academy of Education and a fellow of the International Academy of Education.

Scott L. Thomas is Associate Professor of Higher Education at the Institute of Higher Education at the University of Georgia. His current research is on issues of access and stratification in higher education, with a focus on economic outcomes and indebtedness related to college quality and choice of major. His writings have examined topics in the areas of the sociology of education, labor economics, and student persistence. His work has appeared in journals such as *Sociology of Education, Economics of Education Review,* the *American Journal of Education,* the *Journal of Higher Education,* and *Research in Higher Education.* His methodological work includes a recent book (co-authored with Ronald H. Heck), *An Introduction to Multilevel Modeling Techniques.* He currently chairs the Council for Public Policy in Higher Education for the Association for the Study of Higher Education.

John C. Weidman is Professor of Education and of Sociology at the University of Pittsburgh and Director of the Institute for International Studies in Education. He has published both conceptual and empirical research on the socialization of students in higher education at both the undergraduate and graduate levels. Since the early 1990s, he has also been working on comparative education management, reform, and policy analysis at the national level in Mongolia, Laos, Uzbekistan, and Kyrgyzstan through consulting assignments with the Asian Development Bank. He has also worked on institutional reform and strategic planning in higher education in Kenya and South Africa on projects funded by USAID. His visiting professorships include the UNESCO Chair of Higher Education Research at Maseno University College in Kenya and Fulbright Professor of the Sociology of Education at Augsburg University in Germany.

About the Contributors

Vonzell Agosto, a former high school teacher, is currently a Ph.D. student at the University of Wisconsin–Madison in the Department of Curriculum and Instruction. Her areas of interest are multicultural education, teacher education, and curriculum theory. She serves as a program adviser for the Multicultural Learning Community and as a program assistant for the multicultural seminar at UW–Madison. She has made presentations at the National Association for Multicultural Education and the American Educational Research Association.

Juliet A. Baxter is Associate Professor in the College of Education at the University of Oregon. Her research focuses on issues of teaching and learning mathematics, teacher education, and teacher professional development. She has conducted more than a decade of research into reform-based mathematics programs for students with learning disabilities and those at risk for special education. She has also directed a professional development project to support teachers' efforts to teach science as inquiry at the elementary and middle school levels. She is currently studying professional development that supports the strategic integration of mathematics and science at the elementary school level. Her work has been published in the *American Educational Research Journal,* the *Elementary School Journal,* and *Learning Disabilities Research and Practice,* among other journals.

John P. Bean is Associate Professor in the Educational Leadership and Policy Studies Department at Indiana University–Bloomington, where for the past 20 years he has taught a seminar in research design for doctoral students. He has chaired the research papers program for the annual meetings of the Association for the Study of Higher Education and Division J of the American Educational Research Association. He is best known for his development and estimation of theoretical models of college student retention and has published articles in the *American Education Research Journal, Review of Educational Research, Research in Higher Education,* and the *Journal of Higher Education.* He co-authored *The Strategic Management of College Enrollments* (1990) and co-edited the *ASHE Reader on College Students* (1996). John Mellencamp purchased one of his oil paintings. He makes Cremonese-style violins and once repaired Joshua Bell's Stradivarius violin.

Brian A. Bottge is Associate Professor in the Department of Rehabilitation Psychology and Special Education at the University of Wisconsin–Madison. He has combined his extensive classroom experience with learning theory to develop and test curricula and teaching methods to improve mathematics learning of students with disabilities. Since joining the faculty at UW–Madison, his research has been funded by the James S. McDonnell Foundation Cognitive Studies in Educational Practice program, the Office of Special Education and Rehabilitative Services, and the Institute of Education Sciences Cognition and Student Learning Research Grant program. He has published numerous articles on this topic in leading journals in special education and is frequently invited to speak at national and international conferences on math education such as the International Conference on Learning Disabilities in Chennai, India.

Gerald W. Bracey is an independent researcher and writer in Alexandria, Virginia. After obtaining a Ph.D. in psychology in 1967, he worked at many levels of education—state department, school district, university, and private company—before becoming an independent researcher in 1991. Since 1984, he has written a monthly "Research" column for *Phi Delta Kappan* to make research accessible to practitioners. Each October since 1991, he has written an annual essay that the editors of *Phi Delta Kappan* named "The Bracey Report on the Condition of Public Education." His most recent book is a compendium of statistical information bearing on the performance of American public schools: *Setting the Record Straight: Responses to Misconceptions About Public Education in the U.S.*

Elizabeth G. Creamer is Associate Professor in the Department of Educational Policy and Leadership at Virginia Tech. Her research interests center on issues related to faculty work and lives, including personal and environmental factors associated with faculty research productivity and how these vary by gender. She is an active scholar who has published more than 45 journal articles and book chapters as well as three authored, co-authored, or co-edited books. She is a principal investigator on four projects funded by the National Science Foundation and is director of research and assessment for the Virginia Tech ADVANCE Grant.

Joyce L. Epstein is Director of the Center on School, Family, and Community Partnerships and the National Network of Partnership Schools, Principal Research Scientist, and Research Professor of Sociology at Johns Hopkins University. She has more than 100 publications on school organization and effects, with many on school, family, and community connections. She serves on many advisory and editorial boards. Her current research focuses on the roles of district and state leaders in guiding schools to develop partnership programs that reach all families and that help students to succeed at high levels. In all of her work, she is interested in the connections of research, policy, and practice.

Kadriye Ercikan is Associate Professor at the University of British Columbia in the area of Measurement, Evaluation, and Research Methods. Her research focuses on construction of data through assessments and the validity of interpretations from large-scale assessment results. In particular, her publications focus on validity and fairness issues in international and multilingual assessments. She combines statistical approaches with think-aloud approaches for examining examinee cognitive processes and validity of interpretations of assessment results. She has published widely in *Educational Measurement: Issues and Practice,* the *Journal of Educational Measurement, Applied Measurement in Education,* and the *International Journal of Testing.* She has served on the National Academy of Sciences' (NAS) Committee on Foundations of Educational and Psychological Assessment and contributed to the NAS book *Knowing What People Know: The Science and Design of Educational Assessments.*

Michael Ford is Assistant Professor in the Department of Instruction and Learning at the University of Pittsburgh. He develops classroom activities that engage students in key scientific practices and examines the learning outcomes from these activities that support scientific literacy. His work also involves preparing future science teachers and exploring the epistemological underpinnings of scientific knowledge in history and philosophy. His recent publications have appeared in *Science & Education* and the *Journal of the Learning Sciences.*

Ellice Ann Forman is Professor in the Department of Instruction and Learning at the University of Pittsburgh. She studies the processes of teacher–student and student–student interactions and problem solving in mathematics and science classrooms. Her research has been published in *Linguistics and Education, Cognition and Instruction, Learning and Instruction,* the *Journal of the Learning Sciences,* and *Educational Studies in Mathematics.* She has co-edited two books: *Contexts for Learning: Sociocultural Dynamics in Children's Development* and *Learning Discourse: Discursive Approaches to Research in Mathematics Education.* From 2000 to 2003, she served as associate editor of the *American Educational Research Journal.*

Robert E. Floden is Professor of Teacher Education, Measurement and Quantitative Methods, Educational Psychology, and Educational Policy at the Michigan State University College of Education. He has an A.B. in philosophy from Princeton University as well as an M.S. in mathematical statistics and a Ph.D. in philosophy of education, both from Stanford University. His work has been published in the *Handbook of Research on Teaching,* the *Handbook of Research on Teacher Education,* and many journals. He has been editor of *Review of Research in Education,* features editor of *Educational Researcher,* and president of the Philosophy of Education Society. He has been studying teacher education and other influences on teaching and learning for nearly three decades. He is currently co-principal investigator of Michigan State University's Teachers for a New Era initiative and co-principal investigator on a project developing measures of teachers' mathematical knowledge for teaching algebra.

R. Evely Gildersleeve is a Ph.D. student in the Graduate School of Education and Information Studies at the University of California, Los Angeles, where he holds a doctoral fellowship funded by the Spencer Foundation. His research interests focus on educational opportunity in P–16 pathways, especially as related to college choice for historically marginalized students. Before coming to UCLA, he worked in student affairs at Iowa State University. He is a graduate of Occidental College.

Carl A. Grant is Hoefs-Bascom Professor of Teacher Education in the Department of Curriculum and Instruction at the University of Wisconsin–Madison. He has written or edited 25 books or monographs in multicultural education and/or teacher education. He has also written more than 125 articles, book chapters, and reviews. Several of his writings and programs he directed have received awards. He is a former classroom teacher and administrator. He served as president of the National Association for Multicultural Education from 1993 to 1999, served as editor of the *Review of Educational Research* from 1996 to 1999, was a member of the National Research Council's Committee on Assessment and Teacher Quality from 1999 to 2001, and is currently the chair of the American Educational Research Association's Publication Committee.

Cheryl Hanley-Maxwell is Chair and Professor in the Department of Rehabilitation Psychology and Special Education at the University of Wisconsin–Madison. Her research interests focus on career development, enhancing family and student participation and power in educational processes and postschool life planning, and preparing adolescents for their adult roles. Recently, she co-directed the Research Institute on Secondary Education Reform for Youth With Disabilities (RISER). The purpose of RISER was to identify and describe educational policies and practices that enhance inclusive and challenging secondary education for all students. She has published numerous articles and chapters related to supported employment and transition. She also has extensive experience in preparing professionals and paraprofessionals to work with students as they move from school to their adult lives and to provide employees with disabilities employment-related services.

Debbi Harris recently received her Ph.D. in educational policy from Michigan State University. Her work has been published in *Educational and Psychological Measurement,* and she has presented at the annual meetings of the American Education Finance Association and the American Educational Research Association. She has also served as a research assistant for the Education Policy Center at Michigan State University and as an intern for the Michigan Department of Education. Her research interests include teacher quality, teacher compensation, and the interplay between educational politics and policy persistence. Prior to beginning her doctoral studies, she was a middle school science teacher.

Susan Harter is Professor of Psychology and Head of the Developmental Psychology Program at the University of Denver. She received her Ph.D. from Yale University in 1966, obtaining a joint degree in developmental and child clinical psychology. She remained at Yale as the first female faculty member in the Department of Psychology until coming to the University of Denver in 1974. While her research has focused on self-esteem, the construction of multiple selves, false self-behavior, classroom motivation, and emotional development, her research interests also include the study of gender issues across the life span and, most recently, school violence and the role of the self-system in provoking both depressive and violent ideation. Her research has resulted in the development of a battery of assessment instruments that are in widespread use in the United States and abroad. In addition to her numerous scholarly articles and chapters, she is the author of *The Construction of the Self: Developmental Perspectives.* At the University of Denver, she has received two major faculty research awards—the University Lecturer of the Year in 1990 and the John Evans Professorship Award in 1993—and has received awards conveying national and international recognition as well.

Ronald H. Heck is Professor of Educational Administration and Policy at the University of Hawaii at Manoa. His research interests include school effects on student learning, school leadership, and student transition to postsecondary education. Recent publications include *Studying Educational and Social Policy: Theoretical Concepts and Research Methods* (2004), *Introduction to Multilevel Modeling Techniques* (2000, with Scott L. Thomas), and "Tracks as Emergent Structures: A Network Analysis of Student Differentiation in a High School" (in *American Journal of Education,* with Carol L. Price and Scott L. Thomas).

Jason N. Johnson is a Ph.D. student in the Department of Educational Leadership and Policy Analysis at the University of Wisconsin–Madison. His research interests include postsecondary education institutional identity, college and university curriculum, leadership within the disciplines, and the rhetoric of education. He earlier studied and worked at the University of Washington, where he earned a bachelor's degree in comparative history of ideas and a master's degree in educational leadership and policy studies and served in a series of professional staff positions in the Office of Undergraduate Education, most recently as the associate director of first-year programs.

Cindy L. Juntunen is Professor in the Department of Counseling at the University of North Dakota. She received her Ph.D. from the University of California, Santa Barbara. Her primary research interests revolve around vocational psychology, with an emphasis on the work and social needs of marginalized groups. Her work has focused on the school-to-work transition, the welfare-to-work transition, and vocational needs of and issues for American Indian populations. Her current research is addressing the integration of vocational and emotional needs among high-risk youth. Other research and teaching interests include counselor supervision, feminist therapy, and ethical decision making.

Mary M. Kennedy is Professor at Michigan State University. From 1986 to 1994, she directed the National Center for Research on Teacher Learning. Her scholarship focuses on the relationship between knowledge and teaching practice, the nature of knowledge used in teaching practice, and how research knowledge and policy initiatives can improve practice. She has published three books addressing the relationship between knowledge and teaching and has won five awards for her work, the most recent being the Margaret B. Lindsey Award for Distinguished Research in Teacher Education. She has consulted with four ministries of education, the World Bank, and a host of national organizations. Prior to joining Michigan State University in 1986, her work focused mainly on policy issues and the role of research in improving policy. She has authored numerous journal articles and book chapters in these areas and has authored reports specifically for policy audiences, including the U.S. Congress.

Jane Clark Lindle is Eugene T. Moore Endowed Professor of Educational Leadership at Clemson University. She has worked as a special education teacher, principal, and professor. She has served in various editorial roles, including editor of *Educational Administration Quarterly* from 1998 to 2004. Her research includes studies of shared governance, micropolitics, and state and national accountability policies. She recently published a study of middle school teaming in the *Journal of Thought* and another on coping with trauma in the principalship in the *Journal of School Leadership*. Her most recent books are *20 Strategies for Collaborative School Leaders* and *Building Spiritually Dispelling Myths About Early Adolescence*.

Shirley J. Magnusson is Cotchett Professor of Science and Mathematics Teacher Education at the California Polytechnic State University in San Luis Obispo. She began her career in education in 1980 as a middle school science teacher and has taught science to students at the elementary, middle, and high school levels as well as at the college level. Her research has focused on both the teaching and learning of science in the context of inquiry-based instruction, drawing on sociocultural perspectives and the philosophy of science to conceptualize teacher and student roles. Along with several books, her work has appeared in the *Journal of the Learning Sciences, Teaching and Teacher Education,* and the *Journal of Science Education and Technology.*

Patricia M. McDonough is Professor of Higher Education in the Graduate School of Education and Information Studies at the University of California, Los Angeles. Her research is on college access, organizational culture, and educational equity. She has conducted research on students' college choice decision making, high school counseling, college rankings, access for African American and Latino students, rural college access, access in historically black colleges, private college counselors, affirmative action, and college admissions officers. She is the author of *Choosing Colleges: How Social Class and Schools Structure Opportunity.*

Mary Lee Nelson is Professor of Counseling Psychology at the University of Wisconsin–Madison. She has conducted research on counselor training and supervision processes; power, gender, and social class issues in counseling and supervision; and the relation of appearance talk to body dissatisfaction in adolescents. She has published articles on these and other topics in the *Journal of Counseling Psychology,* the *Journal of Counseling and Development, Counselor Education and Supervision,* the *Journal of Multicultural Counseling and Development,* the *Journal of Clinical Child and Adolescent Psychology,* the *Journal of Clinical Psychology,* and *Clinical Supervisor* and is currently on the editorial boards of *The Counseling Psychologist* and *Psychotherapy Research.* She has recently co-authored the book *Critical Events in Psychotherapy Supervision: An Interpersonal Approach.*

Anna Neumann is Professor of Higher Education and Coordinator of the Program in Higher and Postsecondary Education at Teachers College, Columbia University. Her research addresses scholarly learning and development within academic careers, intellectual development across the life span, teaching and learning in higher education, the learning of research and development of researchers, and interdisciplinarity in research. Her books include *Learning From Our Lives: Women, Research, and Autobiography in Education* (with Penelope L. Peterson) and *Redesigning Collegiate Leadership: Teams and Teamwork in Higher Education* (with Estela M. Bensimon). Funded by the Spencer Foundation's Major Grants Program, her current research explores professors' intellectual and professional learning through the early posttenure years. She is also co-investigator on a National Institutes of Health grant concerned with interdisciplinary research in public health and medicine. Other work includes studies of doctoral students' learning of research in education and the social sciences and professors as undergraduate teachers.

Aaron M. Pallas is Professor of Sociology and Education in the Department of Human Development at Teachers College, Columbia University. He also holds a courtesy appointment in the Department of Sociology at Columbia University. Since receiving his Ph.D. in sociology from Johns Hopkins University in 1984, he has held positions at the National Center for Education Statistics, Michigan State University, and Teachers College. His intellectual interests converge on the study of stratification within and between schools, school organization, and the life course. He is a former editor of *Sociology of Education* and is a past chair of the American Sociological Association's Section on Sociology of Education.

David Phillips is Professor of Comparative Education and a Fellow of St. Edmund Hall at the University of Oxford. He has written widely on issues in comparative education, with a focus on education in Germany and on educational policy borrowing. He served as chair of the British Association for International and Comparative Education from 1998 to 2000 and is an academician of the British Social Sciences Academy and a fellow of the Royal Historical Association. He was editor of the *Oxford Review of Education* for 20 years and serves on the editorial boards of various journals, including *Comparative Education.* He now edits the online journal *Research in Comparative and International Education* and is series editor of *Oxford Studies in Comparative Education.*

David N. Plank is Co-Director of the Education Policy Center at Michigan State University and Professor in the College of Education. He is a specialist in the areas of educational policy and education finance with both domestic and international research interests. He has worked as a consultant in education policy development for the World Bank, USAID, the United Nations Development Program, the Ford Foundation, and ministries of education in several countries in Africa and Latin America. He has published five books and numerous articles and chapters in a variety of fields, including history of education and economics of education. His most recent book is *Choosing Choice: School Choice in International Perspective* (2003), which he co-edited with

Gary Sykes. He is currently at work on a book on the shifting relationship between schooling and the state.

Mike Rose is on the faculty of the Graduate School of Education and Information Studies at the University of California, Los Angeles, Division of Social Research Methodology. He has written a number of books and articles on language, literacy, schooling, and work and is the recipient of awards from the Spencer Foundation, the McDonnell Foundation, the National Counsel of Teachers of English, and the Guggenheim Foundation. His books include *Lives on the Boundary: The Struggles and Achievements of America's Underprepared, Possible Lives: The Promise of Public Education in America,* and *The Mind at Work: Valuing the Intelligence of the American Worker.*

Wolff-Michael Roth is Lansdowne Professor of Applied Cognitive Science at the University of Victoria. After a 12-year career as a high school science teacher, he first held a position teaching statistics for social scientists at Simon Fraser University before securing his current position in 1997. His interests lie in understanding knowing, learning, and identity related to mathematics and science from kindergarten to professional practice. He actively publishes in the areas of science studies, linguistics, learning sciences, and mathematics and science education. His recent major publications include *Toward an Anthropology of Graphing* (2003), *Rethinking Scientific Literacy* (2004, with A. C. Barton), and *Talking Science: Language and Learning in Science Classrooms* (2005). He has received numerous awards for his journal and book publications, including awards from organizations such as the National Association for Research in Science Teaching, the American Educational Research Association, and the European Association for Research on Learning and Instruction.

Steven Schlossman is Professor of History and Policy at Carnegie Mellon University. His research centers on the history of education, childhood, and juvenile justice. He has taught previously at the University of Chicago, the University of California, Los Angeles, and Harvard University and has been a research fellow at the University of California, Berkeley; Radcliffe College; and Stanford University. He has also held full-time positions at the RAND Corporation, the California State Assembly, and the California State Department of Justice. His recent publications include *Transforming Juvenile Justice: Reform Ideals and Institutional Realities* (2005), "Villain or Savior? The American Discourse on Homework, 1850–2003" (*Theory Into Practice,* Summer 2004, with Brian P. Gill), and "Punishing Serious Juvenile Offenders: Crime, Racial Disparity, and the Incarceration of Adolescents in Adult Prison in Late Nineteenth- and Early Twentieth-Century Pennsylvania" (in *Beyond Empiricism* [Joan McCord, Ed.], 2004, with David Wolcott).

Michael Seltzer is Associate Professor in the Social Research Methodology Division of the Graduate School of Education and Information Studies at the University of California, Los Angeles, where he teaches courses on quantitative methods and on the philosophical underpinnings of inquiry. He received his Ph.D. in education from the University of Chicago. His research activities center on the development of hierarchical modeling techniques and their use in multisite evaluation studies and studies of change. His methodological work has been published in various journals and edited volumes, including the *Journal of Educational and Behavioral Statistics, Evaluation Review, Educational Evaluation and Policy Analysis,* and *The SAGE Handbook of Quantitative Methodology for the Social Sciences.* Various substantive pieces on which he collaborated have appeared in journals such as *Cognition and Learning, Developmental Psychology,* the *Reading Research Quarterly,* and the *American Journal of Psychiatry.*

Steven B. Sheldon is Associate Research Scientist with the Center on School, Family, and Community Partnerships at Johns Hopkins University. He received his Ph.D. in educational psychology from Michigan State University. He conducts research on the influences on parental involvement, including parental beliefs, parents' social relationships, and school outreach. In addition, he studies the development of family and community involvement programs in school and the impact of these programs on student outcomes.

J. Douglas Toma is Associate Professor at the Institute of Higher Education at the University of Georgia, where he also has an appointment on the School of Law faculty and serves as dean of Franklin Residential College. Before his appointment at the University of Georgia in the fall of 2003, he served on the Graduate School of Education faculty at the University of Pennsylvania, where he organized and directed the Executive Doctorate in Higher Education Management. He writes about management and strategy, qualitative research, and law in higher education. He is the author of *Football U.: Spectator Sports in the Life of the American University* (2003). In 1995, he earned his Ph.D. in higher education from the University of Michigan. He also earned his M.A. (1993) in history and his J.D. (1989) from the University of Michigan and earned his B.A. (1986) in public policy and history from James Madison College at Michigan State University.

Kathryn R. Wentzel is Professor of Human Development in the College of Education at the University of Maryland, College Park. Her research interests focus on parents, peers, and teachers as motivators of adolescents' classroom behavior and academic accomplishments. She is currently examining dimensions of students' interpersonal relationships with teachers and peers that promote the adoption of group values and goals and that promote beliefs that the classroom is a safe, responsive, helpful, and emotionally supportive place to learn. Her work has been published in developmental and educational psychology journals such as *Child Development* and the *Journal of Educational Psychology*. She is a past vice president of Division E of the American Educational Research Association.

James Youniss is Wylma R. and James R. Curtin Professor of Psychology at the Catholic University of America. For more than four decades, he has studied cognitive, social, and moral development in children and youth, with his most recent focus being on civic–political participation. His books include *Parents and Peers in Social Development; Adolescent Relations With Mothers, Fathers, and Friends; Community Service and Social Responsibility in Youth;* and *Roots of Civic Identity: International Perspectives on Community Service and Activism in Youth.*

Kenneth M. Zeichner is Hoefs-Bascom Professor of Teacher Education and Associate Dean of the School of Education at the University of Wisconsin–Madison. His research focuses on issues of teacher education and teacher professional development. He was vice president of the American Educational Research Association (Division K), co-chair of the American Educational Research Association's Panel on Research in Teacher Education, a member of the National Academy of Education Committee on Teacher Education, and a member of the board of directors of the American Association of Colleges for Teacher Education (AACTE). In 2002, he received the Margaret B. Lindsey Award for Distinguished Research in Teacher Education from AACTE. He teaches graduate courses in the study of teacher education and directs the Madison Professional Development School Partnership.